ArtScroll® Series

Rabbi Nosson Scherman / Rabbi Meir Zlotowitz

General Editors

SWARTZ FAMILY EDITION

AVOS DeRABBI NASSAN

The ancient Baraisa
that illuminates
the teachings
of Pirkei Avos

Published by

ARTSCROLL®
Mesorah Publications, ltd

The following outstanding Torah scholars contributed to this volume:

Rabbis Nochum Brown, Geilan Grant, Henoch Moshe Levin,
Yosef Levinson, Avraham Y. Morgenstern, and **Moshe Yosef Ruvel**
composed and edited the elucidation;

Rabbi Chaim Zev Malinowitz

reviewed and commented on the edited version,
assisted by **Rabbi Yosaif Asher Weiss;**

Rabbi Moshe Rosenblum reviewed the Hebrew text and vowelization;
Rabbi Hillel Danziger served with distinction as Editorial Director.

FIRST EDITION
Three Impressions ... March 2017 — May 2020
Fourth Impression ... March 2021

Published and Distributed by **MESORAH PUBLICATIONS, Ltd.**
313 Regina Avenue, Rahway, New Jersey 07065

Distributed in Europe by
LEHMANNS
Unit E, Viking Business Park
Rolling Mill Road
Jarrow, Tyne & Wear NE32 3DP
England

Distributed in Australia & New Zealand by
GOLDS WORLD OF JUDAICA
3-13 William Street
Balaclava, Melbourne 3183
Victoria Australia

Distributed in Israel by
SIFRIATI / A. GITLER — BOOKS
POB 2351
Bnei Brak 51122

Distributed in South Africa by
KOLLEL BOOKSHOP
Northfield Centre, 17 Northfield Avenue
Glenhazel 2192, Johannesburg, South Africa

THE ARTSCROLL® SERIES / SWARTZ FAMILY EDITION
AVOS DERABBI NASSAN

Typography by CompuScribe at **ArtScroll Studios,** Ltd.
Custom bound by **Sefercraft, Inc.,** Rahway, NJ

*S*ince the Gemara teaches that we may say only a part of a person's praise in his presence, we embrace this opportunity to dedicate this volume as an expression of intense gratitude to, and recognition of, our friend, our teacher, our inspiration,

Joel Fleishman

*T*o our family, Joel personifies a life of Torah, *chesed*, and *ahavas Yisrael*. He is a dear friend, a mentor, a frequent Shabbos guest in America and Israel, a shul-mate, a role model, and an inspiration.

To countless people from many backgrounds, Joel is a teacher, guide, support, prod, adviser, and much more. Behind the relentless smile and indispensable Southern kindness lies an impregnable core of integrity and principle, based on his constantly nourished roots in our Torah heritage.

As the one who envisioned and nursed the ArtScroll Mesorah Heritage Foundation into existence, he is one of the elite who made possible the enormous upsurge in Torah learning in our generation. This magnificent treatment of **Avos DeRabbi Nassan** is an example of the Torah classics that are opened up to the modern world thanks to the Foundation—and in a very real way, to Joel!

Joel is a leader of one the world's great universities, a premier scholar in the law and in the practice of effective philanthropy and in the process and practice of government, an internationally renowned professor, and a board member of a variety of philanthropic and industrial institutions. His personal hospitality is unexcelled; to be his guest is to experience *hachnassas orchim* in the tradition of Avraham Avinu.

Despite all his international distinctions, the essential Joel Fleishman is the friend and guide of individuals young and old, famous and unknown, the scholar whose Hirsch Chumash is filled with many years of notes, the humble and loyal successor of his father as the *ba'al tefillah* in his native Fayetteville.

It is an honor, therefore, to dedicate this classic in honor of one of the truly unique Jews of our time.

Jeff and Debbie Swartz
and family — all of us
who have *hakaras hatov* in our hearts always for Joel.

PUBLISHER'S PREFACE

It is with great pride that we present the SWARTZ FAMILY EDITION of *Avos DeRabbi Nassan*. This tractate, widely quoted in Talmudic and Rabbinic literature, expands upon the concepts of *Pirkei Avos* and contains a wealth of additional halachic, Aggadic, and historical material. This volume presents the tractate with unprecedented clarity, in both the translation and the notes, in what has come to be known as the Schottenstein Edition-style of elucidation. We have no doubt that readers will find it both enjoyable and enriching.

We are proud to welcome JEFF AND DEBBIE SWARTZ to the ArtScroll/Mesorah family. As patrons of the Swartz Family Edition of *Avos DeRabbi Nassan*, they are introducing the Torah public to a classic Tannaitic work, containing the teachings of some of the greatest sages in our history. The Swartz family is dedicated to Torah life and learning. Mr. Swartz and his three sons are involved in Talmud study every day, and he and Mrs. Swartz are leaders of Jewish day schools and Jewish causes in their native Boston, in America, and in Israel. As the former Chairman and CEO of Timberland, Jeff was renowned in the corporate world as a model of communal responsibility for the needy.

It is typical of their graciousness that they dedicate this volume to our very dear mutual friend, JOEL FLEISHMAN, founding Trustee and Chairman of the Mesorah Heritage Foundation. Joel is a mentor and inspiration to all who know him. That the Swartzes have chosen to honor Professor Fleishman in this way demonstrates their appreciation of a great man.

Avos DeRabbi Nassan is part of the *Mesechtos Ketanos*, popularly, but inaccurately, translated as the "Minor Tractates." No Tannaitic work is "minor." These tractates are important sources of halachah. We look forward to presenting the other tractates of *Mesechtos Ketanos* with similar thoroughness and accuracy.

We hope that this volume will stimulate other visionary, insightful patrons to enable our scholars and editors to present the other volumes of *Mesechtos Ketanos* with the same high literary quality and accuracy as this volume.

We gratefully acknowledge the Torah scholars who composed and edited the elucidation of this classic work, and all the dedicated and skilled ArtScroll/Mesorah editors, readers, designers, and typesetters whose indispensable work has made ArtScroll/Mesorah a respected mark of quality:

We salute RABBI HILLEL DANZIGER, who directed the scholars who produced the translation and commentary. Rabbi Danziger is known to our readers from his exceptional work on the Schottenstein Edition of the Talmud, the Kleinman Edition of the Midrash, the Yad Avraham Mishnah, and other classics.

RABBIS GEILAN GRANT, HENOCH MOSHE LEVIN, and YOSEF LEVINSON wrote the vast majority of the manuscript, with great erudition and skill.

The unique literary talents and great scholarship of RABBIS NOCHUM BROWN, MOSHE YOSEF RUVEL, and AVRAHAM Y. MORGENSTERN converged to make them the ideal editors of this work, roles that they successfully filled with grace, elegance, and keen insight. In addition, Rabbi Ruvel's willing assistance in so many other varied facets of this work has significantly enhanced the finished product.

As usual, RABBI CHAIM ZEV MALINOWITZ, a senior editor of so many of our most difficult projects, reviewed and commented on the entire edited version with his customary incisiveness, vast scholarship, and extraordinary discipline. How he is able to accomplish so much so well in so short a time remains a mystery.

RABBI YOSAIF ASHER WEISS read and commented on the edited version and coordinated many aspects of the proofreading and correcting, with an inimitable eye to detail and timetable.

RABBI ELIYAHU MEIR KLUGMAN of Jerusalem also reviewed a portion of this work with his keen sense of literary and philosophical nuance.

RABBI MOSHE ROSENBLUM reviewed the Hebrew text and vowelization, and made numerous and valuable editorial suggestions.

The contribution of our esteemed colleague RABBI SHEAH BRANDER to this project, and to every other, cannot be overstated. There is virtually no aspect of a project, from the scholarly to the graphical, that does not benefit enormously from his incredibly keen eye and even keener intellect.

SHLOIME BRANDER paginated the book and enhanced countless pages with his signature precision and eye to detail.

MRS. AHUVA WEISS read the entire volume and provided skilled literary editing, as well as insightful comments; MRS. MINDY STERN proofread and made important suggestions; MRS. ESTIE DICKER entered all the proofreader corrections in the pre-paginated stages of the book; MRS. CHUMIE LIPSCHITZ did many of the corrections on the final copy.

ELI KROEN designed the beautiful cover. And as always, the keen eye of YECHEZKEL SOCHACZEWSKI and the exceptional skills of MOISHE DEUTSCH transformed the book into a finished product.

MENDY HERZBERG coordinated the book through its many stages, with unwavering good cheer and efficiency. As usual, AVROHOM BIDERMAN made his store of considerable knowledge and good judgment available whenever needed.

Rabbi Nosson Scherman / Rabbi Meir Zlotowitz

Adar, 5777
March, 2017

⚜ GENERAL INTRODUCTION ⚜
AVOS DERABBI NASSAN

A VOS DERABBI NASSAN [THE AVOS OF R' NASSAN] IS A COLLECTION OF BARAISOS [literally: *outside;* Tannaitic teachings "outside" the Mishnah redacted by Rebbi] that, in the main, parallel, amplify, and elaborate many of the themes in *Pirkei Avos.* Whether *Avos DeRabbi Nassan* is taken as an independent Tannaitic corpus of *Avos*[1] or as an expository work on the Mishnah of *Avos,* the fact remains that its slight changes of expression, different formulations, and additional material open new vistas in understanding even well-known teachings of *Pirkei Avos.* Very often, the Baraisos of *Avos DeRabbi Nassan* add examples and stories that deepen our appreciation of *Pirkei Avos* and its application to our lives. *Avos DeRabbi Nassan* also contains a wealth of Aggadic material not directly related to the teachings of *Avos.*

Who composed *Avos DeRabbi Nassan* is unclear. Some say that it was compiled by the Tanna R' Nassan, an older contemporary of Rebbi, redactor of the Mishnah.[2] In any event, many of its Baraisos are cited and expounded by the Gemara itself, and are cited by the Rishonim, such as *Rambam, Machzor Vitri, R' Yonah,* and *Meiri,* in their commentaries on Mishnah *Avos.*[3]

Some Rishonim refer to *Avos DeRabbi Nassan* as "the Baraisa of *R' Nassan*" or simply "the Baraisa,"[4] while others seem to call it "the *Tosefta* of *Avos.*"[5] R' Avraham Witmond, in his classic commentary *Ahavas Chesed* on *Avos DeRabbi Nassan,* refers to it as "the Gemara." In the present edition, we will refer to it simply as "the Baraisa."

---

1. See *Rashbatz* cited in the next note.

2. *R' Simchah of Vitri,* author of *Machzor Vitri* and disciple of *Rashi,* writes in his commentary on the first Mishnah in *Avos* (ד״ה ונביאים מסרוה לאנשי כנסת הגדולה) about *Avos DeRabbi Nassan* that "I do not know why this Baraisa is called thus ... Perhaps there was a tradition that R' Nassan compiled it, similar to 'the Mishnah of R' Chiya and R' Hoshaya' and 'the Mishnah of Bar Kappara.' and of Shmuel and of Levi ..." *Rashbatz* writes in the introduction to his commentary on *Avos* that *Avos DeRabbi Nassan* is the Baraisa of R' Nassan, who, together with Rebbi, are called by the Gemara "the last [Sages] of the Mishnah" (*Bava Metzia* 86a). "But Rebbi's words [i.e., redaction of *Avos* material] were

more concise than those of R' Nassan, and they were therefore incorporated into the Mishnah due to the beauty of their organization and the elegance of their language."

3. *Meiri* writes in the introduction to his commentary on *Avos:* "This tractate has no Gemara, neither in ... *Bavli* nor in ... *Yerushalmi,* nor [anything] in the arrangements of R' Chiya and R' Hoshaya and Bar Kappara or Baraisa or *Tosefta,* but it does have a major Baraisa by R' Nassan called *Avos DeRabbi Nassan.*"

4. *Meiri* throughout his commentary on *Avos.*

5. See *Tosafos* to *Bava Kamma* 25a, ד״ה קל וחומר.

✍ Versions of Avos DeRabbi Nassan

BESIDES THE STANDARD PRINTED EDITIONS OF AVOS DERABBI NASSAN, ON WHICH this present edition is based, there is another, entirely different, collection of Baraisos also known as *Avos DeRabbi Nassan,* quoted extensively by R' Yom Tov Tzahalon in his monumental commentary *Magen Avos* on the standard version of *Avos DeRabbi Nassan.* While there are numerous parallels between these two works, there are wide divergences, and even many of the same teachings are often presented in dramatically different formulations. When referencing this alternative collection of *Avos DeRabbi Nassan* in the course of this work, we will refer to it as *"Avos DeRabbi Nassan, Nusach 2."*[6]

THE SUBJECT MATTER OF AVOS DERABBI NASSAN FOLLOWS ROUGHLY THE SEQUENCE of the subjects of the five chapters of the Mishnah *Avos,*[7] except that the chap-

Structure ter divisions in *Avos DeRabbi Nassan* are different and more numerous. In the printed editions of *Avos DeRabbi Nassan,* beginning with the first edition, printed in Venice in 1550, the work is divided into forty-one chapters.[8]

AS MENTIONED, AVOS DERABBI NASSAN WAS FIRST PRINTED IN VENICE IN 1550. EXTENsive emendations of that text, based on a manuscript, were printed in a collec-

Text tion called *Tummas Yesharim* in 1622, and many of those emendations were incorporated in later editions of *Avos DeRabbi Nassan.* Nevertheless, the text of *Avos DeRabbi Nassan* remained problematic in many places, and subsequent editions added numerous emendations, placed questionable readings in parentheses, and inserted bracketed additions. We have based the

---

6. This alternative version of *Avos De-Rabbi Nassan* was published under the title מסכת אבות דרבי נתן בשתי נוסחאות (London, 1887), where it appears side-by-side with the standard version. Until then, *Nusach* 2 was largely unknown; the *Magen Avos* commentary of R' Yom Tov Tzahalon on *Avos DeRabbi Nassan,* which quotes *Nusach* 2 extensively, remained in manuscript and was not published until 2010. *Nusach* 2 has recently been published anew from manuscript, under the title אבות דרבי נתן נוסח אחר (Bnei Brak, 2002).

7. [The sixth chapter of *Avos* is not really part of the Mishnah, but is a Baraisa that was added on; it is not contained in most early editions of the Mishnah, and was not commented on by the major early commentators, such as *Rambam, R' Yonah* and *Rav.*] See *Maharatz Chajes, Imrei Binah* §13, who

discusses at length the order of the Baraisos in *Avos DeRabbi Nassan.*

8. The last chapter in the Venice edition appears as "Chapter 40," but that is because the printer mistakenly repeated chapter number "24" for chapter 25, so the chapter numbering is one off from there to the end. In the early edition of *Avos DeRabbi Nassan* that is printed with the commentary of the *Mefaresh* (R' Eliezer Lipman), the printer further compounded this numbering error with additional numbering errors toward the end, so that the last chapter appears as "Chapter 36." In both editions, however, the text is still divided into forty-one sections, despite the errors in the headers. [*Avos DeRabbi Nassan, Nusach* 2 is divided into forty-eight chapters, or in some manuscripts slightly more.] The Baraisa numbers within each chapter were added in later editions.

text of our edition on the Vilna edition (which in turn is apparently based on the Frankfort edition of the Talmud printed in 1720[9]), not because it is necessarily the most accurate, but because it is the most widepsread. The Vilna edition also references the extensive emendations of the *Gra,* and places in parentheses the words that the *Gra* marks for deletion, with marginal notes to that effect.

In the current work, the all-Hebrew text of the Vilna edition appears on top of the page, including all parentheses and brackets (but without the marginal notes indicating which parentheses represent the deletions of the *Gra*), but with the following differences: Our all-Hebrew text is fully vowelized. Abbreviations are expanded, slight additional punctuation has been added, and the Scriptural references have been expanded to include not only the chapter but the verse as well. All Scriptural citations have been enclosed in quotation marks. We have also preserved the *kesiv malei* spellings of extra *yuds* and *vavs* found in Vilna's unvowelized text, except for Scriptural citations, which we have changed to *kesiv chaseir,* exactly as they appear in *Tanach.* Where we have not included bracketed or parenthesized text in the elucidated section (see next paragraph), we have not vowelized those words in the all-Hebrew text. Also, obvious misspellings have been corrected.

Our elucidated section generally follows the all-Hebrew text, except that we sometimes adopt the reading that omits words in parentheses or brackets. Even when those words are included, the parentheses or brackets enclosing them have been removed. In this way, the Hebrew portion of our elucidated section reads smoothly, unencumbered by brackets or parentheses. On occasion, we adopt in our elucidated section a Hebrew reading not found in the Vilna text, based on the emendation of the *Gra* or one of the other commentators, or on a manuscript reading.[10] In those instances, we have a note explaining the source for that change, and we place a degree sign in the all-Hebrew text where the change is being made.

WE HAVE MADE USE OF MANY COMMENTARIES WRITTEN DIRECTLY ON AVOS DERABBI *Nassan.* Below are the ones we used most extensively:

Commentaries Perhaps the most comprehensive of all is *Magen Avos* by R' Yom Tov Tzahalon (1559-1620), who leaves virtually no topic or nuance of language unaddressed. However, as his commentary remained unpublished until 2010, later commentators did not have his work available to them. The earliest major commentary used by subsequent

---

9. This edition, even in facsimile, is not generally available. However, its text is very close to the one printed with the commentary of *Ahavas Chesed* in Amsterdam (1777), which is widely available on HebrewBooks.org and in the Otzar HaHochma.

10. We consulted several manuscripts, which we mention occasionally in the notes to this work. They are: Oxford, Opp. 95; New York, JTS Rab. 10484 (Epstein); and New York, JTS Rab. 25. This latter manuscript was particularly useful, and was recently

commentators was written by R' Eliezer Lipman (author of *Lekach Tov* on various Aggados), printed in the author's lifetime in 1701, and referred to simply as the *"Mefaresh."* This is quoted consistently in *Binyan Yehoshua* by R' Yehoshua Falk of Lisa (printed in 1788), which is the major commentary that appears on the page of the Vilna edition. *Binyan Yehoshua* is therefore the commentary we generally follow by default.

Three additional commentaries that are especially comprehensive and useful are:

Ahavas Chesed by R' Avraham Witmond (1695-1773), printed in Amsterdam in 1777. The author arranges the work in Gemara format, with the text of *Avos DeRabbi Nassan* in the center of the page (which the author indeed calls "the Gemara"), a concise *Rashi*-like commentary in the inner margin called *Ahavas Chesed* (and which the author refers to as "the *Kuntreis*), and *Tosafos*-like comments in the outer margin, called *Machazeh Avraham*.

Ben Avraham by R' Eliyahu ben Avraham, a disciple of the *Gra*, printed in 1833. The commentary is divided into two parts — on the inner margin is *Shenei Eliyahu*, which deals with the *Gra's* text and emendations, and on the outer margin is *Ben Avraham*, in which the author provides a thorough and incisive commentary, often with ingenious and innovative explanations.

Avos HaRosh by R' Rachamim Palagi (1814-1907) is a series of three commentaries on *Avos DeRabbi Nassan* in three volumes. The author often expands at very great length on a single point or topic, and exhibits vast erudition in citing related teachings and statements from the length and breadth of the entire Talmudic and Midrashic literature.

Also of special note are the commentaries *Velo Od Ella* by R' Eliyahu ben R' Avraham Shlomo HaKohen (1659-1729), *Kisei Rachamim* by the *Chida* (1724-1806), and the very useful contemporary work *Meorei Ohr* by R' Meir Zeev Esrog (Bnei Brak, 2001), which provides a thorough commentary, with many quotes from the earlier commentators, a section containing the full text of the *Gra's* emended text of *Avos DeRabbi Nassan,* and additional footnotes entitled *Tosefes Ohr.*

BECAUSE AVOS DERABBI NASSAN IS REALLY A COMPANION TEXT TO PIRKEI AVOS, which many recite and study in several cycles on Sabbath afternoons between

Special features of this Edition

Pesach and Rosh Hashanah, we have provided the full text and translation of *Pirkei Avos* at the beginning of the book,[11] with marginal references to where a particular teaching or topic is discussed in *Avos DeRabbi Nassan.* In this way, one can use

---

published under the title מסכת אבות דרבי נתן מנוסח צרפת (Bnei Brak, 2002), available also on the Otzar HaHochma.

11. There are two popular systems of numbering the individual Mishnahs within each chapter of *Pirkei Avos*: the one that appears

Avos DeRabbi Nassan and our commentary on it as parallel texts that broaden and deepen our understanding of the timeless Torah truths of *Pirkei Avos,* and add further dimensions to our knowledge of the wisdom of *Chazal.*

---

in the standard editions of Mishnayos and the one that appears in the standard editions of the Siddur. For ease of reference, we have provided the reader with both numbering systems in the text of *Pirkei Avos* at the beginning of the book — the Mishnayos numbering system appears in brackets and bold type, the Siddur numbering system appears in parentheses and non-bold type. [Please note that in our *commentary* on *Avos DeRabbi Nassan,* we refer to specific Mishnahs in *Avos* only according to the Mishnayos numbering system.]

פרקי אבות

Pirkei Avos /
Ethics of the Fathers

Avos DeRabbi Nassan elaborates many of the teachings of *Pirkei Avos*. For this reason, we have included *Pirkei Avos* in this volume, and added a reference in the margin to help find where in *Avos DeRabbi Nassan* these teachings are discussed.

The way each chapter of *Pirkei Avos* is subdivided into Mishnahs differs from the Mishnayos to the Siddur. For ease of reference, we have placed the Mishnah number of the Mishnayos in brackets and bold type, and the one of the Siddur in parentheses and light type.

Marginal references show where *Avos DeRabbi Nassan* discusses the Mishnah's teaching.

פרק ראשון

כָּל יִשְׂרָאֵל יֵשׁ לָהֶם חֵלֶק לָעוֹלָם הַבָּא, שֶׁנֶּאֱמַר: "וְעַמֵּךְ כֻּלָּם צַדִּיקִים, לְעוֹלָם יִירְשׁוּ אָרֶץ, נֵצֶר מַטָּעַי, מַעֲשֵׂה יָדַי לְהִתְפָּאֵר."

❈ ❈ ❈

[א] (א) **מֹשֶׁה** קִבֵּל תּוֹרָה מִסִּינַי, וּמְסָרָהּ לִיהוֹשֻׁעַ, וִיהוֹשֻׁעַ לִזְקֵנִים, וּזְקֵנִים לִנְבִיאִים, וּנְבִיאִים מְסָרוּהָ לְאַנְשֵׁי כְנֶסֶת הַגְּדוֹלָה. הֵם אָמְרוּ שְׁלֹשָׁה דְבָרִים, הֱווּ מְתוּנִים בַּדִּין, וְהַעֲמִידוּ תַלְמִידִים הַרְבֵּה, וַעֲשׂוּ סְיָג לַתּוֹרָה.

פרק א־ב
(p. 46)

[ב] (ב) שִׁמְעוֹן הַצַּדִּיק הָיָה מִשְּׁיָרֵי כְנֶסֶת הַגְּדוֹלָה. הוּא הָיָה אוֹמֵר, עַל שְׁלֹשָׁה דְבָרִים הָעוֹלָם עוֹמֵד, עַל הַתּוֹרָה, וְעַל הָעֲבוֹדָה, וְעַל גְּמִילוּת חֲסָדִים.

ד, א־ה
(p. 141)

[ג] (ג) אַנְטִיגְנוֹס אִישׁ סוֹכוֹ קִבֵּל מִשִּׁמְעוֹן הַצַּדִּיק. הוּא הָיָה אוֹמֵר, אַל תִּהְיוּ כַעֲבָדִים הַמְשַׁמְּשִׁין אֶת הָרַב עַל מְנָת לְקַבֵּל פְּרָס, אֶלָּא הֱווּ כַעֲבָדִים הַמְשַׁמְּשִׁין אֶת הָרַב שֶׁלֹּא עַל מְנָת לְקַבֵּל פְּרָס, וִיהִי מוֹרָא שָׁמַיִם עֲלֵיכֶם.

פרק ה
(p. 161)

[ד] (ד) יוֹסֵי בֶן יוֹעֶזֶר אִישׁ צְרֵדָה וְיוֹסֵי בֶן יוֹחָנָן אִישׁ יְרוּשָׁלַיִם קִבְּלוּ מֵהֶם. יוֹסֵי בֶן יוֹעֶזֶר אִישׁ צְרֵדָה אוֹמֵר, יְהִי בֵיתְךָ בֵית וַעַד לַחֲכָמִים, וֶהֱוֵי מִתְאַבֵּק בַּעֲפַר רַגְלֵיהֶם, וֶהֱוֵי שׁוֹתֶה בְצָמָא אֶת דִּבְרֵיהֶם.

פרק ו
(p. 164)

[ה] (ה) יוֹסֵי בֶן יוֹחָנָן אִישׁ יְרוּשָׁלַיִם אוֹמֵר יְהִי בֵיתְךָ פָּתוּחַ לִרְוָחָה, וְיִהְיוּ עֲנִיִּים בְּנֵי בֵיתֶךָ, וְאַל תַּרְבֶּה שִׂיחָה עִם הָאִשָּׁה. בְּאִשְׁתּוֹ אָמְרוּ, קַל וָחֹמֶר בְּאֵשֶׁת חֲבֵרוֹ. מִכָּאן אָמְרוּ חֲכָמִים, כָּל זְמַן שֶׁאָדָם מַרְבֶּה שִׂיחָה עִם הָאִשָּׁה, גּוֹרֵם רָעָה לְעַצְמוֹ, וּבוֹטֵל מִדִּבְרֵי תוֹרָה, וְסוֹפוֹ יוֹרֵשׁ גֵּיהִנֹּם.

פרק ז
(p. 181)

[ו] (ו) יְהוֹשֻׁעַ בֶּן פְּרַחְיָה וְנִתַּאי הָאַרְבֵּלִי קִבְּלוּ מֵהֶם. יְהוֹשֻׁעַ בֶּן פְּרַחְיָה אוֹמֵר, עֲשֵׂה לְךָ רַב, וּקְנֵה לְךָ חָבֵר, וֶהֱוֵי דָן אֶת כָּל הָאָדָם לְכַף זְכוּת.

פרק ח
(p. 189)

[ז] (ז) נִתַּאי הָאַרְבֵּלִי אוֹמֵר, הַרְחֵק מִשָּׁכֵן רָע, וְאַל תִּתְחַבֵּר לָרָשָׁע, וְאַל תִּתְיָאֵשׁ מִן הַפֻּרְעָנוּת.

פרק ט
(p. 202)

AVOS DR"N

Marginal references show where *Avos DeRabbi Nassan*
discusses the Mishnah's teaching.

CHAPTER ONE

All Israel has a share in the World to Come, as it is said: "And your people are all righteous; they shall inherit the land forever; they are the branch of My planting, My handiwork, in which to take pride."

❦ ❦ ❦

ch. 1-2
(p. 46)

[1] (1) **מֹשֶׁה** *Moses received the Torah from Sinai and transmitted it to Joshua; Joshua to the Elders; the Elders to the Prophets; and the Prophets transmitted it to the Men of the Great Assembly. They [the Men of the Great Assembly] said three things: Be deliberate in judgment; develop many disciples; and make a fence for the Torah.*

4 §1-5
(p. 141)

[2] (2) *Shimon the Righteous was among the survivors of the Great Assembly. He used to say: The world depends on three things — on Torah study, on the service [of God], and on kind deeds.*

ch. 5
(p. 161)

[3] (3) *Antigonus, leader of Socho, received the tradition from Shimon the Righteous. He used to say: Be not like servants who serve their master for the sake of receiving a reward; instead be like servants who serve their master not for the sake of receiving a reward. And let the awe of Heaven be upon you.*

ch. 6
(p. 164)

[4] (4) *Yose ben Yoezer, leader of Tz'redah, and Yose ben Yochanan, leader of Jerusalem, received the tradition from them. Yose ben Yoezer, leader of Tz'redah, says: Let your house be a meeting place for sages; sit in the dust of their feet; and drink in their words thirstily.*

ch. 7
(p. 181)

[5] (5) *Yose ben Yochanan, leader of Jerusalem, says: Let your house be open wide; treat the poor as members of your household; and do not converse excessively with a woman. They said this even about one's own wife; surely it applies to another's wife. Consequently, the Sages said: Anyone who converses excessively with a woman causes evil to himself, neglects Torah study, and will eventually inherit Gehinnom.*

ch. 8
(p. 189)

[6] (6) *Yehoshua ben Perachyah and Nittai of Arbel received the tradition from them. Yehoshua ben Perachyah says: Accept a teacher upon yourself, acquire a friend for yourself, and judge everyone favorably.*

ch. 9
(p. 202)

[7] (7) *Nittai of Arbel says: Distance yourself from a bad neighbor; do not associate with a wicked person; and do not despair of retribution.*

[ח] (ח) יְהוּדָה בֶן טַבַּאי וְשִׁמְעוֹן בֶּן שָׁטַח קִבְּלוּ מֵהֶם. יְהוּדָה בֶּן טַבַּאי אוֹמֵר, אַל תַּעַשׂ עַצְמְךָ כְּעוֹרְכֵי הַדַּיָּנִין. וּכְשֶׁיִּהְיוּ בַעֲלֵי דִינִין עוֹמְדִים לְפָנֶיךָ יִהְיוּ בְעֵינֶיךָ כִּרְשָׁעִים. וּכְשֶׁנִּפְטָרִים מִלְּפָנֶיךָ יִהְיוּ בְעֵינֶיךָ כְּזַכָּאִין, כְּשֶׁקִּבְּלוּ עֲלֵיהֶם אֶת הַדִּין.

[ט] (ט) שִׁמְעוֹן בֶּן שָׁטַח אוֹמֵר, הֱוֵי מַרְבֶּה לַחֲקֹר אֶת הָעֵדִים, וֶהֱוֵי זָהִיר בִּדְבָרֶיךָ, שֶׁמָּא מִתּוֹכָם יִלְמְדוּ לְשַׁקֵּר.

[י] (י) שְׁמַעְיָה וְאַבְטַלְיוֹן קִבְּלוּ מֵהֶם. שְׁמַעְיָה אוֹמֵר, אֱהַב אֶת הַמְּלָאכָה, וּשְׂנָא אֶת הָרַבָּנוּת, וְאַל תִּתְוַדַּע לָרָשׁוּת.

[יא] (יא) אַבְטַלְיוֹן אוֹמֵר, חֲכָמִים, הִזָּהֲרוּ בְדִבְרֵיכֶם, שֶׁמָּא תָחוּבוּ חוֹבַת גָּלוּת וְתִגְלוּ לִמְקוֹם מַיִם הָרָעִים, וְיִשְׁתּוּ הַתַּלְמִידִים הַבָּאִים אַחֲרֵיכֶם וְיָמוּתוּ, וְנִמְצָא שֵׁם שָׁמַיִם מִתְחַלֵּל.

[יב] (יב) הִלֵּל וְשַׁמַּאי קִבְּלוּ מֵהֶם. הִלֵּל אוֹמֵר, הֱוֵי מִתַּלְמִידָיו שֶׁל אַהֲרֹן, אוֹהֵב שָׁלוֹם וְרוֹדֵף שָׁלוֹם, אוֹהֵב אֶת הַבְּרִיּוֹת וּמְקָרְבָן לַתּוֹרָה.

[יג] (יג) הוּא הָיָה אוֹמֵר, נְגַד שְׁמָא, אֲבַד שְׁמֵהּ. וּדְלָא מוֹסִיף, יָסֵיף. וּדְלָא יָלִיף, קְטָלָא חַיָּב. וּדְאִשְׁתַּמֵּשׁ בְּתָגָא, חֲלָף.

[יד] (יד) הוּא הָיָה אוֹמֵר, אִם אֵין אֲנִי לִי מִי לִי. וּכְשֶׁאֲנִי לְעַצְמִי מָה אֲנִי. וְאִם לֹא עַכְשָׁיו אֵימָתָי.

[טו] (טו) שַׁמַּאי אוֹמֵר, עֲשֵׂה תוֹרָתְךָ קֶבַע. אֱמוֹר מְעַט וַעֲשֵׂה הַרְבֵּה, וֶהֱוֵי מְקַבֵּל אֶת כָּל הָאָדָם בְּסֵבֶר פָּנִים יָפוֹת.

[טז] (טז) רַבָּן גַּמְלִיאֵל הָיָה אוֹמֵר, עֲשֵׂה לְךָ רַב, וְהִסְתַּלֵּק מִן הַסָּפֵק, וְאַל תַּרְבֶּה לְעַשֵּׂר אֹמָדוֹת.

[יז] (יז) שִׁמְעוֹן בְּנוֹ אוֹמֵר, כָּל יָמַי גָּדַלְתִּי בֵּין הַחֲכָמִים, וְלֹא מָצָאתִי לַגּוּף טוֹב אֶלָּא שְׁתִיקָה. וְלֹא הַמִּדְרָשׁ הוּא הָעִקָּר, אֶלָּא הַמַּעֲשֶׂה. וְכָל הַמַּרְבֶּה דְבָרִים מֵבִיא חֵטְא.

[יח] (יח) רַבָּן שִׁמְעוֹן בֶּן גַּמְלִיאֵל אוֹמֵר, עַל שְׁלֹשָׁה דְבָרִים הָעוֹלָם עוֹמֵד עַל הַדִּין, וְעַל הָאֱמֶת, וְעַל הַשָּׁלוֹם, שֶׁנֶּאֱמַר, אֱמֶת וּמִשְׁפַּט שָׁלוֹם שִׁפְטוּ בְּשַׁעֲרֵיכֶם.

⁂ ⁂ ⁂

[8] (8) *Yehudah ben Tabbai and Shimon ben Shatach received the tradition from them. Yehudah ben Tabbai says: [When serving as a judge] do not act as a lawyer; when the litigants stand before you, consider them both as guilty; but when they are dismissed from you, consider them both as innocent, provided they have accepted the judgment.*

[9] (9) *Shimon ben Shatach says: Interrogate the witnesses extensively; and be cautious with your words, lest they learn to lie.*

[10] (10) *Shemayah and Avtalyon received the tradition from them. Shemayah says: Love work; despise lordliness; and do not become overly familiar with the government.*

[11] (11) *Avtalyon says: Scholars, be cautious with your words, for you may incur the penalty of exile and be banished to a place of evil waters [heresy]. The disciples who follow you there may drink and die, and consequently the Name of Heaven will be desecrated.*

[12] (12) *Hillel and Shammai received the tradition from them. Hillel says: Be among the disciples of Aaron, loving peace and pursuing peace, loving people, and bringing them closer to the Torah.*

[13] (13) *He used to say: He who seeks renown loses his reputation; he who does not increase [his Torah learning] decreases it; he who refuses to teach [Torah] deserves death; and he who exploits the crown of Torah shall fade away.*

[14] (14) *He used to say: If I am not for myself, who will be for me? And if I am for myself, what am I? And if not now, when?*

[15] (15) *Shammai says: Make your Torah study a fixed practice; say little and do much; and receive everyone with a cheerful face.*

[16] (16) *Rabban Gamliel used to say: Accept a teacher upon yourself and remove yourself from uncertainty; and do not give excess tithes by estimating [instead of measuring].*

[17] (17) *Shimon his son says: All my days I have been raised among the Sages and I found nothing better for oneself than silence; not study, but practice is the main thing; and one who talks excessively brings on sin.*

[18] (18) *Rabban Shimon ben Gamliel says: The world endures on three things — justice, truth, and peace, as it is said: "Truth and the verdict of peace are you to adjudicate in your gates."*

❧   ❧   ❧

אבות דר"נ

רַבִּי חֲנַנְיָא בֶּן עֲקַשְׁיָא אוֹמֵר: רָצָה הַקָּדוֹשׁ בָּרוּךְ הוּא לְזַכּוֹת
אֶת יִשְׂרָאֵל, לְפִיכָךְ הִרְבָּה לָהֶם תּוֹרָה וּמִצְוֹת, שֶׁנֶּאֱמַר: „יהוה
חָפֵץ לְמַעַן צִדְקוֹ, יַגְדִּיל תּוֹרָה וְיַאְדִּיר".

פרק שני

כָּל יִשְׂרָאֵל יֵשׁ לָהֶם חֵלֶק לָעוֹלָם הַבָּא, שֶׁנֶּאֱמַר: „וְעַמֵּךְ כֻּלָּם
צַדִּיקִים, לְעוֹלָם יִירְשׁוּ אָרֶץ, נֵצֶר מַטָּעַי, מַעֲשֵׂה יָדַי לְהִתְפָּאֵר".

❋ ❋ ❋

[א] (א) **רַבִּי** אוֹמֵר, אֵיזוֹהִי דֶרֶךְ יְשָׁרָה שֶׁיָּבוֹר לוֹ הָאָדָם, כֹּל
שֶׁהִיא תִפְאֶרֶת לְעוֹשֶׂהָ וְתִפְאֶרֶת לוֹ מִן הָאָדָם.

וֶהֱוֵי זָהִיר בְּמִצְוָה קַלָּה כְּבַחֲמוּרָה, שֶׁאֵין אַתָּה יוֹדֵעַ מַתַּן
שְׂכָרָן שֶׁל מִצְוֹת. וֶהֱוֵי מְחַשֵּׁב הֶפְסֵד מִצְוָה כְּנֶגֶד שְׂכָרָהּ,
וּשְׂכַר עֲבֵרָה כְּנֶגֶד הֶפְסֵדָהּ. וְהִסְתַּכֵּל בִּשְׁלשָׁה דְבָרִים וְאִי
אַתָּה בָא לִידֵי עֲבֵרָה, דַּע מַה לְמַעְלָה מִמְּךָ, עַיִן רוֹאָה, וְאֹזֶן
שׁוֹמַעַת, וְכָל מַעֲשֶׂיךָ בַּסֵּפֶר נִכְתָּבִין.

[ב] (ב) רַבָּן גַּמְלִיאֵל בְּנוֹ שֶׁל רַבִּי יְהוּדָה הַנָּשִׂיא אוֹמֵר, יָפֶה
תַלְמוּד תּוֹרָה עִם דֶּרֶךְ אֶרֶץ, שֶׁיְּגִיעַת שְׁנֵיהֶם מַשְׁכַּחַת
עָוֹן. וְכָל תּוֹרָה שֶׁאֵין עִמָּהּ מְלָאכָה, סוֹפָהּ בְּטֵלָה וְגוֹרֶרֶת עָוֹן.
וְכָל הָעֲמֵלִים עִם הַצִּבּוּר, יִהְיוּ עֲמֵלִים עִמָּהֶם לְשֵׁם שָׁמַיִם,
שֶׁזְּכוּת אֲבוֹתָם מְסַיַּעְתָּן וְצִדְקָתָם עוֹמֶדֶת לָעַד. וְאַתֶּם, מַעֲלֶה
אֲנִי עֲלֵיכֶם שָׂכָר הַרְבֵּה כְּאִלּוּ עֲשִׂיתֶם.

[ג] (ג) הֱווּ זְהִירִין בָּרָשׁוּת, שֶׁאֵין מְקָרְבִין לוֹ לָאָדָם אֶלָּא לְצֹרֶךְ
עַצְמָן, נִרְאִין כְּאוֹהֲבִין בְּשָׁעַת הֲנָאָתָן, וְאֵין עוֹמְדִין לוֹ
לָאָדָם בִּשְׁעַת דָּחְקוֹ.

[ד] (ד) הוּא הָיָה אוֹמֵר, עֲשֵׂה רְצוֹנוֹ כִּרְצוֹנֶךָ, כְּדֵי שֶׁיַּעֲשֶׂה
רְצוֹנְךָ כִּרְצוֹנוֹ. בַּטֵּל רְצוֹנְךָ מִפְּנֵי רְצוֹנוֹ, כְּדֵי שֶׁיְּבַטֵּל
רְצוֹן אֲחֵרִים מִפְּנֵי רְצוֹנֶךָ.

(ה) הִלֵּל אוֹמֵר, אַל תִּפְרֹשׁ מִן הַצִּבּוּר, וְאַל תַּאֲמֵן בְּעַצְמְךָ
עַד יוֹם מוֹתְךָ, וְאַל תָּדִין אֶת חֲבֵרְךָ עַד שֶׁתַּגִּיעַ לִמְקוֹמוֹ,
°וְאַל תֹּאמַר דָּבָר שֶׁאִי אֶפְשָׁר לִשְׁמֹעַ שֶׁסּוֹפוֹ לְהִשָּׁמַע, וְאַל
תֹּאמַר לִכְשֶׁאֶפָּנֶה אֶשְׁנֶה, שֶׁמָּא לֹא תִפָּנֶה.

כח, ח
(p. 406)
ראה כח, ז
(p. 406)
כו, ג
(p. 387)

[ה] (ו) הוּא הָיָה אוֹמֵר, אֵין בּוּר יְרֵא חֵטְא, וְלֹא עַם
הָאָרֶץ חָסִיד, וְלֹא הַבַּיְשָׁן לָמֵד, וְלֹא הַקַּפְּדָן מְלַמֵּד,

AVOS DR"N

Rabbi Chanania ben Akashia says: The Holy One, Blessed is He, wished to confer merit upon Israel; therefore He gave them Torah and mitzvos in abundance, as it is said: "HASHEM desired, for the sake of its [Israel's] righteousness, that the Torah be made great and glorious."

CHAPTER TWO

All Israel has a share in the World to Come, as it is said: "And your people are all righteous; they shall inherit the land forever; they are the branch of My planting, My handiwork, in which to take pride."

❧ ❧ ❧

[1] (1) **רַבִּי** *Rebbi says: Which is the proper path that a man should choose for himself? Whatever is a credit to himself and earns him the esteem of fellow men. Be as scrupulous in performing a "minor" mitzvah as in a "major" one, for you do not know the reward given for the respective mitzvos. Calculate the cost of a mitzvah against its reward, and the reward of a sin against its cost. Consider three things and you will not come into the grip of sin: Know what is above you — a watchful Eye, an attentive Ear, and all your deeds are recorded in a Book.*

[2] (2) *Rabban Gamliel, the son of Rabbi Yehudah HaNassi, says: Torah study is good together with an occupation, for the exertion of them both makes sin forgotten. All Torah study that is not joined with work will cease in the end, and leads to sin. All who exert themselves for the community should exert themselves for the sake of Heaven, for then the merit of the community's forefathers aids them, and their righteousness endures forever. Nevertheless, as for you, I [God] will bestow upon you as great a reward as if you had accomplished it on your own.*

[3] (3) *Beware of rulers, for they befriend someone only for their own benefit; they act friendly when it benefits them, but they do not stand by someone in his time of need.*

[4] (4) *He used to say: Treat His Will as if it were your own will, so that He will treat your will as if it were His Will. Nullify your will before His Will, so that He will nullify the will of others before your will.*

28 §8;
(p. 406)

°see 28 §7
(p. 406)

(5) *Hillel says: Do not separate yourself from the community; do not believe in yourself until the day you die; do not judge your fellow until you have reached his place; °and do not say what cannot be easily understood on the grounds that it will be understood eventually; and do not say, "When I am free I will study," for perhaps you will not become free.*

26 §3
(p. 387)

[5] (6) *He used to say: A boor cannot be fearful of sin; an unlearned person cannot be scrupulously pious; the bashful person cannot learn, and the quick, impatient person cannot teach;*

וְלֹא כָל הַמַּרְבֶּה בִּסְחוֹרָה מַחְכִּים. וּבְמָקוֹם שֶׁאֵין אֲנָשִׁים, הִשְׁתַּדֵּל לִהְיוֹת אִישׁ.

יב, יב (p. 257)

[ו] (ז) אַף הוּא רָאָה גֻלְגֹּלֶת אַחַת שֶׁצָּפָה עַל פְּנֵי הַמָּיִם. אָמַר (לָהּ), עַל דְּאַטֵּפְתְּ, אַטְפוּךְ, וְסוֹף מְטַיְּפַיִךְ, יְטוּפוּן.

ראה כח, ט (p. 407)

[ז] (ח) הוּא הָיָה אוֹמֵר, מַרְבֶּה בָשָׂר, מַרְבֶּה רִמָּה. מַרְבֶּה נְכָסִים, מַרְבֶּה דְאָגָה. מַרְבֶּה נָשִׁים, מַרְבֶּה כְשָׁפִים. מַרְבֶּה שְׁפָחוֹת, מַרְבֶּה זִמָּה. מַרְבֶּה עֲבָדִים, מַרְבֶּה גָזֵל. מַרְבֶּה תוֹרָה, מַרְבֶּה חַיִּים. מַרְבֶּה יְשִׁיבָה, מַרְבֶּה חָכְמָה. מַרְבֶּה עֵצָה, מַרְבֶּה תְבוּנָה. מַרְבֶּה צְדָקָה, מַרְבֶּה שָׁלוֹם. קָנָה שֵׁם טוֹב, קָנָה לְעַצְמוֹ. קָנָה לוֹ דִבְרֵי תוֹרָה, קָנָה לוֹ חַיֵּי הָעוֹלָם הַבָּא.

יד, א-ד (p. 267)

[ח] (ט) רַבָּן יוֹחָנָן בֶּן זַכַּאי קִבֵּל מֵהִלֵּל וּמִשַּׁמַּאי. הוּא הָיָה אוֹמֵר, אִם לָמַדְתָּ תוֹרָה הַרְבֵּה, אַל תַּחֲזִיק טוֹבָה לְעַצְמְךָ, כִּי לְכָךְ נוֹצָרְתָּ.

(י) חֲמִשָּׁה תַלְמִידִים הָיוּ לוֹ לְרַבָּן יוֹחָנָן בֶּן זַכַּאי, וְאֵלּוּ הֵן, רַבִּי אֱלִיעֶזֶר בֶּן הֻרְקָנוֹס, וְרַבִּי יְהוֹשֻׁעַ בֶּן חֲנַנְיָה, וְרַבִּי יוֹסֵי הַכֹּהֵן, וְרַבִּי שִׁמְעוֹן בֶּן נְתַנְאֵל, וְרַבִּי אֶלְעָזָר בֶּן עֲרָךְ.

(יא) הוּא הָיָה מוֹנֶה שְׁבָחָן. רַבִּי אֱלִיעֶזֶר בֶּן הֻרְקָנוֹס, בּוֹר סוּד שֶׁאֵינוֹ מְאַבֵּד טִפָּה. רַבִּי יְהוֹשֻׁעַ בֶּן חֲנַנְיָה, אַשְׁרֵי יוֹלַדְתּוֹ. רַבִּי יוֹסֵי הַכֹּהֵן, חָסִיד. רַבִּי שִׁמְעוֹן בֶּן נְתַנְאֵל, יְרֵא חֵטְא. וְרַבִּי אֶלְעָזָר בֶּן עֲרָךְ, מַעְיָן הַמִּתְגַּבֵּר.

(יב) הוּא הָיָה אוֹמֵר, אִם יִהְיוּ כָל חַכְמֵי יִשְׂרָאֵל בְּכַף מֹאזְנַיִם, וֶאֱלִיעֶזֶר בֶּן הֻרְקָנוֹס בְּכַף שְׁנִיָּה, מַכְרִיעַ אֶת כֻּלָּם. אַבָּא שָׁאוּל אוֹמֵר מִשְּׁמוֹ, אִם יִהְיוּ כָל חַכְמֵי יִשְׂרָאֵל בְּכַף מֹאזְנַיִם, וְרַבִּי אֱלִיעֶזֶר בֶּן הֻרְקָנוֹס אַף עִמָּהֶם, וְרַבִּי אֶלְעָזָר בֶּן עֲרָךְ בְּכַף שְׁנִיָּה, מַכְרִיעַ אֶת כֻּלָּם.

יד, ה (p. 271)

[ט] (יג) אָמַר לָהֶם, צְאוּ וּרְאוּ אֵיזוֹהִי דֶרֶךְ יְשָׁרָה שֶׁיִּדְבַּק בָּהּ הָאָדָם. רַבִּי אֱלִיעֶזֶר אוֹמֵר, עַיִן טוֹבָה. רַבִּי יְהוֹשֻׁעַ אוֹמֵר, חָבֵר טוֹב. רַבִּי יוֹסֵי אוֹמֵר, שָׁכֵן טוֹב. רַבִּי שִׁמְעוֹן אוֹמֵר, הָרוֹאֶה אֶת הַנּוֹלָד. רַבִּי אֶלְעָזָר אוֹמֵר, לֵב טוֹב. אָמַר לָהֶם, רוֹאֶה אֲנִי אֶת דִּבְרֵי אֶלְעָזָר בֶּן עֲרָךְ מִדִּבְרֵיכֶם, שֶׁבִּכְלַל דְּבָרָיו דִּבְרֵיכֶם.

AVOS DR″N anyone excessively occupied in business cannot become a scholar; and in a place where there are no leaders, strive to be a leader.

12 §12
(p. 257) **[6]** (7) He also saw a skull floating on the water; he said to it: "Because you drowned others, they drowned you; and those who drowned you will be drowned eventually."

see 28 §9
(p. 407) **[7]** (8) He used to say: The more flesh, the more worms; the more possessions, the more worry; the more wives, the more witchcraft; the more maidservants, the more lewdness; the more manservants, the more thievery. [However,] the more Torah, the more life; the more study, the more wisdom; the more counsel, the more understanding; the more charity, the more peace. One who has gained a good reputation has gained it for his own benefit; one who has gained himself Torah knowledge has gained himself the life of the World to Come.

14 §1-4
(p. 267) **[8]** (9) Rabban Yochanan ben Zakkai received the tradition from Hillel and Shammai. He used to say: If you have studied much Torah, do not take credit for yourself, because that is what you were created to do.

(10) Rabban Yochanan ben Zakkai had five [primary] disciples. They were: Rabbi Eliezer ben Hyrkanos, Rabbi Yehoshua ben Chanania, Rabbi Yose the Kohen, Rabbi Shimon ben Nesanel, and Rabbi Elazar ben Arach.

(11) He used to enumerate their praises: Rabbi Eliezer ben Hyrkanos is like a cemented cistern that loses not a drop; Rabbi Yehoshua ben Chanania, praiseworthy is she who bore him; Rabbi Yose the Kohen is a scrupulously pious person; Rabbi Shimon ben Nesanel fears sin; and Rabbi Elazar ben Arach is like a spring flowing stronger and stronger.

(12) He used to say: If all the Sages of Israel were on one pan of a balance scale, and Eliezer ben Hyrkanos were on the other, he would outweigh them all. Abba Shaul said in his name: If all the Sages of Israel, with even Rabbi Eliezer ben Hyrkanos among them, were on one pan of the balance scale, and Rabbi Elazar ben Arach were on the other, he would outweigh them all.

14 §5
(p. 271) **[9]** (13) He said to them: Go out and discern which is the proper way to which a man should cling. Rabbi Eliezer says: A good eye. Rabbi Yehoshua says: A good friend. Rabbi Yose says: A good neighbor. Rabbi Shimon says: One who considers the outcome of a deed. Rabbi Elazar says: A good heart. He [Rabban Yochanan ben Zakkai] said to them: I prefer the words of Elazar ben Arach to your words, for your words are included in his words.

(יד) אָמַר לָהֶם, צְאוּ וּרְאוּ אֵיזוֹהִי דֶּרֶךְ רָעָה שֶׁיִּתְרַחֵק מִמֶּנָּה הָאָדָם. רַבִּי אֱלִיעֶזֶר אוֹמֵר, עַיִן רָעָה. רַבִּי יְהוֹשֻׁעַ אוֹמֵר, חָבֵר רָע. רַבִּי יוֹסֵי אוֹמֵר, שָׁכֵן רָע. רַבִּי שִׁמְעוֹן אוֹמֵר, הַלֹּוֶה וְאֵינוֹ מְשַׁלֵּם. אֶחָד הַלֹּוֶה מִן הָאָדָם, כְּלֹוֶה מִן הַמָּקוֹם בָּרוּךְ הוּא, שֶׁנֶּאֱמַר, לֹוֶה רָשָׁע וְלֹא יְשַׁלֵּם, וְצַדִּיק חוֹנֵן וְנוֹתֵן. רַבִּי אֶלְעָזָר אוֹמֵר, לֵב רָע. אָמַר לָהֶם, רוֹאֶה אֲנִי אֶת דִּבְרֵי אֶלְעָזָר בֶּן עֲרָךְ מִדִּבְרֵיכֶם, שֶׁבִּכְלָל דְּבָרָיו דִּבְרֵיכֶם.

[י] (טו) הֵם אָמְרוּ שְׁלֹשָׁה (שְׁלֹשָׁה) דְבָרִים. רַבִּי אֱלִיעֶזֶר אוֹמֵר, יְהִי כְבוֹד חֲבֵרְךָ חָבִיב עָלֶיךָ כְּשֶׁלָּךְ, וְאַל תְּהִי נוֹחַ לִכְעֹס. וְשׁוּב יוֹם אֶחָד לִפְנֵי מִיתָתָךְ. וֶהֱוֵי מִתְחַמֵּם כְּנֶגֶד אוּרָן שֶׁל חֲכָמִים, וֶהֱוֵי זָהִיר בְּגַחַלְתָּן שֶׁלֹּא תִכָּוֶה, שֶׁנְּשִׁיכָתָן נְשִׁיכַת שׁוּעָל, וַעֲקִיצָתָן עֲקִיצַת עַקְרָב, וּלְחִישָׁתָן לְחִישַׁת שָׂרָף, וְכָל דִּבְרֵיהֶם כְּגַחֲלֵי אֵשׁ.

[יא] (טז) רַבִּי יְהוֹשֻׁעַ אוֹמֵר, עַיִן הָרָע, וְיֵצֶר הָרָע, וְשִׂנְאַת הַבְּרִיּוֹת, מוֹצִיאִין אֶת הָאָדָם מִן הָעוֹלָם.

[יב] (יז) רַבִּי יוֹסֵי אוֹמֵר, יְהִי מָמוֹן חֲבֵרְךָ חָבִיב עָלֶיךָ כְּשֶׁלָּךְ. וְהַתְקֵן עַצְמְךָ לִלְמֹד תּוֹרָה, שֶׁאֵינָה יְרֻשָּׁה לָךְ. וְכָל מַעֲשֶׂיךָ יִהְיוּ לְשֵׁם שָׁמָיִם.

[יג] (יח) רַבִּי שִׁמְעוֹן אוֹמֵר, הֱוֵי זָהִיר בִּקְרִיאַת שְׁמַע וּבִתְפִלָּה. וּכְשֶׁאַתָּה מִתְפַּלֵּל, אַל תַּעַשׂ תְּפִלָּתְךָ קֶבַע, אֶלָּא רַחֲמִים וְתַחֲנוּנִים לִפְנֵי הַמָּקוֹם בָּרוּךְ הוּא, שֶׁנֶּאֱמַר, כִּי חַנּוּן וְרַחוּם הוּא אֶרֶךְ אַפַּיִם וְרַב חֶסֶד וְנִחָם עַל הָרָעָה. וְאַל תְּהִי רָשָׁע בִּפְנֵי עַצְמֶךָ.

[יד] (יט) רַבִּי אֶלְעָזָר אוֹמֵר, הֱוֵי שָׁקוּד לִלְמֹד תּוֹרָה, וְדַע מַה שֶּׁתָּשִׁיב לָאֶפִּיקוֹרוֹס. וְדַע לִפְנֵי מִי אַתָּה עָמֵל. וְנֶאֱמָן הוּא בַּעַל מְלַאכְתְּךָ שֶׁיְּשַׁלֵּם לָךְ שְׂכַר פְּעֻלָּתֶךָ.

[טו] (כ) רַבִּי טַרְפוֹן אוֹמֵר, הַיּוֹם קָצָר וְהַמְּלָאכָה מְרֻבָּה, וְהַפּוֹעֲלִים עֲצֵלִים, וְהַשָּׂכָר הַרְבֵּה, וּבַעַל הַבַּיִת דּוֹחֵק.

[טז] (כא) הוּא הָיָה אוֹמֵר, לֹא עָלֶיךָ הַמְּלָאכָה לִגְמֹר, וְלֹא אַתָּה בֶן חוֹרִין לִבָּטֵל מִמֶּנָּה. אִם לָמַדְתָּ תּוֹרָה

AVOS DR"N (14) *He said to them: Go out and discern which is the evil path from which a man should distance himself. Rabbi Eliezer says: An evil eye. Rabbi Yehoshua says: A wicked friend. Rabbi Yose says: A wicked neighbor. Rabbi Shimon says: One who borrows and does not repay; one who borrows from man is like one who borrows from the Omnipresent, as it is said: "The wicked one borrows and does not repay, but the Righteous One is gracious and gives." Rabbi Elazar said: A wicked heart. He [Rabban Yochanan ben Zakkai] said to them: I prefer the words of Elazar ben Arach to your words, for your words are included in his words.*

ch. 15 (p. 279) **[10]** (15) *They each said three things. Rabbi Eliezer says: (a) Let your fellow's honor be as dear to you as your own and do not anger easily; (b) repent one day before your death; and (c) warm yourself by the fire of the Sages, but beware of their glowing coal lest you be burnt — for their bite is the bite of a fox, their sting is the sting of a scorpion, their hiss is the hiss of a serpent, and all their words are like fiery coals.*

ch. 16 (p. 291) **[11]** (16) *Rabbi Yehoshua says: (a) An evil eye, (b) the evil inclination, and (c) hatred of other people remove a person from the world.*

17 §1-3; 7 (p. 306; 314) **[12]** (17) *Rabbi Yose says: (a) Let your fellow's money be as dear to you as your own; (b) apply yourself to study Torah, for it is not yours by inheritance; and (c) let all your deeds be for the sake of Heaven.*

17 §8 (p. 314) **[13]** (18) *Rabbi Shimon says: (a) Be meticulous in reading the Shema and in prayer; (b) when you pray, do not make your prayer a set routine, but rather [beg for] compassion and supplication before the Omnipresent, as it is said: "For He is gracious and compassionate, slow to anger, abounding in kindness, and relentful of punishment"; and (c) do not judge yourself to be a wicked person.*

17 §8 (p. 315) **[14]** (19) *Rabbi Elazar says: (a) Be diligent in the study of Torah and know what to answer a heretic; (b) know before Whom you toil; and (c) know that your Employer can be relied upon to pay you the wage of your labor.*

[15] (20) *Rabbi Tarfon says: The day is short, the task is abundant, the laborers are lazy, the wage is great, and the Master of the house is insistent.*

see 27 §2 (p. 396) **[16]** (21) *He used to say: You are not required to complete the task, yet you are not free to withdraw from it. If you have studied*

אבות ד״ר נ

הַרְבֵּה, נוֹתְנִים לְךָ שָׂכָר הַרְבֵּה. וְנֶאֱמָן הוּא בַּעַל מְלַאכְתְּךָ שֶׁיְּשַׁלֶּם לְךָ שְׂכַר פְּעֻלָּתֶךָ. וְדַע, מַתַּן שְׂכָרָן שֶׁל צַדִּיקִים לֶעָתִיד לָבוֹא.

☙ ☙ ☙

רַבִּי חֲנַנְיָא בֶּן עֲקַשְׁיָא אוֹמֵר: רָצָה הַקָּדוֹשׁ בָּרוּךְ הוּא לְזַכּוֹת אֶת יִשְׂרָאֵל, לְפִיכָךְ הִרְבָּה לָהֶם תּוֹרָה וּמִצְוֹת, שֶׁנֶּאֱמַר: ״יהוה חָפֵץ לְמַעַן צִדְקוֹ, יַגְדִּיל תּוֹרָה וְיַאְדִּיר״.

פרק שלישי

כָּל יִשְׂרָאֵל יֵשׁ לָהֶם חֵלֶק לְעוֹלָם הַבָּא, שֶׁנֶּאֱמַר: ״וְעַמֵּךְ כֻּלָּם צַדִּיקִים, לְעוֹלָם יִירְשׁוּ אָרֶץ, נֵצֶר מַטָּעַי, מַעֲשֵׂה יָדַי לְהִתְפָּאֵר״.

☙ ☙ ☙

יט, א-ג
(p. 325)

[א] (א) **עֲקַבְיָא** בֶּן מַהֲלַלְאֵל אוֹמֵר, הִסְתַּכֵּל בִּשְׁלֹשָׁה דְּבָרִים, וְאִי אַתָּה בָא לִידֵי עֲבֵרָה, דַּע מֵאַיִן בָּאתָ, וּלְאָן אַתָּה הוֹלֵךְ, וְלִפְנֵי מִי אַתָּה עָתִיד לִתֵּן דִּין וְחֶשְׁבּוֹן. מֵאַיִן בָּאתָ, מִטִּפָּה סְרוּחָה, וּלְאָן אַתָּה הוֹלֵךְ, לִמְקוֹם עָפָר רִמָּה וְתוֹלֵעָה. וְלִפְנֵי מִי אַתָּה עָתִיד לִתֵּן דִּין וְחֶשְׁבּוֹן, לִפְנֵי מֶלֶךְ מַלְכֵי הַמְּלָכִים הַקָּדוֹשׁ בָּרוּךְ הוּא.

[ב] (ב) רַבִּי חֲנִינָא סְגַן הַכֹּהֲנִים אוֹמֵר, הֱוֵי מִתְפַּלֵּל בִּשְׁלוֹמָהּ שֶׁל מַלְכוּת, שֶׁאַלְמָלֵא מוֹרָאָהּ אִישׁ אֶת רֵעֵהוּ חַיִּים בְּלָעוֹ.

(ג) רַבִּי חֲנִינָא בֶּן תְּרַדְיוֹן אוֹמֵר, שְׁנַיִם שֶׁיּוֹשְׁבִין, וְאֵין בֵּינֵיהֶן דִּבְרֵי תוֹרָה, הֲרֵי זֶה מוֹשַׁב לֵצִים, שֶׁנֶּאֱמַר, וּבְמוֹשַׁב לֵצִים

°ראה ח, ה
(p. 194)

לֹא יָשָׁב. °אֲבָל שְׁנַיִם שֶׁיּוֹשְׁבִין, וְיֵשׁ בֵּינֵיהֶם דִּבְרֵי תוֹרָה, שְׁכִינָה שְׁרוּיָה בֵינֵיהֶם, שֶׁנֶּאֱמַר, אָז נִדְבְּרוּ יִרְאֵי ה׳ אִישׁ אֶל רֵעֵהוּ, וַיַּקְשֵׁב ה׳ וַיִּשְׁמָע, וַיִּכָּתֵב סֵפֶר זִכָּרוֹן לְפָנָיו לְיִרְאֵי ה׳

°ראה ח, ו
(p. 195)

וּלְחוֹשְׁבֵי שְׁמוֹ. אֵין לִי אֶלָּא שְׁנַיִם, °מִנַּיִן שֶׁאֲפִלּוּ אֶחָד שֶׁיּוֹשֵׁב וְעוֹסֵק בַּתּוֹרָה, שֶׁהַקָּדוֹשׁ בָּרוּךְ הוּא קוֹבֵעַ לוֹ שָׂכָר, שֶׁנֶּאֱמַר, יֵשֵׁב בָּדָד וְיִדֹּם כִּי נָטַל עָלָיו.

[ג] (ד) רַבִּי שִׁמְעוֹן אוֹמֵר, שְׁלֹשָׁה שֶׁאָכְלוּ עַל שֻׁלְחָן אֶחָד, וְלֹא אָמְרוּ עָלָיו דִּבְרֵי תוֹרָה, כְּאִלּוּ אָכְלוּ מִזִּבְחֵי מֵתִים, שֶׁנֶּאֱמַר, כִּי כָּל שֻׁלְחָנוֹת מָלְאוּ קִיא צֹאָה בְּלִי מָקוֹם. אֲבָל שְׁלֹשָׁה שֶׁאָכְלוּ עַל שֻׁלְחָן אֶחָד, וְאָמְרוּ עָלָיו דִּבְרֵי תוֹרָה,

AVOS DR"N

much Torah, they will give you great reward; and your Employer can be relied upon to pay you the wage for your labor, but be aware that the reward of the righteous will be given in the World to Come.

✲ ✲ ✲

Rabbi Chanania ben Akashia says: The Holy One, Blessed is He, wished to confer merit upon Israel; therefore He gave them Torah and mitzvos in abundance, as it is said: "HASHEM desired, for the sake of its [Israel's] righteousness, that the Torah be made great and glorious."

CHAPTER THREE

All Israel has a share in the World to Come, as it is said: "And your people are all righteous; they shall inherit the land forever; they are the branch of My planting, My handiwork, in which to take pride."

✲ ✲ ✲

19 §1-3
(p. 325)

[1] (1) **עֲקַבְיָא** Akavia ben Mahalalel says: Consider three things and you will not come into the grip of sin: Know whence you came, whither you go, and before Whom you will give justification and reckoning. "Whence you came?" — from a putrid drop; "whither you go?" — to a place of dust, worms, and maggots; "and before Whom you will give justification and reckoning?" — before the King Who reigns over kings, the Holy One, Blessed is He.

[2] (2) Rabbi Chanina, the deputy Kohen Gadol [High Priest], says: Pray for the welfare of the government, because if people did not fear it, a person would swallow his fellow alive.

(3) Rabbi Chanina ben Tradyon says: If two sit together and there are no words of Torah between them, it is a session of scorn-°see 8 §5
(p. 194) ers, as it is said: "In the session of scorners he does not sit." °But if two sit together and words of Torah are between them, the Divine Presence rests between them, as it is said: "Then those who fear HASHEM spoke to each other, and HASHEM listened and heard, and a book of remembrance was written before Him for those who °see 8 §6
(p. 195) fear HASHEM and give thought to His Name." °From this verse we would know this only about two people; how do we know that if even one person sits and occupies himself with Torah, the Holy One, Blessed is He, determines a reward for him? For it is said: "Let one sit in solitude and be still, for he will have received [a reward] for it."

[3] (4) Rabbi Shimon says: If three have eaten at the same table and have not spoken words of Torah there, it is as if they have eaten of offerings to dead idols, as it is said: "For all tables are full of vomit and filth, without the Omnipresent." But if three have eaten at the same table and have spoken words of Torah there,

אבות דר"נ כְּאִלּוּ אָכְלוּ מִשֻּׁלְחָנוֹ שֶׁל מָקוֹם בָּרוּךְ הוּא, שֶׁנֶּאֱמַר, וַיְדַבֵּר אֵלַי, זֶה הַשֻּׁלְחָן אֲשֶׁר לִפְנֵי ה'.

ראה כט, ג
(p. 413) [ד] (ה) רַבִּי חֲנִינָא בֶּן חֲכִינַאי אוֹמֵר, הַנֵּעוֹר בַּלַּיְלָה, וְהַמְהַלֵּךְ בַּדֶּרֶךְ יְחִידִי, וְהַמְפַנֶּה לִבּוֹ לְבַטָּלָה, הֲרֵי זֶה מִתְחַיֵּב בְּנַפְשׁוֹ.

[ה] (ו) רַבִּי נְחוּנְיָא בֶּן הַקָּנָה אוֹמֵר, כָּל הַמְקַבֵּל עָלָיו עֹל תּוֹרָה, מַעֲבִירִין מִמֶּנּוּ עֹל מַלְכוּת וְעֹל דֶּרֶךְ אֶרֶץ. וְכָל הַפּוֹרֵק מִמֶּנּוּ עֹל תּוֹרָה, נוֹתְנִין עָלָיו עֹל מַלְכוּת וְעֹל דֶּרֶךְ אֶרֶץ.

ראה ח, ד-יו
(p. 193) [ו] (ז) רַבִּי חֲלַפְתָּא בֶּן דּוֹסָא אִישׁ כְּפַר חֲנַנְיָה אוֹמֵר, עֲשָׂרָה שֶׁיּוֹשְׁבִין וְעוֹסְקִין בַּתּוֹרָה, שְׁכִינָה שְׁרוּיָה בֵּינֵיהֶם, שֶׁנֶּאֱמַר, אֱלֹהִים נִצָּב בַּעֲדַת אֵל. וּמִנַּיִן אֲפִלּוּ חֲמִשָּׁה, שֶׁנֶּאֱמַר, וַאֲגֻדָּתוֹ עַל אֶרֶץ יְסָדָהּ. וּמִנַּיִן אֲפִלּוּ שְׁלֹשָׁה, שֶׁנֶּאֱמַר, בְּקֶרֶב אֱלֹהִים יִשְׁפֹּט. וּמִנַּיִן אֲפִלּוּ שְׁנַיִם, שֶׁנֶּאֱמַר, אָז נִדְבְּרוּ יִרְאֵי ה' אִישׁ אֶל רֵעֵהוּ וַיַּקְשֵׁב ה' וַיִּשְׁמָע וְגוֹ'. וּמִנַּיִן אֲפִלּוּ אֶחָד, שֶׁנֶּאֱמַר, בְּכָל הַמָּקוֹם אֲשֶׁר אַזְכִּיר אֶת שְׁמִי אָבוֹא אֵלֶיךָ וּבֵרַכְתִּיךָ.

[ז] (ח) רַבִּי אֶלְעָזָר אִישׁ בַּרְתּוֹתָא אוֹמֵר, תֶּן לוֹ מִשֶּׁלּוֹ, שֶׁאַתָּה וְשֶׁלְּךָ שֶׁלּוֹ. וְכֵן בְּדָוִד הוּא אוֹמֵר, כִּי מִמְּךָ הַכֹּל, וּמִיָּדְךָ נָתַנּוּ לָךְ.

(ט) רַבִּי יַעֲקֹב אוֹמֵר, הַמְהַלֵּךְ בַּדֶּרֶךְ וְשׁוֹנֶה, וּמַפְסִיק מִמִּשְׁנָתוֹ וְאוֹמֵר, מַה נָּאֶה אִילָן זֶה, וּמַה נָּאֶה נִיר זֶה, מַעֲלֶה עָלָיו הַכָּתוּב כְּאִלּוּ מִתְחַיֵּב בְּנַפְשׁוֹ.

[ח] (י) רַבִּי דּוֹסְתַּאי בְּרַבִּי יַנַּאי מִשּׁוּם רַבִּי מֵאִיר אוֹמֵר, כָּל הַשּׁוֹכֵחַ דָּבָר אֶחָד מִמִּשְׁנָתוֹ, מַעֲלֶה עָלָיו הַכָּתוּב כְּאִלּוּ מִתְחַיֵּב בְּנַפְשׁוֹ, שֶׁנֶּאֱמַר, רַק הִשָּׁמֶר לְךָ וּשְׁמֹר נַפְשְׁךָ מְאֹד פֶּן תִּשְׁכַּח אֶת הַדְּבָרִים אֲשֶׁר רָאוּ עֵינֶיךָ. יָכוֹל אֲפִלּוּ תָקְפָה עָלָיו מִשְׁנָתוֹ, תַּלְמוּד לוֹמַר, וּפֶן יָסוּרוּ מִלְּבָבְךָ כֹּל יְמֵי חַיֶּיךָ, הָא אֵינוֹ מִתְחַיֵּב בְּנַפְשׁוֹ עַד שֶׁיֵּשֵׁב וִיסִירֵם מִלִּבּוֹ.

כב, א
(p. 345) [ט] (יא) רַבִּי חֲנִינָא בֶּן דּוֹסָא אוֹמֵר, כָּל שֶׁיִּרְאַת חֶטְאוֹ קוֹדֶמֶת לְחָכְמָתוֹ, חָכְמָתוֹ מִתְקַיֶּמֶת, וְכָל שֶׁחָכְמָתוֹ קוֹדֶמֶת לְיִרְאַת חֶטְאוֹ, אֵין חָכְמָתוֹ מִתְקַיֶּמֶת.

AVOS DR″N

see 29 §3
(p. 413)

it is as if they have eaten from the table of the Omnipresent, as it is said: "And he said to me, 'This is the table that is before HASHEM.*'"*

[4] (5) *Rabbi Chanina ben Chachinai says: One who stays awake at night or who travels alone on the road, but turns his heart to idleness — indeed, he bears guilt for his soul.*

[5] (6) *Rabbi Nechunia ben Hakanah says: If someone takes upon himself the yoke of Torah — the yoke of government and the yoke of worldly responsibilities are removed from him. But if someone throws off the yoke of Torah from himself — the yoke of government and the yoke of worldly responsibilities are placed upon him.*

see 8 §4-6
(p. 193)

[6] (7) *Rabbi Chalafta ben Dosa of Kfar Chananiah says: If ten people sit together and engage in Torah study, the Divine Presence rests among them, as it is said: "God stands in the assembly of God." How do we know this even of five? For it is said: "He has established His bundle upon earth." How do we know this even of three? For it is said: "In the midst of judges He shall judge." How do we know this even of two? For it is said: "Then those who fear* HASHEM *spoke to each other, and* HASHEM *listened and heard." How do we know this even of one? For it is said: "In every place where I cause My Name to be mentioned, I will come to you and bless you."*

[7] (8) *Rabbi Elazar of Bartosa says: Give Him from His Own, for you and your possessions are His. And so has David said, "For everything is from You, and from Your own we have given You."*

(9) *Rabbi Yaakov says: One who walks on the road while reviewing [a Torah lesson] but interrupts his review and exclaims, "How beautiful is this tree! How beautiful is this plowed field!" — Scripture considers it as if he bears guilt for his soul.*

[8] (10) *Rabbi Dostai bar Yannai says in the name of Rabbi Meir: Whoever forgets anything of his Torah learning, Scripture considers it as if he bears guilt for his soul, for it is said: "But beware and guard your soul exceedingly lest you forget the things your eyes have seen." Does this apply even if [he forgot because] his studies were too difficult for him? [This is not so, for] Scripture says, "And lest they be removed from your heart all the days of your life." Thus, one does not bear guilt for his soul unless he sits [idly] and [through lack of concentration and review] removes them from his consciousness.*

22 §1
(p. 345)

[9] (11) *Rabbi Chanina ben Dosa says: Anyone whose fear of sin takes priority over his wisdom, his wisdom will endure; but anyone whose wisdom takes priority over his fear of sin, his wisdom will not endure.*

אבות דר"נ

(יב) הוּא הָיָה אוֹמֵר, כֹּל שֶׁמַּעֲשָׂיו מְרֻבִּין מֵחָכְמָתוֹ, חָכְמָתוֹ מִתְקַיֶּמֶת, וְכֹל שֶׁחָכְמָתוֹ מְרֻבָּה מִמַּעֲשָׂיו, אֵין חָכְמָתוֹ מִתְקַיֶּמֶת.

[י] (יג) הוּא הָיָה אוֹמֵר, כֹּל שֶׁרוּחַ הַבְּרִיּוֹת נוֹחָה הֵימֶנּוּ, רוּחַ הַמָּקוֹם נוֹחָה הֵימֶנּוּ, וְכֹל שֶׁאֵין רוּחַ הַבְּרִיּוֹת נוֹחָה הֵימֶנּוּ, אֵין רוּחַ הַמָּקוֹם נוֹחָה הֵימֶנּוּ.

פרק כא
(p. 339)

(יד) רַבִּי דוֹסָא בֶּן הָרְכִּינַס אוֹמֵר, שֵׁנָה שֶׁל שַׁחֲרִית, וְיַיִן שֶׁל צָהֳרַיִם, וְשִׂיחַת הַיְלָדִים, וִישִׁיבַת בָּתֵּי כְנֵסִיּוֹת שֶׁל עַמֵּי הָאָרֶץ, מוֹצִיאִין אֶת הָאָדָם מִן הָעוֹלָם.

כו, ד
(p. 389)

[יא] (טו) רַבִּי אֶלְעָזָר הַמּוֹדָעִי אוֹמֵר, הַמְחַלֵּל אֶת הַקֳּדָשִׁים, וְהַמְבַזֶּה אֶת הַמּוֹעֲדוֹת, וְהַמַּלְבִּין פְּנֵי חֲבֵרוֹ בָּרַבִּים, וְהַמֵּפֵר בְּרִיתוֹ שֶׁל אַבְרָהָם אָבִינוּ עָלָיו הַשָּׁלוֹם, וְהַמְגַלֶּה פָנִים בַּתּוֹרָה שֶׁלֹּא כַהֲלָכָה, אַף עַל פִּי שֶׁיֵּשׁ בְּיָדוֹ תוֹרָה וּמַעֲשִׂים טוֹבִים, אֵין לוֹ חֵלֶק לָעוֹלָם הַבָּא.

[יב] (טז) רַבִּי יִשְׁמָעֵאל אוֹמֵר, הֱוֵי קַל לְרֹאשׁ וְנוֹחַ לְתִשְׁחֹרֶת, וֶהֱוֵי מְקַבֵּל אֶת כָּל הָאָדָם בְּשִׂמְחָה.

[יג] (יז) רַבִּי עֲקִיבָא אוֹמֵר, שְׂחוֹק וְקַלּוּת רֹאשׁ מַרְגִּילִין לְעֶרְוָה. מָסֹרֶת, סְיָג לַתּוֹרָה. מַעַשְׂרוֹת, סְיָג לָעֹשֶׁר. נְדָרִים, סְיָג לַפְּרִישׁוּת. סְיָג לַחָכְמָה, שְׁתִיקָה.

°ראה כו, א
(p. 384)

[יד] (יח) הוּא הָיָה אוֹמֵר, חָבִיב אָדָם שֶׁנִּבְרָא בְּצֶלֶם. חִבָּה יְתֵרָה נוֹדַעַת לוֹ שֶׁנִּבְרָא בְּצֶלֶם, שֶׁנֶּאֱמַר, כִּי בְּצֶלֶם אֱלֹהִים עָשָׂה אֶת הָאָדָם. חֲבִיבִין יִשְׂרָאֵל שֶׁנִּקְרְאוּ בָנִים לַמָּקוֹם. חִבָּה יְתֵרָה נוֹדַעַת לָהֶם שֶׁנִּקְרְאוּ בָנִים לַמָּקוֹם, שֶׁנֶּאֱמַר, בָּנִים אַתֶּם לַה' אֱלֹהֵיכֶם. חֲבִיבִין יִשְׂרָאֵל, שֶׁנִּתַּן לָהֶם כְּלִי חֶמְדָּה. חִבָּה יְתֵרָה נוֹדַעַת לָהֶם שֶׁנִּתַּן לָהֶם כְּלִי חֶמְדָּה שֶׁבּוֹ נִבְרָא הָעוֹלָם, שֶׁנֶּאֱמַר, כִּי לֶקַח טוֹב נָתַתִּי לָכֶם, תּוֹרָתִי אַל תַּעֲזֹבוּ.

לט, א
(p. 551)

[טו] (יט) הַכֹּל צָפוּי, וְהָרְשׁוּת נְתוּנָה, וּבְטוֹב הָעוֹלָם נָדוֹן. וְהַכֹּל לְפִי רֹב הַמַּעֲשֶׂה.

ראה לט, א
(p. 552)

[טז] (כ) הוּא הָיָה אוֹמֵר, הַכֹּל נָתוּן בְּעֵרָבוֹן, וּמְצוּדָה פְרוּסָה עַל כָּל הַחַיִּים. הַחֲנוּת פְּתוּחָה, וְהַחֶנְוָנִי מַקִּיף, וְהַפִּנְקָס פָּתוּחַ, וְהַיָּד כּוֹתֶבֶת, וְכָל הָרוֹצֶה לִלְווֹת יָבוֹא וְיִלְוֶה,

לט, א
(p. 553)

AVOS DR"N (12) *He used to say: Anyone whose good deeds exceed his wisdom, his wisdom will endure; but anyone whose wisdom exceeds his good deeds, his wisdom will not endure.*

[10] (13) *He used to say: If the spirit of one's fellows is pleased with him, the spirit of the Omnipresent is pleased with him; but if the spirit of one's fellows is not pleased with him, the spirit of the Omnipresent is not pleased with him.*

ch. 21
(p. 339) (14) *Rabbi Dosa ben Harkinas says: Late morning sleep, midday wine, children's chatter, and sitting in the assemblies of the ignorant remove a man from the world.*

26 §4
(p. 389) **[11]** (15) *Rabbi Elazar the Moda'ite says: One who desecrates sacred things, who disgraces the Festivals, who humiliates his fellow in public, who nullifies the covenant of our forefather Abraham, or who perverts the Torah contrary to the halachah — though he may have Torah and good deeds, he has no share in the World to Come.*

[12] (16) *Rabbi Yishmael says: Be yielding to a superior, pleasant to the young, and receive every person cheerfully.*

°see 26 §1
(p. 384) **[13]** (17) *Rabbi Akiva said: Mockery and levity accustom a man to immorality.* °*The transmitted Oral Torah is a protective fence around the Torah; tithes are a protective fence for wealth; vows are a protective fence for abstinence; a protective fence for wisdom is silence.*

39 §1
(p. 551) **[14]** (18) *He used to say: Beloved is man, for he was created in God's image; it is indicative of a greater love that it was made known to him that he was created in God's image, as it is said: "For in the image of God He made man." Beloved are the people of Israel, for they are described as children of the Omnipresent; it is indicative of a greater love that it was made known to them that they are described as children of the Omnipresent, as it is said: "You are children to HASHEM, Your God." Beloved are the people of Israel, for a cherished utensil was given to them; it is indicative of a greater love that it was made known to them that they were given a cherished utensil, as it is said: "For I have given you a good teaching; do not forsake My Torah."*

see 39 §1
(p. 552) **[15]** (19) *Everything is foreseen, yet the freedom of choice is given. The world is judged with goodness, and everything depends on the abundance of good deeds.*

39 §1
(p. 553) **[16]** (20) *He used to say: Everything is given on collateral and a net is spread over all the living. The shop is open; the Merchant extends credit; the ledger is open; the hand writes; and whoever wishes to borrow, let him come and borrow. The*

אבות דר"נ

וְהַגַּבָּאִים מַחֲזִירִים תָּדִיר בְּכָל יוֹם, וְנִפְרָעִין מִן הָאָדָם מִדַּעְתּוֹ וְשֶׁלֹּא מִדַּעְתּוֹ, וְיֵשׁ לָהֶם עַל מַה שֶׁיִּסְמֹכוּ, וְהַדִּין דִּין אֱמֶת, וְהַכֹּל מְתֻקָּן לַסְּעוּדָה.

כב, א
(p. 346)

[יז] (כא) רַבִּי אֶלְעָזָר בֶּן עֲזַרְיָה אוֹמֵר, אִם אֵין תּוֹרָה, אֵין דֶּרֶךְ אֶרֶץ. אִם אֵין דֶּרֶךְ אֶרֶץ, אֵין תּוֹרָה. אִם אֵין חָכְמָה, אֵין יִרְאָה. אִם אֵין יִרְאָה, אֵין חָכְמָה. אִם אֵין בִּינָה, אֵין דָּעַת. אִם אֵין דַּעַת, אֵין בִּינָה. אִם אֵין בִּינָה, אֵין דָּעַת. אִם אֵין קֶמַח, אֵין תּוֹרָה. אִם אֵין תּוֹרָה, אֵין קֶמַח.

(כב) הוּא הָיָה אוֹמֵר, כֹּל שֶׁחָכְמָתוֹ מְרֻבָּה מִמַּעֲשָׂיו לְמָה הוּא דוֹמֶה, לְאִילָן שֶׁעֲנָפָיו מְרֻבִּין וְשָׁרָשָׁיו מֻעָטִין, וְהָרוּחַ בָּאָה וְעוֹקַרְתּוֹ וְהוֹפַכְתּוֹ עַל פָּנָיו, שֶׁנֶּאֱמַר, וְהָיָה כְּעַרְעָר בָּעֲרָבָה וְלֹא יִרְאֶה כִּי יָבוֹא טוֹב, וְשָׁכַן חֲרֵרִים בַּמִּדְבָּר אֶרֶץ מְלֵחָה וְלֹא תֵשֵׁב. אֲבָל כֹּל שֶׁמַּעֲשָׂיו מְרֻבִּין מֵחָכְמָתוֹ לְמָה הוּא דוֹמֶה, לְאִילָן שֶׁעֲנָפָיו מֻעָטִין וְשָׁרָשָׁיו מְרֻבִּין, שֶׁאֲפִלּוּ כָּל הָרוּחוֹת שֶׁבָּעוֹלָם בָּאוֹת וְנוֹשְׁבוֹת בּוֹ אֵין מְזִיזִין אוֹתוֹ מִמְּקוֹמוֹ, שֶׁנֶּאֱמַר, וְהָיָה כְּעֵץ שָׁתוּל עַל מַיִם, וְעַל יוּבַל יְשַׁלַּח שָׁרָשָׁיו, וְלֹא יִרְאֶה כִּי יָבֹא חֹם, וְהָיָה עָלֵהוּ רַעֲנָן; וּבִשְׁנַת בַּצֹּרֶת לֹא יִדְאָג, וְלֹא יָמִישׁ מֵעֲשׂוֹת פֶּרִי.

כג, ב
(p. 397)

[יח] (כג) רַבִּי אֱלִיעֶזֶר בֶּן חִסְמָא אוֹמֵר, קִנִּין וּפִתְחֵי נִדָּה הֵן הֵן גּוּפֵי הֲלָכוֹת. תְּקוּפוֹת וְגִמַּטְרִיָאוֹת, פַּרְפְּרָאוֹת לַחָכְמָה.

❈ ❈ ❈

רַבִּי חֲנַנְיָא בֶּן עֲקַשְׁיָא אוֹמֵר: רָצָה הַקָּדוֹשׁ בָּרוּךְ הוּא לְזַכּוֹת אֶת יִשְׂרָאֵל, לְפִיכָךְ הִרְבָּה לָהֶם תּוֹרָה וּמִצְוֹת, שֶׁנֶּאֱמַר: "יהוה חָפֵץ לְמַעַן צִדְקוֹ, יַגְדִּיל תּוֹרָה וְיַאְדִּיר".

פרק רביעי

כָּל יִשְׂרָאֵל יֵשׁ לָהֶם חֵלֶק לָעוֹלָם הַבָּא, שֶׁנֶּאֱמַר: "וְעַמֵּךְ כֻּלָּם צַדִּיקִים, לְעוֹלָם יִירְשׁוּ אָרֶץ, נֵצֶר מַטָּעַי, מַעֲשֵׂה יָדַי לְהִתְפָּאֵר".

❈ ❈ ❈

כג, א
(p. 350)

[א] (א) בֶּן זוֹמָא אוֹמֵר, אֵיזֶהוּ חָכָם, הַלּוֹמֵד מִכָּל אָדָם, שֶׁנֶּאֱמַר, מִכָּל מְלַמְּדַי הִשְׂכַּלְתִּי. אֵיזֶהוּ גִּבּוֹר, הַכּוֹבֵשׁ אֶת יִצְרוֹ, שֶׁנֶּאֱמַר, טוֹב אֶרֶךְ אַפַּיִם מִגִּבּוֹר

AVOS DR"N | collectors make their rounds constantly, every day, and collect payment from the person whether he realizes it or not. They have proof to rely upon; the judgment is a truthful judgment; and everything is prepared for the [final festive] banquet.

22 §1
(p. 346) **[17]** (21) *Rabbi Elazar ben Azariah says: If there is no Torah, there is no worldly occupation; if there is no worldly occupation, there is no Torah. If there is no wisdom, there is no fear of God; if there is no fear of God, there is no wisdom. If there is no knowledge, there is no understanding; if there is no understanding, there is no knowledge. If there is no flour, there is no Torah; if there is no Torah, there is no flour.*

(22) *He used to say: Anyone whose wisdom exceeds his good deeds, to what is he likened? — to a tree whose branches are numerous but whose roots are few; then the wind comes and uproots it and turns it upside down; as it is said: "And he shall be like an isolated tree in an arid land and shall not see when good comes; he shall dwell on parched soil in the wilderness, on a salted land, uninhabited." But one whose good deeds exceed his wisdom, to what is he likened? — to a tree whose branches are few but whose roots are numerous; even if all the winds in the world were to come and blow against it, they could not budge it from its place; as it is said: "And he shall be like a tree planted by waters, toward the stream spreading its roots, and it shall not notice the heat's arrival, and its foliage shall be fresh; in the year of drought it shall not worry, nor shall it cease from yielding fruit."*

27 §2
(p. 397) **[18]** (23) *Rabbi Elazar ben Chisma said: The laws of bird-offerings, and the laws regarding the beginning of menstrual periods — these are the essential laws; astronomy and mathematics are like the seasonings of wisdom.*

❧ ❧ ❧

Rabbi Chanania ben Akashia says: The Holy One, Blessed is He, wished to confer merit upon Israel; therefore He gave them Torah and mitzvos in abundance, as it is said: "HASHEM desired, for the sake of its [Israel's] righteousness, that the Torah be made great and glorious."

CHAPTER FOUR

All Israel has a share in the World to Come, as it is said: "And your people are all righteous; they shall inherit the land forever; they are the branch of My planting, My handiwork, in which to take pride."

❧ ❧ ❧

23 §1
(p. 350) **[1]** (1) **בֶּן זוֹמָא** *Ben Zoma says: Who is wise? He who learns from every person, as it is said: "From all my teachers I grew wise." Who is strong? He who subdues his personal inclination, as it is said: "He who is slow to anger is better than the strong man,*

וּמָשָׁל בְּרוּחוֹ מִלֹּכֵד עִיר. אֵיזֶהוּ עָשִׁיר הַשָּׂמֵחַ בְּחֶלְקוֹ, שֶׁנֶּאֱמַר, יְגִיעַ כַּפֶּיךָ כִּי תֹאכֵל אַשְׁרֶיךָ וְטוֹב לָךְ. אַשְׁרֶיךָ בָּעוֹלָם הַזֶּה, וְטוֹב לָךְ לָעוֹלָם הַבָּא. אֵיזֶהוּ מְכֻבָּד, הַמְכַבֵּד אֶת הַבְּרִיּוֹת, שֶׁנֶּאֱמַר, כִּי מְכַבְּדַי אֲכַבֵּד וּבֹזַי יֵקָלּוּ.

[**ב**] (ב) בֶּן עַזַּאי אוֹמֵר, הֱוֵי רָץ לְמִצְוָה קַלָּה (כְּבַחֲמוּרָה), וּבוֹרֵחַ מִן הָעֲבֵרָה. שֶׁמִּצְוָה גוֹרֶרֶת מִצְוָה, וַעֲבֵרָה גוֹרֶרֶת עֲבֵרָה. שֶׁשְּׂכַר מִצְוָה מִצְוָה, וּשְׂכַר עֲבֵרָה עֲבֵרָה.

[**ג**] (ג) הוּא הָיָה אוֹמֵר, אַל תְּהִי בָז לְכָל אָדָם, וְאַל תְּהִי מַפְלִיג לְכָל דָּבָר, שֶׁאֵין לְךָ אָדָם שֶׁאֵין לוֹ שָׁעָה, וְאֵין לְךָ דָּבָר שֶׁאֵין לוֹ מָקוֹם.

[**ד**] (ד) רַבִּי לְוִיטָס אִישׁ יַבְנֶה אוֹמֵר, מְאֹד מְאֹד הֱוֵי שְׁפַל רוּחַ, שֶׁתִּקְוַת אֱנוֹשׁ רִמָּה.

(ה) רַבִּי יוֹחָנָן בֶּן בְּרוֹקָא אוֹמֵר, כָּל הַמְחַלֵּל שֵׁם שָׁמַיִם בַּסֵּתֶר נִפְרָעִין מִמֶּנּוּ בַּגָּלוּי. אֶחָד שׁוֹגֵג וְאֶחָד מֵזִיד בְּחִלּוּל הַשֵּׁם.

[**ה**] (ו) רַבִּי יִשְׁמָעֵאל בְּנוֹ אוֹמֵר, הַלּוֹמֵד עַל מְנָת לְלַמֵּד, מַסְפִּיקִין בְּיָדוֹ לִלְמֹד וּלְלַמֵּד. וְהַלּוֹמֵד עַל מְנָת לַעֲשׂוֹת, מַסְפִּיקִין בְּיָדוֹ לִלְמֹד וּלְלַמֵּד לִשְׁמֹר וְלַעֲשׂוֹת.

(ז) רַבִּי צָדוֹק אוֹמֵר, אַל תַּעֲשֵׂם עֲטָרָה לְהִתְגַּדֵּל בָּהֶם, וְלֹא קַרְדֹּם לַחְפֹּר בָּהֶם. וְכָךְ הָיָה הִלֵּל אוֹמֵר, וּדְאִשְׁתַּמֵּשׁ בְּתָגָא חֲלָף. הָא לָמַדְתָּ, כָּל הַנֶּהֱנֶה מִדִּבְרֵי תוֹרָה נוֹטֵל חַיָּיו מִן הָעוֹלָם.

[**ו**] (ח) רַבִּי יוֹסֵי אוֹמֵר, כָּל הַמְכַבֵּד אֶת הַתּוֹרָה גּוּפוֹ מְכֻבָּד עַל הַבְּרִיּוֹת. וְכָל הַמְחַלֵּל אֶת הַתּוֹרָה גּוּפוֹ מְחֻלָּל עַל הַבְּרִיּוֹת.

[**ז**] (ט) רַבִּי יִשְׁמָעֵאל בְּנוֹ אוֹמֵר, הַחוֹשֵׂךְ עַצְמוֹ מִן הַדִּין פּוֹרֵק מִמֶּנּוּ אֵיבָה וְגָזֵל וּשְׁבוּעַת שָׁוְא. וְהַגַּס לִבּוֹ בְּהוֹרָאָה שׁוֹטֶה, רָשָׁע וְגַס רוּחַ.

[**ח**] (י) הוּא הָיָה אוֹמֵר, אַל תְּהִי דָן יְחִידִי, שֶׁאֵין דָּן יְחִידִי אֶלָּא אֶחָד. וְאַל תֹּאמַר קַבְּלוּ דַעְתִּי, שֶׁהֵן רַשָּׁאִין וְלֹא אָתָּה.

AVOS DR"N

and a master of his passions is better than a conqueror of a city." Who is rich? He who is happy with his lot, as it is said: "When you eat of the labor of your hands, you are praiseworthy and all is well with you." "You are praiseworthy" — in this world; "and all is well with you" — in the World to Come. Who is honored? He who honors others, as it is said: "For those who honor Me I will honor, and those who scorn Me shall be degraded."

25 §4
(p. 380)

[2] (2) *Ben Azzai says: Run to perform even a "minor" mitzvah, and flee from sin; for one mitzvah leads to another mitzvah, and one sin leads to another sin; for the consequence of a mitzvah is a mitzvah, and the consequence of a sin is a sin.*

23 §2
(p. 352)

[3] (3) *He used to say: Do not be scornful of any person and do not be disdainful of anything, for you have no person without his hour and no thing without its place.*

[4] (4) *Rabbi Levitas of Yavneh says: Be exceedingly humble in spirit, for the anticipated end of mortal man is worms.*

(5) *Rabbi Yochanan ben Beroka says: Whoever desecrates the Name of Heaven in secret, they will exact punishment from him in public; unintentional or intentional, both are alike regarding desecration of the Name.*

27 §2
(p. 396)

[5] (6) *Rabbi Yishmael bar Rabbi Yose says: One who studies Torah in order to teach is given the means to study and to teach; and one who studies in order to practice is given the means to study and to teach, to observe and to practice.*

(7) *Rabbi Tzadok says: Do not separate yourself from the community; [when serving as a judge] do not act as a lawyer; do not make the Torah a crown for self-glorification, nor a spade with which to dig. So too Hillel used to say: He who exploits the crown [of Torah for personal benefit] shall fade away. From this you derive that whoever seeks personal benefit from the words of Torah removes his life from the world.*

27 §1
(p. 393)

[6] (8) *Rabbi Yose says: Whoever honors the Torah is himself honored by people; and whoever disgraces the Torah is himself disgraced by people.*

[7] (9) *Rabbi Yishmael his son says: One who withdraws from judgment removes from himself hatred, robbery, and [the responsibility for] an unnecessary oath; but one who is too self-confident in handing down legal decisions is a fool, wicked, and arrogant of spirit.*

[8] (10) *He used to say: Do not act as judge alone, for none judges alone except One; and do not say, "Accept my view," for they are permitted to, but not you.*

אבות דר״נ
ל, א
(p. 422)

[ט] (יא) רַבִּי יוֹנָתָן אוֹמֵר, כָּל הַמְקַיֵּם אֶת הַתּוֹרָה מֵעֹנִי סוֹפוֹ לְקַיְּמָהּ מֵעשֶׁר. וְכָל הַמְבַטֵּל אֶת הַתּוֹרָה מֵעשֶׁר סוֹפוֹ לְבַטְּלָהּ מֵעֹנִי.

כט, ב
(p. 412)

[י] (יב) רַבִּי מֵאִיר אוֹמֵר, הֱוֵי מְמַעֵט בְּעֵסֶק, וַעֲסֹק בַּתּוֹרָה. וֶהֱוֵי שְׁפַל רוּחַ בִּפְנֵי כָל אָדָם. °וְאִם בָּטַלְתָּ מִן הַתּוֹרָה יֶשׁ לְךָ בְּטֵלִים הַרְבֵּה כְּנֶגְדֶּךָ. וְאִם עָמַלְתָּ בַתּוֹרָה יֶשׁ לוֹ שָׂכָר הַרְבֵּה לִתֶּן לָךְ.

[יא] (יג) רַבִּי אֱלִיעֶזֶר בֶּן יַעֲקֹב אוֹמֵר, הָעוֹשֶׂה מִצְוָה אַחַת קוֹנֶה לוֹ פְּרַקְלִיט אֶחָד. וְהָעוֹבֵר עֲבֵרָה אַחַת קוֹנֶה לוֹ קַטֵּיגוֹר אֶחָד. תְּשׁוּבָה וּמַעֲשִׂים טוֹבִים כִּתְרִיס בִּפְנֵי הַפֻּרְעָנוּת.

מ, יז
(p. 574)

(יד) רַבִּי יוֹחָנָן הַסַּנְדְּלָר אוֹמֵר, כָּל כְּנֵסִיָּה שֶׁהִיא לְשֵׁם שָׁמַיִם סוֹפָהּ לְהִתְקַיֵּם. וְשֶׁאֵינָהּ לְשֵׁם שָׁמַיִם אֵין סוֹפָהּ לְהִתְקַיֵּם.

כז, ד
(p. 399)

[יב] (טו) רַבִּי אֶלְעָזָר בֶּן שַׁמּוּעַ אוֹמֵר, יְהִי כְבוֹד תַּלְמִידְךָ חָבִיב עָלֶיךָ כְּשֶׁלָּךְ, וּכְבוֹד חֲבֵרְךָ כְּמוֹרָא רַבָּךְ, וּמוֹרָא רַבְּךָ כְּמוֹרָא שָׁמַיִם.

[יג] (טז) רַבִּי יְהוּדָה אוֹמֵר, הֱוֵי זָהִיר בַּתַּלְמוּד, שֶׁשִּׁגְגַת תַּלְמוּד עוֹלָה זָדוֹן.

מא, א
(p. 575)

(יז) רַבִּי שִׁמְעוֹן אוֹמֵר, שְׁלשָׁה כְתָרִים הֵם, כֶּתֶר תּוֹרָה וְכֶתֶר כְּהֻנָּה וְכֶתֶר מַלְכוּת, וְכֶתֶר שֵׁם טוֹב עוֹלֶה עַל גַּבֵּיהֶן.

כג, ב
(p. 352)

[יד] (יח) רַבִּי נְהוֹרַאי אוֹמֵר, הֱוֵי גוֹלֶה לִמְקוֹם תּוֹרָה, וְאַל שֶׁהִיא תָבוֹא אַחֲרֶיךָ, שֶׁחֲבֵרֶיךָ יְקַיְּמוּהָ בְיָדֶךָ, וְאַל בִּינָתְךָ אַל תִּשָּׁעֵן.

[טו] (יט) רַבִּי יַנַּאי אוֹמֵר, אֵין בְּיָדֵינוּ לֹא מִשַּׁלְוַת הָרְשָׁעִים וְאַף לֹא מִיִּסּוּרֵי הַצַּדִּיקִים.

כט, ז
(p. 421)

(כ) רַבִּי מַתְיָא בֶּן חָרָשׁ אוֹמֵר, הֱוֵי מַקְדִּים בִּשְׁלוֹם כָּל אָדָם. וֶהֱוֵי זָנָב לָאֲרָיוֹת, וְאַל תְּהִי רֹאשׁ לַשּׁוּעָלִים.

[טז] (כא) רַבִּי יַעֲקֹב אוֹמֵר, הָעוֹלָם הַזֶּה דּוֹמֶה לִפְרוֹזְדוֹר בִּפְנֵי הָעוֹלָם הַבָּא, הַתְקֵן עַצְמְךָ בַּפְּרוֹזְדוֹר, כְּדֵי שֶׁתִּכָּנֵס לַטְּרַקְלִין.

AVOS DR"N
30 §1
(p. 422)

[9] (11) *Rabbi Yonasan says: Whoever fulfills the Torah despite poverty will ultimately fulfill it in wealth; but whoever neglects the Torah because of wealth will ultimately neglect it in poverty.*

°29 §2
(p. 412)

[10] (12) *Rabbi Meir says: Reduce your business activities and engage in Torah study. Be of humble spirit before every person. °If you should neglect the [study of] Torah, you will come upon many excuses to neglect it; but if you labor in the Torah, God has ample reward to give you.*

[11] (13) *Rabbi Eliezer ben Yaakov says: He who fulfills even a single mitzvah gains himself a single advocate, and he who commits even a single transgression gains himself a single accuser. Repentance and good deeds are like a shield against retribution.*

40 §17
(p. 574)

(14) *Rabbi Yochanan HaSandler says: Every assembly that is dedicated to the sake of Heaven will have an enduring effect, but one that is not for the sake of Heaven will not have an enduring effect.*

27 §4
(p. 399)

[12] (15) *Rabbi Elazar ben Shamua says: Let the honor of your student be as dear to you as your own; the honor of your colleague as the reverence for your teacher; and the reverence for your teacher as the reverence of Heaven.*

[13] (16) *Rabbi Yehudah says: Be meticulous in study, for a careless misinterpretation is considered tantamount to willful transgression.*

41 §1
(p. 575)

(17) *Rabbi Shimon says: There are three crowns — the crown of Torah, the crown of priesthood, and the crown of kingship; but the crown of a good name surpasses them all.*

23 §2
(p. 352)

[14] (18) *Rabbi Nehorai says: Exile yourself to a place of Torah —and do not assume that it will come after you — for it is your colleagues who will cause it to remain with you; and do not rely on your own understanding.*

[15] (19) *Rabbi Yannai says: It is not in our power to explain either the tranquility of the wicked or the suffering of the righteous.*

29 §7
(p. 421)

(20) *Rabbi Masya ben Charash says: Initiate a greeting to every person; and be a tail to lions rather than a head to foxes.*

[16] (21) *Rabbi Yaakov says: This World is like a corridor before the World to Come; prepare yourself in the corridor so that you may enter the banquet hall.*

אבות דר"נ

[יז] (כב) הוּא הָיָה אוֹמֵר, יָפָה שָׁעָה אַחַת בִּתְשׁוּבָה וּמַעֲשִׂים טוֹבִים בָּעוֹלָם הַזֶּה מִכֹּל חַיֵּי הָעוֹלָם הַבָּא, וְיָפָה שָׁעָה אַחַת שֶׁל קוֹרַת רוּחַ בָּעוֹלָם הַבָּא מִכֹּל חַיֵּי הָעוֹלָם הַזֶּה.

כט, א (p. 410)

[יח] (כג) רַבִּי שִׁמְעוֹן בֶּן אֶלְעָזָר אוֹמֵר, אַל תְּרַצֶּה אֶת חֲבֵרְךָ בִּשְׁעַת כַּעֲסוֹ, וְאַל תְּנַחֲמֶנּוּ בְּשָׁעָה שֶׁמֵּתוֹ מֻטָּל לְפָנָיו, וְאַל תִּשְׁאַל לוֹ בִּשְׁעַת נִדְרוֹ, וְאַל תִּשְׁתַּדֵּל לִרְאוֹתוֹ בִּשְׁעַת קַלְקָלָתוֹ.

[יט] (כד) שְׁמוּאֵל הַקָּטָן אוֹמֵר, בִּנְפֹל אוֹיִבְךָ אַל תִּשְׂמָח וּבִכָּשְׁלוֹ אַל יָגֵל לִבֶּךָ, פֶּן יִרְאֶה ה' וְרַע בְּעֵינָיו וְהֵשִׁיב מֵעָלָיו אַפּוֹ.

כג, ג (p. 354)

[כ] (כה) אֱלִישָׁע בֶּן אֲבוּיָה אוֹמֵר, הַלּוֹמֵד יֶלֶד לְמָה הוּא דוֹמֶה, לִדְיוֹ כְתוּבָה עַל נְיָר חָדָשׁ. וְהַלּוֹמֵד זָקֵן לְמָה הוּא דוֹמֶה, לִדְיוֹ כְתוּבָה עַל נְיָר מָחוּק.

(כו) רַבִּי יוֹסֵי בְּרַבִּי יְהוּדָה אִישׁ כְּפַר הַבַּבְלִי אוֹמֵר, הַלּוֹמֵד מִן הַקְּטַנִּים לְמָה הוּא דוֹמֶה, לְאוֹכֵל עֲנָבִים קֵהוֹת וְשׁוֹתֶה יַיִן מִגִּתּוֹ. וְהַלּוֹמֵד מִן הַזְּקֵנִים לְמָה הוּא דוֹמֶה, לְאוֹכֵל עֲנָבִים בְּשׁוּלוֹת וְשׁוֹתֶה יַיִן יָשָׁן.

(כז) רַבִּי אוֹמֵר, אַל תִּסְתַּכֵּל בַּקַּנְקַן, אֶלָּא בַּמֶּה שֶׁיֵּשׁ בּוֹ, יֵשׁ קַנְקַן חָדָשׁ מָלֵא יָשָׁן, וְיָשָׁן שֶׁאֲפִלּוּ חָדָשׁ אֵין בּוֹ.

[כא] (כח) רַבִּי אֶלְעָזָר הַקַּפָּר אוֹמֵר, הַקִּנְאָה וְהַתַּאֲוָה וְהַכָּבוֹד מוֹצִיאִין אֶת הָאָדָם מִן הָעוֹלָם.

[כב] (כט) הוּא הָיָה אוֹמֵר, הַיִּלּוֹדִים לָמוּת, וְהַמֵּתִים לְהַחֲיוֹת, וְהַחַיִּים לִדּוֹן, לֵידַע לְהוֹדִיעַ וּלְהִוָּדַע שֶׁהוּא אֵל, הוּא הַיּוֹצֵר, הוּא הַבּוֹרֵא, הוּא הַמֵּבִין, הוּא הַדַּיָּן, הוּא עֵד, הוּא בַּעַל דִּין, וְהוּא עָתִיד לָדוּן. בָּרוּךְ הוּא, שֶׁאֵין לְפָנָיו לֹא עַוְלָה וְלֹא שִׁכְחָה וְלֹא מַשּׂוֹא פָנִים וְלֹא מִקַּח שֹׁחַד, שֶׁהַכֹּל שֶׁלּוֹ. וְדַע, שֶׁהַכֹּל לְפִי הַחֶשְׁבּוֹן. וְאַל יַבְטִיחֲךָ יִצְרְךָ שֶׁהַשְּׁאוֹל בֵּית מָנוֹס לָךְ, שֶׁעַל כָּרְחֲךָ אַתָּה נוֹצָר, וְעַל כָּרְחֲךָ אַתָּה נוֹלָד, וְעַל כָּרְחֲךָ אַתָּה חַי, וְעַל כָּרְחֲךָ אַתָּה מֵת, וְעַל כָּרְחֲךָ אַתָּה עָתִיד לִתֵּן דִּין וְחֶשְׁבּוֹן לִפְנֵי מֶלֶךְ מַלְכֵי הַמְּלָכִים הַקָּדוֹשׁ בָּרוּךְ הוּא.

❧ ❧ ❧

AVOS DR″N

[17] (22) *He used to say: Better one hour of repentance and good deeds in This World than the entire life of the World to Come; and better one hour of spiritual bliss in the World to Come than the entire life of This World.*

29 §1
(p. 410)

[18] (23) *Rabbi Shimon ben Elazar says: Do not appease your fellow in the time of his anger; do not console him while his dead lies before him; do not question him about his vow at the time he makes it; and do not attempt to see him at the time of his degradation.*

[19] (24) *Shmuel HaKatan says: "When your enemy falls be not glad, and when he stumbles let your heart not be joyous. Lest HASHEM see and it displease Him, and He will turn His wrath from him [to you]."*

23 §3
(p. 354)

[20] (25) *Elisha ben Avuyah says: One who studies Torah as a child, to what can he be likened? — to ink written on fresh paper. And one who studies Torah as an old man, to what can he be likened? — to ink written on smudged paper.*

(26) *Rabbi Yose bar Yehudah of Kfar HaBavli says: One who learns Torah from the young, to what can he be likened? — to one who eats unripe grapes or drinks unfermented wine from his vat. But one who learns Torah from the old, to what can he be likened? — to one who eats ripe grapes or drinks aged wine.*

(27) *Rabbi Meir says: Do not look at the vessel, but what is in it; there is a new vessel filled with old wine and an old vessel that does not contain even new wine.*

[21] (28) *Rabbi Elazar HaKappar says: Jealousy, lust, and glory remove a man from the world.*

[22] (29) *He used to say: The newborn will die; the dead will live again; the living will be judged — in order that they know, teach, and become aware that He is God, He is the Fashioner, He is the Creator, He is the Discerner, He is the Judge, He is the Witness, He is the Plaintiff, He will judge. Blessed is He, before Whom there is no iniquity, no forgetfulness, no favoritism, and no acceptance of bribery, for everything is His. Know that everything is according to the reckoning. And let not your evil inclination promise you that the grave will be an escape for you — for against your will you were created; against your will you were born; against your will you live; against your will you die, and against your will you are destined to give an account before the King Who rules over kings, the Holy One, Blessed is He.*

☙ ☙ ☙

רַבִּי חֲנַנְיָא בֶּן עֲקַשְׁיָא אוֹמֵר: רָצָה הַקָּדוֹשׁ בָּרוּךְ הוּא לְזַכּוֹת
אֶת יִשְׂרָאֵל, לְפִיכָךְ הִרְבָּה לָהֶם תּוֹרָה וּמִצְוֹת, שֶׁנֶּאֱמַר: „יהוה
חָפֵץ לְמַעַן צִדְקוֹ, יַגְדִּיל תּוֹרָה וְיַאְדִּיר”.

פרק חמישי

כָּל יִשְׂרָאֵל יֵשׁ לָהֶם חֵלֶק לָעוֹלָם הַבָּא, שֶׁנֶּאֱמַר: „וְעַמֵּךְ כֻּלָּם
צַדִּיקִים, לְעוֹלָם יִירְשׁוּ אָרֶץ, נֵצֶר מַטָּעַי, מַעֲשֵׂה יָדַי לְהִתְפָּאֵר”.

❀ ❀ ❀

אבות דר"נ	
	[א] **(א)** **בַּעֲשָׂרָה** מַאֲמָרוֹת נִבְרָא הָעוֹלָם. וּמַה תַּלְמוּד
לא, ב	לוֹמַר, וַהֲלֹא בְּמַאֲמָר אֶחָד יָכוֹל
(p. 432)	לְהִבָּרְאוֹת, אֶלָּא לְהִפָּרַע מִן הָרְשָׁעִים שֶׁמְּאַבְּדִין אֶת הָעוֹלָם

שֶׁנִּבְרָא בַּעֲשָׂרָה מַאֲמָרוֹת, וְלִתֵּן שָׂכָר טוֹב לַצַּדִּיקִים
שֶׁמְּקַיְּמִין אֶת הָעוֹלָם שֶׁנִּבְרָא בַּעֲשָׂרָה מַאֲמָרוֹת.

[ב] **(ב)** עֲשָׂרָה דוֹרוֹת מֵאָדָם וְעַד נֹחַ, לְהוֹדִיעַ כַּמָּה אֶרֶךְ
אַפַּיִם לְפָנָיו, שֶׁכָּל הַדּוֹרוֹת הָיוּ מַכְעִיסִין וּבָאִין עַד
שֶׁהֵבִיא עֲלֵיהֶם אֶת מֵי הַמַּבּוּל.

לב, א
(p. 442)

(ג) עֲשָׂרָה דוֹרוֹת מִנֹּחַ וְעַד אַבְרָהָם, לְהוֹדִיעַ כַּמָּה אֶרֶךְ אַפַּיִם
לְפָנָיו, שֶׁכָּל הַדּוֹרוֹת הָיוּ מַכְעִיסִין וּבָאִין, עַד שֶׁבָּא אַבְרָהָם
וְקִבֵּל (עָלָיו) שְׂכַר כֻּלָּם.

לג, א
(p. 449)

[ג] **(ד)** עֲשָׂרָה נִסְיוֹנוֹת נִתְנַסָּה אַבְרָהָם אָבִינוּ עָלָיו הַשָּׁלוֹם,
וְעָמַד בְּכֻלָּם. לְהוֹדִיעַ כַּמָּה חִבָּתוֹ שֶׁל אַבְרָהָם אָבִינוּ
עָלָיו הַשָּׁלוֹם.

לג, ב
(p. 452)

[ד] **(ה)** עֲשָׂרָה נִסִּים נַעֲשׂוּ לַאֲבוֹתֵינוּ בְּמִצְרַיִם וַעֲשָׂרָה עַל
הַיָּם. עֶשֶׂר מַכּוֹת הֵבִיא הַקָּדוֹשׁ בָּרוּךְ הוּא עַל
הַמִּצְרִיִּים בְּמִצְרַיִם וְעֶשֶׂר עַל הַיָּם.

לג, ב
(p. 454)

(ו) עֲשָׂרָה נִסְיוֹנוֹת נִסּוּ אֲבוֹתֵינוּ אֶת הַמָּקוֹם בָּרוּךְ הוּא
בַּמִּדְבָּר, שֶׁנֶּאֱמַר, וַיְנַסּוּ אֹתִי זֶה עֶשֶׂר פְּעָמִים וְלֹא שָׁמְעוּ
בְּקוֹלִי.

ט, ב; לד, א
(p. 203;
463)

[ה] **(ז)** עֲשָׂרָה נִסִּים נַעֲשׂוּ לַאֲבוֹתֵינוּ בְּבֵית הַמִּקְדָּשׁ, לֹא הִפִּילָה
אִשָּׁה מֵרֵיחַ בְּשַׂר הַקֹּדֶשׁ, וְלֹא הִסְרִיחַ בְּשַׂר הַקֹּדֶשׁ
מֵעוֹלָם, וְלֹא נִרְאָה זְבוּב בְּבֵית הַמִּטְבָּחַיִם, וְלֹא אֵרַע קֶרִי
לְכֹהֵן גָּדוֹל בְּיוֹם הַכִּפּוּרִים, וְלֹא כִבּוּ גְּשָׁמִים אֵשׁ שֶׁל עֲצֵי
הַמַּעֲרָכָה, וְלֹא נָצְחָה הָרוּחַ אֶת עַמּוּד הֶעָשָׁן, וְלֹא נִמְצָא פְּסוּל

לה, א; ה-ח
(p. 484;
496)

AVOS DR"N

Rabbi Chanania ben Akashia says: The Holy One, Blessed is He, wished to confer merit upon Israel; therefore He gave them Torah and mitzvos in abundance, as it is said: "HASHEM desired, for the sake of its [Israel's] righteousness, that the Torah be made great and glorious."

CHAPTER FIVE

All Israel has a share in the World to Come, as it is said: "And your people are all righteous; they shall inherit the land forever; they are the branch of My planting, My handiwork, in which to take pride."

❧ ❧ ❧

31 §2
(p. 432)

[1] (1) בַּעֲשָׂרָה *With ten utterances the world was created. What does this come to teach us? Indeed, could it not have been created with one utterance? This was to exact punishment from the wicked who destroy the world that was created with ten utterances, and to bestow goodly reward upon the righteous who sustain the world that was created by ten utterances.*

32 §1
(p. 442)

[2] (2) *There were ten generations from Adam to Noah — to show the degree of His patience; for all those generations angered Him increasingly, until He brought upon them the waters of the Flood.*

33 §1
(p. 449)

(3) *There were ten generations from Noah to Abraham — to show the degree of His patience; for all those generations angered Him increasingly, until our forefather Abraham came and received the reward of them all.*

33 §2
(p. 452)

[3] (4) *Our forefather Abraham was tested with ten trials, and he withstood them all — to show the degree of our forefather Abraham's love for God.*

33 §2
(p. 454)

[4] (5) *Ten miracles were performed for our ancestors in Egypt and ten at the Sea. Ten plagues did the Holy One, Blessed is He, bring upon the Egyptians in Egypt and ten at the Sea.*

9 §2; 34 §1
(p. 203;
463)

(6) *With ten trials did our ancestors test the Holy One, Blessed is He, in the Wilderness, as it is said: "They have tested Me these ten times and did not heed My voice."*

35 §1; 5-8
(p. 484;
496)

[5] (7) *Ten miracles were performed for our ancestors in the Holy Temple: No woman miscarried because of the aroma of the sacrificial meat; the sacrificial meat never became putrid; no fly was seen in the place where the meat was butchered; no seminal emission occurred to the High Priest on Yom Kippur; the rains did not extinguish the fire on the Altar pyre; the wind did not disperse the vertical column of smoke from the Altar; no disqualification was found*

אבות ד"ר"נ

בָּעֹמֶר וּבִשְׁתֵּי הַלֶּחֶם וּבְלֶחֶם הַפָּנִים, עוֹמְדִים צְפוּפִים וּמִשְׁתַּחֲוִים רְוָחִים, וְלֹא הִזִּיק נָחָשׁ וְעַקְרָב בִּירוּשָׁלַיִם מֵעוֹלָם, וְלֹא אָמַר אָדָם לַחֲבֵרוֹ, צַר לִי הַמָּקוֹם שֶׁאָלִין בִּירוּשָׁלָיִם.

[ו](ח) עֲשָׂרָה דְבָרִים נִבְרְאוּ בְּעֶרֶב שַׁבָּת בֵּין הַשְּׁמָשׁוֹת, וְאֵלּוּ הֵן, פִּי הָאָרֶץ, וּפִי הַבְּאֵר, וּפִי הָאָתוֹן, וְהַקֶּשֶׁת, וְהַמָּן, וְהַמַּטֶּה, וְהַשָּׁמִיר, וְהַכְּתָב, וְהַמִּכְתָּב, וְהַלּוּחוֹת. וְיֵשׁ אוֹמְרִים, אַף הַמַּזִּיקִין, וּקְבוּרָתוֹ שֶׁל מֹשֶׁה, וְאֵילוֹ שֶׁל אַבְרָהָם אָבִינוּ. וְיֵשׁ אוֹמְרִים, אַף צְבָת בִּצְבָת עֲשׂוּיָה.

לז, יא-יג
(p. 529)

[ז](ט) שִׁבְעָה דְבָרִים בְּגֹלֶם וְשִׁבְעָה בְּחָכָם, חָכָם אֵינוֹ מְדַבֵּר בִּפְנֵי מִי שֶׁהוּא גָדוֹל מִמֶּנּוּ בְּחָכְמָה (וּבְמִנְיָן), וְאֵינוֹ נִכְנָס לְתוֹךְ דִּבְרֵי חֲבֵרוֹ, וְאֵינוֹ נִבְהָל לְהָשִׁיב, שׁוֹאֵל כָּעִנְיָן וּמֵשִׁיב כַּהֲלָכָה, וְאוֹמֵר עַל רִאשׁוֹן רִאשׁוֹן וְעַל אַחֲרוֹן אַחֲרוֹן, וְעַל מַה שֶּׁלֹּא שָׁמַע, אוֹמֵר, לֹא שָׁמַעְתִּי, וּמוֹדֶה עַל הָאֱמֶת. וְחִלּוּפֵיהֶן בְּגֹלֶם.

לח, א-ד
(p. 541)

[ח](י) שִׁבְעָה מִינֵי פֻּרְעָנִיּוֹת בָּאִין לָעוֹלָם עַל שִׁבְעָה גוּפֵי עֲבֵרָה, מִקְצָתָן מְעַשְּׂרִין וּמִקְצָתָן אֵינָן מְעַשְּׂרִין, רָעָב שֶׁל בַּצֹּרֶת בָּא, מִקְצָתָן רְעֵבִים וּמִקְצָתָן שְׂבֵעִים. גָּמְרוּ שֶׁלֹּא לְעַשֵּׂר, רָעָב שֶׁל מְהוּמָה וְשֶׁל בַּצֹּרֶת בָּא. וְשֶׁלֹּא לִטּוֹל אֶת הַחַלָּה, רָעָב שֶׁל כְּלָיָה בָּא.

(יא) דֶּבֶר בָּא לָעוֹלָם עַל מִיתוֹת הָאֲמוּרוֹת בַּתּוֹרָה שֶׁלֹּא נִמְסְרוּ לְבֵית דִּין, וְעַל פֵּרוֹת שְׁבִיעִית. חֶרֶב בָּאָה לָעוֹלָם עַל עִנּוּי הַדִּין, וְעַל עִוּוּת הַדִּין, וְעַל הַמּוֹרִים בַּתּוֹרָה שֶׁלֹּא כַהֲלָכָה.

[ט] חַיָּה רָעָה בָּאָה לָעוֹלָם עַל שְׁבוּעַת שָׁוְא, וְעַל חִלּוּל הַשֵּׁם. גָּלוּת בָּאָה לָעוֹלָם עַל (עוֹבְדֵי) עֲבוֹדָה זָרָה, וְעַל גִּלּוּי עֲרָיוֹת, וְעַל שְׁפִיכוּת דָּמִים, וְעַל הַשְׁמָטַת הָאָרֶץ.

(יב) בְּאַרְבָּעָה פְרָקִים הַדֶּבֶר מִתְרַבֶּה, בָּרְבִיעִית, וּבַשְּׁבִיעִית, וּבְמוֹצָאֵי שְׁבִיעִית, וּבְמוֹצָאֵי הֶחָג שֶׁבְּכָל שָׁנָה וְשָׁנָה. בָּרְבִיעִית, מִפְּנֵי מַעְשַׂר עָנִי שֶׁבַּשְּׁלִישִׁית. בַּשְּׁבִיעִית, מִפְּנֵי מַעְשַׂר

AVOS DR"N | *in the Omer, or in the Two Loaves, or in the Show-bread; the people stood crowded together, yet prostrated themselves in ample space; neither serpent nor scorpion ever caused injury in Jerusalem; nor did any man say to his fellow, "The space is insufficient for me to stay overnight in Jerusalem."*

[6] (8) *Ten things were created on Sabbath eve, at twilight. They are: The mouth of the earth; the mouth of the well; the mouth of the donkey; the rainbow [which was Noah's sign that there would be no future floods]; the manna; the staff; the shamir worm; the script; the inscription; and the Tablets. Some say also destructive spirits, Moses' grave, and the ram of our forefather Abraham. And some say also tongs, which are made with tongs.*

37 §11-13 (p. 529) | **[7]** (9) *Seven traits characterize an uncultivated person and seven a learned one. A learned person does not begin speaking before one who is greater than he in wisdom or in years; he does not interrupt the words of his fellow; he does not answer impetuously; he questions with relevance to the subject and he replies accurately; he discusses first things first and last things last; about something he has not heard he says, "I have not heard"; and he acknowledges the truth. And the reverse of these characterize an uncultivated person.*

38 §1-4 (p. 541) | **[8]** (10) *Seven kinds of punishment come to the world for seven kinds of transgressions. (a) If some people tithe and others do not, a famine caused by lack of rain ensues, some go hungry and others are satisfied; (b) if all decided not to tithe, general famine caused by both armed bands and drought ensues; and (c) [if they also decided] not to separate the challah, a famine caused by destructive drought ensues;*

(11) (d) pestilence comes to the world for the death penalties prescribed by the Torah that were not carried out by the court, and for illegally using the fruits of the Sabbatical year; (e) the sword of war comes to the world for the delay of justice, for the perversion of justice, and for interpreting the Torah decision in opposition to the halachah;

[9] *(f) wild beasts come upon the world for vain oaths and for desecration of God's Name; (g) exile comes to the world for idolatry, for immorality, for bloodshed, and for working the earth during the Sabbatical year.*

(12) At four periods [of the seven-year Sabbatical cycle] pestilence increases — in the fourth year, in the seventh year, in the year following the Sabbatical year, and annually following the Succos Festival. In the fourth year, for [neglecting] the tithe of the poor in the third; in the seventh year, for [neglecting] the tithe of the

אבות דר"נ

עֲנִי שֶׁבַּשְּׁשִׁית. וּבְמוֹצָאֵי שְׁבִיעִית, מִפְּנֵי פֵּרוֹת שְׁבִיעִית.
וּבְמוֹצָאֵי הֶחָג שֶׁבְּכָל שָׁנָה וְשָׁנָה, מִפְּנֵי גֶּזֶל מַתְּנוֹת עֲנִיִּים.

מ, ו
(p. 563)

[י] (יג) אַרְבַּע מִדּוֹת בָּאָדָם, הָאוֹמֵר, שֶׁלִּי שֶׁלִּי וְשֶׁלְּךָ שֶׁלָּךְ, זוֹ
מִדָּה בֵּינוֹנִית. וְיֵשׁ אוֹמְרִים, זוֹ מִדַּת סְדוֹם. שֶׁלִּי שֶׁלְּךָ
וְשֶׁלְּךָ שֶׁלִּי, עַם הָאָרֶץ. שֶׁלִּי שֶׁלְּךָ וְשֶׁלְּךָ שֶׁלָּךְ, חָסִיד. שֶׁלִּי
שֶׁלִּי וְשֶׁלְּךָ שֶׁלִּי, רָשָׁע.

[יא] (יד) אַרְבַּע מִדּוֹת בַּדֵּעוֹת, נוֹחַ לִכְעֹס וְנוֹחַ לִרְצוֹת, יָצָא
שְׂכָרוֹ בְהֶפְסֵדוֹ; קָשֶׁה לִכְעֹס וְקָשֶׁה לִרְצוֹת, יָצָא
הֶפְסֵדוֹ בִשְׂכָרוֹ. קָשֶׁה לִכְעֹס וְנוֹחַ לִרְצוֹת, חָסִיד; נוֹחַ לִכְעֹס
וְקָשֶׁה לִרְצוֹת, רָשָׁע.

[יב] (טו) אַרְבַּע מִדּוֹת בַּתַּלְמִידִים, מַהֵר לִשְׁמֹעַ וּמַהֵר לְאַבֵּד,
יָצָא שְׂכָרוֹ בְהֶפְסֵדוֹ; קָשֶׁה לִשְׁמֹעַ וְקָשֶׁה לְאַבֵּד,
יָצָא הֶפְסֵדוֹ בִשְׂכָרוֹ; מַהֵר לִשְׁמֹעַ וְקָשֶׁה לְאַבֵּד, חָכָם. קָשֶׁה
לִשְׁמֹעַ וּמַהֵר לְאַבֵּד, זֶה חֵלֶק רָע.

[יג] (טז) אַרְבַּע מִדּוֹת בְּנוֹתְנֵי צְדָקָה, הָרוֹצֶה שֶׁיִּתֵּן וְלֹא יִתְּנוּ
אֲחֵרִים, עֵינוֹ רָעָה בְּשֶׁל אֲחֵרִים. יִתְּנוּ אֲחֵרִים וְהוּא לֹא
יִתֵּן, עֵינוֹ רָעָה בְּשֶׁלּוֹ. יִתֵּן וְיִתְּנוּ אֲחֵרִים, חָסִיד. לֹא יִתֵּן וְלֹא
יִתְּנוּ אֲחֵרִים, רָשָׁע.

[יד] (יז) אַרְבַּע מִדּוֹת בַּהוֹלְכֵי לְבֵית הַמִּדְרָשׁ, הוֹלֵךְ וְאֵינוֹ
עוֹשֶׂה, שְׂכַר הֲלִיכָה בְיָדוֹ. עוֹשֶׂה וְאֵינוֹ הוֹלֵךְ, שְׂכַר
מַעֲשֶׂה בְיָדוֹ. הוֹלֵךְ וְעוֹשֶׂה, חָסִיד. לֹא הוֹלֵךְ וְלֹא עוֹשֶׂה, רָשָׁע.

מ, ח
(p. 565)

[טו] (יח) אַרְבַּע מִדּוֹת בְּיוֹשְׁבֵי לִפְנֵי חֲכָמִים, סְפוֹג, וּמַשְׁפֵּךְ,
מְשַׁמֶּרֶת, וְנָפָה. סְפוֹג, שֶׁהוּא סוֹפֵג אֶת הַכֹּל. מַשְׁפֵּךְ,
שֶׁמַּכְנִיס בְּזוֹ וּמוֹצִיא בְזוֹ. מְשַׁמֶּרֶת, שֶׁמּוֹצִיאָה אֶת הַיַּיִן וְקוֹלֶטֶת
אֶת הַשְּׁמָרִים. וְנָפָה, שֶׁמּוֹצִיאָה אֶת הַקֶּמַח וְקוֹלֶטֶת אֶת
הַסֹּלֶת.

מ, יז
(p. 573)

[טז] (יט) כָּל אַהֲבָה שֶׁהִיא תְלוּיָה בְדָבָר, בָּטֵל דָּבָר בְּטֵלָה
אַהֲבָה. וְשֶׁאֵינָהּ תְּלוּיָה בְדָבָר אֵינָהּ בְּטֵלָה לְעוֹלָם.
אֵיזוֹ הִיא אַהֲבָה הַתְּלוּיָה בְדָבָר, זוֹ אַהֲבַת אַמְנוֹן וְתָמָר.
וְשֶׁאֵינָהּ תְּלוּיָה בְדָבָר, זוֹ אַהֲבַת דָּוִד וִיהוֹנָתָן.

AVOS DR"N

poor in the sixth; in the year following the Sabbatical year, for [violating the laws of] the Sabbatical produce; annually, at the conclusion of the Festival of Succos, for robbing the poor of their gifts.

40 §6
(p. 563)

[10] (13) *There are four character types among people: (a) One who says, "My property is mine and yours is yours," is an average character type, but some say this is characteristic of Sodom; (b) "Mine is yours, and yours is mine," is an unlearned person; (c) "Mine is yours and yours is yours," is scrupulously pious; (d) "Yours is mine and mine is mine," is wicked.*

[11] (14) *There are four types of temperament: (a) One who is angered easily and pacified easily, his gain is offset by his loss; (b) one who is hard to anger and hard to pacify, his loss is offset by his gain; (c) one who is hard to anger and easy to pacify is pious; (d) one who is easily angered and hard to pacify is wicked.*

[12] (15) *There are four types of students: (a) One who grasps quickly and forgets quickly, his gain is offset by his loss; (b) one who grasps slowly and forgets slowly, his loss is offset by his gain; (c) one who grasps quickly and forgets slowly, [is] a wise person; (d) one who grasps slowly and forgets quickly, this is a bad portion.*

[13] (16) *There are four types of donors to charity: (a) One who wishes to give himself but wants others not to give, he begrudges others; (b) that others should give but that he should not give, he begrudges himself; (c) that he should give and that others should give is pious; (d) that he should not give and that others should not give is wicked.*

[14] (17) *There are four types among those who go to the house of study: (a) One who goes but does not study has the reward for going; (b) one who studies [at home] but does not attend [the house of study] has the reward for accomplishment; (c) one who goes and studies is pious; (d) one who does not go and does not study is wicked.*

40 §8
(p. 565)

[15] (18) *There are four types among students who sit before the sages: A sponge, a funnel, a strainer and a sieve: a sponge, which absorbs everything; a funnel, which lets in from one end and lets out from the other; a strainer, which lets the wine flow through and retains the sediment; and a sieve, which allows the flour dust to pass through and retains the fine flour.*

40 §17
(p. 573)

[16] (19) *Any love that depends on a specific cause, when that cause is gone, the love is gone; but if it does not depend on a specific cause, it will never cease. What sort of love depended upon a specific cause? — The love of Amnon for Tamar. And what did not depend upon a specific cause? — The love of David and Jonathan.*

אבות דר"נ
מ, יז
(p. 574)

[יז] (ב) כָּל מַחֲלוֹקֶת שֶׁהִיא לְשֵׁם שָׁמַיִם סוֹפָה לְהִתְקַיֵּם, וְשֶׁאֵינָה לְשֵׁם שָׁמַיִם אֵין סוֹפָה לְהִתְקַיֵּם. אֵיזוֹ הִיא מַחֲלוֹקֶת שֶׁהִיא לְשֵׁם שָׁמַיִם, זוֹ מַחֲלוֹקֶת הִלֵּל וְשַׁמַּאי, וְשֶׁאֵינָה לְשֵׁם שָׁמַיִם, זוֹ מַחֲלוֹקֶת קֹרַח וְכָל עֲדָתוֹ.

מ, ג
(p. 561)

[יח] (כא) כָּל הַמְזַכֶּה אֶת הָרַבִּים אֵין חֵטְא בָּא עַל יָדוֹ. וְכָל הַמַּחֲטִיא אֶת הָרַבִּים אֵין מַסְפִּיקִין בְּיָדוֹ לַעֲשׂוֹת תְּשׁוּבָה. מֹשֶׁה זָכָה וְזִכָּה אֶת הָרַבִּים זְכוּת הָרַבִּים תָּלוּי בּוֹ, שֶׁנֶּאֱמַר, צִדְקַת ה' עָשָׂה וּמִשְׁפָּטָיו עִם יִשְׂרָאֵל. יָרָבְעָם חָטָא וְהֶחֱטִיא אֶת הָרַבִּים חֵטְא הָרַבִּים תָּלוּי בּוֹ, שֶׁנֶּאֱמַר, עַל חַטֹּאות יָרָבְעָם (בֶּן נְבָט) אֲשֶׁר חָטָא וַאֲשֶׁר הֶחֱטִיא אֶת יִשְׂרָאֵל.

[יט] (כב) כָּל מִי שֶׁיֵּשׁ בְּיָדוֹ שְׁלֹשָׁה דְבָרִים הַלָּלוּ, מִתַּלְמִידָיו שֶׁל אַבְרָהָם אָבִינוּ, וּשְׁלֹשָׁה דְבָרִים אֲחֵרִים, מִתַּלְמִידָיו שֶׁל בִּלְעָם הָרָשָׁע. עַיִן טוֹבָה, וְרוּחַ נְמוּכָה, וְנֶפֶשׁ שְׁפָלָה, מִתַּלְמִידָיו שֶׁל אַבְרָהָם אָבִינוּ. עַיִן רָעָה, וְרוּחַ גְּבֹהָה, וְנֶפֶשׁ רְחָבָה, מִתַּלְמִידָיו שֶׁל בִּלְעָם הָרָשָׁע. מַה בֵּין תַּלְמִידָיו שֶׁל אַבְרָהָם אָבִינוּ לְתַלְמִידָיו שֶׁל בִּלְעָם הָרָשָׁע, תַּלְמִידָיו שֶׁל אַבְרָהָם אָבִינוּ אוֹכְלִין בָּעוֹלָם הַזֶּה וְנוֹחֲלִין בָּעוֹלָם הַבָּא, שֶׁנֶּאֱמַר, לְהַנְחִיל אֹהֲבַי יֵשׁ, וְאֹצְרֹתֵיהֶם אֲמַלֵּא. אֲבָל תַּלְמִידָיו שֶׁל בִּלְעָם הָרָשָׁע יוֹרְשִׁין גֵּיהִנָּם וְיוֹרְדִין לִבְאֵר שַׁחַת, שֶׁנֶּאֱמַר, וְאַתָּה אֱלֹהִים תּוֹרִדֵם לִבְאֵר שַׁחַת, אַנְשֵׁי דָמִים וּמִרְמָה לֹא יֶחֱצוּ יְמֵיהֶם, וַאֲנִי אֶבְטַח בָּךְ.

מא, י
(p. 584)

[כ] (כג) יְהוּדָה בֶן תֵּימָא אוֹמֵר, הֱוֵי עַז כַּנָּמֵר, וְקַל כַּנֶּשֶׁר, וְרָץ כַּצְּבִי, וְגִבּוֹר כָּאֲרִי לַעֲשׂוֹת רְצוֹן אָבִיךָ שֶׁבַּשָּׁמַיִם.

(כד) הוּא הָיָה אוֹמֵר, עַז פָּנִים לְגֵיהִנָּם, וּבֹשֶׁת פָּנִים לְגַן עֵדֶן. יְהִי רָצוֹן מִלְּפָנֶיךָ ה' אֱלֹהֵינוּ שֶׁתִּבְנֶה עִירְךָ בִּמְהֵרָה בְיָמֵינוּ וְתֵן חֶלְקֵנוּ בְּתוֹרָתֶךָ.

[כא] (כה) הוּא הָיָה אוֹמֵר, בֶּן חָמֵשׁ שָׁנִים לַמִּקְרָא, בֶּן עֶשֶׂר לַמִּשְׁנָה, בֶּן שְׁלֹשׁ עֶשְׂרֵה לַמִּצְוֹת, בֶּן חֲמֵשׁ עֶשְׂרֵה לַתַּלְמוּד, בֶּן שְׁמוֹנֶה עֶשְׂרֵה לַחֻפָּה, בֶּן עֶשְׂרִים לִרְדֹּף,

AVOS DR″N
40 §17
(p. 574)

40 §3
(p. 561)

41 §10
(p. 584)

[17] (20) *Any dispute that is for the sake of Heaven will have a constructive outcome; but one that is not for the sake of Heaven will not have a constructive outcome. What sort of dispute was for the sake of Heaven? — The dispute between Hillel and Shammai. And which was not for the sake of Heaven? — The dispute of Korah and his entire company.*

[18] (21) *Whoever influences the masses to become meritorious shall not be the cause of sin; but one who influences the masses to sin will not be given the means to repent. Moses was meritorious and influenced the masses to be meritorious, so the merit of the masses was to his credit, as it is said: "He performed the righteousness of HASHEM, and His laws together with Israel." Jeroboam ben Nebat sinned and caused the masses to sin, so the sin of the masses is charged against him, as it is said: "For the sins of Jeroboam which he committed and which he caused Israel to commit."*

[19] (22) *Whoever has the following three traits is among the disciples of our forefather Abraham; and [whoever has] three different traits is among the disciples of the wicked Balaam. Those who have a good eye, a humble spirit, and a meek soul are among the disciples of our forefather Abraham. Those who have an evil eye, an arrogant spirit, and a greedy soul are among the disciples of the wicked Balaam. How are the disciples of our forefather Abraham different from the disciples of the wicked Balaam? The disciples of our forefather Abraham enjoy [the fruits of their good deeds] in This World and inherit the World to Come, as is said: "To cause those who love Me to inherit an everlasting possession [the World to Come], and I will fill their storehouses [in This World]." But the disciples of the wicked Balaam inherit Gehinnom and descend into the well of destruction, as is said: "And You, O God, shall lower them into the well of destruction, men of bloodshed and deceit shall not live out half their days; but as for me, I will trust in You."*

[20] (23) *Yehudah ben Tema says: Be bold as a leopard, light as an eagle, swift as a deer, and strong as a lion, to carry out the will of your Father in Heaven.*

(24) *He used to say: The brazen goes to Gehinnom, but the shame-faced goes to the Garden of Eden. May it be Your will, HASHEM, our God and the God of our forefathers, that the Holy Temple be rebuilt, speedily in our days, and grant us our share in Your Torah.*

[21] (25) *He used to say: A five-year-old begins Scripture; a ten-year-old begins Mishnah; a thirteen-year-old becomes obliged to observe the commandments; a fifteen-year-old begins the study of Gemara; an eighteen-year-old goes to the marriage canopy; a twenty-year-old begins pursuit [of a livelihood];*

אבות דר"נ בֶּן שְׁלֹשִׁים לַכֹּחַ, בֶּן אַרְבָּעִים לַבִּינָה, בֶּן חֲמִשִּׁים לָעֵצָה, בֶּן שִׁשִּׁים לַזִּקְנָה, בֶּן שִׁבְעִים לַשֵּׂיבָה, בֶּן שְׁמוֹנִים לַגְּבוּרָה, בֶּן תִּשְׁעִים לָשׁוּחַ, בֶּן מֵאָה כְּאִלּוּ מֵת וְעָבַר וּבָטֵל מִן הָעוֹלָם.

יב, יא
(p. 256) **[כב]** (כו) בֶּן בַּג בַּג אוֹמֵר, הֲפָךְ בָּהּ וַהֲפָךְ בָּהּ, דְּכֹלָּא בָהּ. וּבָהּ תֶּחֱזֵי, וְסִיב וּבְלֵה בָהּ, וּמִנַּהּ לָא תָזוּעַ, שֶׁאֵין לְךָ מִדָּה טוֹבָה הֵימֶנָּה.

יב, יא-יב
(p. 256) **[כג]** בֶּן הֵא הֵא אוֹמֵר, לְפוּם צַעֲרָא אַגְרָא.

※ ※ ※

רַבִּי חֲנַנְיָא בֶּן עֲקַשְׁיָא אוֹמֵר: רָצָה הַקָּדוֹשׁ בָּרוּךְ הוּא לְזַכּוֹת אֶת יִשְׂרָאֵל, לְפִיכָךְ הִרְבָּה לָהֶם תּוֹרָה וּמִצְוֹת, שֶׁנֶּאֱמַר: „יהוה חָפֵץ לְמַעַן צִדְקוֹ, יַגְדִּיל תּוֹרָה וְיַאְדִּיר".

פרק ששי

כָּל יִשְׂרָאֵל יֵשׁ לָהֶם חֵלֶק לָעוֹלָם הַבָּא, שֶׁנֶּאֱמַר: „וְעַמֵּךְ כֻּלָּם צַדִּיקִים, לְעוֹלָם יִירְשׁוּ אָרֶץ, נֵצֶר מַטָּעַי, מַעֲשֵׂה יָדַי לְהִתְפָּאֵר".

※ ※ ※

שָׁנוּ חֲכָמִים בִּלְשׁוֹן הַמִּשְׁנָה, בָּרוּךְ שֶׁבָּחַר בָּהֶם וּבְמִשְׁנָתָם.

[א] (א) רַבִּי מֵאִיר אוֹמֵר, כָּל הָעוֹסֵק בַּתּוֹרָה לִשְׁמָהּ, זוֹכֶה לִדְבָרִים הַרְבֵּה. וְלֹא עוֹד אֶלָּא שֶׁכָּל הָעוֹלָם כֻּלּוֹ כְּדַאי הוּא לוֹ. נִקְרָא רֵעַ, אָהוּב, אוֹהֵב אֶת הַמָּקוֹם, אוֹהֵב אֶת הַבְּרִיּוֹת, מְשַׂמֵּחַ אֶת הַמָּקוֹם, מְשַׂמֵּחַ אֶת הַבְּרִיּוֹת, וּמַלְבַּשְׁתּוֹ עֲנָוָה וְיִרְאָה, וּמַכְשַׁרְתּוֹ לִהְיוֹת צַדִּיק, וְחָסִיד, וְיָשָׁר וְנֶאֱמָן, וּמְרַחַקְתּוֹ מִן הַחֵטְא, וּמְקָרַבְתּוֹ לִידֵי זְכוּת, וְנֶהֱנִין מִמֶּנּוּ עֵצָה וְתוּשִׁיָּה, בִּינָה וּגְבוּרָה. שֶׁנֶּאֱמַר, לִי עֵצָה וְתוּשִׁיָּה, אֲנִי בִינָה, לִי גְבוּרָה, וְנוֹתֶנֶת לוֹ מַלְכוּת וּמֶמְשָׁלָה וְחִקּוּר דִּין, וּמְגַלִּין לוֹ רָזֵי תוֹרָה, וְנַעֲשֶׂה כְּמַעְיָן הַמִּתְגַּבֵּר וּכְנָהָר שֶׁאֵינוֹ פוֹסֵק, וְהָוֵי צָנוּעַ וְאֶרֶךְ רוּחַ, וּמוֹחֵל עַל עֶלְבּוֹנוֹ, וּמְגַדַּלְתּוֹ וּמְרוֹמַמְתּוֹ עַל כָּל הַמַּעֲשִׂים.

[ב] (ב) אָמַר רַבִּי יְהוֹשֻׁעַ בֶּן לֵוִי, בְּכָל יוֹם וָיוֹם בַּת קוֹל יוֹצֵאת מֵהַר חוֹרֵב, וּמַכְרֶזֶת וְאוֹמֶרֶת, אוֹי לָהֶם לַבְּרִיּוֹת מֵעֶלְבּוֹנָהּ שֶׁל תּוֹרָה. שֶׁכָּל מִי שֶׁאֵינוֹ עוֹסֵק בַּתּוֹרָה

AVOS DR"N   a thirty-year-old attains full strength; a forty-year-old attains understanding; a fifty-year-old can offer counsel; a sixty-year-old attains
seniority; a seventy-year-old attains a ripe old age; an eighty-year-
old shows strength; a ninety-year-old becomes stooped over; a
hundred-year-old is as if he were dead, passed away, and ceased
from the world.

12 §11
(p. 256)   **[22]** (26) Ben Bag Bag says: Delve in it [the Torah] and continue to
delve in it [the Torah] for everything is in it; look deeply
into it; grow old and gray over it, and do not stir from it, for you can
have no better portion than it.

12 §11-12
(p. 256)   **[23]** Ben Hei Hei says: The reward is in proportion to the exertion.

❀ ❀ ❀

Rabbi Chanania ben Akashia says: The Holy One, Blessed is He,
wished to confer merit upon Israel; therefore He gave them Torah and
mitzvos in abundance, as it is said: "HASHEM desired, for the sake of its
[Israel's] righteousness, that the Torah be made great and glorious."

CHAPTER SIX

All Israel has a share in the World to Come, as it is said: "And your
people are all righteous; they shall inherit the land forever; they are the
branch of My planting, My handiwork, in which to take pride."

❀ ❀ ❀

שָׁנוּ חֲכָמִים The Sages taught [this chapter] in the language of
the Mishnah. Blessed is He Who chose them and
their teaching.

[1] (1) Rabbi Meir says: Whoever engages in Torah study for its
own sake merits many things; furthermore, [the creation
of] the entire world is worthwhile for his sake alone. He is called,
"Friend, Beloved." He loves the Omnipresent, he loves [His] creatures, he gladdens the Omnipresent, he gladdens [His] creatures.
[The Torah] clothes him in humility and fear [of God]; it makes him
fit to be righteous, devout, fair, and faithful. It moves him away from
sin and draws him near to merit. From him people enjoy counsel
and wisdom, understanding and strength, as it is said: "Mine are
counsel and wisdom, I am understanding, mine is strength." [The
Torah] gives him kingship and dominion and analytical judgment; the secrets of the Torah are revealed to him; he becomes like
a steadily strengthening fountain and like an unceasing river. He
becomes modest, patient, and forgiving of insult to himself. [The
Torah] makes him great and exalts him above all things.

[2] (2) Rabbi Yehoshua ben Levi said: Every single day a Heavenly voice emanates from Mount Horeb, proclaiming and
saying, "Woe to them, to the people, because of [their] insult to
the Torah!" For whoever does not occupy himself with the Torah

אבות דר"נ

°ראה ב, ג
(p. 101)

נִקְרָא נָזוּף, שֶׁנֶּאֱמַר, נֶזֶם זָהָב בְּאַף חֲזִיר, אִשָּׁה יָפָה וְסָרַת טָעַם. °וְאוֹמֵר, וְהַלֻּחֹת מַעֲשֵׂה אֱלֹהִים הֵמָּה, וְהַמִּכְתָּב מִכְתַּב אֱלֹהִים הוּא, חָרוּת עַל הַלֻּחֹת, אַל תִּקְרָא חָרוּת אֶלָּא חֵרוּת, שֶׁאֵין לְךָ בֶּן חוֹרִין אֶלָּא מִי שֶׁעוֹסֵק בְּתַלְמוּד תּוֹרָה. וְכָל מִי שֶׁעוֹסֵק בְּתַלְמוּד תּוֹרָה הֲרֵי זֶה מִתְעַלֶּה, שֶׁנֶּאֱמַר, וּמִמַּתָּנָה נַחֲלִיאֵל וּמִנַּחֲלִיאֵל בָּמוֹת.

[ג] (ג) הַלּוֹמֵד מֵחֲבֵרוֹ פֶּרֶק אֶחָד אוֹ הֲלָכָה אַחַת אוֹ פָסוּק אֶחָד אוֹ דִבּוּר אֶחָד אוֹ אֲפִילוּ אוֹת אַחַת, צָרִיךְ לִנְהָג בּוֹ כָּבוֹד, שֶׁכֵּן מָצִינוּ בְּדָוִד מֶלֶךְ יִשְׂרָאֵל, שֶׁלֹּא לָמַד מֵאֲחִיתֹפֶל אֶלָּא שְׁנֵי דְבָרִים בִּלְבַד, קְרָאוֹ רַבּוֹ אַלּוּפוֹ וּמְיֻדָּעוֹ, שֶׁנֶּאֱמַר, וְאַתָּה אֱנוֹשׁ כְּעֶרְכִּי אַלּוּפִי וּמְיֻדָּעִי. וַהֲלֹא דְבָרִים קַל וָחֹמֶר, וּמָה דָוִד מֶלֶךְ יִשְׂרָאֵל, שֶׁלֹּא לָמַד מֵאֲחִיתֹפֶל אֶלָּא שְׁנֵי דְבָרִים בִּלְבַד, קְרָאוֹ רַבּוֹ אַלּוּפוֹ וּמְיֻדָּעוֹ, הַלּוֹמֵד מֵחֲבֵרוֹ פֶּרֶק אֶחָד אוֹ הֲלָכָה אַחַת אוֹ פָסוּק אֶחָד אוֹ דִבּוּר אֶחָד אוֹ אֲפִילוּ אוֹת אַחַת, עַל אַחַת כַּמָּה וְכַמָּה שֶׁצָּרִיךְ לִנְהָג בּוֹ כָּבוֹד. וְאֵין כָּבוֹד אֶלָּא תוֹרָה, שֶׁנֶּאֱמַר, כָּבוֹד חֲכָמִים יִנְחָלוּ, וּתְמִימִים יִנְחֲלוּ טוֹב; וְאֵין טוֹב אֶלָּא תוֹרָה, שֶׁנֶּאֱמַר, כִּי לֶקַח טוֹב נָתַתִּי לָכֶם תּוֹרָתִי אַל תַּעֲזֹבוּ.

[ד] (ד) כָּךְ הִיא דַרְכָּהּ שֶׁל תּוֹרָה, פַּת בַּמֶּלַח תֹּאכֵל, וּמַיִם בִּמְשׂוּרָה תִּשְׁתֶּה, וְעַל הָאָרֶץ תִּישָׁן, וְחַיֵּי צַעַר תִּחְיֶה, וּבַתּוֹרָה אַתָּה עָמֵל, אִם אַתָּה עֹשֶׂה כֵן, אַשְׁרֶיךָ וְטוֹב לָךְ. אַשְׁרֶיךָ בָּעוֹלָם הַזֶּה, וְטוֹב לָךְ לָעוֹלָם הַבָּא.

(ה) אַל תְּבַקֵּשׁ גְּדֻלָּה לְעַצְמְךָ, וְאַל תַּחְמֹד כָּבוֹד. יוֹתֵר מִלִּמּוּדְךָ עֲשֵׂה. וְאַל תִּתְאַוֶּה לְשֻׁלְחָנָם שֶׁל (שָׂרִים) [מְלָכִים], שֶׁשֻּׁלְחָנְךָ גָדוֹל מִשֻּׁלְחָנָם וְכִתְרְךָ גָּדוֹל מִכִּתְרָם. וְנֶאֱמָן הוּא בַּעַל מְלַאכְתְּךָ שֶׁיְּשַׁלֶּם לְךָ שְׂכַר פְּעֻלָּתֶךָ.

[ה] (ו) גְּדוֹלָה תּוֹרָה יוֹתֵר מִן הַכְּהֻנָּה וּמִן הַמַּלְכוּת, שֶׁהַמַּלְכוּת נִקְנֵית בִּשְׁלֹשִׁים מַעֲלוֹת, וְהַכְּהֻנָּה בְּעֶשְׂרִים וְאַרְבַּע, וְהַתּוֹרָה נִקְנֵית בְּאַרְבָּעִים וּשְׁמוֹנָה דְבָרִים. וְאֵלּוּ הֵן, בְּתַלְמוּד, בִּשְׁמִיעַת הָאֹזֶן, בַּעֲרִיכַת שְׂפָתַיִם, בְּבִינַת הַלֵּב, בְּשִׂכְלוּת הַלֵּב, בְּאֵימָה, בְּיִרְאָה, בַּעֲנָוָה, בְּשִׂמְחָה, בְּשִׁמּוּשׁ חֲכָמִים, בְּדִקְדּוּק

AVOS DR″N

°see 2 §3
(p. 101)

is called, "Rebuked," as it is said: "Like a golden ring in a swine's snout is a beautiful woman who turns away from good judgment." °And it says: "The Tablets are God's handiwork and the script was God's script, 'charus' (engraved) on the Tablets." Do not read "charus" (engraved) but "cheirus" (freedom), for you can have no freer man than one who engages in the study of the Torah. And anyone who engages in the study of the Torah becomes elevated, as it is said: "From Mattanah to Nachaliel, and from Nachaliel to Bamos."

[3] (3) He who learns from his fellowman a single chapter, a single halachah, a single verse, a single Torah statement, or even a single letter, must treat him with honor. For thus we find in the case of David, king of Israel, who learned nothing from Achitophel except for two things, yet called him his teacher, his guide, his intimate, as it is said: "You are a man of my measure, my guide and my intimate." One can derive from this the following: If David, king of Israel, who learned nothing from Achitophel except for two things, called him his teacher, his guide, his intimate — one who learns from his fellowman a single chapter, a single halachah, a single verse, a single statement, or even a single letter, how much more must he treat him with honor! And honor is due only for Torah, as it is said: "The wise shall inherit honor," ". . . and the perfect shall inherit good." And only Torah is truly good, as it is said: "I have given you a good teaching, do not forsake My Torah."

[4] (4) This is the way of Torah: Eat bread with salt, drink water in small measure, sleep on the ground, live a life of deprivation — but toil in the Torah! If you do this, "You are praiseworthy, and all is well with you." "You are praiseworthy" — in This World; "and all is well with you" — in the World to Come.

(5) Do not seek greatness for yourself, and do not crave honor; let your performance exceed your learning. Do not lust for the table of kings, for your table is greater than theirs, and your crown is greater than their crown; and your Employer is trustworthy to pay you remuneration for your deeds.

[5] (6) Torah is even greater than priesthood or royalty; for royalty is acquired along with thirty prerogatives, and the priesthood with twenty-four [gifts], but the Torah is acquired by means of forty-eight qualities, which are: Study, attentive listening, articulate speech, intuitive understanding, discernment, awe, reverence, modesty, joy, purity, ministering to the Sages, closeness

חֲבֵרִים, בְּפִלְפּוּל הַתַּלְמִידִים, בְּיִשּׁוּב, בְּמִקְרָא, בְּמִשְׁנָה, בְּמִעוּט שֵׁנָה, בְּמִעוּט שִׂיחָה, בְּמִעוּט תַּעֲנוּג, בְּמִעוּט שְׂחוֹק, בְּמִעוּט דֶּרֶךְ אֶרֶץ, בְּאֶרֶךְ אַפַּיִם, בְּלֵב טוֹב, בֶּאֱמוּנַת חֲכָמִים, וּבְקַבָּלַת הַיִּסּוּרִין.

[ו] הַמַּכִּיר אֶת מְקוֹמוֹ, וְהַשָּׂמֵחַ בְּחֶלְקוֹ, וְהָעוֹשֶׂה סְיָג לִדְבָרָיו, וְאֵינוּ מַחֲזִיק טוֹבָה לְעַצְמוֹ, אָהוּב, אוֹהֵב אֶת הַמָּקוֹם, אוֹהֵב אֶת הַבְּרִיּוֹת, (אוֹהֵב אֶת הַצְּדָקוֹת,) אוֹהֵב אֶת הַתּוֹכָחוֹת, אוֹהֵב אֶת הַמֵּישָׁרִים, מִתְרַחֵק מִן הַכָּבוֹד, וְלֹא מֵגִיס לִבּוֹ בְּתַלְמוּדוֹ, וְאֵינוּ שָׂמֵחַ בְּהוֹרָאָה, נוֹשֵׂא בְעֹל עִם חֲבֵרוֹ, מַכְרִיעוֹ לְכַף זְכוּת, מַעֲמִידוֹ עַל הָאֱמֶת, מַעֲמִידוֹ עַל הַשָּׁלוֹם, מִתְיַשֵּׁב לִבּוֹ בְּתַלְמוּדוֹ, שׁוֹאֵל וּמֵשִׁיב, שׁוֹמֵעַ וּמוֹסִיף, הַלּוֹמֵד עַל מְנָת לְלַמֵּד, וְהַלּוֹמֵד עַל מְנָת לַעֲשׂוֹת, הַמַּחְכִּים אֶת רַבּוֹ, וְהַמְכַוֵּן אֶת שְׁמוּעָתוֹ, וְהָאוֹמֵר דָּבָר בְּשֵׁם אוֹמְרוֹ. הָא לָמַדְתָּ, שֶׁכָּל הָאוֹמֵר דָּבָר בְּשֵׁם אוֹמְרוֹ, מֵבִיא גְאֻלָּה לָעוֹלָם, שֶׁנֶּאֱמַר, וַתֹּאמֶר אֶסְתֵּר לַמֶּלֶךְ בְּשֵׁם מָרְדֳּכָי.

[ז] (ז) גְּדוֹלָה תוֹרָה, שֶׁהִיא נוֹתֶנֶת חַיִּים לְעוֹשֶׂיהָ בָּעוֹלָם הַזֶּה וּבָעוֹלָם הַבָּא, שֶׁנֶּאֱמַר, כִּי חַיִּים הֵם לְמֹצְאֵיהֶם, וּלְכָל בְּשָׂרוֹ מַרְפֵּא, וְאוֹמֵר, רִפְאוּת תְּהִי לְשָׁרֶּךָ, וְשִׁקּוּי לְעַצְמוֹתֶיךָ, וְאוֹמֵר, עֵץ חַיִּים הִיא לַמַּחֲזִיקִים בָּהּ, וְתֹמְכֶיהָ מְאֻשָּׁר, וְאוֹמֵר, כִּי לִוְיַת חֵן הֵם לְרֹאשֶׁךָ, וַעֲנָקִים לְגַרְגְּרֹתֶיךָ, וְאוֹמֵר, תִּתֵּן לְרֹאשְׁךָ לִוְיַת חֵן, עֲטֶרֶת תִּפְאֶרֶת תְּמַגְּנֶךָ. וְאוֹמֵר, אֹרֶךְ יָמִים בִּימִינָהּ, בִּשְׂמֹאולָהּ עשֶׁר וְכָבוֹד, וְאוֹמֵר, כִּי אֹרֶךְ יָמִים וּשְׁנוֹת חַיִּים וְשָׁלוֹם יוֹסִיפוּ לָךְ.

[ח] (ח) רַבִּי שִׁמְעוֹן בֶּן מְנַסְיָא אוֹמֵר מִשּׁוּם רַבִּי שִׁמְעוֹן בֶּן יוֹחַאי, הַנּוֹי, וְהַכֹּחַ, וְהָעשֶׁר, וְהַכָּבוֹד, וְהַחָכְמָה, וְהַזִּקְנָה וְהַשֵּׂיבָה, וְהַבָּנִים, נָאֶה לַצַּדִּיקִים וְנָאֶה לָעוֹלָם, שֶׁנֶּאֱמַר, עֲטֶרֶת תִּפְאֶרֶת שֵׂיבָה, בְּדֶרֶךְ צְדָקָה תִּמָּצֵא, וְאוֹמֵר, עֲטֶרֶת חֲכָמִים עָשְׁרָם, וְאוֹמֵר, עֲטֶרֶת זְקֵנִים בְּנֵי בָנִים, וְתִפְאֶרֶת בָּנִים אֲבוֹתָם, וְאוֹמֵר, תִּפְאֶרֶת בַּחוּרִים כֹּחָם,

AVOS DR"N | *with colleagues, sharp discussion with students, deliberation, [knowledge of] Scripture, Mishnah, limited business activity, limited sexual activity, limited pleasure, limited sleep, limited conversation, limited laughter, slowness to anger, a good heart, faith in the Sages, and acceptance of suffering.*

[6] *Knowing one's place, being happy with one's lot, making a protective fence around his personal matters, claiming no credit for himself, being beloved, loving the Omnipresent, loving [His] creatures, loving righteous ways, loving justice, loving reproof, keeping far from honor, not being arrogant with his learning, not enjoying halachic decision-making, sharing his fellow's yoke, judging him favorably, setting him on the truthful course, setting him on the peaceful course, thinking deliberately in his study, asking and answering, listening and contributing to the discussion, learning in order to teach, learning in order to practice, making his teacher wiser, pondering over what he has learned, and repeating a saying in the name of the one who said it. For you have learned this: Whoever repeats a thing in the name of the one who said it brings redemption to the world, as it is said: "And Esther said to the king in the name of Mordechai."*

[7] (7) *Great is Torah, for it confers life upon its practitioners, both in This World and in the World to Come, as it is said: "For they [the teachings of the Torah] are life to those who find them, and a healing to his entire flesh." And it says: "It shall be healing to your body, and marrow to your bones." And it says: "It is a tree of life to those who grasp it, and its supporters are praiseworthy." And it says: "They are a garland of grace for your head, and necklaces for your neck." And it says: "It will give to your head a garland of grace, a crown of glory it will deliver to you." And it says: "Indeed, through me (the Torah) your days shall be increased, and years of life shall be added to you." And it says: "Lengthy days are at its right, and at its left are wealth and honor." And it says: "For lengthy days and years of life, and peace shall they add to you."*

[8] (8) *Rabbi Shimon ben Yehudah says in the name of Rabbi Shimon ben Yochai: Beauty, strength, wealth, honor, wisdom, old age, hoary age, and children — these befit the righteous and befit the world, as it is said: "Ripe old age is a crown of splendor; it can be found in the path of righteousness." And it says: "The crown of the aged is grandchildren, and the splendor of children is their fathers." And it says: "The splendor of young men is their strength,*

וַהֲדַר זְקֵנִים שֵׂיבָה, וְאוֹמֵר, וְחָפְרָה הַלְּבָנָה וּבוֹשָׁה הַחַמָּה, כִּי מָלַךְ ה' צְבָאוֹת בְּהַר צִיּוֹן וּבִירוּשָׁלַיִם, וְנֶגֶד זְקֵנָיו כָּבוֹד. רַבִּי שִׁמְעוֹן בֶּן מְנַסְיָא אוֹמֵר, אֵלּוּ שֶׁבַע מִדּוֹת שֶׁמָּנוּ חֲכָמִים לַצַּדִּיקִים, כֻּלָּם נִתְקַיְּמוּ בְּרַבִּי וּבְבָנָיו.

[ט](ט) אָמַר רַבִּי יוֹסֵי בֶּן קִסְמָא, פַּעַם אַחַת הָיִיתִי מְהַלֵּךְ בַּדֶּרֶךְ, וּפָגַע בִּי אָדָם אֶחָד וְנָתַן לִי שָׁלוֹם, וְהֶחֱזַרְתִּי לוֹ שָׁלוֹם. אָמַר לִי, רַבִּי, מֵאֵיזֶה מָקוֹם אַתָּה, אָמַרְתִּי לוֹ, מֵעִיר גְּדוֹלָה שֶׁל חֲכָמִים וְשֶׁל סוֹפְרִים אָנִי. אָמַר לִי, רַבִּי, רְצוֹנְךָ שֶׁתָּדוּר עִמָּנוּ בִּמְקוֹמֵנוּ, וַאֲנִי אֶתֵּן לְךָ אֶלֶף אֲלָפִים דִּנְרֵי זָהָב וַאֲבָנִים טוֹבוֹת וּמַרְגָּלִיּוֹת, אָמַרְתִּי לוֹ, בְּנִי, אִם אַתָּה נוֹתֵן לִי כָּל כֶּסֶף וְזָהָב וַאֲבָנִים טוֹבוֹת וּמַרְגָּלִיּוֹת שֶׁבָּעוֹלָם, אֵינִי דָר אֶלָּא בִּמְקוֹם תּוֹרָה, לְפִי שֶׁבִּשְׁעַת פְּטִירָתוֹ שֶׁל אָדָם אֵין מְלַוִּין לוֹ לְאָדָם לֹא כֶסֶף וְלֹא זָהָב וְלֹא אֲבָנִים טוֹבוֹת וּמַרְגָּלִיּוֹת, אֶלָּא תּוֹרָה וּמַעֲשִׂים טוֹבִים בִּלְבַד, שֶׁנֶּאֱמַר, בְּהִתְהַלֶּכְךָ תַּנְחֶה אֹתָךְ, בְּשָׁכְבְּךָ תִּשְׁמֹר עָלֶיךָ, וַהֲקִיצוֹתָ הִיא תְשִׂיחֶךָ, בְּהִתְהַלֶּכְךָ תַּנְחֶה אֹתָךְ בָּעוֹלָם הַזֶּה, בְּשָׁכְבְּךָ תִּשְׁמֹר עָלֶיךָ בַּקֶּבֶר, וַהֲקִיצוֹתָ הִיא תְשִׂיחֶךָ לָעוֹלָם הַבָּא. וְכֵן כָּתוּב בְּסֵפֶר תִּלִּים עַל יְדֵי דָוִד מֶלֶךְ יִשְׂרָאֵל, טוֹב לִי תוֹרַת פִּיךָ, מֵאַלְפֵי זָהָב וָכָסֶף, וְאוֹמֵר, לִי הַכֶּסֶף וְלִי הַזָּהָב נְאֻם ה' צְבָאוֹת.

[י](י) חֲמִשָּׁה קִנְיָנִים קָנָה הַקָּדוֹשׁ בָּרוּךְ הוּא בְּעוֹלָמוֹ, וְאֵלּוּ הֵן, תּוֹרָה קִנְיָן אֶחָד, שָׁמַיִם וָאָרֶץ קִנְיָן אֶחָד, אַבְרָהָם קִנְיָן אֶחָד, יִשְׂרָאֵל קִנְיָן אֶחָד, בֵּית הַמִּקְדָּשׁ קִנְיָן אֶחָד. תּוֹרָה מִנַּיִן, דִּכְתִיב, ה' קָנָנִי רֵאשִׁית דַּרְכּוֹ קֶדֶם מִפְעָלָיו מֵאָז. שָׁמַיִם וָאָרֶץ מִנַּיִן, דִּכְתִיב, כֹּה אָמַר ה', הַשָּׁמַיִם כִּסְאִי וְהָאָרֶץ הֲדֹם רַגְלָי, אֵי זֶה בַיִת אֲשֶׁר תִּבְנוּ לִי, וְאֵי זֶה מָקוֹם מְנוּחָתִי, וְאוֹמֵר, מָה רַבּוּ מַעֲשֶׂיךָ ה' כֻּלָּם בְּחָכְמָה עָשִׂיתָ, מָלְאָה הָאָרֶץ קִנְיָנֶךָ. אַבְרָהָם מִנַּיִן, דִּכְתִיב, וַיְבָרְכֵהוּ וַיֹּאמַר, בָּרוּךְ אַבְרָם לְאֵל עֶלְיוֹן קֹנֵה שָׁמַיִם וָאָרֶץ. יִשְׂרָאֵל מִנַּיִן, דִּכְתִיב, עַד יַעֲבֹר עַמְּךָ ה' עַד יַעֲבֹר עַם זוּ קָנִיתָ, וְאוֹמֵר, לִקְדוֹשִׁים אֲשֶׁר בָּאָרֶץ הֵמָּה,

AVOS DR"N

and the glory of old men is hoary age." And it says: "The moon will grow pale and the sun be shamed, when HASHEM, Master of Legions, will have reigned on Mount Zion and in Jerusalem, and honor shall be before His elders." Rabbi Shimon ben Menasya says: These seven qualities that the Sages attributed to the righteous were all realized in Rebbi and his sons.

[9] (9) *Rabbi Yose ben Kisma said: Once I was walking on the road, when a certain man met me. He greeted me and I returned his greeting. He said to me, "Rabbi, from what place are you?" I said to him, "I am from a great city of scholars and sages." He said to me, "Rabbi, would you be willing to live with us in our place? I would give you thousands upon thousands of golden dinars, precious stones, and pearls." I replied, "Even if you were to give me all the silver and gold, precious stones and pearls in the world, I would dwell nowhere but in a place of Torah." And so it is written in the Book of Psalms by David, king of Israel: "I prefer the Torah of Your mouth above thousands in gold and silver." Furthermore, when a man departs from This World, neither silver, nor gold, nor precious stones, nor pearls escort him, but only Torah study and good deeds, as it is said: "When you walk, it shall guide you; when you lie down, it shall guard you; and when you awake, it shall speak on your behalf." "When you walk, it shall guide you" — in This World; "when you lie down, it shall guard you" — in the grave; "and when you awake, it shall speak on your behalf" — in the World to Come. And it says: "Mine is the silver, and Mine is the gold, says HASHEM, Master of Legions."*

[10] (10) *Five possessions did the Holy One, Blessed is He, acquire [for Himself] in His world, and they are: Torah, one possession; heaven and earth, one possession; Abraham, one possession; Israel, one possession; the Holy Temple, one possession. From where do we know this about the Torah? Since it is written: "HASHEM acquired me [the Torah] at the beginning of His way, before His works in time of yore." From where do we know this about heaven and earth? Since it is written: "So says HASHEM. The heaven is My throne, and the earth is My footstool; what House can you build for Me, and where is the place of My rest?" And it says: "How abundant are Your works, HASHEM, with wisdom You made them all, the earth is full of Your possessions." From where do we know this about Abraham? Since it is written: "And He blessed him and said: Blessed is Abram of God the Most High, Who acquired heaven and earth." From where do we know this about the people of Israel? Since it is written: "Until Your people passes through, HASHEM, until it passes through — this people You acquired," and it [also] says: "But for the holy ones who are in the earth and for the mighty —*

אבות דר"נ

וְאַדִּירֵי כָל חֶפְצִי בָם. בֵּית הַמִּקְדָּשׁ מִנַּיִן, דִּכְתִיב, מָכוֹן לְשִׁבְתְּךָ פָּעַלְתָּ ה׳ מִקְדָּשׁ אֲדֹנָי כּוֹנֲנוּ יָדֶיךָ, וְאוֹמֵר, וַיְבִיאֵם אֶל גְּבוּל קָדְשׁוֹ הַר זֶה קָנְתָה יְמִינוֹ.

מא, טז
(p. 591)

[יא] (יא) כָּל מַה שֶּׁבָּרָא הַקָּדוֹשׁ בָּרוּךְ הוּא בְּעוֹלָמוֹ, לֹא בָּרָא אֶלָּא לִכְבוֹדוֹ, שֶׁנֶּאֱמַר, כֹּל הַנִּקְרָא בִשְׁמִי, וְלִכְבוֹדִי בְּרָאתִיו, יְצַרְתִּיו אַף עֲשִׂיתִיו, וְאוֹמֵר, ה׳ יִמְלֹךְ לְעֹלָם וָעֶד.

🙢 🙢 🙢

רַבִּי חֲנַנְיָא בֶּן עֲקַשְׁיָא אוֹמֵר: רָצָה הַקָּדוֹשׁ בָּרוּךְ הוּא לְזַכּוֹת אֶת יִשְׂרָאֵל, לְפִיכָךְ הִרְבָּה לָהֶם תּוֹרָה וּמִצְוֹת, שֶׁנֶּאֱמַר: „יהוה חָפֵץ לְמַעַן צִדְקוֹ, יַגְדִּיל תּוֹרָה וְיַאְדִּיר".

AVOS DR"N

all my desires are due to them." From where do we know this about the Holy Temple? Since it is written: "Your dwelling-place which You, HASHEM, have made; the Sanctuary, my Lord, that Your hands established." And it says: "And He brought them to His sacred boundary, to this mountain which His right hand acquired."

41 §16
(p. 591)

[11] (11) *All that the Holy One, Blessed is He, created in His world, He created solely for His glory, as it is said: "All that is called by My Name, indeed, it is for My glory that I have created it, formed it, and made it." And it says: "HASHEM shall reign for all eternity."*

᎚ ᎚ ᎚

Rabbi Chanania ben Akashia says: The Holy One, Blessed is He, wished to confer merit upon Israel; therefore He gave them Torah and mitzvos in abundance, as it is said: "HASHEM desired, for the sake of its [Israel's] righteousness, that the Torah be made great and glorious."

אבות דרבי נתן ✑

Avos DeRabbi Nassan

Please note that throughout our commentary, the word "Baraisa," unless otherwise noted, refers to the statement of *Avos DeRabbi Nassan* that is being discussed.

‎‏ פֶּרֶק א ‏

א. מֹשֶׁה[1] נִתְקַדֵּשׁ בֶּעָנָן וְקִבֵּל תּוֹרָה מִסִּינַי[2], שֶׁנֶּאֱמַר (שמות כד, טז) "וַיִּשְׁכֹּן
כְּבוֹד ה' עַל הַר סִינַי", לְמֹשֶׁה לְטַהֲרוֹ, זֶה הָיָה אַחַר עֲשֶׂרֶת הַדִּבְּרוֹת[3],

‎‏ CHAPTER 1 ‏

§1 The Mishnah in *Pirkei Avos* begins with a statement about the Torah's origin: "Moses received the Torah from Sinai." *Avos DeRabbi Nassan* begins by focusing on one aspect of this historic event.[1]

מֹשֶׁה נִתְקַדֵּשׁ בֶּעָנָן — After ascending Mount Sinai, **Moses became sanctified in the cloud** of God's presence hovering at the top of the mountain, וְקִבֵּל תּוֹרָה מִסִּינַי — **and he received the Torah from Sinai**,[2] שֶׁנֶּאֱמַר "וַיִּשְׁכֹּן כְּבוֹד ה' עַל הַר סִינַי", לְמֹשֶׁה as it is stated, *And the glory of HASHEM rested upon Mount Sinai, and the cloud covered him* — that is, it covered **Moses** — *for six days* לְטַהֲרוֹ — **to purify him** in preparation for receiving the Torah. זֶה הָיָה אַחַר עֲשֶׂרֶת הַדִּבְּרוֹת — **This occurred after** the giving of **the Ten Commandments**.[3]

---

1. *Binyan Yehoshua.* [This Baraisa is cited in *Yoma* 4b with some variations; *Gra* considers the Gemara's version to be the correct one (see note in *Avos DeRabbi Nassan im Hagahos HaGra*, p. 1).]

The following background helps us understand this Baraisa: The events of *Mattan Torah* [the Giving of the Torah] unfolded in three stages. On Rosh Chodesh Sivan, when the nation arrived at the foot of Mount Sinai, Moses ascended the mountain, and God, speaking through Moses, began the process of offering Israel the Torah and preparing the people to hear His voice. On the sixth or seventh day of the month (opinions differ — see below, note 6), God revealed Himself to the entire nation and proclaimed the Ten Commandments amid lightning, thunder, and shofar blasts. On the following day, Moses reascended the mountain and, over the next forty days and nights, God taught him the rest of the Torah and gave him the first set of Tablets (*Luchos*).

In the Scriptural account of these events, the Torah says at one point that when Moses ascended the mountain, *the glory of Hashem rested upon Mount Sinai, and the cloud covered "him/it"* (וַיְכַסֵּהוּ הֶעָנָן) *for six days. He called to Moses on the seventh day from the midst of the cloud* (Exodus 24:16).

From the context of the verse, it is not clear what six-day period is meant. Were these the first six days of Sivan, when Moses and the people were preparing to receive the Ten Commandments? Or perhaps the six days mentioned here began *after* the giving of the Ten Commandments, when Moses went up for his forty-day stay on Mount Sinai? [Also not clear from the verse is whether the suffix הוּ in וַיְכַסֵּהוּ means "him" or "it." This will depend on which six-day period the verse refers to, as will be seen below.] The Baraisa will present different opinions on this matter.

2. Meaning, from the One Who revealed Himself at Sinai (*Binyan Yehoshua*), or, owing to the lesson Moses learned from Mount Sinai — for at first Moses shrank from receiving the Torah on behalf of the nation, thinking himself unworthy of the task. Only when he contemplated God's choice of humble Mount Sinai for this momentous event, precisely because it was ordinary and unpretentious, was Moses able to justify accepting the role of intermediary for himself (*Ahavas Chesed* in marginal note, citing *Kli Yakar*).

3. At the beginning of Moses' forty-day sojourn on Mount Sinai, where he was taught the remainder of the Torah (*Binyan Yehoshua*; see above, note 1).

דִּבְרֵי רַבִּי יוֹסֵי הַגְּלִילִי⁴. (משום) רַבִּי עֲקִיבָא אוֹמֵר: (שם) "וַיְכַסֵּהוּ הֶעָנָן
שֵׁשֶׁת יָמִים" °לְמֹשֶׁה⁵, (ההי"ד) (שם) "וַיִּקְרָא אֶל מֹשֶׁה בַּיּוֹם הַשְּׁבִיעִי מִתּוֹךְ
הֶעָנָן" לַחֲלוֹק לוֹ כָּבוֹד לְמֹשֶׁה⁷·⁶. אָמַר רַבִּי נָתָן: מִפְּנֵי מָה נִתְעַכֵּב מֹשֶׁה
כָּל שֵׁשֶׁת יָמִים וְלֹא שָׁרָה עָלָיו דִּבּוּר. בִּשְׁבִיל שֶׁיְּמָרֵק מִכָּל אֲכִילָה וּשְׁתִיָּה

דִּבְרֵי רַבִּי יוֹסֵי הַגְּלִילִי — **These are the words of R' Yose HaGlili.**[4]

Another opinion:

"וַיְכַסֵּהוּ הֶעָנָן שֵׁשֶׁת יָמִים" לָהָר וְלֹא לְמֹשֶׁה — R' Akiva says: רַבִּי עֲקִיבָא אוֹמֵר
— When the verse says *and the cloud covered* "הוּ" *for six days,* it means that
it covered **the mountain, not Moses.**[5] וַיִּקְרָא אֶל מֹשֶׁה בַּיּוֹם הַשְּׁבִיעִי מִתּוֹךְ
הֶעָנָן" — Accordingly, when the verse goes on to say that *He called to Moses
on the seventh day* — the day of the Revelation[6] — *from the midst of the
cloud,* it cannot mean that He called to Moses alone, for God addressed all of
Israel when He gave them the Ten Commandments. לַחֲלוֹק לוֹ כָּבוֹד לְמֹשֶׁה —
Rather, the Torah merely wishes **to accord honor to Moses** by singling him out
from among all of Israel.[7]

Two other sages comment on this matter:

מִפְּנֵי מָה נִתְעַכֵּב מֹשֶׁה כָּל שֵׁשֶׁת יָמִים וְלֹא — **R' Nassan said:** אָמַר רַבִּי נָתָן
Why was Moses kept waiting for six whole days be- שָׁרָה עָלָיו דִּבּוּר
fore God's word rested upon him? בִּשְׁבִיל שֶׁיְּמָרֵק מִכָּל אֲכִילָה וּשְׁתִיָּה

---

4. Why was it necessary at this point to
confine Moses in the cloud for six days? According to R' Yose HaGlili, the reason is that
anyone seeking to enter the Camp of the
Divine Presence needs to undergo a period
of isolation (*perishah*). From this he derives
the rule that the Kohen Gadol needs to be
isolated for a week's time before Yom Kippur, when he is required to enter the Holy
of Holies as part of the Yom Kippur sacrificial service (*Rashi, Yoma* 4a). [This is what
the Baraisa means by לְטַהֲרוֹ, *to purify him.*
Some, however, omit this word from the
Baraisa (see *Binyan Yehoshua*).]

5. [Emendation follows *Gra* and many other
commentators.] This Baraisa is found in an
expanded form in *Yoma* 4a-b, where the
Baraisa introduces R' Akiva's opinion with
his understanding that the "six days" of this
verse began from Rosh Chodesh Sivan, with
the seventh day being the day of *Mattan
Torah.* According to this approach, the
phrase וַיְכַסֵּהוּ הֶעָנָן cannot mean *and the
cloud covered "him,"* i.e., Moses (as R' Yose

HaGlili explained it), for Moses did not stay
on the mountain for all those six days; rather,
he went up and down the mountain, carrying
messages back and forth between God and
the people in preparation for *Mattan Torah*
(see *Rashi* to *Yoma* ad loc.). It means, rather,
and the cloud covered "it" — the mountain.

6. This accords with R' Akiva's opinion that
the Revelation took place on 7 Sivan. R'
Yose HaGlili, on the other hand, holds that
the Revelation occurred on 6 Sivan. He is
therefore compelled to say that the six days
of our passage took place *after* the Revelation (*Yoma* 4b).

7. This is contrast to the first opinion (that
of R' Yose HaGlili), which upholds the more
straightforward reading of the verse that
God called *only* to Moses: After six days
of confining Moses within the cloud, God
called him, and only him, to learn the rest
of the Torah. [See *Ramban* (commentary on
Exodus 24:1), who accepts as primary the
opinion that the entire narrative of that passage occurred after the Revelation.]

שֶׁהָיָה בִּמְעָיו עַד שָׁעָה שֶׁנִּתְקַדֵּשׁ וִיהֵא כְּמַלְאֲכֵי הַשָּׁרֵת[8]. אָמַר לוֹ רַבִּי מַתְיָא
בֶּן חָרָשׁ: רַבִּי, לֹא אָמְרוּ אֶלָּא לְאַיֵּם עָלָיו, כְּדֵי שֶׁיְּקַבֵּל עָלָיו דִּבְרֵי תוֹרָה
בְּאֵימָה בְּיִרְאָה בְּרֶתֶת וּבְזִיעַ, שֶׁנֶּאֱמַר (תהלים ב, יא) "עִבְדוּ אֶת ה' בְּיִרְאָה
וְגִילוּ בִּרְעָדָה"[10]. מַעֲשֶׂה שֶׁאֵירַע בְּרַבִּי יֹאשִׁיָּה וּבְרַבִּי מַתְיָא בֶּן חָרָשׁ

שֶׁהָיָה בִּמְעָיו — So that he could be cleansed of all the food and drink that remained in his innards, עַד שָׁעָה שֶׁנִּתְקַדֵּשׁ וִיהֵא כְּמַלְאֲכֵי הַשָּׁרֵת — until the moment came that he was sanctified and would be like one of the ministering angels.[8] אָמַר לוֹ רַבִּי מַתְיָא בֶּן חָרָשׁ — R' Masya ben Charash said to him: רַבִּי לֹא אָמְרוּ אֶלָּא לְאַיֵּם עָלָיו — My teacher, the Sages did not say this explanation. Rather, they said that God kept Moses waiting in the cloud to instill fear in him, כְּדֵי שֶׁיְּקַבֵּל עָלָיו דִּבְרֵי תוֹרָה בְּאֵימָה בְּיִרְאָה בְּרֶתֶת וּבְזִיעַ — so that he would accept on himself the words of Torah with fear, awe, trembling, and quaking.[9] שֶׁנֶּאֱמַר "עִבְדוּ אֶת ה' בְּיִרְאָה וְגִילוּ בִּרְעָדָה" — Such reverence is necessary for receiving the Torah, as it is stated, *Serve HASHEM with awe, and rejoice with trepidation* (*Psalms* 2:11). By speaking of awe and rejoicing in the same sentence, the verse implies that in the place of rejoicing — that is, when receiving the Torah, whose mitzvos gladden the heart — there should be trepidation.[10]

An incident concerning the last sage mentioned:[11]

מַעֲשֶׂה שֶׁאֵירַע בְּרַבִּי יֹאשִׁיָּה וּבְרַבִּי מַתְיָא בֶּן חָרָשׁ — An incident occurred with

---

8. R' Nassan agrees with R' Yose HaGlili that it was Moses who was covered by the cloud for six days after the Revelation. However, unlike R' Yose HaGlili, who maintains that this verse establishes a general rule that anyone entering the Camp of the Divine Presence, such as the Kohen Gadol on Yom Kippur, requires isolation in advance (see *Yoma* ibid.), R' Nassan holds that the isolation of Moses applied only to him, to cleanse his innards of any remnant of food and drink, so that he would resemble an angel. This sublime readiness was not required of the Kohen Gadol before entering the Holy of Holies (*Rashi, Yoma* 4b).

Why, then, was it required of Moses? Because in ascending to heaven and claiming the Torah for Israel, Moses would have to overcome the opposition of the angels, who would protest the giving of such a Heavenly treasure to a man of flesh and blood. *"What is a mortal,"* they would ask of God in wonderment, *"that You should remember him, or*

the son of man that You should recall him?" To deflect their arguments, it was necessary that Moses resemble an angel as much as possible (*Mefaresh* and *Ben Avraham*, based on *Shabbos* 88b).

9. R' Masya, too, agrees with R' Yose HaGlili that it was Moses whom the cloud covered. This instilled in Moses the awe and trepidation necessary to enter the Heavenly realm.

10. *Yoma* 4b with *Rashi.*

The lesson to take away from this discussion concerns the proper attitude toward Torah study. If Moses, the greatest of prophets and humblest of men, needed to undergo a program of sanctification before receiving the Torah, then how much more necessary is it for us ordinary mortals to sanctify ourselves in order to absorb the Torah's holy teachings! (*Magen Avos*).

11. *Binyan Yehoshua.* For more on the relevance of this incident, see below, end of note 15.

שֶׁהָיוּ שְׁנֵיהֶם יוֹשְׁבִים וְעוֹסְקִין בְּדִבְרֵי תוֹרָה, פֵּירַשׁ רַבִּי יֹאשִׁיָּה לְדֶרֶךְ
אֶרֶץ, אָמַר לוֹ רַבִּי מַתְיָא בֶּן חָרָשׁ: רַבִּי, מַה לְךָ לַעֲזוֹב דִּבְרֵי אֱלֹהִים
חַיִּים וְלִשְׁטוֹף בְּדֶרֶךְ אֶרֶץ, (וְאַף עַל פִּי שֶׁאַתָּה רַבִּי וַאֲנִי תַּלְמִידְךָ)[14]
אֵין טוֹב לַעֲזוֹב דִּבְרֵי אֱלֹהִים חַיִּים וְלִשְׁטוֹף בְּדֶרֶךְ אֶרֶץ,)[15] וְאָמְרוּ:

שֶׁהָיוּ שְׁנֵיהֶם יוֹשְׁבִים וְעוֹסְקִין בְּדִבְרֵי — R' Yoshiyah and R' Masya ben Charash,
תוֹרָה — who had both been devoting their lives to sitting and studying the
words of Torah study. פֵּירַשׁ רַבִּי יֹאשִׁיָּה לְדֶרֶךְ אֶרֶץ — There came a time,
however, when R' Yoshiyah, out of severe financial distress,[12] left the study
hall to take up a worldly occupation. אָמַר לוֹ רַבִּי מַתְיָא בֶּן חָרָשׁ — R' Masya
ben Charash said to him: רַבִּי, מַה לְךָ לַעֲזוֹב דִּבְרֵי אֱלֹהִים חַיִּים וְלִשְׁטוֹף בְּדֶרֶךְ
אֶרֶץ — My teacher, why would you abandon the words of the Living God and
become absorbed[13] in a worldly occupation? וְאַף עַל פִּי שֶׁאַתָּה רַבִּי וַאֲנִי
תַּלְמִידְךָ — And even though you are my teacher and I am your student,[14]
אֵין טוֹב לַעֲזוֹב דִּבְרֵי אֱלֹהִים חַיִּים וְלִשְׁטוֹף בְּדֶרֶךְ אֶרֶץ — it is still my duty to point
out respectfully that it is not good to abandon the words of the Living God
and become absorbed in a worldly occupation.[15] וְאָמְרוּ — And they (those

12. Mefaresh

13. Ahavas Chesed, Kisei Rachamim.

14. R' Masya was actually a talmid chaver,
part disciple and part colleague, of R' Yoshiyah, which is why the story begins and
ends by describing them as sitting together
and studying Torah, as if they were equals
(ibid.).

15. What was the basis of their dispute?
Some maintain that they differed over the
same issue that was disputed by Ilfa and
R' Yochanan, another pair of Torah students who became unbearably poor, in a
later generation. The Talmud (Taanis 21a)
relates that at first Ilfa and R' Yochanan resolved to undertake a joint business venture
to fulfill the verse that states, But among
you there shall be no destitute, taking that
verse as teaching that an individual should
work rather than live in severe poverty. But
then R' Yochanan, prompted by a Heavenly sign, had a change of heart. He said
to Ilfa, "I have decided to go back to studying Torah, and I will thereby fulfill another
Scriptural verse, The poor will never cease
from the midst of the land — which offers an
exemption, presumably to Torah scholars,
from the obligation to avoid poverty." Ilfa,

unconvinced by this argument, continued
on his way, while R' Yochanan returned to
the yeshivah, and eventually rose to become its leading light (Binyan Yehoshua,
quoting Mefaresh).

[Interestingly, the similarly persistent R'
Masya ben Charash also attained great
prominence in the Torah world. He was a
Rosh Yeshivah in Rome (Sanhedrin 32b et
al.; see, though, Avos HaRosh [Vol. 2] here),
and his court of Torah law was considered
the leading Beis Din of his time (Hagahos
Maimoniyos, Hil. Sanhedrin 6:10).]

How much deprivation should a Torah
student endure? According to Chida, both
sages agreed that one must have at least
enough to cover his most basic needs.
Their disagreement arose only because
they (barely) cleared that threshold. R'
Yoshiyah advocated leaving full-time study
to reduce the stress of an impoverished
lifestyle and to support one's family more
generously, whereas R' Masya opposed this
(Kisei Rachamim). [For a practical discussion of this subject, see Igros Moshe, Yoreh
Deah IV 36:5.]

In any case, R' Masya's stringent view on
the question of a worldly occupation stems

כָּל זְמַן שֶׁיּוֹשְׁבִין וְעוֹסְקִין בַּתּוֹרָה הָיוּ עוֹשִׂין מְקַנְאִין זֶה לָזֶה, וּכְשֶׁנִּפְטָרִין דּוֹמִין כְּשֶׁהֵן אוֹהֲבִים מִנְּעוּרֵיהֶם:[16]

ב. עַל יְדֵי מֹשֶׁה נִתְּנָה תוֹרָה בְּסִינַי, שֶׁנֶּאֱמַר (דברים ה, יט) "וַיִּכְתְּבֵם עַל שְׁנֵי לֻחֹת אֲבָנִים וַיִּתְּנֵם אֵלָי" וּלְהַלָּן הוּא אוֹמֵר (ויקרא כו, מו) "אֵלֶּה הַחֻקִּים וְהַמִּשְׁפָּטִים וְהַתּוֹרֹת אֲשֶׁר נָתַן ה' בֵּינוֹ וּבֵין בְּנֵי יִשְׂרָאֵל בְּהַר סִינַי בְּיַד מֹשֶׁה"[17]. תּוֹרָה שֶׁנָּתַן הַקָּדוֹשׁ בָּרוּךְ הוּא לְיִשְׂרָאֵל לֹא נִתְּנָה אֶלָּא עַל יְדֵי מֹשֶׁה,

familiar with these two sages) **said:** כָּל זְמַן שֶׁיּוֹשְׁבִין וְעוֹסְקִין בַּתּוֹרָה הָיוּ עוֹשִׂין מְקַנְאִין זֶה לָזֶה — **As long as they were sitting and studying Torah, they would make** themselves **as rivals with each other,** וּכְשֶׁנִּפְטָרִין דּוֹמִין כְּשֶׁהֵן אוֹהֲבִים מִנְּעוּרֵיהֶם — **yet when they would part** from each other, **they would be like friends from their youth.**[16]

§2 The Baraisa now returns to the discussion of its opening line, which said that Moses became sanctified in the cloud of the Divine Presence and received the Torah on Mount Sinai. The Baraisa now highlights various ways in which Moses helped shape Israel's destiny for all time: עַל יְדֵי מֹשֶׁה נִתְּנָה תוֹרָה בְּסִינַי — **It was through Moses that the Torah was given** to Israel **at Sinai,** שֶׁנֶּאֱמַר "וַיִּכְתְּבֵם עַל שְׁנֵי לֻחֹת אֲבָנִים וַיִּתְּנֵם אֵלָי" — **as it is stated,** *And [God] inscribed them on two Tablets of stone and gave them to me* (Deuteronomy 5:19), וּלְהַלָּן הוּא אוֹמֵר — **and elsewhere it says,** "אֵלֶּה הַחֻקִּים וְהַמִּשְׁפָּטִים וְהַתּוֹרֹת אֲשֶׁר נָתַן ה' בֵּינוֹ וּבֵין בְּנֵי יִשְׂרָאֵל בְּהַר סִינַי בְּיַד מֹשֶׁה" — *These are the laws, statutes, and teachings that HASHEM gave between Him and the Children of Israel at Mount Sinai, by the hand of Moses* (Leviticus 26:46).[17] תּוֹרָה שֶׁנָּתַן הַקָּדוֹשׁ בָּרוּךְ הוּא לְיִשְׂרָאֵל לֹא נִתְּנָה אֶלָּא עַל יְדֵי מֹשֶׁה — **And from this second verse we see an added point: The Torah that the Holy One, Blessed is He, gave to Israel, He gave only through Moses,**

---

from his previously mentioned teaching that Torah study requires "fear, awe, trembling, and quaking." In his judgment, it is not possible to maintain such a reverent attitude while one is occupied with material pursuits. This is why the Baraisa introduces this story precisely at this point (*Magen Avos*).

16. In accordance with the Gemara's teaching: "Even a father and his son, or a teacher and his student, who are studying Torah together at first become 'enemies' of one another [in the contentious atmosphere of Talmudic debate]; yet, they do not move

from there until they become devoted friends of one another [bonded by their shared pursuit of the Divine truth]" (*Kiddushin* 30b).

17. Thus, the verses state that Moses was the intermediary not only for the Ten Commandments but also for the entire Torah, including its written and oral elements. This is alluded to not only by the multiple terms (*laws, statutes, and teachings*), but also by the expression תּוֹרֹת, *Torahs*, which refers (as *Sifra* to the verse explains) to two distinct sections of Torah knowledge, one written and one oral (*Magen Avos, Binyan Yehoshua*).

שֶׁנֶּאֱמַר °"בֵּינִי וּבֵין בְּנֵי יִשְׂרָאֵל"[18], זָכָה מֹשֶׁה לִהְיוֹת שָׁלִיחַ בֵּין בְּנֵי יִשְׂרָאֵל
לַמָּקוֹם.[19] מֹשֶׁה (עָשָׂה אֶת אֵיל הַמִּלּוּאִים[20] וְאֶת) שֶׁמֶן הַמִּשְׁחָה[21] וּמִשַׁח
בּוֹ אַהֲרֹן וּבָנָיו כָּל שִׁבְעַת יְמֵי הַמִּלּוּאִים[22], מִמֶּנּוּ נִמְשְׁחוּ כֹּהֲנִים גְּדוֹלִים
וּמְלָכִים. וְאֶלְעָזָר שָׂרַף פָּרַת הַחַטָּאת שֶׁמִּמֶּנּוּ טְמֵאִים מְטַהֲרִים לְדוֹרוֹת.[24]

שֶׁנֶּאֱמַר "בֵּינוֹ וּבֵין בְּנֵי יִשְׂרָאֵל" — as it is stated in this verse, *between Him and the Children of Israel*,[18] זָכָה מֹשֶׁה לִהְיוֹת שָׁלִיחַ בֵּין בְּנֵי יִשְׂרָאֵל לַמָּקוֹם — for only Moses had the merit to serve as the intermediary between the Children of Israel and the Omnipresent.[19]

The Baraisa continues with other examples of Moses' everlasting legacy: מֹשֶׁה עָשָׂה אֶת אֵיל הַמִּלּוּאִים — Moses performed the service of the *Miluim* ram[20] וְאֶת שֶׁמֶן הַמִּשְׁחָה — and made the Anointing Oil.[21] וּמִשַׁח בּוֹ אַהֲרֹן וּבָנָיו כָּל שִׁבְעַת יְמֵי הַמִּלּוּאִים — With this oil, he anointed Aaron and his sons throughout the Seven Days of Inauguration,[22] מִמֶּנּוּ נִמְשְׁחוּ כֹּהֲנִים גְּדוֹלִים וּמְלָכִים — and from this oil, high priests and kings were anointed for many generations.[23] וְאֶלְעָזָר שָׂרַף פָּרַת הַחַטָּאת — In another example of Moses' far-reaching influence, **Elazar**, son of Aaron, burned the purification cow, the first פָרָה אֲדֻמָּה, *Red Cow,* שֶׁמִּמֶּנּוּ טְמֵאִים מְטַהֲרִים לְדוֹרוֹת — from which people who are *tamei* with corpse *tumah* become *tahor* throughout the generations,

---

18. Since the verse could have said simply, *These are the laws ... that Hashem gave to the Children of Israel,* the Baraisa understands the added phrase *between Him and the Children of Israel* as making an extra point — that *all* Torah laws and thoughts that help define the relationship between God and His people — even those that will be "discovered" by the Torah scholars of the future — were actually revealed to Moses and given to Israel through him (*Ben Avraham*).

19. As the result of a lifelong effort to sanctify his mind, heart, and body, and to erase all traces of pride and self-interest, Moses achieved an unmatched level of spiritual purity and identification with his people. [His soul, Kabbalistic sources tell us, encompassed the souls of all 600,000 Jews.] This made him uniquely qualified to serve both as God's representative to Israel and Israel's representative before God (*Binyan Yehoshua,* quoting *Mefaresh*).

20. The *Miluim* offerings were part of the seven-day inaugural process that consecrated Aaron and his sons as Kohanim (see

Leviticus Ch. 8). During this period Moses had the status of Kohen Gadol, and performed all parts of the sacrificial service, one of which was אֵיל הַמִּלּאִים, *the Miluim ram.* The Baraisa mentions the *Miluim* ram as a way of referring to the entire process, since that offering alone was truly מָלֵא, "complete," in the sense that it was divided among all the "parties" involved — the Altar, Moses, and Aaron (*Ahavas Chesed*).

21. A special mixture of oil and spices made by Moses, as commanded by the verse: *Now you, take for yourself choice spices ... and a "hin" of olive oil ...* (*Exodus* 30:23).

22. Through his efforts during the *Miluim* period, Moses consecrated the family of Aaron as Kohanim forever. Until the end of time, any male born into this family automatically takes on the status of a Kohen (*Binyan Yehoshua*).

23. Though the Anointing Oil consisted of only one *hin* of oil (approximately 1-2 gallons), it was used to anoint the Tabernacle with its vessels, as well as Aaron and his sons, every day during the *Miluim* period,

אָמַר רַבִּי אֱלִיעֶזֶר: גְּדוֹלָה מִדָּה זוֹ שֶׁהִיא נוֹהֶגֶת לְדוֹרוֹת, שֶׁאַהֲרֹן וּבָנָיו
נִתְקַדְּשׁוּ בְּשֶׁמֶן הַמִּשְׁחָה, שֶׁנֶּאֱמַר (שמות ל, ל) "וְאֶת אַהֲרֹן וְאֶת בָּנָיו
תִּמְשָׁח וְקִדַּשְׁתָּ אֹתָם לְכַהֵן":[25]

‎**ג.** יְהוֹשֻׁעַ קִבֵּל מִמֹּשֶׁה[26], שֶׁנֶּאֱמַר (במדבר כז, כ) "וְנָתַתָּה מֵהוֹדְךָ עָלָיו

---

by being sprinkled with a mixture of its ashes and water.[24]   אָמַר רַבִּי
אֱלִיעֶזֶר — R' Eliezer said: גְּדוֹלָה מִדָּה זוֹ שֶׁהִיא נוֹהֶגֶת לְדוֹרוֹת — Great is
this capacity of the Anointing Oil, for it remains in force for all generations,
שֶׁאַהֲרֹן וּבָנָיו נִתְקַדְּשׁוּ בְּשֶׁמֶן הַמִּשְׁחָה — as Aaron and his sons were consecrated for all time with the Anointing Oil,   שֶׁנֶּאֱמַר "וְאֶת אַהֲרֹן וְאֶת בָּנָיו תִּמְשָׁח
וְקִדַּשְׁתָּ אֹתָם לְכַהֵן" — as it is stated, You shall anoint Aaron and his sons and
sanctify them to minister to Me (Exodus 30:30).[25]

§3 The Baraisa proceeds to outline how the Torah was passed down from
Moses all the way to the the Men of the Great Assembly, who arose a
thousand years later.
שֶׁנֶּאֱמַר Joshua received the Torah from Moses,[26]   יְהוֹשֻׁעַ קִבֵּל מִמֹּשֶׁה —
"וְנָתַתָּה מֵהוֹדְךָ עָלָיו — as it is stated, You shall place some of your majesty

---

and then to anoint high priests and kings for
over eight hundred years until it was hidden
away, alongside the Holy Ark, during the
reign of Josiah. Miraculously, the oil prepared by Moses never diminished, so that
the entire hin remains intact, waiting to be
discovered for use in the Messianic future
(Horayos 11b). This is another way in which
Moses' work was everlasting.

24. Although Elazar oversaw the preparation of the Red Cow (and, according to
our Baraisa, burned it as well; see Avos
HaRosh [Vol. 1], pp. 50-51), he did so in
Moses' name. Thus, the Mishnah speaks of
the "Cow that Moses prepared" (Parah 3:5),
as if he had performed the service himself
(see Rashi to Numbers 19:2). And we know
that some ashes of this Cow endured forever
(Bamidbar Rabbah 19 §6). These ashes
were used to sanctify the ashes of all eight
Red Cows prepared during the Second Temple era (see Parah 3:3 with Tos. Yom Tov and
Rashi to Numbers 19:9), and will be used to
sanctify the Red Cow that will be prepared in
the Messianic era (Tos. Yom Tov ibid.; Maharzu to Bamidbar Rabbah ibid.).
  Why was such importance attached to

the ashes of Moses' Red Cow? Because
Moses was the only human being ever to
understand the Red Cow's inner meaning
(Bamidbar Rabbah ibid.), of which King
Solomon said in despair, I thought I could
become wise, but it is distant from me. Thus,
only Moses could prepare the ashes with all
the proper intentions (kavanos) and infuse
them with the greatest possible sanctity. For
this reason, the ashes of his Red Cow were
used to transfer a measure of that sanctity
to all subsequent Red Cows (Yedei Moshe
to Bamidbar Rabbah ibid., cited by Kisei
Rachamim here).

25. It is thus their orginal anointment that
consecrated their descendants for all time
(see Ben Avraham).

26. Certainly, Moses taught the Torah
thoroughly to the entire nation, not just to
Joshua (see Eruvin 54b). So what does
the Baraisa mean when it says that it was
Joshua specifically who received the Torah
from Moses? Some explain that it refers to
the esoteric portions, which may not be
revealed to the public [see Chagigah 2:1
with Gemara 11b and 13a] (R' Yitzchak
Abohab, cited by Midrash Shmuel on Avos

לְמַעַן יִשְׁמְעוּ כָּל עֲדַת בְּנֵי יִשְׂרָאֵל"‏[27]. זְקֵנִים קִבְּלוּ מִיהוֹשֻׁעַ[28], שֶׁנֶּאֱמַר (שופטים
ב, ז) "וַיַּעַבְדוּ הָעָם אֶת ה'‏ כֹּל יְמֵי יְהוֹשֻׁעַ וְכֹל יְמֵי הַזְּקֵנִים אֲשֶׁר הֶאֱרִיכוּ יָמִים
אַחֲרֵי יְהוֹשֻׁעַ אֲשֶׁר רָאוּ אֵת כָּל מַעֲשֵׂה ה'‏ הַגָּדוֹל אֲשֶׁר עָשָׂה לְיִשְׂרָאֵל"‏[29].
שׁוֹפְטִים קִבְּלוּ °מִיהוֹשֻׁעַ[30], שֶׁנֶּאֱמַר (רות א, א) "וַיְהִי בִּימֵי שְׁפֹט הַשֹּׁפְטִים"‏[31].
נְבִיאִים קִבְּלוּ מִשּׁוֹפְטִים, שֶׁנֶּאֱמַר (ירמיה ז, כה) "וָאֶשְׁלַח אֲלֵיכֶם אֶת כָּל
עֲבָדַי הַנְּבִיאִים יוֹם הַשְׁכֵּם וְשָׁלֹחַ"‏[32]. חַגַּי זְכַרְיָה וּמַלְאָכִי קִבְּלוּ מִנְּבִיאִים[33].

---

upon him, "לְמַעַן יִשְׁמְעוּ כָּל עֲדַת בְּנֵי יִשְׂרָאֵל" — *so that the entire assembly of the Children of Israel will pay heed* (Numbers 27:20).[27] זְקֵנִים קִבְּלוּ מִיהוֹשֻׁעַ — The Elders[28] received the Torah from Joshua, שֶׁנֶּאֱמַר "וַיַּעַבְדוּ הָעָם אֶת ה'‏ כֹּל יְמֵי יְהוֹשֻׁעַ — *as it is stated, The people served HASHEM all the days of Joshua,* וְכֹל יְמֵי הַזְּקֵנִים אֲשֶׁר הֶאֱרִיכוּ יָמִים אַחֲרֵי יְהוֹשֻׁעַ אֲשֶׁר רָאוּ אֵת כָּל מַעֲשֵׂה ה'‏ הַגָּדוֹל אֲשֶׁר עָשָׂה לְיִשְׂרָאֵל" — *and all the days of the Elders who outlived Joshua, who had seen all the great work of HASHEM, which He had done for Israel* (Judges 2:7).[29] שׁוֹפְטִים קִבְּלוּ מִזְּקֵנִים — The Judges received the Torah from the Elders,[30] שֶׁנֶּאֱמַר "וַיְהִי בִּימֵי שְׁפֹט הַשֹּׁפְטִים" — *as it is stated, And it happened in the days when the Judges judged ...* (Ruth 1:1).[31] נְבִיאִים קִבְּלוּ מִשּׁוֹפְטִים — The Prophets received the Torah from the Judges, שֶׁנֶּאֱמַר "וָאֶשְׁלַח אֲלֵיכֶם אֶת כָּל עֲבָדַי הַנְּבִיאִים יוֹם הַשְׁכֵּם וְשָׁלֹחַ" — *as it is stated, I sent to you all My servants, the prophets, daily, rising early and sending forth* (Jeremiah 7:25).[32] חַגַּי זְכַרְיָה וּמַלְאָכִי קִבְּלוּ מִנְּבִיאִים — **Haggai, Zechariah, and Malachi,** who were among the Men of the Great Assembly, **received**

1:1; see also *Sforno* there). Alternatively, it means that Joshua succeeded Moses as the acknowledged leader of the nation, whose responsibility it is to ensure that they follow the Torah's precepts and who is empowered to enact legislation, if necessary, for this purpose (*Shem Tov ibn Shem Tov,* cited by *Midrash Shmuel* there; see also *Meiri* there).

27. Moses' "majesty" was the Heavenly radiance that emanated from his face (*Ahavas Chesed,* from *Rashi* to verse). [The fact that the Baraisa cites this verse to prove its contention that "Joshua received from Moses" would seem to support the second approach cited in the preceding note. However,] it may refer to the exalted understanding of esoteric wisdom that Joshua alone received from Moses (see *Binyan Yehoshua*).

28. These were not the seventy Elders who served under Moses in the Wilderness. They were a later set of national officers who

helped keep law and order in Israel after Joshua's passing (*Binyan Yehoshua,* quoting *Rashi* to *Pirkei Avos*).

29. Since the verse attributes the people's religious loyalty to "the Elders who outlived Joshua," implying that the Elders were perpetuating Joshua's legacy, it is apparent that Joshua had bequeathed that legacy to them (see *Ahavas Chesed*).

30. [This reading follows *Nuschas HaGra* and several manuscripts.]

31. This verse does not show that the Judges received the Torah from the Elders, but it does show that there was a period in which a succession of leaders known as the Judges guided the people in matters of Torah law and practice (see *Kisei Rachamim*).

32. Here, too, the verse merely shows that there was a class of spiritual guides who were prophets, dedicated to teaching and disciplining the people (*Ben Avraham*).

אַנְשֵׁי כְנֶסֶת הַגְּדוֹלָה[34] קִבְּלוּ מֵחַגַּי זְכַרְיָה וּמַלְאָכִי[35]. וְהֵם אָמְרוּ שְׁלֹשָׁה דְבָרִים[36]: הֱווּ מְתוּנִין בַּדִּין[37] וְהַעֲמִידוּ תַלְמִידִים הַרְבֵּה וַעֲשׂוּ סְיָיג לַתּוֹרָה[38]:

ד. הֱווּ מְתוּנִין בַּדִּין, כֵּיצַד, מְלַמֵּד שֶׁיְּהֵא אָדָם מַמְתִּין בַּדִּין[39], שֶׁכָּל הַמַּמְתִּין בַּדִּין מְיוּשָׁב בַּדִּין, שֶׁנֶּאֱמַר (משלי כה, א) "גַּם אֵלֶּה מִשְׁלֵי שְׁלֹמֹה אֲשֶׁר הֶעְתִּיקוּ אַנְשֵׁי חִזְקִיָּה מֶלֶךְ יְהוּדָה", וְלֹא שֶׁהֶעְתִּיקוּ אֶלָּא שֶׁהִמְתִּינוּ[40].

---

the Torah from the earlier Prophets.[33]   אַנְשֵׁי כְנֶסֶת הַגְּדוֹלָה קִבְּלוּ מֵחַגַּי זְכַרְיָה וּמַלְאָכִי — **The Men of the Great Assembly**[34] received the Torah from Haggai, Zechariah, and Malachi,[35]   וְהֵם אָמְרוּ שְׁלֹשָׁה דְבָרִים — and they of the Great Assembly said three things:[36]   הֱווּ מְתוּנִין בַּדִּין — Be deliberate in judgment;[37]   וְהַעֲמִידוּ תַלְמִידִים הַרְבֵּה — raise up many disciples;   וַעֲשׂוּ סְיָיג לַתּוֹרָה — and make a fence around the Torah.[38]

§4   The Baraisa examines each of the Great Assembly's three teachings, beginning with the first.

מְלַמֵּד   הֱווּ מְתוּנִין בַּדִּין, כֵּיצַד — **"Be deliberate in judgment"** — how so?   שֶׁיְּהֵא אָדָם מַמְתִּין בַּדִּין — This teaches that a person should be patient in judgment,[39]   שֶׁכָּל הַמַּמְתִּין בַּדִּין מְיוּשָׁב בַּדִּין — for whoever is patient in judgment is settled in judgment.   שֶׁנֶּאֱמַר "גַּם אֵלֶּה מִשְׁלֵי שְׁלֹמֹה אֲשֶׁר הֶעְתִּיקוּ אַנְשֵׁי חִזְקִיָּה מֶלֶךְ יְהוּדָה" — As it is stated (*Proverbs* 25:1), *These, too, are the proverbs of King Solomon, that the men of Hezekiah, king of Judah, "he'etiku,"*   וְלֹא שֶׁהֶעְתִּיקוּ אֶלָּא שֶׁהִמְתִּינוּ — which does not mean that *they copied,* but *with*

---

33. Haggai, Zechariah, and Malachi were themselves prophets, but the Baraisa lists them separately because, unlike their predecessors, they witnessed the rebuilding of the Temple, served as members of the Great Assembly, and thus belonged to a different, new era in Jewish history (*Magen Avos*).

34. A Sanhedrin consisting of 120 Sages who led the Jewish settlement in the early years of the Second Temple era (see *Yoma* 69b).

35. Although the three prophets mentioned were also part of the Great Assembly, they stood apart as the founders and guiding lights of that body of Jewish leaders (*Magen Avos*).

36. Three things aimed at preserving the nation's Jewish integrity at a time of spiritual

decline (*Binyan Yehoshua,* quoting *Derech Chaim* and *Mefaresh*).

The Baraisa will go on to elaborate — on the first and third teachings in this chapter and the next, and on the second teaching in Chapter 3 (*Binyan Yehoshua*).

37. Do not be hasty in reaching decisions, for "the fruit of haste is remorse," especially when it comes to judicial rulings, which can deeply affect people's lives (*Magen Avos*).

38. That is, establish safeguards in the form of Rabbinic ordinances to distance people from violating Torah law.

39. Rather than reaching a decision quickly, a judge should slowly and methodically explore every aspect of the case before him before arriving at a well-considered conclusion (*Binyan Yehoshua*).

אַבָּא שָׁאוּל אוֹמֵר: לֹא שֶׁהִמְתִּינוּ אֶלָּא שֶׁפֵּירְשׁוּ.[41] בָּרִאשׁוֹנָה הָיוּ אוֹמְרִים:
מִשְׁלֵי וְשִׁיר הַשִּׁירִים וְקֹהֶלֶת גְּנוּזִים הָיוּ, שֶׁהֵם הָיוּ אוֹמְרִים: מְשָׁלוֹת וְאֵינָן
מִן הַכְּתוּבִים,[43] וְעָמְדוּ וְגָנְזוּ אוֹתָם עַד שֶׁבָּאוּ אַנְשֵׁי כְּנֶסֶת הַגְּדוֹלָה[44] וּפֵירְשׁוּ
אוֹתָם,[45] שֶׁנֶּאֱמַר (משלי ז,ז,י-כ) "וָאֵרֶא בַפְּתָאיִם אָבִינָה בַבָּנִים נַעַר חֲסַר לֵב [וְגוֹ']"

---

which they were patient in judgment.[40]   אַבָּא שָׁאוּל אוֹמֵר: לֹא שֶׁהִמְתִּינוּ
אֶלָּא שֶׁפֵּירְשׁוּ — Alternatively, **Abba Shaul said:** It does not mean that *they
were patient,* but that *they explained* the puzzling teachings of Solomon.[41]
בָּרִאשׁוֹנָה הָיוּ אוֹמְרִים: מִשְׁלֵי וְשִׁיר הַשִּׁירִים וְקֹהֶלֶת גְּנוּזִים הָיוּ — Abba Shaul elaborates: **At first [the Sages]**[42] had said that *Proverbs, Song of Songs,* and *Ecclesiastes* should be hidden away,   שֶׁהֵם הָיוּ אוֹמְרִים: מְשָׁלוֹת וְאֵינָן מִן הַכְּתוּבִים
— for they said, "These are merely **parables,**[43] and they do not belong **among
the Writings** of Scripture."   וְעָמְדוּ וְגָנְזוּ אוֹתָם — With that, **they arose and
hid them away.**   עַד שֶׁבָּאוּ אַנְשֵׁי כְּנֶסֶת הַגְּדוֹלָה וּפֵירְשׁוּ אוֹתָם — This situation
persisted **until the Men of the Great Assembly;** that is, the men of Hezekiah,[44]
came and explained the difficult passages in **these Books.**[45]

The Baraisa identifies some of the problems presented by Solomon's writings.
שֶׁנֶּאֱמַר — Among these passages is **that which is stated** in *Proverbs:*   "וָאֵרֶא
בַפְּתָאיִם אָבִינָה בַבָּנִים נַעַר חֲסַר לֵב וְגוֹ' — *And I saw among the fools, I discerned*

---

40. The plain meaning of the verse is that
the men of Hezekiah "copied" these latter proverbs from other works of Solomon
that they had (see *Radak, Shorashim*
עתק). עתק in Scripture often means to
"move." One who copies "moves" what
he copies from one document to another
(ibid.). Cf. *Rashi* on *Proverbs* ad loc.] The
Baraisa, however, expounds the word to
mean that "they were patient" (as עתק in
Scripture sometimes mean "old"; that is,
they allowed the words to "age," and were
not quick to judge them as inappropriate)
as the Baraisa proceeds to explain (see
Ben Avraham).

41. As the Baraisa will explain. According
to Abba Shaul, the word הֶעְתִּיקוּ means *they
removed* the puzzling parables from their
superficial meaning, and explained their
deeper and proper meaning (*Ben Avraham,*
citing his son).

42. Who lived between the times of Solomon
and Hezekiah (*Ahavas Chesed*).

43. [So there is no need to find in them a
deeper, proper meaning.]

44. Having numerous members, the council
formed by the colleagues of Hezekiah was
also known as a "Great Assembly" (*Binyan
Yehoshua*). Some commentators emend the
text to read אַנְשֵׁי חִזְקִיָּה, *the men of Hezekiah*
(*Ahavas Chesed; Kisei Rachamim*).

In any case, the "men of Hezekiah"
referred to here are the same as those
mentioned in the Talmud: "Hezekiah and
his colleagues wrote the Books of *Isaiah,
Proverbs, Song of Songs,* and *Ecclesiastes*"
(*Bava Basra* 15a; *Rashi* there clarifies that
Hezekiah himself died before his colleagues,
and was the inspiration for, but not directly
involved in, these endeavors). In light of our
Baraisa, we can see that the Talmud does not
mean that Hezekiah's men actually *wrote* the
last three Books (as some have understood).
Rather, it means that they ended the sup-
pression of these Books and brought them
into public use (*Ahavas Chesed*).

45. In doing so, they showed that these
Books were actually filled with profound
wisdom and written with Divine Inspiration
(*Mefaresh*).

וְהִנֵּה אִשָּׁה לִקְרָאתוֹ שִׁית זוֹנָה וּנְצֻרַת לֵב. הֹמִיָּה הִיא וְסֹרָרֶת בְּבֵיתָה לֹא יִשְׁכְּנוּ רַגְלֶיהָ. פַּעַם בַּחוּץ פַּעַם בָּרְחֹבוֹת וְאֵצֶל כָּל פִּנָּה תֶאֱרֹב. וְהֶחֱזִיקָה בּוֹ וְנָשְׁקָה לוֹ הֵעֵזָה פָנֶיהָ וַתֹּאמַר לוֹ. זִבְחֵי שְׁלָמִים עָלַי הַיּוֹם שִׁלַּמְתִּי נְדָרָי. עַל כֵּן יָצָאתִי לִקְרָאתֶךָ לְשַׁחֵר פָּנֶיךָ וָאֶמְצָאֶךָּ. מַרְבַדִּים רָבַדְתִּי עַרְשִׂי חֲטֻבוֹת אֵטוּן מִצְרָיִם. נַפְתִּי מִשְׁכָּבִי מֹר אֲהָלִים וְקִנָּמוֹן. לְכָה נִרְוֶה דֹדִים עַד הַבֹּקֶר נִתְעַלְּסָה בָּאֳהָבִים. כִּי אֵין הָאִישׁ בְּבֵיתוֹ הָלַךְ בְּדֶרֶךְ מֵרָחוֹק. צְרוֹר הַכֶּסֶף לָקַח בְּיָדוֹ לְיוֹם הַכֵּסֶא יָבֹא בֵיתוֹ"[46].

וּכְתִיב בְּשִׁיר הַשִּׁירִים (ז, יב-יג) "לְכָה דוֹדִי נֵצֵא הַשָּׂדֶה נָלִינָה בַּכְּפָרִים נַשְׁכִּימָה לַכְּרָמִים נִרְאֶה אִם פָּרְחָה הַגֶּפֶן [פִּתַּח הַסְּמָדַר] הֵנֵצוּ הָרִמּוֹנִים

among the youths, a lad who lacked [an understanding] heart, etc. וְהִנֵּה אִשָּׁה לִקְרָאתוֹ שִׁית זוֹנָה וּנְצֻרַת לֵב — *Then behold, a woman approached him, bedecked as a harlot and with siege in [her] heart.* הֹמִיָּה הִיא וְסֹרָרֶת בְּבֵיתָה לֹא יִשְׁכְּנוּ רַגְלֶיהָ — *She coos and she entices, her feet do not dwell at home.* פַּעַם בַּחוּץ פַּעַם בָּרְחֹבוֹת וְאֵצֶל כָּל פִּנָּה תֶאֱרֹב — *Sometimes in the courtyard, sometimes in the streets, she lurks at every corner.* וְהֶחֱזִיקָה בּוֹ וְנָשְׁקָה לוֹ הֵעֵזָה פָנֶיהָ וַתֹּאמַר לוֹ — *She seized him and kissed him; she was brazen-faced and said to him:* זִבְחֵי שְׁלָמִים עָלַי הַיּוֹם שִׁלַּמְתִּי נְדָרָי — *"I have vowed to bring peace offerings, and today I have fulfilled my vow.* עַל כֵּן יָצָאתִי לִקְרָאתֶךָ לְשַׁחֵר פָּנֶיךָ וָאֶמְצָאֶךָּ — *That is why I went out toward you, to seek your countenance, and I have found you!* מַרְבַדִּים רָבַדְתִּי עַרְשִׂי חֲטֻבוֹת אֵטוּן מִצְרָיִם — *I have decked my bed with spreads; carved bed poles are hung with Egyptian linen.* נַפְתִּי מִשְׁכָּבִי מֹר אֲהָלִים וְקִנָּמוֹן — *I have perfumed my bed with myrrh, aloes, and cinnamon.* לְכָה נִרְוֶה דֹדִים עַד הַבֹּקֶר נִתְעַלְּסָה בָּאֳהָבִים — *Come, let us sate ourselves with love until the morning; let us rejoice with acts of love,* כִּי אֵין הָאִישׁ בְּבֵיתוֹ הָלַךְ בְּדֶרֶךְ מֵרָחוֹק — *for [my] husband is not at home; he has gone on a distant journey.* צְרוֹר הַכֶּסֶף לָקַח — *He has taken the money-pouch with him; he will* בְּיָדוֹ לְיוֹם הַכֵּסֶא יָבֹא בֵיתוֹ" — *come home at the appointed time"* (Proverbs 7:7,10-20).[46]

An example from *Song of Songs:*

וּכְתִיב בְּשִׁיר הַשִּׁירִים — *And in Song of Songs it is written,* "לְכָה דוֹדִי נֵצֵא — *Come, my Beloved, let us go forth into the field, let us* הַשָּׂדֶה נָלִינָה בַּכְּפָרִים — *lodge in the villages.* נַשְׁכִּימָה לַכְּרָמִים — *Let us rise early for the vineyards,* נִרְאֶה אִם פָּרְחָה הַגֶּפֶן [פִּתַּח הַסְּמָדַר] הֵנֵצוּ הָרִמּוֹנִים — *let us see if the vine has*

---

46. This graphic description of a temptress at work seems out of place in a holy book of proverbial wisdom and moral guidance. The Baraisa does not elaborate on how the colleagues of Hezekiah explained this passage to put such objections to rest, but the Midrash (*Bereishis Rabbah* 87 §1) interprets the passage as a detailed study of Joseph's encounter with the wife of Potiphar in Egypt; see there (*Ahavas Chesed*).

שָׁם אֶתֵּן אֶת דֹּדַי לָךְ"⁴⁷, וּכְתִיב בְּקֹהֶלֶת (יא, ט) "שְׂמַח בָּחוּר בְּיַלְדוּתֶיךָ
וִיטִיבְךָ לִבְּךָ בִּימֵי בְחוּרוֹתֶיךָ וְהַלֵּךְ בְּדַרְכֵי לִבְּךָ וּבְמַרְאֵי עֵינֶיךָ וְדַע
כִּי עַל כָּל אֵלֶּה יְבִיאֲךָ הָאֱלֹהִים בַּמִּשְׁפָּט"⁴⁸, וּכְתִיב בְּשִׁיר הַשִּׁירִים
(ז, יא) "אֲנִי לְדוֹדִי וְעָלַי תְּשׁוּקָתוֹ"⁴⁹, הֱוֵי לֹא שֶׁהִמְתִּינוּ אֶלָּא שֶׁפֵּירְשׁוּ.

שָׁם budded, if the blossom has opened, if the pomegranates are in bloom.
אֶתֵּן אֶת דֹּדַי לָךְ" — *There I will give my love to You* (*Song of Songs* 7:12-13).[47]

Two more examples:

"שְׂמַח בָּחוּר בְּיַלְדוּתֶיךָ — And in *Ecclesiastes* it is written, **וּכְתִיב בְּקֹהֶלֶת**
וִיטִיבְךָ לִבְּךָ בִּימֵי בְחוּרוֹתֶיךָ — *Rejoice, young man, in your childhood; let your
heart cheer you in the days of your youth;* **וְהַלֵּךְ בְּדַרְכֵי לִבְּךָ וּבְמַרְאֵי עֵינֶיךָ** —
follow the path of your heart and the sight of your eyes, **וְדַע כִּי עַל כָּל אֵלֶּה**
יְבִיאֲךָ הָאֱלֹהִים בַּמִּשְׁפָּט" — *but be aware that for all these things God will call
you to account* (*Ecclesiastes* 11:9).[48] **וּכְתִיב בְּשִׁיר הַשִּׁירִים "אֲנִי לְדוֹדִי וְעָלַי**
תְּשׁוּקָתוֹ" — And finally, in *Song of Songs* it is written, *I am my Beloved's and
His longing is upon me* (*Song of Songs* 7:11).[49]

The Baraisa sums up:

הֱוֵי לֹא שֶׁהִמְתִּינוּ אֶלָּא שֶׁפֵּירְשׁוּ — Conclude, then, that the meaning of the *Proverbs* verse is as we have said: **Not that** *they* (the men of Hezekiah) *were*
merely *patient* in judgment, **but that they explained** Solomon's works so as
to restore them to their proper place in Scripture.

---

47. Here, too, the Baraisa does not give us
the explanation. According to the Talmud
(*Eruvin* 21b), the "Beloved" in this passage
is God, the speaker is Israel, and the idea is
to draw a contrast between the ingratitude
of the prosperous but idol-worshiping descendants of Esau, and the loving devotion
displayed by the long-suffering people of the
Torah. In this context, the passage means as
follows: *Come, my Beloved, let us go to the
field where Your children serve You in want,
let us lodge there with Esau's children, who
are blessed with plenty, yet still deny You.
Let us wake at dawn in vineyards of prayer
and study. Let us see if students of the Written Torah have budded, if students of the
Oral Law have blossomed, if ripened scholars
have bloomed; there I will display my finest
products to You.*

48. This verse is difficult because it appears
to encourage people to follow their hearts
and eyes, whereas the Torah warns, *And
do not explore after your heart and after your*
eyes (*Numbers* 15:39). The Baraisa does
not record the explanation, but according to
the Midrash, the Sages resolved the problem
by pointing to the end of the verse, which
states clearly: *but be aware that for all these
things God will call you to account.* From
the verse's conclusion it is evident that the
previous call for partaking of all that youth
has to offer was meant to be tempered by
his warning to do so responsibly, considering that God will hold a person accountable
for improper indulgences (*Koheles Rabbah*
1 §4 with *Eitz Yosef*; as for what the Sages
originally thought, see *Yefeh Anaf* there,
cited in the Kleinman edition of *Koheles Rabbah*, note 81).

49. Like the earlier quote from *Song of
Songs*, this poetic description of mutual
love is understood as referring to the relationship between God and His people. "*I
am my Beloved's,*" sings Israel, "*and His
longing is upon me*" (*Yalkut Shimoni* on the
verse).

דָּבָר אַחֵר, הֱווּ מְתוּנִים בַּדִּין כֵּיצַד, מְלַמֵּד שֶׁיְּהֵא אָדָם מַמְתִּין בִּדְבָרָיו
וְאַל יְהִי מַקְפִּיד עַל דְּבָרָיו, שֶׁכָּל הַמַּקְפִּיד עַל דְּבָרָיו מְשַׁכֵּחַ אֶת דְּבָרָיו,[51]
(וְהֵיכָן) [שֶׁכֵּן] מָצִינוּ בְּמשֶׁה רַבֵּינוּ שֶׁשָּׁכַח אֶת דְּבָרָיו, שֶׁנֶּאֱמַר (במדבר לא, כא)
"וַיֹּאמֶר אֶלְעָזָר הַכֹּהֵן אֶל אַנְשֵׁי הַצָּבָא הַבָּאִים לַמִּלְחָמָה זֹאת חֻקַּת הַתּוֹרָה
אֲשֶׁר צִוָּה ה' אֶת משֶׁה",[52] משֶׁה צִוָּה וְלֹא אוֹתִי (צִוָּה), אֶת משֶׁה אֲחִי אַבָּא
צִוָּה וְאוֹתִי לֹא צִוָּה). וְהֵיכָן מָצִינוּ בְּמשֶׁה שֶׁהִקְפִּיד עַל דְּבָרָיו, הֲרֵי הוּא

A different aspect of being "deliberate in judgment":

דָּבָר אַחֵר — Another understanding: **הֱווּ מְתוּנִים בַּדִּין, כֵּיצַד — "Be deliberate in judgment" — how so?** **מְלַמֵּד שֶׁיְּהֵא אָדָם מַמְתִּין בִּדְבָרָיו — This teaches** that a person should be patient in his matters, **וְאַל יְהִי מַקְפִּיד עַל דְּבָרָיו** and should not be overly **particular in his matters,**[50] **שֶׁכָּל הַמַּקְפִּיד עַל דְּבָרָיו מְשַׁכֵּחַ אֶת דְּבָרָיו — for whoever is** overly **particular in his matters,** so that he is angered if things go wrong, **will forget** important things regarding **his matters.**[51] **שֶׁכֵּן מָצִינוּ בְּמשֶׁה רַבֵּינוּ שֶׁשָּׁכַח אֶת דְּבָרָיו — For so we find with our teacher Moses, that** because he was overly particular and became angry (as the Baraisa will detail further), **he forgot** important things **regarding his matters.** **שֶׁנֶּאֱמַר "וַיֹּאמֶר אֶלְעָזָר הַכֹּהֵן אֶל אַנְשֵׁי הַצָּבָא הַבָּאִים לַמִּלְחָמָה — How do** we know that Moses forgot? **As it is stated,** *Elazar the Kohen said to the men of the legion who came to battle,* **זֹאת חֻקַּת הַתּוֹרָה אֲשֶׁר צִוָּה ה' אֶת משֶׁה"** — *"This is the decree of the Torah, which HASHEM commanded Moses"* (Numbers 31:21).[52] **משֶׁה צִוָּה וְלֹא אוֹתִי צִוָּה — In announcing these laws,** Elazar emphasized that it was to **Moses** that **God had commanded** them, **but** to **me He did not command** them. **אֶת משֶׁה אֲחִי אַבָּא צִוָּה וְאוֹתִי לֹא צִוָּה — It** was to **Moses, my father's brother,** that **He commanded** them, **but to me He did not command** them. Why, then, did Elazar announce them and not Moses himself? It is because Moses had forgotten them in his moment of anger. **וְהֵיכָן מָצִינוּ בְּמשֶׁה שֶׁהִקְפִּיד עַל דְּבָרָיו — And where do we find that Moses was** overly **particular about his matters** and became angered as a result? **הֲרֵי הוּא**

---

50. According to this approach, being "deliberate in judgment" is a precept that everyone must follow, not only judges in the courtroom. All people make judgments in their everyday lives; they reach decisions about what to say and how to act, and they draw conclusions about people and events in the world around them. The point of our Baraisa is that one should be patient in making these judgments, even when frustrated by people who have disobeyed or offended him. If he reacts angrily, he is bound to make some embarrassing or harmful mistake (*Ben Avraham*).

51. In the words of the Talmud: "Concerning anyone who becomes angry: If he is a wise man, his wisdom deserts him; if he is a prophet, his prophecy deserts him (*Pesachim* 66b).

52. This incident occurred when the Israelite army returned from their successful war of vengeance against the people of Midian, who had sent their women to lure the Israelites into the sins of immorality and idolatry (see below). Among the booty, the victors brought back cooking utensils, and Elazar announced to them the laws of the Torah regarding how to purify these utensils

אוֹמֵר בִּפְקוּדֵי הֶחָיִל (שם פסוקים יד־טו)" וַיִּקְצֹף מֹשֶׁה עַל פְּקוּדֵי הֶחָיִל ...
וַיֹּאמֶר אֲלֵיהֶם מֹשֶׁה הַחִיִּיתֶם כָּל נְקֵבָה"53. אִם כֵּן מַה תַּלְמוּד לוֹמַר "כָּל
נְקֵבָה"54. אֶלָּא זוֹ עֵצָה שֶׁיָּעַץ בִּלְעָם הָרָשָׁע עַל יִשְׂרָאֵל, דִּכְתִיב (שם כד,
יד) "וְעַתָּה הִנְנִי הוֹלֵךְ לְעַמִּי לְכָה אִיעָצְךָ אֲשֶׁר יַעֲשֶׂה הָעָם הַזֶּה לְעַמְּךָ
בְּאַחֲרִית הַיָּמִים"55. אָמַר לוֹ: עַם זוֹ שֶׁאַתָּה שׂוֹנֵא רָעֵב הוּא לַאֲכִילָה וְצָמֵא
הוּא לִשְׁתִיָּה וְאֵין לָהֶם שֶׁיֹּאכְלוּ וְשֶׁיִּשְׁתּוּ אֶלָּא מָן בִּלְבַד, לֵךְ וְתַקֵּן לָהֶם
קוּבּוֹת וְהַנַּח לָהֶם מַאֲכָל וּמִשְׁתֶּה וְהוֹשֵׁב בָּהֶן נָשִׁים יָפוֹת בְּנוֹת מְלָכִים57

אוֹמֵר בִּפְקוּדֵי הֶחָיִל — **For it says** in the verse, **regarding the commanders of the army** who returned from the successful campaign against Midian with the female and minor captives, ... וַיִּקְצֹף מֹשֶׁה עַל פְּקוּדֵי הֶחָיִל — *Moses became angry with the commanders of the army ...* וַיֹּאמֶר אֲלֵיהֶם מֹשֶׁה הַחִיִּיתֶם כָּל נְקֵבָה" — *and Moses said to them, "Did you let every female live?"* (ibid. vv. 14-15).[53]

Having quoted Moses' words of rebuke, the Baraisa proceeds to examine them in more detail.

אִם כֵּן מַה תַּלְמוּד לוֹמַר "כָּל נְקֵבָה" — **If so, what does the verse teach by saying,** *Did you let every female live?*[54] *Behold! — it was they who caused the Children of Israel, by the word of Balaam, to commit a betrayal against Hashem regarding the matter of Peor; and the plague occurred in the assembly of Hashem.* אֶלָּא זוֹ עֵצָה שֶׁיָּעַץ בִּלְעָם הָרָשָׁע עַל יִשְׂרָאֵל — **Rather, this** entire incident **was the strategy that the wicked Balaam had proposed for** defeating Israel, דִּכְתִיב "וְעַתָּה הִנְנִי הוֹלֵךְ לְעַמִּי — **as it is written** that Balaam said to Balak, *"And now, behold! I go to my people.* לְכָה אִיעָצְךָ אֲשֶׁר יַעֲשֶׂה הָעָם הַזֶּה לְעַמְּךָ בְּאַחֲרִית הַיָּמִים" — *Come, I shall advise you what this people will do to your people in the End of Days"* (ibid. 24:14). What advice did Balaam offer Balak?[55] אָמַר לוֹ: עַם זוֹ שֶׁאַתָּה שׂוֹנֵא רָעֵב הוּא לַאֲכִילָה וְצָמֵא הוּא לִשְׁתִיָּה — **He said to him, "This people that you hate** and wish to destroy **is hungry for food and thirsty for drink,** וְאֵין לָהֶם שֶׁיֹּאכְלוּ וְשֶׁיִּשְׁתּוּ אֶלָּא מָן בִּלְבַד — **for they have nothing to eat or drink except for the manna alone.** לֵךְ וְתַקֵּן לָהֶם קוּבּוֹת וְהַנַּח לָהֶם מַאֲכָל וּמִשְׁתֶּה — **Go set up harlots' booths**[56] **for them and put out food and drink for them.** וְהוֹשֵׁב בָּהֶן נָשִׁים יָפוֹת בְּנוֹת מְלָכִים — **And station beautiful women of royal descent**[57] in these booths,

---

for kosher use (as the verses there detail).

53. The Baraisa will proceed to explain Moses' complaint.

54. The commentators struggle to explain this line of the Baraisa. *Gra* deletes this line, and replaces it with the full quote of Moses's rebuke (as we have done in the English text), followed by: מַאי "בִּדְבַר בִּלְעָם", *What is [meant by] "by the word of Balaam"?* What

was it that Balaam said to bring this about?

55. As rendered by Onkelos, the words *I shall advise you* and *what this people will do to your people in the End of Days* are two distinct things. Our Baraisa proceeds to explain what Balaam advised Balak.

56. *Ahavas Chesed*, based on *Numbers* 25:8.

57. To attract the greatest, highest-ranking men in Israel (*Magen Avos*).

כְּדֵי שֶׁיִּזְנוּ הָעָם לְבַעַל פְּעוֹר וְיִפְּלוּ בְּיַד הַמָּקוֹם.[58] מִיָּד הָלַךְ וְעָשָׂה בָלָק
כָּל מַה שֶׁאָמַר לוֹ בִּלְעָם הָרָשָׁע, רְאֵה מַה גָּרַם לוֹ בִּלְעָם הָרָשָׁע לְיִשְׂרָאֵל
שֶׁנָּפְלוּ מֵהֶן עֶשְׂרִים וְאַרְבָּעָה אֶלֶף, שֶׁנֶּאֱמַר (שם כה, ט) "וַיִּהְיוּ הַמֵּתִים
בַּמַּגֵּפָה אַרְבָּעָה וְעֶשְׂרִים אָלֶף". וַהֲלֹא דְבָרִים קַל וָחֹמֶר, וּמַה מֹשֶׁה רַבֵּינוּ
חָכָם גָּדוֹל שֶׁבַּגְּדוֹלִים אָב לַנְּבִיאִים בְּשָׁעָה שֶׁהִקְפִּיד עַל דְּבָרָיו שָׁכַח אֶת
דְּבָרָיו, אָנוּ עַל אַחַת כַּמָּה וְכַמָּה, מְלַמֵּד שֶׁיְּהֵא אָדָם מַמְתִּין בִּדְבָרָיו וְלֹא
יִהְיֶה מַקְפִּיד עַל דְּבָרָיו. בֶּן עַזַּאי אוֹמֵר: הֱוֵי זָהִיר בִּדְבָרֶיךָ מִבַּטָּלָה:[59]

כְּדֵי שֶׁיִּזְנוּ הָעָם לְבַעַל פְּעוֹר וְיִפְּלוּ בְּיַד הַמָּקוֹם — so that the people of Israel who come in to eat and drink will stray and come to worship Baal-peor.[58] When that happens, they will surely fall by the wrathful hand of the Omnipresent!" מִיָּד הָלַךְ וְעָשָׂה בָלָק כָּל מַה שֶׁאָמַר לוֹ בִּלְעָם הָרָשָׁע — Immediately, Balak took this advice and went and did everything the wicked Balaam told him to do. רְאֵה מַה גָּרַם לוֹ בִּלְעָם הָרָשָׁע לְיִשְׂרָאֵל — See what great harm the wicked Balaam caused to befall Israel, שֶׁנָּפְלוּ מֵהֶן עֶשְׂרִים וְאַרְבָּעָה אֶלֶף — in that twenty-four thousand of them fell in the plague God brought upon them as a punishment, שֶׁנֶּאֱמַר "וַיִּהְיוּ הַמֵּתִים בַּמַּגֵּפָה אַרְבָּעָה וְעֶשְׂרִים אָלֶף" — as it is stated, *Those who died in the plague were twenty-four thousand* (ibid. 25:9).

The Baraisa concludes by reinforcing its lesson.

וַהֲלֹא דְבָרִים קַל וָחֹמֶר — Is the matter not, then, a *kal va'chomer*? וּמַה מֹשֶׁה רַבֵּינוּ חָכָם גָּדוֹל שֶׁבַּגְּדוֹלִים אָב לַנְּבִיאִים — If Moses, our teacher, the greatest of sages, the father of all subsequent prophets, בְּשָׁעָה שֶׁהִקְפִּיד עַל דְּבָרָיו שָׁכַח אֶת דְּבָרָיו — when he was overly particular about his matters he forgot important things regarding his matters, אָנוּ עַל אַחַת כַּמָּה וְכַמָּה — then how much more are we ordinary people vulnerable to forgetting our wisdom or losing our senses in a moment of anger. מְלַמֵּד שֶׁיְּהֵא אָדָם מַמְתִּין בִּדְבָרָיו וְלֹא יִהְיֶה מַקְפִּיד עַל דְּבָרָיו — This teaches that a person should be patient in his matters and should not be overly particular about his matters.

A related teaching:

בֶּן עַזַּאי אוֹמֵר — Ben Azzai says: הֱוֵי זָהִיר בִּדְבָרֶיךָ מִבַּטָּלָה — Be careful with your words, lest they go to waste.[59]

---

58. The Gemara relates that when a Midianite woman succeeded in ensnaring an Israelite, she would take out an idol of Baalpeor and refuse to submit to him until he worshiped the idol (*Sanhedrin* 106a; see there for a fuller account of how the Midianites enticed the Israelites into sinning).

59. Since the Baraisa taught earlier that a person should be patient in his matters so as not to become angry, it adds here a related teaching from Ben Azzai: that a person should be patient in choosing his words, so as to speak wisely and constructively without speaking empty words and nonsense (*Kisei Rachamim*).

Alternatively, Ben Azzai is deriving an additional lesson from the incident just mentioned. Moses had told the commanders going out to war *to inflict Hashem's vengeance against Midian,* without making clear

ה. וַעֲשׂוּ[60] סְיָיג לַתּוֹרָה. וַעֲשֵׂה סְיָיג לִדְבָרֶיךָ כְּדֶרֶךְ שֶׁעָשָׂה הַקָּדוֹשׁ
בָּרוּךְ הוּא סְיָיג לִדְבָרָיו וְאָדָם הָרִאשׁוֹן עָשָׂה סְיָיג לִדְבָרָיו. תּוֹרָה
עָשְׂתָה סְיָיג לִדְבָרֶיהָ[61]. מֹשֶׁה עָשָׂה סְיָיג לִדְבָרָיו וְאַף אִיּוֹב וְאַף נְבִיאִים
וַחֲכָמִים כּוּלָּם עָשׂוּ סְיָיג לִדְבָרֵיהֶם. אֵיזֶהוּ סְיָיג שֶׁעָשָׂה הַקָּדוֹשׁ בָּרוּךְ הוּא
לִדְבָרָיו, הֲרֵי הוּא אוֹמֵר (דברים כט, כג) "וְאָמְרוּ כָּל הַגּוֹיִם עַל מֶה עָשָׂה ה׳
כָּכָה לָאָרֶץ הַזֹּאת"[62], מְלַמֵּד שֶׁגָּלוּי הָיָה לִפְנֵי מִי שֶׁאָמַר וְהָיָה הָעוֹלָם

---

§5 The Baraisa turns now to the third practice encouraged by the Men of the
Great Assembly:[60]

וַעֲשֵׂה סְיָיג לִדְבָרֶיךָ — "And make a fence around the Torah." וַעֲשׂוּ סְיָיג לַתּוֹרָה
— This means to say: **Make a fence around your words** of Torah instruction,
just as the Holy One, Blessed is He, — כְּדֶרֶךְ שֶׁעָשָׂה הַקָּדוֹשׁ בָּרוּךְ הוּא סְיָיג לִדְבָרָיו
made a fence around His words, וְאָדָם הָרִאשׁוֹן עָשָׂה סְיָיג לִדְבָרָיו — **and just
as Adam, the first** man, **made a fence around his words.** תּוֹרָה עָשְׂתָה סְיָיג
לִדְבָרֶיהָ — **The Torah,** too, **made a fence around its words;**[61] מֹשֶׁה עָשָׂה סְיָיג
לִדְבָרָיו — **and Moses made a fence around his words;** וְאַף אִיּוֹב וְאַף נְבִיאִים
וַחֲכָמִים — **and also Job and also the Prophets and the Sages —** כּוּלָּם עָשׂוּ סְיָיג
לִדְבָרֵיהֶם — **all of them made a fence around their words** of Torah instruction.
The Baraisa cites sources that all of them made fences around their words:
אֵיזֶהוּ סְיָיג שֶׁעָשָׂה הַקָּדוֹשׁ בָּרוּךְ הוּא לִדְבָרָיו — **What was the fence that the Holy
One, Blessed is He, made around His words?** הֲרֵי הוּא אוֹמֵר "וְאָמְרוּ כָּל
הַגּוֹיִם עַל מֶה עָשָׂה ה׳ כָּכָה לָאָרֶץ הַזֹּאת" — **You see that it states,** *And all the
nations will say, "For what reason did* HASHEM *do so to this land; why this
wrathfulness and great anger?"* (*Deuteronomy* 29:23).[62] מְלַמֵּד שֶׁגָּלוּי הָיָה
לִפְנֵי מִי שֶׁאָמַר וְהָיָה הָעוֹלָם — **This teaches** explicitly **that it was revealed** and

---

what this mission entailed. Were they to kill
only the opposing troops, or the Midianite
civilians as well? If the latter, were they to
kill every member of the offending tribe —
male and female, adults and children — or
perhaps only one or more segments of the
population? Phinehas and the commanders
were left to decide on their own, and when
they erred, Moses' command, as he meant it
to be understood, went for naught. Ben Azzai therefore warns us all not to repeat this
mistake: "Be careful with your words and
clarify what you mean, for if your words are
misunderstood, they will fail to have their
intended effect" (see *Magen Avos*).

60. For now, the Baraisa skips the second
teaching, which is to "raise up many disciples"

— either because its meaning is self-evident,
or because the first and third teachings belong together, since they both call for a person to tread carefully and beware of pitfalls
that could be lying in his path (*Magen Avos*).
In Chapter 3, however, the Baraisa will return
to the theme of raising many disciples.

61. The Torah is the actual word of God,
and the Baraisa has already stated that
God made a fence around His words. Nevertheless, the Baraisa states "the Torah"
separately to indicate that even the actual
laws of the Torah can contain an element of
"making a fence" (see *Magen Avos* below, to
the beginning of Chapter 2).

62. The previous verse there describes what
"your children who will arise after you and

שֶׁעֲתִידִין הַדּוֹרוֹת כָּךְ לוֹמַר "עַל מֶה עָשָׂה ה׳ כָּכָה לָאָרֶץ הַזֹּאת"[63], לְפִיכָךְ אָמַר
לוֹ הַקָּדוֹשׁ בָּרוּךְ הוּא לְמֹשֶׁה: מֹשֶׁה, כְּתוֹב וְהַנַּח לַדּוֹרוֹת הַבָּאִים[64] (שם פסוקים
כד־כה) "וְאָמְרוּ עַל אֲשֶׁר עָזְבוּ אֶת בְּרִית ה׳ [וְגוֹ'] וַיֵּלְכוּ וַיַּעַבְדוּ אֱלֹהִים אֲחֵרִים
וַיִּשְׁתַּחֲווּ לָהֶם אֱלֹהִים אֲשֶׁר לֹא יְדָעוּם וְלֹא חָלַק לָהֶם"[65]. הָא לָמַדְתָּ (שֶׁעָשָׂה
הַקָּדוֹשׁ בָּרוּךְ הוּא סְיָיג לִדְבָרָיו, וּכְתִיב בַּתְרֵיה מַה שֶׁהָיוּ עֲתִידִין לוֹמַר עֲדַיִין,)

שֶׁעֲתִידִין — known before the One Who spoke and the world came into being
הַדּוֹרוֹת כָּךְ לוֹמַר "עַל מֶה עָשָׂה ה׳ כָּכָה לָאָרֶץ הַזֹּאת" — that the later generations were destined to say this — *for what reason did HASHEM do so to
this land; why this wrathfulness and great anger?*[63]   לְפִיכָךְ אָמַר לוֹ הַקָּדוֹשׁ
בָּרוּךְ הוּא לְמֹשֶׁה — Therefore, to preempt them, the Holy One, Blessed is
He, said to Moses,   מֹשֶׁה — "Moses — write
down this verse and leave it for the coming generations:[64]   "וְאָמְרוּ עַל
אֲשֶׁר עָזְבוּ אֶת בְּרִית ה׳ וְגוֹ׳ — *They will say, "Because they forsook the covenant of HASHEM, etc.,*   וַיֵּלְכוּ וַיַּעַבְדוּ אֱלֹהִים אֲחֵרִים וַיִּשְׁתַּחֲווּ לָהֶם — *and they
went and served the gods of others and prostrated themselves to them,*
אֱלֹהִים אֲשֶׁר לֹא יְדָעוּם וְלֹא חָלַק לָהֶם" — *gods they did not know and that
He did not apportion to them"* (ibid., vv. 24-25).[65]   הָא לָמַדְתָּ — Thus
you learn   שֶׁעָשָׂה הַקָּדוֹשׁ בָּרוּךְ הוּא סְיָיג לִדְבָרָיו, וּכְתִיב בַּתְרֵיה מַה שֶׁהָיוּ עֲתִידִין
לוֹמַר עֲדַיִין — that the Holy One, Blessed is He, made a fence around His
words, and recorded what is written after it [i.e., after the detailed punishment
He would bring upon them][66] what they were destined to say in the future,

---

the foreigner who will come from a distant
land" will see when they lay eyes upon the
once fertile and prosperous land of milk and
honey: *Sulfur and salt, a conflagration of the
entire Land, it cannot be sown and it cannot sprout, and no grass shall rise up on it;
like the upheaval of Sodom and Gomorrah,
Admah and Zeboiim, which Hashem overturned in His anger and wrath.*

63. Implicit in their question is: How could
God, after promising to give Israel this land
and shower them with blessings of all kinds,
not continue to fulfill His promise? Does this
not call into question His trustworthiness?
(*Ahavas Chesed*).

64. To forestall any such doubts about His
actions, God recorded these ominous pre-
dictions in the Torah. It would then be plain
for all to see that He had warned Israel of
the calamities that would befall them if they
turned away from Him, that the blame for

their downfall rested exclusively on them,
and that a return to virtue would revive their
faded fortunes, for God's promises remain
eternally in force.

In this way, God "made a fence around His
words," that is, He took measures to protect
the credibility of His promises in human
eyes (*Ahavas Chesed, Ben Avraham*).

65. They will say this answer to their question because the Torah has already written
that this is the answer to their question.
Thus, by stating from the outset the answer
to the question on His trustworthiness, God
made a protective fence around His words of
promise. For those who will ask the question
will then answer that the answer is already
recorded in the Torah (*Ahavas Chesed*).

66. *Ahavas Chesed.* [*Magen Avos* suggests
that the word בַּתְרֵיה should be emended to
read: בַּתּוֹרָה, *in the Torah.* This is also the
emendation of *Nuschas HaGra.*]

שֶׁהוֹצִיא הַקָּדוֹשׁ בָּרוּךְ הוּא שְׂכַר בְּרִיּוֹתָיו בְּשָׁלוֹם[67]. אֵיזֶהוּ סְיָיג שֶׁעָשָׂה
אָדָם הָרִאשׁוֹן לִדְבָרָיו, הֲרֵי הוּא אוֹמֵר (בראשית ב, טז-יז) "וַיְצַו ה' אֱלֹהִים
עַל הָאָדָם [לֵאמֹר] מִכֹּל עֵץ הַגָּן אָכֹל תֹּאכֵל וּמֵעֵץ הַדַּעַת טוֹב וָרָע לֹא
תֹאכַל מִמֶּנּוּ כִּי בְּיוֹם אֲכָלְךָ מִמֶּנּוּ מוֹת תָּמוּת". לֹא רָצָה אָדָם הָרִאשׁוֹן
לוֹמַר לְחַוָּה כְּדֶרֶךְ שֶׁאָמַר לוֹ הַקָּדוֹשׁ בָּרוּךְ הוּא, אֶלָּא כָּךְ אָמַר לָהּ וְעָשָׂה
סְיָיג לִדְבָרָיו יוֹתֵר מִמַּה שֶּׁאָמַר לוֹ הַקָּדוֹשׁ בָּרוּךְ הוּא (שם ג, ג): "וּמִפְּרִי
הָעֵץ אֲשֶׁר בְּתוֹךְ הַגָּן אָמַר אֱלֹהִים לֹא תֹאכְלוּ מִמֶּנּוּ וְלֹא תִגְּעוּ בּוֹ פֶּן
תְּמֻתוּן"[68], שֶׁרָצָה לִשְׁמוֹר אֶת עַצְמוֹ וְאֶת חַוָּה מִן הָעֵץ אֲפִילוּ בִּנְגִיעָה.

שֶׁהוֹצִיא הַקָּדוֹשׁ בָּרוּךְ הוּא שְׂכַר בְּרִיּוֹתָיו בְּשָׁלוֹם — so that the Holy One, Blessed is He, will have paid out his creatures' wages for sin in accord with what is right and proper.[67]

Adam's fence:

אֵיזֶהוּ סְיָיג שֶׁעָשָׂה אָדָם הָרִאשׁוֹן לִדְבָרָיו — What was the fence that Adam, the first man, made around his words? הֲרֵי הוּא אוֹמֵר "וַיְצַו ה' אֱלֹהִים עַל הָאָדָם לֵאמֹר — See that [Scripture] states, *And HASHEM God commanded the man, saying,* מִכֹּל עֵץ הַגָּן אָכֹל תֹּאכֵל — *"Of every tree of the garden you may freely eat;* וּמֵעֵץ הַדַּעַת טוֹב וָרָע לֹא תֹאכַל מִמֶּנּוּ — *but of the Tree of Knowledge of Good and Bad, you must not eat thereof,* כִּי בְּיוֹם אֲכָלְךָ מִמֶּנּוּ מוֹת תָּמוּת" — *for on the day you eat of it, you shall surely die"* (*Genesis* 2:16-17). לֹא רָצָה אָדָם הָרִאשׁוֹן לוֹמַר לְחַוָּה כְּדֶרֶךְ שֶׁאָמַר לוֹ הַקָּדוֹשׁ בָּרוּךְ הוּא — Adam, the first man, did not want to tell Eve about the prohibition in the same way that the Holy One, Blessed is He, told it to him, prohibiting only "eating" from the tree and nothing else; אֶלָּא כָּךְ אָמַר לָהּ וְעָשָׂה סְיָיג לִדְבָרָיו יוֹתֵר מִמַּה שֶּׁאָמַר לוֹ הַקָּדוֹשׁ בָּרוּךְ הוּא — rather, he told her as follows, making a fence around his words by saying more than what the Holy One, Blessed is He, told him: "וּמִפְּרִי הָעֵץ אֲשֶׁר בְּתוֹךְ הַגָּן אָמַר אֱלֹהִים לֹא תֹאכְלוּ מִמֶּנּוּ וְלֹא תִגְּעוּ בּוֹ פֶּן תְּמֻתוּן" — *"Of the fruit of the tree that is in the center of the garden God has said, 'You shall neither eat of it nor touch it, lest you die'"* (ibid. 3:3), implying that both aspects of the prohibition were God-given, and that both carried the death penalty.[68] שֶׁרָצָה לִשְׁמוֹר אֶת עַצְמוֹ וְאֶת חַוָּה מִן הָעֵץ אֲפִילוּ בִּנְגִיעָה — For he wanted to protect himself and Eve from approaching the tree even by means of touching.

---

67. All will realize that the punishment is deserved, and does not pose a challenge to His trustworthiness (*Ahavas Chesed*; see *Binyan Yehoshua* for a completely different understanding of this line). [Some suggest emending the text to read: בְּשָׁלֵם, *in full* (*Mefaresh*).]

68. The verse quoted actually contains *Eve's* words in her response to the serpent. But since Eve had no source for this statement other than Adam himself, the Baraisa infers that this is how Adam had transmitted the commandment to her (*Ben Avraham*).

בְּאוֹתָהּ שָׁעָה הָיָה נָחָשׁ הָרָשָׁע, נָטַל עֵצָה בְּלִבּוֹ, אָמַר: הוֹאִיל וְאֵינִי יָכוֹל
לְהַכְשִׁיל אֶת הָאָדָם[70] אֵלֵךְ וְאַכְשִׁיל אֶת חַוָּה. הָלַךְ וְיָשַׁב אֶצְלָהּ וְהִרְבָּה
שִׂיחָה עִמָּהּ[71], אָמַר לָהּ: אִם לִנְגִיעָה אַתְּ אוֹמֶרֶת צִוָּה עָלֵינוּ הַקָּדוֹשׁ בָּרוּךְ
הוּא, הֲרֵינִי נוֹגֵעַ בּוֹ וְאֵינִי מֵת, אַף אַתְּ אִם תִּגְּעִי בּוֹ אִי אַתְּ מֵתָה. מֶה עָשָׂה
הַנָּחָשׁ הָרָשָׁע בְּאוֹתָהּ שָׁעָה, עָמַד וְנָגַע בָּאִילָן בְּיָדָיו וּבְרַגְלָיו[72] וְהִרְתִּיעוֹ
עַד שֶׁנָּשְׁרוּ פֵּירוֹתָיו לָאָרֶץ[73], (וְיֵשׁ אוֹמְרִים: לֹא נָגַע בּוֹ כָּל עִיקָר, אֶלָּא)

While Adam was correct in his desire to enact a safeguard, he unwittingly provided the serpent with an opening for his evil plan, as the Baraisa proceeds to detail:

בְּאוֹתָהּ שָׁעָה הָיָה נָחָשׁ הָרָשָׁע — **At that moment** that God spoke to Adam and Adam to Eve, **the evil serpent was** present and overheard what had been said.[69] נָטַל עֵצָה בְּלִבּוֹ — **So he devised a plan,** אָמַר: הוֹאִיל וְאֵינִי יָכוֹל לְהַכְשִׁיל אֶת הָאָדָם, אֵלֵךְ וְאַכְשִׁיל אֶת חַוָּה — and said to himself, "**Since I am not able to entrap Adam,**[70] **I will go and entrap Eve.**" הָלַךְ וְיָשַׁב אֶצְלָהּ וְהִרְבָּה שִׂיחָה עִמָּהּ — **He went and sat beside her and engaged her in much casual conversation.**[71] אָמַר לָהּ: אִם לִנְגִיעָה אַתְּ אוֹמֶרֶת צִוָּה עָלֵינוּ הַקָּדוֹשׁ בָּרוּךְ הוּא — **He said to her, "If what you say is true, that even with regard to touching, the Holy One, Blessed is He, has commanded us** to avoid the Tree of Knowledge (as Adam had said to her), הֲרֵינִי נוֹגֵעַ בּוֹ וְאֵינִי מֵת — **then how do you explain** this? **Behold, I will touch the tree, and I will not die.** אַף אַתְּ אִם תִּגְּעִי בּוֹ אִי אַתְּ מֵתָה — **And then you can be assured that if you, too, touch it you will not die.**" מֶה עָשָׂה הַנָּחָשׁ הָרָשָׁע בְּאוֹתָהּ שָׁעָה — **What did the evil serpent do at** **that moment** to prove his point? עָמַד וְנָגַע בָּאִילָן בְּיָדָיו וּבְרַגְלָיו וְהִרְתִּיעוֹ עַד שֶׁנָּשְׁרוּ פֵּירוֹתָיו לָאָרֶץ — **He stood up and touched the tree with his hands and feet,**[72] **and shook it until its fruit fell off** and dropped **to the ground.**[73] וְיֵשׁ אֶלָּא אוֹמְרִים: לֹא נָגַע בּוֹ כָּל עִיקָר — **Some say that he did not touch it at all;**

---

69. *Ben Avraham.*

70. By exploiting the "fence" that he added to God's command, since he knows that God did not say that (*Binyan Yehoshua, Rishon LeTzion*).

71. That is, he drew her into an exchange of small talk, to relax her defenses before steering the conversation to his real topic of interest (*Magen Avos*).

How did the serpent communicate with Eve? Some say that he had, before being cursed over this incident, a human-like power of speech to go along with his ability to walk about on two feet (*Devarim Rabbah* 5 §10). Others say that his patron angel

spoke for him (*Pirkei DeRabbi Eliezer* §13), or that Eve understood his primitive serpentine language (*Rabbeinu Ephraim;* see *Avos HaRosh* for a comprehensive discussion).

72. Since the serpent at this point had an upright posture like that of human beings (as the Baraisa will teach below), it had hands and feet (*Binyan Yehoshua*).

73. He thus touched it in the most complete way possible (*Ben Avraham*). This proved to Eve that the death penalty of which she had been warned would not come to pass.

The Baraisa does not say whether Eve followed the serpent's example and touched the tree, but other sources say that she did,

כֵּיוָן שֶׁרָאָהוּ אוֹתוֹ אִילָן הָיָה צוֹוֵחַ עָלָיו וְאָמַר לוֹ: רָשָׁע רָשָׁע, אַל תִּגַּע
בִּי שֶׁנֶּאֱמַר (תהלים לו, יב) "אַל תְּבוֹאֵנִי רֶגֶל גַּאֲוָה וְיַד רְשָׁעִים אַל תְּנִדֵנִי":

ו. דָּבָר אַחֵר, (תהלים לו, יב) "אַל תְּבוֹאֵנִי רֶגֶל גַּאֲוָה", זֶה טִיטוֹס הָרָשָׁע
שֶׁנִּשְׁחֲקוּ עַצְמוֹתָיו, שֶׁהָיָה מוֹרֶה בְּיָדוֹ וְהָיָה מַכֶּה עַל גַּבֵּי הַמִּזְבֵּחַ,
וְאוֹמֵר: לָקוֹס לָקוֹס, אַתְּ מֶלֶךְ וַאֲנִי מֶלֶךְ, בּוֹא וַעֲשֵׂי עִמִּי מִלְחָמָה,[77]

כֵּיוָן שֶׁרָאָהוּ אוֹתוֹ אִילָן — rather, **as soon as the tree saw him** approaching הָיָה צוֹוֵחַ עָלָיו וְאָמַר לוֹ: רָשָׁע רָשָׁע אַל תִּגַּע בִּי — **it began shouting at him saying,** "**Evil one, evil one, do not touch me!**"[74]   שֶׁנֶּאֱמַר "אַל תְּבוֹאֵנִי רֶגֶל גַּאֲוָה וְיַד רְשָׁעִים אַל תְּנִדֵנִי" — **All this is as it is stated,** *Let not the foot of arrogance come to me, and let not the hand of the wicked move me* (*Psalms* 36:12).[75]

§6 The Baraisa interrupts its discussion to offer an alternative exposition of the verse just cited.

דָּבָר אַחֵר "אַל תְּבוֹאֵנִי רֶגֶל גַּאֲוָה" — **Another explanation:** *Let not the foot of arrogance come to me* — זֶה טִיטוֹס הָרָשָׁע שֶׁנִּשְׁחֲקוּ עַצְמוֹתָיו — **this refers to the wicked Titus, whose bones were ground up,**[76]   שֶׁהָיָה מוֹרֶה בְּיָדוֹ וְהָיָה מַכֶּה עַל גַּבֵּי הַמִּזְבֵּחַ — **who pointed** accusingly **with his hand, banged on the Altar,** וְאוֹמֵר: לָקוֹס לָקוֹס אַתְּ מֶלֶךְ וַאֲנִי מֶלֶךְ, בּוֹא וַעֲשֵׂי עִמִּי מִלְחָמָה — **and said,** "**Wolf! Wolf!**[77] **You are a king and I am a king. Come and wage war with me!**"

---

either of her own volition (*Pirkei DeRabbi Eliezer* §13), or only after the serpent pushed her against the tree (*Bereishis Rabbah* 19 §3). Either way, the serpent drove his point home by saying, "Just as you did not die for touching it, so will you not die for eating of it."

74. The "shouting" of the tree is a metaphor for its shuddering at the prospect of the snake's attempt to touch it, and it is that shuddering that caused its fruits to fall to the ground (*Ben Avraham*).

75. According to the first opinion, this verse represents the tree's prayer that it should never again endure the kind of abuse to which the serpent subjected it — grasping it with hands and feet and shaking it. According to the second opinion, the verse represents the tree's prayer that the plan of the approaching serpent to grasp and shake it not succeed (*Ben Avraham*).

76. This or a similar curse was commonly appended to the names of wicked people,

as in אַנְדְּרְיָינוּס שְׁחִיק עֲצָמוֹת, *Hadrian, may his bones be ground up* (*Vayikra Rabbah* 18 §1 and 25 §5). Alternatively, the phrase, which here is in the past tense, refers to Titus' self-imposed fate, as described in the Talmud (*Gittin* 56b): "When Titus was dying, he said to the people around him, 'Burn my corpse and scatter my ashes over the seven seas, so that the God of the Jews will not find me and bring me to judgment in Heaven' " (*Magen Avos*).

77. By calling the Altar a "wolf" (*lukos* in Greek), Titus was accusing it of devouring Israel's abundant and expensive offerings, like a wolf preying on unsuspecting sheep, without protecting them in return, as evidenced by his own conquest of Judea and triumphant entry into the Holy Temple (*Binyan Yehoshua,* based on *Succah* 56b with *Maharsha*).

In any case, Titus did not think the Altar was an independent being capable of acting greedily or of waging war with him. Rather, he was allusively addressing himself to God,

כַּמָּה שְׁוָורִים נִשְׁחֲטוּ עָלֶיךָ[78] כַּמָּה עוֹפוֹת נִמְלְקוּ עָלֶיךָ כַּמָּה יֵינוֹת
נִסְכּוּ עָלֶיךָ[79] כַּמָּה בְשָׂמִים קָטְרוּ עָלֶיךָ, אַתָּה הוּא שֶׁמַּחֲרִיב אֶת כָּל
הָעוֹלָם,[80] שֶׁנֶּאֱמַר (ישעיה כט, א) "הוֹי אֲרִיאֵל אֲרִיאֵל קִרְיַת חָנָה דָוִד סְפוּ
שָׁנָה עַל שָׁנָה חַגִּים יִנְקֹפוּ"[81]. וְשׁוּב אָמַר לָהּ: אִם לַאֲכִילָה אַתְּ °אוֹמֶר
צִוָּה עָלֵינוּ הַקָּדוֹשׁ בָּרוּךְ הוּא[83], הֲרֵינִי (אוֹמֵר) אוֹכֵל מִמֶּנּוּ °וְאֵינוּ

כַּמָּה שְׁוָורִים נִשְׁחֲטוּ עָלֶיךָ — How many bulls were slaughtered on you!
כַּמָּה עוֹפוֹת נִמְלְקוּ עָלֶיךָ — How many birds had *melikah* on you![78] כַּמָּה
יֵינוֹת נִסְכּוּ עָלֶיךָ — How many wine libations were poured on you! כַּמָּה
בְשָׂמִים קָטְרוּ עָלֶיךָ — How much incense did they cause to go up in smoke on
you![79] אַתָּה הוּא שֶׁמַּחֲרִיב אֶת כָּל הָעוֹלָם — You are the one destroying the
entire world!"[80] שֶׁנֶּאֱמַר "הוֹי אֲרִיאֵל אֲרִיאֵל קִרְיַת חָנָה דָוִד סְפוּ שָׁנָה עַל שָׁנָה
חַגִּים יִנְקֹפוּ" — As it is stated, *Oh, Ariel, Ariel, [in] the city where David
encamped! You add [sins] year after year, so that the sheep are being axed*
(*Isaiah* 29:1).[81]

The Baraisa returns to the narrative of the serpent and Eve:
וְשׁוּב אָמַר לָהּ — Seeing that Eve was still not convinced by his touching of
the tree without mishap,[82] he said to her further: אִם לַאֲכִילָה אַתְּ אוֹמֶרֶת
צִוָּה עָלֵינוּ הַקָּדוֹשׁ בָּרוּךְ הוּא — "If you say, 'It is primarily eating that the Holy
One, Blessed is He, has commanded us about,'[83] הֲרֵינִי אוֹכֵל מִמֶּנּוּ וְאֵינִי

---

to Whom the Altar was dedicated, which is
why he continued, "You are a king and I am
a king ..." (*Ben Avraham*).

78. *Melikah* is the special slaughter (with the
Kohen's thumbnail) used for bird offerings in
the Temple.

79. The reference is apparently to private,
voluntary frankincense offerings (see *Shekalim* 6:4; *Yoma* 55b with *Rashi* ד״ה כולן
עולות)because the communal *ketoress*
offering was brought only on the Inner (or
Golden) Altar; the Roman general's tirade,
however, was directed at the Outer Altar,
where nearly all the sacrificial services
were performed (*Ahavas Chesed, Kisei Rachamim*). Alternatively, it may refer not to
incense but to the burning of the offerings in
general, which are called רֵיחַ נִיחוֹחַ, *a satisfying aroma* (*Leviticus* 1:9, et al.). Alternatively, it may refer to the frankincense that was
part of nearly all *minchah* offerings, which
were offered on the Outer Altar (see *Binyan
Yehoshua*).

80. [By consuming all the offerings yet doing nothing to protect your people.]

81. The verse explains *why* the anticipated protection of the sacrificial service
noted by Titus was not forthcoming — it
is because the people continue to sin year
after year. It is thus as if they "ax" the sacrificial sheep instead of actually sacrificing
them (*Magen Avos*). [*Ariel*, "lion of God,"
is another name for the Altar in the First
Temple, which was graced by a lion-like
flame that descended from Heaven when
the Temple was inaugurated in the time of
King Solomon (*Yoma* 21b, cited by *Binyan
Yehoshua*).]

82. As will become evident, this part of the
Baraisa accords with the first view above,
that the serpent *did* actually touch the tree
(*Binyan Yehoshua*, from *Mefaresh*).

83. [Even though Adam had told her that
both touching and eating were prohibited
(as taught above),] surely touching the forbidden fruit is not as grievous as eating

מֵת,[84] וְאַף אַתְּ תֹּאכְלִי וְאִי אַתְּ מֵתָה. מַה אָמְרָה חַוָּה בְּדַעְתָּהּ, (אָמְרָה חַוָּה בְּדַעְתָּהּ:) כָּל הַדְּבָרִים שֶׁפְּקָדַנִי רַבִּי מִתְּחִלָּה שֶׁקֶר הֵם, לְפִי שֶׁאֵין חַוָּה קוֹרֵא לְאָדָם הָרִאשׁוֹן מִתְּחִלָּה אֶלָּא רַבִּי.[85] מִיָּד נָטְלָה וְאָכְלָה וְנָתְנָה לְאָדָם וְאָכַל,[86] שֶׁנֶּאֱמַר (בראשית ג, ו) "וַתֵּרֶא הָאִשָּׁה כִּי טוֹב הָעֵץ לְמַאֲכָל וְכִי תַאֲוָה הוּא לָעֵינַיִם [וְגוֹ']":[87]

וְאַף אַתְּ תֹּאכְלִי וְאִי מֵת — behold, I will eat of the tree and I will not die![84] אַתְּ מֵתָה — And then you can be assured that **you, too, can eat of it and you will not die.**" מַה אָמְרָה חַוָּה בְּדַעְתָּהּ, אָמְרָה חַוָּה בְּדַעְתָּהּ — **What did Eve say in her mind** when she saw the serpent eating the forbidden fruit without being harmed? **Eve said in her mind:** כָּל הַדְּבָרִים שֶׁפְּקָדַנִי רַבִּי מִתְּחִלָּה שֶׁקֶר הֵם — **Everything that my master (Adam) originally commanded me** in God's **Name is false!** לְפִי שֶׁאֵין חַוָּה קוֹרֵא לְאָדָם הָרִאשׁוֹן מִתְּחִלָּה אֶלָּא רַבִּי — **Eve** referred to her husband in this way **because at first**[85] Eve did not call Adam, the first man, anything but "my master." מִיָּד נָטְלָה וְאָכְלָה וְנָתְנָה לְאָדָם — **Immediately, she took** some of the fruit **and she ate, and** then she **gave** some **to Adam and he ate,**[86] שֶׁנֶּאֱמַר "וַתֵּרֶא הָאִשָּׁה כִּי טוֹב הָעֵץ לְמַאֲכָל וְכִי תַאֲוָה הוּא לָעֵינַיִם וְגוֹ' " — **as it is stated,** *And the woman perceived that the tree was good for eating and that it was a delight for the eyes, etc. ... and she took of its fruit and ate; and she gave also to her husband with her and he ate* (Genesis 3:6).[87]

them [and perhaps that is why the serpent did not die by touching the tree] (*Magen Avos*).

84. The serpent was not afraid to do this because he thought, as Eve did, that God banned the tree because it was poisonous (see *Ramban* to 3:6). Accordingly, the serpent reasoned that it was poisonous only to humans, while Eve assumed that if it was poisonous to humans, it would be poisonous to all creatures (*Ahavas Chesed*). And since the serpent did not immediately die, he was able to persuade Eve that the tree was not poisonous at all, and that the real reason God had forbidden it was to prevent them from becoming like Him: *for God knows that on the day you eat of it ... you will be like God, knowing good and bad* (see *Magen Avos*).

85. Before Adam sinned and while the

angels were still treating him like a king, ministering to his every need (*Ahavas Chesed* [see *Sanhedrin* 59b]). Alternatively, she called him "my master," because he was her source for everything she knew about God's Will, including the Seven Noahide Laws (which were actually given to Adam) and the prohibition against the Tree of Knowledge (*Magen Avos*).

86. As to how she persuaded him to eat, see *Bereishis Rabbah* 19 §5 (quoted by *Ahavas Chesed* here) with commentaries.

87. This verse proves that the serpent first ate from the fruit. Otherwise, how did Eve perceive that the tree was good for eating? (*Ben Avraham*). The balance of the verse also states clearly that Eve then ate and also gave the fruit to Adam, who ate as well, as the Baraisa states.

ז. עֶשֶׂר קְלָלוֹת נִתְקַלְלָה חַוָּה בְּאוֹתָהּ שָׁעָה. שֶׁנֶּאֱמַר (שם פסוק טז) "אֶל
הָאִשָּׁה אָמַר הַרְבָּה אַרְבֶּה עִצְּבוֹנֵךְ וְהֵרֹנֵךְ בְּעֶצֶב תֵּלְדִי בָנִים וְאֶל אִישֵׁךְ
תְּשׁוּקָתֵךְ וְהוּא יִמְשָׁל בָּךְ". אֵלּוּ שְׁתֵּי רְבִיעִיּוֹת (נ"א רְבִיּוֹת) דָּם,[88] אַחַת דַּם
צַעַר נִדָּה[89] וְאַחַת דַּם צַעַר בְּתוּלִים.[90] ["עִצְּבוֹנֵךְ" זֶה צַעַר גִּדּוּל בָּנִים.[91]]
"וְהֵרֹנֵךְ" זֶה צַעַר הָעִבּוּר.[92] "בְּעֶצֶב תֵּלְדִי בָנִים" כְּמַשְׁמָעוֹ. "וְאֶל אִישֵׁךְ
תְּשׁוּקָתֵךְ" מְלַמֵּד שֶׁהָאִשָּׁה מִשְׁתּוֹקֶקֶת עַל בַּעְלָהּ בְּשָׁעָה שֶׁהוּא יוֹצֵא
לַדֶּרֶךְ.[93] "וְהוּא יִמְשָׁל בָּךְ" שֶׁהָאִישׁ תּוֹבֵעַ בַּפֶּה וְהָאִשָּׁה תּוֹבַעַת בַּלֵּב.[94]

---

§7 The Baraisa details the consequences of Eve's sinful behavior: עֶשֶׂר קְלָלוֹת נִתְקַלְלָה חַוָּה בְּאוֹתָהּ שָׁעָה — Eve was cursed with ten curses at that time because of her sin. שֶׁנֶּאֱמַר "אֶל הָאִשָּׁה אָמַר הַרְבָּה אַרְבֶּה עִצְּבוֹנֵךְ וְהֵרֹנֵךְ — As it is stated, *To the woman He said, "I will greatly increase your suffering and [what is associated with] your pregnancy;* בְּעֶצֶב תֵּלְדִי בָנִים — *in pain you shall give birth to children,* וְאֶל אִישֵׁךְ תְּשׁוּקָתֵךְ וְהוּא יִמְשָׁל בָּךְ" — *yet your craving shall be for your husband and he shall rule over you* (ibid. v. 16). אֵלּוּ שְׁתֵּי רְבִיּוֹת דָּם — These double words, הַרְבָּה אַרְבֶּה (literally, *Increase I will increase*), are a reference to the two increases[88] of blood to which a woman is subject, and which are the first of her two curses: אַחַת דַּם צַעַר נִדָּה וְאַחַת דַּם צַעַר בְּתוּלִים — (i) one is the blood of menstrual pain[89] and (ii) one is the blood of virginal pain.[90] "עִצְּבוֹנֵךְ" זֶה צַעַר גִּדּוּל בָּנִים — *Your suffering*: This refers to (iii) the pain of raising children.[91] "וְהֵרֹנֵךְ" זֶה צַעַר הָעִבּוּר — *And [the pain of] your pregnancy*: This is (iv) the pain of pregnancy.[92] "בְּעֶצֶב תֵּלְדִי בָנִים" כְּמַשְׁמָעוֹ — *In pain you shall give birth to children*: This is as its meaning suggests, (v) the pain of actual childbirth; "וְאֶל אִישֵׁךְ תְּשׁוּקָתֵךְ" — *yet your craving shall be for your husband*: מְלַמֵּד שֶׁהָאִשָּׁה מִשְׁתּוֹקֶקֶת עַל בַּעְלָהּ בְּשָׁעָה שֶׁהוּא יוֹצֵא לַדֶּרֶךְ — This teaches that (vi) a woman yearns for intimacy with her husband, especially when he is about to leave on a journey.[93] "וְהוּא יִמְשָׁל בָּךְ" — *And he shall rule over you*: שֶׁהָאִישׁ תּוֹבֵעַ בַּפֶּה וְהָאִשָּׁה תּוֹבַעַת בַּלֵּב — This means that (vii) the man petitions

---

88. We have followed here the alternative reading in the text: רְבִיּוֹת.

89. Menstrual bleeding, which is often accompanied by pain (*Binyan Yehoshua*).

90. The bleeding caused by the painful rupture of the hymen (*Binyan Yehoshua*).

91. Emendation based on *Binyan Yehoshua* and *Kisei Rachamim*.

Although shared by the father, the trials and tribulations of raising children are primarily borne by the mother (*Binyan*

Yehoshua, quoting *Maharsha*).

92. The malaise a woman often feels during pregnancy (*Binyan Yehoshua*, quoting *Rashi*).

93. *Binyan Yehoshua*, quoting *Mefaresh*.

The Baraisa uses the word "teaches" here because this observation of a wife's yearning results in a halachic obligation on her husband: Before leaving on a journey, a husband is duty-bound to accommodate his wife's yearning for him (*Kisei Rachamim*).

עֲטוּפָה כְּאָבֵל[96] וַחֲבוּשָׁה מִכָּל אָדָם בְּבֵית הָאֲסוּרִין[97] וּמְנוּדָּה מִכָּל אָדָם. מִי
גָּרַם לִנְגִיעָה זוֹ, סְיָיג שֶׁסָּג אָדָם הָרִאשׁוֹן שֶׁעָשָׂה לִדְבָרָיו[99]. מִכָּאן אָמְרוּ:

---

his wife for marital relations **verbally, whereas the woman,** who is naturally shy
in this respect, **petitions** her husband **in her heart,** i.e., wordlessly.[94]   **עֲטוּפָה**
כְּאָבֵל — In addition to those seven, there are three more not alluded to in the
verse:[95] (viii) **She is wrapped up** in a head-covering **like a mourner,** who pulls
his cloak over his head.[96]   **וַחֲבוּשָׁה מִכָּל אָדָם בְּבֵית הָאֲסוּרִין** — (ix) **She is**
confined to her home, **away from all** other **people,** as if **in a prison.**[97]   **וּמְנוּדָּה**
מִכָּל אָדָם — And finally, (x) **she is cut off from all people** besides her husband,
in the sense that she may not marry more than one man, whereas a man may
take multiple wives.[98]

The Baraisa returns to its original point — that Adam "made a fence around
his words":

מִי גָּרַם לִנְגִיעָה זוֹ — **What caused this touching** that led Eve and then Adam
to eat the forbidden fruit?   **סְיָיג שֶׁסָּג אָדָם הָרִאשׁוֹן שֶׁעָשָׂה לִדְבָרָיו** — **It was the**
fence that Adam, the first man, made around his words.[99]   **מִכָּאן אָמְרוּ** —

---

94. By acting in an affectionate manner
(Rashi, Eruvin 100b), or by adorning herself
(Rabbeinu Chananel there). The imbalance
in this arrangement gives the husband more
control over their relationship, and thus is
contained in the "curse" he shall rule over
you. [Nevertheless, the Gemara (Eruvin
ibid.) characterizes the woman's reticence
in this matter as a mark of refinement.]

95. Magen Avos, first explanation; see there
for a second approach.

96. [By Talmudic law, a mourner is required
to cloak his head (see Moed Katan 15a;
Yoreh Deah 386). Rama (ad loc.), however,
writes that this is not the custom nowadays.]
A woman, too, is naturally embarrassed to
appear in public with her head uncovered
(Binyan Yehoshua, quoting Rashi).

97. Because the entire honor of the king's
daughter is inside: A princess does not venture out of her palace and circulate among
the masses without a special need to do
so (ibid.). Although this is a matter of up-
holding her majestic dignity, it nevertheless
places limitations on her freedom.

98. Ibid., quoting Eruvin 100b. [Having
more than one wife is allowed under Biblical

and Talmudic law. Almost 1,000 years ago,
however, a ban against the practice was
introduced by the Rabbinic leaders of Ash-
kenazic Jewry.]

99. As explained earlier (§5), Adam's decision to add touching the Tree of Knowledge to God's prohibition against eating its
fruit gave the serpent a way to persuade
Eve that the entire prohibition could be
ignored.

There is, however, a difficulty here: The
Baraisa stated earlier that the serpent demonstrated not only that it could touch the
tree without any ill effects but also that it
could eat of its fruit. If so, it would seem that
the serpent could have persuaded Eve even
if Adam had told her precisely what God had
told him — that it was only eating the fruit
that was forbidden!

Magen Avos suggests that the serpent
could not have begun with a discussion
about eating the forbidden fruit, because
Eve would not have been open to considering such a blatant transgression. He had to
begin with the more subtle transgression of
touching the tree, and progress from there
to eating of its fruit. [See Mefaresh for a more
intricate resolution to this difficulty.]

אִם סָג אָדָם לִדְבָרָיו אֵין יָכוֹל לַעֲמוֹד בִּדְבָרָיו[100]. מִכָּאן אָמְרוּ: אַל יוֹסִיף אָדָם
עַל דְּבָרִים שֶׁשּׁוֹמֵעַ[101]. רַבִּי יוֹסֵי אוֹמֵר: טוֹב עֲשָׂרָה טְפָחִים וְעוֹמֵד מִמֵּאָה
אַמָּה[102] וְנוֹפֵל[103]. מֶה חָשַׁב נָחָשׁ (הָרִאשׁוֹן) [הָרָשָׁע] בְּאוֹתָהּ שָׁעָה. אֵלֵךְ
וְאֶהֱרוֹג אֶת אָדָם וְאֶשָּׂא אֶת אִשְׁתּוֹ[104] וְאֶהְיֶה מֶלֶךְ עַל כָּל הָעוֹלָם כּוּלּוֹ[105]

From here, based on this precedent, [the Sages] said: אֵין לִדְבָרָיו אָדָם סָג אִם — **If a person makes a fence around his words, he will not be able to uphold his words.**[100] מִכָּאן אָמְרוּ — **From here they said** along the same lines: אַל יוֹסִיף אָדָם עַל דְּבָרִים שֶׁשּׁוֹמֵעַ — **A person should not add to the words that he hears** from others.[101] טוֹב עֲשָׂרָה טְפָחִים וְעוֹמֵד מִמֵּאָה אַמָּה וְנוֹפֵל — **R' Yose said: Better** a wall **ten handbreadths** high **that will stand than** a wall **one hundred cubits**[102] high **that will fall.**[103]

The Baraisa details the serpent's overreaching designs and the "measure for measure" punishments that he incurred as a result: מֶה חָשַׁב נָחָשׁ הָרָשָׁע בְּאוֹתָהּ שָׁעָה — **What was the evil serpent thinking at that time,** when he set out to persuade Adam and Eve to sin? אֵלֵךְ וְאֶהֱרוֹג אֶת אָדָם — **He was thinking, "I shall go kill Adam and marry his wife.**[104] וְאֶהְיֶה מֶלֶךְ עַל כָּל הָעוֹלָם כּוּלּוֹ — **I will then be king over the entire world;**[105]

---

100. Certainly there is a place for erecting safeguards to protect one's mitzvah observance. The Talmud is replete with Rabbinic enactments of this sort, and our Baraisa itself has advocated building a "fence" around one's words (above, §5). There is, however, an important rule for creating these safeguards: One must clearly distinguish between the Divine core of the mitzvah and the man-made "fence" surrounding it. Had Adam made this distinction, the serpent would not have been able to persuade Eve (Binyan Yehoshua, quoting Mefaresh; Hagahos Yaavetz).

101. If he presents his addition as an integral part of the original.

102. A cubit equals six handbreadths. Thus, a hundred-cubit wall is sixty times higher than a ten-handbreadth wall.

103. It is better to devise a smaller safeguard ("fence") that will endure than to reach for a more ambitious one, like that of Adam, and see it collapse and be trampled underfoot (Ben Avraham).

Alternatively, R' Yose's comment is not the conclusion of the preceding but an introduction to what follows: Better to be ten handbreadths tall, i.e., to curb your ambition and be satisfied with what you have, than to strive to be one hundred amos tall, i.e., to strive for what is not coming to you and end up with less than you had to begin with. As the Sages teach elsewhere: "Anyone who sets his eyes [covetously] on what is not his — what he wants he will not get, and what he has will be taken from him" (Sotah 9a; see below, 3:3). The Baraisa goes on to show how the serpent exemplified this folly of overreaching (Magen Avos).

104. How would the serpent marry Eve if, as per his plan, she would eat from the forbidden fruit and die? It must be that he expected her to serve the fruit first to Adam, in deference to him, and he alone would die (see Binyan Yehoshua, and Rashi to Genesis 3:15 with Gur Aryeh). [See Mefaresh here for a more complex resolution; see also Magen Avos, and Maharsha to Sotah 9b.]

105. By virtue of my superior intelligence (as Scripture says: Now, the serpent was cunning beyond any beast of the field) and power of speech (Mefaresh).

וְאֵלֵךְ בְּקוֹמָה זְקוּפָה וְאוֹכַל כָּל מַעֲדַנֵּי עוֹלָם[106], אָמַר לוֹ הַקָּדוֹשׁ בָּרוּךְ
הוּא: אַתָּה אָמַרְתָּ אֶהֱרוֹג אֶת אָדָם וְאֶשָּׂא אֶת חַוָּה, לְפִיכָךְ (בראשית ג,
טו) "אֵיבָה אָשִׁית"[107]. אַתָּה אָמַרְתָּ: אֶהְיֶה מֶלֶךְ עַל כָּל הָעוֹלָם, לְפִיכָךְ
(שם פסוק יד) "אָרוּר אַתָּה מִכָּל הַבְּהֵמָה"[108]. אַתָּה אָמַרְתָּ: אֵלֵךְ בְּקוֹמָה
זְקוּפָה, לְפִיכָךְ (שם) "עַל גְּחֹנְךָ תֵלֵךְ". אַתָּה אָמַרְתָּ: אוֹכַל כָּל מַעֲדַנֵּי
עוֹלָם, לְפִיכָךְ (שם) "עָפָר תֹּאכַל כָּל יְמֵי חַיֶּיךָ". רַבִּי שִׁמְעוֹן בֶּן מְנַסְיָא
אוֹמֵר: חֲבָל עַל שַׁמָּשׁ גָּדוֹל שֶׁאָבַד מִן הָעוֹלָם, שֶׁאִלְמָלֵא (לֹא) נִתְקַלֵּל
הַנָּחָשׁ הָיָה לוֹ לְכָל אֶחָד וְאֶחָד מִיִּשְׂרָאֵל (הָיוּ לוֹ) שְׁנֵי נְחָשִׁים בְּתוֹךְ
בֵּיתוֹ, אֶחָד מְשַׁגְּרוֹ לַמַּעֲרָב וְאֶחָד מְשַׁגְּרוֹ לַמִּזְרָח וּמְבִיאִים לָהֶם
סַנְדְּלַכִּים טוֹבִים אֲבָנִים טוֹבוֹת וּמַרְגָּלִיּוֹת וְכָל כְּלִי חֶמֶד טוֹב שֶׁבָּעוֹלָם

וְאֵלֵךְ בְּקוֹמָה זְקוּפָה וְאוֹכַל כָּל מַעֲדַנֵּי עוֹלָם — **I will walk about,** like a human being, with an upright posture and eat all the delicacies of the world."[106] אָמַר לוֹ הַקָּדוֹשׁ בָּרוּךְ הוּא — **Said the Holy One, Blessed is He,** to him in response, אַתָּה אָמַרְתָּ: אֶהֱרוֹג אֶת אָדָם וְאֶשָּׂא אֶת חַוָּה — "**You said, 'I shall kill Adam and marry Eve';** לְפִיכָךְ "אֵיבָה אָשִׁית" — **therefore,** *I will put enmity between you and the woman,* to ensure that you never have any meaningful contact with her.[107] אַתָּה אָמַרְתָּ: אֶהְיֶה מֶלֶךְ עַל כָּל הָעוֹלָם — **You said, 'I will be king over the entire world';** לְפִיכָךְ "אָרוּר אַתָּה מִכָּל הַבְּהֵמָה" — **therefore,** *accursed are you beyond all the animals,* making you lower, not higher, than your fellow beasts.[108] אַתָּה אָמַרְתָּ: אֵלֵךְ בְּקוֹמָה זְקוּפָה — **You said, 'I will walk with an upright posture';** לְפִיכָךְ "עַל גְּחֹנְךָ תֵלֵךְ" — **therefore,** *upon your belly shall you go,* adopting an even less dignified posture than that of most other animals, which have legs to lift them off the ground. אַתָּה אָמַרְתָּ: אוֹכַל כָּל מַעֲדַנֵּי עוֹלָם — Finally, **you said, 'I will eat all the delicacies of the world';** לְפִיכָךְ "עָפָר תֹּאכַל כָּל יְמֵי חַיֶּיךָ" — **therefore,** *dust you shall eat all the days of your life.*" The Baraisa notes that the serpent's curse was also a loss for mankind: רַבִּי שִׁמְעוֹן בֶּן מְנַסְיָא אוֹמֵר — **R' Shimon ben Menasya says:** חֲבָל עַל שַׁמָּשׁ גָּדוֹל שֶׁאָבַד מִן הָעוֹלָם — **What a shame that such a great servant was lost to the world!** שֶׁאִלְמָלֵא נִתְקַלֵּל הַנָּחָשׁ — **For had the serpent not been cursed,** הָיָה לוֹ לְכָל אֶחָד וְאֶחָד מִיִּשְׂרָאֵל שְׁנֵי נְחָשִׁים בְּתוֹךְ בֵּיתוֹ — **each and every Jew would have had two serpents in his house,** אֶחָד מְשַׁגְּרוֹ לַמַּעֲרָב וְאֶחָד מְשַׁגְּרוֹ לַמִּזְרָח — **one he would send to the** distant **west and the other he would send to the** distant **east,** וּמְבִיאִים לָהֶם סַנְדְּלַכִּים טוֹבִים — **and they would bring** back to their owners *sandelakim* gems, אֲבָנִים טוֹבוֹת וּמַרְגָּלִיּוֹת וְכָל כְּלִי חֶמֶד — **precious stones and pearls, and every kind of good, desirable** טוֹב שֶׁבָּעוֹלָם

---

106. Of the kind that Adam was enjoying, as described below [§8] (*Magen Avos*).
107. The punishment of "enmity between

them" indicates that the serpent had desired closeness with her (*Ben Avraham*).
108. Included in this punishment is the loss

וְאֵין כָּל בְּרִיָּה יְכוֹלָה לְהַחֲזִיק אוֹתָן[109], וְלֹא עוֹד אֶלָּא שֶׁהָיוּ מַכְנִיסִין אוֹתָן
תַּחַת גָּמָל תַּחַת חֲמוֹר תַּחַת פֶּרֶד וּמוֹצִיאִין זְבָלִים לַגַּנּוֹת וְלַפַּרְדֵּסוֹת:

ח. רַבִּי יְהוּדָה בֶּן בְּתֵירָה אוֹמֵר: אָדָם הָרִאשׁוֹן הָיָה מֵיסֵב בְּגַן עֵדֶן
וּמַלְאֲכֵי הַשָּׁרֵת עוֹמְדִין בְּגַן עֵדֶן לִקְרָאתוֹ וְצוֹלִין לוֹ בָּשָׂר[111] וּמְצַנְּנִין
לוֹ יַיִן[112] בָּא נָחָשׁ וְרָאָה אוֹתוֹ וְהֵצִיץ בִּכְבוֹדוֹ וְנִתְקַנֵּא בּוֹ. כֵּיצַד נִבְרָא
אָדָם הָרִאשׁוֹן. שָׁעָה רִאשׁוֹנָה הוּצְבַּר עֲפָרוֹ[114]. שְׁנִיָּה נִבְרָא צוּרָתוֹ[115].

---

thing in the world; וְאֵין כָּל בְּרִיָּה יְכוֹלָה לְהַחֲזִיק אוֹתָן — and no creature
would be able to hold them back.[109] וְלֹא עוֹד אֶלָּא שֶׁהָיוּ מַכְנִיסִין אוֹתָן תַּחַת
גָּמָל תַּחַת חֲמוֹר תַּחַת פֶּרֶד — Not only that, but people would have substituted
them for donkeys and mules, which are not intelligent enough to work independently,[110] וּמוֹצִיאִין זְבָלִים לַגַּנּוֹת וְלַפַּרְדֵּסוֹת — and they would carry out
manure to fertilize the gardens and the orchards. In short, mankind would
have benefited greatly from having highly intelligent beasts at its disposal.

§8 The Baraisa identifies another cause for the serpent's jealousy:

רַבִּי יְהוּדָה בֶּן בְּתֵירָה אוֹמֵר — R' Yehudah ben Beseirah says: אָדָם
הָרִאשׁוֹן הָיָה מֵיסֵב בְּגַן עֵדֶן — Adam, the first man, would recline in the Garden of Eden, וּמַלְאֲכֵי הַשָּׁרֵת עוֹמְדִין בְּגַן עֵדֶן לִקְרָאתוֹ — and the ministering
angels would stand opposite him וְצוֹלִין לוֹ בָּשָׂר וּמְצַנְּנִין לוֹ יַיִן — and roast
meat for him[111] and cool wine for him.[112] בָּא נָחָשׁ וְרָאָה אוֹתוֹ — The serpent came along and saw him, וְהֵצִיץ בִּכְבוֹדוֹ וְנִתְקַנֵּא בּוֹ — and gazed at
the honor accorded to him, and became jealous of him.

The Baraisa shows how despite all this honor, it was only a matter of hours
before Adam sinned, as the Baraisa proceeds to detail the events of the day
of Adam's creation:[113]

כֵּיצַד נִבְרָא אָדָם הָרִאשׁוֹן — How was Adam, the first man, created?
שָׁעָה רִאשׁוֹנָה הוּצְבַּר עֲפָרוֹ — In the first hour of the day, his dust was
gathered.[114] שְׁנִיָּה נִבְרָא צוּרָתוֹ — In the second hour, his form was

---

of those special qualities (see note 105) that
had until now raised the serpent above, and
made him fit to rule over, all other "beasts of
the field" (*Mefaresh*).

109. *Ben Avraham*, second explanation.
Alternatively, no creature would be able to
overpower the serpents and *grab hold* of the
valuables under their care (*Magen Avos*).
[Some texts, however, read here "לְהַזִּיק אוֹתָן,
to harm them. That is, no creature would be
able to harm these serpentine couriers or
wrest away what they carried (see *Nuschas
HaGra* and *Magen Avos*).]

110. *Ben Avraham*.

111. According to the Talmud, this was not
ordinary animal meat, because that was not
permitted for consumption until after the
Great Flood. Rather, this was meat that descended from Heaven (*Ben Avraham*, from
Sanhedrin 59b).

112. I.e., to chill the wine, or, alternatively,
to dilute it by mixing it with water (*Magen
Avos*).

113. *Magen Avos*.

114. From all over the world, as the Sages
teach elsewhere: The dust for his head was

שְׁלִישִׁית נַעֲשָׂה גוֹלֶם.‏[116] רְבִיעִית נִתְקַשְׁרוּ אֵבְרָיו.‏[117] חֲמִישִׁית נִתְפַּתְּחוּ נְקָבָיו. שִׁשִּׁית נִתְּנָה בּוֹ נְשָׁמָה.‏[118] שְׁבִיעִית עָמַד עַל רַגְלָיו.‏[119] שְׁמִינִית נִזְדַּוְּוגָה לוֹ חַוָּה. תְּשִׁיעִית הִכְנִיסוֹ לְגַן עֵדֶן. עֲשִׂירִית צִוָּהוּ.‏[120] אַחַד עָשָׂר סָרַח. שְׁתֵּים עָשָׂר נִטְרַד וְהָלַךְ לוֹ, לְקַיֵּים מַה שֶּׁנֶּאֱמַר (תהלים מט, יג) ‏"וְאָדָם בִּיקָר בַּל יָלִין".

created.‏[115] שְׁלִישִׁית נַעֲשָׂה גוֹלֶם — In the third hour, he was made into an unfinished bodily form.‏[116] רְבִיעִית נִתְקַשְׁרוּ אֵבְרָיו — In the fourth hour, his limbs were connected.‏[117] חֲמִישִׁית נִתְפַּתְּחוּ נְקָבָיו — In the fifth hour, his orifices were opened. שִׁשִּׁית נִתְּנָה בּוֹ נְשָׁמָה — In the sixth hour, a soul was placed within him.‏[118] שְׁבִיעִית עָמַד עַל רַגְלָיו — In the seventh hour, he stood up on his feet.‏[119] שְׁמִינִית נִזְדַּוְּוגָה לוֹ חַוָּה — In the eighth hour, Eve was paired with him. תְּשִׁיעִית הִכְנִיסוֹ לְגַן עֵדֶן — In the ninth hour, [God] brought him into the Garden of Eden. עֲשִׂירִית צִוָּהוּ — In the tenth hour, [God] commanded him not to eat from the Tree of Knowledge.‏[120] אַחַד עָשָׂר סָרַח — In the eleventh hour, he soured, i.e., sinned, by eating from it. שְׁתֵּים עָשָׂר נִטְרַד וְהָלַךְ לוֹ — In the twelfth hour, he was expelled from the Garden of Eden and he went on his way. לְקַיֵּים מַה שֶּׁנֶּאֱמַר "וְאָדָם בִּיקָר בַּל יָלִין" — This outcome served to fulfill that which is stated, *But as for man, he does not remain in a state of glory overnight* (*Psalms* 49:13). For by nightfall, Adam had sinned and descended from his glory.

taken from the Land of Israel; the dust for his torso was taken from Babylonia, etc. (*Magen Avos* and *Ahavas Chesed*, quoting *Sanhedrin* 38b).

115. That is, the form of his head and face (*Magen Avos, Ahavas Chesed*). [Alternatively, this means that the gathered dust was made into the form of a human body, but not fused into a single entity (*Ben Avraham*).]

116. That is, the rest of his body was shaped into the lifeless image of a human being (*Magen Avos, Ahavas Chesed*). [Alternatively, this means that the shaped dust became fused into a single entity (*Ben Avraham*).]

117. His limbs were connected by the various systems that integrate all of them into one living organism (*Magen Avos*).

118. Many commentators wonder: In creating the world, God brought all other creatures into being instantaneously, in their complete and final form (*Rosh Hashanah* 11a). Only when it came to man did He use this slow, gradual method, adding another element

every hour. Why the difference? Some explain that God wished to demonstrate that man's task in life is to develop his character and sanctify his being slowly and gradually, acquiring perfection step by laborious step. This is in contrast to all other creatures (even angels), which invariably remain as they were made. They have no obligation, and indeed no ability, to raise themselves up to ever higher levels of Divine service (*Binyan Yehoshua*, quoting *Mefaresh*).

Alternatively, in order to demonstrate the special nature of man, God made a point of creating man "patiently," in the way a human craftsman would perform important work, with patience and care (*Ahavas Chesed* [in marginal note], quoting *Yefeh To'ar* to *Vayikra Rabbah* 29 §1).

119. See below, note 155.

120. Here, the Baraisa indicates that Eve's creation preceded God's command, unlike a simple reading of the Scriptural account, which implies the opposite (see *Ahavas Chesed*).

יוֹם רִאשׁוֹן מַהוּ אוֹמֵר[121], (שם כד, א) "לַה' הָאָרֶץ וּמְלוֹאָהּ תֵּבֵל וְיֹשְׁבֵי בָהּ"[122], כִּי הוּא קָנָה וַיִּקְנֶהָ[123] וְהוּא יָדִין אֶת הָעוֹלָם. בְּיוֹם שֵׁנִי מַהוּ אוֹמֵר, (שם מח, ב) "גָּדוֹל ה' וּמְהֻלָּל מְאֹד בְּעִיר אֱלֹהֵינוּ", חִלֵּק אֶת כָּל מַעֲשָׂיו וְנַעֲשָׂה °כֻּלּוֹ עַל עוֹלָמוֹ[125]. בִּשְׁלִישִׁי מַהוּ אוֹמֵר (שם פב, א) "אֱלֹהִים נִצָּב בַּעֲדַת אֵל בְּקֶרֶב אֱלֹהִים יִשְׁפֹּט", בָּרָא אֶת הַיָּם וְאֶת הַיַּבָּשָׁה

Having mentioned the progressive creation of the human being hour by hour, the Baraisa deals with the progressive creation of the world day by day: יוֹם רִאשׁוֹן מַהוּ אוֹמֵר — **On the first day** of the week, Sunday (which was the first day of Creation), **what** hymn **does one recite?**[121] "לַה' הָאָרֶץ וּמְלוֹאָהּ תֵּבֵל וְיֹשְׁבֵי בָהּ" — One recites the psalm that begins, *HASHEM's is the earth and its fullness, the inhabited land and those who dwell in it* (*Psalms* 24:1).[122] כִּי הוּא קָנָה וַיִּקְנֶהָ וְהוּא יָדִין אֶת הָעוֹלָם — This selection is appropriate **because** on the first day of Creation **He acquired** the universe by creating it from nothing, **and granted** it to "those who dwell in it,"[123] **and He will** eventually **judge** these human masters of **the world** based on how they used the gift that He granted to them.[124] בְּיוֹם שֵׁנִי מַהוּ אוֹמֵר — **On the second day** of the week, Monday, **what** hymn **does one recite?** "גָּדוֹל ה' וּמְהֻלָּל מְאֹד בְּעִיר אֱלֹהֵינוּ" — **One** recites the psalm that begins, *Great is HASHEM and much praised, in the city of our God ...* (ibid. 48:2). חִלֵּק אֶת כָּל מַעֲשָׂיו וְנַעֲשָׂה מֶלֶךְ עַל עוֹלָמוֹ — This selection is appropriate because on the second day of Creation **He separated all of His works and became King over His world.**[125] בִּשְׁלִישִׁי מַהוּ אוֹמֵר — **On the third** day of the week, Tuesday, **what does one recite?** "אֱלֹהִים נִצָּב בַּעֲדַת אֵל בְּקֶרֶב אֱלֹהִים יִשְׁפֹּט" — One recites the psalm that begins, *God stands in the Divine assembly, in the midst of judges He shall judge* (ibid. 82:1). בָּרָא אֶת הַיָּם וְאֶת הַיַּבָּשָׁה — This selection is appropriate because on the third

---

121. Originally, these hymns were sung by the Levites in the Temple. With the Temple in ruins, that is no longer possible, but as a remembrance of the Temple service it is proper for every individual to recite each psalm on its day (*Ben Avraham*). Hence the Baraisa's use of the singular מַהוּ אוֹמֵר, *What does "one" recite?* (ibid.).

Alternatively, the singular form is used because these daily hymns were introduced by Adam, just as the Sabbath-day song was first sung by him (as described below, end of chapter). Accordingly, the phrase מַהוּ אוֹמֵר should be rendered "What did he recite?" (*Avos HaRosh;* cf. *Ben Avraham*).

122. One recites not just the verse quoted,

but the entire psalm containing that verse (*Binyan Yehoshua,* quoting *Rashi* to *Rosh Hashanah* 31a).

123. No creatures existed on the first day (even the angels were not created until the second day), but the idea is that God acquired the world for no other purpose than to pass it on to its future inhabitants (*Binyan Yehoshua,* quoting *Rashi*).

124. *Magen Avos,* second explanation.

125. [Emendation of כֻּלּוֹ to מֶלֶךְ follows *Magen Avos,* and is indeed the reading found in several manuscripts.] That is, He created the firmament to divide between the upper and lower strata of creation, established His royal "court" in the heavens above, and took up the

וְנִכְפֶּלֶת אֶרֶץ לִמְקוֹמָהּ[126] וְנַעֲשָׂה מָקוֹם לַעֲדָתוֹ[127]. בִּרְבִיעִי מַהוּ אוֹמֵר (שם
צד, א) "אֵל נְקָמוֹת ה' אֵל נְקָמוֹת הוֹפִיעַ", בָּרָא אֶת הַחַמָּה וְאֶת הַלְּבָנָה
וְהַכּוֹכָבִים וְהַמַּזָּלוֹת שֶׁהֵן מְאִירִין בָּעוֹלָם וְעָתִיד לִיפָּרַע מֵעוֹבְדֵיהֶם[128].
בַּחֲמִישִׁי מַהוּ אוֹמֵר (שם פא, ב) "הַרְנִינוּ לֵאלֹהִים עוּזֵּנוּ הָרִיעוּ לֵאלֹהֵי
יַעֲקֹב", בָּרָא עוֹפוֹת וְדָגִים וְאֶת הַתַּנִּינִים שֶׁהֵם מְרַנְּנִים בָּעוֹלָם[129].
בַּשִּׁשִּׁי מַהוּ אוֹמֵר (שם צג, א) "ה' מָלָךְ גֵּאוּת לָבֵשׁ ה' עֹז הִתְאַזָּר

---

day of Creation He created the sea and the dry land, וְנִכְפֶּלֶת אֶרֶץ לִמְקוֹמָהּ — and the earth was folded back to its place,[126] וְנַעֲשָׂה מָקוֹם לַעֲדָתוֹ — and a place was made for His assembly to live.[127] בִּרְבִיעִי מַהוּ אוֹמֵר — On the fourth day of the week, Wednesday, what does one recite? אֵל נְקָמוֹת ה' "אֵל נְקָמוֹת הוֹפִיעַ" — One recites the psalm that begins, A God of vengeance is HASHEM, the God of vengeance has appeared (ibid. 94:1). בָּרָא אֶת הַחַמָּה וְאֶת הַלְּבָנָה וְהַכּוֹכָבִים וְהַמַּזָּלוֹת — This selection is appropriate because on the fourth day of Creation He created the sun, moon, stars, and constellations, שֶׁהֵן מְאִירִין בָּעוֹלָם — which give light to the world and are therefore liable to be revered as great cosmic powers, וְעָתִיד לִיפָּרַע מֵעוֹבְדֵיהֶם — and in the future He will exact punishment from those who worship them.[128] בַּחֲמִישִׁי מַהוּ אוֹמֵר — On the fifth day of the week, Thursday, what does one recite? "הַרְנִינוּ לֵאלֹהִים עוּזֵּנוּ הָרִיעוּ לֵאלֹהֵי יַעֲקֹב" — One recites the psalm that begins, Sing joyously to the God of our might, call out to the God of Jacob (ibid. 81:2). בָּרָא עוֹפוֹת וְדָגִים וְאֶת הַתַּנִּינִים — This selection is appropriate because on the fifth day of Creation He created the birds, fish, and sea-giants, שֶׁהֵם מְרַנְּנִים בָּעוֹלָם — which sing glad songs of praise in the world.[129] בַּשִּׁשִּׁי מַהוּ אוֹמֵר — On the sixth day of the week, Friday, what does one recite? "ה' מָלָךְ גֵּאוּת לָבֵשׁ — One recites the psalm that begins, HASHEM has reigned, He has donned grandeur; לָבֵשׁ ה' עֹז הִתְאַזָּר — HASHEM has donned strength

---

reins of kingship over the world. The hymn of Monday speaks of a similar division on earth: the separation of Jerusalem and the Temple Mount from the rest of the world, and God's choice of the former as His resting place on earth (Binyan Yehoshua, quoting Rashi).

126. Originally, the entire globe was under water. In order to gather the water into a smaller area, God excavated part the earth's surface to create a low-lying seabed and deposited the extra soil on the surrounding area, raising it above sea level to keep it dry and suitable for habitation. In that sense, then, the earth's surface was peeled away from the seabed and folded back onto its place — the

place meant to be dry land (Ben Avraham; see Magen Avos for a similar explanation).

127. In order for God to "stand" over the Divine assembly, He had to first make a place for that assembly to rest (Magen Avos).

128. Recognizing the luminaries as esteemed servants of God, man began [mistakenly] to revere them as a way of honoring God, and eventually lost sight of their subordinate nature and slid into pure idol worship (see Rambam, Hil. Avodas Kochavim 1:1-2).

129. That is, they inspire human beings who observe them in their great variety to give praise to the One Who created them all (Ben Avraham, based on Rashi; see Magen Avos).

אַף תִּכּוֹן תֵּבֵל בַּל תִּמּוֹט״, גָּמַר אֶת כָּל מַעֲשָׂיו וְנִתְעַלָּה וְיָשַׁב בִּמְרוֹמָיו
שֶׁל עוֹלָם.[130] בַּשְּׁבִיעִי מַהוּ אוֹמֵר (שם צב, א) ״מִזְמוֹר שִׁיר לְיוֹם הַשַּׁבָּת״,
יוֹם שֶׁכֻּלּוֹ שַׁבָּת שֶׁאֵין בּוֹ לֹא אֲכִילָה וְלֹא שְׁתִיָּה וְלֹא מַשָּׂא וּמַתָּן[131], אֶלָּא
צַדִּיקִים יוֹשְׁבִין וְעַטְרוֹתֵיהֶן בְּרָאשֵׁיהֶן וְנִזּוֹנִין מִזִּיו שְׁכִינָה[132], שֶׁנֶּאֱמַר
(שמות כד, יא) ״וַיֶּחֱזוּ אֶת הָאֱלֹהִים וַיֹּאכְלוּ וַיִּשְׁתּוּ״[132], כְּמַלְאֲכֵי הַשָּׁרֵת,

and girded Himself; ‫אַף תִּכּוֹן תֵּבֵל בַּל תִּמּוֹט״‬ — *even the world of men is firm, it shall not falter* (ibid. 93:1). ‫גָּמַר אֶת כָּל מַעֲשָׂיו וְנִתְעַלָּה וְיָשַׁב בִּמְרוֹמָיו‬ ‫שֶׁל עוֹלָם‬ — This selection is appropriate because on the sixth day of Creation He completed all of His works, ascended Heavenward, and sat on His throne in the heights of the world.[130] ‫בַּשְּׁבִיעִי מַהוּ אוֹמֵר‬ — On the seventh day of the week, the Sabbath, **what does one recite?** ‫מִזְמוֹר שִׁיר לְיוֹם הַשַּׁבָּת״‬ — One recites the psalm that begins, *A song, a hymn for the Sabbath day* (ibid. 92:1). ‫יוֹם שֶׁכֻּלּוֹ שַׁבָּת‬ — This hymn refers to a future **day that is entirely Sabbath,** ‫שֶׁאֵין בּוֹ לֹא אֲכִילָה וְלֹא שְׁתִיָּה וְלֹא מַשָּׂא וּמַתָּן‬ — a day on which there **is no eating, no drinking, and no business dealings,**[131] ‫אֶלָּא צַדִּיקִים יוֹשְׁבִין‬ ‫וְעַטְרוֹתֵיהֶן בְּרָאשֵׁיהֶן וְנִזּוֹנִין מִזִּיו שְׁכִינָה‬ — nothing except **righteous people sitting with their crowns on their heads, being nourished by the radiance of the Divine Presence.**[132] ‫שֶׁנֶּאֱמַר ״וַיֶּחֱזוּ אֶת הָאֱלֹהִים וַיֹּאכְלוּ וַיִּשְׁתּוּ‬ — The idea that it is possible to derive life-giving nourishment by drawing close to God's presence is found in Scripture, **for it is stated,** *They gazed at [the glory of] God, and [it was as if] they ate and drank* (Exodus 24:11),[133] ‫כְּמַלְאֲכֵי הַשָּׁרֵת‬ —

---

130. On the sixth day, after creating man in His final and most important act of creation, God "retreated" to the Heavenly realm and installed man as master of the earthly world, in keeping with the verse (*Psalms* 115:16): *As for the heavens, the heavens are Hashem's; but the earth He has given to mankind* (*Ben Avraham*). Nevertheless, God did not abandon this lower sphere. With all His grandeur, He continues to supervise and sustain the earthly world and its inhabitants, as the verse concludes, *even the world of men is firm, it shall not falter,* as cited by the Baraisa (*Magen Avos*).

131. Nor is there any conjugal activity, envy, hatred, or rivalries (*Binyan Yehoshua,* from *Berachos* 17a).

132. As most commentators understand it, this means that when six millennia have passed from the time of Creation, the world as we know it will cease to exist, leaving a

void for one millennium, after which the world will be reconstructed on a much higher spiritual level. During this seventh millennium, there will be no man on earth, all activity will cease, and the righteous will endure in a semi-angelic state, deriving nourishment from the radiance of God's presence. The "hymn for the Sabbath day" refers to that seventh millennium, when all of creation will be in a restful state of "Sabbath" (based on *Rashi* to *Rosh Hashanah* 31a). [For a closer examination of this esoteric subject, see Schottenstein ed. of *Sanhedrin,* 97a note 59.]

In keeping with its futuristic outlook, the "hymn for the Sabbath day" goes on to depict the harmony that will exist in the end of days, the destruction of the wicked, and the reward of the righteous (*Maharsha, Aruch LaNer* to *Rosh Hashanah* ibid.; see *Arachin* 13b).

133. This verse describes how the elders of Israel saw the glory of God on Mount Sinai

כָּל כָּךְ לָמָּה, כְּדֵי שֶׁיָּבֵּנֶס לִסְעוּדַת שַׁבָּת מִיָּד[136]). רַבִּי שִׁמְעוֹן בֶּן אֶלְעָזָר
אוֹמֵר: אֶמְשׁוֹל [לְךָ מָשָׁל] לְמָה הַדָּבָר דּוֹמֶה, (אָדָם הָרִאשׁוֹן דּוֹמֶה) לְאָדָם
אֶחָד שֶׁנָּשָׂא אֶת הַגִּיּוֹרֶת[137] הָיָה יוֹשֵׁב מְפַקְּדָה, אָמַר לָהּ: בִּתִּי[138], אַל תֹּאכְלִי
פַת בְּשָׁעָה שֶׁיָּדֵךְ טְמֵאוֹת[139], וְאַל תֹּאכְלִי פֵּירוֹת שֶׁאֵינָן מְעוּשָּׂרִין, אַל
תְּחַלְּלִי שַׁבָּתוֹת, וְאַל תִּפְרְצִי בִּנְדָרִים[140], וְאַל תֵּלְכִי עִם אִישׁ אַחֵר, הָא אִם

---

just like the ministering angels, who also derive nourishment from the radiance of the Divine Presence.[134]

The Baraisa asks:

כָּל כָּךְ לָמָּה — And why to such an extent? Why did God wait so long, until the sixth day, to create man, the most important element of the created world?[135] כְּדֵי שֶׁיָּבֵּנֶס לִסְעוּדַת שַׁבָּת מִיָּד — So that he, Adam, should enter into the Sabbath banquet immediately.[136]

The Baraisa returns to its discussion of the eating from the Tree of Knowledge: אֶמְשׁוֹל לְךָ מָשָׁל — R' Shimon ben Elazar said: רַבִּי שִׁמְעוֹן בֶּן אֶלְעָזָר אוֹמֵר — I will give you a parable. לְמָה הַדָּבָר דּוֹמֶה — To what is the matter comparable? אָדָם הָרִאשׁוֹן דּוֹמֶה — Adam, the first man, was comparable לְאָדָם אֶחָד שֶׁנָּשָׂא אֶת הַגִּיּוֹרֶת — to a certain man who married a convert.[137] הָיָה יוֹשֵׁב מְפַקְּדָה — Knowing that his wife was not well-versed in Jewish law, he would sit down patiently and instruct her. אָמַר לָהּ: בִּתִּי אַל תֹּאכְלִי פַת — He would say to her, "My daughter,[138] do not eat bread בְּשָׁעָה שֶׁיָּדֵךְ טְמֵאוֹת — when your hands are impure.[139] וְאַל תֹּאכְלִי פֵּירוֹת שֶׁאֵינָן מְעוּשָּׂרִין — Do not eat produce that has not been tithed. אַל תְּחַלְּלִי שַׁבָּתוֹת — Do not desecrate the Sabbath days. וְאַל תִּפְרְצִי בִּנְדָרִים — Do not make vows freely.[140] הָא אִם וְאַל תֵּלְכִי עִם אִישׁ אַחֵר — And do not walk with another man.[141]

---

in connection with the Giving of the Torah. As *Rashi* (to *Berachos* 17a) explains it, the verse means that these elders were sated from the radiance of the Divine Presence as if they had partaken of food and drink (*Binyan Yehoshua*).

134. *Ben Avraham.*

135. *Binyan Yehoshua*, quoting *Mefaresh.*

136. The Baraisa seems to be combining two answers into one, because the Talmud offers two reasons for putting off Adam's creation until Friday: (i) so that he would proceed directly to performing a mitzvah by observing the Sabbath; (ii) so that he could enter immediately into the "banquet" of God's finished world, replete with all the amenities it has to offer. Our Baraisa alludes

to both of these reasons by fusing their key points ("Sabbath" and "banquet") into one phrase (*Magen Avos, Ahavas Chesed*).

137. R' Shimon ben Elazar compares Eve to a convert. Just as a fresh convert is unfamiliar with basic Jewish law and practice, so was Eve unfamiliar with God's command regarding the Tree of Knowledge (see *Binyan Yehoshua*, quoting *Mefaresh*).

138. This was once a common and affectionate way of addressing one's wife (*Binyan Yehoshua, Avos HaRosh*).

139. Rather, you should purify your hands first through *netilas yadayim.*

140. See *Demai* 2:3.

141. This potential interloper of the parable represents the serpent. Like the husband in

עָבַרְתְּ עַל אַחַת מֵהֶן הֲרֵי אַתְּ מֵתָה. (מֶה עָשָׂה הָאִישׁ הַהוּא, עָמַד) וְאָכַל
פַּת בְּפָנֶיהָ בְּשָׁעָה שֶׁיָּדָיו טְמֵאוֹת וְאָכַל פֵּירוֹת שֶׁאֵינָן מְעוּשָּׂרִין וְחִלֵּל
שַׁבָּתוֹת וּפָרַץ בִּנְדָרִים, [וְהוֹצִיא לָהּ] מֶה אָמְרָה גִּיוֹרֶת הַהִיא בְּלִבָּהּ: כָּל
הַדְּבָרִים שֶׁפְּקָדַנִי בַּעְלִי מִתְּחִלָּה שֶׁקֶר הֵם, מִיָּד עָמְדָה וְעָבְרָה עַל כּוּלָם.
רַבִּי ‎143 שִׁמְעוֹן בֶּן יוֹחַאי אוֹמֵר: אֶמְשׁוֹל לְךָ מָשָׁל לְמָה (הַדָּבָר דּוֹמֶה,) אָדָם
הָרִאשׁוֹן דּוֹמֶה לְאֶחָד שֶׁהָיָה לוֹ אִשָּׁה בְּתוֹךְ בֵּיתוֹ‎144, מֶה עָשָׂה אוֹתוֹ הָאִישׁ,
הָלַךְ וְהֵבִיא אֶת הֶחָבִית וְהִנִּיחַ בּוֹ תְּאֵנִים בְּמִנְיָן וֶאֱגוֹזִים בְּמִנְיָן‎145 וְצָד אֶת
הָעַקְרָב וּנְתָנוֹ עַל פִּי הֶחָבִית וְהִקִּיפָה בְּצָמִיד פָּתִיל וְהִנִּיחָהּ בְּקֶרֶן זָוִית,

---

עָבַרְתְּ עַל אַחַת מֵהֶן הֲרֵי אַתְּ מֵתָה — But if you transgress one of these prohibitions, you will incur God's wrath and die." מֶה עָשָׂה הָאִישׁ הַהוּא — What did that other man (whom the husband had warned his wife about)[142] do? עָמַד He got up and ate bread in front of her while his hands were impure, וְאָכַל פַּת בְּפָנֶיהָ בְּשָׁעָה שֶׁיָּדָיו טְמֵאוֹת — He got up and ate bread in front of her while his hands were impure, וְאָכַל פֵּירוֹת שֶׁאֵינָן מְעוּשָּׂרִין — he ate produce that was not tithed, וְחִלֵּל שַׁבָּתוֹת וּפָרַץ בִּנְדָרִים — and he desecrated the Sabbath days and made vows freely. מֶה אָמְרָה גִּיוֹרֶת הַהִיא בְּלִבָּהּ — What did that convert say in her heart when she saw the apparent emptiness of her husband's warnings? כָּל הַדְּבָרִים שֶׁפְּקָדַנִי בַּעְלִי מִתְּחִלָּה שֶׁקֶר הֵם — Everything that my husband instructed me earlier was false! מִיָּד עָמְדָה וְעָבְרָה עַל כּוּלָם — Immediately she got up and transgressed them all.

Another parable on the subject:[143] אֶמְשׁוֹל לְךָ מָשָׁל — R' Shimon ben Yochai says: רַבִּי שִׁמְעוֹן בֶּן יוֹחַאי אוֹמֵר I will give you a parable. לְמָה הַדָּבָר דּוֹמֶה — To what is the matter comparable? אָדָם הָרִאשׁוֹן דּוֹמֶה לְאֶחָד — Adam, the first man, was comparable to someone who had a wife in his home.[144] שֶׁהָיָה לוֹ אִשָּׁה בְּתוֹךְ בֵּיתוֹ — to someone who had a wife in his home.[144] מֶה עָשָׂה אוֹתוֹ הָאִישׁ — What did this man do? הָלַךְ וְהֵבִיא אֶת הֶחָבִית — He went and brought a barrel, וְהִנִּיחַ בּוֹ תְּאֵנִים בְּמִנְיָן וֶאֱגוֹזִים בְּמִנְיָן — and placed in it a certain number of figs and a certain number of walnuts.[145] וְצָד אֶת הָעַקְרָב וּנְתָנוֹ עַל פִּי הֶחָבִית — He then caught a scorpion and placed it near the opening of the barrel on the inside וְהִקִּיפָה בְּצָמִיד פָּתִיל וְהִנִּיחָהּ בְּקֶרֶן זָוִית — and sealed it all around with a tight seal and placed it in a corner.

---

the parable, Adam warned his wife to stay away from outsiders who might exert an evil influence on her (Avos HaRosh).

142. Binyan Yehoshua; Magen Avos, third explanation; Avos HaRosh.

143. The coming parable has a different focus: Whereas the previous parable illustrates the relationship between Adam and Eve, this one illustrates the relationship

between God and Adam (Magen Avos, Ahavas Chesed).

144. Just as God ("the husband" in the parable) hosted Adam ("the wife" in the parable) in the Garden of Eden, close to His earthly presence (Ben Avraham).

145. See Avos HaRosh for a lengthy discussion of why the Baraisa specifies these two kinds of fruit.

אָמַר לָהּ: בִּתִּי, כָּל שֶׁיֵּשׁ לִי בַּבַּיִת הַזֶּה מָסוּר בְּיָדֵךְ חוּץ מֵחָבִית זוֹ
שֶׁלֹא תִּגְּעִי בָהּ כָּל עִיקָר. מֶה עָשְׂתָה הָאשָּׁה הַהִיא, כֵּיוָן שֶׁיָּצָא בַּעְלָהּ
לַשּׁוּק עָמְדָה וּפָתְחָה אֶת הֶחָבִית וְהוֹשִׁיטָה יָדָהּ לְתוֹכָהּ וַעֲקָצַתָּה עַקְרָב,
הָלְכָה לָהּ וְנָפְלָה עַל הַמִּטָּה. כֵּיוָן שֶׁבָּא בַעְלָהּ מִן הַשּׁוּק, אָמַר לָהּ: מַה
זֶּה, אָמְרָה לוֹ: יָדִי הֵשַׁטְתִּי עַל הֶחָבִית‎[146]‎ וַעֲקָצַתְנִי עַקְרָב וַהֲרֵינִי מֵתָה,
אָמַר לָהּ: לֹא כָּךְ אָמַרְתִּי לָךְ מִתְּחִלָּה, כָּל מַה שֶׁיֵּשׁ לִי בְּבַיִת זֶה מָסוּר
בְּיָדֵךְ חוּץ מֵחָבִית זוֹ שֶׁלֹא תִּגְּעִי בָהּ כָּל עִקָר, מִיָּד כָּעַס עָלֶיהָ וְהוֹצִיאָהּ,
כָּךְ אָדָם הָרִאשׁוֹן (דּוֹמֶה), בְּשָׁעָה שֶׁאָמַר לוֹ הַקָּדוֹשׁ בָּרוּךְ הוּא (בראשית
ב, טז-יז) "מִכֹּל עֵץ הַגָּן אָכֹל תֹּאכֵל וּמֵעֵץ הַדַּעַת טוֹב וָרָע לֹא תֹאכַל
מִמֶּנּוּ כִּי בְּיוֹם אֲכָלְךָ מִמֶּנּוּ מוֹת תָּמוּת", כֵּיוָן שֶׁאָכַל מִמֶּנּוּ נִטְרַד‎[147]‎,

אָמַר לָהּ כָּל בִּתִּי שֶׁיֵּשׁ לִי בַּבַּיִת הַזֶּה מָסוּר בְּיָדֵךְ — With that done, he said to her, "My daughter, everything that I have in this house is handed to you to do with as you please, חוּץ מֵחָבִית זוֹ שֶׁלֹא תִּגְּעִי בָהּ כָּל עִיקָר — except for this barrel, which you are not to touch at all." מֶה עָשְׂתָה הָאִשָּׁה הַהִיא — What did that woman do? כֵּיוָן שֶׁיָּצָא בַּעְלָהּ לַשּׁוּק — When her husband left to the marketplace, עָמְדָה וּפָתְחָה אֶת הֶחָבִית וְהוֹשִׁיטָה יָדָהּ לְתוֹכָהּ וַעֲקָצַתָּה עַקְרָב — she got up, opened the barrel, and stuck her hand inside, whereupon the scorpion stung her. הָלְכָה לָהּ וְנָפְלָה עַל הַמִּטָּה — Sickened by the scorpion's venom, she went and fell onto the bed. כֵּיוָן שֶׁבָּא בַעְלָהּ מִן הַשּׁוּק — When her husband came back from the marketplace, אָמַר לָהּ מַה זֶּה — he said to her, "What is this all about? Why do you look so ill?" אָמְרָה לוֹ יָדִי הֵשַׁטְתִּי עַל הֶחָבִית — She said to him, "I stretched my hand over the barrel,‎[146]‎ וַעֲקָצַתְנִי עַקְרָב וַהֲרֵינִי מֵתָה — and a scorpion stung me and now I am dying." אָמַר לָהּ — He said to her, לֹא כָּךְ אָמַרְתִּי לָךְ מִתְּחִלָּה — "Did I not tell you from the beginning, כָּל מַה שֶׁיֵּשׁ לִי בְּבַיִת זֶה מָסוּר בְּיָדֵךְ — that everything that I have in this house is handed to you, חוּץ מֵחָבִית זוֹ שֶׁלֹא תִּגְּעִי בָהּ כָּל עִקָר — except for this barrel, which you are not to touch at all?!" מִיָּד כָּעַס עָלֶיהָ וְהוֹצִיאָהּ — With that he became angry at her and banished her from the house. כָּךְ אָדָם הָרִאשׁוֹן דּוֹמֶה — This is what Adam, the first man, was like בְּשָׁעָה שֶׁאָמַר לוֹ הַקָּדוֹשׁ בָּרוּךְ הוּא — when the Holy One, Blessed is He, said to him, "מִכֹּל עֵץ הַגָּן אָכֹל תֹּאכֵל וּמֵעֵץ הַדַּעַת טוֹב וָרָע לֹא תֹאכַל מִמֶּנּוּ — "Of every tree of the garden you may freely eat; but of the Tree of Knowledge of Good and Bad, you must not eat; כִּי בְּיוֹם אֲכָלְךָ מִמֶּנּוּ מוֹת תָּמוּת" — for on the day you eat of it, you shall surely die" (Genesis 2:16-17). כֵּיוָן שֶׁאָכַל מִמֶּנּוּ נִטְרַד — As soon as he ate from it, he was expelled from God's "house," the Garden of Eden.‎[147]‎

---

146. Some manuscripts read here instead בֶּחָבִית, "into" the barrel.
147. Which prepared the way for God to carry out His threat that you shall surely die, for death cannot occur in the Garden of Eden (Avos HaRosh, based on Yalkut Reuveni).

לְקַיֵּם מַה שֶּׁנֶּאֱמַר (תהלים מט, יג) "וְאָדָם בִּיקָר בַּל יָלִין נִמְשַׁל כַּבְּהֵמוֹת נִדְמוּ"[148]. (בּוֹ בַיּוֹם נוֹצַר[150].) בּוֹ בַיּוֹם נִבְרָא[151]. בּוֹ בַיּוֹם נוֹצְרָה צוּרָתוֹ[152]. בּוֹ בַיּוֹם נַעֲשָׂה גוֹלֶם[153]. בּוֹ בַיּוֹם נִתְקַשְׁרוּ אֲבָרָיו[154] וְנִתְפַּתְּחוּ נְקָבָיו. בּוֹ בַיּוֹם נִתְּנָה נְשָׁמָה בּוֹ. בּוֹ בַיּוֹם עָמַד עַל רַגְלָיו[155]. בּוֹ בַיּוֹם נִזְדַּוְּגָה

"לְקַיֵּם מַה שֶּׁנֶּאֱמַר "וְאָדָם בִּיקָר בַּל יָלִין נִמְשַׁל כַּבְּהֵמוֹת נִדְמוּ" — This outcome served to fulfill that which is stated, *As for man, he does not remain in a state of glory overnight; he is likened to the animals* (Psalms 49:13).[148]

Having mentioned the verse, *As for man, he does not remain in a state of glory overnight*, R' Shimon ben Yochai reviews the events of the day of Adam's creation to show how the verse was fulfilled:[149]

בּוֹ בַיּוֹם נוֹצַר — On that day the dust from which [Adam] was made was gathered;[150] בּוֹ בַיּוֹם נִבְרָא — on that day he was created;[151] בּוֹ בַיּוֹם נוֹצְרָה צוּרָתוֹ — on that day his form was formed;[152] בּוֹ בַיּוֹם נַעֲשָׂה גוֹלֶם — on that day he was made into an unfinished bodily form;[153] בּוֹ בַיּוֹם נִתְקַשְׁרוּ אֲבָרָיו וְנִתְפַּתְּחוּ נְקָבָיו — on that day his limbs were connected[154] and his orifices were opened; בּוֹ בַיּוֹם נִתְּנָה נְשָׁמָה בּוֹ — on that day a soul was placed within him; בּוֹ בַיּוֹם עָמַד עַל רַגְלָיו — on that day he stood up on his feet;[155] בּוֹ בַיּוֹם נִזְדַּוְּגָה

---

148. [As the Baraisa stated above. Here, the Baraisa adds the end of the verse, *he is likened to the animals*.] Compared to his lofty pre-sin status, in which the Garden of Eden was his palace and the angels were his servants, man's condition after the sin is animal-like (*Avos HaRosh*).

What does R' Shimon ben Yochai come to teach with this parable? One explanation is that he is addresses the question of why Adam and Eve were given multiple curses after eating from the Tree of Knowledge. Wasn't death, or being subject to death, enough of a punishment for their sin? From the carefully woven parable, we learn the answer: Ingesting the forbidden fruit was like being stung by a scorpion. Death was not a punishment, but a natural consequence, just as in any case of lethal poisoning. It would therefore not gain them atonement. Only the other punishments would atone (*Binyan Yehoshua*, quoting *Mefaresh*; see *Derashos HaRan* §1).

Alternatively, R' Shimon ben Yochai was addressing a different question: We know that Adam worked long and hard at repenting of his sin — for no less than 130 years (*Eruvin* 18b)! Why did this earnest *teshuvah*

fail to exempt him from the punishment of death? Here, too, the answer is that the fate of death was a natural consequence of eating the "poisonous" fruit. As such, it was not something that could be be reversed by *teshuvah* (*Kisei Rachamim*; see *R' Elchanan Wasserman* in *Kovetz Maamarim,* end of *Maamar al HaTeshuvah*).

149. The Baraisa above (with some differences) did this as well (see *Ahavas Chesed*).

150. R' Shimon ben Yochai means the same thing here that the Baraisa said above (at note 114). The root יצר used here by R' Shimon ben Yochai can mean "gather," as we find in certain verses (*Binyan Yehoshua*; see also *Avos HaRosh* [Vol. 1] and *Radak* to *Amos* 7:1).

151. The dust was kneaded into the mass that would become Adam's body (*Avos Ha-Rosh* [Vol. 1]).

152. I.e., the facial form (*Binyan Yehoshua,* as explained by *Avos HaRosh*; see above, note 115).

153. See above, note 116.

154. See above, note 117.

155. Unlike ordinary human beings, who

לוֹ חַוָּה. בּוֹ בַּיּוֹם קָרָא שֵׁמוֹת[156]. בּוֹ בַּיּוֹם הִכְנִיסוֹ לְגַן עֵדֶן. בּוֹ בַּיּוֹם
צִוָּהוּ. בּוֹ בַּיּוֹם סָרַח. בּוֹ בַּיּוֹם נִטְרַד, לְקַיֵּים מַה שֶּׁנֶּאֱמַר "וְאָדָם בִּיקָר
בַּל יָלִין". (בּוֹ בַּיּוֹם עָלוּ לַמִּטָּה שְׁנַיִם וְיָרְדוּ [אַרְבָּעָה][157]. רַבִּי יְהוּדָה בֶּן
בְּתֵירָה אוֹמֵר: בּוֹ בַּיּוֹם עָלוּ לַמִּטָּה שְׁנַיִם וְיָרְדוּ] שִׁשָּׁה[158].) בּוֹ בַּיּוֹם נִגְזְרוּ
עַל אָדָם שָׁלֹשׁ גְּזֵרוֹת, שֶׁנֶּאֱמַר (בראשית ג, יז־יח) "וּלְאָדָם אָמַר כִּי שָׁמַעְתָּ
לְקוֹל אִשְׁתֶּךָ וְגו' אֲרוּרָה הָאֲדָמָה בַּעֲבוּרֶךָ[159] בְּעִצָּבוֹן תֹּאכְלֶנָּה[160]

לוֹ חַוָּה — on that day Eve was paired with him; בּוֹ בַּיּוֹם קָרָא שֵׁמוֹת — on that day he called the animals by their names;[156] בּוֹ בַּיּוֹם הִכְנִיסוֹ לְגַן עֵדֶן — on that day [God] brought him into the Garden of Eden; בּוֹ בַּיּוֹם צִוָּהוּ — on that day He commanded him not to eat from the Tree of Knowledge; בּוֹ בַּיּוֹם סָרַח — on that day [Adam] soured, i.e., sinned; בּוֹ בַּיּוֹם נִטְרַד — and on that day he was expelled from the Garden of Eden. לְקַיֵּים מַה שֶּׁנֶּאֱמַר "וְאָדָם בִּיקָר בַּל יָלִין" — This outcome served to fulfill that which is stated, As for man, he does not remain in a state of glory overnight.

The Baraisa continues to list other things that occurred on the day of Adam's creation:

בּוֹ בַּיּוֹם עָלוּ לַמִּטָּה שְׁנַיִם וְיָרְדוּ אַרְבָּעָה — On that day they went up into the bed as two individuals and came down as four.[157] רַבִּי יְהוּדָה בֶּן בְּתֵירָה אוֹמֵר — R' Yehudah ben Beseirah says: בּוֹ בַּיּוֹם עָלוּ לַמִּטָּה שְׁנַיִם וְיָרְדוּ שִׁשָּׁה — On that day they went up into into bed as two individuals and they came down as six.[158] בּוֹ בַּיּוֹם נִגְזְרוּ עַל אָדָם שָׁלֹשׁ גְּזֵרוֹת — On that day three decrees were passed against Adam for his sin, שֶׁנֶּאֱמַר "וּלְאָדָם אָמַר כִּי שָׁמַעְתָּ לְקוֹל אִשְׁתֶּךָ וְגו' — as it is stated, And to Adam He said, "Because you listened to the voice of your wife, etc., אֲרוּרָה הָאֲדָמָה בַּעֲבוּרֶךָ בְּעִצָּבוֹן תֹּאכְלֶנָּה — accursed is the land because of you;[159] (i) through suffering shall you

cannot stand or otherwise function independently until long after birth, Adam "stood up on his feet" as soon as life pulsed within him. According to Ibn Ezra and others, this is what Scripture means when it says, and man became a נֶפֶשׁ חַיָּה. The latter phrase can be translated a beastly being, meaning that Adam was able to stand and walk immediately, like newborn animals can, in contrast to helpless human infants (Avos HaRosh).

156. See Genesis 2:20.

157. I.e., Adam and Eve cohabited, and two children were conceived, developed, and born immediately — Cain and a twin sister. Abel was born later, as it is stated, And she

continued to give birth, [bearing] his brother, Abel (Mefaresh).

158. R' Yehudah ben Beseirah holds that Abel and his sister were born at the same time as Cain and his sister (Binyan Yehoshua). [Some emend the text to read "seven," for the Midrash (Bereishis Rabbah 22 §2) states that Abel was born with two sisters (Nuschas HaGra, as explained by Ben Avraham; see Avos HaRosh at length).

159. The Baraisa does not count this phrase as one of the decrees against Adam, since it is the land's curse, not Adam's (Magen Avos). [See, however, Avos HaRosh (Vol. 1), who counts the three decrees differently.]

... וְקוֹץ וְדַרְדַּר תַּצְמִיחַ לָךְ 161 וְאָכַלְתָּ אֶת עֵשֶׂב הַשָּׂדֶה"163,162. כֵּיוָן
שֶׁשָּׁמַע אָדָם הָרִאשׁוֹן שֶׁאָמַר לוֹ הַקָּדוֹשׁ בָּרוּךְ הוּא "וְאָכַלְתָּ אֶת
עֵשֶׂב הַשָּׂדֶה", מִיָּד נִזְדַּעְזְעוּ אֵבָרָיו, אָמַר לְפָנָיו: רִבּוֹנוֹ שֶׁל עוֹלָם,
אֲנִי וּבְהֶמְתִּי נֹאכַל בְּאֵבוּס אֶחָד164. אָמַר לוֹ הַקָּדוֹשׁ בָּרוּךְ הוּא:
הוֹאִיל וְנִזְדַּעְזְעוּ אֵבָרֶיךָ, (שם פסוק יט) "בְּזֵעַת אַפֶּיךָ תֹּאכַל לֶחֶם"165.

---

eat of it ...;[160] "וְקוֹץ וְדַרְדַּר תַּצְמִיחַ לָךְ וְאָכַלְתָּ אֶת עֵשֶׂב הַשָּׂדֶה" — (ii) *Thorns and thistles shall it sprout for you;*[161] and (iii) *you shall eat the herbs of the field*" (Genesis 3:17-18).[162]

The Baraisa addresses the meaning of the next verse — *by the sweat of your brow shall you eat bread:*[163]

כֵּיוָן שֶׁשָּׁמַע אָדָם הָרִאשׁוֹן שֶׁאָמַר לוֹ הַקָּדוֹשׁ בָּרוּךְ הוּא "וְאָכַלְתָּ אֶת עֵשֶׂב הַשָּׂדֶה" — *When Adam, the first man, heard the Holy One, Blessed is He, say to him, "And you shall eat the herbs of the field,"* מִיָּד נִזְדַּעְזְעוּ אֵבָרָיו — *his limbs immediately began trembling.* אָמַר לְפָנָיו: רִבּוֹנוֹ שֶׁל עוֹלָם — *He said before [God], "Master of the Universe!* אֲנִי וּבְהֶמְתִּי נֹאכַל בְּאֵבוּס אֶחָד — *Shall I and my animal feed from the same trough?!"*[164] אָמַר לוֹ הַקָּדוֹשׁ בָּרוּךְ הוּא — *Said the Holy One, Blessed is He, to him in reply,* הוֹאִיל וְנִזְדַּעְזְעוּ אֵבָרֶיךָ "בְּזֵעַת אַפֶּיךָ תֹּאכַל לֶחֶם" — *"Since your limbs trembled at the prospect of being like an animal, you are hereby absolved from eating the herbs of the field; rather, by the sweat of your brow shall you eat bread"* (ibid. v. 19).[165]

---

160. That is, you will have to expend much effort to get the earth to yield whatever food it does produce for you (see *Bereishis Rabbah* 20 §9).

161. That is, although you will plant food-producing seeds, the ground that was cursed because of you will produce thorns and thistles instead (*Rashi* on the verse; *Ahavas Chesed*).

162. Although God had told Adam from the beginning that he was to subsist on vegetation (*Behold, I have given you all herbage ... that is on the surface of the earth ... it shall be yours for food*), at that time God was referring to the herbs of Gan Eden. Those herbs were of a different quality; according to the Midrash (*Bereishis Rabbah* 20 §10), they would have allowed Adam a taste of all the delights in the world. Now, however, he would suffer the disgrace of eating what was essentially animal food (*Binyan Yehoshua*, quoting *Mefaresh*). Alternatively, the word

"field" in the phrase *you shall eat the herbs of the field* implied to Adam that he would be relegated to grazing in the field, feeding directly on living vegetation like an animal (*Magen Avos*; cf. *Rashi* on the verse).

163. [If the land was to produce thorns and thistles for Adam instead of wheat, and he was to eat the herbs of the field (see above), then how was he to eat "bread" by the sweat of his brow?]

164. Adam's concern was not just one of dignity. He feared that by sharing the eating habits of an animal he would acquire the nature and intelligence of an animal. He was relieved only when God promised him that he would eat bread after all, for he knew that grain products have the capacity to nourish the human mind (*Binyan Yehoshua*, quoting *Maharsha, Pesachim* 118b).

165. Hence, this pronouncement was not a curse but a blessing that he would indeed

וּכְשֵׁם שֶׁנִּגְזְרוּ עַל אָדָם הָרִאשׁוֹן שָׁלֹשׁ גְּזֵרוֹת כָּךְ נִגְזְרוּ עַל חַוָּה שָׁלֹשׁ
גְּזֵרוֹת[166], שֶׁנֶּאֱמַר (שם פסוק טז) "אֶל הָאִשָּׁה אָמַר הַרְבָּה אַרְבֶּה עִצְּבוֹנֵךְ
וְהֵרֹנֵךְ בְּעֶצֶב תֵּלְדִי בָנִים", בִּזְמַן שֶׁהָאִשָּׁה רוֹאָה דַם נִדָּתָהּ בִּתְחִלַּת וְסִתָּהּ
קָשֶׁה לָהּ. ("הַרְבָּה אַרְבֶּה",) בִּזְמַן שֶׁהָאִשָּׁה נִבְעֶלֶת בִּתְחִלַּת בְּעִילָתָהּ
קָשֶׁה לָהּ[167]. "עִצְּבוֹנֵךְ", בִּזְמַן שֶׁהָאִשָּׁה מִתְעַבֶּרֶת פָּנֶיהָ מְכוֹעָרוֹת
וּמוֹרִיקוֹת כָּל שְׁלֹשָׁה חֳדָשִׁים הָרִאשׁוֹנִים. כֵּיוָן שֶׁבָּא (אָדָם הָרִאשׁוֹן)
לְעֵת עֶרֶב, רָאָה אָדָם הָרִאשׁוֹן אֶת הָעוֹלָם כְּלַפֵּי מַעֲרָב שֶׁמַּחֲשִׁיךְ וּבָא,

---

The Baraisa continues:

וּכְשֵׁם שֶׁנִּגְזְרוּ עַל אָדָם הָרִאשׁוֹן שָׁלֹשׁ גְּזֵרוֹת — **And just as three decrees were passed against Adam, the first man,** כָּךְ נִגְזְרוּ עַל חַוָּה שָׁלֹשׁ גְּזֵרוֹת — **so were three decrees passed against Eve,**[166] שֶׁנֶּאֱמַר "אֶל הָאִשָּׁה אָמַר הַרְבָּה אַרְבֶּה עִצְּבוֹנֵךְ וְהֵרֹנֵךְ בְּעֶצֶב תֵּלְדִי בָנִים" — **as it is stated, And to the woman He said, "I will greatly increase** [literally, Increase I will increase] **your suffering and [what is associated with] your pregnancy; in pain you shall bear children"** (ibid. v. 16). בִּזְמַן שֶׁהָאִשָּׁה רוֹאָה דַם נִדָּתָהּ בִּתְחִלַּת וְסִתָּהּ קָשֶׁה לָהּ — (i) **The** first word, הַרְבָּה, *Increase,* **refers to the fact that when a woman discharges her menstrual blood, at the beginning of her period, it is uncomfortable for her.** "הַרְבָּה אַרְבֶּה" בִּזְמַן שֶׁהָאִשָּׁה נִבְעֶלֶת בִּתְחִלַּת בְּעִילָתָהּ קָשֶׁה לָהּ — **The fact** that the verse uses the double expression, *Increase I will increase,* indicates a second decree as well, and refers to the fact that (ii) **when a woman cohabits for the first time, at the beginning of cohabitation it is uncomfortable for her.**[167] "עִצְּבוֹנֵךְ" בִּזְמַן שֶׁהָאִשָּׁה מִתְעַבֶּרֶת פָּנֶיהָ מְכוֹעָרוֹת וּמוֹרִיקוֹת — **And the** next expression, *your suffering,* refers to the fact that (iii) **when a woman becomes pregnant, her face becomes uncomely and sallow** כָּל שְׁלֹשָׁה חֳדָשִׁים הָרִאשׁוֹנִים — for **the entire first three months** of her pregnancy.[168]

The Baraisa highlights the humility and remorse Adam displayed after committing his sin.[169]

כֵּיוָן שֶׁבָּא לְעֵת עֶרֶב — **When it approached evening time** of that day, רָאָה אָדָם הָרִאשׁוֹן אֶת הָעוֹלָם כְּלַפֵּי מַעֲרָב שֶׁמַּחֲשִׁיךְ וּבָא — **Adam, the first man, saw the world getting progressively darker,** with the sun descending **toward the**

---

eat bread — a reprieve from a much harsher fate (*Magen Avos*).

166. Although an earlier passage (in §6) listed ten curses, the Baraisa here refers only to those three that cannot be seen in a positive light. The other seven curses can also be viewed as blessings or as expressions of her modesty and dignity (*Magen Avos,* first explanation; cf. *Binyan Yehoshua*).

167. This refers to "the blood of virginal

pain" the first time a woman cohabits [see above at note 90] (*Ben Avraham*).

168. *Ahavas Chesed* counts the three decrees differently: (i) the pain of menstrual blood and the blood of virginal pain (both alluded to in the double expression *Increase I will increase your suffering*); (ii) the pain of pregnancy; (iii) the pain of childbirth (mentioned next in the verse).

169. *Magen Avos.*

אָמַר: אוֹי לִי, כִּי בִּשְׁבִיל שֶׁסָּרַחְתִּי הַקָּדוֹשׁ בָּרוּךְ הוּא מַחְשִׁיךְ עָלַי
אֶת הָעוֹלָם[171], וְהוּא אֵינוֹ יוֹדֵעַ שֶׁבֵּן דֶּרֶךְ הָעוֹלָם[172]. לְשַׁחֲרִית כֵּיוָן
שֶׁרָאָה הָעוֹלָם שֶׁמֵּאִיר וּבָא לַמִּזְרָח שָׂמַח שִׂמְחָה גְדוֹלָה, עָמַד וּבָנָה
מִזְבְּחוֹת[173] וְהֵבִיא שׁוֹר שֶׁקַּרְנָיו קוֹדְמוֹת לְפַרְסוֹתָיו וְהֶעֱלָהוּ עוֹלָה[174],

---

horizon in the west.   אָמַר: אוֹי לִי כִּי בִּשְׁבִיל שֶׁסָּרַחְתִּי הַקָּדוֹשׁ בָּרוּךְ הוּא מַחְשִׁיךְ
עָלַי אֶת הָעוֹלָם — Fearing that God had begun to implement the death sentence
against him,[170] he said, "Woe is to me! Because I have sinned, the Holy One,
Blessed is He, is making the world dark for me!"[171]   וְהוּא אֵינוֹ יוֹדֵעַ שֶׁבֵּן
דֶּרֶךְ הָעוֹלָם — Since he had never experienced night, he did not know that this
was the way of the world.[172]   לְשַׁחֲרִית, כֵּיוָן שֶׁרָאָה הָעוֹלָם שֶׁמֵּאִיר וּבָא לַמִּזְרָח
— Toward morning, when he saw that the world was becoming progres-
sively lighter from the east,   שָׂמַח שִׂמְחָה גְדוֹלָה — he became exceedingly
happy, realizing that the darkness he had feared was simply part of the daily
cycle.   עָמַד וּבָנָה מִזְבְּחוֹת — To express his joy and gratitude, he got up and
built altars,[173]   וְהֵבִיא שׁוֹר שֶׁקַּרְנָיו קוֹדְמוֹת לְפַרְסוֹתָיו וְהֶעֱלָהוּ עוֹלָה — and then
brought an ox whose horns had preceded its hooves[174] and offered it up on

---

170. Avodah Zarah 8a.

171. The Gemara (ibid.) adds that Adam,
thinking that his end was near, fasted and
wept in contrition the entire night; Eve sat
opposite him and wept as well.

172. Some wonder how Adam, who was
angel-like in his greatness and wisdom,
could be ignorant of such a basic natural
phenomenon as nightfall (Ritva, Avodah
Zarah ad loc., quoted in Ein Yaakov). Chida
finds an explanation in the Midrashic teaching that the original Heavenly light, brought
forth on the first day of Creation, kept the
world illuminated from Friday morning until
the conclusion of the Sabbath, for thirty-six
consecutive hours (Bereishis Rabbah 11
§2). Thus, while Adam certainly knew that
the world alternated between night and day
during the six days of Creation, he inferred
from the absence of darkness on Friday
night that from then on, with the work of creation completed, the world had moved into
a state of perpetual day. If so, the darkening
night could only be a result of his sin and a
sign of doom (Kisei Rachamim).

[This explanation assumes that the incident recorded here took place on Saturday
night and Sunday morning, not on Friday

night and Saturday morning, as some commentators (e.g., Regel Yesharah) understand
it; see Ahavas Chesed in marginal note.]

173. One for the olah offering, and one
for incense, as in the Tabernacle and Holy
Temple (Avos HaRosh [Vol. 2], p. 4b; cf.
Magen Avos). [Some texts have here instead
מִזְבֵּחַ, an altar, in the singular. This is also the
reading of Gra.]

174. That is, the ox that was created by God
during the seven days of Creation. Normally,
when a calf is born, its hooves are already
present but its horns do not emerge until
much later. The first ox, however, was different, since the Sages teach that all the
creatures from the six days of Creation were
brought into being in their fully mature state
(Rosh Hashanah 11a). Hence, when the
first ox was created, it already had horns.
Furthermore, since God drew the ox out
from the ground head first, it follows that
the horns emerged first and the hooves last
(Rashi, Avodah Zarah ad loc.).

As for the significance of this particular
ox, some say that, since the idea of a sacrificial offering is to symbolically give oneself
up to God, Adam sought to bring an offering
that was similar to him, a direct creation of

שֶׁנֶּאֱמַר (תהלים סט, לב) "וְתִיטַב לַה' מִשּׁוֹר פָּר מַקְרִן מַפְרִיס"[175]. שׁוֹר שֶׁהֶעֱלָה אָדָם הָרִאשׁוֹן וּפָר שֶׁהֶעֱלָה נֹחַ[176] וְאַיִל שֶׁהֶעֱלָה אַבְרָהָם אָבִינוּ תַּחַת בְּנוֹ עַל גַּבֵּי הַמִּזְבֵּחַ (כּוּלָּם קַרְנוֹתֵיהֶן קוֹדְמוֹת לְפַרְסוֹתֵיהֶן), שֶׁנֶּאֱמַר (בראשית כב, יג) "וַיִּשָּׂא אַבְרָהָם אֶת עֵינָיו וַיַּרְא וְהִנֵּה אַיִל אַחַר נֶאֱחַז"[177].

as — שֶׁנֶּאֱמַר "וְתִיטַב לַה' מִשּׁוֹר פָּר מַקְרִן מַפְרִיס" it is stated, *I shall praise the Name of God with song, and I shall magnify it with thanksgiving*, **and this should be more pleasing before HASHEM than the** *"shor-par"* [literally, *ox-bull*], **horned and hoofed** (*Psalms* 69:32).[175] שׁוֹר שֶׁהֶעֱלָה אָדָם הָרִאשׁוֹן וּפָר שֶׁהֶעֱלָה נֹחַ וְאַיִל שֶׁהֶעֱלָה אַבְרָהָם אָבִינוּ תַּחַת בְּנוֹ עַל גַּבֵּי הַמִּזְבֵּחַ — This was the first of three such primeval animals brought as offerings to God; namely, **the ox that Adam, the first man, brought** after his first night gave way to morning, **and the bull that Noah brought** after he survived the Great Flood,[176] **and the ram that our forefather Abraham brought instead of his son,** Isaac, **on the altar** — כּוּלָּם קַרְנוֹתֵיהֶן קוֹדְמוֹת לְפַרְסוֹתֵיהֶן — all of **them** were drawn out of the ground during the six days of Creation, so that **their horns preceded their hooves,** שֶׁנֶּאֱמַר "וַיִּשָּׂא אַבְרָהָם אֶת עֵינָיו וַיַּרְא וְהִנֵּה אַיִל אַחַר נֶאֱחַז" — **as it is stated,** *And Abraham raised his eyes and saw — behold, a ram! — afterward, caught* in the thicket ... (*Genesis* 22:13).[177]

God (*Iyun Yaakov, Avodah Zarah* ad loc.). Other suggest that the point is to explain how Adam could ignore the Scriptural law that an animal offering must be at least eight days old, to ensure that it is viable. And the answer is that since this ox was born as a mature adult, there was no reason to suspect that it would not live (*Avos HaRosh* [Vol. 1], p. 81a). Many sources explore the deeper meaning of this ox; see, for example, *Rashba al HaAggados, Chullin* 60a; *Maharal, Avodah Zarah* ad loc.; and *Nefesh HaChaim* 1:20).

175. "Horned and hoofed" implies that the animal in question had horns before it had hooves. Since an ordinary calf is born with hooves and does not grow horns until it is older, the verse must be referring to the ox of Creation, which was created fully grown, complete with horns (*Yalkut Shimoni, Tehillim* §802). King David, in referring to this *shor-par* used by Adam for his first offering, was asking that his own praise be found even more pleasing before God (*Rashi, Avodah Zarah* ad loc.).

176. Scripture (*Genesis* 8:20) records that Noah brought sacrificial offerings (*from every clean animal and every clean bird*) after the Flood, but it does not single out a bull. Our Baraisa infers from the double term *shor-par* (*ox-bull*), that Adam was not the only one who brought a primeval animal as an offering. Whereas he brought a *shor* (defined as a male bovine less than three years old), Noah brought a *par,* a bull over three (*Magen Avos*). [It would emerge, then, that more than one male bovine was created in the beginning — one that Adam offered and another that Noah offered. Alternatively, *Avos HaRosh* (Vol. 1, p. 83a) suggests that the primeval "ox" offered by Adam was the female, whereas the bull offered by Noah was the male.]

177. The Baraisa expounds the apparently superfluous word אַחַר, *afterward,* as if it were vowelized אַחֵר, *different.* The verse thus indicates that this was different from other rams — viz., it was the primeval ram (see *Binyan Yehoshua;* cf. *Matnos Kehunah* to *Bamidbar Rabbah* 17 §2).

בְּאוֹתָהּ שָׁעָה יָרְדוּ שָׁלֹש כִּתּוֹת שֶׁל מַלְאֲכֵי הַשָּׁרֵת וּבִידֵיהֶם כִּנּוֹרוֹת וּנְבָלִים
וְכָל כְּלֵי שִׁיר, הָיוּ אוֹמְרִים שִׁירָה עִמּוֹ179, שֶׁנֶּאֱמַר (תהלים צב, א-ג) ״מִזְמוֹר
שִׁיר לְיוֹם הַשַּׁבָּת טוֹב לְהֹדוֹת לַה׳ וְגוֹ׳ לְהַגִּיד בַּבֹּקֶר חַסְדֶּךָ וֶאֱמוּנָתְךָ
בַּלֵּילוֹת״180, ״לְהַגִּיד בַּבֹּקֶר חַסְדֶּךָ״ זֶה הָעוֹלָם הַבָּא שֶׁנִּמְשַׁל כַּבְּקָרִים,
שֶׁנֶּאֱמַר (איכה ג, כג) ״חֲדָשִׁים לַבְּקָרִים רַבָּה אֱמוּנָתֶךָ״181. ״וֶאֱמוּנָתְךָ
בַּלֵּילוֹת״ זֶה הָעוֹלָם הַזֶּה שֶׁנִּמְשַׁל בַּלֵּילוֹת, שֶׁנֶּאֱמַר (ישעיה כא, יא) ״מַשָּׂא

In the wake of Adam's repentance and offering, a sign of Divine mercy was shown to him:[178]

בְּאוֹתָהּ שָׁעָה יָרְדוּ שָׁלֹש כִּתּוֹת שֶׁל מַלְאֲכֵי הַשָּׁרֵת — At that moment, three groups of ministering angels descended from Heaven. וּבִידֵיהֶם כִּנּוֹרוֹת וּנְבָלִים וְכָל כְּלֵי שִׁיר — In their hands were harps, lyres, and all types of musical instruments, הָיוּ אוֹמְרִים שִׁירָה עִמּוֹ — and they recited song along with him over his offering,[179] שֶׁנֶּאֱמַר ״מִזְמוֹר שִׁיר לְיוֹם הַשַּׁבָּת טוֹב לְהֹדוֹת לַה׳ וְגוֹ׳ — as it is stated, *A psalm, a song for the Sabbath day. It is good to thank HASHEM, etc.,* לְהַגִּיד בַּבֹּקֶר חַסְדֶּךָ וֶאֱמוּנָתְךָ בַּלֵּילוֹת — *to relate Your kindness in the dawn and Your faith in the nights. Upon a ten-stringed instrument and upon lyre, with singing accompanied by a harp* (Psalms 92:1-3).[180]

The Baraisa expounds the verses of this song:

״לְהַגִּיד בַּבֹּקֶר חַסְדֶּךָ״ זֶה הָעוֹלָם הַבָּא שֶׁנִּמְשַׁל כַּבְּקָרִים — *To relate Your kindness in the dawn* — this refers to the World to Come, which is compared to morning, שֶׁנֶּאֱמַר ״חֲדָשִׁים לַבְּקָרִים רַבָּה אֱמוּנָתֶךָ״ — as it is stated, *[His kindnesses] are new every morning; great is Your faithfulness!* (Lamentations 3:23).[181] ״וֶאֱמוּנָתְךָ בַּלֵּילוֹת״ זֶה הָעוֹלָם הַזֶּה שֶׁנִּמְשַׁל בַּלֵּילוֹת — *And Your faith in the nights* — this refers to the present world, which is compared to night, שֶׁנֶּאֱמַר ״מַשָּׂא

While the *Psalms* verse alludes to the special offerings of Adam and Noah (*shor-par*), it does not allude to that of Abraham, because King David could not ask that his praises be found more pleasing than the *Akeidah*, the Binding of Isaac, whose merit has sustained Israel for all generations (*Magen Avos*).

178. See *Binyan Yehoshua*.

179. The offerings in the Holy Temple were accompanied by Levite song. Adam did the same, and was assisted by the angels from Heaven (see *Meorei Ohr*).

180. *Pirkei DeRabbi Eliezer* §19 teaches that it was Adam who sang this song. [Assuming that Adam experienced his first period of darkness on Friday night (see above,

note 172). then he indeed sang this song on the Sabbath. If, however, his first night was delayed until after the Sabbath (see there), then Adam sang this song on Sunday (*Ahavas Chesed,* in marginal note).]

The Baraisa finds support in this verse for its assertion that the angels joined Adam in his singing, for otherwise where did Adam obtain the musical instruments mentioned in the verse? It must be that the angels brought them down from Heaven, as stated above (*Magen Avos*).

181. "Morning" in this verse refers to the World to Come, where for the first time God's faithfulness — His commitment to fulfilling His promises of reward for moral virtue — will become evident to all (*Ahavas Chesed*).

דּוּמָה אֵלַי קֹרֵא מִשֵּׂעִיר שֹׁמֵר מַה מִלַּיְלָה שֹׁמֵר מַה מִלֵּיל"[182]. בְּאוֹתָהּ
שָׁעָה אָמַר הַקָּדוֹשׁ בָּרוּךְ הוּא: אִם אֵינִי דָן אֶת הַנָּחָשׁ נִמְצֵאתִי מַחֲרִיב
אֶת כָּל הָעוֹלָם כֻּלּוֹ[183], וְאָמַר: זֶה שֶׁהִמְלַכְתִּי וַעֲשִׂיתִיו מֶלֶךְ עַל כָּל
הָעוֹלָם כֻּלּוֹ הֵיאַךְ נִשְׁתַּבֵּשׁ וְאָכַל פֵּירוֹת הָאִילָן. מִיָּד נִפְנָה אֵלָיו וְקִלְּלוֹ,
שֶׁנֶּאֱמַר(בראשית ג, יד) "וַיֹּאמֶר ה' אֱלֹהִים אֶל הַנָּחָשׁ וְגוֹ' ". רַבִּי יוֹסֵי
אוֹמֵר: אִלְמָלֵא (לא) נִכְתַּב [קִלְלָתוֹ] בְּסוֹפָן כְּבָר הֶחֱרִיב אֶת כָּל הָעוֹלָם.

דּוּמָה אֵלַי קֹרֵא מִשֵּׂעִיר שֹׁמֵר מַה מִלַּיְלָה שֹׁמֵר מַה מִלֵּיל" — as it is stated, *A prophecy concerning Duma: He calls out to me because of Seir, "Watchman, what of the night? Watchman, what of the night?"* (Isaiah 21:11).[182]

The Midrash returns to its discussion of the punishments meted out for the sin of eating from the Tree of Knowledge:

בְּאוֹתָהּ שָׁעָה אָמַר הַקָּדוֹשׁ בָּרוּךְ הוּא — At that moment, the Holy One, Blessed is He, said, אִם אֵינִי דָן אֶת הַנָּחָשׁ, נִמְצֵאתִי מַחֲרִיב אֶת כָּל הָעוֹלָם כֻּלּוֹ — "If I do not punish the serpent immediately, I will effectively be destroying the entire world,"[183] וְאָמַר: זֶה שֶׁהִמְלַכְתִּי וַעֲשִׂיתִיו מֶלֶךְ עַל כָּל הָעוֹלָם כֻּלּוֹ הֵיאַךְ נִשְׁתַּבֵּשׁ וְאָכַל פֵּירוֹת הָאִילָן — and He said, "This serpent whom I have crowned and made king over all the beasts of the world,[184] how can he have erred so egregiously and eaten from the fruit of the forbidden tree?" מִיָּד נִפְנָה אֵלָיו וְקִלְּלוֹ — Immediately, without giving the serpent a chance to defend himself,[185] He turned to him and cursed him, שֶׁנֶּאֱמַר "וַיֹּאמֶר ה' אֱלֹהִים אֶל הַנָּחָשׁ וְגוֹ' " — as it is said, *And HASHEM God said to the serpent, etc. Because you have done this, accursed are you beyond all the cattle and beyond all beasts of the field* ... (Genesis 3:14). רַבִּי יוֹסֵי אוֹמֵר — R' Yose says: אִלְמָלֵא נִכְתַּב קִלְלָתוֹ בְּסוֹפָן — Had [the serpent's] curse been delayed and written only at the end, after those of Adam and Eve,[186] thus prolonging his term as the most clever of animals, כְּבָר הֶחֱרִיב אֶת כָּל הָעוֹלָם — he would have already managed to spread his evil ideas further[187] and **destroyed the entire world.**

---

182. "Duma" is a reference to Edom (*Rashi*), the nation that launched Israel into its longest exile. This prophecy describes Israel as crying out to God, its Watchman, for relief from the oppression of the night, i.e., the exile which was inflicted by Edom, whose homeland was Seir (*Ahavas Chesed,* quoting *Yerushalmi Taanis* 1:1).

183. For the smooth-talking serpent will go on and persuade all the world's creatures to eat from the Tree of Knowledge (*Mefaresh*).

184. *Ahavas Chesed*; see also *Binyan Yehoshua.*

185. If given the chance, the serpent could

have argued that Adam and Eve should not have ignored God's word and listened to him (as the Talmud puts it: If the master says one thing and the student says another, whose words must one obey?). God did not grant him a hearing, however, for by this logic, he would be free to corrupt the entire world with impunity (*Mefaresh*).

186. *Binyan Yehoshua, Ahavas Chesed.* [According to the rule set forth by *Tosafos, Megillah* 21a, the spelling here should not be אִלְמָלֵא, but rather אִלְמָלֵי, as indeed emended here by *Gra*.]

187. *Binyan Yehoshua.*

כְּשֶׁבְּרָאוֹ הַקָּדוֹשׁ בָּרוּךְ הוּא לְאָדָם הָרִאשׁוֹן צָר אוֹתוֹ פָּנִים וְאָחוֹר,
שֶׁנֶּאֱמַר (תהלים קלט, ה) "אָחוֹר וָקֶדֶם צַרְתָּנִי וַתָּשֶׁת עָלַי כַּפֶּכָה"188. וְיָרְדוּ
מַלְאֲכֵי הַשָּׁרֵת (לְשָׁרְתוֹ189) וּנְטָלוֹ הַקָּדוֹשׁ בָּרוּךְ הוּא וּנְתָנוֹ תַּחַת כְּנָפָיו190,
שֶׁנֶּאֱמַר "וַתָּשֶׁת עָלַי כַּפֶּכָה". דָּבָר אַחֵר, "וַתָּשֶׁת עָלַי כַּפֶּכָה", (כֵּיוָן
שֶׁסָּרַח נָטַל לוֹ הַקָּדוֹשׁ בָּרוּךְ הוּא אֶחָד מֵהֶן). מִכָּאן לְאָדָם וְלַמִּקְדָּשׁ
כְּשֶׁנִּבְרְאוּ בִּשְׁתֵּי יָדָיו נִבְרָאוּ192. מִנַּיִן לְאָדָם שֶׁנִּבְרָא בִּשְׁתֵּי יָדָיו,

The Baraisa presents a pair of teachings about Adam, the second of which reveals another unfortunate result of his sin.

כְּשֶׁבְּרָאוֹ הַקָּדוֹשׁ בָּרוּךְ הוּא לְאָדָם הָרִאשׁוֹן, צָר אוֹתוֹ פָּנִים וְאָחוֹר — When the Holy One, Blessed is He, created Adam, the first man, He shaped him front and back, שֶׁנֶּאֱמַר "אָחוֹר וָקֶדֶם צַרְתָּנִי וַתָּשֶׁת עָלַי כַּפֶּכָה" — as it is stated, *Back and front You have shaped me, and You have laid Your hand upon me* (Psalms 139:5).[188] וְיָרְדוּ מַלְאֲכֵי הַשָּׁרֵת לְשָׁרְתוֹ וּנְטָלוֹ הַקָּדוֹשׁ בָּרוּךְ הוּא וּנְתָנוֹ תַּחַת כְּנָפָיו — The ministering angels descended from Heaven to serve him,[189] so to indicate that Adam was a mere mortal, God took him and placed him underneath His wings,[190] שֶׁנֶּאֱמַר "וַתָּשֶׁת עָלַי כַּפֶּכָה" — as it is stated, *and You have laid Your hand upon me,* a reference to being sheltered under God's wings. דָּבָר אַחֵר "וַתָּשֶׁת עָלַי כַּפֶּכָה" — Another interpretation of the words, *and you have laid Your hand upon me:* כֵּיוָן שֶׁסָּרַח נָטַל לוֹ הַקָּדוֹשׁ בָּרוּךְ הוּא אֶחָד מֵהֶן — Once [Adam] soured, i.e., once he sinned, the Holy One, Blessed is He, took away one of his two [facial figures], leaving him in his present-day form.

A final teaching about man's creation:

מִכָּאן לְאָדָם וְלַמִּקְדָּשׁ כְּשֶׁנִּבְרְאוּ בִּשְׁתֵּי יָדָיו נִבְרָאוּ — From the verses that will be cited[191] here, we can infer that when Adam and the Temple were created, they were created with both of [God's] hands, as it were.[192] מִנַּיִן לְאָדָם שֶׁנִּבְרָא בִּשְׁתֵּי יָדָיו — From where can we learn that Adam was created with

188. That is, He created Adam with two facial figures, each one facing the opposite way (*Binyan Yehoshua*). This double-faced form symbolized that man's power and influence extended in all directions, and that wherever he would turn, he would succeed. However, this striking mark of human mastery made such a strong impression on the angels that they came down from heaven to enter into his service (*Magen Avos*). [This Baraisa has a different understanding of the double-faced form of Adam than that found in several places in the Gemara (see *Ahavas Chesed*).]

189. Preparing meat and wine for him, as mentioned in the beginning of this section

(*Binyan Yehoshua*). Alternatively, the word לְשָׁרְתוֹ here means "to sing before him," for the angels were so awed by Adam's greatness that they mistook him for an eternal being and prepared themselves to sing his praises (ibid., from *Mefaresh,* based on *Bereishis Rabbah* 8 §10).

190. As if to say that with all of man's intellect and abilities, he still must cling to God for life, sustenance, protection, and success; therefore, it is God alone that the angels should serve (*Magen Avos*).

191. *Ahavas Chesed;* cf. *Magen Avos* and *Avos HaRosh* (Vol. 1), p. 88b.

192. Since God is described as having

שֶׁנֶּאֱמַר (שם קיט, עג) "יָדֶיךָ עָשׂוּנִי וַיְכוֹנְנוּנִי". מִנַּיִן לַמִּקְדָּשׁ שֶׁנִּבְרָא בִּשְׁתֵּי

יָדָיו, שֶׁנֶּאֱמַר (שמות טו, יז) "מִקְּדָשׁ אֲדֹנָי כּוֹנְנוּ יָדֶיךָ". (וְאוֹמֵר (תהלים עח, נד)

"וַיְבִיאֵם אֶל גְּבוּל קָדְשׁוֹ הַר זֶה קָנְתָה יְמִינוֹ". ¹⁹³ וְאוֹמֵר (שמות טו, יח) "ה׳

יִמְלֹךְ לְעוֹלָם וָעֶד"¹⁹⁴):

---

both of His hands? "יָדֶיךָ עָשׂוּנִי וַיְכוֹנְנוּנִי" שֶׁנֶּאֱמַר — **For it is stated,** *Your hands made me and prepared me* (ibid. 119:73). מִנַּיִן לַמִּקְדָּשׁ שֶׁנִּבְרָא בִּשְׁתֵּי יָדָיו — **And from where** can we learn **that the Temple was created with both of His hands?** "מִקְּדָשׁ אֲדֹנָי כּוֹנְנוּ יָדֶיךָ" שֶׁנֶּאֱמַר — **For it is stated,** ... *the Sanctuary, my Lord, that Your hands established* (*Exodus* 15:17). וְאוֹמֵר "וַיְבִיאֵם אֶל גְּבוּל קָדְשׁוֹ הַר זֶה קָנְתָה יְמִינוֹ" — **And it states** further, *He brought them to His sacred boundary, this mountain that His right hand acquired* (*Psalms* 78:54).[193] וְאוֹמֵר "ה׳ יִמְלֹךְ לְעוֹלָם וָעֶד" — **And it states** immediately after the *Exodus* verse itself about the Temple, *HASHEM shall reign for all eternity,* implying that the "Sanctuary" mentioned previously will endure forever.[194]

---

created the earth with one hand and the heavens with another (as it is written, *My hand has laid the foundation of the earth, and My right hand has measured out the heavens* — *Isaiah* 48:13), to say that He created something with *both* hands indicates that it is rooted in both the physical and spiritual worlds. This is true of the Temple, for the Sages teach that the Heavenly Temple is aligned with the earthly Temple (*Midrash Tanchuma, Shemos* §18). And it is true of man as well, for his actions are of cosmic significance, building or destroying in both the earthly and Heavenly spheres (*Kli Yakar* to *Exodus* 15:17).

193. The Baraisa cites this verse (and the next one) to address an unspoken difficulty: How can the verse say that *God* created the Temple with two hands, when we know that it was King Solomon who built the Temple?

The answer lies in the verse now cited: The reference is not so much to the Temple itself but to the *place* of the Temple — the Temple Mount, *"this mountain"* that His right hand *acquired*. True, the verse speaks only of the mountain that His "right" hand acquired, but this is in addition to the "left" hand that He used to create the earthly world at large, as it states: *My hand has laid the foundation of the earth, and My right hand has measured out the heavens* (*Isaiah* 48:13). We may conclude, then, that God created the Temple mount with both His right and left hands (*Avos HaRosh* [Vol. 1], p. 88b).

194. This, too, proves that "the Temple" built by God's "hands" (mentioned in the preceding verse) is really a reference to the *place* of the Temple. For the Temple itself did not last "forever," but rather went through periods of destruction (see *Ben Avraham*).

✿ פֶּרֶק ב }▸

א. אֵיזֶהוּ סְיָיג שֶׁעָשְׂתָה תוֹרָה לִדְבָרֶיהָ. הֲרֵי הוּא אוֹמֵר (ויקרא יח, יט) "וְאֶל
אִשָּׁה בְּנִדַּת טֻמְאָתָהּ לֹא תִקְרַב"[1], יָכוֹל יְחַבְּקֶנָּה וִינַשְּׁקֶנָּה וִידַבֵּר עִמָּהּ
דְּבָרִים בְּטֵלִים. תַּלְמוּד לוֹמַר, "לֹא תִקְרַב". יָכוֹל יִשַּׁן עִמָּהּ בִּבְגָדֶיהָ עַל
הַמִּטָּה. תַּלְמוּד לוֹמַר "לֹא תִקְרַב". יָכוֹל תִּרְחוֹץ בְּפָנֶיהָ וְתִכְחוֹל עֵינֶיהָ.
תַּלְמוּד לוֹמַר (שם טו, לג) "וְהַדָּוָה בְּנִדָּתָהּ", כָּל יָמִים שֶׁבְּנִדָּתָהּ תִּהְיֶה בְּנִדּוּי.
מִכָּאן אָמְרוּ: כָּל הַמְנַוֶּולֶת עַצְמָהּ בִּימֵי נִדָּתָהּ רוּחַ חֲכָמִים נוֹחָה הֵימֶנָּה,

---

✿ CHAPTER 2 }▸

§1 The Baraisa continues expounding the list of those who made fences
around their words:

אֵיזֶהוּ סְיָיג שֶׁעָשְׂתָה תוֹרָה לִדְבָרֶיהָ — **What was the fence that the Torah made
around its words?** הֲרֵי הוּא אוֹמֵר "וְאֶל אִשָּׁה בְּנִדַּת טֻמְאָתָהּ לֹא תִקְרַב" — **It says**
in Scripture, *You shall not approach a woman in her time of unclean sepa-
ration,*[1] *to uncover her nakedness* (*Leviticus* 18:19). יָכוֹל יְחַבְּקֶנָּה וִינַשְּׁקֶנָּה
— Now, had Scripture simply written, "You shall not uncover the nakedness of
a woman in her time of unclean separation," **one might have thought that he
can hug her, kiss her,** וִידַבֵּר עִמָּהּ דְּבָרִים בְּטֵלִים — **and speak with her idle
chatter,** of the kind that can lead to physical intimacy;[2] תַּלְמוּד לוֹמַר "לֹא
תִקְרַב" — Scripture therefore teaches otherwise and **says**, *You shall not approach ... to uncover her nakedness,* which implies *any* behavior that can lead
to uncovering her nakedness. יָכוֹל יִשַּׁן עִמָּהּ בִּבְגָדֶיהָ עַל הַמִּטָּה — **One might
think that he can sleep next to her on the** same **bed while she is clothed.**
תַּלְמוּד לוֹמַר לֹא תִקְרַב — Scripture therefore teaches otherwise and **says**, *You
shall not approach;* sleeping next to her even while she is clothed is also a
form of "approach." יָכוֹל תִּרְחוֹץ בְּפָנֶיהָ וְתִכְחוֹל עֵינֶיהָ — **One might think
that she may** nevertheless **wash her face and apply makeup to her eyes** to
make herself attractive to her husband during this time. תַּלְמוּד לוֹמַר "וְהַדָּוָה
בְּנִדָּתָהּ — Scripture therefore **teaches** otherwise and **says** in a different passage, *and concerning a woman who suffers through her separation* (ibid.
15:33), כָּל יָמִים שֶׁבְּנִדָּתָהּ תִּהְיֶה בְּנִדּוּי — which indicates: **all the days of her
separation** [נִדָּה] period, **she is to be** considered as if **excommunicated** [נִדּוּי]
from her husband. מִכָּאן אָמְרוּ: כָּל הַמְנַוֶּולֶת עַצְמָהּ בִּימֵי נִדָּתָהּ רוּחַ חֲכָמִים נוֹחָה
הֵימֶנָּה — Based on this, [the Sages] said: **The Sages are pleased with any**

---

1. Each time a woman's period begins, she
immediately becomes *tamei* (halachically
"unclean") for seven days, after which she

immerses herself in a *mikveh* to become
tahor (see further below, note 12).
2. *Avos HaRosh* [Vol. 1].

וְכָל הַמִּתְקַשֶּׁטֶת עַצְמָהּ בִּימֵי נִדָּתָהּ אֵין רוּחַ חֲכָמִים נוֹחָה הֵימֶנָּה:[3]

ב. מַעֲשֶׂה בְּאָדָם אֶחָד שֶׁקָּרָא הַרְבֵּה וְשָׁנָה הַרְבֵּה וְשִׁמֵּשׁ תַּלְמִידֵי חֲכָמִים הַרְבֵּה,[5] וּמֵת בַּחֲצִי יָמָיו. וְהָיְתָה אִשְׁתּוֹ נוֹטֶלֶת תְּפִילָּיו[6] וְחוֹזֶרֶת בְּבָתֵּי כְנֵסִיּוֹת וּבְבָתֵּי מִדְרָשׁוֹת וְהָיְתָה צוֹעֶקֶת וּבוֹכָה, וְאָמְרָה לָהֶם: רַבּוֹתַי, כְּתִיב בְּתוֹרַתְכֶם (דברים ל, כ) "כִּי הוּא חַיֶּיךָ וְאֹרֶךְ יָמֶיךָ", בַּעְלִי שֶׁקָּרָא הַרְבֵּה וְשָׁנָה הַרְבֵּה וְשִׁמֵּשׁ תַּלְמִידֵי חֲכָמִים הַרְבֵּה, מִפְּנֵי מָה מֵת

---

woman **who makes herself unattractive** to her husband **during her separation period,** וְכָל הַמִּתְקַשֶּׁטֶת עַצְמָהּ בִּימֵי נִדָּתָהּ אֵין רוּחַ חֲכָמִים נוֹחָה הֵימֶנָּה — **and the Sages are not pleased with any** woman **who adorns herself during her separation period.**[3]

§2 The Baraisa records a story that illustrates the severity of transgressing even one of the protective fences discussed above:[4]

מַעֲשֶׂה בְּאָדָם אֶחָד שֶׁקָּרָא הַרְבֵּה וְשָׁנָה הַרְבֵּה וְשִׁמֵּשׁ תַּלְמִידֵי חֲכָמִים הַרְבֵּה — **It once happened that** there was **a certain man who had read Scripture extensively, studied Mishnah extensively, and served Torah scholars extensively,**[5] וּמֵת בַּחֲצִי יָמָיו — **and yet, he died in the middle of his life.** וְהָיְתָה אִשְׁתּוֹ נוֹטֶלֶת תְּפִילָּיו וְחוֹזֶרֶת בְּבָתֵּי כְנֵסִיּוֹת וּבְבָתֵּי מִדְרָשׁוֹת — **And his wife would take his tefillin**[6] **and go around to** various **synagogues and study halls,** וְהָיְתָה צוֹעֶקֶת וּבוֹכָה וְאָמְרָה לָהֶם — **and cry out and weep** before those assembled there **and say to them,** "רַבּוֹתַי, כְּתִיב בְּתוֹרַתְכֶם "כִּי הוּא חַיֶּיךָ וְאֹרֶךְ יָמֶיךָ" — **"My masters! It is written in your Torah** regarding it, *For it is your life and the length of your days* (*Deuteronomy* 30:20). בַּעְלִי שֶׁקָּרָא הַרְבֵּה וְשָׁנָה הַרְבֵּה וְשִׁמֵּשׁ תַּלְמִידֵי חֲכָמִים הַרְבֵּה — **My husband, who read Scripture extensively, studied Mishnah extensively, and served Torah scholars extensively —** מִפְּנֵי מָה מֵת

---

3. The halachah follows the view of R' Akiva (*Shabbos* 64b), who expounds the verse וְהַדָּוָה בְּנִדָּתָהּ differently, and rules that a woman is *not* forbidden to adorn herself during her time of *niddah,* for there is the concern that she might become repulsive to her husband (see *Rambam, Hil. Issurei Biah* 11:19, and *Binyan Yehoshua* here). However, *Tur* and *Shulchan Aruch* (*Yoreh Deah* 195:9) write that this is permitted "reluctantly." Apparently, they understood that this last part of the Baraisa, which speaks only of whether or not the Sages are "pleased" with such behavior [indicating that it is not a matter of actual *law*], can accord even with the view of R' Akiva [and is meant to restrain the

niddah from adorning herself *extensively*] (*Beur HaGra* to *Shulchan Aruch* ibid.; see also *Eitz Yosef* on *Bamidbar Rabbah* 10 §8, and *Divrei Malkiel* 5:103).

4. See *Magen Avos.*

5. "Serving Torah scholars," in this context, means learning from them the various ways of analyzing Mishnahs. All these studies were later included in the Gemara (*Binyan Yehoshua*).

6. In order to evoke the sympathy of those to whom she would lament her husband's untimely passing. Alternatively, since she was questioning the shortness of his life (as described below), she brought his tefillin, which are supposed to earn a person long

בַּחֲצִי יָמָיו. לֹא הָיָה אָדָם שֶׁהֵשִׁיב דָּבָר. פַּעַם אַחַת נִזְדַּמֵּן לָהּ אֵלִיָּהוּ זָכוּר
לַטּוֹב. אָמַר לָהּ: בִּתִּי, מִפְּנֵי מָה אַתְּ בּוֹכָה וְצוֹעֶקֶת. אָמְרָה לוֹ: רַבִּי בַּעְלִי
שֶׁקָּרָא הַרְבֵּה וְשָׁנָה הַרְבֵּה וְשִׁמֵּשׁ תַּלְמִידֵי חֲכָמִים הַרְבֵּה וּמֵת בַּחֲצִי
יָמָיו. אָמַר לָהּ: כְּשֶׁבָּאת בְּנִדָּתֵךְ, כָּל אוֹתָן (שְׁלֹשָׁה) יָמִים הָרִאשׁוֹנִים
מַהוּ אֶצְלֵךְ[7]. אָמְרָה לוֹ: רַבִּי, חַס וְשָׁלוֹם שֶׁלֹּא נָגַע בִּי אֲפִילוּ בְּאֶצְבַּע
קְטַנָּה שֶׁלּוֹ. אֶלָּא כָּךְ אָמַר לִי: אַל תִּגְּעִי בַּכֵּלִים שֶׁמָּא °תָּבִיאִי (לִי) לִידֵי
סָפֵק[8]. כָּל אוֹתָן יָמִים הָאַחֲרוֹנִים מַהוּ אֶצְלֵךְ[9]. אָמְרָה לוֹ: רַבִּי, אָכַלְתִּי
עִמּוֹ וְשָׁתִיתִי עִמּוֹ וְיָשַׁנְתִּי עִמּוֹ בִּבְגָדַי עַל הַמִּטָּה, וּבְשָׂרוֹ נָגַע בִּבְשָׂרִי,[10]

בַּחֲצִי יָמָיו — why did he die in the middle of his life?!" לֹא הָיָה אָדָם שֶׁהֵשִׁיב
דָּבָר — And there was never anyone there who could give her an answer.
פַּעַם אַחַת נִזְדַּמֵּן לָהּ אֵלִיָּהוּ זָכוּר לַטּוֹב — One time, Elijah — who is remembered
for good — encountered her. אָמַר לָהּ בִּתִּי מִפְּנֵי מָה אַתְּ בּוֹכָה וְצוֹעֶקֶת — He
said to her, "My daughter, why are you weeping and crying out?" אָמְרָה
לוֹ: רַבִּי, בַּעְלִי שֶׁקָּרָא הַרְבֵּה וְשָׁנָה הַרְבֵּה וְשִׁמֵּשׁ תַּלְמִידֵי חֲכָמִים הַרְבֵּה וּמֵת בַּחֲצִי יָמָיו
— She replied, "My master! My husband, who read Scripture extensively,
studied Mishnah extensively, and served Torah scholars extensively, and despite all that, died in the middle of his life!" אָמַר לָהּ כְּשֶׁבָּאת בְּנִדָּתֵךְ כָּל אוֹתָן
יָמִים הָרִאשׁוֹנִים מַהוּ אֶצְלֵךְ — [Elijah] asked her, "When you would begin your
niddah period, how did he act with you during those first days?"[7] אָמְרָה
לוֹ: רַבִּי חַס וְשָׁלוֹם שֶׁלֹּא נָגַע בִּי אֲפִילוּ בְּאֶצְבַּע קְטַנָּה שֶׁלּוֹ — She answered him,
"My master, God forbid to think that he would behave with me improperly,
for he never touched me during that time, even with his little finger! אֶלָּא
כָּךְ אָמַר לִי אַל תִּגְּעִי בַּכֵּלִים שֶׁמָּא תָּבִיאִי לִי לִידֵי סָפֵק — On the contrary, he was
so scrupulous in this matter that he would even say to me, 'Do not touch
the utensils, for perhaps you will cause me a doubt of tumah.'"[8] כָּל אוֹתָן
יָמִים הָאַחֲרוֹנִים מַהוּ אֶצְלֵךְ — Elijah asked her further, "And how did he act with
you during the last days of your separation period?"[9] אָמְרָה לוֹ רַבִּי אָכַלְתִּי
עִמּוֹ — She replied, "My master, during that time I ate with him
and drank with him, וְיָשַׁנְתִּי עִמּוֹ בִּבְגָדַי עַל הַמִּטָּה וּבְשָׂרוֹ נָגַע בִּבְשָׂרִי — and I
slept next to him on the bed in my clothes, and his skin touched mine,[10]

---

life [see Menachos 44a] (Ben Avraham, two
approaches).

7. "The first days" are what the Gemara
(Shabbos 13b) calls "the niddah days." See
below, note 12.

8. I.e., do not hand me anything, lest I touch
you inadvertently in the process and become tamei (Ahavas Chesed; see also Ben
Avraham).

9. "The last days" are what the Gemara
(Shabbos ibid.) calls "the clean days." See
below, note 12.

10. If she was clothed, how would their skin
touch? Some explain that she meant that
she would wear a garment around and below
her waist, but their skin touched elsewhere
(Ahavas Chesed and Ben Avraham). Binyan
Yehoshua emends the text and deletes the

אֲבָל לֹא נִתְכַּוֵּן לְדָבָר אַחֵר¹¹. אָמַר לָהּ: בָּרוּךְ הַמָּקוֹם שֶׁהֲרָגוּ, שֶׁכָּךְ כָּתוּב
בַּתּוֹרָה (ויקרא יח, יט) "וְאֶל אִשָּׁה בְּנִדַּת טֻמְאָתָהּ לֹא תִקְרַב"¹², הֲרֵי הוּא אוֹמֵר
(שם פסוק ו) "אִישׁ אִישׁ אֶל כָּל שְׁאֵר בְּשָׂרוֹ לֹא תִקְרְבוּ", מִכָּאן אָמְרוּ: אַל
יִתְיַחֵד אָדָם עִם (כָּל) הַנָּשִׁים בְּפוּנְדָק¹³, אֲפִילוּ עִם אֲחוֹתוֹ וְעִם בִּתּוֹ, מִפְּנֵי דַעַת

אֲבָל לֹא נִתְכַּוֵּן לְדָבָר אַחֵר — but he did not have any thought of the 'other
thing.' "¹¹ אָמַר לָהּ: בָּרוּךְ הַמָּקוֹם שֶׁהֲרָגוּ — He said to her, "If that is the case,
then blessed be the Omnipresent Who killed him! שֶׁכָּךְ כָּתוּב בַּתּוֹרָה "וְאֶל
אִשָּׁה בְּנִדַּת טֻמְאָתָהּ לֹא תִקְרַב" — For so is it written in the Torah, *You shall not
approach a woman in her time of unclean separation*" (*Leviticus* 18:19),
which teaches us (as mentioned above in the Baraisa) that *no* intimate behavior is permitted while the woman remains unclean.[12]

Other protective fences in the general area of distancing oneself from forbidden relations:

הֲרֵי הוּא אוֹמֵר "אִישׁ אִישׁ אֶל כָּל שְׁאֵר בְּשָׂרוֹ לֹא תִקְרְבוּ" — It says in Scripture, *Any
man shall not approach his close relative to uncover nakedness* (ibid. v. 6).
מִכָּאן אָמְרוּ אַל יִתְיַחֵד אָדָם עִם כָּל הַנָּשִׁים בְּפוּנְדָק — Based on this, [the Sag-
es] said: A man should not be secluded in an inn with any woman forbid-
den to him, lest they come to sin.[13] אֲפִילוּ עִם אֲחוֹתוֹ וְעִם בִּתּוֹ — And he
should not do so **even with his sister or with his daughter**, מִפְּנֵי דַעַת

---

word בִּבְגָדַי, *in my clothes* [and this is indeed
the reading in one of the manuscripts]. *Meorei Ohr* cites the reading of *Raavad*, who has
here "לֹא" נָגַע בִּבְשָׂרִי, *and his skin did
"not" touch mine.* [See *Shabbos* 13b, where
the Gemara cites three different versions of
how he had slept on the same bed as she.]

11. I.e., of conjugal relations.

12. The commentators wonder how an accomplished scholar such as this woman's
husband could have erred so grievously.
Surely a *niddah* is just as forbidden during
the last days as during the first days, and
for any time thereafter, as long as she has
not immersed herself in the *mikveh*! *Tosafos*
(to *Shabbos* ibid.) explain as follows: As is
well known, with the onset of her period a
woman becomes a *niddah* for seven days.
Biblically, she may immerse herself in the
mikveh and become *tahor* on the eighth
day (assuming her period has ended within
the seven days). However, the practice ad-
opted by Jewish women [and subsequently
mandated by the Rabbis] is for the woman

to continue to conduct herself as a *niddah*
until she counts seven clean days *after* the
end of her period, whereupon she immerses
herself in the *mikveh* and becomes *tahor*
(see *Niddah* 66a; the reasons for this stringency are complex). *Tosafos* maintain that
the custom was for the woman to immerse
herself in the *mikveh* twice — once at the
end of "the first (or 'niddah') days," whereupon she would become Biblically *tahor*,
and a second time at the end of "the last
(or 'clean') days," whereupon she would
become *tahor* even Rabbinically. Thus, the
scholar under discussion was scrupulous
in distancing himself from his wife during
her days of Biblical *tumah*, but not during
her days of Rabbinic *tumah*, though even
then he never entertained a thought of
actually cohabiting with her. [For other explanations, see *Binyan Yehoshua, Ben Avraham*, and the commentators to *Shabbos*
ad loc.]

13. As the verse says, *Any man shall not approach* ... (*Ben Avraham*). [This law applies

הַבְּרִיּוֹת.[14] לֹא יְסַפֵּר עִם הָאִשָּׁה בַּשּׁוּק, וַאֲפִילוּ עִם אִשְׁתּוֹ, וְאֵין צָרִיךְ לוֹמַר עִם אִשָּׁה אַחֶרֶת מִפְּנֵי טַעֲנַת הַבְּרִיּוֹת.[15] לֹא יֵלֵךְ אָדָם אַחַר הָאִשָּׁה בַּשּׁוּק וַאֲפִילוּ עִם אִשְׁתּוֹ וְאֵין צָרִיךְ לוֹמַר עִם אִשָּׁה אַחֶרֶת מִפְּנֵי טַעֲנַת הַבְּרִיּוֹת.[16] נֶאֱמַר כָּאן "לֹא תִקְרְבוּ" וְנֶאֱמַר לְהַלָּן (שם פסוק יט) "לֹא תִקְרַב", לְדָבָר הַמֵּבִיא לִידֵי עֲבֵירָה לֹא תִקְרַב, הַרְחֵק מִן הַכִּיעוּר וּמִן הַדּוֹמֶה לַכִּיעוּר.

לֹא יְסַפֵּר עִם הָאִשָּׁה — **because of what people might think.**[14] **הַבְּרִיּוֹת** **בַּשּׁוּק** — Similarly, **a man should not converse with a woman in the market-place** — **וַאֲפִילוּ עִם אִשְׁתּוֹ וְאֵין צָרִיךְ לוֹמַר עִם אִשָּׁה אַחֶרֶת** — **not even with his wife, and it goes without saying with a different woman** — **מִפְּנֵי טַעֲנַת** **הַבְּרִיּוֹת** — **because of people's suspicions** that this is an improper association.[15] **לֹא יֵלֵךְ אָדָם אַחַר הָאִשָּׁה בַּשּׁוּק** — Similarly, **a man should not walk behind a woman in the marketplace** — **וַאֲפִילוּ עִם אִשְׁתּוֹ וְאֵין צָרִיךְ לוֹמַר עִם** **אִשָּׁה אַחֶרֶת** — **and this is true even with his own wife, and needless to mention with a different woman** — **מִפְּנֵי טַעֲנַת הַבְּרִיּוֹת** — **because of what people might claim.**[16] **נֶאֱמַר כָּאן "לֹא תִקְרְבוּ" וְנֶאֱמַר לְהַלָּן "לֹא תִקְרַב"** — **From where is all of this derived? For it is stated here** with regard to the *niddah, You shall not approach* (ibid. v. 19), **and it is stated there** with regard to other forbidden women, *You shall not approach* (ibid. v. 6), **לְדָבָר הַמֵּבִיא לִידֵי עֲבֵירָה לֹא** **תִקְרַב** — the implication being that **anything that might lead to sin you should not approach; הַרְחֵק מִן הַכִּיעוּר וּמִן הַדּוֹמֶה לַכִּיעוּר** — **keep far from what is morally repulsive, and even from** what **appears repulsive.**

to seclusion with an *ervah* of the type that a person might be improperly attracted to. It does not apply to an *ervah* that a person would not naturally be attracted to, such as his mother, sister, or daughter; see next note.]

14. [Even though there is no concern that a person might sin with his sister or daughter,] since not everyone [in an inn, where people in transit lodge (see *Hagahos Yaavetz*)] knows who this man's relatives are, his seclusion with this "unknown" woman might be misconstrued as forbidden (*Binyan Yehoshua*).

15. Here, both in the case of one's wife and in the case of another woman, the matter is not forbidden in and of itself; the concern is only what people will say (*Ben Avraham*).

16. Walking "behind a woman" — even one's own wife — is considered unseemly (see *Berachos* 66a). In context, our Baraisa

seems to be dealing with the more serious concern of sexual impropriety: One should not walk behind a woman so as not to evoke thoughts that might lead to sexual impropriety. And while this should not apply in the case of one's wife, one must be concerned of "what people might claim" — that on-lookers will not realize that she is his wife (see *Ahavas Chesed*).

In our text (and most others), the Baraisa begins here by speaking about walking "אַחַר" הָאִשָּׁה, "behind" a woman, and then shifts to "עִם" אִשְׁתּוֹ, "with" his wife, and "עִם" אִשָּׁה אַחֶרֶת, "with" another woman. See *Magen Avos* for a novel explanation of this reading. [In one manuscript, however, the Baraisa speaks both times of אַחַר, after.] *Gra* emends the text to read עִם, with, even the first time. Accordingly, the Baraisa speaks here not of *following* a woman but of walking *alongside* her, which is forbidden because

(לְפִיכָךְ) אָמְרוּ חֲכָמִים: הַרְחֵק מֵחֵטְא הַקַּל, שֶׁמָּא יְבִיאֲךָ לְחֵטְא
חָמוּר[17]. הֱוֵי רָץ לְמִצְוָה קַלָּה, שֶׁיְּבִיאֲךָ לְמִצְוָה רַבָּה[18]. הֲרֵי הוּא אוֹמֵר
(שיר השירים ז, ג) "בִּטְנֵךְ עֲרֵמַת חִטִּים סוּגָה בַּשּׁוֹשַׁנִּים", "בִּטְנֵךְ עֲרֵמַת
חִטִּים" זוֹ כְּנֶסֶת יִשְׂרָאֵל, "סוּגָה בַּשּׁוֹשַׁנִּים" אֵלּוּ שִׁבְעִים זְקֵנִים[19]. דָּבָר
אַחֵר, "בִּטְנֵךְ עֲרֵמַת חִטִּים" אֵלּוּ מִצְוֹת קַלּוֹת הָרַכּוֹת, "סוּגָה בַּשּׁוֹשַׁנִּים",
בִּזְמַן שֶׁיִּשְׂרָאֵל עוֹשִׂין אוֹתָן הָיוּ מְבִיאִים אוֹתָן לְחַיֵּי הָעוֹלָם הַבָּא.
הָא כֵּיצַד, אִשְׁתּוֹ נִדָּה עִמּוֹ בַּבַּיִת, רָצָה מְשַׁמֵּשׁ רָצָה אֵינוֹ מְשַׁמֵּשׁ,

---

A general rule derived from the above:

לְפִיכָךְ אָמְרוּ חֲכָמִים הַרְחֵק מֵחֵטְא הַקַּל שֶׁמָּא יְבִיאֲךָ לְחֵטְא חָמוּר — Therefore, the Sages said: Keep far from even **a small sin, lest it lead you to a grave sin.**[17] **הֱוֵי רָץ לְמִצְוָה קַלָּה שֶׁיְּבִיאֲךָ לְמִצְוָה רַבָּה — And conversely, run to perform** even **a** seemingly **small mitzvah, for** performing it **will lead you to** perform **a great mitzvah.**[18]

The Baraisa will cite and expound a verse in a way that relates to the earlier discussion of distancing oneself from a *niddah*:

הֲרֵי הוּא אוֹמֵר "בִּטְנֵךְ עֲרֵמַת חִטִּים סוּגָה בַּשּׁוֹשַׁנִּים" — See that it says, *Your stomach is like a heap of wheat, hedged about with roses* (*Song of Songs* 7:3). **"בִּטְנֵךְ עֲרֵמַת חִטִּים" זוֹ כְּנֶסֶת יִשְׂרָאֵל — *Your stomach is like a heap of wheat* refers to the Assembly of Israel;** **"סוּגָה בַּשּׁוֹשַׁנִּים" אֵלּוּ שִׁבְעִים זְקֵנִים — *hedged about with roses* refers to the seventy Elders** of Israel.[19] **דָּבָר אַחֵר: "בִּטְנֵךְ** **עֲרֵמַת חִטִּים" אֵלּוּ מִצְוֹת קַלּוֹת הָרַכּוֹת "סוּגָה בַּשּׁוֹשַׁנִּים"–Alternatively: *Your stomach is like a heap of wheat* refers to the mitzvos that are easy** to transgress, **and** protected by only a **soft fence, as if** *hedged about with roses,* which is easily breached[20] (as the Baraisa will soon explain); **בִּזְמַן שֶׁיִּשְׂרָאֵל עוֹשִׂין** **אוֹתָן הָיוּ מְבִיאִים אוֹתָן לְחַיֵּי הָעוֹלָם הַבָּא — when** the people of **Israel perform** [such mitzvos], **they bring them to the life of the World to Come.** **הָא כֵּיצַד —** **How is this?** The Baraisa illustrates: **אִשְׁתּוֹ נִדָּה עִמּוֹ בַּבַּיִת — When his wife is a** *niddah* **and alone with him in the house,** **רָצָה מְשַׁמֵּשׁ רָצָה אֵינוֹ מְשַׁמֵּשׁ —** he

---

people might suspect them of impropriety (see *Ben Avraham*).

17. From the fact that the Torah itself imposed protective fences around some of its laws, the Sages understood that this was the manner by which God wanted them to safeguard all other areas of the Torah as well (*Mesillas Yesharim* Ch. 11).

18. For if a minor sin can lead to a greater one, all the more so that a small mitzvah has the power to beget an even greater mitzvah, as the force of good is more far-reaching

than that of bad [see below, 30 §2] (*Ben Avraham*).

19. The people of Israel are treasured by God like wheat is by a farmer [unlike his less important grains (see *Shir HaShirim Rabbah* 7 §7)]. Just as wheat is protected by a fence, so are the Jewish people protected from transgressing the Torah's prohibitions by the safeguards enacted by the great men of the Sanhedrin, whose ways are beautiful like roses (see *Kisei Rachamim*).

20. *Mefaresh.*

וְכִי אָדָם רוֹאֵהוּ אוֹ אָדָם יוֹדֵעַ בּוֹ שֶׁיֹּאמַר לוֹ כְּלוּם, הָא אֵינוֹ מִתְיָרֵא אֶלָּא מִמִּי שֶׁפּוֹקֵד עַל הַטְּבִילָה. וְכֵן אַתָּה אוֹמֵר בַּחַלָּה²¹, וְכֵן אַתָּה אוֹמֵר בְּרֵאשִׁית הַגֵּז²². (אָמַר לֵיהּ) [נ״א אֵלּוּ] מִצְוֹת קַלּוֹת הָרַבּוֹת כַּשּׁוֹשַׁנִּים, שֶׁבִּזְמַן שֶׁיִּשְׂרָאֵל עוֹשִׂין אוֹתָן מְבִיאוֹת אוֹתָן לְחַיֵּי הָעוֹלָם הַבָּא²³:

ג. אֵיזוֹ סְיָיג שֶׁעָשָׂה מֹשֶׁה לִדְבָרָיו, הֲרֵי הוּא אוֹמֵר (שמות יט, י) "וַיֹּאמֶר ה' אֶל מֹשֶׁה לֵךְ אֶל הָעָם וְקִדַּשְׁתָּם הַיּוֹם וּמָחָר"²⁴, לֹא רָצָה מֹשֶׁה הַצַּדִּיק לוֹמַר לָהֶם לְיִשְׂרָאֵל כְּדֶרֶךְ שֶׁאָמַר (לָהֶם) [לוֹ] הַקָּדוֹשׁ בָּרוּךְ הוּא,

is free to choose **whether or not to cohabit with her,** yet he refrains. **וְכִי** — Now, **is there anybody** there who **אָדָם רוֹאֵהוּ אוֹ אָדָם יוֹדֵעַ בּוֹ שֶׁיֹּאמַר לוֹ כְּלוּם** would see him, or anybody who would know what he is doing that would say anything to him should he wish to transgress? **הָא אֵינוֹ מִתְיָרֵא אֶלָּא מִמִּי שֶׁפּוֹקֵד עַל הַטְּבִילָה** — Why, he is afraid only of the One Who commanded that a *niddah* shall not cohabit until her **immersion** in the *mikveh,* and that is the sole reason he refrains! **וְכֵן אַתָּה אוֹמֵר בַּחַלָּה** — And so can you say regarding the obligation to separate *challah* for the Kohen from one's dough,[21] **וְכֵן אַתָּה אוֹמֵר בְּרֵאשִׁית הַגֵּז** — and so can you say regarding the obligation to give **the first shearings** of one's flock to a Kohen.[22] **אֵלּוּ מִצְוֹת קַלּוֹת הָרַבּוֹת כַּשּׁוֹשַׁנִּים** — These are some of the mitzvos that are easy to transgress in private and are protected by fences **soft like roses,** **שֶׁבִּזְמַן שֶׁיִּשְׂרָאֵל עוֹשִׂין אוֹתָן** **מְבִיאוֹת אוֹתָן לְחַיֵּי הָעוֹלָם הַבָּא** — and that when the people of Israel perform them, they bring them to the life of the World to Come.[23]

§3 The Baraisa discusses the next one in its list of those who made fences around their words:

אֵיזוֹ סְיָיג שֶׁעָשָׂה מֹשֶׁה לִדְבָרָיו — What is an example of **a protective fence that Moses made around his words?** **הֲרֵי הוּא אוֹמֵר "וַיֹּאמֶר ה' אֶל מֹשֶׁה לֵךְ אֶל הָעָם וְקִדַּשְׁתָּם הַיּוֹם וּמָחָר"** — It says in Scripture, *HASHEM said to Moses, "Go to the people and sanctify them today and tomorrow"* (Exodus 19:10).[24] **לֹא רָצָה מֹשֶׁה הַצַּדִּיק לוֹמַר לָהֶם לְיִשְׂרָאֵל כְּדֶרֶךְ שֶׁאָמַר לוֹ הַקָּדוֹשׁ בָּרוּךְ הוּא** — The **righteous Moses did not want to tell** the message **to the people of Israel**

---

21. See *Numbers* 15:17-21.

22. See *Deuteronomy* 18:4.

Neither of these gifts needs to be given to a specific Kohen, so no one would know if the person did not give them at all. The fact that the Jewish people are, nonetheless, meticulous to keep these easily transgressed mitzvos attests to their fear of God, Who commanded them (see further in *Ben Avraham*).

23. The fear of God demonstrated by the performance of each of these mitzvos is, in its own right, enough to earn a person a share in the World to Come (*Kisei Rachamim*).

24. That is, they are to purify themselves from *tumah* and also abstain from conjugal relations, which cause both husband and wife to become *tamei.* By purifying themselves as commanded, they would all receive the Torah in a state of purity.

[A variant version of this Baraisa is

אֶלָּא כָּךְ אָמַר לָהֶם: (שם פסוק טו) "הֱיוּ נְכֹנִים לִשְׁלֹשֶׁת יָמִים אַל תִּגְּשׁוּ
אֶל אִשָּׁה", וְהוֹסִיף לָהֶם מֹשֶׁה יוֹם אֶחָד מֵעַצְמוֹ.[25] (אֶלָּא כָּךְ) אָמַר
מֹשֶׁה: יֵלֵךְ אִישׁ אֵצֶל אִשְׁתּוֹ וְתֵצֵא מִמֶּנָּה שִׁכְבַת זֶרַע בַּיּוֹם הַשְּׁלִישִׁי[26]
וְיִהְיוּ טְמֵאִים וְנִמְצָא יִשְׂרָאֵל מְקַבְּלִים דִּבְרֵי תוֹרָה בְּטוּמְאָה מֵהַר
סִינַי, אֶלָּא אוֹסִיף לָהֶם יוֹם שְׁלִישִׁי[27] (כְּדֵי שֶׁלֹּא יֵלֵךְ אִישׁ אֵצֶל אִשְׁתּוֹ

in exactly the same way that the Holy One, Blessed is He, told it to him;
אֶלָּא כָּךְ אָמַר לָהֶם "הֱיוּ נְכֹנִים לִשְׁלֹשֶׁת יָמִים אַל תִּגְּשׁוּ אֶל אִשָּׁה" — rather, this
is what he said to them: *Be prepared for after a three-day period; do not
draw near a woman* (ibid. v. 15). וְהוֹסִיף לָהֶם מֹשֶׁה יוֹם אֶחָד מֵעַצְמוֹ — And
in this way Moses added one day on his own to the simple meaning of God's
words.[25] אָמַר מֹשֶׁה — Moses reasoned as follows: יֵלֵךְ אִישׁ אֵצֶל אִשְׁתּוֹ
וְתֵצֵא מִמֶּנָּה שִׁכְבַת זֶרַע בַּיּוֹם הַשְּׁלִישִׁי — "If I tell them exactly the words that God
said, perhaps a man will go and cohabit with his wife today, and contaminat-
ing semen might issue from her on the third day after cohabitation — on
the day that the Torah is given.[26] וְיִהְיוּ טְמֵאִים — Then [these women] will
be *tamei*, וְנִמְצָא יִשְׂרָאֵל מְקַבְּלִים דִּבְרֵי תוֹרָה בְּטוּמְאָה מֵהַר סִינַי — and it will
emerge that some of the women of Israel will receive the words of the Torah
in a state of *tumah* at Mount Sinai! אֶלָּא אוֹסִיף לָהֶם יוֹם שְׁלִישִׁי — Rather
than have this occur, I will add a third day,[27] כְּדֵי שֶׁלֹּא יֵלֵךְ אִישׁ אֵצֶל אִשְׁתּוֹ
— so that no man will go and cohabit with his wife during the remainder of

---

discussed at length by the Gemara in *Shabbos* (87a ff.). We will explain the Baraisa, as it
appears here, according to the commentary
of *Ahavas Chesed*.] Moses was to tell this
command to them on Wednesday; the Torah
would be given on the Sabbath (see Gemara
there).

25. God's actual words, הַיּוֹם וּמָחָר, *today
and tomorrow*, imply only two days of abstinence. Moses, however, told them to be prepared *for after a three-day period*, so that his
way of relaying the command would make
them abstain for three days, not only two.

26. Semen that issues from a woman within
72 hours after cohabitation renders her *tamei*. [After 72 hours, the semen in her body
is considered rancid and no longer viable,
and its issuing from her does not render her
tamei.]
   Moses reasoned that God's words הַיּוֹם
וּמָחָר, *today and tomorrow*, told to the people on Wednesday morning (see *Shabbos*

86a), would be construed (correctly) by
the people to mean two *full* days (night followed by day), meaning the entire Thursday
and the entire Friday, for just as "tomorrow"
is a full day, so too "today" (*Shabbos* ibid.).
"Today" could not refer to Wednesday, the
day the command was announced, because
the first half of that day (the preceding
night) had already passed. Understood this
way, the people would think (incorrectly)
that conjugal relations were permitted for
the remainder of Wednesday. And if so, a
woman who had conjugal relations during
the remainder of Wednesday might emit
semen toward the end of 72 hours and thus
be *tamei* when the Torah was given on Sabbath morning.

27. I.e., I will phrase God's command as *be
prepared for after a three-day period*, which
will indicate to the people that they are to
abstain *from this point forward*, even for the
remainder of this day, Wednesday.

וְלֹא תֵצֵא מִמֶּנָּה שִׁכְבַת זֶרַע בַּיּוֹם הַשְּׁלִישִׁי וְיִהְיוּ טְהוֹרִים (וְנִמְצְאוּ
מְקַבְּלִין תּוֹרָה בְּטָהֳרָה מֵהַר סִינַי)[28]. זֶה אֶחָד מֵהַדְּבָרִים שֶׁעָשָׂה מֹשֶׁה
מִדַּעְתּוֹ (דִּין ק״ו) וְהִסְכִּימָה דַּעְתּוֹ לְדַעַת הַמָּקוֹם. שָׁבַר אֶת הַלּוּחוֹת
וְהִסְכִּימָה דַּעְתּוֹ לְדַעַת הַמָּקוֹם. פֵּירֵשׁ [מִן] אֹהֶל מוֹעֵד וְהִסְכִּימָה
דַּעְתּוֹ לְדַעַת הַמָּקוֹם. פֵּירֵשׁ מִן הָאִשָּׁה וְהִסְכִּימָה דַּעְתּוֹ לְדַעַת הַמָּקוֹם.
כֵּיצַד, אָמַר: מָה אִם יִשְׂרָאֵל שֶׁלֹּא נִתְקַדְּשׁוּ אֶלָּא לְפִי שָׁעָה וְלֹא
נִזְדַּמְּנוּ אֶלָּא כְּדֵי לְקַבֵּל עֲלֵיהֶם עֲשֶׂרֶת הַדִּבְּרוֹת מֵהַר סִינַי, אָמַר לִי
הַקָּדוֹשׁ בָּרוּךְ הוּא: (שם פסוק י) "לֵךְ אֶל הָעָם וְקִדַּשְׁתָּם הַיּוֹם וּמָחָר",

וְלֹא תֵצֵא מִמֶּנָּה שִׁכְבַת זֶרַע בַּיּוֹם הַשְּׁלִישִׁי וְיִהְיוּ the day the command is given, **and then no viable semen will issue from [any woman]** on the third day, when the Torah is given, **and they will all be** *tahor,* וְנִמְצְאוּ מְקַבְּלִין תּוֹרָה בְּטָהֳרָה מֵהַר סִינַי — **and it will** thus **emerge that all of Israel will receive the words of the Torah in purity at Mount Sinai.**"[28]

The Baraisa notes:

זֶה אֶחָד מֵהַדְּבָרִים שֶׁעָשָׂה מֹשֶׁה מִדַּעְתּוֹ — **This** "addition" of a third day **was one of the things that Moses did on the basis of his own understanding** (i.e., without having been explicitly commanded to do so), וְהִסְכִּימָה דַּעְתּוֹ לְדַעַת הַמָּקוֹם — **and** in each case, **his understanding agreed with God's Will.** The other instances are: שָׁבַר אֶת הַלּוּחוֹת וְהִסְכִּימָה דַּעְתּוֹ לְדַעַת הַמָּקוֹם — **(i) He smashed the First Tablets, and his understanding** in this matter **agreed with God's Will;** פֵּירֵשׁ מִן אֹהֶל מוֹעֵד וְהִסְכִּימָה דַּעְתּוֹ לְדַעַת הַמָּקוֹם — **(ii) he separated from the Tent of Meeting, and his understanding** in this matter **agreed with God's Will;** פֵּירֵשׁ מִן הָאִשָּׁה וְהִסְכִּימָה דַּעְתּוֹ לְדַעַת הַמָּקוֹם — **(iii) and he separated from his wife, and his understanding** in this matter **agreed with God's Will.**

The Baraisa elaborates on these three things, beginning with the last:

כֵּיצַד — "**He separated from his wife, and his understanding agreed with God's Will**" — **how so?** אָמַר — [Moses] **reasoned:** מָה אִם יִשְׂרָאֵל שֶׁלֹּא נִתְקַדְּשׁוּ אֶלָּא לְפִי שָׁעָה — "**If** regarding **the people of Israel** — who were commanded to be **sanctified only temporarily,** וְלֹא נִזְדַּמְּנוּ אֶלָּא כְּדֵי לְקַבֵּל עֲלֵיהֶם עֲשֶׂרֶת הַדִּבְּרוֹת מֵהַר סִינַי — **as they were being prepared only to be able to accept upon themselves the Ten Commandments at Mount Sinai** — אָמַר לִי הַקָּדוֹשׁ בָּרוּךְ הוּא — **the Holy One, Blessed is He, told me,** *Go* "לֵךְ אֶל הָעָם וְקִדַּשְׁתָּם הַיּוֹם וּמָחָר" — *the Holy One, Blessed is He, told me, Go*

---

28. Thus, Moses "added" a day to God's command, by phrasing it in such a way that the people would realize that they were to abstain from that point forward until the Giving of the Torah. And he thus made "a fence" around the words of God that he was to relay to the people, so that they not be misunderstood. [Note that the Gemara in *Shabbos* 87a (as explained by *Rashi*) understands "Moses added a day on his own" differently, and not in the sense of "a protective fence."]

וַאֲנִי שֶׁאֲנִי מְזוּמָּן לְךָ בְּכָל יוֹם וָיוֹם וּבְכָל שָׁעָה, וְאֵינִי יוֹדֵעַ אֵימָתַי מְדַבֵּר
עִמִּי אוֹ בַּיּוֹם אוֹ בַּלַּיְלָה²⁹, עַל אַחַת כַּמָּה וְכַמָּה שֶׁאֶפְרוֹשׁ מִן הָאִשָּׁה³⁰,
וְהִסְכִּימָה דַעְתּוֹ לְדַעַת הַמָּקוֹם³¹. רַבִּי יְהוּדָה בֶּן בְּתֵירָא אוֹמֵר: לֹא פֵּירֵשׁ
מֹשֶׁה מִן הָאִשָּׁה אֶלָּא³² שֶׁנֶּאֶמְרָה לוֹ מִפִּי הַגְּבוּרָה, שֶׁנֶּאֱמַר (במדבר יב, ח)
"פֶּה אֶל פֶּה אֲדַבֶּר בּוֹ", פֶּה אֶל פֶּה אָמַרְתִּי לוֹ פְּרוֹשׁ מִן הָאִשָּׁה וּפֵירַשׁ³³.

---

to the people and sanctify them today and tomorrow (ibid. v. 10), meaning that they should purify themselves and abstain from conjugal relations, **וַאֲנִי** **שֶׁאֲנִי מְזוּמָּן לְךָ בְּכָל יוֹם וָיוֹם וּבְכָל שָׁעָה** — then I, who must be prepared for this level of God's revelation **every single day and every single moment,** **וְאֵינִי יוֹדֵעַ** **אֵימָתַי מְדַבֵּר עִמִּי אוֹ בַּיּוֹם אוֹ בַּלַּיְלָה** — and am unsure of when He will speak to me next, **whether by day or by night,**[29] **עַל אַחַת כַּמָּה וְכַמָּה שֶׁאֶפְרוֹשׁ מִן הָאִשָּׁה** — all the more so that I should separate from my wife!"[30] **וְהִסְכִּימָה דַעְתּוֹ** **לְדַעַת הַמָּקוֹם** — And his understanding in this matter agreed with God's Will.[31]

The Baraisa continues:

לֹא פֵּירֵשׁ מֹשֶׁה — R' Yehudah ben Beseira says: **רַבִּי יְהוּדָה בֶּן בְּתֵירָא אוֹמֵר** **מִן הָאִשָּׁה אֶלָּא שֶׁנֶּאֶמְרָה לוֹ מִפִּי הַגְּבוּרָה** — Moses did not separate from his wife on his own; rather,[32] he was expressly told to do so from the mouth of the Almighty, **שֶׁנֶּאֱמַר "פֶּה אֶל פֶּה אֲדַבֶּר בּוֹ"** — as it says, *Mouth to mouth do I speak to him* (*Numbers* 12:8), **פֶּה אֶל פֶּה אָמַרְתִּי לוֹ פְּרוֹשׁ מִן הָאִשָּׁה וּפֵירַשׁ** — which means, "From My mouth to his mouth (i.e., explicitly), I said to him, 'Separate from your wife,' and he separated."[33]

---

29. All other prophets needed to prepare themselves prior to receiving prophecy, and would therefore always know when God might come to speak with them. Moses, however, was *always* on such a high level that he did not need such preparation, and could receive prophecy unexpectedly at any time (see *Avos HaRosh* [Vol. 1]; see also *Ramban* to *Numbers* 24:4).

30. "Permanent" sanctity is higher than "temporary" sanctity (*Ben Avraham*). Since I must be ready for Divine revelation at any time, that should preclude conjugal relations with my wife.

31. [The verses that the Baraisa cites next indicate that this was God's intent.]

32. Some texts have here עַד, *until* [as in the Baraisa further] and this is the reading of *Gra* as well. We have preserved the reading אֶלָּא, *rather,* but explained it to mean essentially the same thing as עַד, *until.* (See, though,

Ben Avraham and *Magen Avos* at length.)

33. Miriam and Aaron criticized Moses for separating from his wife, saying (*Numbers* 12:2): *Was it only to Moses that HASHEM spoke? Did He not speak to us, as well?* (i.e., we, too, are prophets, yet we did not separate from our spouses). God reprimanded them and said (ibid. vv. 6-8): *Hear now My words. If there shall be prophets among you, in a vision shall I, HASHEM, make Myself known to him; in a dream shall I speak with him. Not so is My servant Moses; in My entire house he is the trusted one. Mouth to mouth do I speak to him ...* R' Yehudah ben Beseira expounds that God was telling them that what Moses did in separating from his wife was something He had instructed Moses "mouth to mouth" to do (see *Maharsha* to *Shabbos* 87a).

Thus, R' Yehudah ben Beseira says that although Moses did indeed arrive on his own

יֵשׁ אוֹמְרִים: לֹא פֵּירַשׁ מֹשֶׁה מִן הָאִשָּׁה עַד שֶׁנֶּאֱמַר לוֹ מִפִּי הַגְּבוּרָה, שֶׁנֶּאֱמַר
(דברים ה, כז) "לֵךְ אֱמֹר לָהֶם שׁוּבוּ לָכֶם לְאָהֳלֵיכֶם", וּכְתִיב בַּתְרֵיהּ (שם פסוק
כח) "וְאַתָּה פֹּה עֲמֹד עִמָּדִי"[34], חָזַר לַאֲחוֹרָיו וּפֵירַשׁ וְהִסְכִּימָה דַעְתּוֹ לְדַעַת
הַמָּקוֹם. פֵּירַשׁ מֵאֹהֶל מוֹעֵד, כֵּיצַד, אָמַר: וּמָה אַהֲרֹן אָחִי שֶׁמָּשׁוּחַ בְּשֶׁמֶן
הַמִּשְׁחָה וּמְרוּבֶּה בִּבְגָדִים וּמִשְׁתַּמֵּשׁ בָּהֶם בִּקְדוּשָׁה[35], אָמַר לוֹ הַקָּדוֹשׁ
בָּרוּךְ הוּא: (ויקרא טז, ב) "דַּבֵּר אֶל אַהֲרֹן אָחִיךָ וְאַל יָבֹא בְכָל עֵת אֶל הַקֹּדֶשׁ",
אֲנִי שֶׁאֵינִי מְזוּמָּן לְכָךְ עַל אַחַת כַּמָּה וְכַמָּה שֶׁאֶפְרוֹשׁ מֵאֹהֶל מוֹעֵד.

A different source:

יֵשׁ אוֹמְרִים: לֹא פֵּירַשׁ מֹשֶׁה מִן הָאִשָּׁה עַד שֶׁנֶּאֱמַר לוֹ מִפִּי הַגְּבוּרָה — And some say: Moses did not separate from his wife until he was expressly **told** to do so from the mouth of the Almighty, **שֶׁנֶּאֱמַר "לֵךְ אֱמֹר לָהֶם שׁוּבוּ לָכֶם לְאָהֳלֵיכֶם"** — as it says that God told him after the Giving of the Torah at Sinai, *Go say to [the people], "Return to your tents"* (Deuteronomy 5:27), **וּכְתִיב בַּתְרֵיהּ** **"וְאַתָּה פֹּה עֲמֹד עִמָּדִי"** — and it is written immediately after that, *But as for you, stand here with Me* (ibid. v. 28).[34] **חָזַר לַאֲחוֹרָיו וּפֵירַשׁ וְהִסְכִּימָה דַעְתּוֹ לְדַעַת הַמָּקוֹם** — So after conveying God's message to the Jewish people, [Moses] turned back toward Mount Sinai, and from then on remained separated from his wife; thus, it emerges that his earlier understanding in this matter agreed with God's Will.

The Baraisa expounds the second thing that Moses did on his own: **פֵּירַשׁ מֵאֹהֶל מוֹעֵד, כֵּיצַד** – "He separated from the Tent of Meeting, and his understanding agreed with God's Will" — how so? **אָמַר: וּמָה אַהֲרֹן אָחִי** — [Moses] reasoned: "If regarding my brother Aaron — **שֶׁמָּשׁוּחַ בְּשֶׁמֶן הַמִּשְׁחָה** — who has been sanctified through being anointed with the holy Anointing Oil **וּמְרוּבֶּה בִּבְגָדִים** — and through being robed with more priestly vestments than are standard Kohanim, **וּמִשְׁתַּמֵּשׁ בָּהֶם בִּקְדוּשָׁה** — and who may use them only during the sacred Tabernacle service[35] — **אָמַר לוֹ הַקָּדוֹשׁ בָּרוּךְ הוּא** — the Holy One, Blessed is He, told me, *Speak to Aaron, your brother* — he shall not come at all times into the Sanctuary* (Leviticus 16:2), **"דַּבֵּר אֶל אַהֲרֹן אָחִיךָ וְאַל יָבֹא בְכָל עֵת אֶל הַקֹּדֶשׁ"** — then I — who **אֲנִי שֶׁאֵינִי מְזוּמָּן לְכָךְ** am not privileged to this level of sanctity — **עַל אַחַת כַּמָּה וְכַמָּה שֶׁאֶפְרוֹשׁ** — all the more so that I should separate myself from the Tent of **מֵאֹהֶל מוֹעֵד**

---

at the idea of separating from his wife, he did not implement it until God specifically instructed him to do so (*Ben Avraham* [according to the reading עַד]).

34. That is, while the rest of the people could "return to their tents" (i.e., resume conjugal

relations), Moses was not to do so, but rather was to remain with God on Mount Sinai.

35. Wearing clothing that was used exclusively for the sacred service, as well as donning extra priestly garments and being anointed with holy oil, all increased Aaron's personal

פֵּירַשׁ מֵאֹהֶל מוֹעֵד, וְהִסְכִּימָה דַעְתּוֹ לְדַעַת הַמָּקוֹם. שָׁבַר אֶת הַלּוּחוֹת,
כֵּיצַד, אָמְרוּ: בְּשָׁעָה שֶׁעָלָה מֹשֶׁה לַמָּרוֹם לְקַבֵּל אֶת הַלּוּחוֹת שֶׁהֵן כְּתוּבוֹת
וּמוּנָּחוֹת מְשֵׁשֶׁת יְמֵי בְרֵאשִׁית‎[37], שֶׁנֶּאֱמַר (שמות לב, טז) ״וְהַלֻּחֹת מַעֲשֵׂה
אֱלֹהִים הֵמָּה וְהַמִּכְתָּב מִכְתַּב אֱלֹהִים הוּא חָרוּת עַל הַלֻּחֹת״‎[38], אַל תִּקְרֵי
״חָרוּת״ אֶלָּא ״חֵירוּת״, שֶׁכָּל מִי שֶׁעוֹסֵק בַּתּוֹרָה הֲרֵי הוּא בֶן חוֹרִין
לְעַצְמוֹ‎[39], בְּאוֹתָהּ שָׁעָה הָיוּ מַלְאֲכֵי הַשָּׁרֵת קוֹשְׁרִין קַטֵיגוֹר עַל מֹשֶׁה,

---

פֵּירַשׁ מֵאֹהֶל מוֹעֵד וְהִסְכִּימָה Meeting and not just enter it whenever I wish."
דַעְתּוֹ לְדַעַת הַמָּקוֹם — So he separated himself from the Tent of Meeting, and
his understanding in this matter agreed with God's Will, as evidenced by the
fact that God never reprimanded him for doing so.[36]

The Baraisa expounds the third thing that Moses did on his own:
שָׁבַר אֶת הַלּוּחוֹת, כֵּיצַד — "He smashed the First Tablets, and his understanding agreed with God's Will" — how so? **אָמְרוּ בְּשָׁעָה שֶׁעָלָה מֹשֶׁה לַמָּרוֹם לְקַבֵּל**
אֶת הַלּוּחוֹת — [The Sages] said: When Moses ascended to heaven to receive
the Tablets, **שֶׁהֵן כְּתוּבוֹת וּמוּנָּחוֹת מְשֵׁשֶׁת יְמֵי בְרֵאשִׁית** — which were written
and stored away from the Six Days of Creation,[37] **שֶׁנֶּאֱמַר ״וְהַלֻּחֹת מַעֲשֵׂה**
אֱלֹהִים הֵמָּה וְהַמִּכְתָּב מִכְתַּב אֱלֹהִים הוּא חָרוּת עַל הַלֻּחֹת״ — as it says, *The Tab-*
lets were God's handiwork, and the script was the script of God, engraved
[חָרוּת] *on the Tablets* (*Exodus* 32:16).[38]

The Baraisa interrupts its narrative to offer a homiletical interpretation of the
verse just cited:
אַל תִּקְרֵי ״חָרוּת״ אֶלָּא ״חֵירוּת״ — For purposes of exposition, do not read the
word as *charus* [חָרוּת], which means "engraved," but as *cheirus* [חֵרוּת], which
means "freedom." **שֶׁכָּל מִי שֶׁעוֹסֵק בַּתּוֹרָה הֲרֵי הוּא בֶן חוֹרִין לְעַצְמוֹ** — This
indicates that anyone who involves himself in the study of Torah is a truly free
person for himself.[39]

The Baraisa resumes its narrative:
בְּאוֹתָהּ שָׁעָה הָיוּ מַלְאֲכֵי הַשָּׁרֵת קוֹשְׁרִין קַטֵיגוֹר עַל מֹשֶׁה — At that time, the
ministering angels came together to begin prosecution against Moses in

---

sanctity, and should have reasonably permitted him to enter any part of the Tabernacle
whenever he so desired (*Ben Avraham*).

36. *Binyan Yehoshua.*

37. The Baraisa mentions the glorious origin
of the Tablets so that we should appreciate how impressive it was that Moses was
ready to smash them for the sole purpose of
sparing his brethren from punishment (see
further). It is for this same reason that the
Baraisa below describes how strongly the

angels protested against the Tablets being
given to mere mortals (*Ben Avraham*).

38. Calling them "God's handiwork" shows
that the Tablets were created during the Six
Days of Creation, for after that time, God
did not form any new creations in His world
(*Binyan Yehoshua*).

39. The Torah allows one's true identity
— his soul — to be free, and not enslaved
by the whims of his body (*Tiferes Yisrael* to
Pirkei Avos 6:2).

וְהָיוּ אוֹמְרִים: רִבּוֹנוֹ שֶׁל עוֹלָם, (תהלים ח, ה־ט) "מָה אֱנוֹשׁ כִּי תִזְכְּרֶנּוּ וּבֶן
אָדָם כִּי תִפְקְדֶנּוּ וַתְּחַסְּרֵהוּ מְּעַט מֵאֱלֹהִים וְכָבוֹד וְהָדָר תְּעַטְּרֵהוּ תַּמְשִׁילֵהוּ
בְּמַעֲשֵׂי יָדֶיךָ כֹּל שַׁתָּה תַחַת רַגְלָיו צֹנֶה וַאֲלָפִים כֻּלָּם וְגַם בַּהֲמוֹת שָׂדָי
צִפּוֹר שָׁמַיִם וּדְגֵי הַיָּם"[40], הָיוּ מְרַנְּנִים אַחֲרָיו שֶׁל מֹשֶׁה, וְהָיוּ אוֹמְרִים: מַה
טִּיבוֹ שֶׁל יְלוּד אִשָּׁה שֶׁעָלָה לַמָּרוֹם, שֶׁנֶּאֱמַר (שם סח, יט) "עָלִיתָ לַמָּרוֹם
שָׁבִיתָ שֶּׁבִי לָקַחְתָּ מַתָּנוֹת"[41]. נְטָלָן וְיָרַד וְהָיָה שָׂמֵחַ שִׂמְחָה גְדוֹלָה, כֵּיוָן
שֶׁרָאָה אוֹתוֹ סִרְחוֹן שֶׁסֵּרְחוּ בְּמַעֲשֵׂה הָעֵגֶל, אָמַר: הֵיאַךְ אֲנִי נוֹתֵן לָהֶם אֶת
הַלּוּחוֹת, מַזְקִיקְנִי אוֹתָן לְמִצְוֹת חֲמוּרוֹת, וּמְחַיְּבָנִי אוֹתָן מִיתָה לַשָּׁמַיִם,

---

וְהָיוּ אוֹמְרִים: רִבּוֹנוֹ שֶׁל — order to prevent him from being given the Tablets,
עוֹלָם — claiming before God, "Master מָה אֱנוֹשׁ כִּי תִזְכְּרֶנּוּ וּבֶן אָדָם כִּי תִפְקְדֶנּוּ
of the Universe! *What is frail man that You should remember him, and the
son of mortal man that You should be mindful of him?* וַתְּחַסְּרֵהוּ מְּעַט
Yet, You have made him but slightly less than — מֵאֱלֹהִים וְכָבוֹד וְהָדָר תְּעַטְּרֵהוּ
the angels, and crowned him with soul and splendor. תַּמְשִׁילֵהוּ בְּמַעֲשֵׂי
יָדֶיךָ — *You give him dominion over Your handiwork, You* כֹּל שַׁתָּה תַחַת רַגְלָיו
placed everything under his feet: צֹנֶה וַאֲלָפִים כֻּלָּם וְגַם בַּהֲמוֹת שָׂדָי — *sheep
and cattle, all of them, even the beasts of the field;* צִפּוֹר שָׁמַיִם וּדְגֵי הַיָּם" —
the birds of the sky and the fish of the sea" (Psalms 8:5-9).[40] הָיוּ מְרַנְּנִים
— They were murmuring about Moses וְהָיוּ אוֹמְרִים: מַה טִּיבוֹ
שֶׁל יְלוּד אִשָּׁה שֶׁעָלָה לַמָּרוֹם — and they were saying, "What is the exalted
nature of this man born of woman, that he should have ascended on High?,"
שֶׁנֶּאֱמַר "עָלִיתָ לַמָּרוֹם שָׁבִיתָ שֶּׁבִי לָקַחְתָּ מַתָּנוֹת" — as it says, *You ascended on
High, You have taken captives, You took gifts* (ibid. 68:19).[41] נְטָלָן וְיָרַד
וְהָיָה שָׂמֵחַ שִׂמְחָה גְדוֹלָה — Moses then took [the Tablets] and descended with
them from on High feeling great joy. כֵּיוָן שֶׁרָאָה אוֹתוֹ סִרְחוֹן שֶׁסֵּרְחוּ בְּמַעֲשֵׂה
הָעֵגֶל — But as soon as he saw the blunder of the Israelites into which they had
fallen by making the Golden Calf, אָמַר: הֵיאַךְ אֲנִי נוֹתֵן לָהֶם אֶת הַלּוּחוֹת — he
said to himself, "How can I give the Tablets to them? מַזְקִיקְנִי אוֹתָן לְמִצְוֹת
חֲמוּרוֹת — I will thereby be making them subject to its many strict commandments, such as the one against idolatry that they have just violated, וּמְחַיְּבָנִי
אוֹתָן מִיתָה לַשָּׁמַיִם — and making them liable to death at the hand of Heaven

---

40. [*You give him dominion over "Your
handiwork"* is an allusion to the Tablets,
which are called *God's handiwork* in the
verse cited above.]

41. An allusion to Moses, who ascended
to the Heavens, "captured" the Torah, and
then took it with him down to earth in order

to present it as a gift to the Jewish people
(*Rashi* ad loc.).

Referring to the Tablets as "captives" indicates that Moses faced strong opposition
when taking them; hence, the proof that the
angels protested (*Ahavas Chesed*, first approach; *Ben Avraham*).

שֶׁכֵּן כָּתוּב בָּהֶן (שמות כ, ג) "לֹא יִהְיֶה לְךָ אֱלֹהִים אֲחֵרִים עַל פָּנָי".⁴² חָזַר
לַאֲחוֹרָיו וְרָאוּ אוֹתוֹ שִׁבְעִים זְקֵנִים וְרָצוּ אַחֲרָיו, הוּא אָחַז בְּרֹאשׁ הַלּוּחַ וְהֵן
אָחֲזוּ בְּרֹאשׁ הַלּוּחַ, חָזַק כֹּחוֹ שֶׁל מֹשֶׁה מִכּוּלָן,⁴³ שֶׁנֶּאֱמַר (דברים לד, יב) "וּלְכֹל
הַיָּד הַחֲזָקָה וּלְכֹל הַמּוֹרָא הַגָּדוֹל אֲשֶׁר עָשָׂה מֹשֶׁה לְעֵינֵי כָּל יִשְׂרָאֵל".⁴⁴
(נִסְתַּכֵּל בָּהֶן וְרָאָה שֶׁפָּרַח כְּתָב מֵעֲלֵיהֶן,⁴⁵ אָמַר: הֵיאַךְ אֲנִי נוֹתֵן לָהֶם
לְיִשְׂרָאֵל אֶת הַלּוּחוֹת שֶׁאֵין בָּהֶם מַמָּשׁ, אֶלָּא אָאֱחוֹז וַאֲשַׁבְּרֵם, שֶׁנֶּאֱמַר
(שם ט, יז) "וָאֶתְפֹּשׂ בִּשְׁנֵי הַלֻּחֹת וָאַשְׁלִכֵם מֵעַל שְׁתֵּי יָדָי וָאֲשַׁבְּרֵם").⁴⁶

for that violation! שֶׁכֵּן כָּתוּב בָּהֶן "לֹא יִהְיֶה לְךָ אֱלֹהִים אֲחֵרִים עַל פָּנָי" — **For so it is written in [the Tablets],** *You shall not recognize the gods of others in My presence" (Exodus 20:3).*[42] חָזַר לַאֲחוֹרָיו — **Whereupon [Moses] turned back** with the Tablets so as to keep them from the Jewish people. וְרָאוּ אוֹתוֹ שִׁבְעִים זְקֵנִים וְרָצוּ אַחֲרָיו — **But the Seventy Elders saw him retreating and ran after him** to prevent him from withholding the Tablets from the people. הוּא אָחַז בְּרֹאשׁ הַלּוּחַ וְהֵן אָחֲזוּ בְּרֹאשׁ הַלּוּחַ — **A struggle ensued. He grasped one end of the Tablet and they grasped the other end of the Tablet.** חָזַק כֹּחוֹ שֶׁל מֹשֶׁה מִכּוּלָן — **Finally, Moses' strength overpowered all of theirs,**[43] שֶׁנֶּאֱמַר "וּלְכֹל הַיָּד הַחֲזָקָה וּלְכֹל הַמּוֹרָא הַגָּדוֹל אֲשֶׁר עָשָׂה מֹשֶׁה לְעֵינֵי כָּל יִשְׂרָאֵל" — **as it says,** *And by all the strong hand and awesome power that Moses performed before the eyes of all Israel (Deuteronomy 34:12).*[44] נִסְתַּכֵּל בָּהֶן וְרָאָה שֶׁפָּרַח כְּתָב מֵעֲלֵיהֶן — **But though Moses had wrested control of the Tablets, he looked carefully at them and saw that the writing had flown from them.**[45] אָמַר הֵיאַךְ אֲנִי נוֹתֵן לָהֶם לְיִשְׂרָאֵל אֶת הַלּוּחוֹת שֶׁאֵין בָּהֶם מַמָּשׁ — **He said, "How can I give the people of Israel these Tablets that have nothing of substance on them?** אֶלָּא אָאֱחוֹז וַאֲשַׁבְּרֵם — **Rather, I shall take hold of them and cast them down to smash them,"** שֶׁנֶּאֱמַר "וָאֶתְפֹּשׂ בִּשְׁנֵי הַלֻּחֹת וָאַשְׁלִכֵם מֵעַל שְׁתֵּי יָדָי וָאֲשַׁבְּרֵם" — **as it is stated,** *I grasped the two Tablets and threw them from my two hands, and I smashed them (ibid. 9:17-18).*[46]

---

42. [And by not giving them the Tablets, which symbolize the covenant that binds them to those laws, it will be as if the covenant with them was never sealed, as in the Baraisa's parable below.]

43. [In one manuscript, the reading is מִכֹּחָן, *their strength.*]

44. That is, with the strength of his hand, Moses overpowered the "eyes of all Israel," i.e., the Elders, who are like the "eyes" of the Jewish people [for just as the body follows its eyes, so do the Jewish people follow their spiritual leaders; see *Shir HaShirim Rabbah*

1 §63] (*Avos HaRosh* [Vol. 1]).

45. For the Divine inscription departed as soon as it came in close proximity with idolatry, for holiness cannot abide depravity (ibid.).

Possibly, the meaning is that the Tablets became entirely blank. Alternatively, it may be that the engraving was still present, but the spiritual element that had suffused it was gone (see *Magen Avos* and *Avos HaRosh* [Vol. 1]).

46. By saying that he first "grasped" the Tablets before smashing them, Moses

רַבִּי יוֹסֵי הַגְּלִילִי אוֹמֵר: אֶמְשׁוֹל לְךָ מָשָׁל לְמָה הַדָּבָר דּוֹמֶה, לְמֶלֶךְ בָּשָׂר
וָדָם שֶׁאָמַר לִשְׁלוּחוֹ: צֵא וְקַדֵּשׁ לִי נַעֲרָה יָפָה וַחֲסוּדָה[48] וּמַעֲשֶׂיהָ נָאִין.
הָלַךְ אוֹתוֹ שָׁלִיחַ וְקִדְּשָׁהּ, לְאַחַר שֶׁקִּדְּשָׁהּ הָלַךְ וּמְצָאָהּ שֶׁזִּינְּתָה תַּחַת
אַחֵר[49], מִיָּד הָיָה דָן (קַל וָחוֹמֶר) מֵעַצְמוֹ[50], וְאָמַר: אִם אֲנִי נוֹתֵן לָהּ כְּתוּבָּה
מֵעַכְשָׁיו נִמְצָא מְחַיְּבָהּ מִיתָה °וְנִפְטְרוּהוּ מֵאֲדוֹנִי לְעוֹלָם[51,52]. כָּךְ הָיָה
מֹשֶׁה הַצַּדִּיק דָן (קַל וָחוֹמֶר) מֵעַצְמוֹ, אָמַר: הֵיאַךְ אֲנִי נוֹתֵן לָהֶם לְיִשְׂרָאֵל
אֶת הַלּוּחוֹת הַלָּלוּ, מַזְקִיקְנִי אוֹתָן לְמִצְוֹת חֲמוּרוֹת וּמְחַיְּבָנִי אוֹתָן מִיתָה,

---

The above narrative describes why Moses wanted to withhold the Tablets from the Jewish people. Now the Baraisa illustrates why he also felt it necessary to smash them:[47]

רַבִּי יוֹסֵי הַגְּלִילִי אוֹמֵר אֶמְשׁוֹל לְךָ מָשָׁל לְמָה הַדָּבָר דּוֹמֶה — R' Yose HaGlili says: I shall give you an analogy: To what is this matter comparable? לְמֶלֶךְ בָּשָׂר וָדָם שֶׁאָמַר לִשְׁלוּחוֹ — To a human king who said to his messenger, צֵא וְקַדֵּשׁ לִי נַעֲרָה יָפָה וַחֲסוּדָה וּמַעֲשֶׂיהָ נָאִין — "Go out and betroth on my behalf a girl who is beautiful and charming[48] and whose behavior is proper." הָלַךְ אוֹתוֹ שָׁלִיחַ וְקִדְּשָׁהּ — The messenger went and found such a girl, and betrothed her on behalf of the king. לְאַחַר שֶׁקִּדְּשָׁהּ הָלַךְ וּמְצָאָהּ שֶׁזִּינְּתָה תַּחַת אַחֵר — However, after he betrothed her, he went and found that she committed adultery with another man![49] מִיָּד הָיָה דָן קַל וָחוֹמֶר מֵעַצְמוֹ — Immediately, [the messenger] reasoned deductively on his own,[50] וְאָמַר: אִם אֲנִי נוֹתֵן לָהּ כְּתוּבָּה מֵעַכְשָׁיו — and said: If I give her the marriage contract now, נִמְצָא מְחַיְּבָהּ מִיתָה וְנִפְטְרָה מֵאֲדוֹנִי לְעוֹלָם[51] — it will emerge that I am making her liable to the death penalty for her infidelity, and she will also be lost from my master forever![52] כָּךְ הָיָה מֹשֶׁה הַצַּדִּיק דָן קַל וָחוֹמֶר מֵעַצְמוֹ — In the same way, the righteous Moses reasoned deductively on his own, אָמַר הֵיאַךְ אֲנִי נוֹתֵן לָהֶם לְיִשְׂרָאֵל אֶת הַלּוּחוֹת הַלָּלוּ — and said: How can I give the people of Israel these Tablets? מַזְקִיקְנִי אוֹתָן לְמִצְוֹת חֲמוּרוֹת וּמְחַיְּבָנִי אוֹתָן מִיתָה — I will thereby be making them subject to its many strict commandments, such as the one against idolatry that they have just violated, and making them liable to the

---

implies that he had to pull them away from someone who was trying to seize them. This refers to the struggle he had with the Elders (Ben Avraham, Binyan Yehoshua).

47. Ben Avraham.

48. Some texts read here וַחֲסִידָה, and pious. [See also Magen Avos and Ben Avraham.]

49. [The expression תַּחַת" "אַחֵר does not seem to fit here; Gra emends it to read ".אַחֵר "עִם.]

50. Literally, reasoned a kal va'chomer from himself. See below, end of note 52, regarding this expression here.

51. Emendation follows Kisei Rachamim and some manuscripts.

52. This contract was proof to her marriage, and would thus show that she deserved death for her unfaithfulness. And even if she could somehow escape this fate, the king would surely never take her back (see Avos

שֶׁכָּךְ כָּתוּב בָּהֶן ⁵³ (שמות כב, יט) "זֹבֵחַ לָאֱלֹהִים יָחֳרָם בִּלְתִּי לַה' לְבַדּוֹ",
אֶלָּא (אֶאֱחֹז בָּהֶן וַאֲשַׁבְּרֵם⁵⁴ וְחִזְרָן לַמּוּטָב, שֶׁמָּא יֹאמְרוּ יִשְׂרָאֵל:
הֵיכָן הַלּוּחוֹת הָרִאשׁוֹנוֹת אֲשֶׁר הוֹרַדְתָּ, אֵין דְּבָרִים אֶלָּא בַּדַּאי.⁵⁵

---

death penalty for that violation!   שֶׁכָּךְ כָּתוּב בָּהֶן "זֹבֵחַ לָאֱלֹהִים יָחֳרָם בִּלְתִּי לַה'
לְבַדּוֹ" — **For so it is written in** [the Tablets],[53] *One who brings offerings
to the gods shall be destroyed — only to HASHEM alone!* (*Exodus* 22:19).
אֶלָּא אֶאֱחֹז בָּהֶן וַאֲשַׁבְּרֵם — **Rather, I shall grasp them and smash them** to
the ground![54]   וְחִזְרָן לַמּוּטָב — **And** in that way, **he would return them to**
the good **and proper path,**   שֶׁמָּא יֹאמְרוּ יִשְׂרָאֵל הֵיכָן הַלּוּחוֹת הָרִאשׁוֹנוֹת אֲשֶׁר
הוֹרַדְתָּ — for perhaps they would now be able to say, "Moses, **where are those
Tablets that you brought down** from Mount Sinai? They are nowhere to be
found!   אֵין דְּבָרִים אֶלָּא בַּדַּאי — So all **the words** of the covenant **are nothing
more than** something **void!**" And with this claim they will be able to exonerate
themselves.[55]

HaRosh [Vol. 1]). Pitying the young girl, the
messenger therefore destroyed her marriage
contract (see *Avos DeRabbi Nassan, Nusach
2, Ch. 2*) so that there would be no evidence
of her marriage to the king (see below,
note 54).

This reasoning does not seem to contain
any element of *kal va'chomer*. *Magen Avos*
suggests several explanations, one of which
is that the messenger quite literally "reasoned a *kal va'chomer* from himself" — from
how *he* would feel if this happened to him:
If I, a mere commoner, would be angered by
my bride's disloyalty to me, how much more
so will the king be angered by the disloyalty
of his bride to him. [*Gra*, however, removes
the words קַל וָחֹמֶר.]

53. Although the verse cited afterward is
not written in the Ten Commandments, it
[like all the mitzvos of the Torah] is *alluded*
to in the words of the Ten Commandments
written on the Tablets. Thus, the Baraisa
uses the expression "כָּתוּב בָּהֶן", *written "in
them"* (*Binyan Yehoshua*; *Ahavas Chesed*).
[Some texts, however, omit the word בָּהֶן, *in
them,* and have only: שֶׁכָּךְ כָּתוּב, *For so it is
written.*]

54. One may ask: What did the messenger
accomplish by destroying the contract? Was
it not still true that the bride had breached

the marriage? *Ben Avraham* suggests an ingenious explanation: The king's instruction
that his messenger betroth him a girl whose
"behavior is proper" had the legal status of
a stipulation. Thus, when it emerged that
her behavior was *improper*, the stipulation
was not fulfilled and the marriage would be
void retroactively, in which case she could
not be considered an adulteress. Giving her
the contract at that point, however, would
have constituted a waiver of the stipulation,
which would have validated the marriage
retroactively and rendered her an adulteress. To avoid this, the messenger destroyed
the contract. Similarly, the pledge of the
people of Israel to keep the commandments
was the condition on which God made His
covenant with them at Sinai. When they
sinned with the Golden Calf, the covenant
was voided retroactively. If, however, Moses
would have then given them the Tablets of
the Covenant, that would have been deemed
a waiver of the condition, which would have
validated the covenant retroactively and
thereby rendered them liable to death for
violating it.

55. *Ahavas Chesed.* And with this mitiga-
tion of their guilt, they would not despair of
returning to God, and would repent (*Binyan
Yehoshua*).

רַבִּי יְהוּדָה בֶּן בְּתֵירָא אוֹמֵר: לֹא שִׁבֵּר מֹשֶׁה אֶת הַלּוּחוֹת אֶלָּא [56] שֶׁנֶּאֱמַר לוֹ מִפִּי הַגְּבוּרָה, שֶׁנֶּאֱמַר (במדבר יב, ח) "פֶּה אֶל פֶּה אֲדַבֶּר בּוֹ'", פֶּה אֶל פֶּה אָמַרְתִּי לוֹ: שַׁבֵּר אֶת הַלּוּחוֹת.[57]) וְיֵשׁ אוֹמְרִים: לֹא שִׁבֵּר מֹשֶׁה אֶת הַלּוּחוֹת אֶלָּא שֶׁנֶּאֱמַר לוֹ מִפִּי הַגְּבוּרָה, שֶׁנֶּאֱמַר (דברים ט, טז) "וָאֵרֶא וְהִנֵּה חֲטָאתֶם לַה' אֱלֹהֵיכֶם", אֵינוֹ אוֹמֵר "וָאֵרֶא" אֶלָּא שֶׁרָאָה[58] שֶׁפָּרַח כְּתָב מֵעֲלֵיהֶם.[59] אֲחֵרִים אוֹמְרִים: לֹא שִׁבֵּר מֹשֶׁה אֶת הַלּוּחוֹת אֶלָּא שֶׁנֶּאֱמַר לוֹ מִפִּי הַגְּבוּרָה, שֶׁנֶּאֱמַר (שם י, ה) "וַיִּהְיוּ שָׁם כַּאֲשֶׁר צִוַּנִי ה' ",

Here, too (as above), the Baraisa records those who say that Moses did not act on his own reasoning until it was approved by God:

לֹא שִׁבֵּר מֹשֶׁה — רַבִּי יְהוּדָה בֶּן בְּתֵירָא אוֹמֵר — R' Yehudah ben Beseira says: אֶת הַלּוּחוֹת אֶלָּא שֶׁנֶּאֱמַר לוֹ מִפִּי הַגְּבוּרָה — Moses did not smash the Tablets on his own; rather,[56] he was expressly told to do so from the mouth of the Almighty, שֶׁנֶּאֱמַר "פֶּה אֶל פֶּה אֲדַבֶּר בּוֹ'" — as it is stated in God's words, *Mouth to mouth do I speak to him* (Numbers 12:8), פֶּה אֶל פֶּה אָמַרְתִּי לוֹ שַׁבֵּר אֶת הַלּוּחוֹת — which can be expounded to mean, "From My mouth to his mouth (i.e., explicitly), I said to him, 'Smash the Tablets,' and he smashed them."[57]

A second source:

וְיֵשׁ אוֹמְרִים — And some say: Moses did not smash the Tablets on his own; rather, he was expressly told to do so from the mouth of the Almighty, שֶׁנֶּאֱמַר "וָאֵרֶא וְהִנֵּה חֲטָאתֶם לַה' אֱלֹהֵיכֶם" — as it says that Moses said to the people when recalling their sin of the Golden Calf, *"Then I saw and behold! you had sinned to HASHEM, your God"* (Deuteronomy 9:16). אֵינוֹ אוֹמֵר "וָאֵרֶא" אֶלָּא שֶׁרָאָה שֶׁפָּרַח כְּתָב מֵעֲלֵיהֶם — It says *Then I saw*[58] only to indicate that he saw that the writing had flown from them.[59]

A third source:

אֲחֵרִים אוֹמְרִים — Others say: Moses did not smash the Tablets on his own; rather, he was expressly told to do so from the mouth of the Almighty, שֶׁנֶּאֱמַר "וַיִּהְיוּ שָׁם כַּאֲשֶׁר צִוַּנִי ה' " — as it says in his description of how he received the Second Tablets, *And I placed the Tablets in the Ark that I had made,* **and they remained there as HASHEM**

---

56. Here, too, as well as in the subsequent occurrences below, some texts have עַד, *until*, instead of אֶלָּא; see above, note 32.

57. See above, note 33.

58. The verse tells exactly what confronted Moses when he came down from the mountain. What, then, is the point of saying "and I saw"? It must be referring to something else

that Moses saw, something not specified in the verse (see *Ahavas Chesed*; see also *Ben Avraham*).

59. This was a clear sign that God wanted him to smash the Tablets, for why would he give the people Tablets that had nothing of substance on them, as above [at note 45] (*Binyan Yehoshua*).

אֵינוֹ אוֹמֵר ״צִוַּנִי״ אֶלָּא שֶׁנִּצְטַוָּה וְשִׁבְּרָן‎60. רַבִּי אֶלְעָזָר בֶּן עֲזַרְיָה
אוֹמֵר: לֹא שָׁבַר מֹשֶׁה אֶת הַלּוּחוֹת אֶלָּא שֶׁנֶּאֱמַר לוֹ מִפִּי הַגְּבוּרָה,
שֶׁנֶּאֱמַר (שם לד, יב) ״אֲשֶׁר עָשָׂה מֹשֶׁה לְעֵינֵי כָּל יִשְׂרָאֵל״‎61, מַה לְּהַלָּן
נִצְטַוָּה וְעָשָׂה, אַף כָּאן נִצְטַוָּה וְעָשָׂה. (רַבִּי עֲקִיבָא אוֹמֵר: לֹא שָׁבַר
מֹשֶׁה אֶת הַלּוּחוֹת אֶלָּא שֶׁנֶּאֱמַר לוֹ מִפִּי הַגְּבוּרָה, שֶׁנֶּאֱמַר (שם ט,
יז) ״וָאֶתְפֹּשׂ בִּשְׁנֵי הַלֻּחֹת״, בַּמֶּה אָדָם תּוֹפֵס בְּמַה שֶׁיָּכוֹל לְבוֹרְאָן‎62.

had commanded me (ibid. 10:5).   אֵינוֹ אוֹמֵר ״צִוַּנִי״ אֶלָּא שֶׁנִּצְטַוָּה וְשִׁבְּרָן — It
says *as HASHEM had commanded me* only to indicate that with regard to the
First Tablets, he was first commanded, and only then did he break them.[60]

A fourth source:

רַבִּי אֶלְעָזָר בֶּן עֲזַרְיָה אוֹמֵר: לֹא שָׁבַר מֹשֶׁה אֶת הַלּוּחוֹת אֶלָּא שֶׁנֶּאֱמַר לוֹ מִפִּי הַגְּבוּרָה —
R' Elazar ben Azaryah says: Moses did not smash the Tablets on his own; rather,
he was expressly told to do so from the mouth of the Almighty, שֶׁנֶּאֱמַר ״אֲשֶׁר
עָשָׂה מֹשֶׁה לְעֵינֵי כָּל יִשְׂרָאֵל״ — as it says in the Torah's tribute to Moses, *And by
all the strong hand and awesome power that Moses performed before the eyes
of all Israel* (ibid. 34:12); the Torah thereby groups *"all" the strong hand* ... and
that Moses performed ... together,[61]   מַה לְּהַלָּן נִצְטַוָּה וְעָשָׂה, אַף כָּאן נִצְטַוָּה וְעָשָׂה
— which teaches: Just as there with regard to all the signs and wonders (*all the
strong hand and awesome power*), he was obviously first commanded and only
then did he do, so too here, with regard to the smashing of the Tablets (*performed
before the eyes of all Israel*), he was first commanded and only then did he do.

A fifth source:

רַבִּי עֲקִיבָא אוֹמֵר — R' Akiva
says: Moses did not smash the Tablets on his own; rather, he was expressly
told to do so from the mouth of the Almighty, ״וָאֶתְפֹּשׂ בִּשְׁנֵי הַלֻּחֹת״ —
as it says in Moses' own description of this incident: *I grasped the two Tablets
and threw them from my two hands, and I smashed them* (ibid. 9:17).   בַּמֶּה
אָדָם תּוֹפֵס — What does a person grasp?   בְּמַה שֶׁיָּכוֹל לְבוֹרְאָן — Only those
which he is able to create, i.e., that over which he has dominion. The fact that
Moses grasped and thus had dominion over the Tablets indicates that God had
granted him that dominion by commanding him to smash them.[62]

---

60. The earlier phrase, *And I placed the
Tablets in the Ark,* refers to the Second Tablets. The seemingly extraneous phrase, *and
they remained there,* must therefore refer
to the shattered pieces of the First Tablets.
[Indeed, our Sages teach that both sets
were placed in the Ark (*Bava Basra* 14a).]
Accordingly, when Moses says that he
placed the smashed Tablets there "as God

commanded me," it intimates that even
the original *smashing* of those Tablets was
commanded by God (*Magen Avos*).
61. Which includes the smashing of the Tablets, alluded to in the words *before the eyes of
all Israel* — see above, at note 44.
62. *Magen Avos,* first explanation. Alternatively, a person can grasp only physical
things (which he can create). The First

רַבִּי מֵאִיר אוֹמֵר: לֹא שָׁבַר מֹשֶׁה אֶת הַלּוּחוֹת אֶלָּא שֶׁנֶּאֱמַר לוֹ מִפִּי
הַגְּבוּרָה, שֶׁנֶּאֱמַר (שם י, ב) ״אֲשֶׁר שִׁבַּרְתָּ״, יִישַׁר כֹּחֲךָ שֶׁשִּׁבַּרְתָּ[63]:

ד. יְחִזְקִיָּהוּ מֶלֶךְ יְהוּדָה עָשָׂה אַרְבָּעָה דְבָרִים וְהִסְכִּימָה דַעְתּוֹ לְדַעַת
הַמָּקוֹם. גָּנַז סֵפֶר רְפוּאוֹת, וְהִסְכִּימָה דַעְתּוֹ לְדַעַת הַמָּקוֹם[65]. כִּתֵּת נְחַשׁ

A sixth and final source:

רַבִּי מֵאִיר אוֹמֵר: לֹא שָׁבַר מֹשֶׁה אֶת הַלּוּחוֹת אֶלָּא שֶׁנֶּאֱמַר לוֹ מִפִּי הַגְּבוּרָה — **R' Meir says:** Moses did not smash the Tablets on his own; rather, he was expressly told to do so from the mouth of the Almighty, שֶׁנֶּאֱמַר ״אֲשֶׁר שִׁבַּרְתָּ״ — as it says in God's words to Moses, *And I shall inscribe on the [Second] Tablets the words that were on the first Tablets that* [אֲשֶׁר] *you smashed* (ibid. 10:2), יִישַׁר כֹּחֲךָ שֶׁשִּׁבַּרְתָּ — which we expound to mean, **"Your strength should be reinforced [**יִישַׁר**] because you smashed them!"**[63] God would not have approved the smashing of the Tablets in this way had He not explicitly instructed Moses to smash them.[64]

§4 Having discussed the things Moses did on his own and with which God concurred, the Baraisa discusses the things another great Biblical personality did that met with God's approval:

יְחִזְקִיָּהוּ מֶלֶךְ יְהוּדָה עָשָׂה אַרְבָּעָה דְבָרִים — In a similar way, **Hezekiah king of Judah did four things,** וְהִסְכִּימָה דַעְתּוֹ לְדַעַת הַמָּקוֹם — **and** in each case, **his understanding** in the matter **agreed with God's will.** גָּנַז סֵפֶר רְפוּאוֹת וְהִסְכִּימָה דַעְתּוֹ לְדַעַת הַמָּקוֹם — They are as follows: (i) **He hid the Book of Remedies, and his understanding** in this matter **agreed with God's Will.**[65] כִּתֵּת נְחַשׁ

Tablets, however, had been spiritual things [see *Exodus* 32:16], which Moses could not have "grasped" were it not that their spiritual essence had departed, indicating to him that he was to smash them [see above, note 59] (see *Magen Avos,* second explanation; see also *Binyan Yehoshua*).

Ahavas Chesed, however, adopts an alternative reading: בְּמַה שֶׁיָּכוֹל לְ"שַׁבְּרָן", *what he is able to break* by letting go of them. That is, if Moses "grasped" the Tablets, he was trying to *prevent* them from falling and being smashed. How then does that verse state next *and I threw them ...*? It must be that after grasping them to prevent them from falling, he was commanded by God to throw them down and smash them.

63. The words אֲשֶׁר שִׁבַּרְתָּ are expounded this way because they are apparently superfluous; the verse could have said simply *the*

words that were on the first Tablets (*Maharsha* to *Yevamos* 62a).

64. *Magen Avos,* second explanation. Alternatively, the words אֲשֶׁר שִׁבַּרְתָּ might indicate God's approval only after the fact. And R' Meir's proof is from the earlier part of the verse, which states: *the words that "were" on the Tablets that you smashed.* "Were" implies that the words *were* on the Tablets, but are not there any longer — the disappearance of the letters being tantamount to a Divine command to smash the Tablets, as above [see note 59] (*Magen Avos,* first explanation).

65. This book included cures for virtually all illnesses. King Hezekiah saw that because of this book people were not humbled by their sicknesses [to return to God], as they found immediate relief and cure in the remedies of this book (*Binyan Yehoshua,* from *Rashi* to *Pesachim* 56a). Some say that King

הַנְּחוֹשֶׁת, וְהִסְכִּימָה דַעְתּוֹ לְדַעַת הַמָּקוֹם.⁶⁶ וְהֵסִיר אֶת הַבָּמוֹת וְהַמִּזְבְּחוֹת,
(וְהִסְכִּימָה דַעְתּוֹ לְדַעַת הַמָּקוֹם)[⁶⁷], שֶׁנֶּאֱמַר (דה״ב לב, יב) ״יְחִזְקִיָּהוּ הֵסִיר
אֶת בָּמֹתָיו וְאֶת מִזְבְּחֹתָיו וַיֹּאמֶר לִיהוּדָה וְלִירוּשָׁלַיִם לֵאמֹר לִפְנֵי מִזְבֵּחַ
אֶחָד תִּשְׁתַּחֲווּ וְעָלָיו תַּקְטִירוּ״.⁶⁸ סָתַם מֵי גִיחוֹן ⁶⁹ (וְהִסְכִּימָה דַעְתּוֹ לְדַעַת

הַנְּחוֹשֶׁת וְהִסְכִּימָה דַעְתּוֹ לְדַעַת הַמָּקוֹם — (ii) **He ground up the copper serpent,
and his understanding** in this matter **agreed with God's Will.**[66] וְהֵסִיר אֶת
הַבָּמוֹת וְהַמִּזְבְּחוֹת וְהִסְכִּימָה דַעְתּוֹ לְדַעַת הַמָּקוֹם — (iii) **And he removed the high
places and altars** upon which the Jewish people had brought offerings, **and
his understanding** in this matter **agreed with God's Will.**[67] שֶׁנֶּאֱמַר ״יְחִזְקִיָּהוּ
הֵסִיר אֶת בָּמֹתָיו וְאֶת מִזְבְּחֹתָיו וַיֹּאמֶר לִיהוּדָה וְלִירוּשָׁלַיִם לֵאמֹר לִפְנֵי מִזְבֵּחַ אֶחָד
תִּשְׁתַּחֲווּ וְעָלָיו תַּקְטִירוּ״ — That he removed these high places is **as it says:** *Is
this not the same **Hezekiah who removed [HASHEM's] high places and altars,
telling Judah and Jerusalem, "You must prostrate yourselves before only
one Altar and burn offerings upon it"?*** (*II Chronicles* 32:12).[68] סָתַם מֵי
גִיחוֹן וְהִסְכִּימָה דַעְתּוֹ לְדַעַת הַמָּקוֹם — (iv) And **he stopped up the waters of**

Solomon was the author of this book. Others
say that one of Noah's sons wrote it, based
on what an angel had shown him in Gan
Eden (see *Binyan Yehoshua*).

That God agreed with this decision is indicated in Hezekiah's prayer to God, where he
declares, *and I have done what is good in Your
eyes* (*Isaiah* 38:3), which the Gemara (*Berachos* 10b), according to one opinion, understands as a reference to his having concealed
the Book of Remedies. For the words "what
is good in *Your* eyes" implies that it was *not*
good in the eyes of men (*Maharsha* there).
Moreover, the implication is that what he did
was *good* — but not required (*Ben Avraham*).

Rambam (Commentary to *Pesachim* 4:10)
disagrees vehemently with the explanation
that Hezekiah would have concealed a book
of natural remedies so that people would rely
instead on God. According to *Rambam* there,
natural remedies are no different from the food
God gives us to "cure" our hunger. Rather, the
book's author had included remedies containing some religiously problematic elements
(which he included because one is permitted
to study — although not employ — them),
or had listed poisons and their antidotes.
When these lists became misused, Hezekiah
concealed the book (see *Binyan Yehoshua*).

66. As it states regarding Hezekiah: *He did
what was proper in the eyes of HASHEM ...
he ground up the copper serpent that Moses
had made — for until those days the Children
of Israel used to burn incense before it ...* (*II
Kings* 18:3-4). The words of preface — *He
did what was proper in the eyes of HASHEM*
— indicate that God agreed with Hezekiah's
understanding in this matter (*Ben Avraham*).

This serpent had once been a vehicle for
the Divine healing sent to the people whom
God had punished with the bite of venom-
ous snakes (see *Numbers* 21:4-9). For a
long time after, this copper serpent was
preserved because it commemorated that
miraculous incident, and also reminded the
Jewish people that their suffering comes
only from their sins, and this was a reason
not to grind it up (see *Binyan Yehoshua*,
from *Maharsha*). After the passage of time,
however, people erroneously attributed
healing powers to the serpent itself and began to stray after it (*Rashi* to *Pesachim* 56a).

67. See end of next note.

68. These were the words of Sennacherib,
king of Assyria, who declared that Judah's
resistance to his invasion was futile because
Hezekiah their king had removed "His" high
places. These were the *bamos* on which

הַמָּקוֹם), שֶׁנֶּאֱמַר (שם פסוק ל) "יְחִזְקִיָּהוּ סָתַם [אֶת מוֹצָא מֵימֵי] גִּיחוֹן
[הָעֶלְיוֹן] וַיִּישְׁרֵם לְמַטָּה מַּעְרָבָה לְעִיר דָּוִיד וַיַּצְלַח יְחִזְקִיָּהוּ בְּכָל מַעֲשֵׂהוּ"[70]:

ה. אֵיזֶהוּ סְיָיג שֶׁעָשָׂה אִיּוֹב לִדְבָרָיו[71], הֲרֵי הוּא אוֹמֵר (איוב א, ח) "אִישׁ
תָּם וְיָשָׁר °וִירֵא אֱלֹהִים וְסָר מֵרָע", מְלַמֵּד שֶׁהִרְחִיק אִיּוֹב אֶת

---

the **Gihon**[69] in order to deny water to the enemy forces who were about to
besiege Jerusalem, **and his understanding** in this matter **agreed with God's
Will,**   שֶׁנֶּאֱמַר "יְחִזְקִיָּהוּ סָתַם אֶת מוֹצָא מֵימֵי גִּיחוֹן הָעֶלְיוֹן וַיִּישְׁרֵם לְמַטָּה מַּעְרָבָה
לְעִיר דָּוִיד וַיַּצְלַח יְחִזְקִיָּהוּ בְּכָל מַעֲשֵׂהוּ" — as it is stated, *He, Hezekiah, stopped
up the upper source of the waters of Gihon, diverting them underground
westward, to the city of David. Hezekiah was successful in all his endeavors* (*II Chronicles 32:30*).[70]

§5 The Baraisa discusses the next one in the list of those who made protective fences around their words:

אֵיזֶהוּ סְיָיג שֶׁעָשָׂה אִיּוֹב לִדְבָרָיו — **What is** an example of **a fence that Job made
around his words?**[71]   הֲרֵי הוּא אוֹמֵר "אִישׁ תָּם וְיָשָׁר יְרֵא אֱלֹהִים וְסָר מֵרָע"
— **It says** about Job that he was *a wholesome and upright man, who fears
God and shuns evil* (*Job 1:8; 2:3; see also 1:1*).   מְלַמֵּד שֶׁהִרְחִיק אִיּוֹב אֶת

---

people brought offerings to Hashem. [There
were periods in Jewish history when offering to Hashem at a *bamah* was permitted. Once the Temple was built in Jerusalem,
however, offering on a *bamah* became forbidden for all time (see Mishnah, *Zevachim*
112b).] The Temple in Jerusalem had been
built hundreds of years before Hezekiah; yet
the practice of offering on a *bamah* endured
stubbornly, despite many efforts to eradicate
it. Hezekiah did much to destroy the *bamos,*
an endeavor that Sennacherib mistakenly
thought must have surely incurred God's
displeasure by reducing the places in which
He would be worshiped through sacrificial
service (see *Rashi* ad loc.).

[It seems superfluous to state with regard
to this matter that Hezekiah's understanding agreed with God's Will — obviously
this is so, as *bamos* were clearly forbidden
at this time. (Indeed, for this reason some
texts omit here the words "and his opinion
agreed with God's Will" — *Ahavas Chesed
[Machazeh Avraham]* and *Kisei Rachamim*.)
Nevertheless, it might be that these words
are justified here, because in practice *bamos*

were widespread, so that they were widely
thought to be permitted.]

69. Gihon here refers to the Shiloah spring in
Jerusalem, not to the river Gihon mentioned
in *Genesis* 2:13 (*Binyan Yehoshua,* from
Rashi to *Berachos* 10b).

70. The verse's mention of Hezekiah's abundant success immediately after stating that
he stopped up the waters of the Gihon suggests that God approved of his decision in
that matter (*Binyan Yehoshua*).

The Baraisa cited by the Gemara (*Berachos* 10b and *Pesachim* 56a) lists Hezekiah's
stopping up of the Gihon as one of the things
that the Sages did *not* approve of, for (as the
Gemara explains) God had promised that
He would protect the city. Our Baraisa, however, maintains that the Divine assurance of
protection did not absolve Hezekiah from
the need to employ the defensive tactics
available to him (*Ahavas Chesed [Machazeh
Avraham]*; see also *Magen Avos,* who elaborates on the dispute between our Baraisa
and the one cited in the Gemara).

71. [In this context, לִדְבָרָיו is perhaps more
accurately rendered as "his matters." See,

עַצְמוֹ מִדְּבָר הַמֵּבִיא לַעֲבֵירָה, וּמִן הַכִּיעוּר וּמִן הַדּוֹמֶה לַכִּיעוּר.[72]
אִם כֵּן מַה תַּלְמוּד לוֹמַר "אִישׁ תָּם וְיָשָׁר", אֶלָּא מְלַמֵּד שֶׁיָּצָא אִיּוֹב
מָהוּל.[73] אַף אָדָם הָרִאשׁוֹן יָצָא מָהוּל, שֶׁנֶּאֱמַר (בראשית א, כז) "וַיִּבְרָא
אֱלֹהִים אֶת הָאָדָם בְּצַלְמוֹ".[74] אַף שֵׁת יָצָא מָהוּל, שֶׁנֶּאֱמַר (שם ה, ג)
"וַיּוֹלֶד בִּדְמוּתוֹ כְּצַלְמוֹ". אַף נֹחַ יָצָא מָהוּל, שֶׁנֶּאֱמַר (שם ו, ט) "אִישׁ
צַדִּיק תָּמִים הָיָה בְּדֹרֹתָיו".[75] אַף שֵׁם יָצָא מָהוּל, שֶׁנֶּאֱמַר (שם יד, יח)

עַצְמוֹ מִדְּבָר הַמֵּבִיא לַעֲבֵירָה — This teaches that Job kept far even from anything that might lead to sin, וּמִן הַכִּיעוּר וּמִן הַדּוֹמֶה לַכִּיעוּר — and from what is morally repulsive or even from what appears repulsive.[72] אִם כֵּן מַה תַּלְמוּד לוֹמַר "אִישׁ תָּם וְיָשָׁר" — If so, what additional point is Scripture teaching by saying that he was a wholesome and upright man? אֶלָּא מְלַמֵּד שֶׁיָּצָא אִיּוֹב מָהוּל — Rather, it teaches that Job emerged from his mother's womb already circumcised.[73]

The Baraisa interrupts its discussion to list numerous other Scriptural personalities who were born circumcised:

אַף אָדָם הָרִאשׁוֹן יָצָא מָהוּל — Adam, the first man, also emerged into the world already circumcised, שֶׁנֶּאֱמַר "וַיִּבְרָא אֱלֹהִים אֶת הָאָדָם בְּצַלְמוֹ" — as it says, So God created Man in his image (Genesis 1:27).[74] אַף שֵׁת יָצָא מָהוּל — Adam's son Seth, too, emerged from his mother's womb already circumcised, שֶׁנֶּאֱמַר "וַיּוֹלֶד בִּדְמוּתוֹ כְּצַלְמוֹ" — as it says, He (Adam) begot in his likeness and his image, and he named him Seth (ibid. 5:3), implying that Adam's son was born the same way that he was, i.e., already circumcised. אַף נֹחַ יָצָא מָהוּל — Noah, too, emerged from his mother's womb already circumcised, שֶׁנֶּאֱמַר "אִישׁ צַדִּיק תָּמִים הָיָה בְּדֹרֹתָיו" — as it says, Noah was a righteous man, perfect in his generations (ibid. 6:9).[75] אַף שֵׁם יָצָא מָהוּל — Noah's son Shem, too, emerged from his mother's womb already circumcised, שֶׁנֶּאֱמַר

---

however, Magen Avos below at the beginning of §6, who explains how it might mean here as well "his words."]

72. [See Baraisa above, after note 16.] Once the verse says that Job feared God, the additional phrase, וְסָר מֵרָע, and shunned evil, must mean more than that he did not sin. Thus, it means that he took pains to avoid evil by making safeguards for himself that would keep him far away from sin (Binyan Yehoshua).

The Baraisa here does not give a specific example of how Job distanced himself from sin, but it does below. (See, however, Magen Avos here.)

73. The Sages often understand Scripture's

use of the adjective תָּם, wholesome, or תָּמִים, perfect, as an allusion to being circumcised (Binyan Yehoshua, based on Nedarim 32a).

The foreskin on a man's body is a blemish, which is removed to perfect his creation. A tzaddik who is born circumcised has thus been born already perfected in this way, and is to use this as a springboard to rise to even greater heights (Ahavas Chesed [marginal addendum]).

74. Meaning, in the exact form that God had intended for him, which implies that he needed no further "improvement," including circumcision (Binyan Yehoshua).

75. See above, note 73.

"וּמַלְכִּי צֶדֶק מֶלֶךְ שָׁלֵם"[76]. אַף יַעֲקֹב יָצָא מָהוּל, שֶׁנֶּאֱמַר (שם כה,
כז) "וְיַעֲקֹב אִישׁ תָּם ישֵׁב אֹהָלִים"[77]. אַף יוֹסֵף יָצָא מָהוּל, שֶׁנֶּאֱמַר
(שם לז, ב) "אֵלֶּה תֹּלְדוֹת יַעֲקֹב יוֹסֵף", וַהֲלֹא אֵין רָאוּי לוֹמַר [אֶלָּא]
"אֵלֶּה תֹּלְדוֹת יַעֲקֹב רְאוּבֵן", וּמַה תַּלְמוּד לוֹמַר "יוֹסֵף", אֶלָּא כְּשֵׁם
שֶׁיָּצָא יַעֲקֹב מָהוּל (אַף) כָּךְ יָצָא יוֹסֵף מָהוּל[78]. אַף מֹשֶׁה יָצָא מָהוּל,
שֶׁנֶּאֱמַר (שמות ב, ב) "וַתֵּרֶא אֹתוֹ כִּי טוֹב הוּא", וְכִי מָה רָאֲתָה אִמּוֹ בּוֹ
שֶׁנָּאֶה וּמְשׁוּבָּח מִכָּל אָדָם[79], אֶלָּא שֶׁיָּצָא מָהוּל[80]. אַף בִּלְעָם הָרָשָׁע

"וּמַלְכִּי צֶדֶק מֶלֶךְ שָׁלֵם" — as it says, *And Malchizedek, king of Salem* (ibid. 14:18).[76] אַף יַעֲקֹב יָצָא מָהוּל — Our forefather **Jacob, too, emerged** from his mother's womb **already circumcised,** שֶׁנֶּאֱמַר "וְיַעֲקֹב אִישׁ תָּם ישֵׁב אֹהָלִים" — **as it says,** *but Jacob was a wholesome man, abiding in tents* (ibid. 25:27).[77] אַף יוֹסֵף יָצָא מָהוּל — **Jacob's son Joseph, too, emerged** from his mother's womb **already circumcised,** שֶׁנֶּאֱמַר "אֵלֶּה תֹּלְדוֹת יַעֲקֹב יוֹסֵף" — **as it says,** *These are the offspring of Jacob: Joseph* (ibid. 37:2). וַהֲלֹא אֵין רָאוּי לוֹמַר אֶלָּא 'אֵלֶּה תֹּלְדוֹת יַעֲקֹב רְאוּבֵן' — **Now, would it not have been more correct to state** first, **"***These are the offspring of Jacob: Reuben* ...," as Reuben, not Joseph, was Jacob's firstborn? וּמַה תַּלְמוּד לוֹמַר יוֹסֵף — **What then is Scripture teaching by saying,** *These are the offspring of Jacob: "Joseph"*? אֶלָּא כְּשֵׁם שֶׁיָּצָא יַעֲקֹב מָהוּל כָּךְ יָצָא יוֹסֵף מָהוּל — **It is** only to tell you that **just as Jacob emerged** from his mother's womb **already circumcised, so did Joseph emerge** from his mother's womb **already circumcised.**[78] אַף מֹשֶׁה יָצָא מָהוּל — **Moses, too, emerged** from his mother's **womb already circumcised,** שֶׁנֶּאֱמַר "וַתֵּרֶא אֹתוֹ כִּי טוֹב הוּא" — **as it says** that when he was born, *[his mother] saw that he was good* (Exodus 2:2). וְכִי מָה רָאֲתָה אִמּוֹ בּוֹ שֶׁנָּאֶה וּמְשׁוּבָּח מִכָּל אָדָם — **Now, what did his mother see in him that** made him **more comely and better than any other person** that is born?[79] אֶלָּא שֶׁיָּצָא מָהוּל — **It was nothing other than that** he emerged from her womb **already circumcised.**[80] אַף בִּלְעָם הָרָשָׁע

---

76. "Malchizedek" was in fact Shem the son of Noah (*Midrash Shocher Tov, Tehillim* 76; see also *Nedarim* 32b). The term מֶלֶךְ שָׁלֵם [lit., *king of Salem*] can be rendered "a complete king," which implies that he was blessed with physical perfection, i.e., he was born already circumcised (*Binyan Yehoshua*).

77. See above, note 73.

78. The verse mentions Joseph (instead of a chronological list of Jacob's sons) because of *many* parallels between Jacob and Joseph (see *Bereishis Rabbah* 84 §6). Our Baraisa

sees this specific parallel (being born circumcised) indicated because of the verse's use of the word תֹּלְדוֹת, which suggests a similarity that existed *from birth* (*Magen Avos, Ahavas Chesed* [marginal addendum]).

79. The verse must refer to *uncommon* good that she saw in him when he was born.

80. Hence, Scripture is stating that Moses was born in his full "goodness," meaning that he was complete – an allusion to being born circumcised [see above, note 73] (*Binyan Yehoshua*).

יָצָא מָהוּל, שֶׁנֶּאֱמַר (במדבר כד, ד) "נְאֻם שֹׁמֵעַ אִמְרֵי אֵל".[81] [אַף
שְׁמוּאֵל יָצָא מָהוּל, שֶׁנֶּאֱמַר (שמואל א ב, כו) "וְהַנַּעַר שְׁמוּאֵל הֹלֵךְ °וְגָדֵל
וָטוֹב"].[82] אַף דָּוִד יָצָא מָהוּל, שֶׁנֶּאֱמַר (תהלים טז, א) "מִכְתָּם לְדָוִד
(שָׁמְרֵנִי אֵל כִּי חָסִיתִי בָךְ)".[83] אַף יִרְמְיָה יָצָא מָהוּל, שֶׁנֶּאֱמַר (ירמיה
א, ה) "בְּטֶרֶם אֶצָּרְךָ בַבֶּטֶן יְדַעְתִּיךָ וּבְטֶרֶם תֵּצֵא מֵרֶחֶם הִקְדַּשְׁתִּיךָ".[84]
אַף זְרוּבָּבֶל יָצָא מָהוּל, שֶׁנֶּאֱמַר (חגי ב, כג) "בַּיּוֹם הַהוּא (אֶקָּחֲךָ אֶת)
[נְאֻם ה' צְבָאוֹת אֶקָּחֲךָ] זְרֻבָּבֶל בֶּן שְׁאַלְתִּיאֵל עַבְדִּי נְאֻם ה'".[85]

יָצָא מָהוּל — The wicked **Balaam, too, emerged** from his mother's womb already **circumcised,** שֶׁנֶּאֱמַר "נְאֻם שֹׁמֵעַ אִמְרֵי אֵל" — **as it says** in Balaam's preface to his own words of prophecy: *The words of the one who hears the sayings of God (Numbers* 24:4).[81] אַף שְׁמוּאֵל יָצָא מָהוּל — **The prophet Samuel, too, emerged** from his mother's womb already **circumcised** שֶׁנֶּאֱמַר "וְהַנַּעַר שְׁמוּאֵל הֹלֵךְ וְגָדֵל וָטוֹב" — **as it says,** *But the boy Samuel kept growing and was good (I Samuel* 2:26).[82] אַף דָּוִד יָצָא מָהוּל — **King David, too, emerged** from his mother's womb already **circumcised,** שֶׁנֶּאֱמַר "מִכְתָּם לְדָוִד שָׁמְרֵנִי אֵל כִּי חָסִיתִי בָךְ" — **as it says,** *A michtam by David. Protect me O God, for I have sought refuge in You (Psalms* 16:1).[83] אַף יִרְמְיָה יָצָא מָהוּל — **The prophet Jeremiah, too, emerged** from his mother's womb already **circumcised,** שֶׁנֶּאֱמַר "בְּטֶרֶם אֶצָּרְךָ בַבֶּטֶן יְדַעְתִּיךָ וּבְטֶרֶם תֵּצֵא מֵרֶחֶם הִקְדַּשְׁתִּיךָ" — **as it says** in God's words to Jeremiah, *Before I formed you in the belly I knew you, and before you left the womb I sanctified you (Jeremiah* 1:5).[84] אַף זְרוּבָּבֶל יָצָא מָהוּל — **Zerubbabel, too, emerged** from his mother's womb already **circumcised,** שֶׁנֶּאֱמַר "בַּיּוֹם הַהוּא נְאֻם ה' צְבָאוֹת אֶקָּחֲךָ זְרֻבָּבֶל בֶּן שְׁאַלְתִּיאֵל עַבְדִּי נְאֻם ה'" — **as it says,** *On that day — the word of HASHEM, Master of Legions — I will take you, Zerubbabel son of Shealtiel, my servant — the word of HASHEM — and I made you like the seal ... (Haggai* 2:23).[85]

---

81. He could not have merited that degree of prophecy had he been uncircumcised [see *Pirkei DeRabbi Eliezer* Ch. 29]. And since it was not his father who circumcised him as a child [as he was not descended from Abraham], it must be that Balaam was *born* circumcised (see *Magen Avos, Mefaresh*; see also *Binyan Yehoshua*).

82. Just as טוֹב, *good,* written with regard to Moses indicates that he was born circumcised (as in the Baraisa above), so too does וָטוֹב, *and was good,* written with regard to Samuel indicate the same (*Ahavas Chesed; Ben Avraham,* second explanation).

83. A *michtam* is a type of psalm. The Baraisa here expounds מִכְתָּם as a contraction of מַכָּתוֹ תַּמָּה, *his wound was whole,* an allusion to being born circumcised, so that the wound he would have suffered during circumcision was already whole (*Binyan Yehoshua,* from *Sotah* 10b with *Rashi*).

84. One who is uncircumcised has an element of *tumah.* Jeremiah could not therefore have been considered "sanctified" in the womb were it not that he was already circumcised (see *Mefaresh* and *Binyan Yehoshua*).

85. The continuation of the verse, וְשַׂמְתִּיךָ

הֲרֵי הוּא אוֹמֵר (איוב לא, א) "בְּרִית כָּרַתִּי לְעֵינָי וּמָה אֶתְבּוֹנֵן עַל בְּתוּלָה",
מְלַמֵּד שֶׁהֶחֱמִיר אִיּוֹב עַל עַצְמוֹ, וְלֹא נִסְתַּכֵּל אֲפִילוּ בִּבְתוּלָה, וַהֲלֹא
דְּבָרִים קַל וָחוֹמֶר, וּמָה אִם בְּתוּלָה זוֹ, שֶׁאִם יִרְצֶה יִשָּׂאֶנָּה לְעַצְמוֹ (לִבְנוֹ
לְאָחִיו וְלִקְרוֹבוֹ) הֶחֱמִיר אִיּוֹב עַל עַצְמוֹ וְלֹא נִסְתַּכֵּל בָּהּ, אֵשֶׁת אִישׁ עַל
אַחַת כַּמָּה וְכַמָּה. וּמִפְּנֵי מָה הֶחֱמִיר אִיּוֹב עַל עַצְמוֹ וְלֹא נִסְתַּכֵּל אֲפִילוּ
בִּבְתוּלָה, מִפְּנֵי שֶׁאָמַר אִיּוֹב: שֶׁמָּא אֶסְתַּכֵּל אֲנִי הַיּוֹם, וּלְמָחָר יָבֹא אִישׁ
אַחֵר וְיִשָּׂאֶנָּה, וְנִמְצָא שֶׁאֲנִי מִסְתַּכֵּל בְּאֵשֶׁת אִישׁ[87]:

The Baraisa resumes its discussion of Job and gives a specific example of how he made a protective fence to distance himself from sin:[86]

הֲרֵי הוּא אוֹמֵר "בְּרִית כָּרַתִּי לְעֵינָי וּמָה אֶתְבּוֹנֵן עַל בְּתוּלָה" — It says that Job declared, *I forged a covenant for my eyes, and I would not gaze at a maiden* (*Job* 31:1). מְלַמֵּד שֶׁהֶחֱמִיר אִיּוֹב עַל עַצְמוֹ וְלֹא נִסְתַּכֵּל אֲפִילוּ בִּבְתוּלָה — This teaches that Job was strict with himself, and did not gaze at any woman, even **a maiden.** וַהֲלֹא דְּבָרִים קַל וָחוֹמֶר — Now, is it not then a *kal va'chomer?* וּמָה אִם בְּתוּלָה זוֹ שֶׁאִם יִרְצֶה יִשָּׂאֶנָּה לְעַצְמוֹ לִבְנוֹ לְאָחִיו וְלִקְרוֹבוֹ — If with regard to **a maiden** — whom, if he wanted, he could marry her **to himself** or **to his son** or **to his brother** or **to** some other **relative,** and it would therefore have been acceptable for him to gaze at her to see if she was fitting for one of them — הֶחֱמִיר אִיּוֹב עַל עַצְמוֹ וְלֹא נִסְתַּכֵּל בָּהּ — **Job was strict with himself, and did not gaze at her,** אֵשֶׁת אִישׁ עַל אַחַת כַּמָּה וְכַמָּה — then with regard to **a married woman** — for whom there would be no acceptable reason to gaze at her — **all the more so** that he would certainly not gaze at her. וּמִפְּנֵי מָה הֶחֱמִיר אִיּוֹב עַל עַצְמוֹ וְלֹא נִסְתַּכֵּל אֲפִילוּ בִּבְתוּלָה — And why was Job strict with himself and did not gaze even at even **a maiden?** מִפְּנֵי שֶׁאָמַר אִיּוֹב — Because Job said to himself, שֶׁמָּא אֶסְתַּכֵּל אֲנִי הַיּוֹם וּלְמָחָר יָבֹא אִישׁ אַחֵר וְיִשָּׂאֶנָּה — "Perhaps I will gaze at her today, and tomorrow another man will come along and marry her, וְנִמְצָא שֶׁאֲנִי מִסְתַּכֵּל בְּאֵשֶׁת אִישׁ — and it will emerge that I am gazing at a married woman!"[87]

כְּחוֹתָם, *and I made you like the seal,* indicates that God caused him to be circumcised before birth, as circumcision is called the "seal" on a Jewish man's body [as we say in the blessing on circumcision, and in the second blessing of *Bircas HaMazon*] (*Yaavetz*).

86. *Ahavas Chesed.*

87. A person is likely to continue what he has done previously, even if it has now become forbidden. Alternatively, it means that the image of her that became fixed in his mind before she was married will remain, and his thinking of that image now that she is married would be tantamount to gazing at a married woman (*Magen Avos*).

ו. אֵיזֶהוּ סְיָיג שֶׁעָשׂוּ נְבִיאִים לְדִבְרֵיהֶם, הֲרֵי הוּא אוֹמֵר (ישעיה מב,
יג) "ה' כַּגִּבּוֹר יֵצֵא כְּאִישׁ מִלְחָמוֹת יָעִיר קִנְאָה יָרִיעַ אַף יַצְרִיחַ",
לֹא כְּגִבּוֹר אֶחָד אֶלָּא כְּכָל הַגִּבּוֹרִים שֶׁבָּעוֹלָם. כַּיּוֹצֵא בּוֹ, (עמוס ג, ח)
"אַרְיֵה שָׁאָג מִי לֹא יִירָא ה' אֱלֹהִים דִּבֶּר מִי לֹא יִנָּבֵא", לֹא כְּאַרְיֵה
אֶחָד בִּלְבַד אֶלָּא כְּכָל אֲרָיוֹת שֶׁבָּעוֹלָם. כַּיּוֹצֵא בּוֹ (יחזקאל מג, ב) "וְהִנֵּה
כְּבוֹד אֱלֹהֵי יִשְׂרָאֵל בָּא מִדֶּרֶךְ הַקָּדִים וְקוֹלוֹ כְּקוֹל מַיִם רַבִּים וְהָאָרֶץ
הֵאִירָה מִכְּבֹדוֹ", "כְּקוֹל מַיִם רַבִּים" זֶה גַּבְרִיאֵל הַמַּלְאָךְ[88], "וְהָאָרֶץ
הֵאִירָה מִכְּבֹדוֹ" אֵלּוּ פְּנֵי הַשְּׁכִינָה, וַהֲלֹא דְבָרִים קַל וָחֹמֶר, מַה
גַּבְרִיאֵל שֶׁהוּא אֶחָד מֵאֶלֶף אַלְפֵי אֲלָפִים וְרִבֵּי רְבָבוֹת שֶׁעוֹמְדִים לְפָנָיו,

§6 The next of those who made protective fences around their words: אֵיזֶהוּ סְיָיג שֶׁעָשׂוּ נְבִיאִים לְדִבְרֵיהֶם — What is an example of a fence that the prophets made around their words? הֲרֵי הוּא אוֹמֵר "ה' כַּגִּבּוֹר יֵצֵא כְּאִישׁ מִלְחָמוֹת יָעִיר קִנְאָה יָרִיעַ אַף יַצְרִיחַ" — It says in *Isaiah*, *HASHEM will go forth like a mighty warrior, He will arouse vengeance like a man of war; He will shout triumphantly, even roar; He will overpower His enemies* (Isaiah 42:13). לֹא כְּגִבּוֹר אֶחָד אֶלָּא כְּכָל הַגִּבּוֹרִים שֶׁבָּעוֹלָם — Now, God's power is not merely like that of *one* warrior, but like that of *all* the warriors in the world combined, and even more! Why then does the prophet describe Him in such a limited way?

The same question with regard to other verses in the Prophets: כַּיּוֹצֵא בּוֹ "אַרְיֵה שָׁאָג מִי לֹא יִירָא ה' אֱלֹהִים דִּבֶּר מִי לֹא יִנָּבֵא" — Similarly, the prophet Amos says, *A lion has roared; who will not fear? The Lord HASHEM/ ELOHIM has spoken; who will not prophesy?* (Amos 3:8). לֹא כְּאַרְיֵה אֶחָד בִּלְבַד אֶלָּא כְּכָל אֲרָיוֹת שֶׁבָּעוֹלָם — Now, the "roar" of God is not merely like that of *one* lion, but like that of *all* the lions in the world combined, and even more! Why then does the prophet describe Him in such a limited way? כַּיּוֹצֵא בּוֹ "וְהִנֵּה כְּבוֹד אֱלֹהֵי יִשְׂרָאֵל בָּא מִדֶּרֶךְ הַקָּדִים וְקוֹלוֹ כְּקוֹל מַיִם רַבִּים וְהָאָרֶץ הֵאִירָה מִכְּבֹדוֹ" — Similarly, the prophet Ezekiel says, *And behold, the glory of the God of Israel was coming from the east. Its sound was like the sound of a multitude of waters, and the earth shone with His glory* (Ezekiel 43:2). "כְּקוֹל מַיִם רַבִּים" זֶה גַּבְרִיאֵל הַמַּלְאָךְ — The Baraisa expounds the verse: *Like the sound of a multitude of waters* refers to the voice of the angel Gabriel;[88] "וְהָאָרֶץ הֵאִירָה מִכְּבֹדוֹ" אֵלּוּ פְּנֵי הַשְּׁכִינָה — and *the earth shone with His glory* refers to the radiance of the Divine Presence. וַהֲלֹא דְבָרִים קַל וָחֹמֶר — Now, is it not a *kal va'chomer*? מַה גַּבְרִיאֵל שֶׁהוּא אֶחָד מֵאֶלֶף אַלְפֵי אֲלָפִים וְרִבֵּי רְבָבוֹת שֶׁעוֹמְדִים לְפָנָיו — If Gabriel — who is merely one of the thousands of thousands upon thousands and myriads upon myriads of angels who stand

88. Whose body is likened elsewhere [*Daniel* 10:6] to that of a sea (see *Ahavas Chesed*).

קוֹלוֹ הוֹלֵךְ מִסּוֹף הָעוֹלָם וְעַד סוֹפוֹ[89], מֶלֶךְ מַלְכֵי הַמְּלָכִים הַקָּדוֹשׁ בָּרוּךְ הוּא שֶׁבָּרָא אֶת כָּל הָעוֹלָם כּוּלּוֹ, בָּרָא הָעֶלְיוֹנִים וּבָרָא אֶת הַתַּחְתּוֹנִים עַל אַחַת כַּמָּה וְכַמָּה. אֶלָּא מַרְאִין אֶת הָעַיִן מַה שֶׁיְכוֹלָה לִרְאוֹת, וּמַשְׁמִיעִין אֶת הָאוֹזֶן מַה שֶׁיְכוֹלָה לִשְׁמוֹעַ[90]:

ז. אֵיזֶהוּ סְיָיג שֶׁעָשׂוּ כְּתוּבִים לְדִבְרֵיהֶם[91], הֲרֵי הוּא אוֹמֵר (משלי ה, ח) "הַרְחֵק מֵעָלֶיהָ דַרְכֶּךָ וְאַל תִּקְרַב אֶל פֶּתַח בֵּיתָהּ", "הַרְחֵק מֵעָלֶיהָ דַרְכֶּךָ" זוֹ אֶפִּיקוֹרְסִים, שֶׁאוֹמְרִים לוֹ לָאָדָם: אַל תֵּלֵךְ בֵּין הָאֶפִּיקוֹרְסִים[92],

---

קוֹלוֹ הוֹלֵךְ מִסּוֹף הָעוֹלָם וְעַד סוֹפוֹ — his voice travels from one end of the world to the other,[89]   before [God] — מֶלֶךְ מַלְכֵי הַמְּלָכִים הַקָּדוֹשׁ בָּרוּךְ הוּא — then the King of all kings, the Holy One, Blessed is He אֶת כָּל הָעוֹלָם כּוּלּוֹ — Who created the entire world, and — בָּרָא הָעֶלְיוֹנִים וּבָרָא אֶת הַתַּחְתּוֹנִים — Who created both the upper and lower spheres — עַל אַחַת כַּמָּה וְכַמָּה — how much more so is His voice infinitely greater! Why then does Scripture limit its description of God's voice by likening it to that of Gabriel's? אֶלָּא מַרְאִין אֶת הָעַיִן מַה שֶׁיְכוֹלָה לִרְאוֹת — The answer to all of these questions is the same: It is only because they show the eye only what it is able to see, וּמַשְׁמִיעִין אֶת הָאוֹזֶן מַה שֶׁיְכוֹלָה לִשְׁמוֹעַ — and they let the ear hear only what it is able to hear.[90]

§7 The next of those who made protective fences around their words: אֵיזֶהוּ סְיָיג שֶׁעָשׂוּ כְּתוּבִים לְדִבְרֵיהֶם — What is an example of a protective fence that the authors of the Writings made around their words?[91] הֲרֵי הוּא אוֹמֵר — It says in the Writings, "הַרְחֵק מֵעָלֶיהָ דַרְכֶּךָ וְאַל תִּקְרַב אֶל פֶּתַח בֵּיתָהּ" Distance your way from her, and do not come near the door of her house (Proverbs 5:8). "הַרְחֵק מֵעָלֶיהָ דַרְכֶּךָ" זוֹ אֶפִּיקוֹרְסִים — The Baraisa expounds the verse: Distance your way from her refers to keeping away from heretics. שֶׁאוֹמְרִים לוֹ לָאָדָם אַל תֵּלֵךְ בֵּין הָאֶפִּיקוֹרְסִים — For we tell a person, "Do not

---

89. The Baraisa does not subtantiate this assertion. *Magen Avos* writes that our Sages say this elsewhere. [Perhaps the Baraisa here refers to *the sound of a multitude of waters* mentioned in the verse — i.e., the sound of the oceans that span the earth and whose sound thus travels "from one end of the world to the other."]

90. To express God's might, roar, or sound in much greater terms would overwhelm the human mind. Therefore, the prophets placed "fences" around their words to limit them to what people can grasp (see *Ahavas Chesed*). Alternatively, comparing God to any or all of His creatures is fundamentally

impossible. We do so only as a way of conveying to the human mind what it is able to comprehend. Had the prophets described God in terms of the highest magnitude, one might have mistakenly thought that the description was accurate. Therefore, they "made a fence" to guard against such mistaken notions by deliberately *limiting* their descriptions, thereby indicating that such comparisons are by their very nature inadequate (*Kisei Rachamim*).

91. Our Baraisa's inclusion here of the fence that "the Writings" made around their words would suggest that "the Writings" were included in the Baraisa's list above (1 §5) of

וְאַל תִּכָּנֵס לְשָׁם, שֶׁמָּא תְּבֻשַׁל בָּם.94,93 וְאִם אָמַר: בּוֹטֵחַ אֲנִי בְּעַצְמִי שֶׁאַף
עַל פִּי שֶׁאֲנִי הוֹלֵךְ שָׁם אֵינִי נִכְשָׁל בָּם, שֶׁמָּא תֹאמַר: שׁוֹמֵעַ אֲנִי אֶת דִּבְרֵיהֶם
וְחוֹזֵר בִּי95, תַּלְמוּד לוֹמַר (שם ב, יט) "כָּל בָּאֶיהָ לֹא יְשׁוּבוּן וְלֹא יַשִּׂיגוּ אָרְחוֹת
חַיִּים"96. כְּתִיב (שם ט, ב) "טָבְחָה טִבְחָה מָסְכָה יֵינָהּ אַף עָרְכָה שֻׁלְחָנָהּ",

---

walk among the heretics,[92] וְאַל תִּכָּנֵס לְשָׁם שֶׁמָּא תְּבֻשַׁל בָּם — **and do not**
even **enter** a place if they are there,[93] for **perhaps you will stumble with them**
and be led astray."[94] וְאִם אָמַר: בּוֹטֵחַ אֲנִי בְּעַצְמִי שֶׁאַף עַל פִּי שֶׁאֲנִי הוֹלֵךְ שָׁם
אֵינִי נִכְשָׁל בָּם — **And perhaps one will say, "I am confident that even if I go**
there, I will not stumble with them. שֶׁמָּא תֹאמַר שׁוֹמֵעַ אֲנִי אֶת דִּבְרֵיהֶם וְחוֹזֵר
בִּי — **And even if you will say** to me that my confidence is misplaced and that
I *will* **listen to their words** and find them compelling, even then **I will** eventually reject them **and return** to the proper beliefs."[95] תַּלְמוּד לוֹמַר "כָּל בָּאֶיהָ
לֹא יְשׁוּבוּן וְלֹא יַשִּׂיגוּ אָרְחוֹת חַיִּים" — **Scripture** elsewhere **teaches** otherwise **by**
saying, *And all who come to her do not return, nor do they attain the paths*
of life (ibid. 2:19).[96]

The Baraisa speaks further about those who are ensnared by the heretics:
כְּתִיב "טָבְחָה טִבְחָה מָסְכָה יֵינָהּ אַף עָרְכָה שֻׁלְחָנָהּ" — **It is written** in Scripture,
She prepared her meat, mixed her wine, and also set her table (ibid. 9:2).

---

those who made fences around their words.
Our texts of 1 §5, however, do not list "the
Writings." It may be that the Baraisa there
felt it unnecessary to specify "the Writings,"
considering them to be a subcategory of
"the Prophets" listed there. It is more likely,
though, that our texts there are corrupted
and should be emended to include "the
Writings" as well [a reading found there in at
least one manuscript] (*Magen Avos*).

92. As indicated by the verse's first exhortation, *Distance your way from her* (*Ben*
Avraham).

93. As indicated by the verse's second ex-
horation, *and do not come near the door of*
her house (*Ben Avraham*).

94. Thus, the verse cautions us to avoid
even the proximity of heretics, lest you
come to mingle with them (*Mefaresh*).

The first part of the verse, *Distance your*
way from her, is the primary warning; *and*
do not come near the door of her house is the
"fence" that the verse made to distance us
even further (see *Magen Avos*, second approach). Alternatively, the Baraisa does not

mean literally that the Writings made a fence
around *their* words; rather, the entire verse
is a fence made for *us,* to avoid not only
heresy, but even contact with those who
embrace it (*Magen Avos,* first approach).

95. Explanation follows *Mefaresh,* cited in
part by *Binyan Yehoshua.*

96. Both claims of this overconfident person are erroneous: A person who involves
himself in heretical ideas will *not* avoid
stumbling, and will likely be forever ensnared by them [*all who come to her do not*
return]. And even if he *will* subsequently try
to return and repent, the pain and struggle
of doing so will cause his early demise
[*nor do they attain the paths of life*]; this is
a Divine decree as punishment for his sin
(*Binyan Yehoshua,* from *Avodah Zarah* 17a
with *Rashi*). [*Rashi* on the verse implies that
while repentance in this matter is exceedingly difficult, it is not impossible; see also
Metzudos there.]

[See *Magen Avos* here, who writes that our
Baraisa does *not* refer to one who contends
with heretics in order to refute them.]

אֵלּוּ רְשָׁעִים, שֶׁבִּזְמַן שֶׁאָדָם נִכְנָס בֵּינֵיהֶם מַאֲכִילִין אוֹתוֹ וּמַשְׁקִין אוֹתוֹ
וּמַלְבִּישִׁין אוֹתוֹ וּמְכַסִּין אוֹתוֹ וְנוֹתְנִין לוֹ מָמוֹן הַרְבֵּה. כֵּיוָן שֶׁהָיָה כְּאֶחָד
מֵהֶם כָּל אֶחָד וְאֶחָד מַכִּיר אֶת שֶׁלּוֹ וְנוֹטְלוֹ. וַעֲלֵיהֶם נֶאֱמַר (שם ז, כג)
"עַד יְפַלַּח חֵץ כְּבֵדוֹ [כְּמַהֵר] צִפּוֹר אֶל פָּח וְלֹא יָדַע"‎98. דָּבָר אַחֵר,
"הַרְחֵק מֵעָלֶיהָ דַרְכֶּךְ" זוֹ זוֹנָה, שֶׁאוֹמְרִים לוֹ לָאָדָם: אַל תֵּלֵךְ בְּשׁוּק
זֶה, וְאַל תִּכָּנֵס בְּמָבוֹי זֶה, שֶׁזּוֹנָה יֵשׁ שָׁם נָאָה וּמְשׁוּבַּחַת. וְהוּא אוֹמֵר:
בּוֹטֵחַ אֲנִי בְּעַצְמִי שֶׁאַף עַל פִּי שֶׁאֲנִי הוֹלֵךְ לְשָׁם אֵינִי נִכְשָׁל בָּהּ. אָמְרוּ
לוֹ: אַף עַל פִּי שֶׁאַתָּה בּוֹטֵחַ בְּעַצְמְךָ אַל תֵּלֵךְ לְשָׁם שֶׁמָּא תִּבָּשֵׁל
בָּהּ, (שֶׁהֲרֵי אָמְרוּ חֲכָמִים שֶׁלֹּא יַרְגִּיל אָדָם לַעֲבוֹר עַל פֶּתַח זוֹנָה,)

אֵלּוּ רְשָׁעִים — Who is "she" in this verse? These are the wicked heretics.[97]
שֶׁבִּזְמַן שֶׁאָדָם נִכְנָס בֵּינֵיהֶם — For when a person enters among them, מַאֲכִילִין
אוֹתוֹ וּמַשְׁקִין אוֹתוֹ וּמַלְבִּישִׁין אוֹתוֹ וּמְכַסִּין אוֹתוֹ — they feed him, give him to
drink, clothe him, give him covering, וְנוֹתְנִין לוֹ מָמוֹן הַרְבֵּה — and give him
much money, all in an effort to influence him to join them. כֵּיוָן שֶׁהָיָה כְּאֶחָד
מֵהֶם — However, once he becomes like one of them, כָּל אֶחָד וְאֶחָד מַכִּיר אֶת
שֶׁלּוֹ וְנוֹטְלוֹ — each one of them identifies what was originally his and takes it
back from the apostate. וַעֲלֵיהֶם נֶאֱמַר "עַד יְפַלַּח חֵץ כְּבֵדוֹ כְּמַהֵר צִפּוֹר אֶל פָּח
וְלֹא יָדַע" — And regarding those who are ensnared in this way by the heretics,
it says in another verse, *Until the arrow splits his liver; he is like a bird
hurrying to the trap, unaware that its life will be lost* (ibid. 7:23).[98]

A different explanation of the *Proverbs* verse cited above, which shows yet
another protective fence that the Writings made around their words:
דָּבָר אַחֵר, "הַרְחֵק מֵעָלֶיהָ דַרְכֶּךְ" זוֹ זוֹנָה — Alternatively: *Distance your way
from her* and do not come near the door of her house (ibid. 5:8) refers to keeping one's distance from a harlot. שֶׁאוֹמְרִים לוֹ לָאָדָם: אַל תֵּלֵךְ בְּשׁוּק זֶה וְאַל
תִּכָּנֵס בְּמָבוֹי זֶה — Accordingly, Scripture is telling us that we should say to a
person, "Do not walk in this market, and do not enter this alley, שֶׁזּוֹנָה יֵשׁ
שָׁם נָאָה וּמְשׁוּבַּחַת — for a harlot is there who is attractive and acclaimed."
וְהוּא אוֹמֵר: בּוֹטֵחַ אֲנִי בְּעַצְמִי שֶׁאַף עַל פִּי שֶׁאֲנִי הוֹלֵךְ לְשָׁם אֵינִי נִכְשָׁל בָּהּ — And if
he replies, "I am confident that even if I go there, I will not stumble and sin
with her," אָמְרוּ לוֹ: אַף עַל פִּי שֶׁאַתָּה בּוֹטֵחַ בְּעַצְמְךָ — then say to him, "Even
though you are confident that you will not fall prey, אַל תֵּלֵךְ לְשָׁם שֶׁמָּא תִּבָּשֵׁל
בָּהּ — still do not go there, for perhaps you *will* stumble and sin with her!"
שֶׁהֲרֵי אָמְרוּ חֲכָמִים שֶׁלֹּא יַרְגִּיל אָדָם לַעֲבוֹר עַל פֶּתַח זוֹנָה — For indeed our Sages
have said that one should not be accustomed to pass the door of a harlot,

---

97. [Translation follows the various texts
that have here "מִינֵי" רְשָׁעִים.]
98. Like a bird lured by bait in a trap, so too

is the one enticed by the gifts of the heretics,
unaware that they will only lure him to his
downfall.

שֶׁנֶּאֱמַר (שם פסוק כו) "כִּי רַבִּים חֲלָלִים הִפִּילָה וַעֲצֻמִים כָּל הֲרֻגֶיהָ"‎‎[99]:

ח. אֵיזֶהוּ סְיָיג שֶׁעָשׂוּ חֲכָמִים לְדִבְרֵיהֶם, שֶׁחֲכָמִים אוֹמְרִים: קְרִיאַת שְׁמַע שֶׁל עַרְבִית עַד חֲצוֹת. (רַבָּן גַּמְלִיאֵל אוֹמֵר: עַד קְרוֹת הַגֶּבֶר.) כֵּיצַד‎[100], אָדָם בָּא מִמְּלַאכְתּוֹ אַל יֹאמַר: אוֹכַל קִימְעָא וְאֶשְׁתֶּה קִימְעָא וְאִישַׁן קִימְעָא וְאַחַר כָּךְ אֶקְרָא קְרִיאַת שְׁמַע, נִמְצָא יָשֵׁן כָּל הַלַּיְלָה וְאֵינוֹ קוֹרֵא, אֶלָּא אָדָם בָּא מִמְּלַאכְתּוֹ בָּעֶרֶב, יֵלֵךְ לְבֵית הַכְּנֶסֶת אוֹ לְבֵית הַמִּדְרָשׁ, אִם רָגִיל לִקְרוֹת קוֹרֵא‎[101], וְאִם רָגִיל לִשְׁנוֹת שׁוֹנֶה, וְאִם לָאו קוֹרֵא

"כִּי רַבִּים חֲלָלִים הִפִּילָה וַעֲצֻמִים כָּל הֲרֻגֶיהָ" שֶׁנֶּאֱמַר — as it is stated, *For she has felled many victims, and all her slain are "mighty"* (ibid. 7:26).[99]

§8 The last in the list of those who made protective fences around their words: אֵיזֶהוּ סְיָיג שֶׁעָשׂוּ חֲכָמִים לְדִבְרֵיהֶם — What is an example of a fence that the Sages made around their words? שֶׁחֲכָמִים אוֹמְרִים: קְרִיאַת שְׁמַע שֶׁל עַרְבִית עַד חֲצוֹת — It is that which we are taught in the Mishnah (*Berachos* 2a): The Sages say that the reciting of the evening *Shema* may be done only until midnight. רַבָּן גַּמְלִיאֵל אוֹמֵר: עַד קְרוֹת הַגֶּבֶר — Rabban Gamliel disagrees and says: It can be done until the rooster crows (i.e., the entire night). כֵּיצַד — How is this?[100] אָדָם בָּא מִמְּלַאכְתּוֹ — When a person comes home in the evening from his work, אַל יֹאמַר: אוֹכַל קִימְעָא וְאֶשְׁתֶּה קִימְעָא וְאִישַׁן קִימְעָא — the Sages wanted to ensure that he should not say, "First I will eat a bit, drink a bit, and sleep a bit, וְאַחַר כָּךְ אֶקְרָא קְרִיאַת שְׁמַע — and afterward I will recite the *Shema*," נִמְצָא יָשֵׁן כָּל הַלַּיְלָה וְאֵינוֹ קוֹרֵא — for then it will likely emerge that he will sleep through the entire night and not recite the *Shema*. אֶלָּא אָדָם בָּא מִמְּלַאכְתּוֹ בָּעֶרֶב — Rather, when a person comes home in the evening from his work, יֵלֵךְ לְבֵית הַכְּנֶסֶת אוֹ לְבֵית הַמִּדְרָשׁ — he should go straight to the synagogue or to the study hall; אִם רָגִיל לִקְרוֹת קוֹרֵא – if he is accustomed to recite Scripture, he should recite Scripture until nightfall;[101] וְאִם רָגִיל לִשְׁנוֹת שׁוֹנֶה — and if he is accustomed to learning Mishnah, then he should learn Mishnah until nightfall. וְאִם לָאו קוֹרֵא

---

99. Indicating that even the most strong-willed and principled among men were not able to withstand the lure of such women (see *Binyan Yehoshua*). [The word עֲצֻמִים, *mighty,* in the verse is being understood as meaning "mighty in character" rather than "mighty in number" (see *Ralbag* on the verse).]

100. This question refers back to the view of the Sages that *Shema* must be recited before midnight. And the question is: Since we know that the Sages agree in principle with Rabban

Gamliel's interpretation of the Torah's command to recite *Shema* "*when you lie down*" (*Deuteronomy* 6:7) as meaning *any* time during the night, which is "the time when people are lying down," why did they insist that one recite it before midnight? (*Binyan Yehoshua*; see, however, below, note 103).

101. *Binyan Yehoshua.* [Studying Torah during the twilight period is especially important, so as to connect the day to the night through Torah study (ibid., from *Shelah*).]

קְרִיאַת שְׁמַע וּמִתְפַּלֵּל[102,103], וְכָל הָעוֹבֵר עַל דִּבְרֵי [חֲכָמִים] חַיָּב מִיתָה[104].

קְרִיאַת שְׁמַע וּמִתְפַּלֵּל — **And if** he is **not** accustomed to studying either Scripture or Mishnah, **he should recite the** Shema **and pray** Shemoneh Esrei.[102] The Sages' insistence that the Shema be recited before midnight is a protective fence that they made for their words.[103] וְכָל הָעוֹבֵר עַל דִּבְרֵי חֲכָמִים חַיָּב מִיתָה — **And anyone who transgresses the words of the Sages is liable to death!**[104]

---

102. The words וְאִם לָאו, and if not, do not seem to fit here: If it is not yet nightfall, then why is the person being told to pray early? Magen Avos suggests that these words be omitted; indeed, they do not appear in the Gemara's citation of our Baraisa (Berachos 4b), and Nuschas HaGra omits them as well. If these words are to be retained (they indeed appear in the available manuscripts), Magen Avos suggests the following explanation: If a person is unable to learn until nightfall, he should recite Shema and pray Shemoneh Esrei immediately; he fulfills his prayer obligation even though it is not yet night [see Berachos 27a], and his prior recitation of the Shema is not in fulfillment of that obligation (as it is not yet night), but in order that he pray after reciting words of Torah. By the time he finishes praying, night will have already fallen, and he will then recite the Shema again to fulfill that obligation. Alternatively, Avos HaRosh [Vol. 1] suggests a novel explanation: The Baraisa refers to where a person comes in from work when night has already fallen. When it says if he is accustomed to recite ..., it is teaching not a recommended practice but rather a permit — even though it is forbidden to engage before Shema and prayer in any activity that is liable to become prolonged (such as eating, drinking, and sleeping), it is permitted to study Torah if he is accustomed to do so, i.e., if this is his set time for doing so. For in that case, there is no concern that his learning will become drawn out beyond his set time (see Taz, Orach Chaim 431:2).

103. Thinking that one has the entire night to fulfill his obligation is likely to lead to delay upon delay, until one becomes involved in eating and sleeping until morning. By insisting that one recite the Shema before midnight, the Sages accomplished that a person will feel the time constraint and recite the Shema immediately when night falls, before involving himself in anything else (see Binyan Yehoshua, from Berachos 4b, as explained by Re'ah there). [What is somewhat difficult, however, is that the "fence" our Baraisa speaks of (to recite the Shema before midnight) is not so much a fence that the Sages made for their words, but rather for the Torah's words that one must recite the Shema sometime during the night.]

Some Rishonim, however, explain that the Baraisa's words, How? When a person comes from his work, he should not say ..., teach us a Rabbinic directive (true according to both Rabban Gamliel and the Sages) against involving ourselves in eating, drinking, and sleeping before reciting the nighttime Shema. This "fence" — that Shema be recited right away, before involving ourselves in other things — was made so that one not come to miss the deadline for the Shema (Rashba to Berachos 9a, in explanation of Rif). Now, according to Rabban Gamliel, who sets dawn as the deadline for reciting the Shema, this decree that one recite the Shema immediately at nightfall is a fence to protect against missing the Biblical deadline of dawn. According to the Sages, who say that there is a Rabbinic deadline of "midnight" for reciting the Shema, however, this additional decree that one recite the Shema immediately upon nightfall is a fence that the Rabbis made for their words — so that one not come to miss even the Rabbinic deadline of midnight (see R' Yonah to Berachos 2a; see Ahavas Chesed and Avos HaRosh [Vol. 1] here).

104. The Gemara in Berachos (4b) explains that the Sages made this harsh statement particularly in this case because the urge to

רַבָּן גַּמְלִיאֵל אוֹמֵר: פְּעָמִים שֶׁאָדָם קוֹרֵא אוֹתָהּ [שְׁתֵּי פְּעָמִים] בַּלַּיְלָה,
אַחַת עַד שֶׁלֹּא יַעֲלֶה עַמּוּד הַשַּׁחַר וְאַחַת מִשֶּׁיַּעֲלֶה עַמּוּד הַשַּׁחַר, וְנִמְצָא
יוֹצֵא בָהּ יְדֵי חוֹבָתוֹ שֶׁל יוֹם וְשֶׁל לַיְלָה[105]. (עָמְדוּ חֲכָמִים וְהִרְבּוּ וְעָשׂוּ
סְיָיג לְדִבְרֵיהֶם[106]):

ט. [וְהַעֲמִידוּ[107] תַּלְמִידִים הַרְבֵּה,] שֶׁבֵּית שַׁמַּאי אוֹמְרִים: אַל יִשְׁנֶה

The Baraisa records a related teaching, which highlights the need for the protective fence in this matter:

רַבָּן גַּמְלִיאֵל אוֹמֵר: פְּעָמִים שֶׁאָדָם קוֹרֵא אוֹתָהּ שְׁתֵּי פְּעָמִים בַּלַּיְלָה — **Rabban Gamliel says: There are times that a person will recite [the Shema] twice at night in close succession —** אַחַת עַד שֶׁלֹּא יַעֲלֶה עַמּוּד הַשַּׁחַר וְאַחַת מִשֶּׁיַּעֲלֶה עַמּוּד הַשַּׁחַר — **once just before dawn and once right after dawn,** וְנִמְצָא יוֹצֵא בָהּ יְדֵי חוֹבָתוֹ שֶׁל יוֹם וְשֶׁל לַיְלָה — **and it will emerge that he has thereby fulfilled** both **his obligation of** reciting the Shema by **day and** his obligation of reciting the Shema by **night.**[105] עָמְדוּ חֲכָמִים וְהִרְבּוּ וְעָשׂוּ סְיָיג לְדִבְרֵיהֶם — **The Sages** therefore **arose and made many a** protective **fence around their words.**[106]

§9 The Baraisa expounds the second saying of the men of the Great Assembly, cited in the previous chapter (§3):[107]

וְהַעֲמִידוּ תַּלְמִידִים הַרְבֵּה — **"Develop many disciples"** — how is this to be understood? שֶׁבֵּית שַׁמַּאי אוֹמְרִים — In the sense that while **Beis Shammai say**

---

sleep at night is particularly strong. Alternatively, it is to reinforce the notion that praying Shemoneh Esrei at night is obligatory, and not merely optional, as other opinions maintain (Binyan Yehoshua). [According to the latter explanation, the "transgression of the words of the Sages" meant here is not transgressing their directive to recite Shema early, but rather transgressing their directive to "recite the Shema **and pray Shemoneh Esrei"** (Emes LeYaakov to the Gemara there).]

105. Although the two recitations are made in quick succession, each one fulfills a different obligation, because one is recited at the time of "lying down" and the other at the time of "arising" (see Binyan Yehoshua, from Berachos 8b; see Rishonim there for considerable discussion; see also Orach Chaim 58:3-5 and 235:3-4). [Rabban Gamliel is following his view that the time for the nighttime Shema is until dawn (see Magen Avos).]

106. [Since we see from this law that

(Biblically) the last time for the evening Shema and the first time for the morning Shema are in close succession "at night," the Sages were concerned that the times might be confused, and made a fence that one should recite the nighttime Shema before midnight. According to the second approach in note 103, even Rabban Gamliel makes a fence in this matter and agrees that one must strive to recite the Shema when night falls before involving himself in other things.]

The expression "וְהִרְבּוּ", which implies that there was more than one fence made in this matter, fits well according to the opinion of the Sages, as explained by the second approach in note 103, who hold that a double fence was made — one to recite the Shema before midnight, and another to recite it even earlier, at the beginning of the night (Ahavas Chesed, Avos HaRosh [Vol. 1]).

107. [See above, Chapter 1 note 60, for why the Baraisa expounds the last two sayings of the men of the Great Assembly out of order.]

אָדָם אֶלָּא לְמִי שֶׁהוּא חָכָם, וְעָנָיו, וּבֶן אָבוֹת, וְעָשִׁיר[108]. וּבֵית הִלֵּל
אוֹמְרִים: לְכָל אָדָם יִשְׁנֶה, שֶׁהַרְבֵּה פוֹשְׁעִים הָיוּ בָהֶם בְּיִשְׂרָאֵל וְנִתְקָרְבוּ
לְתַלְמוּד תּוֹרָה וְיָצְאוּ מֵהֶם צַדִּיקִים, וַחֲסִידִים, וּכְשֵׁרִים[109]:

אַל יִשְׁנֶה אָדָם אֶלָּא לְמִי שֶׁהוּא חָכָם וְעָנָיו וּבֶן אָבוֹת וְעָשִׁיר — a person should teach Torah only to a student who is wise, humble, of noble lineage, and wealthy,[108]　וּבֵית הִלֵּל אוֹמְרִים: לְכָל אָדָם יִשְׁנֶה — Beis Hillel, however, say that one should teach Torah to any person.　שֶׁהַרְבֵּה פוֹשְׁעִים הָיוּ בָהֶם בְּיִשְׂרָאֵל — For there were many sinners among the Jewish people who were brought close to the study of Torah,　וְיָצְאוּ מֵהֶם צַדִּיקִים — and there came forth from them people who were righteous, pious, and worthy.[109]

---

108. All of these traits are necessary, according to Beis Shammai, to allow a student to succeed in his Torah studies: Wisdom is needed to grasp what is taught; humility is needed to retain what is taught [for an arrogant person forgets his Torah learning (Pesachim 66b)]; good lineage is needed to merit the Divine assistance earned by the righteous deeds of his ancestors; and wealth is needed so that the student will not resort to using his Torah for monetary gain [see Avos 4:5] (Avos HaRosh [Vol. 1], citing Pesach Einayim).

109. [I.e., not only were they themselves righteous and worthy people, but their offspring were as well (Binyan Yehoshua).] One should therefore not discriminate among the various types of students coming to study Torah, for those who seem the most unworthy may ultimately prove to be the most valuable.

Beis Shammai surely do not argue on a directive of the men of the Great Assembly. Rather, Beis Shammai interpret that directive as encouraging one to have many students within the guidelines that Beis Shammai set forth. Beis Hillel, however, interpret that directive as an invitation to open the doors of the study hall to one and all (Avos HaRosh [Vol. 1]). [The Baraisa, which cites both the views of Beis Shammai and Beis Hillel, obviously intends us to adopt the view of Beis Hillel as authoritative, as is nearly always the case.]

Alternatively, the Baraisa means that [while Beis Shammai do not see themselves at being at odds with the directive of the men of the Great Assembly], the plain meaning of the directive to "develop many disciples" tends to support Beis Hillel's position (Ben Avraham).

﴾ פֶּרֶק ג ﴿

א. רַבִּי עֲקִיבָא אוֹמֵר כָּל הַנּוֹטֵל פְּרוּטָה מִן הַצְּדָקָה בִּזְמַן שֶׁאֵינוֹ צָרִיךְ אֵינוֹ נִפְטָר מִן הָעוֹלָם עַד שֶׁיִּצְטָרֵךְ לַבְּרִיּוֹת. הוּא הָיָה אוֹמֵר הַמַּכְרִיךְ סְמַרְטוּטִין עַל עֵינָיו וְעַל שׁוֹקָיו וְאוֹמֵר תְּנוּ לְסוּמָא, לְמוּכֵּה שְׁחִין זֶה סוֹף

﴾ CHAPTER 3 ﴿

§1 R' Akiva warns against three wrongful practices for which one is liable to be reduced to poverty:[1]

רַבִּי עֲקִיבָא אוֹמֵר — R' Akiva says: כָּל הַנּוֹטֵל פְּרוּטָה מִן הַצְּדָקָה בִּזְמַן שֶׁאֵינוֹ צָרִיךְ — Anyone who takes even a *perutah* from charity when he does not need such assistance אֵינוֹ נִפְטָר מִן הָעוֹלָם עַד שֶׁיִּצְטָרֵךְ לַבְּרִיּוֹת — will not leave the world until he loses his money and becomes genuinely **dependent on** other **people.**[2]

הוּא הָיָה אוֹמֵר — In a similar vein, he used to say: הַמַּכְרִיךְ סְמַרְטוּטִין עַל עֵינָיו וְעַל שׁוֹקָיו — Someone who wraps bandages over his eyes or legs to pretend that he is disabled, וְאוֹמֵר: תְּנוּ לְסוּמָא, לְמוּכֵּה שְׁחִין זֶה — and calls out, "Give charity to this blind man," or "to this man plagued with boils!" סוֹף

---

1. This chapter seems out of place. It does not seem to follow the earlier chapters chronologically (as R' Akiva lived much later than the *Anshei Knesses HaGedolah*) or thematically.

Ben Avraham gives an insightful explanation. This chapter relates to the end of the previous chapter, which detailed the dispute between Beis Shammai and Beis Hillel regarding what kind of students are included in the directive of the *Anshei Knesses HaGedolah* to "raise up many students." Beis Shammai limited this to students who are wise and modest, of good family and of adequate means. Beis Hillel insisted that one should teach *any* student, because there were many sinners in Israel who were then drawn close to Torah study and became righteous and pious. Our chapter follows with the pious teachings of one of the greatest successes of Beis Hillel's approach — R' Akiva. The shepherd Akiva exhibited none of the qualities described by Beis Shammai. He was completely ignorant (below, 6 §2) with a haughty disdain for Torah

scholars (*Pesachim* 49b), he was of exceedingly humble origins (*Rambam,* Introduction to *Mishneh Torah*) and poor. And yet when ignited by the fire of Torah study, he became one of the greatest masters of Torah and piety of all time. This piety is seen in his maxims that begin our chapter — maxims that he not only uttered but that "he used to say," meaning, they were always on his lips and informed his teaching and way of life. Moreover, our chapter extols the virtues of persistent effort, which were key to transforming an unaccomplished youth into one of the Mishnah's greatest sages. Thus, our chapter is the ultimate vindication of Beis Hillel's opinion in the last chapter that we must "raise up many students" of all kinds.

2. Conversely, if a person needs charity and does not take it (but rather finds a way to make do with less), he will not leave the world before he becomes wealthy enough to help others (*Mishnah, Peah* 8:8).

שֶׁהוּא אוֹמֵר לַאֲמִתּוֹ.³ הוּא הָיָה אוֹמֵר: הַחוֹבֵט פִּתּוֹ בַּקַּרְקַע וְהַמְפַזֵּר
מְעוֹתָיו בַּחֲמָתוֹ⁴ אֵינוֹ נִפְטָר מִן הָעוֹלָם עַד שֶׁיִּצְטָרֵךְ לַבְּרִיּוֹת:⁵

ב. הוּא הָיָה אוֹמֵר: הַקּוֹרֵעַ אֶת בְּגָדָיו בַּחֲמָתוֹ וְהַמְשַׁבֵּר כֵּלָיו בַּחֲמָתוֹ
סוֹף שֶׁיַּעֲבוֹד עֲבוֹדַת כּוֹכָבִים, שֶׁכָּךְ אוּמָּנָתוֹ שֶׁל יֵצֶר הָרַע הַיּוֹם
אוֹמֵר לוֹ קְרַע אֶת בְּגָדֶיךָ וּלְמָחָר אוֹמֵר לוֹ עֲבוֹד עֲבוֹדַת כּוֹכָבִים:⁶

שֶׁהוּא אוֹמֵר לַאֲמִתּוֹ — in the end will become disabled in that way and have to
say the same appeal in truth.[3]

הוּא הָיָה אוֹמֵר — He also used to say: הַחוֹבֵט פִּתּוֹ בַּקַּרְקַע — Someone who
throws his bread down on the ground,   וְהַמְפַזֵּר מְעוֹתָיו בַּחֲמָתוֹ — or who
scatters his money in his anger,[4] thereby showing disregard for the blessings
God has given him,   אֵינוֹ נִפְטָר מִן הָעוֹלָם עַד שֶׁיִּצְטָרֵךְ לַבְּרִיּוֹת — will not leave
the world until he loses his money and becomes financially dependent on
other people.[5]

§2 Additional sayings of R' Akiva concerning disregard for one's property:

הוּא הָיָה אוֹמֵר — He used to say: הַקּוֹרֵעַ אֶת בְּגָדָיו בַּחֲמָתוֹ — Someone
who tears his clothing in his anger,   וְהַמְשַׁבֵּר כֵּלָיו בַּחֲמָתוֹ — or who breaks
his utensils in his anger,   סוֹף שֶׁיַּעֲבוֹד עֲבוֹדַת כּוֹכָבִים — in the end will go so
far as to worship idols.   שֶׁכָּךְ אוּמָּנָתוֹ שֶׁל יֵצֶר הָרַע — For such are the work-
ings of the evil inclination: הַיּוֹם אוֹמֵר לוֹ קְרַע אֶת בְּגָדֶיךָ — Today it tells him,
"Tear your clothing,"   וּלְמָחָר אוֹמֵר לוֹ עֲבוֹד עֲבוֹדַת כּוֹכָבִים — and the next day
it tells him, "Worship idols."[6]

§3 R' Akiva returns to the theme of the justice that eventually catches up
with schemers:[7]

---

3. This applies even if he is truly poor (for
otherwise he is no different from the im-
postor of the previous teaching who takes
charity he does not need). Though he is
poor, it is wrong for him to pretend that he
is disabled and unable to take a job to support himself (Magen Avos), or to imply that
he deserves more sympathy and a larger
donation than his fellow paupers (Mefaresh,
Binyan Yehoshua).

4. Some omit the word בַּחֲמָתוֹ, in his anger
(Binyan Yehoshua, Kisei Rachamim).

5. He is punished measure for measure.
Since he treated his food and money as if
he had no need for them, he ends up so desperate for food and money that he must go
begging (Magen Avos).

The commentators seem to differ on

whether R' Akiva refers here to where the
person actually ruined his food or squandered his money, and thereby violated the
prohibition against wastefulness (Mefaresh,
Ahavas Chesed), or whether he refers even
to someone who treats his possessions
with disrespect without ruining them (Ben
Avraham).

6. Once the evil inclination accustoms a
person to lose self-control and act irratio-
nally, even if only in relatively small matters
[and only in regard to his own property], it
can induce him to commit any sin in a fit of
rage, even a sin as severe as idolatry (Mesillas Yesharim Ch. 11).

7. Which he mentioned above regarding
those who pretend to have disabilities in order to arouse sympathy (Magen Avos).

ג. הוּא הָיָה אוֹמֵר: הַנּוֹתֵן עֵינָיו בְּאִשְׁתּוֹ שֶׁתָּמוּת וְיִירָשֶׁנָה אוֹ שֶׁתָּמוּת
וְיִשָּׂא אֶת אֲחוֹתָהּ[8] וְכָל הַנּוֹתֵן עֵינָיו בְּאָחִיו שֶׁיָּמוּת וְיִשָּׂא אֶת אִשְׁתּוֹ[9]
סוֹף קוֹבְרִין אוֹתוֹ בְּחַיֵּיהֶן, עָלָיו הַכָּתוּב אוֹמֵר (קהלת י, ח) "חֹפֵר גּוּמָץ בּוֹ
יִפּוֹל וּפֹרֵץ גָּדֵר יִשְּׁכֶנּוּ נָחָשׁ"[10]:

ד. מַעֲשֶׂה בְּאָדָם אֶחָד (שֶׁעָבַר עַל דִּבְרֵי רַבִּי עֲקִיבָא[12]) וּפָרַע רֹאשָׁהּ
שֶׁל אִשָּׁה בַּשּׁוּק וּבָאתָה לִפְנֵי רַבִּי עֲקִיבָא וְחִיְּבוּ לִתֵּן לָהּ

הַנּוֹתֵן עֵינָיו בְּאִשְׁתּוֹ שֶׁתָּמוּת וְיִירָשֶׁנָה — **He used to say:** הוּא הָיָה אוֹמֵר —
Someone who evilly **sets his eyes on his wife,** hoping for her to die so that
he will then **inherit her wealth,** אוֹ שֶׁתָּמוּת וְיִשָּׂא אֶת אֲחוֹתָהּ — **or that she will
die and he will** then **marry her sister;**[8] וְכָל הַנּוֹתֵן עֵינָיו בְּאָחִיו שֶׁיָּמוּת — **and,**
similarly, someone who **sets his eyes on his brother,** hoping for him to die
without children וְיִשָּׂא אֶת אִשְׁתּוֹ — so that **he will,** then be able to **marry**
the brother's wife,[9] סוֹף קוֹבְרִין אוֹתוֹ בְּחַיֵּיהֶן — **in the end it is he who will
be buried in their lifetime,** rather than the other way around. עָלָיו הַכָּתוּב
אוֹמֵר — **Regarding** such a person **Scripture says,** "חֹפֵר גּוּמָץ בּוֹ יִפּוֹל וּפֹרֵץ
גָּדֵר יִשְּׁכֶנּוּ נָחָשׁ" — **He who digs a pit will fall into it, and he who breaks down
a wall will be bitten by a snake** (Ecclesiastes 10:8).[10]

§4 An example of a schemer whose tricks did not succeed:[11]

מַעֲשֶׂה בְּאָדָם אֶחָד שֶׁעָבַר עַל דִּבְרֵי רַבִּי עֲקִיבָא — **There was an incident with
a certain man** (**who violated the words of R' Akiva**[12]) וּפָרַע רֹאשָׁהּ שֶׁל אִשָּׁה
בַּשּׁוּק — **and he uncovered the head of a woman in the street.** וּבָאתָה לִפְנֵי רַבִּי
עֲקִיבָא — **She came** to complain **before** the court of **R' Akiva,** וְחִיְּבוּ לִתֵּן לָהּ

---

8. Which he cannot do while his wife is alive,
even if he divorces her (see *Leviticus* 18:18).

9. In accordance with the law of *yibum*,
which calls for the widow of the childless
man to be wed to his brother (*Deuteronomy*
25:5), a union that is otherwise forbidden
(*Leviticus* 18:16).

10. Although in this case, the evil-eyed offender did not act on his wish — he did not
"dig any pit" — and God does not generally equate an evil thought with a deed,
here the selfish thought was not merely a
passing whim. It was a longstanding ob-
session, which surely expressed itself over
time in some malicious word or deed (*Kisei
Rachamim*).

Alternatively, R' Akiva speaks of where
the schemer fixed an "evil eye" on his wife
or brother, hoping that in this mystical way

he could hasten their deaths and obtain the
wealth or woman that he covets. Thus, he
did "dig a pit" (*Magen Avos, Ben Avraham*).
[For a brief treatment of the concept of
"the evil eye" and how it causes harm, see
Schottenstein edition of *Bava Metzia* 84a,
note 16.]

[Seemingly, even though our Baraisa cites
the entire verse of *Eccleisastes* 10:8, it means
to refer only to the first part — *He who digs a
pit will fall into it.* See, however, *Magen Avos*
for a suggestion as to how the second part of
the verse is relevant here as well.]

11. *Magen Avos.*

12. Which words of R' Akiva did he violate?
It is not immediately clear, and indeed, some
(including *Gra*) omit this phrase from the
text. Others, however, defend the standard
text; see below, note 16.

אַרְבַּע מֵאוֹת זוּז. אָמַר לוֹ: רַבִּי, תֶּן לִי זְמַן. נָתַן לוֹ זְמַן. (כֵּיצַד) אָמַר
לוֹ חֲבֵרוֹ: אֲנִי אֶתֵּן לְךָ עֵצָה שֶׁלֹּא תִתֵּן לָהּ אֲפִילּוּ שָׁוֶה פְּרוּטָה. אָמַר
לוֹ: תֶּן לִי. [אָמַר לוֹ:] לֵךְ טוֹל שֶׁמֶן בִּכְאִיסָר¹³ וּשְׁבוֹר אֶת הַצְּלוֹחִית עַל
פִּתְחָהּ שֶׁל הָאִשָּׁה. מֶה עָשְׂתָה הָאִשָּׁה, יָצְאתָה מִתּוֹךְ בֵּיתָהּ וּפֵרְעָה
רֹאשָׁהּ בַּשּׁוּק וְהָיְתָה מְטַפַּחַת וּמַנַּחַת יָדָהּ עַל רֹאשָׁהּ¹⁴. וְהֶעֱמִיד לָהּ
עֵדִים וּבָא לִפְנֵי רַבִּי עֲקִיבָא, אָמַר לוֹ: לִבְזוּיָה זוֹ אֲנִי אֶתֵּן אַרְבַּע מֵאוֹת
זוּז, וּמָה עַל שֶׁמֶן בִּכְאִיסָר לֹא חָסָה עַל כְּבוֹד עַצְמָהּ אֶלָּא שֶׁיָּצְתָה מִתּוֹךְ
בֵּיתָהּ וּפֵרְעָה אֶת רֹאשָׁהּ בַּשּׁוּק וְהָיְתָה מְטַפַּחַת וּמַנַּחַת יָדָהּ עַל רֹאשָׁהּ.

אַרְבַּע מֵאוֹת זוּז — who obligated [the man] to pay her four hundred *zuz* as compensation for shaming her in public. אָמַר לוֹ: רַבִּי תֶּן לִי זְמָן — He said to [R' Akiva], "My teacher, give me time to pay her." נָתַן לוֹ זְמָן — [R' Akiva] complied and gave him some time. אָמַר לוֹ חֲבֵרוֹ — After the defendant left the courtroom, his friend said to him, אֲנִי אֶתֵּן לְךָ עֵצָה שֶׁלֹּא תִתֵּן לָהּ אֲפִילּוּ שָׁוֶה פְּרוּטָה — "I will advise you on how to arrange it that you will not have to give her even a *perutah*'s worth of payment! אָמַר לוֹ: תֶּן לִי — [The defendant] said to him, "Give me your advice!" אָמַר לוֹ: לֵךְ טוֹל שֶׁמֶן בִּכְאִיסָר — [The friend] said to him, "Go take a bottle with an *issar*'s worth of oil,[13] וּשְׁבוֹר אֶת הַצְּלוֹחִית עַל פִּתְחָהּ שֶׁל הָאִשָּׁה — and break the bottle near the woman's front door. You will see how she debases herself for this little bit of oil. מֶה עָשְׂתָה הָאִשָּׁה — What did the woman do when she saw the spilled oil in front of her door? יָצְאתָה מִתּוֹךְ בֵּיתָהּ וּפֵרְעָה רֹאשָׁהּ בַּשּׁוּק — She came out of her house, uncovered her head in the street to expose her hair, וְהָיְתָה מְטַפַּחַת וּמַנַּחַת יָדָהּ עַל רֹאשָׁהּ — and kept moistening her hand with the oil and placing her hand on her head, so that the oil would be absorbed in her hair and not go to waste.[14] וְהֶעֱמִיד לָהּ עֵדִים וּבָא לִפְנֵי רַבִּי עֲקִיבָא — And [the defendant] stationed witnesses to observe her unbecoming behavior, and he came armed with this evidence before R' Akiva. אָמַר לוֹ: לִבְזוּיָה זוֹ אֲנִי אֶתֵּן אַרְבַּע מֵאוֹת זוּז — He said to [R' Akiva], "To this debased woman I shall give four hundred *zuz* for uncovering her hair in public?! וּמָה עַל שֶׁמֶן בִּכְאִיסָר לֹא חָסָה עַל כְּבוֹד עַצְמָהּ — If for a *issar*'s worth of oil she does not care about her own dignity, אֶלָּא שֶׁיָּצְתָה — but rather she came out of her house, מִתּוֹךְ בֵּיתָהּ וּפֵרְעָה אֶת רֹאשָׁהּ בַּשּׁוּק — uncovered her head in the street, וְהָיְתָה מְטַפַּחַת וּמַנַּחַת יָדָהּ עַל רֹאשָׁהּ — and kept moistening her hand with the oil and placing her hand on her head, is it fair that you should assess the humiliation I caused her at the huge sum of four hundred *zuz*? Why, she shamed herself publicly in exactly the same way for

---

13. An *issar* is a small coin, worth 1/24 of a *zuz*.
14. She would have had to anoint her hair at some point anyway. She used this

opportunity to save a few pennies, and anoint her hair with the spilled oil that would soon be absorbed into the ground.

אָמַר לוֹ: לֹא אָמַרְתָּ כְּלוּם, שֶׁהַחוֹבֵל בְּעַצְמוֹ אַף עַל פִּי שֶׁאֵינוֹ רַשַּׁאי
פָּטוּר[15] וַאֲחֵרִים שֶׁחָבְלוּ בּוֹ חַיָּיבִין, הִיא שֶׁחָבְלָה בְּעַצְמָהּ פְּטוּרָה וְאַתָּה
שֶׁחָבַלְתָּ בָּהּ צֵא וְתֵן לָהּ אַרְבַּע מֵאוֹת זוּז[16]:

ה. רַבִּי דּוֹסְתַּאי בְּרַבִּי יַנַּאי אוֹמֵר: אִם בֵּרַרְתָּ וְזָרַעְתָּ בִּרְבִיעָה
רִאשׁוֹנָה[18] שׁוּב וָלֵךְ וּזְרַע[19] בִּרְבִיעָה שְׁנִיָּה שֶׁמָּא יֵרֵד בָּרָד לָעוֹלָם

---

mere pennies!" אָמַר לוֹ: לֹא אָמַרְתָּ כְּלוּם — Dismissing the man's argument,
[R' Akiva] said to him, "You have said nothing of any merit. שֶׁהַחוֹבֵל בְּעַצְמוֹ
אַף עַל פִּי שֶׁאֵינוֹ רַשַּׁאי פָּטוּר — For someone who wounds himself, although he
is not permitted to do so,[15] is exempt from any penalty; וַאֲחֵרִים שֶׁחָבְלוּ בּוֹ
חַיָּיבִין — whereas others who wound him are liable. הִיא שֶׁחָבְלָה בְּעַצְמָהּ
פְּטוּרָה — Here, too, she who "wounded" herself is exempt, וְאַתָּה שֶׁחָבַלְתָּ בָּהּ
צֵא וְתֵן לָהּ אַרְבַּע מֵאוֹת זוּז — whereas you who "wounded" her are liable. And
therefore I say as I said earlier: Go and give her four hundred zuz."[16]

§5 The Baraisa presents a series of teachings on the importance of repeated
effort:
רַבִּי דּוֹסְתַּאי בְּרַבִּי יַנַּאי אוֹמֵר — R' Dostai the son of R' Yannai says: אִם
בֵּרַרְתָּ וְזָרַעְתָּ בִּרְבִיעָה רִאשׁוֹנָה — If you cleared your field[17] and planted it in
time for the first period of rain,[18] שׁוּב וָלֵךְ וּזְרַע בִּרְבִיעָה שְׁנִיָּה — go again and
plant another area[19] in time for the second period of rain, and do not rely on
the first planting as sufficient; שֶׁמָּא יֵרֵד בָּרָד לָעוֹלָם — perhaps a hailstorm

---

15. The commentators cite various sources
for this prohibition against self-injury: *However, your blood of your souls I will demand*
(Mefaresh, citing Genesis 9:5); *But you
shall greatly beware for your souls* (Binyan
Yeshoshua, citing Deuteronomy 4:15); "If a
nazir, who deprived himself only of wine, is
called a sinner, someone who [undertakes a
fast] and deprives himself of all things, how
much more so is he considered a sinner?"
(ibid., citing Bava Kamma 91b).

16. Some commentators defend the reading
of our text (that the man in this case had "violated the words of R' Akiva" — see above, note
14) by referring to the Mishnah (Bava Kamma
90a-b) in which this story also appears.
There, the story is preceded by a disagreement about how payments for humiliation
are assessed. The Sages say, "Everything depends on the victim's level of honor"; people
of lower stature receive less compensation. R'
Akiva counters that "even the poorest among

Israel must be viewed like aristocrats who
have lost their wealth, for they are all children
of Abraham, Isaac and Jacob." According to
R' Akiva's view, a poor Jew is assessed not
as an unrefined commoner, but as a respect-
able noble who has fallen on hard times.

The assailant in our case sought to have
his victim appraised according to her diminished sense of dignity, adopting the opinion
of the Sages. He thus "violated" the words of
R' Akiva, who insists on viewing every person
according to the exalted potential of his birth-
right, and not according to the debased level
of his current status (Magen Avos; Mefaresh,
cited by Binyan Yehoshua; Kisei Rachamim;
cf. Ben Avraham).

17. Mefaresh. [Some versions have אִם בְּכַרְתָּ,
if you started early.]

18. In the Holy Land there are typically three
periods of rain during the growing season
(see Taanis 6a).

19. If you have additional land (Regel

וְיִלְכְּדוּ רִאשׁוֹנִים וְיִתְקַיְּימוּ אַחֲרוֹנִים,²⁰ כִּי אֵינְךָ יוֹדֵעַ אֵיזֶה יִכְשַׁר הֲזֶה אוֹ
זֶה²¹ אוֹ שְׁנֵיהֶם נִתְקַיְּימוּ בְּיָדְךָ (וְהֵם כְּאַחַת טוֹבִים) (וְאִם שְׁנֵיהֶם כְּאַחַת
רעים) שֶׁנֶּאֱמַר (קהלת יא, י) "בַּבֹּקֶר זְרַע אֶת זַרְעֶךָ וְלָעֶרֶב אַל תַּנַּח יָדֶךָ".
אִם בֵּרַרְתָּ וְזָרַעְתָּ בִּרְבִיעָה רִאשׁוֹנָה וּשְׁנִיָּה²² שׁוּב לְךָ וּזְרַע בִּרְבִיעָה
שְׁלִישִׁית שֶׁמָּא יָבֹא שִׁדָּפוֹן לָעוֹלָם וְיִשָּׁדְפוּ רִאשׁוֹנוֹת וְיִתְקַיְּימוּ אַחֲרוֹנוֹת²³
(שנאמר) כִּי אֵינְךָ יוֹדֵעַ אֵיזֶה יִכְשַׁר הֲזֶה אוֹ זֶה אוֹ שְׁנֵיהֶם כְּאֶחָד טוֹבִים,
שֶׁנֶּאֱמַר "בַּבֹּקֶר זְרַע אֶת זַרְעֶךָ [וְגוֹ']":

---

will descend upon the world וְיִלְכְּדוּ רִאשׁוֹנִים וְיִתְקַיְּימוּ אַחֲרוֹנִים — **and the** seedlings planted first, which will have begun to harden, **will be caught** in the hail and ruined, **while the latter,** still pliant, seedlings **will survive.**[20] כִּי אֵינְךָ יוֹדֵעַ אֵיזֶה יִכְשַׁר הֲזֶה אוֹ זֶה — **For you cannot know which** planting **will succeed — this one or that one,**[21] אוֹ שְׁנֵיהֶם נִתְקַיְּימוּ בְּיָדְךָ וְהֵם כְּאַחַת טוֹבִים — **or** perhaps **both will remain with you, and they will be equally good,** שֶׁנֶּאֱמַר "בַּבֹּקֶר זְרַע אֶת זַרְעֶךָ וְלָעֶרֶב אַל תַּנַּח יָדֶךָ" — **as it is stated,** *In the morning sow your seed, and in the evening do not be idle, for you cannot know which will succeed — this or that — or whether both are equally good* (Ecclesiastes 11:6).

The Baraisa adds that even further efforts are encouraged: אִם בֵּרַרְתָּ וְזָרַעְתָּ בִּרְבִיעָה רִאשׁוֹנָה וּשְׁנִיָּה — **If you cleared** your field **and planted** it in time for **the first and second** periods of rain,[22] שׁוּב לְךָ וּזְרַע בִּרְבִיעָה שְׁלִישִׁית — **go again and plant** additional acreage in time for **the third** period of rain; שֶׁמָּא יָבֹא שִׁדָּפוֹן לָעוֹלָם וְיִשָּׁדְפוּ רִאשׁוֹנוֹת וְיִתְקַיְּימוּ אַחֲרוֹנוֹת — **perhaps a** blight will come upon the world and the first seedlings will become blighted, **while the latter,** still dormant seeds **will survive.**[23] כִּי אֵינְךָ יוֹדֵעַ אֵיזֶה יִכְשַׁר הֲזֶה אוֹ זֶה — **For you cannot know which** planting will succeed — this one or that one, אוֹ שְׁנֵיהֶם כְּאֶחָד טוֹבִים — **or** perhaps **both will be equally good,** שֶׁנֶּאֱמַר "בַּבֹּקֶר זְרַע אֶת זַרְעֶךָ וְגוֹ' " — **as it is stated,** *In the morning sow your seed, etc.* and in the evening do not be idle, for you cannot know which will succeed — this or that — or whether both are equally good (ibid.).

Yesharah, Avos HaRosh).

20. As happened in Egypt during the Plague of Hail: *The flax and barley were struck, for the barley was ripe and the flax was in its stalk. But the wheat and spelt were not struck, for they ripened later* (Exodus 9:31-32). The hail broke the mature, hardened plants, but merely bent the immature, softer ones, which then sprang back (see *Rashi* ad loc.).

21. For it is also possible that the first planting will fare better than the second, as the

story told below (§8) illustrates.

22. [That is, you planted twice, as recommended earlier in the Baraisa.]

23. Blight is ruinous primarily to tender young plants (see below, §8). The blight might strike while the second planting will have already produced such vulnerable seedlings, while the seeds of the third planting will hardly have sprouted and thus be less susceptible to disease (see *Magen Avos* and *Ben Avraham*).

ו. רַבִּי יִשְׁמָעֵאל בְּרַבִּי יוֹסֵי אוֹמֵר: (למוד תורה בזקנותך) אִם לָמַדְתָּ תוֹרָה בְּיַלְדוּתֶךָ, אַל תֹּאמַר: אֵינִי לוֹמֵד בְּזִקְנוּתִי[24]. אֶלָּא לְמוֹד תּוֹרָה כִּי אֵינְךָ יוֹדֵעַ אֵיזֶה יִכְשָׁר. אִם לָמַדְתָּ תוֹרָה בִּשְׁעַת הָעֹשֶׁר אַל תָּשׁוּב לָךְ בִּשְׁעַת הָעוֹנִי. אִם לָמַדְתָּ תוֹרָה בִּשְׁעַת שְׂבִיעָה אַל תָּשׁוּב לָךְ בִּשְׁעַת רַעֲבָה[25]. אִם לָמַדְתָּ תוֹרָה בִּשְׁעַת הָרֶיוַח אַל תָּשׁוּב לָךְ בִּשְׁעַת הַדְּחָק[26]. לְפִי שֶׁטוֹב לוֹ לָאָדָם דָּבָר אֶחָד בְּצַעַר מִמֵּאָה בְּרֶיוַח[28], (שֶׁנֶּאֱמַר כִּי אֵינְךָ יוֹדֵעַ אִם שְׁנֵיהֶם כְּאֶחָת טוֹבִים) שֶׁנֶּאֱמַר "בַּבֹּקֶר זְרַע אֶת זַרְעֶךָ וְלָעֶרֶב אַל תַּנַּח יָדֶךָ". רַבִּי עֲקִיבָא אוֹמֵר: לָמַדְתָּ תוֹרָה בְּיַלְדוּתֶךָ (למוד תורה בזקנותך),

---

§6 Diligence is no less important in the realm of Torah study:

אם — **R' Yishmael son of R' Yose said:** רַבִּי יִשְׁמָעֵאל בְּרַבִּי יוֹסֵי אוֹמֵר — לָמַדְתָּ תוֹרָה בְּיַלְדוּתֶךָ אַל תֹּאמַר אֵינִי לוֹמֵד בְּזִקְנוּתִי — **If you learned Torah in your youth, do not say, "I will not learn in my old age."[24]** אֶלָּא לְמוֹד תּוֹרָה כִּי אֵינְךָ — **Rather, learn Torah** in your old age as well, **for you cannot** יוֹדֵעַ אֵיזֶה יִכְשָׁר — **know which** course of study **will succeed.** אִם לָמַדְתָּ תוֹרָה בִּשְׁעַת הָעֹשֶׁר — **If you learned Torah at a time of prosperity,** אַל תָּשׁוּב לָךְ בִּשְׁעַת הָעוֹנִי — **do not turn away** from it **at a time of poverty.** אִם לָמַדְתָּ תוֹרָה בִּשְׁעַת שְׂבִיעָה — **If you learned Torah at a time of satiety,** אַל תָּשׁוּב לָךְ בִּשְׁעַת רַעֲבָה — **do not turn away** from it **at a time of hunger.[25]** אִם לָמַדְתָּ תוֹרָה בִּשְׁעַת הָרֶיוַח — **If you learned Torah at a time of ease,** אַל תָּשׁוּב לָךְ בִּשְׁעַת הַדְּחָק — **do not turn away** from it **at a time of hardship.[26]** מִמֵּאָה בְּרֶיוַח — **Do not say that your adversity will prevent you from learning** as much or as well as you did in better times,[27] **for one word** of Torah learned **in distress is more beneficial to a person than one hundred** words learned in ease.[28] שֶׁנֶּאֱמַר "בַּבֹּקֶר זְרַע אֶת זַרְעֶךָ וְלָעֶרֶב אַל תַּנַּח יָדֶךָ" — **This lesson, too, is** implicit in Scripture, **as it is stated,** *In the morning sow your seed, and in the evening do not be idle, for you cannot know which will succeed, etc.* (ibid.).

Another sage reinforces this lesson.

רַבִּי עֲקִיבָא אוֹמֵר — **R' Akiva said:** לָמַדְתָּ תוֹרָה בְּיַלְדוּתֶךָ — **If you learned Torah**

---

24. An older person might be inclined to say, "I hardly have any strength. How much can I accomplish with my learning anyway?" But that is a mistake, for the Torah is a Jew's spiritual sustenance — "your life and the length of your days" — and besides, as R' Yishmael goes on to explain, you really cannot know which period of study will be more productive for you, or more valuable in God's eyes (*Binyan Yehoshua*).

25. A state of "hunger," in which a person lacks his basic dietary needs, is worse than

"poverty." Nevertheless, even in this state, a person should not neglect the study of Torah (*Magen Avos*).

26. Such as illness, physical pain and other troubles (ibid.).

27. *Mefaresh, Binyan Yehoshua.*

28. Both in terms of Heavenly reward, which is paid in proportion to the effort involved, and in terms of scholarly attainment, for Torah study is most fruitful when it is pursued amid difficulties, as the Sages taught

אבות דרבי נתן   130

אַל תֹּאמַר אֵינִי לָמֵד תּוֹרָה בְּזִקְנוּתִי כִּי אֵינְךָ יוֹדֵעַ אֵיזֶה יִכְשָׁר אִם שְׁנֵיהֶם
יִתְקַיְּימוּ בְּיָדֶךָ אוֹ שְׁנֵיהֶם כְּאַחַת טוֹבִים, שֶׁנֶּאֱמַר: "בַּבֹּקֶר זְרַע אֶת זַרְעֶךָ
[וְגוֹ']"29. רַבִּי מֵאִיר אוֹמֵר: אִם לָמַדְתָּ מֵרַב אֶחָד, אַל תֹּאמַר: דַּיִּי. אֶלָּא לֵךְ אֵצֶל
חָכָם וּלְמוֹד תּוֹרָה30, וְאַל תֵּלֵךְ אֵצֶל הַכֹּל אֶלָּא לְמִי שֶׁהוּא קָרוֹב לְךָ מִתְּחִלָּה31,

---

אַל תֹּאמַר: אֵינִי לָמֵד תּוֹרָה בְּזִקְנוּתִי — do not say, "I will not learn Torah in my old age." in your youth, כִּי אֵינְךָ יוֹדֵעַ אֵיזֶה יִכְשָׁר — For you cannot know which course of study will succeed, אִם שְׁנֵיהֶם יִתְקַיְּימוּ בְּיָדֶךָ, אוֹ שְׁנֵיהֶם כְּאַחַת טוֹבִים — or whether both of them will remain with you, or "whether both are equally good," שֶׁנֶּאֱמַר "בַּבֹּקֶר זְרַע אֶת זַרְעֶךָ וְגוֹ'" — as it is stated, *In the morning sow your seed, etc. and in the evening do not be idle, for you cannot know which will succeed* — this or that — or whether both are equally good (ibid.)[29]

Perseverance in Torah study also means continually expanding one's Torah horizons:

רַבִּי מֵאִיר אוֹמֵר — R' Meir said: אִם לָמַדְתָּ מֵרַב אֶחָד אַל תֹּאמַר דַּיִּי — If you learned Torah from one teacher, do not say, "That is enough for me." אֶלָּא לֵךְ אֵצֶל חָכָם וּלְמוֹד תּוֹרָה — Rather, go to a different scholar and learn Torah from him as well.[30] וְאַל תֵּלֵךְ אֵצֶל הַכֹּל — But do not go to just anyone; אֶלָּא לְמִי שֶׁהוּא קָרוֹב לְךָ מִתְּחִלָּה — go at first only to someone who is close and known to you as exemplary in behavior as well as in scholarship,[31]

(*Nedarim* 81a): "Be heedful of the sons of the poor, because from them Torah will emerge" (*Magen Avos*).

29. R' Akiva seems to be saying the same thing as R' Yishmael, quoted above. What, then, does the Baraisa add by including this paragraph?

Some commentators suggest that R' Akiva is referring here to *teaching* rather than private learning. [This approach requires a slight adjustment to the text: לָמַדְתָּ, *you learned,* becomes לִמַּדְתָּ, *you taught;* and אֵינִי לָמֵד, *I will not learn,* becomes אֵינִי מְלַמֵּד, *I will not teach.*] Even if one raised many disciples in his youth, he should continue to teach in his old age, for there is no telling which group of disciples will succeed in passing down his teachings to the next generation. This is a lesson that R' Akiva exemplified in his own life. After his original group of twelve thousand students (or twelve thousand *pairs*) died in an epidemic due to their lack of respect for one another, R' Akiva recruited and taught a handful of new students who proceeded to become central figures in

disseminating the Torah, and vital links in the transmission of the Oral Law (*Mefaresh* and *Ben Avraham,* based on *Bereishis Rabbah* 61 §3; see also *Ahavas Chesed*).

30. For "whoever learns Torah from a single master never sees a sign of blessing [from his learning]" (*Avodah Zarah* 19a). The Gemara there clarifies that this is true only with regard to "reasoning," i.e., analyzing the text and delving in the theoretical underpinnings of the law. When it comes to acquiring fluency in the Talmudic text itself, the opposite is true: It is better to confine oneself to one master and avoid becoming confused by the textual variants used in different schools (*Binyan Yehoshua*).

31. As the Sages teach elsewhere (*Chagigah* 15b): If a Torah teacher resembles an angel of God, then people may seek Torah instruction from him (*Binyan Yehoshua,* from *Mefaresh*).

Why does the Baraisa speak of exercising such caution only "at first"? Because the speaker, R' Meir, held that once a student is an accomplished scholar and well developed

שֶׁנֶּאֱמַר (משלי ה, טו) "שְׁתֵה מַיִם מִבּוֹרֶךָ וְנֹזְלִים מִתּוֹךְ בְּאֵרֶךָ"[32]. חוֹבָה הוּא
לְאָדָם שֶׁיְּשַׁמֵּשׁ שְׁלֹשָׁה תַּלְמִידֵי חֲכָמִים, כְּגוֹן רַבִּי אֱלִיעֶזֶר וְרַבִּי יְהוֹשֻׁעַ
וְרַבִּי עֲקִיבָא[33], שֶׁנֶּאֱמַר (משלי ח, לד) "אַשְׁרֵי אָדָם שֹׁמֵעַ לִי לִשְׁקֹד עַל דַּלְתֹתַי
יוֹם יוֹם לִשְׁמֹר מְזוּזֹת פְּתָחָי", אַל תִּקְרֵי "דַּלְתֹתַי" אֶלָּא 'דֶלֶת דַּלְתֹתַי". כִּי
אֵינְךָ יוֹדֵעַ אִם שְׁנֵיהֶם יִתְקַיְּימוּ בְּיָדֶךָ, "אִם שְׁנֵיהֶם כְּאֶחָד טוֹבִים", שֶׁנֶּאֱמַר
"בַּבֹּקֶר זְרַע אֶת זַרְעֶךָ"[35]. רַבִּי יְהוֹשֻׁעַ אוֹמֵר: שָׂא אִשָּׁה בְּיַלְדוּתֶךָ וְשָׂא אִשָּׁה

שֶׁנֶּאֱמַר "שְׁתֵה מַיִם מִבּוֹרֶךָ וְנֹזְלִים מִתּוֹךְ בְּאֵרֶךָ" — as it is stated, *Drink water from your own cistern and flowing water from your own well* (*Proverbs* 5:15).[32]   חוֹבָה הוּא לְאָדָם שֶׁיְּשַׁמֵּשׁ שְׁלֹשָׁה תַּלְמִידֵי חֲכָמִים — Moreover, it is incumbent on a person to serve (i.e., study under) not only two but even **three Torah scholars,** כְּגוֹן רַבִּי אֱלִיעֶזֶר וְרַבִּי יְהוֹשֻׁעַ וְרַבִּי עֲקִיבָא — such as **R' Eliezer, R' Yehoshua and R' Akiva,**[33]   שֶׁנֶּאֱמַר "אַשְׁרֵי אָדָם שֹׁמֵעַ לִי לִשְׁקֹד עַל דַּלְתֹתַי יוֹם יוֹם לִשְׁמֹר מְזוּזֹת פְּתָחָי" — as it is stated (*Proverbs* 8:34), *Praiseworthy is the person who listens to me, to hasten to my doors* (דַּלְתֹתַי) *every day, to the doorposts of my entranceways* (פְּתָחָי). אַל תִּקְרֵי "דַּלְתֹתַי" אֶלָּא 'דֶלֶת דַּלְתֹתַי" — Do not read the word as דַּלְתֹתַי; rather, break it down and read it דֶלֶת דַּלְתֹתַי, indicating three doors,[34] and hence, three teachers.   כִּי אֵינְךָ יוֹדֵעַ אִם שְׁנֵיהֶם יִתְקַיְּימוּ בְּיָדֶךָ — Such diversity is necessary **because you cannot know if both [courses of study] will remain with you,** "אִם שְׁנֵיהֶם כְּאֶחָד טוֹבִים" — in the words of King Solomon, *whether both are equally good,* שֶׁנֶּאֱמַר "בַּבֹּקֶר זְרַע אֶת זַרְעֶךָ" — as it is stated, *In the morning sow your seed,* and in the evening do not be idle, for you cannot know which will succeed — this or that — or whether both are equally good (*Ecclesiastes* 11:6).[35]

A call for diligence in the matter of having children: שָׂא אִשָּׁה בְּיַלְדוּתֶךָ וְשָׂא אִשָּׁה רַבִּי יְהוֹשֻׁעַ אוֹמֵר — **R' Yehoshua said:**

---

in his fear of God, he can seek out teachers who have important traditions or insights to share even if they do not "resemble an angel of God." True to this opinion, R' Meir continued to study under Elisha ben Avuyah even after the latter had abandoned his faith (*Magen Avos*).

32. "Drinking water" is a common metaphor for learning Torah (*Ben Avraham*). Thus, the verse is saying: At first quench your thirst from the still waters in a cistern, which lie entirely in the reservoir before you, and therefore symbolize the Torah wisdom of a teacher close to you. Later, you can draw flowing water from a well, which may come from a faraway source and therefore represents the

wisdom of a more distant and less familiar Torah scholar (*Binyan Yehoshua*).

33. The speaker, R' Meir, chose for his example three Torah greats who were close to his time. R' Akiva was R' Meir's own teacher, while R' Eliezer and R' Yehoshua were R' Akiva's teachers (*Magen Avos, Ben Avraham*).

34. The verse could have said דְלָתַי, *My doors* (on the pattern of פְּתָחָי, *My entranceways*), which would already have connoted plurality. By using דַּלְתֹתַי with its extra letter, the verse hints at an additional door, yielding a total of three (ibid.).

35. Perhaps this verse is being cited to support the *first* part of R' Meir's teaching — that

בְּזִקְנוּתֶךָ, הוֹלֵיד בָּנִים בְּיַלְדוּתֶךָ וְהוֹלֵיד בָּנִים בְּזִקְנוּתֶךָ.[36] אַל תֹּאמַר: אֵינִי נוֹשֵׂא אִשָּׁה, אֶלָּא שָׂא אִשָּׁה וְהוֹלֵיד בָּנִים וּבָנוֹת וְהַרְבֵּה פְּרִיָּה וּרְבִיָּה בָּעוֹלָם, כִּי אֵינְךָ יוֹדֵעַ אִם שְׁנֵיהֶם יִתְקַיְּמוּ בְּיָדֶךָ[37] "אִם שְׁנֵיהֶם כְּאֶחָד טוֹבִים", שֶׁנֶּאֱמַר "בַּבֹּקֶר זְרַע אֶת זַרְעֶךָ":

ז. הוּא הָיָה אוֹמֵר: אִם נָתַתָּ פְּרוּטָה לְעָנִי שַׁחֲרִית וּבָא עָנִי אַחֵר וְעָמַד לְפָנֶיךָ

בְּזִקְנוּתֶךָ — **Marry a woman in your youth and marry a woman in your old age.** הוֹלֵיד בָּנִים בְּיַלְדוּתֶךָ וְהוֹלֵיד בָּנִים בְּזִקְנוּתֶךָ — **Have children in your youth and have children in your old age.**[36] אַל תֹּאמַר אֵינִי נוֹשֵׂא אִשָּׁה — **Do not say, "I will not take a wife."** אֶלָּא שָׂא אִשָּׁה וְהוֹלֵיד בָּנִים וּבָנוֹת וְהַרְבֵּה פְּרִיָּה וּרְבִיָּה בָּעוֹלָם — **Rather, take a wife, have sons and daughters, and increase the birth of children in the world,** כִּי אֵינְךָ יוֹדֵעַ אִם שְׁנֵיהֶם יִתְקַיְּמוּ בְּיָדֶךָ — **for you cannot know whether both broods of children will remain with you,**[37] אִם שְׁנֵיהֶם כְּאֶחָד טוֹבִים — **in the words of King Solomon, *if both will be equally good,*** שֶׁנֶּאֱמַר "בַּבֹּקֶר זְרַע אֶת זַרְעֶךָ" — **as it is stated, *In the morning sow your seed, and in the evening do not be idle, etc.*** (ibid.).

§7 R' Yehoshua counsels persistence in regard to giving charity as well. אִם נָתַתָּ פְּרוּטָה לְעָנִי שַׁחֲרִית — **If you gave a *perutah* to a poor person in the morning,** הוּא הָיָה אוֹמֵר — **He used to say:** וּבָא עָנִי אַחֵר וְעָמַד לְפָנֶיךָ

---

if one studied under one teacher, he should not say that is enough, but he should study under another teacher as well. It is not a source for R' Meir's additional comment that even two are not sufficient (*Magen Avos,* first approach). Alternatively, R' Meir is indeed citing this to elaborate his additional comment that even two teachers are insufficient, and he is using the words אִם שְׁנֵיהֶם כְּאֶחָד טוֹבִים in the sense of "if they are both equally good — or neither is" (see *Magen Avos,* second approach).

36. For you cannot know which child will turn out to be worthy and God-fearing, or which child will survive (*Rashi* to *Yevamos* 62b).

According to some, the concern here is about fulfilling the Biblical obligation to procreate. Torah law requires a man to procreate until he fathers at least one boy and one girl. If the death of one's children brings him back under the minimum, he must father other children until he has the requisite son and daughter. Since there is no way to know

whether one's children will survive him [and since, if they die late in his life, he may then be unable to have children], R' Yehoshua calls for a man to father children beyond the minimum and thereby increase the likelihood that he will have fulfilled the mitzvah by the end of his life (*She'iltos* §165; see *Even HaEzer* 1:8).

In any case, *Rambam* points out that adding even one soul to the Jewish people is like building an entire world (*Hil. Ishus* 15:16).

37. A case in point: The Jewish leader Boaz, also known as Ivtzan, originally had thirty sons and thirty daughters (*Judges* 12:9). All of these children died in his lifetime. At the end of his life, he married Ruth, the Moabite convert, and fathered a son. This son became the grandfather of King David, as recorded at the end of the Book of Ruth. From this dramatic turn of events arose a popular saying: If in your life you beget sixty, what good are these sixty? Carry on and beget one more, who may accomplish more than all sixty (*Bava Basra* 91a).

עַרְבִית, תֶּן לוֹ, כִּי אֵינְךָ יוֹדֵעַ אִם שְׁנֵיהֶם יִתְקַיְּימוּ בְּיָדֶךָ "אִם שְׁנֵיהֶם
כְּאֶחָד טוֹבִים"[38] שֶׁנֶּאֱמַר, "בַּבֹּקֶר זְרַע אֶת זַרְעֶךָ":

ח. מַעֲשֶׂה בְּחָסִיד אֶחָד[39] שֶׁנָּתַן דִּינָר אֶחָד לְעָנִי אֶחָד בִּשְׁנֵי בַּצּוֹרֶת[40],
הִקְנִיטַתּוּ אִשְׁתּוֹ[41], הָלַךְ וְלָן בְּבֵית הַקְּבָרוֹת [בְּעֶרֶב רֹאשׁ הַשָּׁנָה][42]
וְשָׁמַע שְׁתֵּי רוּחוֹת שֶׁמְּסַפְּרוֹת זוֹ עִם זוֹ[43] וְאוֹמֶרֶת חֲדָא לַחֲבֶרְתָּהּ:

עַרְבִית — and another poor person comes and stands expectantly before you in the evening, תֶּן לוֹ — give charity to him as well. כִּי אֵינְךָ יוֹדֵעַ אִם שְׁנֵיהֶם יִתְקַיְּימוּ בְּיָדֶךָ, אִם שְׁנֵיהֶם כְּאֶחָד טוֹבִים — For you cannot know whether both of [these charitable acts] will remain with you, in the words of King Solomon, *if both will be equally good*,[38] שֶׁנֶּאֱמַר "בַּבֹּקֶר זְרַע אֶת זַרְעֶךָ" — as it is stated, *In the morning sow your seed, and in the evening do not be idle, etc.* (ibid.).

§8 The Baraisa illustrates the great merit of giving charity, as well as the difference between early and late plantings, as taught by R' Dostai above (§5): מַעֲשֶׂה בְּחָסִיד אֶחָד — There was an incident with a certain pious man[39] שֶׁנָּתַן דִּינָר אֶחָד לְעָנִי אֶחָד בִּשְׁנֵי בַּצּוֹרֶת — who gave a dinar as charity to a poor person in a year of famine.[40] הִקְנִיטַתּוּ אִשְׁתּוֹ — His wife, distraught over the "loss" of such a coin when food and money were both scarce, provoked him over it.[41] הָלַךְ וְלָן בְּבֵית הַקְּבָרוֹת בְּעֶרֶב רֹאשׁ הַשָּׁנָה — So he went and spent the night in a cemetery on the eve of Rosh Hashanah.[42] וְשָׁמַע שְׁתֵּי רוּחוֹת שֶׁמְּסַפְּרוֹת זוֹ עִם זוֹ — While there, he heard two spirits of deceased children[43] conversing with each other. וְאוֹמֶרֶת חֲדָא לַחֲבֶרְתָּהּ — One said

---

38. You cannot know if both the paupers you helped are equally good (*Magen Avos*). If one of the paupers is unworthy, you will get little reward for helping him (*Mefaresh, Magen Avos, Ahavas Chesed*; see *Bava Kamma* 16b).

39. Stories that begin with these words refer either to R' Yehudah bar Il'ai or R' Yehudah ben Bava (*Binyan Yehoshua,* from *Temurah* 15b). In this case, there is some evidence that the pious man was the former, usually referred to simply as R' Yehudah (*Tosafos, Rosh Hashanah* 16a; see *Ahavas Chesed*).

40. The Talmud, which quotes this Baraisa (in *Berachos* 18b), specifies that the incident occurred on the eve of Rosh Hashanah.

41. Considering that R' Yehudah bar Il'ai was very poor (*Nedarim* 49b), it is likely that he had given away his last dinar (*Maharsha* to *Berachos* ibid.)

42. Many ask the question: Can it be that a great Jew would spend the night of Rosh Hashanah in a cemetery? This question has led some to say that this entire episode in the cemetery, as well as those that follow later, occurred only in the pious man's dreams (ibid., citing *Ritva*; *Ahavas Chesed,* citing *R' Yehoshua ibn Shuib*). Others suggest that he slept near the cemetery, not inside it (*Kisei Rachamim*).

43. They were the spirits of two young girls who had died (*Binyan Yehoshua,* from *Rashi* to *Berachos* ibid.).

What were these "spirits," and why would they be in a cemetery? *Maharsha* (ibid.) explains: The human soul consists of several different elements. The *nefesh*, the lowest part of the soul, remains with the body after death; the *neshamah*, the most elevated part of the soul, separates from the body after death and ascends to higher realms; the

חֲבֶרְתִּי, בּוֹאִי וְנָשׁוּט בָּעוֹלָם וְנִרְאֶה מַה פּוּרְעָנוּת בָּאָה לָעוֹלָם.[44] אָמְרָה
לָהּ: חֲבֶרְתִּי, אֵינִי יְכוֹלָה לָצֵאת מִפְּנֵי שֶׁקְּבוּרָה אֲנִי בְּמַחְצֶלֶת שֶׁל קָנִים.[45]
אֶלָּא לְכִי אַתְּ וּמַה שֶׁאַתְּ שׁוֹמַעַת אִמְרִי לִי. הָלְכָה וּבָאתָה אֶצְלָהּ אָמְרָה
לָהּ: חֲבֶרְתִּי, כְּלוּם שָׁמַעַתְּ מֵאֲחוֹרֵי הַפַּרְגוֹד[46] מַה פּוּרְעָנוּת בָּאָה לָעוֹלָם.
אָמְרָה לָהּ: שָׁמַעְתִּי שֶׁכָּל הַזּוֹרֵעַ בִּרְבִיעָה רִאשׁוֹנָה בָּרָד מַלְקֶה אוֹתוֹ. הָלַךְ
הוּא וְזָרַע בִּרְבִיעָה שְׁנִיָּה, שֶׁל כָּל הָעוֹלָם בָּרָד לָקָה אוֹתוֹ, וְשֶׁלּוֹ לֹא לָקָה.[47]

---

to the other, חֲבֶרְתִּי בּוֹאִי וְנָשׁוּט בָּעוֹלָם — "Come, my friend, let us roam
the world, וְנִרְאֶה מַה פּוּרְעָנוּת בָּאָה לָעוֹלָם — and see what misfortune is
coming to the world this year."[44] אָמְרָה לָהּ — [The other] replied, חֲבֶרְתִּי
— אֵינִי יְכוֹלָה לָצֵאת מִפְּנֵי שֶׁקְּבוּרָה אֲנִי בְּמַחְצֶלֶת שֶׁל קָנִים — "My friend, I cannot
leave my place, because I am buried in a matting of reeds.[45] אֶלָּא לְכִי אַתְּ
— וּמַה שֶׁאַתְּ שׁוֹמַעַת אִמְרִי לִי Rather, you go, and then come back and relate
to me whatever you hear." הָלְכָה וּבָאתָה אֶצְלָהּ — So [the first spirit] went
and came back to her confined friend. אָמְרָה לָהּ — Said [the latter] to her,
חֲבֶרְתִּי כְּלוּם שָׁמַעַתְּ מֵאֲחוֹרֵי הַפַּרְגוֹד מַה פּוּרְעָנוּת בָּאָה לָעוֹלָם — "My friend, did
you hear anything from behind the curtain[46] about what misfortune is com-
ing to the world?" אָמְרָה לָהּ — She replied, שָׁמַעְתִּי שֶׁכָּל הַזּוֹרֵעַ בִּרְבִיעָה
רִאשׁוֹנָה בָּרָד מַלְקֶה אוֹתוֹ — "I heard that the crops of anyone who plants this
winter in time for the first period of rain will be destroyed by hail." הָלַךְ הוּא
וְזָרַע בִּרְבִיעָה שְׁנִיָּה — Hearing this, [the pious man] went and planted in time for
the second period of rain. שֶׁל כָּל הָעוֹלָם בָּרָד לָקָה אוֹתוֹ וְשֶׁלּוֹ לֹא לָקָה — And
indeed, everyone's crops were destroyed, while his were not destroyed.[47]

---

ruach, "spirit," being intermediate in status,
sometimes remains with the dead body and
sometimes roams free, ascending to the
higher realms where the neshamah is found.

44. This conversation took place on the
second night of Rosh Hashanah (Chidushei
HaGra, Imrei Noam to Berachos ibid.). Thus,
the spirit wanted to find out what harsh decrees had already been issued during the
[first] Day of Judgment (Rashi ad loc.).

45. Her family was too poor to afford proper
linen shrouds (Tzlach ad loc.), and she was
ashamed to be seen in such poor attire
(Ritva, Mosad HaRav Kook ed. ad loc.). Although the first spirit was not proposing that
they bodily leave the grave, a disembodied
spirit appears "dressed" in the same manner as the body itself (ibid.; see also Michtav
MeiEliyahu vol. 2 p. 62).

Alternatively, Tzlach explains that as long

as the body has not decomposed, the spirit
cannot fully disengage from it (see Shabbos
152b). For this reason the dead are buried in
linen shrouds, which disintegrate quickly and
thus do not retard the body's decomposition.
Because this girl was buried in sturdy reed
matting, her body was unable to decompose
quickly and her spirit could not roam freely.

A third approach is that the "reed matting"
is a metaphor for the restrictions placed on
a spirit burdened by sin. Such a spirit is not
worthy of approaching the vicinity of the
Divine presence, at least not close enough
to overhear the decrees being issued there
(Magen Avos).

46. That is, the curtain that partitions off the
Divine presence (Binyan Yehoshua, from
Rashi).

47. As we have seen (above §5, with note
20), mature, hardened stalks are vulnerable

לְשָׁנָה אַחֶרֶת הָלַךְ וְלָן בְּבֵית הַקְּבָרוֹת וְשָׁמַע שְׁתֵּי רוּחוֹת שֶׁמְּסַפְּרוֹת
זוֹ אֶת זוֹ וְאוֹמֶרֶת אַחַת לַחֲבֶרְתָּהּ: בּוֹאִי וְנָשׁוּט בָּעוֹלָם וְנִרְאֶה מַה
פּוּרְעָנוּת בָּאָה לָעוֹלָם. אָמְרָה לָהּ: חֲבֶרְתִּי, [לֹא כָּךְ אָמַרְתִּי לָךְ], אֵינִי
יְכוֹלָה לָצֵאת מִפְּנֵי שֶׁאֲנִי קְבוּרָה בְּמַחְצֶלֶת שֶׁל קָנִים. אֶלָּא לְכִי אַתְּ וּמַה
שֶּׁאַתְּ שׁוֹמַעַת אִמְרִי לִי. הָלְכָה וּבָאתָה אֶצְלָהּ, אָמְרָה לָהּ: כְּלוּם שָׁמַעַתְּ
מֵאֲחוֹרֵי הַפַּרְגּוֹד. [אָמְרָה לָהּ:] שָׁמַעְתִּי שֶׁכָּל הַזּוֹרֵעַ בִּרְבִיעָה שְׁנִיָּה שֶׁדָּפוֹן
מַלְקֶה אוֹתוֹ[48]. הָלַךְ וְזָרַע בִּרְבִיעָה רִאשׁוֹנָה, בָּא שִׁדָּפוֹן לָעוֹלָם, שֶׁל כָּל
הָעוֹלָם נִשְׁדַּף וְשֶׁלּוֹ לֹא נִשְׁדַּף. אָמְרָה לוֹ אִשְׁתּוֹ: מִפְּנֵי מָה (פּוּרְעָנִיּוֹת
שֶׁבָּא לָעוֹלָם) שֶׁל כָּל הָעוֹלָם לָקֶה וְנִשְׁדַּף וְשֶׁלְּךָ לֹא לָקֶה וְלֹא נִשְׁדַּף.

The pious man's good fortune continues:

לְשָׁנָה אַחֶרֶת הָלַךְ וְלָן בְּבֵית הַקְּבָרוֹת — **The next year, [the pious man] again went and spent the night of Rosh Hashanah in the cemetery,** וְשָׁמַע שְׁתֵּי רוּחוֹת שֶׁמְּסַפְּרוֹת זוֹ אֶת זוֹ — **and he heard the same two spirits conversing with each other.** וְאוֹמֶרֶת אַחַת לַחֲבֶרְתָּהּ — **One was saying to the other,** בּוֹאִי וְנָשׁוּט בָּעוֹלָם — **"Come, let us roam the world,** וְנִרְאֶה מַה פּוּרְעָנוּת בָּאָה לָעוֹלָם — **and see what misfortune is coming to the world this year."** אָמְרָה לָהּ — **[The other] replied,** חֲבֶרְתִּי לֹא כָּךְ אָמַרְתִּי לָךְ, אֵינִי יְכוֹלָה לָצֵאת מִפְּנֵי שֶׁאֲנִי קְבוּרָה בְּמַחְצֶלֶת שֶׁל קָנִים — **"My friend, have I not told you that I cannot leave my place, because I am buried in a matting of reeds?** אֶלָּא לְכִי אַתְּ וּמַה שֶּׁאַתְּ שׁוֹמַעַת אִמְרִי לִי — **Rather, you go, and then come back and relate to me whatever you hear."** הָלְכָה וּבָאתָה אֶצְלָהּ — **So she went and came back to her friend.** אָמְרָה לָהּ — **Said [the latter] to her,** כְּלוּם שָׁמַעַתְּ מֵאֲחוֹרֵי הַפַּרְגּוֹד — **"Did you hear anything from behind the curtain?"** אָמְרָה לָהּ — **[The first spirit] replied,** שָׁמַעְתִּי שֶׁכָּל הַזּוֹרֵעַ בִּרְבִיעָה שְׁנִיָּה שֶׁדָּפוֹן מַלְקֶה אוֹתוֹ — **"I heard that the crops of anyone who plants this winter in time for the second period of rain will be afflicted by blight.[48]** הָלַךְ וְזָרַע בִּרְבִיעָה רִאשׁוֹנָה — **Hearing this, [the pious man] went and planted in time for the first period of rain.** בָּא שֶׁל כָּל הָעוֹלָם נִשְׁדַּף שִׁדָּפוֹן לָעוֹלָם — **And indeed, a blight came to the world:** וְשֶׁלּוֹ לֹא נִשְׁדַּף — **Everyone's crops were blighted, while his were not blighted.**

An indiscreet remark brought these valuable revelations to an end:

אָמְרָה לוֹ אִשְׁתּוֹ — **At this point, his wife began wondering and said to him,** מִפְּנֵי מָה פּוּרְעָנִיּוֹת שֶׁבָּא לָעוֹלָם — **"Why is it that when misfortune came to the world,** שֶׁל כָּל הָעוֹלָם לָקֶה וְנִשְׁדַּף — **everyone's crops were destroyed by hail and blighted by disease,** וְשֶׁלְּךָ לֹא לָקֶה וְלֹא נִשְׁדַּף — **while yours were neither**

---

to hail, while soft, pliant seedlings are not (*Binyan Yehoshua*, from *Rashi*).

The blessing of a successful harvest during a time of widespread crop failures was a reward to the pious man for giving away his dinar to charity (*Iyun Yaakov* to *Berachos* 18b).

48. Which primarily affects soft plants that have recently sprouted (*Rashi* ad loc.).

סִפֵּר לָהּ כָּל הַמַּעֲשֶׂה. לְיָמִים נָפְלָה קְטָטָה בֵּין אִשְׁתּוֹ שֶׁל אוֹתוֹ חָסִיד לְבֵין אִמָּהּ שֶׁל [אוֹתָהּ] רִיבָה, אָמְרָה לָהּ: לְכִי [וְאַרְאֵךְ] בְּתֵךְ שֶׁהִיא קְבוּרָה בְּמַחֲצֶלֶת שֶׁל קָנִים. לְשָׁנָה אַחֶרֶת הָלַךְ וְלָן בְּבֵית הַקְּבָרוֹת וְשָׁמַע אוֹתָן שְׁתֵּי רוּחוֹת שֶׁמְּסַפְּרוֹת זוֹ אֶת זוֹ. אָמְרָה לָהּ: חֲבֶרְתִּי, בּוֹאִי וְנָשׁוּט בָּעוֹלָם וְנִשְׁמַע מַה שֶׁאוֹמְרִים אֲחוֹרֵי הַפַּרְגּוֹד. אָמְרָה לָהּ: חֲבֶרְתִּי, הַנִּיחִי לִי, דְּבָרִים שֶׁבֵּינֵךְ לְבֵינִי כְּבָר נִשְׁמְעוּ לְבֵין הַחַיִּים:

ט. מַעֲשֶׂה בְּחָסִיד אֶחָד שֶׁהָיָה רָגִיל בִּצְדָקָה,[50] פַּעַם אַחַת הָלַךְ וְיָשַׁב בִּסְפִינָה בָּא הָרוּחַ וְטָבַע סְפִינָתוֹ בַּיָּם. רָאָהוּ רַבִּי עֲקִיבָא

---

destroyed nor blighted?" סִפֵּר לָהּ כָּל הַמַּעֲשֶׂה — In answer to her question, he told her the whole story. לְיָמִים נָפְלָה קְטָטָה —After some time, a quarrel broke out בֵּין אִשְׁתּוֹ שֶׁל אוֹתוֹ חָסִיד לְבֵין אִמָּהּ שֶׁל אוֹתָהּ רִיבָה — between the pious man's wife and the mother of that young girl whose spirit was confined to her grave. אָמְרָה לָהּ — In the course of that quarrel, [the wife] said to her, לְכִי וְאַרְאֵךְ בְּתֵךְ שֶׁהִיא קְבוּרָה בְּמַחֲצֶלֶת שֶׁל קָנִים — "Come, I will show you your daughter buried shamefully in a matting of reeds." לְשָׁנָה אַחֶרֶת — The next year, הָלַךְ וְלָן בְּבֵית הַקְּבָרוֹת — [the pious man] went and spent the night in the cemetery, וְשָׁמַע אוֹתָן שְׁתֵּי רוּחוֹת שֶׁמְּסַפְּרוֹת זוֹ אֶת זוֹ — and he heard the same two spirits conversing with each other. אָמְרָה לָהּ — Said [one] to [the other], חֲבֶרְתִּי בּוֹאִי וְנָשׁוּט בָּעוֹלָם — "Come, my friend, let us roam the world, וְנִשְׁמַע מַה שֶׁאוֹמְרִים אֲחוֹרֵי הַפַּרְגּוֹד — and let us hear what they are saying behind the curtain." אָמְרָה לָהּ — [The other] replied, חֲבֶרְתִּי — הַנִּיחִי לִי — "My friend, leave me be. דְּבָרִים שֶׁבֵּינֵךְ לְבֵינִי — The words spoken between you and me כְּבָר נִשְׁמְעוּ לְבֵין הַחַיִּים — have already been heard among the living."

§9 Charity pays — not only through material gain (as in the previous story), but also through the gift of life itself:[49]

מַעֲשֶׂה בְּחָסִיד אֶחָד — There was an incident with a certain pious man שֶׁהָיָה רָגִיל בִּצְדָקָה — who was habitual in performing acts of charity.[50] פַּעַם אַחַת הָלַךְ וְיָשַׁב בִּסְפִינָה — One time he went and took a seat in a boat that was embarking on a voyage. בָּא הָרוּחַ וְטָבַע סְפִינָתוֹ בַּיָּם — A stormy wind came along and sank his boat at sea. רָאָהוּ רַבִּי עֲקִיבָא — R' Akiva saw him

---

49. *Magen Avos.*

50. By using this unusual expression instead of saying simply that he gave charity generously, the Baraisa indicates that in addition to supporting the poor himself, he would prevail on others to contribute as well. As the Sages

teach (*Bava Basra* 9a), "he who causes others to perform charitable deeds is greater than one who performs the deed himself," since the former brings merit to the public, and generally provides more assistance to the needy than a single, private donor (*Magen Avos*).

וּבָא לִפְנֵי בֵית דִּין לְהָעִיד עַל אִשְׁתּוֹ לְהִנָּשֵׂא[51]. עַד שֶׁלֹּא הִגִּיעַ עֵת לַעֲמוֹד בָּא אוֹתוֹ הָאִישׁ וְעָמַד לְפָנָיו. אָמַר לוֹ: אַתְּ הוּא שֶׁטָּבַעְתָּ בַּיָּם. אָמַר לוֹ: הֵן. וּמִי הֶעֱלְךָ מִן הַיָּם. אָמַר לוֹ: צְדָקָה שֶׁעָשִׂיתִי הִיא הֶעֱלִיתַנִי מִן הַיָּם. אָמַר לוֹ: מֵאַיִן אַתָּה יוֹדֵעַ. אָמַר לוֹ: כְּשֶׁיָּרַדְתִּי לְמַעֲמַקֵּי מְצוּלָה שָׁמַעְתִּי קוֹל רַעַשׁ גָּדוֹל מִגַּלֵּי הַיָּם[53] שֶׁוּוֹ אוֹמֵר לָזוֹ וְזוֹ אוֹמֵר לָזוֹ: רוּצוּ וְנַעֲלֶה אֶת הָאִישׁ הַזֶּה מִן הַיָּם, שֶׁעָשָׂה צְדָקָה כָּל יָמָיו. בְּאוֹתָהּ שָׁעָה פָּתַח רַבִּי עֲקִיבָא וְאָמַר: בָּרוּךְ אֱלֹהִים אֱלֹהֵי יִשְׂרָאֵל שֶׁבָּחַר בְּדִבְרֵי תוֹרָה

וּבָא לִפְנֵי בֵית דִּין לְהָעִיד עַל אִשְׁתּוֹ לְהִנָּשֵׂא — and he came before a rabbinical court to testify about his wife that she was permitted to remarry.[51] עַד שֶׁלֹּא הִגִּיעַ עֵת לַעֲמוֹד — Before the time came for him to stand as a witness in court,[52] בָּא אוֹתוֹ הָאִישׁ וְעָמַד לְפָנָיו — the man in question suddenly came in and stood before [R' Akiva]. אָמַר לוֹ — Astonished, [R' Akiva] said to him, Are you not the one who drowned at sea?!" אַתְּ הוּא שֶׁטָּבַעְתָּ בַּיָּם: הֵן — He replied, "Yes, I am the one." וּמִי הֶעֱלְךָ מִן הַיָּם — Asked R' Akiva, "And who lifted you out of the sea?" אָמַר לוֹ: צְדָקָה שֶׁעָשִׂיתִי הִיא הֶעֱלִיתַנִי מִן הַיָּם — He replied, "The charity that I performed — that is what lifted me out of the sea." אָמַר לוֹ: מֵאַיִן אַתָּה יוֹדֵעַ — Asked [R' Akiva], How do you know this to be true?" אָמַר לוֹ: כְּשֶׁיָּרַדְתִּי לְמַעֲמַקֵּי מְצוּלָה — [The man] replied, שָׁמַעְתִּי קוֹל רַעַשׁ גָּדוֹל מִגַּלֵּי הַיָּם "When I was sinking into the watery depths, — I heard a great, thunderous voice emanating from the waves of the sea,[53] שֶׁוּוֹ אוֹמֵר לָזוֹ וְזוֹ אוֹמֵר לָזוֹ — and I heard that this one was saying to that one, and that one was saying to this one, רוּצוּ וְנַעֲלֶה אֶת הָאִישׁ הַזֶּה מִן הַיָּם — 'Hurry, let us lift this man out of the sea, שֶׁעָשָׂה צְדָקָה כָּל יָמָיו — for he has performed acts of charity all throughout his life.'" בְּאוֹתָהּ שָׁעָה פָּתַח רַבִּי עֲקִיבָא וְאָמַר — At that moment, R' Akiva opened his mouth and said, בָּרוּךְ אֱלֹהִים אֱלֹהֵי יִשְׂרָאֵל — "Blessed is God, the God of Israel, שֶׁבָּחַר בְּדִבְרֵי תוֹרָה

---

51. The halachah is that if a man falls into a body of water that "has an end" — i.e., it is small enough for a witness to see its banks all around and note that the man did not emerge soon enough to survive — the man is presumed dead and his wife is free to re-marry. But if the body of water "has no end" — that is, its boundaries extend beyond the witness's range of sight, it is possible that the current swept the man to the far end and enabled him to emerge safely. In that scenario, as long as no further information is available, the missing man's wife is not permitted to remarry (Yevamos 121a).

In our case, the body of water in question apparently had "an end." R' Akiva, who had seen the pious man go under and fail to emerge in time, was therefore able to free his wife from the shackles of uncertainty by testifying to what he saw (Ahavas Chesed; cf. Binyan Yeshoshua).

52. Ben Avraham (see there). Or "before the time came for the court to get up from their session" (Regel Yesharah, Binyan Yehoshua).

53. That is, from the angels assigned to preside over the waves (Ahavas Chesed, based on Rashbam, Bava Basra 73a and Tosafos, Chullin 7a).

וּבְדִבְרֵי חֲכָמִים, שֶׁדִּבְרֵי תוֹרָה וְדִבְרֵי חֲכָמִים קַיָּמִין הֵם לְעוֹלָם וּלְעוֹלְמֵי
עוֹלָמִים[54], שֶׁנֶּאֱמַר (קהלת יא, א) "שַׁלַּח לַחְמְךָ עַל פְּנֵי הַמָּיִם כִּי בְרֹב הַיָּמִים
תִּמְצָאֶנּוּ". וְעוֹד כְּתִיב (משלי י, ב) "וּצְדָקָה תַּצִּיל מִמָּוֶת"[55]:

י. מַעֲשֶׂה[56] בְּבִנְיָמִין הַצַּדִּיק שֶׁהָיָה מְמוּנֶּה עַל קוּפָּה שֶׁל צְדָקָה, וּבָאתָה
אִשָּׁה אַחַת לְפָנָיו[57], אָמְרָה לוֹ: רַבִּי פַּרְנְסֵנִי. אָמַר לָהּ: הָעֲבוֹדָה שֶׁאֵין

וּבְדִבְרֵי חֲכָמִים — **Who chose the words of the Torah** (to be quoted shortly) **and the words of the Sages,** who set forth guidelines for confirming the death of a husband and permitting his wife to remarry. שֶׁדִּבְרֵי תוֹרָה וְדִבְרֵי חֲכָמִים קַיָּמִין הֵם לְעוֹלָם וּלְעוֹלְמֵי עוֹלָמִים — **For the words of the Torah and the words of the Sages endure forever and ever,**[54] שֶׁנֶּאֱמַר "שַׁלַּח לַחְמְךָ עַל פְּנֵי הַמָּיִם — **as it is stated,** *Send your bread upon the waters,* i.e., distribute your bread to the needy, *for after many days you will find it* (*Ecclesiastes* 11:1). וְעוֹד כְּתִיב "וּצְדָקָה תַּצִּיל מִמָּוֶת" — **Moreover, it is written,** *And charity saves from death* (*Proverbs* 10:2).[55]

§10 Charity saves a person not only from a physical threat like the depths of the sea, but also from a Heavenly decree of death.[56] מַעֲשֶׂה בְּבִנְיָמִין הַצַּדִּיק — **There was an incident with Benjamin the Righteous,** שֶׁהָיָה מְמוּנֶּה עַל קוּפָּה שֶׁל צְדָקָה — **who was appointed** to oversee the communal charity fund. וּבָאתָה אִשָּׁה אַחַת לְפָנָיו — **One time a woman came before him** during a famine[57] and requested assistance. אָמְרָה לוֹ: רַבִּי פַּרְנְסֵנִי — **She said to him, "My master, sustain me!"** אָמַר לָהּ הָעֲבוֹדָה שֶׁאֵין

54. When considered together with the "words of the Torah," the "words of the Sages" shine forth as enduring and true — even when they seem to be refuted by the evidence. Here, for example, a man who had been submerged at length in "water that has an end" lived to tell the story. One might have thought that his survival belied the Sages' ruling that discounts the likelihood of such an occurrence (see above, note 51). The "words of the Torah," however, deflect the challenge: If the man of our story had been like most people, he would surely have perished. But unlike most people, he had an extraordinary reserve of lifesaving merit from his activities on behalf of the poor, and he was therefore able to defy the laws of nature (*Ahavas Chesed*).

55. Since the first verse does not specify what benefit one will "find" after "many days," this second verse is cited to clarify the matter: It is the unparalleled benefit of life itself (*Ben Avraham*).

56. In the previous incident, there may not have been a prior decree that the pious man should die (though he still needed a great merit to be saved from the danger he was in), whereas in the following case, there clearly was a decree that Benjamin the Righteous should die, either because his time had come or for some other reason (*Magen Avos*).

57. The Talmudic version of this story (in *Bava Bara* 11a) specifies that it took place during a famine, which helps explain why the charity fund's coffers were empty and why Benjamin's private donation was considered so meritorious.

בַּקּוּפָּה שֶׁל צְדָקָה כְּלוּם[58]. אָמְרָה לוֹ: רַבִּי, אִם אֵין אַתָּה מְפַרְנְסֵנִי הִנְנִי מֵתָה וְאַרְבָּעָה בָנִים. עָמַד וּפִרְנְסָהּ מִשֶּׁלּוֹ[59]. לְיָמִים חָלָה בִּנְיָמִין הַצַּדִּיק וְהָיָה מִצְטַעֵר עַל הַמִּטָּה. אָמְרוּ מַלְאֲכֵי הַשָּׁרֵת לִפְנֵי הַקָּדוֹשׁ בָּרוּךְ הוּא: רִבּוֹנוֹ שֶׁל עוֹלָם, אַתָּה אָמַרְתָּ[60] כָּל הַמְקַיֵּים נֶפֶשׁ אַחַת מִיִּשְׂרָאֵל (מַעֲלֶה עָלָיו הַכָּתוּב) כְּאִלּוּ קִיֵּים עוֹלָם מָלֵא[61], בִּנְיָמִין הַצַּדִּיק שֶׁקִּיֵּים אַלְמָנָה וְאַרְבָּעָה בָנִים עַל אַחַת כַּמָּה וְכַמָּה, וְהוּא מִצְטַעֵר בְּצַעַר חוֹלִי זֶה עַל הַמִּטָּה.

בַּקּוּפָּה שֶׁל צְדָקָה כְּלוּם — He said to her, "I swear by the Holy Temple service[58] that there is nothing in the charity fund for me to distribute to you." אָמְרָה לוֹ — But the woman persisted. She said to him, רַבִּי אִם אֵין אַתָּה מְפַרְנְסֵנִי הִנְנִי מֵתָה וְאַרְבָּעָה בָנִים — My master, if you do not sustain me, I will surely perish — and my four sons as well. עָמַד וּפִרְנְסָהּ מִשֶּׁלּוֹ — Moved by the woman's plea, [Benjamin] got up and provided her with sustenance from his own pocket.[59]

Benjamin's generosity served to sustain him as well: לְיָמִים חָלָה בִּנְיָמִין הַצַּדִּיק — After a time Benjamin the Righteous took seriously ill, וְהָיָה מִצְטַעֵר עַל הַמִּטָּה — and he was reduced to suffering in bed. אָמְרוּ מַלְאֲכֵי הַשָּׁרֵת לִפְנֵי הַקָּדוֹשׁ בָּרוּךְ הוּא — The ministering angels thereupon said to the Holy One, Blessed is He, רִבּוֹנוֹ שֶׁל עוֹלָם — "Master of the universe! אַתָּה אָמַרְתָּ, כָּל הַמְקַיֵּים נֶפֶשׁ אַחַת מִיִּשְׂרָאֵל כְּאִלּוּ קִיֵּים עוֹלָם מָלֵא — You have said[60] that whoever preserves one Jewish soul is regarded as if he preserved an entire world.[61] בִּנְיָמִין הַצַּדִּיק שֶׁקִּיֵּים אַלְמָנָה וְאַרְבָּעָה בָנִים עַל אַחַת כַּמָּה — If that is true, it is all the more so regarding Benjamin the Righteous, וְכַמָּה — who preserved many souls by sustaining a widow and her four sons. וְהוּא מִצְטַעֵר בְּצַעַר חוֹלִי זֶה עַל הַמִּטָּה — And yet he is suffering in bed from the pain

---

58. [It was common in those times for a person taking an oath to mention the Holy Temple, or something connected to it, instead of explicitly invoking the Name of God.]

59. At first, Benjamin did not realize that the woman's situation was critical, and therefore held back his limited resources for his own basic needs, in accordance with halachah. Had he understood from the beginning how desperate she was, he would have given her the money anonymously, as if it were coming from the charity fund, so as to avoid causing her embarrassment (*Maharsha* to *Bava Basra* 11a).

60. Through the Torah You have given Israel (*Binyan Yehoshua,* from *Rashi* ad loc.).

61. The Mishnah (*Sanhedrin* 37a) states that

God initially created a solitary human being (Adam) who would then become the father of all mankind, to teach that preserving a single Jew's life is tantamount to preserving an entire world.

Furthermore, after Cain killed Abel, God reprimanded him by saying (*Genesis* 4:10): *The voice of your brother's bloods cry out to me.* The word *bloods* is in plural form, explains the Mishnah (ibid.), because it refers to the "bloods" of Abel and his unborn descendants. Evidently, a murderer is condemned not only for snuffing out the life of his victim, but also for destroying all of his future generations. If so, it is all the more true that one who preserves a life is regarded as preserving all of that person's unborn

מִיָּד בִּקְּשׁוּ עָלָיו רַחֲמִים וְקָרְעוּ לוֹ גְזַר דִּינוֹ וְהוֹסִיפוּ לוֹ עֶשְׂרִים וּשְׁתַּיִם
שָׁנָה עַל שְׁנוֹתָיו:[62]

---

of this illness that he has!" **מִיָּד בִּקְּשׁוּ עָלָיו רַחֲמִים** — On the strength of this argument, **the angels promptly solicited Divine mercy for him** and they were successful. **וְקָרְעוּ לוֹ גְזַר דִּינוֹ** — [The Heavenly Court] tore up [Benjamin's] decree, **וְהוֹסִיפוּ לוֹ עֶשְׂרִים וּשְׁתַּיִם שָׁנָה עַל שְׁנוֹתָיו**—and [the Court] added **twenty-two years to his lifetime** in the merit of this single instance of charity.[62]

---

progeny — for there is a general principle that God rewards good more abundantly than He punishes evil (*Binyan Yehoshua,* from *Rashi, Bava Basra* 11a.).

62. Although a person's lifespan is not ordinarily fixed according to his moral worth, an exceptional merit can nevertheless add years to one's original allotment (*Ahavas Chesed,* from *Tosafos, Yevamos* 50a).

The twenty-two extra years awarded to

Benjamin correspond to the twenty-two Hebrew letters from which the Torah is composed (*Binyan Yehoshua*). This correspondence alludes to *why* saving one soul in Israel is like preserving the world: Because that rescued soul can go on to study the Torah and observe its laws, thus living a life that upholds the world, for the world was created, and continues to exist, only for the sake of the Torah (*Magen Avos*).

﴾ פֶּרֶק ד ﴿

א. שִׁמְעוֹן הַצַּדִּיק הָיָה מִשְּׁיָרֵי אַנְשֵׁי כְּנֶסֶת הַגְּדוֹלָה‎[1], הוּא הָיָה אוֹמֵר‎[2]: עַל שְׁלֹשָׁה דְבָרִים הָעוֹלָם עוֹמֵד, עַל הַתּוֹרָה, וְעַל הָעֲבוֹדָה וְעַל גְּמִילוּת חֲסָדִים. עַל הַתּוֹרָה, כֵּיצַד‎[3] הֲרֵי הוּא אוֹמֵר (הושע ו, ו) "חֶסֶד חָפַצְתִּי וְלֹא זָבַח וְדַעַת אֱלֹהִים מֵעֹלוֹת"‎[4], מִכָּאן לְעוֹלָה שֶׁהִיא חֲבִיבָה מִזְּבָחִים‎[5], מִפְּנֵי שֶׁהָעוֹלָה כּוּלָהּ כָּלִיל לָאִישִׁים, שֶׁנֶּאֱמַר (ויקרא א, ט) "וְהִקְטִיר הַכֹּהֵן אֶת הַכֹּל הַמִּזְבֵּחָה"‎[6] וּבְמָקוֹם אַחֵר

﴾ CHAPTER 4 ﴿

§1 The Baraisa proceeds to elaborate Avos 1:2, which states:

שִׁמְעוֹן הַצַּדִּיק הָיָה מִשְּׁיָרֵי אַנְשֵׁי כְּנֶסֶת הַגְּדוֹלָה — **Shimon HaTzaddik was one of the last members of the Great Assembly.**[1] הוּא הָיָה אוֹמֵר עַל שְׁלֹשָׁה — **He used to say:**[2] The world stands upon three things: דְּבָרִים הָעוֹלָם עוֹמֵד עַל הַתּוֹרָה וְעַל הָעֲבוֹדָה וְעַל גְּמִילוּת חֲסָדִים — **upon Torah, upon the sacrificial service, and upon acts of kindness.**

The Baraisa expands upon each part of this teaching:

הֲרֵי הוּא אוֹמֵר "חֶסֶד חָפַצְתִּי וְלֹא עַל הַתּוֹרָה, כֵּיצַד — **"Upon Torah"** — **how so?**[3] זָבַח וְדַעַת אֱלֹהִים מֵעֹלוֹת" — **It says, For I** [God] **desire kindness, not sacrifice; and knowledge of God more than "olos"**[4] (Hosea 6:6). מִכָּאן לְעוֹלָה שֶׁהִיא חֲבִיבָה מִזְּבָחִים — **First, we may infer from here that an olah is more beloved before God than** other **offerings,**[5] מִפְּנֵי שֶׁהָעוֹלָה כּוּלָהּ כָּלִיל לָאִישִׁים — **and that is because the olah is** burnt **entirely upon the** Altar **fires,** שֶׁנֶּאֱמַר "וְהִקְטִיר הַכֹּהֵן אֶת הַכֹּל הַמִּזְבֵּחָה" — **as it says** regarding the olah, **and the Kohen shall cause it all to go up in smoke on the Altar** (Leviticus 1:9);[6] וּבְמָקוֹם אַחֵר

---

1. Shimon HaTzaddik was a legendary Kohen Gadol of the early Second Temple era. He was one of the last surviving members of the אַנְשֵׁי כְּנֶסֶת הַגְּדוֹלָה, *the Men of the Great Assembly*, a group of 120 Sages that included Ezra, Haggai, Zechariah, Malachi, Daniel, Nehemiah, and Mordechai (see *Pirkei Avos* 1:2 with commentaries). For further discussion of Shimon HaTzaddik, see Appendix to Schottenstein ed. of *Yoma*, Vol. I.

2. He was *accustomed* to say this. This is the meaning of the phrase, *Rabbi [So-and-so] used to say,* throughout this tractate (*Binyan Yehoshua*, citing *Rav*).

3. The Baraisa is asking how the world stands on Torah. Does it stand on Torah and the other pillars (sacrificial service and kindness) equally, or does it lean more heavily on the pillar of Torah? Also, is the intention that the world was created for the sake of these things, or that the world continues to exist in the merit of these things? (see *Ben Avraham,* preferred explanation).

4. *Olos* (sing. *olah*) are often referred to as "burnt offerings" for reasons that will soon become clear.

5. Since the verse speaks first of offerings in general, and then singles out the *olah*, it indicates that the *olah* is the most precious of all offerings (*Binyan Yehoshua*, citing *Mefaresh*).

6. By contrast, other animal offerings have only certain parts burned on the Altar. The

הוּא אוֹמֵר (שמואל א ז, ט) "וַיִּקַּח שְׁמוּאֵל טְלֵה חָלָב אֶחָד °וַיַּעֲלֶה עוֹלָה כָלִיל לַה׳ "[7]. וְתַלְמוּד תּוֹרָה חֲבִיבָה לִפְנֵי הַמָּקוֹם מֵעוֹלוֹת, לְפִי שֶׁאִם אָדָם לָמַד תּוֹרָה יוֹדֵעַ דַּעְתּוֹ שֶׁל מָקוֹם, שֶׁנֶּאֱמַר (משלי ב, ה) "אָז תָּבִין יִרְאַת ה׳ וְדַעַת אֱלֹהִים תִּמְצָא"[8] מִכָּאן לְחָכָם שֶׁיּוֹשֵׁב וְדוֹרֵשׁ בַּקָּהָל שֶׁמַּעֲלֶה עָלָיו הַכָּתוּב כְּאִלּוּ הִקְרִיב חֵלֶב וָדָם לְגַבֵּי מִזְבֵּחַ[9].

הוּא אוֹמֵר "וַיִּקַּח שְׁמוּאֵל טְלֵה חָלָב אֶחָד וַיַּעֲלֵהוּ עוֹלָה כָלִיל לַה׳ " — and elsewhere it says, *Samuel took a suckling lamb and offered it up as an olah entirely to HASHEM* (*I Samuel* 7:9).[7]   וְתַלְמוּד תּוֹרָה חֲבִיבָה לִפְנֵי הַמָּקוֹם מֵעוֹלוֹת — And, second, we see that **Torah study is more beloved before the Omnipresent than *olos,*** לְפִי שֶׁאִם אָדָם לָמַד תּוֹרָה יוֹדֵעַ דַּעְתּוֹ שֶׁל מָקוֹם — **because if a person studies Torah he** thereby **understands the knowledge of the Omnipresent,** שֶׁנֶּאֱמַר "אָז תָּבִין יִרְאַת ה׳ וְדַעַת אֱלֹהִים תִּמְצָא" — **as it says,** *If you seek it [the wisdom of the Torah] as [if it were] silver, if you search for it as [if it were] hidden treasures —* **then you will understand the fear of HASHEM, and discover the knowledge of God** (*Proverbs* 2:4-5).[8]

The Baraisa comments:

מִכָּאן לְחָכָם שֶׁיּוֹשֵׁב וְדוֹרֵשׁ בַּקָּהָל שֶׁמַּעֲלֶה עָלָיו הַכָּתוּב כְּאִלּוּ הִקְרִיב חֵלֶב וָדָם לְגַבֵּי מִזְבֵּחַ — **From here we may infer that a sage who sits and teaches the**

---

rest is eaten or, in some cases, burned outside the Temple.

7. [In this verse, the pronounced form of the word (*kri*) is וַיַּעֲלֵהוּ. The Vilna ed. has the written form (*kesiv*) וַיַּעֲלֶה.] This second verse, with its characterization of the *olah* as being *entirely to HASHEM,* is more explicit than the first, which does not specify that even the innards and the feet are burned on the Altar (see *Ben Avraham*). Alternatively, *Binyan Yehoshua* explains that the Baraisa cites the *Samuel* verse because the end of that verse and those that follow tell how in the merit of this *olah* God gave the Israelites a miraculous victory over their Philistine enemies. It is this great merit that indicates the superiority of the *olah* over other offerings.

8. We see from this verse that Torah study leads to "knowledge of God" (familiarity with His ways of conducting the world, and other hidden branches of the Torah's wisdom — *Magen Avos*). And from the *Hosea* verse we see that knowledge of God is more favored than *olos.* It emerges, then, that Torah study

is greater than *olos,* the highest of offerings.

Thus, the Baraisa's question of "how so?" (see above, note 3) — or at least the first part of that question — is answered: Torah study is superior to, and therefore a more important cosmic pillar than, *olos* and other offerings (*Ben Avraham*). [*Avos DeRabbi Nassan, Nusach* 2 (Ch. 8) comments on the *Hosea* verse: הַקֵּשׁ הַקַּל לַקַּל וְהֶחָמוּר לֶחָמוּר, *it compares the lighter item to the lighter item* (i.e., kindness to the lesser offerings) *and the weightier item to the weightier item* (i.e., knowledge of God to the *olah*). This indicates that Torah is superior to kindness as well; see further in the Baraisa regarding one forced to choose between Torah study and performing kindness.]

As for the second part of the Baraisa's question — whether the world was created merely for the sake of Torah, Divine service, and kindness, or it continues at all times to exist only in their merit — the answer will become clear when the Baraisa (below, §4) turns its focus to the sacrificial service (*Ben Avraham*).

שְׁנֵי תַּלְמִידֵי חֲכָמִים שֶׁיּוֹשְׁבִים וְעוֹסְקִים בַּתּוֹרָה וְעָבְרָה לִפְנֵיהֶם כַּלָּה אוֹ
מִטָּה שֶׁל מֵת, אִם בְּיָדָן כְּדֵי צָרְכָּן[10] אַל יְבַטְּלוּ מִמִּשְׁנָתָן, וְאִם לָאו יַעַמְדוּ
וְיִשְׁנוּ[11] וִיקַלְּסוּ לַכַּלָּה וִילַוּוּ לַמֵּת[12].°

Torah **to the public is considered by Scripture as if he offered** sacrificial **fats
and blood upon the Altar.**[9]

The verse in *Hosea* extols both kindness and Torah study; but what is one to
do when he must choose between the two? The Baraisa teaches:
שְׁנֵי תַּלְמִידֵי חֲכָמִים שֶׁיּוֹשְׁבִים וְעוֹסְקִים בַּתּוֹרָה — **When two Torah scholars are
sitting and engrossing themselves in Torah study** וְעָבְרָה לִפְנֵיהֶם כַּלָּה
אוֹ מִטָּה שֶׁל מֵת — **and a bride passes before them** on the way to her wedding, **or the bier of a deceased person** on the way to burial, the rule is as
follows: אִם בְּיָדָן כְּדֵי צָרְכָּן אַל יְבַטְּלוּ מִמִּשְׁנָתָן — **If** [the wedding party or
the funeral party] **has sufficient participation,**[10] **then** [the scholars] **should
not interrupt their studies;** וְאִם לָאו יַעַמְדוּ וְיִשַׁנְּנוּ וִיקַלְּסוּ לַכַּלָּה וִילַוּוּ לַמֵּת —
but if there **is not sufficient participation, then they should rise** from their
studies **and speak the praises of the bride,**[11] or **accompany the deceased
to burial.**[12]

---

9. [The words "from here (we may infer)
that," do not appear in manuscripts or in the
first printed edition, but were inserted based
on the emendation of *Tumas Yesharim*. It is
not readily clear, however, how this teaching is *derived* from the verse cited earlier.
See *Binyan Yehoshua*.] The public teacher
is considered as if he were the Kohen who
places the fats and blood of other people's
offerings on the Altar. Just as that Kohen
gains atonement for the people bringing the
offering, so too does the public teacher of
Torah gain atonement for them by moving
them to repentance through the Torah that
he teaches them (*Velo Od Ella*, referenced
by *Avos HaRosh*; *Magen Avos* explains in a
similar vein).

Indeed, Reish Lakish expounds the verse,
*This is the "Torah" of the olah, of the minchah,
of the chatas, and of the asham* ... (*Leviticus*
7:37) to mean that whoever engages in Torah study is considered as if he brought all of
these offerings (*Menachos* 110a, referenced
here by *Binyan Yehoshua*). [It emerges,
then, that the public teacher of Torah is considered as if he brought all these offerings on
behalf of his listeners.] Even though the *olah*

was offered in its entirety on the Altar [and
our Baraisa has taught that Torah study is
superior even to the *olah*], our Baraisa mentions only "the fats and the blood" because
these are common to all animal offerings
(*Binyan Yehoshua*).

10. See *Kesubos* 17a for several views as to
the participation required for a funeral. The
Gemara does not, however, define the term
sufficient with regard to a bride, because
it depends on the particular bride and her
stature (*Talmidei Rabbeinu Yonah*, cited in
Shitah Mekubetzes; cf. *Likkutei HaGeonim*
cited there and *Meiri*).

11. וְיִשַׁנְּנוּ means *they should speak compre-
hensively,* similar to the word וְשִׁנַּנְתָּם that we
say in *Shema* (*Mefaresh*). [The Vilna text,
which our all-Hebrew section follows, has
וְיִשְׁנוּ in error.] The Gemara (*Kesubos* ibid.)
discusses the praises one should say when
dancing before the bride (*Binyan Yehoshua*).

12. *Kisei Rachamim* points us to the rule
that Torah study takes precedence over all
other mitzvos, unless it is a mitzvah that
cannot be fulfilled [properly] by others, in
which case the law is that we interrupt our

ב. מַעֲשֶׂה בְּרַבִּי יְהוּדָה בְּרַבִּי אֶלְעָאי[13] שֶׁהָיָה יוֹשֵׁב וְשׁוֹנֶה לְתַלְמִידָיו וְעָבְרָה כַלָּה, וְאָחַז בְּיָדוֹ כְּדֵי צָרְכּוֹ, וְהָיָה מְשַׁנֶּין בָּהּ עַד שֶׁעָבְרָה הַכַּלָּה מִלְּפָנָיו.[14]

ג. שׁוּב מַעֲשֶׂה בְּרַבִּי יְהוּדָה בְּרַבִּי אֶלְעָאי שֶׁהָיָה יוֹשֵׁב וְשׁוֹנֶה לְתַלְמִידָיו וְעָבְרָה כַלָּה לְפָנָיו, אָמַר: מַהוּ זֶה. אָמְרוּ לוֹ: כַּלָּה שֶׁעָבְרָה. אָמַר לָהֶם: בָּנַי, עִמְדוּ וְהִתְעַסְּקוּ בַּכַּלָּה, שֶׁכֵּן מָצִינוּ בְּהַקָּדוֹשׁ בָּרוּךְ הוּא שֶׁנִּתְעַסֵּק בְּכַלָּה, (שֶׁנֶּאֱמַר (בראשית ב, כב) "וַיִּבֶן ה' אֱלֹהִים אֶת הַצֵּלָע",) הוּא נִתְעַסֵּק בְּכַלָּה, °אֲנִי עַל אַחַת כַּמָּה וְכַמָּה.[15] וְהֵיכָן מָצִינוּ שֶׁהַקָּדוֹשׁ

---

§2 The Baraisa continues on the above theme:

מַעֲשֶׂה בְּרַבִּי יְהוּדָה בְּרַבִּי אֶלְעָאי — **There was an incident involving R' Yehudah bar Il'ai:**[13] שֶׁהָיָה יוֹשֵׁב וְשׁוֹנֶה לְתַלְמִידָיו וְעָבְרָה כַלָּה — **As he was sitting and teaching his students, a bride passed by,** וְאָחַז בְּיָדוֹ כְּדֵי צָרְכּוֹ וְהָיָה מְשַׁנֶּין בָּהּ עַד שֶׁעָבְרָה הַכַּלָּה מִלְּפָנָיו — **and it was in his hands to complete** her entourage, so he **arose and spoke of her** wonderful qualities **until the bride passed from before him.**[14]

§3 The Baraisa cites another, similar incident:

שׁוּב מַעֲשֶׂה בְּרַבִּי יְהוּדָה בְּרַבִּי אֶלְעָאי — **There was another incident involving R' Yehudah bar Il'ai.** שֶׁהָיָה יוֹשֵׁב וְשׁוֹנֶה לְתַלְמִידָיו וְעָבְרָה כַלָּה לְפָנָיו — **He was sitting and teaching his students and a bride passed before him.** R' Yehudah recognized that there was some commotion, but did not know what it was. אָמַר מַהוּ זֶה — **He said** to his students, **"What is this?"** אָמְרוּ לוֹ כַּלָּה שֶׁעָבְרָה — **They said to him** in reply, **"It is a bride** and her entourage **that has passed."** אָמַר לָהֶם בָּנַי עִמְדוּ וְהִתְעַסְּקוּ בַּכַּלָּה — **He said to them, "My sons, arise and participate in** the wedding party of this **bride.** Make the procession joyful! שֶׁכֵּן מָצִינוּ בְּהַקָּדוֹשׁ בָּרוּךְ הוּא שֶׁנִּתְעַסֵּק בְּכַלָּה — **For so we find regarding the Holy One, Blessed is He** — that He participated in the wedding party of a bride. הוּא נִתְעַסֵּק בְּכַלָּה אֲנוּ עַל אַחַת כַּמָּה וְכַמָּה — **And if He participated** in the wedding party of a **bride, then we must certainly do so!"**[15] וְהֵיכָן מָצִינוּ

---

study to perform the mitzvah (*Yoreh Deah* 246:18).

Although there is a principle that being occupied with one mitzvah exempts one from performing another mitzvah (הָעוֹסֵק בְּמִצְוָה פָּטוּר מִן הַמִּצְוָה, Torah study is an exception. Since the basic purpose of studying Torah is to apply its teachings in practice, being involved in such study cannot absolve one from acting to fulfill the very purpose of that

study! (*Meiri, Shabbos* 9b; *Kehillos Yaakov, Berachos* §25 and *Shabbos* §11).

13. Who is known simply as "R' Yehudah" throughout the Mishnah.

14. *Kesubos* 17a teaches: They said about R' Yehudah bar Il'ai that he would take a branch of myrtle and dance before the bride, saying, כַּלָּה נָאָה וַחֲסוּדָה, "A beautiful and charming bride!" (see *Ahavas Chesed*).

15. Emendation follows *Nuschas HaGra*.

בָּרוּךְ הוּא נִתְעַסֵּק בְּכַלָּה, שֶׁנֶּאֱמַר (בראשית ב, כב) "וַיִּבֶן ה' אֱלֹהִים אֶת
הַצֵּלָע" שֶׁכֵּן קוֹרִין בִּכְרַכֵּי הַיָּם °לְכַלָּה "בְּנָאִיתָה"[16], מִכָּאן שֶׁתִּקְנָהּ
הַקָּדוֹשׁ בָּרוּךְ הוּא לְחַוָּה וְקִשְּׁטָהּ כְּכַלָּה וֶהֱבִיאָהּ אֵצֶל אָדָם, שֶׁנֶּאֱמַר
(שם) "וַיְבִאֶהָ אֶל הָאָדָם"[17], פַּעַם אַחַת נַעֲשָׂה הַקָּדוֹשׁ בָּרוּךְ הוּא שׁוֹשְׁבִין
לְאָדָם[18], מִכָּאן וְאֵילָךְ אָדָם קוֹנֶה שׁוֹשְׁבִין לְעַצְמוֹ, (שֶׁנֶּאֱמַר (בראשית ב, כג)
"עֶצֶם מֵעֲצָמַי וּבָשָׂר מִבְּשָׂרִי") פַּעַם אַחַת נִטְּלָה חַוָּה מֵאָדָם, מִכָּאן וְאֵילָךְ
מְקַדֵּשׁ אָדָם אֶת בַּת חֲבֵירוֹ.

שֶׁהַקָּדוֹשׁ בָּרוּךְ הוּא נִתְעַסֵּק בְּכַלָּה — And where do we find that the Holy One,
Blessed is He, participated in the wedding party of a bride? שֶׁנֶּאֱמַר "וַיִּבֶן
ה'—אֱלֹהִים אֶת הַצֵּלָע" — For it says, *Then HASHEM God fashioned the side
that He had taken from the man into a woman* (Genesis 2:22). Now, this term,
וַיִּבֶן, *vayiven,* refers to braiding hair, שֶׁכֵּן בִּכְרַכֵּי הַיָּם קוֹרִין לְקֶלַע בְּנָאִיתָא
— for in the cities by the sea, they call a braided hairdo a *bena'isa*.[16]
מִכָּאן שֶׁתִּקְנָהּ הַקָּדוֹשׁ בָּרוּךְ הוּא לְחַוָּה וְקִשְּׁטָהּ כְּכַלָּה וֶהֱבִיאָהּ אֵצֶל אָדָם — We can
thus learn from here that the Holy One, Blessed is He, prepared Eve and
adorned her as befits a bride and brought her to Adam, שֶׁנֶּאֱמַר "וַיְבִאֶהָ
אֶל הָאָדָם" — as it says, *and He brought her to Adam* (ibid.).[17] פַּעַם
אַחַת נַעֲשָׂה הַקָּדוֹשׁ בָּרוּךְ הוּא שׁוֹשְׁבִין לְאָדָם — For this one time, the Holy
One, Blessed is He, acted as the wedding attendant for a man;[18] מִכָּאן
וְאֵילָךְ אָדָם קוֹנֶה שׁוֹשְׁבִין לְעַצְמוֹ — from then on, a man must procure a
wedding attendant for himself. פַּעַם אַחַת נִטְּלָה חַוָּה מֵאָדָם — Similarly, for this **one time,** a match was made when **Eve** was **taken** from the
body of **Adam** and made his wife. מִכָּאן וְאֵילָךְ מְקַדֵּשׁ אָדָם אֶת בַּת חֲבֵירוֹ
— From then on, a man needs to betroth the daughter of his fellow
man.

---

16. Emendation follows *Nuschas HaGra.*

17. This verse indicates that God brought
her to Adam in a beautified state, adorned
with all twenty-four types of ornaments associated with a bride (see *Isaiah* 3:18-24
and *Shir HaShirim Rabbah* 4 §22). *Zohar*
explains the allusion: The word וַיְבִאֶהָ, *and
He brought her,* has the numerical value
of twenty-four [ו=6, י=10, ב=2, א=1, ה=5],
corresponding to the twenty-four bridal
ornaments (quoted by *Matnos Kehunah* to
Bereishis Rabbah 18 §1).

18. This term refers to the individual who

accepts the responsibilities that pertain
to the wedding, to the match (*Binyan Yehoshua,* from *Rashi, Berachos* 61a), and
to making the wedding a joyous occasion
(*Rashi, Eruvin* 18b). In the case of Adam,
God Himself acted as the wedding attendant. The Gemara in *Berachos* comments:
"Here the Torah teaches us proper conduct,
that an important person should make the
wedding arrangements even for a person of
lower rank, and this should not disturb him."
He should not feel it beneath his dignity, for
God did it for man, whose rank is insignificant compared to His.

ד. עַל הָעֲבוֹדָה, כֵּיצַד¹⁹, כָּל זְמַן שֶׁעֲבוֹדַת בֵּית הַמִּקְדָּשׁ קַיֶּמֶת
הָעוֹלָם מִתְבָּרֵךְ עַל יוֹשְׁבָיו וּגְשָׁמִים יוֹרְדִין בִּזְמַנָּן, שֶׁנֶּאֱמַר (דברים
יא, יג-טו) "(לְאַהֲבָה אֶת ה' אֱלֹהֵיכֶם) וּלְעָבְדוֹ בְּכָל לְבַבְכֶם וּבְכָל נַפְשְׁכֶם²⁰,
וְנָתַתִּי מְטַר אַרְצְכֶם בְּעִתּוֹ יוֹרֶה וּמַלְקוֹשׁ [וְגו']], וְנָתַתִּי עֵשֶׂב בְּשָׂדְךָ
לִבְהֶמְתֶּךָ"²¹. וּבִזְמַן שֶׁאֵין עֲבוֹדַת בֵּית הַמִּקְדָּשׁ קַיֶּמֶת, אֵין הָעוֹלָם
מִתְבָּרֵךְ עַל יוֹשְׁבָיו, וְאֵין הַגְּשָׁמִים יוֹרְדִין בִּזְמַנָּן, שֶׁנֶּאֱמַר (שם, טז-יז)
"הִשָּׁמְרוּ לָכֶם פֶּן יִפְתֶּה לְבַבְכֶם וְגו'²², וְעָצַר אֶת הַשָּׁמַיִם וְלֹא יִהְיֶה מָטָר",

---

§4 The Baraisa turns to the pillar of Divine service:

עַל הָעֲבוֹדָה, כֵּיצַד — The world stands "upon the sacrificial service" —
how so?[19] כָּל זְמַן שֶׁעֲבוֹדַת בֵּית הַמִּקְדָּשׁ קַיֶּמֶת — As long as the Temple
service endures, הָעוֹלָם מִתְבָּרֵךְ עַל יוֹשְׁבָיו וּגְשָׁמִים יוֹרְדִין בִּזְמַנָּן — the world
is blessed on behalf of its inhabitants and the rains fall at the right time,
שֶׁנֶּאֱמַר "לְאַהֲבָה אֶת ה' אֱלֹהֵיכֶם וּלְעָבְדוֹ בְּכָל לְבַבְכֶם וּבְכָל נַפְשְׁכֶם — as it says, It
will be that if you hearken to My commandments that I command you today, to
love HASHEM, your God, and to serve Him[20] with all your heart and with all
your soul, וְנָתַתִּי מְטַר אַרְצְכֶם בְּעִתּוֹ יוֹרֶה וּמַלְקוֹשׁ וְגו' וְנָתַתִּי עֵשֶׂב בְּשָׂדְךָ לִבְהֶמְתֶּךָ"
— then I shall provide rain for your Land in its proper time, the early and
the late rains, etc. And I shall provide grass in your field for your cattle
(Deuteronomy 11:13-15).[21] וּבִזְמַן שֶׁאֵין עֲבוֹדַת בֵּית הַמִּקְדָּשׁ קַיֶּמֶת — But
when there is no Temple service, אֵין הָעוֹלָם מִתְבָּרֵךְ עַל יוֹשְׁבָיו וְאֵין הַגְּשָׁמִים
יוֹרְדִין בִּזְמַנָּן — the world is not blessed on behalf of its inhabitants and the
rains do not fall at the right time, שֶׁנֶּאֱמַר "הִשָּׁמְרוּ לָכֶם פֶּן יִפְתֶּה לְבַבְכֶם וְגו'
וְעָצַר אֶת הַשָּׁמַיִם וְלֹא יִהְיֶה מָטָר" — as it says, Beware for yourselves, lest your
heart be seduced and you turn astray[22] and serve gods of others, etc. Then ...

---

19. Is the intention that the world was *created* for the sacrificial service, or that the world continues to endure in its merit? The answer, provided in the next sentence, is that the world continually benefits from the sacrificial service. If so, we may conclude that the same is true for the pillar of Torah, thus completing the answer to the Baraisa's first question, as explained above in notes 3 and 8 (*Ben Avraham*).

20. To serve Him, that is, through the sacrificial service in the Temple. The verse adds *with all your heart* because one bringing an offering must do so in the proper frame of mind, without any disqualifying intentions (*Ben Avraham*).

21. Why does the sacrificial service bring

material blessing in its wake? *Binyan Yehoshua* explains that it is only natural for God to provide the needs of His servants, in the same way He provides for all His other creatures. The only difference is that man, with his free will and consequent ability to sin, often forfeits his claim to God's loving care (*Kiddushin* 82b). Thus, when the Divine service in the Temple brings atonement — the morning *tamid* offering for the night's sins, the afternoon *tamid* for the day's sins, and various other offerings for specific sins — we return to the ranks of God's creatures, who are entitled by that very fact to all the Divine blessings necessary for them to flourish.

22. From serving God through the Temple service, as mentioned earlier in the passage

וְכֵן בְּחַגַּי (ב, טו-טז) הוּא אוֹמֵר:[23] "שִׂימוּ נָא לְבַבְכֶם מִן הַיּוֹם הַזֶּה וָמָעְלָה מִטֶּרֶם שׂוֹם אֶבֶן אֶל אֶבֶן בְּהֵיכַל ה'",[24] מִהְיוֹתָם בָּא אֶל עֲרֵמַת עֶשְׂרִים וְהָיְתָה עֲשָׂרָה בָּא אֶל הַיֶּקֶב לַחְשֹׂף חֲמִשִּׁים פּוּרָה וְהָיְתָה עֶשְׂרִים", מִפְּנֵי מָה לֹא נֶאֱמַר בַּיֶּקֶב "עֶשְׂרִים וְהָיוּ עֲשָׂרָה" כְּשֵׁם שֶׁנֶּאֱמַר בַּחִטִּים "עֶשְׂרִים וְהָיוּ עֲשָׂרָה"?[25], לְפִי שֶׁיֶּקֶב סִימָן טוֹב יוֹתֵר מֵחִטִּים,

He will restrain the heaven so there will be no rain, and the ground will not yield its produce; and you will be swiftly banished from the goodly Land that HASHEM gives you (ibid. vv. 16,17).

The connection between the Temple service and material blessing is found in the Prophets as well: וְכֵן בְּחַגַּי הוּא אוֹמֵר — And similarly in Haggai it says regarding the first years of the Second Temple era:[23] "שִׂימוּ נָא לְבַבְכֶם מִן הַיּוֹם הַזֶּה וָמָעְלָה מִטֶּרֶם שׂוֹם "אֶבֶן אֶל אֶבֶן בְּהֵיכַל ה' — Haggai spoke up and said ... Consider [the situation] from this day and previously, before stone was placed upon stone in the Sanctuary of HASHEM,[24] מִהְיוֹתָם בָּא אֶל עֲרֵמַת עֶשְׂרִים וְהָיְתָה עֲשָׂרָה בָּא אֶל "הַיֶּקֶב לַחְשֹׂף חֲמִשִּׁים פּוּרָה וְהָיְתָה עֶשְׂרִים — when they would come to a grain heap of [what should have been] twenty [units] but was [only] ten; [when one would come] to the winepress to draw out fifty [units] from the pit, but there were [only] twenty (Haggai 2:14,15-16). In previous years, Haggai reminds the people, grain harvests were half, and wine yields only two-fifths, of what was expected.

The Baraisa interrupts the quotation to comment on the last verse. מִפְּנֵי מָה לֹא נֶאֱמַר בַּיֶּקֶב עֶשְׂרִים וְהָיוּ עֲשָׂרָה כְּשֵׁם שֶׁנֶּאֱמַר בַּחִטִּים עֶשְׂרִים וְהָיוּ עֲשָׂרָה — Why does the verse ascribe a greater shortfall to the wine yields than to the grain harvests? Why does it not say "[what should have been] twenty [units] but was [only] ten" regarding the winepress, just as it says "[what should have been] twenty [units] but was [only] ten" regarding the wheat?[25] לְפִי שֶׁיֶּקֶב סִימָן טוֹב יוֹתֵר מֵחִטִּים — Because the wine vat is more of a good omen

(Mefaresh, Ben Avraham; see above, note 20).

23. Haggai the Prophet sanctioned and encouraged the construction of the Second Temple, which had begun in the days of Cyrus (Ezra Ch. 3), but was subsequently discontinued for eighteen years. The Baraisa cites one of Haggai's prophecies, in which he points to the lack of prosperity in the renewed Jewish settlement, and predicts a turnaround with the construction of the Temple.

24. Haggai told the people: We are placing

our stone upon the original stone of the returnees who heeded Cyrus' call for the Jews to resettle the Holy Land and rebuild the Temple. At this historic moment, pause and contemplate the disappointing harvests of the recent past, and consider how these "stones" will affect the harvests of the near future.

25. Since wheat is more of a necessity than wine, the greater misfortune would have been the reverse — if the shortage of wheat were greater than the shortage of wine (Magen Avos).

לְלַמֶּדְךָ שֶׁכָּל זְמַן שֶׁהַיַּיִן לוֹקֶה, סִימָן רַע לְכָל הַשָּׁנָה כּוּלָהּ‎[26], אָמְרוּ יִשְׂרָאֵל לִפְנֵי הַקָּדוֹשׁ בָּרוּךְ הוּא: רִבּוֹנוֹ שֶׁל עוֹלָם, מִפְּנֵי מָה אַתָּה עָשִׂיתָ לָנוּ כָּךְ, הֱשִׁיבָן רוּחַ הַקּוֹדֶשׁ: (שם א, ט) "פָּנֹה אֶל הַרְבֵּה וְהִנֵּה לִמְעָט [וְגוֹ'] יַעַן בֵּיתִי אֲשֶׁר הוּא חָרֵב, וְאַתֶּם רָצִים אִישׁ לְבֵיתוֹ‎[27]", וְאִם אַתֶּם תַּעַסְקוּ בַּעֲבוֹדַת בֵּית הַמִּקְדָּשׁ, אֲנִי אֲבָרֵךְ אֶתְכֶם כְּבַתְּחִילָה‎[28], שֶׁנֶּאֱמַר (שם ב, יח-יט) "שִׂימוּ נָא לְבַבְכֶם [וְגוֹ'], מִיּוֹם עֶשְׂרִים וְאַרְבָּעָה לַתְּשִׁיעִי לְמִן הַיּוֹם אֲשֶׁר יֻסַּד הֵיכַל ה' [וְגוֹ'], הַעוֹד הַזֶּרַע בַּמְּגוּרָה וְעַד הַגֶּפֶן וְהַתְּאֵנָה וְהָרִמּוֹן וְעֵץ הַזַּיִת לֹא נָשָׂא. מִן הַיּוֹם הַזֶּה אֲבָרֵךְ"‎

---

than wheat. — לְלַמֶּדְךָ שֶׁכָּל זְמַן שֶׁהַיַּיִן לוֹקֶה סִימָן רַע לְכָל הַשָּׁנָה כּוּלָהּ The verse thus comes to teach you that when a year's vintage is ruined, it is a bad omen for all the crops of the entire year.[26]

The Baraisa discusses the cause of this economic downturn.

אָמְרוּ יִשְׂרָאֵל לִפְנֵי הַקָּדוֹשׁ בָּרוּךְ הוּא — At that time, the Jewish people said before the Holy One, Blessed is He, רִבּוֹנוֹ שֶׁל עוֹלָם מִפְּנֵי מָה אַתָּה עָשִׂיתָ לָנוּ כָּךְ — "Master of the Universe! Why did You do this to us? Why did You give us such poor harvests of wheat and wine?" הֱשִׁיבָן רוּחַ הַקּוֹדֶשׁ — The Divine Spirit, speaking through Haggai, responded to them, "פָּנֹה אֶל הַרְבֵּה וְהִנֵּה לִמְעָט וְגוֹ' יַעַן בֵּיתִי אֲשֶׁר הוּא חָרֵב וְאַתֶּם רָצִים אִישׁ לְבֵיתוֹ" — "You looked for much [produce] but, behold, it is little ... because of My Temple, which is ruined, while you run, each to his own house (ibid. 1:9).[27] וְאִם אַתֶּם תַּעַסְקוּ בַּעֲבוֹדַת בֵּית הַמִּקְדָּשׁ אֲנִי אֲבָרֵךְ אֶתְכֶם כְּבַתְּחִילָה — So, if you occupy yourselves with the Temple service, I will bless you with prosperity as I did in the beginning,"[28] שֶׁנֶּאֱמַר "שִׂימוּ נָא לְבַבְכֶם וְגוֹ' מִיּוֹם עֶשְׂרִים וְאַרְבָּעָה לַתְּשִׁיעִי לְמִן הַיּוֹם אֲשֶׁר יֻסַּד הֵיכַל ה' וְגוֹ' — as it says, Set now your heart [to consider] from this day and before, from the twenty-fourth of the ninth [month], [back] to the day when the foundations of the Sanctuary were laid; הַעוֹד הַזֶּרַע בַּמְּגוּרָה — set your heart [to consider]: Is there וְעַד הַגֶּפֶן וְהַתְּאֵנָה וְהָרִמּוֹן וְעֵץ הַזַּיִת לֹא נָשָׂא — any more seed in the silo? Even the grapevine and the fig tree and the pomegranate tree and the olive tree have not borne [their fruit]. מִן הַיּוֹם הַזֶּה אֲבָרֵךְ — But from this day on I will provide a blessing (ibid. 2:18-19).

---

26. The wine shortage was a more significant curse than the wheat shortage, because the poor grape harvest was a bad omen for all the harvests of the year (ibid.)

27. God alludes to the question and then answers it: Why was the harvest so short of expectations? Because My house is in ruins, and you do not take it to heart, instead running each to his own house (*Binyan Yehoshua*).

28. Indeed, the people responded to the prophet's rebuke and applied themselves to the holy task they had neglected: *And so Zerubbabel son of Shealtiel [the governor of Judea] and Joshua son of Jehozadak, the Kohen Gadol, and the entire remnant of the people listened to the voice of HASHEM their God, and to the words of Haggai the prophet ... and the people feared before HASHEM ...*

הָא לָמַדְתָּ שֶׁאֵין עֲבוֹדָה שֶׁהִיא חֲבִיבָה לִפְנֵי הַקָּדוֹשׁ בָּרוּךְ הוּא יוֹתֵר מֵעֲבוֹדַת בֵּית הַמִּקְדָּשׁ.[29]

ה. עַל גְּמִילוּת חֲסָדִים, כֵּיצַד[30], הֲרֵי הוּא אוֹמֵר (הושע ו,ו) "כִּי חֶסֶד חָפַצְתִּי וְלֹא זָבַח"[31]. הָעוֹלָם מִתְחִלָּה לֹא נִבְרָא אֶלָּא בְּחֶסֶד, שֶׁנֶּאֱמַר (תהלים פט, ג) "כִּי אָמַרְתִּי עוֹלָם חֶסֶד יִבָּנֶה שָׁמַיִם תָּכִן אֱמוּנָתְךָ בָהֶם"[32], פַּעַם אַחַת הָיָה רַבָּן יוֹחָנָן בֶּן זַכַּאי יוֹצֵא מִירוּשָׁלַיִם וְהָיָה רַבִּי יְהוֹשֻׁעַ הוֹלֵךְ אַחֲרָיו וְרָאָה בֵּית הַמִּקְדָּשׁ חָרֵב, [אָמַר רַבִּי יְהוֹשֻׁעַ: אוֹי לָנוּ עַל זֶה שֶׁהוּא חָרֵב]

הָא לָמַדְתָּ שֶׁאֵין עֲבוֹדָה שֶׁהִיא חֲבִיבָה לִפְנֵי הַקָּדוֹשׁ בָּרוּךְ הוּא יוֹתֵר מֵעֲבוֹדַת בֵּית הַמִּקְדָּשׁ — Thus, you have learned from [this passage] that there is no service more beloved before the Holy One, Blessed is He, than the Temple service.[29]

§5 The Baraisa turns to the pillar of kindness:

עַל גְּמִילוּת חֲסָדִים, כֵּיצַד — The world stands "**upon kindness**" — how so?[30] הֲרֵי הוּא אוֹמֵר "כִּי חֶסֶד חָפַצְתִּי וְלֹא זָבַח" — Scripture provides the answer when it says, *For I desire kindness, not sacrifice* (Hosea 6:6), implying that acts of kindness are superior to the Temple service.[31] הָעוֹלָם מִתְחִלָּה לֹא נִבְרָא אֶלָּא בְּחֶסֶד שֶׁנֶּאֱמַר "כִּי אָמַרְתִּי עוֹלָם חֶסֶד יִבָּנֶה שָׁמַיִם תָּכִן אֱמוּנָתְךָ בָהֶם" — Moreover, the world was created from the very beginning through kindness alone, as it says, *For I said, the world was built with kindness; the heavens, You establish your faithfulness in them* (Psalms 89:3).[32]

Kindness can even be a substitute for the Temple service, as the following anecdote shows:

פַּעַם אַחַת הָיָה רַבָּן יוֹחָנָן בֶּן זַכַּאי יוֹצֵא מִירוּשָׁלַיִם — Once, Rabban Yochanan ben Zakkai was leaving Jerusalem. וְהָיָה רַבִּי יְהוֹשֻׁעַ הוֹלֵךְ אַחֲרָיו וְרָאָה בֵּית הַמִּקְדָּשׁ חָרֵב — R' Yehoshua, his student, was following him, and as they walked, he saw the recently destroyed Temple. אָמַר רַבִּי יְהוֹשֻׁעַ אוֹי לָנוּ עַל זֶה שֶׁהוּא חָרֵב

---

and they came and did work on the Temple of HASHEM, *Master of Legions, their God* (Haggai 1:12,14).

29. That is, for the purpose of atonement. Although Torah study and acts of kindness also provide a measure of atonement (see, for example, §1 above and §5 below), the Temple service is more effective in this regard. In other respects, however, the sacrificial service does not equal the other two pillars, as the Baraisa demonstrated earlier (§1) from Scripture: כִּי חֶסֶד חָפַצְתִּי וְלֹא זָבַח וְדַעַת אֱלֹהִים מֵעֹלוֹת, *For I desire kindness, not sacrifice; and knowledge of God more than "olos"* (Ben Avraham).

30. Is the intention that the world was created with kindness (or for the sake of kindness), or is the intention that the world continues to exist in the merit of kindness? (Magen Avos, Ben Avraham).

31. Thus, if the world continually benefits from the sacrificial service, as established above, it certainly benefits in a similar way from acts of kindness (ibid.).

32. This is a second explanation for what it means that the world stands on kindness: Not only does the world endure and thrive in the merit of kindness, but it originally came into being through kindness (Magen Avos)

מָקוֹם שֶׁמְּכַפְּרִים בּוֹ עֲוֹנוֹתֵיהֶם שֶׁל יִשְׂרָאֵל. אָמַר לוֹ: בְּנִי, אַל יֵרַע לְךָ,
יֵשׁ לָנוּ כַּפָּרָה אַחַת שֶׁהִיא כְּמוֹתָהּ, וְאֵיזֶה, זֶה גְמִילוּת חֲסָדִים, שֶׁנֶּאֱמַר
"כִּי חֶסֶד חָפַצְתִּי וְלֹא זָבַח"[33], שֶׁכֵּן מָצִינוּ בְּדָנִיֵּאל אִישׁ חֲמוּדוֹת שֶׁהָיָה
מִתְעַסֵּק בִּגְמִילוּת חֲסָדִים[34]. וּמָה הֵן גְּמִילוּת חֲסָדִים שֶׁהָיָה דָנִיֵּאל מִתְעַסֵּק
בָּהֶם[35], אִם תֹּאמַר עוֹלוֹת וּזְבָחִים מַקְרִיב בְּבָבֶל, וַהֲלֹא כְּבָר נֶאֱמַר (דברים
יב, יג-יד) "הִשָּׁמֶר לְךָ פֶּן תַּעֲלֶה עֹלֹתֶיךָ בְּכָל מָקוֹם אֲשֶׁר תִּרְאֶה. כִּי אִם
בַּמָּקוֹם אֲשֶׁר יִבְחַר ה' בְּאַחַד שְׁבָטֶיךָ, שָׁם תַּעֲלֶה עֹלֹתֶיךָ"[36]. אֶלָּא מָה הֵן

מָקוֹם שֶׁמְּכַפְּרִים בּוֹ עֲוֹנוֹתֵיהֶם שֶׁל יִשְׂרָאֵל — R' Yehoshua exclaimed, "Woe is to us regarding this Temple that has been destroyed, for it is the place where the sins of Israel are atoned!" **אָמַר לוֹ בְּנִי אַל יֵרַע לְךָ יֵשׁ לָנוּ כַּפָּרָה אַחַת שֶׁהִיא כְּמוֹתָהּ** — [Rabban Yochanan ben Zakkai] said to him, "My son, do not let it trouble you on that account; we have one other, comparable form of atonement. **וְאֵיזֶה זֶה גְמִילוּת חֲסָדִים שֶׁנֶּאֱמַר "כִּי חֶסֶד חָפַצְתִּי וְלֹא זָבַח"** — And what is this alternative source of atonement? Acts of kindness, as it says: *For I desire kindness, not sacrifice*" (Hosea 6:6).[33]

The Baraisa finds additional support for this idea.

שֶׁכֵּן מָצִינוּ בְּדָנִיֵּאל אִישׁ חֲמוּדוֹת שֶׁהָיָה מִתְעַסֵּק בִּגְמִילוּת חֲסָדִים — For so we find with Daniel, the greatly beloved man, that he engaged in acts of kindness, and those acts were characterized as a "service" to God.[34] **וּמָה הֵן גְּמִילוּת חֲסָדִים שֶׁהָיָה דָנִיֵּאל מִתְעַסֵּק בָּהֶם** — And what were those acts of kindness that Daniel engaged in?[35] **אִם תֹּאמַר עוֹלוֹת וּזְבָחִים מַקְרִיב בְּבָבֶל** — If you will say that he was offering olos and other sacrifices in Babylonia, **וַהֲלֹא** that cannot be, **כְּבָר נֶאֱמַר "הִשָּׁמֶר לְךָ פֶּן תַּעֲלֶה עֹלֹתֶיךָ בְּכָל מָקוֹם אֲשֶׁר תִּרְאֶה** — for surely it already says in the Torah that such a thing is forbidden: *Beware for yourself, lest you bring up your burnt offerings in any place that you see;* **כִּי אִם בַּמָּקוֹם אֲשֶׁר יִבְחַר ה' בְּאַחַד שְׁבָטֶיךָ שָׁם תַּעֲלֶה עֹלֹתֶיךָ"** — *only in the place that HASHEM will choose, among one of your tribes, there shall you bring up your burnt offerings* (Deuteronomy 12:13-14).[36] **אֶלָּא מָה הֵן**

— that is, through God's desire to share His goodness with others.

33. According to this interpretation, the verse apparently means, *For I desire kindness [when there is] not sacrifice* — i.e., when the Temple is in ruins and no sacrifices can be brought (see *Binyan Yehoshua*, cting *Mefaresh*).

34. The book of *Daniel* refers to the fact that Daniel engaged in the service of God. So said King Darius to his favored minister before throwing him unwillingly into a lion's den, *"May your God, Whom you*

serve continually, save you!" Since this cannot mean that Daniel performed any kind of sacrificial service, as the Baraisa goes on to say, it must mean that he served God by engaging in acts of kindness (*Kisei Rachamim*).

35. *Gra* emends the text here to read וְכִי מַה עֲבוֹדָה שֶׁהָיָה דָנִיֵּאל מִתְעַסֵּק בָּהּ, "What 'service' did Daniel engage in?"

36. In these verses, the Torah prohibits bringing offerings in any place other than the Temple site in Jerusalem. This prohibition

גְּמִילוּת חֲסָדִים שֶׁהָיָה מִתְעַסֵּק בָּהֶן, הָיָה מְתַקֵּן אֶת הַכַּלָּה וּמְשַׂמְּחָהּ, וּמְלַוֶּה אֶת הַמֵּת, וְנוֹתֵן פְּרוּטָה לֶעָנִי[37], וּמִתְפַּלֵּל שָׁלֹשׁ פְּעָמִים בְּכָל יוֹם, וּתְפִלָּתוֹ מִתְקַבֶּלֶת בְּרָצוֹן[38], שֶׁנֶּאֱמַר (דניאל ו, יא) "וְדָנִיֵּאל כְּדִי יְדַע דִּי רְשִׁים כְּתָבָא עַל לְבַיְתֵהּ וְכַוִּין פְּתִיחָן לֵהּ בְּעִלִּיתֵהּ נֶגֶד יְרוּשְׁלֶם וְזִמְנִין תְּלָתָה בְיוֹמָא הוּא בָּרֵךְ עַל בִּרְכוֹהִי וּמְצַלֵּא וּמוֹדֵא קֳדָם אֱלָהֵהּ כָּל קֳבֵל דִּי הֲוָא עָבֵד מִן קַדְמַת דְּנָה", וּכְשֶׁבָּא אַסְפַּסְיָינוֹס לְהַחֲרִיב אֶת יְרוּשָׁלַיִם, אָמַר לָהֶם: שׁוֹטִים, מִפְּנֵי מָה אַתֶּם מְבַקְשִׁים לְהַחֲרִיב אֶת הָעִיר הַזֹּאת וְאַתֶּם

גְּמִילוּת חֲסָדִים שֶׁהָיָה מִתְעַסֵּק בָּהֶן — Rather, what were the acts of kindness that [Daniel] engaged in? הָיָה מְתַקֵּן אֶת הַכַּלָּה וּמְשַׂמְּחָהּ וּמְלַוֶּה אֶת הַמֵּת וְנוֹתֵן פְּרוּטָה לֶעָנִי — He would take care of a bride and gladden her, escort a dead person to his grave, and give a *perutah* (a small coin) to a pauper.[37] וּמִתְפַּלֵּל שָׁלֹשׁ פְּעָמִים בְּכָל יוֹם וּתְפִלָּתוֹ מִתְקַבֶּלֶת בְּרָצוֹן — In addition, he would pray three times every day, and because of his charitable activities, his prayer would be accepted with favor,[38] שֶׁנֶּאֱמַר "וְדָנִיֵּאל כְּדִי יְדַע דִּי רְשִׁים כְּתָבָא עַל לְבַיְתֵהּ — as it says, *When Daniel learned that the writing had been inscribed, he went home.* וְכַוִּין פְּתִיחָן לֵהּ בְּעִלִּיתֵהּ נֶגֶד יְרוּשְׁלֶם וְזִמְנִין תְּלָתָה בְיוֹמָא הוּא בָּרֵךְ עַל בִּרְכוֹהִי וּמְצַלֵּא וּמוֹדֵא קֳדָם אֱלָהֵהּ — *He had windows open in his upper story, facing Jerusalem, and three times a day he fell to his knees and prayed and gave thanks before his God,* כָּל קֳבֵל דִּי הֲוָא עָבֵד מִן קַדְמַת דְּנָה" — exactly as *he used to do before this* (Daniel 6:11).

Having recounted an exchange between Rabban Yochanan ben Zakkai and a disciple soon after the Temple's destruction, the Baraisa turns to another incident involving the same sage and his disciples just before that destruction. [39] וּכְשֶׁבָּא אַסְפַּסְיָינוֹס לְהַחֲרִיב אֶת יְרוּשָׁלַיִם — When Vespasian came to destroy Jerusalem, אָמַר לָהֶם שׁוֹטִים — he said to [the people walled up in the city], "Fools! מִפְּנֵי מָה אַתֶּם מְבַקְשִׁים לְהַחֲרִיב אֶת הָעִיר הַזֹּאת וְאַתֶּם

---

took permanent effect when the the First Temple was built, and therefore remained in force after that Temple was destroyed and throughout the Babylonian exile, when the events recorded in *Daniel* occurred. Clearly, then, Daniel did not perform any kind of sacrificial service in Babylonia.

37. Some combine this phrase with the next one and take the combination to mean that Daniel was careful to give charity before praying, in fulfillment of the verse (*Psalms* 17:15), אֲנִי בְּצֶדֶק אֶחֱזֶה פָנֶיךָ, *And I — amid charity shall I behold Your face* (*Binyan Yehoshua*, citing *Mefaresh*, and *Ahavas*

Chesed; see also *Magen Avos*).

38. For anyone who treats other people with compassion is treated by Heaven with compassion (*Mefaresh*, citing *Shabbos* 151b). The Midrash states: "He who performs acts of kindness will be informed that his prayers have been answered, as it says (*Hosea* 10:12), *Sow for yourselves charity and you will reap according to kindness ... and [set] a time to seek* HASHEM (*Avos HaRosh*, citing *Midrash Tehillim* §65).

39. *Ben Avraham.* [Much of this story appears, with many variations, in *Gittin* 55b-56b.]

מְבַקְשִׁים לִשְׂרוֹף אֶת בֵּית הַמִּקְדָּשׁ. וְכִי מָה אֲנִי מְבַקֵּשׁ מִכֶּם אֶלָּא שֶׁתְּשַׁגְּרוּ לִי קֶשֶׁת אַחַת אוֹ חֵץ אַחַת,[40] וְאֵלֵךְ [לִי] מִכֶּם. אָמְרוּ לוֹ: כְּשֵׁם שֶׁיָּצָאנוּ עַל שְׁנַיִם רִאשׁוֹנִים שֶׁהֵם לְפָנֶיךָ וַהֲרַגְנוּם, כָּךְ נֵצֵא לְפָנֶיךָ וְנַהַרְגֶךָ.[41] כֵּיוָן שֶׁשָּׁמַע רַבָּן יוֹחָנָן בֶּן זַכַּאי, שָׁלַח וְקָרָא לְאַנְשֵׁי יְרוּשָׁלַיִם וְאָמַר לָהֶם: בָּנַי, מִפְּנֵי מָה אַתֶּם מַחֲרִיבִין אֶת הָעִיר הַזֹּאת וְאַתֶּם מְבַקְשִׁים לִשְׂרוֹף אֶת בֵּית הַמִּקְדָּשׁ.[42] וְכִי מַהוּ מְבַקֵּשׁ מִכֶּם, הָא אֵינוּ מְבַקֵּשׁ מִכֶּם אֶלָּא קֶשֶׁת אַחַת אוֹ חֵץ אַחַת, וְיֵלֵךְ לוֹ מִכֶּם. אָמְרוּ לוֹ: כְּשֵׁם שֶׁיָּצָאנוּ עַל שְׁנַיִם שֶׁלְּפָנָיו וַהֲרַגְנוּם, כָּךְ נֵצֵא עָלָיו וְנַהַרְגֵהוּ. הָיוּ לְאַסְפַּסְיָינוֹס אֲנָשִׁים שְׁרוּיִין

מְבַקְשִׁים לִשְׂרוֹף אֶת בֵּית הַמִּקְדָּשׁ — Why do you want to destroy this city, and why do you want to burn down the Temple?! וְכִי מָה אֲנִי מְבַקֵּשׁ מִכֶּם אֶלָּא — What, after all, am I asking שֶׁתְּשַׁגְּרוּ לִי קֶשֶׁת אַחַת אוֹ חֵץ אַחַת וְאֵלֵךְ לִי מִכֶּם of you? Only that you send me one bow or one arrow as a symbolic display of submission,[40] and then I will go away from you." אָמְרוּ לוֹ כְּשֵׁם שֶׁיָּצָאנוּ עַל שְׁנַיִם רִאשׁוֹנִים שֶׁהֵם לְפָנֶיךָ וַהֲרַגְנוּם כָּךְ נֵצֵא לְפָנֶיךָ וְנַהַרְגֶךָ — [The armed defenders of Jerusalem] said to him defiantly, "Just as we sallied out against the first two who came before you and killed them, so shall we sally out against you and kill you."[41] כֵּיוָן שֶׁשָּׁמַע רַבָּן יוֹחָנָן בֶּן זַכַּאי שָׁלַח וְקָרָא לְאַנְשֵׁי יְרוּשָׁלַיִם וְאָמַר לָהֶם — As soon as Rabban Yochanan ben Zakkai heard of this provocative response, he sent a messenger to summon the people of Jerusalem, and said to them, בָּנַי מִפְּנֵי מָה אַתֶּם מַחֲרִיבִין אֶת הָעִיר הַזֹּאת וְאַתֶּם מְבַקְשִׁים לִשְׂרוֹף אֶת בֵּית הַמִּקְדָּשׁ — "My sons, why are you destroying this city and why are you seeking to burn down the Holy Temple?[42] וְכִי מַהוּ מְבַקֵּשׁ מִכֶּם — What, after all, is he asking of you? הָא אֵינוּ מְבַקֵּשׁ מִכֶּם אֶלָּא קֶשֶׁת אַחַת אוֹ חֵץ אַחַת וְיֵלֵךְ לוֹ מִכֶּם — He is asking you only for a single bow or a single arrow, and he will leave you alone!" אָמְרוּ לוֹ כְּשֵׁם שֶׁיָּצָאנוּ עַל שְׁנַיִם שֶׁלְּפָנָיו וַהֲרַגְנוּם כָּךְ נֵצֵא עָלָיו וְנַהַרְגֵהוּ — They told [Rabban Yochanan ben Zakkai], "Just as we sallied out against the two before him and killed them, so shall we sally out against him and kill him." הָיוּ לְאַסְפַּסְיָינוֹס אֲנָשִׁים שְׁרוּיִין

---

40. *Binyan Yehoshua*. Included in this gesture was a commitment to pay tribute to the conqueror (*Magen Avos*).

41. It is not clear who these "first two" were. Some explain that the reference is to the Syrian-Greeks who fell to the Hasmoneans and (generations later) a Roman force, led by Cestius Gallus and Agrippa II, whose failed attack on Jerusalem is recorded by Josephus (*Binyan Yehoshua*). Alternatively, the reference is to the two leaders of the

latter attack (*Ahavas Chesed*).

42. Rabban Yochanan ben Zakkai was opposed to the aggressive tactics of the zealots and other extreme factions in Jerusalem, who were agitating for open war with the Romans rather than appeasing them or even outlasting them passively by waiting out the siege. One fateful measure taken by the extremists, in an effort to silence the moderates, was to burn the vast storehouses of food and supplies that would have sustained the populace

כְּנֶגֶד חוֹמוֹתֶיהָ שֶׁל יְרוּשָׁלַיִם,[43] וְכָל דָּבָר וְדָבָר שֶׁהָיוּ שׁוֹמְעִין הָיוּ כּוֹתְבִין עַל הַחֵצִי וְזוֹרְקִין חוּץ לַחוֹמָה, לוֹמַר שֶׁרַבָּן יוֹחָנָן בֶּן זַכַּאי מֵאוֹהֲבֵי קֵיסָר הוּא, [וְכָךְ הָיָה מַזְכִּיר לְאַנְשֵׁי יְרוּשָׁלַיִם.] וְכֵיוָן שֶׁאָמַר [לָהֶם] רַבִּי יוֹחָנָן בֶּן זַכַּאי יוֹם אֶחָד וּשְׁנַיִם וּשְׁלֹשָׁה וְלֹא קִבְּלוּ מִמֶּנּוּ, שָׁלַח וְקָרָא לְתַלְמִידָיו, לְרַבִּי אֱלִיעֶזֶר וְרַבִּי יְהוֹשֻׁעַ, אָמַר לָהֶם: בָּנַי, עִמְדוּ וְהוֹצִיאוּנִי מִכָּאן, עֲשׂוּ לִי אָרוֹן וְאִישַׁן בְּתוֹכוֹ. רַבִּי אֱלִיעֶזֶר אָחַז בְּרֹאשׁוֹ, רַבִּי יְהוֹשֻׁעַ אָחַז (בְּרַגְלָיו,

---

יְרוּשָׁלַיִם שֶׁל חוֹמוֹתֶיהָ כְּנֶגֶד — **Vespasian had certain men** among the populace who were loyal to him[43] and **who lived just inside the walls of Jerusalem.** These men provided intelligence for the Roman forces. וְדָבָר דָּבָר וְכָל לַחוֹמָה חוּץ וְזוֹרְקִין כּוֹתְבִין הָיוּ שׁוֹמְעִין שֶׁהָיוּ — **They would write down anything** of value **they would hear,** attach the note **to an arrow, and** then, pretending to act against the enemy,[44] **shoot it outside the wall.** Vespasian's soldiers would retrieve these missives and learn what was happening within the city. הוּא קֵיסָר מֵאוֹהֲבֵי זַכַּאי בֶּן יוֹחָנָן שֶׁרַבָּן לוֹמַר — On this occasion, they sent a note **to say that Rabban Yochanan ben Zakkai was one of the people friendly to the Caesar,** יְרוּשָׁלַיִם לְאַנְשֵׁי מַזְכִּיר הָיָה וְכָךְ — **and** that **he would remind the Jerusalemites of the same** words and logic that Vespasian used in his attempt to dissuade the Jewish patriots from continuing their resistance.[45]

Rabban Yochanan ben Zakkai, fearing the worst, acts boldly to preserve the future of the Jewish people:

מִמֶּנּוּ קִבְּלוּ וְלֹא וּשְׁלֹשָׁה וּשְׁנַיִם אֶחָד יוֹם זַכַּאי בֶּן יוֹחָנָן רַבִּי לָהֶם שֶׁאָמַר וְכֵיוָן — **Once Rabban Yochanan ben Zakkai spoke to the [people] for one, two, and three days** about the wisdom of appeasing the Romans **and** found **that they would not listen to him,** יְהוֹשֻׁעַ וְרַבִּי אֱלִיעֶזֶר לְרַבִּי לְתַלְמִידָיו וְקָרָא שָׁלַח — **he sent** a messenger **to summon his disciples, R' Eliezer and R' Yehoshua.** אָמַר מִכָּאן וְהוֹצִיאוּנִי עִמְדוּ בָּנַי לָהֶם — When they arrived, **he said to them, "My sons, arise and take me out of [the city].** בְּתוֹכוֹ וְאִישַׁן אָרוֹן לִי עֲשׂוּ — **Make a coffin for me and I will sleep within it,** i.e., I will pretend to lie dead within it." After the coffin was made and Rabban Yochanan ben Zakkai lay down inside, the two students lifted it up. יְהוֹשֻׁעַ רַבִּי בְּרֹאשׁוֹ אָחַז אֱלִיעֶזֶר רַבִּי — **R' Eliezer held the head of [the coffin] and R' Yehoshua held** בְּרַגְלָיו אָחַז —

---

for twenty-one years. This action brought on a famine (as they intended) and made the siege far less bearable (see *Gittin* 56a and below, 6 §3). Rabban Yochanan therefore accused them of actively destroying the city through arson and effectively seeking to burn down the Temple by instigating a battle

the Romans were sure to win (*Magen Avos*).

43. These were Jews who supported Vespasian's goal of ruling Jerusalem (*Ben Avraham*).

44. Ibid.

45. Ibid.

וְהָיוּ מוֹלִיכִין אוֹתוֹ עַד שְׁקִיעַת הַחַמָּה, עַד שֶׁהִגִּיעוּ אֵצֶל שַׁעֲרֵי יְרוּשָׁלַיִם.[46]
אָמְרוּ לָהֶם הַשּׁוֹעֲרִים: מִי הוּא זֶה. אָמְרוּ לָהֶן: מֵת הוּא. וְכִי אֵין אַתֶּם יוֹדְעִים
שֶׁאֵין מְלִינִים אֶת הַמֵּת בִּירוּשָׁלַיִם[47]. אָמְרוּ לָהֶן: אִם מֵת הוּא הוֹצִיאוּהוּ.)
וְהוֹצִיאוּהוּ, (וְהָיוּ מוֹלִיכִין אוֹתוֹ עַד שְׁקִיעַת הַחַמָּה) עַד שֶׁהִגִּיעוּ אֵצֶל
אַסְפַּסְיָינוֹס[48], פָּתְחוּ הָאָרוֹן וְעָמַד לְפָנָיו. אָמַר לוֹ: אַתָּה הוּא רַבָּן יוֹחָנָן
בֶּן זַכַּאי, שְׁאַל מָה אֶתֵּן לָךְ[49]. אָמַר לוֹ: אֵינִי מְבַקֵּשׁ מִמְּךָ אֶלָּא יַבְנֶה, אֵלֵךְ
וְאֶשְׁנֶה בָהּ לְתַלְמִידַי, וְאֶקְבַּע בָּהּ תְּפִלָּה, וְאֶעֱשֶׂה בָהּ כָּל מִצְוֹת [הָאֲמוּרוֹת
בַּתּוֹרָה]. אָמַר לוֹ: לֵךְ, וְכָל מַה שֶּׁאַתָּה רוֹצֶה לַעֲשׂוֹת, עֲשֵׂה.[50] אָמַר לוֹ:

---

the foot of [the coffin],　　　וְהָיוּ מוֹלִיכִין אוֹתוֹ עַד שְׁקִיעַת הַחַמָּה עַד שֶׁהִגִּיעוּ אֵצֶל
שַׁעֲרֵי יְרוּשָׁלַיִם — and they carried it until sunset, until they reached the gates
of Jerusalem.[46] אָמְרוּ לָהֶם הַשּׁוֹעֲרִים מִי הוּא זֶה — The gatekeepers said to
them, "Who is this?"　　　אָמְרוּ לָהֶן מֵת הוּא וְכִי אֵין אַתֶּם יוֹדְעִים שֶׁאֵין מְלִינִים אֶת
הַמֵּת בִּירוּשָׁלַיִם — [The "pallbearers"] said to them. "It is a deceased person.
Please let us hurry on. Do you not know that we may not harbor a corpse
overnight in Jerusalem?"[47] אָמְרוּ לָהֶן אִם מֵת הוּא הוֹצִיאוּהוּ — [The gate-
keepers] said to them, "If it is a corpse, take it out," and they opened the
gate.　וְהוֹצִיאוּהוּ עַד שֶׁהִגִּיעוּ אֵצֶל אַסְפַּסְיָינוֹס — So they took [the coffin] out
of Jerusalem, and carried it until they reached the vicinity of Vespasian.[48]
פָּתְחוּ הָאָרוֹן וְעָמַד לְפָנָיו — They opened the coffin and [Rabban Yochanan ben
Zakkai] stood up before [Vespasian].　　　אָמַר לוֹ אַתָּה הוּא רַבָּן יוֹחָנָן בֶּן זַכַּאי
שְׁאַל מָה אֶתֵּן לָךְ — [Vespasian] said to him, "You are Rabban Yochanan ben
Zakkai? Ask me for something I can give to you."[49] אָמַר לוֹ אֵינִי מְבַקֵּשׁ
מִמְּךָ אֶלָּא יַבְנֶה אֵלֵךְ וְאֶשְׁנֶה בָהּ לְתַלְמִידַי וְאֶקְבַּע בָּהּ תְּפִלָּה וְאֶעֱשֶׂה בָהּ כָּל מִצְוֹת
הָאֲמוּרוֹת בַּתּוֹרָה — [Rabban Yochanan ben Zakkai] replied to him, "I ask noth-
ing of you other than to spare the city of Yavneh, so that I may go there and
teach my students, establish a house of prayer there and observe all of the
Torah's commandments there."　　　אָמַר לוֹ לֵךְ וְכָל מַה שֶּׁאַתָּה רוֹצֶה לַעֲשׂוֹת עֲשֵׂה
— [Vespasian] said to him, "Go, and all that you wish to do, do."[50] אָמַר לוֹ

---

46. They timed their progress to reach the
gates at sunset, so that there would be no
time for the gatekeepers to check what was
in the coffin (Magen Avos, Ben Avraham).

47. See below, 35 §2.

48. They waited until the last minute before
opening the coffin so that Vespasian would
see how difficult it was to come meet him,
and how loyal Rabban Yochanan must be to
undertake such a venture (Ben Avraham).

49. Because I have heard that you are

my friend and you desire peace (Binyan
Yehoshua).

50. Rabban Yochanan ben Zakkai did not
want to risk asking Vespasian to lift the
siege and return to Rome; he feared that if
he asked for too much he would get nothing (Gittin 56b). In Eichah Rabbah (1 §31),
however, the Midrash states that Rabban
Yochanan ben Zakkai did in fact ask the
Roman general to suspend his military campaign, but the latter rejected that proposal

רְצוֹנְךָ שֶׁאוֹמַר לְפָנֶיךָ דָּבָר אֶחָד⁵¹. אָמַר לוֹ: אֱמוֹר. אָמַר לוֹ: הֲרֵי אַתָּה עוֹמֵד
בַּמַּלְכוּת⁵². מִנַּיִן אַתָּה יוֹדֵעַ. אָמַר לוֹ: כָּךְ מָסוּר לָנוּ שֶׁאֵין בֵּית הַמִּקְדָּשׁ
נִמְסָר בְּיַד הֶדְיוֹט אֶלָּא בְּיַד הַמֶּלֶךְ, שֶׁנֶּאֱמַר (ישעיה י, לד) "וְנִקַּף סָבְכֵי
הַיַּעַר בַּבַּרְזֶל וְהַלְּבָנוֹן בְּאַדִּיר יִפּוֹל"⁵³. אָמְרוּ: לֹא הָיָה (יוֹם אֶחָד שְׁנַיִם)
שְׁלֹשָׁה יָמִים עַד שֶׁבָּא אֵלָיו דְּיוֹפְלָא מֵעִירוֹ שֶׁמֵּת קֵיסָר וְנִמְנוּ עָלָיו לַעֲמוֹד
בַּמַּלְכוּת, ⁵⁴ הֵבִיאוּ לוֹ קֶשֶׁת שֶׁל זֵירִים וְתִיפָ"א כְּנֶגֶד הַחוֹמָה שֶׁל יְרוּשָׁלַיִם,

---

רְצוֹנְךָ שֶׁאוֹמַר לְפָנֶיךָ דָּבָר אֶחָד — [Rabban Yochanan ben Zakkai] then said to him, "With your permission, may I say one thing before you?"[51] אָמַר לוֹ — He said to him, "Speak." אֱמוֹר — [Rabban Yochanan ben Zakkai] said to him, אָמַר לוֹ הֲרֵי אַתָּה עוֹמֵד בַּמַּלְכוּת "Behold, you stand at the head of the empire."[52] אָמַר — Said Vespasian, "How do you know?" מִנַּיִן אַתָּה יוֹדֵעַ [Rabban Yochanan ben Zakkai] said to him, לוֹ כָּךְ מָסוּר לָנוּ שֶׁאֵין בֵּית הַמִּקְדָּשׁ נִמְסָר בְּיַד הֶדְיוֹט אֶלָּא בְּיַד הַמֶּלֶךְ "This tradition has been passed down to us, that the Temple will not be delivered into the hands of a commoner, but only into the hands of a king, שֶׁנֶּאֱמַר "וְנִקַּף סָבְכֵי הַיַּעַר בַּבַּרְזֶל וְהַלְּבָנוֹן בְּאַדִּיר יִפּוֹל" — as it says, *Forest thickets will be hewn by iron, and the Lebanon will fall by a mighty one*" (Isaiah 10:34).[53] אָמְרוּ לֹא הָיָה שְׁלֹשָׁה יָמִים עַד שֶׁבָּא אֵלָיו דְּיוֹפְלָא מֵעִירוֹ שֶׁמֵּת קֵיסָר — [The Sages] said: It was not yet three days before a delegation of two men came from his city to tell him that the emperor had died, וְנִמְנוּ עָלָיו לַעֲמוֹד בַּמַּלְכוּת — and that [the Romans] had elected him to stand at the helm of the empire.

The Baraisa describes the assault on Jerusalem:[54] הֵבִיאוּ לוֹ קֶשֶׁת שֶׁל זֵירִים וְתִיפָ"א כְּנֶגֶד הַחוֹמָה שֶׁל יְרוּשָׁלַיִם — They brought him

---

and told him to ask for something else (*Ahavas Chesed*).

In any case, Rabban Yochanan ben Zakkai used this seemingly minor imperial grant to build up a center of learning and leadership that set the pace for Torah life and Jewish continuity under foreign rule, in the absence of the Temple.

51. Rabban Yochanan may have been extra cautious here because what he was about to say, if unfounded, could be taken as an attempt to poke fun at Vespasian (*Magen Avos,* based on *Gittin* 56a with *Rashi*).

52. [Rabban Yochanan said this at a time when the Roman succession was in doubt after the death of Nero. In this turbulent "Year of the Four Emperors," Vespasian was contending for the throne against three other

generals. After each of his rivals served briefly before meeting his death, Vespasian was chosen as emperor, whereupon he began a ten-year reign.]

53. *Lebanon* refers to the Temple, because it is there that the Jewish nation finds atonement and the stain of their sins is whitened (לְבָנוֹן from לָבָן, *white*) and cleansed. *Mighty one* refers to a king (*Gittin* 56b with *Rashi;* see *Maharal, Netzach Yisrael* §5). Although Vespasian had not yet captured Jerusalem, his three-and-a-half year siege had already brought its inhabitants to the brink of starvation. Thus, he had *virtually* conquered the city and destroyed the Temple (*Tosafos, Gittin* 56b).

54. This next part of the story apparently took place after a long interval, during which

הֵבִיאוּ לוֹ נְסָרִים שֶׁל אֶרֶז וְנָתַן לְתוֹךְ קֶשֶׁת שֶׁל זֵירִים, וְהָיָה מַכֶּה בָּהֶן עַל הַחוֹמָה עַד שֶׁפּוֹרֵץ בּוֹ פִּירְצָה. הֵבִיאוּ רֹאשׁ חֲזִיר וְנָתְנוּ לְתוֹךְ קֶשֶׁת שֶׁל זֵירִים וְהָיָה מַשְׁלִיךְ אוֹתוֹ כְּלַפֵּי אֵיבָרִים שֶׁעַל גַּבֵּי הַמִּזְבֵּחַ[57]. בְּאוֹתָהּ שָׁעָה נִלְכְּדָה יְרוּשָׁלַיִם, וְהָיָה רַבָּן יוֹחָנָן בֶּן זַכַּאי יוֹשֵׁב וּמְצַפֶּה וְחָרֵד (כְּנֶגֶד מָקוֹם) ° שֶׁהָיָה עֵלִי יוֹשֵׁב וּמְצַפֶּה[58], שֶׁנֶּאֱמַר (ש"א ד, יג) "וְהִנֵּה עֵלִי יֹשֵׁב עַל הַכִּסֵּא יַד דֶּרֶךְ מְצַפֶּה, כִּי הָיָה לִבּוֹ חָרֵד עַל אֲרוֹן הָאֱלֹהִים". כֵּיוָן שֶׁשָּׁמַע רַבָּן יוֹחָנָן בֶּן זַכַּאי שֶׁהֶחֱרִיב אֶת יְרוּשָׁלַיִם וְשָׂרַף אֶת בֵּית הַמִּקְדָּשׁ בָּאֵשׁ,

---

a ballista[55] and incendiary projectiles[56] to be shot at the wall of Jerusalem. הֵבִיאוּ לוֹ נְסָרִים שֶׁל אֶרֶז וְנָתַן לְתוֹךְ קֶשֶׁת שֶׁל זֵירִים — **They brought him cedar blocks and loaded the ballista with them,** וְהָיָה מַכֶּה בָּהֶן עַל הַחוֹמָה עַד שֶׁפּוֹרֵץ בּוֹ פִּירְצָה — **and the [ballista] would launch these projectiles with great force, pummeling the wall with them until it smashed through.** הֵבִיאוּ רֹאשׁ חֲזִיר וְנָתְנוּ לְתוֹךְ קֶשֶׁת שֶׁל זֵירִים — **They also brought the head of a pig and loaded the ballista with it,** וְהָיָה מַשְׁלִיךְ אוֹתוֹ כְּלַפֵּי אֵיבָרִים שֶׁעַל גַּבֵּי הַמִּזְבֵּחַ — **and the [ballista] hurled it toward the limbs on the Altar.**[57]

The downfall of Jerusalem: בְּאוֹתָהּ שָׁעָה נִלְכְּדָה יְרוּשָׁלַיִם וְהָיָה — **At that time, Jerusalem was captured,** רַבָּן יוֹחָנָן בֶּן זַכַּאי יוֹשֵׁב וּמְצַפֶּה וְחָרֵד כְּשֵׁם שֶׁהָיָה עֵלִי יוֹשֵׁב וּמְצַפֶּה — **and Rabban Yochanan ben Zakkai sat and waited in trepidation, just as** hundreds of years before,[58] **Eli the Kohen, the nation's leader at the end of the era of the Judges, had sat and waited in trepidation for news about the Holy Ark, which had been sent to escort the Jewish army into battle against the Philistines,** שֶׁנֶּאֱמַר "וְהִנֵּה עֵלִי יֹשֵׁב עַל הַכִּסֵּא יַד דֶּרֶךְ מְצַפֶּה כִּי הָיָה לִבּוֹ חָרֵד עַל אֲרוֹן הָאֱלֹהִים" — **as it says,** Eli was seated in a chair next to the road, looking out, for his heart was fearful about the Ark of God **(I Samuel 4:13).** כֵּיוָן שֶׁשָּׁמַע רַבָּן יוֹחָנָן בֶּן זַכַּאי שֶׁהֶחֱרִיב אֶת יְרוּשָׁלַיִם וְשָׂרַף אֶת בֵּית הַמִּקְדָּשׁ בָּאֵשׁ — **Once Rabban Yochanan ben Zakkai heard that [the Roman enemy] had destroyed**

Vespasian returned to Rome to assume his new position as emperor (*Ben Avraham;* see *Avos HaRosh*). At any rate, the Baraisa implies that Vespasian himself saw his campaign through to its successful conclusion, whereas the Talmud (*Gittin* 56b) states that upon leaving for Rome, he appointed his son Titus to finish the task he had started (see *Avos HaRosh*).

55. A ballista was a form of catapult. It resembled a giant crossbow and was used to shoot heavy, damaging projectiles

— including bundles of arrows or darts — at the enemy or its fortifications.

56. See *Binyan Yehoshua*, citing *Aruch*.

57. This tactic had symbolic significance, since the pig represents Esau, the forefather of Edom-Rome. Heaving a pig's head onto the Altar therefore symbolized the imposition of Esau's rule over Jacob (*Binyan Yehoshua* [in 1788 edition], based on *Maharsha* to *Sotah* 49a).

58. Emendation based on *Nuschas HaGra* and *R' Yeshayah Berlin*.

קָרַע בְּגָדָיו וְקָרְעוּ תַּלְמִידָיו אֶת בִּגְדֵיהֶם, וְהָיוּ בּוֹכִין וְצוֹעֲקִין וְסוֹפְדִין,
וְאוֹמֵר (זכריה יא, א) "פְּתַח לְבָנוֹן דְּלָתֶיךָ", [זֶה בֵּית הַמִּקְדָּשׁ,] "וְתֹאכַל
אֵשׁ בַּאֲרָזֶיךָ", אֵלּוּ כֹּהֲנִים (גְּדוֹלִים) שֶׁהָיוּ בַּמִּקְדָּשׁ, שֶׁהָיוּ [נוֹטְלִים]
מַפְתְּחוֹתָן בְּיָדָן וְזוֹרְקִין כְּלַפֵּי מַעֲלָה, וְאוֹמְרִים לִפְנֵי הַקָּדוֹשׁ בָּרוּךְ
הוּא: רִבּוֹנוֹ שֶׁל עוֹלָם, הֵילָךְ מַפְתְּחוֹתֶיךָ שֶׁמָּסַרְתָּ לָנוּ, הוֹאִיל וְלֹא
הָיִינוּ גִזְבָּרִין נֶאֱמָנִין לַעֲשׂוֹת מְלָאכֶת הַמֶּלֶךְ וְלֶאֱכוֹל מִשֻּׁלְחַן הַמֶּלֶךְ[60].
אַבְרָהָם יִצְחָק וְיַעֲקֹב, וּשְׁנֵים עָשָׂר שְׁבָטִים, הָיוּ בּוֹכִין וְצוֹעֲקִין וְסוֹפְדִין
וְאוֹמְרִים: (שם, ב) "הֵילֵל בְּרוֹשׁ כִּי נָפַל אֶרֶז אֲשֶׁר אַדִּירִים שֻׁדָּדוּ".

קָרַע בְּגָדָיו וְקָרְעוּ תַּלְמִידָיו אֶת Jerusalem and burned down the Holy Temple, בִּגְדֵיהֶם — he rent his garments, and his students rent their garments after him, וְהָיוּ בּוֹכִין וְצוֹעֲקִין וְסוֹפְדִין — and they were all weeping, crying out, and eulogizing.

The Baraisa cites a sample eulogy for the Temple.

וְאוֹמֵר "פְּתַח לְבָנוֹן דְּלָתֶיךָ" זֶה בֵּית הַמִּקְדָּשׁ — And [the Prophet Zechariah] says about this moment:[59] *Open your doors, O Lebanon* (Zechariah 11:1) — this refers to the Holy Temple; "וְתֹאכַל אֵשׁ בַּאֲרָזֶיךָ" אֵלּוּ כֹּהֲנִים גְּדוֹלִים שֶׁהָיוּ בַּמִּקְדָּשׁ — *and let fire consume your cedars!* — these refer to the High Priests who were in the Temple as it was being engulfed in flames, שֶׁהָיוּ נוֹטְלִים מַפְתְּחוֹתָן בְּיָדָן וְזוֹרְקִין כְּלַפֵּי מַעֲלָה — who took their Temple keys in hand, threw them up Heavenward, וְאוֹמְרִים לִפְנֵי הַקָּדוֹשׁ בָּרוּךְ הוּא רִבּוֹנוֹ שֶׁל עוֹלָם הֵילָךְ מַפְתְּחוֹתֶיךָ שֶׁמָּסַרְתָּ לָנוּ — and said before the Holy One, Blessed is He, "Master of the Universe! Here are Your keys that You entrusted to us. הוֹאִיל וְלֹא הָיִינוּ גִזְבָּרִין נֶאֱמָנִין לַעֲשׂוֹת מְלָאכֶת הַמֶּלֶךְ וְלֶאֱכוֹל מִשֻּׁלְחַן הַמֶּלֶךְ — We are returning them, since we were obviously not trustworthy custodians to do the King's work and eat from the King's table."[60]

Further reaction to the tragedy:

אַבְרָהָם יִצְחָק וְיַעֲקֹב וּשְׁנֵים עָשָׂר שְׁבָטִים הָיוּ בּוֹכִין וְצוֹעֲקִין וְסוֹפְדִין — Abraham, Isaac, Jacob, the Twelve Tribes, and other leaders of our nation were weeping, crying out, and eulogizing; וְאוֹמְרִים "הֵילֵל בְּרוֹשׁ כִּי נָפַל אֶרֶז אֲשֶׁר אַדִּירִים שֻׁדָּדוּ" — and they were saying as the prophet Zechariah said, *Wail, O cypress, for the cedar has fallen, for the mighty ones have been vanquished; wail, O oaks of Bashan, because the impregnable forest has come down. There is a sound of the shepherds' wailing, for their power has been vanquished; there is a sound of the young lions' roar, for the heights of the Jordan have been vanquished* (ibid. vv. 2-3).

---

59. *Ben Avraham.*

60. And something resembling the palm of

a hand emerged [from Heaven] and received [the keys] from them (*Binyan Yehosua*, citing *Taanis* 29a).

["הֵילֵל בְּרוֹשׁ כִּי נָפַל אֶרֶז", זֶה בֵּית הַמִּקְדָּשׁ[61], "אֲשֶׁר אַדִּירִים שֻׁדָּדוּ",
זֶה אַבְרָהָם יִצְחָק וְיַעֲקֹב וּשְׁנֵים עָשָׂר שְׁבָטִים[62], (שם) "הֵילִילוּ אַלּוֹנֵי
בָשָׁן", זֶה מֹשֶׁה אַהֲרֹן וּמִרְיָם[63], (שם) "כִּי יָרַד יַעַר הַבָּצִיר", זֶה קוֹדֶשׁ
הַקֳּדָשִׁים[64], (שם, ג) "קוֹל יִלְלַת הָרֹעִים כִּי [שֻׁדְּדָה] אַדַּרְתָּם", זֶה דָוִד
וּשְׁלֹמֹה בְנוֹ[65], (שם) "קוֹל שַׁאֲגַת כְּפִירִים כִּי שֻׁדַּד גְּאוֹן הַיַּרְדֵּן", זֶה אֵלִיָּהוּ
וֶאֱלִישָׁע[66].

The Baraisa explains these verses, phrase by phrase:
"הֵילֵל בְּרוֹשׁ כִּי נָפַל אֶרֶז" זֶה בֵּית הַמִּקְדָּשׁ — *Wail, O cypress, for the cedar has
fallen* — this refers to the Holy Temple;[61] "אֲשֶׁר אַדִּירִים שֻׁדָּדוּ" זֶה אַבְרָהָם
יִצְחָק וְיַעֲקֹב וּשְׁנֵים עָשָׂר שְׁבָטִים — *for the mighty ones have been vanquished* —
this refers to Abraham, Isaac and Jacob, and the Twelve Tribes;[62] "הֵילִילוּ
אַלּוֹנֵי בָשָׁן" זֶה מֹשֶׁה אַהֲרֹן וּמִרְיָם — *wail O oaks of Bashan* — this refers to
Moses, Aaron, and Miriam;[63] "כִּי יָרַד יַעַר הַבָּצִיר" זֶה קוֹדֶשׁ הַקֳּדָשִׁים — *because the impregnable forest has come down* — this refers to the Holy of
Holies. [64] "קוֹל יִלְלַת הָרֹעִים כִּי שֻׁדְּדָה אַדַּרְתָּם" זֶה דָוִד וּשְׁלֹמֹה בְנוֹ — *There is
a sound of the shepherds' wailing, for their power has been vanquished* —
this refers to David and his son Solomon;[65] "קוֹל שַׁאֲגַת כְּפִירִים כִּי שֻׁדַּד גְּאוֹן
הַיַּרְדֵּן" זֶה אֵלִיָּהוּ וֶאֱלִישָׁע — *there is a sound of the young lions' roar, for the
heights of the Jordan have been vanquished* — this refers to the prophets
Elijah and Elisha.[66]

§6 This chapter about the three pillars of the world concludes with a list of
three phenomena that are in their own way indispensable to a properly
functioning world:[67]

---

61. In whose structure cedarwood was a major component (ibid., citing *I Kings* 6:9-10).

62. Who are called *mighty ones* in *Psalms*
16:3 (ibid., citing *Menachos* 53a).

63. Who led the Jewish people in receiving the Torah at Mount Sinai, which is also
called Mount Bashan (*Midrash Tanchuma,
Bamidbar* §7). Hence, the "oaks of Bashan"
are the greats of Sinai (*Ben Avraham*).

64. The Temple is referred to as a "forest"
(*I Kings* 10:21) — because just as a forest
blooms, so the Temple bloomed (i.e., its
gold fruit trees would bloom in season and
produce golden fruit — *Yoma* 39b) — and
its most impregnable stronghold was the
Holy of Holies (*Binyan Yehoshua, Ben
Avraham*).

65. Who lovingly cared for their Jewish
flock, and who epitomized the royal power
of Israel (ibid.).

66. *Ben Avraham* sees this as a two-tiered
metaphor. The Jordan River area was a habitat for lions (*Jeremiah* 49:19: *... will ascend
like a lion from the heights of the Jordan*),
which would therefore roar in distress if their
territory were taken from them. This area
was also frequented by the "lions" of Israel,
the great prophets Elijah and Elisha (representative of the nation's spiritual leaders in
every generation) who accordingly "roared"
when their beloved Jordan (symbolic of the
Holy Temple, the "habitat" of any Jew seeking a close relationship with God) was taken
from them (*Ben Avraham*).

67. See *Ben Avraham*.

ו. בִּשְׁלֹשָׁה דְבָרִים שִׁינָה הַקָּדוֹשׁ בָּרוּךְ הוּא אֶת בְּנֵי אָדָם זֶה מִזֶּה, אֵלּוּ
הֵן: בַּקּוֹל, בַּנְּעִימָה, וּבַמַּרְאֶה. כֵּיצַד, מְלַמֵּד שֶׁשִּׁינָה הַקָּדוֹשׁ בָּרוּךְ
הוּא קוֹלוֹת בְּנֵי אָדָם זֶה מִזֶּה, שֶׁאִלְמָלֵא (לֹא) שִׁינָה הַקָּדוֹשׁ הוּא
קוֹלוֹת בְּנֵי אָדָם זֶה מִזֶּה כְּבָר הָיְתָה זְנוּת הַרְבֵּה בָּעוֹלָם. כֵּיוָן שֶׁאָדָם
יוֹצֵא מִתּוֹךְ בֵּיתוֹ [יָבֹא אַחֵר] וְיִכְבֹּשׁ אֶת אִשְׁתּוֹ בְּתוֹךְ בֵּיתוֹ. לְפִיכָךְ שִׁינָה
הַקָּדוֹשׁ בָּרוּךְ הוּא קוֹלוֹת בְּנֵי אָדָם זֶה מִזֶּה, קוֹלוֹ שֶׁל זֶה אֵינוֹ דוֹמֶה
לְקוֹלוֹ שֶׁל זֶה. בַּנְּעִימָה כֵּיצַד, [מְלַמֵּד שֶׁשִּׁינָה הַקָּדוֹשׁ בָּרוּךְ הוּא נְעִימוֹת
בְּנֵי אָדָם זֶה מִזֶּה[68,69,70,] שֶׁאִלְמָלֵא שִׁינָה הַקָּדוֹשׁ בָּרוּךְ הוּא [71] נְעִימוֹת
בְּנֵי אָדָם זֶה מִזֶּה הָיוּ מִתְקַנְּאִין זֶה בָּזֶה, לְפִיכָךְ שִׁינָה הַקָּדוֹשׁ בָּרוּךְ

בִּשְׁלֹשָׁה דְבָרִים שִׁינָה הַקָּדוֹשׁ בָּרוּךְ הוּא אֶת בְּנֵי אָדָם זֶה מִזֶּה — There are three primary **ways in which the Holy One, Blessed is He, differentiated people from one another,**   אֵלּוּ הֵן בַּקּוֹל בַּנְּעִימָה וּבַמַּרְאֶה — **and they are these: in voice, in temperament, and in appearance.**

The Baraisa elaborates:

מְלַמֵּד שֶׁשִּׁינָה כֵּיצַד — **"In voice" — how so?** — What is meant by "in voice"?   הַקָּדוֹשׁ בָּרוּךְ הוּא קוֹלוֹת בְּנֵי אָדָם זֶה מִזֶּה — **This teaches that the Holy One, Blessed is He, made people's voices different from one another,**   שֶׁאִלְמָלֵא — שִׁינָה הַקָּדוֹשׁ בָּרוּךְ הוּא קוֹלוֹת בְּנֵי אָדָם זֶה מִזֶּה כְּבָר הָיְתָה זְנוּת הַרְבֵּה בָּעוֹלָם — **for if the Holy One, Blessed is He, had not varied people's voices from one another, there would have been much promiscuity in the world.**   כֵּיוָן שֶׁאָדָם יוֹצֵא מִתּוֹךְ בֵּיתוֹ יָבֹא אַחֵר וְיִכְבֹּשׁ אֶת אִשְׁתּוֹ בְּתוֹךְ בֵּיתוֹ — **Once a man would leave his house,** another person **would come** in the dark of the night, pretend to be the husband **and violate his wife within his house.**   לְפִיכָךְ שִׁינָה הַקָּדוֹשׁ בָּרוּךְ הוּא קוֹלוֹת בְּנֵי אָדָם זֶה מִזֶּה — **Therefore, the Holy One, Blessed is He, made people's voices different from one another,**   קוֹלוֹ שֶׁל זֶה אֵינוֹ דוֹמֶה לְקוֹלוֹ שֶׁל זֶה — **such that this one's voice does not resemble that one's voice.**   מְלַמֵּד שֶׁשִּׁינָה הַקָּדוֹשׁ בָּרוּךְ בַּנְּעִימָה כֵּיצַד — **"In temperament" — how so?**   הוּא נְעִימוֹת בְּנֵי אָדָם זֶה מִזֶּה — **This teaches that the Holy One, Blessed is He, made people's temperaments** — i.e., their preferences regarding which line of work to choose, which possessions to acquire,[68] which spouses to seek,[69] and which life goals to pursue[70] — **different from one another.** This diversity is important for a smoothly functioning society,   שֶׁאִלְמָלֵא שִׁינָה הַקָּדוֹשׁ בָּרוּךְ הוּא — נְעִימוֹת בְּנֵי אָדָם זֶה מִזֶּה הָיוּ מִתְקַנְּאִין זֶה בָּזֶה — **for if the Holy One, Blessed is He, had not varied people's temperaments from one other, they would compete** constantly **with each other** for the same thing.[71]   לְפִיכָךְ שִׁינָה הַקָּדוֹשׁ בָּרוּךְ

---

68. *Binyan Yehoshua.*
69. *Magen Avos.*

70. *Ahavas Chesed.*
71. Cf. *Sanhedrin* 38a; see *Ahavas Chesed.*

הוּא נְעִימוֹת בְּנֵי אָדָם שֶׁל זֶה מִזֶּה, נְעִימָה שֶׁל זֶה אֵינוֹ דוֹמֶה לָזֶה וְשֶׁל זֶה אֵינוֹ דוֹמֶה לָזֶה. בַּמַּרְאֶה כֵּיצַד, מְלַמֵּד שֶׁשִּׁנָּה הַקָּדוֹשׁ בָּרוּךְ הוּא מַרְאֵה בְּנֵי אָדָם זֶה מִזֶּה, שֶׁאִלְמָלֵא (לֹא) שִׁנָּה הַקָּדוֹשׁ בָּרוּךְ הוּא מַרְאֵה פָּנִים זֶה מִזֶּה לֹא הָיוּ בְּנוֹת יִשְׂרָאֵל מַכִּירוֹת אֶת בַּעֲלֵיהֶן, וְאֵין הַזְּכָרִים מַכִּירִין אֶת נְשׁוֹתֵיהֶן, לְפִיכָךְ שִׁנָּה הַקָּדוֹשׁ בָּרוּךְ הוּא אֶת מַרְאֵה פָּנִים זֶה מִזֶּה.

הוּא נְעִימוֹת בְּנֵי אָדָם שֶׁל זֶה מִזֶּה — Therefore, the Holy One, Blessed is He, made people's temperaments different from one another, נְעִימָה שֶׁל זֶה אֵינוֹ דוֹמֶה לָזֶה וְשֶׁל זֶה אֵינוֹ דוֹמֶה לָזֶה — such that this one's temperament does not resemble that one's temperament, and vice versa. בַּמַּרְאֶה, כֵּיצַד — "In appearance" — how so? מְלַמֵּד שֶׁשִּׁנָּה הַקָּדוֹשׁ בָּרוּךְ הוּא מַרְאֵה בְּנֵי אָדָם זֶה מִזֶּה — This teaches that the Holy One, Blessed is He, made people's looks different from one another, שֶׁאִלְמָלֵא שִׁנָּה הַקָּדוֹשׁ בָּרוּךְ הוּא מַרְאֵה פָּנִים זֶה מִזֶּה — for if the Holy One, Blessed is He, had not varied the appearance of people's faces from one other, לֹא הָיוּ בְּנוֹת יִשְׂרָאֵל מַכִּירוֹת אֶת בַּעֲלֵיהֶן וְאֵין הַזְּכָרִים מַכִּירִין אֶת נְשׁוֹתֵיהֶן — the daughters of Israel would not recognize their husbands, and the males would not recognize their wives. לְפִיכָךְ שִׁנָּה הַקָּדוֹשׁ בָּרוּךְ הוּא אֶת מַרְאֵה פָּנִים זֶה מִזֶּה — Therefore, the Holy One, blessed is He, made the appearance of people's faces different from one another.

⤝ פֶּרֶק ה ⤞

א. אַנְטִיגְנוֹס אִישׁ סוֹכוֹ[1] קִבֵּל מִשִּׁמְעוֹן הַצַּדִּיק, הוּא הָיָה אוֹמֵר: אַל
תִּהְיוּ כַּעֲבָדִים הַמְשַׁמְּשִׁים אֶת הָרַב עַל מְנָת לְקַבֵּל פְּרָס אֶלָּא הֱווּ
כַּעֲבָדִים הַמְשַׁמְּשִׁים אֶת הָרַב שֶׁלֹּא עַל מְנָת לְקַבֵּל פְּרָס[2] וִיהִי מוֹרָא
שָׁמַיִם עֲלֵיכֶם[3] כְּדֵי שֶׁיִּהְיֶה שְׂכַרְכֶם כָּפוּל לֶעָתִיד לָבֹא:[4]

⤝ CHAPTER 5 ⤞

§1 The Baraisa cites and elaborates upon *Avos* 1:3:

אַנְטִיגְנוֹס אִישׁ סוֹכוֹ קִבֵּל מִשִּׁמְעוֹן הַצַּדִּיק — Antigonus, the leader of Socho,[1] received the tradition from Shimon the Righteous. הוּא הָיָה אוֹמֵר —
He used to say: אַל תִּהְיוּ כַּעֲבָדִים הַמְשַׁמְּשִׁים אֶת הָרַב עַל מְנָת לְקַבֵּל פְּרָס — In
your service of God, be not as servants who serve the master for the sake
of receiving a reward, אֶלָּא הֱווּ כַּעֲבָדִים הַמְשַׁמְּשִׁים אֶת הָרַב שֶׁלֹּא עַל מְנָת לְקַבֵּל
פְּרָס — but rather, be like servants who serve the master not for the sake of
receiving a reward,[2] וִיהִי מוֹרָא שָׁמַיִם עֲלֵיכֶם — and let the fear of Heaven be
upon you,[3] כְּדֵי שֶׁיִּהְיֶה שְׂכַרְכֶם כָּפוּל לֶעָתִיד לָבֹא — so that your reward will
be doubled in the Future Era.[4]

---

1. Socho was a city in Eretz Yisrael (see *Joshua* 15:35). The term אִישׁ is used in the sense of lord or leader, as in *Yoma* 1:3: אִישִׁי כֹהֵן גָּדוֹל, *my lord, Kohen Gadol* (*Binyan Yehoshua*, citing *Tos. Yom Tov* to *Avos* here).

2. That is, serve God purely out of love, without any expectation of reward (*Binyan Yehoshua*, citing *Rav*). [Antigonus did not mean to discount serving God for the sake of reward, for that is certainly an acceptable practice. Antigonus urged his students, however, to choose a *more devout* form of service (*Binyan Yehoshua*, citing *Maharal* in *Derech Chaim*).]

3. I.e., in addition to serving God out of love [a manner of service that is demonstrated by serving Him not for the sake of receiving a reward; see previous note], you should also serve God out of fear (ibid.), i.e., reverence (*R' Yonah* and *Tos. Yom Tov* to *Avos* here).

4. Service of God that incorporates both love and fear is a complete one, and therefore earns a greater reward (*Binyan*

Yehoshua). Alternatively, this is going back to Antigonus' main point — that one should serve God without expectation of reward. As indicated in note 2, serving God for the sake of reward is also an acceptable practice, and one will surely receive reward for it. The Baraisa therefore concludes that if one serves *not* for the sake of reward, but purely out of love for God and a desire to do His will, his reward will actually increase twofold (*Ben Avraham*). [*Binyan Yehoshua* emends the text to read וִיהְיֶה שְׂכַרְכֶם כָּפוּל לֶעָתִיד לָבֹא, "*And*" your reward will be doubled in the Future Era. Presumably, he does this because the phrase שֶׁ...כְּדֵי, *so that*, makes it sound as though one's intention should be to earn double reward, but Antigonus' entire point is that this should *not* be one's intention!]

[The term לֶעָתִיד לָבֹא, *the Future Era*, is at times used in reference to the World to Come, i.e., the life of reward after death; see *Meiri* and *Rav* to *Avos* 2:16.] For further exposition and discussion of Antigonus' teaching, see commentators to the Mishnah here.

ב. אַנְטִיגְנוֹס אִישׁ סוֹכוֹ הָיוּ לוֹ שְׁנֵי תַלְמִידִים שֶׁהָיוּ שׁוֹנִין בִּדְבָרָיו וְהָיוּ
שׁוֹנִים לְתַלְמִידִים⁵ וְתַלְמִידִים לְתַלְמִידֵיהֶם, עָמְדוּ וְדִקְדְּקוּ אַחֲרֵיהֶן
וְאָמְרוּ: מָה רָאוּ אֲבוֹתֵינוּ⁶ לוֹמַר [דָּבָר זֶה]⁷ אֶפְשָׁר שֶׁיַּעֲשֶׂה פּוֹעֵל מְלָאכָה
כָּל הַיּוֹם וְלֹא יִטּוֹל שְׂכָרוֹ עַרְבִית, אֶלָּא אִילּוּ הָיוּ יוֹדְעִין אֲבוֹתֵינוּ שֶׁיֵּשׁ עוֹלָם
[אַחֵר] וְיֵשׁ תְּחִיַּית הַמֵּתִים לֹא הָיוּ אוֹמְרִים כָּךְ⁸. עָמְדוּ וּפֵירְשׁוּ מִן הַתּוֹרָה⁹

§2 The Baraisa relates the historical repercussions of a misunderstanding of the above teaching:

אַנְטִיגְנוֹס אִישׁ סוֹכוֹ הָיוּ לוֹ שְׁנֵי תַלְמִידִים שֶׁהָיוּ שׁוֹנִין בִּדְבָרָיו — Antigonus, leader of Socho, had two students, Zadok and Boethus, who studied these words of his, וְהָיוּ שׁוֹנִים לְתַלְמִידִים וְתַלְמִידִים לְתַלְמִידֵיהֶם — and they taught them to their own students,[5] and those students, in turn, taught Antigonus' words to their own students. עָמְדוּ וְדִקְדְּקוּ אַחֲרֵיהֶן וְאָמְרוּ — [The third-generation students] rose up and examined the words of [their teachers], saying: מָה רָאוּ אֲבוֹתֵינוּ לוֹמַר דָּבָר זֶה — "Why would our fathers (i.e., our teachers)[6] say such a thing, that one should not expect reward for serving God?[7] אֶפְשָׁר שֶׁיַּעֲשֶׂה פּוֹעֵל מְלָאכָה כָּל הַיּוֹם וְלֹא יִטּוֹל שְׂכָרוֹ עַרְבִית — Is it conceivable that a worker should labor the entire day and not receive his pay in the evening?! אֶלָּא אִילּוּ הָיוּ יוֹדְעִין אֲבוֹתֵינוּ שֶׁיֵּשׁ עוֹלָם אַחֵר וְיֵשׁ תְּחִיַּית הַמֵּתִים לֹא הָיוּ אוֹמְרִים כָּךְ — We must conclude that, indeed, had our fathers known for certain that there is another world after one dies (i.e., the World to Come), and that there will be a Resurrection of the Dead in the Future Era, they would not have said such a thing. However, they realized there is *no* other world after this one, and there will *not* be a Resurrection of the Dead in the future, and for this reason they said to serve God without expecting reward!"[8] עָמְדוּ וּפֵירְשׁוּ מִן הַתּוֹרָה — Having concluded that their teachers had rejected the basic tenets of Judaism, [the students] arose and separated themselves from the Torah.[9]

5. But they were not careful to convey Antigonus' words with precision (see *Ben Avraham* and *Avos HaRosh* [Vol. 1]; see further, note 8).

6. *Binyan Yehoshua*. [A teacher of Torah is like a father to his students (*Ben Avraham*, citing *Sanhedrin* 99b).]

7. The students understood Antigonus' statement to mean that a person must serve God even though he will not receive any reward [as opposed to Antigonus' true intention, that there *is* reward, but that it should not be the focus of one's service of God] (see *Rashbam* to *Bava Basra* 115b, s.v. עם בת הבן).

8. Evidently, the students were not taught the end of Antigonus' statement, "so that your reward will be doubled in the Future Era" (*Avos HaRosh* [Vol. 1]). Alternatively, that last statement is not Antigonus' words [indeed, it does not appear in the Mishnah in *Avos*], but rather an elaboration of the Baraisa (*Ben Avraham*).

9. The Baraisa implies that the students forsook the *entire* Torah, both Written and Oral. This seems difficult, however, for it is evident throughout the Talmud that the Sadducees and Boethusians rejected *only* the Oral Torah, i.e., the interpretation of the Sages, while still observing the Written Torah [as

וְנִפְרְצוּ מֵהֶם שְׁתֵּי פְרָצוֹת צְדוֹקִין וּבַיְתּוֹסִין, צְדוֹקִים עַל שׁוּם צָדוֹק, בַּיְתּוֹסִין עַל שׁוּם בַּיְתּוֹס.[11] וְהָיוּ מִשְׁתַּמְּשִׁין בִּכְלֵי כֶסֶף וּבִכְלֵי זָהָב כָּל יְמֵיהֶם שֶׁלֹּא הָיְתָה דַעְתָּן גַּסָּה עֲלֵיהֶם אֶלָּא צְדוֹקִים אוֹמְרִים מָסוֹרֶת הוּא בְּיַד פְּרוּשִׁים[12] שֶׁהֵן מְצַעֲרִין עַצְמָן בָּעוֹלָם הַזֶּה וּבָעוֹלָם הַבָּא אֵין לָהֶם כְּלוּם:[13]

────────────────────────

וְנִפְרְצוּ מֵהֶם שְׁתֵּי פְרָצוֹת צְדוֹקִין וּבַיְתּוֹסִין — Two corrupt sects emanated from them:[10] *Tzadokim* (Sadducees) and *Boethusim* (Boethusians) — צְדוֹקִים עַל שׁוּם צָדוֹק, בַּיְתּוֹסִין עַל שׁוּם בַּיְתּוֹס — the *Tzadokim* were named after Tzadok, and the *Boethusim* were named after Boethus.[11] וְהָיוּ מִשְׁתַּמְּשִׁין בִּכְלֵי — [The members of these sects] would use silver כֶסֶף וּבִכְלֵי זָהָב כָּל יְמֵיהֶם and golden vessels all their lives, שֶׁלֹּא הָיְתָה דַעְתָּן גַּסָּה עֲלֵיהֶם — not out of vanity, אֶלָּא צְדוֹקִים אוֹמְרִים: מָסוֹרֶת הוּא בְּיַד פְּרוּשִׁים — but rather, it was a matter of principle, for the *Tzadokim* and the *Boethusim* would say, "There must be a tradition in the hands of the *Perushim* (Pharisees)[12] שֶׁהֵן מְצַעֲרִין עַצְמָן בָּעוֹלָם הַזֶּה — that they should cause themselves suffering in this world, וּבָעוֹלָם הַבָּא אֵין לָהֶם כְּלוּם — even though they will get nothing as reward in the World to Come!"[13]

────────────────────────

they understood it]. *Rambam* (to *Avos* ad loc., cited by *Magen Avos*) explains that originally they *did* reject the Written Torah as well, but they were unable to convince the masses of this heresy, so they modified their positions and began to profess belief in the Written Torah, while still rejecting the Oral Torah. This still allowed them "freedom" from the Written Torah, as they could interpret its words however they saw fit and release themselves from any laws they considered burdensome. See also *Hagahos Yaavetz*.

10. Literally, *two breaches* [in Torah Judaism] *came about through them* (see Mishnah, *Kilayim* 4:4).

11. That is, the *Tzadokim* were the students of the school of Tzadok and the *Boethusim* were the students of the school of Boethus.

From our Baraisa it is clear that it was *not* Tzadok and Boethus themselves who went astray, but rather the students of their students. [See further, *Avos HaRosh* (Vol. 1), who discusses this point at length.] Nonetheless, these groups were associated with Tzadok and Boethus, because it was due to their unclear transmittal of Antigonus'

words that their students' students were led to make such a gross error [see note 5] (*Ben Avraham*).

12. [After the rise of the *Tzadokim* and *Boethusim*, the true Torah scholars were called *Perushim* (פְּרוּשִׁים), which literally means "the separate ones."] This name represented the fact that they would "separate" themselves from the indulgences of this world, so that they could focus on Torah study (*Magen Avos, Ben Avraham*). [For alternative explanations of this name, see *Avos HaRosh* [Vol. 1] here, and below, Ch. 37 note 16.]

13. The *Tzadokim* and *Boethusim*, who had come to the heretical conclusion that there is no reward after death, viewed the *Perushim* as fools for denying themselves physical pleasures in order to study the Torah. After all, their self-denial would gain them nothing in the World to Come, and they would be left without any enjoyment whatsoever! Consistent with their beliefs, these sects chose to spend their lives in this world enjoying it to the fullest (based on *Magen Avos* ד"ה אלא צדוקים, though he explains somewhat differently based on an alternative reading in the text).

‎פֶּרֶק ו

א. ‎[יוֹסֵי בֶּן יוֹעֶזֶר אוֹמֵר:] יְהִי בֵיתְךָ בֵית וַעַד לַחֲכָמִים. כֵּיצַד,
‎מְלַמֵּד שֶׁיִּהְיֶה בֵיתוֹ שֶׁל אָדָם מְזוּמָּן לַחֲכָמִים וְתַלְמִידִים וְתַלְמִידֵי
‎תַלְמִידֵיהֶם, כְּאָדָם שֶׁאוֹמֵר לַחֲבֵירוֹ הֲרֵינִי מְשַׁמֵּר לְךָ בְּמָקוֹם פְּלוֹנִי.[1] דָּבָר
‎אַחֵר: יְהִי בֵיתְךָ בֵית וַעַד לַחֲכָמִים, כֵּיצַד, בִּזְמַן שֶׁתַּלְמִיד חָכָם נִכְנָס
‎אֶצְלְךָ לוֹמַר לְךָ [שְׁנֵה לִי], אִם יֵשׁ בְּיָדְךָ לִשְׁנוֹת, שְׁנֵה לוֹ, וְאִם לָאו פְּטָרֵהוּ
‎מִיָּד.[3] וְאַל יֵשֵׁב לְפָנֶיךָ לֹא עַל הַמִּטָּה וְלֹא עַל הַכִּסֵּא וְלֹא עַל סַפְסָל,

CHAPTER 6

§1 The leading disciples of Antigonus of Socho were Yose ben Yoezer and
Yose ben Yochanan. In this chapter, the Baraisa will examine the sayings
of Yose ben Yoezer, which appear in *Avos* 1:4, and in the next chapter those of
Yose ben Yochanan.

‎יְהִי בֵיתְךָ בֵית וַעַד לַחֲכָמִים — **Let
your house be a meeting place for sages.** ‎כֵּיצַד — **How so?** The Baraisa
explains: ‎מְלַמֵּד שֶׁיִּהְיֶה בֵיתוֹ שֶׁל אָדָם מְזוּמָּן לַחֲכָמִים וְתַלְמִידִים וְתַלְמִידֵי תַלְמִידֵיהֶם
— **[This] teaches that a person's house should be available to Torah scholars
and students, and the students of their students,** ‎כְּאָדָם שֶׁאוֹמֵר לַחֲבֵירוֹ
‎הֲרֵינִי מְשַׁמֵּר לְךָ בְּמָקוֹם פְּלוֹנִי — **such that a person might tell his friend, "I will
wait for you in this-and-this place,"** since it is such a recognizable landmark
and so frequently used as a meeting place by Torah scholars and students.[1]

The preceding explanation was addressed to laymen; the next is addressed
to Torah scholars:[2]
‎דָּבָר אַחֵר — **Another explanation:** ‎יְהִי בֵיתְךָ בֵית וַעַד לַחֲכָמִים, כֵּיצַד — **"Let
your house be a meeting place for sages"** — **how so?** ‎בִּזְמַן שֶׁתַּלְמִיד חָכָם
‎נִכְנָס אֶצְלְךָ לוֹמַר לְךָ שְׁנֵה לִי — **When a Torah student visits you, asking you,
"Teach me about this-and-this subject"** — ‎אִם יֵשׁ בְּיָדְךָ לִשְׁנוֹת שְׁנֵה לוֹ — **if you
are capable of teaching** that subject, then **teach** it **to him;** ‎וְאִם לָאו פְּטָרֵהוּ
‎מִיָּד — **if not, send him off immediately** and let him find someone else who can
teach him.[3] ‎וְאַל יֵשֵׁב לְפָנֶיךָ לֹא עַל הַמִּטָּה וְלֹא עַל הַכִּסֵּא וְלֹא עַל סַפְסָל — **And**
if you do teach him, **he should not sit before you on a couch, nor on a chair,**

---

1. *Binyan Yehoshua.*
In this way, even if you are not a scholar,
you will inevitably absorb some Torah wisdom from the scholars that frequent your
house, just as someone who spends time
in a spice shop will pick up and retain the
fragrance even after he leaves (ibid., from

Rav to *Avos* 1:4).

2. *Ahavas Chesed, Ben Avraham.*

3. Be forthright about your inability to teach
him, for if you are not, you will discourage
other students from turning to you, and your
house will cease to be a haven for Torah
scholars (*Ben Avraham*).

אֶלָּא יֵשֵׁב לְפָנֶיךָ עַל הָאָרֶץ‏[4], וְכָל דָּבָר וְדָבָר שֶׁיֵּצֵא מִפִּיךְ יְקַבְּלֵהוּ עָלָיו
בְּאֵימָה בְּיִרְאָה בְּרֶתֶת וּבְזִיעַ‏[5]:

ב. וֶהֱוֵי מִתְאַבֵּק בַּעֲפַר רַגְלֵיהֶם, כֵּיצַד, בִּזְמַן שֶׁתַּלְמִיד חָכָם נִכְנָס לָעִיר
אַל תֹּאמַר אֵינִי צָרִיךְ לוֹ אֶלָּא לֵךְ אֶצְלוֹ‏[6], וְאַל תֵּשֵׁב עִמּוֹ לֹא עַל
גַּבֵּי הַמִּטָּה וְלֹא עַל גַּבֵּי הַכִּסֵּא וְלֹא עַל הַסַּפְסָל, אֶלָּא שֵׁב לְפָנָיו עַל
הָאָרֶץ‏[7], וְכָל דָּבָר שֶׁיֵּצֵא מִפִּיו קַבְּלֵהוּ עָלֶיךָ בְּאֵימָה בְּיִרְאָה בְּרֶתֶת וּבְזִיעַ,

אֶלָּא יֵשֵׁב לְפָנֶיךָ עַל הָאָרֶץ — rather, he should sit before you nor on a bench; on the ground.[4] וְכָל דָּבָר וְדָבָר שֶׁיֵּצֵא מִפִּיךְ יְקַבְּלֵהוּ עָלָיו בְּאֵימָה בְּיִרְאָה בְּרֶתֶת וּבְזִיעַ — And he should accept each and every word that emerges from your mouth with dread, awe, trembling, and fear.[5]

§2 Yose ben Yoezer's next teaching:

וֶהֱוֵי מִתְאַבֵּק בַּעֲפַר רַגְלֵיהֶם — "And become dusty in the dust of their feet." בִּזְמַן שֶׁתַּלְמִיד חָכָם נִכְנָס לָעִיר — How so? The Baraisa explains: אַל תֹּאמַר אֵינִי צָרִיךְ לוֹ — When a Torah scholar comes to town, do not say, "I have no need for him." אֶלָּא לֵךְ אֶצְלוֹ — Rather, go to him and learn from him.[6] וְאַל תֵּשֵׁב עִמּוֹ לֹא עַל גַּבֵּי הַמִּטָּה וְלֹא עַל גַּבֵּי הַכִּסֵּא וְלֹא עַל הַסַּפְסָל אֶלָּא שֵׁב לְפָנָיו עַל הָאָרֶץ — And when you do, do not sit *with* him on a couch, nor on a chair, nor on a bench, but rather sit *before* him on the ground.[7] וְכָל דָּבָר שֶׁיֵּצֵא מִפִּיו קַבְּלֵהוּ עָלֶיךָ בְּאֵימָה בְּיִרְאָה בְּרֶתֶת וּבְזִיעַ — And accept every word that emerges from his mouth with dread, awe, trembling, and fear,

---

4. As if to say, "I am not conversant in Torah works and do not even reach the ankles of my teacher in scholarship" (*Mefaresh*). Even King David sat on the ground when he studied under his teachers (*Binyan Yehoshua* on the following section, citing *Moed Katan* 16b).

5. This is a directive to the teacher, who is charged with "casting fear upon the students" (*Kesubos* 103b), because an attitude of laxness and levity is not conducive to Torah study (see above, 1 §1). A measure of trepidation can stretch a student's abilities and enable him to learn a great deal from his teacher in a short time. At first, however, before the teacher has actually begun the lecture, the mood should be one of joy (*Ahavas Chesed*, citing *Shabbos* 30b).

[See *Chidushei HaGra* to *Berachos* 22a for a commentary on the seemingly redundant terms "dread, awe, trembling, and fear."]

6. This teaching highlights two prerequisites for success in Torah study: humility and hard work. When a person sets aside his own reputation for scholarship to seek instruction from, and sit at the feet of, a visiting Torah scholar, he gains merit for success by exercising the trait of humility ("Who is wise? He who learns from every person" — *Avos* 4:1; below, 23 §1). And when he goes out of his way to do so, he gains additional merit by investing toil in his quest for Torah knowledge (*Binyan Yehoshua*, from *Maharsha* to *Sotah* 21b).

7. The Baraisa thus offers two interpretations of the call to "become dusty in the dust of their feet." One is to follow after them and get dusty from the dust kicked up by their feet, and the other is to sit before them on the dusty ground while receiving Torah instruction from them (see *Ahavas Chesed* and *Ben Avraham*, based on *Rav* to *Avos* 1:4).

כְּדֶרֶךְ שֶׁקִּבְּלוּ אֲבוֹתֵינוּ מֵהַר סִינַי בְּאֵימָה בְּיִרְאָה בְּרֶתֶת וּבְזִיעַ[8]. דָּבָר
אַחֵר: הֱוֵי מִתְאַבֵּק בַּעֲפַר רַגְלֵיהֶם, זֶה רַבִּי אֱלִיעֶזֶר. וְשׁוֹתֶה בַּצָּמָא אֶת
דִּבְרֵיהֶם, זֶה רַבִּי עֲקִיבָא[9]. מֶה הָיָה תְּחִלָּתוֹ שֶׁל רַבִּי עֲקִיבָא, אָמְרוּ: בֶּן
אַרְבָּעִים שָׁנָה הָיָה וְלֹא שָׁנָה כְּלוּם[10]. פַּעַם אַחַת הָיָה עוֹמֵד עַל פִּי הַבְּאֵר,
אָמַר: מִי חָקַק אֶבֶן זוֹ, אָמְרוּ: לֹא הַמַּיִם שֶׁתָּדִיר [נוֹפְלִים] עָלֶיהָ בְּכָל
יוֹם, אָמְרוּ [לוֹ]: עֲקִיבָא אִי אַתָּה קוֹרֵא (איוב יד, יט) "אֲבָנִים שָׁחֲקוּ מַיִם"[11].

כְּדֶרֶךְ שֶׁקִּבְּלוּ אֲבוֹתֵינוּ מֵהַר סִינַי בְּאֵימָה בְּיִרְאָה בְּרֶתֶת וּבְזִיעַ — in the same way
our ancestors accepted every word emerging from God at **Mount Sinai, with
dread, awe, trembling, and fear.**[8]

The Baraisa points to two exemplary students of Torah:

דָּבָר אַחֵר — **Another interpretation:** הֱוֵי מִתְאַבֵּק בַּעֲפַר רַגְלֵיהֶם, זֶה רַבִּי אֱלִיעֶזֶר
— "And become dusty in the dust of their feet" — this refers to the way R'
Eliezer conducted himself; וְשׁוֹתֶה בַּצָּמָא אֶת דִּבְרֵיהֶם, זֶה רַבִּי עֲקִיבָא — "and
drink their words with thirst" — this refers to the way R' **Akiva** conducted
himself.[9]

The Baraisa begins with the story of R' Akiva:

מֶה הָיָה תְּחִלָּתוֹ שֶׁל רַבִּי עֲקִיבָא — **What was R' Akiva's origin** as a Torah scholar?
אָמְרוּ: בֶּן אַרְבָּעִים שָׁנָה הָיָה וְלֹא שָׁנָה כְּלוּם — [The Sages] said: **He was forty
years old and had not studied anything.**[10] פַּעַם אַחַת הָיָה עוֹמֵד עַל פִּי הַבְּאֵר
— **Once he was standing next to a well** and saw a stone within the well that
had been hollowed out. אָמַר: מִי חָקַק אֶבֶן זוֹ — **He said, "Who hollowed out
this stone?"** אָמְרוּ: לֹא הַמַּיִם שֶׁתָּדִיר נוֹפְלִים עָלֶיהָ בְּכָל יוֹם — **They said to him,
"Was it not the water that drips upon it constantly, every day?"** אָמְרוּ לוֹ:
עֲקִיבָא אִי אַתָּה קוֹרֵא "אֲבָנִים שָׁחֲקוּ מַיִם" — **They said to him** further, **"Akiva, have
you never read the verse, Stones are worn away by water?!"** (Job 14:19).[11]

---

8. *Berachos* 22a, based on the Torah's statement that the Jewish people were awestruck
by the Revelation at Mount Sinai (*Rashi* ad
loc., citing *Exodus* 20:15).

9. R' Eliezer's example teaches that even
someone from a prominent, wealthy family (see *Pirkei DeRabbi Eliezer* Ch. 1) should
lower himself and sit in the dust before his
Torah teacher; and R' Akiva's example
shows that even a needy, "thirsty" person
should ignore his material deprivation and
drink from the Torah wisdom of the Sages
(*Magen Avos*). Alternatively, R' Akiva's
example of starting to learn Torah at forty
years old shows that even someone who is
"thirsty" for Torah after remaining ignorant

for much of his life can begin to "drink" from
the wellspring of God's wisdom and aspire
to achieve great success, as R' Akiva did
(ibid.; *Ahavas Chesed* and *Avos HaRosh*, citing *R' Eliyahu ibn Chaim*).

10. Some understand this to mean that he
had not even learned the *aleph-beis* (*Ben
Avraham, Avos HaRosh*), while others
say that while he did not learn Mishnah (as
implied by the phrase לֹא שָׁנָה), he did have
a grounding in the Written Torah (*Binyan
Yehoshua, Kisei Rachamim*).

11. If R' Akiva had no Torah background
whatsoever (see previous note), the bystand-
ers meant this not as a question but as a

מִיָּד הָיָה רַבִּי עֲקִיבָא דָן קַל וָחוֹמֶר בְּעַצְמוֹ[12]: מָה רַךְ פָּסַל אֶת הַקָּשֶׁה, דִּבְרֵי
תוֹרָה שֶׁקָּשֶׁה כַּבַּרְזֶל עַל אַחַת כַּמָּה וְכַמָּה שֶׁיַּחְקְקוּ אֶת לִבִּי שֶׁהוּא בָּשָׂר
וָדָם. מִיָּד חָזַר לִלְמוֹד תּוֹרָה[13]. הָלַךְ הוּא וּבְנוֹ וְיָשְׁבוּ אֵצֶל מְלַמְּדֵי תִּינוֹקוֹת[14],
אָמַר לוֹ: רַבִּי לַמְּדֵנִי תוֹרָה. אָחַז רַבִּי עֲקִיבָא בְּרֹאשׁ הַלּוּחַ וּבְנוֹ בְּרֹאשׁ הַלּוּחַ,
כָּתַב לוֹ אָלֶף בֵּית וּלְמָדָהּ[15], (אָלֶף תָּיו וּלְמָדָהּ[16] תּוֹרַת כֹּהֲנִים וּלְמָדָהּ[17]) הָיָה

מִיָּד הָיָה רַבִּי עֲקִיבָא דָן קַל וָחוֹמֶר בְּעַצְמוֹ — Immediately, R' Akiva thought of a
kal va'chomer argument[12] regarding himself: מָה רַךְ פָּסַל אֶת הַקָּשֶׁה — "If
something soft, like water, can sculpt something hard, like a stone, דִּבְרֵי
תוֹרָה שֶׁקָּשֶׁה כַּבַּרְזֶל עַל אַחַת כַּמָּה וְכַמָּה שֶׁיַּחְקְקוּ אֶת לִבִּי שֶׁהוּא בָּשָׂר וָדָם — then
words of Torah, which are hard as iron, are all the more capable of hol-
lowing out my heart, which is flesh and blood." מִיָּד חָזַר לִלְמוֹד תּוֹרָה —
Immediately, he turned away from his mundane pursuits[13] to learn Torah.
הָלַךְ הוּא וּבְנוֹ וְיָשְׁבוּ אֵצֶל מְלַמְּדֵי תִּינוֹקוֹת — He went with his son,[14] and they
sat before the teachers of schoolchildren. אָמַר לוֹ: רַבִּי לַמְּדֵנִי תוֹרָה [R'
Akiva] said to [the teacher], "My master, teach me Torah." אָחַז רַבִּי עֲקִיבָא
בְּרֹאשׁ הַלּוּחַ וּבְנוֹ בְּרֹאשׁ הַלּוּחַ — R' Akiva held one end of the tablet upon
which it was customary to write, and his son held the other end of the tablet. כָּתַב לוֹ אָלֶף בֵּית וּלְמָדָהּ — [The teacher] wrote out *aleph, beis,* etc.,
for him, and he learned it;[15] אָלֶף תָּיו וּלְמָדָהּ — *aleph, tav,* and he learned
it;[16] תּוֹרַת כֹּהֲנִים וּלְמָדָהּ — the Book of *Leviticus,*[17] and he learned it. הָיָה

statement: Akiva, you ask this question because you are not familiar with the *Job* verse.
Had you known the verse, you would have
had no cause to wonder (*Avos HaRosh*).

12. [An *a fortiori* argument, which reasons
from a weaker proposition to a stronger one.]

13. *Avos HaRosh;* cf. *Kisei Rachamim.*

Other sources credit R' Akiva's wife with
sending him to learn Torah (see *Kesubos*
62b, *Nedarim* 50a; see further below, with
note 38). *Avos HaRosh* suggests that both
together prompted him to proceed. Originally, he followed his wife's counsel, but God
arranged for him to see the water-shaped
stone so that he might have the insight
about the Torah's ability to shape his heart.
With new confidence and enthusiasm, he
dedicated himself to Torah study.

14. This was apparently a son from a previous marriage, alluded to in *Yadayim* 3:5
(*Hagahos HaGriv,* cited by *Binyan Yehoshua; Kisei Rachamim*).

15. According to the view that until this point
R' Akiva was a complete ignoramus, this
statement is meant literally (*Avos HaRosh*).
But if R' Akiva already knew Scripture, the
intention here is that he learned the Midrashic teachings that center on the Hebrew
alphabet (*Binyan Yehoshua,* from *Mefaresh*).

16. Here the reference is to the א"ת ב"ש system
of letter substitution, used for Midrashic interpretation. Under this system, the first letter
(א) is interchangeable with the last letter (ת),
the second letter (ב) is interchangeable with
the second to last letter (ש), and so on (*Magen Avos; Binyan Yehoshua,* from *Mefaresh*).

17. Literally, "the Law of Kohanim," which
is the primary subject of *Leviticus.* It is an
ancient custom to begin the teaching of
Scripture to children with *Leviticus* rather
than *Genesis.* Since innocent children are
pure, and the sacrificial offerings (discussed
in *Leviticus* and meant to purify their offer-
ers of sin) are pure, it is fitting that the pure

לוֹמֵד וְהוֹלֵךְ עַד שֶׁלָּמַד כָּל הַתּוֹרָה כּוּלָהּ.[18] הָלַךְ וְיָשַׁב לִפְנֵי רַבִּי אֱלִיעֶזֶר
וְלִפְנֵי רַבִּי יְהוֹשֻׁעַ, אָמַר לָהֶם: רַבּוֹתַי, פִּתְחוּ לִי טַעַם מִשְׁנָה.[19] כֵּיוָן ֹשֶׁאָמַר
לוֹ הֲלָכָה אַחַת[20] הָלַךְ וְיָשַׁב לוֹ בֵּינוֹ לְבֵין עַצְמוֹ, אָמַר: (אָלֶף זוֹ לְמָה נִכְתְּבָה
בֵּית זוֹ לְמָה נִכְתְּבָה) דָּבָר זֶה לְמָה נֶאֱמַר[21]. חָזַר וּשְׁאָלָן וְהֶעֱמִידָן בִּדְבָרִים[22].

לוֹמֵד וְהוֹלֵךְ עַד שֶׁלָּמַד כָּל הַתּוֹרָה כּוּלָהּ — [R' Akiva] continued learning, until he had learned the whole Torah in its entirety.[18]

R' Akiva then progressed to the next stage of his development. **הָלַךְ וְיָשַׁב לִפְנֵי רַבִּי אֱלִיעֶזֶר וְלִפְנֵי רַבִּי יְהוֹשֻׁעַ** — He went and sat before R' Eliezer and R' Yehoshua, two of the generation's leading sages. **אָמַר לָהֶם: רַבּוֹתַי** **פִּתְחוּ לִי טַעַם מִשְׁנָה** — He said to them, "My masters! Reveal to me the Mishnah's reasoning."[19] **כֵּיוָן שֶׁאָמְרוּ לוֹ הֲלָכָה אַחַת** — Once they told[20] [R' Akiva] the explanation behind **one halachah,** i.e., one Mishnah, **הָלַךְ וְיָשַׁב לוֹ בֵּינוֹ לְבֵין עַצְמוֹ** — he went and sat by himself. **אָמַר: אָלֶף זוֹ לְמָה נִכְתְּבָה בֵּית זוֹ לְמָה נִכְתְּבָה** — He analyzed the subject he had learned and said, "Why was this *aleph* written, why was this *beis* written, why was this matter stated?"[21] **חָזַר וּשְׁאָלָן וְהֶעֱמִידָן בִּדְבָרִים** — He went back, asked them his questions, **and** ultimately **brought them to a standstill with his words.**[22]

---

should come and engross themselves in the study of that which is pure (*Avos HaRosh,* citing *Vayikra Rabbah* 7 §3).

18. That is, he learned the entire Written Torah (*Magen Avos*) — not only the Five Books of Moses, but also the Prophets and Writings; hence the added words "in its entirety" (*Ben Avraham*) — before going on to learn Mishnah under R' Eliezer and R' Yehoshua. Alternatively, he learned the Oral Law as well, but only superficially, in preparation for the in-depth study he would pursue under R' Eliezer and R' Yehoshua. This was in keeping with the Talmudic principle (*Shabbos* 63a) that one should first learn [by rote to become fluent in the text] and then reason [as to the logical underpinnings of what he has learned] (*Ahavas Chesed*).

19. He was referring to the sources for the Mishnah's rulings and the logic behind them — the body of Mishnah commentary known as Talmud (*Avos HaRosh*).

[Although this incident took place long before the Mishnaic text (as we know it) was redacted by R' Yehudah HaNasi, an essential form of the Mishnah had been passed down for many generations, since the time of the Men of the Great Assembly. For general discussion of this topic, see *Maharatz Chayes, Mevo HaTalmud* §33; *R' Yitzchak Isaac HaLevi, Doros HaRishonim,* Vols. 3 and 4; *R' Reuven Margaliyos, Yesod HaMishnah VeArichasah.*]

20. Emendation follows *Binyan Yehoshua.*

21. He searched for meaning in the most subtle nuances in the Torah text. He even delved into the mysteries behind the shape and spelling of the Hebrew letters, such as why the *aleph* is formed by two *yuds* on top and bottom with a *vav* in between, and why the letter's name consists of the letters א-ל-ף. This was an early sign of the attention to detail, that, with time, enabled R' Akiva (as recorded in *Menachos* 29b) to derive "mounds and mounds of halachos from each and every *kotz* [thorn-like projection in the Torah's letters]" (*Binyan Yehoshua,* from *Mefaresh; Ahavas Chesed*).

22. As his knowledge and understanding grew, his questions became more keen and penetrating, until eventually even his great and illustrious teachers could not reslove them.

23רַבִּי שִׁמְעוֹן בֶּן אֶלְעָזָר אוֹמֵר: אֶמְשׁוֹל לְךָ מָשָׁל לְמָה הַדָּבָר דּוֹמֶה, לְסַתָּת
שֶׁהָיָה מְסַתֵּת בֶּהָרִים, פַּעַם אַחַת נָטַל קַרְדּוּמוֹ בְּיָדוֹ וְהָלַךְ וְיָשַׁב עַל הָהָר וְהָיָה
מַכֶּה מִמֶּנּוּ צְרוֹרוֹת דַּקּוֹת וּבָאוּ בְּנֵי אָדָם וְאָמְרוּ לוֹ: מָה אַתָּה עוֹשֶׂה. אָמַר
לָהֶם: הֲרֵי אֲנִי עוֹקֵר וּמְטִילוֹ בְּתוֹךְ הַיַּרְדֵּן, אָמְרוּ לוֹ: אִי אַתָּה יָכוֹל לַעֲקוֹר
אֶת כָּל הָהָר, הָיָה מְסַתֵּת וְהוֹלֵךְ עַד שֶׁהִגִּיעַ אֵצֶל סֶלַע גָּדוֹל, נִכְנַס תַּחְתָּיו
סְתָרוֹ וַעֲקָרוֹ וֶהֱטִילוֹ אֶל הַיַּרְדֵּן וְאָמַר לוֹ: אֵין זֶה מְקוֹמְךָ אֶלָּא מָקוֹם זֶה. כָּךְ
עָשָׂה לָהֶם רַבִּי עֲקִיבָא לְרַבִּי אֱלִיעֶזֶר וְרַבִּי יְהוֹשֻׁעַ.24 אָמַר לוֹ רַבִּי טַרְפוֹן:

The Baraisa expresses the wonder of that moment:[23]

אֶמְשׁוֹל לְךָ מָשָׁל אוֹמֵר רַבִּי שִׁמְעוֹן בֶּן אֶלְעָזָר — R' Shimon ben Elazar says: I will offer you a parable: To what is this comparable? לְמָה הַדָּבָר דּוֹמֶה — To a stonecutter who was quarrying in the mountains. לְסַתָּת שֶׁהָיָה מְסַתֵּת בֶּהָרִים — Once, he took his ax in his hand, and went and sat on the mountain, פַּעַם אַחַת נָטַל קַרְדּוּמוֹ בְּיָדוֹ וְהָלַךְ וְיָשַׁב עַל הָהָר וְהָיָה מַכֶּה מִמֶּנּוּ צְרוֹרוֹת — and he was dislodging small pebbles from it. דַּקּוֹת — People came, observed him, and said to him, "What are you doing?" וּבָאוּ בְּנֵי אָדָם וְאָמְרוּ לוֹ: מָה אַתָּה עוֹשֶׂה — [The stonecutter] said to them, "I am uprooting this mountain and casting it into the Jordan River." אָמַר לָהֶם: הֲרֵי אֲנִי עוֹקֵר וּמְטִילוֹ בְּתוֹךְ הַיַּרְדֵּן — They replied to him, "You cannot uproot the whole mountain!" אָמְרוּ לוֹ: אִי אַתָּה יָכוֹל לַעֲקוֹר אֶת כָּל הָהָר — Nevertheless, he continued quarrying until he reached, i.e., exposed, a huge slab of rock. הָיָה מְסַתֵּת וְהוֹלֵךְ עַד שֶׁהִגִּיעַ אֵצֶל סֶלַע גָּדוֹל — He got under it, detached and uprooted it, and cast it into the Jordan River, נִכְנַס תַּחְתָּיו סְתָרוֹ וַעֲקָרוֹ וֶהֱטִילוֹ אֶל הַיַּרְדֵּן — and said to it, "This is not your place; rather, that is your place." וְאָמַר לוֹ: אֵין זֶה מְקוֹמְךָ אֶלָּא מָקוֹם זֶה — That is what R' Akiva did to R' Eliezer and R' Yehoshua.[24] כָּךְ עָשָׂה לָהֶם רַבִּי עֲקִיבָא לְרַבִּי אֱלִיעֶזֶר וְרַבִּי יְהוֹשֻׁעַ

The Baraisa resumes its narrative.

אָמַר לוֹ רַבִּי טַרְפוֹן — Later, after R' Akiva had discovered parts of the Torah that had previously been known to no one,[25] his colleague **R' Tarfon said to him,**

---

23. After an extremely late start and just a short period of study under two of the greatest sages of the generation, R' Akiva was able to pose questions that even they could not answer. How was this possible? It is this question that the following parable comes to address (see *Mefaresh*).

24. Like the stonecutter in the parable, R' Akiva approached the enormous task before him patiently and methodically. Despite the naysayers, he knew that he could master the entire Torah, one fine point at a time, if only he would be dedicated enough. He began by asking relatively simple questions, such as, "Why was this matter stated?," and advanced until he posed such immense and challenging questions that even R' Eliezer and R' Yehoshua could not answer them (*Ahavas Chesed*).

25. See *Ahavas Chesed*, who cites *Bamidbar Rabbah* 19 §6 to this effect.

עֲקִיבָא, עָלֶיךָ הַכָּתוּב אוֹמֵר (איוב כח, יא) "מִבְּכִי נְהָרוֹת חִבֵּשׁ וְתַעֲלֻמָה
יֵצֵא אוֹר" דְּבָרִים הַמְסוּתָּרִים מִבְּנֵי אָדָם הוֹצִיאָם רַבִּי עֲקִיבָא לָאוֹרָה[26].
בְּכָל יוֹם וָיוֹם הָיָה מֵבִיא חֲבִילָה שֶׁל עֵצִים, חֶצְיָה מוֹכֵר וּמִתְפַּרְנֵס וְחֶצְיָה
מִתְקַשֵּׁט בָּהּ, עָמְדוּ עָלָיו שְׁכֵנָיו וְאָמְרוּ לוֹ: עֲקִיבָא, אִבַּדְתָּנוּ בְּעָשָׁן, מְכוֹר
אוֹתָן לָנוּ וְטוֹל שֶׁמֶן בִּדְמֵיהֶן וּשְׁנֵה לְאוֹר הַנֵּר, אָמַר לָהֶם: הַרְבֵּה סְפוּקִים
אֲנִי מִסְתַּפֵּק בָּהֶן, אֶחָד שֶׁאֲנִי שׁוֹנֶה בָּהֶן[27] וְאֶחָד שֶׁאֲנִי מִתְחַמֵּם כְּנֶגְדָּן וְאֶחָד
שֶׁאֲנִי יָכוֹל לִישַׁן [בָּהֶם][28]. עָתִיד רַבִּי עֲקִיבָא לְחַיֵּיב אֶת כָּל הָעֲנִיִּים בַּדִּין[29],

---

"מִבְּכִי נְהָרוֹת חִבֵּשׁ וְתַעֲלֻמָה יֵצֵא אוֹר" — "Akiva, it is
about you that Scripture states, *From the waters of the deep he harnessed
rivers; he brings secret things out into the light* (*Job* 28:11).   דְּבָרִים
הַמְסוּתָּרִים מִבְּנֵי אָדָם הוֹצִיאָם רַבִּי עֲקִיבָא לָאוֹרָה — Things that were concealed
from people, R' Akiva has brought out into the light."[26]

The Baraisa continues with a description of R' Akiva's poverty:
בְּכָל יוֹם וָיוֹם הָיָה מֵבִיא חֲבִילָה שֶׁל עֵצִים — Each and every day, R' Akiva would
bring a bundle of twigs that he had gathered.   חֶצְיָה מוֹכֵר וּמִתְפַּרְנֵס וְחֶצְיָה
מִתְקַשֵּׁט בָּהּ — Half [the wood] he would sell and thereby sustain himself, and
half he would make use of for his own needs.   עָמְדוּ עָלָיו שְׁכֵנָיו וְאָמְרוּ לוֹ: עֲקִיבָא
אִבַּדְתָּנוּ בְּעָשָׁן — His neighbors confronted him and told him, "Akiva, you are
destroying us with the smoke! Here is a better idea: מְכוֹר אוֹתָן לָנוּ וְטוֹל שֶׁמֶן
בִּדְמֵיהֶן וּשְׁנֵה לְאוֹר הַנֵּר — Sell [the extra twigs] to us, buy oil with the money,
and study by the light of an oil lamp."   אָמַר לָהֶם: הַרְבֵּה סְפוּקִים אֲנִי מִסְתַּפֵּק
בָּהֶן — [R' Akiva] told them, "I make many different uses of [the twigs]:   אֶחָד
שֶׁאֲנִי שׁוֹנֶה בָּהֶן וְאֶחָד שֶׁאֲנִי מִתְחַמֵּם כְּנֶגְדָּן וְאֶחָד שֶׁאֲנִי יָכוֹל לִישַׁן בָּהֶם — One, that
I learn by [their light];[27] another, that I warm myself opposite them, and yet
another, that I sleep on them.[28] So no, I do not want to sell those bundles."

The Baraisa draws a moral lesson from R' Akiva's devotion to Torah study
in spite of his financial difficulties:
עָתִיד רַבִּי עֲקִיבָא לְחַיֵּיב אֶת כָּל הָעֲנִיִּים בַּדִּין — The standard set by **R' Akiva is**

---

26. *Ben Avraham* suggests that R' Tarfon
was interpreting the verse as follows: מִבְּכִי
נְהָרוֹת, *From the crying by the river,* that is,
from the tearful repentance that R' Akiva
performed by the well, where he saw how
the dripping water bore a hole in the stone;
חִבֵּשׁ, *he girded* himself to begin studying the
Torah and have it penetrate his own heart;
וְתַעֲלֻמָה יֵצֵא אוֹר, *and he* not only became
a Torah scholar, but even *brought secret
things,* hidden Torah insights, *out into the*

light (see also *Magen Avos*).

27. A wood fire lasts longer and produces
more light and heat than the flame of a lamp
filled with oil of equivalent value (see *Magen
Avos*).

28. By making a bed frame out of them
(*Ben Avraham*). Alternatively, he meant to
say, "I can sleep through them," because
the warmth they provide allows me to sleep
soundly and regain my strength for further
study (*Magen Avos*).

שֶׁאִם אוֹמֵר לָהֶם מִפְּנֵי מָה לֹא לְמַדְתֶּם [וְהֵם אָמְרוּ מִפְּנֵי] שֶׁעֲנִיִּים
הָיִינוּ, אוֹמְרִים לָהֶם: וַהֲלֹא רַבִּי עֲקִיבָא עָנִי בְּיָתֵר וּמְדוּלְדָּל הָיָה[30],
[וְהֵם אָמְרוּ: מִפְּנֵי טַפֵּינוּ, אוֹמְרִים לָהֶם: וַהֲלֹא רַבִּי עֲקִיבָא] הָיוּ לוֹ בָּנִים
וּבָנוֹת[31], (אֶלָּא אוֹמְרִים לָהֶם: מִפְּנֵי) שֶׁזָּכְתָה רָחֵל אִשְׁתּוֹ[32]. בֶּן אַרְבָּעִים
שָׁנָה הָלַךְ לִלְמוֹד תּוֹרָה, סוֹף שָׁלֹשׁ עֶשְׂרֵה שָׁנָה[33] לִימֵּד תּוֹרָה בָּרַבִּים[34],
אָמְרוּ: לֹא נִפְטַר מִן הָעוֹלָם עַד שֶׁהָיוּ לוֹ שׁוּלְחָנוֹת שֶׁל כֶּסֶף וְשֶׁל זָהָב

---

destined to condemn all the poor people in their final judgment.[29] שֶׁאִם
אוֹמֵר לָהֶם מִפְּנֵי מָה לֹא לְמַדְתֶּם — For if [the Heavenly Court] says to them,
"Why did you not study Torah?," וְהֵם אָמְרוּ מִפְּנֵי שֶׁעֲנִיִּים הָיִינוּ — and they
answer, "Because we were poor and preoccupied with supporting ourselves,"
אוֹמְרִים לָהֶם: וַהֲלֹא רַבִּי עֲקִיבָא עָנִי בְּיָתֵר וּמְדוּלְדָּל הָיָה — [the prosecutors] will
respond to them, "But was R' Akiva not extremely poor and destitute?[30]
Yet he found a way to study Torah!" וְהֵם אָמְרוּ מִפְּנֵי טַפֵּינוּ — So [the poor]
will change their argument and say, "But we could not study because we were
busy with the needs of our little children!" אוֹמְרִים לָהֶם: וַהֲלֹא רַבִּי עֲקִיבָא הָיוּ
לוֹ בָּנִים וּבָנוֹת — [The prosecutors] will respond, "But did R' Akiva not also
have sons and daughters to support?"[31] אֶלָּא אוֹמְרִים לָהֶם: מִפְּנֵי שֶׁזָּכְתָה רָחֵל
אִשְׁתּוֹ — Rather, what will [the poor] say in response to them? "R' Akiva was
different, because his wife, Rachel, was especially meritorious."[32]

The Baraisa concludes the narrative of R' Akiva:
בֶּן אַרְבָּעִים שָׁנָה הָלַךְ לִלְמוֹד תּוֹרָה — [R' Akiva] went to learn Torah when he
was forty years old, סוֹף שָׁלֹשׁ עֶשְׂרֵה שָׁנָה לִימֵּד תּוֹרָה בָּרַבִּים — and at the end
of thirteen years,[33] he taught Torah publicly.[34] אָמְרוּ: לֹא נִפְטַר מִן הָעוֹלָם
עַד שֶׁהָיוּ לוֹ שׁוּלְחָנוֹת שֶׁל כֶּסֶף וְשֶׁל זָהָב — [The Sages] said: Despite his earlier

---

29. Although the Sages elsewhere cite Hillel,
an earlier sage, as setting the moral standard for poor people, R' Akiva's example
goes further, because, as the Baraisa goes
on to say, he is known to have had many
children to support (Ahavas Chesed), and
because he was originally poor in Torah
learning as well as in material assets (Magen
Avos). Hence, the Baraisa emphasizes that
R' Akiva will condemn all the poor people.

30. R' Akiva was "poor" in a spiritual sense,
having learned nothing (or very little) of the
Torah until age forty; and he was "destitute"
in a material sense, having to engage in
menial labor for the most paltry of incomes
(Magen Avos).

31. From a previous marriage (Kisei

Rachamim); see above, note 14.

32. Binyan Yehoshua. Regarding Rachel's
great merit, see below with note 38.

According to this version of the text, it
would appear that the poor who did not engage in Torah study will not be condemned,
for they will be able to vindicate themselves
with this last argument. See Magen Avos,
who understands the following line of the
Baraisa as explaining why this defense will
not be accepted; see Nuschas HaGra for an
alternative version.

33. One year with the teachers of little children, and twelve years with R' Eliezer and R'
Yehoshua (Ben Avraham)

34. See Kesubos 62b, where the Gemara

וְעַד שֶׁעָלָה לְמִטָּתוֹ בְּסוּלָמוֹת שֶׁל זָהָב.[35] הָיְתָה אִשְׁתּוֹ יוֹצְאָה בְּקַרְדְּמִין
וּבְעִיר שֶׁל זָהָב,[36] אָמְרוּ לוֹ תַּלְמִידָיו: רַבִּי, בְּיִישַׁתָּנוּ מִמַּה שֶׁעָשִׂיתָ לָהּ,[37]
אָמַר לָהֶם: הַרְבֵּה צַעַר נִצְטַעֲרָה עִמִּי בַּתּוֹרָה[38]:

ג. מֶה הָיָה תְּחִלָּתוֹ שֶׁל רַבִּי אֱלִיעֶזֶר בֶּן [הוֹרְקָנוֹס, בֶּן] עֶשְׂרִים וּשְׁתַּיִם
שָׁנָה הָיָה וְלֹא לָמַד תּוֹרָה. פַּעַם אַחַת [אָמַר: אֵלֵךְ וְאֶלְמוֹד] תּוֹרָה
לִפְנֵי רַבָּן יוֹחָנָן בֶּן זַכַּאי, אָמַר לוֹ אָבִיו הוֹרְקָנוֹס: אִי אַתָּה טוֹעֵם עַד

---

poverty, he did not depart from the world until he had tables of silver and gold, וְעַד שֶׁעָלָה לְמִטָּתוֹ בְּסוּלָמוֹת שֶׁל זָהָב — and until he would ascend to his bed upon golden ladders, for he became extremely wealthy.[35] הָיְתָה אִשְׁתּוֹ יוֹצְאָה בְּקַרְדְּמִין וּבְעִיר שֶׁל זָהָב — His wife would go out wearing a *kardemin* and a "city of gold" that he had bought for her.[36] אָמְרוּ לוֹ תַּלְמִידָיו — His students told him, רַבִּי בְּיִישַׁתָּנוּ מִמַּה שֶׁעָשִׂיתָ לָהּ — "Master, because of what you have done for her, you have shamed us before our wives, for we do not provide them with such fine jewelry."[37] אָמַר לָהֶם: הַרְבֵּה צַעַר נִצְטַעֲרָה עִמִּי — He said to them, "My wife is different from other wives: She has בַּתּוֹרָה suffered together with me through much travail in the pursuit of Torah."[38]

§3 The Baraisa earlier held up R' Eliezer as a model for becoming "dusty in the dust of [the Torah sages'] feet." It now elaborates with the story of his rise to greatness:

מֶה הָיָה תְּחִלָּתוֹ שֶׁל רַבִּי אֱלִיעֶזֶר בֶּן הוֹרְקָנוֹס — What was R' Eliezer ben Hyrkanos' origin? בֶּן עֶשְׂרִים וּשְׁתַּיִם שָׁנָה הָיָה וְלֹא לָמַד תּוֹרָה — He was twenty-two years old and had not yet studied Torah. פַּעַם אַחַת אָמַר אֵלֵךְ וְאֶלְמוֹד תּוֹרָה לִפְנֵי — Once, he said in his father's presence, "I shall travel to רַבָּן יוֹחָנָן בֶּן זַכַּאי — Jerusalem and study Torah before Rabban Yochanan ben Zakkai." אָמַר לוֹ אָבִיו הוֹרְקָנוֹס — His father, Hyrkanos, said to him, אִי אַתָּה טוֹעֵם עַד

---

says that at this point R' Akiva already had 12,000 students.

35. This illustrates the principle that "whoever fulfills the Torah amid poverty will ultimately fulfill it amid wealth" (*Avos HaRosh*, citing *Pirkei Avos* 4:9). *Nedarim* 50a-b lists six different incidents that enriched R' Akiva later in life.

36. A *kardemin* is an ornament, possibly one that was wide on one end and tapered toward the other end, thus resembling the head of an ax (*kardom*), as it was commonly shaped in those times (*Ahavas Chesed*; see *Kisei Rachamim*).

A "city of gold" was a gold ornament

engraved with a likeness of the city of Jerusalem (*Binyan Yehoshua,* from *Shabbos* 59a with *Tosafos*). R' Akiva had promised to buy his wife this ornament when, early in their marriage, they had nothing but straw to sleep on, and he had to pick the straw out of her hair every morning (*Nedarim* 50a).

37. *Binyan Yehoshua.* We do not treat our wives even at our own economic level the way you treat your wife at yours (*Avos HaRosh*, quoting *Chida, Maris HaAyin, Bava Kamma* 41b).

38. Despite their abject poverty, R' Akiva's wife encouraged him to leave home and

שֶׁתַּחֲרוֹשׁ מְלֹא מַעֲנָה[39], הִשְׁכִּים וְחָרַשׁ מְלֹא מַעֲנָה. אָמְרוּ: אוֹתוֹ הַיּוֹם
עֶרֶב שַׁבָּת הָיָה, הָלַךְ וְסָעַד אֵצֶל חָמִיו, וְיֵשׁ אוֹמְרִים לֹא טָעַם כְּלוּם
מִשֵּׁשׁ שָׁעוֹת שֶׁל עֶרֶב שַׁבָּת עַד שֵׁשׁ שָׁעוֹת שֶׁל מוֹצָאֵי שַׁבָּת, כְּשֶׁהוּא
הוֹלֵךְ בַּדֶּרֶךְ רָאָה אֶבֶן שֶׁדִּימָה וּנְטָלָהּ וּנְתָנָהּ לְתוֹךְ פִּיו, וְיֵשׁ אוֹמְרִים
גֶּלְלֵי הַבָּקָר הָיָה, הָלַךְ וְלָן בָּאַכְסַנְיָא שֶׁלּוֹ, הָלַךְ וְיָשַׁב לוֹ לִפְנֵי רַבָּן
יוֹחָנָן בֶּן זַכַּאי בִּירוּשָׁלַיִם עַד שֶׁיָּצָא רֵיחַ רַע מִפִּיו[43], אָמַר לוֹ רַבִּי יוֹחָנָן
בֶּן זַכַּאי: אֱלִיעֶזֶר בְּנִי, כְּלוּם סָעַדְתָּ הַיּוֹם, שָׁתַק. שׁוּב אָמַר לוֹ וְשָׁתַק.
שָׁלַח וְקָרָא לָאַכְסַנְיָא שֶׁלּוֹ, אָמַר לָהֶם: כְּלוּם סָעַד אֱלִיעֶזֶר אֶצְלְכֶם,

שֶׁתַּחֲרוֹשׁ מְלֹא מַעֲנָה — "You will not taste a thing before you plow a furrow's length!"[39] הִשְׁכִּים וְחָרַשׁ מְלֹא מַעֲנָה — In obedience to his father, [R' Eliezer] arose early and plowed a furrow's length. אָמְרוּ: אוֹתוֹ הַיּוֹם עֶרֶב שַׁבָּת הָיָה — They said: That day was Sabbath eve. Rather than encountering his father and discussing the matter again, הָלַךְ וְסָעַד אֵצֶל חָמִיו he went and ate the Sabbath meal at the table of his father-in-law.[40] וְיֵשׁ אוֹמְרִים: לֹא טָעַם כְּלוּם — But some say: He did מִשֵּׁשׁ שָׁעוֹת שֶׁל עֶרֶב שַׁבָּת עַד שֵׁשׁ שָׁעוֹת שֶׁל מוֹצָאֵי שַׁבָּת not taste a thing from noon of Sabbath eve until noon of Sunday, the day after the Sabbath.[41] He left his town and began walking to Jerusalem, without food or money. כְּשֶׁהוּא הוֹלֵךְ בַּדֶּרֶךְ רָאָה אֶבֶן שֶׁדִּימָה וּנְטָלָהּ וּנְתָנָהּ לְתוֹךְ פִּיו — As he was walking along the road, he saw a stone that appeared to him as an old, decayed piece of bread,[42] and in his great hunger, he took it and put it in his mouth. וְיֵשׁ אוֹמְרִים גֶּלְלֵי הַבָּקָר הָיָה — Some say: It was actually a dried piece of cow dung. הָלַךְ וְלָן בָּאַכְסַנְיָא שֶׁלּוֹ — When R' Eliezer reached Jerusalem, he went and lodged at the home of his hosts. הָלַךְ וְיָשַׁב לוֹ לִפְנֵי רַבָּן יוֹחָנָן בֶּן זַכַּאי בִּירוּשָׁלַיִם עַד שֶׁיָּצָא רֵיחַ רַע מִפִּיו — The next day, he went and sat before Rabban Yochanan ben Zakkai in Jerusalem until, at some point, a bad odor emerged from his mouth.[43] אָמַר לוֹ רַבִּי יוֹחָנָן בֶּן זַכַּאי: אֱלִיעֶזֶר בְּנִי, כְּלוּם סָעַדְתָּ הַיּוֹם — Rabban Yochanan ben Zakkai said to him, "Eliezer, my son, did you eat anything today?" שָׁתַק — [R' Eliezer] remained silent. שׁוּב אָמַר לוֹ וְשָׁתַק — Again he asked him and again he remained silent. שָׁלַח וְקָרָא לָאַכְסַנְיָא שֶׁלּוֹ — [Rabban Yochanan] summoned [the new student's] hosts. אָמַר לָהֶם: כְּלוּם — He asked them, "Did Eliezer eat anything with you?" סָעַד אֱלִיעֶזֶר אֶצְלְכֶם

study Torah for twelve years, and upon his return home, she encouraged him to go back for another twelve years, as stated in the well-known narrative recorded in *Kesubos* 62b-63a and *Nedarim* 50a.

39. This was Hyrkanos's way of expressing displeasure at his son's idea. He doubted that a grown man with such a weak background

in learning could make up for lost time and become an accomplished scholar (*Magen Avos, Ben Avraham*).

40. *Magen Avos.*

41. *Ben Avraham.*

42. *Binyan Yehoshua,* from *Mefaresh.*

43. Because he had not eaten for a long time,

אָמְרוּ לוֹ: אָמַרְנוּ שֶׁמָּא אֵצֶל רַבִּי הָיָה סוֹעֵד, אָמַר לָהֶם: [אַף אֲנִי] אָמַרְתִּי
שֶׁמָּא אֶצְלְכֶם הָיָה סוֹעֵד, בֵּינִי וּבֵינֵיכֶם אִבַּדְנוּ אֶת רַבִּי אֱלִיעֶזֶר מִן הָאֶמְצַע.
אָמַר לוֹ: כְּשֵׁם שֶׁיָּצָא לְךָ רֵיחַ רַע מִפִּיךָ כָּךְ יֵצֵא לְךָ שֵׁם טוֹב בַּתּוֹרָה.
שָׁמַע עָלָיו הוֹרְקָנוֹס אָבִיו שֶׁהָיָה לוֹמֵד תּוֹרָה אֵצֶל רַבָּן יוֹחָנָן בֶּן זַכַּאי,
אָמַר: אֵלֵךְ (וְאַדִּיר) אֱלִיעֶזֶר בְּנִי מִנְּכָסָי.[44] אָמְרוּ: אוֹתוֹ הַיּוֹם רַבָּן יוֹחָנָן
בֶּן זַכַּאי יוֹשֵׁב וְדוֹרֵשׁ בִּירוּשָׁלַיִם וְכָל גְּדוֹלֵי יִשְׂרָאֵל יוֹשְׁבִין לְפָנָיו. שָׁמַע
עָלָיו שֶׁבָּא, הוֹשִׁיב לוֹ שׁוֹמְרִין, אָמַר לָהֶם: אִם בָּא לֵישֵׁב אַל תְּנִיחוּהוּ,[45]
הוּא בָּא לֵישֵׁב וְלֹא הֱנִיחוּהוּ. הָיָה מְדַלֵּג וְעוֹלֶה [וְהוֹלֵךְ] עַד שֶׁהִגִּיעַ
אֵצֶל בֶּן צִיצִית הַכֶּסֶת וְאֵצֶל נַקְדִּימוֹן בֶּן גּוּרְיוֹן וְאֵצֶל בֶּן כַּלְבָּא שָׂבוּעַ,

---

אָמְרוּ לוֹ: אָמַרְנוּ שֶׁמָּא אֵצֶל רַבִּי הָיָה סוֹעֵד — **They said to him,** "No. We noticed his absence, but we thought that perhaps he is dining with the master (i.e., with you)." אָמַר לָהֶם: אַף אֲנִי אָמַרְתִּי שֶׁמָּא אֶצְלְכֶם הָיָה סוֹעֵד — **[Rabban Yochanan] replied,** "I, too, thought that perhaps he is dining with you. בֵּינִי וּבֵינֵיכֶם אִבַּדְנוּ — אֶת רַבִּי אֱלִיעֶזֶר מִן הָאֶמְצַע — **Between me and the two of you, we nearly eliminated R' Eliezer!"** אָמַר לוֹ: כְּשֵׁם שֶׁיָּצָא לְךָ רֵיחַ רַע מִפִּיךָ כָּךְ יֵצֵא לְךָ שֵׁם טוֹב בַּתּוֹרָה — **He then said to R' Eliezer,** "Just as a bad odor emerged from your mouth, so should a good name for Torah scholarship one day emerge from you!" שָׁמַע עָלָיו הוֹרְקָנוֹס אָבִיו שֶׁהָיָה לוֹמֵד תּוֹרָה אֵצֶל רַבָּן יוֹחָנָן בֶּן זַכַּאי — **His father, Hyrkanos, heard** that he was studying Torah under Rabban Yochanan ben Zakkai. אָמַר אֵלֵךְ וְאַדִּיר אֱלִיעֶזֶר בְּנִי מִנְּכָסָי — **At the instigation of his other sons, [Hyrkanos] said,** "I will go to Jerusalem and disinherit Eliezer, my son, from my estate."[44] אָמְרוּ: אוֹתוֹ הַיּוֹם רַבָּן יוֹחָנָן בֶּן זַכַּאי יוֹשֵׁב וְדוֹרֵשׁ בִּירוּשָׁלַיִם — **They said: On that day,** when Hyrkanos arrived, Rabban Yochanan ben Zakkai was sitting and giving a Torah discourse in Jerusalem, וְכָל גְּדוֹלֵי יִשְׂרָאֵל יוֹשְׁבִין לְפָנָיו — **and all the dignitaries of Israel were sitting before him.** שָׁמַע עָלָיו שֶׁבָּא הוֹשִׁיב לוֹ שׁוֹמְרִין — **[Rabban Yochanan] heard that [Hyrkanos] had come,** so he designated special ushers for him. אָמַר לָהֶם: אִם בָּא לֵישֵׁב אַל תְּנִיחוּהוּ — **He told them,** "If [Hyrkanos] tries to sit anywhere but the front, do not let him."[45] הוּא בָּא לֵישֵׁב וְלֹא הֱנִיחוּהוּ — **Indeed, he tried to sit** at the back and the [ushers] did not let him. הָיָה מְדַלֵּג וְעוֹלֶה וְהוֹלֵךְ עַד שֶׁהִגִּיעַ אֵצֶל בֶּן צִיצִית הַכֶּסֶת וְאֵצֶל נַקְדִּימוֹן בֶּן גּוּרְיוֹן וְאֵצֶל בֶּן כַּלְבָּא שָׂבוּעַ — **He kept advancing**

---

or because he had eaten dung (*Magen Avos*).

44. Literally, *make a vow [banning him] from my estate.* Hyrkanos's sons had protested to him, "Our brother Eliezer abandoned you in your old age, yet when the time comes to inherit you, he will receive an equal share with us!" (*Rashi* to *Bereishis Rabbah* 42 §1; see *Pirkei DeRabbi Eliezer* Ch. 2).

Hyrkanos could have made this vow at home, but he wished to consult with Rabban Yochanan ben Zakkai before doing so (*Magen Avos*).

45. Because Hyrkanos deserves a seat of honor on account of his son, Eliezer, who has become one of the great sages of the generation (*Binyan Yehoshua*).

הָיָה יוֹשֵׁב בֵּינֵיהֶם וּמַרְתֵּת. אָמְרוּ: אוֹתוֹ הַיּוֹם נָתַן עֵינָיו רַבָּן יוֹחָנָן בֶּן
זַכַּאי בְּרַבִּי אֱלִיעֶזֶר וְאָמַר לוֹ: פְּתַח [וּדְרֹשׁ], אָמַר לוֹ: אֵינִי יָכוֹל לִפְתּוֹחַ[46],
דָּחַק עָלָיו וּדְחָקוּהוּ הַתַּלְמִידִים, עָמַד (וּפָתַח) וְדָרַשׁ בִּדְבָרִים שֶׁלֹּא
שְׁמָעָתַן אֹזֶן מֵעוֹלָם. כָּל דָּבָר וְדָבָר שֶׁיָּצָא מִפִּיו עָמַד רַבָּן יוֹחָנָן בֶּן
זַכַּאי ([עַל רַגְלָיו]) וּנְשָׁקוֹ עַל רֹאשׁוֹ (וְאָמַר לוֹ רַבִּי אֱלִיעֶזֶר: רַבִּי, אֱמֶת
לִמַּדְתַּנִי[47]). עַד שֶׁלֹּא הִגִּיעַ [זְמַן] לָצֵאת עָמַד הוּרְקְנוֹס אָבִיו עַל רַגְלָיו
וְאָמַר: רַבּוֹתַי, אֲנִי לֹא בָּאתִי אֶלָּא לְהַדִּיר אֱלִיעֶזֶר בְּנִי מִנְּכָסַי, עַכְשָׁיו כָּל
נְכָסַי יִהְיוּ נְתוּנִין לֶאֱלִיעֶזֶר בְּנִי וְכָל אֶחָיו פְּטוּרִין [וְאֵין לָהֶם בָּהֶן כְּלוּם][48].

toward the front, trying to find a place to sit, **until he reached** a seat at the head, **next to Ben Tzitzis HaKesses, Nakdimon ben Guryon, and Ben Kalba Savua,** the three wealthiest men in Jerusalem.   הָיָה יוֹשֵׁב בֵּינֵיהֶם וּמַרְתֵּת — **He sat between them and trembled,** feeling very out of place.   אָמְרוּ: אוֹתוֹ הַיּוֹם — **They said: On that day** נָתַן עֵינָיו רַבָּן יוֹחָנָן בֶּן זַכַּאי בְּרַבִּי אֱלִיעֶזֶר וְאָמַר לוֹ פְּתַח וּדְרֹשׁ **Rabban Yochanan ben Zakkai cast his eyes** lovingly **upon R' Eliezer and told him, "Open a discourse. Expound** upon what you know!"   אָמַר לוֹ: אֵינִי יָכוֹל לִפְתּוֹחַ — **He replied, "I cannot open** a discourse in your presence!"[46]   דָּחַק עָלָיו וּדְחָקוּהוּ הַתַּלְמִידִים — **[Rabban Yochanan] and the other disciples pressured him** until he relented.   עָמַד וְדָרַשׁ בִּדְבָרִים שֶׁלֹּא שְׁמָעָתַן אֹזֶן מֵעוֹלָם — **He arose and expounded** wondrous things that no ear had ever heard.   כָּל דָּבָר וְדָבָר שֶׁיָּצָא מִפִּיו עָמַד רַבָּן יוֹחָנָן בֶּן זַכַּאי וּנְשָׁקוֹ עַל רֹאשׁוֹ — **After each and every teaching that emerged from his mouth, Rabban Yochanan ben Zakkai stood up and kissed him on his head.**   וְאָמַר לוֹ רַבִּי אֱלִיעֶזֶר: רַבִּי, אֱמֶת לִמַּדְתַּנִי — **And R' Eliezer said to him, "My teacher, you have taught me the truth!"**[47]   עַד שֶׁלֹּא הִגִּיעַ זְמַן לָצֵאת עָמַד הוּרְקְנוֹס אָבִיו עַל רַגְלָיו — **Before it was time to leave, Hyrkanos, his father, stood up on his feet**   וְאָמַר: רַבּוֹתַי — and declared to everyone, "**My masters,** אֲנִי לֹא בָּאתִי אֶלָּא לְהַדִּיר אֱלִיעֶזֶר בְּנִי מִנְּכָסַי **I must confess that I came here only** in order **to disinherit Eliezer, my son, from my estate.**   עַכְשָׁיו כָּל נְכָסַי יִהְיוּ נְתוּנִין לֶאֱלִיעֶזֶר בְּנִי וְכָל אֶחָיו פְּטוּרִין וְאֵין לָהֶם בָּהֶן כְּלוּם — **But now** that I have witnessed this spectacle, I have changed my mind: **All my possessions shall be given to Eliezer, my son;** whereas **all of his brothers,** who urged me to punish him, **shall be disregarded, and will receive no** portion of [my property] at all!"[48]

46. R' Eliezer was awed by the presence of his teacher, and felt that he could not lecture in front of him (*Radal, Pirkei DeRabbi Eliezer* 2:11).

47. As if to say, "Everything I know I learned from you." Although he expounded on this occasion "things that no ear had ever heard,"

he nevertheless credited all his knowledge to Rabban Yochanan, who had helped him to reach this level (*Ben Avraham*).

48. In *Bereishis Rabbah* 42 §1, the Midrash relates that R' Eliezer respectfully declined this gift and resolved to accept only an equal share among his brothers, as was his entitlement.

וְלָמָּה נִקְרָא שְׁמוֹ צִיצִית הַכֶּסֶת, שֶׁהָיָה מוּסָב עַל מִטָּה שֶׁל כֶּסֶף בְּרֹאשׁ
כָּל גְּדוֹלֵי יִשְׂרָאֵל[49]. אָמְרוּ עַל בִּתּוֹ שֶׁל נַקְדִּימוֹן בֶּן גּוּרְיוֹן שֶׁהָיְתָה מִטָּתָהּ
מוּצַעַת בִּשְׁנֵים עָשָׂר אֲלָפִים דִּינְרֵי זָהָב וְדִינָר צוֹרִי[50] שֶׁל דִּינַר זָהָב הָיָה
יוֹצֵא לָהּ מֵעֶרֶב שַׁבָּת לְעֶרֶב שַׁבָּת לְצִיקֵי קְדֵירָה וְשׁוֹמֶרֶת יָבָם הָיְתָה[51].
וְלָמָּה נִקְרָא שְׁמוֹ נַקְדִּימוֹן בֶּן גּוּרְיוֹן, מִפְּנֵי שֶׁנָּקְדָה לוֹ חַמָּה בַּעֲבוּרוֹ,

---

The Baraisa mentioned, in passing, three wealthy citizens of Jerusalem. Since these were not their real names, the Baraisa explains how these names arose, beginning with the first one.

וְלָמָּה נִקְרָא שְׁמוֹ צִיצִית הַכֶּסֶת — And why was he called by the name Ben Tzitzis HaKesses? — שֶׁהָיָה מוּסָב עַל מִטָּה שֶׁל כֶּסֶף בְּרֹאשׁ כָּל גְּדוֹלֵי יִשְׂרָאֵל — Because he would recline upon the seat cushion (kesses) of a silver couch at the head of all the lay dignitaries of Israel.[49]

The Baraisa mentions another luxurious couch, belonging to a child of one of the other wealthy men named above:

אָמְרוּ עַל בִּתּוֹ שֶׁל נַקְדִּימוֹן בֶּן גּוּרְיוֹן שֶׁהָיְתָה מִטָּתָהּ מוּצַעַת בִּשְׁנֵים עָשָׂר אֲלָפִים דִּינְרֵי זָהָב — They said about the daughter of Nakdimon ben Guryon, that her couch was spread with cushions and linens worth twelve thousand gold dinars. וְדִינָר — Additionally, צוֹרִי שֶׁל דִּינַר זָהָב הָיָה יוֹצֵא לָהּ מֵעֶרֶב שַׁבָּת לְעֶרֶב שַׁבָּת לְצִיקֵי קְדֵירָה — a Tyrian gold dinar[50] was expended from Sabbath eve to Sabbath eve just for the spices she needed to season her pot. וְשׁוֹמֶרֶת יָבָם הָיְתָה — And she was a woman awaiting yibum when this amount was awarded to her.[51]

The Baraisa explains Nakdimon's name:

וְלָמָּה נִקְרָא שְׁמוֹ נַקְדִּימוֹן בֶּן גּוּרְיוֹן — Why was he called by the name Nakdimon ben Guryon? — מִפְּנֵי שֶׁנָּקְדָה לוֹ חַמָּה בַּעֲבוּרוֹ — Because the sun pierced (nakdah) the clouds on his behalf in the following incident.[52]

---

49. According to this explanation, "Ben Tzitzis" was his real name, and "HaKesses" was added as a tribute to his eminence (see Rashi to Gittin 56a).

50. [Tyrian currency is far more valuable than provincial currency; see Kiddushin 11a with Rashi s.v. ושל דבריהם, and elsewhere.]

51. A widow is entitled to a stipend from the estate of her deceased husband for as long as she is living in his house and expresses no intention of remarrying (Kesubos 52b). Nakdimon's daughter was a widow whose husband had died childless, and as such was subject to the law of yibum, which dictates that if a man dies childless, his brother must perform either yibum (by

marrying his brother's widow) or chalitzah; until then, the widow may not remarry (see Deuteronomy 25:5-10). Accordingly, as long as Nakdimon's daughter was awaiting yibum and thus could not remarry, she was entitled to a stipend from her deceased husband's estate. The Sages of the Rabbinic Court awarded her a gold dinar just for the spices to season her pot, in accordance with her financial standing (see Kesubos 65a; see Magen Avos for discussion regarding the discrepancies between our Baraisa and the Gemara's version of this episode).

52. Rashi to Gittin 56a; see Avos HaRosh. ["Nakdimon" contains the root letters of nakdah (נ-ק-ד).]

פַּעַם אַחַת עָלוּ יִשְׂרָאֵל לָרֶגֶל לִירוּשָׁלַיִם⁵³ וְלֹא הָיָה לָהֶם מַיִם לִשְׁתּוֹת, הָלַךְ אֵצֶל שַׂר אֶחָד⁵⁴ וְאָמַר לוֹ: הַלְוֵינִי שְׁתֵּים עֶשְׂרֵה עֲיָנוֹת מַיִם מִכָּאן וְעַד יוֹם פְּלוֹנִי, אִם אֵינִי נוֹתֵן לְךָ שְׁתֵּים עֶשְׂרֵה מַעְיָנוֹת מַיִם אֲנִי נוֹתֵן לְךָ שְׁתֵּים עָשָׂר כִּכַּר כֶּסֶף⁵⁵, וְקָבַע לוֹ זְמַן. כֵּיוָן שֶׁהִגִּיעַ זְמַן שָׁלַח לוֹ: שַׁגֵּר לִי שְׁתֵּים עֶשְׂרֵה מַעְיָנוֹת מַיִם אוֹ שְׁתֵּים עָשָׂר כִּכַּר כֶּסֶף. אָמַר לוֹ: עֲדַיִין שָׁהוּת בַּיּוֹם. לִגְלֵג עָלָיו אוֹתוֹ הַשַּׂר וְאָמַר: כָּל הַשָּׁנָה כּוּלָהּ לֹא יָרְדוּ גְּשָׁמִים וְעַכְשָׁיו יֵרְדוּ גְּשָׁמִים. נִכְנַס אוֹתוֹ הַשַּׂר לְבֵית הַמֶּרְחָץ שָׂמֵחַ⁵⁶.

The Baraisa recounts the full story:

פַּעַם אַחַת עָלוּ יִשְׂרָאֵל לָרֶגֶל לִירוּשָׁלַיִם — It once happened that the Jewish people went up to Jerusalem for a Pilgrimage Festival,[53] וְלֹא הָיָה לָהֶם מַיִם לִשְׁתּוֹת — and, due to a drought, there was not enough water for them to drink. הָלַךְ אֵצֶל שַׂר אֶחָד וְאָמַר לוֹ — [Nakdimon ben Guryon] went to a non-Jewish minister[54] and said to him, הַלְוֵינִי שְׁתֵּים עֶשְׂרֵה עֲיָנוֹת מַיִם מִכָּאן — "Lend me twelve wells of water for the pilgrims' use from now וְעַד יוֹם פְּלוֹנִי — until such-and-such a date. אִם אֵינִי נוֹתֵן לְךָ שְׁתֵּים עֶשְׂרֵה מַעְיָנוֹת מַיִם אֲנִי נוֹתֵן — And if I do not give you back twelve wells of water, I לְךָ שְׁתֵּים עָשָׂר כִּכַּר כֶּסֶף — will give you twelve talents of silver instead."[55] וְקָבַע לוֹ זְמַן — The minister agreed, and he set for him a time for the repayment of the water.

כֵּיוָן שֶׁהִגִּיעַ זְמַן שָׁלַח לוֹ — When the time for repayment arrived, [the minister] sent him a message, שַׁגֵּר לִי שְׁתֵּים עֶשְׂרֵה מַעְיָנוֹת מַיִם אוֹ שְׁתֵּים עֶשְׂרֵה כִּכַּר כֶּסֶף — saying, "Send me either the twelve wells of water or the twelve talents of silver that you owe me." אָמַר לוֹ: עֲדַיִין שָׁהוּת בַּיּוֹם — [Nakdimon] responded, "There is still time left in the day to repay the water, for the loan is not due until the day's end." לִגְלֵג עָלָיו אוֹתוֹ הַשַּׂר — The minister mocked him, וְאָמַר: כָּל הַשָּׁנָה כּוּלָהּ לֹא יָרְדוּ גְּשָׁמִים וְעַכְשָׁיו יֵרְדוּ גְּשָׁמִים — saying, "No rain has fallen the entire year, and now he expects that rain will fall in the short time left before the end of the day?" נִכְנַס אוֹתוֹ הַשַּׂר לְבֵית הַמֶּרְחָץ שָׂמֵחַ — The minister entered the bathhouse in joy, confident that he would collect the twelve talents of silver.[56]

---

53. One of the three Pilgrimage Festivals (Pesach, Shavuos, and Succos), for which every Jewish man is obliged to come to Jerusalem and appear in the Temple.

54. This story took place at the end of the Second Temple era, when non-Jews [primarily Romans] wielded great power in the Land of Israel (Maharsha to Taanis 19b).

55. The underground streams feeding these wells were not strong enough to refill them; only rainwater would replenish them. Nakdimon was hoping that rain would come and

refill the wells in time (Binyan Yehoshua, from Rashi to Taanis 19b). He asked for twelve wells to invoke the merit of the Twelve Tribes of Israel to help him repay the loan (Binyan Yehoshua, from Maharsha ibid.).

[A talent (kikar) is equivalent to 6,000 silver dinars. Thus, he pledged 72,000 silver dinars, an enormous sum, as security for the water.]

56. By bathing at this time, he was further mocking Nakdimon. While the Jews did not have enough water to drink, he himself had enough even to bathe (Binyan Yehoshua,

וְנַקְדִּימוֹן בֶּן גּוּרְיוֹן לְבֵית הַמִּדְרָשׁ, נִתְעַטֵּף וְעָמַד בִּתְפִלָּה וְאָמַר לְפָנָיו: רִבּוֹנוֹ
שֶׁל עוֹלָם, גָּלוּי וְיָדוּעַ לְפָנֶיךָ שֶׁלֹּא לִכְבוֹדִי עָשִׂיתִי וְלֹא לִכְבוֹד בֵּית אַבָּא עָשִׂיתִי
אֶלָּא לִכְבוֹדְךָ עָשִׂיתִי כְּדֵי שֶׁיִּהְיֶה מַיִם לְעוֹלֵי הָרֶגֶל. מִיָּד נִתְקַשְּׁרוּ שָׁמַיִם
בְּעָבִים וְיָרְדוּ גְשָׁמִים עַד שֶׁנִּתְמַלְּאוּ שְׁתֵּים עֶשְׂרֵה מַעֲיָנוֹת מַיִם וְהוֹתִירוּ.
שָׁלַח לְאוֹתוֹ הַשַּׂר: שַׁגֵּר לִי דְמֵי מַיִם יְתֵירִים שֶׁיֵּשׁ לִי בְּיָדְךָ.57 אָמַר לוֹ: כְּבָר
שָׁקְעָה חַמָּה58 וּמַיִם בִּרְשׁוּתִי יָרְדוּ.59 חָזַר וְנִכְנַס לְבֵית הַמִּדְרָשׁ וְנִתְעַטֵּף וְעָמַד
בִּתְפִלָּה, אָמַר לְפָנָיו: רִבּוֹנוֹ שֶׁל עוֹלָם, עֲשֵׂה לִי נֵס בָּאַחֲרוֹנָה כְּבָרִאשׁוֹנָה.
מִיָּד נָשְׁבָה הָרוּחַ וְנִתְפַּזְּרוּ הֶעָבִים וְזָרְחָה חַמָּה. (וּפָגְעוּ זֶה בָּזֶה וְאָמַר לוֹ: יוֹדֵעַ

וְנַקְדִּימוֹן בֶּן גּוּרְיוֹן לְבֵית הַמִּדְרָשׁ נִתְעַטֵּף וְעָמַד בִּתְפִלָּה — In the meantime, Nakdimon entered the study hall, wrapped himself in his garment, and stood in prayer. וְאָמַר לְפָנָיו: רִבּוֹנוֹ שֶׁל עוֹלָם — He said before [God], "Master of the Universe! גָּלוּי וְיָדוּעַ לְפָנֶיךָ שֶׁלֹּא לִכְבוֹדִי עָשִׂיתִי וְלֹא לִכְבוֹד בֵּית אַבָּא עָשִׂיתִי — It is clearly known before You that I did not act this way and put my fortune at risk for my personal honor, nor did I act for the honor of my father's house. אֶלָּא לִכְבוֹדְךָ עָשִׂיתִי כְּדֵי שֶׁיִּהְיֶה מַיִם לְעוֹלֵי הָרֶגֶל — Rather, I acted for Your honor, so that there would be water for the festival pilgrims." מִיָּד נִתְקַשְּׁרוּ שָׁמַיִם בְּעָבִים וְיָרְדוּ גְשָׁמִים — Immediately, the sky became overcast with clouds, and rain fell עַד שֶׁנִּתְמַלְּאוּ שְׁתֵּים עֶשְׂרֵה מַעֲיָנוֹת מַיִם וְהוֹתִירוּ — until all twelve wells borrowed from the minister were filled with water to their original level and beyond. שָׁלַח לְאוֹתוֹ הַשַּׂר: שַׁגֵּר לִי דְמֵי מַיִם יְתֵירִים שֶׁיֵּשׁ לִי בְּיָדְךָ — After Nakdimon saw that he had "overpaid," he sent a message to the minister, saying, "Send me the money for the extra water that you now owe me."[57] אָמַר לוֹ: כְּבָר שָׁקְעָה חַמָּה וּמַיִם בִּרְשׁוּתִי יָרְדוּ — [The minister] said to him in reply, "Actually, the sun had already set before the rain fell,[58] so the rain has fallen in my possession, i.e., past the deadline."[59] חָזַר וְנִכְנַס לְבֵית הַמִּדְרָשׁ וְנִתְעַטֵּף וְעָמַד בִּתְפִלָּה — [Nakdimon] then re-entered the study hall. He wrapped himself in his garment, stood in prayer, אָמַר לְפָנָיו: רִבּוֹנוֹ שֶׁל עוֹלָם, עֲשֵׂה לִי נֵס בָּאַחֲרוֹנָה כְּבָרִאשׁוֹנָה — and said before [God], "Master of the Universe! Perform a miracle for me again, just as You did before." מִיָּד נָשְׁבָה הָרוּחַ וְנִתְפַּזְּרוּ הֶעָבִים וְזָרְחָה חַמָּה — Immediately, the wind blew, the clouds dispersed, and the sun shone through, demonstrating that the day had not yet ended, and that Nakdimon had repaid the water on time. וּפָגְעוּ זֶה בָּזֶה וְאָמַר לוֹ: יוֹדֵעַ — When they later encountered each other,

from *Maharsha* ibid.).

57. Nakdimon did not mean this seriously; he was merely responding in kind to the minister's earlier mockery of him (*Ben Avraham*, citing *Maharsha* ibid.).

58. He did not actually see the sun set,

because the clouds were blocking his view. He meant only that the time for sunset had passed.

59. And since you did not repay the loan before the deadline, you are obligated to pay me the twelve silver talents, as agreed.

אֲנִי שֶׁלֹּא הִרְעִישׁ הַקָּדוֹשׁ בָּרוּךְ הוּא אֶת עוֹלָמוֹ אֶלָּא בִּשְׁבִילְךָ). וְלָמָּה נִקְרָא
שְׁמוֹ כַּלְבָּא שָׂבוּעַ, שֶׁכָּל הַנִּכְנָס לְבֵיתוֹ רָעֵב כְּכֶלֶב הָיָה יוֹצֵא מִבֵּיתוֹ שָׂבֵעַ.[60]
וּכְשֶׁבָּא אַסְפַּסְיָינוֹס קֵיסָר לְהַחֲרִיב אֶת יְרוּשָׁלַיִם בִּקְּשׁוּ קַנָּאִים לִשְׂרוֹף כָּל
הַטּוֹב הַהוּא בָּאֵשׁ. אָמַר לָהֶם כַּלְבָּא שָׂבוּעַ: מִפְּנֵי מָה אַתֶּם מַחֲרִיבִים אֶת הָעִיר
הַזֹּאת וְאַתֶּם מְבַקְּשִׁים כָּל הַטּוֹב הַזֶּה לִשְׂרוֹף בָּאֵשׁ. הַמְתִּינוּ לִי עַד שֶׁאֶכָּנֵס
וְאֶרְאֶה מַה יֵּשׁ לִי בְּתוֹךְ הַבַּיִת. הָלַךְ וּמָצָא שֶׁיֵּשׁ לוֹ מְזוֹן עֶשְׂרִים וּשְׁתַּיִם
שָׁנָה סְעוּדָה לְכָל אֶחָד וְאֶחָד מִירוּשָׁלַיִם. מִיָּד צִוָּה גְּרָשׁוּ וּבְרְרוּ וְטָחֲנוּ וְרִקְּדוּ
וְלָשׁוּ וְאָפוּ וְהִתְקִינוּ מְזוֹן עֶשְׂרִים וּשְׁתַּיִם שָׁנָה לְכָל אֶחָד וְאֶחָד מִירוּשָׁלַיִם[62]

אֲנִי שֶׁלֹּא הִרְעִישׁ הַקָּדוֹשׁ בָּרוּךְ הוּא אֶת עוֹלָמוֹ אֶלָּא בִּשְׁבִילְךָ — [the minister] said
to him, "I know that the Holy One, Blessed is He, agitated His world, by
sending a drought-ending rainstorm so late in the season, only for your sake."

The Baraisa explains the name of the third wealthy person:
וְלָמָּה נִקְרָא שְׁמוֹ כַּלְבָּא שָׂבוּעַ — And why was he called by the name Kalba
Savua? שֶׁכָּל הַנִּכְנָס לְבֵיתוֹ רָעֵב כְּכֶלֶב הָיָה יוֹצֵא מִבֵּיתוֹ שָׂבֵעַ — Because anyone
who entered his house as hungry as a dog (kalba) left satisfied (savua).[60]

The Gemara (Gittin 56a) relates that during the Roman campaign against Jerusalem that preceded the destruction of the Second Temple, the three wealthy
men named above had enough supplies to enable the inhabitants of the city
to hold out against a Roman siege for many years. The zealots among them,
however, favored open battle with the Romans.[61] In an attempt to force the
residents of the city to join them, they burned the storehouses of supplies to the
ground, and a famine ensued. The Baraisa relates some details of this episode:
וּכְשֶׁבָּא אַסְפַּסְיָינוֹס קֵיסָר לְהַחֲרִיב אֶת יְרוּשָׁלַיִם — When Vespasian Caesar
came to destroy Jerusalem, בִּקְּשׁוּ קַנָּאִים לִשְׂרוֹף כָּל הַטּוֹב הַהוּא בָּאֵשׁ — the
zealots sought to burn all of that bounty by fire. אָמַר לָהֶם כַּלְבָּא שָׂבוּעַ —
Kalba Savua said to them, מִפְּנֵי מָה אַתֶּם מַחֲרִיבִים אֶת הָעִיר הַזֹּאת וְאַתֶּם
מְבַקְּשִׁים כָּל הַטּוֹב הַזֶּה לִשְׂרוֹף בָּאֵשׁ — "Why are you destroying this city and
seeking to burn all this bounty by fire? הַמְתִּינוּ לִי עַד שֶׁאֶכָּנֵס וְאֶרְאֶה מַה
יֵּשׁ לִי בְּתוֹךְ הַבַּיִת — Wait for me while I go inside and see what I have in the
house." הָלַךְ וּמָצָא שֶׁיֵּשׁ לוֹ מְזוֹן עֶשְׂרִים וּשְׁתַּיִם שָׁנָה סְעוּדָה לְכָל אֶחָד וְאֶחָד
מִירוּשָׁלַם — He went and found enough food to supply twenty-two years'
worth of meals to each and every person in Jerusalem. מִיָּד צִוָּה גְּרָשׁוּ וּבְרְרוּ
וְטָחֲנוּ וְרִקְּדוּ וְלָשׁוּ וְאָפוּ וְהִתְקִינוּ מְזוֹן עֶשְׂרִים וּשְׁתַּיִם שָׁנָה לְכָל אֶחָד וְאֶחָד מִירוּשָׁלַיִם

---

60. Ownerless dogs typically have less access to food than other animals (Shabbos
155b). This tribute to Ben Kalba Savua
highlights the fact that he did not just give
his petitioners money or food and send

them off. Rather, he welcomed them into
his home, served them food and drink, and
made sure they were fully satisfied before
they left (Magen Avos).

61. See above, 4 §5, with note 42.

וְלֹא הִשְׁגִּיחוּ עָלָיו. מֶה הָיוּ אַנְשֵׁי יְרוּשָׁלַיִם עוֹשִׂין, הָיוּ מְבִיאִין הָעֲגָלִים וְגוֹרְרִים
אוֹתָם בַּמְּגֵרִים וְטוֹחִים אוֹתָם בַּטִּיט. וְעוֹד עָשׂוּ אַנְשֵׁי יְרוּשָׁלַם שׁוֹלְקִין אֶת
הַתֶּבֶן וְאוֹכְלִין אוֹתָם וְכָל אֶחָד וְאֶחָד מִיִּשְׂרָאֵל שָׁרוּוִי[64] נֶגֶד חוֹמוֹתֶיהָ שֶׁל
יְרוּשָׁלַיִם, אָמַר: מִי יִתֶּן לִי חָמֵשׁ תְּמָרִים וְאֵרֵד וְאֶטּוֹל חֲמִשָּׁה רָאשִׁים. נָתְנוּ
לוֹ חֲמִשָּׁה תְּמָרִים, יָרַד וְנָטַל חֲמִשָּׁה רָאשִׁים מֵאַנְשֵׁי אַסְפַּסְיָינוֹס. הֵצִיץ
אַסְפַּסְיָינוֹס בְּצוֹאָתָן וְרָאָה שֶׁאֵין בָּהֶן מִין דָּגָן, וְאָמַר לַחֲיָילוֹת שֶׁלּוֹ: וּמָה
אֵלּוּ שֶׁאֵין אוֹכְלִין אֶלָּא כָּךְ תֶּבֶן בָּךְ הוֹרְגִין בָּהֶן, אִילּוּ הָיוּ אוֹכְלִין כָּל מַה
שֶׁאַתֶּם אוֹכְלִין וְשׁוֹתִין עַל אַחַת כַּמָּה וְכַמָּה שֶׁהָיוּ הוֹרְגִין אֶתְכֶם:

— At that moment, he gave the order and [his workers] piled the grain up, cleansed, ground, sifted, kneaded, and baked it into bread, and he thereby prepared twenty-two years' worth of meals for each and every person in Jerusalem.[62] וְלֹא הִשְׁגִּיחוּ עָלָיו — But the zealots were eager for battle, whatever the costs, and they paid no heed to him. They burned the supplies and a famine ensued.

The Baraisa describes how desperate the people became: מֶה הָיוּ אַנְשֵׁי יְרוּשָׁלַיִם עוֹשִׂין — What would the people of Jerusalem do to ward off starvation? הָיוּ מְבִיאִין הָעֲגָלִים וְגוֹרְרִים אוֹתָם בַּמְּגֵרִים וְטוֹחִים אוֹתָם בַּטִּיט — They would bring calf hides, cut them into small pieces with saws, place them in an oven, and plaster them with clay to soften them. After cleaning them off, they would eat them.[63] וְעוֹד עָשׂוּ אַנְשֵׁי יְרוּשָׁלַם שׁוֹלְקִין אֶת הַתֶּבֶן וְאוֹכְלִין אוֹתָם — Additionally, the people of Jerusalem would boil straw and eat it. וְכָל אֶחָד וְאֶחָד מִיִּשְׂרָאֵל שֶׁשָּׁרוּוִי נֶגֶד חוֹמוֹתֶיהָ שֶׁל יְרוּשָׁלַיִם אָמַר — And each and every Jewish man who was positioned[64] opposite the wall of Jerusalem for defense would say, מִי יִתֶּן לִי חָמֵשׁ תְּמָרִים וְאֵרֵד וְאֶטּוֹל חֲמִשָּׁה רָאשִׁים — "If only someone would give me five dates with which to rally my strength,[65] I would go down to the Romans and take five of their heads." נָתְנוּ לוֹ חֲמִשָּׁה תְּמָרִים — They would give him five dates and, יָרַד וְנָטַל חֲמִשָּׁה רָאשִׁים מֵאַנְשֵׁי אַסְפַּסְיָינוֹס — indeed, he would go down and take five heads off Vespasian's men. הֵצִיץ אַסְפַּסְיָינוֹס בְּצוֹאָתָן וְרָאָה שֶׁאֵין בָּהֶן מִין דָּגָן — Intrigued, Vespasian examined the excrement of [the Jerusalem warriors] that they had left behind, and he noted that they contained no sort of grain. וְאָמַר לַחֲיָילוֹת שֶׁלּוֹ: וּמָה אֵלּוּ שֶׁאֵין אוֹכְלִין — He said to his soldiers, "If these people who eat אֶלָּא כָּךְ תֶּבֶן בָּךְ הוֹרְגִין בָּהֶן nothing but straw are killing so many of [our men], אִילּוּ הָיוּ אוֹכְלִין כָּל מַה שֶׁאַתֶּם אוֹכְלִין וְשׁוֹתִין עַל אַחַת כַּמָּה וְכַמָּה שֶׁהָיוּ הוֹרְגִין אֶתְכֶם — if they were to eat all that you eat and drink, how much more of you would they be able to kill!"

---

62. That is, they baked enough to meet the city's short-term needs and put the rest in storage to be used as necessary (Magen Avos).

63. Hagahos Yaavetz.

64. Emendation follows Nuschas HaGra.

65. Magen Avos.

﴾ פֶּרֶק ז ﴿

א. יוֹסֵף[1] בֶּן יוֹחָנָן אִישׁ יְרוּשָׁלַיִם אוֹמֵר: יְהִי בֵיתְךָ פָּתוּחַ לִרְוָחָה, וְיִהְיוּ
עֲנִיִּים בְּנֵי בֵיתֶךָ, וְאַל תַּרְבֶּה שִׂיחָה עִם הָאִשָּׁה. יְהִי בֵיתְךָ פָּתוּחַ
לִרְוָחָה, כֵּיצַד, מְלַמֵּד שֶׁיְּהֵא בֵיתוֹ שֶׁל אָדָם פָּתוּחַ לִרְוָחָה לַדָּרוֹם וְלַמִּזְרָח
וְלַמַּעֲרָב וְלַצָּפוֹן, כְּגוֹן (שֶׁעָשָׂה) אִיּוֹב, שֶׁעָשָׂה אַרְבָּעָה פְתָחִים לְבֵיתוֹ[2].
וְלָמָּה עָשָׂה אִיּוֹב אַרְבָּעָה פְתָחִים לְבֵיתוֹ. כְּדֵי שֶׁלֹּא יִהְיוּ עֲנִיִּים מִצְטַעֲרִים
לְהַקִּיף אֶת כָּל הַבַּיִת. הַבָּא מִן הַצָּפוֹן יִכָּנֵס כְּדַרְכּוֹ, הַבָּא מִן הַדָּרוֹם
יִכָּנֵס כְּדַרְכּוֹ, וְכֵן לְכָל רוּחַ. לְכָךְ עָשָׂה אִיּוֹב אַרְבָּעָה פְתָחִים לְבֵיתוֹ.

﴾ CHAPTER 7 ﴿

§1 This chapter elaborates the teachings in *Avos* 1:5:

יוֹסֵף בֶּן יוֹחָנָן אִישׁ יְרוּשָׁלַיִם אוֹמֵר: יְהִי בֵיתְךָ פָּתוּחַ לִרְוָחָה וְיִהְיוּ עֲנִיִּים בְּנֵי בֵיתֶךָ
וְאַל תַּרְבֶּה שִׂיחָה עִם הָאִשָּׁה — Yosef[1] ben Yochanan, leader of Jerusalem, says:
Let your house be open wide; let people be members of your household;
and do not converse excessively with the woman.

The Baraisa will expound each of Yosef ben Yochanan's sayings. The first
saying:

יְהִי בֵיתְךָ פָּתוּחַ לִרְוָחָה, כֵּיצַד — "Let your house be open wide" — how so?
מְלַמֵּד שֶׁיְּהֵא בֵיתוֹ שֶׁל אָדָם פָּתוּחַ לִרְוָחָה לַדָּרוֹם וְלַמִּזְרָח וְלַמַּעֲרָב וְלַצָּפוֹן — This
teaches that a person's house should be open wide — to the south, to the
east, to the west, and to the north, כְּגוֹן שֶׁעָשָׂה אִיּוֹב שֶׁעָשָׂה אַרְבָּעָה פְתָחִים
לְבֵיתוֹ — as done by Job, who made four entrances to his house, one on each
side.[2] וְלָמָּה עָשָׂה אִיּוֹב אַרְבָּעָה פְתָחִים לְבֵיתוֹ — And why did Job make four
entrances to his house? כְּדֵי שֶׁלֹּא יִהְיוּ עֲנִיִּים מִצְטַעֲרִים לְהַקִּיף אֶת כָּל הַבַּיִת
— So that the poor people coming to his house from a direction other than the
front should not have to trouble themselves to walk around his entire house
before entering. הַבָּא מִן הַצָּפוֹן יִכָּנֵס כְּדַרְכּוֹ — Rather, one coming from the
north could enter Job's house directly, הַבָּא מִן הַדָּרוֹם יִכָּנֵס כְּדַרְכּוֹ — and
one coming from the south could enter directly, וְכֵן לְכָל רוּחַ — and so with
respect to every other direction. לְכָךְ עָשָׂה אִיּוֹב אַרְבָּעָה פְתָחִים לְבֵיתוֹ — For
this reason Job made four entrances to his house.

---

1. This sage was also called *Yose ben Yo-chanan*; see, for example, *Avos* 1:5, *Shab-bos* 14b. ("Yose" is a diminutive of "Yosef.")
2. Scripture does not state explicitly that Job made four entrances to his house. But this can be deduced from Job's declaration, *No sojourner ever slept outside; I opened*

my doors to the street (*Job* 31:32). If "no sojourner ever slept outside," is it not then obvious "that he opened his doors to the street"? The added declaration, *I opened my doors to the street,* as well as the plural *doors,* must mean that he opened his home in an *expansive* way — by making multiple

וְיִהְיוּ עֲנִיִּים בְּנֵי בֵיתֶךְ. וְלֹא בְּנֵי בֵיתֶךְ מַמָּשׁ[3], אֶלָּא שֶׁיִּהְיוּ [עֲנִיִּים] מְשִׂיחִין
מַה שֶׁאוֹכְלִים וְשׁוֹתִים בְּתוֹךְ בֵּיתֶךְ, כְּדֶרֶךְ שֶׁהָיוּ עֲנִיִּים מְשִׂיחִין מַה שֶׁאוֹכְלִים
וְשׁוֹתִין בְּתוֹךְ בֵּיתוֹ שֶׁל אִיּוֹב. וּכְשֶׁנִּפְגְּשׁוּ זֶה בָּזֶה אָמַר אֶחָד לַחֲבֵרוֹ: מֵאַיִן
אַתָּה בָא, מִתּוֹךְ בֵּיתוֹ שֶׁל אִיּוֹב. וּלְאָן אַתָּה הוֹלֵךְ, לְבֵיתוֹ שֶׁל אִיּוֹב[4].
וּכְשֶׁבָּא עָלָיו הַהוּא פֻּרְעָנִיּוֹת גָּדוֹל אָמַר לִפְנֵי הַקָּדוֹשׁ בָּרוּךְ הוּא[5]: רִבּוֹנוֹ
שֶׁל עוֹלָם, לֹא הָיִיתִי מַאֲכִיל רְעֵבִים וּמַשְׁקֶה צְמֵאִים, שֶׁנֶּאֱמַר (איוב לא, יז)
"וְאֹכַל פִּתִּי לְבַדִּי וְלֹא אָכַל יָתוֹם מִמֶּנָּה". וְלֹא הָיִיתִי מַלְבִּישׁ עֲרוּמִים,

---

The Baraisa expounds Yosef ben Yochanan's second saying:

וְיִהְיוּ עֲנִיִּים בְּנֵי בֵיתֶךְ — "Let poor people be members of your household" — וְלֹא בְּנֵי בֵיתֶךְ מַמָּשׁ — now, this does not mean that they should literally become members of your household.[3]   אֶלָּא שֶׁיִּהְיוּ עֲנִיִּים מְשִׂיחִין מַה שֶׁאוֹכְלִים וְשׁוֹתִים בְּתוֹךְ בֵּיתֶךְ — Rather, it means that poor people should talk about what they eat and drink in your house,   כְּדֶרֶךְ שֶׁהָיוּ עֲנִיִּים מְשִׂיחִין מַה שֶׁאוֹכְלִים וְשׁוֹתִין בְּתוֹךְ בֵּיתוֹ שֶׁל אִיּוֹב — in the way the poor people would talk about what they ate and drank in the house of Job. וּכְשֶׁנִּפְגְּשׁוּ זֶה בָּזֶה אָמַר אֶחָד לַחֲבֵרוֹ: מֵאַיִן אַתָּה בָא — And when they would meet one another in the street, one would say to his friend, "From where are you coming?,"   and — מִתּוֹךְ בֵּיתוֹ שֶׁל אִיּוֹב the other would answer, "From the house of Job — וּלְאָן אַתָּה הוֹלֵךְ, לְבֵיתוֹ שֶׁל אִיּוֹב — and where are you going?" to which the first would reply, "I am going to the house of Job!"[4]

The Baraisa presents another aspect of Job's charitableness and contrasts it with the even greater hospitality of Abraham, which will yield yet another understanding of "let poor people be members of your household":

וּכְשֶׁבָּא — And when עָלָיו הַהוּא פֻּרְעָנִיּוֹת גָּדוֹל אָמַר לִפְנֵי הַקָּדוֹשׁ בָּרוּךְ הוּא that great punishment befell [Job], he said before the Holy One, Blessed is He,[5] רִבּוֹנוֹ שֶׁל עוֹלָם, לֹא הָיִיתִי מַאֲכִיל רְעֵבִים וּמַשְׁקֶה צְמֵאִים — "Master of the Universe! Did I not feed the hungry and give drink to the thirsty?" שֶׁנֶּאֱמַר "וְאֹכַל פִּתִּי לְבַדִּי וְלֹא אָכַל יָתוֹם מִמֶּנָּה" — as it is stated, *Nor did I eat my bread in solitude, so that an orphan could not eat from it* (*Job* 31:17). וְלֹא הָיִיתִי מַלְבִּישׁ עֲרוּמִים — "And did I not clothe the naked?,"

---

entrances, one on each side (*Ben Avraham*).

3. This would place an unsustainable drain on one's resources, and result in his actual family members being deprived of their needs (*Ahavas Chesed*, based on *Kesubos* 50a; see also *Binyan Yehoshua*).

4. The point is that the hospitality of your home to the poor should be so commonplace that it becomes a topic of conversation

among the poor, to the point that it seems as if they actually live there; this is the meaning of "let poor people be members of your household" (*Meiri* to *Avos* 1:5).

5. As described in *Job* Chs. 1-2, Job endured extraordinary suffering. The Baraisa now describes Job's questions before God as to why his exceptional righteousness did not spare him from that intense suffering.

שֶׁנֶּאֱמַר (שם שם כ) "וּמִגֵּז כְּבָשַׂי יִתְחַמָּם". אַף עַל פִּי כֵן אָמַר לוֹ הַקָּדוֹשׁ
בָּרוּךְ הוּא לְאִיּוֹב: אִיּוֹב, עֲדַיִין לֹא הִגַּעְתָּ [לַחֲצִי שִׁעוּר] שֶׁל אַבְרָהָם.[6]
אַתָּה יוֹשֵׁב וְשׁוֹהֶה בְּתוֹךְ בֵּיתְךָ וְאוֹרְחִין נִכְנָסִים אֶצְלְךָ. אֶת שֶׁדַּרְכּוֹ
לֶאֱכוֹל פַּת חִטִּים °הֶאֱכִילְתּוֹ פַּת חִטִּים. אֶת שֶׁדַּרְכּוֹ לֶאֱכוֹל בָּשָׂר
הֶאֱכִילְתּוֹ בָּשָׂר. אֶת שֶׁדַּרְכּוֹ לִשְׁתּוֹת יַיִן הִשְׁקִיתוֹ יַיִן. אֲבָל אַבְרָהָם
לֹא עָשָׂה כֵן, אֶלָּא יוֹשֵׁב וּמְהַדֵּר בָּעוֹלָם, וּכְשֶׁיִּמְצָא אוֹרְחִין מַכְנִיסָן
בְּתוֹךְ בֵּיתוֹ. אֶת שֶׁאֵין דַּרְכּוֹ לֶאֱכוֹל פַּת חִטִּין הֶאֱכִילְהוּ פַּת חִטִּין. אֶת
שֶׁאֵין דַּרְכּוֹ לֶאֱכוֹל בָּשָׂר הֶאֱכִילְהוּ בָּשָׂר. וְאֶת שֶׁאֵין דַּרְכּוֹ לִשְׁתּוֹת יַיִן
הִשְׁקָהוּ יַיִן. וְלֹא עוֹד, אֶלָּא עָמַד וּבָנָה פַּלְטֵרִין גְּדוֹלִים עַל הַדְּרָכִים,

שֶׁנֶּאֱמַר "וּמִגֵּז כְּבָשַׂי יִתְחַמָּם" — as it is stated, *Did I ever see a forlorn person
without a garment, or was there ever a destitute person without clothing, whose
loins would not bless me, who would [not] warm himself by the shearings
of my sheep?* (ibid. vv. 19-20). אַף עַל פִּי כֵן אָמַר לוֹ הַקָּדוֹשׁ בָּרוּךְ הוּא לְאִיּוֹב:
אִיּוֹב, עֲדַיִין לֹא הִגַּעְתָּ לַחֲצִי שִׁעוּר שֶׁל אַבְרָהָם — And despite all that, the Holy
One, Blessed is He, said to Job in reply, "Job! You have still not reached even
half the measure of kindness performed by Abraham![6] אַתָּה יוֹשֵׁב וְשׁוֹהֶה
בְּתוֹךְ בֵּיתְךָ וְאוֹרְחִין נִכְנָסִים אֶצְלְךָ — You would sit and wait in your house for
guests to come to you. אֶת שֶׁדַּרְכּוֹ לֶאֱכוֹל פַּת חִטִּים הֶאֱכַלְתּוֹ פַּת חִטִּים — And
after they would come, one accustomed to eat wheat bread you would feed
wheat bread, אֶת שֶׁדַּרְכּוֹ לֶאֱכוֹל בָּשָׂר הֶאֱכַלְתּוֹ בָּשָׂר — one accustomed to
eat meat you would feed meat, אֶת שֶׁדַּרְכּוֹ לִשְׁתּוֹת יַיִן הִשְׁקִיתוֹ יַיִן — and one
accustomed to drink wine you would give wine to drink. Only such people
would you provide with these superior foods and beverages, whereas to the
others you would give only the coarser fare to which they were accustomed.
אֲבָל אַבְרָהָם לֹא עָשָׂה כֵן, אֶלָּא יוֹשֵׁב וּמְהַדֵּר בָּעוֹלָם — However, Abraham did
not act this way. Rather, he would go searching the world outside his house,
וּכְשֶׁיִּמְצָא אוֹרְחִין מַכְנִיסָן בְּתוֹךְ בֵּיתוֹ — and when he would find guests whom he
could host, he would bring them into his house. אֶת שֶׁאֵין דַּרְכּוֹ לֶאֱכוֹל פַּת חִטִּין
הֶאֱכִילְהוּ פַּת חִטִּין — Then, even one *not* accustomed to eat wheat bread he
would feed wheat bread, אֶת שֶׁאֵין דַּרְכּוֹ לֶאֱכוֹל בָּשָׂר הֶאֱכִילְהוּ בָּשָׂר — even one
not accustomed to eat meat he would feed meat, וְאֶת שֶׁאֵין דַּרְכּוֹ לִשְׁתּוֹת יַיִן
הִשְׁקָהוּ יַיִן — and even one *not* accustomed to drink wine he would give wine to
drink. He gave these delicacies to all! וְלֹא עוֹד, אֶלָּא עָמַד וּבָנָה פַּלְטֵרִין גְּדוֹלִים עַל
הַדְּרָכִים — Not only that, but he even built a large mansion at the crossroads,[7]

6. We are taught elsewhere that Job thought
to equate himself with Abraham (see *Tanchuma HaYashan, Vayishlach* §8). Therefore,
God responded to Job that he was mistaken

in believing so (*Ahavas Chesed*). [See also
Avos DeRabbi Nassan, Nusach 2, Ch. 14.]
7. Some understand this in the plural: He
built *several* mansions on *several* roads (see

וְהִנִּיחַ מַאֲכָל וּמַשְׁקֶה, וְכָל הַבָּא וְנִכְנָס אָכַל וְשָׁתָה וּבֵרַךְ לַשָּׁמַיִם8, לְפִיכָךְ
נַעֲשֵׂית לוֹ נַחַת רוּחַ9. וְכָל שֶׁהַפֶּה שׁוֹאֵל מָצוּי בְּתוֹךְ בֵּיתוֹ שֶׁל אַבְרָהָם10,
שֶׁנֶּאֱמַר (בראשית כא, לב) "וַיִּטַּע אֶשֶׁל בִּבְאֵר שָׁבַע"11:

ב • לַמֵּד בְּנֵי בֵיתְךָ עֲנָוָה12, שֶׁבִּזְמַן שֶׁאָדָם עָנָו וּבְנֵי בֵיתוֹ עֲנָוְתָנִין13,

---

וְכָל **וְהִנִּיחַ מַאֲכָל וּמַשְׁקֶה** — and placed food and drink there for passersby. **וְכָל הַבָּא וְנִכְנָס אָכַל וְשָׁתָה וּבֵרַךְ לַשָּׁמַיִם** — And whoever came and entered ate and drank and then gave thanks to God in Heaven.[8] **לְפִיכָךְ נַעֲשֵׂית לוֹ נַחַת רוּחַ** — Therefore, a great satisfaction was given to him.[9] **וְכָל שֶׁהַפֶּה שׁוֹאֵל מָצוּי** **בְּתוֹךְ בֵּיתוֹ שֶׁל אַבְרָהָם** — Moreover, anything that the mouth could ask for was available in the house of Abraham,"[10] **שֶׁנֶּאֱמַר "וַיִּטַּע אֶשֶׁל בִּבְאֵר שָׁבַע"** — as it is stated, [Abraham] planted an "eshel" in Beer-sheba (Genesis 21:32).[11]

§2 The Baraisa presents an additional understanding of Yosef ben Yochanan's second saying:

לַמֵּד בְּנֵי בֵיתְךָ עֲנָוָה — Teach the members of your household humility.[12] **שֶׁבִּזְמַן שֶׁאָדָם עָנָו וּבְנֵי בֵיתוֹ עֲנָוְתָנִין** — For when a person is humble, and

---

Magen Avos and Avos HaRosh [Vol. 1]).

8. How did this occur? The same scenario would repeat itself time and again: After enjoying their meal, Abraham's guests wished to bless him, to which he would respond, "Do you think that it was *my* food that you ate? It was actually the food belonging to the God of the World that you ate. Therefore, thank, praise, and bless the One Who spoke and the world came into being" (*Binyan Yehoshua*, from *Sotah* 10a). In this way, Abraham managed not only to offer kind hospitality, but also to make God's Name known and loved throughout the world.

9. Since Abraham provided his guests with great satisfaction, and additionally utilized that opportunity to spread the recognition of God, God provided him, too, with great satisfaction, which came in the form of bearing a son in his old age, receiving many other blessings, and being spared from suffering any painful tribulations [as did Job, who had *not* provided his guests with such satisfaction] (*Binyan Yehoshua*). Similarly, we are taught in *Midrash Tanchuma* (*Parashas Ki Seitzei* §2) that one merits to have children in reward for hosting guests (*Avos HaRosh* [Vol. 1]).

Alternatively, the Baraisa means that a great satisfaction was given to Abraham's

guest. That is, because the guest enjoyed himself and blessed God, God reciprocated by blessing the food the guest had eaten so that it satisfied him greatly (*Magen Avos*, preferred explanation).

10. Abraham had such foresight in caring for his guests that he would stock his house with whatever they might request (*Magen Avos*, final approach).

11. In *Bereishis Rabbah* (ad loc.), R' Yehudah explains that the term אֶשֶׁל, *eshel*, of this *Genesis* verse means an orchard, and it alludes to the fact that Abraham would say to his guests, "Ask for anything you would like: figs, grapes, or pomegranates" [as the letters of אֶשֶׁל can be rearranged to spell שְׁאַל, *ask* (*Matnos Kehunah* ad loc.)]. Hence, the Baraisa proves from this verse that anything one could request was available in Abraham's house (*Binyan Yehoshua*).

We now have another understanding of the directive, "Let poor people be members of your household": be so hospitable to the poor people entering your home as guests, that they feel as at home there as members of your own household do (*Meiri* to *Avos* 1:5).

12. Accordingly, וְיִהְיוּ עֲנִיִּים בְּנֵי בֵיתֶךָ, is rendered, "Let the members of your household

כְּשֶׁבָּא עָנִי וְעָמַד עַל פִּתְחוֹ שֶׁל בַּעַל הַבַּיִת וְאָמַר לָהֶם: אֲבִיכֶם יֵשׁ בְּכָאן,
יֹאמְרוּ לוֹ: הֵן, בֹּא וְהִכָּנֵס. עַד שֶׁלֹּא נִכְנָס, וְשֻׁלְחָן [הָיָה עָרוּךְ] לְפָנָיו. נִכְנָס,
וְאָכַל וְשָׁתָה, וּבֵרֵךְ לְשֵׁם שָׁמַיִם[14], נַעֲשֵׂית לוֹ נַחַת רוּחַ גְּדוֹלָה[15]. וּבִזְמַן
שֶׁאָדָם עִנְוְותָן[16] וּבְנֵי בֵיתוֹ קַפְּדָנִין[17], וּבָא עָנִי וְעָמַד עַל פִּתְחוֹ וְאָמַר לָהֶם:

---

the members of his household are humble,[13]   כְּשֶׁבָּא עָנִי וְעָמַד עַל פִּתְחוֹ
שֶׁל בַּעַל הַבַּיִת וְאָמַר לָהֶם: אֲבִיכֶם יֵשׁ בְּכָאן — then when a poor person comes
and stands at the householder's door and asks them, "Is your father
here?,"   יֹאמְרוּ לוֹ: הֵן, בֹּא וְהִכָּנֵס — they cordially answer him, "Yes, he
is. Come in!"   עַד שֶׁלֹּא נִכְנָס וְשֻׁלְחָן הָיָה עָרוּךְ לְפָנָיו — And even before he
enters, the table is already set before him.   נִכְנָס וְאָכַל וְשָׁתָה וּבֵרֵךְ לְשֵׁם
שָׁמַיִם — Then, he enters, eats and drinks, and gives thanks to the Name
of God in Heaven.[14]   נַעֲשֵׂית לוֹ נַחַת רוּחַ גְּדוֹלָה — And through this, a great
satisfaction is given to him.[15]   וּבִזְמַן שֶׁאֵין אָדָם עִנְוְותָן וּבְנֵי בֵיתוֹ קַפְּדָנִין
— However, when a person is not humble,[16] and as a result, the members of
his household are short-tempered,[17]   וּבָא עָנִי וְעָמַד עַל פִּתְחוֹ וְאָמַר לָהֶם:

---

be humble people," interpreting עֲנִיִּים not as
the plural of עָנִי, poor man, but as the plural
of עָנָו, humble man (Meiri to Avos 1:5; Binyan Yehoshua).

Alternatively, עֲנִיִּים is still understood to
mean poor people, but וְיִהְיוּ עֲנִיִּים בְּנֵי בֵיתֶךָ, is
now interpreted to mean, "Let the members
of your household be [like] poor people [who
are humble]" (see Magen Avos, Ahavas
Chesed, and Ben Avraham). For humility is
a trait commonly seen in poor people, as it
states in Proverbs (18:12): A pauper utters
supplications, but a rich one responds with
brazen words (Magen Avos, second approach; Ahavas Chesed, Ben Avraham).

[Perhaps, the reason the Baraisa does not
introduce this new interpretation with the
words דָּבָר אַחֵר, another explanation, is that
the two interpretations are not independent,
but complementary: If one wishes to allow
poor people to be welcome in his home, he
must be sure to teach his family the trait of
humility, as illustrated below (Ben Avraham).]

13. Since the head of the house conducts
himself with humility, it is natural that his
family members will behave the same way.
Conversely, when he lacks this trait (as in the
next scenario), his family will likely follow suit
(Mefaresh). The Baraisa is subtly teaching us
that the truly best way to foster humility in

the home is to practice it ourselves (Magen
Avos). [Possibly, that is why the Baraisa uses
the term לִמּוֹד, which literally means learn,
instead of the word, לַמֵּד, teach (ibid.).]

14. What an extraordinary kindness to this
poor man. Even without having to shame
himself by asking, his unspoken request for
food is granted in full! (Magen Avos).

15. I.e., to the poor person, who surely en-
joys the generous hospitality much more
than he would have enjoyed a simple hand-
out. Alternatively, a satisfying feeling is
given to the householder, for the reward for
the charity done in his home is far greater
than the monetary benefit received by the
poor person (Ben Avraham).

The Baraisa views the kindness displayed
in this scenario as a direct outgrowth of humility. When one is humble, he can receive
guests — especially poor ones — without
any airs, and be ready to serve them graciously (Magen Avos).

16. [We have restored the word אֵין, not, which
was omitted from the Vilna text, but appears
in many earlier editions and manuscripts,
and in the words of the commentators.]

17. [See note 13.] Lack of humility breeds
intolerance and insensitivity to the needs
and feelings of others.

אֲבִיכֶם יֵשׁ בְּכָאן, וְאוֹמְרִים לוֹ: לֹא, וְגוֹעֲרִים בּוֹ וְהוֹצִיאוּ בִּנְזִיפָה.[18] דָּבָר אַחֵר, לְמוֹד בְּנֵי בֵיתְךָ עֲנָוָה, כֵּיצַד, בִּזְמַן שֶׁאָדָם עִנְוְותָן, וּבְנֵי בֵיתוֹ עִנְוְותָנִין, וְהָלַךְ לוֹ לִמְדִינַת הַיָּם וְאָמַר: מוֹדֶה אֲנִי לְפָנֶיךָ ה' אֱלֹהַי שֶׁאִשְׁתִּי אֵינָה עוֹשָׂה מְרִיבָה אֵצֶל אֲחֵרִים.[19] לִבּוֹ אֵין מִתְפַּחֵד עָלָיו וְדַעְתּוֹ מְיוּשֶׁבֶת בִּמְקוֹמוֹ, עַד שָׁעָה שֶׁיַּחֲזוֹר.[20] וּבִזְמַן שֶׁאֵין אָדָם עִנְוְותָן, וּבְנֵי בֵיתוֹ קַפְּדָנִין, וְהָלַךְ לוֹ לִמְדִינַת הַיָּם וְאוֹמֵר: יְהִי רָצוֹן מִלְּפָנֶיךָ ה' אֱלֹהַי שֶׁאֵין אִשְׁתִּי עוֹשָׂה מְרִיבָה אֵצֶל אֲחֵרִים וּבָנַי אַל יַעֲשׂוּ מְרִיבָה. לִבּוֹ מִתְפַּחֵד עָלָיו וְדַעְתּוֹ אֵינָה מְיוּשֶׁבֶת, עַד שֶׁיַּחֲזוֹר.[21]

אֲבִיכֶם יֵשׁ בְּכָאן — then when a poor person comes and stands by the opening of his house and asks [his children], "Is your father here?," וְאוֹמְרִים לוֹ: לֹא, — they reply to him discourteously, "No, he is not!" וְגוֹעֲרִים בּוֹ וְהוֹצִיאוּ בִּנְזִיפָה — and then they scold him, and send him away with reproach.[18]

Another application of this last interpretation of Yosef ben Yochanan's second saying:

דָּבָר אַחֵר, לְמוֹד בְּנֵי בֵיתְךָ עֲנָוָה, כֵּיצַד — Alternatively: "Teach the members of your household humility" — how so? בִּזְמַן שֶׁאָדָם עִנְוְותָן וּבְנֵי בֵיתוֹ עִנְוְותָנִין — When a person is humble and the members of his household are humble, וְאָמַר: מוֹדֶה אֲנִי לְפָנֶיךָ — then when he travels overseas וְהָלַךְ לוֹ לִמְדִינַת הַיָּם ה' אֱלֹהַי — and says before God, "I gratefully thank you, Hashem, my God, שֶׁאִשְׁתִּי אֵינָה עוֹשָׂה מְרִיבָה אֵצֶל אֲחֵרִים — that my wife is not quarreling with others,"[19] לִבּוֹ אֵין מִתְפַּחֵד עָלָיו וְדַעְתּוֹ מְיוּשֶׁבֶת בִּמְקוֹמוֹ — he says so because his heart is not afraid and his mind is at ease, confident that peace and humility reign back home, עַד שָׁעָה שֶׁיַּחֲזוֹר — until the time that he returns home.[20] וּבִזְמַן שֶׁאֵין אָדָם עִנְוְותָן וּבְנֵי בֵיתוֹ קַפְּדָנִין — However, when a person is not humble, and as a result, the members of his household are short-tempered, וְאוֹמֵר: יְהִי רָצוֹן מִלְּפָנֶיךָ — then when he travels overseas וְהָלַךְ לוֹ לִמְדִינַת הַיָּם ה' אֱלֹהַי — and says imploringly before God, "May it be Your will, Hashem, my God, שֶׁאֵין אִשְׁתִּי עוֹשָׂה מְרִיבָה אֵצֶל אֲחֵרִים — that my wife is not quarreling with others," וּבָנַי אַל יַעֲשׂוּ מְרִיבָה — and that my children shall not quarrel with others," לִבּוֹ מִתְפַּחֵד עָלָיו וְדַעְתּוֹ אֵינָה מְיוּשֶׁבֶת — his heart is afraid and his mind is ill at ease, concerned that strife prevails back home, עַד שֶׁיַּחֲזוֹר — until he returns home.[21]

---

18. In essence, then, Yosef ben Yochanan teaches that if one truly wishes to make poor people feel like members of his household, he must cultivate humility in his home, so that no needy person is ever made to feel unwelcome there (*Ben Avraham, Avos Ha-Rosh* [Vol. 1]; see note 12).

19. That is, with the poor people who visit

his home (*Magen Avos*).

20. It is because of this confidence that he thanks God for the peace that reigns back home, even though he has no direct knowledge that this is so.

21. It is because of this unease that he prays to God that peace *shall* reign back home. [Thus, the Baraisa says that when he is

וְאַל תַּרְבֶּה שִׂיחָה עִם הָאִשָּׁה, וַאֲפִילוּ הִיא אִשְׁתּוֹ[22], וְאֵין צָרִיךְ לוֹמַר
בְּאֵשֶׁת חֲבֵרוֹ[23], שֶׁכָּל זְמַן שֶׁאָדָם מַרְבֶּה שִׂיחָה עִם הָאִשָּׁה גּוֹרֵם רָעָה
לְעַצְמוֹ[24], וּבוֹטֵל מִדִּבְרֵי תוֹרָה, וְסוֹפוֹ יוֹרֵשׁ גֵּיהִנֹּם:

ג. (דָּבָר אַחֵר,) אַל תַּרְבֶּה שִׂיחָה עִם הָאִשָּׁה, כֵּיצַד[26], בִּזְמַן שֶׁאָדָם בָּא לְבֵית
הַמִּדְרָשׁ וְלֹא הָיוּ נוֹהֲגִין בּוֹ כָּבוֹד אוֹ שֶׁעִרְעֵר עִם חֲבֵרוֹ, אַל יֵלֵךְ וְיֹאמַר
לְאִשְׁתּוֹ: כָּךְ וְכָךְ עִרְעַרְתִּי עִם חֲבֵירִי כָּךְ וְכָךְ אָמַר לִי כָּךְ וְכָךְ אָמַרְתִּי לוֹ,

The Baraisa expounds Yosef ben Yochanan's third saying:

וְאַל תַּרְבֶּה שִׂיחָה עִם הָאִשָּׁה — "And do not converse excessively with the woman" — וַאֲפִילוּ הִיא אִשְׁתּוֹ — this means even if she is his wife,[22] וְאֵין צָרִיךְ
לוֹמַר בְּאֵשֶׁת חֲבֵרוֹ — and needless to say that it is certainly true regarding his
friend's wife.[23] שֶׁכָּל זְמַן שֶׁאָדָם מַרְבֶּה שִׂיחָה עִם הָאִשָּׁה — For any time that
a person converses excessively with the woman, גּוֹרֵם רָעָה לְעַצְמוֹ וּבוֹטֵל
מִדִּבְרֵי תוֹרָה — he causes evil to himself,[24] and neglects
Torah study; and he will eventually inherit Gehinnom for both of those sins.[25]

§3 An alternative approach to Yosef ben Yochanan's third saying:

דָּבָר אַחֵר, אַל תַּרְבֶּה שִׂיחָה עִם הָאִשָּׁה, כֵּיצַד — Another explanation of the
caution, "Do not converse excessively with the woman" — how so?[26] בִּזְמַן
שֶׁאָדָם בָּא לְבֵית הַמִּדְרָשׁ וְלֹא הָיוּ נוֹהֲגִין בּוֹ כָּבוֹד — When a man comes to the
study hall and they do not treat him there with respect, אוֹ שֶׁעִרְעֵר עִם
חֲבֵרוֹ — or when he has a dispute with his friend, אַל יֵלֵךְ וְיֹאמַר לְאִשְׁתּוֹ: כָּךְ
וְכָךְ עִרְעַרְתִּי עִם חֲבֵירִי — he should not then go and tell his wife, "I had such-
and-such a dispute with my friend; כָּךְ וְכָךְ אָמַר לִי כָּךְ וְכָךְ אָמַרְתִּי לוֹ — such-
and-such is what he said to me and such-and-such is what I replied to him,"

---

away overseas, the humble person "gives
thanks" that peace reigns back home (as he
is confident that this is so), whereas the person who is not humble "prays" that peace
shall reign back home (as he fears that this
is not the case).]

22. As "*the woman*" implies the one who
is specific to him (*Ben Avraham*, from
Rav).

23. Because when one idly converses with
another man's wife, there is the added worry
that onlookers may suspect him of illicit
behavior (*Binyan Yehoshua*, from *Rashi* to
Avos ibid.). Alternatively, excessive conversation with another man's wife is not only
ill-advised, but even forbidden (*Ahavas
Chesed, Avos HaRosh* [Vol. 1]).

Meiri (ibid.) notes that this "excessive
conversation" refers exclusively to *idle* chatter. Purposeful discussion, however, is not
included in Yosef ben Yochanan's injunction.
(See also *Binyan Yehoshua*.)

24. When one chatters excessively with his
wife, he will almost inevitably share with
her his grievances toward others. This will
lead her to incite him to become involved
in controversy (*Ahavas Chesed,* from first
explanation of *Rav* on *Avos* 1:5), which is
a great evil.

25. *Ben Avraham.*

26. What follows is the second explanation given by *Rav* on *Avos* 1:5 (*Ahavas
Chesed*).

מִפְּנֵי שֶׁבּוֹזֶה אֶת עַצְמוֹ (וּבוֹזֶה אֶת אִשְׁתּוֹ) וּבוֹזֶה אֶת חֲבֵרוֹ, וְאִשְׁתּוֹ,
שֶׁהָיְתָה נוֹהֶגֶת בּוֹ כָּבוֹד, עוֹמֶדֶת וּמְשַׂחֶקֶת עָלָיו[27]. כֵּיוָן שֶׁשָּׁמַע חֲבֵרוֹ,
אָמַר: אוֹי לִי, דְּבָרִים שֶׁבֵּינוֹ לְבֵינִי הָלַךְ וְשָׂחָן לְאִשְׁתּוֹ. וְנִמְצָא אוֹתוֹ
הָאִישׁ בּוֹזֶה אֶת עַצְמוֹ וְאֶת אִשְׁתּוֹ וְאֶת חֲבֵירוֹ:

מִפְּנֵי שֶׁבּוֹזֶה אֶת עַצְמוֹ וּבוֹזֶה אֶת חֲבֵרוֹ — because by doing so, he debases him-self and debases his friend.   וְאִשְׁתּוֹ שֶׁהָיְתָה נוֹהֶגֶת בּוֹ כָּבוֹד עוֹמֶדֶת וּמְשַׂחֶקֶת עָלָיו — And his wife, who had previously acted toward him with respect, now rises up and makes fun of him.[27]   כֵּיוָן שֶׁשָּׁמַע חֲבֵרוֹ, אָמַר: אוֹי לִי — Then his friend hears about this and says, "Woe is me!   דְּבָרִים שֶׁבֵּינוֹ לְבֵינִי הָלַךְ וְשָׂחָן לְאִשְׁתּוֹ — The disparaging words that were traded between us in private he went and told them to his wife!"   וְנִמְצָא אוֹתוֹ הָאִישׁ בּוֹזֶה אֶת עַצְמוֹ וְאֶת אִשְׁתּוֹ וְאֶת חֲבֵירוֹ — It thus emerges that that man who told his wife about his dispute has debased himself and his wife and his friend!

---

27. And this is obviously a disgrace to him. In addition, it also causes a disgrace to his wife, because after hearing about his feud, she very likely will go and feud with the other man's wife (*Binyan Yehoshua*, from *Rashi* ad loc.; *Avos* DeRabbi Nassan, Nusach 2, Ch. 15); or alternatively, because it is very probable that he will respond to his wife's insulting comments by shaming her with some biting comments of his own (*Magen Avos, Ben Avraham*).

﴾ פֶּרֶק ח ﴿

א. יְהוֹשֻׁעַ בֶּן פְּרַחְיָה וְנִתַּאי הָאַרְבֵּלִי קִבְּלוּ מֵהֶם, יְהוֹשֻׁעַ בֶּן פְּרַחְיָה אוֹמֵר: עֲשֵׂה לְךָ רַב, וּקְנֵה לְךָ חָבֵר, וֶהֱוֵי דָן אֶת כָּל הָאָדָם לְכַף זְכוּת.[1] עֲשֵׂה לְךָ רַב, כֵּיצַד, מְלַמֵּד שֶׁיַּעֲשֶׂה לוֹ אֶת רַבּוֹ קֶבַע, וְיִלְמַד מִמֶּנּוּ מִקְרָא וּמִשְׁנָה מִדְרָשׁ הֲלָכוֹת וְאַגָּדוֹת,[3] טַעַם שֶׁהִנִּיחַ לוֹ בַּמִּקְרָא סוֹף שֶׁיֹּאמַר לוֹ בַּמִּשְׁנָה,[4] טַעַם שֶׁהִנִּיחַ לוֹ בַּמִּדְרָשׁ סוֹף שֶׁיֹּאמַר לוֹ בַּהֲלָכוֹת,

﴾ CHAPTER 8 ﴿

§1 The Baraisa proceeds to elaborate *Avos* 1:6, which states: יְהוֹשֻׁעַ בֶּן פְּרַחְיָה וְנִתַּאי הָאַרְבֵּלִי קִבְּלוּ מֵהֶם — **Yehoshua ben Perachyah and Nittai of Arbel received** the tradition **from them,** i.e, from Yose ben Yoezer and Yose ben Yochanan, the previous pair of Sages, mentioned in Mishnah 4. יְהוֹשֻׁעַ בֶּן פְּרַחְיָה אוֹמֵר — **Yehoshua ben Perachyah says:** עֲשֵׂה לְךָ רַב — **Appoint a teacher for yourself;** וּקְנֵה לְךָ חָבֵר — **acquire a friend for yourself;** וֶהֱוֵי דָן אֶת כָּל הָאָדָם לְכַף זְכוּת — **and judge every person favorably.**[1]

The Baraisa elucidates the first teaching of Yehoshua ben Perachyah: עֲשֵׂה לְךָ רַב, כֵּיצַד — **"Appoint a teacher for yourself" — how so?** מְלַמֵּד שֶׁיַּעֲשֶׂה לוֹ אֶת רַבּוֹ קֶבַע — **This teaches that one should choose for himself a steady teacher,**[2] וְיִלְמַד מִמֶּנּוּ מִקְרָא וּמִשְׁנָה מִדְרָשׁ הֲלָכוֹת וְאַגָּדוֹת — **and study** all branches of the Torah from him — **Scripture, Mishnah, Midrash, Halachos, and Aggados.**[3] טַעַם שֶׁהִנִּיחַ לוֹ בַּמִּקְרָא סוֹף שֶׁיֹּאמַר לוֹ בַּמִּשְׁנָה — **The benefit** of studying under a single teacher is that **the explanation** of a particular verse **that he might omit during** their study of **Scripture, he will eventually explain to him during** their study of **the** relevant **Mishnah;**[4] the explanation of something that he might omit during their study of Mishnah, he will eventually explain to him during their study of the relevant Midrash; טַעַם שֶׁהִנִּיחַ לוֹ בַּמִּדְרָשׁ סוֹף שֶׁיֹּאמַר לוֹ בַּהֲלָכוֹת — **the explanation** of something **that he might omit during** their study of **Midrash, he will eventually explain to him during**

---

1. I.e., give him the benefit of the doubt (*Binyan Yehoshua,* from *Rashi* on *Avos*).

2. [Literally, *make his teacher steady for himself.*] Our translation fits precisely with the emendation of *Gra:* שֶׁיַּעֲשֶׂה לוֹ ״רַב קָבוּעַ״, and this seems to have been the reading of the *Mefaresh* as well.

3. "Scripture" is the entire Bible; "Mishnah" is a general term for the Oral Tradition explaining the laws of the Torah; "Midrash" refers to the [Halachic] expositions of

Scripture; "Halachos" are the various rulings and halachic discussions; and "Aggados" are the ethical and homiletic teachings (see *Magen Avos*). In short, one should choose a single teacher from whom to learn the entire range of Torah subjects.

4. If one's teacher did not explain a particular verse while they were learning Scripture, he will have to explain it when they study the Mishnah that is relevant to that verse. [Indeed, it is quite possible that the teacher's

טַעַם שֶׁהִנִּיחַ לוֹ בַּהֲלָכוֹת סוֹף שֶׁיֹּאמַר לוֹ בַּהַגָּדָה, נִמְצָא הָאָדָם הַהוּא
[יוֹשֵׁב בִּמְקוֹמוֹ] וּמָלֵא טוֹב וּבְרָכָה:[6]

ב. הָיָה[7] רַבִּי מֵאִיר אוֹמֵר: הַלּוֹמֵד תּוֹרָה מֵרַב אֶחָד לְמָה הוּא דוֹמֶה,

their study of the relevant **Halachos**; טַעַם שֶׁהִנִּיחַ לוֹ בַּהֲלָכוֹת סוֹף שֶׁיֹּאמַר לוֹ
בַּהַגָּדָה — and **the explanation** of something that he might omit during their
study of **Halachos**, he will eventually explain to him during their study of the
relevant **Aggadah**. נִמְצָא הָאָדָם הַהוּא יוֹשֵׁב בִּמְקוֹמוֹ — It emerges that this
person remains in his place[5] וּמָלֵא טוֹב וּבְרָכָה — and is filled with good and
blessing.[6]

§2 The Baraisa cites a parable that further illustrates Yehoshua ben Perachyah's teaching:[7]

הַלּוֹמֵד תּוֹרָה מֵרַב אֶחָד לְמָה הוּא — **R' Meir used to say:** הָיָה רַבִּי מֵאִיר אוֹמֵר
דוֹמֶה — **To what can one who learns from a single teacher be compared?**

---

initial intention was to delay explaining that particular verse until they would reach the relevant Mishnah, when that verse would be more readily understood.] Should he choose another teacher under whom to learn Mishnah, however, he might never hear the interpretation of that verse. The clauses of the Baraisa that follow are to be interpreted in the same manner (*Magen Avos,* first approach).

5. Since he continuously studies under the same teacher, he is spared the difficulties of traveling from place to place to study with different teachers (*Avos HaRosh,* Vol. 1).

6. For he will be fluent in all branches of the Torah without having missed even one explanation (see *Magen Avos*).

The Gemara (*Avodah Zarah* 19a-b) states that having one teacher is preferable only during the initial study of the text (known as גְּמָרָא). A person should first learn the entire Torah from the same teacher (for the reason given above, and additionally), because each teacher transmits the material to his students in a particular style (see the following section). If the lessons of two teachers differ in their wording, even if they are identical in meaning, a student who is taught some parts of the Torah by one teacher and others by a different teacher may grow

confused. However, after a student is fluent in the text and is ready to learn the process of analyzing the rulings (known as סְבָרָא), he should seek various teachers to learn different styles of logic and analysis. *Binyan Yehoshua* notes that this accounts for an apparent contradiction in our Baraisa; for whereas here it states that one should learn from one teacher, earlier (3 §6) it states that one should not suffice with the Torah that he has studied from one teacher, but should go to another teacher to learn from him as well. The answer is that here it is referring to the initial study of the text, whereas there it is referring to the subsequent analysis of the material one has already mastered.

Avos HaRosh (Vol. 1) cites *Abarbanel* (*Nachalos Avos* 1:6), who suggests that this teaching of Yehoshua ben Perachyah is meant as a qualification of the teaching of his teacher, Yose ben Yoezer, who said (Mishnah 1:4; above 6 §1), "Let your house be a meeting place for Torah scholars." Nevertheless, cautions Yehoshua ben Perachyah, do not *study* under all of them; appoint for yourself but one teacher.

7. In the previous section, the Baraisa stated that the benefit of learning the entire Torah from the same teacher is that one will thereby

לְאֶחָד שֶׁהָיָה לוֹ שָׂדֶה אַחַת וְזָרַע מִקְצָתָהּ חִטִּים וּמִקְצָתָהּ שְׂעוֹרִים [וּבְמִקְצָתָהּ זֵיתִים וּבְמִקְצָתָהּ אִילָנוֹת, וְנִמְצָא הָאָדָם הַהוּא מָלֵא טוֹבָה וּבְרָכָה,8 וּבִזְמַן שֶׁלּוֹמֵד מִשְּׁנַיִם שְׁלֹשָׁה, דּוֹמֶה לְמִי שֶׁיֵּשׁ לוֹ שָׂדוֹת הַרְבֵּה, אַחַת זָרַע חִטִּין וְאַחַת זָרַע שְׂעוֹרִים] וְנָטַע אַחַת זֵיתִים וְאַחַת אִילָנוֹת, וְנִמְצָא אָדָם הַהוּא מְפוּזָּר בֵּין הָאֲרָצוֹת בְּלֹא טוֹב וּבְרָכָה:9

ג. וּקְנֵה לְךָ חָבֵר, כֵּיצַד, מְלַמֵּד שֶׁיִּקְנֶה הָאָדָם חָבֵר לְעַצְמוֹ שֶׁיֹּאכַל עִמּוֹ וְיִשְׁתֶּה עִמּוֹ וְיִקְרָא עִמּוֹ וְיִשְׁנֶה עִמּוֹ וְיִישַׁן עִמּוֹ

לְאֶחָד שֶׁהָיָה לוֹ שָׂדֶה אַחַת וְזָרַע מִקְצָתָהּ חִטִּים וּמִקְצָתָהּ שְׂעוֹרִים וּבְמִקְצָתָהּ זֵיתִים וּבְמִקְצָתָהּ אִילָנוֹת — To someone who owned a single field, part of which he sowed with wheat, part of it with barley, part of it with olive trees, and part of it with other fruit trees. וְנִמְצָא הָאָדָם הַהוּא מָלֵא טוֹבָה וּבְרָכָה — It emerges that this person is filled with good and blessing.[8] וּבִזְמַן שֶׁלּוֹמֵד מִשְּׁנַיִם שְׁלֹשָׁה דּוֹמֶה לְמִי שֶׁיֵּשׁ לוֹ שָׂדוֹת הַרְבֵּה — But when one learns from two or three teachers, he may be compared to someone who has many different fields, אַחַת זָרַע חִטִּין וְאַחַת זָרַע שְׂעוֹרִים וְנָטַע אַחַת זֵיתִים וְאַחַת אִילָנוֹת — one of which he sowed with wheat, another one with barley, another one with olive trees, and another one with other fruit trees. וְנִמְצָא אָדָם הַהוּא מְפוּזָּר בֵּין הָאֲרָצוֹת בְּלֹא טוֹב וּבְרָכָה — It emerges that the mind of this person is dispersed among his various fields, and he is lacking good and blessing.[9]

§3 The Baraisa goes on to the second teaching of Yehoshua ben Perachyah cited in §1:

מְלַמֵּד שֶׁיִּקְנֶה וּקְנֵה לְךָ חָבֵר, כֵּיצַד — "Acquire a friend for yourself" — how so? הָאָדָם חָבֵר לְעַצְמוֹ שֶׁיֹּאכַל עִמּוֹ וְיִשְׁתֶּה עִמּוֹ — This teaches that a person should acquire a friend for himself who will eat and drink with him, וְיִקְרָא עִמּוֹ וְיִשְׁנֶה עִמּוֹ — read Scripture and study Mishnah with him, וְיִישַׁן עִמּוֹ — and reside

---

avoid missing any explanations. R' Meir will note another advantage of this practice, one that conforms with the explanation given by the Gemara in *Avodah Zarah* (cited in the previous note).

8. Since all his crops are located in a single field, he is able to manage them effectively. In a similar fashion, one who studies the various branches of Torah from one teacher can easily focus on and retain what he has learned, since he was taught the entire

Torah in a uniform style of expression (*Ben Avraham*).

9. Since his crops are distant from one another, he is unable to remain focused on any one crop, and he cannot manage his fields properly. Similarly, since each teacher transmits his lessons using a different wording, one who seeks a different teacher for each Torah subject will have difficulty focusing on what he has learned, and will be left in confusion (ibid.).

וִיגַלֶּה לוֹ כָּל סְתָרָיו, סֵתֶר תּוֹרָה וְסֵתֶר דֶּרֶךְ אֶרֶץ[10], שֶׁבְּשֶׁיּוֹשְׁבִין וְעוֹסְקִין בַּתּוֹרָה, וְטָעָה אֶחָד מֵהֶם הֲלָכָה אוֹ רֹאשׁ הַפֶּרֶק[11], אוֹ שֶׁיֹּאמַר עַל טָמֵא טָהוֹר אוֹ עַל טָהוֹר טָמֵא [וְעַל אָסוּר מוּתָּר וְעַל מוּתָּר אָסוּר, חֲבֵירוֹ מַחֲזִירוֹ, וּמִנַּיִין] שֶׁבְּשֶׁחֲבֵירוֹ מַחֲזִירוֹ וְקוֹרֵא עִמּוֹ שֶׁיֵּשׁ לָהֶם שָׂכָר טוֹב בַּעֲמָלָן, שֶׁנֶּאֱמַר (קהלת ד, ט) ״טוֹבִים הַשְּׁנַיִם מִן הָאֶחָד אֲשֶׁר יֵשׁ לָהֶם שָׂכָר טוֹב בַּעֲמָלָם[12]״:

with him; וִיגַלֶּה לוֹ כָּל סְתָרָיו סֵתֶר תּוֹרָה וְסֵתֶר דֶּרֶךְ אֶרֶץ — and he should reveal to [this friend] all his secrets: both **secrets concerning** matters of **Torah** and **secrets concerning mundane matters.**[10]

The Baraisa elaborates on the benefit of studying with a friend:
שֶׁבְּשֶׁיּוֹשְׁבִין וְעוֹסְקִין בַּתּוֹרָה וְטָעָה אֶחָד מֵהֶם הֲלָכָה אוֹ רֹאשׁ הַפֶּרֶק — **For when** [**two friends**] **sit and engage in Torah** study together, **and one of them errs** regarding **a halachah or a chapter heading**[11] אוֹ שֶׁיֹּאמַר עַל טָמֵא טָהוֹר אוֹ עַל טָהוֹר טָמֵא — **or he says that** something *tamei* (ritually contaminated) **is** *tahor* (ritually pure), **or that** something *tahor* **is** *tamei;* וְעַל אָסוּר מוּתָּר וְעַל מוּתָּר אָסוּר — **that** something **forbidden is permitted or that** something **permitted is forbidden,** חֲבֵירוֹ מַחֲזִירוֹ — **his friend can correct him.**

The Baraisa cites Scriptural proof for its assertion that studying with a partner who can correct one's mistakes is preferable to studying alone:
וּמִנַּיִין שֶׁבְּשֶׁחֲבֵירוֹ מַחֲזִירוֹ וְקוֹרֵא עִמּוֹ שֶׁיֵּשׁ לָהֶם שָׂכָר טוֹב בַּעֲמָלָן — **And from where** do we derive **that when his friend corrects him, and reads the material together with him, they both receive a good reward for their labor?** שֶׁנֶּאֱמַר — **For it is stated,** *Two are better than one, for they receive a good reward for their labor* (Ecclesiastes 4:9).[12]

---

10. Yehoshua ben Perachyah is not discussing a friendship formed merely for the purpose of companionship, but one whose purpose is to enhance the spiritual level of both parties. It is for this reason that he urges a person to "acquire," or literally, "buy," a friend: for even if one must spend money in order to obtain such a friend, it is worthwhile (see *Rambam* and *R' Yonah* to *Avos* 1:6).

The ideal arrangement for this sort of friendship is one in which the two companions dine together, study together, and reside together, and neither of them has any hesitation about revealing his innermost secrets to the other. This will enable each of them to look out for the spiritual growth of the other;

and if either of them does anything unwise or improper, his colleague will take notice and offer constructive criticism (see ibid.).

11. I.e., he makes a mistake as a result of having forgotten a halachah or the general outline of a chapter that he has studied. See 24 § 6 below.

12. That is, two that study Torah together will receive a greater reward than one who studies alone. The next verse explains, *For should they fall, one can lift the other; but woe to him who is alone when he falls and there is no one to lift him!* I.e., two that study together will receive a greater reward because if one of them "falls" and errs in his understanding of the material, his colleague

ד. שְׁלֹשָׁה[13] שֶׁיּוֹשְׁבִין וְעוֹסְקִין בַּתּוֹרָה, מַעֲלֶה עֲלֵיהֶם הַקָּדוֹשׁ בָּרוּךְ הוּא כְּאִילּוּ נַעֲשִׂים אֲגוּדָה אַחַת לְפָנָיו[14], שֶׁנֶּאֱמַר (עמוס ט, ו) "הַבּוֹנֶה בַשָּׁמַיִם מַעֲלוֹתָיו וַאֲגֻדָּתוֹ עַל אֶרֶץ יְסָדָהּ (הַקֹּרֵא לְמֵי הַיָּם וַיִּשְׁפְּכֵם עַל פְּנֵי הָאָרֶץ ה' שְׁמוֹ[15])", הָא לָמַדְתָּ שְׁלֹשָׁה שֶׁיּוֹשְׁבִין וְעוֹסְקִין בַּתּוֹרָה מַעֲלֶה עֲלֵיהֶם כְּאִילּוּ נַעֲשׂוּ אֲגוּדָה אַחַת לִפְנֵי הַקָּדוֹשׁ בָּרוּךְ הוּא[16]:

§4 The following sections (§4-6) discuss the virtues of learning Torah in groups of three or two, and of studying by oneself:[13]

שְׁלֹשָׁה שֶׁיּוֹשְׁבִין וְעוֹסְקִין בַּתּוֹרָה — Three people who sit together and engage in Torah study מַעֲלֶה עֲלֵיהֶם הַקָּדוֹשׁ בָּרוּךְ הוּא כְּאִילּוּ נַעֲשִׂים אֲגוּדָה אַחַת לְפָנָיו are regarded by the Holy One, Blessed is He, as if they had formed a single group before Him,[14] שֶׁנֶּאֱמַר "הַבּוֹנֶה בַשָּׁמַיִם מַעֲלוֹתָיו וַאֲגֻדָּתוֹ עַל אֶרֶץ יְסָדָהּ הַקֹּרֵא לְמֵי הַיָּם וַיִּשְׁפְּכֵם עַל פְּנֵי הָאָרֶץ ה' שְׁמוֹ" — as it is stated, *Who built His strata in the heavens and founded His group upon the earth; Who calls to the waters of the sea and pours them out upon the face of the earth — HASHEM is His Name* (Amos 9:6).[15] הָא לָמַדְתָּ שְׁלֹשָׁה שֶׁיּוֹשְׁבִין וְעוֹסְקִין בַּתּוֹרָה — You may thus derive that three people who sit and engage in Torah study מַעֲלֶה עֲלֵיהֶם כְּאִילּוּ נַעֲשׂוּ אֲגוּדָה אַחַת לִפְנֵי הַקָּדוֹשׁ בָּרוּךְ הוּא — are regarded by the Holy One, Blessed is He, as if they had formed a single group.[16]

---

will "lift him" by pointing out his mistake, whereas if one studies alone and errs, his error will remain with him (see *Ahavas Chesed*, citing *Rashi* ad loc.).

13. These teachings parallel *Avos* 3:6, where the Mishnah discusses the virtues of studying in groups of five and ten, as well.

14. The literal meaning of the term אֲגֻדָּה is *bundle*, and is used in reference to a cluster of three elements. One example of this is the *lulav*, which is *bundled* together with the *hadassim* and *aravos* on Succos (see *Succcah* 36b). Another example is the *bundle* of hyssop used in Egypt to place the blood of the *pesach* offering on the doorposts, which was composed of three stalks [see *Exodus* 12:22 and *Rashi* ad loc.] (*Binyan Yehoshua*, from *Rashi* to *Avos* 3:6).

[Our Baraisa conforms with one reading of the Mishnah cited by *Rashi* and *Rav*. According to our version of the Mishnah, however, it is *five* people who study together that are called a "group."]

15. One of God's purposes in creating the world was that the Jewish people engage in the study of Torah (see *Shabbos* 88a). Hence, the world is sustained by their Torah study, provided that they are united in their goal of arriving at the correct interpretation of the law. Thus, the Amos verse states regarding God: *Who built His strata in the heavens and founded His group upon the earth ... HASHEM is His Name*, meaning that God's kingship over the world (*His strata in the heavens ... HASHEM is His Name*) is confirmed when His people engage in Torah study as a unified group (*founded His group upon the earth*). Our Baraisa informs us that even three people who study in unity qualify as a group, thereby sustaining the world (*Mefaresh*).

16. *Ben Avraham* explains the advantage that three people who Torah study together have over two: Should two study partners reach an impasse in a dispute, the position taken by the third individual will be accepted, since that opinion is shared by two people, while the second view is held by a single person. Alternatively, he may suggest a third opinion, incorporating aspects of the two opposing sides.

ה. שְׁנַיִם שֶׁיּוֹשְׁבִין וְעוֹסְקִין בַּתּוֹרָה שְׂכָרָם מִתְקַבֵּל בַּמָּרוֹם[17], שֶׁנֶּאֱמַר
(מלאכי ג, טז) "אָז נִדְבְּרוּ יִרְאֵי ה' אִישׁ אֶל רֵעֵהוּ וַיַּקְשֵׁב ה'"[18],
אֵלּוּ הֵן "יִרְאֵי ה'"[19], אֵלּוּ שֶׁגּוֹזְרִים גְּזֵרָה וְאוֹמְרִים: נֵלֵךְ וְנַתִּיר אֶת
הָאֲסוּרִים, וְנִפְדֶּה אֶת הַשְּׁבוּיִים. וְהִסְפִּיק הַקָּדוֹשׁ בָּרוּךְ הוּא בִּידֵיהֶם,
וְהוֹלְכִין וְעוֹשִׂין מִיָּד[20]. וְאֵלּוּ הֵן "וּלְחֹשְׁבֵי שְׁמוֹ", אֵלּוּ שֶׁמְּחַשְּׁבִין
בְּלִבָּם וְאוֹמְרִים: נֵלֵךְ וְנַתִּיר אֶת הָאֲסוּרִים, וְנִפְדֶּה אֶת הַשְּׁבוּיִים.

---

§5 Continuing its discussion from the previous section, the Baraisa addresses the case of two people who study Torah together:

שְׁנַיִם שֶׁיּוֹשְׁבִין וְעוֹסְקִין בַּתּוֹרָה — Two people who sit together and engage in Torah study שְׂכָרָם מִתְקַבֵּל בַּמָּרוֹם — will receive their due reward from God on High,[17] שֶׁנֶּאֱמַר "אָז נִדְבְּרוּ יִרְאֵי ה' אִישׁ אֶל רֵעֵהוּ וַיַּקְשֵׁב ה' " — as it is stated, *Then those who fear HASHEM spoke to one another, and HASHEM listened and heard, and a book of remembrance was written before Him for those who fear HASHEM and those who give thought to His Name* (Malachi 3:16).[18]

The Baraisa goes on to explain the end of the *Malachi* verse, *for those who fear HASHEM and those who give thought to His Name:*

אֵלּוּ הֵן "יִרְאֵי ה' " — Who are *those who fear HASHEM?*[19] אֵלּוּ שֶׁגּוֹזְרִים גְּזֵרָה וְאוֹמְרִים — They are those who issue a proclamation, saying, נֵלֵךְ וְנַתִּיר אֶת הָאֲסוּרִים וְנִפְדֶּה אֶת הַשְּׁבוּיִים — "We shall go and liberate prisoners!," or, "We shall go and redeem captives!" וְהִסְפִּיק הַקָּדוֹשׁ בָּרוּךְ הוּא בִּידֵיהֶם וְהוֹלְכִין — And the Holy One, Blessed is He, grants them success and they go and carry out the deed immediately.[20] וְעוֹשִׂין מִיָּד וְאֵלּוּ הֵן "וּלְחֹשְׁבֵי שְׁמוֹ" — And who are *those who give thought to His Name?* אֵלּוּ שֶׁמְּחַשְּׁבִין בְּלִבָּם — They are those who think to themselves: נֵלֵךְ וְנַתִּיר אֶת הָאֲסוּרִים וְאוֹמְרִים — "We shall go and liberate prisoners!," or, "We shall go וְנִפְדֶּה אֶת הַשְּׁבוּיִים

---

17. That is, aside from the individual reward that each of them will receive for engaging in Torah study, they will receive additional reward for studying together. This is because when two people discuss a Torah topic with each other, each one improves the understanding of his colleague, and they are better equipped to arrive at the correct interpretation of the law (*Mefaresh* here and in the following section; see §3 above).

18. The verse speaks of two people, as indicated by the phrase *to one another* [lit., *one man to his fellow*] (*Binyan Yehoshua*). When two people who fear God discuss

Torah matters together, God inscribes their merit before Him and determines a reward for them (*Magen Avos*).

19. It cannot be speaking about the pair of study partners discussed previously, for then this phrase would be redundant, as they were already described in the first half of the verse as *those who fear HASHEM*. Rather, it must be speaking of another category of God-fearing individuals who are likewise inscribed in God's book and rewarded (see *Mefaresh*).

20. Thus, the term *those who fear HASHEM* means that they demonstrate their fear of Him by performing His mitzvos (ibid.).

וְלֹא הִסְפִּיק הַקָּדוֹשׁ בָּרוּךְ הוּא בִּידֵיהֶם, וּבָא מַלְאָךְ וַחֲבָטָן בַּקַּרְקַע[22,21]:

ו. יָחִיד יוֹשֵׁב וְעוֹסֵק בַּתּוֹרָה, שְׂכָרוֹ מִתְקַבֵּל בַּמָּרוֹם, שֶׁנֶּאֱמַר (איכה ג, כח)
"יֵשֵׁב בָּדָד וְיִדֹּם כִּי נָטַל עָלָיו"[23], מִשְׁלוּ[24] מָשָׁל לְמָה הַדָּבָר דּוֹמֶה,
לְאֶחָד שֶׁהָיָה לוֹ בֵּן קָטָן, הִנִּיחוֹ וְיָצָא לַשּׁוּק, עָמַד וְנָטַל אֶת הַמְּגִילָה
וְהִנִּיחָהּ בֵּין בִּרְכָּיו וְהָיָה יוֹשֵׁב וְהוֹגֶה בָּהּ, כֵּיוָן שֶׁבָּא אָבִיו מִן הַשּׁוּק,

---

and redeem captives!" וְלֹא הִסְפִּיק הַקָּדוֹשׁ בָּרוּךְ הוּא בִּידֵיהֶם וּבָא מַלְאָךְ וַחֲבָטָן
בַּקַּרְקַע — **But the Holy One, Blessed is He, did not grant them the opportunity** to carry out the deed; rather, **an angel came and knocked them to the ground.**[21] Although circumstances beyond their control prevented them from performing the mitzvah, they are rewarded for their good intentions.[22]

§6 The Baraisa resumes its discussion regarding the Heavenly reward of those who study Torah, addressing the case of a person who studies alone: יָחִיד יוֹשֵׁב וְעוֹסֵק בַּתּוֹרָה שְׂכָרוֹ מִתְקַבֵּל בַּמָּרוֹם — **Even one person who sits and occupies himself with Torah will receive his** due **reward** from God **on High,** שֶׁנֶּאֱמַר "יֵשֵׁב בָּדָד וְיִדֹּם כִּי נָטַל עָלָיו" — **as it is stated,** *Let one sit in solitude and whisper, for he has taken [a reward] for himself* (Lamentations 3:28).[23]

The Baraisa presents a parable to clarify when solitary Torah study is appreciated in God's eyes and will be rewarded:[24] מָשְׁלוּ מָשָׁל לְמָה הַדָּבָר דּוֹמֶה — **An analogy was made: To what may the matter be compared?** לְאֶחָד שֶׁהָיָה לוֹ בֵּן קָטָן הִנִּיחוֹ וְיָצָא לַשּׁוּק — **To someone who had a young son, whom he left alone and went out to the marketplace.** עָמַד וְנָטַל אֶת הַמְּגִילָה וְהִנִּיחָהּ בֵּין בִּרְכָּיו וְהָיָה יוֹשֵׁב וְהוֹגֶה בָּהּ — **While the father** was gone, **[the son] arose and took a scroll and placed it between his knees, and he sat and read it.** כֵּיוָן שֶׁבָּא אָבִיו מִן הַשּׁוּק — **When his father came**

---

21. I.e., an angel struck them dead, thus preventing them from carrying out their noble intentions. Alternatively, the angel struck down the people whom they had intended to rescue (*Magen Avos*).

22. See *Berachos* 6a. The term *and those who give thought to His Name* implies that they had intention to fulfill God's will but were unsuccessful.

In the previous case, where they succeeded in carrying out their mission, the Baraisa says that they issued a proclamation, *saying* that they would release the prisoners, whereas in this case, where they did not succeed, it says only that they *thought* it to themselves. *Binyan Yehoshua* suggests

that this is because if one verbalizes a commitment to perform a mitzvah, it is more likely that God will grant him success, in accordance with the rule that God fulfills the decree of a righteous person (see *Job* 22:28; *Taanis* 23a).

23. Translation of the verse follows *Midrash Shmuel* to *Avos* 3:2, cited by *Tos. Yom Tov.* It is the habit of those studying alone to do so in a whisper (*Binyan Yehoshua*, citing *Rav* to *Avos* ibid.).

24. The Gemara (*Berachos* 63b) states that Torah students who study in solitude will become foolish and are deserving of punishment, for a person must study with a partner or as part of a group in order to arrive at

אָמַר: רְאוּ בְּנִי קָטָן שֶׁהֻנַּחְתִּיו וְיָצָאתִי לַשּׁוּק, מֶה עָשָׂה, מֵעַצְמוֹ לָמַד
וְנָטַל אֶת הַמְּגִילָה וְהֶנִּיחָהּ בֵּין בִּרְכָּיו וְהָיָה יוֹשֵׁב וְלוֹמֵד בָּהּ. הָא לָמַדְתָּ
שֶׁאַף יָחִיד שֶׁיּוֹשֵׁב וְעוֹסֵק בַּתּוֹרָה שְׂכָרוֹ מִתְקַבֵּל בַּמָּרוֹם:25

ז. "וֶהֱוֵי דָן אֶת כָּל הָאָדָם לְכַף זְכוּת", מַעֲשֶׂה בְּרִיבָה אַחַת שֶׁנִּשְׁבֵּית,
וְהָלְכוּ אַחֲרֶיהָ שְׁנֵי חֲסִידִים לִפְדּוֹתָהּ, נִכְנַס אֶחָד מֵהֶם לְקוּבָּה שֶׁל זוֹנוֹת,

---

back **from the marketplace** and saw his son studying alone, **אָמַר רְאוּ בְּנִי** — **קָטָן שֶׁהֻנַּחְתִּיו וְיָצָאתִי לַשּׁוּק מֶה עָשָׂה** he said proudly, "See what my young son did when I left him alone and went out to the marketplace! **מֵעַצְמוֹ לָמַד** — He studied by himself; **וְנָטַל אֶת הַמְּגִילָה וְהֶנִּיחָהּ בֵּין בִּרְכָּיו וְהָיָה יוֹשֵׁב וְלוֹמֵד בָּהּ** — he took a scroll and placed it between his knees, and he sat and studied from it!" **הָא לָמַדְתָּ** — You may thus derive **שֶׁאַף יָחִיד שֶׁיּוֹשֵׁב וְעוֹסֵק בַּתּוֹרָה שְׂכָרוֹ** — **מִתְקַבֵּל בַּמָּרוֹם** that even an individual who sits and occupies himself with Torah will receive his due reward from God **on High.**[25]

§7 In the following two sections, the Baraisa expounds upon the third and final teaching of Yehoshua ben Perachyah (quoted in §1), citing two incidents to highlight his point:

מַעֲשֶׂה "And judge every person favorably." **וֶהֱוֵי דָן אֶת כָּל הָאָדָם לְכַף זְכוּת** — **בְּרִיבָה אַחַת שֶׁנִּשְׁבֵּית** There was an incident involving a certain young girl who was captured, **וְהָלְכוּ אַחֲרֶיהָ שְׁנֵי חֲסִידִים לִפְדּוֹתָהּ** — and two pious men went after her to ransom her. **נִכְנַס אֶחָד מֵהֶם לְקוּבָּה שֶׁל זוֹנוֹת** — At one point during their attempts to free her, **one of them entered the house of harlots**

---

the correct interpretation of the law. Accordingly, when it states that God is pleased with one who studies Torah in solitude, it must be referring to someone who does not have the option of studying with another person. The Baraisa will illustrate this with a parable (*Mefaresh*, cited by *Binyan Yehoshua*).

25. The child was too young to study without his father. Nonetheless, the father was pleased to see that when he was not available to teach his son, the boy did not waste his time, but attempted to read from the scroll on his own. Similarly, although a true understanding of the Torah is acquired only by learning together with others, if one learns by himself when there is no one available to learn with him, God appreciates it and will reward him accordingly (see ibid.).

This is not to say that one is obligated to learn with others whenever there are people available to learn with him. There are times and situations in which a person will arrive at a clearer understanding of the subject if he studies alone than if he does so with others. In such cases, solitary Torah study is ideal (Responsa *Salmas Chaim, Yoreh Deah* §67). Others note that *Rashi* to *Avos* (1:6) explains the statement, "Acquire a friend for yourself," to mean that one should purchase Torah books from which to study, which can be viewed as his colleagues. Accordingly, they maintain that in our times, when all areas of the Torah can be learned from books, one may study alone (Responsa *Teshuvos VeHanhagos* [R' Moshe Sternbuch], Vol. 1, §542). However, it is still preferable to study Torah with others when this is possible (ibid.; see *Beur Halachah* 155:1).

כְּשֶׁיָּצָא אָמַר לַחֲבֵרוֹ: בַּמֶּה חֲשַׁדְתַּנִי[26]. אָמַר: שֶׁמָּא לֵידַע בְּכַמָּה דָמִים הִיא מְהוֹרְהֶנֶת. אָמַר לוֹ: הָעֲבוֹדָה[27], כָּךְ הָיָה. אָמַר לוֹ: כְּשֵׁם שֶׁדַּנְתַּנִי לְכַף זְכוּת, כָּךְ הַקָּדוֹשׁ בָּרוּךְ הוּא יָדִין אוֹתְךָ לְכַף זְכוּת[28]:

ח. שׁוּב מַעֲשֶׂה בְּרִיבָה אַחַת שֶׁנִּשְׁבֵּית, וְהָלְכוּ אַחֲרֶיהָ שְׁנֵי חֲסִידִים לִפְדּוֹתָהּ, וְנִתְפַּס אֶחָד מֵהֶם לְשׁוּם לִסְטוֹס וַחֲבָשׁוּהוּ בְּבֵית הָאֲסוּרִין, בְּכָל יוֹם וָיוֹם הָיְתָה אִשְׁתּוֹ מְבִיאָה לוֹ לֶחֶם וּמַיִם, יוֹם אֶחָד אָמַר לָהּ: לְכִי אֵצֶל פְּלוֹנִי וְאִמְרִי לוֹ שֶׁאֲנִי חָבוּשׁ בְּבֵית אֲסוּרִין [(מִפְּנֵי הַזְּנוּת)[29], הוּא

where the girl was being held. כְּשֶׁיָּצָא אָמַר לַחֲבֵרוֹ בַּמֶּה חֲשַׁדְתַּנִי — **When he emerged, he said to his colleague, "Of what did you suspect me?"**[26] אָמַר שֶׁמָּא לֵידַע בְּכַמָּה דָמִים הִיא מְהוֹרְהֶנֶת — **[His colleague] replied, "I thought that perhaps you entered in order to determine how much money she was being held for, so that we would know how much to raise in order to ransom her."** אָמַר לוֹ הָעֲבוֹדָה כָּךְ הָיָה — **[The first man] replied, "By the Divine service!**[27] **So it was!"** אָמַר לוֹ כְּשֵׁם שֶׁדַּנְתַּנִי לְכַף זְכוּת כָּךְ הַקָּדוֹשׁ בָּרוּךְ הוּא יָדִין אוֹתְךָ לְכַף זְכוּת — **He then said to him, "Just as you have judged me favorably, so shall the Holy One, Blessed is He, judge you favorably."**[28]

§8 Another incident regarding judging people favorably: שׁוּב מַעֲשֶׂה בְּרִיבָה אַחַת שֶׁנִּשְׁבֵּית — **There was another incident involving a certain young girl who was captured,** וְהָלְכוּ אַחֲרֶיהָ שְׁנֵי חֲסִידִים לִפְדּוֹתָהּ — **and two pious men went after her to ransom her.** וְנִתְפַּס אֶחָד מֵהֶם לְשׁוּם לִסְטוֹס וַחֲבָשׁוּהוּ בְּבֵית הָאֲסוּרִין — **One of them was apprehended on charges of robbery and confined in prison.** בְּכָל יוֹם וָיוֹם הָיְתָה אִשְׁתּוֹ מְבִיאָה לוֹ לֶחֶם וּמַיִם — **Each day, his wife would bring him bread and water** in prison. יוֹם אֶחָד אָמַר לָהּ לְכִי אֵצֶל פְּלוֹנִי — **One day he said to [his wife], "Go to So-and-so** (the other pious man) וְאִמְרִי לוֹ שֶׁאֲנִי חָבוּשׁ בְּבֵית אֲסוּרִין מִפְּנֵי הַזְּנוּת — **and tell him that I am confined in prison as a result of** my efforts to rescue the captive

---

26. I.e., did you suspect me of entering for sinful purposes, or did you judge me favorably?

27. This is a form of oath. One swears by linking his words to an object of sanctity (see *Binyan Yehoshua*).

28. The Gemara (*Shabbos* 127b) states that if a person judges his fellow man favorably, he too is judged favorably. Now obviously, this does not mean that God will give him the benefit of the doubt, as such a concept does not apply to God, Who knows a person's innermost thoughts. Rather, what it

means is that if one has an equal number of merits and sins, the merit of judging his fellow man favorably will tip the balance to the side of merit. He will then be judged as one whose merits exceed his sins, who is considered a completely righteous person (*Mefaresh*, based on *Shabbos* 127a-b and *Kiddushin* 39b). This is in accordance with the principle that God repays people measure for measure; thus, just as he judged his fellow man favorably, so will God judge him favorably (*Binyan Yehoshua*; see further there). See *Shemiras HaLashon, Shaar HaTevunah* Ch. 4, for a different approach.

יוֹשֵׁב (וְשׂוֹחֵק) בְּבֵיתוֹ וְאֵינוֹ מַשְׁגִּיחַ עַל הָרִיבָה[30]. אָמְרָה לוֹ: לֹא דַיֶּיךָ
שֶׁאַתָּה חָבוּשׁ בְּבֵית הָאֲסוּרִים, אֶלָּא שֶׁהָיִיתָ מִתְעַסֵּק בִּדְבָרִים בְּטֵלִים[31].
לֹא °הָלְכָה (אֶלָּא הָיְתָה מִתְעַסֶּקֶת בִּדְבָרִים בְּטֵלִים[32]) אָמַר לָהּ: בְּבַקָּשָׁה
מִמֵּךְ לְכִי וְאִמְרִי לוֹ. הָלְכָה וְאָמְרָה לוֹ, מֶה עָשָׂה אוֹתוֹ הָאִישׁ, הָלַךְ וְהֵבִיא
כֶּסֶף וְזָהָב וּבְנֵי אָדָם עִמּוֹ וְהוֹצִיאוּ אֶת שְׁנֵיהֶם, כְּשֶׁיָּצָא, אָמַר לָהֶם: תְּנוּ לִי
רִיבָה זוֹ שֶׁתִּישַׁן עִמִּי בִּבְגָדֶיהָ עַל הַמִּטָּה[34]. לַשַּׁחֲרִית, אָמַר לָהֶם: הַטְבִּילוּנִי
וְהַטְבִּילוּהָ. וְהִטְבִּילוּם, אָמַר לְטוֹבְלֵיהֶם: לַטְבִילָה שֶׁלִּי בַּמֶּה חֲשַׁדְתּוּנִי[35].

---

girl from **promiscuity**,[29]   **הוּא יוֹשֵׁב בְּבֵיתוֹ וְאֵינוֹ מַשְׁגִּיחַ עַל הָרִיבָה** — while he
sits at home and pays no heed to the plight of the young girl!"[30]   **אָמְרָה לוֹ**
[His — **לֹא דַיֶּיךָ שֶׁאַתָּה חָבוּשׁ בְּבֵית הָאֲסוּרִים אֶלָּא שֶׁהָיִיתָ מִתְעַסֵּק בִּדְבָרִים בְּטֵלִים**
wife] replied to him, "Is it not enough that you are confined to prison — but
you have involved yourself in idle matters?!"[31]   **אָמַר לָהּ בְּבַקָּשָׁה מִמֵּךְ לְכִי**
וְאִמְרִי לוֹ — He[32] said to her, "I implore you, go and say to him as I have
told you."   **הָלְכָה וְאָמְרָה לוֹ** — So she went and conveyed her husband's
words to [his colleague].   **מֶה עָשָׂה אוֹתוֹ הָאִישׁ** — So what did that man
do?   **הָלַךְ וְהֵבִיא כֶּסֶף וְזָהָב וּבְנֵי אָדָם עִמּוֹ וְהוֹצִיאוּ אֶת שְׁנֵיהֶם** — He went and
procured silver and gold with which to ransom his colleague and the young
girl, and enlisted other **people** to join **with him, and** together, **they secured**
the release of both of them.   **כְּשֶׁיָּצָא אָמַר לָהֶם** — When he was released
and they arrived at the inn where they were to spend the night,[33] [the pious
man] who had been freed from prison **said to those** who were with him,   **תְּנוּ**
לִי רִיבָה זוֹ שֶׁתִּישַׁן עִמִּי בִּבְגָדֶיהָ עַל הַמִּטָּה — "Entrust this young **girl to me,**
that she should sleep in her clothing at the foot of my bed."[34]   **לַשַּׁחֲרִית**
אָמַר לָהֶם הַטְבִּילוּנִי וְהַטְבִּילוּהָ וְהִטְבִּילוּם — In the morning, he told them, "Have
me and her immersed in a *mikveh*," and they had them immersed.   **אָמַר**
לְטוֹבְלֵיהֶם לַטְבִילָה שֶׁלִּי בַּמֶּה חֲשַׁדְתּוּנִי — He then **said to those who had them**
immersed, "Regarding my immersion, of what did you suspect me?"[35]

---

29. *Binyan Yehoshua.*

30. [Emendation follows *Nuschas HaGra.*]
When the man was arrested, his colleague
had returned home and discontinued his efforts to ransom the captive girl. The impris-
oned man therefore urged him take up her
cause once again (*Ben Avraham*).

31. His wife was arguing that instead of
wasting his efforts asking his colleague to
ransom the girl, he should be appealing to
him to obtain his own release (ibid.).

32. Emendation follows *Binyan Yehoshua,*
and conforms with *Tummas Yesharim.*

33. Based on the parallel incident cited in
Shabbos 127b.

34. *Avos HaRosh* (Vol. 1), citing *Shabbos*
ibid. The pious man feared that among the
people who were accompanying him, there
might be one man who could not be trusted
to refrain from sinning with the girl. Therefore, he told them to entrust her to his care,
so that he could guard her properly (*Ahavas*
Chesed, citing *Shabbos* ibid.).

35. Ezra enacted that a man who experienced a seminal emission, or a man or
woman who had relations, must immerse

אָמְרוּ לוֹ: אָמַרְנוּ כָּל אוֹתָן יָמִים שֶׁהָיָה חָבוּשׁ בְּבֵית הָאֲסוּרִין הָיָה רָעֵב
וְצָמֵא, וְעַכְשָׁיו יָצָא לַאֲוִיר הָעוֹלָם, וְחַם בִּשָׂרְךָ עָלֶיךָ וְשֶׁמָּא רָאִיתָ קֶרִי.‏[36]
אָמַר לָהֶם: לַטְבִילָה שֶׁל רִיבָה זוֹ בַּמֶּה חֲשַׁדְתּוּהָ?‏[37] אָמְרוּ לוֹ: שֶׁכָּל אוֹתָן
הַיָּמִים שֶׁהָיְתָה שְׁרוּיָה בֵּין הָעוֹבְדֵי כּוֹכָבִים הָיְתָה אוֹכֶלֶת מִשֶׁלָּהֶם וְשׁוֹתָה
מִשֶׁלָּהֶם, עַכְשָׁיו אָמַרְתָּ הַטְבִּילוּהָ כְּדֵי שֶׁתִּטְהַר.‏[38] אָמַר לָהֶם: הָעֲבוֹדָה,
כָּךְ הָיָה, וְאַתֶּם שֶׁדַּנְתּוּנִי לְכַף זְכוּת, הַמָּקוֹם יָדִין אֶתְכֶם לְכַף זְכוּת.

They — אָמְרוּ לוֹ אָמַרְנוּ כָּל אוֹתָן יָמִים שֶׁהָיָה חָבוּשׁ בְּבֵית הָאֲסוּרִין הָיָה רָעֵב וְצָמֵא answered him, "We reasoned that all those days that you were confined to prison, you were hungry and thirsty, **וְעַכְשָׁיו יָצָא לַאֲוִיר הָעוֹלָם וְחַם בִּשָׂרְךָ עָלֶיךָ** — and now that you emerged into the open air and ate and drank, your body was warmed; **וְשֶׁמָּא רָאִיתָ קֶרִי** — and perhaps as a result of the sudden increase in your body temperature, **you experienced an** involuntary emission, and that is why you immersed yourself."[36] **אָמַר לָהֶם לַטְבִילָה שֶׁל רִיבָה זוֹ בַּמֶּה חֲשַׁדְתּוּהָ** — He then **asked them,** "And **as for the immersion of this young girl, of what did you suspect her?**"[37] **אָמְרוּ לוֹ שֶׁכָּל אוֹתָן הַיָּמִים שֶׁהָיְתָה שְׁרוּיָה בֵּין הָעוֹבְדֵי כּוֹכָבִים** — **They replied to him,** "We reasoned **that all those days that she was staying among the idolaters, הָיְתָה אוֹכֶלֶת מִשֶׁלָּהֶם וְשׁוֹתָה מִשֶׁלָּהֶם** — **she was eating and drinking of their** nonkosher food **items.** **עַכְשָׁיו אָמַרְתָּ הַטְבִּילוּהָ כְּדֵי שֶׁתִּטְהַר** — **Therefore, now** that she was redeemed, **you told** us to have her immersed so that she would be purified from this contamination."[38] **אָמַר לָהֶם הָעֲבוֹדָה כָּךְ הָיָה** — He replied to them, "By the Divine **service! So it was! וְאַתֶּם שֶׁדַּנְתּוּנִי לְכַף זְכוּת הַמָּקוֹם יָדִין אֶתְכֶם לְכַף זְכוּת** — And as for **you, who have judged me favorably, so shall the Omnipresent judge you favorably."**

---

in a *mikveh* before uttering words of Torah or prayer (*Bava Kamma* 82b; see *Berachos* 26a). [In later generations, Ezra's enactment was rescinded (*Berachos* 22a); see *Ahavas Chesed* for further discussion.] Thus, the pious man's request that both he and the girl be immersed lent credence to the suspicion that he had sinned with her during the previous night.

36. In other words, not only did we not suspect you of immoral behavior, but we did not even suspect that you experienced an emission as a result of having improper thoughts (*Magen Avos*; see further there).

37. I.e., how did you rationalize my request that she be immersed if I had not sinned with her?

38. Our Baraisa indicates that one who ate nonkosher foods should immerse himself in a *mikveh* (*Haamek Davar* to *Leviticus* 17:16), even if he did so under duress — as was the case with the girl in this narrative — although in that case he is innocent of any wrongdoing (see Responsa *Minchas Yitzchak*, Vol. 4 §100:12). Others derive from here that anyone who repents of a sin must immerse himself in a *mikveh* (see *Or Zarua*, Vol. 1 §112; and see *Rama* to *Yoreh Deah* 268:12 [referenced by *Binyan Yehoshua*] with *Beur HaGra* §30). See also *Maharil, Hil. Erev Yom Kippur*, and *Tanya Rabbasi* §72, who cite this teaching as the source for the custom to immerse in a *mikveh* on Erev Yom Kippur as part of the repentance process.

כְּשֵׁם שֶׁהַצַּדִּיקִים הָרִאשׁוֹנִים הָיוּ חֲסִידִים, כָּךְ בְּהֶמְתָּן הָיוּ חֲסִידוֹת,[39]
אָמְרוּ: גְּמַלָּיו שֶׁל אַבְרָהָם אָבִינוּ לֹא נִכְנְסוּ לְבַיִת שֶׁיֵּשׁ בּוֹ עֲבוֹדַת
כּוֹכָבִים, שֶׁנֶּאֱמַר (בראשית כד, לא) "וְאָנֹכִי פִּנִּיתִי הַבַּיִת וּמָקוֹם לַגְּמַלִּים",
["וְאָנֹכִי פִּנִּיתִי הַבַּיִת" מִתְּרָפִים, וּמַה תַּלְמוּד לוֹמַר "וּמָקוֹם לַגְּמַלִּים,"]
מְלַמֵּד שֶׁלֹּא נִכְנְסוּ לְבֵית לָבָן הָאֲרַמִּי עַד שֶׁפִּנּוּ כָּל הָעֲבוֹדַת כּוֹכָבִים
מִפְּנֵיהֶם,[40] מַעֲשֶׂה בַּחֲמוֹרוֹ שֶׁל רַבִּי חֲנִינָא בֶּן דּוֹסָא שֶׁגְּנָבוּהוּ
לִסְטִים, וְחָבְשׁוּ אֶת הַחֲמוֹר בֶּחָצֵר וְהִנִּיחוּ לוֹ תֶּבֶן וּשְׂעוֹרִין וּמַיִם,

---

Tangentially, the Baraisa cites additional incidents regarding pious individuals: כְּשֵׁם שֶׁהַצַּדִּיקִים הָרִאשׁוֹנִים הָיוּ חֲסִידִים כָּךְ בְּהֶמְתָּן הָיוּ חֲסִידוֹת — Just as the righteous men of earlier generations were pious, so were their animals pious.[39] אָמְרוּ גְּמַלָּיו שֶׁל אַבְרָהָם אָבִינוּ לֹא נִכְנְסוּ לְבַיִת שֶׁיֵּשׁ בּוֹ עֲבוֹדַת כּוֹכָבִים — For example, [the Sages] said: The camels of our patriarch Abraham did not enter a house that contained idols, שֶׁנֶּאֱמַר "וְאָנֹכִי פִּנִּיתִי הַבַּיִת וּמָקוֹם לַגְּמַלִּים" — as it says that Laban told Abraham's servant, *"Come, O blessed of HASHEM! Why should you stand outside when I have cleared the house, and place for the camels?"* (*Genesis* 24:31). "וְאָנֹכִי פִּנִּיתִי הַבַּיִת" מִתְּרָפִים — When it says, *"I have cleared the house,"* it means that Laban had cleansed the house of idols. וּמַה תַּלְמוּד לוֹמַר "וּמָקוֹם לַגְּמַלִּים" — And what is [the verse] teaching us by saying subsequently, *"and place for the camels"*? מְלַמֵּד שֶׁלֹּא נִכְנְסוּ לְבֵית לָבָן הָאֲרַמִּי עַד שֶׁפִּנּוּ כָּל הָעֲבוֹדַת כּוֹכָבִים מִפְּנֵיהֶם — It is teaching us that it was necessary to cleanse the house of idols in order to provide a place for the camels, for [the camels] of Abraham would not enter the house of Laban the Aramean until all the idols were cleared away from before them.[40]

Another instance in which the animal of a pious individual displayed piety: מַעֲשֶׂה בַּחֲמוֹרוֹ שֶׁל רַבִּי חֲנִינָא בֶּן דּוֹסָא שֶׁגְּנָבוּהוּ לִסְטִים — There was an incident in which the donkey of R' Chanina ben Dosa was stolen by bandits. וְחָבְשׁוּ אֶת הַחֲמוֹר בֶּחָצֵר וְהִנִּיחוּ לוֹ תֶּבֶן וּשְׂעוֹרִין וּמַיִם — [The bandits] harnessed the donkey and placed it in [their] courtyard, and put straw, barley, and water in front of

---

39. Piety (חֲסִידוּת) is a higher level than righteousness. A righteous person fulfills all the mitzvos meticulously and guards himself from any form of sin; a pious person goes beyond the letter of the law in his performance of the mitzvos and distances himself from anything even remotely connected to sin (see *Mesillas Yesharim* Ch. 13). The virtuous men of old attained not only the basic level of righteousness, but the lofty level of piety as well. When it states that their animals were "pious," it means that

God miraculously spared not only them, but even their animals from anything resembling transgression, as the Baraisa will go on to explain (see *Yefeh Mareh* to *Yerushalmi Demai* 1:3).

40. There is no prohibition against entering a house that contains an idol (and certainly not against bringing one's animal into such a house). However, because of Abraham's extraordinary piety, God caused his camels to be stringent in this matter (see *Magen Avos, Lehoros Nassan*).

וְלֹא הָיָה אוֹכֵל וְשׁוֹתֶה[41], אָמְרוּ: לָמָה אָנוּ מַנִּיחִין אוֹתוֹ שֶׁיָּמוּת וְיַבְאִישׁ
לָנוּ אֶת הֶחָצֵר. עָמְדוּ וּפָתְחוּ לָהּ אֶת הַדֶּלֶת וְהוֹצִיאוּהָ, וְהָיְתָה מוֹשֶׁכֶת
וְהוֹלֶכֶת עַד שֶׁהִגִּיעָה אֵצֶל רַבִּי חֲנִינָא בֶּן דּוֹסָא, כֵּיוָן שֶׁהִגִּיעָה אֶצְלוֹ,
שָׁמַע בְּנוֹ קוֹלָה, אָמַר לוֹ: אַבָּא, דּוֹמֶה קוֹלָהּ לְקוֹל בְּהֶמְתֵּנוּ. אָמַר לוֹ:
בְּנִי, פְּתַח לָהּ אֶת הַדֶּלֶת, שֶׁכְּבָר מֵתָה בְּרָעָב[42]. עָמַד וּפָתַח לָהּ הַדֶּלֶת,
וְהִנִּיחַ לָהּ תֶּבֶן וּשְׂעוֹרִים וּמַיִם וְהָיְתָה אוֹכֶלֶת וְשׁוֹתָה[43], לְפִיכָךְ אָמְרוּ:
כְּשֵׁם שֶׁהַצַּדִּיקִים הָרִאשׁוֹנִים הָיוּ חֲסִידִים כָּךְ בְּהֶמְתָּן חֲסִידוֹת כְּמוֹתָן:

אָמְרוּ לָמָה אָנוּ — וְלֹא הָיָה אוֹכֵל וְשׁוֹתֶה — but it would not eat or drink.[41] it;
מַנִּיחִין אוֹתוֹ שֶׁיָּמוּת וְיַבְאִישׁ לָנוּ אֶת הֶחָצֵר — [The bandits] said, "Why should we let [the donkey] die of starvation and emit a foul odor in our courtyard?" עָמְדוּ וּפָתְחוּ לָהּ אֶת הַדֶּלֶת וְהוֹצִיאוּהָ — So they arose and opened the door for it, and removed it from their courtyard, וְהָיְתָה מוֹשֶׁכֶת וְהוֹלֶכֶת עַד שֶׁהִגִּיעָה אֵצֶל רַבִּי חֲנִינָא בֶּן דּוֹסָא — whereupon it pulled itself along until it arrived at the home of R' Chanina ben Dosa. כֵּיוָן שֶׁהִגִּיעָה אֶצְלוֹ שָׁמַע בְּנוֹ קוֹלָה — When it arrived at his door, it began to bray and [R' Chanina's] son heard its voice. אָמַר לוֹ אַבָּא דּוֹמֶה קוֹלָהּ לְקוֹל בְּהֶמְתֵּנוּ — He said to [R' Chanina], "Father, its voice resembles that of our animal!" אָמַר לוֹ בְּנִי פְּתַח לָהּ אֶת הַדֶּלֶת שֶׁכְּבָר מֵתָה בְּרָעָב — [R' Chanina] replied, "My son, open the door for it, for I thought that it had already died of hunger, as it has not eaten anything all this time!"[42] עָמַד וּפָתַח לָהּ הַדֶּלֶת וְהִנִּיחַ לָהּ תֶּבֶן וּשְׂעוֹרִים וּמַיִם — So he arose and opened the door for it, and put straw, barley, and water in front it; וְהָיְתָה אוֹכֶלֶת וְשׁוֹתָה — and then it ate and drank.[43]

The Baraisa concludes with regard to both narratives:

לְפִיכָךְ אָמְרוּ כְּשֵׁם שֶׁהַצַּדִּיקִים הָרִאשׁוֹנִים הָיוּ חֲסִידִים — Therefore, [the Sages] said: Just as the righteous men of earlier generations were pious, כָּךְ בְּהֶמְתָּן חֲסִידוֹת כְּמוֹתָן — so were their animals pious like them.

---

41. The animal did not eat the food that it was offered because it was untithed (Tos. HaRosh to Shabbos 112a; see Ahavas Chesed). [It is forbidden to feed an animal untithed food. See further, Bavli Chullin 7b and Yerushalmi Demai 1:3).] However, this explains only why the donkey did not eat the barley; it does not account for its refusal to eat the straw and drink the water, which do not require tithing. Magen Avos suggests that perhaps everything was placed before the animal together, and therefore it was

stringent and refrained from eating or drinking at all, lest it inadvertently eat an untithed barley kernel.

42. R' Chanina knew that the donkey would not eat the food of the bandits, and he therefore assumed that by now it had surely starved to death (Ahavas Chesed).

43. See Yerushalmi Demai 1:3 and Bereishis Rabbah 60 §8 for a different version of this incident; see Bavli Chullin 7a-b for a similar narrative involving the donkey of R' Pinchas ben Yair.

﴾ פֶּרֶק ט ﴿

א. (יהושע בן פרחיה ו) נִתַּאי הָאַרְבֵּלִי אוֹמֵר: הַרְחֵק מִשָּׁכֵן רַע וְאַל תִּתְחַבֵּר לְרָשָׁע וְאַל תִּתְיָאֵשׁ מִן הַפּוּרְעָנוּת. הַרְחֵק מִשָּׁכֵן רַע, אֶחָד שָׁכֵן שֶׁבַּבַּיִת וְאֶחָד שָׁכֵן שֶׁבַּחוּץ וְאֶחָד שָׁכֵן שֶׁבַּשָּׂדֶה[1]. (מלמד) שֶׁאֵין הַנְּגָעִים בָּאִין [אֶלָּא עַל בֵּיתוֹ שֶׁל רָשָׁע, שֶׁנֶּאֱמַר (משלי ה, כב) "עֲווֹנוֹתָיו יִלְכְּדֻנוֹ אֶת הָרָשָׁע", מְלַמֵּד שֶׁאֵין הַנְּגָעִים בָּאִים] אֶלָּא בַּעֲווֹנוֹ שֶׁל רָשָׁע.[2] עֲווֹנוֹתָיו שֶׁל רָשָׁע גָּרְמוּ לוֹ לִסְתּוֹר כָּתְלוֹ שֶׁל צַדִּיק. [כֵּיצַד,] כָּתְלוֹ שֶׁבֵּין רָשָׁע לְבֵין צַדִּיק,

---

﴾ CHAPTER 9 ﴿

§1 This chapter cites and elaborates the teaching of *Avos* 1:7, which states: נִתַּאי הָאַרְבֵּלִי אוֹמֵר: הַרְחֵק מִשָּׁכֵן רַע וְאַל תִּתְחַבֵּר לְרָשָׁע וְאַל תִּתְיָאֵשׁ מִן הַפּוּרְעָנוּת — **Nittai of Arbel says: Distance yourself from a bad neighbor; do not associate with a wicked person; and do not despair of retribution.**

The Baraisa will expound each of Nittai's sayings. The first saying: הַרְחֵק מִשָּׁכֵן רַע — **"Distance yourself from a bad neighbor"** — אֶחָד שָׁכֵן שֶׁבַּבַּיִת וְאֶחָד שָׁכֵן שֶׁבַּחוּץ וְאֶחָד שָׁכֵן שֶׁבַּשָּׂדֶה — this applies **whether it is a neighbor in the house, a neighbor outside** the house, **or a neighbor in the field.**[1]

The Baraisa illustrates its point by demonstrating just one of the many possible negative effects of living next to a bad person: שֶׁאֵין הַנְּגָעִים בָּאִין אֶלָּא עַל בֵּיתוֹ שֶׁל רָשָׁע — **For** *tzaraas* **afflictions come only upon the house of a wicked person,** שֶׁנֶּאֱמַר "עֲווֹנוֹתָיו יִלְכְּדֻנוֹ אֶת הָרָשָׁע" — **as it is stated,** *The iniquities of the wicked one will trap him* (Proverbs 5:22), מְלַמֵּד שֶׁאֵין הַנְּגָעִים בָּאִים אֶלָּא בַּעֲווֹנוֹ שֶׁל רָשָׁע — **which teaches us that** *tzaraas* **afflictions come only on account of the sins of a wicked person.**[2] עֲווֹנוֹתָיו שֶׁל רָשָׁע גָּרְמוּ לוֹ לִסְתּוֹר כָּתְלוֹ שֶׁל צַדִּיק — Nonetheless, **the sins of a wicked person** can **cause the wall of a righteous person to be dismantled** because of *tzaraas* afflictions. כֵּיצַד — **How so?** כָּתְלוֹ שֶׁבֵּין רָשָׁע לְבֵין צַדִּיק — Suppose there is a

---

1. Meaning, whether his house is next to your house, his store is next to your store, or his field is next to your field (*Magen Avos*). The Baraisa stresses that you must be careful not only with regard to those who are near your house and with whom you are thus in frequent contact. You must keep your distance even from less-common encounters with bad people who might be near your store, and even the least-common encounters with bad people, who might be near your field (*Binyan Yehoshua*).

2. The end of the *Proverbs* verse reads, *and*

he will be suspended in the cords of his sins, referring to the fact that the wicked man's sins ultimately lead to his hanging ["*suspended in the cords*"], or some other form of death. Now, because God is kind and merciful, He usually brings retribution upon a person's possessions [to give him a chance to repent] before attacking his actual body; it follows that the "trapping" mentioned in the beginning of the verse alludes to some punishment brought upon his property, namely, a *tzaraas* affliction of the house (*Ahavas Chesed*).

נִרְאָה נֶגַע בְּבֵיתוֹ שֶׁל רָשָׁע בְּכָתְלוֹ [שֶׁבֵּינוֹ לְבֵין הַצַּדִּיק,[3] נִמְצָא סוֹתְרִין
כָּתְלוֹ] שֶׁל צַדִּיק בַּעֲוֹנוֹ שֶׁל רָשָׁע.[4] (רַבִּי יִשְׁמָעֵאל בְּנוֹ שֶׁל רַבִּי יוֹחָנָן בֶּן
בְּרוֹקָה אוֹמֵר:) אוֹי לָרָשָׁע אוֹי לִשְׁבֵינוֹ, (עֲוֹנוֹתָיו שֶׁל רָשָׁע גָּרְמוּ לִסְתּוֹר
כָּתְלוֹ שֶׁל צַדִּיק):

ב. עֲשָׂרָה נִסְיוֹנוֹת נִסּוּ אֲבוֹתֵינוּ אֶת הַקָּדוֹשׁ בָּרוּךְ הוּא[5] וְלֹא נֶעֶנְשׁוּ
אֶלָּא עַל לָשׁוֹן הָרַע ([שֶׁהוּא אֶחָד מֵהֶם]). וְאֵלּוּ הֵן: אֶחָד עַל
הַיָּם[6] וְאֶחָד בִּתְחִלַּת הַמָּן[7] וְאֶחָד בְּסוֹף הַמָּן[8] וְאֶחָד בַּשְּׁלָיו הָרִאשׁוֹן[9]

wall that is between the house of **a wicked person and** that of his neighbor, who
is **a righteous person.** נִרְאָה נֶגַע בְּבֵיתוֹ שֶׁל רָשָׁע בְּכָתְלוֹ שֶׁבֵּינוֹ לְבֵין הַצַּדִּיק — **If a**
tzaraas **affliction appears in the house of the wicked person on the shared wall
that is between his** house **and** that of **the righteous person, and the affected
stone of the common wall must be removed,**[3] נִמְצָא סוֹתְרִין כָּתְלוֹ שֶׁל צַדִּיק
בַּעֲוֹנוֹ שֶׁל רָשָׁע — **it emerges that** when they dismantle the wall of the wicked
person, **they** also **dismantle the wall of the righteous person, because of the
sins of the wicked person.**[4] רַבִּי יִשְׁמָעֵאל בְּנוֹ שֶׁל רַבִּי יוֹחָנָן בֶּן בְּרוֹקָה אוֹמֵר: אוֹי
לָרָשָׁע אוֹי לִשְׁבֵינוֹ — **R' Yishmael son of R' Yochanan ben Berokah says:** This
case is an illustration of the principle: **"Woe to a wicked person, woe to his
neighbor";** עֲוֹנוֹתָיו שֶׁל רָשָׁע גָּרְמוּ לִסְתּוֹר כָּתְלוֹ שֶׁל צַדִּיק — **the sins of a wicked
person have caused the wall of the righteous** neighbor **to be dismantled.**

§2 The Baraisa just mentioned *tzaraas* afflictions, which are caused by the
sin of *lashon hara* (as the Baraisa will state soon). The Baraisa therefore
proceeds to demonstrate the great severity of *lashon hara*:
עֲשָׂרָה נִסְיוֹנוֹת נִסּוּ אֲבוֹתֵינוּ אֶת הַקָּדוֹשׁ בָּרוּךְ הוּא — With **ten trials did our ancestors "test" the Holy One, Blessed is He,** while they were in the Wilderness,[5]
וְלֹא נֶעֶנְשׁוּ אֶלָּא עַל לָשׁוֹן הָרַע — **but they were punished** with the severe sentence of not being allowed entry into the Land of Israel **only on account of
the** sin of *lashon hara.* וְאֵלּוּ הֵן — **Those** ten trials are **as follows:** אֶחָד
עַל הַיָּם — **(i) One at the Sea** of Reeds,[6] וְאֶחָד בִּתְחִלַּת הַמָּן — **(ii) one at
the beginning of** the falling of **the manna,**[7] וְאֶחָד בְּסוֹף הַמָּן — **(iii) one at
the end of** the falling of **the manna,**[8] וְאֶחָד בַּשְּׁלָיו הָרִאשׁוֹן — **(iv) one on**

---

3. See *Leviticus* 14:40.

4. See *Negaim* 12:6 with *Rav.*

5. I.e., on ten occasions they exhibited a lack
of faith in Him (see *Binyan Yehoshua,* citing
Tos. Yom Tov to *Avos* 5:4, which our Baraisa
elaborates).

6. The Israelites, trapped between the pursuing
Egyptians and the sea that stood before them,
brazenly said to Moses (*Exodus* 14:11), *"Were*

there no graves in Egypt that you took us to
die in the Wilderness?"* (*Avos HaRosh* [Vol. 1]).

7. When the manna first fell, God commanded the people not to leave over any manna
until the morning, and they disobeyed Him
[see *Exodus* 16:19-20] (*Binyan Yehoshua*).
[This was a lack of faith that God would provide for them on the next day as well.]

8. After the manna had fallen for several days

וְאֶחָד בַּשְּׂלָיו הָאַחֲרוֹן[10] אֶחָד בְּמָרָה[11] וְאֶחָד בִּרְפִידִים[12] וְאֶחָד °בְּחֹרֵב[13]
וְאֶחָד [בָּעֵגֶל[14] וְאֶחָד] בַּמְרַגְּלִים[15]. זֶה שֶׁל מְרַגְּלִים קָשֶׁה מִכּוּלָם,
שֶׁנֶּאֱמַר (במדבר יד, כב) ״וַיְנַסּוּ אֹתִי זֶה עֶשֶׂר פְּעָמִים וְלֹא שָׁמְעוּ בְּקוֹלִי״.[16]

the occasion of **the first** provision of quail,[9]   **וְאֶחָד בַּשְּׂלָיו הָאַחֲרוֹן** — (v) **one**
on the occasion of **the second** provision of quail,[10]   **אֶחָד בְּמָרָה** — (vi) **one**
in Marah,[11]   **וְאֶחָד בִּרְפִידִים** — (vii) **one** in Rephidim,[12]   **וְאֶחָד בִּתְבְעֵרָה**
— (viii) **one** in Taberah,[13]   **וְאֶחָד בָּעֵגֶל** — (ix) **one** with the Golden Calf,[14]
וְאֶחָד בַּמְרַגְּלִים — and (x) **one** in the incident of the Spies.[15]   **זֶה שֶׁל מְרַגְּלִים**
קָשֶׁה מִכּוּלָם — This sin that was committed during the incident of **the Spies**
was worse than all the others,   **שֶׁנֶּאֱמַר ״וַיְנַסּוּ אֹתִי זֶה עֶשֶׂר פְּעָמִים וְלֹא שָׁמְעוּ**
בְּקוֹלִי״ — as it is stated, *and they have tested Me these ten times and have*
not heeded My voice (Numbers 14:22).[16]

and the Sabbath approached, God commanded the people not to go out and look
for the manna on the Sabbath because
it would not fall on that day, and they disobeyed Him [see *Exodus* 16:25-27] (ibid.).

Alternatively, the "beginning" and "end" of
the manna refer to the two times the people
complained about the manna: the first time
in the second year from the Exodus, when
they said, *But now, our life is parched, there
is nothing; we have nothing to anticipate but
the manna!* (*Numbers* 11:6) and the second
time, in the fortieth year, when, *The people
spoke against God and Moses, "Why did you
bring us up from Egypt to die in this Wilderness, for there is no food and no water, and
our soul is disgusted with the insubstantial
food [that is the manna]"* [ibid. 21:5] (*Avos
HaRosh* [Vol. 1]).

9. At the beginning of their sojourn in the
Wilderness, they lamented leaving Egypt,
where they "sat by the pot of meat" and "ate
bread to satiety," to be taken to the Wilderness to face famine [see *Exodus* 16:3] (*Binyan Yehoshua*). In response to this grievance, God supplied them with quail [see v.
13 there].

10. In the Wildnerness of Paran, when they
complained about their lack of proper food,
as recounted in *Numbers* Ch. 11 (*Binyan
Yehoshua*). This occasioned their second
provision of quail (see v. 31 there). [These
two provisions of quail took place a little

more than a year apart (see Schottenstein
ed. of *Arachin* 15b note 5).]

11. After encamping in the city of Marah,
they complained that there was no water for
them to drink [see *Exodus* 15:23-24] (*Binyan Yehoshua*, from *Arachin* 15a).

12. Upon reaching Rephidim, they contended
against God, and they said to Moses, *"Why is
this that you have brought us up from Egypt
to kill me and my children and my livestock
through thirst?"* [*Exodus* 17:3] (ibid.).

13. [Emendation follows *Gra* and *Ben
Avraham*; see also *Ahavas Chesed*.] In the
place subsequently named Taberah, Scripture tells us, *The people took to seeking
complaints; it was evil in the ears of HASHEM*
(*Numbers* 11:1-3).

14. When the people despaired of Moses's
return from Mount Sinai and made the
Golden Calf to lead them, as described in
Exodus Ch. 32.

15. When the Spies sent to the Land of Israel
returned and slandered it, causing the rest
of the nation to despair about ever taking
possession of it (see *Numbers* Chs. 13-14).
In addition to "testing" God, this sin was one
of terrible *lashon hara*.

16. The seemingly extraneous word זֶה [lit.,
this] implies that it was for *this* sin alone
that God issued their verdict to die in the
Wilderness [stated in the next verse] (*Magen
Avos*). This is the Baraisa's proof that this

כַּיוֹצֵא בוֹ, (שם פסוק לז) "וַיָּמֻתוּ הָאֲנָשִׁים מוֹצִאֵי דִבַּת הָאָרֶץ רָעָה בַּמַּגֵּפָה לִפְנֵי
ה' "[17]. וַהֲלֹא דְבָרִים קַל וָחֹמֶר וּמַה אֶרֶץ שֶׁאֵין לָהּ לֹא פֶּה לְדַבֵּר[18] וְלֹא פָּנִים
וְלֹא בֹשֶׁת בִּקֵּשׁ הַקָּדוֹשׁ בָּרוּךְ הוּא עֶלְבּוֹנָהּ מִן הַמְרַגְּלִים, הַמְדַבֵּר דְּבָרִים
כְּנֶגֶד חֲבֵירוֹ וּמְבַיֵּישׁ אוֹתוֹ עַל אַחַת כַּמָּה וְכַמָּה שֶׁיְּבַקֵּשׁ הַקָּדוֹשׁ בָּרוּךְ הוּא
עֶלְבּוֹנוֹ. רַבִּי שִׁמְעוֹן אוֹמֵר: עַל מְסַפְּרֵי לָשׁוֹן הָרָע נְגָעִים בָּאִים עָלָיו[19], שֶׁכֵּן
מָצִינוּ בְּאַהֲרֹן וּמִרְיָם שֶׁסִּפְּרוּ לָשׁוֹן הָרָע בְּמֹשֶׁה וּבָא עֲלֵיהֶם אֶת הַפּוּרְעָנוּת,

The Baraisa supports its contention that the sin of the Spies was considered most severe because it involved *lashon hara*:

Similarly, — כַּיוֹצֵא בוֹ, "וַיָּמֻתוּ הָאֲנָשִׁים מוֹצִאֵי דִבַּת הָאָרֶץ רָעָה בַּמַּגֵּפָה לִפְנֵי ה' " you find that the verse states about the Spies, *The people who spread the evil report about the Land died in a plague before HASHEM* (ibid. v. 37). This verse indicates that the main reason they died in the plague was that they spread an evil report about the Land.[17]

A further lesson regarding *lashon hara* that can be drawn from this:

Now, is the matter — וַהֲלֹא דְבָרִים קַל וָחֹמֶר of *lashon hara* against a person, then, **not** one that can be shown to be even more severe, through a *kal va'chomer*? **If in the case of a land, — וּמַה אֶרֶץ שֶׁאֵין לָהּ לֹא פֶּה לְדַבֵּר וְלֹא פָּנִים וְלֹא בֹשֶׁת** which **has no mouth to speak,**[18] **nor face** to redden, **nor feelings of humiliation, — בִּקֵּשׁ הַקָּדוֹשׁ בָּרוּךְ הוּא עֶלְבּוֹנָהּ מִן הַמְרַגְּלִים** the **Holy One, Blessed is He, sought** redress for **its insult from the Spies,** who spoke disparagingly against it, **— הַמְדַבֵּר דְּבָרִים כְּנֶגֶד חֲבֵירוֹ וּמְבַיֵּישׁ אוֹתוֹ** then if **someone speaks** evil **words against his fellow** — who *does* have a mouth to speak, a face to redden, and feelings of humiliation — **and** thereby **embarrasses him, עַל אַחַת כַּמָּה וְכַמָּה שֶׁיְּבַקֵּשׁ הַקָּדוֹשׁ בָּרוּךְ הוּא עֶלְבּוֹנוֹ —** how much more so will the **Holy One, Blessed is He, seek** redress for **the insult to him!**

The Baraisa demonstrates the connection between *lashon hara* and *tzaraas*: **R' Shimon says: On — רַבִּי שִׁמְעוֹן אוֹמֵר: עַל מְסַפְּרֵי לָשׁוֹן הָרָע נְגָעִים בָּאִים עָלָיו** those who speak *lashon hara, tzaraas* afflictions come upon him.[19] **שֶׁכֵּן מָצִינוּ בְּאַהֲרֹן וּמִרְיָם שֶׁסִּפְּרוּ לָשׁוֹן הָרָע בְּמֹשֶׁה וּבָא עֲלֵיהֶם אֶת הַפּוּרְעָנוּת — For thus** do we find in the case of **Aaron and Miriam** that they spoke *lashon hara*

"test" was worse than all the others. And the reason it was worse is that it involved the sin of *lashon hara*.

17. Similarly, the Gemara (*Arachin* 15a) proves from this verse that *lashon hara* was considered the defining sin of the Spies, and not that they had doubted God's power to overcome the inhabitants of the Land (*Magen Avos*).

18. So its silence after being shamed is not embarrassing (see *Ben Avraham* ד"ה כנגד חברו).

19. [The word עָלָיו, *upon him,* seems redundant; moreover, its singular tense does not agree with the plural antecedent מְסַפְּרֵי, *those who speak.* See *Magen Avos,* who suggests several explanations for this peculiar wording.]

שֶׁנֶּאֱמַר (שם יב, א) ״וַתְּדַבֵּר מִרְיָם וְאַהֲרֹן בְּמֹשֶׁה״.[20] [לָמָּה הִקְדִּים
הַכָּתוּב מִרְיָם לְאַהֲרֹן].[21] מְלַמֵּד שֶׁהָלְכָה] צִפּוֹרָה וְשָׂחָה לָהּ לְמִרְיָם.[22]
הָלְכָה מִרְיָם וְשָׂחָה לוֹ לְאַהֲרֹן. עָמְדוּ שְׁנֵיהֶם וְדִבְּרוּ בַּצַּדִּיק הַהוּא.

about Moses, and the punishment of *tzaraas* befell them,   שֶׁנֶּאֱמַר ״וַתְּדַבֵּר
מִרְיָם וְאַהֲרֹן בְּמֹשֶׁה״ — as it is stated, *Miriam and Aaron spoke against Moses*
(ibid. 12:1).[20]

In developing its proof, the Baraisa analyzes this verse:
לָמָּה הִקְדִּים הַכָּתוּב מִרְיָם לְאַהֲרֹן — Why did Scripture mention Miriam here before Aaron?[21]   מְלַמֵּד שֶׁהָלְכָה צִפּוֹרָה וְשָׂחָה לָהּ לְמִרְיָם — This teaches us that
Zipporah, Moses's wife, **had gone and told Miriam** that Moses had separated
from her,[22]   הָלְכָה מִרְיָם וְשָׂחָה לוֹ לְאַהֲרֹן — then **Miriam went and told** it to
Aaron,   עָמְדוּ שְׁנֵיהֶם וְדִבְּרוּ בַּצַּדִּיק הַהוּא — and then **both** Miriam and Aaron
arose and spoke against that righteous man, Moses (as the Baraisa will soon
elaborate). Thus, because Miriam was the instigator of the *lashon hara*, she is
mentioned before Aaron in this verse.

---

20. [As will be seen below, the *tzaraas* initially affected Aaron as well.] We present
here the entire passage (much of which will
be expounded by the Baraisa below):
[1] *Miriam and Aaron spoke against Moses
regarding the Cushite woman he had married, for he had married a Cushite woman.*
[As the Baraisa will explain, they criticized
him for having ceased to have conjugal relations with her.] [2] *They said, "Was it only to
Moses that HASHEM spoke? Did He not speak
to us, as well?" And HASHEM heard.* [3] *Now the
man Moses was exceedingly humble, more
than any person on the face of the earth!*
[4] *HASHEM said suddenly to Moses, to Aaron,
and to Miriam, "You three, go out to the Tent
of Meeting." And the three of them went out.*
[5] *HASHEM descended in a pillar of cloud and
stood at the entrance to the Tent, and He summoned Aaron and Miriam; the two of them
went out.* [6] *He said, "Hear now My words. If
there shall be prophets among you, in a vision shall I, HASHEM, make Myself known to
him; in a dream shall I speak with him.* [7] *Not
so is My servant Moses; in My entire house
he is the trusted one.* [8] *Mouth to mouth do
I speak to him, in a clear vision and not in
riddles, at the image of HASHEM does he gaze.
Why did you not fear to speak against My
servant Moses?"* [9] *The wrath of HASHEM flared*

up against them, and He left. [10] *The cloud
had departed from atop the Tent, and behold!
Miriam was afflicted with tzaraas, like snow!
Aaron turned to Miriam and behold! she was
afflicted with tzaraas.* [11] *Aaron said to Moses,
"I beg you, my lord, do not cast a sin upon us,
for we have been foolish and we have sinned.*
[12] *Let her not be like a corpse, like one who
leaves his mother's womb with half his flesh
having been consumed!"* [13] *Moses cried out to
HASHEM, saying, "Please, God, heal her now."*
[14] *HASHEM said to Moses, "Were her father to
spit in her face, would she not be humiliated for seven days? Let her be quarantined
outside the camp for seven days, and then
she may be brought in."* [15] *So Miriam was
quarantined outside the camp for seven days,
and the people did not journey until Miriam
was brought in.*

21. Miriam would not be accustomed to
speak before her brother Aaron [who was
the Kohen Gadol]. Why then does Scripture
here place her first? (*Ahavas Chesed*).

22. When Zipporah heard about certain
men who were prophesying, she exclaimed, "Woe to the wives of these men if
they become prophets, for their husbands
will separate from them just as my husband
separated from me!" Miriam overheard this

מִתּוֹךְ שֶׁעָמְדוּ שְׁנֵיהֶם וְדִבְּרוּ בַּצַּדִּיק בָּא עֲלֵיהֶם אֶת הַפּוּרְעָנוּת, שֶׁנֶּאֱמַר
(שם פסוק ט) "וַיִּחַר אַף ה' בָּם וַיֵּלַךְ"[23]. מַה תַּלְמוּד לוֹמַר "וַיֵּלַךְ", מְלַמֵּד
שֶׁנִּסְתַּלֵּק מֵאַהֲרֹן וְדָבַק בְּמִרְיָם[24] מִפְּנֵי שֶׁלֹּא הָיָה אַהֲרֹן עַסְקָן בַּדְּבָרִים,
אֲבָל מִרְיָם שֶׁהָיְתָה עוֹסֶקֶת בַּדְּבָרִים (מִיָּד) נֶעֶנְשָׁה יוֹתֵר[26]. מִרְיָם
אָמְרָה: אֵלַי הָיָה דִבּוּר וְלֹא פֵּרַשְׁתִּי מֵאֵצֶל בַּעְלִי. אַהֲרֹן אָמַר: אֵלַי הָיָה
דִבּוּר וְלֹא פֵּרַשְׁתִּי מֵאֵצֶל אִשְׁתִּי. וְאַף אֲבוֹתֵינוּ הָרִאשׁוֹנִים הָיָה דִבּוּר

The Baraisa continues:

מִתּוֹךְ שֶׁעָמְדוּ שְׁנֵיהֶם וְדִבְּרוּ בַּצַּדִּיק בָּא עֲלֵיהֶם אֶת הַפּוּרְעָנוּת — And because both of them arose and spoke against that righteous man, the punishment of tzaraas afflictions came upon them, שֶׁנֶּאֱמַר "וַיִּחַר אַף ה' בָּם וַיֵּלַךְ" — as it is stated, The wrath of HASHEM flared up against "them," and He left (ibid. v. 9).[23] מַה תַּלְמוּד לוֹמַר "וַיֵּלַךְ" — Now, what is Scripture teaching us by saying further, and He left? מְלַמֵּד שֶׁנִּסְתַּלֵּק מֵאַהֲרֹן וְדָבַק בְּמִרְיָם — It teaches us that [the tzaraas affliction] departed from Aaron and clung to Miriam.[24] Why did it cling to Miriam and not to Aaron? מִפְּנֵי שֶׁלֹּא הָיָה אַהֲרֹן עַסְקָן בַּדְּבָרִים — Because Aaron was not the instigator in the matter, and he was therefore cured immediately.[25] אֲבָל מִרְיָם שֶׁהָיְתָה עוֹסֶקֶת בַּדְּבָרִים מִיָּד נֶעֶנְשָׁה יוֹתֵר — But Miriam, who was the instigator in the matter, was punished immediately, and more than Aaron.[26]

The Baraisa recounts the particulars of their criticism of Moses:

מִרְיָם אָמְרָה: אֵלַי הָיָה דִבּוּר וְלֹא פֵּרַשְׁתִּי מֵאֵצֶל בַּעְלִי — First, Miriam said, "I received prophecy as well, and I did not separate from my husband." אַהֲרֹן אָמַר: אֵלַי הָיָה דִבּוּר וְלֹא פֵּרַשְׁתִּי מֵאֵצֶל אִשְׁתִּי — Then Aaron said, "I received prophecy as well, and I did not separate from my wife." וְאַף אֲבוֹתֵינוּ הָרִאשׁוֹנִים הָיָה דִבּוּר

---

comment, and in this way, Zipporah "told" her about what Moses had done (Binyan Yehoshua).

23. The Godly "wrath" that flared up against them is the tzaraas affliction. And the verse says that it flared up against "them," indicating that Aaron, too, became afflicted with tzaraas (see Magen Avos).

24. The word וַיֵּלַךְ is now rendered, not and "He" left, but and "it" [the wrath] left [i.e., the tzaraas affliction] (see Ben Avraham). The tzaraas left only Aaron, but it clung to Miriam, as it states in the next verse that Aaron turned to Miriam and saw that she was afflicted with tzaraas (Avos HaRosh [Vol. 1]).

25. Avos HaRosh [Vol. 1].

26. Avos HaRosh [Vol. 1]. "Immediately" means that the tzaraas afflicted her body to begin with, in contrast to other times, when the tzaraas punishment for lashon hara comes in stages — first to the house, then to the clothing, and only afterward to the body (ibid., based on Rambam, Hil. Tzaraas 16:10).

Alternatively, Ahavas Chesed suggests that the word מִיָּד, immediately, is part of the preceding clause: Miriam "was the instigator in the matter immediately." Aaron, however, did not pursue the matter so vigorously. [Gra removes the word מִיָּד, immediately, from the text.]

עֲלֵיהֶם וְלֹא פֵּרְשׁוּ מֵאֵצֶל נְשׁוֹתֵיהֶן. אֲבָל הוּא מִפְּנֵי שֶׁדַּעְתּוֹ גָּסָה עָלָיו
פֵּירֵשׁ הוּא מֵאֵצֶל אִשְׁתּוֹ.[27] וְלֹא הָיוּ דָנִין אוֹתוֹ בְּפָנָיו אֶלָּא שֶׁלֹּא בְּפָנָיו,[28]
וְלֹא הָיוּ דָנִין אוֹתוֹ בְּוַדַּאי אֶלָּא בְּסָפֵק, סָפֵק שֶׁדַּעְתּוֹ גָּסָה עָלָיו[29] סָפֵק
שֶׁאֵין דַּעְתּוֹ גָּסָה עָלָיו. וַהֲרֵי דְבָרִים קַל וָחֹמֶר, וּמַה מִרְיָם שֶׁלֹּא דִבְּרָה
אֶלָּא בְּאָחִיהָ [וְלֹא דִבְּרָה אֶלָּא בְּהֶחְבֵּא] וְלֹא דִבְּרָה אֶלָּא שֶׁלֹּא בְּפָנָיו
שֶׁל מֹשֶׁה נֶעֶנְשָׁה, אָדָם הֶדְיוֹט הַמְדַבֵּר דְּבָרִים בִּפְנֵי חֲבֵירוֹ וּמְבַיְּישׁוֹ

עֲלֵיהֶם וְלֹא פֵּרְשׁוּ מֵאֵצֶל נְשׁוֹתֵיהֶן — Then both Miriam and Aaron said, "And similarly, our ancestors, Abraham, Isaac, and Jacob, received prophecy, and they did not separate from their wives. אֲבָל הוּא מִפְּנֵי שֶׁדַּעְתּוֹ גָּסָה עָלָיו פֵּירֵשׁ הוּא מֵאֵצֶל אִשְׁתּוֹ — However, he (our brother, Moses), it is apparently because he has become haughty that he has separated from his wife."[27]

The Baraisa examines this incident more closely and draws an important lesson from it:

וְלֹא הָיוּ דָנִין אוֹתוֹ בְּפָנָיו אֶלָּא שֶׁלֹּא בְּפָנָיו — Now, they did not judge him in this matter in his presence, but rather in his absence, so he was not embarrassed as a result of their discussion.[28] וְלֹא הָיוּ דָנִין אוֹתוֹ בְּוַדַּאי אֶלָּא בְּסָפֵק — Moreover, they did not judge him as definitely guilty of their charge of haughtiness against him, but rather only as possibly guilty of it — that is, סָפֵק שֶׁדַּעְתּוֹ גָּסָה עָלָיו סָפֵק שֶׁאֵין דַּעְתּוֹ גָּסָה עָלָיו — their accusation was only that possibly he was haughty, possibly he was not haughty.[29] And despite all this, they were punished for their lashon hara. וַהֲרֵי דְבָרִים קַל וָחֹמֶר — Now, is the matter of ordinary lashon hara spoken by people, then, not one that can be shown to be even more severe through a kal va'chomer? וּמַה מִרְיָם שֶׁלֹּא דִבְּרָה אֶלָּא בְּאָחִיהָ — If Miriam (who was righteous), who spoke only about her brother (whom she loved), וְלֹא דִבְּרָה אֶלָּא בְּהֶחְבֵּא — and who spoke about him only in private, so that other people (except for her brother Aaron, to whom she spoke) did not hear it,[30] וְלֹא דִבְּרָה אֶלָּא שֶׁלֹּא בְּפָנָיו שֶׁל מֹשֶׁה — and who spoke only in Moses's absence, so he was not embarrassed by what she said, נֶעֶנְשָׁה — was nevertheless punished for speaking lashon hara, אָדָם הֶדְיוֹט הַמְדַבֵּר דְּבָרִים בִּפְנֵי חֲבֵירוֹ וּמְבַיְּישׁוֹ

---

27. [Thinking that his prophecy is somehow superior to that of all other prophets, and therefore he requires separation from his wife, so that he will remain in a state of perpetual purity. That they attributed this to haughtiness is indicated by the Torah's stating immediately afterward, *Now the man Moses was exceedingly humble ...*, to negate what they had accused him of.]

28. [See *Magen Avos*.] That Moses was not present is indicated by the verse there (v. 2),

and HASHEM heard, which implies that *only* God heard, and no one else (*Ben Avraham*, from *Sifrei* ad loc.).

29. [Their attribution of his separation to haughtiness was merely conjecture; it is not something they could have known with certainty. (See *Ben Avraham*, who sees an indication of their uncertainty in the wording of the verse.)

30. Alternatively, *Ben Avraham* suggests that בְּהֶחְבֵּא, *in hiding*, is a reference to the

עַל אַחַת כַּמָּה וְכַמָּה שֶׁיְּהֵא עוֹנְשׁוֹ מְרוּבֶּה. בְּאוֹתָהּ שָׁעָה אָמַר לוֹ
אַהֲרֹן לְמֹשֶׁה: מֹשֶׁה אָחִי, כִּסָּבוּר אַתָּה בְּעַצְמְךָ שֶׁצָּרַעַת זוֹ עַל מִרְיָם
נְתוּנָה, אֵינָהּ נְתוּנָה אֶלָּא עַל בְּשָׂרוֹ שֶׁל אַבָּא שֶׁל עַמְרָם.[32] אֶמְשׁוֹל לְךָ מָשָׁל
לְמָה הַדָּבָר דּוֹמֶה, לְאֶחָד שֶׁנָּתַן גַּחֶלֶת בְּתוֹךְ יָדוֹ, אַף עַל פִּי שֶׁהוֹפְכָהּ
מִמָּקוֹם לְמָקוֹם מִכָּל מָקוֹם בְּשָׂרוֹ נִכְוֶית, שֶׁנֶּאֱמַר (שם פסוק יב) "אַל נָא
תְהִי כַּמֵּת.[33]" בְּאוֹתָהּ שָׁעָה הִתְחִיל אַהֲרֹן לְפַיֵּיס בְּמֹשֶׁה. אָמַר לוֹ:
מֹשֶׁה אָחִי, כְּלוּם עָשִׂינוּ רָעָה עִם אֶחָד בָּעוֹלָם.[34] אָמַר לוֹ: לָאו. וּמַה עִם

עַל אַחַת כַּמָּה וְכַמָּה שֶׁיְּהֵא עוֹנְשׁוֹ מְרוּבֶּה — then **an ordinary person, who speaks words** of *lashon hara* about his fellow **in the presence of his fellow and** who thereby **embarrasses him, how much more so that his punishment is great!**

The Baraisa continues its elaboration of this incident:

בְּאוֹתָהּ שָׁעָה אָמַר לוֹ אַהֲרֹן לְמֹשֶׁה — **At that time,** when Aaron begged Moses to pray for their stricken sister,[31] **Aaron said to Moses,** **מֹשֶׁה אָחִי, כִּסָּבוּר אַתָּה** — "**Moses my brother, do you think that this** **בְּעַצְמְךָ שֶׁצָּרַעַת זוֹ עַל מִרְיָם נְתוּנָה** *tzaraas* **affliction has been placed** on *Miriam*? **אֵינָהּ נְתוּנָה אֶלָּא עַל בְּשָׂרוֹ שֶׁל** **אַבָּא עַמְרָם** — Not so! In effect, **it has been placed on the flesh of none other than** our deceased **father Amram!**[32] **אֶמְשׁוֹל לְךָ מָשָׁל לְמָה הַדָּבָר דּוֹמֶה** — **I will give you an analogy: To what is this matter comparable?** **לְאֶחָד שֶׁנָּתַן** **גַּחֶלֶת בְּתוֹךְ יָדוֹ** — **To someone who placed** a fiery **coal in his hand;** **אַף עַל** **פִּי שֶׁהוֹפְכָהּ מִמָּקוֹם לְמָקוֹם מִכָּל מָקוֹם בְּשָׂרוֹ נִכְוֶית** — **even though he shifts it from one place to another** in his hand, **it is nevertheless his flesh that is burned!**" **שֶׁנֶּאֱמַר** "**אַל נָא תְהִי כַּמֵּת**" — This analogy is **as it is stated** that Aaron said to Moses, "*Let her not be like a corpse, like one who leaves his mother's womb with half his flesh having been consumed!*" (ibid. v. 12).[33] **בְּאוֹתָהּ שָׁעָה** **הִתְחִיל אַהֲרֹן לְפַיֵּיס בְּמֹשֶׁה** — **At that time, Aaron began to appease Moses** **אָמַר לוֹ: מֹשֶׁה אָחִי** — **and said to him, "Moses my brother, have we** — Miriam or I — **ever done evil to anyone** else **in the world?**"[34] **אָמַר לוֹ: לָאו** — [Moses] **answered** him, "**No,** you have not." **וּמַה עִם**

"uncertainty of guilt" spoken of earlier by the Baraisa.

31. As related there in Scripture and cited in part below.

32. That is, since we are all children of the same father, we are like one body; an affliction to our sister is like an affliction to us all (*Binyan Yehoshua,* citing *Mefaresh*).

33. The Baraisa's proof is from the end of the verse [whose translation we have added to the text] (*Binyan Yehoshua*). A person

afflicted with *tzaraas* is like a corpse. If Miriam our sister, who came from the same womb as we, is like a corpse, then it is as if half our own body has been consumed (*Rashi* on the verse). [This analogy is identical to the one stated in the Baraisa, except that the Baraisa describes their common bond in terms of being of the same father, whereas the verse describes it in terms of being of the same mother.]

34. This is alluded to in the verse 11, where Aaron says to Moses, "*I beg you, my lord,*

אֶחָד בָּעוֹלָם לֹא עָשִׂינוּ רָעָה אַתָּה שֶׁאָחִינוּ אַתָּה הֵיאַךְ נַעֲשֶׂה רָעָה עִמְּךָ,
אֲבָל מָה אֶעֱשֶׂה, שְׁגָגָה הִיא בֵּינוֹתֵינוּ[35], בְּרִית שֶׁבֵּינֵינוּ לְבֵינְךָ[36°], (מִפְּנֵי
שֶׁהַבְּרִית כְּרוּתָה לְאַהֲרֹן וּלְבָנָיו) שֶׁנֶּאֱמַר (עמוס א, ט) "וְלֹא זָכְרוּ בְּרִית
אַחִים". בְּאוֹתָהּ שָׁעָה עָג מֹשֶׁה עוּגָה קְטַנָּה וְעָמַד בְּתוֹכָהּ וּבִקֵּשׁ רַחֲמִים
עָלֶיהָ, וְאָמַר: אֵינִי זָז מִכָּאן עַד שֶׁתִּתְרַפֵּא מִרְיָם אֲחוֹתִי[38], שֶׁנֶּאֱמַר (במדבר יב,
יג) "אֵל נָא רְפָא נָא לָהּ"[39]. בְּאוֹתָהּ שָׁעָה אָמַר לוֹ הַקָּדוֹשׁ בָּרוּךְ הוּא לְמֹשֶׁה:
אִילּוּ מֶלֶךְ נָזַף בָּהּ, אִילּוּ אָבִיהָ נָזַף בָּהּ, כִּרְאוּי הָיָה לָהּ שֶׁתִּכָּלֵם שִׁבְעַת יָמִים,

---

אֶחָד בָּעוֹלָם לֹא עָשִׂינוּ רָעָה, אַתָּה שֶׁאָחִינוּ אַתָּה הֵיאַךְ נַעֲשֶׂה רָעָה עִמְּךָ — Aaron continued, "If we have never done evil to anyone else in the world, then you, who
are our brother, how could we have meant to do evil to you? אֲבָל מָה אֶעֱשֶׂה,
שְׁגָגָה הִיא בֵּינוֹתֵינוּ — But what shall I do? Although we meant no malice, it was
a careless remark that was made between us.[35] בְּרִית שֶׁבֵּינֵינוּ לְבֵינְךָ בִּטַּלְנוּ
— Indeed, we have violated the brotherly covenant that is naturally between
us and you."[36] שֶׁנֶּאֱמַר "וְלֹא זָכְרוּ בְּרִית אַחִים" — That there is such a natural
covenant among siblings is as it is stated, Not remembering the covenant
of brothers (Amos 1:9). מִפְּנֵי הַבְּרִיתָה הַכְּרוּתָה בֵּינֵינוּ שֶׁבְּטַלְנוּ נְאַבֵּד אֶת אֲחוֹתֵינוּ
— "But shall it be that because of the covenant that exists between us that
we have violated, we shall lose our sister?"[37] בְּאוֹתָהּ שָׁעָה עָג מֹשֶׁה עוּגָה
בְּתוֹכָהּ קְטַנָּה וְעָמַד — At that time, Moses accepted Aaron's words of appease-
ment, and immediately drew a small circle on the ground and stood inside it,
וּבִקֵּשׁ רַחֲמִים עָלֶיהָ — and prayed to God on her behalf for mercy, וְאָמַר: אֵינִי
זָז מִכָּאן עַד שֶׁתִּתְרַפֵּא מִרְיָם אֲחוֹתִי — saying, "I will not move from here inside
this circle until my sister Miriam is cured!,"[38] שֶׁנֶּאֱמַר "אֵל נָא רְפָא נָא לָהּ"
— as it is stated, Moses cried out to HASHEM, saying, "Please, God, heal her
now" (Numbers 12:13).[39] בְּאוֹתָהּ שָׁעָה אָמַר לוֹ הַקָּדוֹשׁ בָּרוּךְ הוּא לְמֹשֶׁה — At
that time, the Holy One, Blessed is He, said to Moses, אִילּוּ מֶלֶךְ נָזַף בָּהּ,
אִילּוּ אָבִיהָ נָזַף בָּהּ, כִּרְאוּי הָיָה לָהּ שֶׁתִּכָּלֵם שִׁבְעַת יָמִים — "If a king were to scold
her or if her father were to scold her, it would be fitting for her to be humiliated

---

do not cast a sin upon us, for "we have been
foolish" [נוֹאַלְנוּ] and we have sinned. The
word נוֹאַלְנוּ can mean "we have begun" [see
Onkelos on Genesis 18:27 and Rashi on
Deuteronomy 1:5]. That is, this is the first
time we have ever spoken lashon hara (Ben
Avraham).

35. This is indicated by the term, and we
have "sinned" [חָטָאנוּ]. The root חטא generally refers to inadvertent sin (Ben Avraham).

36. [Emendation of this line and the next is
in accordance with the alternative version

cited by Tumas Yesharim, and is followed by
Gra.]

37. Aaron was imploring Moses to forgive
Miriam's sin against him and entreat God to
remove her affliction.

38. This is a way of indicating that he was
praying for immediate relief [since he could
remain in the circle for only a relatively short
time] (Ben Avraham).

39. Which indicates that Moses indeed
prayed for her immediate relief (ibid.).

אֲנִי שֶׁאֲנִי מֶלֶךְ מַלְכֵי הַמְּלָכִים עַל אַחַת כַּמָּה וְכַמָּה, לֹא דִין הוּא שֶׁתִּכָּלֵם אַרְבָּעָה עָשָׂר יוֹם[40], אֶלָּא לְמַעֲנֵךְ מָחוּל לָהּ, שֶׁנֶּאֱמַר (שם פסוק יד) "וַיֹּאמֶר ה' אֶל מֹשֶׁה וְאָבִיהָ יָרֹק יָרַק בְּפָנֶיהָ וְגוֹ' "[41] (שם פסוק ג). "וְהָאִישׁ מֹשֶׁה עָנָו מְאֹד", יָכוֹל שֶׁהָיָה עָנָו וְלֹא נָאֶה וּמְשׁוּבָּח[43], תַּלְמוּד לוֹמַר (שמות מ, יט) "וַיִּפְרֹשׂ אֶת הָאֹהֶל עַל הַמִּשְׁכָּן". מַה מִּשְׁכָּן עֶשֶׂר אַמּוֹת אַף מֹשֶׁה עֶשֶׂר אַמּוֹת קוֹמָתוֹ[44].

I, Who am — אֲנִי שֶׁאֲנִי מֶלֶךְ מַלְכֵי הַמְּלָכִים עַל אַחַת כַּמָּה וְכַמָּה   **for seven days.** the King Who reigns over kings, all the more so that she should be humiliated from My scolding for that length of time.   לֹא דִין הוּא שֶׁתִּכָּלֵם אַרְבָּעָה עָשָׂר יוֹם — **Is it not arguable,** then, **that she should** therefore **be humiliated for** not seven but *fourteen* **days?**[40]   אֶלָּא לְמַעֲנֵךְ מָחוּל לָהּ — **However, for your sake, she is pardoned** with regard to the additional seven days."   שֶׁנֶּאֱמַר "וַיֹּאמֶר ה' אֶל מֹשֶׁה וְאָבִיהָ יָרֹק יָרַק בְּפָנֶיהָ וְגוֹ' " — **This is the meaning of that which is stated,** HASHEM *said to Moses, "Were her father to spit in her face, would she not be humiliated for seven days? Let her be quarantined outside the camp for seven days, and then she may be brought in"* (ibid. v. 14).[41]

In response to Miriam and Aaron's suspicion that Moses had become haughty, Scripture asserts, *Now the man Moses was exceedingly humble, more than any person on the face of the earth* (ibid. v. 3). The Baraisa now expounds that verse:[42] "וְהָאִישׁ מֹשֶׁה עָנָו מְאֹד" — **The verse states,** *Now the man Moses was exceedingly humble* (ibid. v. 3).   יָכוֹל שֶׁהָיָה עָנָו וְלֹא נָאֶה וּמְשׁוּבָּח — **One might think that he was humble, but not splendid and admirable.**[43]   תַּלְמוּד לוֹמַר "וַיִּפְרֹשׂ אֶת הָאֹהֶל עַל הַמִּשְׁכָּן" — **Scripture,** however, **teaches** otherwise **by saying,** *[Moses] spread the Tent over the Tabernacle* (*Exodus* 40:19),   מַה מִּשְׁכָּן עֶשֶׂר אַמּוֹת אַף מֹשֶׁה עֶשֶׂר אַמּוֹת קוֹמָתוֹ — **which suggests that just as the Tabernacle was ten** *amos* **high, so was Moses ten** *amos* **tall.**[44]

---

40. Since I am both her King *and* her Father, it would be fitting for her to be humiliated seven days on each count, for a total of fourteen days (*Ben Avraham*). These two counts of fourteen are what *Tosafos* in *Bava Kamma* 25b, ד"ה ק"ו, refer to as the explanation of "the *Tosefta* of Tractate *Avos*" (*Ben Avraham*; see, however, *Tosafos* to *Bava Basra* 111a, ד"ה ק"ו, who seem to understand our Baraisa differently; see also *Magen Avos* here at length).

41. [The "humiliation" in Miriam's case is her being quarantined outside the camp until her *tzaraas* is healed. (See, however, *Magen Avos*.)]

42. *Ben Avraham*.

43. I.e., had the verse said only that Moses was "exceedingly humble," one might have thought that it means he was *physically* humble and unimposing, not humble in spirit (*Magen Avos*, based on *Sifrei* to the verse; see also *Ben Avraham*). Alternatively, we would know that "humble" here means humble in spirit. But perhaps that is because he did not have anything to be arrogant about — because he was not physically imposing or possessed of admirable qualities (*Yaavetz, Avos HaRosh* [Vol. 1]).

44. For otherwise, he would have been unable to spread the Tent over the Tabernacle, which was ten *amos* high [as stated in *Exodus* 26:16] (*Binyan Yehoshua*). This proves that

יָכוֹל שֶׁהָיָה עָנָו כְּמַלְאֲכֵי הַשָּׁרֵת,[45] תַּלְמוּד לוֹמַר (במדבר יב ג) "מִכֹּל
הָאָדָם", מֵאָדָם אָמְרוּ וְלֹא מִמַּלְאֲכֵי הַשָּׁרֵת. יָכוֹל שֶׁהָיָה עָנָו כַּדּוֹרוֹת
הָרִאשׁוֹנִים, תַּלְמוּד לוֹמַר (שם) "עַל פְּנֵי הָאֲדָמָה", מִדּוֹרוֹ אָמְרוּ וְלֹא
מִדּוֹרוֹת הָרִאשׁוֹנִים.[47] שְׁלֹשָׁה מִינֵי מוּכֵּי שְׁחִין נִבְרְאוּ בָּעוֹלָם: לַח יָבֵשׁ
בַּעַל פּוֹלִיפּוֹס,[48] וְהָיְתָה נַפְשׁוֹ שֶׁל מֹשֶׁה נְמוּכָה מִכּוּלָּם:[49]

יָכוֹל שֶׁהָיָה עָנָו כְּמַלְאֲכֵי הַשָּׁרֵת — Now, being that Scripture describes Moses as
"exceedingly" humble, **one might** make a different mistake and **think that
he was as humble as the ministering angels.**[45] תַּלְמוּד לוֹמַר "מִכֹּל הָאָדָם"
— Scripture, however, **teaches** otherwise by saying, *more than any person,*
מֵאָדָם אָמְרוּ וְלֹא מִמַּלְאֲכֵי הַשָּׁרֵת — implying that he **was only said** to be more
humble **than** any other *person,* **but not** more humble **than the ministering
angels.** For they are indeed more humble than he. יָכוֹל שֶׁהָיָה עָנָו כַּדּוֹרוֹת
הָרִאשׁוֹנִים — But **one might** still **think that he was as humble as** those great
men who lived in **the previous generations,** namely, Abraham, Isaac, and
Jacob.[46] תַּלְמוּד לוֹמַר "עַל פְּנֵי הָאֲדָמָה" — Scripture, however, **teaches** otherwise by saying, *on the face of the earth,* מִדּוֹרוֹ אָמְרוּ וְלֹא מִדּוֹרוֹת הָרִאשׁוֹנִים
— implying that he **was only said** to be more humble **than** those who were still
on the face of the earth in *his* generation, **but not** more **than** those great men
who lived in **previous generations.**[47]

The Baraisa gives us an idea of the great extent of Moses' humility:
שְׁלֹשָׁה מִינֵי מוּכֵּי שְׁחִין נִבְרְאוּ בָּעוֹלָם — **Three types of people afflicted with boils
were created in the world:** לַח יָבֵשׁ בַּעַל פּוֹלִיפּוֹס — one with a **moist** affliction, one with **a dry** affliction, and **one who has *polypus;*[48]** and due to their
physical inferiority, they are extremely humble of spirit. וְהָיְתָה נַפְשׁוֹ שֶׁל מֹשֶׁה
נְמוּכָה מִכּוּלָּם — But nonetheless, **Moses' spirit was more humble than any of
them.**[49]

---

he was indeed tall and physically imposing.
45. [See below, 12 §6, regarding the extraordinary humility of the ministering angels.]
46. See *Sifrei* on the verse.
47. For they were indeed even more humble
than he. [So it would emerge from our reading in the Baraisa — יָכוֹל שֶׁהָיָה עָנָו "כַּ"דּוֹרוֹת
הָרִאשׁוֹנִים, *one might think that he was "as
humble as" those of the previous generations,* which implies that the next words, *on
the face of the earth,* then teach us that he
was *not* as humble as they. In the Epstein
manuscript, however, the reading is: יָכוֹל
שֶׁהָיָה עָנָו "מִ"דּוֹרוֹת הָרִאשׁוֹנִים, *one might think
that he was humble "more than" those of the*

previous generations. Accordingly, the words
on the face of the earth would teach only that
he was not *more* humble than they.]
In any event, this is but one opinion in *Sifrei* there. However, R' Yose's opinion there is
that Moses was even more humble than the
Patriarchs. [See also *Chullin* 89a.]
48. A bad odor emitting from either the
mouth or the nose (see *Kesubos* 77a),
caused by an affliction of boils in one of
those areas (see *Ben Avraham*).
49. As the verse testifies that Moses was
more humble than *any person on the face of
the earth,* which includes even these people
(*Mefaresh*).

ג. רַבִּי שִׁמְעוֹן בֶּן אֶלְעָזָר אוֹמֵר: אַף⁵⁰ עַל מְסַפְּרֵי לָשׁוֹן הָרַע נְגָעִים
בָּאִין, שֶׁכֵּן מָצִינוּ בְּגֵחֲזִי שֶׁסִּפֵּר לָשׁוֹן הָרַע בְּרַבּוֹ⁵¹ וְדָבְקָה בּוֹ צָרַעַת
עַד יוֹם מוֹתוֹ, שֶׁנֶּאֱמַר (מלכים ב ה, כז) "וְצָרַעַת נַעֲמָן תִּדְבַּק בְּךָ [וְגוֹ'] וַיֵּצֵא
מִלְּפָנָיו מְצֹרָע כַּשָּׁלֶג". הוּא הָיָה אוֹמֵר: עַל גַּס הָרוּחַ נְגָעִים בָּאִין עָלָיו,
שֶׁכֵּן מָצִינוּ בְּעוּזִּיָּהוּ, שֶׁנֶּאֱמַר (דברי הימים ב כו, טז-יט) "וּבְחֶזְקָתוֹ גָּבַהּ לִבּוֹ
עַד לְהַשְׁחִית וַיִּמְעַל מַעַל בַּה' [אֱלֹהָיו וַיָּבֹא אֶל הֵיכַל ה' לְהַקְטִיר עַל
מִזְבַּח הַקְּטֹרֶת וַיָּבֹא אַחֲרָיו] עֲזַרְיָהוּ הַכֹּהֵן וְעִמּוֹ כֹהֲנִים לַה' שְׁמוֹנִים
בְּנֵי חָיִל וַיַּעַמְדוּ עַל עֻזִּיָּהוּ הַמֶּלֶךְ וַיֹּאמְרוּ לוֹ לֹא לְךָ עֻזִּיָּהוּ לְהַקְטִיר לַה'

---

§3 The Baraisa continues its presentation of sources that connect *tzaraas* to
the sin of *lashon hara*:

רַבִּי שִׁמְעוֹן בֶּן אֶלְעָזָר אוֹמֵר: אַף עַל מְסַפְּרֵי לָשׁוֹן הָרַע נְגָעִים בָּאִין — R' Shimon ben
Elazar says: *Tzaraas* afflictions come upon even[50] those who speak *lashon
hara.* שֶׁכֵּן מָצִינוּ בְּגֵחֲזִי שֶׁסִּפֵּר לָשׁוֹן הָרַע בְּרַבּוֹ וְדָבְקָה בּוֹ צָרַעַת עַד יוֹם מוֹתוֹ
— For thus we find in the case of **Gehazi** that he spoke *lashon hara* about
his teacher, **Elisha,**[51] and a *tzaraas* affliction subsequently befell him and
clung to him until the day of his death, שֶׁנֶּאֱמַר "וְצָרַעַת נַעֲמָן תִּדְבַּק בְּךָ [וְגוֹ']
— as it is stated, *Elisha then said to him, "Naaman's
tzaraas affliction shall therefore cleave to you and to your children forever!"
When [Gehazi] left his presence, he was [white] as snow with tzaraas*
(*II Kings* 5:27).

Another teaching of R' Shimon ben Elazar about *tzaraas*:

הוּא הָיָה אוֹמֵר: עַל גַּס הָרוּחַ נְגָעִים בָּאִין עָלָיו — He used to say: *Tzaraas* afflictions come upon one of haughty spirit. שֶׁכֵּן מָצִינוּ בְּעוּזִּיָּהוּ — For thus do
we find in the case of **Uzziah,** שֶׁנֶּאֱמַר "וּבְחֶזְקָתוֹ גָּבַהּ לִבּוֹ עַד לְהַשְׁחִית — as it
is stated, *But as he became strong, his heart became haughty to the point
of destructiveness,* וַיִּמְעַל מַעַל בַּה' אֱלֹהָיו וַיָּבֹא אֶל הֵיכַל ה' לְהַקְטִיר עַל מִזְבַּח
הַקְּטֹרֶת — *and he betrayed HASHEM his God — he entered the Sanctuary of
HASHEM to burn incense upon the Incense Altar.* וַיָּבֹא אַחֲרָיו עֲזַרְיָהוּ הַכֹּהֵן
— *Azariah the Kohen went after him, along
with eighty strong Kohanim of HASHEM.* וְעִמּוֹ כֹהֲנִים לַה' שְׁמוֹנִים בְּנֵי חָיִל
— וַיַּעַמְדוּ עַל עֻזִּיָּהוּ הַמֶּלֶךְ וַיֹּאמְרוּ לוֹ
They stood next to King Uzziah and said to him, לֹא לְךָ עֻזִּיָּהוּ לְהַקְטִיר לַה'

---

50. [See *Magen Avos,* who discusses the
meaning of אַף, *even,* here. *Avos HaRosh*
[Vol. 1, p. 139a], however, deletes the word
אַף from the text.]

51. Gehazi fabricated a story, making it
seem as if Elisha had changed his mind
and decided to accept the payment he had

previously refused for a miracle he had performed [see *II Kings* Ch. 5] (*Ahavas Chesed,
Magen Avos*). Alternatively, the Baraisa
refers to the account in *Yerushalmi Sanhedrin* 10:2, where Gehazi ridiculed Elisha's
plans to bring a dead boy back to life (see
Mefaresh).

כִּי לַכֹּהֲנִים בְּנֵי אַהֲרֹן הַמְקֻדָּשִׁים לְהַקְטִיר צֵא מִן הַמִּקְדָּשׁ כִּי מָעַלְתָּ וְלֹא
לְךָ לְכָבוֹד מֵה' אֱלֹהִים וַיִּזְעַף עֻזִּיָּהוּ וּבְיָדוֹ מִקְטֶרֶת לְהַקְטִיר וּבְזַעְפּוֹ עִם
הַכֹּהֲנִים וְהַצָּרַעַת זָרְחָה בְמִצְחוֹ". בְּאוֹתָהּ שָׁעָה נִבְקַע הֵיכָל אֵילָךְ וְאֵילָךְ
שְׁנֵים עָשָׂר מִיל [52] עַל שְׁנֵים עָשָׂר מִיל וְהָיוּ הַכֹּהֲנִים מְבֹהֲלִים לָצֵאת [53],
(שם פסוקים כ-כב) "וְגַם הוּא נִבְהַל לָצֵאת כִּי נְגָעוֹ ה' וַיְהִי מְצֹרָע עַד יוֹם
מוֹתוֹ וַיֵּשֶׁב בֵּית הַחָפְשִׁית מְצֹרָע כִּי נִגְזַר מִבֵּית ה' וְיוֹתָם בְּנוֹ עַל בֵּית
הַמֶּלֶךְ שׁוֹפֵט אֶת עַם הָאָרֶץ":

כִּי לַכֹּהֲנִים בְּנֵי אַהֲרֹן הַמְקֻדָּשִׁים לְהַקְטִיר — *"It is not for you, Uzziah, to burn incense to HASHEM, but it is for the Kohanim, the descendants of Aaron, who are consecrated, to burn incense.* צֵא מִן הַמִּקְדָּשׁ כִּי מָעַלְתָּ וְלֹא לְךָ לְכָבוֹד מֵה' אֱלֹהִים — *Leave the Temple, for you have been treacherous, and this will not bring you honor from HASHEM, God."* וַיִּזְעַף עֻזִּיָּהוּ וּבְיָדוֹ מִקְטֶרֶת לְהַקְטִיר — *Uzziah became enraged, and he already had a censer in his hand to burn incense.* וּבְזַעְפּוֹ עִם הַכֹּהֲנִים וְהַצָּרַעַת זָרְחָה בְמִצְחוֹ" — *As he was becoming enraged with the Kohanim, a leprous growth appeared on his forehead ...* (II Chronicles 26:16-19).

The Baraisa interjects:

בְּאוֹתָהּ שָׁעָה נִבְקַע הֵיכָל אֵילָךְ וְאֵילָךְ שְׁנֵים עָשָׂר מִיל עַל שְׁנֵים עָשָׂר מִיל — At that moment, the Sanctuary split this way and that way, creating a chasm of twelve *mil* by twelve *mil*.[52]

The Baraisa continues its (slightly abbreviated) citation of the Scriptural narrative:

וְהָיוּ הַכֹּהֲנִים מְבֹהֲלִים לָצֵאת — So the Kohanim were rushing him to leave,[53] "וְגַם הוּא נִבְהַל לָצֵאת כִּי נְגָעוֹ ה' — and he, too, hastened to leave, for HASHEM had afflicted him וַיְהִי ... מְצֹרָע עַד יוֹם מוֹתוֹ — King Uzziah was a leper until the day of his death. וַיֵּשֶׁב בֵּית הַחָפְשִׁית מְצֹרָע כִּי נִגְזַר מִבֵּית ה' — He dwelt in his leprosy in a place of asylum, for he was banished from the Temple of HASHEM. וְיוֹתָם בְּנוֹ עַל בֵּית הַמֶּלֶךְ שׁוֹפֵט אֶת עַם הָאָרֶץ" — His son Jotham took charge of the royal house and judged the people of the land (ibid. vv. 20-22). Hence, we see that haughtiness is punished with *tzaraas*.

---

52. The ground upon which Uzziah was standing split open, preparing itself to swallow him, just as it did centuries before to those who similarly contended against the Kehunah during Korah's uprising [see Numbers Ch. 16]. God, however, told the ground that Uzziah's punishment would not be carried out this way, but rather through *tzaraas* (see *Midrash Tanchuma, Tzav* §13).

Twelve *mil* by twelve *mil* were the exact dimensions of the Israelite camp [during their sojourn in the Wilderness; see *Eruvin* 55b]. That chasm thus symbolized that Uzziah would be banished from the entire Jewish community for the rest of his life, due to the *tzaraas* that was about to come upon him (*Ben Avraham*).

53. [This is the Baraisa's paraphrase of the middle of v. 20 there.]

ד. וְאַל תִּתְחַבֵּר לָרָשָׁע. מְלַמֵּד שֶׁלֹּא יִתְחַבֵּר אָדָם עִם אָדָם רַע וְלֹא
עִם אָדָם רָשָׁע, שֶׁכֵּן מָצִינוּ בִּיהוֹשָׁפָט שֶׁנִּתְחַבֵּר בְּאַחְאָב וְעָלָה עִמּוֹ
רָמוֹת גִּלְעָד⁵⁵ וְיָצָא עָלָיו קֶצֶף (מֵאֵת) ה׳⁵⁶. שׁוּב נִתְחַבֵּר לַאֲחַזְיָה [וַיַּעֲשׂוּ
אֳנִיּוֹת בְּעֶצְיוֹן גָּבֶר⁵⁷ וּפָרַץ ה׳ אֶת מַעֲשָׂיו, שֶׁנֶּאֱמַר] (דברי הימים ב כ, לז)
"בְּהִתְחַבֶּרְךָ⁵⁸ עִם אֲחַזְיָהוּ פָּרַץ ה׳ אֶת מַעֲשֶׂיךָ וַיִּשָּׁבְרוּ אֳנִיּוֹת". וְכֵן מָצִינוּ
בְּאַמְנוֹן שֶׁנִּתְחַבֵּר עִם יוֹנָדָב וְיָעַץ לוֹ עֵצָה רָעָה, שֶׁנֶּאֱמַר (שמואל ב יג, ג)

---

§4 The Baraisa now expounds Nittai's second saying:

מְלַמֵּד — "Do not associate with a wicked person." — וְאַל תִּתְחַבֵּר לָרָשָׁע
שֶׁלֹּא יִתְחַבֵּר אָדָם עִם אָדָם רַע וְלֹא עִם אָדָם רָשָׁע — This teaches that a person should not associate with a person who is bad (i.e., who sins against his fellow man as well as against God), **and not** even **with a person who is wicked** (i.e., who sins only against God, but not against his fellow man).[54]

The Baraisa presents several incidents in Scripture where negative consequences befell those who associated with the wicked:

שֶׁכֵּן מָצִינוּ בִּיהוֹשָׁפָט — **For thus do we find in** the case of **Jehoshaphat,** the righteous king of Judah, — שֶׁנִּתְחַבֵּר בְּאַחְאָב וְעָלָה עִמּוֹ רָמוֹת גִּלְעָד — that he **associated with Ahab,** the wicked king of Israel, **and went up with him** to wage war **in Ramoth-gilead,**[55] וְיָצָא עָלָיו קֶצֶף מֵאֵת ה׳ — **and** as a result, **fury went out upon him from** before **God.**[56]

Another instance:

שׁוּב נִתְחַבֵּר לַאֲחַזְיָה וַיַּעֲשׂוּ אֳנִיּוֹת בְּעֶצְיוֹן גָּבֶר[57] — **Afterward,** [Jehoshaphat] **associated with** another wicked king, Ahab's son **Ahaziah,** to make a joint fleet of ships to go to Tarshish, **and they built ships** together **in Ezion-geber,**[57] וּפָרַץ ה׳ אֶת מַעֲשָׂיו — **and God wrecked his undertakings,** שֶׁנֶּאֱמַר "בְּהִתְחַבֶּרְךָ[58] עִם אֲחַזְיָהוּ פָּרַץ ה׳ אֶת מַעֲשֶׂיךָ וַיִּשָּׁבְרוּ אֳנִיּוֹת" — **as it is stated,** *The prophet said to Jehoshaphat, "Because you have allied yourself with Ahaziah, HASHEM has wrecked your undertakings!" The ships broke down and did not succeed in going to Tarshish (II Chronicles 20:37).*

Another instance:

וְכֵן מָצִינוּ בְּאַמְנוֹן שֶׁנִּתְחַבֵּר עִם יוֹנָדָב — **And similarly do we find in** the case of King David's son, **Amnon, that he associated with** his cousin, the wicked **Jonadab,** וְיָעַץ לוֹ עֵצָה רָעָה — who ultimately **gave him bad advice,** שֶׁנֶּאֱמַר

---

54. *Binyan Yehoshua.* From the fact that Nittai mentioned a *wicked* person, the Baraisa extrapolates that the same is certainly true regarding a *bad* person, who is even worse (ibid.).

[*Meiri* on the Mishnah connects this teaching with the Baraisa below, 30 §3, which discusses the harm that befalls "one who

attaches himself to sinners."]

55. See *I Kings* 22:4, *II Chronicles* 18:3.

56. This is a paraphrase of *II Chronicles* 19:2.

57. As recounted there, 20:35-36, which the Baraisa has just paraphrased.

58. [The standard texts of *Chronicles* have כְּהִתְחַבֶּרְךָ, and it might be a simple

"וּלְאַמְנוֹן רֵעַ וּשְׁמוֹ יוֹנָדָב בֶּן שִׁמְעָה אֲחִי דָוִד וְיוֹנָדָב אִישׁ חָכָם מְאֹד",
חָכָם לְרֵעַ59,60. דָּבָר אַחֵר, אַל תִּתְחַבֵּר לְרָשָׁע וַאֲפִילוּ לַתּוֹרָה61:

ה. וְאַל תִּתְיָאֵשׁ מִן הַפּוּרְעָנוּת, כֵּיצַד. מְלַמֵּד שֶׁיְּהֵא לִבּוֹ שֶׁל אָדָם
מִתְפַּחֵד בְּכָל יוֹם, [וַיֹּאמַר: אוֹי לִי, שֶׁמָּא יָבֹא עָלַי פּוּרְעָנוּת הַיּוֹם
וְשֶׁמָּא לְמָחָר, וְנִמְצָא מִתְפַּחֵד בְּכָל יוֹם,] שֶׁנֶּאֱמַר בֶּן בְּאִיּוֹב (איוב ג, כד)
"פַּחַד פָּחַדְתִּי"62:

"וּלְאַמְנוֹן רֵעַ וּשְׁמוֹ יוֹנָדָב בֶּן שִׁמְעָה אֲחִי דָוִד וְיוֹנָדָב אִישׁ חָכָם מְאֹד" — as it is stated,
*Amnon had a friend named Jonadab, the son of David's brother Shimeah,
and Jonadab was a very wise man* (II Samuel 13:3), חָכָם לְרֵעַ — by which
Scripture means **wise for** purposes **of evil.**[59] Indeed, it was this advice that led
Amnon to an early death.[60] This is another instance in which a person suffered
from his association with the wicked.

Another explanation of Nittai's second saying:
דָּבָר אַחֵר, אַל תִּתְחַבֵּר לְרָשָׁע וַאֲפִילוּ לַתּוֹרָה — Alternatively, "**Do not associate
with a wicked person**" means **even for** the purpose of studying **Torah** together.[61]

§5 The Baraisa expounds Nittai's third saying:
וְאַל תִּתְיָאֵשׁ מִן הַפּוּרְעָנוּת, כֵּיצַד — "**And do not despair of retribution**" —
how so? מְלַמֵּד שֶׁיְּהֵא לִבּוֹ שֶׁל אָדָם מִתְפַּחֵד בְּכָל יוֹם — **This teaches that the
heart of a person** who has sinned **should be in fear every day,** וַיֹּאמַר: אוֹי
לִי, שֶׁמָּא יָבֹא עָלַי פּוּרְעָנוּת הַיּוֹם וְשֶׁמָּא לְמָחָר — **and he should** constantly **say** to
himself, "**Woe is me! Perhaps** the Divine **retribution** for my sins **will befall me
today, or perhaps** it will be **tomorrow!**" וְנִמְצָא מִתְפַּחֵד בְּכָל יוֹם — Thus, **it
emerges that he is in fear** of retribution **every day,** and this will dissuade him
from sinning any further. שֶׁנֶּאֱמַר בֶּן בְּאִיּוֹב "פַּחַד פָּחַדְתִּי" — **For so is it stated
regarding Job:** *[Job said,]* "*Because I feared a fright*" (*Job* 3:24).[62] Thus, Nittai exhorts us not to become complacent in this world, as retribution even in
this world could come at any time.

---

copyist's error here in *Avos DeRabbi Nassan,*
but *Minchas Shai* there does note that some
Biblical texts indeed have בְּ"הִתְחַבֶּרְךָ".]

59. [A paraphrase of the expression in *Jer-
emiah* 4:22: חֲכָמִים הֵמָּה לְהָרַע וּלְהֵיטִיב לֹא יָדָעוּ,
*they are wise at doing evil, but know not
how to do good.*]

60. Jonadab had advised Amnon on how
to maneuver Tamar into his chambers in
order to violate her, which led to Amnon's
eventual death at the hands of her brother,
Absalom (see *II Samuel* Ch. 13).

61. *Rashbatz* on the Mishnah in *Avos* quotes
Avos DeRabbi Nassan as saying: אֲפִילוּ לִדְבַר
מִצְוָה, *even for a mitzvah purpose.*

[*Nuschas HaGra* has here: "אֲפִילוּ "לְקָרְבוֹ,
לַתּוֹרָה, *even "in order to bring him close"* to
Torah, which is a reading found in *Mechilta,
Yisro, Parashah* 1, and in *Yalkut Shimoni* on
Exodus §169 (see *Tosefes Ohr* here).]

62. Scripture's double expression suggests
a constant state of fear. And indeed, it was
precisely this constant fear that deterred Job
from sinning, as the verse (*Job* 1:1) says

ו. דָּבָר אַחֵר, אַל תִּתְיָיאֵשׁ מִן הַפּוּרְעָנוּת, כֵּיצַד. בִּזְמַן שֶׁאָדָם רוֹאֶה
מַה שֶׁבְּיָדוֹ מַצְלִיחַ, אַל יֹאמַר: בִּשְׁבִיל שֶׁזָּכִיתִי נָתַן לִי הַמָּקוֹם מַאֲכָל
וּמִשְׁתֶּה בָּעוֹלָם הַזֶּה וְהַקֶּרֶן קַיֶּימֶת לָעוֹלָם הַבָּא, אֶלָּא יֹאמַר: אוֹי לִי,
שֶׁמָּא לֹא נִמְצָא לִי לְפָנָיו אֶלָּא זְכוּת אֶחָד בִּלְבַד, נָתַן לִי מַאֲכָל וּמִשְׁתֶּה
בָּעוֹלָם הַזֶּה כְּדֵי שֶׁיְּאַבְּדֵנִי לָעוֹלָם הַבָּא:[63]

---

§6 An alternative interpretation of Nittai's third saying:

דָּבָר אַחֵר, אַל תִּתְיָיאֵשׁ מִן הַפּוּרְעָנוּת, כֵּיצַד — Another explanation of "and do not despair of retribution" — how so?   בִּזְמַן שֶׁאָדָם רוֹאֶה מַה שֶׁבְּיָדוֹ מַצְלִיחַ — When a person sees his endeavors succeeding, אַל יֹאמַר: בִּשְׁבִיל שֶׁזָּכִיתִי — he should not say to himself, "Because I am worthy, God has given me food and drink in this world,   נָתַן לִי הַמָּקוֹם מַאֲכָל וּמִשְׁתֶּה בָּעוֹלָם הַזֶּה וְהַקֶּרֶן קַיֶּימֶת לָעוֹלָם הַבָּא — but the principal reward for my good deeds remains intact for me to enjoy in the World to Come."   אֶלָּא יֹאמַר: אוֹי לִי, שֶׁמָּא לֹא נִמְצָא לִי לְפָנָיו אֶלָּא זְכוּת אֶחָד בִּלְבַד — Rather, he should say to himself, "Woe is me! Perhaps only one merit was found for me before Him,   נָתַן לִי מַאֲכָל וּמִשְׁתֶּה בָּעוֹלָם הַזֶּה כְּדֵי שֶׁיְּאַבְּדֵנִי לָעוֹלָם הַבָּא — and He has already rewarded me for it in full by giving me food and drink in this world, leaving me with no more merits, so that He can destroy me in the World to Come!"[63]

---

about him, *That man was wholesome and upright, he feared God and shunned evil*, implying that his shunning of evil resulted directly from his fearing of God (ibid.).

[In some versions of this Baraisa, the *Job* verse is replaced with a verse from *Proverbs* (28:14): *Praiseworthy is the man who always fears* (see *Meiri* to *Avos* here and *Nuschas HaGra*; see also *Binyan Yehoshua*).]

63. Accordingly, the retribution Nittai warns about refers to punishment in the World to Come.

﴾ פֶּרֶק י ﴿

א. יְהוּדָה בֶּן טַבַּאי וְשִׁמְעוֹן בֶּן שָׁטַח קִבְּלוּ מֵהֶם. יְהוּדָה בֶּן טַבַּאי אוֹמֵר: אַל תַּעַשׂ עַצְמְךָ כְּעוֹרְכֵי הַדַּיָּינִין. וּכְשֶׁיִּהְיוּ בַּעֲלֵי דִינִין עוֹמְדִין לְפָנֶיךָ יִהְיוּ בְּעֵינֶיךָ כִּרְשָׁעִים, וּכְשֶׁנִּפְטָרִים מִלְּפָנֶיךָ יִהְיוּ בְּעֵינֶיךָ כְּזַכָּאִין כְּשֶׁקִּבְּלוּ עֲלֵיהֶם אֶת הַדִּין:

ב. אַל תַּעַשׂ עַצְמְךָ כְּעוֹרְכֵי הַדַּיָּינִין, כֵּיצַד, מְלַמֵּד שֶׁאִם בָּאתָ לְבֵית הַמִּדְרָשׁ וְשָׁמַעְתָּ דָּבָר אוֹ הֲלָכָה אַל תְּבַהֵל בְּרוּחֲךָ לְהָשִׁיב, אֶלָּא הֱוֵי יוֹשֵׁב וְשׁוֹאֵל בְּאֵיזֶה טַעַם אָמְרוּ [דָּבָר זֶה וּמֵאֵיזֶה עִנְיָן הָיָה לָהֶם דִּין זֶה.[3]

﴾ CHAPTER 10 ﴿

§1 This chapter first elaborates on *Avos* 1:8, and then on 1:9:

יְהוּדָה בֶּן טַבַּאי וְשִׁמְעוֹן בֶּן שָׁטַח קִבְּלוּ מֵהֶם — Yehudah ben Tabbai and Shimon ben Shatach received the tradition from them. יְהוּדָה בֶּן טַבַּאי אוֹמֵר — Yehudah ben Tabbai says: אַל תַּעַשׂ עַצְמְךָ כְּעוֹרְכֵי הַדַּיָּינִין — Do not make yourself like those who arrange cases before the judges;[1] וּכְשֶׁיִּהְיוּ בַּעֲלֵי — while the litigants stand before you, דִינִין עוֹמְדִין לְפָנֶיךָ יִהְיוּ בְּעֵינֶיךָ כִּרְשָׁעִים — consider them both as guilty; וּכְשֶׁנִּפְטָרִים מִלְּפָנֶיךָ יִהְיוּ בְּעֵינֶיךָ כְּזַכָּאִין כְּשֶׁקִּבְּלוּ — but when they are dismissed from you, consider them both עֲלֵיהֶם אֶת הַדִּין as innocent, provided they have accepted the judgment.

§2 The Baraisa expounds Yehudah ben Tabbai's first saying:

אַל תַּעַשׂ עַצְמְךָ כְּעוֹרְכֵי הַדַּיָּינִין, כֵּיצַד — "Do not make yourself like those who arrange cases before the judges" — how so? מְלַמֵּד שֶׁאִם בָּאתָ — This teaches that if you come into the study hall וְשָׁמַעְתָּ לְבֵית הַמִּדְרָשׁ — דָּבָר אוֹ הֲלָכָה — and you hear presented to you a question about a monetary matter or a halachah in some other area of Torah,[2] אַל תְּבַהֵל — do not be hasty to offer an opinion. אֶלָּא הֱוֵי יוֹשֵׁב וְשׁוֹאֵל בְּרוּחֲךָ לְהָשִׁיב — Rather, first dwell on the matter, and ask, בְּאֵיזֶה טַעַם אָמְרוּ דָּבָר זֶה "Based on what reason did they say this thing, וּמֵאֵיזֶה עִנְיָן הָיָה לָהֶם דִּין זֶה — and what were the circumstances surrounding this question of law?"[3]

---

1. Alternatively: "like the chief judges"; see below, note 3.

2. *Magen Avos.*

3. Investigate the matter thoroughly, so that the verdict you finally issue is true and correct (see *Ben Avraham*). To answer immediately without careful consideration of the particulars and different opinions, however, is to act like those who arrange cases before

the court, who are not interested in the truth of the matter, but only in advancing the interests of their clients. So, too, one who answers immediately will simply seek to maintain and reinforce his initial judgment of the matter rather than to ascertain the truth (see *Meiri* to *Avos* ad loc. [though he explains that the Baraisa refers to a student rather than to a teacher]). Alternatively,

אוֹמֵר הֲלָכָה, שָׁאַל לָהֶם תְּחִלָּה עִיקַּר הַדִּין וַהֲלָכָה[4] בִּזְמַן] שֶׁשְּׁאָלוּנִי.[5]
וּבִזְמַן שֶׁשְּׁנֵי בַּעֲלֵי דִינִין בָּאִין לְפָנֶיךָ לַדִּין אֶחָד עָנִי וְאֶחָד עָשִׁיר, אַל
תֹּאמַר: הֵיאַךְ אֲזַכֶּה אֶת הֶעָנִי וַאֲחַיֵּיב אֶת הֶעָשִׁיר וְהֵיאַךְ (אֲזַכֶּה אֶת
הֶעָשִׁיר וַאֲחַיֵּיב אֶת הֶעָנִי, וְאִם אֲחַיֵּיב אֶת הֶעָנִי נִמְצָא עָנִי אוֹיְבִי וְאִם
אֲזַכֶּה אֶת הֶעָנִי נִמְצָא הֶעָשִׁיר אוֹיְבִי). וְאַל תֹּאמַר: הֵיאַךְ) אֶטוֹל מָמוֹנוֹ

אוֹמֵר הֲלָכָה, שָׁאַל לָהֶם תְּחִלָּה עִיקַּר הַדִּין וַהֲלָכָה בִּזְמַן שֶׁשְּׁאָלוּנִי — Similarly, **if you**
wish to **say a** decision **in halachah,** be sure to **first ask them** (i.e., the people
presenting the query) all **the important details of the case,**[4] **and** also remind
yourself, "I should render **a decision in halachah** *only* **at a time that they** actually **ask me** for one."[5]

The Baraisa expounds Yehudah ben Tabbai's second saying — "While the
litigants stand before you, consider them both as guilty":

וּבִזְמַן שֶׁשְּׁנֵי בַּעֲלֵי דִינִין בָּאִין לְפָנֶיךָ לַדִּין — **This can be understood as follows:**
When you are sitting as a judge, **and two litigants come before you for judg-**
ment, אֶחָד עָנִי וְאֶחָד עָשִׁיר — **one** of whom is **poor and one** of whom is
rich, אַל תֹּאמַר: הֵיאַךְ אֲזַכֶּה אֶת הֶעָנִי וַאֲחַיֵּיב אֶת הֶעָשִׁיר — **do not say,** "**How**
can I vindicate the poor man and obligate the rich man to pay, when that will
disgrace the rich man?"; וְהֵיאַךְ אֲזַכֶּה אֶת הֶעָשִׁיר וַאֲחַיֵּיב אֶת הֶעָנִי — **or,** "**How**
can I vindicate the rich man and obligate the poor man to pay, when that
will embarrass the poor man?" וְאִם אֲחַיֵּיב אֶת הֶעָנִי נִמְצָא עָנִי אוֹיְבִי — **Nor**
should you say, "**If I obligate the poor man** to pay, **then the poor man will**
become my enemy, for he will assume that I showed favor to the rich man
because of his wealth"; וְאִם אֲזַכֶּה אֶת הֶעָנִי נִמְצָא הֶעָשִׁיר אוֹיְבִי — **or,** "**If I**
vindicate the poor man, then the rich man will become my enemy, for he will
assume that I showed favor to the poor man." וְאַל תֹּאמַר: הֵיאַךְ אֶטוֹל מָמוֹנוֹ

עוֹרְכֵי הַדַּיָּנִים means "the chief judges," whose
great expertise and experience enables
them to penetrate to the heart of a matter
immediately (see *Machzor Vitri* on *Avos* ad
loc.; *Ben Avraham*; see also *Rav* to *Avos* ad
loc.).

4. This is essentially a restatement of the
previous line regarding the obligation to
thoroughly investigate a matter before ruling on it.

5. Do not render a decision for a theoretical
situation, but only when an actual case is
presented. For only when one's ruling has
practical implications will a scholar do his
utmost to plumb the depths of a given topic
(see *Ahavas Chesed*, second approach).

[We have explained this line of text according to the reading found in the Vilna
edition, which is not found in the available
manuscripts or early editions, but is based on
a bracketed interpolation in the Frankfort ed.
of 1720. *Ben Avraham* notes that this reading
is exceedingly difficult, and he emends it to
read: אַל תִּבָּהֵל בְּרוּחֲךָ לְהָשִׁיב אֶלָּא הֱוֵי יוֹשֵׁב וְשׁוֹאֵל
עִיקַּר הַדָּבָר וְהַהֲלָכָה וּבְאֵיזֶה טַעַם אָמְרוּ דָּבָר זֶה וּמֵאֵיזֶה
עִנְיָן הָיָה לָהֶם דִּין זֶה שֶׁשְּׁאָלוּנִי, *Do not be hasty to*
offer an opinion; rather, dwell and ask about
the root of the matter and the law, and what
were the circumstances surrounding this law
that they asked me. This emendation closely
approximates the reading found in the Venice
edition and several of the manuscripts.]

שֶׁל זֶה וְאֶתֵּן לָזֶה. וְהַתּוֹרָה אָמְרָה (דברים א, יז) "לֹא תַכִּירוּ פָנִים
בַּמִּשְׁפָּט"[8]. (הָיָה רַבִּי מֵאִיר אוֹמֵר: מַה תַּלְמוּד לוֹמַר) (שם) "כַּקָּטֹן כַּגָּדֹל
תִּשְׁמָעוּן", שֶׁלֹּא יְהֵא אָדָם אֶחָד עוֹמֵד וְאֶחָד יוֹשֵׁב, אֶחָד מְדַבֵּר כָּל
צָרְכּוֹ וְאֶחָד אוֹמֵר לוֹ קַצֵּר דְּבָרֶיךָ[9]. (אָמַר רַבִּי יְהוּדָה: שָׁמַעְתִּי שֶׁאִם
רָצוּ לְהוֹשִׁיב שְׁנֵיהֶם כְּאֶחָד מוֹשִׁיבִין וְאֵין זֶה אָסוּר. אֵי זֶה אָסוּר, שֶׁלֹּא
יְהֵא אֶחָד יוֹשֵׁב וְאֶחָד עוֹמֵד. [אֶלָּא מַה תַּלְמוּד לוֹמַר) "כַּקָּטֹן כַּגָּדֹל",]

שֶׁל זֶה וְאֶתֵּן לָזֶה — And even if they are both of equal financial and social status,[6] do not say, "How can I take the money of this one who is my friend and give it to this other one?"[7]   **וְהַתּוֹרָה אָמְרָה "לֹא תַכִּירוּ פָנִים בַּמִּשְׁפָּט"** — For with regard to all these situations the Torah says, *You shall not show favoritism in judgment* (Deuteronomy 1:17).[8]

The Baraisa expounds the continuation of the *Deuteronomy* verse just cited: **הָיָה רַבִּי מֵאִיר אוֹמֵר: מַה תַּלְמוּד לוֹמַר "כַּקָּטֹן כַּגָּדֹל תִּשְׁמָעוּן"** — R' Meir used to say: What is Scripture teaching us by saying, *Small and great alike shall you hear* (ibid.)?   **שֶׁלֹּא יְהֵא אָדָם אֶחָד עוֹמֵד וְאֶחָד יוֹשֵׁב** — It is teaching that one litigant should not stand while the other one sits; **אֶחָד מְדַבֵּר כָּל צָרְכּוֹ** **וְאֶחָד אוֹמֵר לוֹ קַצֵּר דְּבָרֶיךָ** — one should not be allowed to speak as much as he needs while the other one is told, "Keep your words short!"[9]

Another sage derives this from a different verse: **אָמַר רַבִּי יְהוּדָה** — R' Yehudah said: I have heard (with reference to the verse, *Then the two men who have the grievance shall stand before HASHEM*, which would seem to imply that both parties must stand)[10] **שָׁמַעְתִּי שֶׁאִם רָצוּ לְהוֹשִׁיב שְׁנֵיהֶם כְּאֶחָד מוֹשִׁיבִין** that if [the judges] want to have both litigants sit in the same manner, they may do so, **וְאֵין זֶה אָסוּר** — and this is not prohibited.   **אֵי זֶה אָסוּר** — What then is the prohibition implied by the verse? **שֶׁלֹּא יְהֵא אֶחָד יוֹשֵׁב וְאֶחָד עוֹמֵד** — Only that one litigant should not stand while the other one sits. ..... **אֶלָּא מַה תַּלְמוּד לוֹמַר "כַּקָּטֹן כַּגָּדֹל"** — But if this lesson is derived from the words *the two men ... shall stand,* then what is Scripture teaching us by saying, *Small and great alike shall you hear?*[11]

---

6. *Ahavas Chesed.*

7. Ibid.

8. Accordingly, the statement, "While the litigants stand before you, consider them both as guilty," means that the judge should view both litigants as *equally* guilty, so that he will not hesitate to obligate the truly guilty party to pay (see *Magen Avos*).

9. In each of these scenarios, the party treated less respectfully feels at a disadvantage

and, as a result, becomes too flustered to present his case in a cogent manner (*Binyan Yehoshua*).

Accordingly, *Small and great alike you hear,* means that you should give equal treatment to all litigants, regardless of their social status (*Ben Avraham*).

10. This is the verse R' Yehudah was commenting upon, as stated explicitly in *Shevuos* 30a (*Binyan Yehoshua, Ahavas Chesed*).

11. It is no longer necessary to expound

וִיהֵא עָלֶיךָ דִין קָטָן כְּדִין גָּדוֹל, [דִין] שֶׁל פְּרוּטָה כְּדִין שֶׁל מֵאָה מָנֶה:[12]

ג. (הוּא הָיָה אוֹמֵר: כָּל מִי שֶׁיֹּאמַר לִי קוֹדֶם שֶׁאֶכָּנֵס לִגְדוּלָה זוֹ: הִכָּנֵס, רוֹצֶה אֲנִי [שֶׁאֶרֵד עִמּוֹ עַד לְחַיָּיו[13]. עַכְשָׁיו שֶׁנִּכְנַסְתִּי, כָּל מִי שֶׁיֹּאמַר לִי רֵד הֵימֶנָּה רוֹצֶה אֲנִי] שֶׁאַפִּיל עָלָיו קוּמְקוּמוֹס שֶׁל חַמִּין. שֶׁהַגְּדוּלָה קָשָׁה הִיא לְהַעֲלוֹתָהּ, וּכְשֵׁם שֶׁקָּשָׁה הִיא לְהַעֲלוֹתָהּ כָּךְ קָשָׁה לְהוֹרִידָהּ[14]. שֶׁכֵּן מָצִינוּ בְּשָׁאוּל, בְּשָׁעָה שֶׁאָמַר לוֹ: עֲמוֹד בַּמַּלְכוּת, הָיָה מִתְחַבֵּא, שֶׁנֶּאֱמַר

וִיהֵא עָלֶיךָ דִין קָטָן כְּדִין גָּדוֹל — It teaches that **the case brought by a small person shall be in your eyes as** important as **the case brought by a great person,** דִין שֶׁל פְּרוּטָה כְּדִין שֶׁל מֵאָה מָנֶה — and that **a case concerning a** *perutah* **shall be in your eyes as** important as **a case concerning** the vast sum of **one hundred** *maneh*.[12]

§3 The Baraisa cites another saying of Yehudah ben Tabbai: הוּא הָיָה אוֹמֵר — **He** also used to say: כָּל מִי שֶׁיֹּאמַר לִי קוֹדֶם שֶׁאֶכָּנֵס לִגְדוּלָה זוֹ: הִכָּנֵס — "**Whoever would have said to me before I had assumed this position of authority** that I now occupy, '**Assume** that position of authority,' רוֹצֶה אֲנִי שֶׁאֶרֵד עִמּוֹ עַד לְחַיָּיו — **I would have wanted to damage his livelihood.**[13] עַכְשָׁיו שֶׁנִּכְנַסְתִּי, כָּל מִי שֶׁיֹּאמַר לִי רֵד הֵימֶנָּה — **However, now that I have assumed** that position, **whoever would say to me, 'Descend from it!'** רוֹצֶה אֲנִי שֶׁאַפִּיל עָלָיו קוּמְקוּמוֹס שֶׁל חַמִּין — **I would want to drop a kettleful of hot water on him!**" שֶׁהַגְּדוּלָה קָשָׁה הִיא לְהַעֲלוֹתָהּ — The Baraisa explains: For **an ascent to authority is difficult** for a person to accept upon himself, וּכְשֵׁם שֶׁקָּשָׁה הִיא לְהַעֲלוֹתָהּ כָּךְ קָשָׁה לְהוֹרִידָהּ — **but just as it is difficult to ascend to it, so is it difficult to descend from it.**[14] שֶׁכֵּן מָצִינוּ בְּשָׁאוּל — **For so do we find in** the case of **Saul:** בְּשָׁעָה שֶׁאָמַר לוֹ: עֲמוֹד בַּמַּלְכוּת, הָיָה מִתְחַבֵּא — **When** the prophet [Samuel] first **said to him, "Rise to** the position of **kingship," he** went and **hid himself** in order to avoid receiving the position, שֶׁנֶּאֱמַר

these words to teach this same lesson, as R' Meir did above.

12. Accordingly, *small and great alike shall you hear* means that you should give equal consideration to all cases, whether of a small person or a great person, whether about a small sum or a great sum.

13. As he would be trying to ruin *my* life. For the Gemara advises, "Stay out of the limelight and live" [*Sanhedrin* 92a] for "a position of authority buries the one who holds it" [*Yoma* 86b] (*Ahavas Chesed*). [A

high-ranking position distinguishes a person from the rest of his community, and therefore places him in a precarious situation (see *Pesachim* 87b), as this distinction makes his actions more subject to Divine scrutiny (see *Derech HaChaim* to *Avos* 1:10).]

14. Loss of power humiliates a person and reddens his face. For this reason, if anyone would have requested this of Yehudah ben Tabbai, he would have wanted to scald that person with boiling hot water, which also burns ["reddens"] the skin (see ibid.).

(שמואל א י, כב) "וַיֹּאמֶר ה' הִנֵּה הוּא נֶחְבָּא אֶל הַכֵּלִים". וּבְשָׁעָה שֶׁאָמַר
לֵיהּ: רֵד הֵימֶנָּה, הָיָה מַחֲזִיר אַחֲרֵי דָוִד לְהָרְגוֹ[16]:

ד. שִׁמְעוֹן בֶּן שָׁטַח אוֹמֵר: הֱוֵי מַרְבֶּה לַחֲקוֹר אֶת הָעֵדִים. מִתּוֹךְ שֶׁאַתָּה
חוֹקְרָן (הֱוֵי זָהִיר בִּדְבָרֶיךָ), שֶׁמָּא מִתּוֹךְ דְּבָרֶיךָ יִשְׁמְעוּ הַשּׁוֹמְעִין[17]
וְיוֹסִיפוּ עָלֶיךָ שֶׁקֶר מִפְּנֵי הָרַמָּאִין[18]:

"וַיֹּאמֶר ה' הִנֵּה הוּא נֶחְבָּא אֶל הַכֵּלִים" — as it is stated that when the people
inquired as to the whereabouts of their new king, *And HASHEM replied, "He
is hidden among the baggage"* (*I Samuel* 10:22). וּבְשָׁעָה שֶׁאָמַר לֵיהּ: רֵד
הֵימֶנָּה, הָיָה מַחֲזִיר אַחֲרֵי דָוִד לְהָרְגוֹ — And yet, when [Samuel] told him to descend from [his kingship] because David was to be the next king,[15] he went
looking for his rival **David in order to kill him.**[16]

§4 The Baraisa now expounds *Avos* 1:9:

שִׁמְעוֹן בֶּן שָׁטַח אוֹמֵר: הֱוֵי מַרְבֶּה לַחֲקוֹר אֶת הָעֵדִים — **Shimon ben Shatach
says: Interrogate the witnesses excessively;** yet be careful with your words,
lest they learn from them to lie.

The Baraisa explains the connection between the two parts of Shimon ben
Shatach's saying:

מִתּוֹךְ שֶׁאַתָּה חוֹקְרָן הֱוֵי זָהִיר בִּדְבָרֶיךָ — **Because you must interrogate them
thoroughly, you must be** especially **careful with your words —** שֶׁמָּא מִתּוֹךְ
דְּבָרֶיךָ יִשְׁמְעוּ הַשּׁוֹמְעִין — **for perhaps through your** many **words** of interroga-
tion, **those who are listening will realize** what they need to say in order to
obtain their desired outcome[17] — וְיוֹסִיפוּ עָלֶיךָ שֶׁקֶר מִפְּנֵי הָרַמָּאִין — **and then
they will tell you even more lies — because of the deceivers.**[18]

---

15. See *I Samuel* 15:28.

16. See ibid. 18:29, et al. Hence the proof
that both ascending to and descending from
a position of power are difficult for a person
to accept (*Ben Avraham*).

17. This refers not only to the witnesses,
but to the litigants as well; they, too, might
learn what to claim in order to win (*Binyan*

Yehoshua, from *Rav* and *Tos. Yom Tov* to
Avos ad loc.).

18. We have explained that the words "because of the deceivers" refer back to "be
careful with your words." *Gra* emends the
text and moves the words "because of the
deceivers" above, so that the text reads:
"Interrogate the witnesses excessively because of the deceivers."

∗{ פֶּרֶק יא {∗

א. שְׁמַעְיָה וְאַבְטַלְיוֹן קִבְּלוּ מֵהֶם. שְׁמַעְיָה אוֹמֵר: אֱהוֹב אֶת הַמְּלָאכָה,
וּשְׂנָא אֶת הָרַבָּנוּת, וְאַל תִּתְוַדַּע לָרָשׁוּת. אֱהוֹב אֶת הַמְּלָאכָה, כֵּיצַד,
מְלַמֵּד שֶׁיְּהֵא אָדָם אוֹהֵב אֶת הַמְּלָאכָה וְאַל יְהִי שׂוֹנֵא אֶת הַמְּלָאכָה², כְּשֵׁם
שֶׁהַתּוֹרָה נִתְּנָה בִּבְרִית³ כָּךְ הַמְּלָאכָה נִתְּנָה בִּבְרִית, שֶׁנֶּאֱמַר (שמות כ, ט-י)
"שֵׁשֶׁת יָמִים תַּעֲבֹד וְעָשִׂיתָ כָּל מְלַאכְתֶּךָ וְיוֹם הַשְּׁבִיעִי שַׁבָּת לַה' אֱלֹהֶיךָ".⁴

∗{ CHAPTER 11 {∗

§1 This chapter first elaborates on *Avos* 1:10, and then on 1:11:[1]
שְׁמַעְיָה וְאַבְטַלְיוֹן קִבְּלוּ מֵהֶם — **Shemayah and Avtalyon received the tradi-**
tion from them. שְׁמַעְיָה אוֹמֵר — **Shemayah says:** אֱהוֹב אֶת הַמְּלָאכָה —
Love work; וּשְׂנָא אֶת הָרַבָּנוּת — **despise positions of power;** וְאַל תִּתְוַדַּע
לָרָשׁוּת — **and do not make yourself known to the government.**

The Baraisa expounds each of Shemayah's sayings. The first saying:
אֱהוֹב אֶת הַמְּלָאכָה — **"Love work":** כֵּיצַד — **How** is this to be understood?
מְלַמֵּד שֶׁיְּהֵא אָדָם אוֹהֵב אֶת הַמְּלָאכָה וְאַל יְהִי שׂוֹנֵא אֶת הַמְּלָאכָה — **This teaches**
us that a person should love work and not despise it.[2] כְּשֵׁם שֶׁהַתּוֹרָה נִתְּנָה
בִּבְרִית כָּךְ הַמְּלָאכָה נִתְּנָה בִּבְרִית — **For just as the Torah was given** to the Jewish people **with a covenant,**[3] so was the directive to **work given** to them **with a**
covenant, שֶׁנֶּאֱמַר "שֵׁשֶׁת יָמִים תַּעֲבֹד וְעָשִׂיתָ כָּל מְלַאכְתֶּךָ וְיוֹם הַשְּׁבִיעִי שַׁבָּת לַה'
אֱלֹהֶיךָ" — as it is stated, *Six days shall you work and accomplish all your*
work; but the seventh day is the Sabbath to HASHEM, your God (*Exodus*
20:9-10).[4]

---

1. [Because the Baraisa does not comment
much on *Avos* 1:11, it therefore does not
designate a separate chapter to expounding that Mishnah (*Ben Avraham*, end of
chapter).]

2. Were it not for the Baraisa, one might
have explained the Mishnah's exhortation
to "love work" as teaching simply that one
should not shun the work he must do, but
he may despise it as a necessarily evil that
takes time away from Torah study. The
Baraisa therefore teaches "and not despise
it." A person is to consider working not only
necessary but virtuous (*Magen Avos*). He
should not consider any form of work beneath his dignity (*Binyan Yehoshua*).

3. As it is stated, *HASHEM said to Moses,*
"Write these words for yourself, for ac-
cording to these words have I sealed a cov-
enant with you and Israel" [*Exodus 34:27*]
(*Avos HaRosh*). Moreover, the verse states,
Thus said HASHEM: If My covenant with the
night and with the day would not be ...
(*Jeremiah 33:25*), which the Gemara
explains in several places (*Shabbos 33a*
et al.) as referring to the Torah (*Binyan*
Yehoshua).

4. The verse directs a person to work for the
six days of the workweek. This directive is
what the Baraisa refers to, in an expository
sense, as a "covenant" (*Meiri* to *Avos* 1:10;
Avos HaRosh).

רַבִּי עֲקִיבָא אוֹמֵר: עִתִּים שֶׁאָדָם עוֹשֶׂה מְלָאכָה וּמִתְנַצֵּל מִן הַמִּיתָה וְעִתִּים שֶׁאֵין אָדָם עוֹשֶׂה מְלָאכָה וּמִתְחַיֵּיב מִיתָה לַשָּׁמַיִם. כֵּיצַד, יָשַׁב אָדָם כָּל הַשָּׁבוּעַ וְלֹא עָשָׂה מְלָאכָה וּלְעֶרֶב שַׁבָּת אֵין לוֹ מַה יֹּאכַל[6] הָיוּ לוֹ מָעוֹת שֶׁל הֶקְדֵּשׁ בְּתוֹךְ בֵּיתוֹ וְנָטַל מֵהֶם וְאָכַל מִתְחַיֵּיב מִיתָה לַשָּׁמַיִם[7]. אֲבָל אִם הָיָה פּוֹעֵל וְהוֹלֵךְ בְּבִנְיַן בֵּית הַמִּקְדָּשׁ אַף עַל פִּי שֶׁנָּתְנוּ לוֹ מָעוֹת שֶׁל הֶקְדֵּשׁ בִּשְׂכָרוֹ וְנָטַל מֵהֶם וְאָכַל מִתְנַצֵּל מִן הַמִּיתָה[8,9].

The Baraisa records the comments of numerous sages, each extolling the virtues of work:

רַבִּי עֲקִיבָא אוֹמֵר: עִתִּים שֶׁאָדָם עוֹשֶׂה מְלָאכָה וּמִתְנַצֵּל מִן הַמִּיתָה — R' Akiva says: There are times when **a person does work and** thereby **saves himself from being liable to death,**[5] וְעִתִּים שֶׁאֵין אָדָם עוֹשֶׂה מְלָאכָה וּמִתְחַיֵּיב מִיתָה לַשָּׁמַיִם — and there are times when a person does not do work and thereby makes himself liable to a Divine punishment of death. כֵּיצַד — How so? יָשַׁב אָדָם כָּל הַשָּׁבוּעַ וְלֹא עָשָׂה מְלָאכָה — Suppose **a person sat** idly **all week, and did not do work.** וּלְעֶרֶב שַׁבָּת אֵין לוֹ מַה יֹּאכַל — When **the eve of the Sabbath** comes, **he does not have what to eat on the Sabbath.**[6] הָיוּ לוֹ מָעוֹת שֶׁל הֶקְדֵּשׁ בְּתוֹךְ בֵּיתוֹ — It so happens that **he has consecrated money in his house,** וְנָטַל מֵהֶם וְאָכַל — **and he takes some of it** to buy food **to eat** on the Sabbath. מִתְחַיֵּיב מִיתָה לַשָּׁמַיִם — **He has** thereby **made himself liable to a** Divine **punishment of death** for intentionally benefiting from sacred funds.[7] It thus emerges that by not working during the week, he effectively caused himself to be liable to death. אֲבָל אִם הָיָה פּוֹעֵל וְהוֹלֵךְ בְּבִנְיַן בֵּית הַמִּקְדָּשׁ — **But if he would be continuously working on building** something **for the Holy Temple,** אַף עַל פִּי שֶׁנָּתְנוּ לוֹ מָעוֹת שֶׁל הֶקְדֵּשׁ בִּשְׂכָרוֹ — then **even though they paid him his wages from consecrated money,** וְנָטַל מֵהֶם וְאָכַל — **and he takes some of it** to buy food **to eat,** מִתְנַצֵּל מִן הַמִּיתָה — **he is saved from** a Divine punishment of **death** by his work.[8] Thus, being idle can make one

---

5. *Ahavas Chesed, Ben Avraham.*

6. Because he was idle during the week, he did not have much to eat then either. But during the week, he is content to get by with very little; on the Sabbath, he seeks something more substantial (*Binyan Yehoshua*).

7. R' Akiva here follows the opinion that one is liable to the Heavenly death penalty for intentionally benefiting improperly from sacred funds [see *Sanhedrin* 83a, et al.] (*Binyan Yehoshua*).

8. When sacred funds are given as payment for work done for the Temple, that money is

deconsecrated on the work that was done. The money thereby loses its sanctity and may be spent any way one wishes (*Binyan Yehoshua*).

Magen Avos wonders why the Baraisa uses the expression "פּוֹעֵל וְהוֹלֵךְ", *"continuously" working.* He suggests that it teaches us a novel law — namely, that if the Temple official contracted with the worker a set price for the complete job (rather than an hourly or daily rate) and paid him the full amount before the job is complete, he is permitted to use the entire amount even

רַבִּי דּוֹסְתַּאי אוֹמֵר: מִנַּיִן שֶׁאִם לֹא עָשָׂה מְלָאכָה כָּל שִׁשָּׁה שֶׁיַּעֲשֶׂה
כָּל שִׁבְעָה, הֲרֵי שֶׁיָּשַׁב כָּל יְמוֹת הַשַּׁבָּת וְלֹא עָשָׂה מְלָאכָה וּלְעֶרֶב
שַׁבָּת אֵין לוֹ מַה שֶׁיֹּאכַל הָלַךְ וְנָפַל בֵּין הַגַּיָּיסוֹת וּתְפָשׂוּהוּ וְאָחֲזוּ
אוֹתוֹ בְּקוֹלָר וְעָשׂוּ בּוֹ מְלָאכָה בְּשַׁבָּת כָּל זֹאת שֶׁלֹּא עָשָׂה כָּל
שִׁשָּׁה. רַבִּי שִׁמְעוֹן בֶּן אֶלְעָזָר אוֹמֵר: אַף אָדָם הָרִאשׁוֹן לֹא טָעַם
כְּלוּם עַד שֶׁעָשָׂה מְלָאכָה, שֶׁנֶּאֱמַר (בראשית ב, טו) "וַיַּנִּחֵהוּ בְגַן עֵדֶן
לְעָבְדָהּ וּלְשָׁמְרָהּ" וְהָדַר (שם פסוק טז) "מִכֹּל עֵץ הַגָּן אָכֹל תֹּאכֵל".

liable to death for using sacred money, whereas working can save one from that penalty.[9]

The second sage:

רַבִּי דּוֹסְתַּאי אוֹמֵר: מִנַּיִן שֶׁאִם לֹא עָשָׂה מְלָאכָה כָּל שִׁשָּׁה — R' Dostai says: From where do we see that if one did not do work all six days of the workweek, **שֶׁיַּעֲשֶׂה כָּל שִׁבְעָה** — that he may end up having to do work all *seven* days of a different week? It can be seen from the following scenario: **הֲרֵי שֶׁיָּשַׁב כָּל יְמוֹת הַשַּׁבָּת וְלֹא עָשָׂה מְלָאכָה** — Here you have someone who sat idly all the days of the week, and did not do work. **וּלְעֶרֶב שַׁבָּת אֵין לוֹ מַה שֶׁיֹּאכַל** — And as a result, when the eve of the Sabbath comes, he does not have what to eat on the Sabbath. **הָלַךְ וְנָפַל בֵּין הַגַּיָּיסוֹת** — In desperation, he goes out on the road to rob someone and as a result wanders into the area of bandits,[10] **וּתְפָשׂוּהוּ וְאָחֲזוּ אוֹתוֹ בְּקוֹלָר וְעָשׂוּ בּוֹ מְלָאכָה בְּשַׁבָּת** — who seize him, lock a collar upon him, and then force him to do work even on the Sabbath. **כָּל זֹאת שֶׁלֹּא עָשָׂה כָּל שִׁשָּׁה** — All this befell him because he did not do work all six days of the week.

The third sage:

רַבִּי שִׁמְעוֹן בֶּן אֶלְעָזָר אוֹמֵר: אַף אָדָם הָרִאשׁוֹן לֹא טָעַם כְּלוּם עַד שֶׁעָשָׂה מְלָאכָה — R' Shimon ben Elazar says: So great is work that even Adam, the first man, did not taste any food until he did work, **שֶׁנֶּאֱמַר "וַיַּנִּחֵהוּ בְגַן עֵדֶן לְעָבְדָהּ וּלְשָׁמְרָהּ"** — as it is stated, *HASHEM God took the man and placed him in the Garden of Eden, to work it and to guard it* (Genesis 2:15), **וְהָדַר "מִכֹּל עֵץ הַגָּן אָכֹל תֹּאכֵל"** — and only afterward does it state, *And HASHEM God commanded the*

---

before he completes the job, as long as he is "continuously working" at it. This highlights the value of "working" quite apart from the job's completion.

9. [Actually, R' Akiva's first scenario already illustrates how work can save one from the death penalty: If failing to work can lead one to misuse sacred funds, then the converse is that working would lead one to avoid using such funds! However, R' Akiva wishes to

show how working can save one from death even if he *does* use the funds that had been consecrated. (The explanation of *Magen Avos* mentioned at the end of the previous note would also account for why R' Akiva presents this second scenario.)]

10. *Binyan Yehoshua.* Alternatively, he sets out not to rob, but to throw himself at the mercy of the bandits who, he hopes, will sustain him (*Magen Avos; Avos HaRosh*).

רַבִּי טַרְפוֹן אוֹמֵר: אַף הַקָּדוֹשׁ בָּרוּךְ הוּא לֹא הִשְׁרָה שְׁכִינָתוֹ עַל יִשְׂרָאֵל
עַד שֶׁעָשׂוּ מְלָאכָה, שֶׁנֶּאֱמַר (שמות כה, ח) "וְעָשׂוּ לִי מִקְדָּשׁ וְשָׁכַנְתִּי
בְּתוֹכָם". רַבִּי יְהוּדָה בֶּן בְּתֵירָא אוֹמֵר: מִי שֶׁאֵין לוֹ מְלָאכָה לַעֲשׂוֹת
מַה יַּעֲשֶׂה[11], אִם יֶשׁ לוֹ חָצֵר חֲרֵבָה אוֹ שָׂדֶה חֲרֵבָה יֵלֵךְ וְיִתְעַסֵּק בָּהּ,
שֶׁנֶּאֱמַר (שמות כ, ט) "שֵׁשֶׁת יָמִים תַּעֲבֹד וְעָשִׂיתָ כָּל מְלַאכְתֶּךָ" וּמָה
תַּלְמוּד לוֹמַר "וְעָשִׂיתָ כָּל מְלַאכְתֶּךָ" לְהָבִיא אֶת מִי שֶׁיֵּשׁ לוֹ חֲצֵרוֹת אוֹ
שָׂדוֹת חֲרֵבוֹת יֵלֵךְ וְיִתְעַסֵּק בָּהֶן[12], רַבִּי [טַרְפוֹן] אוֹמֵר: (אֵין אָדָם מֵת)
אֶלָּא מִתּוֹךְ הַבַּטָּלָה (שֶׁנֶּאֱמַר (בראשית מט, לג) "וַיִּגְוַע וַיֵּאָסֶף אֶל עַמָּיו"[13],

---

man, saying, *"Of every tree of the garden you may freely eat"* (ibid. v. 16),
implying that Adam was permitted to eat only *after* he worked.

The fourth sage:

רַבִּי טַרְפוֹן אוֹמֵר: אַף הַקָּדוֹשׁ בָּרוּךְ הוּא לֹא הִשְׁרָה שְׁכִינָתוֹ עַל יִשְׂרָאֵל עַד שֶׁעָשׂוּ
מְלָאכָה — R' Tarfon says: So great is work that **even the Holy One, Blessed is
He, did not rest His Presence among the people of Israel until they did work,**
שֶׁנֶּאֱמַר "וְעָשׂוּ לִי מִקְדָּשׁ וְשָׁכַנְתִּי בְּתוֹכָם" — as it is stated, *They shall make a
Sanctuary for Me — and I shall dwell among them* (*Exodus* 25:8), implying
that only *after* the people of Israel would do the work of building the Tabernacle
would God rest His Presence in their midst.

The fifth sage:

רַבִּי יְהוּדָה בֶּן בְּתֵירָא אוֹמֵר: מִי שֶׁאֵין לוֹ מְלָאכָה לַעֲשׂוֹת מַה יַּעֲשֶׂה — R' Yehudah
ben Beseira says: **Someone who does not have work to do, what shall he
do?**[11] אִם יֶשׁ לוֹ חָצֵר חֲרֵבָה אוֹ שָׂדֶה חֲרֵבָה יֵלֵךְ וְיִתְעַסֵּק בָּהּ — **If he has a vacant
yard or a vacant field,** which he does not need for his living area or livelihood,
he should still **go and work on it,** so as to avoid the curse of idleness, שֶׁנֶּאֱמַר
— "שֵׁשֶׁת יָמִים תַּעֲבֹד וְעָשִׂיתָ כָּל מְלַאכְתֶּךָ" — as it is stated, *Six days shall you
work and accomplish all your work* (ibid. 20:9). וּמָה תַּלְמוּד לוֹמַר "וְעָשִׂיתָ"
"כָּל מְלַאכְתֶּךָ" — Now, what is Scripture teaching us by saying the inclusive
phrase *and accomplish "all" your work?* לְהָבִיא אֶת מִי שֶׁיֵּשׁ לוֹ חֲצֵרוֹת אוֹ
שָׂדוֹת חֲרֵבוֹת — It comes **to include even someone who has vacant yards or
vacant fields,** יֵלֵךְ וְיִתְעַסֵּק בָּהֶן — and teaches that **he should still go and
work on them.**[12] Thus, we see the superiority of work over idleness.

The sixth sage:

רַבִּי טַרְפוֹן אוֹמֵר: אֵין אָדָם מֵת אֶלָּא מִתּוֹךְ הַבַּטָּלָה — R' Tarfon says: **A person dies
only because of idleness,** שֶׁנֶּאֱמַר "וַיִּגְוַע וַיֵּאָסֶף אֶל עַמָּיו" — as it is stated, *[Jacob]*

---

11. He has servants to take care of all his
needs. What shall he do to avoid the immorality and anxiety that are the negative
consequences of leisure? (*Mefaresh, Ahavas*

Chesed, based on *Kesubos* 59b).

12. This refers to one who is not learned. But
a learned person should instead toil in Torah
study. Alternatively, even a learned person

[רַבִּי יוֹסֵי הַגְּלִילִי אוֹמֵר:] הֲרֵי שֶׁנִּכְפָּה וְנָפַל עַל אוֹמֶן שֶׁלּוֹ וּמֵת¹⁴ הָא
אֵינוֹ מֵת אֶלָּא מִתּוֹךְ הַבַּטָּלָה). הָיָה עוֹמֵד עַל רֹאשׁ הַגַּג [וְעַל רֹאשׁ
הַבִּירָה וְעַל רֹאשׁ הַבִּנְיָן] [(וְעַל שְׂפַת הַנָּהָר)] וְנָפַל וָמֵת אֵינוֹ מֵת אֶלָּא
מִתּוֹךְ הַבַּטָּלָה. (שֶׁכֵּן) שָׁמַעְנוּ לָאֲנָשִׁים וּלְנָשִׁים, מִנַּיִן, שֶׁנֶּאֱמַר (שמות לו, ו)
"אִישׁ וְאִשָּׁה אַל יַעֲשׂוּ עוֹד מְלָאכָה לִתְרוּמַת הַקֹּדֶשׁ"¹⁷, לִטְפָלִים מִנַּיִן,

---

רַבִּי יוֹסֵי הַגְּלִילִי — *expired and was gathered to his people* (*Genesis* 49:33).[13]
אוֹמֵר הֲרֵי שֶׁנִּכְפָּה וְנָפַל עַל אוֹמֶן שֶׁלּוֹ וּמֵת — R' Yose HaGlili says: Here you have
someone who had a seizure and fell while on his job, and died;[14]   הָא אֵינוֹ מֵת
עַל מִתּוֹךְ הַבַּטָּלָה — he has thus died only because of idleness.   הָיָה עוֹמֵד עַל
רֹאשׁ הַגַּג וְעַל רֹאשׁ הַבִּירָה וְעַל רֹאשׁ הַבִּנְיָן וְעַל שְׂפַת הַנָּהָר וְנָפַל וָמֵת — Or one was
standing idly atop a roof or on top of a mansion or on top of a building or on the
bank of a river, and he fell to the ground or into the river and died,   אֵינוֹ מֵת אֶלָּא
מִתּוֹךְ הַבַּטָּלָה — he has died only because of idleness; for if he would have had
work to do, he would not have been standing idly in those dangerous places.[15]

Above, R' Tarfon (the fourth sage) showed the value of work from the fact that
God did not rest His Presence on the Jewish people until they had done work in
building the Tabernacle. The Baraisa now continues to show from that same context that work is important not only for men and women, but for children as well:
שֶׁכֵּן שָׁמַעְנוּ לָאֲנָשִׁים וּלְנָשִׁים — We have thus far learned from the building of
the Tabernacle about the importance of work for men and women.[16]   מִנַּיִן,
שֶׁנֶּאֱמַר "אִישׁ וְאִשָּׁה אַל יַעֲשׂוּ עוֹד מְלָאכָה לִתְרוּמַת הַקֹּדֶשׁ" — From where? For it
is stated, *Moses commanded that they proclaim throughout the camp, saying,
"Man and woman shall not do more work toward the gift for the Sanctuary!"*
(*Exodus* 36:6). Thus, we see that the men and women had both been involved in
the work for the Tabernacle.[17]   לִטְפָלִים מִנַּיִן — From where do we know that

---

must do some work, for Torah without work
will not endure [*Avos* 2:2] (*Ben Avraham*).

13. The Sages expound the glaring omission
of the expression וַיָּמָת, *and he died,* here as
teaching that, in a sense, "Jacob our father
did not die" (see *Taanis* 5b). The Baraisa
understands that this is because he never
sat idly, but rather worked hard his whole
life [see, e.g., *Genesis* 31:40] (*Magen Avos*).
Perhaps this is because hard work does not
allow one's soul to become the prisoner of
physical pleasures. To such a person, the
separation of the soul from the body at the
end of life is not so wrenching an experience,
and is not referred to with the usual term
"death" (ibid.).

14. [Several days later (see *Avos DeRabbi
Nassan, Nusach* 2, Ch. 21)] because he could
not work and sustain himself (*Binyan Yehoshua*). Alternatively, the meaning is that he
had been idle and unused to working; when
he finally worked, the strain was too much for
him, and he had a seizure and died (*Ahavas
Chesed,* based on *R' Yonah*). [*Ben Avraham*
renders נָפַל עַל אוֹמֶן שֶׁלּוֹ as *fell on his temple.*]

15. *Ahavas Chesed, Avos HaRosh* [Vol. 1]).

16. We have rendered this line according to
Avos HaRosh [Vol. 1], in explanation of our
reading.

17. Earlier verses demonstrate this as well.
The Baraisa, however, cites this verse because it explicitly uses the word מְלָאכָה,

שֶׁנֶּאֱמַר (שם) "וַיִּכָּלֵא הָעָם מֵהָבִיא"18. אָמַר רַבִּי נָתָן: בְּשָׁעָה שֶׁנִּתְעַסֵּק
מֹשֶׁה בִּמְלֶאכֶת הַמִּשְׁכָּן לֹא רָצָה לִיטוֹל עֵצָה מִנְּשִׂיאֵי יִשְׂרָאֵל20 וְהָיוּ
נְשִׂיאֵי יִשְׂרָאֵל יוֹשְׁבִין וְשׁוֹתְקִין וְאוֹמְרִים: עַכְשָׁיו יִצְטָרֵךְ לָנוּ מֹשֶׁה21.
כֵּיוָן שֶׁשָּׁמְעוּ שֶׁהֶעֱבִירוּ קוֹל בַּמַּחֲנֶה, שֶׁנֶּאֱמַר (שם פסוק ז) "וְהַמְּלָאכָה
הָיְתָה דַיָּם" אָמְרוּ: אוֹי לָנוּ שֶׁלֹּא הָיָה לָנוּ שׁוּתָּפוּת בִּמְלֶאכֶת הַמִּשְׁכָּן,

the young children were involved as well?   שֶׁנֶּאֱמַר "וַיִּכָּלֵא הָעָם מֵהָבִיא" — As
it is stated at the end of the verse just cited, and *"the nation" was restrained
from bringing,* which includes even the young children.[18]

The Baraisa now shows that even a prominent figure should not refrain from
work:[19]

אָמַר רַבִּי נָתָן: בְּשָׁעָה שֶׁנִּתְעַסֵּק מֹשֶׁה בִּמְלֶאכֶת הַמִּשְׁכָּן — R' Nassan said: At the
time that Moses was occupied in the work of the Tabernacle,   לֹא רָצָה לִיטוֹל
עֵצָה מִנְּשִׂיאֵי יִשְׂרָאֵל — he did not wish to consult the tribal leaders (*nesiim*) of
Israel as to which materials they would donate.[20]   וְהָיוּ נְשִׂיאֵי יִשְׂרָאֵל יוֹשְׁבִין
וְשׁוֹתְקִין — And so the tribal leaders of Israel sat quietly without donating anything,   וְאוֹמְרִים עַכְשָׁיו יִצְטָרֵךְ לָנוּ מֹשֶׁה — saying to themselves, "Soon, Moses
will need us to donate what the people do not."[21]   כֵּיוָן שֶׁשָּׁמְעוּ שֶׁהֶעֱבִירוּ קוֹל
בַּמַּחֲנֶה — However, when they heard the proclamation sent throughout the
camp saying that nothing more was needed for the Tabernacle,   שֶׁנֶּאֱמַר
"וְהַמְּלָאכָה הָיְתָה דַיָּם" — as it is stated, *Moses commanded that they proclaim
throughout the camp, saying, "Man and woman shall not do more work toward
the gift for the Sanctuary!" And the people were restrained from bringing.* **But
the work had been enough** *for all the work, to do it — and there was extra* (ibid.
vv. 6-7),   אָמְרוּ אוֹי לָנוּ שֶׁלֹּא הָיָה לָנוּ שׁוּתָּפוּת בִּמְלֶאכֶת הַמִּשְׁכָּן — they said,
"Woe is to us, that we did not have a share in the work of the Tabernacle!"

---

work, with reference to both men and
women, and because it must in any case
cite this verse to include children, as it does
next (see *Ben Avraham* and *Avos HaRosh*
[Vol. 1]).

18. The verse should have concluded simply
and "they" were restrained from bringing.
The otherwise unnecessary expression "the
nation" comes to include *all* its members
— even the young children (*Magen Avos,
Ahavas Chesed*).

19. *Magen Avos.*

20. This is evident from the fact that Moses
requested donations for the Tabernacle from
the people in general — *everyone whose
heart motivates him* (ibid. 35:5) — and not

specifically from the leaders (*Binyan Yehoshua,* from *Bamidbar Rabbah* 12 §16).
Moses did so in order to allow all the people
a share in this great merit, or alternatively,
so that the leaders would not be able to
claim that the Tabernacle belonged to them
more than it did to the rest of the nation
(*Magen Avos*).

21. The leaders assumed that the rest of the
nation would bring only the materials necessary for the construction of the Tabernacle,
and they would be left the opportunity to
supply all the other materials [required for
the various services and upkeep of the Tab-
ernacle] (*Binyan Yehoshua,* citing *Yalkut
Shimoni* to *Numbers* 7:2 [§713]).

עָמְדוּ וְהוֹסִיפוּ דָבָר גָּדוֹל מֵעַצְמָם, שֶׁנֶּאֱמַר (שמות לה, כז) "וְהַנְּשִׂאָם הֵבִיאוּ אֵת אַבְנֵי הַשֹּׁהַם"[22]:

ב. וּשְׂנָא אֶת הָרַבָּנוּת, כֵּיצַד, מְלַמֵּד שֶׁלֹּא יַנִּיחַ אָדָם עֲטָרָה מֵעַצְמוֹ בְּרֹאשׁוֹ. אֲבָל אֲחֵרִים יַנִּיחוּ לוֹ, שֶׁנֶּאֱמַר (משלי כז, ב) "יְהַלֶּלְךָ זָר וְלֹא פִיךָ נָכְרִי וְאַל שְׂפָתֶיךָ"[23]. אָמַר רַבִּי עֲקִיבָא: כָּל הַמַּגְבִּיהַּ עַצְמוֹ עַל דִּבְרֵי תוֹרָה לְמָה הוּא דוֹמֶה, לִנְבֵלָה מוּשְׁלֶכֶת בַּדֶּרֶךְ, כָּל עוֹבֵר וְשָׁב מַנִּיחַ יָדוֹ

עָמְדוּ וְהוֹסִיפוּ דָבָר גָּדוֹל מֵעַצְמָם — Immediately, **they arose and added a great donation of their own,** שֶׁנֶּאֱמַר "וְהַנְּשִׂאָם הֵבִיאוּ אֵת אַבְנֵי הַשֹּׁהַם" — **as it is stated,** *The leaders brought the shoham stones* (ibid. 35:27).[22] Thus, we see that even a prominent figure should not refrain from involving himself when work is called for.

§2 The Baraisa now expounds Shemayah's second saying: וּשְׂנָא אֶת הָרַבָּנוּת — **"Despise positions of power":** כֵּיצַד — **How is this to be understood?** מְלַמֵּד שֶׁלֹּא יַנִּיחַ אָדָם עֲטָרָה מֵעַצְמוֹ בְּרֹאשׁוֹ — **This teaches** only **that a person should not** be the one to **place a crown on his own head,** אֲבָל אֲחֵרִים יַנִּיחוּ לוֹ — **but** he may allow **others to place it on him,** שֶׁנֶּאֱמַר "יְהַלֶּלְךָ זָר וְלֹא פִיךָ נָכְרִי וְאַל שְׂפָתֶיךָ" — **as it is stated,** *Let another praise you, not your own mouth; a stranger, not your own lips* (Proverbs 27:2). Thus, Shemayah means that one should avoid *seizing* a position of power, but he may accept it if offered to him.[23]

Having mentioned that it is improper for a person to bestow honor on himself, the Baraisa cites a similar teaching: אָמַר רַבִּי עֲקִיבָא — **R' Akiva said:** כָּל הַמַּגְבִּיהַּ עַצְמוֹ עַל דִּבְרֵי תוֹרָה לְמָה הוּא דוֹמֶה — **Someone who holds himself high because of the words of Torah** that he has studied — **to what can he be compared?** לִנְבֵלָה מוּשְׁלֶכֶת בַּדֶּרֶךְ — **To a rotting carcass that has been abandoned on the road;** כָּל עוֹבֵר וְשָׁב מַנִּיחַ יָדוֹ

---

22. Although this verse is written *before* the verse regarding the proclamation, R' Nassan must have had a tradition that it actually occurred after the proclamation (*Magen Avos*). Although all the materials for the Tabernacle itself had already been brought, as stated in the verse, these stones were not for the Tabernacle itself, but rather for the vestments of the Kohen Gadol, and were still needed (ibid., based on *Bamidbar Rabbah* ibid.).

23. Our Baraisa comes to resolve an apparent contradiction: Shemayah teaches that one is to "despise a position of power." Yet elsewhere the Sages are critical of a scholar

who is capable of rendering halachic decisions to the public but does not do so (see *Sotah* 22a, *Avodah Zarah* 19b). Our Baraisa therefore explains that Shemayah never meant for a person to shirk the responsibilities of an office thrust upon him; it is only that he should not seek the office on his own (*Avos HaRosh* [Vol. 1]).

The verse cited, however, does not seem to correspond exactly to what the Baraisa is teaching. Some suggest a different explanation: The Baraisa is taking שְׂנָא אֶת הָרַבָּנוּת to mean "despise superiority." Do not declare yourself superior to others. If you are superior

עַל חוֹטְמוֹ וּמִתְרַחֵק מִמֶּנָּה וְהוֹלֵךְ, שֶׁנֶּאֱמַר (שם ל, לב) ״אִם נָבַלְתָּ
בְהִתְנַשֵּׂא וְאִם זַמּוֹתָ יָד לְפֶה״[24] [(אָמַר לוֹ בֶּן עַזַּאי: דְּרָשֵׁהוּ מֵעִנְיָינוֹ[25])]
אִם מְנַבֵּל אָדָם עַצְמוֹ עַל דִּבְרֵי תוֹרָה וְאוֹכֵל תְּמָרִים חֲרוּבִים[26] וְלוֹבֵשׁ
בְּגָדִים צוֹאִים וְיוֹשֵׁב וּמְשַׁמֵּר עַל פֶּתַח שֶׁל חֲכָמִים[27], כָּל עוֹבֵר וָשָׁב
אוֹמֵר שֶׁמָּא שׁוֹטֶה הוּא זֶה לְסוֹף אַתָּה מוֹצֵא כָּל הַתּוֹרָה כּוּלָּהּ עִמּוֹ[28].

עַל חוֹטְמוֹ וּמִתְרַחֵק מִמֶּנָּה וְהוֹלֵךְ — **every passerby puts his hand on his nose
to avoid the stench, and keeps far away from it as he walks on.** So too the
scholar who exalts himself. People are repelled by his arrogance and keep
their distance from him, שֶׁנֶּאֱמַר — **as it is stated:** ״אִם נָבַלְתָּ בְהִתְנַשֵּׂא
וְאִם זַמּוֹתָ יָד לְפֶה״ — *If you have become like a carcass [נָבַלְתָּ], it is because
of holding [yourself] high; and if you have thoughts, hand to mouth* (ibid.
30:32).[24]

The Baraisa records another interpretation of the *Proverbs* verse just cited:
אָמַר לוֹ בֶּן עַזַּאי: דְּרָשֵׁהוּ מֵעִנְיָינוֹ — **Ben Azzai said to [R' Akiva]: My master, you
should** rather **expound the verse according to its context:**[25] אִם מְנַבֵּל אָדָם
עַצְמוֹ עַל דִּבְרֵי תוֹרָה — It teaches that **if a person debases himself over the
words of Torah,** וְאוֹכֵל תְּמָרִים חֲרוּבִים וְלוֹבֵשׁ בְּגָדִים צוֹאִים — in that **he eats
dry dates**[26] **and wears stained clothing,** focusing on his learning instead of
on acquiring the normal amenities of life, וְיוֹשֵׁב וּמְשַׁמֵּר עַל פֶּתַח שֶׁל חֲכָמִים —
and he waits in attendance at the doorstep of the study hall of the **Sages,** so
that he may hear their every word, from the moment they enter until the moment they leave,[27] כָּל עוֹבֵר וָשָׁב אוֹמֵר שֶׁמָּא שׁוֹטֶה הוּא זֶה — **every passerby
may say, "Perhaps this** man **is deranged,"** as he cares so little for his needs.
לְסוֹף אַתָּה מוֹצֵא כָּל הַתּוֹרָה כּוּלָּהּ עִמּוֹ — But **in the end, you will find the entire
Torah with him.**[28]

---

in some way, you may let others place that
"crown" on your head, but it is not something
you should do on your own. This sentiment is
exactly what is expressed in the verse cited
by the Baraisa (*Binyan Yehoshua*).

24. [According to this exposition, the words
וְאִם זַמּוֹתָ יָד לְפֶה are seemingly expounded as:
*and if you have thoughts [of arrogance, oth-
ers will place] hand to mouth [and nose]* to
avoid the stench of your arrogance.]

25. See below, note 28.

26. Which are inferior food, and also cause
physical discomfort when eaten (*Magen
Avos, Avos HaRosh* [Vol. 1]). Some versions
of the Baraisa read תְּמָרִים וַחֲרוּבִים, *dates and
carobs* (see *Avos HaRosh* [Vol. 1]).

27. *Ben Avraham.*

28. Accordingly, the *Proverbs* verse is rendered: *If you debase yourself [נָבַלְתָּ] [to study
Torah], you will [in the end] be raised up
[with Torah mastery]; if you have thoughts
[of Torah greatness], put your hand to your
mouth* and do not eat unnecessary delicacies, or respond to those who ridicule you
as deranged because of your privations (see
Magen Avos; cf. *Ben Avraham*).

Ben Azzai considers this exposition more in
line with the context of the verse (see above
at note 25), because it then deals exclusively
with the person himself, what he does and his
reactions. [R' Akiva's exposition, however, is
a blend of what the person does and of how

(רַבִּי יוֹסֵי אוֹמֵר: רֵד מַטָּה לְמַעְלָה וּמַעְלָה לְמַטָּה), כָּל הַמַּגְבִּיהַּ עַצְמוֹ עַל
דִּבְרֵי תוֹרָה סוֹף שֶׁמַּשְׁפִּילִין אוֹתוֹ וְכָל הַמַּשְׁפִּיל עַצְמוֹ עַל דִּבְרֵי תוֹרָה
סוֹף שֶׁמַּגְבִּיהִין אוֹתוֹ:

ג. וְאַל תִּתְוַודַּע לָרָשׁוּת, כֵּיצַד, מְלַמֵּד שֶׁלֹּא יֵצֵא לוֹ לְאָדָם שֵׁם בָּרָשׁוּת,29
כֵּיוָן שֶׁיָּצָא לוֹ שֵׁם בָּרָשׁוּת סוֹף נוֹתְנִין בּוֹ עֵינֵיהֶם וְהוֹרְגִים אוֹתוֹ וְנוֹטְלִין
הֵימֶנּוּ כָּל מָמוֹנוֹ30. כֵּיצַד, הָיָה חֲבֵירוֹ בַּשּׁוּק וְאוֹמֵר: הַקָּדוֹשׁ בָּרוּךְ הוּא יְבָרְכֵהוּ
לִפְלוֹנִי31, הַיּוֹם יָצָא מִתּוֹךְ בֵּיתוֹ מֵאָה שְׁוָורִים מֵאָה רְחֵלִים וּמֵאָה עִזִּים,

---

Another sage comments:

רַבִּי יוֹסֵי אוֹמֵר: רֵד מַטָּה לְמַעְלָה — R' Yose says: The teachings of both R' Akiva and Ben Azzai are true: Go down below to eventually be above; וּמַעְלָה לְמַטָּה — and go above to eventually be below. How so? כָּל הַמַּגְבִּיהַּ עַצְמוֹ עַל דִּבְרֵי תוֹרָה סוֹף שֶׁמַּשְׁפִּילִין אוֹתוֹ — Whoever holds himself high because of the words of Torah that he has studied will in the end be brought low; וְכָל הַמַּשְׁפִּיל עַצְמוֹ עַל דִּבְרֵי תוֹרָה סוֹף שֶׁמַּגְבִּיהִין אוֹתוֹ — and whoever lowers himself for the sake of studying the words of Torah will in the end be raised up.

§3 The Baraisa now expounds Shemayah's third saying: וְאַל תִּתְוַודַּע לָרָשׁוּת — "And do not become make yourself known to the government": כֵּיצַד — How is this to be understood? מְלַמֵּד שֶׁלֹּא יֵצֵא לוֹ לְאָדָם שֵׁם בָּרָשׁוּת — This teaches that a person should avoid getting a name for being wealthy in the eyes of the government.[29] כֵּיוָן שֶׁיָּצָא לוֹ שֵׁם בָּרָשׁוּת — For once a person gets a name for being wealthy in the eyes of the government, סוֹף נוֹתְנִין בּוֹ עֵינֵיהֶם — in the end they will set their sights upon him, וְהוֹרְגִים אוֹתוֹ וְנוֹטְלִין הֵימֶנּוּ כָּל מָמוֹנוֹ — and kill him and take from him all his money.[30] כֵּיצַד — How so? The Baraisa illustrates: הָיָה חֲבֵירוֹ — Suppose someone's friend was בַּשּׁוּק וְאוֹמֵר: הַקָּדוֹשׁ בָּרוּךְ הוּא יְבָרְכֵהוּ לִפְלוֹנִי — sitting in the market, and says out loud, "May the Holy One, Blessed is He, bless my friend, So-and-so!"[31] הַיּוֹם יָצָא מִתּוֹךְ בֵּיתוֹ מֵאָה שְׁוָורִים מֵאָה רְחֵלִים — Today, there emerged from his homestead one hundred oxen, one וּמֵאָה עִזִּים —

---

others react to him — see above, note 24] (Ahavas Chesed). [Alternatively, "the context of the verse" refers to the verses that precede it (vv. 29-31). Those verses speak of things that are indeed superior to others of their class: 29 There are three that step securely, and a fourth that walks with confidence: 30 The lion is the strongest of the animals, and does not turn back from anything; 31 the thigh-belted greyhound, the he-goat, and the king against whom none can stand. It stands to

reason, then, that this verse, too, speaks of one who, through his great efforts, rises to great prominence over his peers.]

29. Binyan Yehoshua.

30. [The רְשׁוּת, government, of the Mishnah were the Roman authorities, who were known for their ruthless greed.]

31. He means that he is not jealous of his friend's wealth (which he details next), but wishes that God will bless his friend even further (Magen Avos).

וְשָׁמַע הֵימֶנּוּ סַרְדְּיוֹט אֶחָד וְהָלַךְ וְאָמַר לַשַּׂר, הָלַךְ וְהִקִּיף אֶת כָּל בֵּיתוֹ
וְנָטַל מִמֶּנּוּ כָּל מָמוֹנוֹ, עָלָיו הַכָּתוּב אוֹמֵר (משלי כז, יד) "מְבָרֵךְ רֵעֵהוּ
בְּקוֹל גָּדוֹל ... קְלָלָה תֵּחָשֶׁב לוֹ". דָּבָר אַחֵר: (אַל תִּתְוַדַּע לָרָשׁוּת)
הָיָה חֲבֵרוֹ יוֹשֵׁב בַּשּׁוּק וְאָמַר: הַקָּדוֹשׁ בָּרוּךְ הוּא °יִתְנֶנּוּ³² לִפְלוֹנִי,
אוֹתוֹ הַיּוֹם הִכְנִיס לְתוֹךְ בֵּיתוֹ כַּמָּה כּוֹרִין³³ שֶׁל חִטִּים כַּמָּה כּוֹרִין שֶׁל
שְׂעוֹרִים, שָׁמְעוּ מִמֶּנּוּ לִסְטִים וּבָאוּ וְהִקִּיפוּ אֶת כָּל בֵּיתוֹ נָטְלוּ מִמֶּנּוּ כָּל
מָמוֹנוֹ, לְשַׁחֲרִית אֵין לוֹ כְּלוּם, עָלָיו הַכָּתוּב אוֹמֵר "מְבָרֵךְ רֵעֵהוּ בְּקוֹל
גָּדוֹל וְגוֹ'"³⁴. דָּבָר אַחֵר: אַל תִּתְוַדַּע לָרָשׁוּת, כֵּיצַד, מְלַמֵּד שֶׁלֹּא יְכַוֵּין

---

hundred ewes, and one hundred goats!" וְשָׁמַע הֵימֶנּוּ סַרְדְּיוֹט אֶחָד וְהָלַךְ וְאָמַר — לַשַּׂר **— Now an officer overhears him and goes and tells the governor,** הָלַךְ **— who then goes,** וְהִקִּיף אֶת כָּל בֵּיתוֹ וְנָטַל מִמֶּנּוּ כָּל מָמוֹנוֹ — **surrounds [the wealthy friend's] entire homestead, and takes all his money from him!** עָלָיו הַכָּתוּב **— Regarding him who made** אוֹמֵר "מְבָרֵךְ רֵעֵהוּ בְּקוֹל גָּדוֹל ... קְלָלָה תֵּחָשֶׁב לוֹ" **that indiscreet announcement Scripture states,** *If one blesses his friend loudly from early in the morning, it will be considered a curse to him* (*Proverbs* 27:14).

Another interpretation:

דָּבָר אַחֵר: אַל תִּתְוַדַּע לָרָשׁוּת **— Another explanation and illustration of,** *And do not make yourself known "larashus":* הָיָה חֲבֵרוֹ יוֹשֵׁב בַּשּׁוּק וְאָמַר: הַקָּדוֹשׁ בָּרוּךְ הוּא יְחַנְּנוּ לִפְלוֹנִי **— Suppose someone's friend was sitting in the market and says out loud, "May the Holy One, Blessed is He, be gracious[32] to my friend, So-and-so!** אוֹתוֹ הַיּוֹם הִכְנִיס לְתוֹךְ בֵּיתוֹ כַּמָּה כּוֹרִין שֶׁל חִטִּים כַּמָּה כּוֹרִין שֶׁל שְׂעוֹרִים **— This day he brought into his homestead many** *korim*[33] **of wheat and many** *korim* **of barley."** שָׁמְעוּ מִמֶּנּוּ לִסְטִים וּבָאוּ וְהִקִּיפוּ אֶת כָּל בֵּיתוֹ **— Now robbers overhear him and come and surround [the wealthy friend's] entire homestead** in the night נָטְלוּ מִמֶּנּוּ כָּל מָמוֹנוֹ **— and take all his money from him.** לְשַׁחֲרִית אֵין לוֹ כְּלוּם **— In the morning, he sees that he has nothing left.** עָלָיו הַכָּתוּב אוֹמֵר "מְבָרֵךְ רֵעֵהוּ בְּקוֹל גָּדוֹל וְגוֹ' " **— Regarding him who made that indiscreet announcement Scripture states,** *If one blesses his friend loudly, etc., from early in the morning, it will be considered a curse to him.*[34]

The Baraisa offers an alternative understanding of Shemayah's third saying: דָּבָר אַחֵר: אַל תִּתְוַדַּע לָרָשׁוּת **— Another explanation of,** *And do not make yourself known "larashus":* כֵּיצַד **— How is this to be understood?** מְלַמֵּד שֶׁלֹּא יְכַוֵּין

---

32. [The standard edition has here a spelling mistake, יִתְנֶנּוּ instead of יְחַנְּנוּ, which we have corrected according to the Venice ed.]

33. A *kor* is the volume of 4,320 eggs.

34. This explanation understands אַל תִּתְוַדַּע לָרָשׁוּת to mean "do not become known *as someone of power*" — i.e., of wealth. It is not from fear of government confiscation (as before), but of robbers (*Ahavas Chesed*). Thus, this illustration makes no mention of the one overhearing the comment reporting it to the government. Rather, it is the robbers themselves who overhear the comment and come to rob the man's wealth.

אָדָם לוֹמַר אֲנִי הוּא שַׂר הָעִיר וַאֲנִי הוּא הַמִּשְׁנֶה[35] מִפְּנֵי שֶׁגּוֹזְלִין לְיִשְׂרָאֵל:[36]

ד.[37] דָּבָר אַחֵר: אַל יְכַוֵּין אָדָם לִיטּוֹל אֶת הָרָשׁוּת, אַף עַל פִּי שֶׁבָּרִאשׁוֹנָה פּוֹתְחִין לוֹ פֶּתַח הֲנָאָה בָּאַחֲרוֹנָה, פּוֹתְחִין לוֹ פֶּתַח הַקָּשֶׁה לוֹ:[39]

ה. אַבְטַלְיוֹן אוֹמֵר: חֲכָמִים הִזָּהֲרוּ בְּדִבְרֵיכֶם שֶׁמָּא יוֹרוּ דָבָר מִשְּׁמְכֶם שֶׁלֹּא בְּתַלְמוּד תּוֹרָה וְתָחוּבוּ חוֹבַת גָּלוּת וְתִגְלוּ לִמְקוֹם מַיִם הָרָעִים[40]

אָדָם לוֹמַר אֲנִי הוּא שַׂר הָעִיר וַאֲנִי הוּא הַמִּשְׁנֶה — This teaches that a person should not endeavor to announce, "I am the power behind the officer of the city," or "I am the power behind the viceroy."[35] מִפְּנֵי שֶׁגּוֹזְלִין לְיִשְׂרָאֵל — Because they generally **steal** money **from Jews,** and if he claims to be so influential with the rulers, the people will blame him for the theft.[36]

§4[37] Yet another interpretation of Shemayah's third saying:

דָּבָר אַחֵר — Alternatively: אַל יְכַוֵּין אָדָם לִיטּוֹל אֶת הָרָשׁוּת — A person should not endeavor to take a position in the government, but should rather refuse the offer if he can.[38] אַף עַל פִּי שֶׁבָּרִאשׁוֹנָה פּוֹתְחִין לוֹ פֶּתַח הֲנָאָה — For even though in the beginning they may **open for him the door that is beneficial for him,** בָּאַחֲרוֹנָה פּוֹתְחִין לוֹ פֶּתַח הַקָּשֶׁה לוֹ — in the end they will open for him the door that is difficult for him.[39]

§5 The Baraisa now expounds *Avos* 1:11, which reads:

אַבְטַלְיוֹן אוֹמֵר — Avtalyon says: חֲכָמִים הִזָּהֲרוּ בְּדִבְרֵיכֶם — Scholars, be cautious with your words, etc. [for you may incur the penalty of exile and be banished to a place of bad water. The disciples who come after you may drink and die, and consequently, the Name of Heaven may be desecrated.]

The Baraisa clarifies Avtalyon's statement:

שֶׁמָּא יוֹרוּ דָבָר מִשְּׁמְכֶם שֶׁלֹּא בְּתַלְמוּד תּוֹרָה — This means, if you are not cautious with your words, **perhaps [your disciples] will** misinterpret your words and **teach something** to others **that is not in accordance with the meaning of the** Torah, וְתָחוּבוּ חוֹבַת גָּלוּת וְתִגְלוּ לִמְקוֹם מַיִם הָרָעִים — and **you will become**

The robbers must operate in stealth and thus rob at night. The government, however, is under no such limitations. Thus, the first illustration, which deals with government confiscation, makes no mention of the loss being discovered "in the morning" (*Magen Avos*).

This latter explanation, which illustrates that the fear is of robbers who come in the night and that the man discovers his wealth gone in the morning, sees this in the *Proverbs* verse itself, which it renders: *If one blesses his friend loudly, from early in the morning it will be considered a curse to him*; that is, it is in the morning that the curse becomes

apparent (*Magen Avos*).

35. I.e., they consult me on everything and follow my advice (*Binyan Yehoshua*).

36. *Binyan Yehoshua*, from *Mefaresh*.

Accordingly, the phrase אַל תִּתְוַדַּע לָרָשׁוּת, is rendered, *And do not make yourself known as [influential with] the government.* In other words, do not advertise your affiliation with the government.

37. [The Vilna print has the number "8" here in error and numbers the next section "4".]

38. *Ben Avraham.*

39. That is, initially, they make his position

וְאַף הַתַּלְמִידִים הַבָּאִים אַחֲרֵיכֶם שֶׁמָּא יוֹרוּ דָבָר מִשְּׁמְכֶם שֶׁלֹּא כְּתַלְמוּד
תּוֹרָה[41]. וְתָחוּבוּ חוֹבַת גָּלוּת °וְיִגְלוּ לִמְקוֹם מַיִם הָרָעִים. אֵיזֶהוּ מַיִם הָרָעִים,
הֱוֵי אוֹמֵר: (תהלים קו, לה) ״וַיִּתְעָרְבוּ בַגּוֹיִם וַיִּלְמְדוּ מַעֲשֵׂיהֶם״[44] דָּבָר אַחֵר:
מַיִם הָרָעִים כְּמַשְׁמָעוֹ[45]. וְיֵשׁ אוֹמְרִים: שֶׁמָּא יִגְלוּ לַעֲבוֹדָה קָשָׁה[46]:

---

liable to exile and be exiled to a place of bad waters.[40]   וְאַף הַתַּלְמִידִים
שֶׁמָּא יוֹרוּ דָבָר — And also the disciples who come after you, הַבָּאִים אַחֲרֵיכֶם
מִשְּׁמְכֶם שֶׁלֹּא כְּתַלְמוּד תּוֹרָה — perhaps they will teach something in your name
that is not in accordance with the meaning of the Torah.[41]

The Baraisa explains the term "bad waters."[42]

וְתָחוּבוּ חוֹבַת גָּלוּת וְתִגְלוּ לִמְקוֹם מַיִם הָרָעִים — When Avtalyon said, "and you
will become liable to exile and be exiled[43] to a place of bad waters," אֵיזֶהוּ
מַיִם הָרָעִים — what are these bad waters he was speaking of? הֱוֵי אוֹמֵר:
״וַיִּתְעָרְבוּ בַגּוֹיִם וַיִּלְמְדוּ מַעֲשֵׂיהֶם״ — Say that it is a reference to the idolatrous
nations, as it is stated, *But they mingled with the nations and learned their
deeds* (Psalms 106:35).[44]   דָּבָר אַחֵר: מַיִם הָרָעִים כְּמַשְׁמָעוֹ — Alternatively,
"bad waters" is to be understood in its literal sense — i.e., water that is unfit
for drinking.[45]   וְיֵשׁ אוֹמְרִים: שֶׁמָּא יִגְלוּ לַעֲבוֹדָה קָשָׁה — And some say the
concern is that **perhaps they will be exiled to** a place where they will be forced
to perform **difficult labor.**[46]

---

of authority pleasant for him, but in the end
they will make things difficult for him (*Avos
HaRosh* [Vol. 1]). Accordingly, the phrase
אַל תִּתְוַדַּע לָרָשׁוּת is rendered, *And do not
make yourself known [as available] to the
government,* i.e., avoid accepting government positions (see *Rav* to *Avos* 1:10).

40. You must be careful, Avtalyon warns,
that your words not be misinterpreted as
teaching heretical ideas. Now, this is not so
great a concern in settled times and places,
where you can make sure that your listeners
are not likely to misconstrue what you say.
However, you might (for some unrelated sin)
be exiled to a place of "bad waters" — a place
where heretical ideas abound (see further
below) — where the listeners are likely to
seize upon your ambiguous words as supporting their heretical views (see *Rav* to *Avos*
1:11 [cited by *Binyan Yehoshua*] and *Meiri*
ad loc.).

41. Moreover, Avtalyon adds, upon your

passing, the disciples you leave behind
("who come after you") might perpetuate
the errors that were caused by your insuf-
ficiently considered words (*Rav*, cited by
Binyan Yehoshua).

42. *Binyan Yehoshua*, second approach;
Ben Avraham.

43. Emendation follows some manuscripts
and the reading and explanation of *Ben
Avraham.*

44. Jews living among such nations tend to
assimilate and learn from their evil ways,
making them prone to misunderstand and
misrepresent any Jewish teachings they
hear.

45. Drinking such water [and the other living conditions in exile] makes it difficult
for Torah to penetrate one's heart (*Binyan
Yehoshua*; see there further).

46. Which also makes it difficult for one to
study Torah (ibid.).

﴾ פֶּרֶק יב ﴿

א. הִלֵּל וְשַׁמַּאי קִבְּלוּ מֵהֶם. הִלֵּל אוֹמֵר: הֱוֵי מִתַּלְמִידָיו שֶׁל אַהֲרֹן, אוֹהֵב שָׁלוֹם וְרוֹדֵף שָׁלוֹם וּמֵשִׂים שָׁלוֹם בֵּין אִישׁ לְאִשְׁתּוֹ, [אוֹהֵב אֶת הַבְּרִיּוֹת] וּמְקָרְבָן לַתּוֹרָה. הוּא הָיָה אוֹמֵר: נְגַד שְׁמָא אָבַד שְׁמֵיהּ, וּדְלָא מוֹסִיף יָסֵיף, וּדְלָא יָלֵיף קְטָלָא חַיָּיב, וּדְאִישְׁתַּמַּשׁ בְּתָגָא חֲלָף:

ב. הוּא הָיָה אוֹמֵר: אִם אֵין אֲנִי לִי מִי לִי וּכְשֶׁאֲנִי לְעַצְמִי מָה אֲנִי אִם לֹא עַכְשָׁיו אֵימָתַי:

ג. אוֹהֵב שָׁלוֹם, כֵּיצַד, מְלַמֵּד שֶׁיְּהֵא אָדָם אוֹהֵב שָׁלוֹם בְּיִשְׂרָאֵל בֵּין כָּל אֶחָד וְאֶחָד¹ כְּדֶרֶךְ שֶׁהָיָה אַהֲרֹן אוֹהֵב שָׁלוֹם בֵּין כָּל אֶחָד וְאֶחָד,

﴾ CHAPTER 12 ﴿

§1 The Baraisa will cite, and then elaborate, *Avos* 1:12-14:

הִלֵּל וְשַׁמַּאי קִבְּלוּ מֵהֶם — **Hillel and Shammai** were students of Shemayah and Avtalyon and **received the tradition from them.** First, the teachings of Hillel: הִלֵּל אוֹמֵר: הֱוֵי מִתַּלְמִידָיו שֶׁל אַהֲרֹן — **Hillel says: Be from the disciples of Aaron,** learning from his ways: אוֹהֵב שָׁלוֹם וְרוֹדֵף שָׁלוֹם — **loving peace and pursuing peace;** וּמֵשִׂים שָׁלוֹם בֵּין אִישׁ לְאִשְׁתּוֹ — **making peace between man and wife;** אוֹהֵב אֶת הַבְּרִיּוֹת וּמְקָרְבָן לַתּוֹרָה — **loving people and bringing them closer to the Torah** (see *Avos* 1:12).

The Mishnah continues the teachings of Hillel:

הוּא הָיָה אוֹמֵר: נְגַד שְׁמָא אָבַד שְׁמֵיהּ — **He** also **used to say: He who seeks fame loses his reputation;** וּדְלָא מוֹסִיף יָסֵיף — **he who does not increase** his Torah learning **decreases it;** וּדְלָא יָלֵיף קְטָלָא חַיָּיב — **he who refuses to learn** Torah **deserves to die;** וּדְאִישְׁתַּמַּשׁ בְּתָגָא חֲלָף — **and he who exploits the crown for** personal gain **shall fade away** (ibid. 1:13).

§2 The Mishnah's final group of Hillel's teachings:

הוּא הָיָה אוֹמֵר: אִם אֵין אֲנִי לִי מִי לִי — **He** also **used to say: If I am not for myself, who will be for me?** וּכְשֶׁאֲנִי לְעַצְמִי מָה אֲנִי — **And if I am for myself, what am I?** אִם לֹא עַכְשָׁיו אֵימָתִי — **And if not now, when?** (ibid. 1:14).

§3 The Baraisa begins its elaboration of *Avos* 1:12:

אוֹהֵב שָׁלוֹם, כֵּיצַד — Hillel calls upon us to follow Aaron's example of **"loving peace"** — **how so?** מְלַמֵּד שֶׁיְּהֵא אָדָם אוֹהֵב שָׁלוֹם בְּיִשְׂרָאֵל בֵּין כָּל אֶחָד וְאֶחָד — **This teaches that a person should love** for there to be **peace in Israel between each and every person,**[1] כְּדֶרֶךְ שֶׁהָיָה אַהֲרֹן אוֹהֵב שָׁלוֹם בֵּין כָּל אֶחָד וְאֶחָד —

---

1. [Peaceful relations with the nations of the world is a Jewish ideal as well (see verses cited by *Ben Avraham*). The Baraisa, how-ever, is speaking to Jews who dwell among

שֶׁנֶּאֱמַר (מלאכי ב, ו) ״תּוֹרַת אֱמֶת הָיְתָה בְּפִיהוּ וְעַוְלָה לֹא נִמְצָא בִשְׂפָתָיו
בְּשָׁלוֹם וּבְמִישׁוֹר הָלַךְ אִתִּי וְרַבִּים הֵשִׁיב מֵעָוֹן״[2]. (רַבִּי מֵאִיר אוֹמֵר: מַה
תַּלְמוּד לוֹמַר ״וְרַבִּים הֵשִׁיב מֵעָוֹן״,) כְּשֶׁהָיָה אַהֲרֹן מְהַלֵּךְ בַּדֶּרֶךְ פָּגַע בּוֹ
בְּאָדָם רָשָׁע וְנָתַן לוֹ שָׁלוֹם[3]. לְמָחָר בִּקֵּשׁ אוֹתוֹ הָאִישׁ לַעֲבוֹר עֲבֵירָה.
אָמַר: אוֹי לִי, הֵיאַךְ אֶשָּׂא עֵינַי אַחַר כָּךְ וְאֶרְאֶה אֶת אַהֲרֹן, בּוֹשְׁתִּי
הֵימֶנּוּ שֶׁנָּתַן לִי שָׁלוֹם[4]. נִמְצָא אוֹתוֹ הָאִישׁ מוֹנֵעַ עַצְמוֹ מִן הָעֲבֵירָה[5].

---

in the same way that Aaron loved for there to be **peace between each and ev-**
ery person, שֶׁנֶּאֱמַר ״תּוֹרַת אֱמֶת הָיְתָה בְּפִיהוּ, וְעַוְלָה לֹא נִמְצָא בִשְׂפָתָיו — **as it is**
stated regarding Aaron, *The Torah of truth was in his mouth, and injustice*
was not found on his lips; בְּשָׁלוֹם וּבְמִישׁוֹר הָלַךְ אִתִּי, וְרַבִּים הֵשִׁיב מֵעָוֹן״ — he
walked with Me in peace and with fairness, and turned many away from
sin (Malachi 2:6).[2]

The Baraisa cites a teaching that explains how this verse describes Aaron's
efforts in the pursuit of peace:

רַבִּי מֵאִיר אוֹמֵר: מַה תַּלְמוּד לוֹמַר ״וְרַבִּים הֵשִׁיב מֵעָוֹן״ — **R' Meir says: What does**
the verse mean by, *and turned many away from sin?* כְּשֶׁהָיָה אַהֲרֹן מְהַלֵּךְ
בַּדֶּרֶךְ — It describes the following practice of Aaron: **When Aaron would walk**
in the street, פָּגַע בְּאָדָם רָשָׁע וְנָתַן לוֹ שָׁלוֹם — he would meet a sinful person
and greet him.[3] This friendly greeting from the holy Kohen would make a
deep impression on the sinner. לְמָחָר בִּקֵּשׁ אוֹתוֹ הָאִישׁ לַעֲבוֹר עֲבֵירָה — **The**
next day, when that person was about to commit a sin, אָמַר: אוֹי לִי, הֵיאַךְ
אֶשָּׂא עֵינַי אַחַר כָּךְ וְאֶרְאֶה אֶת אַהֲרֹן — he would say to himself, "**Woe is me if**
I commit this sin! How will I then be able to raise my eyes and look the holy
Aaron in the face? בּוֹשְׁתִּי הֵימֶנּוּ שֶׁנָּתַן לִי שָׁלוֹם — **I would be embarrassed**
to face him, because he greeted me so warmly!"[4] נִמְצָא אוֹתוֹ הָאִישׁ מוֹנֵעַ
עַצְמוֹ מִן הָעֲבֵירָה — **As a result, that person would refrain from the sin** he had
wanted to commit — all because of Aaron's friendly greeting![5]

---

their own nation. Their love of peace should
not be locally confined, but should embrace
the wider nation.]

2. This verse refers to Aaron, as the next
verse continues, *For the lips of the Kohen*
should safeguard knowledge (*Rashi* to *San-*
hedrin 6b).

3. According to *Magen Avos,* this means that
Aaron would deliberately choose a path on
which he would meet the sinful person upon
whom he wished to have an effect (as the
Baraisa continues to describe).

4. "Which," the person thinks, "Aaron would

not have done, had he considered me to be
a sinner (*Binyan Yehoshua*). He would not
have allowed his holy eyes to gaze upon a
wicked person. Since he *did* look at me and
greet me, it must be that he saw me as an
upright person. The least I can do is improve
my ways and live up to the image Aaron has
of me!" (*Meiri* to *Avos* here).

5. In this way, Aaron brought sinners to
repent without having to admonish them
directly. Simply by interacting kindly with
them, he stirred within them an inner urge to
repent on their own (see *Magen Avos*).

וְכֵן שְׁנֵי בְּנֵי אָדָם שֶׁעָשׂוּ מְרִיבָה זֶה עִם זֶה, הָלַךְ אַהֲרֹן וְיָשַׁב אֵצֶל אֶחָד מֵהֶם. אָמַר לוֹ: בְּנִי, רְאֵה חֲבֵרְךָ מַהוּ אוֹמֵר, מְטָרֵף אֶת לִבּוֹ וְקוֹרֵעַ אֶת בְּגָדָיו, אוֹמֵר: אוֹי לִי, הֵיאַךְ אֶשָּׂא אֶת עֵינַי וְאֶרְאֶה אֶת חֲבֵרִי, בּוֹשְׁתִּי הֵימֶנּוּ שֶׁאֲנִי הוּא שֶׁסָּרַחְתִּי עָלָיו. הוּא יוֹשֵׁב אֶצְלוֹ עַד שֶׁמֵּסִיר קִנְאָה מִלִּבּוֹ. וְהוֹלֵךְ אַהֲרֹן וְיוֹשֵׁב אֵצֶל הָאַחֵר, וְאוֹמֵר לוֹ: בְּנִי, רְאֵה חֲבֵרְךָ מַהוּ אוֹמֵר, מְטָרֵף אֶת לִבּוֹ וְקוֹרֵעַ אֶת בְּגָדָיו, וְאוֹמֵר: אוֹי לִי, הֵיאַךְ אֶשָּׂא אֶת עֵינַי וְאֶרְאֶה אֶת חֲבֵרִי, בּוֹשְׁתִּי הֵימֶנּוּ שֶׁאֲנִי הוּא שֶׁסָּרַחְתִּי עָלָיו. הוּא יוֹשֵׁב אֶצְלוֹ עַד שֶׁמֵּסִיר קִנְאָה מִלִּבּוֹ[6]. וּכְשֶׁנִּפְגְּשׁוּ זֶה בָּזֶה גִּפְּפוּ וְנָשְׁקוּ

R' Meir tells us of another way in which Aaron's pleasant ways would "turn many away from sin":

וְכֵן שְׁנֵי בְּנֵי אָדָם שֶׁעָשׂוּ מְרִיבָה זֶה עִם זֶה — And similarly, if there were two people quarreling, הָלַךְ אַהֲרֹן וְיָשַׁב אֵצֶל אֶחָד מֵהֶם. אָמַר לוֹ — Aaron would go seat himself next to one of them and say to him, בְּנִי, רְאֵה חֲבֵרְךָ מַהוּ אוֹמֵר — "My son, do you see what the other fellow is saying in private? מְטָרֵף אֶת לִבּוֹ וְקוֹרֵעַ אֶת בְּגָדָיו — He is beating his chest and tearing his clothing in remorse, וְאוֹמֵר: אוֹי לִי, הֵיאַךְ אֶשָּׂא אֶת עֵינַי וְאֶרְאֶה אֶת חֲבֵרִי — and saying, 'Woe is me! How will I now raise my eyes and look my friend in the face? בּוֹשְׁתִּי הֵימֶנּוּ שֶׁאֲנִי הוּא שֶׁסָּרַחְתִּי עָלָיו — I am embarrassed to face him, for it is I who has wronged him!' " הוּא יוֹשֵׁב אֶצְלוֹ עַד שֶׁמֵּסִיר קִנְאָה מִלִּבּוֹ — And [Aaron] would remain seated next to him, talking in this manner, until he would entirely remove the resentment the man harbored against his fellow from his heart. וְהוֹלֵךְ אַהֲרֹן וְיוֹשֵׁב אֵצֶל הָאַחֵר, וְאוֹמֵר לוֹ — Then, Aaron would go seat himself next to the other one and do the same, and say to him, בְּנִי, רְאֵה חֲבֵרְךָ מַהוּ אוֹמֵר — "My son, do you see what the other fellow is saying in private? מְטָרֵף אֶת לִבּוֹ וְקוֹרֵעַ אֶת בְּגָדָיו — He is beating his chest and tearing his clothing in remorse, וְאוֹמֵר: אוֹי לִי, הֵיאַךְ אֶשָּׂא אֶת עֵינַי וְאֶרְאֶה אֶת חֲבֵרִי — and saying, 'Woe is me! How will I now raise my eyes and look my friend in the face? בּוֹשְׁתִּי הֵימֶנּוּ שֶׁאֲנִי הוּא שֶׁסָּרַחְתִּי עָלָיו — I am embarrassed to face him, for it is I who has wronged him!' " הוּא יוֹשֵׁב אֶצְלוֹ עַד שֶׁמֵּסִיר קִנְאָה מִלִּבּוֹ — And [Aaron] would remain seated next to him, talking in this manner, until he would entirely remove the resentment he harbored against his fellow from his heart.[6] וּכְשֶׁנִּפְגְּשׁוּ זֶה בָּזֶה גִּפְּפוּ וְנָשְׁקוּ

[Thus the verse can perhaps be read: Though the Torah of truth was on his lips — he did not overlook sin in others — injustice was not found on his lips — he did not say hurtful things to the sinner. Rather, he "walked" with Me "in peace" and with

fairness, and turned many away from sin — the greetings of peace he extended to those he encountered on the street are what turned many away from sin.]

6. Aaron implied (or even said explicitly — Avos HaRosh [Vol. 1]) that he had witnessed

זֶה לָזֶה. לְכָךְ נֶאֱמַר (במדבר כ, כט) "וַיִּבְכּוּ אֶת אַהֲרֹן שְׁלֹשִׁים יוֹם כֹּל
בֵּית יִשְׂרָאֵל"[7,8]:

ד. (דָּבָר אַחֵר,) מִפְּנֵי מָה בָּכוּ יִשְׂרָאֵל אֶת אַהֲרֹן שְׁלֹשִׁים יוֹם
[(אֲנָשִׁים וְנָשִׁים)[9]], מִפְּנֵי שֶׁדָּן אַהֲרֹן דִּין אֱמֶת לַאֲמִיתּוֹ[10]. מִנַּיִן[11],

זֶה לָזֶה — Later, when those two former adversaries would meet, they would
embrace and kiss each other, glad that the quarrel was behind them and peace
was restored.   לְכָךְ נֶאֱמַר "וַיִּבְכּוּ אֶת אַהֲרֹן שְׁלֹשִׁים יוֹם כֹּל בֵּית יִשְׂרָאֵל" — Therefore it is stated, *When the entire assembly saw that Aaron had perished, they
wept for Aaron thirty days, the "entire" House of Israel* (Numbers 20:29).
The extra word *entire* implies that *everyone* wept,[7] a testament to the universal
love and admiration his pleasant ways had earned for him.[8]

§4 Another explanation of the *Numbers* verse just cited:

דָּבָר אַחֵר, מִפְּנֵי מָה בָּכוּ יִשְׂרָאֵל אֶת אַהֲרֹן שְׁלֹשִׁים יוֹם אֲנָשִׁים וְנָשִׁים — Alternatively, why was it that the *entire* people of Israel — men and women alike —
wept for Aaron for thirty days?[9]   מִפְּנֵי שֶׁדָּן אַהֲרֹן דִּין אֱמֶת לַאֲמִיתּוֹ — Because
when judging an interpersonal dispute, **Aaron would** always **render a decision
that was absolutely true.**[10]   מִנַּיִן — Whereby did he accomplish this?[11]

---

the other person's regret, which was not true
(see, though, note 7 below). Nevertheless,
the Sages teach us that one is permitted to
speak an untruth — unselfishly — for the
sake of peace (*Meiri* to *Avos* here). [*Rabbeinu Yonah* (in his commentary on *Proverbs* 10:31-32) writes that the mitzvah "to
bring peace between man and his fellow,"
which both Scripture and the Sages praise
so highly, almost invariably requires one to
bend the truth somewhat.]

The Gemara tells us that the disciples of
Hillel would praise even a homely bride as
כַּלָּה נָאָה וַחֲסוּדָה, *a beautiful and charming
bride* (*Kesubos* 17a). They likely learned
this from their master, Hillel, who exhorts
us here to "be from the disciples of Aaron,
loving peace ... making peace between man
and wife" even at the expense of uttering an
untruth! (*Avos HaRosh* [Vol. 1]).

7. Even people less likely to be grieved by
the death of a saintly Kohen, such as sinful
and quarrelsome people, mourned Aaron's
loss. For he had shown a sincere interest in
them and touched their hearts, and thereby
raised them to a higher place.

8. Thus, the verse can be read: *The Torah of
truth was on his lips* — though his words were
factually untrue, it was the *Torah of truth,* which
permits an untruth for the sake of peace, that
was on his lips. Yet on a deeper level, *injustice
was not found on his lips* — he did not really
utter an untruth at all, for people quickly regret their misdeeds, and it was probable that
each of the parties indeed had regrets (*Magen
Avos* s.v. לכך אמר שהכונה). [And the rest of the
verse can perhaps be read: *he walked with
Me in peace and with fairness* ("walking" to sit
with each quarreler and remove the resentment from his heart), *and turned* רבים (which
can be read רָבִים, *quarrelers*) *away from sin.*]

9. As the Baraisa will derive below, the expression *the "entire House" of Israel* means
to emphasize that both men and women
mourned him.

10. See *Magen Avos* and *Ben Avraham.*
[See, however, *Binyan Yehoshua,* who
maintains that the text should be emended,
so that it refers at this point to Moses rather
than to Aaron.]

11. [Some texts have the word מִיָּמָיו, *In all
his life,* instead. See also *Nuschas HaGra.*]

לֹא אָמַר לָאִישׁ שֶׁסָּרַחְתָּ וְלֹא לָאשָׁה שֶׁסָּרַחְתְּ¹². לְכָךְ נֶאֱמַר וַיִּבְכּוּ אוֹתוֹ
(במדבר כ, כט) "כָּל בֵּית יִשְׂרָאֵל". אֲבָל מֹשֶׁה שֶׁמּוֹכִיחָן בִּדְבָרִים קָשִׁים,
נֶאֱמַר (דברים לד, ח) "וַיִּבְכּוּ בְנֵי יִשְׂרָאֵל אֶת מֹשֶׁה"¹³. וְעוֹד, כַּמָּה אֲלָפִים הָיוּ
בְּיִשְׂרָאֵל שֶׁנִּקְרְאוּ שְׁמָם אַהֲרֹן (אהרן), שֶׁאִלְמָלֵא אַהֲרֹן לֹא בָא זֶה לָעוֹלָם,
שֶׁהָיָה מֵשִׂים שָׁלוֹם בֵּין אִישׁ לְאִשְׁתּוֹ וּמִזְדַּוְּוגִין זֶה עִם זֶה וְהָיוּ קוֹרִין שֵׁם
הַיִּלּוֹד עַל שְׁמוֹ. וְיֵשׁ אוֹמְרִים: לְכָךְ נֶאֱמַר (במדבר כ, כט) "וַיִּבְכּוּ אֶת אַהֲרֹן

לֹא אָמַר לָאִישׁ שֶׁסָּרַחְתָּ וְלֹא לָאשָׁה שֶׁסָּרַחְתְּ — In a dispute between husband and wife, he did not ever **say to the man, "You have wronged** your wife!" or to the woman, "You have wronged your husband!"[12] לְכָךְ נֶאֱמַר וַיִּבְכּוּ אוֹתוֹ "כָּל בֵּית יִשְׂרָאֵל" — Therefore, it is stated in the cited verse that *the "entire House" of Israel wept for him* when he died, which implies both men and women alike. אֲבָל מֹשֶׁה שֶׁמּוֹכִיחָן בִּדְבָרִים קָשִׁים — However, regarding **Moses, who would rebuke them with harsh words,** נֶאֱמַר "וַיִּבְכּוּ בְנֵי יִשְׂרָאֵל אֶת מֹשֶׁה" — **it is stated** only that upon his death *"The sons" of Israel wept for Moses* (*Deuteronomy* 34:8).[13]

Other reasons that the mourning for Aaron was more widespread than for Moses:[14]

וְעוֹד, כַּמָּה אֲלָפִים הָיוּ בְּיִשְׂרָאֵל שֶׁנִּקְרְאוּ שְׁמָם אַהֲרֹן — **Moreover, there were many thousands in Israel who were named "Aaron,"** שֶׁאִלְמָלֵא אַהֲרֹן לֹא בָא זֶה לָעוֹלָם — **because** were it not for Aaron the Kohen Gadol, who made peace between their parents, **this one** bearing his name **would not have come into the world.** שֶׁהָיָה מֵשִׂים שָׁלוֹם בֵּין אִישׁ לְאִשְׁתּוֹ — **For he would make peace between a man and his wife,** וּמִזְדַּוְּוגִין זֶה עִם זֶה וְהָיוּ קוֹרִין שֵׁם הַיִּלּוֹד עַל שְׁמוֹ — **and they would** then **unite** and produce a child **and** gratefully **name the newborn after him.** These thousands of families, who were so grateful to Aaron, mourned the death of Aaron intensely, which brought the rest of the nation to tears as well.[15] וְיֵשׁ אוֹמְרִים: לְכָךְ נֶאֱמַר "וַיִּבְכּוּ אֶת אַהֲרֹן

---

12. When resolving disputes between husband and wife, Aaron never criticized them harshly for what they had done wrong. Rather, he spoke to each with softness (*Magen Avos*), implying that the wrong each had done had not been willful or malicious (*Velo Od Ella*).

[That may be what the Baraisa means when it states that Aaron offered a resolution that was אֱמֶת לַאֲמִתּוֹ, *absolutely true*: It was a resolution that both parties *accepted,* so that it became true not only in theory but in practice (see *Rashi* to *Sanhedrin* 23a, ד"ה יצא דין אמת לאמתו).]

13. Not *"the entire House" of Israel,* as it

states with regard to Aaron. For many resented the harsh (albeit justified) criticism that Moses had leveled against them.

Moses did not have the luxury that Aaron had to soften his criticism of a guilty party. For Moses, unlike Aaron, was bidden to *judge* the people, and a judge must present the law in its unvarnished truth (*Ben Avraham*; see *Sanhedrin* 6b with *Tosafos* ד"ה אבל אהרן; see also *Binyan Yehoshua* and *Avos DeRabbi Nassan, Nusach* 2, Ch. 24).

14. See *Avos HaRosh* [Vol. 1].

15. *Ben Avraham*; see also *Avos DeRabbi Nassan, Nusach* 2, Ch. 24.

שְׁלֹשִׁים יוֹם כָּל בֵּית יִשְׂרָאֵל", שֶׁכָּל מִי שֶׁרוֹאֶה מֹשֶׁה רַבֵּינוּ שֶׁיּוֹשֵׁב וּבוֹכֶה
מִי לֹא יִבְכֶּה16. (וְיֵשׁ אוֹמְרִים:) מִי שֶׁרוֹאֶה אֶלְעָזָר וּפִינְחָס שֶׁהֵם שְׁנֵי
כֹּהֲנִים גְּדוֹלִים17 שֶׁעוֹמְדִים וּבוֹכִים מִי לֹא יִבְכֶּה18. בְּאוֹתָהּ שָׁעָה בִּקֵּשׁ
מֹשֶׁה לָמוּת כְּמִיתַת אַהֲרֹן מִפְּנֵי שֶׁרָאָה מִטָּתוֹ מוּצַעַת בְּכָבוֹד גָּדוֹל וְכִתּוֹת
כִּתּוֹת שֶׁל מַלְאֲכֵי הַשָּׁרֵת סוֹפְדוֹת אוֹתוֹ19. וְכִי בֵּינוֹ לְבֵין אָדָם שָׁאַל,

---

שְׁלֹשִׁים יוֹם כָּל בֵּית יִשְׂרָאֵל" — And some say that it is for the following reason that it is stated, *They wept for Aaron thirty days, the entire House of Israel*: שֶׁכָּל מִי שֶׁרוֹאֶה מֹשֶׁה רַבֵּינוּ שֶׁיּוֹשֵׁב וּבוֹכֶה מִי לֹא יִבְכֶּה — For when Aaron died, Moses was still alive, and could anyone see Moses our Teacher sitting and weeping for his deceased brother and not weep along with him?[16] וְיֵשׁ אוֹמְרִים: מִי שֶׁרוֹאֶה אֶלְעָזָר וּפִינְחָס, שֶׁהֵם שְׁנֵי כֹּהֲנִים גְּדוֹלִים שֶׁעוֹמְדִים וּבוֹכִים מִי לֹא יִבְכֶּה — And some say a variation of this explanation, as follows: Could anyone see Aaron's son, Elazar, and Aaron's grandson, Phinehas — who were both Kohanim Gedolim (High Priests)[17] — standing and weeping for their deceased father and grandfather, and not weep along with them?[18]

Having discussed Aaron's death, the Baraisa presents a teaching relating to it: בְּאוֹתָהּ שָׁעָה בִּקֵּשׁ מֹשֶׁה לָמוּת כְּמִיתַת אַהֲרֹן — At that moment, Moses wished that when his time would come, he would merit to die a death like the death of Aaron. מִפְּנֵי שֶׁרָאָה מִטָּתוֹ מוּצַעַת בְּכָבוֹד גָּדוֹל — For he saw how [Aaron's] bier was arrayed in great honor, וְכִתּוֹת כִּתּוֹת שֶׁל מַלְאֲכֵי הַשָּׁרֵת סוֹפְדוֹת אוֹתוֹ — with groups upon groups of angels in Heaven eulogizing him.[19]

The Baraisa shows how we know that this was Moses' request: וְכִי בֵּינוֹ לְבֵין אָדָם שָׁאַל — Now how do we know that Moses asked for this? Did [Moses] perhaps ask for this in front of other men who might have publicized

---

16. The fact that Moses, despite being so complete in every way, felt the loss of Aaron so keenly brought home to them the magnitude of the void that Aaron's death had left (*Velo Od Ella*).

17. Upon Aaron's death, Elazar inherited the position of Kohen Gadol (*Numbers* 20:28). Phinehas was an Associate Kohen Gadol — the Kohen Anointed for Battle (*Sotah* 43a), who escorts the nation's army to war and is subject to some of the unique laws that govern the High Priesthood (*Binyan Yehoshua*). Alternatively, כֹּהֲנִים גְּדוֹלִים here means simply "prominent Kohanim," who inherited the exalted stature of Aaron (*Ben Avraham*).

18. Elazar and Phinehas came into great prominence as Kohanim with the death

of Aaron the Kohen Gadol, and thus had reason to temper their mourning. But they nevertheless wept intensely when he died, which brought home to the people the magnitude of their loss (*Magen Avos*). When Moses died, however, his children and grandchildren did not come into any special prominence, so their weeping did not affect the rest of the nation as deeply.

[With regard to Moses, the Baraisa stated "*sitting*" and weeping. Elazar and Phinehas, however, were "*standing*" and weeping, for it would have been disrespectful for them to sit in the presence of Moses, who was the nation's king (*Ben Avraham*).]

19. The meaning of "groups upon groups" is that each group eulogized a different aspect

וַהֲלֹא בֵּינוֹ לְבֵין עַצְמוֹ שָׁאַל וְשָׁמַע הַקָּדוֹשׁ בָּרוּךְ הוּא לַחֲשִׁיתוֹ,
שֶׁנֶּאֱמַר (דברים לב, נ) "וּמֵת בָּהָר אֲשֶׁר אַתָּה עֹלֶה שָׁמָּה וְהֵאָסֵף אֶל
עַמֶּיךָ כַּאֲשֶׁר מֵת אַהֲרֹן אָחִיךָ בְּהֹר הָהָר". הָא לָמַדְתָּ שֶׁבִּקֵּשׁ לָמוּת
כְּמִיתָתוֹ שֶׁל אַהֲרֹן. בְּאוֹתָהּ שָׁעָה אָמַר לוֹ לְמַלְאַךְ הַמָּוֶת: לֵךְ הָבֵא
לִי נִשְׁמָתוֹ שֶׁל מֹשֶׁה. הָלַךְ מַלְאַךְ הַמָּוֶת וְעָמַד לְפָנָיו. אָמַר לוֹ: מֹשֶׁה,
תֵּן לִי נִשְׁמָתְךָ. גָּעַר בּוֹ. [וְאָמַר לוֹ: בַּמָּקוֹם שֶׁאֲנִי יוֹשֵׁב אֵין נוֹתְנִין לְךָ
רְשׁוּת לַעֲמוֹד, וְאַתָּה אָמַרְתָּ תֵּן לִי נִשְׁמָתְךָ]. גָּעַר בּוֹ] וְהוֹצִיאוֹ בִּנְזִיפָה.
עַד שֶׁאָמַר לוֹ הַקָּדוֹשׁ בָּרוּךְ הוּא לְמֹשֶׁה: מֹשֶׁה, דַּיֶּיךָ הָעוֹלָם הַזֶּה,

---

וַהֲלֹא בֵּינוֹ לְבֵין עַצְמוֹ שָׁאַל — Why, it was only in the privacy of his own heart that he asked this of God, this wish? **וְשָׁמַע הַקָּדוֹשׁ בָּרוּךְ הוּא לַחֲשִׁיתוֹ** — and the Holy One, Blessed is He, heard his silent longing.[20] How do we know all this? **שֶׁנֶּאֱמַר "וּמֵת בָּהָר אֲשֶׁר אַתָּה עֹלֶה שָׁמָּה, וְהֵאָסֵף אֶל עַמֶּיךָ, כַּאֲשֶׁר מֵת אַהֲרֹן אָחִיךָ בְּהֹר הָהָר"** — As it is stated in God's final instructions to Moses, *And die on the mountain where you will ascend, and be gathered to your people, "as Aaron your brother died on Mount Hor"* (Deuteronomy 32:50). What was the point of assuring Moses that he would die "as Aaron had died" if not that Moses had desired this? **הָא לָמַדְתָּ שֶׁבִּקֵּשׁ לָמוּת כְּמִיתָתוֹ שֶׁל אַהֲרֹן** — Thus you learn that [Moses] had wished to die a death like Aaron's death.

The Baraisa turns to describe Moses' death: **בְּאוֹתָהּ שָׁעָה אָמַר לוֹ לְמַלְאַךְ הַמָּוֶת: לֵךְ הָבֵא לִי נִשְׁמָתוֹ שֶׁל מֹשֶׁה** — When the time came for Moses to die, [God] said to the Angel of Death, "Go bring Me the soul of Moses." **הָלַךְ מַלְאַךְ הַמָּוֶת וְעָמַד לְפָנָיו** — The Angel of Death went and stood before Moses. **אָמַר לוֹ: מֹשֶׁה, תֵּן לִי נִשְׁמָתְךָ** — He said to him, "Moses, give me your soul!" **גָּעַר בּוֹ** — [Moses] reprimanded him, **אָמַר לוֹ: בַּמָּקוֹם שֶׁאֲנִי יוֹשֵׁב אֵין נוֹתְנִין לְךָ רְשׁוּת לַעֲמוֹד** — and said to him, "In the place where I sit, you have no permission to stand;[21] **וְאַתָּה אָמַרְתָּ תֵּן לִי נִשְׁמָתְךָ** — and you dare say to me, 'Give me your soul'?" **גָּעַר בּוֹ וְהוֹצִיאוֹ בִּנְזִיפָה** — [Moses] reprimanded him further, and then sent him away disapprovingly. **עַד שֶׁאָמַר לוֹ הַקָּדוֹשׁ בָּרוּךְ הוּא לְמֹשֶׁה: מֹשֶׁה, דַּיֶּיךָ הָעוֹלָם הַזֶּה** — The Angel of Death was

---

of Aaron's greatness. Moreover, the Baraisa alludes to the three groups of angels that, the Gemara teaches, come to greet a righteous person when he passes from this world: One group says to him, "Come in peace" — and satisfy your desire to draw close to God. A second group says, "Here is someone who walks a straight path" — the path laid out by God, which causes one's soul to cleave to God. And a third group says, "He will come

in peace; they will rest upon their resting places" — in the ultimate place of eternal rest, before the Divine Presence (see *Magen Avos*, quoting *Kesubos* 104a; *Maharal, Chidushei Aggados* there; see also *Avos DeRabbi Nassan, Nusach* 2, Ch. 25).

20. *Kisei Rachamim; Ben Avraham.*

21. The Angel of Death also serves as the evil inclination (*Bava Basra* 15a). Since the antidote to the evil inclination is Torah

שֶׁהֲרֵי הָעוֹלָם הַבָּא שָׁמוּר לְךָ מִשֵּׁשֶׁת יְמֵי בְרֵאשִׁית[23], שֶׁנֶּאֱמַר (שמות לג, כא) "וַיֹּאמֶר ה' הִנֵּה מָקוֹם אִתִּי וְנִצַּבְתָּ עַל הַצּוּר"[24]. נָטְלָה הַקָּדוֹשׁ בָּרוּךְ הוּא נִשְׁמָתוֹ שֶׁל מֹשֶׁה וּגְנָזָהּ תַּחַת כִּסֵּא הַכָּבוֹד, שֶׁנֶּאֱמַר (שמואל א כה, כט) "וְהָיְתָה נֶפֶשׁ אֲדֹנִי צְרוּרָה בִּצְרוֹר הַחַיִּים"[25]. כְּשֶׁנְּטָלָהּ לֹא נָטְלָה אֶלָּא בִּנְשִׁיקָה[26],

---

sent back by God numerous other times to claim Moses' soul, but failed every attempt,[22] until finally **the Holy One, Blessed is He,** Himself intervened and said to Moses, "**Moses, you have had enough** of living in **this world,** שֶׁהֲרֵי הָעוֹלָם הַבָּא שָׁמוּר לְךָ מִשֵּׁשֶׁת יְמֵי בְרֵאשִׁית — for **you have a portion** in **the World to Come that has been reserved for you since the Six Days of Creation,**"[23] שֶׁנֶּאֱמַר "וַיֹּאמֶר ה' הִנֵּה מָקוֹם אִתִּי וְנִצַּבְתָּ עַל הַצּוּר" — **as it is stated,** HASHEM said, "Behold! there is a place near Me; you may stand on the rock. When My glory passes by, I shall place you in a cleft of the rock; I shall shield you with My hand until I have passed" (Exodus 33:21-22).[24] נָטְלָה הַקָּדוֹשׁ בָּרוּךְ הוּא — The Holy One, Blessed is He, then **took Moses' soul** נִשְׁמָתוֹ שֶׁל מֹשֶׁה — **and placed it securely under the Throne of Glory,** וּגְנָזָהּ תַּחַת כִּסֵּא הַכָּבוֹד — in the manner of **that which is stated,** שֶׁנֶּאֱמַר When Abigail saw David ... she fell at his feet and said ... "May my lord's soul be bound up in the bond of life, 'with' HASHEM, your God" (I Samuel 25:29), meaning, under His Throne of Glory.[25] כְּשֶׁנְּטָלָהּ לֹא נָטְלָה אֶלָּא בִּנְשִׁיקָה — And **when He took [Moses' soul], He took it only through a "kiss,"**[26]

---

study (*Kiddushin* 30b), in which Moses was constantly engaged, the Angel of Death had no permission to stand in his place (*Binyan Yehoshua*).

22. See detailed account in *Devarim Rabbah* 11 §10 (*Ben Avraham*).

23. The world was created in the merit of Moses (*Bereishis Rabbah* 1 §4), and so his reward had been designated for him since that time. This is another way of saying that his portion in the World to Come is exceedingly great (see *Mefaresh*).

24. Moses had asked to see "God's glory" — a clear understanding of God's grandeur (v. 18 there). God replied that it was not possible for a person to have this clarity while still alive in this world (v. 20), but *there is a place near Me* — i.e., reserved for you in the World to Come near the Throne of Glory, from whose vantage point you will be able to attain the clarity you seek. In this world, however, *I shall place you in a cleft of the*

rock and shield you ..., so that you will have only a partial understanding, which is all that is accessible to you in this world. At any rate, we see from this verse that God told Moses that his place in the World to Come (*a place near Me*) was already reserved for him [though we do not see from here that it was reserved for him *since the Six Days of Creation*] (*Magen Avos*).

25. *Binyan Yehoshua*, from *Rashi* to *Shabbos* 152b. Being a prophetess, Abigail surely spoke these words with Divine Inspiration (*Binyan Yehoshua*).

[Although the souls of *all* righteous people are placed under God's Throne, as stated below, Moses' soul was unique in that it was designated a place there into which no other souls could enter (*Velo Od Ella*); or, alternatively, in that it was taken and placed there by God Himself (*Avos HaRosh* [Vol. 1]).]

26. The Talmud describes this as the most painless form of death, by which the soul

שֶׁנֶּאֱמַר (דברים לד, ה) "עַל פִּי ה' ". לֹא נִשְׁמָתוֹ שֶׁל מֹשֶׁה בִּלְבַד גְּנוּזָה תַּחַת
כִּסֵּא הַכָּבוֹד, אֶלָּא נִשְׁמָתָן שֶׁל צַדִּיקִים גְּנוּזוֹת תַּחַת כִּסֵּא הַכָּבוֹד, שֶׁנֶּאֱמַר
(שמואל א כה, כט) "וְהָיְתָה נֶפֶשׁ אֲדֹנִי צְרוּרָה בִּצְרוֹר הַחַיִּים"‏.27 יָכוֹל אַף שֶׁל
רְשָׁעִים כֵּן,‏28 תַּלְמוּד לוֹמַר (שם) "וְאֵת נֶפֶשׁ אֹיְבֶיךָ יְקַלְּעֶנָּה בְּתוֹךְ כַּף
הַקֶּלַע". [(מָשָׁל לְמָה הַדָּבָר דּוֹמֶה,) לְאֶחָד שֶׁנָּטַל אֶת הָאֶבֶן וּנְתָנוֹ בְּתוֹךְ
הַקֶּלַע,] אַף עַל פִּי שֶׁזּוֹרֵק מִמָּקוֹם לְמָקוֹם אֵינוֹ יוֹדֵעַ עַל מַה שֶׁתִּסְמוֹךְ.

שֶׁנֶּאֱמַר "עַל פִּי ה'" — as it is stated, So Moses, servant of Hashem, died there, in the land of Moab, by the "mouth" of HASHEM (Deuteronomy 34:5).

Having mentioned the destiny that awaited Moses' pure soul, the Baraisa interrupts its narrative with a related teaching regarding the distinct destinies that await the souls of the righteous and the wicked:

לֹא נִשְׁמָתוֹ שֶׁל מֹשֶׁה בִּלְבַד גְּנוּזָה תַּחַת כִּסֵּא הַכָּבוֹד — And not only is the soul of Moses hidden under the Throne of Glory, אֶלָּא נִשְׁמָתָן שֶׁל צַדִּיקִים גְּנוּזוֹת תַּחַת כִּסֵּא הַכָּבוֹד — but the souls of all righteous people are likewise hidden under the Throne of Glory, שֶׁנֶּאֱמַר — as it is stated, "וְהָיְתָה נֶפֶשׁ אֲדֹנִי צְרוּרָה בִּצְרוֹר הַחַיִּים" When Abigail saw David ... she fell at his feet and said ... "May my lord's soul be bound up in the bond of life, with HASHEM, your God" (I Samuel 25:29).[27] יָכוֹל אַף שֶׁל רְשָׁעִים כֵּן — Now, one might think that even regarding the souls of the wicked the same is true.[28] תַּלְמוּד לוֹמַר "וְאֵת נֶפֶשׁ אֹיְבֶיךָ יְקַלְּעֶנָּה בְּתוֹךְ כַּף הַקֶּלַע" — Scripture, however, teaches us otherwise by saying, "And may He hurl away the soul of your enemies as one shoots a stone from a slingshot" (ibid.). מָשָׁל לְמָה הַדָּבָר דּוֹמֶה, לְאֶחָד שֶׁנָּטַל אֶת הָאֶבֶן וּנְתָנוֹ בְּתוֹךְ הַקֶּלַע — This is an analogy: To what can the matter of the wicked person's fate after death be compared? To someone who takes a stone and places it in the pocket of a slingshot; אַף עַל פִּי שֶׁזּוֹרֵק מִמָּקוֹם לְמָקוֹם אֵינוֹ יוֹדֵעַ עַל מַה שֶׁתִּסְמוֹךְ — even though he throws it from one place to another, he still

---

leaves the body without any resistance (Berachos 8a).

[To the extent that people become enmeshed in the physicality of this world, it becomes difficult for them to part from it. For those who become totally attached to physicality, death is a very painful experience; but for someone like Moses, whose soul remained completely pure, there is little resistance or pain when the soul is "kissed" and restored to its Heavenly place (see R' Tzadok HaKohen in Resisei Laylah §56).]

27. Implying that all deserving souls are placed there (Binyan Yehoshua), as בִּצְרוֹר

הַחַיִּים can be rendered, in the bond of the living — an allusion to the righteous [who are called "living" even in their death; Berachos 18a] (see Magen Avos).

28. That is, although the soul will undergo its deserved suffering, it will eventually come to rest in one place (Mefaresh, Binyan Yehoshua). [Alternatively, perhaps it is only the wicked person's body that will endure suffering for his sins, since ultimately it was the bodily urges that led him to sin, but his soul will return after death to its Heavenly place, just like like the souls of the righteous (Magen Avos, Velo Od Ella).]

אַף כֵּן נִשְׁמָתָן שֶׁל רְשָׁעִים זוֹמְמוֹת וְהוֹלְכוֹת וְשׁוֹטְפוֹת בָּעוֹלָם וְאֵינָן יוֹדְעוֹת עַל מַה שֶׁיִּסְמוֹכוּ[29]. שׁוּב אָמַר לוֹ הַקָּדוֹשׁ בָּרוּךְ הוּא לְמַלְאַךְ הַמָּוֶת: לֵךְ וְהָבֵא לִי נִשְׁמָתוֹ שֶׁל מֹשֶׁה[30]. הָלַךְ לִמְקוֹמוֹ בִּקְּשׁוֹ וְלֹא מְצָאוֹ. הָלַךְ אֵצֶל הַיָּם הַגָּדוֹל, אָמַר לוֹ[31]: מֹשֶׁה בָּא לְכָאן. אָמַר לוֹ: מִיּוֹם שֶׁעָבְרוּ יִשְׂרָאֵל בְּתוֹכִי שׁוּב לֹא רְאִיתִיו. הָלַךְ אֵצֶל הָרִים וּגְבָעוֹת, וְאָמַר לָהֶם: מֹשֶׁה בָּא לְכָאן. [אָמְרוּ לוֹ: מִיּוֹם שֶׁקִּבְּלוּ יִשְׂרָאֵל אֶת הַתּוֹרָה בְּהַר סִינַי שׁוּב לֹא רְאִינוּהוּ.

The — אַף כֵּן נִשְׁמָתָן שֶׁל רְשָׁעִים does not know on what it will come to rest. The same is true regarding the souls of the wicked. זוֹמְמוֹת וְהוֹלְכוֹת וְשׁוֹטְפוֹת — **Namely, they are confined and continuously wander about the world** בָּעוֹלָם וְאֵינָן יוֹדְעוֹת עַל מַה שֶׁיִּסְמוֹכוּ searching for a place to rest, **but do not know where they will ultimately rest.**[29]

The Baraisa resumes its account of Moses' death:

Once — שׁוּב אָמַר לוֹ הַקָּדוֹשׁ בָּרוּךְ הוּא לְמַלְאַךְ הַמָּוֶת: לֵךְ וְהָבֵא לִי נִשְׁמָתוֹ שֶׁל מֹשֶׁה **more, the Holy One, Blessed is He, said to the Angel of Death, "Go and bring Me the soul of Moses."**[30] הָלַךְ לִמְקוֹמוֹ בִּקְּשׁוֹ וְלֹא מְצָאוֹ — **So he went to the place** where Moses had previously been sitting, **and searched for him, but could not find him there. So** — הָלַךְ אֵצֶל הַיָּם הַגָּדוֹל, אָמַר לוֹ: מֹשֶׁה בָּא לְכָאן **he went to the ocean and asked it, "Has Moses come here?"** אָמַר לוֹ: מִיּוֹם **It replied to him,**[31] **"Since the day that** שֶׁעָבְרוּ יִשְׂרָאֵל בְּתוֹכִי שׁוּב לֹא רְאִיתִיו **the people of Israel passed through me, I have not seen him again." הָלַךְ אֵצֶל הָרִים וּגְבָעוֹת, וְאָמַר לָהֶם: מֹשֶׁה בָּא לְכָאן — He then went to the mountains and hills and asked them, "Has Moses come here?"** אָמְרוּ לוֹ: מִיּוֹם שֶׁקִּבְּלוּ **They replied to him, "Since the** יִשְׂרָאֵל אֶת הַתּוֹרָה בְּהַר סִינַי שׁוּב לֹא רְאִינוּהוּ **day that the people of Israel accepted the Torah on Mount Sinai, we have**

---

29. *Maharal* (*Chidushei Aggados* to *Shabbos* 152b) interprets this teaching in the following vein: To live a righteous life is to live a life carefully balanced between extremes of behavior. The wicked, on the other hand, lead lives that incline dangerously toward one extreme or another, lacking the discipline to achieve balance. Such lives are characterized by instability and violent shifts from one pole to another. Thus, fittingly, the same applies after their death; even in the grave they will be unable to find stability or lasting repose.

Maharsha (to *Shabbos* ibid.), however, explains this teaching as alluding to גִּלְגּוּל נְשָׁמוֹת, *transmigration of souls,* and means that a wicked person's soul does not rest

after his death, but is placed into the body of a new person, who will hopefully follow the proper path. If not, though, this process could be repeated over and over, with the unfortunate soul being "hurled" from person to person, and from lifetime to lifetime, not knowing where it will finally rest.

30. Although God had already taken Moses' soul, as stated above, He said this to the Angel of Death in order to show him that he truly had no power over the soul of Moses, so much so that he would not even be able to locate it, as described below (*Magen Avos*).

31. When the Baraisa says that the ocean, the hills, and the grave "spoke," it refers to the angels appointed over those particular inanimate things (*Binyan Yehoshua*).

הָלַךְ אֵצֶל שְׁאוֹל וַאֲבַדּוֹן, אָמַר לָהֶם: מֹשֶׁה בָּא לְכָאן. אָמְרוּ לוֹ: שְׁמוֹ
שָׁמַעְנוּ וְאוֹתוֹ לֹא רָאִינוּ.[32] הָלַךְ אֵצֶל מַלְאֲכֵי הַשָּׁרֵת, אָמַר לָהֶם: מֹשֶׁה
בָּא לְכָאן. אָמְרוּ לוֹ: אֱלֹהִים הֵבִין דַּרְכּוֹ וְהוּא יָדַע אֶת מְקוֹמוֹ,[33] אֱלֹהִים
גְּנָזוֹ לְחַיֵּי הָעוֹלָם הַבָּא וְאֵין כָּל בְּרִיָּה יוֹדַעַת, שֶׁנֶּאֱמַר (איוב כח, יב-יד)
"וְהַחָכְמָה מֵאַיִן תִּמָּצֵא וְאֵי זֶה מְקוֹם בִּינָה[34] לֹא יָדַע אֱנוֹשׁ עֶרְכָּהּ וְלֹא
תִמָּצֵא בְּאֶרֶץ הַחַיִּים תְּהוֹם אָמַר לֹא בִי הִיא וְיָם אָמַר אֵין עִמָּדִי אֲבַדּוֹן
וָמָוֶת אָמְרוּ בְּאָזְנֵינוּ שָׁמַעְנוּ שִׁמְעָהּ". אַף יְהוֹשֻׁעַ הָיָה יוֹשֵׁב וּמִצְטַעֵר
עַל מֹשֶׁה [שֶׁלֹּא יָדַע הֵיכָן הוּא,] עַד שֶׁאָמַר לוֹ הַקָּדוֹשׁ בָּרוּךְ הוּא:

He — הָלַךְ אֵצֶל שְׁאוֹל וַאֲבַדּוֹן, אָמַר לָהֶם: מֹשֶׁה בָּא לְכָאן not seen him again." then went to the Netherworld and Doom and asked them, "Has Moses come here?" אָמְרוּ לוֹ: שְׁמוֹ שָׁמַעְנוּ וְאוֹתוֹ לֹא רָאִינוּ — They replied to him, "His name we have heard of, but him we have never seen."[32] הָלַךְ אֵצֶל מַלְאֲכֵי הַשָּׁרֵת, אָמַר לָהֶם: מֹשֶׁה בָּא לְכָאן — He then went to the ministering angels and asked them, "Has Moses come here to Heaven?" אָמְרוּ לוֹ: אֱלֹהִים הֵבִין דַּרְכּוֹ וְהוּא יָדַע אֶת מְקוֹמוֹ — They replied to him, "God alone understands his way, and only He knows his place.[33] אֱלֹהִים גְּנָזוֹ לְחַיֵּי הָעוֹלָם הַבָּא וְאֵין כָּל בְּרִיָּה יוֹדַעַת — God has hidden him away for life in the World to Come, and no creature knows where he is." שֶׁנֶּאֱמַר "וְהַחָכְמָה מֵאַיִן תִּמָּצֵא וְאֵי זֶה מְקוֹם בִּינָה — The various replies given to the Angel of Death in the above account are seen in that which is stated, [But as for] wisdom: Where can it be found? Which is the place of understanding?[34] לֹא יָדַע אֱנוֹשׁ עֶרְכָּהּ וְלֹא תִמָּצֵא בְּאֶרֶץ הַחַיִּים — Mankind does not know its worth; it cannot be found in the land of the living. תְּהוֹם אָמַר לֹא בִי הִיא וְיָם אָמַר אֵין עִמָּדִי" — The depth says, "It is not in me!" and the sea says, "It is not with me!" (Job 28:12-14). "אֲבַדּוֹן וָמָוֶת אָמְרוּ בְּאָזְנֵינוּ שָׁמַעְנוּ שִׁמְעָהּ" — Doom and Death say, "With our ears we have heard of its reputation" (ibid. v. 22). אַף יְהוֹשֻׁעַ הָיָה יוֹשֵׁב וּמִצְטַעֵר עַל מֹשֶׁה שֶׁלֹּא יָדַע הֵיכָן הוּא — Even Moses' prime disciple, Joshua, was sitting, distressed over the fact that he did not know Moses' whereabouts, עַד שֶׁאָמַר לוֹ הַקָּדוֹשׁ בָּרוּךְ הוּא — until the Holy One, Blessed is He, said to him,

32. These places are destined for those who are enmeshed in the physical side of this world, completely neglecting their spiritual duties. That Moses had never even been "seen" by these places symbolizes that he was involved entirely in spiritual pursuits (Avos HaRosh [Vol. 1]).

33. [Cf. Job 28:13.] The Angel of Death was asking whether the great heights achieved by Moses caused him to haughtily consider himself as great as the angels (did he "come to Heaven?"). The angels responded that it most certainly did not, for he was even more humble than they — which is why even they were not privy to where his sublime soul was placed by God (Avos HaRosh [Vol. 1]).

34. "Wisdom" and "understanding" allude to Moses, who was "wise" in Torah (Binyan Yehoshua), and who attained virtually all the levels of "understanding" created in

יְהוֹשֻׁעַ, לָמָּה אַתָּה מִצְטַעֵר עַל מֹשֶׁה, (יהושע א, ב) "מֹשֶׁה עַבְדִּי מֵת":

ו. רוֹדֵף³⁵ שָׁלוֹם, כֵּיצַד, מְלַמֵּד שֶׁיְּהֵא אָדָם רוֹדֵף שָׁלוֹם בְּיִשְׂרָאֵל בֵּין כָּל אֶחָד וְאֶחָד (כְּדֶרֶךְ שֶׁהָיָה אַהֲרֹן רוֹדֵף שָׁלוֹם בְּיִשְׂרָאֵל בֵּין כָּל אֶחָד וְאֶחָד, שֶׁנֶּאֱמַר (תהלים לד, טו) "סוּר מֵרָע וַעֲשֵׂה טוֹב בַּקֵּשׁ שָׁלוֹם וְרָדְפֵהוּ". רַבִּי שִׁמְעוֹן בֶּן אֶלְעָזָר אוֹמֵר:) אִם יוֹשֵׁב אָדָם בִּמְקוֹמוֹ וְשׁוֹתֵק הֵיאַךְ רוֹדֵף שָׁלוֹם בְּיִשְׂרָאֵל בֵּין כָּל אֶחָד וְאֶחָד,³⁶ [אֶלָּא יֵצֵא מִמְּקוֹמוֹ וְיַחֲזוֹר בָּעוֹלָם וְיִרְדּוֹף שָׁלוֹם בְּיִשְׂרָאֵל,] שֶׁנֶּאֱמַר (שם) "בַּקֵּשׁ שָׁלוֹם וְרָדְפֵהוּ". הָא כֵּיצַד, בַּקְּשֵׁהוּ מִמְּקוֹמְךָ רָדְפֵהוּ לְמָקוֹם אַחֵר.³⁷

יְהוֹשֻׁעַ, לָמָּה אַתָּה מִצְטַעֵר עַל מֹשֶׁה — "Joshua, why are you distressed over not knowing **Moses'** whereabouts? "מֹשֶׁה עַבְדִּי מֵת" — Why, he is not lost at all; but rather, *Moses My servant has died* " (*Joshua* 1:2).

§6 [35] The Baraisa continues expounding *Avos* 1:12:

רוֹדֵף שָׁלוֹם, כֵּיצַד — Hillel further exhorts us to follow Aaron's example of not only "loving" peace but also of "pursuing peace" — how so? מְלַמֵּד שֶׁיְּהֵא אָדָם רוֹדֵף שָׁלוֹם בְּיִשְׂרָאֵל בֵּין כָּל אֶחָד וְאֶחָד — This teaches that a person should pursue making **peace in Israel between each and every person** כְּדֶרֶךְ שֶׁהָיָה אַהֲרֹן רוֹדֵף שָׁלוֹם בְּיִשְׂרָאֵל בֵּין כָּל אֶחָד וְאֶחָד — in the same way that Aaron pursued making peace in Israel between each and every person, שֶׁנֶּאֱמַר — as it is stated, *Turn from evil and do good, seek peace and pursue it* (*Psalms* 34:15). "סוּר מֵרָע וַעֲשֵׂה טוֹב בַּקֵּשׁ שָׁלוֹם וְרָדְפֵהוּ"

The Baraisa elaborates:

רַבִּי שִׁמְעוֹן בֶּן אֶלְעָזָר אוֹמֵר — R' Shimon ben Elazar says: אִם יוֹשֵׁב אָדָם בִּמְקוֹמוֹ וְשׁוֹתֵק If a person sits quietly in his place, הֵיאַךְ רוֹדֵף שָׁלוֹם בְּיִשְׂרָאֵל בֵּין כָּל — how is he then "pursuing" making peace in Israel between each אֶחָד וְאֶחָד and every person?[36] אֶלָּא יֵצֵא מִמְּקוֹמוֹ וְיַחֲזוֹר בָּעוֹלָם וְיִרְדּוֹף שָׁלוֹם בְּיִשְׂרָאֵל — Rather, he must even leave his place and go about the larger world to pursue making peace, שֶׁנֶּאֱמַר "בַּקֵּשׁ שָׁלוֹם וְרָדְפֵהוּ" — as it is stated, *Seek peace and pursue it.* הָא כֵּיצַד — How is this verse, which speaks of both "seeking" and "pursuing" peace, to be understood? בַּקְּשֵׁהוּ מִמְּקוֹמְךָ רָדְפֵהוּ — "Seek" it from your place and "pursue" it even if it takes you לְמָקוֹם אַחֵר to another place.[37]

---

this world [*Rosh Hashanah* 21b] (*Ahavas Chesed*).

35. [In numbering the Baraisos of this chapter, the Vilna edition inadvertently skips the number "5."]

36. [Even if he makes peace among people in his own locale, how is he "pursuing" it?]

37. In the words of *Avos DeRabbi Nassan*, *Nusach* 2, Ch. 24: "Even if you must chase after it from town to town, from city to city, or from region to region, do not refrain from making peace, which is equal to all the mitzvos in the Torah."

אַף הַקָּדוֹשׁ בָּרוּךְ הוּא עָשָׂה שָׁלוֹם בַּמָּרוֹם. וְאֵיזֶה שָׁלוֹם עָשָׂה הַקָּדוֹשׁ בָּרוּךְ הוּא בַּמָּרוֹם, שֶׁלֹּא קָרָא עֲשָׂרָה גַּבְרִיאֵל עֲשָׂרָה מִיכָאֵל עֲשָׂרָה אוּרִיאֵל עֲשָׂרָה רְפָאֵל כְּדֶרֶךְ שֶׁבְּנֵי אָדָם קוֹרִין עֲשָׂרָה רְאוּבֵן עֲשָׂרָה שִׁמְעוֹן עֲשָׂרָה לֵוִי עֲשָׂרָה יְהוּדָה[38], שֶׁאִלְמָלֵא עָשָׂה כְּדֶרֶךְ שֶׁבְּנֵי אָדָם עוֹשִׂים, כֵּיוָן שֶׁקָּרָא לְאֶחָד מֵהֶם בָּאִין לְפָנָיו וּמִתְקַנְאִין זֶה בָּזֶה. אֶלָּא קָרָא גַּבְרִיאֵל אֶחָד מִיכָאֵל אֶחָד. כֵּיוָן שֶׁקָּרָא אֶחָד °הֵם בָּאוּ לְפָנָיו וּמְשַׁגְּרוֹ לְכָל מָקוֹם שֶׁיִּרְצֶה. וּמִנַּיִן שֶׁיְּרֵאִים זֶה אֶת זֶה וּמְכַבְּדִין זֶה אֶת זֶה וְעָנְוְתָנִין מִבְּנֵי אָדָם, שֶׁבְּשָׁעָה שֶׁפּוֹתְחִין אֶת פִּיהֶם וְאוֹמְרִים שִׁיר, זֶה אוֹמֵר לַחֲבֵירוֹ: פָּתַח

A lesson in the importance of making peace:
אַף הַקָּדוֹשׁ בָּרוּךְ הוּא עָשָׂה שָׁלוֹם בַּמָּרוֹם — Even the Holy One, Blessed is He, took special measures to **make peace in the heavens.** וְאֵיזֶה שָׁלוֹם עָשָׂה הַקָּדוֹשׁ בָּרוּךְ הוּא בַּמָּרוֹם — And what was the peace that the Holy One, Blessed is He, made in the heavens? שֶׁלֹּא קָרָא עֲשָׂרָה גַּבְרִיאֵל עֲשָׂרָה מִיכָאֵל עֲשָׂרָה אוּרִיאֵל עֲשָׂרָה רְפָאֵל — It was that He did not name ten angels Gabriel, ten Michael, ten Uriel, or ten Raphael, כְּדֶרֶךְ שֶׁבְּנֵי אָדָם קוֹרִין עֲשָׂרָה רְאוּבֵן עֲשָׂרָה שִׁמְעוֹן עֲשָׂרָה לֵוִי עֲשָׂרָה יְהוּדָה — in the same way that people name ten different people Reuben, ten Simeon, ten Levi, and ten Judah.[38] שֶׁאִלְמָלֵא עָשָׂה כְּדֶרֶךְ שֶׁבְּנֵי אָדָם עוֹשִׂים — For were He to have given the same name to numerous angels, the same way that people do, כֵּיוָן שֶׁקָּרָא לְאֶחָד מֵהֶם בָּאִין לְפָנָיו — then whenever He would summon one of them, all who had that name would respond to the summons and come, וּמִתְקַנְאִין זֶה בָּזֶה — and they would become jealous of one another when only one of them was given the mission. אֶלָּא קָרָא גַּבְרִיאֵל אֶחָד מִיכָאֵל אֶחָד — Instead, He named only one angel Gabriel, only one angel Michael, and so on. כֵּיוָן שֶׁקָּרָא אֶחָד הֵם בָּא מֵהֶם לְפָנָיו — Thus, when He calls one of them, he alone comes and stands before Him, וּמְשַׁגְּרוֹ לְכָל מָקוֹם שֶׁיִּרְצֶה — and He sends him wherever He wants without any other angel knowing about it.[39] וּמִנַּיִן שֶׁיְּרֵאִים זֶה אֶת זֶה — Now, perhaps this was necessary only because angels are prone to jealousy?[40] How do we know that this is not so, and that, on the contrary, **they are in awe of one another,** וְעָנְוְתָנִין מִבְּנֵי אָדָם — and are more **humble than are people?** שֶׁבְּשָׁעָה שֶׁפּוֹתְחִין אֶת פִּיהֶם וְאוֹמְרִים שִׁיר — For when **they open up their mouths to say song** before God, זֶה אוֹמֵר לַחֲבֵירוֹ: פָּתַח

---

38. Many people have the same name. One would have thought that among the myriad of angels as well, we would find many with the same name. But this is not the case, and the Baraisa explains why.

39. *Binyan Yehoshua.*

40. *Magen Avos.* [See, however, *Avos DeRabbi Nassan, Nusach 2*, Ch. 26, where the following discussion of the angels' respect for one another is brought in connection with the next words of Hillel, אוֹהֵב אֶת הַבְּרִיּוֹת, *loving people.*]

אַתָּה שֶׁאַתָּה גָּדוֹל מִמֶּנִּי, וְזֶה אוֹמֵר לַחֲבֵירוֹ: פָּתַח אַתָּה שֶׁאַתָּה גָּדוֹל
מִמֶּנִּי. לֹא כְּדֶרֶךְ שֶׁבְּנֵי אָדָם עוֹשִׂין שֶׁזֶּה אוֹמֵר לַחֲבֵירוֹ: אֲנִי גָּדוֹל מִמְּךָ,
וְזֶה אוֹמֵר לַחֲבֵירוֹ: אֲנִי גָּדוֹל מִמְּךָ. וְיֵשׁ אוֹמְרִים: כִּתּוֹת כִּתּוֹת הֵן, כַּת
אַחַת אוֹמֶרֶת לַחֲבֶרְתָּהּ: פִּתְחִי אַתְּ שֶׁאַתְּ גְּדוֹלָה מִמֶּנִּי, שֶׁנֶּאֱמַר (ישעיה ו,
ג) "וְקָרָא זֶה אֶל זֶה וְאָמַר":

ז • אוֹהֵב אֶת הַבְּרִיּוֹת, כֵּיצַד, מְלַמֵּד שֶׁיְּהֵא אָדָם אוֹהֵב אֶת הַבְּרִיּוֹת וְלֹא
יְהֵא שׂוֹנֵא אֶת הַבְּרִיּוֹת.[41] שֶׁכֵּן מָצִינוּ בְּאַנְשֵׁי דוֹר הַפַּלָּגָה שֶׁמִּתּוֹךְ

אַתָּה שֶׁאַתָּה גָּדוֹל מִמֶּנִּי — one angel says to his fellow, "You begin the song, for you are greater than I," וְזֶה אוֹמֵר לַחֲבֵירוֹ: פָּתַח אַתָּה שֶׁאַתָּה גָּדוֹל מִמֶּנִּי — and that one responds, "No! *You* begin the song, for *you* are greater than *I.*" לֹא שֶׁזֶּה אוֹמֵר לַחֲבֵירוֹ: כְּדֶרֶךְ שֶׁבְּנֵי אָדָם עוֹשִׂין — This is unlike the way people act, וְזֶה אוֹמֵר לַחֲבֵירוֹ: אֲנִי גָּדוֹל מִמְּךָ — where one says to his fellow, "I am greater than you," and the other one responds, "No, *I* am greater than *you.*" וְיֵשׁ אוֹמְרִים: כִּתּוֹת כִּתּוֹת הֵן — And some Sages say that it is not between individual angels that the above exchange occurs, but it is rather various groups of angels that have this exchange. כַּת אַחַת אוֹמֶרֶת לַחֲבֶרְתָּהּ: פִּתְחִי אַתְּ שֶׁאַתְּ גְּדוֹלָה מִמֶּנִּי — One group of angels says to the other, "You begin the song, for you are greater than we." שֶׁנֶּאֱמַר "וְקָרָא זֶה אֶל זֶה וְאָמַר" — According to either opinion, the fact that this humble exchange occurs between the angels is known from **that which is stated,** *And one would call to another and say, "Holy, holy, holy is HASHEM, Master of Legions"* (Isaiah 6:3), implying that before praising God, each one calls to the other in a show of deference, as described above. Now, if God took special measures to ensure peace among the angels, who are so respectful of one another, how much more so must we take pains to spread peace among human beings, who are by nature jealous and contentious.

§7 The Baraisa continues its elaboration of *Avos* 1:12:
אוֹהֵב אֶת הַבְּרִיּוֹת, כֵּיצַד — Hillel also tells us to learn from Aaron's example of "loving people" — how so? מְלַמֵּד שֶׁיְּהֵא אָדָם אוֹהֵב אֶת הַבְּרִיּוֹת וְלֹא יְהֵא שׂוֹנֵא אֶת הַבְּרִיּוֹת — This teaches that a person should love people and not hate people.[41] שֶׁכֵּן מָצִינוּ בְּאַנְשֵׁי דוֹר הַפַּלָּגָה — For indeed we find with respect to the people of the Generation of the Dispersion שֶׁמִּתּוֹךְ

---

41. One might think that he fulfills Hillel's dictum by loving *some* people, even if he hates others. The Baraisa therefore makes clear that Hillel exhorts us to love *all* people and not hate anyone.

Accordingly, we are bidden to love even those who are wicked [as evident from the Baraisa's proof below]. We should be

concerned for their spiritual welfare, and pray that they repent (*Ben Avraham*, from *Berachos* 10a), and try to lovingly guide them back to the correct path (*Magen Avos*).

[This lesson can be seen clearly in Hillel's wording, אוֹהֵב אֶת הַבְּרִיּוֹת, literally rendered, *loving the* "*creations*": One should love each of his fellows simply because he is a creation

שֶׁאוֹהֲבִין זֶה אֶת זֶה[42] לֹא רָצָה הַקָּדוֹשׁ בָּרוּךְ הוּא לְאַבְּדָן מִן הָעוֹלָם אֶלָּא
פִּזְּרָן בְּאַרְבַּע רוּחוֹת הָעוֹלָם.[43] אֲבָל אַנְשֵׁי סְדוֹם מִתּוֹךְ שֶׁהָיוּ שׂוֹנְאִים זֶה
אֶת זֶה אִבְּדָן הַקָּדוֹשׁ בָּרוּךְ הוּא מִן הָעוֹלָם הַזֶּה וּמִן הָעוֹלָם הַבָּא,[44]
שֶׁנֶּאֱמַר (בראשית יג, יג) "וְאַנְשֵׁי סְדוֹם רָעִים וְחַטָּאִים לַה' מְאֹד".°."וְחַטָּאִים"
זֶה גִּילּוּי עֲרָיוֹת. "לַה' " זֶה חִילּוּל ה'.[46] "מְאֹד" שֶׁמִּתְכַּוְּונִין וְחוֹטְאִים. הָא
לָמַדְתָּ מִתּוֹךְ שֶׁשּׂוֹנְאִין זֶה אֶת זֶה אִבְּדָן הַקָּדוֹשׁ בָּרוּךְ הוּא מִן הָעוֹלָם
הַזֶּה וּמִן הָעוֹלָם הַבָּא:[47]

שֶׁאוֹהֲבִין זֶה אֶת זֶה — that although they rebelled against God, nonetheless, since they loved one another,[42] לֹא רָצָה הַקָּדוֹשׁ בָּרוּךְ הוּא לְאַבְּדָן מִן הָעוֹלָם — the Holy One, Blessed is He, had mercy on them and did not want to eradicate them from the world. אֶלָּא פִּזְּרָן בְּאַרְבַּע רוּחוֹת הָעוֹלָם — Instead, He merely scattered them to the four corners of the world.[43] אֲבָל אַנְשֵׁי סְדוֹם מִתּוֹךְ שֶׁהָיוּ שׂוֹנְאִים זֶה אֶת זֶה — However, the people of Sodom, because they hated one another, אִבְּדָן הַקָּדוֹשׁ בָּרוּךְ הוּא מִן הָעוֹלָם הַזֶּה וּמִן הָעוֹלָם הַבָּא — the Holy One, Blessed is He, eradicated them from this world and from the World to Come.[44] שֶׁנֶּאֱמַר "וְאַנְשֵׁי סְדוֹם רָעִים וְחַטָּאִים לַה' מְאֹד" — That they hated each other is indicated in that which is stated, *Now the people of Sodom were wicked and sinful toward HASHEM, exceedingly* (Genesis 13:13). The Baraisa expounds the verse: "רָעִים" זֶה עִם זֶה — *Wicked* means in their behavior toward one another;[45] "וְחַטָּאִים" זֶה גִּילּוּי עֲרָיוֹת — and *sinful* means with immorality; "לַה' " זֶה חִילּוּל ה' — *toward HASHEM* means with the desecration of God's Name;[46] "מְאֹד" שֶׁמִּתְכַּוְּונִין וְחוֹטְאִים — and *exceedingly* means that they sinned deliberately, in defiance of God's Will. הָא לָמַדְתָּ מִתּוֹךְ שֶׁשּׂוֹנְאִין זֶה אֶת זֶה — From here you can learn that it was because [the people of Sodom] hated one another אִבְּדָן הַקָּדוֹשׁ בָּרוּךְ הוּא מִן הָעוֹלָם הַזֶּה וּמִן הָעוֹלָם הַבָּא — that the Holy One, Blessed is He, eradicated them from this world and the World to Come.[47]

of God, no matter his conduct (ibid.).]

42. As it is stated regarding them, *The whole earth was of one language and of common purpose* [Genesis 11:1] (*Binyan Yehoshua*). This unity bespeaks the love and harmony that prevailed.

43. [They did, however, lose their share in the World to Come, as taught in the Mishnah, *Sanhedrin* 107b, and derived there in the Gemara, 109a.]

44. As taught and derived in the Mishnah and Gemara ibid.

45. [These words do not appear in the Vilna version, but are found in some manuscripts, and are added by *Magen Avos, Gra,* and others; they also appear in the Baraisa's similar exposition of this verse below, 36 §1.] The fact that they were wicked toward one another proves the Baraisa's assertion that they hated one another. [See, however, *Velo Od Ella* for a different explanation.]

46. I.e., blasphemy (see *Binyan Yehoshua* and *Nuschas HaGra*).

47. For the people of the Generation of the Dispersion — who committed all the same sins as the people of Sodom, except for

ח. וּמְקָרְבָן לַתּוֹרָה, כֵּיצַד, מְלַמֵּד שֶׁיְּהֵא אָדָם מְקַפֵּחַ אֶת הַבְּרִיּוֹת וּמַכְנִיסָן תַּחַת כַּנְפֵי הַשְּׁכִינָה כְּדֶרֶךְ שֶׁהָיָה אַבְרָהָם אָבִינוּ מְקַפֵּחַ אֶת הַבְּרִיּוֹת וּמַכְנִיסָן תַּחַת כַּנְפֵי הַשְּׁכִינָה.[49] [וְלֹא אַבְרָהָם לְבַד עָשָׂה אֶלָּא אַף שָׂרָה, שֶׁנֶּאֱמַר] (בראשית יב, ה) "וַיִּקַּח אַבְרָם אֶת שָׂרַי אִשְׁתּוֹ וְאֶת לוֹט בֶּן אָחִיו וְאֶת כָּל רְכוּשָׁם אֲשֶׁר רָכָשׁוּ וְאֶת הַנֶּפֶשׁ אֲשֶׁר עָשׂוּ בְחָרָן". וַהֲלֹא כָּל בָּאֵי עוֹלָם אֵינָם יְכוֹלִים לִבְרֹאות אֲפִילוּ יַתּוּשׁ אֶחָד, וּמַה תַּלְמוּד לוֹמַר "וְאֶת הַנֶּפֶשׁ אֲשֶׁר עָשׂוּ בְחָרָן", מְלַמֵּד שֶׁהֶעֱלָה עֲלֵיהֶם הַקָּדוֹשׁ בָּרוּךְ הוּא כְּאִילוּ עָשׂוּ אוֹתָם.[51]

---

§8 The Baraisa expounds the final piece of *Avos* 1:12:

וּמְקָרְבָן לַתּוֹרָה, כֵּיצַד — **And finally, Hillel bids us to learn from Aaron's example of "bringing [people] closer to the Torah" — how so?** מְלַמֵּד שֶׁיְּהֵא אָדָם מְקַפֵּחַ אֶת הַבְּרִיּוֹת וּמַכְנִיסָן תַּחַת כַּנְפֵי הַשְּׁכִינָה — **This teaches that a person should remove** sinful **people** from their their evil inclination and deeds,[48] and **bring them under the wings of the Divine Presence,** כְּדֶרֶךְ שֶׁהָיָה אַבְרָהָם אָבִינוּ מְקַפֵּחַ אֶת הַבְּרִיּוֹת וּמַכְנִיסָן תַּחַת כַּנְפֵי הַשְּׁכִינָה — **in the same way that our patriarch Abraham would withdraw the people** of his time **from their evil inclination and deeds, and bring them under the wings of the Divine Presence.**[49] וְלֹא אַבְרָהָם לְבַד עָשָׂה אֶלָּא אַף שָׂרָה — **And it was not Abraham alone who did this** (for the men), **but his wife Sarah too,** did this (for the women).[50] שֶׁנֶּאֱמַר "וַיִּקַּח אַבְרָם אֶת שָׂרַי אִשְׁתּוֹ וְאֶת לוֹט בֶּן אָחִיו וְאֶת כָּל רְכוּשָׁם אֲשֶׁר רָכָשׁוּ וְאֶת הַנֶּפֶשׁ אֲשֶׁר עָשׂוּ בְחָרָן" — **All this is as it is stated,** *Abram took his wife Sarai and Lot, his brother's son, and all their wealth that they had amassed, and the souls "they made" in Haran* (Genesis 12:5). וַהֲלֹא כָּל בָּאֵי עוֹלָם אֵינָם יְכוֹלִים לִבְרֹאות אֲפִילוּ יַתּוּשׁ אֶחָד — **Now, is it not true that all who come to the world** working together **could not create even one gnat,** and certainly not a person?! וּמַה תַּלְמוּד לוֹמַר "וְאֶת הַנֶּפֶשׁ אֲשֶׁר עָשׂוּ בְחָרָן" — **So then what does Scripture mean to say by,** *and the souls "they made" in Haran?* מְלַמֵּד שֶׁהֶעֱלָה עֲלֵיהֶם הַקָּדוֹשׁ בָּרוּךְ הוּא כְּאִילוּ עָשׂוּ אוֹתָם — **It teaches that** because Abraham and Sarah brought those people to faith in Him, **the Holy One, Blessed is He, considered it as if they** had actually *made* them.[51]

---

hating one another — were not eradicated from this world [as the Baraisa taught above] (*Ben Avraham*).

48. *Binyan Yehoshua*. Alternatively, מְקַפֵּחַ אֶת הַבְּרִיּוֹת is to be rendered, *compel people to abandon their sinful ways*, by means of convincing arguments (*Mefaresh, Mesores HaShas, Avos HaRosh* [Vol. 1]), or by force (*Magen Avos*).

49. See *Magen Avos*, who discusses why the Baraisa introduces the practice of Abraham when elaborating how we are to emulate Aaron.

50. *Rashi* on the verse, from *Bereishis Rabbah* 39 §14.

51. And the plural *"they"* made indicates that it was not only Abraham that did so, but Sarah as well (*Ahavas Chesed*).

כְּשֵׁם שֶׁאֵין אָדָם חוֹלֵק שָׂכָר לַחֲבֵירוֹ בְּהָעוֹלָם הַזֶּה 53 כָּךְ (אֵין) חוֹלֵק
שָׂכָר (לַחֲבֵירוֹ) לָעוֹלָם הַבָּא 54, שֶׁנֶּאֱמַר (קהלת ד, א) "וְהִנֵּה דִּמְעַת הָעֲשֻׁקִים
וְאֵין לָהֶם מְנַחֵם וּמִיַּד עֹשְׁקֵיהֶם כֹּחַ וְאֵין לָהֶם מְנַחֵם". לָמָּה נֶאֱמַר "וְאֵין
לָהֶם מְנַחֵם" שְׁנֵי פְעָמִים, אֵלּוּ בְּנֵי אָדָם שֶׁאוֹכְלִין וְשׁוֹתִין וּמַצְלִיחִין
בְּבָנִים וּבְבָנוֹת בָּעוֹלָם הַזֶּה וּבָעוֹלָם הַבָּא אֵין לָהֶם [כְּלוּם, "וְאֵין לָהֶם]
מְנַחֵם". שֶׁאִם נִגְנְבָה לוֹ לְאָדָם גְּנֵיבָה בָּעוֹלָם הַזֶּה אוֹ שֵׁמֵת לוֹ מֵת

The Baraisa now turns to expound Hillel's saying in *Avos* 1:14, "If I am not for myself, who will be for me?"[52]

כְּשֵׁם שֶׁאֵין אָדָם חוֹלֵק שָׂכָר לַחֲבֵירוֹ בְּהָעוֹלָם הַזֶּה — **Just as in this world, a person cannot give his friend a portion of** his **reward** for good deeds,[53] כָּךְ אֵין חוֹלֵק שָׂכָר לַחֲבֵירוֹ לָעוֹלָם הַבָּא — **so too in the World to Come, he cannot give his friend a portion of** his **reward** for good deeds,[54] שֶׁנֶּאֱמַר "וְהִנֵּה דִּמְעַת הָעֲשֻׁקִים וְאֵין לָהֶם מְנַחֵם וּמִיַּד עֹשְׁקֵיהֶם כֹּחַ וְאֵין לָהֶם מְנַחֵם" — **as it is stated,** *Behold! Tears of the oppressed with none to comfort them, and their oppressors have the power — with none to comfort them* (*Ecclesiastes* 4:1), which alludes to the souls of the wicked suffering as they receive their punishment in the World to Come, "oppressed" by their misdeeds in this world.[55]

The Baraisa's exposition of the verse just cited will show how it supports the preceding statement:

לָמָּה נֶאֱמַר "וְאֵין לָהֶם מְנַחֵם" שְׁנֵי פְעָמִים — **Why is** the phrase, *with none to comfort them,* **stated twice** in this verse? אֵלּוּ בְּנֵי אָדָם שֶׁאוֹכְלִין וְשׁוֹתִין וּמַצְלִיחִין בְּבָנִים וּבְבָנוֹת בָּעוֹלָם הַזֶּה — **These** two mentions **are** a reference to two types of people:[56] The first type are **the people who eat and drink and are successful with sons and daughters** and all the trappings of the good life **in this world,** וּבָעוֹלָם הַבָּא אֵין לָהֶם כְּלוּם — **but in the World to Come they have nothing,** for they squandered their earthly lives in mundane pursuits and neglected Torah and mitzvos, which are the only things a person brings along to the World to Come. "וְאֵין לָהֶם מְנַחֵם" — **And they are** *with none to comfort them* in the World to Come. שֶׁאִם נִגְנְבָה לוֹ לְאָדָם גְּנֵיבָה בָּעוֹלָם הַזֶּה אוֹ שֵׁמֵת לוֹ מֵת — **For in this world, if** misfortune befalls **a person,** such as if **something is stolen from**

---

52. *Magen Avos* (based on *Avos DeRabbi Nassan, Nusach* 2, Ch. 27), *Nuschas HaGra,* and *Ben Avraham;* see below, note 62.

53. Since the primary reward for one's good deeds is not given to him in this world, but only in World to Come [see *Kiddushin* 39b]. Surely, he cannot share with his friend that which he does not yet have! (*Mefaresh*).

54. Accordingly, "If I am not for myself, who will be for me?" means that if one does not earn merits for himself, he will have nothing in the World to Come, as he will not be able to share a part of anyone else's reward (see *Avos DeRabbi Nassan, Nusach* 2, Ch. 27).

55. *Binyan Yehoshua,* from *Rashi* to the verse.

56. See *Magen Avos.*

בָּאִין בָּנָיו וְאֶחָיו וּקְרוֹבָיו וּמְנַחֲמִין אוֹתוֹ. יָכוֹל אַף לְעוֹלָם הַבָּא כֵּן, תַּלְמוּד
לוֹמַר (שם פסוק ח) ״גַּם בֵּן וָאָח אֵין לוֹ״,[57] וְכֵן מִי שֶׁעוֹבֵר עֲבֵירָה וְהוֹלִיד
מַמְזֵר,[58] אוֹמְרִים לוֹ: רֵיקָה, חָבַלְתָּ בְּעַצְמְךָ חָבַלְתָּ בּוֹ. [שֶׁאוֹתוֹ מַמְזֵר הָיָה
רוֹצֶה לִלְמוֹד תּוֹרָה עִם אוֹתָן הַתַּלְמִידִים] שֶׁהָיוּ יוֹשְׁבִין וְשׁוֹנִין בִּירוּשָׁלַיִם
וְהָיָה הַמַּמְזֵר הוֹלֵךְ עִמָּהֶן עַד שֶׁהִגִּיעַ לְאַשְׁדּוֹד. עוֹמֵד שָׁם וְאוֹמֵר: אוֹי לִי,
אִילּוּ לֹא הָיִיתִי מַמְזֵר כְּבָר הָיִיתִי יוֹשֵׁב וְשׁוֹנֶה בֵּין הַתַּלְמִידִים שֶׁלָּמַדְתִּי
עַד עַכְשָׁיו, וּלְפִי שֶׁאֲנִי מַמְזֵר אֵינִי יוֹשֵׁב וְשׁוֹנֶה בֵּין הַתַּלְמִידִים.[60]

him or a close relative dies, בָּאִין בָּנָיו וְאֶחָיו וּקְרוֹבָיו וּמְנַחֲמִין אוֹתוֹ — his sons, brothers, and other relatives can come and comfort him. יָכוֹל אַף לְעוֹלָם הַבָּא כֵּן — Now, one might think that the same is true even in the World to Come. תַּלְמוּד לוֹמַר ״גַּם בֵּן וָאָח אֵין לוֹ״ — Scripture teaches otherwise and states several verses later, *There is one ... who has neither son nor brother* (ibid. v. 8). In the World to Come, there is *no one*— not even a son or brother — who can comfort the sinner from his suffering in the World to Come. This is the same as what Scripture alludes to in v. 1, when it states, *with none to comfort them*.[57] וְכֵן מִי שֶׁעוֹבֵר עֲבֵירָה וְהוֹלִיד מַמְזֵר — In a similar vein, the second mention of *with none to comfort them* alludes to someone who transgresses a sin of illicit union and begets from that union a child who is a *mamzer*.[58] אוֹמְרִים לוֹ: רֵיקָה, חָבַלְתָּ בְּעַצְמְךָ חָבַלְתָּ בּוֹ — In the World to Come they of the Heavenly Court say to him, "Empty one! You have injured yourself by bringing into the world a *mamzer*, who will serve as a lasting reminder of your sin,[59] and you have also injured him! שֶׁאוֹתוֹ מַמְזֵר הָיָה רוֹצֶה לִלְמוֹד תּוֹרָה — For when the Messiah comes and the Jewish people return to Israel, that *mamzer* will want to study Torah עִם אוֹתָן הַתַּלְמִידִים שֶׁהָיוּ יוֹשְׁבִין וְשׁוֹנִין בִּירוּשָׁלַיִם — in Jerusalem with those same students who had sat and learned Torah with him previously, while still in exile. וְהָיָה הַמַּמְזֵר הוֹלֵךְ עִמָּהֶן עַד שֶׁהִגִּיעַ לְאַשְׁדּוֹד — And because of your sin, that *mamzer* will walk with them until he reaches the city of Ashdod, עוֹמֵד שָׁם וְאוֹמֵר: אוֹי לִי — where he will stop and say, 'Woe is me! אִילּוּ לֹא הָיִיתִי מַמְזֵר כְּבָר הָיִיתִי יוֹשֵׁב וְשׁוֹנֶה בֵּין הַתַּלְמִידִים שֶׁלָּמַדְתִּי — Had I not been a *mamzer*, I would already be preparing to sit and learn Torah in Jerusalem among those students with whom I had studied עַד עַכְשָׁיו — until now. וּלְפִי שֶׁאֲנִי מַמְזֵר אֵינִי יוֹשֵׁב וְשׁוֹנֶה בֵּין הַתַּלְמִידִים — But because I am a *mamzer*, I am not able to sit and learn Torah among those students!' "[60]

---

57. [The "comfort" in the World to Come would be someone else's sharing of his own reward with the sinner. But this cannot be done. Hence, the proof to the Baraisa's statement above that in the World to Come, one cannot give a portion of his reward to his friend.]

58. [A *mamzer* is the child born of certain forbidden unions.]

59. See *Binyan Yehoshua*, from *Chagigah* 9a [see also *Rashi* ad loc.].

60. This is accounted a greater injury to him

לְפִי שֶׁאֵין מַמְזֵר נִכְנָס לִירוּשָׁלַיִם כָּל עִיקָר, שֶׁנֶּאֱמַר (זכריה ט, ו) "וְיָשַׁב מַמְזֵר בְּאַשְׁדּוֹד (וְהִכְרַתִּי גְאוֹן פְּלִשְׁתִּים)"61:

ט. הוּא הָיָה אוֹמֵר: אִם אֵין אֲנִי לִי מִי לִי.62 אִם אֲנִי לֹא אֶזְכֶּה בְּחַיַּי מִי יִזְכֶּה בִּי. וּכְשֶׁאֲנִי לְעַצְמִי מָה אֲנִי. אִם אֲנִי לֹא זוֹכֶה בְּעַצְמִי מִי יִזְכֶּה בִּי בְּעַצְמִי64). אִם לֹא עַכְשָׁיו אֵימָתַי. אִם אֲנִי לֹא זוֹכֶה בְּחַיַּי מִי יִזְכֶּה בִּי לְאַחַר מִיתָתִי65. וְכֵן הוּא אוֹמֵר (קהלת ט, ד) "כִּי לְכֶלֶב חַי הוּא טוֹב מִן הָאַרְיֵה הַמֵּת".

לְפִי שֶׁאֵין מַמְזֵר נִכְנָס לִירוּשָׁלַיִם כָּל עִיקָר — This is because in the Messianic future, a *mamzer* will not be permitted to enter Jerusalem altogether, שֶׁנֶּאֱמַר "וְיָשַׁב מַמְזֵר בְּאַשְׁדּוֹד וְהִכְרַתִּי גְאוֹן פְּלִשְׁתִּים" — as it is stated, *A mamzer will dwell in Ashdod, and I will eliminate the pride of the Philistines* (Zechariah 9:6).[61] Upon hearing this rebuke from the Heavenly Court, the father of that *mamzer* has no one to comfort him. And this is what Scripture alludes to with the second time that it states, *with none to comfort him.*

§9 The Baraisa now expounds the balance of Hillel's teachings cited above: הוּא הָיָה אוֹמֵר: אִם אֵין אֲנִי לִי מִי לִי — "He also used to say: If I am not for myself, who will be for me?"[62] — אִם אֲנִי לֹא אֶזְכֶּה בְּחַיַּי מִי יִזְכֶּה בִּי — meaning, if I do not earn my eternal life[63] by performing good deeds in this world, then who else will earn it for me? — וּכְשֶׁאֲנִי לְעַצְמִי מָה אֲנִי — "And if I am for myself, what am I?" — אִם אֲנִי לֹא זוֹכֶה בְּעַצְמִי מִי יִזְכֶּה בִּי בְּעַצְמִי — meaning, if I do not take possession of my earthly self, then who *will* take possession of my earthly self?[64] — אִם לֹא עַכְשָׁיו אֵימָתַי — "And if not now, when?" — אִם אֲנִי לֹא זוֹכֶה בְּחַיַּי מִי יִזְכֶּה בִּי לְאַחַר מִיתָתִי — meaning, if I do not earn merit during my lifetime, then who will earn it for me after my death?[65]

The Baraisa cites and expounds a verse in support of Hillel's last statement, "And if not now, when?":

וְכֵן הוּא אוֹמֵר "כִּי לְכֶלֶב חַי הוּא טוֹב מִן הָאַרְיֵה הַמֵּת" — And so does it say in

---

than his inability to marry into the Jewish congregation! (*Mefaresh*).

61. Implying that a *mamzer* will be allowed to dwell *only* in Ashdod, but not in the holy Jerusalem. Because of the intense sanctity that Jerusalem will have at that time, it will not tolerate tainted people, like the *mamzer,* in its midst (*Mefaresh*). [See *Kiddushin* 72b, where the Gemara states that another Tanna has an alternative interpretation of this verse (see *Magen Avos* and *Ahavas Chesed* here).]

62. [Some move these words (and the next ones) to the Baraisa above, where it has already begun to elaborate them; see above,

note 52 (*Magen Avos, Nuschas HaGra, Ben Avraham*).]

63. Translation follows *Magen Avos*.

64. If the person's true identity, his soul, does not take possession of his earthly self to utilize it in the service of God, then who *will* take possession of it? It is the evil inclination, in which case the person's soul will become the slave rather than the master (*Magen Avos*). Thus, Hillel's original statement, וּכְשֶׁאֲנִי לְעַצְמִי מָה אֲנִי, means: "If I will become subservient to my [earthly] self, what am I?" (ibid.).

65. Merit can be earned only in this world, not in the next (*Magen Avos*).

"כִּי לְכֶלֶב חַי הוּא טוֹב" זֶה רָשָׁע הַמִּתְקַיֵּים בָּעוֹלָם הַזֶּה. "מִן הָאַרְיֵה הַמֵּת" אֲפִילוּ מֵאַבְרָהָם יִצְחָק וְיַעֲקֹב שֶׁהֵן שׁוֹכְנֵי עָפָר.[66] (דָּבָר אַחֵר, "כִּי לְכֶלֶב חַי הוּא טוֹב" זֶה) רָשָׁע הַמִּתְקַיֵּים בָּעוֹלָם הַזֶּה, אִם עָשָׂה תְּשׁוּבָה הַקָּדוֹשׁ בָּרוּךְ הוּא מְקַבְּלֵהוּ. אֲבָל צַדִּיק כֵּיוָן שֶׁמֵּת שׁוּב אֵינוֹ מוֹסִיף זְכוּת:[67]

י. הוּא הָיָה אוֹמֵר: אִם תָּבֹא לְבֵיתִי אֲנִי אָבֹא לְבֵיתֶךָ. לַמָּקוֹם שֶׁלִּבִּי אוֹהֵב לְשָׁם רַגְלַי מוֹלִיכוֹת אוֹתִי. אִם תָּבֹא לְבֵיתִי אָבֹא לְבֵיתֶךָ, כֵּיצַד, אֵלּוּ בְּנֵי אָדָם שֶׁמַּשְׁכִּימִים וּמַעֲרִיבִים לְבָתֵּי כְנֵסִיּוֹת וּלְבָתֵּי מִדְרָשׁוֹת,

---

"כִּי   Scripture, *A live dog has it better than a dead lion* (*Ecclesiastes* 9:4). לְכֶלֶב חַי הוּא טוֹב" זֶה רָשָׁע הַמִּתְקַיֵּים בָּעוֹלָם הַזֶּה — The Baraisa explains: *A live dog has it better* — this refers to a wicked person who is still living in this world; מִן הָאַרְיֵה הַמֵּת" אֲפִילוּ מֵאַבְרָהָם יִצְחָק וְיַעֲקֹב שֶׁהֵן שׁוֹכְנֵי עָפָר" — *than a dead lion* — meaning, even better **than Abraham, Isaac, and Jacob, who have already died, and now rest in the earth.**[66] דָּבָר אַחֵר, "כִּי לְכֶלֶב חַי הוּא טוֹב" זֶה רָשָׁע הַמִּתְקַיֵּים בָּעוֹלָם הַזֶּה — Another, expanded, version of this last exposition: *A live dog has it better* — this refers to a wicked person who is still living in this world, אִם עָשָׂה תְּשׁוּבָה הַקָּדוֹשׁ בָּרוּךְ הוּא מְקַבְּלֵהוּ — for if he repents, the Holy One, Blessed is He, accepts him back. אֲבָל צַדִּיק כֵּיוָן שֶׁמֵּת שׁוּב אֵינוֹ מוֹסִיף זְכוּת — Whereas a righteous person, once he dies, he can no longer add any merits.[67]

§10 The Baraisa cites additional sayings of Hillel, which he said when he rejoiced at the Celebration of the Water Drawing in the Temple:[68]

הוּא הָיָה אוֹמֵר: אִם תָּבֹא לְבֵיתִי אֲנִי אָבֹא לְבֵיתֶךָ — He also used to say: God tells the people of Israel, "**If you come to My house, then I will come to your house.**" לַמָּקוֹם שֶׁלִּבִּי אוֹהֵב לְשָׁם רַגְלַי מוֹלִיכוֹת אוֹתִי — And also, "**To the place that my heart loves, there my feet lead me.**"

The Baraisa explains the first of these two sayings:

אִם תָּבֹא לְבֵיתִי אָבֹא לְבֵיתֶךָ, כֵּיצַד — "**If you come to My house, then I will come to your house**" — how so? אֵלּוּ בְּנֵי אָדָם שֶׁמַּשְׁכִּימִים וּמַעֲרִיבִים לְבָתֵּי כְנֵסִיּוֹת — This refers to the people who consistently come morning וּלְבָתֵּי מִדְרָשׁוֹת

---

66. A person who is alive, though he may be wicked, still has the opportunity to repent and gain eternal merit for himself, an opportunity no longer available even to the greatest *tzaddik* who has died. This is made clear by the alternative version presented next in the Baraisa (see *Ben Avraham*; see, however, *Ahavas Chesed*, who suggests that the two versions are in dispute).

67. The only time a person is given the special privilege of performing God's mitzvos is while he is still alive. After death, however — no matter how righteous he might have been during his lifetime — he is no longer granted this opportunity (see *Regel Yesharah*).

68. *Succah* 53a.

הַקָּדוֹשׁ בָּרוּךְ הוּא מְבָרְכָן לָעוֹלָם הַבָּא, כָּעִנְיָן שֶׁנֶּאֱמַר (שמות כ, כא) "בְּכָל
הַמָּקוֹם אֲשֶׁר אַזְכִּיר אֶת שְׁמִי וְגוֹ' ". 69. לַמָּקוֹם שֶׁלִּבִּי אוֹהֵב לְשָׁם רַגְלַי
מוֹלִיכוֹת אוֹתִי, כֵּיצַד, אֵלּוּ בְּנֵי אָדָם שֶׁמַּנִּיחִים כַּסְפָּם וּזְהָבָם וְעוֹלִין
לָרֶגֶל לְהַקְבִּיל פְּנֵי שְׁכִינָה בַּמִּקְדָּשׁ, הַקָּדוֹשׁ בָּרוּךְ הוּא מְשַׁמְּרָם בְּתוֹךְ
מַחֲנֵיהֶם70, שֶׁנֶּאֱמַר (שמות לד, כד) "וְלֹא יַחְמֹד אִישׁ אֶת אַרְצְךָ בַּעֲלֹתְךָ
לֵרָאוֹת אֶת פְּנֵי ה' אֱלֹהֶיךָ"71:

---

and evening to the synagogues and study halls. **הַקָּדוֹשׁ בָּרוּךְ הוּא מְבָרְכָן**
לָעוֹלָם הַבָּא — The Holy One, Blessed is He, says that He will bless them in
the World to Come, **כָּעִנְיָן שֶׁנֶּאֱמַר "בְּכָל הַמָּקוֹם אֲשֶׁר אַזְכִּיר אֶת שְׁמִי וְגוֹ' "** — like
the idea that is stated that God told the people of Israel, *in every place that*
I permit My Name to be mentioned, etc., I shall come to you and bless you
(*Exodus* 20:21).[69] With such a guarantee, it should certainly be easier for us to
make the correct decision as to how we choose to spend our time.

The Baraisa explains the second saying:
לַמָּקוֹם שֶׁלִּבִּי אוֹהֵב לְשָׁם רַגְלַי מוֹלִיכוֹת אוֹתִי, כֵּיצַד — "To the place that my heart
loves, there my feet lead me" — how so? **אֵלּוּ בְּנֵי אָדָם שֶׁמַּנִּיחִים כַּסְפָּם וּזְהָבָם**
וְעוֹלִין לָרֶגֶל — This refers to the people who leave behind their gold and silver
as they go up to Jerusalem for the Pilgrimage Festival **לְהַקְבִּיל פְּנֵי שְׁכִינָה**
בַּמִּקְדָּשׁ — to greet the Divine Presence in the Holy Temple, **הַקָּדוֹשׁ בָּרוּךְ**
הוּא מְשַׁמְּרָם בְּתוֹךְ מַחֲנֵיהֶם — and, Hillel teaches, the Holy One, Blessed is He,
protects them in their camps,[70] **שֶׁנֶּאֱמַר "וְלֹא יַחְמֹד אִישׁ אֶת אַרְצְךָ בַּעֲלֹתְךָ**
לֵרָאוֹת אֶת פְּנֵי ה' אֱלֹהֶיךָ" — as it is stated, *No man will covet your land when*
you go up to appear before HASHEM, *your God* (ibid. 34:24).[71]

---

69. That verse refers to the Holy Temple,
which is the only place in which it is permitted
to mention God's actual Name. The Baraisa,
however, extends this ("like the idea which is
stated") to the synagogues and study halls
as well, since the verse states *in "every"*
place ... And the fact that the verse does not
say simply *I shall come,* but adds *to you,* indicates that God will come "to your house"
(*Ben Avraham*), that is, to your eternal place
in the World to Come (*Binyan Yehoshua*).

70. I.e., on their travels (*Magen Avos;* see,
however, end of next note). With these
words, Hillel qualifies God's promise just
mentioned, "If you come to My house, I will
come to your house," as referring not to
those who simply travel to His house, but to
those who do so because that destination is

the desire of their hearts [as demonstrated
by their willingness to abandon their worldly
possessions to go there]. They must be
those who can say, as Hillel did of his going
to the Temple, "To the place that my heart
loves, there my feet lead me" (*Magen Avos,*
second explanation).

Alternatively, the words the Baraisa now
explains are also what Hillel says in God's
Name — "To the place that My heart loves,
there My feet lead Me (i.e., that is where I will
go to protect them). [That is, God loves the
place of those who love His place, and He
will go there to protect them wherever they
are] (*Magen Avos,* first explanation; *Ben*
Avraham explains in a similar vein).

71. This Scriptural citation proves only that
God will protect the homes that the people

יא. הוּא הָיָה אוֹמֵר: אִם אֲנִי כָאן הַכֹּל כָּאן, אִם אֲנִי לֵית כָּאן מַאן כָּאן[72]. הוֹפְכָהּ וְהוֹפֵךְ [בָּהּ דְּכוֹלָא בָהּ][73]. וּלְכוּלְּהוֹן לְפוּם צַעֲרָא אַגְרָא:

יב. מַעֲשֶׂה בְּהִלֵּל הַזָּקֵן שֶׁהָיָה מְהַלֵּךְ בַּדֶּרֶךְ וּפָגַע בְּנֵי אָדָם שֶׁמְּבִיאִין חִטִּין. אָמַר לָהֶם: סְאָה בְּכַמָּה, אָמְרוּ לוֹ: בִּשְׁנֵי דִינָרִין. וּפָגַע בַּאֲחֵרִים, אָמַר לָהֶם: סְאָה בְּכַמָּה, אָמְרוּ לוֹ: בִּשְׁלֹשָׁה דִינָרִין.

---

§11 The Baraisa cites more sayings of Hillel:

הוּא הָיָה אוֹמֵר: אִם אֲנִי כָאן הַכֹּל כָּאן — He also **used to say** the following three things: (i) "**If I am here, all are here;** אִם אֲנִי לֵית כָּאן מַאן כָּאן — **but if I am not here, then who is here?**"[72] הוֹפְכָהּ וְהוֹפֵךְ בָּהּ דְּכוֹלָא בָהּ — (ii) In regard to the Torah, **turn it over and turn it over** again and again, **for everything of value is in it.**[73] וּלְכוּלְּהוֹן לְפוּם צַעֲרָא אַגְרָא — (iii) **And in all things,** even the mundane,[74] **the payment is in proportion to the effort;** the payment will depend on how hard one had to work to produce the result.

§12 The Baraisa records a story in which Hillel came face to face with this teaching:

מַעֲשֶׂה בְּהִלֵּל הַזָּקֵן שֶׁהָיָה מְהַלֵּךְ בַּדֶּרֶךְ — **It once happened that Hillel the Elder was walking on the road** וּפָגַע בְּנֵי אָדָם שֶׁמְּבִיאִין חִטִּין — **and he met people who were bringing wheat** to sell in the market. אָמַר לָהֶם: סְאָה בְּכַמָּה, אָמְרוּ לוֹ: בִּשְׁנֵי דִינָרִין — **He asked them, "How much** do you charge **for a** se'ah[75] of wheat?," to which **they replied, "Two** dinars." וּפָגַע בַּאֲחֵרִים — **Further** along, **he met others** who were also bringing wheat to sell, אָמַר לָהֶם: סְאָה בְּכַמָּה, אָמְרוּ לוֹ: בִּשְׁלֹשָׁה דִינָרִין — **and he asked them** as well, "**How much** do you charge **for a** se'ah of wheat?," to which **they replied, "Three** dinars."

---

leave behind, not that He will also protect them on their travels. The latter protection, though, is alluded to in the verse's opening words, *For I shall banish nations before you …*, which can be construed as referring to the protection God affords the people as they travel (*Magen Avos*). [Possibly, though, "in their camps" might refer to their homes rather than their caravans, in which case the Baraisa's proof is straightforward. See also *Ben Avraham*.]

72. [This, too, he said at the Celebration of the Water Drawing (*Succah* 53a).] He would say this as God's words to the people of Israel: As long as I desire to rest My Presence here in the Holy Temple ("I am here") because you, people of Israel, have acted properly, then the Temple will remain in its

full glory, and people will continue to throng to it ("all are here"). However, if you sin and thereby cause Me to remove My Presence from here, then the Temple will be devoid of glory, and it will become desolate and empty (*Binyan Yehoshua*, from *Rashi* to *Succah* 53a; see, however, *Tosafos* there).

73. [The Mishnah in *Avos*, end of Ch. 5, has this same statement in the name of Ben Bag Bag.] A person must thoroughly analyze the words of Torah again and again, with all the painstaking care he would apply to sifting through sand in search of gems (*Binyan Yehoshua*, from *Mefaresh*). [See further in the commentators to *Avos* ad loc.]

74. *Ahavas Chesed*.

75. [A volume of 144 eggs.]

[אָמַר לָהֶם: וַהֲלֹא רִאשׁוֹנִים אָמְרוּ בִשְׁנַיִם,] אָמְרוּ לוֹ: בַּבְלָאֵי טִפְּשָׁאֵי, אִי אַתָּה יוֹדֵעַ שֶׁלְּפוּם צַעֲרָא אַגְרָא. אָמַר לָהֶם: שׁוֹטִים (וְרֵיקִים), עַל שֶׁאֲנִי אוֹמֵר לָכֶם אַתֶּם מַחֲזִירִין לִי כָּךְ. מֶה עָשָׂה לָהֶם הִלֵּל הַזָּקֵן, הֶחֱזִירָן לַמּוּטָב[77]. אַף[78] הוּא רָאָה גּוֹלְגּוֹלֶת שֶׁצָּפָה עַל פְּנֵי הַמָּיִם[79], אָמַר לָהּ: עַל דְּאַטֵּפְתְּ אַטְּפוּךְ וּדְאַטְּפוּךְ יְאַטְּפוּנֵיהּ[80]:

יג. אַף הוּא אוֹמֵר בְּלָשׁוֹן בַּבְלִי אַרְבָּעָה דְבָרִים[81]: נְגַד שְׁמָא אָבַד שְׁמֵיהּ.

אָמַר לָהֶם: וַהֲלֹא רִאשׁוֹנִים אָמְרוּ בִשְׁנַיִם — He said to them, "But did the first ones not tell me, 'Two *dinars*'?" אָמְרוּ לוֹ: בַּבְלָאֵי טִפְּשָׁאֵי, אִי אַתָּה I encountered — They answered him, "The Babylonians are fools![76] יוֹדֵעַ שֶׁלְּפוּם צַעֲרָא אַגְרָא Do you not know that the payment is in proportion to the effort? Since we had to expend additional effort in bringing the wheat from farther away, we have to charge more for it." אָמַר לָהֶם: שׁוֹטִים וְרֵיקִים, עַל שֶׁאֲנִי אוֹמֵר לָכֶם אַתֶּם מַחֲזִירִין לִי כָּךְ — Disturbed by their rudeness, he said to them, "Fools and empty ones! In response to what I say to you in a kind way, you respond in this insulting way?!" מֶה עָשָׂה לָהֶם הִלֵּל הַזָּקֵן, הֶחֱזִירָן לַמּוּטָב — What did Hillel then do to them? He guided them back to the path of proper conduct and taught them how to speak with respect. Nevertheless, he learned from them that even with regard to mundane matters, the payment is in proportion to the effort.[77]

A somewhat related incident involving Hillel:[78] אַף הוּא רָאָה גּוֹלְגּוֹלֶת שֶׁצָּפָה עַל פְּנֵי הַמָּיִם — He also saw a skull floating on the water, which he recognized as the skull of a murderer.[79] אָמַר לָהּ: עַל דְּאַטֵּפְתְּ אַטְּפוּךְ — He said to it, "Because you caused your victims to float by drowning them, others caused you to float by drowning you; וּדְאַטְּפוּךְ יְאַטְּפוּנֵיהּ — and eventually, those who caused you to float by drowning you will in turn be made to float by still others." All evil deeds will eventually be repaid measure for measure.[80]

§13 Hillel's last teaching was said in Aramaic, the language of his native Babylonia. The Baraisa therefore returns to cite [with some variations] *Avos* 1:13, which records other Aramaic teachings of Hillel: אַף הוּא אוֹמֵר בְּלָשׁוֹן בַּבְלִי אַרְבָּעָה דְבָרִים — He would also say four other say-ings in the Babylonian language:[81] נְגַד שְׁמָא אָבַד שְׁמֵיהּ — (i) He who seeks

---

76. Hillel was originally from Babylonia, and later immigrated to Eretz Yisrael (*Binyan Yehoshua*, from *Pesachim* 66a).

77. *Ahavas Chesed*. So, too, with regard to Torah study, it is not for the final result that one receives reward, but for the effort he expends on achieving it.

78. [This incident and saying is also found

in *Avos* 2:6.]

79. *Rashi* to *Succah* 53a.

80. This incident is cited here because it is, in a sense, another manifestation of the principle that payment for a deed is propor-tional to the work that produced it (*Binyan Yehoshua*, from *Mefaresh*).

81. Because these lessons are so important

וּדְלָא מְשַׁמֵּשׁ חַכִּימַיָּא קְטָלָא חַיָּיב. וּדְלָא מוֹסִיף פָּסִיד. וּדְיִשְׁתַּמֵּשׁ בְּתָגָא
אָבַד וְאָזִיל לֵיהּ. נָגֵד שְׁמָא אָבַד שְׁמֵיהּ, כֵּיצַד, מְלַמֵּד שֶׁלֹּא יוֹצִיא לוֹ לָאָדָם
שֵׁם בַּמְּדִינָה,[82] שֶׁכֵּיוָן שֶׁיּוֹצִיא לוֹ שֵׁם בַּמְּדִינָה סוֹף שֶׁנּוֹתְנִין בּוֹ עֵינֵיהֶם
וְהוֹרְגִין אוֹתוֹ וְנוֹטְלִין מִמֶּנּוּ אֶת מָמוֹנוֹ. וּדְלָא מְשַׁמֵּשׁ חַכִּימַיָּא קְטָלָא
חַיָּיב, כֵּיצַד, (אָמְרוּ:) מַעֲשֶׂה בְּאָדָם אֶחָד מִבֵּית רָמָה שֶׁהָיָה נוֹהֵג בְּעַצְמוֹ
מִדַּת חֲסִידוּת.[84] שָׁלַח אֵלָיו תַּלְמִיד אֶחָד רַבָּן יוֹחָנָן בֶּן זַכַּאי לְבוֹדְקוֹ.
הָלַךְ וּמְצָאוֹ שֶׁנָּטַל שֶׁמֶן וּנְתָנוֹ עַל גַּבֵּי כִּירַיִם וּנְטָלוֹ מֵעַל הַכִּירַיִם וּנְתָנוֹ

---

fame loses his reputation; וּדְלָא מְשַׁמֵּשׁ חַכִּימַיָּא קְטָלָא חַיָּיב — (ii) **he who does not serve** Torah **scholars** to learn from them **deserves death;** וּדְלָא מוֹסִיף פָּסִיד — (iii) **he who does not increase** his Torah learning **loses it;** וּדְיִשְׁתַּמֵּשׁ בְּתָגָא אָבַד וְאָזִיל לֵיהּ — (iv) **and he who exploits the crown** for personal gain **shall fade away.**

The Baraisa expounds each of these sayings. The first saying: נָגֵד שְׁמָא אָבַד שְׁמֵיהּ, כֵּיצַד — **"He who seeks fame loses his reputation"** — **how so?** מְלַמֵּד שֶׁלֹּא יוֹצִיא לוֹ לָאָדָם שֵׁם בַּמְּדִינָה — This teaches that a person **should not make for himself in the province**[82] **a reputation** of wealth. שֶׁכֵּיוָן שֶׁיּוֹצִיא לוֹ שֵׁם בַּמְּדִינָה — For once a person makes for himself **in the province a reputation** of wealth, סוֹף שֶׁנּוֹתְנִין בּוֹ עֵינֵיהֶם וְהוֹרְגִין אוֹתוֹ — **[the authorities] will eventually set their sights upon him, kill him,** וְנוֹטְלִין מִמֶּנּוּ אֶת מָמוֹנוֹ — and take away all of his money. It is best, then, to keep a low profile and remain inconspicuous.

The second saying: וּדְלָא מְשַׁמֵּשׁ חַכִּימַיָּא קְטָלָא חַיָּיב, כֵּיצַד — **"He who does not serve** Torah **scholars** to learn from them **deserves death"** — **how so?** אָמְרוּ: מַעֲשֶׂה בְּאָדָם אֶחָד מִבֵּית רָמָה שֶׁהָיָה נוֹהֵג בְּעַצְמוֹ מִדַּת חֲסִידוּת — **They said: It once happened that there was a man from Beis Rimah who used to conduct himself with exceptional piety.** שָׁלַח אֵלָיו תַּלְמִיד אֶחָד רַבָּן יוֹחָנָן בֶּן זַכַּאי לְבוֹדְקוֹ — **R' Yochanan ben Zakkai** heard about him and **sent one of his disciples**[83] to investigate him to see if he was as scholarly as he was pious.[84] הָלַךְ וּמְצָאוֹ שֶׁנָּטַל שֶׁמֶן וּנְתָנוֹ עַל גַּבֵּי כִּירַיִם — **[The disciple] went** to the man's house, **and saw that he took** terumah **oil and placed it on top of the stove** to heat up. וּנְטָלוֹ מֵעַל הַכִּירַיִם וּנְתָנוֹ

---

for every Jew, scholarly and unlearned alike, Hillel said them in the vernacular (Binyan Yehoshua, from Midrash Shmuel [to Avos 5:23]).

82. [Most other texts have בַּמַּלְכוּת, in the government, instead of בַּמְּדִינָה, in the province.]

83. Magen Avos, Ahavas Chesed (see also Avos DeRabbi Nassan, Nusach 2, Ch. 27).

[Alternatively, the Baraisa means that R' Yochanan ben Zakkai was the disciple, and Hillel, his teacher, sent him (Ben Avraham).]

84. Magen Avos.

[This Sage was concerned because a pious ignoramus poses a great threat to the community, as his piety may lead others to believe that he is also a scholar and

לְתוֹךְ שֶׁל גְּרִיסִין. אָמַר לוֹ: מָה אַתָּה עוֹשֶׂה, אָמַר לוֹ: כֹּהֵן גָּדוֹל [86] אֲנִי
וּתְרוּמָה בְּטָהֳרָה אֲנִי אוֹכֵל. אָמַר לוֹ: כִּירַיִם זֶה טָמֵא אוֹ טָהוֹר. אָמַר לוֹ:
וְכִי יֵשׁ לָנוּ בַּתּוֹרָה עַל כִּירַיִם שֶׁטָּמֵא, וַהֲלֹא לֹא אָמְרָה תוֹרָה אֶלָּא עַל
תַּנּוּר שֶׁטָּמֵא, שֶׁנֶּאֱמַר (ויקרא יא, לג) "כֹּל אֲשֶׁר בְּתוֹכוֹ יִטְמָא" [87]. אָמַר לוֹ:
כְּשֵׁם שֶׁאָמְרָה תוֹרָה עַל תַּנּוּר שֶׁטָּמֵא כָּךְ אָמְרָה תוֹרָה עַל כִּירַיִם שֶׁטָּמֵא,
שֶׁנֶּאֱמַר (שם פסוק לד) "תַּנּוּר וְכִירַיִם יֻתָּץ טְמֵאִים הֵם". אָמַר לוֹ: אִם כֵּן

לְתוֹךְ שֶׁל גְּרִיסִין — He then took it from on top of the stove and put it into a dish of lentils. **אָמַר לוֹ: מָה אַתָּה עוֹשֶׂה** — [The disciple] asked him, "What are you doing? Why did you heat the oil on top of the stove and not in the oven,[85] where it would get hotter?" **אָמַר לוֹ: כֹּהֵן גָּדוֹל אֲנִי וּתְרוּמָה בְּטָהֳרָה אֲנִי אוֹכֵל** — He replied, "I am a prominent Kohen,[86] who must heed the strict regulations of purity prescribed for Kohanim, and I am therefore careful to **eat** *terumah* **in a pure state.** For this reason, I chose to heat it up specifically on the stove, as the oven is presently contaminated." **אָמַר לוֹ: כִּירַיִם זֶה טָמֵא אוֹ טָהוֹר** — [The disciple] then asked him, "Is this stove on which you heated the oil **contaminated or uncontaminated?**" **אָמַר לוֹ וְכִי יֵשׁ לָנוּ בַּתּוֹרָה עַל כִּירַיִם שֶׁטָּמֵא** — He replied to him, "Is there any mention in the Torah of a stove becoming contaminated? **וַהֲלֹא לֹא אָמְרָה תוֹרָה אֶלָּא עַל תַּנּוּר שֶׁטָּמֵא** — Why, the Torah speaks only about an oven becoming contaminated, **שֶׁנֶּאֱמַר "כֹּל אֲשֶׁר בְּתוֹכוֹ יִטְמָא"** — as it is stated, *Any earthenware utensil into whose interior one of them will fall, everything in it shall become contaminated"* (Leviticus 11:33).[87] **אָמַר לוֹ: כְּשֵׁם שֶׁאָמְרָה תוֹרָה עַל תַּנּוּר שֶׁטָּמֵא כָּךְ אָמְרָה תוֹרָה עַל כִּירַיִם שֶׁטָּמֵא** — [The disciple] said to him, "That is incorrect! For **just as the Torah speaks about an oven becoming contaminated, so does the Torah speak about a stove becoming contaminated, שֶׁנֶּאֱמַר "תַּנּוּר וְכִירַיִם יֻתָּץ טְמֵאִים הֵם"** — as it is stated, *Anything upon which part of their carcass may fall shall be contaminated* — **an oven or a stove shall be smashed — they are contaminated** *and they shall remain contaminated to you"* (ibid. v. 35). **אָמַר לוֹ: אִם כֵּן**

---

then they will come to follow his misguided ways (see *Shabbos* 63a, with *Rashi* there ד״ה אל תדור).]

85. *Mefaresh, Binyan Yehoshua.* [תַּנּוּר, oven, refers to a large cooking unit that tapers at the top; it is used as an oven rather than as a stovetop. כִּירָה, stove, refers to a smaller, cylindrical unit used as a stovetop.]

86. See above, note 17, from *Ben Avraham.* Here, however, *Ben Avraham* takes it to mean literally "a Kohen Gadol."

87. Since the Torah speaks of the things *in* the earthenware utensil becoming contaminated, the Kohen concluded that it must be speaking about an oven, which is indeed used by placing things *in* it, as opposed to a stove, which is used by placing things *on* it [see note 85] (*Binyan Yehoshua*). [See there further, regarding how this mistaken understanding also led the Kohen to misinterpret the verse cited afterward by the disciple.]

הָיִיתָ נוֹהֵג לֹא אָכַלְתָּ תְּרוּמָה טְהוֹרָה מִיָּמֶיךָ. וּדְלָא מוֹסִיף פָּסִיד, כֵּיצַד,
מְלַמֵּד שֶׁאִם שָׁנָה אָדָם מַסֶּכְתָּא אוֹ שְׁתַּיִם אוֹ שָׁלֹשׁ מַסֶּכְתּוֹת וְאֵין מוֹסִיף
עֲלֵיהֶם סוֹף שֶׁמְּשַׁכֵּחַ אֶת הָרִאשׁוֹנוֹת.[89] וּדְאִשְׁתַּמֵּשׁ בְּתָגָא אָבַד וְאָזֵיל
לֵיהּ, כֵּיצַד, שֶׁכָּל הַמִּשְׁתַּמֵּשׁ בַּשֵּׁם הַמְפוֹרָשׁ אֵין לוֹ חֵלֶק לְעוֹלָם הַבָּא:[90]

הָיִיתָ נוֹהֵג לֹא אָכַלְתָּ תְּרוּמָה טְהוֹרָה מִיָּמֶיךָ — [The disciple] **said to him** further, **"If
this is how you** have always **conducted yourself,** considering a stove impervious to *tumah,* then **you** may **have never eaten uncontaminated** *terumah* **in
your life!"** From this incident we can see how despite one's earnest piety, without proper guidance, he can make grave mistakes. For this reason, a person
who does not serve Torah scholars, so he will understand the true meaning of
the Torah's words, is deserving of severe punishment.[88]

The third saying:

וּדְלָא מוֹסִיף פָּסִיד, כֵּיצַד — **"He who does not increase** his Torah learning **loses
it"** — **how so?**   מְלַמֵּד שֶׁאִם שָׁנָה אָדָם מַסֶּכְתָּא אוֹ שְׁתַּיִם אוֹ שָׁלֹשׁ מַסֶּכְתּוֹת — **This
teaches that if a person has learned one tractate or two, or** even **three,**   וְאֵין
מוֹסִיף עֲלֵיהֶם — **and does not add to them** by learning additional tractates,
סוֹף שֶׁמְּשַׁכֵּחַ אֶת הָרִאשׁוֹנוֹת — **then in the end, he will forget the original ones**
that he knew.[89]

The fourth saying:

וּדְאִשְׁתַּמֵּשׁ בְּתָגָא אָבַד וְאָזֵיל לֵיהּ, כֵּיצַד — **"And he who exploits the crown** for
personal gain **shall fade away"** — **how so?**   שֶׁכָּל הַמִּשְׁתַּמֵּשׁ בַּשֵּׁם הַמְפוֹרָשׁ אֵין
לוֹ חֵלֶק לְעוֹלָם הַבָּא — **For anyone who utilizes the Ineffable Name** of God for
his own purposes — he exploits God's "crown" — **has no portion in the World
to Come!**[90]

---

88. *Magen Avos.*

89. The Torah's various parts are all interconnected, so when one studies only a few
of them, he has probably not seen all the
pertinent material on any of the topics he
has studied, and without a full picture of
those topics, he will not retain them for long.
Alternatively, by stopping to increase his
Torah knowledge he has separated himself
from the Torah, and as a result, he no longer
merits Divine assistance to remember what
he has already studied (see *Binyan Yehoshua,* two approaches).

90. The Baraisa would seem to refer to
producing miraculous results through uttering or writing the Ineffable Name (see,
for example, *Succah* 53a-b). Doing so for
personal benefit is like misusing the king's

private seal [or his "crown"] for personal
use — a crime that is surely punishable by
death [and in the case of our Divine King
— *eternal* death] (*Binyan Yehoshua,* citing
Sefer HaIkkarim).

[*Meiri* to *Avos* 1:13 cites our Baraisa as
one explanation of "exploiting the crown,"
but concludes that the primary explanation
is that it refers to having oneself served by
a Torah scholar, who is by definition the
"crown" and glory of the place in which
he lives. Perhaps *Meiri* understood that our
Baraisa means its definition only as an *additional* explanation. Alternatively, he understood the Baraisa to mean that exploiting a
Torah scholar is tantamount to exploiting
the Ineffable Name itself! (see *Pesachim* 22b
et al.).]

❧ פֶּרֶק יג ❧

א. שַׁמַּאי אוֹמֵר: עֲשֵׂה תוֹרָתְךָ קֶבַע. אֱמוֹר מְעַט וַעֲשֵׂה הַרְבֵּה. וֶהֱוֵי מְקַבֵּל אֶת כָּל הָאָדָם בְּסֵבֶר פָּנִים יָפוֹת:

ב. עֲשֵׂה תוֹרָתְךָ קֶבַע, כֵּיצַד, מְלַמֵּד שֶׁאִם שָׁמַע אָדָם דָּבָר מִפִּי חָכָם בְּבֵית הַמִּדְרָשׁ אַל יַעֲשֶׂה אוֹתוֹ עֲרַאי אֶלָּא יַעֲשֶׂה אוֹתוֹ קֶבַע.[1] וּמַה שֶׁלָּמַד אָדָם יַעֲשֶׂה וִילַמֵּד לַאֲחֵרִים וְיַעֲשׂוּ[3], שֶׁנֶּאֱמַר (דברים ה, א) "וּלְמַדְתֶּם אֹתָם וּשְׁמַרְתֶּם לַעֲשֹׂתָם". וְכֵן בְּעֶזְרָא הוּא אוֹמֵר (עזרא ז, י) "כִּי עֶזְרָא הֵכִין (אֶת) לְבָבוֹ לִדְרוֹשׁ אֶת תּוֹרַת ה' וְלַעֲשֹׂת", וְאַחַר כָּךְ

❧ CHAPTER 13 ❧

§1 This chapter cites and elaborates the teachings of *Avos* 1:15, which states: שַׁמַּאי אוֹמֵר: עֲשֵׂה תוֹרָתְךָ קֶבַע — Shammai says: Make your Torah fixed; אֱמוֹר מְעַט וַעֲשֵׂה הַרְבֵּה — say little and do much; וֶהֱוֵי מְקַבֵּל אֶת כָּל הָאָדָם — and receive everyone with a cheerful face. בְּסֵבֶר פָּנִים יָפוֹת

§2 The Baraisa expounds each of Shammai's sayings: עֲשֵׂה תוֹרָתְךָ קֶבַע, כֵּיצַד — "Make your Torah fixed" — how so? מְלַמֵּד שֶׁאִם שָׁמַע אָדָם דָּבָר מִפִּי חָכָם בְּבֵית הַמִּדְרָשׁ — This teaches that if a person hears a Torah thought from the mouth of a Torah scholar in the study hall, אַל יַעֲשֶׂה אוֹתוֹ עֲרַאי — he should not treat it as something temporary; אֶלָּא יַעֲשֶׂה אוֹתוֹ קֶבַע — rather, he should treat it as something permanent.[1]

An additional implication of "make your Torah fixed":[2] וּמַה שֶׁלָּמַד אָדָם יַעֲשֶׂה — Furthermore, whatever a person learns through his Torah study he should practice, וִילַמֵּד לַאֲחֵרִים וְיַעֲשׂוּ — and he should teach others so they should practice what they learn,[3] שֶׁנֶּאֱמַר — as it is stated, "וּלְמַדְתֶּם אֹתָם וּשְׁמַרְתֶּם לַעֲשֹׂתָם" *Moses called all of Israel and said to them: Hear, O Israel, the decrees and the ordinances that I speak in your ears today; **learn them, and be careful to perform them*** (Deuteronomy 5:1). וְכֵן בְּעֶזְרָא הוּא אוֹמֵר "כִּי עֶזְרָא הֵכִין לְבָבוֹ לִדְרוֹשׁ אֶת תּוֹרַת ה' וְלַעֲשֹׂת" — And similarly, regarding Ezra, it first says, *For Ezra set his heart to expound the Torah of HASHEM and to fulfill [it]* (Ezra 7:10), וְאַחַר כָּךְ

---

1. By reviewing it repeatedly, and thereby ensuring that it will be firmly implanted in his heart (*Binyan Yehoshua*). Indeed, the Gemara tells of many Sages who, upon hearing a new Torah thought, would immediately review it forty times [see, for example, *Berachos* 28a] (*Kisei Rachamim*).

2. *Ahavas Chesed.*

3. One should learn Torah with the intent of understanding how to properly practice its laws. He should also teach this fundamental approach to others — that they should learn in order to do (*Binyan Yehoshua*, second approach).

(‏שם‏) ‏"וּלְלַמֵּד בְּיִשְׂרָאֵל חֹק וּמִשְׁפָּט"‏^{4,5}:

ג. ‏אֱמוֹר מְעַט וַעֲשֵׂה הַרְבֵּה, כֵּיצַד, מְלַמֵּד שֶׁהַצַּדִּיקִים אוֹמְרִים מְעַט‏ ‏וְעוֹשִׂים הַרְבֵּה‏⁶ ‏אֲבָל רְשָׁעִים אוֹמְרִים הַרְבֵּה וַאֲפִילּוּ מְעַט אֵינָם‏ ‏עוֹשִׂים. וּמִנַּיִין שֶׁהַצַּדִּיקִים אוֹמְרִים מְעַט וְעוֹשִׁין הַרְבֵּה, שֶׁכֵּן מָצִינוּ‏ ‏בְּאַבְרָהָם אָבִינוּ שֶׁאָמַר לַמַּלְאָכִים: פַּת אַתֶּם סוֹעֲדִים עִמִּי הַיּוֹם,‏ ‏שֶׁנֶּאֱמַר‏ (‏בראשית יח, ה‏) ‏"וְאֶקְחָה פַת לֶחֶם וְסַעֲדוּ לִבְּכֶם", אֲבָל בָּאַחֲרוֹנָה‏ ‏רְאֵה מַה עָשָׂה אַבְרָהָם לְמַלְאֲכֵי הַשָּׁרֵת, שֶׁהָלַךְ וְעָשָׂה לָהֶם שְׁלֹשָׁה‏

‏"וּלְלַמֵּד בְּיִשְׂרָאֵל חֹק וּמִשְׁפָּט"‏ — and afterward it says, *and to teach [its] statute and law in Israel* (ibid.).[4] Accordingly, "make your Torah fixed" means that one should study Torah with plans to implement ("fix") it into his life.[5]

§3 The Baraisa expounds Shammai's second saying:

‏אֱמוֹר מְעַט וַעֲשֵׂה הַרְבֵּה, כֵּיצַד‏ — "Say little and do much" — how so? ‏מְלַמֵּד שֶׁהַצַּדִּיקִים אוֹמְרִים מְעַט וְעוֹשִׂים הַרְבֵּה‏ — This teaches that the way of the righteous is to **say** and promise **little, and to do much** in practice, in excess of what they committed to do.[6] ‏אֲבָל רְשָׁעִים אוֹמְרִים הַרְבֵּה וַאֲפִילּוּ מְעַט אֵינָם‏ ‏עוֹשִׂים‏ — The wicked, however, **say** and promise **much, but do not do** even a **little**, failing to fulfill even a fraction of their exaggerated commitments. ‏וּמִנַּיִין‏ ‏שֶׁהַצַּדִּיקִים אוֹמְרִים מְעַט וְעוֹשִׁין הַרְבֵּה‏ — From where do we know **that the righteous say little and do much?** ‏שֶׁכֵּן מָצִינוּ בְּאַבְרָהָם אָבִינוּ‏ — For thus do we find in the case of **our patriarch Abraham,** ‏שֶׁאָמַר לַמַּלְאָכִים: פַּת אַתֶּם סוֹעֲדִים‏ ‏עִמִּי הַיּוֹם‏ — who said to the angels disguised as guests, "You will favor me and eat a meal of bread with me today," ‏שֶׁנֶּאֱמַר "וְאֶקְחָה פַת לֶחֶם וְסַעֲדוּ לִבְּכֶם"‏ — as it is stated, *I will fetch a morsel of bread that you may sustain yourselves, then go on* (Genesis 18:5), implying that he would offer them only some bread. ‏אֲבָל בָּאַחֲרוֹנָה רְאֵה מַה עָשָׂה אַבְרָהָם לְמַלְאֲכֵי הַשָּׁרֵת‏ — But in the end, see what Abraham did for the ministering angels! ‏שֶׁהָלַךְ וְעָשָׂה לָהֶם שְׁלֹשָׁה‏

---

4. The *Deuteronomy* verse supports the statement that one should learn the Torah's words in order that he may be "careful to perform them." The *Ezra* verse shows that after studying the Torah and practicing it by himself, Ezra then went and taught the rest of the Jewish people to do the same (see *Binyan Yehoshua*).

5. It would seem that according to *Rambam* and *Meiri* (to *Avos* ad loc.), our Baraisa speaks of *additional* implications of the dictum "make your Torah fixed." The fundamental meaning, however, is

that one's Torah should be the *primary* focus of his life; pursuit of one's livelihood should be secondary. According to *Machzor Vitri* (*Avos* ad loc.), it means that one must designate fixed times in the day for Torah study. Otherwise, the demands of one's daily cares will lead him to neglect Torah study.

6. They promise little, so that the beneficiary will not be reluctant to impose upon them. Once their offer is accepted, however, they give far more (*Binyan Yehoshua,* from *Yefeh To'ar*).

שְׁוֹורִים וְתֵשַׁע סְאִין⁷ שֶׁל סוֹלֶת. וּמִנַּיִן שֶׁעָשָׂה לָהֶם תֵּשַׁע סְאִין שֶׁל
סוֹלֶת, שֶׁנֶּאֱמַר (שם פסוק ו) "וַיְמַהֵר אַבְרָהָם הָאֹהֱלָה אֶל שָׂרָה וַיֹּאמֶר
מַהֲרִי שְׁלֹשׁ סְאִים קֶמַח סֹלֶת". "שְׁלֹשׁ" כְּמַשְׁמָעָן. "קֶמַח" הֲרֵי שֵׁשׁ.
"סֹלֶת" הֲרֵי תֵשַׁע⁸. וּמִנַּיִן שֶׁעָשָׂה לָהֶם שְׁלֹשָׁה שְׁוָרִים, שֶׁנֶּאֱמַר
(שם פסוק ז) "וְאֶל הַבָּקָר רָץ אַבְרָהָם". "הַבָּקָר" אֶחָד. "בֶּן בָּקָר"
שְׁנַיִם. "רַךְ" שְׁלֹשָׁה. וְיֵשׁ אוֹמְרִים: "וָטוֹב" אַרְבָּעָה⁹. "וַיִּתֵּן אֶל הַנַּעַר
וַיְמַהֵר לַעֲשׂוֹת אֹתוֹ" (שם), נָתַן בְּיַד יִשְׁמָעֵאל בְּנוֹ כְּדֵי לְחַנְּכוֹ בְּמִצְוֹת.

שְׁוָרִים וְתֵשַׁע סְאִין שֶׁל סוֹלֶת — He went and prepared for them a grand feast of **three oxen and** bread made from **nine se'ahs**[7] of fine flour, which is far more than could be eaten by three guests. וּמִנַּיִן שֶׁעָשָׂה לָהֶם תֵּשַׁע סְאִין שֶׁל סוֹלֶת — **And how do we know that he prepared for them** bread made from **nine se'ahs of fine flour?** שֶׁנֶּאֱמַר "וַיְמַהֵר אַבְרָהָם הָאֹהֱלָה אֶל שָׂרָה וַיֹּאמֶר מַהֲרִי שְׁלֹשׁ סְאִים קֶמַח סֹלֶת" — For it is stated, *So Abraham hastened to the tent to Sarah and said, "Hurry! Three se'ahs of meal, fine flour!"* (ibid. v. 6). "שְׁלֹשׁ" כְּמַשְׁמָעָן — The Baraisa expounds the verse: This gives you *three se'ahs* of flour **from the plain meaning** of the verse; "קֶמַח" הֲרֵי שֵׁשׁ — *meal* alludes to three more, making **six**; "סֹלֶת" הֲרֵי תֵשַׁע — and *fine flour* alludes to yet another three, for a total of nine.[8] וּמִנַּיִן שֶׁעָשָׂה לָהֶם שְׁלֹשָׁה שְׁוָרִים — **And how do we know that he prepared for them three oxen?** שֶׁנֶּאֱמַר "וְאֶל הַבָּקָר רָץ אַבְרָהָם" — For it is stated, *Then Abraham ran to the cattle, took a calf, tender and good* (ibid. v. 7), which is expounded as follows: "הַבָּקָר" אֶחָד "בֶּן בָּקָר" שְׁנַיִם "רַךְ" שְׁלֹשָׁה — *cattle* is **one** ox; *a calf* implies **a second**; and *tender* implies **a third.** וְיֵשׁ אוֹמְרִים: "וָטוֹב" אַרְבָּעָה — **And some say** that *good* implies **a fourth.**[9] Here we have a clear example of how a righteous person spoke of his intent to do a modest deed (serve a morsel of bread), and in the end performed a much greater one.

The Baraisa explains the next part of the verse just cited:
"וַיִּתֵּן אֶל הַנַּעַר וַיְמַהֵר לַעֲשׂוֹת אֹתוֹ" — **The verse continues, and [he] gave it to the youth who hurried to prepare it** (ibid.). Why did Abraham delegate this part of the mitzvah? נָתַן בְּיַד יִשְׁמָעֵאל בְּנוֹ כְּדֵי לְחַנְּכוֹ בְּמִצְוֹת — **He gave** it into **the hands of his son Ishmael in order to train him** while still young **in the performance of mitzvos,** such as welcoming guests.

---

7. A se'ah is the volume of 144 eggs.

8. Since Abraham concluded his words by saying, *knead and make cakes*, it was understood that the three se'ahs were to be of flour. Therefore, the Baraisa interprets each of the extra two terms, *meal* and *fine flour*,

as alluding to an *additional* three se'ahs (see *Ben Avraham*).

9. Although *tender* and *good* are both adjectives, and could very well be describing the same animal, nevertheless, since each of the other terms was interpreted as alluding

אַף הַקָּדוֹשׁ בָּרוּךְ הוּא אָמַר מְעַט וְעָשָׂה הַרְבֵּה, שֶׁנֶּאֱמַר (שם טו, יג-יד)
"וַיֹּאמֶר לְאַבְרָם יָדֹעַ תֵּדַע כִּי גֵר יִהְיֶה זַרְעֲךָ בְּאֶרֶץ לֹא לָהֶם וַעֲבָדוּם וְעִנּוּ
אֹתָם אַרְבַּע מֵאוֹת שָׁנָה וְגַם אֶת הַגּוֹי אֲשֶׁר יַעֲבֹדוּ דָּן אָנֹכִי וְאַחֲרֵי כֵן יֵצְאוּ
בִּרְכֻשׁ גָּדוֹל". לֹא אָמַר לוֹ אֶלָּא בְּדָלֵי"ת וְנוּ"ן אֲבָל בָּאַחֲרוֹנָה כְּשֶׁפָּרַע
הַקָּדוֹשׁ בָּרוּךְ הוּא מִשּׂוֹנְאֵיהֶם שֶׁל יִשְׂרָאֵל לֹא פָּרַע אֶלָּא בְּשִׁבְעִים וּשְׁתַּיִם
אוֹתִיּוֹת, שֶׁנֶּאֱמַר (דברים ד, לד) "אוֹ הֲנִסָּה אֱלֹהִים לָבוֹא לָקַחַת לוֹ גוֹי מִקֶּרֶב
גּוֹי בְּמַסֹּת בְּאֹתֹת וּבְמוֹפְתִים ... וּבְמוֹרָאִים גְּדֹלִים". הָא לָמַדְתָּ כְּשֶׁנִּפְרַע
בְּשׂוֹנְאֵיהֶם שֶׁל יִשְׂרָאֵל לֹא נִפְרַע אֶלָּא בְּשִׁבְעִים וּשְׁתַּיִם אוֹתִיּוֹת.[10]

The Baraisa brings another proof that the righteous say little and do much:

אַף הַקָּדוֹשׁ בָּרוּךְ הוּא אָמַר מְעַט וְעָשָׂה הַרְבֵּה — **The Holy One, Blessed is He, too, said little and did much.** שֶׁנֶּאֱמַר "וַיֹּאמֶר לְאַבְרָם יָדֹעַ תֵּדַע כִּי גֵר יִהְיֶה — **For it is stated,** *And He said to Abram, "Know with certainty that your offspring shall be aliens* זַרְעֲךָ בְּאֶרֶץ לֹא לָהֶם וַעֲבָדוּם וְעִנּוּ אֹתָם אַרְבַּע מֵאוֹת שָׁנָה — *in a land not their own — and they will serve them, and they will oppress them — four hundred years.* וְגַם אֶת הַגּוֹי אֲשֶׁר יַעֲבֹדוּ דָּן אָנֹכִי וְאַחֲרֵי כֵן יֵצְאוּ בִּרְכֻשׁ גָּדוֹל" — *But also the nation that they will serve, I shall judge* [דָּן] *and afterward they will leave with great wealth"* (ibid. 15:13-14). לֹא אָמַר לוֹ אֶלָּא בְּדָלֵי"ת וְנוּ"ן — **We have here that He said to [Abraham] in only two letters** — *dalet and nun* [דָּן] — **that he would punish those who oppress his descendants.** אֲבָל בָּאַחֲרוֹנָה כְּשֶׁפָּרַע הַקָּדוֹשׁ בָּרוּךְ הוּא מִשּׂוֹנְאֵיהֶם שֶׁל יִשְׂרָאֵל — **However, in the end, when the Holy One, Blessed is He,** actually punished the Egyptian enemies of Israel who enslaved them, לֹא פָּרַע אֶלָּא בְּשִׁבְעִים — **He punished them with no less than seventy-two letters,** וּשְׁתַּיִם אוֹתִיּוֹת שֶׁנֶּאֱמַר "אוֹ הֲנִסָּה אֱלֹהִים לָבוֹא לָקַחַת לוֹ גוֹי מִקֶּרֶב גּוֹי בְּמַסֹּת בְּאֹתֹת וּבְמוֹפְתִים ... וּבְמוֹרָאִים גְּדֹלִים" — **as it is stated,** *Or has any god ever miraculously come to take for himself a nation from amidst a nation, with challenges, with signs ... and with greatly awesome deeds* (Deuteronomy 4:34). הָא לָמַדְתָּ כְּשֶׁנִּפְרַע בְּשׂוֹנְאֵיהֶם שֶׁל יִשְׂרָאֵל לֹא נִפְרַע אֶלָּא בְּשִׁבְעִים וּשְׁתַּיִם אוֹתִיּוֹת — **From here you can learn that when He punished the enemies of Israel, He punished them with no less than seventy-two letters.**[10] Here we have clear illustration of how the Most Righteous One said little but did much.

---

to a separate animal, this opinion maintains that the term *good* should be expounded in a similar way (*Binyan Yehoshua,* from *Bava Metzia* 86b).

10. This verse (cited only in part by the Baraisa) contains seventy-two Hebrew letters, starting with לָבוֹא and ending with גְּדֹלִים. [The words that the Baraisa leaves out are: וּבְמִלְחָמָה וּבְיָד חֲזָקָה וּבִזְרֹעַ נְטוּיָה, *and with war, and with a strong hand, and with an outstretched arm.*]

Actually, there are seventy-*five* letters in

וּמִנַּיִן שֶׁהָרְשָׁעִים אוֹמְרִים הַרְבֵּה וַאֲפִילוּ מְעַט אֵינָם עוֹשִׂים, שֶׁכֵּן מָצִינוּ
בְּעֶפְרוֹן שֶׁאָמַר לְאַבְרָהָם: (בראשית כג, טו) "אֶרֶץ אַרְבַּע מֵאוֹת שֶׁקֶל כֶּסֶף".
אֲבָל בָּאַחֲרוֹנָה כְּשֶׁשָּׁקַל לוֹ אֶת הַכֶּסֶף, (שם פסוק טז) "וַיִּשְׁמַע אַבְרָהָם אֶל
עֶפְרוֹן וַיִּשְׁקֹל אַבְרָהָם לְעֶפְרֹן וְגו' "12:

The Baraisa now brings support for its statement above that the wicked act
in an opposite way:

וּמִנַּיִן שֶׁהָרְשָׁעִים אוֹמְרִים הַרְבֵּה וַאֲפִילוּ מְעַט אֵינָם עוֹשִׂים — **And from where do
we know that the wicked say much but do not do even a little?** שֶׁכֵּן
מָצִינוּ בְּעֶפְרוֹן שֶׁאָמַר לְאַבְרָהָם: "אֶרֶץ אַרְבַּע מֵאוֹת שֶׁקֶל כֶּסֶף" — **For thus do we
find in** the case of **Ephron,** who sold the Cave of Machpelah to Abraham
as a gravesite, **that** initially **he said to Abraham,** *"My lord, heed me! Land
worth four hundred silver shekels; between me and you — what is it?"*
(Genesis 23:15), implying that the value was so insignificant that he would
not request from Abraham any payment whatsoever.[11] אֲבָל בָּאַחֲרוֹנָה
כְּשֶׁשָּׁקַל לוֹ אֶת הַכֶּסֶף — **However, in the end, when [Abraham] weighed out
the money for him,** "וַיִּשְׁמַע אַבְרָהָם אֶל עֶפְרוֹן וַיִּשְׁקֹל אַבְרָהָם לְעֶפְרֹן וְגו' "
— Scripture tells us, **Abraham heeded Ephron, and Abraham weighed out
to Ephron** the price which he had mentioned in the hearing of the children
of Heth, four hundred silver shekels in negotiable currency (ibid. v. 16).[12]
Hence, the wicked Ephron promised much generosity, but did not do even
a little.

---

those words. The Midrash (Bereishis Rabbah
44 §19) asks this question, and answers
that the second word גּוֹי is not counted;
thus, we must remove three letters from the
count, leaving us with seventy-two (Ahavas
Chesed). The second word גּוֹי is not counted
because it refers to the Egyptians, whereas
the other seventy-two letters there represent
the Seventy-two-letter Name of God, and
it is not appropriate that the three letters
representing the Egyptians be associated
with the seventy-two letters representing the
Name of God (Ahavas Chesed, from Yefeh
To'ar ad loc.).
Our Baraisa (and the Midrash) mean that
whereas God promised to punish the Egyptians only with His Name alluded to by the
letters in the word דָּן, He in fact punished
them with His Seventy-two-letter Name (see
Magen Avos and Ahavas Chesed). See the
Kleinman ed. of Bereishis Rabbah there for
further elaboration.

11. Magen Avos, Ben Avraham, Avos Ha-
Rosh [Vol. 1]; see also Rashi and Rashbam
on the verse. [Our Baraisa considers this
verse a better proof of Ephron's declared
"generosity" than verse 11 there (in which
Ephron says: No, my lord; heed me! I have
given you the field ... bury your dead), since
the meaning there might be "bury your dead
— and we will discuss payment afterward"
(Magen Avos).]

12. The term negotiable currency suggests
that Ephron's insistence — which Abraham
heeded (i.e., which he perceived to be Ephron's true intent, even though Ephron had
ostensibly not meant that; Magen Avos) —
was on being paid with exceptionally large
coins, the type that would be accepted
anywhere. This made his price a great deal
higher than the land's actual worth (see
Meiri to Avos ad loc.; see also Bava Metzia
87a).

ד ‏ . וֶהֱוֵי מְקַבֵּל אֶת כָּל הָאָדָם בְּסֵבֶר פָּנִים יָפוֹת, כֵּיצַד, מְלַמֵּד שֶׁאִם נָתַן
אָדָם לַחֲבֵירוֹ כָּל מַתָּנוֹת טוֹבוֹת שֶׁבָּעוֹלָם וּפָנָיו (זְעוּמוֹת) [כְּבוּשִׁים]
בָּאָרֶץ מַעֲלֶה עָלָיו הַכָּתוּב כְּאִילוּ לֹא נָתַן לוֹ כְּלוּם.[13] אֲבָל הַמְקַבֵּל אֶת
חֲבֵירוֹ בְּסֵבֶר פָּנִים יָפוֹת אֲפִילוּ לֹא נָתַן לוֹ כְּלוּם מַעֲלֶה עָלָיו הַכָּתוּב
כְּאִילוּ נָתַן לוֹ כָּל מַתָּנוֹת טוֹבוֹת שֶׁבָּעוֹלָם:[14]

§4 The Baraisa expounds Shammai's third saying:

וֶהֱוֵי מְקַבֵּל אֶת כָּל הָאָדָם בְּסֵבֶר פָּנִים יָפוֹת, כֵּיצַד — "And receive everyone with a cheerful face" — how so? מְלַמֵּד שֶׁאִם נָתַן אָדָם לַחֲבֵירוֹ כָּל מַתָּנוֹת טוֹבוֹת שֶׁבָּעוֹלָם — This teaches that even if a person gives his friend all the fine gifts in the world, וּפָנָיו כְּבוּשִׁים בָּאָרֶץ — but with his face buried in the ground, i.e., with a downcast look on his face, מַעֲלֶה עָלָיו הַכָּתוּב כְּאִילוּ לֹא נָתַן לוֹ כְּלוּם — Scripture considers it as if he had not given him anything at all![13] אֲבָל — However, הַמְקַבֵּל אֶת חֲבֵירוֹ בְּסֵבֶר פָּנִים יָפוֹת — someone who receives his friend with a cheerful face — אֲפִילוּ לֹא נָתַן לוֹ כְּלוּם — even if he gave him nothing tangible — מַעֲלֶה עָלָיו הַכָּתוּב כְּאִילוּ נָתַן לוֹ כָּל מַתָּנוֹת טוֹבוֹת שֶׁבָּעוֹלָם — has done his friend such a great kindness that it **is considered by Scripture as if he had given him all the best gifts in the world.**[14] From here we can see the greatness of receiving others with a cheerful face, and thus, Shammai advises us to follow this practice always.

---

13. It is unusual for the Baraisa to say "Scripture considers it" without mentioning which verse it means. It would seem that this is why *Rav* (on the Mishnah ad loc.) quotes this teaching as saying simply מַעֲלִין עָלָיו כְּאִילוּ, *it is considered as if,* without the world הַכָּתוּב, *Scripture* (*Ben Avraham*). However, *Midrash Shmuel* (to the Mishnah) does present us with a verse that indicates this. Scripture states, *You shall surely give him* (your destitute fellow), *and let your heart not feel bad when you give him, for in return for this matter* [דָּבָר], *HASHEM, your God, will bless you in all your deeds and in your every undertaking* (*Deuteronomy* 15:10). In this verse, דָּבָר [lit., *matter*] can also be interpreted as *word,* and accordingly, the verse is saying that in

return for the kind *words* that accompany your charity and raise the poor man's spirit, God will bless you for your warm generosity. The implication, then, is that if one *does* let his heart feel bad, and does *not* offer gracious words when he gives the charity, then he will *not* be blessed by God. The Baraisa understands that the reason he receives no blessing must be that Scripture considers it as if he gave the poor person *nothing* at all (*Ben Avraham*).

14. The *Deuteronomy* verse [see previous note] can also be understood as saying that it is *solely* in return for the kind words spoken to a fellow that God blesses the one who offered them, irrespective of whether he gave anything else (ibid.).

❧ פֶּרֶק יד ❧

א. רַבָּן יוֹחָנָן בֶּן זַכַּאי קִבֵּל מֵהִלֵּל וּמִשַּׁמַּאי. שְׁמוֹנִים תַּלְמִידִים הָיוּ לְהִלֵּל הַזָּקֵן[1]. שְׁלֹשִׁים מֵהֶן רְאוּיִין שֶׁתִּשְׁרֶה שְׁכִינָה עֲלֵיהֶן כְּמשֶׁה רַבֵּינוּ אֶלָּא שֶׁאֵין דּוֹרָן רָאוּי לְכָךְ, שְׁלֹשִׁים מֵהֶן רְאוּיִין לְעַבֵּר שָׁנָה[2], וְעֶשְׂרִים בֵּינוֹנִיִּים[3]. גָּדוֹל שֶׁבְּכוּלָם[4] יוֹנָתָן בֶּן עוּזִּיאֵל[5], קָטָן שֶׁבְּכוּלָן רַבָּן יוֹחָנָן בֶּן זַכַּאי. וְאָמְרוּ עָלָיו עַל רַבָּן יוֹחָנָן בֶּן זַכַּאי שֶׁלֹּא הִנִּיחַ מִקְרָא וּמִשְׁנָה גְּמָרָא הֲלָכוֹת וְאַגָּדוֹת תּוֹסְפָתוֹת[6] דְּקְדּוּקֵי תוֹרָה[7] וְדִקְדּוּקֵי סוֹפְרִים[8]

❧ CHAPTER 14 ❧

§1 This chapter elaborates *Avos* 2:8-9. The Baraisa begins with an elaboration of *Avos* 2:8:

רַבָּן יוֹחָנָן בֶּן זַכַּאי קִבֵּל מֵהִלֵּל וּמִשַּׁמַּאי — "**Rabban Yochanan ben Zakkai received** the tradition **from Hillel and Shammai**": שְׁמוֹנִים תַּלְמִידִים הָיוּ לְהִלֵּל הַזָּקֵן — The Baraisa tells us about Rabban Yochanan ben Zakkai: **Hillel the Elder had eighty** primary **disciples.**[1] שְׁלֹשִׁים מֵהֶן רְאוּיִין שֶׁתִּשְׁרֶה שְׁכִינָה עֲלֵיהֶן כְּמשֶׁה רַבֵּינוּ — **The thirty** who were greatest **among them were worthy of having the Divine Presence rest upon them as it did upon our teacher Moses,** אֶלָּא שֶׁאֵין דּוֹרָן רָאוּי לְכָךְ — **but** it did not because **their generation was not worthy of it.** שְׁלֹשִׁים מֵהֶן רְאוּיִין לְעַבֵּר שָׁנָה — **The thirty** who were smallest **among them were** so scholarly that they were **qualified to declare a leap year** based on their calculations.[2] וְעֶשְׂרִים בֵּינוֹנִיִּים — **And** the remaining **twenty** ranked **in between.**[3] גָּדוֹל שֶׁבְּכוּלָם יוֹנָתָן בֶּן עוּזִּיאֵל — **The greatest of them all**[4] was Yonasan ben Uzziel,[5] קָטָן שֶׁבְּכוּלָן רַבָּן יוֹחָנָן בֶּן זַכַּאי — **and the smallest of them all was Rabban Yochanan ben Zakkai.** וְאָמְרוּ עָלָיו עַל רַבָּן יוֹחָנָן בֶּן זַכַּאי — **They said of Rabban Yochanan ben Zakkai** שֶׁלֹּא הִנִּיחַ מִקְרָא וּמִשְׁנָה — that he was so great a scholar that **he did not leave** unmastered any part of **Scripture, Mishnah,** גְּמָרָא הֲלָכוֹת וְאַגָּדוֹת תּוֹסְפָתוֹת — **Gemara, Halachos, Aggados, *Toseftos*,**[6] דְּקְדּוּקֵי תוֹרָה וְדִקְדּוּקֵי סוֹפְרִים

---

1. Hillel had thousands of disciples, but these were his primary ones (*Ben Avraham*, from *Kuzari* 3:65).

2. Being so skilled in such a complex area of Torah testifies to their great Torah scholarship.

3. They were less great than the first thirty, but greater than the second thirty.

4. Of those twenty intermediate disciples (*Rabbeinu Gershom* to *Bava Basra* 134a). Alternatively, of all eighty of Hillel's primary

disciples (see *Ritva* ad loc.).

5. The famed author of the Targum on the Books of the Prophets (*Megillah* 3a).

6. ["Gemara" are the teachings that explain the Mishnah.] Halachos are the laws that are not alluded to in the Written Torah, but were taught to Moses at Sinai and transmitted orally through the generations (*Rashi* to *Succah* 28a). Aggados are the Midrashim [that expound the Torah homiletically,] such as *Midrash Rabbah* and *Midrash Tanchuma*

וְכָל הַמִּדּוֹת שֶׁל חֲכָמִים[9] וְכָל דָּבָר וְדָבָר שֶׁבַּתּוֹרָה[10] לֹא הִנִּיחַ שֶׁלֹּא לָמַד,
לְקַיֵּם מַה שֶּׁנֶּאֱמַר (משלי ח, כא) "לְהַנְחִיל אֹהֲבַי יֵשׁ וְאֹצְרֹתֵיהֶם אֲמַלֵּא"[12]:

ב. הוּא הָיָה אוֹמֵר: אִם עָשִׂיתָ תּוֹרָתְךָ הַרְבֵּה[13] אַל תַּחֲזִיק טוֹבָה לְעַצְמְךָ כִּי
לְכָךְ נוֹצָרְתָּ. לְפִי שֶׁלֹּא נוֹצְרוּ הַבְּרִיּוֹת אֶלָּא עַל מְנָת שֶׁיִּתְעַסְּקוּ בַּתּוֹרָה[14]:

וְכָל הַמִּדּוֹת שֶׁל חֲכָמִים — Scriptural exactitudes,[7] Rabbinic exactitudes,[8] and
all the rules of the Sages[9] — וְכָל דָּבָר וְדָבָר שֶׁבַּתּוֹרָה לֹא הִנִּיחַ שֶׁלֹּא לָמַד — not
one matter in the Torah[10] did he neglect and not study. לְקַיֵּם מַה שֶּׁנֶּאֱמַר
"לְהַנְחִיל אֹהֲבַי יֵשׁ וְאֹצְרֹתֵיהֶם אֲמַלֵּא" — The vast collective wisdom of Hillel's
disciples[11] served to fulfill that which is stated, *To bequeath to those who
love Me there is [enough], and I will fill their storehouses* (*Proverbs 8:21*).[12]

§2 *Avos 2:8* cites a teaching of Rabban Yochanan ben Zakkai:
הוּא הָיָה אוֹמֵר — He used to say: אִם עָשִׂיתָ תּוֹרָתְךָ הַרְבֵּה אַל תַּחֲזִיק טוֹבָה
לְעַצְמְךָ — If you have made your Torah considerable,[13] do not take credit
for yourself, כִּי לְכָךְ נוֹצָרְתָּ — because this is what you were created to do.
לְפִי שֶׁלֹּא נוֹצְרוּ הַבְּרִיּוֹת אֶלָּא עַל מְנָת שֶׁיִּתְעַסְּקוּ בַּתּוֹרָה — For people were created
only on condition that they involve themselves in Torah study and perform
its laws.[14]

(*Rashbam* to *Bava Basra 134a*). *Toseftos*
are collections of Baraisos that parallel, and
elaborate, the Mishnah.

7. These expositions, which derive laws
from the seemingly extra letters in the Torah,
are so named because they are based on
the "exactness" of "Scripture's" language,
which uses even single letters to teach laws
(*Binyan Yehoshua*).

8. I.e., safeguards enacted by the Sages to
prevent people from transgressing the laws
of the Torah. They are called Rabbinic exactitudes because the "Rabbis" made an "exact"
assessment of human behavior to determine
which safeguards are appropriate (ibid.).

9. The interpretive principles used by the
Sages to expound the words of Scripture
(*Magen Avos*, first approach). Alternatively,
the rules of ethics taught by the Sages (*Ben
Avraham*).

10. This alludes to the additional areas of
Torah wisdom listed in the Gemara [*Succah
28a, Bava Basra 134a*] (*Magen Avos*).

11. [So it would seem from *Ritva* to *Succah
28a*, referenced by *Binyan Yehoshua*.]

12. The Baraisa interprets the verse to
mean: In order to be able *to bequeath to
those who love Me the three hundred and ten
[the numerical value of יֵשׁ] worlds promised
to the righteous in the Next World (see *Uk-
tzin 3:12*), *I will fill their* mental *storehouses*
with Torah and wisdom in this world (*Magen
Avos; Rashbam* to *Bava Basra 134a*).

13. The Mishnah has this as אִם לָמַדְתָּ תּוֹרָה
הַרְבֵּה, *If you have studied much Torah.* While
one might say that the difference is simply
stylistic, many commentators explain that
the Baraisa is making a subtantive addition.
According to *Binyan Yehoshua,* the Baraisa
adds that even when one has done considerable good with the Torah he has studied,
such as by practicing its laws and raising
up many disciples, he *still* should not take
credit for himself. See also *Magen Avos,* who
explains our Baraisa in a similar vein. [Note,
however, that many Rishonim have the
Baraisa's reading (עָשִׂיתָ) in the Mishnah as
well (see *Mishnas Reuven* on *Avos* ad loc.).]

14. God made the world conditional on
Israel's acceptance and continued study and
fulfillment of the Torah; should they cease

ג. חֲמִשָּׁה תַלְמִידִים הָיוּ לוֹ לְרַבָּן יוֹחָנָן בֶּן זַכַּאי, לְכוּלָּן קָרָא לָהֶן שֵׁמוֹת.
לְאֱלִיעֶזֶר[15] בֶּן הוֹרְקָנוֹס קָרָא בּוֹר סִיד שֶׁאֵינוֹ מְאַבֵּד טִיפָּה, קַנְקַן
זְפוּתָה שֶׁמְּשַׁמֶּרֶת אֶת יֵינָהּ.[16] לִיהוֹשֻׁעַ בֶּן חֲנַנְיָה קָרָא לוֹ (קהלת ד, יב) "חוּט
הַמְשׁוּלָּשׁ לֹא בִמְהֵרָה יִנָּתֵק".[17] וּלְיוֹסֵי הַכֹּהֵן קָרָא לוֹ חָסִיד שֶׁבַּדּוֹר.[18]
°וּלְיִשְׁמָעֵאל בֶּן °חֲנַנְיָה[19] קָרָא לוֹ גָּרוּעַ בַּמִּדְבָּר שֶׁמַּחֲזֶקֶת מֵימֶיהָ.[21]

§3 The Baraisa goes on to discuss the next teaching of *Avos* 2:8 (with variations):
חֲמִשָּׁה תַלְמִידִים הָיוּ לוֹ לְרַבָּן יוֹחָנָן בֶּן זַכַּאי — **Rabban Yochanan ben Zakkai had five** primary **disciples,** לְכוּלָּן קָרָא לָהֶן שֵׁמוֹת — **and he gave** each one of them a unique **description:** לְאֱלִיעֶזֶר בֶּן הוֹרְקָנוֹס קָרָא בּוֹר סִיד שֶׁאֵינוֹ מְאַבֵּד טִיפָּה — **Eliezer**[15] **ben Hyrkanos he described as a cemented cistern that does not lose** even **one drop** to absorption, קַנְקַן זְפוּתָה שֶׁמְּשַׁמֶּרֶת אֶת יֵינָה — **and as a tarred barrel that keeps** all **its wine.**[16] לִיהוֹשֻׁעַ בֶּן חֲנַנְיָה קָרָא לוֹ "חוּט הַמְשׁוּלָּשׁ לֹא בִמְהֵרָה יִנָּתֵק" — **Yehoshua ben Chananyah he described as a *three-ply cord [that] is not easily severed* (*Ecclesiastes* 4:12).**[17] וּלְיוֹסֵי הַכֹּהֵן קָרָא לוֹ חָסִיד שֶׁבַּדּוֹר — **Yose HaKohen he described as the pious one of the generation.**[18] וּלְשִׁמְעוֹן בֶּן נְתַנְאֵל קָרָא לוֹ גָּרוּעַ בַּמִּדְבָּר שֶׁמַּחֲזֶקֶת מֵימֶיהָ — **Shimon ben Nesanel**[19] **he described as a depression in the desert floor**[20]

doing so, the world would return to nothingness (*Avodah Zarah* 3a). Therefore, a person should not view his occupation with Torah learning as something extraordinary, for it is part of his basic duty to keep the world in existence (*Binyan Yehoshua*).

In *Avos DeRabbi Nassan, Nusach* 2, Ch. 28 (cited by *Magen Avos*), the reading is: *for people were not created for frivolous matters but [for] Torah matters, as it is stated, "for it is your life and your length of days"* in the World to Come.

15. Rabban Yochanan ben Zakkai was their teacher, and therefore referred to these five Sages by their first names, without adding any honorific titles (*Rashi* to *Avos* 2:8).

16. Like a cemented cistern, he did not forget one drop of his Torah learning (*Rashi* ibid.), and like a tarred barrel, he retained every drop in its full quality, without deterioration (*Magen Avos*).

17. I.e., his mind had three elements that made it ideally suited for success in learning — a quick and clear grasp, a powerful memory, and analytical facility (*Meiri* to

Avos 2:8). Alternatively, it alludes to three exceptional attributes: he was expert in all disciplines, gave wise counsel, and had close government connections (*Binyan Yehoshua*).

18. A *chassid* is one who is careful to go beyond the letter of the law (*Binyan Yehoshua*). Alternatively, it refers to the most complete refinement of character (*Meiri* to *Avos* ad loc.).

19. The standard texts of *Avos DeRabbi Nassan* have here יִשְׁמָעֵאל בֶּן חֲנַנְיָה, *Yishmael ben Chananyah,* but many commentators emend the text to שִׁמְעוֹן בֶּן נְתַנְאֵל, *Shimon ben Nesanel,* to conform to the text in *Avos* 2:8 (see *Magen Avos, Hagahos HaGra, Ben Avraham,* and *Avos HaRosh* [Vol. 1]).

20. *Ben Avraham;* see also *Meiri* to *Avos* here.

Some texts have instead: עֲרוּגָה בַּמִּדְבָּר, which might be rendered "a patch (or oasis) in the desert" (see *Magen Avos;* see, however, *Ahavas Chesed,* who [based on *Aruch*] explains this reading, too, to mean "a ditch" in which water collects).

(אַשְׁרֵי תַלְמִיד שֶׁרַבּוֹ מוֹדֶה לוֹ וּמֵעִיד עָלָיו[22]). וּלְאֶלְעָזָר בֶּן עֲרָךְ
קָרָא לוֹ נַחַל שׁוֹטֵף וּמַעְיָן הַמִּתְגַּבֵּר שֶׁמֵּימָיו מִתְגַּבְּרִין וְיוֹצְאִין לַחוּץ,
לְקַיֵּים מַה שֶּׁנֶּאֱמַר (משלי ה, טז) "יָפוּצוּ מַעְיְנוֹתֶיךָ חוּצָה בָּרְחֹבוֹת פַּלְגֵי
מָיִם"[23]:

that retains its water.[21]   אַשְׁרֵי תַלְמִיד שֶׁרַבּוֹ מוֹדֶה לוֹ וּמֵעִיד עָלָיו — Fortunate is the disciple whose teacher acknowledges him and testifies about
him.[22]   וּלְאֶלְעָזָר בֶּן עֲרָךְ קָרָא לוֹ נַחַל שׁוֹטֵף — And Elazar ben Arach he
described as a rushing stream   וּמַעְיָן הַמִּתְגַּבֵּר שֶׁמֵּימָיו מִתְגַּבְּרִין וְיוֹצְאִין
לַחוּץ — and a spring that grows constantly stronger, whose waters increase
and overflow its borders,   לְקַיֵּים מַה שֶּׁנֶּאֱמַר "יָפוּצוּ מַעְיְנוֹתֶיךָ חוּצָה בָּרְחֹבוֹת
פַּלְגֵי מָיִם" — thus a fulfillment of that which is stated, [Then] your springs
will spread outward, streams of water in the thoroughfares (Proverbs
5:16).[23]

---

21. He was an outstanding receptacle for
words of Torah (Meiri ibid.), who thirsted
for them like the parched desert thirsts for
water, and absorbed every drop as does the
thirsty patch (Magen Avos).

22. One might have thought that the master's praise of Shimon ben Nesanel is less
than his praise of Eliezer ben Hyrkanos, who
"never lost a drop." The Baraisa therefore
adds that someone praised in Shimon's way
is indeed fortunate. True, he was not as great
a scholar as Eliezer, but he absorbed and
internalized all the Torah that he learned,
and was thus truly pious. The praise given
him is thus the equivalent of the alternative
version recorded in Avos — "he fears sin"
(see Magen Avos). R' Yosef ibn Aknin (on
Avos ad loc.) writes that "fear of sin" was
the source of R' Shimon's great scholarship
— he feared the sin of allowing difficulties
or complacency to interfere with further
Torah study. Therefore, he did not consider
any study of Torah wisdom too difficult to
undertake. Fortunate, then, is he, whose
master perceived and attested to the source
of his great scholarship. [Gra, however,
moves this line, "Praised is the disciple ...,"
and places it below at the end of §5, after
Rabban Yochanan ben Zakkai approves of
R' Elazar ben Arach's opinion over those of
his colleagues.]

Ben Avraham suggests a different explanation of "like a depression in the desert that retains its water." R' Shimon ben
Nesanel was not naturally pious; he became that way through great effort. What
he achieved was thus as remarkable as
a puddle in the desert, which is unnatu-
ral, as water on the desert floor is quickly
absorbed and disappears. Thus, his "fear
of sin" (as per the version in Avos — see
above) was in a sense a greater praise than
Yose the Kohen's "the pious one of the generation," for Yose was naturally disposed to
piety, whereas R' Shimon had to struggle
mightily to attain his "fear of sin."

23. That is, he is an unending source of wisdom, and his wisdom grows ever stronger,
in that his powers of analysis enable him to
mine from the wealth he received from his
teachers things that were hitherto unseen
(see Binyan Yehoshua; see also Rav and
R' Yonah to Avos ad loc.). Alternatively, the
"overflowing" refers to the spreading of his
Torah to others, as the beauty of his wisdom was studied in all places, "his springs
spreading outward, streams of water in the
thoroughfares" (Magen Avos). [According
to R' Yosef ibn Aknin (on Avos ad loc.), the
Baraisa's metaphor of "a rushing stream"
refers to the many proofs and defenses he
brought for his opinions.]

ד. הוּא הָיָה אוֹמֵר: אִם יִהְיוּ כָּל חַכְמֵי יִשְׂרָאֵל בְּכַף מֹאזְנַיִם וְרַבִּי אֱלִיעֶזֶר בֶּן הוֹרְקָנוֹס בְּכַף שְׁנִיָּיה מַכְרִיעַ אֶת כּוֹלָם. אַבָּא שָׁאוּל אוֹמֵר מִשְּׁמוֹ: אִם יִהְיוּ כָּל חַכְמֵי יִשְׂרָאֵל בְּכַף מֹאזְנַיִם וְרַבִּי אֱלִיעֶזֶר בֶּן הוֹרְקָנוֹס אַף עִמָּהֶם וְרַבִּי אֶלְעָזָר בֶּן עֲרָךְ בְּכַף שְׁנִיָּה מַכְרִיעַ אֶת כּוֹלָם:[24]

ה. אָמַר לָהֶם: צְאוּ וּרְאוּ[25] אֵיזוֹהִי דֶרֶךְ טוֹבָה שֶׁיִּדְבַּק בָּהּ הָאָדָם כְּדֵי שֶׁיִּכָּנֵס בָּהּ לָעוֹלָם הַבָּא[26]. נִכְנַס רַבִּי אֱלִיעֶזֶר וְאָמַר: עַיִן טוֹבָה.

---

§4 The Baraisa cites, without elaboration, the final part of Rabban Yochanan ben Zakkai's sayings in *Avos* 2:8:

הוּא הָיָה אוֹמֵר — **He** also **used to say:** אִם יִהְיוּ כָּל חַכְמֵי יִשְׂרָאֵל בְּכַף מֹאזְנַיִם — **If all the Sages of Israel were on one pan of a balance scale,** וְרַבִּי אֱלִיעֶזֶר בֶּן הוֹרְקָנוֹס בְּכַף שְׁנִיָּיה — **and R' Eliezer ben Hyrkanos were on the other pan,** מַכְרִיעַ אֶת כּוֹלָם — **he would outweigh them all."** אַבָּא שָׁאוּל אוֹמֵר מִשְּׁמוֹ — **Abba Shaul said in [Rabban Yochanan ben Zakkai's] name:** אִם יִהְיוּ כָּל חַכְמֵי יִשְׂרָאֵל בְּכַף מֹאזְנַיִם — **"If all the Sages of Israel were on one pan of a balance scale,** וְרַבִּי אֱלִיעֶזֶר בֶּן הוֹרְקָנוֹס אַף עִמָּהֶם — **with even R' Eliezer ben Hyrkanos among them,** וְרַבִּי אֶלְעָזָר בֶּן עֲרָךְ בְּכַף שְׁנִיָּה — **and R' Elazar ben Arach were on the other pan,** מַכְרִיעַ אֶת כּוֹלָם — **he would outweigh them all.**[24]

§5 The Baraisa cites the two questions, recorded in *Avos* 2:9 [with slight variation], that Rabban Yochanan ben Zakkai asked his five disciples to explore. The first question:

אָמַר לָהֶם: צְאוּ וּרְאוּ אֵיזוֹהִי דֶרֶךְ טוֹבָה שֶׁיִּדְבַּק בָּהּ הָאָדָם — **He said to them: Go out** of the study hall **and discern**[25] **what is the proper path to which a man should cling,** כְּדֵי שֶׁיִּכָּנֵס בָּהּ לָעוֹלָם הַבָּא — **so that through it he may** merit to **enter the World to Come.**[26] The disciples did as they were instructed and returned with their responses. נִכְנַס רַבִּי אֱלִיעֶזֶר וְאָמַר: עַיִן טוֹבָה — **R' Eliezer entered** the study hall with his reply **and said, "A good eye,"** meaning, a charitable and

---

24. Some explain that Abba Shaul and the first Tanna are not in dispute: Rabban Yochanan ben Zakkai said that each of these two disciples was greater than all the Sages (including the other one) together — R' Eliezer ben Hyrkanos in range of knowledge, and R' Elazar ben Arach in analytical reasoning (*Binyan Yehoshua* from *Rav*).

Alternatively, the first Tanna and Abba Shaul are in dispute with regard to which is greater, a "Sinai" [one who has encyclopedic mastery of all the Torah, given at Mount Sinai] or an "uprooter of mountains" [one with keen analytical skills] (see *Horayos*

14a, where this matter is debated). The first Tanna holds that Rabban Yochanan ben Zakkai considered the Sinai (and hence, R' Eliezer ben Hyrkanos) greater, whereas Abba Shaul maintains that he considered the "uprooter of mountains" (and hence, R' Elazar ben Arach) greater (*Machzor Vitri* to *Avos* ad loc.; *Mefaresh*).

25. That is, as soon as you "go out" of the study hall, turn your attention to this question (*Binyan Yehoshua*, from *Midrash Shmuel*).

26. That is, what single trait will bring a person to all other good traits (*Mefaresh*). Perfection in one area is preferable to partial success in

נִכְנַס רַבִּי יְהוֹשֻׁעַ וְאָמַר: חָבֵר טוֹב.[27] נִכְנַס רַבִּי יוֹסֵי וְאָמַר: שָׁכֵן טוֹב יֵצֶר
טוֹב וְאִשָׁה טוֹבָה.[29] רַבִּי שִׁמְעוֹן אוֹמֵר: הָרוֹאֶה אֶת הַנּוֹלָד[30] (נ"א כגון
מרדכי יהודי שראה את הנולד). נִכְנַס רַבִּי אֶלְעָזָר וְאָמַר: לֵב טוֹב
לַשָׁמַיִם וְלֵב טוֹב לַבְּרִיּוֹת.[31] אָמַר לָהֶם: רוֹאֶה אֲנִי אֶת דִּבְרֵי רַבִּי אֶלְעָזָר
בֶּן עֲרָךְ מִדִּבְרֵיכֶם שֶׁבִּכְלַל דְּבָרָיו דִּבְרֵיכֶם.[32] אָמַר לָהֶם: צְאוּ וּרְאוּ
אֵיזֶה דֶּרֶךְ רָעָה שֶׁיִּרְחַק מִמֶּנָּה הָאָדָם[33] כְּדֵי שֶׁיִּכָּנֵס בָּהּ לָעוֹלָם הַבָּא.[34]

---

kind attitude toward others.   נִכְנַס רַבִּי יְהוֹשֻׁעַ וְאָמַר: חָבֵר טוֹב — R' Yehoshua
entered and said, "A good friend."[27]   נִכְנַס רַבִּי יוֹסֵי וְאָמַר: שָׁכֵן טוֹב יֵצֶר טוֹב
וְאִשָׁה טוֹבָה — R' Yose entered and said, "A good neighbor, by which I mean[28]
a good inclination and a good wife."[29]   רַבִּי שִׁמְעוֹן אוֹמֵר: הָרוֹאֶה אֶת הַנּוֹלָד —
R' Shimon entered and said, "One who considers the outcome of a deed."[30]
נִכְנַס רַבִּי אֶלְעָזָר וְאָמַר: לֵב טוֹב לַשָׁמַיִם וְלֵב טוֹב לַבְּרִיּוֹת — R' Elazar entered and
said, "A good heart toward Heaven and a good heart toward people."[31]
אָמַר לָהֶם: רוֹאֶה אֲנִי אֶת דִּבְרֵי רַבִּי אֶלְעָזָר בֶּן עֲרָךְ מִדִּבְרֵיכֶם — [Rabban Yochanan]
said to them, "I see the superiority of R' Elazar ben Arach's words to your
words,   שֶׁבִּכְלַל דְּבָרָיו דִּבְרֵיכֶם — for all of your words are included in his
words."[32]

The second question:

אָמַר לָהֶם: צְאוּ וּרְאוּ אֵיזֶה דֶּרֶךְ רָעָה שֶׁיִּרְחַק מִמֶּנָּה הָאָדָם — He said to them further:
Go out and discern what is the bad path from which a man should distance
himself,[33]   כְּדֵי שֶׁיִּכָּנֵס בָּהּ לָעוֹלָם הַבָּא — so that by doing this he may merit

---

multiple areas, and even one perfected trait
can start a person on the road to perfecting
all of his other traits (Binyan Yehoshua, from
R' Yonah to Avos ad loc.).

27. Who is willing to offer constructive criticism and corrective advice (Meiri ibid.; Binyan Yehoshua, from Rav).

28. Magen Avos, Ben Avraham, Avos Ha-
Rosh [Vol. 1].

29. Who are always near a person, affecting
his decisions (Binyan Yehoshua).

R' Yose maintains that even better for
one's personal growth than having a good
friend, who is around only occasionally, is
having a good "neighbor," who is always
nearby, and is therefore more able to have a
positive influence (ibid., from Rashi to Avos
ad loc.).

30. This person will find it easy to follow the
Sages' advice to assess the relatively small

loss of time or money incurred by doing a
mitzvah against its everlasting reward, and
the temporary gain of committing a sin
against its eternal cost [see Avos 2:1] (Binyan Yehoshua, from Rav to Avos ad loc.).

31. That is, one who makes God's Name
beloved to others by the way he is involved
in Torah study, and how he deals with
others in a pleasant and refined manner
(Avos HaRosh [Vol. 1], based on Yoma 86a).

32. Everything in life depends on the heart
because it is home to all of the person's
emotions and strengths. Therefore, with a
good heart, one can achieve any worthwhile
goal, including all those mentioned by R'
Elazar's colleagues (Rav to Avos ad loc.).

33. This question seems perplexing: Isn't
the improper path simply the exact opposite of the correct path, which was already
discussed above? Rav (to Avos ad loc.)
explains that Rabban Yochanan wanted to

נִכְנַס רַבִּי אֱלִיעֶזֶר וְאָמַר: עַיִן רָעָה. נִכְנַס רַבִּי יְהוֹשֻׁעַ וְאָמַר: חָבֵר רָע.
נִכְנַס רַבִּי יוֹסֵי וְאָמַר: °עַיִן רָע וְשָׁכֵן רָע וְאִשָּׁה רָעָה נִכְנַס רַבִּי שִׁמְעוֹן
וְאָמַר: הַלֹּוֶה וְאֵינוֹ מְשַׁלֵּם,³⁶ שֶׁהַלֹּוֶה מִן הָאָדָם כְּלֹוֶה מִן הַמָּקוֹם, שֶׁנֶּאֱמַר
(תהלים לז, כא) "לֹוֶה רָשָׁע וְלֹא יְשַׁלֵּם וְצַדִּיק חוֹנֵן וְנוֹתֵן". נִכְנַס רַבִּי אֶלְעָזָר

to enter the World to Come.[34] Again, the disciples followed their teacher's request and returned with their responses. **נִכְנַס רַבִּי אֱלִיעֶזֶר וְאָמַר: עַיִן רָעָה** — R' Eliezer entered the study hall with his reply and said, "A bad eye," meaning, a stingy and jealous attitude toward others. **נִכְנַס רַבִּי יְהוֹשֻׁעַ וְאָמַר: חָבֵר רָע** — R' Yehoshua entered and said, "A bad friend," meaning, one who serves as a bad influence. **נִכְנַס רַבִּי יוֹסֵי וְאָמַר: יֵצֶר רָע וְשָׁכֵן רָע וְאִשָּׁה רָעָה** — R' Yose entered and said, "A bad inclination, a bad neighbor, and a bad wife."[35] **נִכְנַס רַבִּי שִׁמְעוֹן וְאָמַר: הַלֹּוֶה וְאֵינוֹ מְשַׁלֵּם** — R' Shimon entered and said, "One who borrows and does not repay,[36] **שֶׁהַלֹּוֶה מִן הָאָדָם כְּלֹוֶה מִן הַמָּקוֹם** for — one who borrows from a man is like one who borrows from God," **שֶׁנֶּאֱמַר** **"לֹוֶה רָשָׁע וְלֹא יְשַׁלֵּם וְצַדִּיק חוֹנֵן וְנוֹתֵן"** — as it is stated, *The wicked one borrows but does not repay, while the Righteous One is generous and gives* (*Psalms* 37:21), which can be understood to mean that when a wicked person does not repay his loan, then God, Who is the epitome of righteousness, graciously repays the loan in his place. Thus, the wicked person is now indebted to God Himself, as if he had borrowed directly from Him.[37] **נִכְנַס רַבִּי אֶלְעָזָר**

teach his students that while the opposite of a good trait is not necessarily a bad trait, that is not the case regarding the particular traits enumerated above. Rather, with *these* traits, the opposite of the good path is not merely neutral but bad. He therefore tested them to see if they would realize this point and indeed say the opposite of what they had responded to the first question.

34. When a person refrains from doing what is negative, he is rewarded as if he had actively done what is positive (*Kiddushin* 39b). Thus, by distancing oneself from the improper path, one has *actively* earned entry into the World to Come (*Binyan Yehoshua*).

35. We have emended the text in accordance with *Binyan Yehoshua* and *Avos HaRosh* [Vol. 1]. *Gra* emends the text further so that שָׁכֵן רָע, a bad neighbor, comes first, as in R' Yose's parallel, opposite answer above. [Accordingly, the meaning here, as above (at note 29), is that "inclination" and "wife" are what he meant by "neighbor."]

36. This is essentially the opposite of the good path that R' Shimon described above (seeing the outcome of a deed). For when one borrows and does not repay, he is closing his eyes to the consequence of his actions — that no one will lend him money in the future, and he will be without means to obtain his needs. R' Shimon did not, however, say simply, "One who does not see the outcome of a deed," because it is conceivable that someone may not have seen the outcome of his deed, and was still fortunate enough to rescue himself from the negative consequence. He therefore gave the specific example of borrowing without repaying, where the negative consequence is almost inevitable (*Binyan Yehoshua*, from *Rav* to *Avos* ad loc.).

37. *Rashi* to *Avos* ad loc., first approach. [Thus, the sin of the borrower's default on his loan is compounded by his unpaid indebtedness to God! See the commentators to *Avos* ad loc. on why this point is added.]

וְאָמַר: לֵב רַע לַשָּׁמַיִם וְלֵב רַע לַמִּצְוֹת וְלֵב רַע לַבְּרִיּוֹת.‏[38] וְאָמַר לָהֶם:
רוֹאֶה אֲנִי אֶת דִּבְרֵי רַבִּי אֶלְעָזָר מִדִּבְרֵיכֶם שֶׁבִּכְלָל דְּבָרָיו דִּבְרֵיכֶם:‏[39]

ו. כְּשֶׁמֵּת בְּנוֹ שֶׁל רַבָּן יוֹחָנָן בֶּן זַכַּאי נִכְנְסוּ תַּלְמִידָיו לְנַחֲמוֹ. נִכְנַס רַבִּי
אֱלִיעֶזֶר וְיָשַׁב לְפָנָיו וְאָמַר לוֹ: רַבִּי, רְצוֹנְךָ אוֹמֵר דָּבָר אֶחָד לְפָנֶיךָ.‏[40]
אָמַר לוֹ: אֱמוֹר. אָמַר לוֹ: אָדָם הָרִאשׁוֹן הָיָה לוֹ בֵן וּמֵת[41] וְקִבֵּל עָלָיו
תַּנְחוּמִין. וּמִנַּיִן שֶׁקִּבֵּל עָלָיו תַּנְחוּמִין, שֶׁנֶּאֱמַר (בראשית ד, כה) "וַיֵּדַע אָדָם
עוֹד אֶת אִשְׁתּוֹ".‏[42] אַף אַתָּה קַבֵּל תַּנְחוּמִין. אָמַר לוֹ: לֹא דַי לִי שֶׁאֲנִי

וְאָמַר: לֵב רַע לַשָּׁמַיִם וְלֵב רַע לַמִּצְוֹת וְלֵב רַע לַבְּרִיּוֹת — **R' Elazar entered and said, "A bad heart toward Heaven, a bad heart toward mitzvos, and a bad heart toward people."**[38] וְאָמַר לָהֶם רוֹאֶה אֲנִי אֶת דִּבְרֵי רַבִּי אֶלְעָזָר מִדִּבְרֵיכֶם — **[Rabban Yochanan] said to the other four of them, "I see the superiority of R' Elazar ben Arach's words to your words,** שֶׁבִּכְלָל דְּבָרָיו דִּבְרֵיכֶם — **for all of your words are included in his words."**[39]

§6 The Baraisa relates another incident in which Rabban Yochanan ben Zakkai preferred the words of R' Elazar ben Arach to those of the other four disciples:

כְּשֶׁמֵּת בְּנוֹ שֶׁל רַבָּן יוֹחָנָן בֶּן זַכַּאי — **When Rabban Yochanan ben Zakkai's son died,** נִכְנְסוּ תַּלְמִידָיו לְנַחֲמוֹ — **his five primary disciples entered the house of mourning to comfort him.** נִכְנַס רַבִּי אֱלִיעֶזֶר וְיָשַׁב לְפָנָיו — **R' Eliezer entered first and sat before him** וְאָמַר לוֹ: רַבִּי, רְצוֹנְךָ אוֹמֵר דָּבָר אֶחָד לְפָנֶיךָ — **and said to him, "My master, do I have permission to say something in your presence?"**[40] אָמַר לוֹ: אֱמוֹר — **He replied, "Yes, you may speak."** אָמַר לוֹ — **So [R' Eliezer] said to him, "Adam, the first man, had a son who died,**[41] **and he accepted condolences for him.** וּמִנַּיִן שֶׁקִּבֵּל עָלָיו תַּנְחוּמִין — **And how do we know that [Adam] accepted condolences for him?** שֶׁנֶּאֱמַר "וַיֵּדַע אָדָם עוֹד אֶת אִשְׁתּוֹ" — **For it is stated, Adam knew his wife again and she bore a son and named him Seth, because: 'God has provided me another child in place of Abel, for Cain had killed him' (Genesis 4:25).**[42] אַף אַתָּה קַבֵּל תַּנְחוּמִין — **So too should you accept condolences and be comforted."** אָמַר לוֹ: לֹא דַי לִי שֶׁאֲנִי

---

38. That is, he transgresses the negative commandments ["toward Heaven"], neglects to fulfill the positive commandments ["toward mitzvos"] (*Binyan Yehoshua*), and deals with his fellow people in an unfriendly way ["toward people"].

39. See above, note 32.

40. Those coming to comfort a mourner are

not permitted to speak before the mourner opens the discussion [see *Moed Katan* 28b] or gives them permission to speak (*Magen Avos*; *Ben Avraham*, second approach).

41. Namely, Abel, who was killed by Adam's other son, Cain (see *Genesis* 4:8).

42. The verse implies that Adam and his wife finally found consolation over the death

מִצְטַעֵר בְּעַצְמִי אֶלָּא שֶׁהִזְכַּרְתָּ לִי צַעֲרוֹ שֶׁל אָדָם הָרִאשׁוֹן. נִכְנַס רַבִּי
יְהוֹשֻׁעַ וְאָמַר לוֹ: רְצוֹנְךָ אוֹמַר דָּבָר אֶחָד לְפָנֶיךָ. אָמַר לוֹ: אֱמוֹר. אָמַר לוֹ:
אִיּוֹב הָיוּ לוֹ בָּנִים וּבָנוֹת וּמֵתוּ כּוּלָּם בְּיוֹם אֶחָד[43] וְקִבֵּל עֲלֵיהֶם תַּנְחוּמִין.
אַף אַתָּה קַבֵּל תַּנְחוּמִין. וּמִנַּיִן שֶׁקִּבֵּל אִיּוֹב תַּנְחוּמִין, שֶׁנֶּאֱמַר (איוב א, כא)
"ה' נָתַן וַה' לָקַח יְהִי שֵׁם ה' מְבֹרָךְ". אָמַר לוֹ: לֹא דַי לִי שֶׁאֲנִי מִצְטַעֵר
בְּעַצְמִי אֶלָּא שֶׁהִזְכַּרְתָּ לִי צַעֲרוֹ שֶׁל אִיּוֹב. נִכְנַס רַבִּי יוֹסֵי וְיָשַׁב לְפָנָיו,
אָמַר לוֹ: רַבִּי, רְצוֹנְךָ אוֹמַר דָּבָר אֶחָד לְפָנֶיךָ. אָמַר לוֹ: אֱמוֹר. אָמַר לוֹ:
אַהֲרֹן הָיוּ לוֹ שְׁנֵי בָנִים גְּדוֹלִים וּמֵתוּ שְׁנֵיהֶם בְּיוֹם אֶחָד[44] וְקִבֵּל עֲלֵיהֶם
תַּנְחוּמִין, שֶׁנֶּאֱמַר (ויקרא י, ג) "וַיִּדֹּם אַהֲרֹן", אֵין שְׁתִיקָה אֶלָּא תַּנְחוּמִין.

מִצְטַעֵר בְּעַצְמִי — [Rabban Yochanan] said to him, "Is it not enough for me that I am suffering with my own pain, אֶלָּא שֶׁהִזְכַּרְתָּ לִי צַעֲרוֹ שֶׁל אָדָם הָרִאשׁוֹן — but you had to remind me of the pain of Adam, the first man, too?!"

The second disciple's attempt:

נִכְנַס רַבִּי יְהוֹשֻׁעַ וְאָמַר לוֹ: רְצוֹנְךָ אוֹמַר דָּבָר אֶחָד לְפָנֶיךָ — R' Yehoshua then entered and said to him, "My master, do I have permission to say something in your presence?" אָמַר לוֹ: אֱמוֹר — He replied, "Yes, you may speak." אָמַר לוֹ: אִיּוֹב הָיוּ לוֹ בָּנִים וּבָנוֹת וּמֵתוּ כּוּלָּם בְּיוֹם אֶחָד — So [R' Yehoshua] said to him, "Job had many sons and daughters, who all died on the same day,[43] וְקִבֵּל עֲלֵיהֶם and he accepted condolences for them. תַּנְחוּמִין — So too should you accept condolences and be comforted. וּמִנַּיִן שֶׁקִּבֵּל אִיּוֹב — And how do we know that Job accepted condolences for them? תַּנְחוּמִין שֶׁנֶּאֱמַר "ה' נָתַן וַה' לָקַח יְהִי שֵׁם ה' מְבֹרָךְ" — For it is stated, *Job said, '...HASHEM has given, and HASHEM has taken away, blessed be the Name of HASHEM'* (*Job* 1:21). אָמַר לוֹ: לֹא דַי לִי שֶׁאֲנִי מִצְטַעֵר בְּעַצְמִי — [Rabban Yochanan] said to him, "Is it not enough for me that I am suffering with my own pain, אֶלָּא שֶׁהִזְכַּרְתָּ לִי צַעֲרוֹ שֶׁל אִיּוֹב — but you had to remind me of Job's pain too?!"

The third disciple's attempt:

אָמַר לוֹ: נִכְנַס רַבִּי יוֹסֵי וְיָשַׁב לְפָנָיו — Then R' Yose entered and sat before him רַבִּי, רְצוֹנְךָ אוֹמַר דָּבָר אֶחָד לְפָנֶיךָ — and said to him, "My master, do I have permission to say something in your presence?" אָמַר לוֹ: אֱמוֹר — He replied, "Yes, you may speak." אָמַר לוֹ: אַהֲרֹן הָיוּ לוֹ שְׁנֵי בָנִים גְּדוֹלִים וּמֵתוּ שְׁנֵיהֶם בְּיוֹם אֶחָד — So [R' Yose] said to him, "Aaron had two great and righteous sons, who both died on the same day,[44] וְקִבֵּל עֲלֵיהֶם תַּנְחוּמִין — and he accepted condolences for them, שֶׁנֶּאֱמַר "וַיִּדֹּם אַהֲרֹן" — as it is stated after describing how they died, *and Aaron was silent* (*Leviticus* 10:3), אֵין שְׁתִיקָה אֶלָּא תַּנְחוּמִין — with 'silence' in this context referring only to the fact that he accepted

---

of their son Abel (*Magen Avos, Ahavas Chesed*).

43. See *Job* 1:18.

44. See *Leviticus* 10:2.

וְאַף אַתָּה קַבֵּל תַּנְחוּמִין. אָמַר לוֹ: לֹא דַי לִי שֶׁאֲנִי מִצְטַעֵר בְּעַצְמִי אֶלָּא
שֶׁהִזְכַּרְתַּנִי צַעֲרוֹ שֶׁל אַהֲרֹן. נִכְנַס רַבִּי שִׁמְעוֹן וְאָמַר לוֹ: רַבִּי, רְצוֹנְךָ
אוֹמַר דָּבָר אֶחָד לְפָנֶיךָ. אָמַר לוֹ: אֱמוֹר. אָמַר לוֹ: דָּוִד הַמֶּלֶךְ הָיָה לוֹ בֵּן
וּמֵת[45] וְקִבֵּל עָלָיו תַּנְחוּמִין. וְאַף אַתָּה קַבֵּל תַּנְחוּמִין. וּמִנַּיִן שֶׁקִּבֵּל דָּוִד
תַּנְחוּמִין, שֶׁנֶּאֱמַר (שמואל ב יב, כד) "וַיְנַחֵם דָּוִד אֵת בַּת שֶׁבַע אִשְׁתּוֹ וַיָּבֹא
אֵלֶיהָ וַיִּשְׁכַּב עִמָּהּ וַתֵּלֶד בֵּן וַיִּקְרָא אֶת שְׁמוֹ שְׁלֹמֹה". אַף אַתָּה רַבִּי,
קַבֵּל תַּנְחוּמִין. אָמַר לוֹ: לֹא דַי שֶׁאֲנִי מִצְטַעֵר בְּעַצְמִי אֶלָּא שֶׁהִזְכַּרְתַּנִי
צַעֲרוֹ שֶׁל דָּוִד הַמֶּלֶךְ[46]. נִכְנַס רַבִּי אֶלְעָזָר בֶּן °עֲזַרְיָה[47] כֵּיוָן שֶׁרָאָהוּ

---

condolences. ‎ וְאַף אַתָּה קַבֵּל תַּנְחוּמִין —**So too should you accept condolences
and be comforted."** ‎ אָמַר לוֹ: לֹא דַי לִי שֶׁאֲנִי מִצְטַעֵר בְּעַצְמִי —**[Rabban Yochan-
an] said to him, "Is it not enough for me that I am suffering with my own pain,**
‎ אֶלָּא שֶׁהִזְכַּרְתַּנִי צַעֲרוֹ שֶׁל אַהֲרֹן —**but you had to remind me of Aaron's pain too?!"**

The fourth disciple's attempt:

נִכְנַס רַבִּי שִׁמְעוֹן וְאָמַר לוֹ: רַבִּי, רְצוֹנְךָ אוֹמַר דָּבָר אֶחָד לְפָנֶיךָ —**Then R' Shimon
entered and said to him, "My master, do I have permission to say something
in your presence?"** ‎ אָמַר לוֹ: אֱמוֹר —**He replied, "Yes, you may speak."**
‎ אָמַר לוֹ: דָּוִד הַמֶּלֶךְ הָיָה לוֹ בֵּן וּמֵת וְקִבֵּל עָלָיו תַּנְחוּמִין —**So [R' Shimon] said
to him, "King David had a son who died,[45] and he accepted condolences
for him.** ‎ וְאַף אַתָּה קַבֵּל תַּנְחוּמִין —**So too should you accept condolences
and be comforted.** ‎ וּמִנַּיִן שֶׁקִּבֵּל דָּוִד תַּנְחוּמִין —**And how do we know that
David accepted condolences?** ‎ שֶׁנֶּאֱמַר "וַיְנַחֵם דָּוִד אֵת בַּת שֶׁבַע אִשְׁתּוֹ וַיָּבֹא
אֵלֶיהָ וַיִּשְׁכַּב עִמָּהּ וַתֵּלֶד בֵּן וַיִּקְרָא אֶת שְׁמוֹ שְׁלֹמֹה" —**For after recounting the
child's death, it is stated in Scripture,** *David comforted his wife Bath-sheba,
and he came to her and lay with her; she gave birth to a boy and called his
name Solomon* (II Samuel 12:24). ‎ אַף אַתָּה רַבִּי, קַבֵּל תַּנְחוּמִין —**So, too, my
master, should you accept condolences and be comforted."** ‎ אָמַר לוֹ: לֹא דַי
‎ שֶׁאֲנִי מִצְטַעֵר בְּעַצְמִי —**[Rabban Yochanan] said to him, "Is it not enough that
I am suffering with my own pain,** ‎ אֶלָּא שֶׁהִזְכַּרְתַּנִי צַעֲרוֹ שֶׁל דָּוִד הַמֶּלֶךְ —**but
you had to remind me of King David's pain too?!"[46]**

The final disciple's successful attempt:

כֵּיוָן שֶׁרָאָהוּ נִכְנַס רַבִּי אֶלְעָזָר בֶּן עֲרָךְ —**Then R' Elazar ben Arach[47] entered.**

---

45. See II Samuel 12:18.

46. As to why each subsequent disciple tried
comforting Rabban Yochanan in a way that
he had apparently already rejected, see *Magen Avos* and *Velo Od Ella* who expand on
this at length. [On a simple level, perhaps
there is a simple progression here: Adam
was the progenitor of the human race; that

he lost a child indicates that this is part of the
way of the world. Job lost all his children in
one day, and still he was consoled. Aharon
lost two *great* sons and still he was consoled.
David lost a child and was consoled, and
fathered the great King Solomon as a result.]

47. We have emended the text in accordance with the alternative version, and

אָמַר לְשַׁמָּשׁוֹ: טוֹל לְפָנַי כֵּלַי וְלֵךְ אַחֲרַי לְבֵית הַמֶּרְחָץ, לְפִי שֶׁאָדָם גָּדוֹל הוּא
וְאֵינִי יָכוֹל לַעֲמוֹד בּוֹ[48]. נִכְנַס וְיָשַׁב לְפָנָיו וְאָמַר לוֹ[49]: אֶמְשׁוֹל לְךָ מָשָׁל לְמָה
הַדָּבָר דּוֹמֶה, לְאָדָם שֶׁהִפְקִיד אֶצְלוֹ הַמֶּלֶךְ פִּקָּדוֹן. בְּכָל יוֹם וָיוֹם הָיָה בּוֹכֶה
וְצוֹעֵק וְאוֹמֵר: אוֹי לִי, אֵימָתַי אֵצֵא מִן הַפִּקָּדוֹן הַזֶּה בְּשָׁלוֹם. אַף אַתָּה רַבִּי,
הָיָה לְךָ בֵּן. קָרָא תוֹרָה מִקְרָא נְבִיאִים וּכְתוּבִים מִשְׁנָה הֲלָכוֹת וְאַגָּדוֹת[51]
וְנִפְטַר מִן הָעוֹלָם בְּלֹא חֵטְא. [וְיֵשׁ לְךָ לְקַבֵּל עָלֶיךָ תַּנְחוּמִים כְּשֶׁהֶחֱזַרְתָּ
פִּקְדוֹנְךָ שָׁלֵם.] אָמַר לוֹ: רַבִּי אֶלְעָזָר בְּנִי, נִחַמְתַּנִי כְּדֶרֶךְ שֶׁבְּנֵי אָדָם מְנַחֲמִין.[52]

אָמַר לְשַׁמָּשׁוֹ: טוֹל לְפָנַי כֵּלַי וְלֵךְ אַחֲרַי לְבֵית הַמֶּרְחָץ — As soon as [Rabban Yochanan] saw him approaching, he said to his attendant, "Get ready to take my clothing and follow me to the bathhouse. לְפִי שֶׁאָדָם גָּדוֹל הוּא וְאֵינִי יָכוֹל לַעֲמוֹד בּוֹ — For he who has come to comfort me now is a great man, and after hearing his words, I will not be able to remain in this pain."[48] נִכְנַס וְיָשַׁב לְפָנָיו וְאָמַר לוֹ: אֶמְשׁוֹל לְךָ מָשָׁל לְמָה הַדָּבָר דּוֹמֶה — [R' Elazar] entered and sat before him and said to him,[49] "I will give you an analogy: To what is this comparable? לְאָדָם שֶׁהִפְקִיד אֶצְלוֹ הַמֶּלֶךְ פִּקָּדוֹן — To a man with whom the king entrusted an article for safekeeping. בְּכָל יוֹם וָיוֹם הָיָה בּוֹכֶה וְצוֹעֵק וְאוֹמֵר: אוֹי לִי, — Every day, overcome with the awesome responsibility of guarding the king's article, he would cry and call out and say, 'Woe is me! אֵימָתַי אֵצֵא מִן הַפִּקָּדוֹן הַזֶּה בְּשָׁלוֹם — When will I have successfully discharged the awesome responsibility of guarding this article entrusted to me by the king?' אַף אַתָּה רַבִּי, הָיָה לְךָ בֵּן — So, too, you, my master: you had a son, קָרָא תוֹרָה מִקְרָא נְבִיאִים וּכְתוּבִים מִשְׁנָה הֲלָכוֹת וְאַגָּדוֹת — and he studied the entirety of the Written and Oral Torah[50] — the Chumash, the Prophets, the Writings, the Mishnah, the Halachos, and the Aggados.[51] וְנִפְטַר מִן הָעוֹלָם בְּלֹא חֵטְא — Now he has left the world without sin, וְיֵשׁ לְךָ לְקַבֵּל עָלֶיךָ תַּנְחוּמִים כְּשֶׁהֶחֱזַרְתָּ פִּקְדוֹנְךָ שָׁלֵם — and you should be comforted with the knowledge that you have returned what was entrusted to you to its Owner intact." אָמַר לוֹ: רַבִּי אֶלְעָזָר בְּנִי, — [Rabban Yochanan] said to him, "R' Elazar, נִחַמְתַּנִי כְּדֶרֶךְ שֶׁבְּנֵי אָדָם מְנַחֲמִין — my son, you have comforted me the way people should comfort others."[52]

Gra, cited in *Mesores HaShas*. See also *Ben Avraham*, who proves that this version is the correct one.

48. *Ben Avraham*.
R' Yochanan was sure that after hearing the words of his wise disciple, he would be ready to move past his sorrow and bathe in the bathhouse (ibid.). [See there further about how he would be halachically permitted to bathe during his period of mourning.]

49. After hearing the comment R' Yochanan made to his attendant, R' Elazar understood that he had permission to speak, and therefore did not request it as his peers did (ibid.).

50. *Avos HaRosh* [Vol. 2].

51. See note 6 above.

52. *Magen Avos*, citing *Baal HaAkeidah*.
While the other disciples tried comforting their teacher by mentioning the pain of other great figures, R' Elazar provided him with a

כְּשֶׁיָּצְאוּ מִלְּפָנָיו, הוּא אָמַר: אֵלֵךְ לְדַמְסִית לְמָקוֹם יָפֶה וּמַיִם יָפִים וְנָאִים[55]. וְהֵם אָמְרוּ: נֵלֵךְ לְיַבְנֶה לְמָקוֹם שֶׁתַּלְמִידֵי חֲכָמִים מְרוּבִּים אוֹהֲבִים אֶת הַתּוֹרָה[56]. הוּא שֶׁהָלַךְ לְדַמְסִית לְמָקוֹם יָפֶה וּמַיִם יָפִים וְנָאִים נִתְמַעֵט שְׁמוֹ בַּתּוֹרָה[57]. הֵם שֶׁהָלְכוּ לְיַבְנֶה לְמָקוֹם שֶׁתַּלְמִידֵי חֲכָמִים מְרוּבִּים וְאוֹהֲבִים אֶת הַתּוֹרָה נִתְגַּדֵּל שְׁמָם בַּתּוֹרָה:

The Baraisa recounts the incident that explains why, despite his superiority to his peers, R' Elazar ben Arach did not ultimately become the most famous:[53] כְּשֶׁיָּצְאוּ מִלְּפָנָיו הוּא אָמַר — After R' Yochanan ben Zakkai died[54] and they left [his academy], these five disciples were discussing where they would settle. [R' Elazar ben Arach] said, אֵלֵךְ לְדַמְסִית לְמָקוֹם יָפֶה וּמַיִם יָפִים וְנָאִים — "I shall go to a town along the river Damsis, to a beautiful place with beautiful and pleasant waters."[55] וְהֵם אָמְרוּ: נֵלֵךְ לְיַבְנֶה — However, the others said, "We shall go to Yavneh — לְמָקוֹם שֶׁתַּלְמִידֵי חֲכָמִים מְרוּבִּים אוֹהֲבִים אֶת הַתּוֹרָה — to a place where the Torah scholars are many and the people love the Torah."[56] הוּא שֶׁהָלַךְ לְדַמְסִית לְמָקוֹם יָפֶה וּמַיִם יָפִים וְנָאִים — He, R' Elazar ben Arach, who went to the river Damsis, to a beautiful place that had beautiful and pleasant waters, נִתְמַעֵט שְׁמוֹ בַּתּוֹרָה — his reputation in Torah scholarship diminished.[57] הֵם שֶׁהָלְכוּ לְיַבְנֶה לְמָקוֹם שֶׁתַּלְמִידֵי חֲכָמִים מְרוּבִּים וְאוֹהֲבִים אֶת הַתּוֹרָה — They, who went to Yavneh, to a place where the Torah scholars are many and the people love the Torah, נִתְגַּדֵּל שְׁמָם בַּתּוֹרָה — their reputations in Torah scholarship grew.

---

valid reason why he, personally, should be consoled (Ahavas Chesed).

53. Magen Avos; see Avos DeRabbi Nassan, Nusach 2, Ch. 29.

54. Avos HaRosh, from Koheles Rabbah 7 §15.

55. The waters of this river were famed for their medicinal and soothing qualities, and the nearby areas were known for their fine wines (see Shabbos 147b, with Rashi there).

Elsewhere, it is clear that it was not R' Elazar ben Arach's personal inclination that drew him to this location, but rather that he wanted to join his wife, who was already living there (Koheles Rabbah 7 §15). Moreover, R' Elazar ben Arach reasoned that his Torah studies would truly be enhanced by the favorable conditions of the area (see Avos DeRabbi Nassan, Nusach 2, Ch. 29).

56. See Avos DeRabbi Nassan, Nusach 2 ibid.

Yavneh was home to the Sanhedrin at that time [see Rosh Hashanah 29b], and these Sages were simply living by the principle that one should exile himself to a place of Torah [Avos 4:14] (Binyan Yehoshua; see Shabbos ibid.).

57. As evident from the limited number of times he is quoted in the Talmud (Ben Avraham). The Gemara also tells us that he forgot the Torah to such a great extent that when asked to read from a Torah scroll, he completely mispronounced an entire phrase. His Torah learning was restored only when his peers prayed on his behalf [Shabbos ibid.] (Binyan Yehoshua).

The explanation for this tragic phenomenon is simple: the Torah does not remain with someone who seeks luxuries (see Sanhedrin 111a); to succeed in Torah, one must limit his pursuit of pleasure (Avos 6:6). One who chooses not to minimize his pleasure, however, will have his Torah knowledge minimized instead, measure for measure (Avos HaRosh [Vol. 1]).

﷽ פֶּרֶק טו ﷽

א. וְהֵם אָמְרוּ שְׁלֹשָׁה דְבָרִים, רַבִּי אֱלִיעֶזֶר אוֹמֵר: יְהִי כְּבוֹד חֲבֵירְךָ
חָבִיב עָלֶיךָ כְּשֶׁלָּךְ, אַל תְּהִי נוֹחַ לִכְעוֹס, שׁוּב יוֹם אֶחָד לִפְנֵי מִיתָתְךָ.
יְהִי כְּבוֹד חֲבֵירְךָ חָבִיב עָלֶיךָ כְּשֶׁלָּךְ, כֵּיצַד, מְלַמֵּד שֶׁכְּשֵׁם שֶׁרוֹאֶה אֶת
כְּבוֹדוֹ כָּךְ יְהֵא אָדָם רוֹאֶה אֶת כְּבוֹד חֲבֵירוֹ, וּכְשֵׁם שֶׁאֵין אָדָם רוֹצֶה
שֶׁיְּהֵא שֵׁם רַע עַל כְּבוֹדוֹ, כָּךְ יְהֵא אָדָם רוֹצֶה שֶׁלֹּא לְהוֹצִיא שֵׁם רַע עַל
כְּבוֹדוֹ שֶׁל חֲבֵרוֹ², דָּבָר אַחֵר, יְהִי כְּבוֹד חֲבֵירְךָ חָבִיב עָלֶיךָ כְּשֶׁלָּךְ, כֵּיצַד,
בִּזְמַן שֶׁיֵּשׁ לוֹ לְאָדָם מֵאָה רִבּוֹא וְנוֹטְלִים אֶת כָּל מָמוֹנוֹ, אַל יִפְגּוֹם אֶת
עַצְמוֹ בִּשְׁוֵה פְרוּטָה³:

﷽ CHAPTER 15 ﷽

§1 Having discussed the five primary disciples of Rabban Yochanan ben
Zakkai, the coming chapters of the Baraisa expound the sayings of each
one of them. This chapter elaborates *Avos* 2:10, where R' Eliezer's sayings
are cited:

רַבִּי אֱלִיעֶזֶר אוֹמֵר: יְהִי — **They each said three things.** וְהֵם אָמְרוּ שְׁלֹשָׁה דְבָרִים
כְּבוֹד חֲבֵירְךָ חָבִיב עָלֶיךָ כְּשֶׁלָּךְ — R' Eliezer says: (i) **Let your fellow's honor be
as dear to you as your own;** אַל תְּהִי נוֹחַ לִכְעוֹס — (ii) **do not anger easily;**
שׁוּב יוֹם אֶחָד לִפְנֵי מִיתָתְךָ — (iii) **and repent one day before your death.**

The Baraisa expounds each of R' Eliezer's sayings. The first saying:
יְהִי כְּבוֹד חֲבֵירְךָ חָבִיב עָלֶיךָ כְּשֶׁלָּךְ, כֵּיצַד — **"Let your fellow's honor be as dear
to you as your own"** — **how so?** מְלַמֵּד שֶׁכְּשֵׁם שֶׁרוֹאֶה אֶת כְּבוֹדוֹ כָּךְ יְהֵא אָדָם
רוֹאֶה אֶת כְּבוֹד חֲבֵירוֹ — **This teaches that just as a person** desires to see his
own honor, so should he desire to see his **fellow's honor.**[1] וּכְשֵׁם שֶׁאֵין אָדָם
רוֹצֶה שֶׁיֵּצֵא שֵׁם רַע עַל כְּבוֹדוֹ — **And just as a person does not wish that there
should be a slander undermining his** own honor, כָּךְ יְהֵא אָדָם רוֹצֶה שֶׁלֹּא
לְהוֹצִיא שֵׁם רַע עַל כְּבוֹדוֹ שֶׁל חֲבֵרוֹ — **so should a person wish to avoid issuing
a slander undermining his fellow's honor.**[2]

Another explanation of R' Eliezer's saying:
דָּבָר אַחֵר, יְהִי כְּבוֹד חֲבֵירְךָ חָבִיב עָלֶיךָ כְּשֶׁלָּךְ, כֵּיצַד — **Another explanation: "Let
your fellow's honor be as dear to you as your own"** — **how so?** The Baraisa illustrates: בִּזְמַן שֶׁיֵּשׁ לוֹ לְאָדָם מֵאָה רִבּוֹא — **If a person has one million** *dinars,*
וְנוֹטְלִים אֶת כָּל מָמוֹנוֹ — **and then all his money is stolen,** אַל יִפְגּוֹם אֶת עַצְמוֹ
בִּשְׁוֵה פְרוּטָה — **he will not devalue himself even a** *perutah's* **worth!**[3]

---

1. *Binyan Yehoshua.*

2. Rather, he should always give his fellow
the benefit of the doubt, just as he would

want others to do for him (ibid.).

3. Even if his entire fortune would be
stolen from him, a millionaire's sense of

ב. וְאַל תְּהִי נוֹחַ לִכְעוֹס, כֵּיצַד, מְלַמֵּד שֶׁיְּהֵא עָנָיו כְּהִלֵּל הַזָּקֵן וְאַל
יְהִי קַפְּדָן כְּשַׁמַּאי הַזָּקֵן, מֶה הָיָה עִנְוְתָנוּתוֹ שֶׁל הִלֵּל הַזָּקֵן, אָמְרוּ:
מַעֲשֶׂה בִּשְׁנֵי בְּנֵי אָדָם שֶׁעָמְדוּ וְהִמְרוּ זֶה אֶת זֶה וְזֶה אֶת זֶה בְּאַרְבַּע
מֵאוֹת זוּז, אָמְרוּ: כָּל שֶׁיֵּלֵךְ וְיַקְנִיט אֶת הִלֵּל יִטֹּל אַרְבַּע מֵאוֹת זוּז. הָלַךְ
אֶחָד מֵהֶם, וְאוֹתוֹ הַיּוֹם עֶרֶב שַׁבָּת הָיָה עִם חֲשִׁיכָה, וְקָא חָיֵיף רֵישֵׁיהּ, בָּא
וְטָפַח לוֹ עַל הַדֶּלֶת, אָמַר: הֵיכָן הִלֵּל הֵיכָן הִלֵּל,[5] נִתְעַטֵּף וְיָצָא לִקְרָאתוֹ,
אָמַר לוֹ: בְּנִי, מֶה אַתָּה צָרִיךְ. אָמַר לוֹ: שְׁאֵלָה (זוֹ) אֲנִי צָרִיךְ לִשְׁאוֹל.

---

§2 The Baraisa expounds R' Eliezer's second saying:

מְלַמֵּד — כֵּיצַד, וְאַל תְּהִי נוֹחַ לִכְעוֹס — "**Do not anger easily**" — **how so?** — שֶׁיְּהֵא עָנָיו כְּהִלֵּל הַזָּקֵן וְאַל יְהִי קַפְּדָן כְּשַׁמַּאי הַזָּקֵן — **This teaches that one should strive to be humble** and forbearing **like Hillel the Elder, and not strict like Shammai the Elder.**

The Baraisa records a story that illustrates Hillel's admirable ways:

מֶה הָיָה עִנְוְתָנוּתוֹ שֶׁל הִלֵּל הַזָּקֵן — **What is** an example of **the humility of Hillel the Elder?** — אָמְרוּ: מַעֲשֶׂה בִּשְׁנֵי בְּנֵי אָדָם שֶׁעָמְדוּ וְהִמְרוּ זֶה אֶת זֶה וְזֶה אֶת זֶה — **They said:** It once **happened that two people got up and made a wager with each other**[4] **for four hundred** *zuz.* — בְּאַרְבַּע מֵאוֹת זוּז — אָמְרוּ: כָּל שֶׁיֵּלֵךְ וְיַקְנִיט אֶת הִלֵּל יִטֹּל אַרְבַּע מֵאוֹת זוּז — **They said** to each other, "**Whichever one of us goes and provokes Hillel to anger shall take four hundred** *zuz!*" הָלַךְ אֶחָד מֵהֶם — **One of them** then **went** to try **to provoke Hillel,** וְאוֹתוֹ הַיּוֹם עֶרֶב שַׁבָּת הָיָה עִם חֲשִׁיכָה — **and it was on a Friday when dark was approaching,** וְקָא חָיֵיף רֵישֵׁיהּ — **and [Hillel] was** in the middle of **washing his hair** in preparation for the Sabbath that was soon to begin. בָּא וְטָפַח לוֹ עַל הַדֶּלֶת — **[The man] came and knocked on the door** of Hillel's house אָמַר: הֵיכָן הִלֵּל הֵיכָן הִלֵּל — **and called out, "Where is Hillel? Where is Hillel?"**[5] נִתְעַטֵּף וְיָצָא לִקְרָאתוֹ — Thinking that some emergency was at hand, Hillel interrupted his washing and **he wrapped himself** in his cloak **and went out to meet him,** אָמַר לוֹ: בְּנִי, מֶה — **and said to him, "My son, what** אַתָּה צָרִיךְ — **do you need?"** אָמַר לוֹ: שְׁאֵלָה — זוֹ אֲנִי צָרִיךְ לִשְׁאוֹל — **He replied, "I need to ask** you **this question** that I have."

---

self-worth would not be diminished in the least. He would still view and conduct himself like a wealthy man. Similarly, one should view even his poor fellow man as if he were a millionaire whose wealth was taken from him, and respect and deal with him accordingly (*Binyan Yehoshua*, citing *Mefaresh*).

4. [Literally, *they bet one with the other, and one with the other.* See below, note 17.]

5. The man deliberately chose this harried moment when Hillel's time would be short and he would likely be short-tempered with the disturbance and the trivial question the man was about to ask. He also called out for the *Nasi* in a disrespectful way. All this was intended to provoke the legendarily patient Hillel into some display of angry annoyance (*Maharsha* to *Shabbos* 31a).

אָמַר לוֹ: אֱמוֹר. אָמַר לוֹ: מִפְּנֵי מָה עֵינֵיהֶם שֶׁל תַּרְמוֹדִים תְּרוּטוֹת. אָמַר
לוֹ: מִפְּנֵי שֶׁדָּרִין בֵּין חוֹל בַּמִּדְבָּר, וּבָאוֹת רוּחוֹת וּמְפַזְּרוֹת אוֹתוֹ עַל
עֵינֵיהֶם, לְפִיכָךְ עֵינֵיהֶם תְּרוּטוֹת.7 הָלַךְ וְהִמְתִּין שָׁעָה אַחַת וְחָזַר וְטָפַח לוֹ
עַל הַדֶּלֶת, אָמַר: הֵיכָן הִלֵּל הֵיכָן הִלֵּל. נִתְעַטֵּף וְיָצָא, אָמַר לוֹ: בְּנִי, מָה
אַתָּה צָרִיךְ. אָמַר לוֹ: הֲלָכָה אֲנִי צָרִיךְ לִשְׁאוֹל.9 אָמַר לוֹ: אֱמוֹר. אָמַר לוֹ:
מִפְּנֵי מָה רַגְלֵיהֶם שֶׁל אַפְרִקִיִּים רְחָבוֹת. אָמַר לוֹ: מִפְּנֵי שֶׁהֵם יוֹשְׁבִין °עִם
בִּצְעֵי הַמַּיִם, וּבְכָל יוֹם וָיוֹם הֵם הוֹלְכִים בַּמַּיִם, לְפִיכָךְ רַגְלֵיהֶם רְחָבוֹת.10

אָמַר לוֹ: אֱמוֹר — [Hillel] said to him, "Tell me your question." אָמַר לוֹ: מִפְּנֵי מָה עֵינֵיהֶם שֶׁל תַּרְמוֹדִים תְּרוּטוֹת — [The man] said to him, "Why is it that the eyes of the people from Tarmod are especially round?"[6] אָמַר לוֹ: מִפְּנֵי שֶׁדָּרִין בֵּין חוֹל בַּמִּדְבָּר — [Hillel] answered him, "Because they live among the sands of the desert, וּבָאוֹת רוּחוֹת וּמְפַזְּרוֹת אוֹתוֹ עַל עֵינֵיהֶם — and the winds come and blow [the sand] into their eyes, לְפִיכָךְ עֵינֵיהֶם תְּרוּטוֹת — that is why their eyes are round."[7] הָלַךְ וְהִמְתִּין שָׁעָה אַחַת — [The man] left and waited for a time, until he was sure that Hillel had resumed washing his hair,[8] וְחָזַר וְטָפַח לוֹ עַל הַדֶּלֶת — and he again knocked on the door of Hillel's house אָמַר: הֵיכָן הִלֵּל הֵיכָן הִלֵּל — and called out, "Where is Hillel? Where is Hillel?" נִתְעַטֵּף וְיָצָא אָמַר לוֹ: בְּנִי, מָה אַתָּה צָרִיךְ — Once again, [Hillel] wrapped himself in his cloak, went out to meet [the man], and said to him, "My son, what do you need?" אָמַר לוֹ: הֲלָכָה אֲנִי צָרִיךְ לִשְׁאוֹל — He replied, "I need to ask a question of halachah."[9] אָמַר לוֹ: אֱמוֹר — [Hillel] said to him, "Tell me your question." אָמַר לוֹ: מִפְּנֵי מָה רַגְלֵיהֶם שֶׁל אַפְרִקִיִּים רְחָבוֹת — [The man] said to him, "Why are the feet of the Africans so wide?" אָמַר לוֹ: מִפְּנֵי שֶׁהֵם יוֹשְׁבִין עַל בִּצְעֵי הַמַּיִם — [Hillel] answered him, "Because they dwell along the swamps, וּבְכָל יוֹם וָיוֹם הֵם הוֹלְכִים בַּמַּיִם — and every day they must walk through the swampy waters, לְפִיכָךְ רַגְלֵיהֶם רְחָבוֹת — that is why their feet are so wide."[10]

---

6. See *Binyan Yehoshua*, citing *Rashi*.

7. Had their eyes been more oblong, like ours, the blowing sands would lodge in the corners of their eyes. Therefore, God made their eyes rounder, so that there would be no corners in which the sands could lodge (ibid.).

8. So that Hillel should become further irritated by the new interruption (*Ben Avraham*).

9. Actually, the matter that this man wanted to ask Hillel (both here and below) was not related to halachah at all. Introducing it as a matter of Jewish law — implying that it needed to be answered without delay — was just another ploy to aggravate Hillel (*Ben Avraham*; see also *Magen Avos*).

10. God made them with wide feet so that they would not sink so readily into the swamps through which they must walk. Alternatively, it is not that they are born with wide feet. But since they walk through swamps, they do not wear shoes, and their feet are thus free to expand naturally (*Binyan Yehoshua*, from *Rashi*, second explanation; see also *Avos DeRabbi Nassan*, *Nusach* 2, Ch. 29).

הָלַךְ וְהִמְתִּין שָׁעָה אַחַת וְחָזַר וְטָפַח עַל הַדֶּלֶת, אָמַר: הֵיכָן הִלֵּל הֵיכָן
הִלֵּל. נִתְעַטֵּף וְיָצָא, אָמַר לוֹ: מָה אַתָּה צָרִיךְ לִשְׁאוֹל. אָמַר לוֹ: הֲלָכָה
אֲנִי צָרִיךְ לִשְׁאוֹל. אָמַר לוֹ: אֱמוֹר. נִתְעַטֵּף וְיָשַׁב לְפָנָיו[11]. אָמַר לוֹ: [מָה
אַתָּה צָרִיךְ. אָמַר לוֹ: כָּךְ נְשִׂיאִים מְשִׁיבִים,] אַל יִרְבּוּ כְּמוֹתְךָ בְּיִשְׂרָאֵל.
(אָמַר לוֹ: חַס וְשָׁלוֹם, הֱוֵי זָהִיר בְּרוּחֲךָ. מָה אַתָּה צָרִיךְ[13].) אָמַר לוֹ:
מִפְּנֵי מָה (רָאשֵׁיהֶם שֶׁל בַּבְלִיִּים אֲרוּכִים[14]. אָמַר לוֹ: בְּנִי, הֲלָכָה גְּדוֹלָה
שָׁאַלְתָּ[15]. לְפִי שֶׁאֵין שָׁם חָיוֹת פִּקְחוֹת, כְּשֶׁנּוֹלָד הַוָּלָד מְגַדְּלוֹת אוֹתָם עַל

הָלַךְ וְהִמְתִּין שָׁעָה אַחַת — [The man] left and again **waited for a time** until he
was sure that Hillel had once again resumed washing his hair, **וְחָזַר וְטָפַח**
עַל הַדֶּלֶת — and he again **knocked on the door** of Hillel's house **הֵיכָן :אָמַר**
הֵיכָן הִלֵּל הִלֵּל — and **called out, "Where is Hillel? Where is Hillel?"** **נִתְעַטֵּף**
וְיָצָא אָמַר לוֹ: מָה אַתָּה צָרִיךְ לִשְׁאוֹל — Once again [Hillel] **wrapped himself,**
went out, and said to him, "My son, what do you need to ask?" **אָמַר לוֹ:**
הֲלָכָה אֲנִי צָרִיךְ לִשְׁאוֹל — He replied, **"I need to ask** a question **of halachah."**
נִתְעַטֵּף וְיָשַׁב [Hillel] said to him, **"Tell** me your question." **אָמַר לוֹ: אֱמוֹר -**
לְפָנָיו[11] — And [Hillel] **wrapped himself** well in his cloak **and sat down in front**
of him,[11] **אָמַר לוֹ: מָה אַתָּה צָרִיךְ** — and said to him, **"What do you need?"**
אָמַר לוֹ: כָּךְ נְשִׂיאִים מְשִׁיבִים — Seeing that his **persistent**
efforts to anger Hillel were not succeeding, **he replied** in frustration, **"If this is**
how Nesiim respond to provocation, then **let there not be many** others **like**
you in Israel!" **אָמַר לוֹ: חַס וְשָׁלוֹם, הֱוֵי זָהִיר בְּרוּחֲךָ** — [Hillel] said to him,
"Heaven forbid! On the contrary, may there be many like this in Israel! **Control**
your temper.[12] **מָה אַתָּה צָרִיךְ** — Now, tell me **what you need** to ask?"[13]
אָמַר לוֹ: מִפְּנֵי מָה שֶׁל בַּבְלִיִּים אֲרוּכִים — So [the man] asked him, **"Why**
are the heads of the Babylonians elongated?"[14] **אָמַר לוֹ: בְּנִי, הֲלָכָה גְּדוֹלָה**
שָׁאַלְתָּ — [Hillel] responded, **"My son, you have asked** a question regarding
an important halachah.[15] **לְפִי שֶׁאֵין שָׁם חָיוֹת פִּקְחוֹת** — The answer is that
since there are no skilled midwives there, **כְּשֶׁנּוֹלָד הַוָּלָד מְגַדְּלוֹת אוֹתָם עַל**

---

11. Hillel knew that there would no longer
be time to resume washing his hair before
the Sabbath. So he indicated to the man that
there was no longer any need to rush and he
was free to ask his questions (*Ben Avraham*).

12. Ibid.

13. [*Gra* removes this phrase and the man's
next question from the text.]

14. Some explain that this question was
meant to insult and provoke Hillel, who was
originally from Babylonia. A sphere is the

most efficient shape for a container. Accordingly, the man was asking why the heads
of Babylonians are oblong and thus have
smaller brains than people with spherical
heads (*Ahavas Chesed*). [In the version cited
in *Shabbos* 31a, however, the man's question was why the heads of the Babylonians
are *round* (*Ahavas Chesed*).]

15. Although the question asked by this
man was not at all connected to halachah,
Hillel referred to it this way so as not to embarrass the man for wrongly introducing it

אֵבָרִים שֶׁל עֲבָדִים וְשֶׁל שְׁפָחוֹת, לְפִיכָךְ רָאשֵׁיהֶם אֲרוּכוֹת, אֲבָל כָּאן
שֶׁיֵּשׁ חַיּוֹת פִּקְחוֹת, כְּשֶׁנּוֹלָד הַוָּלָד מְגַדְּלוֹת אוֹתוֹ בַּעֲרִיסָה וּמְשַׁפְשְׁפוֹת
אֶת רֹאשׁוֹ[16], לְפִיכָךְ רָאשֵׁיהֶם סְגַלְגַּלִּין). אָמַר לוֹ: אִיבַּדְתָּ מִמֶּנִּי אַרְבַּע
מֵאוֹת זוּז. אָמַר לוֹ: כְּדַי הוּא הִלֵּל שֶׁתִּתְאַבֵּד עַל יָדוֹ אַרְבַּע מֵאוֹת זוּז
[וְאַרְבַּע מֵאוֹת זוּז[17]] וְהִלֵּל אַל יַקְפִּיד:

ג. מֶה הָיָה קַפְּדָנוּתוֹ שֶׁל שַׁמַּאי הַזָּקֵן, אָמְרוּ: מַעֲשֶׂה בְּאָדָם אֶחָד שֶׁעָמַד
לִפְנֵי שַׁמַּאי, אָמַר לוֹ: רַבִּי, כַּמָּה תוֹרוֹת יֵשׁ לָכֶם. אָמַר לוֹ: שְׁתַּיִם,

---

אֵבָרִים שֶׁל עֲבָדִים וְשֶׁל שְׁפָחוֹת — when a baby is born they raise him on the laps of inexperienced servants and maidservants, לְפִיכָךְ רָאשֵׁיהֶם אֲרוּכוֹת — there-fore, the heads of [the people there] are oblong. אֲבָל כָּאן שֶׁיֵּשׁ חַיּוֹת פִּקְחוֹת — However, here in the Land of Israel, since there are skilled midwives, כְּשֶׁנּוֹלָד הַוָּלָד מְגַדְּלוֹת אוֹתוֹ בַּעֲרִיסָה — when a baby is born, they raise him in a cradle לְפִיכָךְ רָאשֵׁיהֶם סְגַלְגַּלִּין וּמְשַׁפְשְׁפוֹת אֶת רֹאשׁוֹ — and rub his head with oil,[16] and therefore when the babies here grow up their heads are round." אָמַר לוֹ: אִיבַּדְתָּ מִמֶּנִּי אַרְבַּע מֵאוֹת זוּז — Unable to provoke the humble Hillel, he said to him in frustration, "You have made me lose four hundred zuz!" אָמַר לוֹ: כְּדַי הוּא הִלֵּל שֶׁתִּתְאַבֵּד עַל יָדוֹ אַרְבַּע מֵאוֹת זוּז וְאַרְבַּע מֵאוֹת זוּז — He replied, "Hillel is fitting that you should lose on his account four hundred zuz and another four hundred zuz,[17] וְהִלֵּל אַל יַקְפִּיד — as long as Hillel does not become angry."

§3 In addition to urging one to be humble like Hillel, R' Eliezer had also said above that one should *not* be strict like Shammai. The Baraisa now elaborates:

מֶה הָיָה קַפְּדָנוּתוֹ שֶׁל שַׁמַּאי הַזָּקֵן — What is an example of the strictness of Shammai the Elder? אָמְרוּ: מַעֲשֶׂה בְּאָדָם אֶחָד שֶׁעָמַד לִפְנֵי שַׁמַּאי — They said: It once happened that a non-Jewish man (considering converting to Judaism) came and stood before Shammai, אָמַר לוֹ: רַבִּי, כַּמָּה תוֹרוֹת יֵשׁ לָכֶם — and said to him, "My teacher, how many Torahs do you Jews have?" אָמַר לוֹ: שְׁתַּיִם

---

as a matter of halachah [see note 9] (see *Avos HaRosh* [Vol. 1] and *Ben Avraham*).

16. An infant in the cradle is rocked back and forth, and the rolling motion enables its head to develop a rounder shape. The head of a baby raised primarily on someone's lap, however, does not get as much steady movement, and is thus more likely to end up oblong (*Magen Avos*). [Similarly, rubbing the head with oil massages the pliable head of the infant, inducing it to assume a rounder shape.]

17. According to *Maharsha* (*Shabbos* 31a), the wager had indeed involved *eight* hundred zuz: Whoever would go and succeed in provoking Hillel would take 400 zuz from the other; but if he failed, he would have to *pay* the other one 400 zuz. The man's failed attempt, then, effectively cost him 800 zuz — the 400 that he failed to win, and the 400 that he now had to pay the other one. [Having learned of the terms of the bet,] Hillel used this double expression to allude to the 800 zuz the fellow had lost. [*Ben Avraham*

אַחַת בִּכְתָב וְאַחַת בְּעַל פֶּה. אָמַר לוֹ: אֶת שֶׁבִּכְתָבָה אֲנִי מַאֲמִין לְךָ, אֶת
שֶׁבְּעַל פֶּה אֵינִי מַאֲמִין לְךָ. גָּעַר בּוֹ וְהוֹצִיאוֹ בִּנְזִיפָה[18], בָּא לִפְנֵי הִלֵּל,
אָמַר לוֹ: רַבִּי, כַּמָּה תוֹרוֹת נִתְּנוּ. אָמַר לוֹ: שְׁתַּיִם, אַחַת בִּכְתָב וְאַחַת
בְּעַל פֶּה. אָמַר לוֹ: בִּכְתָב אֲנִי מַאֲמִינְךָ, בְּעַל פֶּה אֵין אֲנִי מַאֲמִינְךָ[19].
אָמַר לוֹ: בְּנִי, שֵׁב, °כְּתַב °לִי אָלֶף בֵּית. אָמַר לוֹ: מַה זֶּה. אָמַר לוֹ:
אָלֶף. אָמַר לוֹ: אֵין זֶה אָלֶף אֶלָּא בֵּית. אָמַר לוֹ: מַהוּ זֶה. אָמַר לוֹ: בֵּית.

אָמַר אַחַת בִּכְתָב וְאַחַת בְּעַל פֶּה — He replied, "Two: one written and one oral." **לוֹ** — [The man] said to him, **אֶת שֶׁבִּכְתָבָה אֲנִי מַאֲמִין לְךָ אֶת שֶׁבְּעַל פֶּה אֵינִי מַאֲמִין לְךָ** "As for the written one, I believe you that it is from God, but as for the oral one I do not believe you that it is from God." **גָּעַר בּוֹ וְהוֹצִיאוֹ בִּנְזִיפָה** — [Shammai] censured him for his comment and sent him away disapprovingly.[18] **בָּא** **אָמַר לוֹ: רַבִּי, כַּמָּה תוֹרוֹת נִתְּנוּ לִפְנֵי הִלֵּל** — [The man] then came before Hillel — and said to him, "My teacher, how many Torahs were given to you Jews?" **אָמַר לוֹ: שְׁתַּיִם אַחַת בִּכְתָב וְאַחַת בְּעַל פֶּה** — He replied, "Two: one written and one oral." **אָמַר לוֹ: בִּכְתָב אֲנִי מַאֲמִינְךָ בְּעַל פֶּה אֵין אֲנִי מַאֲמִינְךָ** — [The man] said to him, "As for the written one I believe you, but as for the oral one I do not believe you."[19] **אָמַר לוֹ: בְּנִי, שֵׁב** - [Hillel] said to him, "My son, sit down," **כְּתַב לוֹ אָלֶף בֵּית** — and he wrote out for him the Hebrew alphabet and taught it to him.[20] **אָמַר לוֹ: מַה זֶּה, אָמַר לוֹ: אָלֶף** — Afterward, he pointed to the *aleph* and asked [the man], "What is this?," to which he replied, "An *aleph*." **אָמַר לוֹ: אֵין זֶה אָלֶף אֶלָּא בֵּית** — [Hillel] said to him, "Actually, this is not an *aleph*, but a *beis*." **אָמַר לוֹ: מַהוּ זֶה, אָמַר לוֹ: בֵּית** — Then [Hillel] pointed to the *beis* and asked him, "What is this?," to which he replied, "A *beis*."

---

sees this explanation of *Maharsha* indicated in the Baraisa's double expression above, "they bet one with the other, and one with the other (see above, note 4).]

18. As evident from his comment, this non-Jew sought to convert to Judaism *on condition* that he be bound only by the rules of the Written Torah and not by those of the Oral Torah (*Shabbos* 31a). Shammai rejected him because the halachah states that if a candidate for conversion specifically refuses to accept any part of the Torah, he must be rejected [*Bechoros* 30b] (*Binyan Yehoshua*, from *Rashi* to *Shabbos* ad loc.).

19. According to the version of this incident as recounted in *Shabbos* 31a (as explained by *Rashi* there; see, however, *Ben Avraham* cited at the end of this note), Hillel

converted the man to Judaism at this point, confident that he would then succeed in convincing the man of the authenticity of the Oral Torah, as the Baraisa proceeds to recount. [See *Rashi* and *Rashash* there as to why the man's current non-acceptance of the Oral Torah did not disqualify his conversion.]

[*Ben Avraham*, however, maintains that the Gemara in *Shabbos* does not mean that Hillel converted the non-Jew *at that point*, but rather that he did so *eventually* (after he succeeded in convincing him of the authenticity of the Oral Torah). And that is the apparent meaning of our Baraisa as well, where no mention is made of Hillel converting him at this point.]

20. See *Shabbos* ibid.

‫אָמַר לוֹ: אֵין זֶה בֵּית אֶלָּא גִימֶל. אָמַר לוֹ: מִנַּיִן אַתָּה יוֹדֵעַ שֶׁזֶּה אֶלֶף וְזֶה‬
‫בֵּית וְזֶה גִימֶל. אָמַר לוֹ: כָּךְ מָסְרוּ לָנוּ אֲבוֹתֵינוּ הָרִאשׁוֹנִים שֶׁזֶּה אֶלֶף וְזֶה‬
‫בֵּית וְזֶה גִימֶל, כְּשֵׁם שֶׁקִּבַּלְתָּ זוֹ בֶּאֱמוּנָה כָּךְ קַבֵּל עָלֶיךָ זוֹ בֶּאֱמוּנָה23,22.‬
‫מַעֲשֶׂה בְּנָכְרִי אֶחָד שֶׁהָיָה עוֹבֵר אֲחוֹרֵי בֵית הַכְּנֶסֶת, וְשָׁמַע תִּינוֹק שֶׁקּוֹרֵא‬
(‫שמות כח, ד‬) ‫"וְאֵלֶּה הַבְּגָדִים אֲשֶׁר יַעֲשׂוּ חֹשֶׁן וְאֵפוֹד וּמְעִיל", בָּא לִפְנֵי‬
‫שַׁמַּאי, אָמַר לוֹ: רַבִּי, כָּל הַכָּבוֹד הַזֶּה לְמִי. אָמַר: לְכֹהֵן גָּדוֹל שֶׁעוֹמֵד‬
‫וּמְשַׁמֵּשׁ עַל גַּבֵּי הַמִּזְבֵּחַ. אָמַר לוֹ: גַּיְּירֵנִי עַל מְנָת שֶׁתְּשִׂימֵנִי כֹהֵן גָּדוֹל.‬

‫אָמַר לוֹ: אֵין זֶה בֵּית אֶלָּא גִימֶל‬ — [Hillel] said to him, "Actually, this is not a *beis*, but a *gimmel*." ‫אָמַר לוֹ: מִנַּיִן אַתָּה יוֹדֵעַ שֶׁזֶּה אֶלֶף וְזֶה בֵּית וְזֶה גִימֶל‬ — [Hillel] continued[21] and said to him, "Now, how do you know that what I just said is wrong and that, in truth, that which you call *aleph* really is an *aleph*, that which you call *beis* really is a *beis*, and that which you call *gimmel* really is a *gimmel*?" ‫אָמַר לוֹ: כָּךְ מָסְרוּ לָנוּ אֲבוֹתֵינוּ הָרִאשׁוֹנִים שֶׁזֶּה אֶלֶף וְזֶה בֵּית וְזֶה גִימֶל‬ — [The man] answered, "Because, as you taught me originally, this is what our ancestors from long ago have transmitted to us — that this is an *aleph*, this is a *beis*, and this is a *gimmel*." ‫כְּשֵׁם שֶׁקִּבַּלְתָּ זוֹ בֶּאֱמוּנָה‬ — Hillel said to him, "So just as you have faithfully accepted that this fact that they have transmitted to us is true, ‫כָּךְ קַבֵּל עָלֶיךָ זוֹ בֶּאֱמוּנָה‬ — so, too, faithfully accept upon yourself as true this fact that they have transmitted to us that the Oral Torah is from God."[22] Thus, the strictness of Shammai distanced this man, whereas the humble patience of Hillel brought him near.[23]

Another story contrasting the different approaches of Shammai and Hillel: ‫מַעֲשֶׂה בְּנָכְרִי אֶחָד שֶׁהָיָה עוֹבֵר אֲחוֹרֵי בֵית הַכְּנֶסֶת‬ — It once happened that a certain non-Jew was passing by the rear of a synagogue ‫וְשָׁמַע תִּינוֹק שֶׁקּוֹרֵא‬ ‫"וְאֵלֶּה הַבְּגָדִים אֲשֶׁר יַעֲשׂוּ חֹשֶׁן וְאֵפוֹד וּמְעִיל"‬ — and heard a child reading aloud the verse, *These are the vestments that they shall make: a Breastplate, an Ephod, a Robe, a Tunic of a box-like knit, a Turban, and a Sash* (*Exodus* 28:4). ‫בָּא לִפְנֵי שַׁמַּאי‬ — [The man] then came before Shammai and related to him the verse that he had overheard, ‫אָמַר לוֹ: רַבִּי, כָּל הַכָּבוֹד הַזֶּה לְמִי‬ — and said to him, "My teacher, all this great honor of wearing such lavish vestments — to whom is it given?" ‫אָמַר: לְכֹהֵן גָּדוֹל שֶׁעוֹמֵד וּמְשַׁמֵּשׁ עַל גַּבֵּי הַמִּזְבֵּחַ‬ — [Shammai] answered, "It is given to the Kohen Gadol (High Priest), who stands and performs the service upon the Altar." ‫אָמַר לוֹ: גַּיְּירֵנִי עַל מְנָת שֶׁתְּשִׂימֵנִי כֹהֵן גָּדוֹל‬

---

21. See *Avos DeRabbi Nassan, Nusach 2*, Ch. 29, and *Ahavas Chesed*.

22. Hillel was showing this man that accepting the Written Torah but not the Oral Torah does not make sense. For even the Written Torah rests on the oral tradition that identifies each of the Hebrew letters, without which the words would mean completely different things (*Ben Avraham*; see also *Ahavas Chesed*).

23. See *Magen Avos*, who discusses why the Baraisa introduced this story only as an illustration of Shammai's strict approach

אָמַר לוֹ: אֵין כֹּהֵן בְּיִשְׂרָאֵל וְאֵין לָנוּ כֹּהֲנִים גְּדוֹלִים שֶׁיַּעַמְדוּ וְיִשְׁתַּמְּשׁוּ
בִּכְהוּנָּה גְדוֹלָה, אֶלָּא גֵּר הַקַּל שֶׁלֹּא בָא אֶלָּא בְּמַקְלוֹ וּבְתַרְמִילוֹ[24]
וְיָבֹא וְיִשְׁתַּמֵּשׁ בִּכְהוּנָה גְדוֹלָה. גָּעַר בּוֹ וְהוֹצִיאוּ בִּנְזִיפָה, בָּא לְהִלֵּל,
אָמַר לוֹ: רַבִּי, גַּיְּירֵנִי עַל מְנָת שֶׁתְּשִׂימֵנִי כֹּהֵן גָּדוֹל שֶׁאֶעֱמוֹד וַאֲשַׁמֵּשׁ
עַל גַּבֵּי הַמִּזְבֵּחַ[25]. אָמַר לוֹ: שֵׁב וְאוֹמַר לְךָ דָבָר אֶחָד, מִי שֶׁמְּבַקֵּשׁ
לְהַקְבִּיל פְּנֵי מֶלֶךְ בָּשָׂר וָדָם, לֹא דִין הוּא שֶׁיִּלְמוֹד אֵיךְ יִכָּנֵס וְאֵיךְ יֵצֵא.
אָמַר לוֹ: הֵן. אַתָּה שֶׁמְּבַקֵּשׁ לְהַקְבִּיל פְּנֵי מֶלֶךְ מַלְכֵי הַמְּלָכִים הַקָּדוֹשׁ
בָּרוּךְ הוּא, לֹא דִין הוּא שֶׁתִּלְמוֹד אֵיךְ תִּכָּנֵס לְבֵית קָדֶשׁ הַקָּדָשִׁים,

— Hearing this, [the man] said to him, "Convert me to Judaism on condition that you have me appointed as Kohen Gadol!" אָמַר לוֹ: אֵין כֹּהֵן בְּיִשְׂרָאֵל — Annoyed by this brazen וְאֵין לָנוּ כֹּהֲנִים גְּדוֹלִים שֶׁיַּעַמְדוּ וְיִשְׁתַּמְּשׁוּ בִּכְהוּנָה גְדוֹלָה request, [Shammai] replied, "Is there no Kohen among the people of Israel, and do we not have Kohanim Gedolim who can stand and serve in the High Priesthood, אֶלָּא גֵּר הַקַּל שֶׁלֹּא בָא אֶלָּא בְּמַקְלוֹ וּבְתַרְמִילוֹ וְיָבֹא וְיִשְׁתַּמֵּשׁ בִּכְהוּנָה גְדוֹלָה — except for a simple convert who comes into the Jewish people with no more than his staff and sack,[24] and he would think that he can come and serve in the High Priesthood?!" גָּעַר בּוֹ וְהוֹצִיאוּ בִּנְזִיפָה — [Shammai] censured him for his brazenness and sent him away disapprovingly. בָּא אָמַר לוֹ: רַבִּי, גַּיְּירֵנִי עַל מְנָת שֶׁתְּשִׂימֵנִי — [The man] then came to Hillel לְהִלֵּל כֹּהֵן גָּדוֹל — and said to him, "Convert me to Judaism on condition that you have me appointed as Kohen Gadol, שֶׁאֶעֱמוֹד וַאֲשַׁמֵּשׁ עַל גַּבֵּי הַמִּזְבֵּחַ — so that I may stand and perform the service upon the Altar."[25] אָמַר לוֹ: שֵׁב — [Hillel] then said to him, "Sit and I will tell you something וְאוֹמַר לְךָ דָבָר אֶחָד concerning your desire to be appointed Kohen Gadol. מִי שֶׁמְּבַקֵּשׁ לְהַקְבִּיל פְּנֵי מֶלֶךְ בָּשָׂר וָדָם — Someone who seeks to greet the presence of a human king, לֹא דִין הוּא שֶׁיִּלְמוֹד אֵיךְ יִכָּנֵס וְאֵיךְ יֵצֵא — is it not only reasonable that he should first learn the protocol as to how he is to enter the king's presence and how he is to leave it?" אָמַר לוֹ: הֵן — [The man] replied, "Yes, it is only reasonable." אַתָּה שֶׁמְּבַקֵּשׁ לְהַקְבִּיל פְּנֵי מֶלֶךְ מַלְכֵי הַמְּלָכִים הַקָּדוֹשׁ בָּרוּךְ הוּא — Hillel continued, "Then you, who seek to greet the presence of the King Who reigns over kings, the Holy One, Blessed is He, by serving in His Temple, לֹא דִין הוּא שֶׁתִּלְמוֹד אֵיךְ תִּכָּנֵס לְבֵית קֹדֶשׁ הַקָּדָשִׁים — is it not even more reasonable that

rather than as an illustration of Hillel's humble approach as well.

24. That is, he enters as a newcomer, without any special merit or impressive ancestry.

25. Here, too, according to the version of this incident recounted in Shabbos 31a (as explained by Rashi there; see, however, Ben Avraham cited in note 19 above), Hillel converted the man to Judaism at this point, confident that he would succeed in convincing him that the condition he sought to impose on his conversion was misguided.

אֵיךְ תֵּיטִיב אֶת הַנֵּרוֹת, אֵיךְ תִּקְרַב לְגַבֵּי מִזְבֵּחַ, אֵיךְ תַּעֲרוֹךְ אֶת הַשֻּׁלְחָן,
אֵיךְ תְּסַדֵּר אֶת הַמַּעֲרָכָה. אָמַר לוֹ: הַטּוֹב בְּעֵינֶיךָ עֲשֵׂה. כָּתַב לוֹ תְּחִלָּה אָלֶף
בֵּית, וְלִמְּדוּ תּוֹרַת כֹּהֲנִים,²⁶ וְהָיָה לוֹמֵד וְהוֹלֵךְ עַד שֶׁהִגִּיעַ (במדבר ג, י; יח, ז)
"וְהַזָּר הַקָּרֵב יוּמָת",²⁷ נָשָׂא אוֹתוֹ גֵּר קַל וָחֹמֶר בְּעַצְמוֹ וְאָמַר: מָה אִם יִשְׂרָאֵל
שֶׁנִּקְרְאוּ בָּנִים לַמָּקוֹם,²⁸ וַעֲלֵיהֶם אָמְרָה שְׁכִינָה (שמות יט, ו) "וְאַתֶּם תִּהְיוּ לִי
מַמְלֶכֶת כֹּהֲנִים וְגוֹי קָדוֹשׁ", אַף עַל פִּי כֵן הִזְהִיר עֲלֵיהֶם הַכָּתוּב "וְהַזָּר
הַקָּרֵב יוּמָת", אֲנִי גֵּר הַקַּל לֹא בָּאתִי אֶלָּא בְּתַרְמִילִי, עַל אַחַת כַּמָּה וְכַמָּה.

אֵיךְ תֵּיטִיב — you should first learn how you are to enter the Holy of Holies,
אֶת הַנֵּרוֹת — אֵיךְ תִּקְרַב לְגַבֵּי — how you are to clean the lamps of the Menorah,
מִזְבֵּחַ — how you are to approach the Altar, אֵיךְ תַּעֲרוֹךְ אֶת הַשֻּׁלְחָן — how
you are to prepare the Show-bread on the Table, אֵיךְ תְּסַדֵּר אֶת הַמַּעֲרָכָה —
and how you are to arrange the pyre on the Altar?" אָמַר לוֹ: הַטּוֹב בְּעֵינֶיךָ עֲשֵׂה
— Trusting the sage who was so obviously guiding him with care, [the man]
said, "Whatever you see fit for me, do." כָּתַב לוֹ תְּחִלָּה אָלֶף בֵּית — So [Hillel]
first wrote down the Hebrew alphabet for him and taught it to him, וְלִמְּדוּ
תּוֹרַת כֹּהֲנִים — and then taught him the Book of Leviticus.[26] וְהָיָה לוֹמֵד
וְהוֹלֵךְ עַד שֶׁהִגִּיעַ "וְהַזָּר הַקָּרֵב יוּמָת" — [The proselyte] continued learning more
and more Torah, until he reached the verse that states, And an alien who
approaches shall die (Numbers 3:10, 18:7), which refers to one who serves in
the Sanctuary when he is disqualified from the position.[27] נָשָׂא אוֹתוֹ גֵּר קַל
וָחֹמֶר בְּעַצְמוֹ — Seeing these words, [the proselyte] reasoned a kal va'chomer
with regard to himself, וְאָמַר: מָה אִם יִשְׂרָאֵל שֶׁנִּקְרְאוּ בָּנִים לַמָּקוֹם — and said,
"If born Israelites, who are called sons of the Ominipresent,[28] וַעֲלֵיהֶם
אָמְרָה שְׁכִינָה "וְאַתֶּם תִּהְיוּ לִי מַמְלֶכֶת כֹּהֲנִים וְגוֹי קָדוֹשׁ" — and regarding whom
the Divine Presence declared, You shall be to Me a kingdom of ministers
and a holy nation (Exodus 19:6), אַף עַל פִּי כֵן הִזְהִיר עֲלֵיהֶם הַכָּתוּב "וְהַזָּר
הַקָּרֵב יוּמָת" — have nonetheless been warned by Scripture, And an alien
who approaches shall die, אֲנִי גֵּר הַקַּל לֹא בָּאתִי אֶלָּא בְּתַרְמִילִי עַל אַחַת כַּמָּה
וְכַמָּה — then I, a simple convert, who is coming into the Jewish people with

---

26. When teaching Torah for the first time
to a student, it is a common custom to begin with the Book of Leviticus [see Vayikra
Rabbah 7 §3, et al.] (Ben Avraham; see
also above, 6 §2). [It is not simply that Hillel
taught him this Book because it details the
laws of the Temple service, for it is evident
from the course of the narrative that he had
taught him other Books of the Torah as
well.]

27. [These words appear as well in Numbers 1:51, but there they do not refer to an
alien who comes to perform the sacrificial
service, but rather the Levite service of dis-
mantling and erecting the Tabernacle; see
Torah Temimah on Numbers 1:51.]

28. As it is stated, So said HASHEM, "My firstborn son is Israel" (Exodus 4:22) and, You
are sons to HASHEM, your God (Deuteronomy
14:1).

מִיָּד נִתְפַּיֵּיס אוֹתוֹ גֵּר מֵאֵלָיו[29], בָּא לוֹ אֵצֶל הִלֵּל הַזָּקֵן, אָמַר לוֹ: כָּל
הַבְּרָכוֹת שֶׁבַּתּוֹרָה יָנוּחוּ עַל רֹאשְׁךָ, שֶׁאִם הָיִיתָ כְּשַׁמַּאי הַזָּקֵן לֹא בָּאתִי
(לְהַקָּהֵל) בְּיִשְׂרָאֵל, קַפְּדָנוּתוֹ שֶׁל שַׁמַּאי הַזָּקֵן בִּקֵּשׁ לְאַבְּדֵנִי מִן הָעוֹלָם
הַזֶּה וּמִן הָעוֹלָם הַבָּא[30], עִנְוְתָנוּתְךָ הֱבִיאַנִי לְחַיֵּי הָעוֹלָם הַזֶּה וְהַבָּא. אָמְרוּ:
לְאוֹתוֹ גֵּר נוֹלְדוּ שְׁנֵי בָנִים, לְאֶחָד קָרְאוּ הִלֵּל וּלְאֶחָד קָרְאוּ גַּמְלִיאֵל וְהָיוּ
קוֹרְאִין אוֹתָם גֵּרִים שֶׁל הִלֵּל[32]:

ד. שׁוּב יוֹם אֶחָד לִפְנֵי מִיתָתְךָ, שָׁאֲלוּ תַּלְמִידָיו אֶת רַבִּי אֱלִיעֶזֶר:

מִיָּד no more than my sack, all the more so am I included in this warning!"
נִתְפַּיֵּיס אוֹתוֹ גֵּר מֵאֵלָיו — Immediately, that convert came to terms on his own
with the fact that he could never be appointed Kohen Gadol.[29] בָּא לוֹ אֵצֶל
הִלֵּל הַזָּקֵן אָמַר לוֹ — Subsequently, he came to Hillel the Elder and said to him,
כָּל הַבְּרָכוֹת שֶׁבַּתּוֹרָה יָנוּחוּ עַל רֹאשְׁךָ — "All of the blessings in the Torah should
rest upon your head! שֶׁאִם הָיִיתָ כְּשַׁמַּאי הַזָּקֵן לֹא בָּאתִי לְהַקָּהֵל בְּיִשְׂרָאֵל — For
if you had been strict like Shammai the Elder, I would not have come to join
in the congregation of Israel. קַפְּדָנוּתוֹ שֶׁל שַׁמַּאי הַזָּקֵן בִּקֵּשׁ לְאַבְּדֵנִי מִן הָעוֹלָם
הַזֶּה וּמִן הָעוֹלָם הַבָּא — The strictness of Shammai the Elder sought to banish
me from this world and from the World to Come.[30] עִנְוְתָנוּתְךָ הֱבִיאַנִי לְחַיֵּי
הָעוֹלָם הַזֶּה וְהַבָּא — But your humility and forbearance brought me to the life
of this world and and the next."

The gratitude of this convert remained for future generations:
אָמְרוּ: לְאוֹתוֹ גֵּר נוֹלְדוּ שְׁנֵי בָּנִים — They said: Two sons were subsequently
born to that proselyte; לְאֶחָד קָרְאוּ "הִלֵּל" וּלְאֶחָד קָרְאוּ "גַּמְלִיאֵל" — one he
named Hillel, after Hillel the Elder, and the other he named Gamliel, after Hillel's grandson, Rabban Gamliel,[31] וְהָיוּ קוֹרְאִין אוֹתָם "גֵּרִים שֶׁל הִלֵּל" — and
[people] would call them "Hillel's converts."[32]

§4 The Baraisa expounds R' Eliezer's third saying:
שׁוּב יוֹם אֶחָד לִפְנֵי מִיתָתְךָ — "And repent one day before your death."
שָׁאֲלוּ תַּלְמִידָיו אֶת רַבִּי אֱלִיעֶזֶר — The disciples asked their teacher, R' Eliezer,

---

29. [The convert's realization of his disqualification echoed the very words with
which Shammai had censured him earlier.
But whereas Shammai had sought to force
this idea on the convert, Hillel allowed him
to come to this realization — and accept its
implications — on his own.]

30. Had I not become a Jew, it is likely that
my life in this world would have been without true meaning, and that I would not have
earned a share in the World to Come.

31. *Mefaresh* and *Binyan Yehoshua*, citing
Shabbos 15a.

Hillel's grandson, Rabban Gamliel, was a
more widely known scion of Hillel's dynasty
than was Hillel's son, Rabban Shimon. The
convert therefore felt that naming the second son Gamliel would be a greater honor
to Hillel than naming him Shimon (*Avos
HaRosh* [Vol. 1]).

32. [Although those children were born
Jews, the title was meant to convey the idea

וְכִי אָדָם יוֹדֵעַ בְּאֵיזֶה יוֹם יָמוּת שֶׁיַּעֲשֶׂה תְּשׁוּבָה. אָמַר לָהֶם: כָּל שֶׁכֵּן
שֶׁיַּעֲשֶׂה תְּשׁוּבָה הַיּוֹם שֶׁמָּא יָמוּת לְמָחָר, יָשׁוּב לְמָחָר שֶׁמָּא יָמוּת
לְמָחֳרָתוֹ, וְנִמְצָא כָּל יָמָיו בִּתְשׁוּבָה³³. רַבִּי³⁴ יוֹסֵי בַּר יְהוּדָה אָמַר
מִשּׁוּם רַבִּי יְהוּדָה בְּרַבִּי אֶלְעָאי שֶׁאָמַר מִשּׁוּם רַבִּי אֶלְעָאי אָבִיו שֶׁאָמַר
מִשּׁוּם רַבִּי אֱלִיעֶזֶר הַגָּדוֹל³⁵: (שׁוּב יוֹם אֶחָד לִפְנֵי מִיתָתְךָ³⁶, וֶהֱוֵי
מִתְחַמֵּם כְּנֶגֶד אוּרָן שֶׁל חֲכָמִים³⁷, הֱוֵי זָהִיר בְּגַחַלְתָּן שֶׁלֹּא תִכָּוֶה³⁸,

---

regarding this: וְכִי אָדָם יוֹדֵעַ בְּאֵיזֶה יוֹם יָמוּת שֶׁיַּעֲשֶׂה תְּשׁוּבָה — **"But does a
person know on which day he will die, that he should** know to **repent one day
in advance?"**   אָמַר לָהֶם: כָּל שֶׁכֵּן שֶׁיַּעֲשֶׂה תְּשׁוּבָה הַיּוֹם שֶׁמָּא יָמוּת לְמָחָר — **He
replied, "All the more** reason **that one should repent today, for perhaps he
will die tomorrow;**   יָשׁוּב לְמָחָר שֶׁמָּא יָמוּת לְמָחֳרָתוֹ — and **he should likewise repent tomorrow, for perhaps he will die the next day.**   וְנִמְצָא כָּל יָמָיו
בִּתְשׁוּבָה — **And** if one always conducts himself in this way, **it emerges** that **all
his days are** lived **in a state of repentance."** Hence, R' Eliezer urges each and
every person to constantly repent for any sins he may have committed, as it
may indeed be just one day before his death.[33]

The Baraisa continues to present sayings of R' Eliezer:[34]

רַבִּי יוֹסֵי בַּר יְהוּדָה אָמַר מִשּׁוּם רַבִּי יְהוּדָה בְּרַבִּי אֶלְעָאי שֶׁאָמַר מִשּׁוּם רַבִּי אֶלְעָאי
אָבִיו שֶׁאָמַר מִשּׁוּם רַבִּי אֱלִיעֶזֶר הַגָּדוֹל — **R' Yose bar Yehudah said in the name
of R' Yehudah bar R' Il'ai, who said in the name of his father, R' Il'ai, who
in turn, said in the name of R' Eliezer the Great:**[35]   שׁוּב יוֹם אֶחָד לִפְנֵי
מִיתָתְךָ — **Repent one day before your death;**[36]   וֶהֱוֵי מִתְחַמֵּם כְּנֶגֶד אוּרָן
שֶׁל חֲכָמִים — **warm yourself by the fire of the Sages,**[37]   הֱוֵי זָהִיר בְּגַחַלְתָּן
שֶׁלֹּא תִכָּוֶה — and **beware of their glowing coal, lest you be scorched,**[38]

---

that they were Jewish only by virtue of Hillel's patience and wisdom, which are what
brought about their father's conversion to
Judaism.]

33. Possibly, this lesson is already alluded to
in R' Eliezer's original wording, which can be
construed as, "Repent! [Today might be] one
day before your death!" (*Rif* [in *Ein Yaakov*]
to *Shabbos* 153a).

34. [See below, note 36 and end of note 40,
for how the sayings that follow relate to the
ones cited above.]

35. [R' Eliezer ben Hyrkanos, the disciple
of Rabban Yochanan ben Zakkai, was also
known as R' Eliezer the Great.]

36. This teaching was already mentioned.
See *Magen Avos*, who suggests that it is

repeated because the ones that follow are
meant to amplify it, as follows: Do not think
that the directive to "repent one day before
your death" is directed to people who sin
regularly. It is also directed to righteous
people who may occasionally commit a
sin, as evidenced by the fact that R' Eliezer
goes on to urge them to warm themselves
by the fire of the Sages, etc. [*Gra*, however,
removes this repetition of "repent one day
before your death."]

37. That is, heed their wise words (*Binyan
Yehoshua*, from *Rashi* to *Avos* ad loc.).

38. I.e., be careful to guard their words so
that you are not punished for transgressing
them (ibid.; see below, note 40, for an alternative understanding).

שֶׁנְּשִׁיכָתָן נְשִׁיכַת שׁוּעָל, וַעֲקִיצָתָן עֲקִיצַת עַקְרָב,[39] אַף כָּל דִּבְרֵיהֶם
כְּגַחֲלֵי אֵשׁ:[40]

וַעֲקִיצָתָן עֲקִיצַת — שֶׁנְּשִׁיכָתָן נְשִׁיכַת שׁוּעָל — for their bite is the bite of a fox,
נְשִׁיכַת שׁוּעָל — their sting is the sting of a scorpion,[39]
עַקְרָב — אַף כָּל דִּבְרֵיהֶם כְּגַחֲלֵי אֵשׁ
and even *any* of their words are like fiery coals.[40]

---

39. A fox's teeth are sharp and slanted, making its bite all the more painful and difficult to heal than that of other animals. The harm of a scorpion's bite is magnified by the injection of the scorpion's poison. Similar is the pain and harm that result from violating the words of the Sages (*Binyan Yehoshua*, from *Rashi* and *Rav*).

40. The word "any" warns a person not to ignore even those Rabbinic enactments that may seem minor to him (ibid.).

Alternatively, R' Eliezer's teachings, from "beware of their glowing coal" and on, do not shift focus to the *words* of the Sages, but rather continue his teaching regarding "warm yourself by the fire of the Sages": Yes, draw close to their fire enough to be warmed, but be careful not to draw *too* close to the fire — to be overly familiar with and disrespectful toward them — lest you be burned by it. For their bite is the bite of a fox, etc. (*Binyan Yehoshua*, from *Rambam* to *Avos* ad loc.; *Rav* and *R' Yonah* there).

At the beginning of the chapter, we enumerated the three sayings of R' Eliezer as (i) Let your fellow's honor be as dear to you as your own; (ii) do not anger easily; and (iii) repent one day before your death. This is how *Rambam* (on *Avos* loc. cit.) enumerates them; and he writes that the additional sayings of R' Eliezer quoted by the Mishnah [and our Baraisa] were, in contrast to the first three, not his original sayings, but those that he had heard from others. [*Magen Avos* (cited above in note 36) follows *Rambam's* enumeration, but considers the rest of the sayings cited by the Baraisa as an elaboration of the third saying rather than as independent ones.] *Rashi* and *Rav* (on *Avos* loc. cit.), however, count the three sayings of R' Eliezer as: (i) Let your fellow's honor be as dear to you as your own [which will be possible if you] do not anger easily; (ii) repent one day before your death; (iii) and warm yourself by the fire of the Sages, etc. [Our Baraisa, which elaborates R' Eliezer's sayings immediately after citing "repent one day before your death," seems to follow *Rambam's* enumeration.]

﴾ פֶּרֶק טז ﴿

א. רַבִּי יְהוֹשֻׁעַ אוֹמֵר: עַיִן הָרַע וְיֵצֶר הָרַע וְשִׂנְאַת הַבְּרִיּוֹת מוֹצִיאִין אֶת הָאָדָם מִן הָעוֹלָם. עַיִן הָרַע, כֵּיצַד, מְלַמֵּד שֶׁכְּשֵׁם שֶׁאָדָם רוֹאֶה אֶת בֵּיתוֹ שֶׁל עַצְמוֹ, כָּךְ יְהֵא רוֹאֶה בֵּיתוֹ שֶׁל חֲבֵירוֹ[1], וּכְשֵׁם שֶׁאָדָם רוֹצֶה שֶׁלֹּא לְהוֹצִיא שֵׁם רַע עַל אִשְׁתּוֹ וּבָנָיו, כָּךְ יְהֵא אָדָם רוֹצֶה שֶׁלֹּא לְהוֹצִיא שֵׁם רַע עַל אֵשֶׁת חֲבֵירוֹ וְעַל בָּנָיו שֶׁל חֲבֵירוֹ[2]. דָּבָר אַחֵר, עַיִן הָרַע, כֵּיצַד, שֶׁלֹּא תְּהֵא עֵינוֹ שֶׁל אָדָם צַר בְּמִשְׁנָתוֹ שֶׁל חֲבֵירוֹ[3],

﴾ CHAPTER 16 ﴿

§1 The Baraisa continues expounding the sayings of Rabban Yochanan ben Zakkai's primary disciples. This chapter elaborates the three things spoken of by R' Yehoshua (cited in *Avos* 2:11):

רַבִּי יְהוֹשֻׁעַ אוֹמֵר: עַיִן הָרַע וְיֵצֶר הָרַע וְשִׂנְאַת הַבְּרִיּוֹת מוֹצִיאִין אֶת הָאָדָם מִן הָעוֹלָם — R' Yehoshua says: (i) An evil eye, (ii) the evil inclination, and (iii) the hatred of other people remove a person from the world.

The Baraisa elaborates:

עַיִן הָרַע, כֵּיצַד — The first thing that removes a person from the world is "an evil eye" — how so? מְלַמֵּד שֶׁכְּשֵׁם שֶׁאָדָם רוֹאֶה אֶת בֵּיתוֹ שֶׁל עַצְמוֹ — This teaches that just as a person views his own home, כָּךְ יְהֵא רוֹאֶה בֵּיתוֹ שֶׁל חֲבֵירוֹ — so should he view the home of his fellow.[1] וּכְשֵׁם שֶׁאָדָם רוֹצֶה שֶׁלֹּא לְהוֹצִיא שֵׁם רַע עַל אִשְׁתּוֹ וּבָנָיו — And just as a person wants that there should be no slander spread against his wife and children, כָּךְ יְהֵא אָדָם רוֹצֶה שֶׁלֹּא לְהוֹצִיא שֵׁם רַע עַל אֵשֶׁת חֲבֵירוֹ וְעַל בָּנָיו שֶׁל חֲבֵירוֹ — so should a person want that there should be no slander spread against his fellow's wife or children.[2]

Another explanation:

דָּבָר אַחֵר, עַיִן הָרַע, כֵּיצַד — Another explanation: "An evil eye" — how so? שֶׁלֹּא תְּהֵא עֵינוֹ שֶׁל אָדָם צַר בְּמִשְׁנָתוֹ שֶׁל חֲבֵירוֹ — This teaches that a person

---

1. "The evil eye" might refer simply to a stingy or jealous attitude toward others (as explained above in 14 §5) or to the metaphysical harm one's jealousy of others' good fortune can bring upon them (*Binyan Yehoshua*, from *Rav*). Either way, R' Yehoshua exhorts a person to rejoice in his fellow's good fortune (just as he would rejoice in his own) and not view it with "an evil eye" (see *Avos HaRosh* [Vol. 1]). Conversely, R' Yehoshua here also exhorts us to feel the pain of our fellow's misfortune. Just as a person

would feel about his own home were it to be in disrepair, so too should he feel about the home of his fellow, and seek to assist him in any way possible (*Ben Avraham*).

2. One who *does* view his friend's home, family, or success with an evil eye, however, is punished by having his *own* prosperity suffer. And he destroys even his own self, as it is stated, *But envy [brings] rotting of the bones* (*Proverbs* 14:30). Thus, an evil eye "removes a person from the world" (*Machzor Vitri* to *Avos* ad loc.).

מַעֲשֶׂה בְּאָדָם אֶחָד שֶׁהָיָה עֵינוֹ צָרָה בְּמִשְׁנָתוֹ שֶׁל חֲבֵירוֹ, נִתְקַצְּרוּ חַיָּיו
וְנִפְטַר וְהָלַךְ לוֹ:[4]

ב. יֵצֶר הָרָע, כֵּיצַד[5], אָמְרוּ: שָׁלֹשׁ עֶשְׂרֵה שָׁנָה גָּדוֹל יֵצֶר הָרָע מִיֵּצֶר טוֹב[6],
מִמְּעֵי אִמּוֹ שֶׁל אָדָם הָיָה גָּדֵל וּבָא עִמּוֹ[7], וְהִתְחִיל מְחַלֵּל שַׁבָּתוֹת

מַעֲשֶׂה should not begrudge his fellow's attainments in **Torah learning.**[3]
בְּאָדָם אֶחָד שֶׁהָיָה עֵינוֹ צָרָה בְּמִשְׁנָתוֹ שֶׁל חֲבֵירוֹ — It happened with a certain
person who begrudged his fellow's Torah learning **נִתְקַצְּרוּ חַיָּיו וְנִפְטַר וְהָלַךְ**
לוֹ — that his life was shortened and he passed and left this world prematurely.[4] Indeed, his evil eye toward his fellow's Torah learning removed him
from the world.

§2 The Baraisa expounds R' Yehoshua's second saying:

יֵצֶר הָרָע, כֵּיצַד — The second thing that removes a person from the
world is "the evil inclination" — how so?[5] **אָמְרוּ: שָׁלֹשׁ עֶשְׂרֵה שָׁנָה גָּדוֹל**
יֵצֶר הָרָע מִיֵּצֶר טוֹב — [The Sages] said: The evil inclination in a person is
thirteen years older than the good inclination that is in him.[6] **מִמְּעֵי אִמּוֹ**
שֶׁל אָדָם הָיָה גָּדֵל וּבָא עִמּוֹ — From the time he leaves his mother's womb,
[the evil inclination] continually grows with him.[7] **וְהִתְחִיל מְחַלֵּל שַׁבָּתוֹת**

---

3. The Midrash teaches that R' Akiva had
12,000 students who died prematurely within a short period of time. The Sages explain
that the reason for this tragedy was that
they all begrudged one another's success
in Torah; each one viewed his colleague's
prominence as a threat to his own, and was
therefore unwilling to assist the other by
sharing his own Torah thoughts (see *Bereishis Rabbah* 61 §3). Our Baraisa warns us
against this begrudging attitude toward the
Torah successes of others (*Avos HaRosh*
[Vol. 1]).

4. A severe punishment, but one that is
meted out measure for measure: He did not
want his friend to succeed in Torah, which
lengthens one's life [see *Proverbs* 3:1-2, et
al.], so his own life was shortened (*Ahavas
Chesed*). Alternatively, his begrudging attitude toward his friend's learning indicates
that, on some level, his own learning was for
self-aggrandizement. Thus, he is one who
seeks to profit from his Torah, about whom
the Mishnah teaches (*Avos* 4:5) that "he
takes his life from the world" (*Sifsei Chaim,*

Moadim III, p. 47). [See also *Shaarei Teshuvah* 3:160.]

5. It is self-understood that one who allows
himself to be led astray by his evil inclination
thereby removes himself from the world.
The Baraisa's question, however, is *how*
the evil inclination is able to mislead a person. Why shouldn't one's good inclination
naturally be an opposite and equal force for
good? (*Magen Avos*).

6. For the evil inclination enters into a person at birth, while the good inclination enters
into him only when he becomes thirteen, as
the Baraisa explains below.

7. Some say that the good and evil inclinations are external forces that enter and
operate upon a person, while others say
that they are innate — the physical side of
the person is his "evil inclination" (as it inclines the person to overindulge in material
things), while his spiritual side is his "good
inclination." Our Baraisa, which speaks of
the evil inclination continually growing with
a person from birth, seems to take the latter
approach (*Avos HaRosh* [Vol. 1], p. 161a).

אֵין מְמַחֶה בְּיָדוֹ‪[9]‬, [הוֹרֵג נְפָשׁוֹת אֵין מְמַחֶה בְּיָדוֹ, הוֹלֵךְ לִדְבַר עֲבֵירָה אֵין
מְמַחֶה בְּיָדוֹ‪[10]‬,] לְאַחַר שָׁלֹשׁ עֶשְׂרֵה שָׁנָה נוֹלַד יֵצֶר טוֹב, כֵּיוָן שֶׁמְּחַלֵּל
שַׁבָּתוֹת, אוֹמֵר לוֹ: רֵיקָה, הֲרֵי הוּא אוֹמֵר (שמות לא, יד) "מְחַלְלֶיהָ מוֹת
יוּמָת". הוֹרֵג נְפָשׁוֹת, אוֹמֵר לוֹ: רֵיקָה, הֲרֵי הוּא אוֹמֵר (בראשית ט, ו) "שֹׁפֵךְ
דַּם הָאָדָם בָּאָדָם דָּמוֹ יִשָּׁפֵךְ". הוֹלֵךְ לִדְבַר עֲבֵירָה, אוֹמֵר לוֹ: רֵיקָה, הֲרֵי
הוּא אוֹמֵר (ויקרא כ, י) "מוֹת יוּמַת הַנֹּאֵף וְהַנֹּאָפֶת". בִּזְמַן שֶׁאָדָם מְחַמֵּם אֶת

אֵין מְמַחֶה בְּיָדוֹ — As time goes by, **if he begins to desecrate the Sabbath,**[8] [the evil inclination] **does not protest against his** doing so.[9] הוֹרֵג נְפָשׁוֹת אֵין מְמַחֶה בְּיָדוֹ — **If he commits murder,** [the evil inclination] **does not protest against his** doing so. הוֹלֵךְ לִדְבַר עֲבֵירָה אֵין מְמַחֶה בְּיָדוֹ — **If he goes to** commit **a sin** of immorality, [the evil inclination] **does not protest against him.**[10] לְאַחַר שָׁלֹשׁ עֶשְׂרֵה שָׁנָה נוֹלַד יֵצֶר טוֹב — **After thirteen years** have passed since the evil inclination first entered him, **the good inclination is "born"** inside of him, and it tries to wean him from the sins to which he has grown accustomed. כֵּיוָן שֶׁמְּחַלֵּל שַׁבָּתוֹת אוֹמֵר לוֹ: רֵיקָה, הֲרֵי הוּא אוֹמֵר "מְחַלְלֶיהָ מוֹת יוּמָת" — Now, **when he** is about to **desecrate the Sabbath** as he has become accustomed to doing, [the good inclination] **says to him, "Empty one! It is stated** in Scripture, *You shall observe the Sabbath, for it is holy to you; its desecrators shall be put to death!"* (*Exodus* 31:14). הוֹרֵג נְפָשׁוֹת אוֹמֵר לוֹ: רֵיקָה, הֲרֵי הוּא אוֹמֵר "שֹׁפֵךְ דַּם הָאָדָם בָּאָדָם דָּמוֹ יִשָּׁפֵךְ" — Now, **when he is** about **to commit murder** as he has become accustomed to doing, [the good inclination] **says to him, "Empty one! It is stated** in Scripture, *Whoever sheds the blood of man, by man shall his blood be shed!"* (*Genesis* 9:6). הוֹלֵךְ לִדְבַר עֲבֵירָה אוֹמֵר לוֹ: רֵיקָה, הֲרֵי הוּא אוֹמֵר "מוֹת יוּמַת הַנֹּאֵף וְהַנֹּאָפֶת" — Now, **when he goes to** commit **a sin** of immorality as he has become accustomed to doing, [the good inclination] **says to him, "Empty one! It is stated** in Scripture, *The adulterer and the adulteress shall be put to death!"* (*Leviticus* 20:10). בִּזְמַן שֶׁאָדָם מְחַמֵּם אֶת

---

8. [*Avos HaRosh* [Vol. 1]; see, however, *Ben Avraham.*]

9. [At this point, the person is a minor and not obligated to observe the Sabbath or any of the commandments. Nevertheless, his evil inclination's tolerance of what will eventually be deemed sinful behavior fosters in him a relaxed attitude toward sin which will accompany him into adulthood, as the Baraisa proceeds to explain.]

10. The Baraisa does not mean that every child inclines toward these particular sins.

It means simply that without the restraint of his good inclination (which is yet to come) he is liable to be drawn to sinful behavior, of which the Baraisa mentions the three most egregious examples. The three cardinal sins are idolatry, immorality, and murder. But since the desire for idolatry is no longer strong [see *Yoma* 69b], the Baraisa substitutes for it desecration of the Sabbath, which is, in some ways, tantamount to idolatry [see *Chullin* 5a (end) with *Rashi*] (*Ben Avraham*).

עַצְמוֹ וְהוֹלֵךְ לִדְבַר זִימָה, כָּל אֵבָרָיו נִשְׁמָעִין לוֹ, מִפְּנֵי שֶׁיֵּצֶר הָרַע מֶלֶךְ
הוּא עַל מָאתַיִם וְאַרְבָּעִים וּשְׁמוֹנָה אֵבָרִים, כְּשֶׁהוּא הוֹלֵךְ לִדְבַר מִצְוָה,
הִתְחִילוּ מִתְעַנִּין (לוֹ) כָּל אֵבָרָיו[11], מִפְּנֵי שֶׁיֵּצֶר הָרַע שֶׁבְּמֵעָיו מֶלֶךְ הוּא
עַל מָאתַיִם וְאַרְבָּעִים וּשְׁמוֹנָה אֵבָרִים שֶׁבְּאָדָם, וְיֵצֶר טוֹב אֵינוֹ דוֹמֶה אֶלָּא
לְמִי שֶׁהוּא חָבוּשׁ בְּבֵית הָאֲסוּרִין, שֶׁנֶּאֱמַר (קהלת ד, יד) "[כִּי] מִבֵּית הָסוּרִים
יָצָא לִמְלֹךְ", זֶה יֵצֶר טוֹב[12], וְיֵשׁ אוֹמְרִים: זֶה יוֹסֵף הַצַּדִּיק[13], כְּשֶׁבָּאתָה
אוֹתָהּ רְשָׁעָה הָיְתָה מְעַנָּה אוֹתוֹ בִּדְבָרֶיהָ[14], אָמְרָה לוֹ: אֲנִי אֶחְבָּשְׁךָ בְּבֵית

עַצְמוֹ וְהוֹלֵךְ לִדְבַר זִימָה — Moreover, when a person arouses himself and goes to commit a matter of immorality, כָּל אֵבָרָיו נִשְׁמָעִין לוֹ — all of his limbs stand ready to obey him in his sinful desire, מִפְּנֵי שֶׁיֵּצֶר הָרַע מֶלֶךְ הוּא עַל מָאתַיִם וְאַרְבָּעִים וּשְׁמוֹנָה אֵבָרִים — because the evil inclination is like a king over all of a person's two hundred and forty-eight limbs. כְּשֶׁהוּא הוֹלֵךְ לִדְבַר מִצְוָה — However, when he goes to perform a mitzvah matter, הִתְחִילוּ מִתְעַנִּין לוֹ כָּל אֵבָרָיו — then all of his limbs begin to become burdensome on him.[11] מִפְּנֵי שֶׁיֵּצֶר הָרַע שֶׁבְּמֵעָיו מֶלֶךְ הוּא עַל מָאתַיִם וְאַרְבָּעִים וּשְׁמוֹנָה אֵבָרִים שֶׁבְּאָדָם — Because the evil inclination that is in one's innards is like a king over all of a person's two hundred and forty-eight limbs, וְיֵצֶר טוֹב אֵינוֹ דוֹמֶה אֶלָּא לְמִי שֶׁהוּא חָבוּשׁ בְּבֵית הָאֲסוּרִין — whereas the good inclination is like nothing more than someone who is bound in a prison, שֶׁנֶּאֱמַר "כִּי מִבֵּית הָסוּרִים יָצָא לִמְלֹךְ" — as it is stated, *Because from the prison he emerged to reign* (*Ecclesiastes* 4:14) — זֶה יֵצֶר טוֹב — this refers to the good inclination.[12]

Another interpretation of the *Ecclesiastes* verse just cited: וְיֵשׁ אוֹמְרִים: זֶה יוֹסֵף הַצַּדִּיק — And some say that this verse refers to the righteous Joseph.[13] כְּשֶׁבָּאתָה אוֹתָהּ רְשָׁעָה הָיְתָה מְעַנָּה אוֹתוֹ בִּדְבָרֶיהָ — When that evil woman, Potiphar's wife, would approach Joseph,[14] she would threaten him with her words. אָמְרָה לוֹ: אֲנִי אֶחְבָּשְׁךָ בְּבֵית

---

11. From the root ענוי, *oppressed* or *burdened* (*Shenei Eliyahu*; see also *Magen Avos*, final approach). [Other texts have מִתְעַדְּנִין לוֹ, *become pampered upon him*, unwilling to exert themselves.]

12. At first, the good inclination is like a prisoner, who has little power to influence a person's decisions. But as time goes on and the person realizes that the good inclination is actually his true friend, it can rise to be "king" over the person's decisions, thus "emerging from prison to reign" (*Ben Avraham*).

The Baraisa thus answers its original question [see note 5]: because of the evil inclination's earlier and longer association with the person, it naturally has more influence over his decisions than does the good inclination, and that is how the evil inclination is able to "remove a person from the world."

13. Who, quite literally, emerged from an Egyptian prison cell to become a ruler over the entire Egypt. See *Genesis* Ch. 41. [See also below, note 18.]

14. The wife of Potiphar, Joseph's Egyptian master, tried relentlessly to entice Joseph

הָאֲסוּרִין. אָמַר לָהּ: (תהלים קמו, ז) ״ה׳ מַתִּיר אֲסוּרִים״. אָמְרָה לוֹ: אֲנִי אֲנַקֵּר
אֶת עֵינֶיךָ. אָמַר לָהּ: (שם, ח) ״ה׳ פֹּקֵחַ עִוְרִים״. אָמְרָה לוֹ: אֲנִי אֶכְפּוֹף אֶת
קוֹמָתְךָ. אָמַר לָהּ: (שם) ״ה׳ זֹקֵף כְּפוּפִים״ (אָמְרָה לוֹ: אֲנִי עוֹשָׂה אוֹתְךָ
רָשָׁע״[15]. אָמַר לָהּ: (שם) ״ה׳ אֹהֵב צַדִּיקִים״[16]. אָמְרָה לוֹ: אֲנִי עוֹשָׂה אוֹתְךָ
אֲרַמַאי. אָמַר לָהּ: (שם, ט) ״ה׳ שֹׁמֵר אֶת גֵּרִים״[17]. עַד שֶׁאָמַר: (בראשית לט,
ט) ״אֵיךְ אֶעֱשֶׂה הָרָעָה הַגְּדֹלָה הַזֹּאת״[18].) אַל תִּתְמַהּ עַל יוֹסֵף הַצַּדִּיק,

---

הָאֲסוּרִין — She said to him, "If you do not yield to me, **I will lock you in prison!**," אָמַר לָהּ: ״ה׳ מַתִּיר אֲסוּרִים״ — to which he replied, "*HASHEM releases the bound*" (*Psalms* 146:7). אָמְרָה לוֹ: אֲנִי אֲנַקֵּר אֶת עֵינֶיךָ — She said to him, "**I will gouge out your eyes**," אָמַר לָהּ: ה׳ פֹּקֵחַ עִוְרִים״ — to which he replied, "*HASHEM gives sight to the blind*" (ibid. v. 8). אָמְרָה לוֹ: אֲנִי אֶכְפּוֹף אֶת קוֹמָתְךָ — She said to him, "**I will make you bent over** and unable to stand erect!," אָמַר לָהּ: ״ה׳ זֹקֵף כְּפוּפִים״ — to which he replied, "*HASHEM straightens the bent*" (ibid.). אָמְרָה לוֹ: אֲנִי עוֹשָׂה אוֹתְךָ רָשָׁע — She said to him, "**I will make you wicked!**,"[15] אָמַר לָהּ: ״ה׳ אֹהֵב צַדִּיקִים״ — to which he replied, "*HASHEM loves the righteous*" (ibid.).[16] אָמְרָה לוֹ: אֲנִי עוֹשָׂה אוֹתְךָ אֲרַמַאי — She said to him, "**I will make you** act like **a non-Jew,** by coercing you until you transgress the laws of your God!," אָמַר לָהּ: ״ה׳ שֹׁמֵר אֶת גֵּרִים״ — to which **he** replied, "*HASHEM protects strangers*" (ibid. v. 9).[17] עַד שֶׁאָמַר ״אֵיךְ אֶעֱשֶׂה הָרָעָה הַגְּדֹלָה הַזֹּאת״ — All this transpired **until** he finally said to her, as recorded in Scripture, "*How* then **can I perpetrate this great evil** and *have sinned against God!*" (*Genesis* 39:9). This declaration made it absolutely clear that no argument could induce him to sin with her.[18]

The Baraisa notes that even greater feats of self-mastery were exhibited by great individuals in our storied past: אַל תִּתְמַהּ עַל יוֹסֵף הַצַּדִּיק — **Do not wonder about Joseph the Righteous** that he

---

to sin with her (see *Genesis* 39:7 ff.). The Baraisa relates some of the ways in which she harassed him.

15. I.e., I will slander you publicly as someone wicked (*Binyan Yehoshua,* second explanation).

16. And because I am righteous, He will protect me from your slander, and people will not believe it.

17. And since I am a stranger here in Egypt, God will protect me from your evil designs (*Magen Avos,* second approach; *Ahavas Chesed*).

Because Joseph did *not* listen to her

requests, God decreed that he would merit being appointed ruler over Egypt, to whom everyone else *would* listen (*Midrash Tanchuma, Nasso* §28). Moreover, for each distinct way that he displayed his moral fortitude during this ordeal, as the Baraisa has described, he was given an extra honor after being appointed ruler (see *Bereishis Rabbah* 90 §3).

18. *Magen Avos.* [Perhaps, the Baraisa means to interpret the verse, *Because from the prison he emerged to reign,* with regard to Joseph not only in the literal sense (that he emerged from the Egyptian prison to become viceroy), but in a metaphorical sense

שֶׁהֲרֵי רַבִּי צָדוֹק הָיָה גְּדוֹל הַדּוֹר[19], כְּשֶׁנִּשְׁבָּה נְטָלַתּוּ מַטְרוֹנִיתָא אַחַת
וְשִׁגְּרָה לוֹ שִׁפְחָה אַחַת יָפָה, כֵּיוָן שֶׁרָאָה אוֹתָהּ נָתַן עֵינָיו בַּכּוֹתֶל שֶׁלֹּא
יִרְאֶנָּה וְהָיָה יוֹשֵׁב וְשׁוֹנֶה כָּל הַלַּיְלָה[21], לְשַׁחֲרִית הָלְכָה וְהִקְבִּילָה אֵצֶל
גְּבִירְתָּהּ, אָמְרָה לָהּ: שָׁוֶה לִי הַמָּוֶת מִשֶּׁתִּתְּנֵנִי לָאִישׁ הַזֶּה. שָׁלְחָה
וְקָרְאָה לוֹ וְאָמְרָה לוֹ: מִפְּנֵי מָה לֹא עָשִׂיתָ עִם אִשָּׁה זֹאת כְּדֶרֶךְ
שֶׁיַּעֲשׂוּ בְּנֵי אָדָם. אָמַר לָהּ: וּמָה אֶעֱשֶׂה, מִכְּהוּנָּה גְּדוֹלָה אֲנִי מִמִּשְׁפָּחָה
גְּדוֹלָה אֲנִי, אָמַרְתִּי, שֶׁמָּא אַבָּא עָלֶיהָ וְהִרְבֵּיתִי מַמְזֵרִים בְּיִשְׂרָאֵל[22].

שֶׁהֲרֵי רַבִּי צָדוֹק הָיָה — should have had such mastery over his evil inclination,
גְּדוֹל הַדּוֹר — for in later times, R' Tzadok, who was the greatest of his generation, exhibited an even greater mastery, as seen in the following incident:[19]
כְּשֶׁנִּשְׁבָּה נְטָלַתּוּ מַטְרוֹנִיתָא אַחַת — When he was captured and brought to
Rome,[20] a certain matron took him as a slave, וְשִׁגְּרָה לוֹ שִׁפְחָה אַחַת יָפָה —
and sent a beautiful maidservant of hers to be with him. כֵּיוָן שֶׁרָאָה אוֹתָהּ
נָתַן עֵינָיו בַּכּוֹתֶל שֶׁלֹּא יִרְאֶנָּה — When he saw [the maidservant] in his room, he
fixed his eyes on the wall so that he would not look at her, וְהָיָה יוֹשֵׁב וְשׁוֹנֶה
כָּל הַלַּיְלָה — and, ignoring her entirely, he sat and learned Torah by heart
the entire night.[21] לְשַׁחֲרִית הָלְכָה וְהִקְבִּילָה אֵצֶל גְּבִירְתָּהּ — In the morning,
she went and complained bitterly to her mistress אָמְרָה לָהּ: שָׁוֶה לִי הַמָּוֶת
מִשֶּׁתִּתְּנֵנִי לָאִישׁ הַזֶּה — and said to her, "I would prefer death to your giving me
to his man, who ignored me completely!" שָׁלְחָה וְקָרְאָה לוֹ — Upon hearing
this, [the matron] sent and summoned him וְאָמְרָה לוֹ: מִפְּנֵי מָה לֹא עָשִׂיתָ עִם
אִשָּׁה זֹאת כְּדֶרֶךְ שֶׁיַּעֲשׂוּ בְּנֵי אָדָם — and asked him, "Why did you not act with
this woman the way normal human beings would?" אָמַר לָהּ: וּמָה אֶעֱשֶׂה
— He replied, "What could I do? מִכְּהוּנָּה גְּדוֹלָה אֲנִי מִמִּשְׁפָּחָה גְּדוֹלָה אֲנִי
— I descend from the High Priesthood, and I am thus from a prominent Jewish
family. אָמַרְתִּי שֶׁמָּא אַבָּא עָלֶיהָ וְהִרְבֵּיתִי מַמְזֵרִים בְּיִשְׂרָאֵל — So I reasoned, 'I
am afraid that if I do not ignore her, I might consort with her, and she will bear

---

as well: He broke free of the shackles of his
evil inclination, to rule over it and overcome,
in an almost superhuman way, the temptation to sin.]

19. The commentators wonder how the
Baraisa proves its point by describing R'
Tzadok as "the greatest of his generation."
On the contrary, one would *expect* the greatest sage of his generation to behave in so
noble a manner! Some explain the Baraisa
on the basis of the Gemara in *Succah* (52a),
which teaches that the greater the person,
the greater his evil inclination (see *Magen*

Avos and *Kisei Rachamim*; *Binyan Yehoshua*
below, s.v. שהרי ר"ע, from *Mefaresh*). *Gra*,
however, emends our text to read: שֶׁהֲרֵי
"מַעֲשֶׂה דְּרַבִּי צָדוֹק הָיָה גָּדוֹל מִמֶּנּוּ", for what
happened with R' Tzadok was greater than
that [see below, with note 23], and this is
indeed the reading found in several manuscript versions.

20. [As per the text of *Magen Avos* and other
versions.]

21. For, as the Gemara teaches (*Kiddushin* 30b), Torah is the primary antidote
to the evil inclination (*Magen Avos*), and

כֵּיָן שֶׁשָּׁמְעָה דְּבָרָיו צִוְּתָה עָלָיו וּפְטָרַתּוּ בְּכָבוֹד גָּדוֹל. (א"ל) אַל
תִּתְמַהּ עַל רַבִּי צָדוֹק שֶׁהֲרֵי רַבִּי עֲקִיבָא גָּדוֹל מִמֶּנּוּ, כְּשֶׁהָלַךְ לְאָרֶץ
אוֹכִילוּ קוּרְצָא אֵצֶל שִׁלְטוֹן אֶחָד וְשִׁגֵּר לוֹ שְׁתֵּי נָשִׁים יָפוֹת, רְחָצוּם
וְסָכוּם וְקִשְׁטוּם כְּכַלּוֹת חֲתָנִים וְהָיוּ מִתְנַפְּלוֹת עָלָיו כָּל הַלַּיְלָה,
זֹאת אוֹמֶרֶת חֲזוֹר אֶצְלִי, וְזֹאת אוֹמֶרֶת חֲזוֹר אֶצְלִי, וְהָיָה יוֹשֵׁב
בֵּינֵיהֶם וּמְרַקֵּק וְלֹא פָנָה אֲלֵיהֶן, הָלְכוּ לָהֶן וְהִקְבִּילוּ פְּנֵי הַשִּׁלְטוֹן
וְאָמְרוּ לוֹ: שָׁוֶה לָנוּ מָוֶת מִשֶּׁתִּתְּנֵנּוּ לָאִישׁ הַזֶּה. שָׁלַח וְקָרָא לוֹ,

me a child **and I will** have thus **increased the** amount of *mamzerim* among
the people of Israel.' "[22]   כֵּיָן שֶׁשָּׁמְעָה דְּבָרָיו צִוְּתָה עָלָיו — When [the matron]
heard his noble **words, she** immediately **issued a** command regarding him
וּפְטָרַתּוּ בְּכָבוֹד גָּדוֹל — **and sent him free with great honor.**

An even greater display of self-mastery:

אַל תִּתְמַהּ עַל רַבִּי צָדוֹק שֶׁהֲרֵי רַבִּי עֲקִיבָא גָּדוֹל מִמֶּנּוּ — **Do not wonder about R'**
Tzadok that he should have had such mastery over his evil inclination, **for**
what happened with R' Akiva was even greater than that.[23]   כְּשֶׁהָלַךְ לְאָרֶץ
אוֹכִילוּ קוּרְצָא אֵצֶל שִׁלְטוֹן אֶחָד — **When [R' Akiva] went to a** certain **country,**
there were those who slandered him to the ruler, who had R' Akiva confined.
וְשִׁגֵּר לוֹ שְׁתֵּי נָשִׁים יָפוֹת — He then **sent to [R' Akiva] two beautiful women,**
רְחָצוּם וְסָכוּם וְקִשְׁטוּם כְּכַלּוֹת חֲתָנִים — **who had been bathed, anointed, and**
adorned like brides for their **grooms.**   וְהָיוּ מִתְנַפְּלוֹת עָלָיו כָּל הַלַּיְלָה — **And**
they threw themselves on [R' Akiva] the entire night.   זֹאת אוֹמֶרֶת: חֲזוֹר
אֶצְלִי, וְזֹאת אוֹמֶרֶת: חֲזוֹר אֶצְלִי — **This** one was saying, "**Turn to me,**" and
that one was saying, "**Turn to me.**"   וְהָיָה יוֹשֵׁב בֵּינֵיהֶם וּמְרַקֵּק — But he just
sat between them and spat in disgust   וְלֹא פָנָה אֲלֵיהֶן — **and did not turn**
toward them at all.   הָלְכוּ לָהֶן וְהִקְבִּילוּ פְּנֵי הַשִּׁלְטוֹן — **They** finally **left and**
went to **complain bitterly before the ruler**   וְאָמְרוּ לוֹ: שָׁוֶה לָנוּ מָוֶת מִשֶּׁתִּתְּנֵנּוּ
לָאִישׁ הַזֶּה — **and said to him, "We would prefer death to your giving us to**
this man, who seemed repelled by us!"   שָׁלַח וְקָרָא לוֹ — Upon hearing this,

---

particularly when it comes to avoiding the
sin of immorality [*Avodah Zarah* 17b] (*Avos*
HaRosh [Vol. 1]). R' Tzadok did not want to
rely solely on his willpower to battle his evil
inclination, so he employed the power of
Torah as well.

22. A *mamzer* is a Jewish child born from
certain forbidden unions. Even if R' Tzadok
had fathered a child with the non-Jewish
maidservant, that child would not have been
Jewish and thus not technically a *mamzer*
(see *Magen Avos* and *Hagahos Yaavetz*).

Perhaps he meant that his male, non-Jewish
child from the maidservant might then
marry a Jewish woman and *their* offspring
would then be (according to some opinions)
a *mamzer* (ibid.). [Possibly, R' Tzadok used
mamzer in a non-technical sense to refer to
the illegitimate offspring of a noble family, a
consideration that a Roman matron would
find compelling.]

23. Translation follows *Magen Avos*, second
explanation. [Cf. his first explanation, and
Binyan Yehoshua.]

אָמַר לוֹ: מִפְּנֵי מָה לֹא עָשִׂיתָ עִם הַנָּשִׁים הַלָּלוּ כְּדֶרֶךְ שֶׁבְּנֵי אָדָם עוֹשִׂים
לְנָשִׁים, לֹא יָפוֹת הֵמָּה לֹא בְּנוֹת אָדָם כְּמוֹתְךָ הֵן מִי שֶׁבָּרָא אוֹתְךָ לֹא
בָּרָא אוֹתָם. אָמַר לוֹ: מָה אֶעֱשֶׂה, רֵיחָן בָּא עָלַי מְבַשֵּׂר נְבֵלוֹת וּטְרֵפוֹת
וּשְׁרָצִים.[24] אַל תִּתְמַהּ עַל רַבִּי עֲקִיבָא שֶׁהֲרֵי רַבִּי אֱלִיעֶזֶר הַגָּדוֹל גָּדוֹל
מִמֶּנּוּ, שֶׁגִּדֵּל אֶת בַּת אֲחוֹתוֹ שָׁלֹשׁ עֶשְׂרֵה שָׁנָה עִמּוֹ בַּמִּטָּה עַד שֶׁבָּאוּ
לָהּ סִימָנִים,[25] אָמַר לָהּ: צְאִי וְהִתְנַשְּׂאִי לְאִישׁ. אָמְרָה לוֹ: הֲלֹא אֲמָתְךָ
(אָנֹכִי) לְשִׁפְחָה לִרְחוֹץ רַגְלֵי תַּלְמִידֶיךָ.[26] אָמַר לָהּ: בִּתִּי, כְּבָר זָקַנְתִּי,

---

אָמַר לוֹ: מִפְּנֵי מָה לֹא עָשִׂיתָ עִם הַנָּשִׁים הַלָּלוּ כְּדֶרֶךְ — [the ruler] summoned him
and asked him, "Why did you not act with these — שֶׁבְּנֵי אָדָם עוֹשִׂים לְנָשִׁים
women the way normal human beings act with women? לֹא יָפוֹת הֵמָּה לֹא
Are they not beautiful? Are they not human beings just — בְּנוֹת אָדָם כְּמוֹתְךָ הֵן
like you? מִי שֶׁבָּרָא אוֹתְךָ לֹא בָּרָא אוֹתָם — Did the same One Who created
you not create them as well?" אָמַר לוֹ: מָה אֶעֱשֶׂה, רֵיחָן בָּא עָלַי מְבַשֵּׂר נְבֵלוֹת
וּטְרֵפוֹת וּשְׁרָצִים — [R' Akiva] replied, "What could I do? Their odor seemed
foul to me as from the meat of carrion, carcasses, and creeping things, and
this filled me with disgust!"[24]

An even greater display of self-mastery:
אַל תִּתְמַהּ עַל רַבִּי עֲקִיבָא שֶׁהֲרֵי רַבִּי אֱלִיעֶזֶר הַגָּדוֹל גָּדוֹל מִמֶּנּוּ — Do not wonder
about R' Akiva that he should have had such mastery over his evil inclination,
for what happened with R' Eliezer the Great was even greater than that.
שֶׁגִּדֵּל אֶת בַּת אֲחוֹתוֹ שָׁלֹשׁ עֶשְׂרֵה שָׁנָה עִמּוֹ בַּמִּטָּה — For he raised his sister's
daughter for thirteen years, even allowing her to sleep next to him in the bed,
עַד שֶׁבָּאוּ לָהּ סִימָנִים — until she developed signs of puberty.[25] אָמַר לָהּ: צְאִי
וְהִתְנַשְּׂאִי לְאִישׁ — At that point, he said to her, "The time has come for you to
go out of my house and get married." אָמְרָה לוֹ: הֲלֹא אֲמָתְךָ לְשִׁפְחָה לִרְחוֹץ
רַגְלֵי תַּלְמִידֶיךָ — She replied, "Were it that your maidservant could be a handmaid to wash even the feet of your students!"[26] אָמַר לָהּ: בִּתִּי כְּבָר זָקַנְתִּי

---

24. Some commentators take this to mean
that he smelled the nonkosher meat these
women had eaten (*Magen Avos; Binyan Yehoshua*, second approach).

25. And he never entertained the slightest
improper thought about her (see end of note
27). This was a greater exhibition of self-
mastery than the previous ones described,
for R' Eliezer's niece was someone he was
permitted to marry, and she was with him
in the same bed for so many years (*Magen
Avos*). [A father is permitted to sleep in the
same bed as his daughter until she matures,

as there is surely no concern of improper
thoughts (see Mishnah, *Kiddushin* 80b and
Even HaEzer 21:7). Perhaps, R' Eliezer did
so to the niece he was raising to demonstrate to her that she was exactly like his
daughter.]

26. This is a paraphrase of *I Samuel* 25:41
(*Ben Avraham*). In other words, it would be
a great merit for me to serve even your holy
students (*Binyan Yehoshua*), and certainly
you, their master. She was telling him, in effect, that she wished to marry no one other
than her saintly uncle (*Ben Avraham*).

צְאִי וְהִתְנַשְּׂאִי לְבָחוּר שֶׁכְּמוֹתֵךְ. אָמְרָה לוֹ: לֹא כָּךְ אָמַרְתִּי לְפָנֶיךָ, הֲלֹא
אֲמָתְךָ לְשִׁפְחָה לִרְחוֹץ רַגְלֵי תַלְמִידֶךָ. כֵּיוָן שֶׁשָּׁמַע אֶת דְּבָרֶיהָ נָטַל
מִמֶּנָּה רְשׁוּת לְקַדְּשָׁהּ וּבָא עָלֶיהָ:[27]

ג. רַבִּי רְאוּבֵן בֶּן אִצְטְרוּבֵּלִי אוֹמֵר: הֵיאַךְ מִתְרַחֵק אָדָם מִיֵּצֶר הָרַע
שֶׁבְּמֵעָיו,[28] לְפִי שֶׁטִּפָּה רִאשׁוֹנָה שֶׁאָדָם מֵטִיל בְּאִשָּׁה הוּא יֵצֶר
הָרַע,[29] וְיֵצֶר הָרַע אֵינוֹ שָׁרוּי אֶלָּא עַל מִפְתְּחֵי הַלֵּב, שֶׁנֶּאֱמַר (בראשית ד, ז)

— He said to her, "My daughter, I am not a suitable husband for you, as I
have already grown old. צְאִי וְהִתְנַשְּׂאִי לְבָחוּר שֶׁכְּמוֹתֵךְ — Go out and marry
someone young like yourself." אָמְרָה לוֹ: לֹא כָּךְ אָמַרְתִּי לְפָנֶיךָ — She replied,
"Did I not already tell you הֲלֹא אֲמָתְךָ לְשִׁפְחָה לִרְחוֹץ רַגְלֵי תַלְמִידֶךָ — 'Were
it that your maidservant could be a handmaid to wash even the feet of your
students'?" כֵּיוָן שֶׁשָּׁמַע אֶת דְּבָרֶיהָ נָטַל מִמֶּנָּה רְשׁוּת לְקַדְּשָׁהּ וּבָא עָלֶיהָ — When
he heard the conviction expressed by her words, he requested her permission
to betroth her and he married her and came unto her.[27]

§3 The Baraisa resumes discussing the evil inclination's influence over a
person:
רַבִּי רְאוּבֵן בֶּן אִצְטְרוּבֵּלִי אוֹמֵר — R' Reuven ben Itztrubeli says: הֵיאַךְ מִתְרַחֵק
אָדָם מִיֵּצֶר הָרַע שֶׁבְּמֵעָיו — How shall a person distance himself from the evil
inclination that resides inside him?![28] Why is the challenge so great? לְפִי
שֶׁטִּפָּה רִאשׁוֹנָה שֶׁאָדָם מֵטִיל בְּאִשָּׁה הוּא יֵצֶר הָרַע — For the initial drop of semen that a man deposits into a woman is the result of his desire created
by the evil inclination,[29] and thus, the evil inclination begins to form in a
child from his very inception.[30] וְיֵצֶר הָרַע אֵינוֹ שָׁרוּי אֶלָּא עַל מִפְתְּחֵי הַלֵּב
— Moreover, the evil inclination does not reside in any place other than at
the gateways of the person's heart, and motivates his decisions, שֶׁנֶּאֱמַר

---

27. [The available manuscripts and first-
print editions omit here the ל from
"לְקַדְשָׁהּ". Accordingly, this should be rendered: *He
asked her permission and betrothed her* ...]
Magen Avos explains that since R' Eliezer
was already old, he needed her to understand that he would be unable to fulfill a
husband's conjugal obligations to her to the
extent that a younger husband would, and
he obtained her permission to absolve him
from any greater obligations.
The Baraisa concludes with the words וּבָא
עָלֶיהָ, *and he came unto her,* to indicate that it
was *only* at this point that he did so, and never

in all the years that he raised her; something
that the Baraisa already implied but did not
yet state explicitly (*Ben Avraham*).

28. I.e., the challenge is great, and each
person must devise means as to how he will
combat his evil inclination (*Ahavas Chesed,
Ben Avraham*).

29. This is the explanation of *Midrash Ha-
Gadol* on *Genesis* 4:7.

30. Alternatively, the meaning is that what
makes the challenge so difficult is that one
must battle his evil inclination without elimi-
nating it completely, for if he were to do so
he would not join with his wife and bear any

‏"לִפְתַּח חַטָּאת רֹבֵץ"‎‏³¹‎, ‏אוֹמֵר לוֹ לָאָדָם בְּשָׁעָה שֶׁהַתִּינוֹק מוּטָל בַּעֲרִיסָה:‎
‏(הָאִישׁ) מְבַקֵּשׁ לְהוֹרְגֶךָ, הוּא רוֹצֶה שֶׁיִּתְלוֹשׁ מִמֶּנּוּ בִּשְׂעָרוֹ. תִּינוֹק מוּטָל‎
‏בַּעֲרִיסָה, הִנִּיחַ יָדוֹ עַל גַּבֵּי נָחָשׁ אוֹ עַל גַּבֵּי עַקְרָב וַעֲקָצַתּוּ, לֹא גָרַם לוֹ‎
‏אֶלָּא יֵצֶר הָרַע שֶׁבְּמֵעָיו, הִנִּיחַ יָדוֹ עַל גַּבֵּי גֶחָלִים וְנִכְוָה, לֹא גָרַם לוֹ אֶלָּא‎
‏יֵצֶר הָרַע שֶׁבְּמֵעָיו‎‏³²‎, (‏לְפִי שֶׁיֵּצֶר הָרַע זוֹרַקְתּוֹ בֵּית רֹאשׁ‎‏³³‎, אֲבָל) בָּא וּרְאֵה‎
‏בִּגְדִי אוֹ בְטָלֶה כֵּיוָן שֶׁהוּא רוֹאֶה אֶת הַבְּאֵר הוּא חוֹזֵר לַאֲחוֹרָיו לְפִי שֶׁאֵין‎

‏"לִפְתַּח חַטָּאת רֹבֵץ"‎ — as it is stated, *Sin rests at the door* (*Genesis* 4:7).[31]

The Baraisa proceeds to show how various behaviors we see in infants are evidence of the evil inclination at work even at that early age: ‏אוֹמֵר לוֹ לָאָדָם בְּשָׁעָה שֶׁהַתִּינוֹק מוּטָל בַּעֲרִיסָה‎ — [The evil inclination] says to a person while he is still **an infant lying in the cradle**, ‏הָאִישׁ מְבַקֵּשׁ לְהוֹרְגֶךָ‎ — "**The man** who is now **approaching you wants to kill you!**" ‏הוּא רוֹצֶה‎ ‏שֶׁיִּתְלוֹשׁ מִמֶּנּוּ בִּשְׂעָרוֹ‎ — That is why [the infant] **wants to pull** [that person] **by his hair,** as we so often see. ‏תִּינוֹק מוּטָל בַּעֲרִיסָה‎ — **An infant who lies in the cradle** ‏הִנִּיחַ יָדוֹ עַל גַּבֵּי נָחָשׁ אוֹ עַל גַּבֵּי עַקְרָב וַעֲקָצַתּוּ‎ — **reaches out and puts his hand on a snake or on a scorpion, and it bites him.** ‏לֹא גָרַם‎ ‏לוֹ אֶלָּא יֵצֶר הָרַע שֶׁבְּמֵעָיו‎ — **This** reckless behavior **is caused only by the evil inclination that resides inside him.** ‏הִנִּיחַ יָדוֹ עַל גַּבֵּי גֶחָלִים וְנִכְוָה‎ — Similarly, he reaches out and **puts his hands on coals and gets burnt.** ‏לֹא גָרַם לוֹ‎ ‏אֶלָּא יֵצֶר הָרַע שֶׁבְּמֵעָיו‎ — **This** reckless behavior **is caused only by the evil inclination that resides inside him.**[32] ‏לְפִי שֶׁיֵּצֶר הָרַע זוֹרַקְתּוֹ בֵּית רֹאשׁ‎ — **For** **the evil inclination that is injected into** [a person] is injected in him **from his inception.**[33] ‏אֲבָל בָּא וּרְאֵה בִּגְדִי אוֹ בְטָלֶה‎ — **In contrast to such human behavior, however, come and see** the behavior **of a young goat or lamb:** ‏כֵּיוָן שֶׁהוּא רוֹאֶה אֶת הַבְּאֵר הוּא חוֹזֵר לַאֲחוֹרָיו‎ — **When it sees an** open **well** in front, **it** instinctively **retreats backward** so as not to fall in, ‏לְפִי שֶׁאֵין‎

---

children [see *Yoma* 69b] (*Magen Avos*, second explanation).

31. Which can be interpreted to mean that the evil inclination, the source of "sin," rests at the "door" of a man's heart (see *Ben Avraham*).

The "heart" is the seat of a person's thoughts (see *Berachos* 61a), so saying that the evil inclination "resides near the gateways of the heart" is akin to saying that the evil inclination is involved in a person's every decision.

32. The young of *animals* (who do not have an evil inclination) will instinctively recoil from such dangerous things, as the Baraisa states next. It must be, then, that the evil inclination is what motivates the infant to aggression — pulling at a person's hair, trying to hit a scorpion or a coal — even when such behavior ends up harming the infant himself (*Magen Avos*).

33. Rendering follows *Ahavas Chesed*. Other texts have: ‏זוֹרַקְתּוֹ "בָּאֵשׁ"‎, *[for it is the evil inclination that] casts him into the fire* (and this emendation of our texts is suggested as well by *Magen Avos*). Other texts have ‏זוֹרַקְתּוֹ "בְּבֵת" רֹאשׁ‎ (*Mesoras HaShas*), which could mean "impels him to rush headlong."

יֵצֶר הָרַע בִּבְהֵמָה,[34] רַבִּי שִׁמְעוֹן בֶּן אֶלְעָזָר אוֹמֵר: אֶמְשׁוֹל לְךָ מָשָׁל לְמָה (הַדָּבָר דּוֹמֶה,) יֵצֶר הָרַע דּוֹמֶה לְבַרְזֶל שֶׁהֱטִילוּהוּ בְּתוֹךְ הָאוֹר, כָּל זְמַן שֶׁהוּא בְּתוֹךְ הָאוֹר עוֹשִׂין מִמֶּנּוּ כָּל כֵּלִים שֶׁיִּרְצוּ, אַף כָּךְ יֵצֶר הָרַע אֵין לוֹ תַּקָּנָה אֶלָּא בְּדִבְרֵי תוֹרָה (שֶׁהוּא כָּאֵשׁ]) בִּלְבַד, שֶׁנֶּאֱמַר (משלי כה, כא-כב) "אִם רָעֵב שֹׂנַאֲךָ הַאֲכִלֵהוּ לָחֶם וְאִם צָמֵא הַשְׁקֵהוּ מָיִם כִּי גֶחָלִים אַתָּה חֹתֶה עַל רֹאשׁוֹ וַה' יְשַׁלֶּם לָךְ"[35] אַל תִּקְרֵי "יְשַׁלֶּם לָךְ" אֶלָּא "יַשְׁלִים לָךְ",[36]

יֵצֶר הָרַע בִּבְהֵמָה — **because animals do not have an evil inclination.** Evidently, then, all the reckless actions of young humans are induced by their evil inclination.[34]

The Baraisa teaches us how to properly combat the evil inclination:

רַבִּי שִׁמְעוֹן בֶּן אֶלְעָזָר אוֹמֵר: אֶמְשׁוֹל לְךָ מָשָׁל לְמָה הַדָּבָר דּוֹמֶה — **R' Shimon ben Elazar says: I will give you an analogy: To what is this comparable?** יֵצֶר הָרַע דּוֹמֶה לְבַרְזֶל שֶׁהֱטִילוּהוּ בְּתוֹךְ הָאוֹר — **The evil inclination is comparable to iron that was cast into the fire.** כָּל זְמַן שֶׁהוּא בְּתוֹךְ הָאוֹר עוֹשִׂין מִמֶּנּוּ כָּל כֵּלִים שֶׁיִּרְצוּ — **As long as it remains in the fire, people can shape it into whatever implements they wish.** אַף כָּךְ יֵצֶר הָרַע — **So too the evil inclination.** אֵין לוֹ תַּקָּנָה אֶלָּא בְּדִבְרֵי תוֹרָה, שֶׁהוּא כָּאֵשׁ, בִּלְבַד — **It can be remedied only through the words of Torah, which is likened to fire,** שֶׁנֶּאֱמַר "אִם רָעֵב שֹׂנַאֲךָ הַאֲכִלֵהוּ לָחֶם וְאִם צָמֵא הַשְׁקֵהוּ מָיִם כִּי גֶחָלִים אַתָּה חֹתֶה עַל רֹאשׁוֹ וַה' יְשַׁלֶּם לָךְ" — **as it is stated,** *If your foe is hungry, feed him bread; and if he is thirsty, give him water to drink, for you will be scooping coals [to heap] on his head, and* HASHEM *"yeshalem lach"* [literally, *will reward you*] (*Proverbs 25:21-22*).[35] אַל תִּקְרֵי "יְשַׁלֶּם לָךְ" אֶלָּא "יַשְׁלִים לָךְ" — **The Baraisa expounds: Do not read** the phrase as *yeshalem lach* [יְשַׁלֶּם לָךְ], **but as** *yashlim lach* [יַשְׁלִים לָךְ], **meaning:** *He will conciliate [him] toward you.*[36]

---

34. The Gemara states that animals, too, have an evil inclination, which is why they damage, bite, and kick (*Berachos* 61a). What our Baraisa means, however, is that animals do not have the impulse to do things that are dangerous to their own well-being, whereas human beings do (*Binyan Yehoshua*).

35. The simple meaning of the verse is that instead of repaying your enemy in kind, be noble in character and act charitably toward him. And if you find it difficult to repay evil with kindness, know that your kindness to him is not only the noble course of action but also a form of revenge, because the burning shame he will feel when he sees how you

have repaid his evil with kindness will be like coals on his head; moreover, God will repay you for your noble kindness (*Ralbag* on the verse).

36. According to this exposition, the verse means that if you see that your greatest enemy — the evil inclination — is "hungry" for sin, burden it with Torah, which is compared to bread, water, and fire (in *Proverbs* 9:5, *Isaiah* 55:1, and *Jeremiah* 23:29, respectively). And then God will conciliate the evil inclination toward you, making it your friend, rather than your enemy who wishes to destroy you through sin (*Rashi* to *Succah* 52a and *Ben Avraham;* see also *Magen Avos*).

רַבִּי יְהוּדָה הַנָּשִׂיא אוֹמֵר: אֶמְשׁוֹל לְךָ מָשָׁל לְמָה (הַדָּבָר דּוֹמֶה), יֵצֶר
הָרָע דּוֹמֶה לִשְׁנֵי בְּנֵי אָדָם שֶׁנִּכְנְסוּ לְפוּנְדָּק אֶחָד, נִתְפַּס אֶחָד מֵהֶם מִשּׁוּם
לִסְטוּת, אָמְרוּ לוֹ: מִי עִמְּךָ. יָכוֹל הוּא שֶׁיֹּאמַר: לֹא הָיָה עִמִּי חֲבֵרִי. אֶלָּא
אוֹמֵר: הוֹאִיל וַאֲנִי נֶהֱרָג, יֵהָרֵג חֲבֵרִי עִמִּי. אַף כָּךְ אוֹמֵר יֵצֶר הָרָע:
הוֹאִיל וַאֲנִי אָבוּד לָעוֹלָם הַבָּא,[38] (אֲנִי) אֲאַבֵּד אֶת (כָּל) הַגּוּף. רַבִּי
שִׁמְעוֹן בֶּן יוֹחַי אוֹמֵר: מִכָּאן שֶׁאֵין יִשְׂרָאֵל רוֹאִים פְּנֵי גֵּיהִנֹּם לְעוֹלָם,[40]
מָשְׁלוּ מָשָׁל לְמָה הַדָּבָר דּוֹמֶה, לְמֶלֶךְ בָּשָׂר וָדָם שֶׁהָיָה לוֹ שָׂדֶה זְבוּרִית,

---

The Baraisa explains the evil inclination's motive in urging a person to sin:[37]
רַבִּי יְהוּדָה הַנָּשִׂיא אוֹמֵר: אֶמְשׁוֹל לְךָ מָשָׁל לְמָה הַדָּבָר דּוֹמֶה — R' Yehudah the
Prince says: I shall give you an analogy: To what is this comparable? יֵצֶר
הָרָע דּוֹמֶה לִשְׁנֵי בְּנֵי אָדָם שֶׁנִּכְנְסוּ לְפוּנְדָּק אֶחָד — The ways of the evil inclination can be compared to the arrested man in the following parable: Two men
entered a certain inn together, נִתְפַּס אֶחָד מֵהֶם מִשּׁוּם לִסְטוּת — where one of
them was arrested on charges of banditry. אָמְרוּ לוֹ: מִי עִמְּךָ — They asked
him upon his arrest, "Who else was involved with you in this crime?" יָכוֹל
הוּא שֶׁיֹּאמַר: לֹא הָיָה עִמִּי חֲבֵרִי — If he wants he can say, "My companion was
not involved with me in this crime." אֶלָּא אוֹמֵר: הוֹאִיל וַאֲנִי נֶהֱרָג יֵהָרֵג חֲבֵרִי
עִמִּי — But instead he says, "Since I will be killed, let my companion be killed
with me!" אַף כָּךְ אוֹמֵר יֵצֶר הָרָע: הוֹאִיל וַאֲנִי אָבוּד לָעוֹלָם הַבָּא — So, too, the
evil inclination says, "Since I am destined to be lost in the World to Come,[38]
אֲנִי אֲאַבֵּד אֶת כָּל הַגּוּף — I will cause the entire body of the person (i.e., the
soul as well)[39] to be lost along with me, by persuading him to sin while he is
still in this world."

The Baraisa notes that when judging us, God takes into account the difficulty in overcoming the evil inclination He has implanted in us:
רַבִּי שִׁמְעוֹן בֶּן יוֹחַי אוֹמֵר — R' Shimon
ben Yochai says: מִכָּאן שֶׁאֵין יִשְׂרָאֵל רוֹאִים פְּנֵי גֵּיהִנֹּם לְעוֹלָם It is based on this reality that the people of Israel do not see
the face of Gehinnom forever, but are eventually redeemed from it.[40] מָשְׁלוּ
מָשָׁל לְמָה הַדָּבָר דּוֹמֶה — [The Sages] offered an analogy to illustrate: To what
is this comparable? לְמֶלֶךְ בָּשָׂר וָדָם שֶׁהָיָה לוֹ שָׂדֶה זְבוּרִית — To a human king

---

37. *Magen Avos, Ben Avraham.*

38. As it is stated regarding the Messianic
era, *[HASHEM] will eliminate death forever*
[*Isaiah* 25:8] (*Binyan Yehoshua*, from *Mefaresh*), meaning that the *Angel of Death* —
who is also the evil inclination (*Bava Basra*
16a) — will be destroyed forever.

39. *Ben Avraham.*

40. By rights, those who sin against God
should never be forgiven, but should be
consigned eternally to Gehinnom. However,
in light of how difficult it is to overcome the
evil inclination, as the Baraisa has just explained, we can understand why our Sages
teach us that the wicked among Israel suffer
in Gehinnom for up to twelve months, and
no longer [*Eduyos* 2:10] (see *Magen Avos*).

בָּאוּ בְּנֵי אָדָם וְהִשְׂכִּירוּהָ בַּעֲשֶׂרֶת כּוֹרִין חִטִּים בְּשָׁנָה,[41] וְזִבְּלוּהָ עֲדָרוּהָ
הַשְׁקוּהָ וְכִסְּחוּהָ וְלֹא הַכְנִיסוּ מִמֶּנָּה אֶלָּא כּוֹר אֶחָד חִטִּים בְּשָׁנָה, אָמַר
לָהֶם הַמֶּלֶךְ: מַהוּ זֶה. אָמְרוּ לוֹ: אֲדוֹנֵינוּ הַמֶּלֶךְ, אַתָּה יוֹדֵעַ בַּשָּׂדֶה שֶׁנְּתַתָּ
לָנוּ שֶׁמִּתְּחִלָּה לֹא הַכְנַסְתְּ מִמֶּנָּה כְּלוּם, וְעַכְשָׁיו שֶׁזִּבַּלְנוּהָ וְכִסַּחְנוּהָ
וְהִשְׁקִינוּהָ מַיִם לֹא הַכְנַסְנוּ מִמֶּנָּה אֶלָּא כּוֹר אֶחָד חִטִּים בִּלְבָד. כָּךְ עֲתִידִים
יִשְׂרָאֵל לוֹמַר לִפְנֵי הַקָּדוֹשׁ בָּרוּךְ הוּא: רִבּוֹנוֹ שֶׁל עוֹלָם, אַתָּה יוֹדֵעַ בְּיֵצֶר
הָרָע שֶׁהוּא מֵסִית בָּנוּ, שֶׁנֶּאֱמַר (תהלים קג, יד) "כִּי הוּא יָדַע יִצְרֵנוּ":

בָּאוּ בְּנֵי אָדָם וְהִשְׂכִּירוּהָ בַּעֲשֶׂרֶת כּוֹרִין חִטִּים who had a field of inferior quality.
בְּשָׁנָה — People came to the king and leased it from him as sharecroppers for
a return of ten *kors* of wheat per year on his field.[41]   זִבְּלוּהָ עֲדָרוּהָ הַשְׁקוּהָ
וְכִסְּחוּהָ — They then fertilized it, hoed it, watered it, and weeded it,   וְלֹא
הַכְנִיסוּ מִמֶּנָּה אֶלָּא כּוֹר אֶחָד חִטִּים בְּשָׁנָה — but despite all their efforts, they harvested from it only one *kor* of wheat in the first year. When they were therefore
unable to pay him his due,   אָמַר לָהֶם הַמֶּלֶךְ: מַהוּ זֶה — the king said to them,
"What is the meaning of this?"   אָמְרוּ לוֹ: אֲדוֹנֵינוּ הַמֶּלֶךְ, אַתָּה יוֹדֵעַ בַּשָּׂדֶה שֶׁנְּתַתָּ
לָנוּ — They answered him, "Our master the king, you know the nature of this
inferior field that you gave us to farm   שֶׁמִּתְּחִלָּה לֹא הַכְנַסְתְּ מִמֶּנָּה כְּלוּם — that
originally you were harvesting nothing from it.   וְעַכְשָׁיו שֶׁזִּבַּלְנוּהָ וְכִסַּחְנוּהָ
וְהִשְׁקִינוּהָ מַיִם — And now that we have fertilized it, weeded it, and watered it,
לֹא הַכְנַסְנוּ מִמֶּנָּה אֶלָּא כּוֹר אֶחָד חִטִּים בִּלְבָד — we have harvested from it only
one single *kor* of wheat! True, we have fallen far short of your expectations,
but we have succeeded in producing *something*."   כָּךְ עֲתִידִים יִשְׂרָאֵל לוֹמַר
לִפְנֵי הַקָּדוֹשׁ בָּרוּךְ הוּא — In the same vein, the people of Israel are destined to
say before the Holy One, Blessed is He, at the time of judgment,   רִבּוֹנוֹ שֶׁל
עוֹלָם, אַתָּה יוֹדֵעַ בְּיֵצֶר הָרָע שֶׁהוּא מֵסִית בָּנוּ — "Master of the Universe! You know
the nature of the evil inclination that You gave us, that it constantly incites
us to sin,   שֶׁנֶּאֱמַר "כִּי הוּא יָדַע יִצְרֵנוּ" — as it is stated, *For He knew our
inclination*" (*Psalms* 103:14). Thus, we will say before God: Despite our true
desire to fulfill Your Will and study Torah and perform good deeds, it is the evil
inclination You have implanted within us that has prevented us from reaching
our potential. We beseech You, however, to look not at how far we have fallen
short, but at how much we have accomplished.[42]

---

41. The sharecroppers agreed to farm the
field and give the king ten *kors* of its produce
each year. Whatever it produced beyond
that would be theirs.

42. *Ben Avraham*. [Like the sharecroppers working the inferior field, performing
any amount of good during one's lifetime,
despite the evil inclination's persistent opposition, is a meritorious feat. Therefore, a
person can ask God to look at his merits and
not his misdeeds.]

ה. וְשִׂנְאַת[43] הַבְּרִיּוֹת כֵּיצַד, מְלַמֵּד שֶׁלֹּא יְכַוֵּין אָדָם לוֹמַר: אֱהוֹב אֶת הַחֲכָמִים וּשְׂנוֹא אֶת הַתַּלְמִידִים, אֱהוֹב אֶת הַתַּלְמִידִים וּשְׂנוֹא אֶת עַמֵּי הָאָרֶץ, [אֶלָּא אֱהוֹב אֶת כֻּלָּם] וּשְׂנוֹא אֶת הָאֶפִּיקוֹרְסִין וְהַמְּסִיתִים וּמַדִּיחִין[44] וְכֵן הַמָּסוֹרוֹת, וְכֵן דָּוִד אָמַר (תהלים קלט, כא-כב) "מְשַׂנְאֶיךָ ה' אֶשְׂנָא וּבִתְקוֹמְמֶיךָ אֶתְקוֹטָט תַּכְלִית שִׂנְאָה שְׂנֵאתִים לְאוֹיְבִים הָיוּ לִי". הֲלֹא הוּא אוֹמֵר (ויקרא יט, יח) "וְאָהַבְתָּ לְרֵעֲךָ כָּמוֹךָ אֲנִי ה' ", [מַה טַעַם, כִּי אֲנִי] בְּרָאתִיו[46], וְאִם עוֹשֶׂה מַעֲשֶׂה עַמְּךָ אַתָּה אוֹהֲבוֹ, וְאִם לָאו אִי אַתָּה

---

§5 [43] The Baraisa expounds R' Yehoshua's third saying:

וְשִׂנְאַת הַבְּרִיּוֹת כֵּיצַד — And the third thing that removes a person from the world is "the hatred of other people" — how so? מְלַמֵּד שֶׁלֹּא יְכַוֵּין אָדָם לוֹמַר: אֱהוֹב אֶת הַחֲכָמִים וּשְׂנוֹא אֶת הַתַּלְמִידִים — This teaches that a person should not be particular and say, "Love the Sages, but hate the students," who are as yet only aspiring sages, אֱהוֹב אֶת הַתַּלְמִידִים וּשְׂנוֹא אֶת עַמֵּי הָאָרֶץ — or "Love the students, but hate the unlearned masses." אֶלָּא אֱהוֹב אֶת כֻּלָּם — Rather, one should say, "Love all of them, for they are all God's people, וּשְׂנוֹא אֶת הָאֶפִּיקוֹרְסִין וְהַמְּסִיתִים וּמַדִּיחִין וְכֵן הַמָּסוֹרוֹת — and hate only the heretics, the inciters, and subverters,[44] and also the informers." וְכֵן דָּוִד אָמַר "מְשַׂנְאֶיךָ ה' אֶשְׂנָא וּבִתְקוֹמְמֶיךָ אֶתְקוֹטָט תַּכְלִית שִׂנְאָה שְׂנֵאתִים לְאוֹיְבִים הָיוּ לִי" — And thus does King David say, For indeed those who hate You, O HASHEM, I hate them, and I quarrel with those who rise up against You! With the utmost hatred, I hate them; they have become enemies unto me (Psalms 139:21-22).

A different source for the commandment to love all, except for Hashem's enemies:[45]

הֲלֹא הוּא אוֹמֵר "וְאָהַבְתָּ לְרֵעֲךָ כָּמוֹךָ אֲנִי ה' " — Does it not say in Scripture, You shall love "your fellow" as yourself — "I am HASHEM"? (Leviticus 19:18). מַה טַעַם, כִּי אֲנִי בְּרָאתִיו — By adding the seemingly extra words I am HASHEM, the verse means to say: What is the reason that you should love your fellow? Because I, Hashem, have created him![46] וְאִם עוֹשֶׂה מַעֲשֶׂה עַמְּךָ אַתָּה אוֹהֲבוֹ — However, the verse also says that you are to love your fellow, which indicates: only if he conducts himself in the ways of your (Jewish) people, by heeding the Torah's laws, must you love him, וְאִם לָאו אִי אַתָּה

---

43. [The earlier notation for §4 is missing in the Vilna edition.]

44. "Inciter" in this context refers to one who tries to persuade one or two others to worship idols; a "subverter" is one who persuades a group of people to do so [see

Deuteronomy 13:7,14] (Ben Avraham; see Minchas Chinuch on Mitzvah 462).

45. Ahavas Chesed; cf. Binyan Yehoshua and Magen Avos.

46. Thus, you are commanded to love everyone — sage and unlearned alike, as taught

אוֹהֲבוֹ[47], רַבִּי שִׁמְעוֹן בֶּן אֶלְעָזָר אוֹמֵר: °בְּשָׁעָה °שֶׁל גְּדוּלָה[48] נֶאֱמַר דָּבָר זֶה, "וְאָהַבְתָּ לְרֵעֲךָ כָּמוֹךָ אֲנִי ה' " בְּרָאתִיו, אִם אַתָּה אוֹהֲבוֹ אֲנִי נֶאֱמָן לְשַׁלֵּם לְךָ שָׂכָר טוֹב, וְאִם לָאו אֲנִי דַּיָּין לִפְרוֹעַ[50]:

אוֹהֲבוֹ — but if he does **not** conduct himself in the Torah ways of the Jewish people, then **you are** *not* **to love him.**[47]

The Baraisa presents another exposition of the *Leviticus* verse just cited, which also sheds light on R' Yehoshua's third saying:

רַבִּי שִׁמְעוֹן בֶּן אֶלְעָזָר אוֹמֵר: בִּשְׁבוּעָה גְדוּלָה נֶאֱמַר דָּבָר זֶה — R' Shimon ben Elazar **says: It was with a great oath**[48] **that this matter** of commanding love for one's fellow **was said:** "וְאָהַבְתָּ לְרֵעֲךָ כָּמוֹךָ אֲנִי ה' " בְּרָאתִיו — *You shall love your fellow as yourself* — **I am** HASHEM **Who has created him!** The expression *I am* HASHEM is one of an oath.[49] אִם אַתָּה אוֹהֲבוֹ אֲנִי נֶאֱמָן לְשַׁלֵּם לְךָ שָׂכָר טוֹב — Moreover, this expression indicates that **if you love him, it is I Who can be trusted to repay you a good reward!** וְאִם לָאו אֲנִי דַּיָּין לִפְרוֹעַ — **And if** you do *not* **love him, it is I Who is the Judge that will exact punishment** against you![50]

---

earlier in the Baraisa — for I have created them all (*Ben Avraham*).

47. This lesson is inferred from the expression רֵעֲךָ, *your fellow*, which denotes someone who is your "fellow" in the performance of God's commandments (see *Meiri* to *Avos* ad loc.).

Thus, the hatred that "removes a person from the world" is only that which is directed at those who obey God's will, but not that which is directed at those who hate Him.

48. [We have followed the reading in several other texts, and this is also the reading in *Machzor Vitri* (to *Avos* ad loc.; see also

Nuschas HaGra here). The standard reading בְּשָׁעָה שֶׁל גְּדוּלָה, *at a time of greatness,* is problematic, and *Magen Avos* is at a loss to explain it.]

49. *Ahavas Chesed.*

50. The expression *I am* HASHEM, is often used to mean "I can be trusted to give reward" or "to mete out punishment" (see *Rashi* to *Leviticus* 19:16, and elsewhere).

Hence, hating other people can, quite literally, remove a person from the world through the punishment that it brings (see *Machzor Vitri* to *Avos* ad loc.).

﴾ פֶּרֶק יז ﴿

א. רַבִּי יוֹסֵי אוֹמֵר: יְהִי מָמוֹן חֲבֵירְךָ חָבִיב עָלֶיךָ כְּשֶׁלָּךְ[1] (וְהַתְקֵן עצמך ללמוד תורה שאינה ירושה לך):

ב. כֵּיצַד, מְלַמֵּד בְּשֵׁם שֶׁאָדָם רוֹאֶה אֶת מָמוֹנוֹ כָּךְ יְהֵא רוֹאֶה אֶת מָמוֹן חֲבֵירוֹ.[2] וּכְמוֹ שֶׁאָדָם רוֹצֶה שֶׁלֹּא יֵצֵא שֵׁם (רַע) עַל מָמוֹן שֶׁלוֹ כָּךְ יִהְיֶה רוֹצֶה שֶׁלֹּא יֵצֵא שֵׁם (רַע) עַל מָמוֹן חֲבֵירוֹ.[3] דָּבָר אַחֵר, יְהִי מָמוֹן חֲבֵירְךָ חָבִיב עָלֶיךָ כְּשֶׁלָּךְ,] כֵּיצַד, בִּזְמַן שֶׁתַּלְמִיד חָכָם נִכְנָס אֶצְלְךָ (לוֹמַר: שְׁנֵה לִי), אִם יֵשׁ בְּיָדְךָ לִשְׁנוֹת שְׁנֵה לוֹ, וְאִם לָאו פָּטְרֵהוּ מִיָּד וְאַל תִּקַּח מִמֶּנּוּ

﴾ CHAPTER 17 ﴿

§1 The Baraisa continues discussing the sayings of Rabban Yochanan ben Zakkai's disciples. In the greater part of this chapter, it will examine the teachings of the third disciple, R' Yose HaKohen. It begins with his first teaching, quoting from *Avos* 2:12:

רַבִּי יוֹסֵי אוֹמֵר: יְהִי מָמוֹן חֲבֵירְךָ חָבִיב עָלֶיךָ כְּשֶׁלָּךְ — R' Yose says: Let your fellow's money be as dear to you as your own.[1]

§2 The Baraisa expounds the above teaching:

מְלַמֵּד בְּשֵׁם שֶׁאָדָם רוֹאֶה אֶת מָמוֹנוֹ — This teaches that כֵּיצַד — How so? כָּךְ יְהֵא רוֹאֶה אֶת מָמוֹן חֲבֵירוֹ — so just as a person views his own money, should he view his fellow's money.[2] וּכְמוֹ שֶׁאָדָם רוֹצֶה שֶׁלֹּא יֵצֵא שֵׁם רַע עַל מָמוֹן שֶׁלוֹ — And just as a person desires that no bad rumor should spread about his own money, כָּךְ יִהְיֶה רוֹצֶה שֶׁלֹּא יֵצֵא שֵׁם רַע עַל מָמוֹן חֲבֵירוֹ — so should he desire that no bad rumor should spread about his fellow's money.[3] דָּבָר אַחֵר — Another explanation: יְהִי מָמוֹן חֲבֵירְךָ חָבִיב עָלֶיךָ כְּשֶׁלָּךְ, כֵּיצַד — "Let your fellow's money be as dear to you as your own" — how so? בִּזְמַן שֶׁתַּלְמִיד חָכָם נִכְנָס אֶצְלְךָ לוֹמַר: שְׁנֵה לִי — When a Torah student approaches you, saying, "Teach me Torah and I will pay you for it,"[4] אִם יֵשׁ בְּיָדְךָ — if you are capable of teaching that subject, then שְׁנֵה לוֹ teach it to him; וְאִם לָאו פָּטְרֵהוּ מִיָּד — if not, send him off immediately, וְאַל תִּקַּח מִמֶּנּוּ

---

1. The following line has been removed from the text based on many old prints. [In the Vilna print, this correction is erroneously attributed to *Nuschas HaGra*.]

2. No one wants their possessions to be damaged or stolen. In the same way, one should take care that his fellow's possessions are not damaged or stolen. This obligation to prevent a loss to another's property is a derivative of the mitzvah to return another's property after it has already been lost (*Binyan Yehoshua*, from *Mefaresh*).

3. People never want their money to be viewed by others as having been amassed illegally. Similarly, one should defend the reputation of his fellow's wealth against any such rumor (ibid.).

4. See *Magen Avos* and *Ahavas Chesed*, who

אֶת מָמוֹנוֹ‏5, שֶׁנֶּאֱמַר (משלי ג, כח) ‏״אַל תֹּאמַר לְרֵעֲךָ לֵךְ וָשׁוּב וּמָחָר אֶתֵּן וְיֵשׁ אִתָּךְ״‏7:

ג. הַתְקֵן עַצְמְךָ לִלְמוֹד תּוֹרָה שֶׁאֵינָהּ יְרוּשָּׁה לְךָ‏8, כֵּיצַד, בְּשָׁעָה שֶׁרָאָה מֹשֶׁה רַבֵּינוּ [אֶת בָּנָיו] שֶׁאֵין בָּהֶן (תּוֹרָה) שֶׁיַּעַמְדוּ בִּנְשִׂיאוּת אַחֲרָיו‏10, נִתְעַטֵּף וְעָמַד בִּתְפִילָה, אָמַר לְפָנָיו: רִבּוֹנוֹ שֶׁל עוֹלָם, הוֹדִיעֵנִי (אֶת) מִי

אֶת מָמוֹנוֹ — and do not take his money from him.[5]

The Baraisa cites a verse to prove that when one *is* capable of teaching Torah to a student who approaches him, he should do so without delay:[6] **שֶׁנֶּאֱמַר ״אַל תֹּאמַר לְרֵעֲךָ לֵךְ וָשׁוּב וּמָחָר אֶתֵּן וְיֵשׁ אִתָּךְ״** — This is derived from that which it says, *Do not tell your neighbor, "Leave and come back; tomorrow I will give it," when it is by you* (Proverbs 3:28).[7]

§3 The Baraisa cites and elaborates on R' Yose's second teaching: **הַתְקֵן עַצְמְךָ לִלְמוֹד תּוֹרָה שֶׁאֵינָהּ יְרוּשָּׁה לְךָ** — "Apply yourself to study the Torah, for it is not yours by inheritance."[8] **כֵּיצַד** — How do we see this? It may be derived from the case of Moses' sons.[9] **בְּשָׁעָה שֶׁרָאָה מֹשֶׁה רַבֵּינוּ אֶת בָּנָיו שֶׁאֵין בָּהֶן תּוֹרָה** — For when our teacher Moses saw that his sons did not possess sufficient Torah knowledge **שֶׁיַּעַמְדוּ בִּנְשִׂיאוּת אַחֲרָיו** — to allow them to assume his position of leadership after [his death],[10] **נִתְעַטֵּף וְעָמַד בִּתְפִילָה** — he wrapped himself in his garment and stood in prayer before God. **אָמַר לְפָנָיו: רִבּוֹנוֹ שֶׁל עוֹלָם, הוֹדִיעֵנִי אֶת מִי יִכָּנֵס**

discuss the permissibility of accepting payment for teaching Torah.

5. I.e., do not take money from him if you are unable to fulfill his request [just as you would not want anyone to take your money without giving you what you need] (*Binyan Yehoshua*, from *Mefaresh*). Alternatively, the Baraisa means to say that even if you do teach him, you should forgo the payment, as it is considered pious behavior to refrain from accepting payment for teaching Torah even when one is permitted to do so (see *Shocher Tov* to *Psalms* 15:5). According to this approach, when it says, "Let your fellow's money be as dear to you as your own," it means that a teacher of Torah should view the money that the student is supposed to pay him as if he has already received it, and thus he should teach him free of charge (*Ahavas Chesed*).

6. *Binyan Yehoshua*, from *Mefaresh*.

7. The "giving" in the verse alludes to the teaching of Torah to one who requests it.

Thus, the verse exhorts the Torah scholar to teach the student who comes before him immediately, and not to put him off until the following day (ibid.).

8. A scion of a dynasty of Torah scholars should not think that he does not need to toil excessively in Torah study, since he is destined for Torah greatness anyway (*Rav* to *Avos* 2:12). There is indeed a concept that the Torah "seeks to reside in its established lodgings" — i.e., it settles more readily in members of families long steeped in Torah study (*Bava Metzia* 85a) — but that phenomenon is helpful only for those who invest the proper degree of toil in their Torah studies (*Binyan Yehoshua*, citing *Tos. Yom Tov* to *Avos* ibid.).

9. Who did not inherit their father's greatness in Torah, as is evident in the following episode.

10. They were in fact great Torah scholars, but not great enough to be the new leaders of the Jewish people (*Hagahos Yaavetz*).

יִכָּנֵס אֶת מִי יֵצֵא בְּרֹאשׁ כָּל הָעָם הַזֶּה"[11], שֶׁנֶּאֱמַר (במדבר כז, טו-יז) "וַיְדַבֵּר
מֹשֶׁה אֶל ה' לֵאמֹר יִפְקֹד ה' אֱלֹהֵי הָרוּחֹת לְכָל בָּשָׂר אִישׁ עַל הָעֵדָה
אֲשֶׁר יֵצֵא לִפְנֵיהֶם וַאֲשֶׁר יָבֹא לִפְנֵיהֶם". אָמַר לוֹ הַקָּדוֹשׁ בָּרוּךְ הוּא
לְמֹשֶׁה: מֹשֶׁה, [קַח לְךָ יְהוֹשֻׁעַ][12]. אָמַר הַקָּדוֹשׁ בָּרוּךְ הוּא לְמֹשֶׁה:]
לֵךְ וַעֲמוֹד לוֹ תּוּרְגְּמָן וְיִדְרוֹשׁ לְפָנֶיךָ בְּרֹאשׁ גְּדוֹלֵי יִשְׂרָאֵל[13]. בְּאוֹתָהּ
שָׁעָה אָמַר לוֹ מֹשֶׁה לִיהוֹשֻׁעַ: יְהוֹשֻׁעַ, עַם זֶה שֶׁאֲנִי מוֹסֵר לְךָ אֵינִי
מוֹסֵר לְךָ תְּיָישִׁים אֶלָּא גְּדָיִים (וּכְבָשִׂים), אֵינִי מוֹסֵר לְךָ אֶלָּא טְלָאִים

אֶת מִי יֵצֵא בְּרֹאשׁ כָּל הָעָם הַזֶּה — He said before Him, "Master of the Universe,
let me know who will come in and who will go out at the head of this na-
tion,"[11]   שֶׁנֶּאֱמַר "וַיְדַבֵּר מֹשֶׁה אֶל ה' לֵאמֹר יִפְקֹד ה' אֱלֹהֵי הָרוּחֹת לְכָל בָּשָׂר אִישׁ
עַל הָעֵדָה אֲשֶׁר יֵצֵא לִפְנֵיהֶם וַאֲשֶׁר יָבֹא לִפְנֵיהֶם" — as it is stated, *Moses spoke
to HASHEM, saying, "May HASHEM, God of the spirits of all flesh, appoint a
man over the assembly, who shall go out before them and come in before
them"* (Numbers 27:15-17).   אָמַר לוֹ הַקָּדוֹשׁ בָּרוּךְ הוּא לְמֹשֶׁה: מֹשֶׁה, קַח לְךָ
יְהוֹשֻׁעַ — The Holy One, Blessed is He, replied to Moses, "Moses, take to
yourself Joshua and designate him as your successor."[12]   אָמַר הַקָּדוֹשׁ בָּרוּךְ
הוּא לְמֹשֶׁה: לֵךְ וַעֲמוֹד לוֹ תּוּרְגְּמָן — With these words, the Holy One, Blessed is
He, was telling Moses, "Go and appoint a spokesman for [Joshua], וְיִדְרוֹשׁ
לְפָנֶיךָ בְּרֹאשׁ גְּדוֹלֵי יִשְׂרָאֵל — and have him lecture on Torah subjects in your
presence while standing at the head of the great [Sages] of Israel."[13]

Having appointed Joshua as his successor, Moses shared with him a piece
of advice:

בְּאוֹתָהּ שָׁעָה אָמַר לוֹ מֹשֶׁה לִיהוֹשֻׁעַ — At that time, Moses said to Joshua,
יְהוֹשֻׁעַ, עַם זֶה שֶׁאֲנִי מוֹסֵר לְךָ — "Joshua, there is something you should know
about this nation that I am passing on to you: אֵינִי מוֹסֵר לְךָ תְּיָישִׁים אֶלָּא
גְּדָיִים — I am not passing on to you matured goats, but undeveloped kids;
וּכְבָשִׂים אֵינִי מוֹסֵר לְךָ אֶלָּא טְלָאִים — and it is not grown sheep that I am passing on to you, but undeveloped lambs. Therefore, you must provide them

---

11. [I.e., who will be its new leader.] Realizing that his own children did not necessarily
qualify for the leadership by their own merit,
Moses was unsure if they would still be allowed to inherit his position because of *his*
merit, or if it would have to be transferred to
someone who was truly worthy on his own
account (*Ben Avraham*).

12. As it states subsequently (*Numbers*
27:18), *HASHEM said to Moses, "Take to yourself Joshua son of Nun, a man in whom there
is spirit, etc."*

13. [When a leading sage would address
the masses, he would customarily relate
his words to a spokesman, who would then
project them to the crowd.] God wanted
Moses to grant Joshua this honor during his
lifetime, so that when the time would later
come for Joshua to lead the people, no one
would say to him, "While Moses was alive
you did not have the courage to speak, but
now that he has passed away, you feel free
to speak" (*Binyan Yehoshua*, from *Sifrei* to
the verse).

שֶׁעֲדַיִין לֹא נִתְעַסְּקוּ בַּמִּצְוֹת וַעֲדַיִין לֹא הִגִּיעוּ לִתְיָשִׁים[15] , שֶׁנֶּאֱמַר (שיר
השירים א, ח) "אִם לֹא תֵדְעִי לָךְ הַיָּפָה בַּנָּשִׁים צְאִי לָךְ בְּעִקְבֵי הַצֹּאן וּרְעִי
אֶת גְּדִיֹּתַיִךְ עַל מִשְׁכְּנוֹת הָרֹעִים"[16]:

ד. פַּעַם אַחַת הָיָה רַבָּן יוֹחָנָן בֶּן זַכַּאי מְהַלֵּךְ בַּשּׁוּק, רָאָה רִיבָה אַחַת
שֶׁמְּלַקֶּטֶת שְׂעוֹרִים מִתַּחַת רַגְלֵי בְהֶמְתָּן שֶׁל עַרְבִיִּים. אָמַר לָהּ: בִּתִּי,
מִי אַתְּ, שָׁתְקָה.[18] שׁוּב אָמַר לָהּ: בִּתִּי, מִי אַתְּ, שָׁתְקָה. אָמְרָה לוֹ: הַמְתֵּן לִי.

with spiritual guidance, and you should not be overly strict when responding to their mistakes,[14] שֶׁעֲדַיִין לֹא נִתְעַסְּקוּ בַּמִּצְוֹת — for they have not yet involved themselves sufficiently in the performance of mitzvos, וַעֲדַיִין לֹא הִגִּיעוּ לִתְיָשִׁים וּכְבָשִׂים — and they have thus not yet reached the level of mature goats and sheep."[15] שֶׁנֶּאֱמַר "אִם לֹא תֵדְעִי לָךְ הַיָּפָה בַּנָּשִׁים צְאִי לָךְ בְּעִקְבֵי הַצֹּאן וּרְעִי אֶת גְּדִיֹּתַיִךְ עַל מִשְׁכְּנוֹת הָרֹעִים" — This is the meaning of that which it says, If you do not know, O fairest of women, follow the footsteps of the sheep and graze your kids by the shepherds' tents (Song of Songs 1:8).[16]

§4 A story relating to the Song of Songs verse just cited: פַּעַם אַחַת הָיָה רַבָּן יוֹחָנָן בֶּן זַכַּאי מְהַלֵּךְ בַּשּׁוּק — Rabban Yochanan ben Zakkai was once walking in the marketplace, רָאָה רִיבָה אַחַת שֶׁמְּלַקֶּטֶת שְׂעוֹרִים מִתַּחַת רַגְלֵי בְהֶמְתָּן שֶׁל עַרְבִיִּים — when he saw a certain girl gathering kernels of barley from the excrement[17] under the feet of animals belonging to Arabians. אָמַר לָהּ: בִּתִּי, מִי אַתְּ, שָׁתְקָה — He said to her, "My daughter, who are you?," but she remained silent.[18] שׁוּב אָמַר לָהּ: בִּתִּי, מִי אַתְּ, שָׁתְקָה — Again he said to her, "My daughter, who are you?," but once more she remained silent. אָמְרָה לוֹ: הַמְתֵּן לִי — When he asked a third time,[19] she said to him, "Wait a moment for me to do something before I respond."

---

14. *Magen Avos.*

15. Emendation is from *Tummas Yesharim.*

16. In this context, the verse is interpreted as Moses' words to Joshua. He was saying to him, "In case you do not know (*if you do not know*) how to lead the Jewish people, O greatest of prophets (*O fairest of women;* see *Shir HaShirim Rabbah* 1 §44), then I will instruct you: Do not treat them haughtily, as if you are above them, but walk behind them (*follow the footsteps of the sheep*). Guide the people, who are like young goats (*and graze your kids*), with care and compassion, as loving shepherds do for their

flocks (*by the shepherds' tents*)."

Hence, the verse shows that Moses told Joshua that the Jewish people were still like undeveloped young goats and lambs, and advised him to treat them accordingly (*Magen Avos,* first approach).

17. *Binyan Yehoshua,* based on *Kesubos* 66b.

18. Ashamed of the stark difference between her previous wealth (see below) and her present poverty, she was too humiliated to divulge her identity (*Magen Avos*).

19. Ibid.

נִתְעַטְּפָה בִּשְׂעָרָהּ וְיָשְׁבָה לְפָנָיו. אָמְרָה לוֹ: רַבִּי, בִּתּוֹ שֶׁל נַקְדִּימוֹן בֶּן גּוּרְיוֹן
אֲנִי[21]. אָמַר לָהּ: בִּתִּי, וּמָמוֹן שֶׁל אָבִיךְ הֵיכָן הוּא. אָמְרָה לוֹ: רַבִּי, לָאו כְּדֵין
מַתְלָא מָתְלִין בִּירוּשָׁלַיִם, מֶלַח מָמוֹן חַסֵּר[22], וְאָמְרֵי לָהּ חֶסֶד[23]. אָמַר לָהּ:
שֶׁל בֵּית חָמִיךְ הֵיכָן הוּא[24]. אָמְרָה לוֹ: רַבִּי, בָּא זֶה וְאִבֵּד זֶה[25]. בְּאוֹתָהּ שָׁעָה
אָמַר לָהֶן רַבָּן יוֹחָנָן בֶּן זַכַּאי לְתַלְמִידָיו: כָּל יָמַי הָיִיתִי קוֹרֵא מִקְרָא הַזֶּה
(שיר השירים א, ח) "אִם לֹא תֵדְעִי לָךְ הַיָּפָה בַּנָּשִׁים צְאִי לָךְ בְּעִקְבֵי הַצֹּאן",

נִתְעַטְּפָה בִּשְׂעָרָהּ וְיָשְׁבָה לְפָנָיו — Then, in an effort to present herself in a more modest and honorable manner,[20] she wrapped herself with her hair and sat before him. אָמְרָה לוֹ: רַבִּי, בִּתּוֹ שֶׁל נַקְדִּימוֹן בֶּן גּוּרְיוֹן אֲנִי — She said to him, "My master, I am the daughter of Nakdimon ben Guryon."[21] אָמַר לָהּ: בִּתִּי, וּמָמוֹן שֶׁל אָבִיךְ הֵיכָן הוּא — He asked her, "My daughter; but where is all of your father's wealth? Why do I find you in such an impoverished state?" אָמְרָה לוֹ: רַבִּי, לָאו כְּדֵין מַתְלָא מָתְלִין בִּירוּשָׁלַיִם — She answered him, "My master, do they not say this proverb in Jerusalem: מֶלַח מָמוֹן חַסֵּר — 'The salt (i.e., preservation) of money is deducting from it and giving to charity'?"[22]

The Baraisa interjects:

וְאָמְרֵי לָהּ חֶסֶד — And some say that the proverb she cited to him states, "The salt of money is kindness."[23]

The Baraisa resumes its narrative:

אָמַר לָהּ: שֶׁל בֵּית חָמִיךְ הֵיכָן הוּא — [Rabban Yochanan] asked her further, "And where is all the wealth of your father-in-law's house?"[24] אָמְרָה לוֹ: רַבִּי, בָּא זֶה וְאִבֵּד זֶה — She answered him, "My master, this one came and wiped out that one."[25] בְּאוֹתָהּ שָׁעָה אָמַר לָהֶן רַבָּן יוֹחָנָן בֶּן זַכַּאי לְתַלְמִידָיו — At that time, Rabban Yochanan ben Zakkai said to his disciples, כָּל יָמַי הָיִיתִי קוֹרֵא מִקְרָא הַזֶּה "אִם לֹא תֵדְעִי לָךְ הַיָּפָה בַּנָּשִׁים צְאִי לָךְ בְּעִקְבֵי הַצֹּאן" — "All my life, I read the following verse numerous times, If you do not know, O fairest of women,

20. Ibid.

21. A man famed for his wealth and philanthropy. See below; see also above, 6 §3.

22. Salt is used as a preservative. The proverb's intent is that one who wishes to preserve his wealth should continually give some of it to charity (Binyan Yehoshua, from Rashi to Kesubos 66b).

23. I.e., to preserve one's money, one must spend part of it on acts of kindness for others. Either way, Nakdimon's daughter was telling Rabban Yochanan that her father's fortune had been forfeited because charity had not been given from it properly (ibid.).

The Gemara (Kesubos 66b-67a) explains that although Nakdimon gave generously of his money to charity, his giving did not protect his money because he did it for his own honor, or because he did not give as much charity as was expected of him in accordance with his wealth.

24. Her father-in-law had been known as a wealthy person who did give charity in the proper way (Magen Avos, Kisei Rachamim).

25. Because my father-in-law's wealth was intermingled with my father's, it too was lost (Binyan Yehoshua, from Rashi to Kesubos 66b).

וְלֹא לָמַדְתִּי מַה שֶּׁכָּתַב בּוֹ [שֶׁנִּתְחַיְּיבוּ]26, עַד שֶׁבָּאתִי הַיּוֹם וְאָמַרְתִּי מַה שֶּׁכָּתַב שֶׁנִּתְחַיְּיבוּ יִשְׂרָאֵל לְאוּמָה שְׁפָלָה27, [וְלֹא בְּאוּמָה שְׁפָלָה בִּלְבַד אֶלָּא לְגַלְלֵי בְהֶמְתָּן].28 שׁוּב אָמְרָה לוֹ: רַבִּי, זָכוּר אַתָּה כְּשֶׁחָתַמְתָּ עַל כְּתוּבָתִי. אָמַר לָהּ: הֵן. אָמַר לְתַלְמִידָיו: הָעֲבוֹדָה29, אֲנִי חָתַמְתִּי עַל כְּתוּבָתָהּ שֶׁל רִיבָה זוֹ וְהָיוּ קוֹרִין בָּהּ אֶלֶף אֲלָפִים דִּינָרֵי זָהָב בְּדִינָרֵי צוֹרִי30. מִימֵיהֶם שֶׁל בֵּית אָבִיהָ שֶׁל רִיבָה זוֹ לֹא הָיוּ נִכְנָסִים מִבָּתֵּיהֶם

---

follow the footsteps of the sheep and graze your kids by the shepherds' tents (*Song of Songs* 1:8); וְלֹא לָמַדְתִּי מַה שֶּׁכָּתַב בּוֹ שֶׁנִּתְחַיְּיבוּ — but I never perceived what [King Solomon] wrote in it regarding the type of punishment to which [the people of Israel] would become liable,[26] עַד שֶׁבָּאתִי הַיּוֹם וְאָמַרְתִּי מַה שֶּׁכָּתַב שֶׁנִּתְחַיְּיבוּ יִשְׂרָאֵל לְאוּמָה שְׁפָלָה — until I came here today and I finally realized what he wrote in this verse; namely, that the people of Israel would become liable to be punished by being delivered into the hand of a lowly nation.[27] וְלֹא בְּאוּמָה שְׁפָלָה בִּלְבַד אֶלָּא לְגַלְלֵי בְהֶמְתָּן — And not just to a lowly nation itself, but to the degrading act of rummaging through the excrement of its animals!"[28] שׁוּב אָמְרָה לוֹ: רַבִּי, זָכוּר אַתָּה כְּשֶׁחָתַמְתָּ עַל כְּתוּבָתִי — [The girl] then said to him, "My master, do you remember when you signed on my *kesubah*?" אָמַר לָהּ: הֵן — He answered her, "Yes, I do." אָמַר לְתַלְמִידָיו: — He said to his disciples, "By the Divine service![29] הָעֲבוֹדָה, אֲנִי חָתַמְתִּי עַל כְּתוּבָתָהּ שֶׁל רִיבָה זוֹ I signed on the *kesubah* of this girl, וְהָיוּ קוֹרִין בָּהּ אֶלֶף אֲלָפִים דִּינָרֵי זָהָב בְּדִינָרֵי צוֹרִי and when it was read aloud, they read in it that she was bringing into the marriage a dowry of one million golden *dinars* in Tyrian currency!"[30] מִימֵיהֶם שֶׁל בֵּית אָבִיהָ שֶׁל רִיבָה זוֹ — Moreover, in all the days of the household members of this girl's father, לֹא הָיוּ נִכְנָסִים מִבָּתֵּיהֶם

---

26. The verse, taken allegorically, is God's warning to the nation of Israel (*O fairest of women*), telling them what their punishment will be if they do not put their minds (*if you do not know*) to guarding the Torah's words (see *Rashi* to *Kesubos* ibid.). Rabban Yochanan ben Zakkai had never before understood the exact allegorical implication of the next part of the verse, *follow the footsteps of the sheep and graze your kids*, which describes what their actual punishment would be.

27. I.e., a primitive nation that dwells in tents in the desert (*Binyan Yehoshua*, from *Rashi* ibid.). [The Arabians found in the Holy Land at this point in history were largely pagan nomads.]

28. The *Song of Songs* verse is being interpreted by reading the word גְּדִיֹּתַיִךְ, *your kids*, as גְּוִיֹּתַיִךְ, *your bodies*. Accordingly, the verse is saying that if the Jewish people do not keep the Torah, their punishment will be that they will have to search through excrement found between the feet of animals (*the footsteps of the sheep*) to find food to sustain their bodies (*and graze your bodies*) — as Nakdimon ben Guryon's daughter was seen doing (*Kesubos* 67a with *Rashi* ad loc.).

29. This is a form of oath. One swears by linking his words to an object of sanctity (see *Binyan Yehoshua*).

30. [Tyrian currency is far more valuable than provincial currency; see *Kiddushin* 11a with *Rashi* s.v. ושל דבריהם, and elsewhere.]

‫לְבֵית הַמִּקְדָּשׁ עַד שֶׁפּוֹרְסִין לוֹ כְּלֵי מֵילָת:³¹‬

‫ה. מַעֲשֶׂה בְּרִיבָה אַחַת שֶׁנִּשְׁבֵּית הִיא וְעֶשֶׂר שִׁפְחוֹתֶיהָ, וּנְטָלָהּ כּוּתִי‬
‫אֶחָד וְהָיְתָה מִתְגַּדֶּלֶת וּבָאת בְּתוֹךְ בֵּיתוֹ. יוֹם אֶחָד נָתַן לָהּ כַּדָּה‬
‫וְאָמַר לָהּ: צְאִי וְהָבֵא לִי מַיִם. עָמְדָה אַחַת מִשִּׁפְחוֹתֶיהָ וּנְטָלַתּוּ מִמֶּנָּה.‬
‫אָמַר לָהּ: מָהוּ? אָמְרָה לוֹ: חַיֵּי רֹאשְׁךָ אֲדוֹנִי, אֲנִי הָיִיתִי מֵחֲמֵשׁ מֵאוֹת‬
‫שְׁפָחוֹת שֶׁל אִמָּהּ שֶׁל רִיבָה זוֹ. כֵּיוָן שֶׁשָּׁמַע אֶת דְּבָרֶיהָ שִׁגְּרָהּ בַּת חוֹרִין‬
‫הִיא וְעֶשֶׂר שִׁפְחוֹתֶיהָ:‬

‫ו. שׁוּב מַעֲשֶׂה בְּרִיבָה אַחַת שֶׁנִּשְׁבֵּית וּנְטָלָהּ כּוּתִי אֶחָד וְהָיְתָה‬

‫לְבֵית הַמִּקְדָּשׁ עַד שֶׁפּוֹרְסִין לוֹ כְּלֵי מֵילָת‬ — they would never go from their house to the Holy Temple until [their servants] would roll out fine woolen garments for [them] to walk on!"[31]

§5 The story of another wealthy Jewish family that met a similar fate.[32] ‫מַעֲשֶׂה בְּרִיבָה אַחַת שֶׁנִּשְׁבֵּית הִיא וְעֶשֶׂר שִׁפְחוֹתֶיהָ‬ — There was an incident with a certain Jewish girl who was taken captive along with her ten maidservants, ‫וּנְטָלָהּ כּוּתִי אֶחָד‬ — and a certain idolater bought her and her maidservants from their captors. ‫וְהָיְתָה מִתְגַּדֶּלֶת וּבָאת בְּתוֹךְ בֵּיתוֹ‬ — She was being raised in his house as a slave ‫יוֹם אֶחָד נָתַן לָהּ כַּדָּה וְאָמַר לָהּ: צְאִי וְהָבֵא לִי מַיִם‬ — until one day he gave her a jug and said to her, "Go out and bring me water." ‫עָמְדָה אַחַת מִשִּׁפְחוֹתֶיהָ וּנְטָלַתּוּ מִמֶּנָּה‬ — Immediately, one of her maidservants arose and took [the jug] from her hand. ‫אָמַר לָהּ: מָהוּ‬ — [The idolater] said to [the maidservant], "What is the meaning of this? Why did you take the jug out of her hand?" ‫אָמְרָה לוֹ: חַיֵּי רֹאשְׁךָ אֲדוֹנִי‬ — She answered him, "My master, I swear by the life of your head ‫אֲנִי הָיִיתִי מֵחֲמֵשׁ מֵאוֹת שְׁפָחוֹת שֶׁל אִמָּהּ שֶׁל רִיבָה זוֹ‬ — that I was one of five hundred maidservants belonging to the mother of this girl, and I could not stand by and allow her to perform slave labor." ‫כֵּיוָן שֶׁשָּׁמַע אֶת דְּבָרֶיהָ שִׁגְּרָהּ בַּת חוֹרִין הִיא וְעֶשֶׂר שִׁפְחוֹתֶיהָ‬ — As soon as [the idolater] heard her words, he was so moved by them that he sent [the girl] free along with her ten maidservants.

§6 Yet another story depicting how Jewish people are occasionally punished by being delivered into the hands of other nations:[33] ‫שׁוּב מַעֲשֶׂה בְּרִיבָה אַחַת שֶׁנִּשְׁבֵּית‬ — There was another incident with a certain Jewish girl who was taken captive, ‫וּנְטָלָהּ כּוּתִי אֶחָד‬ — and a certain idolater

---

31. Obviously, then, Nakdimon ben Guryon had once been a man of exceptional wealth. Nevertheless, his family was reduced to utter poverty — and all because he did not

give charity properly.

32. See *Ben Avraham*.

33. See ibid.

מִתְגַּדֶּלֶת וּבָאת בְּתוֹךְ בֵּיתוֹ. בָּא לוֹ בַּעַל הַחֲלוֹם[34] וְאָמַר לוֹ: הוֹצֵא רִיבָה זוֹ מִתּוֹךְ בֵּיתְךָ. אָמְרָה לוֹ אִשְׁתּוֹ: אַל תּוֹצִיאֶנָּה. שׁוּב בָּא לוֹ בַּעַל הַחֲלוֹם, אָמַר לוֹ: אִם אֵין אַתָּה מוֹצִיאָהּ הֲרֵינִי הוֹרְגֶךָ. עָמַד וְהוֹצִיאָהּ וְהָיָה מְהַלֵּךְ אַחֲרֶיהָ. אָמַר: אֵלֵךְ וְאֶרְאֶה מַה יְּהֵא בְּסוֹפָהּ שֶׁל רִיבָה זוֹ. כְּשֶׁהִיא הוֹלֶכֶת בַּדֶּרֶךְ צָמְאַתָה וְיָרְדָה לִשְׁתּוֹת מַיִם עַל הַמַּעְיָין. כֵּיוָן שֶׁהִנִּיחָה יָדָהּ עַל הַכּוֹתֶל יָצָא עָלֶיהָ נָחָשׁ וּנְשָׁכָהּ וָמֵתָה וְהָיְתָה צָפָה עַל פְּנֵי הַמַּיִם. יָרַד וּנְטָלָהּ וְהֶעֱלָהּ וּקְבָרָהּ. וּבָא וְאָמַר לְאִשְׁתּוֹ: עַם זוֹ שֶׁאַתָּה רוֹאָה לֹא כָּעַס עֲלֵיהֶם אֶלָּא אֲבִיהֶם שֶׁבַּשָּׁמַיִם[37]:

---

bought her from her captors. וְהָיְתָה מִתְגַּדֶּלֶת וּבָאת בְּתוֹךְ בֵּיתוֹ — **She was being raised in his house** as a slave בָּא לוֹ בַּעַל הַחֲלוֹם — **until one time the Master of Dreams**[34] **came to him** וְאָמַר לוֹ: הוֹצֵא רִיבָה זוֹ מִתּוֹךְ בֵּיתְךָ — **and said to him, "Send this girl out of your house** to freedom!" אָמְרָה לוֹ אִשְׁתּוֹ: אַל תּוֹצִיאֶנָּה — **When the man related his dream to his wife, she said to him, "Do not let her go;** dreams are meaningless!"[35] שׁוּב בָּא לוֹ בַּעַל הַחֲלוֹם — **The Master of Dreams came to him again,** אָמַר לוֹ: אִם אֵין אַתָּה מוֹצִיאָהּ — הֲרֵינִי הוֹרְגֶךָ — **and this time said to him, "If you do not send her out** of your house, **I shall kill you!"** עָמַד וְהוֹצִיאָהּ — **So he arose and sent** [the girl] **out** to freedom. וְהָיָה מְהַלֵּךְ אַחֲרֶיהָ — **But** realizing that God obviously had something planned for her, **he followed her** as she left his house, אָמַר: אֵלֵךְ וְאֶרְאֶה מַה יְּהֵא בְּסוֹפָהּ שֶׁל רִיבָה זוֹ — **saying** to himself, **"I shall go and see what will be the fate of this girl."** כְּשֶׁהִיא הוֹלֶכֶת בַּדֶּרֶךְ צָמְאַתָה — **While she was walking on the road she became thirsty,** וְיָרְדָה לִשְׁתּוֹת מַיִם עַל הַמַּעְיָין — **so she climbed down** into a well **to drink** some **water from the spring** at the bottom. כֵּיוָן שֶׁהִנִּיחָה יָדָהּ עַל הַכּוֹתֶל — **After taking a drink, she began to climb back up.**[36] **However, as soon as she placed her hand on the wall,** יָצָא עָלֶיהָ נָחָשׁ וּנְשָׁכָהּ וָמֵתָה — **a snake emerged** from the wall **and bit her, and she died** right then and there. וְהָיְתָה צָפָה עַל פְּנֵי הַמַּיִם — **As a result, her body was left floating on top of the water.** יָרַד וּנְטָלָהּ וְהֶעֱלָהּ וּקְבָרָהּ — **Witnessing all this,** [her former master] **climbed down** into the well, **took her** body, **brought it up** from the well, **and buried it.** וּבָא וְאָמַר לְאִשְׁתּוֹ: עַם זוֹ שֶׁאַתָּה רוֹאָה — **And when he came** home, **he said to his wife, "This nation** — of the girl **whom you have seen** here — לֹא כָּעַס עֲלֵיהֶם אֶלָּא אֲבִיהֶם שֶׁבַּשָּׁמַיִם — **it is none other than their Father in Heaven Who has become angry with them."**[37]

---

34. The angel appointed over relaying Divine messages to people through dreams (*Rashi* to *Sanhedrin* 30a).

35. *Avos HaRosh* [Vol.1].

36. *Ben Avraham.*

37. And it is not by our strength and the might of our hands that we defeated them (*Magen Avos*). When the idolater saw how God had compelled him to remove the girl from his house in order for her to meet her

ז. וְכָל מַעֲשֶׂיךָ יִהְיוּ לְשֵׁם שָׁמַיִם, לְשֵׁם תּוֹרָה,‎38 שֶׁנֶּאֱמַר (משלי ג, ו) "בְּכָל דְּרָכֶיךָ דָעֵהוּ וְהוּא יְיַשֵּׁר אֹרְחֹתֶיךָ"‎:39

ח. רַבִּי שִׁמְעוֹן אוֹמֵר: הֱוֵי זָהִיר בִּקְרִיאַת שְׁמַע וּבַתְּפִלָּה.‎40 וּכְשֶׁאַתָּה מִתְפַּלֵּל אַל תַּעֲשֶׂה תְּפִלָּתְךָ שִׂיחָה‎41 אֶלָּא תַּחֲנוּנִים לִפְנֵי הַקָּדוֹשׁ בָּרוּךְ הוּא,‎42 שֶׁנֶּאֱמַר (יונה ד, ב) "כִּי אַתָּה אֵל חַנּוּן וְרַחוּם אֶרֶךְ אַפַּיִם וְרַב חֶסֶד

§7 R' Yose's third teaching:

וְכָל מַעֲשֶׂיךָ יִהְיוּ לְשֵׁם שָׁמַיִם — "And let all your deeds be for the sake of Heaven": לְשֵׁם תּוֹרָה — This means for the sake of Torah.[38] שֶׁנֶּאֱמַר "בְּכָל דְּרָכֶיךָ דָעֵהוּ וְהוּא יְיַשֵּׁר אֹרְחֹתֶיךָ" — That a person's deeds must all be for the sake of Heaven is derived from that which it says, In all your ways know Him, and He will smooth your paths (Proverbs 3:6).[39]

§8 The Baraisa quotes the three teachings of Rabban Yochanan ben Zakkai's fourth disciple, R' Shimon ben Nesanel, citing a variation of Avos 2:13. רַבִּי שִׁמְעוֹן אוֹמֵר — R' Shimon says: (i) Be הֱוֵי זָהִיר בִּקְרִיאַת שְׁמַע וּבַתְּפִלָּה — meticulous about reciting the Shema (ii) and prayer in their proper time.[40] וּכְשֶׁאַתָּה מִתְפַּלֵּל אַל תַּעֲשֶׂה תְּפִלָּתְךָ שִׂיחָה אֶלָּא תַּחֲנוּנִים לִפְנֵי הַקָּדוֹשׁ בָּרוּךְ הוּא — (iii) And when you pray, do not make your prayer mere speech,[41] but a supplication before the Holy One, Blessed is He,[42] שֶׁנֶּאֱמַר "כִּי אַתָּה אֵל חַנּוּן — as it says, For You are a gracious וְרַחוּם אֶרֶךְ אַפַּיִם וְרַב חֶסֶד וְנִחָם עַל הָרָעָה" —

bitter end, he realized that any misfortune that happens to the Jewish people is a direct act of God.

38. Whatever one does should be done in accordance with the Torah's guidelines ("for the sake of Torah"), and in this way, all his actions will be for the sake of Heaven [i.e., God], since God is one, so to speak, with His Torah [see Zohar, Vol. 3, 73a] (Ben Avraham).

39. This verse teaches us that even the mundane acts one performs, such as eating, walking, etc. (in all your ways), should be done for the purpose of better serving God (know Him). And if a person follows this prescription, then God will give him success in all his endeavors (and He will smooth your paths) (Binyan Yehoshua).

40. Binyan Yeshoshua, from Rav to Avos 2:13.

The Shema, as well as the morning prayer, must be recited during the early hours of the day. It is therefore common to face the

temptation to sleep late or stay warm in bed when the time comes to perform these mitzvos. R' Shimon therefore urges a person to overcome his evil inclination and arise to say these prayers in their proper times (Ben Avraham, from Midrash Shmuel ad loc.).

Earlier (15 §1), the Baraisa prefaced its discussion of these teachings by saying that each of Rabban Yochanan's disciples said three things. It is thus apparent that the Baraisa counts this sentence as two distinct sayings — one for Shema and one for prayer, so that together with the following teaching, R' Shimon said a total of three things. In Avos, however, these two are counted as one, and a third saying is added to the ones recorded here: "Do not judge yourself to be a wicked person" (Magen Avos; see further there).

41. Which is often uttered with no prior thought or consideration (Binyan Yehoshua).

42. By adding the words "before the Holy One, Blessed is He," the Tanna reminds us

וְנִחָם עַל הָרָעָה"[43]. רַבִּי אֶלְעָזָר אוֹמֵר: הֱוֵי שָׁקוּד לִלְמוֹד תּוֹרָה. וְדַע מַה
שֶׁתָּשִׁיב לָאֶפִּיקוֹרוֹס, וְדָבָר אֶחָד בַּתּוֹרָה אַל °תִּשְׁתַּכַּח מִמְּךָ[44]. דַּע לִפְנֵי
מִי אַתָּה עָמֵל וּמִי הוּא בַּעַל בְּרִיתֶךָ, [וְנֶאֱמָן הוּא בַּעַל בְּרִיתֶךָ שֶׁיְּשַׁלֵּם
לְךָ שְׂכַר פְּעוּלָתֶךָ][45]:

_and merciful God, slow to anger, abundant in kindness, and One Who re-
lents from doing harm_ (Jonah 4:2).[43]

The fifth disciple of Rabban Yochanan ben Zakkai was R' Elazar ben Arach.
The Baraisa quotes the three sayings attributed to him, citing a variation of
Avos 2:14:

רַבִּי אֶלְעָזָר אוֹמֵר — R' Elazar says: הֱוֵי שָׁקוּד לִלְמוֹד תּוֹרָה — (i) Be diligent in
the study of Torah. וְדַע מַה שֶׁתָּשִׁיב לָאֶפִּיקוֹרוֹס וְדָבָר אֶחָד בַּתּוֹרָה אַל תִּשְׁכָּחֶה
מִמְּךָ — (ii) Know what to answer a heretic, and do not allow one word of
Torah to be forgotten from you.[44] דַּע לִפְנֵי מִי אַתָּה עָמֵל וּמִי הוּא בַּעַל בְּרִיתֶךָ,
וְנֶאֱמָן הוּא בַּעַל בְּרִיתֶךָ שֶׁיְּשַׁלֵּם לְךָ שְׂכַר פְּעוּלָתֶךָ — (iii) Know before Whom you
toil, Who it is that has made a covenant with you, and that He Who has made
a covenant with you can be trusted to pay you the wage of your labor.[45]

that when one prays, he must view himself
as standing before the Divine Presence [see
Orach Chaim 98:1] (_Avos HaRosh_ [Vol.1]).

43. From this verse we can see that God is
gracious and responds favorably to one who
begs sincerely for mercy (_Binyan Yehoshua_,
from _Rashi_ to _Avos_ 2:13).

44. This is a second part of the advice to
know what to answer a heretic, for one must
be very careful not to be led to stray even
minimally from any Torah principles due

to conversing with such a person (_Binyan
Yehoshua_).

45. All of these can be considered one point.
Namely, a person must realize that it is before God that he toils to study the Torah and
perform its mitzvos. This knowledge will spur
a person to better deeds if he will also reflect
on the fact that each and every Jew entered
a covenant with God at Sinai obligating him
to keep His Torah, and that God can certainly
be relied on to reward him for his labor.

﴾ פֶּרֶק יח ﴿

א. וּלְנֶגְדָּן הָיָה רַבִּי יְהוּדָה הַנָּשִׂיא מוֹנֶה שִׁבְחָן שֶׁל חֲכָמִים, שֶׁל רַבִּי טַרְפוֹן שֶׁל רַבִּי עֲקִיבָא וְשֶׁל רַבִּי אֶלְעָזָר בֶּן עֲזַרְיָה וְשֶׁל רַבִּי יוֹחָנָן בֶּן נוּרִי וְשֶׁל רַבִּי יוֹסֵי הַגְּלִילִי. לְרַבִּי טַרְפוֹן קָרָא לוֹ גַּל שֶׁל אֲבָנִים. וְיֵשׁ אוֹמְרִים: גַּל שֶׁל אֱגוֹזִים. כֵּיוָן שֶׁנּוֹטֵל אָדָם אֶחָד מֵהֶן כֻּלָּן מִתְקַשְׁקְשִׁין וּבָאִין זֶה עַל זֶה. כָּךְ הָיָה רַבִּי טַרְפוֹן דּוֹמֶה, בְּשָׁעָה שֶׁתַּלְמִיד חָכָם נִכְנַס אֶצְלוֹ וְאוֹמֵר לוֹ: שְׁנֵה לִי, מֵבִיא לוֹ מִקְרָא וּמִשְׁנָה מִדְרָשׁ הֲלָכוֹת וְאַגָּדוֹת.[2]

﴾ CHAPTER 18 ﴿

§1 Earlier (14 §3), the Baraisa related how Rabban Yochanan ben Zakkai enumerated the praises of his five primary disciples. Now that the Baraisa has completed its selection of wise sayings from those disciples, it presents two other lists of similarly distinctive praises:

וּלְנֶגְדָּן הָיָה רַבִּי יְהוּדָה הַנָּשִׂיא מוֹנֶה שִׁבְחָן שֶׁל חֲכָמִים — **Corresponding to those** praises devised by Rabban Yochanan ben Zakkai, **R' Yehudah HaNasi** ("the Prince") **would enumerate the praises of** five other **scholars:** שֶׁל רַבִּי טַרְפוֹן שֶׁל רַבִּי עֲקִיבָא וְשֶׁל רַבִּי אֶלְעָזָר בֶּן עֲזַרְיָה וְשֶׁל רַבִּי יוֹחָנָן בֶּן נוּרִי וְשֶׁל רַבִּי יוֹסֵי הַגְּלִילִי — **of R' Tarfon, of R' Akiva, of R' Elazar ben Azaryah, of R' Yochanan ben Nuri, and of R' Yose HaGlili.**

The Baraisa records the tributes one by one.

לְרַבִּי טַרְפוֹן קָרָא לוֹ גַּל שֶׁל אֲבָנִים — **Speaking** of R' Tarfon, he described him as a **pile of stones;** וְיֵשׁ אוֹמְרִים: גַּל שֶׁל אֱגוֹזִים — **and some say,** as a **pile of nuts.** כֵּיוָן שֶׁנּוֹטֵל אָדָם אֶחָד מֵהֶן כֻּלָּן מִתְקַשְׁקְשִׁין וּבָאִין זֶה עַל זֶה — **According to either** version, the metaphor draws on the fact that **as soon as someone takes one of them** (a stone or a nut) from the pile, **they all come tumbling down, one upon another.** כָּךְ הָיָה רַבִּי טַרְפוֹן דּוֹמֶה בְּשָׁעָה שֶׁתַּלְמִיד חָכָם נִכְנַס אֶצְלוֹ וְאוֹמֵר לוֹ: שְׁנֵה לִי — **This was what R' Tarfon was like: Whenever a Torah student would enter his presence and say to him, "Teach me Torah,"** מֵבִיא לוֹ מִקְרָא וּמִשְׁנָה מִדְרָשׁ הֲלָכוֹת וְאַגָּדוֹת — **[R' Tarfon] would** tell him a novel thought and then, calling on his exceptional breadth of knowledge, would **bring him** proofs to it[1] from **Scripture, Mishnah, Midrash, Halachos, and Aggados.**[2]

---

1. *Ben Avraham*, from *Rashi* to *Gittin* 67a; *Ahavas Chesed*.

2. Thus allowing the Torah sources to "tumble" out of his mouth, one upon another, just like the stones (or nuts) in the metaphor. ["Scripture" is the entire Bible. "Mishnah"

is a general term for the Oral Tradition explaining the laws of the Torah; "Midrash" refers to the [Halachic] expositions of Scripture; "Halachos" are the various rulings and halachic discussions; and "Aggados" are the ethical and homiletic teachings.]

כֵּיוָן שֶׁיָּצָא מִלְּפָנָיו הָיָה יוֹצֵא מָלֵא בְּרָכָה וָטוֹב.³ לְרַבִּי עֲקִיבָא קָרָא לוֹ
אוֹצָר בָּלוּם. לְמָה רַבִּי עֲקִיבָא דוֹמֶה, לְפוֹעֵל שֶׁנָּטַל קוּפָּתוֹ וְיָצָא לַחוּץ,
מָצָא חִטִּים מַנִּיחַ בָּהּ⁴ מָצָא שְׁעוֹרִים מַנִּיחַ בָּהּ כּוּסְמִין מַנִּיחַ בָּהּ פּוֹלִין
מַנִּיחַ בָּהּ עֲדָשִׁים מַנִּיחַ בָּהּ, כֵּיוָן שֶׁנִּכְנַס לְבֵיתוֹ מְבָרֵר חִטִּים בִּפְנֵי עַצְמָן
שְׁעוֹרִים בִּפְנֵי עַצְמָן כּוּסְמִין בִּפְנֵי עַצְמָן פּוֹלִין בִּפְנֵי עַצְמָן עֲדָשִׁים
בִּפְנֵי עַצְמָן. כָּךְ עָשָׂה רַבִּי עֲקִיבָא וְעָשָׂה כָּל הַתּוֹרָה טַבָּעוֹת טַבָּעוֹת.⁵

כֵּיוָן שֶׁיָּצָא מִלְּפָנָיו הָיָה יוֹצֵא מָלֵא בְּרָכָה וָטוֹב — Then, when leaving his presence, [the petitioner] would leave full of blessing and goodness from all the Torah he had just learned.[3]

R' Yehudah HaNasi's praise of the next scholar:

לְרַבִּי עֲקִיבָא קָרָא לוֹ אוֹצָר בָּלוּם — As for R' Akiva, he described him as a storehouse with compartments, and gave the following explanation: לְמָה רַבִּי עֲקִיבָא דוֹמֶה — To what is R' Akiva comparable? לְפוֹעֵל שֶׁנָּטַל קוּפָּתוֹ וְיָצָא לַחוּץ — To a worker who takes his basket and goes outside to find work. מָצָא חִטִּים מַנִּיחַ בָּהּ — When he finds wheat he puts it in [the basket],[4] שְׁעוֹרִים מַנִּיחַ בָּהּ — when he finds barley he puts it in, כּוּסְמִין מַנִּיחַ בָּהּ — when he finds spelt he puts it in, פּוֹלִין מַנִּיחַ בָּהּ — when he finds beans he puts them in, עֲדָשִׁים מַנִּיחַ בָּהּ — and when he finds lentils, he puts them in. כֵּיוָן שֶׁנִּכְנַס לְבֵיתוֹ מְבָרֵר חִטִּים בִּפְנֵי עַצְמָן שְׁעוֹרִים בִּפְנֵי עַצְמָן כּוּסְמִין בִּפְנֵי עַצְמָן פּוֹלִין בִּפְנֵי עַצְמָן עֲדָשִׁים בִּפְנֵי עַצְמָן — Then, when he comes home, he sorts the wheat by itself, the barley by itself, the spelt by itself, the beans by themselves, and the lentils by themselves, so that whatever he collected randomly is now arranged in an orderly manner. כָּךְ עָשָׂה רַבִּי עֲקִיבָא וְעָשָׂה כָּל הַתּוֹרָה טַבָּעוֹת טַבָּעוֹת — R Akiva did the same with his learning, and in this way, he made the entire Torah into a system of organized teachings, sorted out as one would sort out various types of coins.[5]

3. This conclusion is a separate tribute to R' Tarfon's rare skill as a teacher, for it indicates that he was able to impart a vast amount of information in a way that the petitioner could understand and absorb it — and walk away feeling "full of blessing and goodness" (Magen Avos).

4. That is, when he finds a job involving wheat (or barley, or spelt, etc.), he is paid with a portion of the corresponding produce (Ben Avraham). Rashi (to Gittin 67a) cites this Baraisa as reading: לֶעָנִי" שֶׁנָּטַל קֻפָּתוֹ", To "a poor person" who took his basket, which would mean that he went to the various fields to

collect the gifts designated for the poor (Ben Avraham).

5. [Magen Avos, first approach; Tummas Yesharim; Ben Avraham.] Rather than devote himself to one area of Torah at a time, R' Akiva was receptive to every piece of Torah he would hear from his teachers — whether it related to Scripture, Halachah, etc. — and he would then review his studies constantly until he knew it all proficiently. Later, when he became a great sage and wanted to teach his students in the most effective way possible, he organized his knowledge according to subject and taught each subject separately (Binyan Yehoshua, quoting Rashi to Gittin

לְרַבִּי אֶלְעָזָר בֶּן עֲזַרְיָה קָרָא לוֹ קוּפָּה שֶׁל רוֹכְלִים. וְלָמָּה הָיָה רַבִּי
אֶלְעָזָר דּוֹמֶה, לְרוֹכֵל שֶׁנָּטַל קוּפָּתוֹ וְנִכְנַס לַמְּדִינָה וּבָאוּ בְּנֵי הַמְּדִינָה
וְאָמְרוּ לוֹ: שֶׁמֶן טוֹב יֵשׁ עִמְּךָ, פְּלָיִיטוֹן יֵשׁ עִמְּךָ, אַפַּרְסְמוֹן יֵשׁ עִמְּךָ,
וּמוֹצְאִין הַכֹּל עִמּוֹ. כָּךְ הָיָה רַבִּי אֶלְעָזָר בֶּן עֲזַרְיָה, בִּזְמַן שֶׁתַּלְמִיד חָכָם
נִכְנָס אֶצְלוֹ שְׁאָלוֹ בַּמִּקְרָא אוֹמֵר לוֹ בַּמִּשְׁנָה אוֹמֵר לוֹ בַּמִּדְרָשׁ אוֹמֵר
לוֹ בַּהֲלָכוֹת אוֹמֵר לוֹ בַּהַגָּדוֹת אוֹמֵר לוֹ. כֵּיוָן שֶׁיָּצָא מִלְּפָנָיו הוּא מָלֵא
טוֹב וּבְרָכָה:[6]

R' Yehudah HaNasi's praise of the next scholar:
לְרַבִּי אֶלְעָזָר בֶּן עֲזַרְיָה קָרָא לוֹ קוּפָּה שֶׁל רוֹכְלִים — As for R' Elazar ben Azaryah,
he described him as a spice-peddler's basket. וְלָמָּה הָיָה רַבִּי אֶלְעָזָר דּוֹמֶה
— And he gave the following explanation: To what is R' Elazar ben Azaryah
comparable? לְרוֹכֵל שֶׁנָּטַל קוּפָּתוֹ וְנִכְנַס לַמְּדִינָה — To a spice-peddler who
takes his basket and enters a town. וּבָאוּ בְּנֵי הַמְּדִינָה וְאָמְרוּ לוֹ: שֶׁמֶן טוֹב יֵשׁ
עִמְּךָ — The townsfolk come over and ask him, "Do you have any fragrant oil
with you? פְּלָיִיטוֹן יֵשׁ עִמְּךָ אַפַּרְסְמוֹן יֵשׁ עִמְּךָ — Do you have any musk with
you? Do you have any balsam with you?" וּמוֹצְאִין הַכֹּל עִמּוֹ — And they
indeed find that he has with him everything they request. כָּךְ הָיָה רַבִּי אֶלְעָזָר
בֶּן עֲזַרְיָה — This is what R' Elazar ben Azaryah
was like: Anytime a Torah student would enter his presence, שְׁאָלוֹ בַּמִּקְרָא
אוֹמֵר לוֹ — if [the student] would ask him a question regarding Scripture,
he would answer him; בַּמִּשְׁנָה אוֹמֵר לוֹ — regarding Mishnah, he would
answer him; בַּמִּדְרָשׁ אוֹמֵר לוֹ — regarding Midrash, he would answer him;
בַּהֲלָכוֹת אוֹמֵר לוֹ — regarding Halachos, he would answer him; בַּהַגָּדוֹת
אוֹמֵר לוֹ — regarding Aggados, he would answer him. כֵּיוָן שֶׁיָּצָא מִלְּפָנָיו
הוּא מָלֵא טוֹב וּבְרָכָה — Then, when [the student] would leave his presence, he
would be full of goodness and blessing, having received answers to all of his
questions.[6]

67a). It was in this later stage of his development that R' Akiva resembled a "storehouse
with compartments" (Magen Avos).

[Ben Avraham suggests that the five foods
enumerated in the analogy (wheat, barley,
spelt, beans, and lentils) represent the
five areas of Torah — Scripture, Mishnah,
Midrash, Halachos, and Aggados — mentioned earlier by the Baraisa with reference
to R' Tarfon.]

6. Like a spice-peddler, who has all his different spices wrapped and ready to sell,
R' Elazar ben Azaryah had ready answers

for any questions that could be asked of
him.

This praise is different from the preceding ones. Although he answered questions
as readily and cogently as R' Tarfon, R'
Elazar ben Azaryah did not embellish his
answers with material from all branches of
Torah wisdom; rather, he kept to the area in
which the question was asked. And unlike R'
Akiva, he did not study the various branches
of Torah simultaneously, but mastered each
one separately (Binyan Yehoshua, based on
Rashi to Gittin 67a).

ב. לְעֵת זִקְנָתוֹ שֶׁל רַבִּי יְהוֹשֻׁעַ נִכְנְסוּ תַּלְמִידָיו לְבַקְּרוֹ. אָמַר לָהֶם בָּנַי, מַה חִדּוּשׁ לָכֶם בְּבֵית הַמִּדְרָשׁ. אָמְרוּ לוֹ: תַּלְמִידֶיךָ אָנוּ וּמֵימֶיךָ[8] אָנוּ שׁוֹתִים[9]. אָמַר לָהֶם: חַס וְשָׁלוֹם שֶׁאֵין דּוֹר יָתוֹם [שֶׁל חֲכָמִים], שַׁבָּת שֶׁל מִי הָיְתָה[11]. אָמְרוּ לוֹ: שַׁבָּת שֶׁל רַבִּי אֶלְעָזָר בֶּן עֲזַרְיָה הָיְתָה. אָמַר לָהֶם: וּבַמֶּה הָיְתָה הַהַגָּדָה הַיּוֹם[12]. אָמְרוּ: בְּפָרָשַׁת (דברים לא, יב) "הַקְהֵל[13] אֶת הָעָם הָאֲנָשִׁים וְהַנָּשִׁים וְהַטַּף". אָמַר לָהֶם: וּמַה דָּרַשׁ בָּהּ. אָמְרוּ לוֹ:

---

§2 The Baraisa cites an anecdote that reflects further on R' Elazar ben Azaryah's Torah wisdom.[7] It will resume its quote of R' Yehudah HaNasi's praises of the Sages at the very end of this section:

לְעֵת זִקְנָתוֹ שֶׁל רַבִּי יְהוֹשֻׁעַ — **In R' Yehoshua's old age**, when he could no longer attend the study hall, נִכְנְסוּ תַּלְמִידָיו לְבַקְּרוֹ — his disciples came in to visit him. אָמַר לָהֶם: בָּנַי, מַה חִדּוּשׁ לָכֶם בְּבֵית הַמִּדְרָשׁ — Upon seeing them, he asked them, "My sons, what novel teaching was taught to you in the study hall?" אָמְרוּ לוֹ: תַּלְמִידֶיךָ אָנוּ וּמֵימֶיךָ אָנוּ שׁוֹתִים — They said to him, "We are your disciples,[8] and we drink *your* waters!"[9] אָמַר לָהֶם: חַס וְשָׁלוֹם שֶׁאֵין דּוֹר יָתוֹם שֶׁל חֲכָמִים — He said to them, "But the generation is not, Heaven forbid, orphaned of worthy Torah scholars who are capable of discovering novel things in the Torah. Thus, you must have heard something new.[10] שַׁבָּת שֶׁל מִי הָיְתָה — Now, whose week was it to lecture in the study hall?"[11] אָמְרוּ לוֹ: שַׁבָּת שֶׁל רַבִּי אֶלְעָזָר בֶּן עֲזַרְיָה הָיְתָה — They replied, "It was R' Elazar ben Azaryah's week to lecture." אָמַר לָהֶם: וּבַמֶּה הָיְתָה הַהַגָּדָה הַיּוֹם — [R' Yehoshua] inquired, "And on what topic was the Aggadah portion of his lecture today?"[12] אָמְרוּ — They answered, "On the Torah בְּפָרָשַׁת "הַקְהֵל אֶת הָעָם הָאֲנָשִׁים וְהַנָּשִׁים וְהַטַּף" portion of *Hakheil*,[13] which states, *Gather together the people — the men, the women, and the small children*" (Deuteronomy 31:12). אָמַר לָהֶם: וּמַה דָּרַשׁ — [R' Yehoshua] asked them, "And what did he expound on it?" בָּהּ אָמְרוּ לוֹ:

---

7. *Magen Avos.*

8. And therefore it is improper for us to speak before you (*Binyan Yehoshua*, citing *Rashi* to *Chagigah* 3a).

9. I.e., it is you who teaches Torah to us, for we are your disciples. [Water is a metaphor for Torah; see *Isaiah* 55:1.]

10. *Magen Avos.*

11. The arrangement at that time was that Rabban Gamliel would lecture three weeks out of every four (or, according to another version, two weeks out of every three), and R' Elazar ben Azaryah would lecture the remaining week (see *Berachos* 27b-28a for what brought about this arrangement).

R' Yehoshua wished to know whose teaching he was about to hear because (as taught in *Avos* 6:6), "whoever relates a Torah thought in the name of its author brings redemption to the world" (*Binyan Yehoshua*, from *Maharsha* to *Chagigah* 3a).

12. It was customary for the lecturer to preface his halachic discussion with a homiletical discourse (see *Rashi* to *Shabbos* 30a, s.v. פתח and 30b, s.v. מוטב). R' Yehoshua asked the students to tell him the homiletical part of R' Elazar ben Azaryah's lecture (see *Derashos Chasam Sofer, Shabbos Shuvah* 5570 [p. 18b]).

13. The mitzvah of *Hakheil* calls on the

כָּךְ דָּרַשׁ בָּהּ: אֲנָשִׁים בָּאִים לִלְמוֹד וְנָשִׁים לִשְׁמוֹעַ[14], טַף לְמָה הֵם בָּאִים, כְּדֵי לָתֵת שָׂכָר טוֹב לִמְבִיאֵיהֶם[15]. אָמַר לָהֶם: מַרְגָּלִית טוֹבָה הָיְתָה בְּיֶדְכֶם וּבִקַּשְׁתֶּם לְאַבְּדָהּ מִמֶּנִּי[16], אִלְמָלֵא (לֹא) בָּאתֶם אֶלָּא לִשְׁמוֹעַ דָּבָר זֶה דַּי. אָמְרוּ לוֹ: וְעוֹד דָּרַשׁ בָּהּ: (קהלת יב, יא) "דִּבְרֵי חֲכָמִים כַּדָּרְבֹנוֹת וּכְמַסְמְרוֹת נְטוּעִים בַּעֲלֵי אֲסֻפּוֹת", מַה דָּרְבָן זֶה[19] מְכַוֵּן אֶת הַפָּרָה לִתְלָמֶיהָ

אֲנָשִׁים כָּךְ דָּרַשׁ בָּהּ — They answered him, "He expounded on it as follows: בָּאִים לִלְמוֹד וְנָשִׁים לִשְׁמוֹעַ — We can understand that the men come to learn and the women come to hear.[14] טַף לְמָה הֵם בָּאִים — Why, however, do the small children come? They are too young to learn or even to hear! כְּדֵי לָתֵת שָׂכָר טוֹב לִמְבִיאֵיהֶם — Rather, it is in order to give a good reward to those who bring them."[15] אָמַר לָהֶם: מַרְגָּלִית טוֹבָה הָיְתָה בְּיֶדְכֶם — Upon hearing his disciples report this insightful exposition, [R' Yehoshua] said to them, "A precious pearl was in your hand, וּבִקַּשְׁתֶּם לְאַבְּדָהּ מִמֶּנִּי — and you sought to withhold it from me?![16] אִלְמָלֵא בָּאתֶם אֶלָּא לִשְׁמוֹעַ דָּבָר זֶה דַּי — Had you come here only to let me hear this teaching, it would have been enough for me!"[17]

R' Yehoshua's disciples share another part of R' Elazar ben Azaryah's homiletical discourse:

אָמְרוּ לוֹ: וְעוֹד דָּרַשׁ בָּהּ — They said to him, "He also expounded in his lecture of [that week]:[18] "דִּבְרֵי חֲכָמִים כַּדָּרְבֹנוֹת וּכְמַסְמְרוֹת נְטוּעִים בַּעֲלֵי אֲסֻפּוֹת" — The verse states, *The words of the wise are like goads, and like nails well planted are the sayings of the masters of assemblies, given from one shepherd* (*Ecclesiastes* 12:11). מַה דָּרְבָן זֶה מְכַוֵּן אֶת הַפָּרָה לִתְלָמֶיהָ — How are the words of Torah like goads?[19] **Just as this goad directs the cow along**

Jewish people to gather in the Temple once every seven years to hear the king read the Book of *Deuteronomy*.

14. When the men listen to the Torah recital, they fulfill their obligation to learn Torah. The women have no obligation to learn Torah for its own sake (according to this opinion; see *Sotah* 20a), but they are still obliged to hear the recital as a source for instruction on how to observe the mitzvos (*Maharsha* to *Chagigah* 3a).

15. Even if there is no purpose in bringing small children who will not understand the Torah reading, God nevertheless commands us to do so. For He knows that since the fathers, mothers, and older children must all come to the gathering, they will have no choice but to bring their younger

children as well, for lack of anyone to watch them. He therefore made it a mitzvah obligation to bring those small children, so that when the parents do so, they will be obeying His command and earning a reward (*Ben Avraham*).

16. [Some explain that this particular teaching moved R' Yehoshua because it was deeply significant to him on a personal level; see *Ben Yehoyada*, *Chagigah* 3a and *Meshech Chochmah* on the verse.]

17. Explanation follows *Magen Avos* (first approach) and *Binyan Yehoshua*.

18. *Magen Avos, Ben Avraham.*

19. A goad is a long stick with a thin nail implanted in its head, and is used to direct and control the animal pulling the plow (*Rav* to *Keilim* 9:6).

כָּךְ דִּבְרֵי תוֹרָה מְכַוְּונִין אֶת הָאָדָם לְדַרְכֵי חַיִּים²⁰. אִי מַה דָּרְבָן זֶה מְטַלְטֵל אַף דִּבְרֵי תוֹרָה מְטַלְטְלִין²¹, תַּלְמוּד לוֹמַר "וּכְמַסְמְרוֹת נְטוּעִים", מַה נְּטוּעִים אֵינָן מִתְעַקְּרִין אַף דִּבְרֵי תוֹרָה אֵינָן מִתְעַקְּרִין²². "בַּעֲלֵי אֲסֻפּוֹת" אֵלּוּ תַּלְמִידֵי חֲכָמִים שֶׁנִּכְנָסִין וְיוֹשְׁבִין אֲסוּפוֹת אֲסוּפוֹת²³, אֵלּוּ אוֹסְרִין וְאֵלּוּ מַתִּירִין²⁴ אֵלּוּ מְטַמְּאִין וְאֵלּוּ מְטַהֲרִין אֵלּוּ פּוֹסְלִין וְאֵלּוּ מַכְשִׁירִין²⁵. [שֶׁמָּא יֹאמַר לְךָ אָדָם:] אֵשֵׁב וְלֹא אֶשְׁנֶה, תַּלְמוּד לוֹמַר (שם) "נִתְּנוּ

---

its furrows, כָּךְ דִּבְרֵי תוֹרָה מְכַוְּונִין אֶת הָאָדָם לְדַרְכֵי חַיִּים — so do the words of Torah direct a person to the paths of life.[20] אִי מַה דָּרְבָן זֶה מְטַלְטֵל אַף דִּבְרֵי תוֹרָה מְטַלְטְלִין — Now, if the words of Torah are like goads, one might think that just as this goad is movable, so too, the words of Torah are movable.[21] תַּלְמוּד לוֹמַר "וּכְמַסְמְרוֹת נְטוּעִים" — [Scripture] therefore teaches us otherwise by saying, *and like nails well planted.* מַה נְּטוּעִים אֵינָן מִתְעַקְּרִין — Just as nails that are well planted are not uprooted, so too, the words of Torah are not uprooted, but remain in place forever.[22] "בַּעֲלֵי אֲסֻפּוֹת" — The verse continues: *and like nails well planted [are the sayings of] the masters of assemblies.* אֵלּוּ תַּלְמִידֵי חֲכָמִים שֶׁנִּכְנָסִין וְיוֹשְׁבִין אֲסוּפוֹת אֲסוּפוֹת — These masters of assemblies are the Torah scholars, who enter the study hall and sit in various groups while studying Torah.[23] אֵלּוּ אוֹסְרִין וְאֵלּוּ מַתִּירִין — These in one group prohibit a certain matter while those in another group permit it;[24] אֵלּוּ מְטַמְּאִין וְאֵלּוּ מְטַהֲרִין — these in one group declare a certain thing *tamei* (ritually impure) while those in another group declare it *tahor* (pure); אֵלּוּ פּוֹסְלִין וְאֵלּוּ מַכְשִׁירִין — these in one group disqualify while those in another group declare fit.[25] שֶׁמָּא יֹאמַר לְךָ אָדָם אֵשֵׁב וְלֹא אֶשְׁנֶה — Now, a person might say to you, 'Since there is so much difference of opinion,[26] I may as well sit idle and not study Torah, for how will I know which position is correct?' תַּלְמוּד לוֹמַר "נִתְּנוּ

---

20. That is, the Rabbinic enactments (*words of the wise*), which are meant to safeguard the Torah's laws, enable Jewry to obey those laws and advance unwaveringly along the path to true, eternal life (see *Ben Avraham,* citing *Maharsha* to *Chagigah* 3b).

21. One might think that just as a goad does not remain permanently in one place, so are the Rabbinic decrees temporary (see *Binyan Yehoshua,* from *Maharsha* ibid.).

22. The words of the Sages remain in force and are observed for all generations (ibid.).

23. They study in groups because the

Torah's wisdom is best acquired through collective study (ibid., based on *Koheles Rabbah* 12 §12; see also *Avos* 6:6).

24. Since the verse alludes to the Sages with the plural אֲסֻפּוֹת, *assemblies,* the Baraisa understands it to be hinting at the divergent Torah views that exist among the various "groups" of Sages (*Binyan Yehoshua,* from *Maharsha* to *Chagigah* 3b).

25. E.g., they debate whether one is fit or disqualified to testify in court, or whether one is fit or disqualified for the priesthood (*Binyan Yehoshua,* from *Rashi* ibid.).

26. *Binyan Yehoshua.*

מַרְעֶה אֶחָד״, אֶל אֶחָד בְּרָאָם²⁷ וּפַרְנָס אֶחָד נְתָנָם²⁸ רִבּוֹן כָּל הַמַּעֲשִׂים אֲמָרָם,²⁹ אַף אַתָּה עֲשֵׂה אָזְנְךָ כְּאַפַּרְכֶּסֶת³⁰ וְהַכְנֵס בָּהֶם דִּבְרֵי אוֹסְרִין וְדִבְרֵי מַתִּירִין דִּבְרֵי מְטַמְּאִים וְדִבְרֵי מְטַהֲרִין דִּבְרֵי פּוֹסְלִין וְדִבְרֵי מַכְשִׁירִין³¹.

מַרְעֶה אֶחָד״ — [Scripture] teaches us otherwise by saying, given from one shepherd, אֶל אֶחָד בְּרָאָם — meaning that although there are two sides in the debate, they are both correct, for one God created them both,[27] וּפַרְנָס אֶחָד נְתָנָם — one leader, Moses, transmitted them both to us,[28] רִבּוֹן כָּל הַמַּעֲשִׂים אֲמָרָם — and the Master of all beings is the One Who said them both.[29] אַף אַתָּה עֲשֵׂה אָזְנְךָ כְּאַפַּרְכֶּסֶת — Therefore, you too should make your ears like a mill-hopper,[30] וְהַכְנֵס בָּהֶם דִּבְרֵי אוֹסְרִין וְדִבְרֵי מַתִּירִין — and gather into them the words of those who prohibit and the words of those who permit, דִּבְרֵי מְטַמְּאִים וְדִבְרֵי מְטַהֲרִין — the words of those who rule tamei and the words of those who rule tahor, דִּבְרֵי פּוֹסְלִין וְדִבְרֵי מַכְשִׁירִין — the words of those who disqualify and the words of those who declare fit."[31]

---

27. Both sides of any dispute adduce proof for their respective positions from the Torah of One God, and not from the "Torah" of any other "god" (Binyan Yehoshua, citing Rashi ibid.).

28. No disputant will ever adduce proof from a prophet who disagrees with Moses (ibid.). Maharsha (ibid.) explains that the phrase given from one shepherd can refer to either God or Moses, since both are called "shepherd" in various places in Scripture (see Koheles Rabbah 12 §12).

29. The Gemara (Chagigah 3b, cited by Binyan Yehoshua) derives this from the verse (Exodus 20:1), God spoke all these words. "All these words" alludes to the two legitimate sides to every issue debated by the Sages, both of which were spoken by God (see below).

The point being made here is that whenever there is a dispute among the Torah scholars, both positions have a basis in, and are derived from, the Torah that God gave us, and thus are, fundamentally, legitimate. This is the concept of, "These and those are the words of the Living God" [Eruvin 13b; Gittin 6b] (Binyan Yehoshua). The Sages explain that in such cases, God transmitted both positions, and the arguments supporting them, to Moses. However, He did not inform him of the final ruling, but left that up to the majority of the Torah scholars who would one day debate the issue (Yerushalmi Sanhedrin 4:2; Shocher Tov, Psalms 12:7). Moreover, it is indeed possible that both opinions are followed in practice, each in a different situation; for in certain cases one argument may be more appropriate, while in other cases a different argument may be more appropriate (Rashi to Kesubos 57a, s.v. הא קמ"ל; see Binyan Yehoshua).

30. A large funnel through which grain is channeled into a mill to be ground (Rashi to Chagigah 3b).

31. [Since all honest Torah views reflect the truth,] one should try to understand every one of them, even when they are on opposite sides of a debate. When one [is qualified and] can discern which position is the proper one, he should decide the halachah accordingly (Binyan Yehoshua, from Rashi ibid.; see note 29). In doing so, a Torah student resembles a mill-hopper, which receives much grain through its mouth, but lets only a small amount flow from its spout (Maharsha ad loc.).

וּלְרַבִּי יוֹחָנָן בֶּן נוּרִי קָרָא לוֹ קוּפָּה שֶׁל הֲלָכוֹת.³² וּלְרַבִּי יוֹסֵי הַגְּלִילִי
מְלַקֵּט יָפֶה בְּלֹא גַסּוּת הָרוּחַ,³³ שֶׁאָחַז בָּהּ מִדַּת חֲכָמִים (מֵהַר סִינַי³⁴ וְהָיָה
מְשַׁנֵּן בָּהּ) כָּל חַכְמֵי יִשְׂרָאֵל:

ג. אִיסִי בֶּן יְהוּדָה הָיָה קוֹרֵא לַחֲכָמִים שֵׁמוֹת. לְרַבִּי מֵאִיר חָכָם
וְסוֹפֵר.³⁶ לְרַבִּי יְהוּדָה חָכָם לִכְשֶׁיִּרְצֶה³⁷. לְרַבִּי אֱלִיעֶזֶר בֶּן יַעֲקֹב קַב
וְנָקִי³⁸. לְרַבִּי יוֹסֵי נִמּוּקוֹ עִמּוֹ³⁹. וּלְרַבִּי יוֹחָנָן בֶּן נוּרִי קוּפָּה שֶׁל הֲלָכוֹת.

The Baraisa returns to R' Yehudah HaNasi's tributes to certain Torah sages:
וּלְרַבִּי יוֹחָנָן בֶּן נוּרִי קָרָא לוֹ קוּפָּה שֶׁל הֲלָכוֹת — As for R' Yochanan ben Nuri, he
described him as a basket of halachos.[32] וּלְרַבִּי יוֹסֵי הַגְּלִילִי מְלַקֵּט יָפֶה בְּלֹא
גַסּוּת הָרוּחַ — As for R' Yose HaGlili, he described him as one who collects
Torah knowledge well, without any arrogance.[33] שֶׁאָחַז בָּהּ מִדַּת חֲכָמִים מֵהַר
סִינַי — For he held onto the trait of humility that the Sages learned from
Mount Sinai,[34] וְהָיָה מְשַׁנֵּן בָּהּ כָּל חַכְמֵי יִשְׂרָאֵל — and he would teach [this
trait] to all the Sages of Israel as well.[35]

§3 Another sage's praiseful descriptions of various scholars:
אִיסִי בֶּן יְהוּדָה הָיָה קוֹרֵא לַחֲכָמִים שֵׁמוֹת — Issi ben Yehudah would refer to
certain **scholars by** descriptive **names** that highlighted the unique strengths of
each one: לְרַבִּי מֵאִיר חָכָם וְסוֹפֵר — He would describe **R' Meir as a sage and
a scribe.**[36] לְרַבִּי יְהוּדָה חָכָם לִכְשֶׁיִּרְצֶה — He would describe **R' Yehudah as**
one who was **a scholar when he chose.**[37] לְרַבִּי אֱלִיעֶזֶר בֶּן יַעֲקֹב קַב וְנָקִי — He
would describe **R' Eliezer ben Yaakov as** one whose teachings were **measured
but pure.**[38] לְרַבִּי יוֹסֵי נִמּוּקוֹ עִמּוֹ — He would describe **R' Yose as** one who
always has **his reasons with him.**[39] וּלְרַבִּי יוֹחָנָן בֶּן נוּרִי קוּפָּה שֶׁל הֲלָכוֹת — He

---

32. He stood out in his ability to clarify issues
of practical halachah (*Avos HaRosh* [Vol. 1]).

33. He would humbly listen to new thoughts
from anyone who would express them, even
if the person was much younger than he (*Binyan Yehoshua*). Alternatively, R' Yose would
pick out (מְלַקֵּט) the best of the Torah insights
he heard, and reject whatever fell short of his
exacting standards. But he did so in a spirit
of humility, without the arrogance typical of
those who pass judgment on the ideas of
others, and without offending or disparaging
anyone (*Ahavas Chesed, Velo Od Ella*).

34. That is, from the fact that God chose
to give the Torah on Mount Sinai, a small,
insignificant mountain, rather than on a
higher, more impressive peak. To the Sages

(*Sotah 5a*), this demonstrated how important the trait of humility is to God (*Binyan
Yehoshua, from Mefaresh*).

35. *Ben Avraham.*

36. See *Sotah 20a*, where R' Meir is quoted
as saying that he worked as a scribe (*Binyan
Yehoshua*, citing *Rashi to Gittin 67a*). [In the
Vilna text, this section is mislabed as §4.]

37. That is, when he chose to be deliberate and methodical, he would surpass even
R' Meir in scholarship (see *Rashi* ibid.,
cited by *Binyan Yehoshua*, and *Tosafos* ibid.
ד"ה חכם לכשירצה).

38. He taught less than his colleagues, but
the law is in accordance with all of his teachings (*Binyan Yehoshua*, citing *Rashi* ibid.).

39. He would always give a clear and

לְרַבִּי יוֹסֵי הַגְּלִילִי מְלַקֵּט יָפֶה יָפֶה בְּלֹא גַסּוּת הָרוּחַ. לְרַבָּן שִׁמְעוֹן בֶּן
גַּמְלִיאֵל חָנוּת מָלֵא אַרְגָּוָן טָב.[40] לְרַבִּי שִׁמְעוֹן שׁוֹנֶה הַרְבֵּה וּמְשַׁבֵּחַ
קִימְעָא. לְאַחַר כָּךְ מְצָאוֹ רַבִּי שִׁמְעוֹן לְאִיסִי בֶּן יְהוּדָה, אָמַר לוֹ: מִפְּנֵי מָה
אַתָּה מְפַטְפֵּט דְּבָרַי בִּפְנֵי תַּלְמִידֵי חֲכָמִים.[41] אָמַר לוֹ: וְכִי אָמַרְתִּי עָלֶיךָ
אֶלָּא שֶׁאַתָּה שׁוֹנֶה הַרְבֵּה וּמְשַׁבֵּחַ קִימְעָא וּמַה שֶׁאַתָּה מְשַׁבֵּחַ סוּבִין שֶׁל
מִשְׁנָתְךָ:[42]

---

would describe R' Yochanan ben Nuri **as a basket of halachos.** לְרַבִּי יוֹסֵי
הַגְּלִילִי מְלַקֵּט יָפֶה יָפֶה בְּלֹא גַסּוּת הָרוּחַ — **He would describe** R' Yose HaGlili **as
one who collects** Torah knowledge **very well, without any arrogance.** לְרַבָּן
שִׁמְעוֹן בֶּן גַּמְלִיאֵל חָנוּת מָלֵא אַרְגָּוָן טָב — **He would describe** Rabban Shimon ben
Gamliel **as a store full of fine purple wool.**[40] לְרַבִּי שִׁמְעוֹן שׁוֹנֶה הַרְבֵּה וּמְשַׁבֵּחַ
קִימְעָא — **And he would describe** R' Shimon ben Yochai **as one who learns
much and forgets little.**

An incident in which the praise of the last scholar is clarified:
לְאַחַר כָּךְ מְצָאוֹ רַבִּי שִׁמְעוֹן לְאִיסִי בֶּן יְהוּדָה — **Subsequently,** R' Shimon ben
Yochai **encountered** Issi ben Yehudah אָמַר לוֹ: מִפְּנֵי מָה אַתָּה מְפַטְפֵּט דְּבָרַי
— **and said to him, "Why do you disparage my words
before other** Torah scholars?"[41] אָמַר לוֹ: וְכִי אָמַרְתִּי עָלֶיךָ אֶלָּא שֶׁאַתָּה שׁוֹנֶה
הַרְבֵּה וּמְשַׁבֵּחַ קִימְעָא — **[**Issi ben Yehudah**] replied to him, "Did I said anything
about you other than that you learn much and forget little,** וּמַה שֶׁאַתָּה
מְשַׁבֵּחַ סוּבִין שֶׁל מִשְׁנָתְךָ — **and that little which you forget is only the 'bran' of
your learning?"**[42]

---

compelling rationale for his view on a given
matter (ibid.).

40. Wool dyed with royal purple was rare
and valuable. Similarly, Rabban Shimon ben
Gamliel possessed novel Torah thoughts
that could not be found anywhere else. Alternatively, it means that his store of Torah
was comprehensive, like a store that stocks
even fine purple wool (*Binyan Yehoshua*).

41. Saying that I forget even one word of

my learning is a great humiliation to me,
for we are taught (*Avos* 3:8) that forgetting
any part of one's Torah learning is a sin of
considerable gravity (*Ben Avraham*).

42. R' Shimon would [sift out] and forget
only those matters that he concluded were
not in accordance with the halachah (*Binyan Yehoshua*, from *Rashi* to *Gittin* 67a),
just as one sifts out the bran in order to produce fine flour.

﴾ פֶּרֶק יט ﴿

א. עֲקַבְיָא בֶּן מַהֲלַלְאֵל אוֹמֵר: כָּל הַנּוֹתֵן אַרְבָּעָה דְבָרִים אֶל לִבּוֹ שׁוּב אֵינוֹ חוֹטֵא[1], מֵאַיִן הוּא בָא וּלְאָן הוּא הוֹלֵךְ וּמֶה עָתִיד לִהְיוֹת וּמִי הוּא דַיָּינוֹ, [מֵאַיִן הוּא בָא מִמְּקוֹם חוֹשֶׁךְ, וּלְאָן הוֹלֵךְ לִמְקוֹם חוֹשֶׁךְ וַאֲפֵילָה, וּמֶה עָתִיד לִהְיוֹת עָפָר רִמָּה וְתוֹלֵעָה, וּמִי הוּא דַיָּינוֹ] מֶלֶךְ מַלְכֵי הַמְּלָכִים הַקָּדוֹשׁ בָּרוּךְ הוּא[3]:

ב. רַבִּי שִׁמְעוֹן אוֹמֵר: בָּא מִמְּקוֹם חוֹשֶׁךְ וְחוֹזֵר לִמְקוֹם חוֹשֶׁךְ, בָּא מִטִּפָּה סְרוּחָה מִמָּקוֹם שֶׁאֵין הָעַיִן יְכוֹלָה לִרְאוֹת, וּמֶה עָתִיד

﴾ CHAPTER 19 ﴿

§1 This chapter cites and elaborates on a variation of *Avos* 3:1:

עֲקַבְיָא בֶּן מַהֲלַלְאֵל אוֹמֵר: כָּל הַנּוֹתֵן אַרְבָּעָה דְבָרִים אֶל לִבּוֹ שׁוּב אֵינוֹ חוֹטֵא — Akavya ben Mahalalel says: Anyone who contemplates the following four points will no longer sin:[1] מֵאַיִן הוּא בָא וּלְאָן הוּא הוֹלֵךְ וּמֶה עָתִיד לִהְיוֹת וּמִי הוּא דַיָּינוֹ — (i) from where he comes; (ii) to where he is going; (iii) what he is destined to be; and (iv) Who his Judge is. מֵאַיִן הוּא בָא מִמְּקוֹם חוֹשֶׁךְ — "From where he comes" — from a place of darkness, i.e., his mother's womb;[2] וּלְאָן הוֹלֵךְ, לִמְקוֹם חוֹשֶׁךְ וַאֲפֵילָה — "to where he is going" — to a place of darkness and gloom, i.e., the grave; וּמֶה עָתִיד לִהְיוֹת, עָפָר רִמָּה — "what he is destined to be" — dust, worms, and maggots; וּמִי וְתוֹלֵעָה — "and Who his Judge is" — the הוּא דַיָּינוֹ, מֶלֶךְ מַלְכֵי הַמְּלָכִים הַקָּדוֹשׁ בָּרוּךְ הוּא — King Who reigns over kings, the Holy One, Blessed is He.[3]

§2 Another sage elaborates further on this idea:

רַבִּי שִׁמְעוֹן אוֹמֵר: בָּא מִמְּקוֹם חוֹשֶׁךְ וְחוֹזֵר לִמְקוֹם חוֹשֶׁךְ — R' Shimon says: [A person] comes from a place of darkness, and ultimately returns to a place of darkness.[4] בָּא מִטִּפָּה סְרוּחָה מִמָּקוֹם שֶׁאֵין הָעַיִן יְכוֹלָה לִרְאוֹת — [A person]

---

1. The speaker, Akavya ben Mahalalel, is addressing a matter that was close to his heart: The Gemara (*Berachos* 19a) asserts that in his generation, he was peerless in his fear of sin (*Magen Avos*).

2. *Binyan Yehoshua* to *Derech Eretz Rabbah* 3:1, first approach.

3. Thinking about one's humble origin is an antidote to haughtiness. Remembering what his unglamorous end will be can help one curb his physical indulgence. And reflecting on the fact that God Himself will eventually judge him for each and every one of his actions deters a person from following his evil inclination (see *Binyan Yehoshua*, citing *Rav* to *Avos* 3:1). [In the Mishnah, Akavya enumerates only three things, as he combines the second and third points into one (*Ben Avraham*, citing *Nachalas Avos* ad loc.).] With such powerful tools at his disposal, a person will find it much less challenging to avoid wrongdoing. Hence, "he will not sin any longer."

4. As explained in the previous section.

לִהְיוֹת עָפָר רִמָּה וְתוֹלֵעָה, שֶׁנֶּאֱמַר (איוב כה, ו) "אַף כִּי אֱנוֹשׁ רִמָּה [וּבֶן אָדָם תּוֹלֵעָה]", רַבִּי °אֶלְעָזָר⁶ בֶּן יַעֲקֹב אוֹמֵר: רִמָּה] בְּחַיָּיו וּבֶן אָדָם תּוֹלֵעָה בְּמוֹתוֹ, אֵיזֶה רִמָּה בְּחַיָּיו [זֶה כִּינִים], וּבֶן אָדָם תּוֹלֵעָה זֶה בְּמוֹתוֹ, זֶה שֶׁמַּרְחִישׁ בְּמוֹתוֹ:⁷

ג. רַבִּי שִׁמְעוֹן בֶּן אֶלְעָזָר אוֹמֵר: אֶמְשׁוֹל לְךָ מָשָׁל לְמָה הַדָּבָר דּוֹמֶה, לְמֶלֶךְ שֶׁבָּנָה פָּלְטְרִין גְּדוֹלִים וְיָשַׁב בְּכוּלָם, וּבִיב שֶׁל בּוּרְסְקִי עוֹבֶרֶת בְּתוֹכָה וְנוֹפֵל עַל פִּתְחָהּ, כָּל עוֹבֵר וְשָׁב אוֹמֵר: כַּמָּה נָאֶה וּמְשׁוּבָּח פָּלְטִין

comes from a putrid drop of semen, which originates from a place that the eye cannot see; and he is going to the grave, which is likewise a place that the eye cannot see.[5]   וּמַה עָתִיד לִהְיוֹת עָפָר רִמָּה וְתוֹלֵעָה — And what is he destined to be? Dust, worms, and maggots,   שֶׁנֶּאֱמַר "אַף כִּי אֱנוֹשׁ רִמָּה וּבֶן אָדָם תּוֹלֵעָה" — as it says, *How much more so man, [who is] a worm; and a mortal, [who is] a maggot!* (*Job* 25:6).   רַבִּי אֱלִיעֶזֶר בֶּן יַעֲקֹב אוֹמֵר "רִמָּה" בְּחַיָּיו — Why does the verse express the same idea twice? To answer this question, R' Eliezer[6] ben Yaakov said: *Man, [who is] a worm,* refers to the creatures that plague a person **during his lifetime;**   "וּבֶן אָדָם תּוֹלֵעָה" בְּמוֹתוֹ — *and a mortal, [who is] a maggot,* refers to the creatures that consume him **after his death.**   אֵיזֶה "רִמָּה" בְּחַיָּיו זֶה כִּינִים — What are the creatures alluded to by the phrase *Man, [who is] a worm,* that plague a person **during his lifetime?** Those are lice.   "וּבֶן אָדָם תּוֹלֵעָה" בְּמוֹתוֹ זֶה שֶׁמַּרְחִישׁ בְּמוֹתוֹ — And what are the creatures alluded to by the phrase *a mortal, [who is] a maggot,* that consume him in death? Those are the ones **that infest** his body **when he is dead.**[7]

§3 The Baraisa discusses another point that is included in Akavya's words: רַבִּי שִׁמְעוֹן בֶּן אֶלְעָזָר אוֹמֵר: אֶמְשׁוֹל לְךָ מָשָׁל — R' Shimon ben Elazar says: I shall give you an analogy: לְמָה הַדָּבָר דּוֹמֶה — To what is the matter of a human being's composition **comparable?**   לְמֶלֶךְ שֶׁבָּנָה פָּלְטְרִין גְּדוֹלִים — To a king who builds a large palace and settles his many servants **throughout.**[8]   וְיָשַׁב בְּכוּלָם — Amid וּבִיב שֶׁל בּוּרְסְקִי עוֹבֶרֶת בְּתוֹכָה וְנוֹפֵל עַל פִּתְחָהּ — the opulence, a tannery's sewage pipe filled with putrid waste water **passes through it and empties right at [the palace] entrance,** where everyone can see it.   כָּל עוֹבֵר וְשָׁב אוֹמֵר כַּמָּה נָאֶה וּמְשׁוּבָּח פָּלְטִין זוֹ — As a result, every passerby says, "**How** much more beautiful and praiseworthy this palace would be

---

5. See *Avos DeRabbi Nassan, Nusach* 2, Ch. 32.

6. The Vilna print (which our all-Hebrew section follows) has "Elazar" in error.

7. Thinking about the unsavory creatures that cling to a person's body during his lifetime — and even more so after his death

— can greatly help a person to avoid feelings of conceit.

8. *Ben Avraham* (see below, note 11).

Others replace the phrase וְיָשַׁב בְּכוּלָם, *and settled throughout,* with the word וְשִׁכְלְלָם, *and perfected it* (*Meiri* to *Avos* 3:1, *Magen Avos, Binyan Yehoshua*).

זוֹ אִלְמָלֵא בִּיב שֶׁל בּוּרְסְקִי לֹא הָיְתָה עוֹבֶרֶת בְּתוֹכָהּ. אַף כָּךְ אָדָם דּוֹמֶה[9],
וּמָה[10] אִם עַכְשָׁיו שֶׁמּוֹצִיאִין מִמֵּעָיו מַעְיָן סָרוּחַ כָּךְ מִתְגָּאֶה עַל הַבְּרִיּוֹת,
אִם הָיָה מוֹצִיא מַעְיָן שֶׁל שֶׁמֶן טוֹב אֲפַרְסְמוֹן וּפַלְיָיטִין עַל אַחַת כַּמָּה
וְכַמָּה שֶׁיִּתְגָּאֶה עַל הַבְּרִיּוֹת:[11]

ד. כְּשֶׁחָלָה רַבִּי אֱלִיעֶזֶר נִכְנְסוּ תַּלְמִידָיו לְבַקְּרוֹ וְיָשְׁבוּ לְפָנָיו, אָמְרוּ
לוֹ: רַבֵּינוּ, לַמְּדֵנוּ דָבָר אֶחָד מִמַּה שֶׁלִּמַּדְתָּנוּ, אָמַר לָהֶם: (מַה
אֲלַמֵּד אֶתְכֶם,) צְאוּ וְהִזָּהֲרוּ אִישׁ בִּכְבוֹד חֲבֵרוֹ[16], וּבְשָׁעָה שֶׁאַתֶּם

אִלְמָלֵא בִּיב שֶׁל בּוּרְסְקִי לֹא הָיְתָה עוֹבֶרֶת בְּתוֹכָהּ — if a tannery's sewage pipe would
not pass through it!"   אַף כָּךְ אָדָם דּוֹמֶה — A person is like this as well.[9]   וּמָה
אִם עַכְשָׁיו שֶׁמּוֹצִיאִין מִמֵּעָיו מַעְיָן סָרוּחַ — And the reason God made him this way
is as follows:[10] If even now that a foul spring of waste pours forth from his innards,   כָּךְ מִתְגָּאֶה עַל הַבְּרִיּוֹת — he still acts arrogantly toward other people,
אִם הָיָה מוֹצִיא מַעְיָן שֶׁל שֶׁמֶן טוֹב אֲפַרְסְמוֹן וּפַלְיָיטִין — then if he would have been
made to produce an aromatic spring of fragrant oil, balsam, or musk,   עַל
אַחַת כַּמָּה וְכַמָּה שֶׁיִּתְגָּאֶה עַל הַבְּרִיּוֹת — how much more so would he have acted
arrogantly toward other people.[11]

§4 The Baraisa records an incident that highlights the importance of humility:[12]
כְּשֶׁחָלָה רַבִּי אֱלִיעֶזֶר — When R' Eliezer became ill with his final illness,
נִכְנְסוּ תַּלְמִידָיו לְבַקְּרוֹ וְיָשְׁבוּ לְפָנָיו — some of his disciples went in to visit him,
and they sat before him.   אָמְרוּ לוֹ: רַבֵּינוּ, לַמְּדֵנוּ דָבָר אֶחָד מִמַּה שֶׁלִּמַּדְתָּנוּ —
They said to him, "Our master, teach us again the one most important thing
from all that you have taught us."[13]   אָמַר לָהֶם: מַה אֲלַמֵּד אֶתְכֶם — He replied
to them, "What can I teach you? There is so much to say and so little time![14]
צְאוּ וְהִזָּהֲרוּ אִישׁ בִּכְבוֹד חֲבֵרוֹ — Nevertheless, I will teach you one lesson about

---

9. The human body is a marvelous creation,
testifying to its Maker's intelligence and
power. Its splendor, however, is marred by
the "sewage pipe" that passes through it and
regularly emits offensive waste materials
(see *Binyan Yehoshua;* but cf. *Derech Eretz
Rabbah* 3:3).

[In this light, it is possible that the "many
servants" that the King "settled throughout
the palace" represent the numerous organs
and physiological systems that God planted
throughout the human body.]

10. Surely the human being would be more
becoming without his unpleasant excretory
function. Nevertheless, the King built him
this way for his own benefit, as the Baraisa
goes on to explain.

11. Reflecting on this humbling aspect of
man is included in Akavya's advice for a
person to remember "from where he comes"
(see *Meiri* to *Avos* here).

12. *Ben Avraham;* see notes 16 and 17.

13. *Magen Avos.*

14. R' Eliezer was disappointed that his disciples did not come earlier to seek his guidance. He knew that he had a vast treasury of
Torah knowledge to impart, and now it was
too late to convey even a small part of that
knowledge (ibid.; see below, 25 §3).

In truth, his disciples had kept their distance because he was under a ban of excommunication; see *Bava Metzia* 59b and
Sanhedrin 68a.

מִתְפַּלְלִין דְּעוּ לִפְנֵי מִי אַתֶּם עוֹמְדִים לְהִתְפַּלֵּל[17], שֶׁמִּתּוֹךְ דָּבָר זֶה
תִּזְכּוּ לְחַיֵּי הָעוֹלָם הַבָּא[18], אָמַר רַבִּי אֶלְעָזָר בֶּן עֲזַרְיָה: חֲמִשָּׁה דְבָרִים
לָמַדְנוּ מֵרַבִּי אֱלִיעֶזֶר וְשָׂמַחְנוּ בָהֶן יוֹתֵר מִמַּה שֶּׁשָּׂמַחְנוּ בָהֶן °בְּחַיָּיוּ[19],
אֵלּוּ הֵן: [כֶּסֶת] עֲגוּלָה וְהַכַּדּוּר וְהָאִימוּם וְהַקָּמֵיעַ וְהַתְּפִלָּה[20] שֶׁנִּקְרְעָה[21]

---

the vital trait of humility in two different ways:[15] **First, go out and be careful
with the honor of one another.**[16]   וּבְשָׁעָה שֶׁאַתֶּם מִתְפַּלְלִין — **And** second,
when you are praying,   דְּעוּ לִפְנֵי מִי אַתֶּם עוֹמְדִים לְהִתְפַּלֵּל — **know before
Whom you are standing to pray.**[17]   שֶׁמִּתּוֹךְ דָּבָר זֶה תִּזְכּוּ לְחַיֵּי הָעוֹלָם הַבָּא —
For through this matter — this pursuit of humility — **you will earn the eternal
life of the World to Come.**"[18]

A halachic lesson from the same visit to R' Eliezer:

אָמַר רַבִּי אֶלְעָזָר בֶּן עֲזַרְיָה: חֲמִשָּׁה דְבָרִים לָמַדְנוּ מֵרַבִּי אֱלִיעֶזֶר — **R' Elazar ben
Azaryah said: On that occasion, we also learned five things from R' Eliezer,**
וְשָׂמַחְנוּ בָהֶן יוֹתֵר מִמַּה שֶּׁשָּׂמַחְנוּ בָהֶן בְּחַיָּיו — **and we rejoiced in them more than
we had rejoiced in them during his lifetime.**[19]   אֵלּוּ הֵן — **These are the five
things** we enumerated in the query we presented to him: כֶּסֶת עֲגוּלָה וְהַכַּדּוּר
וְהָאִימוּם וְהַקָּמֵיעַ וְהַתְּפִלָּה שֶׁנִּקְרְעָה — **A round pillow, a ball, a shoe-form, an**

---

15. *Ben Avraham.*

16. Do not be arrogant toward one another.
Instead, treat everyone with the same respect you covet for yourself. As R' Eliezer
himself taught in *Avos* (2:10, quoted above
15 §1): "Let your fellow's honor be as dear
to you as your own" (*Ben Avraham*). When
one attempts to treat every person with
respect, he will inevitably develop a more
humble attitude.

17. Genuine, submissive prayer is also an
exercise in humility, for it fosters an awareness of one's inability to control his fate as
well as his utter dependence on God for
everything he aspires to in life (see *Ben
Avraham*).

18. No quality like the trait of humility can
set a person squarely on the path to acquiring a share in the World to Come (see *Sanhedrin* 88b).

19. [Emendation of text follows *Magen Avos*
and *Nuschas HaGra*, and is also the reading
found in some manuscripts; see also *Derech
Eretz Rabbah* 3 §5.]

The disciples had heard R' Eliezer's
opinion about the five items on previous

occasions, but thought that he might have
changed his mind over the years and
changed his opinion to the opposing view,
which was held by most other Sages. The
fact that he was staunch in his position even
moments before his passing made them realize that he was firmly convinced of his own
view, and this gave them great joy (*Binyan
Yehoshua* to *Derech Eretz Rabbah* ibid.).

As to what occasioned this joy and why
it exceeded the joy they felt during his
lifetime, *Ben Avraham* suggests that the
disciples had always preferred R' Eliezer's
view on these questions. During his lifetime,
however, they could not accept his view as
halachah because he was under a ban of
excommunication (see note 14). But now
that he was about to die, the disciples were
confident that the ban would be lifted by
Heaven and they could thereupon rule in accordance with his views — provided that R'
Eliezer himself maintained those views until
the end. When they learned that he did, they
had good cause to rejoice (see also *Ahavas
Chesed,* who likewise contends that these
rulings were accepted as halachah after R'
Eliezer's death).

שֶׁאָמַרְתָּ לָנוּ, מָה הֵן, אָמַר לָהֶם: טְמֵאִים הֵם וְהִזָּהֲרוּ בָּהֶן, וְהַטְבִּילוּ אוֹתָן
כְּמָה שֶׁהֵן, שֶׁהֲלָכוֹת קְבוּעוֹת שֶׁנֶּאֶמְרוּ לוֹ לְמשֶׁה בְּסִינַי:[25]

---

amulet, and a *tefillah*[20] that became torn,[21]   שֶׁאָמַרְתָּ לָנוּ מָה הֵן — regarding which you have already told us your opinion in the past — what is your final decision regarding them? Were they susceptible to *tumah* when they were whole?[22] And when they are torn, if they did become *tamei,* can they be purified through immersion in a *mikveh* without being emptied of their contents?"[23]
אָמַר לָהֶם טְמֵאִים הֵם — He answered them, "They are susceptible to *tumah* when whole,   וְהִזָּהֲרוּ בָּהֶן — and be careful about these laws pertaining to them,   וְהַטְבִּילוּ אוֹתָן כְּמָה שֶׁהֵן — and if they contract *tumah,* immerse them in a *mikveh* as they are, i.e., without emptying them, even if they are torn.[24]
שֶׁהֲלָכוֹת קְבוּעוֹת שֶׁנֶּאֶמְרוּ לוֹ לְמשֶׁה בְּסִינַי — For these are established laws that were transmitted to Moses at Sinai."[25]

---

20. *Tefillah* in this context is the singular form of *tefillin.*

21. All of these items consist of a sealed leather casing with some inner component: a round pillow with stuffing, a ball with stuffing, a stuffed foot-shaped form for making shoes ("shoe-form"), a stuffed leather pendant ("amulet"), and a casing for *tefillin* containing the sacred parchments. Two questions arise regarding these items, one for when they are whole and one for when they are torn. Both of these questions had been subject to dispute between R' Eliezer and the other Sages.

[Note: This passage is examined in more detail below, in 25 §3. This note and the ones that follow are abridged from the more extensive commentary we have provided there.]

22. This question centers on the legal premise that a leather article can contract *tumah* only if it has a hollow that can serve as a receptacle. The items specified do have a hollow with something inside, but they are permanently sealed. Does that qualify them as leather receptacles?

23. All agree that when these items are torn and their hollows become exposed, they are susceptible to *tumah.* But then another question arises. How can such articles be purified in a *mikveh?* Do they have to be emptied of their contents to avoid the problem of *chatzitzah* — a barrier between the immersed

item and the *mikveh* water — or can they be immersed as is, based on the assessment that the pouch and its contents make up one integral unit, and are not separate articles that interpose between the water and each other? [When they are whole, however, they are definitely considered one unit, and hence may be immersed as they are (assuming that they are susceptible to *tumah*).]

In the past, R' Eliezer had ruled stringently on the first question (the five items are susceptible to *tumah,* even when whole), and leniently on the second question (they can be immersed as is, without being emptied, even when torn). The disciples were now asking whether he still maintained the same view on each question.

24. Thus, R' Eliezer had remained steadfast in his view on both points.

25. Wanting his students to understand why he was so uncompromising about his opinions on these matters, R' Eliezer explained that he believed them to be laws transmitted to Moses on Mount Sinai directly from God. Clearly then, he had a duty to stand firm and preserve the truth as he saw it (*Magen Avos*).

[*Gra* moves the words וְהִזָּהֲרוּ בָּהֶן, *and be careful about them,* to just before the words שֶׁהֲלָכוֹת קְבוּעוֹת שֶׁנֶּאֶמְרוּ לוֹ לְמשֶׁה בְּסִינַי, *For they are established laws that were transmitted to Moses at Sinai,* and this is also the reading found below in 25 §3.]

﷼ פֶּרֶק ב ﷼

א. רַבִּי חֲנַנְיָה סְגַן הַכֹּהֲנִים אוֹמֵר^[1]: כָּל הַנּוֹתֵן דִּבְרֵי תוֹרָה עַל לִבּוֹ^[2] מְבַטְּלִין מִמֶּנּוּ הִרְהוּרֵי חֶרֶב^[3] הִרְהוּרֵי רָעָב הִרְהוּרֵי שְׁטוּת הִרְהוּרֵי זְנוּת^[4] הִרְהוּרֵי יֵצֶר הָרַע הִרְהוּרֵי אֵשֶׁת אִישׁ^[5] הִרְהוּרֵי דְבָרִים בְּטֵלִים^[6] הִרְהוּרֵי עוֹל בָּשָׂר וָדָם^[7] שֶׁכֵּן כָּתוּב בְּסֵפֶר תִּלִּים עַל יְדֵי דָוִד מֶלֶךְ יִשְׂרָאֵל^[8],

﷼ CHAPTER 20 ﷼

§1 The Baraisa details the peace of mind that results from devotion to Torah study:

כָּל — **R' Chananyah S'gan HaKohanim says:**^[1] רַבִּי חֲנַנְיָה סְגַן הַכֹּהֲנִים אוֹמֵר הַנּוֹתֵן דִּבְרֵי תוֹרָה עַל לִבּוֹ — **Whoever places the words of Torah on his heart**^[2] מְבַטְּלִין מִמֶּנּוּ הִרְהוּרֵי חֶרֶב הִרְהוּרֵי רָעָב — **is assisted from Heaven in being freed from many negative thoughts — thoughts of the enemy's sword,**^[3] **thoughts of famine,** הִרְהוּרֵי שְׁטוּת הִרְהוּרֵי זְנוּת — **thoughts of foolishness, thoughts of immorality;**^[4] הִרְהוּרֵי יֵצֶר הָרַע הִרְהוּרֵי אֵשֶׁת אִישׁ — **thoughts of the evil inclination, thoughts of a married woman;**^[5] הִרְהוּרֵי דְבָרִים בְּטֵלִים — **thoughts of inconsequential matters,**^[6] **thoughts of the yoke of flesh and blood.**^[7] עוֹל בָּשָׂר וָדָם שֶׁכֵּן כָּתוּב בְּסֵפֶר תִּלִּים עַל יְדֵי דָוִד מֶלֶךְ יִשְׂרָאֵל — **For so it**

---

1. [*Nuschas HaGra* has: R' "Chanina" S'gan HaKohanim.] Literally, *Deputy of the Kohanim*. The *s'gan* was deputy to the Kohen Gadol, and held the second highest rank in the Temple hierarchy.

2. That is, he studies in order to fulfill what he learns (*Ahavas Chesed*). Alternatively, he studies Torah with all his heart, for its own sake, and for no ulterior motive (*Ben Avraham*). *Magen Avos* explains our Baraisa to mean that he *takes to heart* the words of the Torah: when he confronts suffering in his life, he seeks to discover what sin he might have committed to have warranted such suffering. *Maharsha* (on *Avodah Zarah* 17b) explains that he always fills his mind with Torah thoughts.

3. The danger of foreign attack.

4. This is akin to what a Baraisa teaches in *Kiddushin* 30b: "The Holy One, Blessed is He, said to Israel, 'My son! I have created the evil inclination and I have created Torah as its antidote' " (*Binyan Yehoshua*).

5. This would seem to be included already in the *thoughts of immorality* mentioned earlier (see *Kisei Rachamim* and *Ben Avraham*). Other texts, however, read here הִרְהוּרֵי "אִשָּׁה רָעָה", *thoughts of a bad wife*. [Living with a bad spouse can seem more bitter than death, because one is forced to live with constant strife (*Responsa, Tashbetz* II §8).]

6. The reference here is not to things of no value whatsoever, which are included in the *thoughts of foolishness* already mentioned. Rather, this refers to things pertaining to one's worldly affairs, which are inconsequential *in comparison to* words of Torah (*Ben Avraham*). One who studies Torah properly will not be burdened by thoughts about such matters.

7. As the Mishnah in *Avos* 3:5 (cited in *Ben Avraham*) teaches: R' Nechunia ben Hakanah says: Anyone who accepts upon himself the yoke of Torah, [then] the yoke of government and the yoke of worldly responsibilities are removed from him.

שֶׁנֶּאֱמַר (תהלים יט, ט) "פִּקּוּדֵי ה' יְשָׁרִים מְשַׂמְּחֵי לֵב מִצְוַת ה' בָּרָה מְאִירַת
עֵינָיִם"9. וְכֹל שֶׁאֵינוֹ נוֹתֵן דִּבְרֵי תוֹרָה עַל לִבּוֹ נוֹתְנִין לוֹ הִרְהוּרֵי חֶרֶב
הִרְהוּרֵי רָעָב הִרְהוּרֵי שְׁטוּת הִרְהוּרֵי זְנוּת הִרְהוּרֵי יֵצֶר הָרָע הִרְהוּרֵי אֵשֶׁת
אִישׁ10 הִרְהוּרֵי דְּבָרִים בְּטֵלִים הִרְהוּרֵי עוֹל בָּשָׂר וָדָם, שֶׁכָּךְ כָּתוּב בְּמִשְׁנֵה
תוֹרָה עַל יְדֵי מֹשֶׁה רַבֵּינוּ (דברים כח, מו-מח) "וְהָיוּ בְךָ לְאוֹת וּלְמוֹפֵת וּבְזַרְעֲךָ
עַד עוֹלָם תַּחַת אֲשֶׁר לֹא עָבַדְתָּ אֶת ה' אֱלֹהֶיךָ בְּשִׂמְחָה וּבְטוֹב לֵבָב מֵרֹב כֹּל

שֶׁנֶּאֱמַר "פִּקּוּדֵי" is written in the Book of *Psalms* by David, King of Israel,[8]
"ה' יְשָׁרִים מְשַׂמְּחֵי לֵב מִצְוַת ה' בָּרָה מְאִירַת עֵינָיִם" — as it is stated, *The laws of
HASHEM are upright, gladdening the heart; the commandment of HASHEM
is clear, enlightening the eyes* (Psalms 19:9).[9] וְכֹל שֶׁאֵינוֹ נוֹתֵן דִּבְרֵי תוֹרָה עַל
לִבּוֹ — But whoever does not place the words of Torah on his heart נוֹתְנִין לוֹ
הִרְהוּרֵי חֶרֶב הִרְהוּרֵי רָעָב — is burdened with thoughts of the enemy's sword,
thoughts of famine, הִרְהוּרֵי שְׁטוּת הִרְהוּרֵי זְנוּת — thoughts of foolishness,
thoughts of immorality; הִרְהוּרֵי יֵצֶר הָרָע הִרְהוּרֵי אֵשֶׁת אִישׁ — thoughts of
the evil inclination and thoughts of a married woman;[10] הִרְהוּרֵי דְּבָרִים
בְּטֵלִים הִרְהוּרֵי עוֹל בָּשָׂר וָדָם — thoughts of inconsequential matters, thoughts
of the yoke of flesh and blood. שֶׁכָּךְ כָּתוּב בְּמִשְׁנֵה תוֹרָה עַל יְדֵי מֹשֶׁה רַבֵּינוּ —
For so it is written in *Deuteronomy* through Moses, our Teacher, regarding
the curses mentioned in the earlier verses of the *Tochachah*: "וְהָיוּ בְךָ לְאוֹת
וּלְמוֹפֵת וּבְזַרְעֲךָ עַד עוֹלָם — *They will be a sign and a wonder, in you and
your offspring, forever,* תַּחַת אֲשֶׁר לֹא עָבַדְתָּ אֶת ה' אֱלֹהֶיךָ בְּשִׂמְחָה וּבְטוֹב לֵבָב
מֵרֹב כֹּל — *because you did not serve HASHEM, your God, amidst gladness*

---

8. In countless other places, *Chazal* cite
proof from *Psalms* without emphasizing that
it was authored by David, King of Israel.
But they emphasize this here because King
David's own life exemplified the teaching of
our Baraisa. King David had every reason
to worry about sword and famine, and to
be plagued by the other negative thoughts
enumerated here, and yet he was able to
overcome them through his devotion to
Torah (see *Magen Avos*).

9. The "gladness of the heart" that comes
from Torah study banishes the worrisome
or sinful thoughts enumerated above (*Kisei
Rachamim*). The "enlightened eyes" that
come from Torah study see clearly the
straight paths that lead to goodness, and the
crookedness of those that lead to sin (*Binyan Yehoshua*).

Ben Avraham (s.v. מבטלין) divides the "ten

negative thoughts" into two groups: One
group is *worry* over possible misfortune
(such as sword, famine, and the yoke of flesh
and blood) and the other group is *thoughts*
that lead to sin (such as foolishness, immorality, and the evil inclination). However, even
with regard to the first group, proper Torah
study not only banishes *worry*, but actually
protects the person from those difficulties, as
the verse states: כִּי חַיִּים הֵם לְמֹצְאֵיהֶם וּלְכָל בְּשָׂרוֹ
מַרְפֵּא, *For they are life to he who finds them,
and healing for all his flesh* (Proverbs 4:22).

Binyan Yehoshua and other commentators cite various other sources in *Chazal*
which teach that Torah study protects a person from the various difficulties enumerated
in our Baraisa.

10. Here, too, other texts have instead:
הִרְהוּרֵי "אִשָּׁה רָעָה", *thoughts of a bad wife;*
see above, note 5.

וְעָבַדְתָּ אֶת אֹיְבֶיךָ אֲשֶׁר יְשַׁלְּחֶנּוּ ה׳ בָּךְ בְּרָעָב וּבְצָמָא וּבְעֵירֹם וּבְחֹסֶר כֹּל״.¹¹
״בְּרָעָב״, כֵּיצַד, (בִּזְמַן שֶׁאָדָם תּוֹאֵב) לֶאֱכוֹל פַּת שְׂעוֹרִים וְאֵינוֹ מוֹצֵא אוֹיְבָיו
מְבַקְשִׁין מִמֶּנּוּ פַּת נְקִיָּה וּבְשַׂר שָׁמֵן. ״וּבְצָמָא״, כֵּיצַד, בִּזְמַן שֶׁאָדָם מִתְאַוֶּה
לִשְׁתּוֹת טִפָּה שֶׁל חֹמֶץ טִפָּה שֶׁל שֵׁכָר וְאֵינוֹ מוֹצֵא וְאוֹיְבָיו מְבַקְשִׁין מִמֶּנּוּ
יַיִן מְשׁוּבָּח שֶׁבְּכָל הַמְּדִינוֹת. ״וּבְעֵירֹם״, כֵּיצַד, בִּזְמַן שֶׁאָדָם יָבֹא לִלְבּוֹשׁ
חָלוּק שֶׁל צֶמֶר אוֹ שֶׁל פִּשְׁתָּן וְאֵינוֹ מוֹצֵא וְאוֹיְבָיו מְבַקְשִׁין מִמֶּנּוּ הַשִּׁירָאִין
וְהַכָּלָךְ שֶׁבְּכָל הַמְּדִינוֹת.¹³ ״וּבְחֹסֶר כֹּל״ בְּלֹא נֵר וּבְלֹא סַכִּין וּבְלֹא שֻׁלְחָן״.¹⁴

וְעָבַדְתָּ אֶת אֹיְבֶיךָ   *and goodness of heart, when everything was abundant.*
So you will serve your — אֲשֶׁר יְשַׁלְּחֶנּוּ ה׳ בָּךְ בְּרָעָב וּבְצָמָא וּבְעֵירֹם וּבְחֹסֶר כֹּל״
enemies whom HASHEM will send against you, in hunger and in thirst, in
nakedness and without anything (Deuteronomy 28:46-48).[11]

    The Baraisa expounds the last few words of the verse just cited:
בִּזְמַן שֶׁאָדָם תּוֹאֵב לֶאֱכוֹל פַּת שְׂעוֹרִים   *In hunger — how so?*   ״בְּרָעָב״, כֵּיצַד
וְאֵינוֹ מוֹצֵא — *At a time when a person craves to eat* coarse *barley bread*
and cannot find any,   אוֹיְבָיו מְבַקְשִׁין מִמֶּנּוּ פַּת נְקִיָּה וּבְשַׂר שָׁמֵן — *his enemies*
among the nations of the world will ask him to provide them with refined
bread and fatty meat.   ״וּבְצָמָא״, כֵּיצַד — *And in thirst — how so?*   בִּזְמַן
שֶׁאָדָם מִתְאַוֶּה לִשְׁתּוֹת טִפָּה שֶׁל חֹמֶץ טִפָּה שֶׁל שֵׁכָר וְאֵינוֹ מוֹצֵא וְאוֹיְבָיו מְבַקְשִׁין
מִמֶּנּוּ יַיִן מְשׁוּבָּח שֶׁבְּכָל הַמְּדִינוֹת — *At a time when a person craves to drink*
even a drop of vinegar or a drop of beer and cannot find any, his enemies
among the nations of the world will ask him to provide them with the fin-
est wine to be found in any country.   ״וּבְעֵירֹם״, כֵּיצַד — *And in naked-*
ness — how so?   בִּזְמַן שֶׁאָדָם יָבֹא לִלְבּוֹשׁ חָלוּק שֶׁל צֶמֶר אוֹ שֶׁל פִּשְׁתָּן וְאֵינוֹ
מוֹצֵא אוֹיְבָיו מְבַקְשִׁין מִמֶּנּוּ הַשִּׁירָאִין וְהַכָּלָךְ שֶׁבְּכָל הַמְּדִינוֹת — *At a time when*
a person comes to put on a shirt of even wool or linen and cannot find
any, his enemies among the nations of the world will ask him to provide
them with the finest silks and kalach fabrics[12] *to be found in any country.*[13]
״וּבְחֹסֶר כֹּל״ — *"And without anything" — how so?*   בְּלֹא נֵר וּבְלֹא סַכִּין וּבְלֹא
שֻׁלְחָן — *It means: without a candle, without a knife, and without a table.*[14]

---

11. All the negative thoughts enumerated by our Baraisa are alluded to in this section of the Torah that deals with curses (see *Magen Avos* at length).

12. See *Shabbos* 20b with *Rashi* and *Tosafos* regarding the definition of *kalach,* and whether it is an inferior or superior grade of silk. Some texts omit the word וְהַכָּלָךְ from the Baraisa here (*Tumas Yesharim*).

13. In short, while we ourselves will crave the basic necessities of food, drink, and

clothing, we will have to serve our enemies and provide them with these luxurious things. Thus, the Baraisa expounds the verse to mean not only that you will serve your enemies *while* you are hungry, thirsty, and naked, but that you will serve them in these very areas in which you are deficient, and you will have to supply them lavishly while you lack even basic necessities.

14. Basic items a person needs (*Magen Avos*).

דָּבָר אַחֵר, "בְּחֹסֶר כֹּל" בְּלֹא חוֹמֶץ וּבְלֹא מֶלַח, זוֹ הִיא קְלָלָה שֶׁמְּקַלְלִין
בְּנֵי אָדָם: אַל יְהֵא לְךָ חוֹמֶץ וּמֶלַח בְּתוֹךְ בֵּיתֶךָ. הוּא הָיָה אוֹמֵר: (שיר
השירים א, ו) "אַל תִּרְאוּנִי שֶׁאֲנִי שְׁחַרְחֹרֶת שֶׁשְּׁזָפַתְנִי הַשָּׁמֶשׁ" אֵלּוּ °כָּל
°בָּנוֹת¹⁶ שֶׁבִּיהוּדָה שֶׁפָּרְקוּ עוּלוֹ שֶׁל הַקָּדוֹשׁ בָּרוּךְ הוּא מֵעֲלֵיהֶם וְהִמְלִיכוּ
עֲלֵיהֶם מֶלֶךְ בָּשָׂר וָדָם¹⁷. דָּבָר אַחֵר, "בְּנֵי אִמִּי נִחֲרוּ בִי", זֶה מֹשֶׁה
שֶׁהָרַג אֶת הַמִּצְרִי, שֶׁנֶּאֱמַר (שמות ב, יא-יב) "וַיְהִי בַּיָּמִים הָהֵם וַיִּגְדַּל מֹשֶׁה
וַיֵּצֵא אֶל אֶחָיו וַיַּרְא בְּסִבְלֹתָם [וְגו'] וַיִּפֶן כֹּה וָכֹה וַיַּרְא כִּי אֵין אִישׁ"¹⁸,

---

דָּבָר אַחֵר "בְּחֹסֶר כֹּל" בְּלֹא חוֹמֶץ וּבְלֹא מֶלַח — Another explanation: *and without anything* means: without vinegar and without salt to flavor our food.[15] זו
הִיא קְלָלָה שֶׁמְּקַלְלִין בְּנֵי אָדָם — And this is indeed a curse that people commonly use: אַל יְהֵא לְךָ חוֹמֶץ וּמֶלַח בְּתוֹךְ בֵּיתֶךָ — "May you have no vinegar or salt within your house!"

The Baraisa cites another teaching from R' Chananyah S'gan HaKohanim: הוּא הָיָה אוֹמֵר — He used to say on the verse, "אַל תִּרְאוּנִי שֶׁאֲנִי שְׁחַרְחֹרֶת שֶׁשְּׁזָפַתְנִי הַשָּׁמֶשׁ"— *Do not look upon me that I am swarthy, because the sun has cast its glance upon me. My mother's sons set anger against me* [בְּנֵי אִמִּי נִחֲרוּ בִי] *and made me keeper of the vineyards; my own vineyard I did not guard* (*Song of Songs* 1:6): Who are *my mother's sons?* אֵלּוּ בּוּלְאוֹת שֶׁבִּיהוּדָה שֶׁפָּרְקוּ עוּלוֹ שֶׁל הַקָּדוֹשׁ בָּרוּךְ הוּא מֵעֲלֵיהֶם וְהִמְלִיכוּ עֲלֵיהֶם מֶלֶךְ בָּשָׂר וָדָם — These are the wealthy ones[16] of Judea who cast off the yoke of the Holy One, Blessed is He, and made sovereign over themselves instead a king of flesh-and-blood.[17] Thus, the verse means: Do not look upon me that I am swarthy with sin; it is those wealthy brethren of mine who made God angry with me by having me serve flesh and blood (*keeper of the vineyards*) instead of Him (*my own vineyard*).

The Baraisa cites a second explanation of this phrase: "בְּנֵי אִמִּי נִחֲרוּ בִי" זֶה מֹשֶׁה שֶׁהָרַג אֶת דָּבָר אַחֵר — Another interpretation: *My mother's sons set anger against me* is a reference to Moses, הַמִּצְרִי who killed the Egyptian who was beating the Israelite man, שֶׁנֶּאֱמַר "וַיְהִי בַּיָּמִים הָהֵם וַיִּגְדַּל מֹשֶׁה וַיֵּצֵא אֶל אֶחָיו וַיַּרְא בְּסִבְלֹתָם וְגו' וַיִּפֶן כֹּה וָכֹה וַיַּרְא כִּי אֵין אִישׁ" — as it is stated, *It happened in those days that Moses grew up and went out to his brethren and observed their burdens, etc.,* and he saw an Egyptian man striking a Hebrew man, of his brethren. *He turned this way and*

---

15. *Magen Avos.*

16. Emendation follows alternative reading cited by *Tummas Yesharim, Binyan Yehoshua,* and *Nuschas HaGra.*

17. [These wealthy Jews willingly accepted the yoke of a foreign ruler because it

benefited them at the time, and they lived a foreign lifestyle.]

The Baraisa's exposition is essentially on the second part of the verse (*My mother's sons set anger against me ...*), which is not cited here explicitly (*Magen Avos,* second explanation). *Mefaresh* suggests that the

מָה תַּלְמוּד לוֹמַר ״כִּי אֵין אִישׁ״, מְלַמֵּד שֶׁהוֹשִׁיב לוֹ מֹשֶׁה
סַנְהֶדְרָאוֹת שֶׁל מַלְאֲכֵי הַשָּׁרֵת וְאָמַר לָהֶם: אֶהֱרוֹג אֶת זֶה, אָמְרוּ
לוֹ: הֲרוֹג[20], וְכִי בַּחֶרֶב הֲרָגוֹ וַהֲלֹא בְּמַאֲמָר הֲרָגוֹ[21], שֶׁנֶּאֱמַר (שם פסוק
יד) ״הַלְהָרְגֵנִי אַתָּה אֹמֵר כַּאֲשֶׁר הָרַגְתָּ אֶת הַמִּצְרִי״[23], מְלַמֵּד שֶׁהֲרָגוֹ
בַּשֵּׁם. (דָּבָר אַחֵר,) ״בְּנֵי אִמִּי נִחֲרוּ בִי״ זֶה מֹשֶׁה שֶׁבָּרַח לְמִדְיָן,

---

that and he saw that there was no man, so he struck down the Egyptian and hid him in the sand (Exodus 2:11-12).[18]

The Baraisa expounds the verse just cited:

מָה תַּלְמוּד לוֹמַר ״כִּי אֵין אִישׁ״ — What does the Torah mean to teach when it says: He saw that there was no man? מְלַמֵּד שֶׁהוֹשִׁיב לוֹ מֹשֶׁה סַנְהֶדְרָאוֹת שֶׁל מַלְאֲכֵי הַשָּׁרֵת וְאָמַר לָהֶם אֶהֱרוֹג אֶת זֶה — This teaches that Moses convened a Sanhedrin of ministering angels, who are sometimes called "men,"[19] and said to them, "Should I kill this one who was striking the Hebrew man?" אָמְרוּ לוֹ הֲרוֹג — They told him, "Kill him!"[20] and Moses did so. וְכִי בַּחֶרֶב הֲרָגוֹ וַהֲלֹא בְּמַאֲמָר הֲרָגוֹ — For did [Moses] kill him with a sword? Why, he killed him with an utterance,[21] שֶׁנֶּאֱמַר ״הַלְהָרְגֵנִי אַתָּה אֹמֵר כַּאֲשֶׁר הָרַגְתָּ אֶת הַמִּצְרִי״ — as it is stated, "Is it to kill me that 'you are saying,' as you killed the Egyptian?" (ibid. v. 14),[22] מְלַמֵּד שֶׁהֲרָגוֹ בַּשֵּׁם — which teaches us that he killed [the Egyptian] by uttering the Name of God.

A third interpretation of this phrase:

דָּבָר אַחֵר — Another interpretation: ״בְּנֵי אִמִּי נִחֲרוּ בִי״ זֶה מֹשֶׁה שֶׁבָּרַח לְמִדְיָן — My mother's sons set anger against me — this phrase is the statement of Moses, who was forced to flee to Midian because his fellow Israelites informed

---

text here be emended to include the second part of the verse. (Cf. *Magen Avos*, first explanation, and *Ahavas Chesed*.)

18. In this interpretation, the Baraisa takes the words בְּנֵי אִמִּי נִחֲרוּ בִי to mean that the Jewish people said "my mother's sons (i.e., Moses) were angry on my behalf" and struck down the Egyptian who was tormenting me (*Mefaresh*; cf. *Magen Avos*). [And the balance of the verse can be explained to mean: for the Egyptians had enslaved me and made me tend their "vineyards" instead of my own.]

19. See, for example, *Daniel* 9:21 and *Genesis* 37:17 (see *Magen Avos*; cf. *Ahavas Chesed*). That Moses was consulting angels is indicated by the words, ״וַיִּפֶן כֹּה וָכֹה״, for another verse (*I Kings* 22:20) states regarding angels who were consulted, וַיֹּאמֶר זֶה ״בְּכֹה״ וְזֶה אֹמֵר ״בְּכֹה״ (*Binyan Yehoshua, Mefaresh*).

20. This is indicated by the words, *and saw that there was no man*, meaning that not one angel argued in defense of the Egyptian aggressor (*Magen Avos, Mefaresh*).

21. The Baraisa is now demonstrating that *He turned this way and that and he saw that there was no man* cannot mean literally that Moses looked both ways to make sure no one would see him kill the Egyptian. For that would make sense only if he killed him with his own hands. But if he killed him with a mere utterance, what would onlookers see? Therefore, it must be that *he saw that there was no man* refers to the court of angels that he convened (*Magen Avos, Mefaresh*).

22. After Moses killed the Egyptian, Moses saw two Israelites fighting and rebuked the aggressor who was striking his fellow. The aggressor said this in retort to Moses.

שֶׁנֶּאֱמַר (שם פסוקים טו-יז) "וַיִּשְׁמַע פַּרְעֹה אֶת הַדָּבָר הַזֶּה וַיְבַקֵּשׁ לַהֲרֹג
אֶת מֹשֶׁה וַיִּבְרַח מֹשֶׁה מִפְּנֵי פַרְעֹה וַיֵּשֶׁב בְּאֶרֶץ מִדְיָן וַיֵּשֶׁב עַל
הַבְּאֵר ... וַיָּבֹאוּ הָרֹעִים וַיְגָרְשׁוּם וַיָּקָם מֹשֶׁה וַיּוֹשִׁעָן וַיַּשְׁקְ אֶת צֹאנָם".
בָּא מֹשֶׁה וְיָשַׁב עֲלֵיהֶם בַּדִּין, אָמַר לָהֶם: מִנְהָגוֹ שֶׁל עוֹלָם אֲנָשִׁים
מְמַלְּאִין וְנָשִׁים מַשְׁקוֹת,[24] כָּאן נָשִׁים דּוֹלוֹת וַאֲנָשִׁים מַשְׁקִין,[25] עִוּוּת
הַדִּין יֵשׁ כָּאן, (°חַיָּיבִין בַּדִּין °חַיָּיבִין לְשָׁעָה,[26]) וְיֵשׁ אוֹמְרִים: כָּל זְמַן
שֶׁהָיָה מֹשֶׁה עוֹמֵד עַל שְׂפַת הַבְּאֵר הָיוּ הַמַּיִם צָפִין וְעוֹלִין לִקְרַאתוֹ

---

on him,[23]   שֶׁנֶּאֱמַר "וַיִּשְׁמַע פַּרְעֹה אֶת הַדָּבָר הַזֶּה וַיְבַקֵּשׁ לַהֲרֹג אֶת מֹשֶׁה וַיִּבְרַח
מֹשֶׁה מִפְּנֵי פַרְעֹה וַיֵּשֶׁב בְּאֶרֶץ מִדְיָן — as it is stated, *Pharaoh heard about this
matter and sought to kill Moses; so Moses fled from before Pharaoh and
settled in the land of Midian;*   וַיֵּשֶׁב עַל הַבְּאֵר ... וַיָּבֹאוּ הָרֹעִים וַיְגָרְשׁוּם וַיָּקָם
מֹשֶׁה וַיּוֹשִׁעָן וַיַּשְׁקְ אֶת צֹאנָם" — *He sat by a well.* The minister of Midian had
seven daughters; they came and drew water and filled the troughs to water their
father's sheep. *The shepherds came and drove them away. Moses got up and
saved them and watered their sheep* (ibid. vv. 15-17).

The Baraisa expounds these verses:

בָּא מֹשֶׁה וְיָשַׁב עֲלֵיהֶם בַּדִּין — What does he *"sat" by a well* mean? It means
that **Moses came and sat in judgment on [the shepherds].**   אָמַר לָהֶם:
מִנְהָגוֹ שֶׁל עוֹלָם אֲנָשִׁים מְמַלְּאִין וְנָשִׁים מַשְׁקוֹת — **"The normal way** when there
are male and female shepherds together **is that the men draw** the water **and
the women water** the flocks;[24]   כָּאן נָשִׁים דּוֹלוֹת וַאֲנָשִׁים מַשְׁקִין — **but here,
the women draw** the water **and the men water the flocks!**[25]   עִוּוּת הַדִּין יֵשׁ
כָּאן — **There is a perversion of justice here!"**   חִיָּיבָן בַּדִּין חִיָּיבָן לְשָׁעָה
— Whereupon **he ruled them guilty in law and ruled them guilty for the moment,
and watered the women's flocks.**[26]   וְיֵשׁ אוֹמְרִים: כָּל זְמַן שֶׁהָיָה מֹשֶׁה עוֹמֵד
עַל שְׂפַת הַבְּאֵר הָיוּ הַמַּיִם צָפִין וְעוֹלִין לִקְרַאתוֹ — **And some say that as long**

---

23. I.e., Dathan and Abiram, who informed Pharaoh that Moses had killed the Egyptian (see *Shemos Rabbah* 1 §29). It was regarding them that Moses said, *My mother's sons set anger against me* (*Magen Avos, Mefaresh*). [See note 28 below for how this interpretation expounds the balance of the verse.]

24. It is less appropriate that the women should have the task of drawing the water, which is laborious and for which they must roll up their sleeves and bend down immodestly before the men (*Magen Avos*).

25. It would make sense for the men to do the laborious and demeaning job of drawing

the water and filling the troughs for everyone, and for the women to guide all the flocks to the water. That would be a reasonable division of labor. Yet, here, the women drew the water and filled the troughs and the men came along and stole that water for their own flocks. That is fundamentally unfair! (see *Magen Avos*).

26. "He ruled them guilty in law" and established that from this day forward, the men should draw the water. And "he ruled them guilty for the moment," for what they had just done was wrong, an injustice that he personally set right by watering the women's flocks himself (*Magen Avos*).

וְכֵיוָן שֶׁחָזַר חָזְרוּ הַמַּיִם לַאֲחוֹרֵיהֶם[27], בְּאוֹתָהּ שָׁﬠָה אָמַר: אוֹי לִי
שֶׁהִנַּחְתִּי אֶת ﬠַמִּי וּבָאתִי לָדוּר ﬠִם כּוּתִים[28]. דָּבָר אַחֵר, "בְּנֵי אִמִּי
נִחֲרוּ בִי" אֵלּוּ יִשְׂרָאֵל שֶׁﬠָשׂוּ אֶת הָﬠֵגֶל, שֶׁבַּתְּחִילָה אָמְרוּ (שם כד,
ז) "כֹּל אֲשֶׁר דִּבֶּר ה' נַﬠֲשֶׂה וְנִשְׁמָﬠ" חָזְרוּ וְאָמְרוּ: (שם לב, ד) "אֵלֶּה
אֱלֹהֶיךָ יִשְׂרָאֵל". דָּבָר אַחֵר, "בְּנֵי אִמִּי נִחֲרוּ בִי" אֵלּוּ מְרַגְּלִים
שֶׁהוֹצִיאוּ דִבַּת הָאָרֶץ[30] וְגָרְמוּ לָהֶם לְיִשְׂרָאֵל שֶׁיִּפְּלוּ פִגְרֵיהֶם בַּמִּדְבָּר,

as Moses was standing at the edge of the well in Midian, the waters would
rise to meet him; וְכֵיוָן שֶׁחָזַר חָזְרוּ הַמַּיִם לַאֲחוֹרֵיהֶם — but once he stepped
back from the well, the waters would recede.[27] בְּאוֹתָהּ שָׁﬠָה אָמַר אוֹי לִי
שֶׁהִנַּחְתִּי אֶת ﬠַמִּי וּבָאתִי לָדוּר ﬠִם כּוּתִים — At that moment, he said, "Woe is
me that I abandoned my own nation and came to live among the nations of
the world!"[28]

A fourth interpretation: דָּבָר אַחֵר, "בְּנֵי אִמִּי נִחֲרוּ בִי" אֵלּוּ יִשְׂרָאֵל שֶׁﬠָשׂוּ אֶת הָﬠֵגֶל — Another interpretation: *My mother's sons set anger against me* refers to the people of Israel,
who made the Golden Calf. שֶׁבַּתְּחִילָה אָמְרוּ "כֹּל אֲשֶׁר דִּבֶּר ה' נַﬠֲשֶׂה וְנִשְׁמָﬠ"
— For at first they said, *"Everything that HASHEM has said, we will do
and we will obey!"* (*Exodus* 24:7), חָזְרוּ וְאָמְרוּ "אֵלֶּה אֱלֹהֶיךָ יִשְׂרָאֵל" — but
then they said, *"This is your god, O Israel,* which brought you up from the
land of Egypt" (ibid. 32:4). Thus, the words בְּנֵי אִמִּי נִחֲרוּ בִי are interpreted
to be the words of God, Who said: *"Bnei imi" angered Me* and abandoned
My covenant.[29]

A fifth interpretation: "בְּנֵי אִמִּי נִחֲרוּ בִי" אֵלּוּ מְרַגְּלִים שֶׁהוֹצִיאוּ
דָּבָר אַחֵר — Another interpretation: דִבַּת הָאָרֶץ וְגָרְמוּ לָהֶם לְיִשְׂרָאֵל שֶׁיִּפְּלוּ פִגְרֵיהֶם בַּמִּדְבָּר — *My mother's sons set
anger against me* refers to the Spies sent by Moses to scout Eretz Yisrael, **who
brought forth an evil report on the Land**[30] and caused the people of Israel to

---

27. Accordingly, it does not mean that
Moses actually drew water and watered their
flocks, but rather that his presence caused
the waters to rise (*Magen Avos*).

28. Moses had just acted as a judge in Midian, and regretted that he was not among
his own brethren in Egypt to fulfill that role,
especially since he saw from the waters that
rose to meet him that God was still with him.
Thus, the verse in *Song of Songs* concludes,
*They made me keeper of the vineyards; my
own vineyard I did not guard* (*Magen Avos*;

see *Shir HaShirim Rabbah* 1 §42).

29. *Magen Avos*, first explanation. The
Baraisa relates the word אִמִּי (*my mother*)
to the similar word אֻמָּתִי, meaning *My nation* (ibid.; see *Shir HaShirim Rabbah* 1
§42). [See further in *Magen Avos* for another explanation, according to which these
are the words of the people of Israel, who
complained that it was the Mixed Multitude
(*eirev rav*) among them who had caused
them to sin.]

30. See *Numbers* Chs. 13-14.

שֶׁנֶּאֱמַר (במדבר יד, כט) "בַּמִּדְבָּר הַזֶּה יִפְּלוּ פִגְרֵיכֶם". (שיר השירים א, ו)
"שָׂמֻנִי נֹטֵרָה אֶת הַכְּרָמִים", אָמַר הַקָּדוֹשׁ בָּרוּךְ הוּא: מִי גָרַם לִי לְהֵיטִיב
לַכּוּתִים אֶלָּא יִשְׂרָאֵל, (שֶׁכָּל זְמַן) שֶׁכּוּתִים שְׁרוּיִין בְּטוֹב הֵם דְּחוּפִים
וּנְזוּפִים וּמְטוּלְטָלִים. דָּבָר אַחֵר, "שָׂמֻנִי נֹטֵרָה אֶת הַכְּרָמִים" אֵלּוּ יִשְׂרָאֵל
שֶׁגָּלוּ לְבָבֶל, עָמְדוּ עֲלֵיהֶם נְבִיאִים שֶׁבֵּינֵיהֶם וְאָמְרוּ לָהֶם: הַפְרִישׁוּ
תְּרוּמוֹת וּמַעַשְׂרוֹת,[33] אָמְרוּ לָהֶם: כָּל עַצְמֵינוּ לֹא גָלִינוּ מֵאַרְצֵנוּ אֶלָּא

שֶׁנֶּאֱמַר "בַּמִּדְבָּר הַזֶּה יִפְּלוּ פִגְרֵיכֶם" — as **fall as carcasses** in the Wilderness, it is stated, *In this Wilderness shall your carcasses drop* (Numbers 14:29). Thus, the Jewish people complain: Certain sons of my nation (the Spies) caused God to be filled with burning wrath against me.[31]

The Baraisa turns to the next phrase of the *Song of Songs* verse:

"שָׂמֻנִי נֹטֵרָה אֶת הַכְּרָמִים" — *They made me keeper of the vineyards; my own vineyard I did not guard.* אָמַר הַקָּדוֹשׁ בָּרוּךְ הוּא: מִי גָרַם לִי לְהֵיטִיב לַכּוּתִים אֶלָּא יִשְׂרָאֵל — The Holy One, Blessed is He, said: **Who caused Me to bring prosperity on the nations of the world? It is none other than Israel!** שֶׁכָּל זְמַן שֶׁכּוּתִים שְׁרוּיִין בְּטוֹב הֵם דְּחוּפִים וּנְזוּפִים וּמְטוּלְטָלִים — **For as long as the nations of the world dwell in prosperity, [the Jewish nation] is pushed away, is in disfavor, and is made to wander.** I make the nations prosperous and ascendant only so that they will be able to subjugate the Jews as punishment for their sins.[32]

Another interpretation of that phrase:

דָּבָר אַחֵר — **Another interpretation:** "שָׂמֻנִי נֹטֵרָה אֶת הַכְּרָמִים" אֵלּוּ יִשְׂרָאֵל שֶׁגָּלוּ לְבָבֶל — *They made me keeper of the vineyards; my own vineyard I did not guard* **refers to the people of Israel, who were exiled to Babylonia.** עָמְדוּ עֲלֵיהֶם נְבִיאִים שֶׁבֵּינֵיהֶם וְאָמְרוּ לָהֶם: הַפְרִישׁוּ תְּרוּמוֹת וּמַעַשְׂרוֹת — **The prophets among them arose and said to them, "Separate *terumos* and *maasros* from the crops that you grow here."**[33] אָמְרוּ לָהֶם: כָּל עַצְמֵינוּ לֹא גָלִינוּ מֵאַרְצֵנוּ אֶלָּא

---

31. Based on *Shir HaShirim Rabbah* ibid. The Midrash continues: *They made me keeper of the vineyards; my own vineyard I did not guard.* Instead of being detained in the Wilderness for forty years, undergoing forty-two journeys, would it not have been better for me to have entered the Land of Israel immediately? *Maharzu* explains there: Through their sin, the Spies caused me to "become the keeper of others' vineyards" by journeying to other places, and not entering the Land of Israel to guard *my own vineyard.*

32. *Magen Avos,* first explanation. [Thus, God says: The people of My nation have angered Me and thereby caused Me to be the keeper of vineyards other than My own.]

33. Biblically, the tithing of crops applies only in Eretz Yisrael. However, when the Jewish people were exiled to Babylonia, the prophets among them enacted that the crops there be tithed (*Yadayim* 4:3; *Rambam, Hil. Terumos* 1:1). This was done so that these laws would not be new to them when they would return to their Land (see *Sifrei, Eikev,* end of §43, with *Rabbeinu Hillel* and *Emek*

עַד שֶׁלֹּא הִפְרַשְׁנוּ תְּרוּמוֹת וּמַעַשְׂרוֹת, וְעַכְשָׁיו אַתֶּם אוֹמְרִים לָנוּ שֶׁנַּפְרִישׁ
תְּרוּמוֹת וּמַעַשְׂרוֹת,[34] [לְכָךְ נֶאֱמַר "שָׂמֻנִי נֹטֵרָה אֶת הַכְּרָמִים"[35]]:

עַד שֶׁלֹּא הִפְרַשְׁנוּ תְּרוּמוֹת וּמַעַשְׂרוֹת — Whereupon [the exiled Jews] said to [the
prophets], "The only reason we were exiled from our Land was that we failed
to separate terumos and maasros there;   וְעַכְשָׁיו אַתֶּם אוֹמְרִים לָנוּ שֶׁנַּפְרִישׁ
תְּרוּמוֹת וּמַעַשְׂרוֹת — and now you are telling us that we should separate terumos and maasros here!"[34]   לְכָךְ נֶאֱמַר "שָׂמֻנִי נֹטֵרָה אֶת הַכְּרָמִים" — Therefore
it says, They made me keeper of the vineyards; my own vineyard I did not
guard.[35] The people of Israel declare: I was made to keep the laws of tithing in
foreign vineyards, because I did not keep them in my own.

HaNetziv). A later Rabbinic enactment extended the tithing obligation to the lands of
Egypt, Ammon, and Moab (Rambam ibid.,
from Yadayim ibid.). [Some Rishonim hold
that this enactment included other lands as
well (see Derech Emunah, Beur HaHalachah,
Hil. Terumos 1:1).] The custom nowadays is
not to tithe produce anywhere outside Eretz
Yisrael, even in Babylonia. [For reasons for
this custom, see Beur HaHalachah loc. cit.]

34. [What did we gain with our sinful behavior? Had we only obeyed these laws — which
we must now obey anyway — when we were
in Eretz Yisrael, we never would have been
exiled!]

35. I kept the tithing laws of "other" vineyards [those in Babylonia, during the exile],
but the tithing obligations of my own vineyard [when I was still in Eretz Yisrael], I did
not keep.

﷽ פֶּרֶק כא ﷽

א. רַבִּי דוֹסָא בֶּן הַרְכִּינַס אוֹמֵר: שֵׁינָה שֶׁל שַׁחֲרִית וְיַיִן שֶׁל צָהֲרִים וְכוּ'.[1]
שֵׁינָה שֶׁל שַׁחֲרִית, כֵּיצַד, מְלַמֵּד שֶׁלֹּא יִתְכַּוֵּן אָדָם לִישַׁן עַד שֶׁתַּעֲבוֹר
עָלָיו זְמַן קְרִיאַת שְׁמַע[2], שֶׁאִם יָשַׁן עַד שֶׁתַּעֲבוֹר עָלָיו זְמַן קְרִיאַת שְׁמַע
נִמְצָא בָּטֵל מִן הַתּוֹרָה[3], שֶׁנֶּאֱמַר (משלי כו, יד) ("הַדֶּלֶת תִּסּוֹב עַל צִירָהּ

﷽ CHAPTER 21 ﷽

§1 The Baraisa discusses the last half of *Avos* 3:10, which states:

שֵׁינָה שֶׁל — **R' Dosa ben Harkinas says:** — רַבִּי דוֹסָא בֶּן הַרְכִּינַס אוֹמֵר
Morning sleep, midday wine, etc.[1] — שַׁחֲרִית וְיַיִן שֶׁל צָהֲרִים וְכוּ'

This teaching enumerates four habits that remove a person from this world, primarily by distancing the person from Torah and its study. The Baraisa proceeds to elaborate each of the four:

מְלַמֵּד שֶׁלֹּא **"Morning sleep" — how so?** — שֵׁינָה שֶׁל שַׁחֲרִית, כֵּיצַד
יִתְכַּוֵּן אָדָם לִישַׁן עַד שֶׁתַּעֲבוֹר עָלָיו זְמַן קְרִיאַת שְׁמַע — **This teaches that a person should not intend to sleep past the time for reciting the** *Shema* **in the morning.**[2] שֶׁאִם יָשַׁן עַד שֶׁתַּעֲבוֹר עָלָיו זְמַן קְרִיאַת שְׁמַע נִמְצָא בָּטֵל מִן הַתּוֹרָה — **For if a person sleeps past the time for reciting the** *Shema,* **he is thereby idle from the Torah.**[3] שֶׁנֶּאֱמַר "הַדֶּלֶת תִּסּוֹב עַל צִירָהּ

---

1. The rest of this teaching reads: וְשִׂיחַת הַיְלָדִים וִישִׁיבַת בָּתֵּי כְנֵסִיּוֹת שֶׁל עַמֵּי הָאָרֶץ מוֹצִיאִים אֶת הָאָדָם מִן הָעוֹלָם, *children's chatter, and sitting at gatherings of the unlearned remove a person from the world.* According to *Rambam* (*Avos* ad loc.), these activities have a negative influence on one's spiritual development and, if unchecked, can rob a person of all he has accomplished over the course of his lifetime.

2. [I.e., the first quarter of the day (see Mishnah, *Berachos* 1:2).] *Magen Avos* explains that the Baraisa here is critical specifically of one *who intends* to oversleep the time for *Shema,* such as where he has been studying all night and wishes to sleep a few hours in the morning to refresh himself for continued study later in the day. However, one who was overcome with sleep (such as where he drank an excess of wine the night before) and missed the time for *Shema* is considered a victim of circumstance [אָנוּס], and is not the subject of our Baraisa's criticism.

[See also below, end of note 15.]

3. The recitation of the *Shema,* morning and evening, represents the minimum fulfillment of the verse cited below (*Joshua* 1:8): *This Book of the Torah shall not depart from your mouth; rather, you should contemplate it day and night.* Scripture reckons these two recitations of *Shema* as if he had toiled in Torah study day and night (*Binyan Yehoshua,* citing *Yalkut Tehillim* §614, end). [In addition to having nullified the mitzvah of reciting the *Shema* in its proper time, one who misses this essential Torah study is thus judged as having idled himself from the Torah.]

Magen Avos (in one of several approaches) explains that the essence of the Torah is to declare God's Oneness and accept His mitzvos, which is embodied by the *Shema.* Therefore, one who neglects to recite the *Shema* in its time has neglected the essence of the Torah, and diminished even the Torah that he studies at other times.

וְעָצֵל עַל מִטָּתוֹ״,) (שם פסוק יג) ״אָמַר עָצֵל שַׁחַל בַּדֶּרֶךְ אֲרִי בֵּין
הָרְחֹבוֹת״4. יַיִן שֶׁל צָהֳרַיִם, כֵּיצַד, מְלַמֵּד שֶׁלֹּא יִתְכַּוֵּן אָדָם לִשְׁתּוֹת יַיִן
בַּצָּהֳרַיִם5, שֶׁכָּל זְמַן שֶׁאָדָם שׁוֹתֶה יַיִן בַּצָּהֳרַיִם נִמְצָא בָּטֵל מִכָּל הַתּוֹרָה
כֻּלָּהּ6, שֶׁנֶּאֱמַר (קהלת י, טז) ״אִי לָךְ אֶרֶץ שֶׁמַּלְכֵּךְ נָעַר וְשָׂרַיִךְ בַּבֹּקֶר
יֹאכֵלוּ״, וְאוֹמֵר (שם פסוק יז) ״אַשְׁרֵיךְ אֶרֶץ שֶׁמַּלְכֵּךְ בֶּן חוֹרִים (וְגוֹ׳)״.

״וְעָצֵל עַל מִטָּתוֹ״ — This phenomenon is **as it is stated,** *The door turns on its hinges, and a lazy person on his bed* (Proverbs 26:14). ״אָמַר עָצֵל שַׁחַל בַּדֶּרֶךְ אֲרִי בֵּין הָרְחֹבוֹת״ — And it says one verse earlier, *A lazy person says, "There is a young lion on the path, a lion between the streets"* (ibid. v. 13).[4]

The Baraisa elaborates the second of the four habits:

יַיִן שֶׁל צָהֳרַיִם, כֵּיצַד, מְלַמֵּד שֶׁלֹּא יִתְכַּוֵּן אָדָם — **"Midday wine" — how so?** לִשְׁתּוֹת יַיִן בַּצָּהֳרַיִם — **This teaches that a person should not intend to drink wine in the middle of the day,**[5] שֶׁכָּל זְמַן שֶׁאָדָם שׁוֹתֶה יַיִן בַּצָּהֳרַיִם נִמְצָא בָּטֵל מִכָּל הַתּוֹרָה כֻּלָּהּ — **for when a person drinks wine in the middle of the day, he is thereby idled from the entire Torah.**[6] שֶׁנֶּאֱמַר ״אִי לָךְ אֶרֶץ שֶׁמַּלְכֵּךְ נָעַר וְשָׂרַיִךְ בַּבֹּקֶר יֹאכֵלוּ״ — **As it is stated,** *Woe to you, O land, whose king acts as an adolescent, and whose ministers dine in the morning* (Ecclesiastes 10:16). וְאוֹמֵר ״אַשְׁרֵיךְ אֶרֶץ שֶׁמַּלְכֵּךְ בֶּן חוֹרִים וְגוֹ׳ — **And it says** in the next verse, *Fortunate are you, O land, whose king is a man of nobility, etc. and whose ministers dine at the [proper] time* [בָּעֵת] — *in strength and not in drink* (ibid., v. 17).[7] The verse speaks of judges who are occupied in the "strength" of Torah.[8] They dine at noon, which is the proper time for a Torah

---

4. The door swings on its hinges, as people leave their houses early for work, but the lazy person remains in bed (*Ibn Ezra*, cited by *Binyan Yehoshua*). He does not want to leave the comforts of home, so he makes excuses about the supposed dangers outside to justify staying indoors, where he remains in bed and sleeps.

The Baraisa cites these two verses in *Proverbs* in reverse order, because it wishes to cite first the verse, *The door turns on its hinges, etc.,* which relates more directly to the person who oversleeps the time of *Shema* and does not learn from the example of the others who "cause the door hinges to turn" and leave the house at the proper time (*Magen Avos*, second explanation).

5. Because wine drunk in the afternoon

(after the morning lethargy has passed and before the morning tiredness sets in) tends to be drunk with gusto and to excess, and makes a person drunk (see *Rav* and *Tos. Yom Tov* to *Avos* ad loc.). [See below, end of note 15, regarding the Baraisa's expression here, *a person should not "intend."*]

6. The "entire" Torah, because one who becomes intoxicated frequently will find any sin to be justifiable in his eyes (*Ahavas Chesed,* citing *Yoma* 74b-75a).

7. The Baraisa's exposition is based on the balance of the verse indicated by וְגוֹ׳, etc., which reads: וְשָׂרַיִךְ בָּעֵת יֹאכֵלוּ בִּגְבוּרָה וְלֹא בַשְׁתִי (*Ahavas Chesed*).

8. *Ahavas Chesed,* from *Shabbos* 10a.

וְאֵיזוֹ אוֹתוֹ עֵת, הֱוֵי אוֹמֵר לֶעָתִיד לָבֹא, שֶׁנֶּאֱמַר (ישעיה ס כב) ״אֲנִי ה׳
בְּעִתָּהּ אֲחִישֶׁנָּה״[12]. וְאוֹמֵר (במדבר כג כג) ״כָּעֵת יֵאָמֵר לְיַעֲקֹב וּלְיִשְׂרָאֵל
וְגוֹ׳ ״, כָּךְ אָמַר הַקָּדוֹשׁ בָּרוּךְ הוּא לְבִלְעָם: ״כָּעֵת״ וְלֹא בָּעֵת, [לֹא]
בָּעֵת שֶׁאַתָּה עוֹמֵד בְּתוֹכָהּ [אֶלָּא] בָּעֵת שֶׁאֲנִי עָתִיד לַעֲשׂוֹת לָהֶם
גְּאוּלָה לְיִשְׂרָאֵל.[13] שִׂיחַת יְלָדִים, כֵּיצַד, מְלַמֵּד שֶׁלֹּא יִתְכַּוֵּן אָדָם
בְּשָׁעָה שֶׁהוּא שׁוֹנֶה בְּבֵיתוֹ לָשׂוּחַ עִם אִשְׁתּוֹ עִם בָּנָיו וְעִם בְּנוֹתָיו,[14]

---

scholar's meal,[9] and even then, it is "not in drink." This verse thus alludes to the Baraisa's criticism of "midday wine."[10]

The Baraisa expounds this verse further, as contrasting the adolescent behavior of those who view this world primarily as a place for physical indulgence with that of the noble ones, who see this world as primarily a place of achievement, and delay their full enjoyment until the Future Era:[11]

וְאֵיזוֹ אוֹתוֹ עֵת — **And what is that** "**proper time**" when the praiseworthy ministers will have full enjoyment? הֱוֵי אוֹמֵר לֶעָתִיד לָבֹא, שֶׁנֶּאֱמַר ״אֲנִי ה׳ בְּעִתָּהּ אֲחִישֶׁנָּה״ — **Say that it is in the Future Era, as it is stated,** *I am* HASHEM, *in its time* [בְּעִתָּהּ] *I will hasten it* (Isaiah 60:22).[12] וְאוֹמֵר ״כָּעֵת יֵאָמֵר לְיַעֲקֹב וּלְיִשְׂרָאֵל וְגוֹ׳ ״ — **And it says** in the prophetic blessings that Balaam uttered, *At the [proper] time it will be said to Jacob and Israel, etc.,* what God has wrought (Numbers 23:23). כָּךְ אָמַר הַקָּדוֹשׁ בָּרוּךְ הוּא לְבִלְעָם — **This is what the Holy One, Blessed is He, was telling Balaam:** ״כָּעֵת״ וְלֹא בָּעֵת — **Israel's full reward will come at the [proper]** time and not "in [this] time," meaning: לֹא בָּעֵת שֶׁאַתָּה עוֹמֵד בְּתוֹכָהּ אֶלָּא בָּעֵת שֶׁאֲנִי עָתִיד לַעֲשׂוֹת לָהֶם גְּאוּלָה לְיִשְׂרָאֵל — **Not in the time in which you stand** now, **but rather at the time that I will bring about a redemption for the Jewish people.**[13]

The Baraisa elaborates the third habit:

מְלַמֵּד שֶׁלֹּא יִתְכַּוֵּן שִׂיחַת יְלָדִים, כֵּיצַד — "**Children's chatter**" — **how so?** אָדָם בְּשָׁעָה שֶׁהוּא שׁוֹנֶה בְּבֵיתוֹ לָשׂוּחַ עִם אִשְׁתּוֹ עִם בָּנָיו וְעִם בְּנוֹתָיו — **This teaches**

---

9. Ibid.

10. Ibid.

11. See *Magen Avos.*

12. Simply, the verse means that the ministers should wait to dine at a normal time, i.e., in the fourth hour of the day (*Targum Yonasan* ad loc., cited in *Maharsha* to *Shabbos* ibid.) or the sixth hour (see *Shabbos* ibid. with *Sfas Emes*). However, if that were the sole meaning, then the word בָּעֵת (literally, *approximately the time*) would have been more appropriate, since the ministers

act properly if they dine at approximately the right time: there is no moral demand on them that they dine at a precise time in the morning, neither earlier nor later. But the verse uses the term בָּעֵת instead, and this alludes to a specific time in the future (*Ahavas Chesed*).

13. This verse, then, is another proof that Scripture sometimes uses the word עֵת, *time,* to refer to the Future Era (*Binyan Yehoshua*).

[Other texts, however, read here in the

שֶׁכָּל זְמַן שֶׁאָדָם יוֹשֵׁב בְּתוֹךְ בֵּיתוֹ וְשׁוֹנֶה וּמֵשִׂיחַ עִם בָּנָיו וּבְנֵי
בֵּיתוֹ נִמְצָא בָּטֵל מִן הַתּוֹרָה, שֶׁנֶּאֱמַר (יהושע א, ח) "לֹא יָמוּשׁ סֵפֶר
הַתּוֹרָה הַזֶּה מִפִּיךָ וְהָגִיתָ בּוֹ יוֹמָם וָלַיְלָה". וִישִׁיבַת בָּתֵּי כְּנֵסִיּוֹת
שֶׁל עַמֵּי הָאָרֶץ, כֵּיצַד, מְלַמֵּד שֶׁלֹּא יֵשֵׁב אָדָם עִם יוֹשְׁבֵי קְרָנוֹת
בַּשּׁוּק וְנִמְצָא בָּטֵל מִן הַתּוֹרָה, שֶׁנֶּאֱמַר (תהלים א, א-ב) "אַשְׁרֵי הָאִישׁ
אֲשֶׁר לֹא הָלַךְ בַּעֲצַת רְשָׁעִים ... [כִּי אִם בְּתוֹרַת ה' חֶפְצוֹ]",[16]

---

that a person should not intend when he sits and studies in his home to
chat with his wife and sons and daughters,[14] — שֶׁכָּל זְמַן שֶׁאָדָם יוֹשֵׁב בְּתוֹךְ
בֵּיתוֹ וְשׁוֹנֶה וּמֵשִׂיחַ עִם בָּנָיו וּבְנֵי בֵּיתוֹ נִמְצָא בָּטֵל מִן הַתּוֹרָה — for whenever a
person sits and studies in his home and chats with his children and other
members of his household, it emerges that he is idled from his Torah study.
And this is something he must avoid, שֶׁנֶּאֱמַר "לֹא יָמוּשׁ סֵפֶר הַתּוֹרָה הַזֶּה
מִפִּיךָ וְהָגִיתָ בּוֹ יוֹמָם וָלַיְלָה" — as it is stated, *This Book of the Torah shall not
depart from your mouth; rather, you should contemplate it day and night*
(*Joshua 1:8*).

The Baraisa elaborates the fourth and final habit:
וִישִׁיבַת בָּתֵּי כְּנֵסִיּוֹת שֶׁל עַמֵּי הָאָרֶץ, כֵּיצַד — "And sitting at gatherings of
the unlearned" — how so? מְלַמֵּד שֶׁלֹּא יֵשֵׁב אָדָם עִם יוֹשְׁבֵי קְרָנוֹת בַּשּׁוּק
— This teaches that a person should not sit in the company of loafers in
the street, וְנִמְצָא בָּטֵל מִן הַתּוֹרָה — for it will then emerge that he is idle
from the Torah,[15] שֶׁנֶּאֱמַר "אַשְׁרֵי הָאִישׁ אֲשֶׁר לֹא הָלַךְ בַּעֲצַת רְשָׁעִים ... כִּי אִם
בְּתוֹרַת ה' חֶפְצוֹ" — as it is stated, *Praiseworthy is the man who walked
not in the counsel of the wicked,* and stood not in the path of the sinful, and

---

"בָּעֵת" וְלֹא "בְּעֵת", כָּעֵת שֶׁאַתָּה עוֹמֵד
בְּתוֹכָם וְלֹא בָּעֵת שֶׁאֲנִי עָתִיד לַעֲשׂוֹת לָהֶם גְּאֻלָּה
לְיִשְׂרָאֵל, [The verse says here] כָּעֵת and not
בָּעֵת; at the present time [כָּעֵת] that you stand
among them, but not at the time [בָּעֵת] that I
am destined to bring about a redemption for
the Jewish people. According to this reading, the Baraisa is bringing another proof
that the specific form בָּעֵת, in contrast to
כָּעֵת, is a reference to the Future Era, which
is why Balaam's prophecy, which speaks
about this world, does *not* use the expression בָּעֵת, but rather כָּעֵת.]

14. [See end of next note, regarding the
Baraisa's expression here, *a person should
not "intend."*]

15. When the unlearned gather, they while
away their time with idle talk (*Rav, Rashi,*

Machzor Vitri to *Avos* ad loc.), or worse (*R'
Yonah* to *Avos* ad loc.).

Here, the Baraisa does not say "a person
should not intend," as it does with regard to
the previous three habits. For the practices
involved in the first three habits certainly
have some value, and are permitted and
even necessary as the need arises; the
Baraisa there is critical only of one who
intends these things [i.e., he plans them as
part of his routine]. This fourth habit (sitting in the company of loafers), however,
is something that a person must *always*
avoid (*Ben Avraham*). [*Magen Avos* explains somewhat differently: In the first
three cases, it is possible that one would do
them deliberately with the intent of doing a
mitzvah; the Baraisa therefore cautions that

רַבִּי מֵאִיר אוֹמֵר: וּמַה תַּלְמוּד לוֹמַר "וּבְמוֹשַׁב לֵצִים (לֹא יָשָׁב)", אֵלּוּ
תַּרְטִיָאוֹת שֶׁל לֵצִים (שֶׁבָּהֶן דָּנִין דִּינֵי נְפָשׁוֹת לְהָמִית[17]). שֶׁנֶּאֱמַר (שם
כו, ה) "שָׂנֵאתִי קְהַל מְרֵעִים וְעִם רְשָׁעִים לֹא אֵשֵׁב". (וְאֵין "מְרֵעִים" אֶלָּא
רְשָׁעִים, שֶׁנֶּאֱמַר (שם לז, ט) "כִּי מְרֵעִים יִכָּרֵתוּן", וּמַה הוּא פּוּרְעָנוּתָן
לֶעָתִיד לָבֹא, שֶׁנֶּאֱמַר (מלאכי ג, יט) "כִּי הִנֵּה הַיּוֹם בָּא בֹּעֵר כַּתַּנּוּר וְהָיוּ כָל
זֵדִים וְכָל עֹשֵׂה רִשְׁעָה קַשׁ". וְאֵין "זֵדִים" אֶלָּא לֵצִים, שֶׁנֶּאֱמַר (משלי כא,
כד) "זֵד יָהִיר לֵץ שְׁמוֹ":

sat not in the session of scorners. **But his desire is in the Torah of HASHEM**
(Psalms 1:1-2).[16]

The Baraisa elaborates further on this verse:

רַבִּי מֵאִיר אוֹמֵר: וּמַה תַּלְמוּד לוֹמַר "וּבְמוֹשַׁב לֵצִים לֹא יָשָׁב" — R' Meir says:
What does Scripture refer to with the phrase, *and sat not in the session of
scorners?* אֵלּוּ תַּרְטִיָאוֹת שֶׁל לֵצִים שֶׁבָּהֶן דָּנִין דִּינֵי נְפָשׁוֹת לְהָמִית — These are
the amphitheaters of the idolatrous scorners [i.e., the Roman stadiums], in
which they sentence people to death,[17] שֶׁנֶּאֱמַר "שָׂנֵאתִי קְהַל מְרֵעִים וְעִם
רְשָׁעִים לֹא אֵשֵׁב" — and this is also as it is stated, *I hated the gathering of
"merei'im"; and I did not sit with the wicked* (ibid. 26:5). וְאֵין "מְרֵעִים"
אֶלָּא רְשָׁעִים, שֶׁנֶּאֱמַר "כִּי מְרֵעִים יִכָּרֵתוּן" — And the word *merei'im* refers to
none other than evildoers, as it is stated, *For the evildoers [מְרֵעִים] shall
be cut off* (ibid. 37:9). וּמַה הוּא פּוּרְעָנוּתָן לֶעָתִיד לָבֹא — And what is the
punishment of [these evildoers] in the Future Era? שֶׁנֶּאֱמַר "כִּי הִנֵּה הַיּוֹם בָּא
בֹּעֵר כַּתַּנּוּר וְהָיוּ כָל זֵדִים וְכָל עֹשֵׂה רִשְׁעָה קַשׁ" — It is as it is stated, *For behold,
the day is coming, burning like an oven, when all the "zeidim" and all the
evildoers will be like straw* (Malachi 3:19). וְאֵין "זֵדִים" אֶלָּא לֵצִים, שֶׁנֶּאֱמַר
"זֵד יָהִיר לֵץ שְׁמוֹ" — And the word *zeidim* in this verse refers to none other
than scorners, as it is stated, *The boastful, willful man ("zeid"), scorner is
his name* (Proverbs 21:24).

---

one should *not* intend to do so (see there for
his elaboration).]

16. [This verse contrasts "one who sits in the
session of scorners" with "one whose desire
is in God's Torah," indicating that the former
leads to neglect of the latter.]

17. The Romans there would hold gladi-
atorial combats, often to the death, pitting
animals against animals, men against animals, and men against men (see *Aruch* ע'
אצטגנין). The gladiators were usually drawn

from among captives of war, criminal prisoners, or slaves. (See also *Avodah Zarah*
18b with *Hagahos HaBach* and *Ran*.)

Our Baraisa emphasizes the murderous
acts committed in these stadiums, and
condemns the *leitzim* who find amusement
in the brutal death of another human being; see the Gemara in *Avodah Zarah* ibid.,
which notes other objectionable features of
these stadiums, and defines the term *leitzim*
more broadly.

ב. מַעֲשֶׂה בְּרַבִּי עֲקִיבָא שֶׁהָיָה יוֹשֵׁב וְשׁוֹנֶה לְתַלְמִידָיו וְנִזְכַּר לוֹ מַה שֶׁעָשָׂה בְּיַלְדוּתוֹ[18], אָמַר: מוֹדֶה אֲנִי לְפָנֶיךָ ה' אֱלֹהַי שֶׁשַּׂמְתָּ חֶלְקִי מִיּוֹשְׁבֵי בֵּית הַמִּדְרָשׁ וְלֹא שַׂמְתָּ חֶלְקִי מִיּוֹשְׁבֵי קְרָנוֹת בַּשּׁוּק:

---

§2 The Baraisa relates a short incident pertaining to the above:

מַעֲשֶׂה בְּרַבִּי עֲקִיבָא שֶׁהָיָה יוֹשֵׁב וְשׁוֹנֶה לְתַלְמִידָיו — It happened once that R' Akiva was sitting and teaching his students, וְנִזְכַּר לוֹ מַה שֶׁעָשָׂה בְּיַלְדוּתוֹ — and, at that moment, he remembered how he had behaved in his youth, before he began to study Torah.[18] אָמַר: מוֹדֶה אֲנִי לְפָנֶיךָ ה' אֱלֹהַי שֶׁשַּׂמְתָּ חֶלְקִי מִיּוֹשְׁבֵי בֵּית הַמִּדְרָשׁ וְלֹא שַׂמְתָּ חֶלְקִי מִיּוֹשְׁבֵי קְרָנוֹת בַּשּׁוּק — Whereupon he said in their presence, "I thank you, O Hashem, my God, that You have placed my portion with those who dwell in the study hall, and You have not placed my portion with the loafers on the street corners!"

---

18. R' Akiva did not study Torah until he was forty, as related above in Ch. 6 (*Binyan Yehoshua*).

﴾ פֶּרֶק כב ﴿

א. רַבִּי חֲנִינָא בֶּן דּוֹסָא אוֹמֵר: כֹּל שֶׁיִּרְאַת חֶטְאוֹ קוֹדֶמֶת לְחָכְמָתוֹ חָכְמָתוֹ מִתְקַיֶּימֶת[1], שֶׁנֶּאֱמַר (תהלים קיא, י) "רֵאשִׁית חָכְמָה יִרְאַת ה'"[2]. הוּא הָיָה אוֹמֵר: כֹּל שֶׁמַּעֲשָׂיו מְרוּבִּין וְכוּ', שֶׁנֶּאֱמַר (שמות כד, ז) "נַעֲשֶׂה וְנִשְׁמָע"[4].

﴾ CHAPTER 22 ﴿

§1 The Baraisa cites *Avos 3:9*:

רַבִּי חֲנִינָא בֶּן דּוֹסָא אוֹמֵר — R' Chanina ben Dosa says: כֹּל שֶׁיִּרְאַת חֶטְאוֹ קוֹדֶמֶת לְחָכְמָתוֹ מִתְקַיֶּימֶת — Anyone whose fear of sin precedes his wisdom, his wisdom will endure.[1]

The Baraisa provides the Scriptural source for R' Chanina ben Dosa's teaching:

שֶׁנֶּאֱמַר "רֵאשִׁית חָכְמָה יִרְאַת ה' " — This is as it is stated, *The beginning of wisdom is the fear of HASHEM (Psalms 111:10)*.[2]

The Baraisa continues citing that Mishnah:

הוּא הָיָה אוֹמֵר — He used to say: כֹּל שֶׁמַּעֲשָׂיו מְרוּבִּין וְכוּ' — Anyone whose actions exceed, etc. [his wisdom, his wisdom will endure;[3] and anyone whose wisdom exceeds his actions, his wisdom will not endure.]

The Baraisa provides the Scriptural source for this teaching:

שֶׁנֶּאֱמַר "נַעֲשֶׂה וְנִשְׁמָע" — This is as it is stated, *We will do and we will listen!* (*Exodus 24:7*).[4]

---

1. The Mishnah begins by describing an individual whose motivation to acquire a fear of sin preceded his motivation to acquire wisdom. That is, his initial goal was to become a person who fears sin, and he seeks to use the acquisition of Torah wisdom as a means of reaching this goal. When he sees how effective Torah is in bringing him closer to his objective, he will derive a great amount of satisfaction from it [and will therefore keep up his studies, ensuring that his wisdom endures] (*Rav* and *Magen Avos* [*Rashbatz*] to *Avos* ad loc.; see *Rambam Commentary, R' Yonah* [second explanation]).

[The Mishnah there concludes with the converse: "And anyone whose wisdom precedes his fear of sin, his wisdom will not endure."]

2. *The beginning* [the original aim of the process] *of* [gaining] *wisdom is* [to achieve through that wisdom] *the fear of Hashem* (*Nachalas Avos*, cited in *Meorei Ohr*).

3. How it is possible for one's actions to exceed his wisdom if he cannot fulfill the commandments he has yet to learn? *R' Yonah* therefore explains that R' Chanina ben Dosa is offering advice to one who lacks Torah wisdom: Accept upon yourself to fulfill God's Will, whatever it may be. And when the person does so, it is accounted immediately as if he has fulfilled all the Torah, even the parts he has not yet learned. His readiness to perform whatever is required of him already defines "his actions" to include even those actions that have yet to occur. Thus, his actions exceed his current learning.

4. Thus did the Israelites accept upon themselves the Torah God gave them at Sinai. They first dedicated themselves to unquestionably carry out whatever God might command them ["We will do"] and were then ready to hear the specifics of the Torah ["we will (now) listen"] (*R' Yonah* loc. cit.).

אָמְרוּ לִפְנֵי רַבָּן יוֹחָנָן בֶּן זַכַּאי: חָכָם וִירֵא חֵטְא מַה הוּא, אָמַר לָהֶם:
הֲרֵי זֶה אוּמָן וּכְלֵי אוּמָנָתוֹ בְּיָדוֹ[5], חָכָם וְאֵין יְרֵא חֵטְא מַהוּ, אָמַר
לָהֶם: הֲרֵי זֶה אוּמָן וְאֵין כְּלֵי אוּמָנָתוֹ בְּיָדוֹ[6]. יְרֵא חֵטְא וְאֵין חָכָם
מַהוּ, אָמַר לָהֶם: אֵין זֶה אוּמָן אֲבָל כְּלֵי אוּמָנָתוֹ בְּיָדוֹ[7]. רַבִּי אֶלְעָזָר
בֶּן עֲזַרְיָה אוֹמֵר: אִם אֵין תּוֹרָה אֵין דֶּרֶךְ אֶרֶץ וְכוּ׳, הוּא הָיָה אוֹמֵר:
אָדָם שֶׁיֵּשׁ בּוֹ מַעֲשִׂים טוֹבִים וְלָמַד תּוֹרָה הַרְבֵּה[8] לְמָה הוּא דּוֹמֶה,

---

The Baraisa speaks further of the relationship between Torah knowledge and fear of sin:

אָמְרוּ לִפְנֵי רַבָּן יוֹחָנָן בֶּן זַכַּאי — They asked the following question in the presence of Rabban Yochanan ben Zakkai: חָכָם וִירֵא חֵטְא מַה הוּא — If a person is both a Torah scholar and one who fears sin, what is he like? אָמַר לָהֶם: — He said to them: This is a craftsman with the tool of his craft in his hand.[5] חָכָם וְאֵין יְרֵא חֵטְא מַהוּ — They asked Rabban Yochanan ben Zakkai further: If a person is a Torah scholar but not one who fears sin, what is he like? אָמַר לָהֶם: הֲרֵי זֶה אוּמָן וְאֵין כְּלֵי אוּמָנָתוֹ בְּיָדוֹ — He said to them: This is a craftsman without the tool of his craft in his hand.[6] יְרֵא חֵטְא וְאֵין חָכָם מַהוּ — They asked him further: If a person is one who fears sin but not a Torah scholar, what is he like? אָמַר לָהֶם: אֵין זֶה אוּמָן אֲבָל כְּלֵי אוּמָנָתוֹ בְּיָדוֹ — He said to them: This is not a craftsman, but he has the tool of his desired craft in his hand.[7]

The Baraisa cites *Avos* 3:17 (with some variations):

רַבִּי אֶלְעָזָר בֶּן עֲזַרְיָה אוֹמֵר — R' Elazar ben Azaryah says: אִם אֵין תּוֹרָה אֵין דֶּרֶךְ אֶרֶץ וְכוּ׳ — If there is no Torah, there is no proper conduct, etc. הוּא הָיָה אוֹמֵר — He used to say: אָדָם שֶׁיֵּשׁ בּוֹ מַעֲשִׂים טוֹבִים וְלָמַד תּוֹרָה הַרְבֵּה לְמָה הוּא דּוֹמֶה — A man who has many good deeds to his credit and has studied much Torah,[8]

---

5. Just as an expert craftsmen with the right tools can take raw materials and produce masterful work, so too a scholar with the fear of sin can instruct and inspire people in the ways of Torah. His scholarship gives him the requisite knowledge, and his fear of sin allows his message to penetrate, as the saying goes, "Words that emerge from the heart enter the heart." Moreover, the Sages teach: *The words of anyone who has fear of sin are listened to* (see *Yalkut Shimoni, Koheles,* end). Conversely, he will not suffer the embarrassment of people accusing him of hypocrisy and of being a greater sinner than they [see *Arachin* 16b] (*Binyan Yehoshua*).

6. He cannot properly instruct people, because they will accuse him of hypocrisy. Elsewhere, the Gemara teaches (*Bava Metzia* 107b): "It is written, הִתְקוֹשְׁשׁוּ וָקוֹשּׁוּ, *Search within yourself, and search [others]*" (*Zephaniah* 2:1), and Reish Lakish explained this to mean: קְשׁוֹט עַצְמְךָ וְאַחַר כַּךְ קְשׁוֹט אֲחֵרִים, *First correct yourself and then correct others* (*Binyan Yehoshua*).

7. His effectiveness is limited because he does not have the requisite knowledge to reprove each person according to his unique nature. On the other hand, he does have the advantage that he cannot be accused of hypocrisy (*Binyan Yehoshua*).

8. [I.e., *whose actions exceed his wisdom,* in the language of the Mishnah.]

לְאִילָן שֶׁעוֹמֵד עַל הַמַּיִם עֲנָפָיו מוּעָטִין וְשָׁרָשָׁיו מְרוּבִּין, אֲפִלּוּ אַרְבַּע
רוּחוֹת הָעוֹלָם בָּאוֹת וְנוֹשְׁבוֹת בּוֹ אֵין מְזִיזִין אוֹתוֹ מִמְּקוֹמוֹ[9], שֶׁנֶּאֱמַר
(ירמיה יז, ח) "וְהָיָה כְּעֵץ שָׁתוּל עַל (פְּלַגֵי) מַיִם וְגוֹ'"[10]. אָדָם שֶׁאֵין
בּוֹ מַעֲשִׂים טוֹבִים וְלָמַד תּוֹרָה[11] לְמָה הוּא דוֹמֶה, לְאִילָן שֶׁעוֹמֵד
בַּמִּדְבָּר עֲנָפָיו מְרוּבִּין וְשָׁרָשָׁיו מוּעָטִין, כְּשֶׁרוּחַ נוֹשֶׁבֶת בּוֹ עוֹקַרְתּוֹ
וְהוֹפַכְתּוֹ עַל פָּנָיו[12], שֶׁנֶּאֱמַר (שם פסוק ו) "וְהָיָה כְּעַרְעָר בָּעֲרָבָה וְגוֹ'".

---

to what is he likened? לְאִילָן שֶׁעוֹמֵד עַל הַמַּיִם — **To a tree that stands near the water,** עֲנָפָיו מוּעָטִין וְשָׁרָשָׁיו מְרוּבִּין — **whose branches are few but whose roots are numerous;** אֲפִלּוּ אַרְבַּע רוּחוֹת הָעוֹלָם בָּאוֹת וְנוֹשְׁבוֹת בּוֹ — **even if the four winds of the world come and blow** against it, אֵין מְזִיזִין אוֹתוֹ מִמְּקוֹמוֹ — **they could not budge it from its place,**[9] שֶׁנֶּאֱמַר "וְהָיָה כְּעֵץ שָׁתוּל עַל מַיִם וְגוֹ'" — **as it is stated,** *He will be like a tree planted near water, etc. which spreads out its roots along a brook and does not perceive when heat comes, whose foliage is ever fresh; it will not worry in a year of drought and will not stop producing fruit (Jeremiah 17:8).*[10] אָדָם שֶׁאֵין בּוֹ מַעֲשִׂים טוֹבִים וְלָמַד תּוֹרָה — **A man who does not have good deeds but has studied Torah,**[11] **to what is he likened?** לְאִילָן שֶׁעוֹמֵד בַּמִּדְבָּר עֲנָפָיו מְרוּבִּין וְשָׁרָשָׁיו מוּעָטִין — **To a tree that stands in the desert, whose branches are numerous but whose roots are few.** כְּשֶׁרוּחַ נוֹשֶׁבֶת בּוֹ עוֹקַרְתּוֹ וְהוֹפַכְתּוֹ עַל פָּנָיו — **When a wind blows upon it, [the wind] uproots it and turns it upside down,**[12] שֶׁנֶּאֱמַר "וְהָיָה כְּעַרְעָר בָּעֲרָבָה וְגוֹ'" — **as it is stated,** *He will be like a lone tree in the desert, etc., and will not see when goodness comes; it dwells in parched lands in the wilderness, in a salty, uninhabited land (ibid. v. 6).*[13]

---

9. Such a man is anchored in his faith like a tree firmly rooted in the earth. Even when confronted by challenges and arguments he does not have the knowledge to refute (*Meiri*) or by the lure of desire and greed (*Tiferes Yisrael* §130), he will remain steadfast in his faith and will not waver.

10. [Most texts have here וְהָיָה כְּעֵץ שָׁתוּל עַל "פַּלְגֵי" מַיִם וְגוֹ', *He will be like a tree planted near "brooks of" water, etc.,* which is a verse in *Psalms* (1:3). We have followed the *Nuschas HaGra,* that the Baraisa here refers to the verse in *Jeremiah,* which is in the same passage as the contrasting verse cited next by the Baraisa. See also *Tos. Yom Tov* to the Mishnah ad loc.]

11. [I.e., *Anyone whose wisdom exceeds his actions,* in the language of the Mishnah.]

12. In this metaphor, the branches of the tree represent man's wisdom: Just as a tree's splendor is distinguished by its branches, man's splendor is his intellectual prowess (*Tiferes Yisrael* §123). The most integral component of the tree, though, is its root system, which bring it sustenance and anchors it; so, too, man's actions are the most important component of his existence, as *Avos* 1:17 teaches: *Study is not the main [objective], rather action [is]* (Rashi; *Machzor Vitri; Tos. Yom Tov*). A tree top-heavy with branches but short of roots is destined to fail; similarly, a man who amasses much knowledge but does not practice what he has studied will be uprooted from the world (*Machzor Vitri*).

13. Since the tree is by itself, it is not shielded by surrounding trees, and the winds

רַבָּן גַּמְלִיאֵל אוֹמֵר: עֲשֵׂה לְךָ רַב וּקְנֵה לְךָ חָבֵר[14]. רַב לַחַכְמָה[15] וְחָבֵר לַלִּמּוּד[16], וְהִסְתַּלֵּק מִן הַסְּפֵיקוֹת[17], וְאַל תַּרְבֶּה לְעַשֵּׂר אוֹמָדוֹת[18]:

The Baraisa cites *Avos* 1:16 (with some variations):

רַבָּן גַּמְלִיאֵל אוֹמֵר — **Rabban Gamliel says:** עֲשֵׂה לְךָ רַב — **Make a teacher for yourself,** וּקְנֵה לְךָ חָבֵר — **and purchase a friend for yourself.**[14]

The Baraisa explains:

רַב לַחַכְמָה — **A teacher for wisdom**[15] וְחָבֵר לַלִּמּוּד — **and a friend with whom to study.**[16]

The Baraisa continues citing Rabban Gamliel's teachings in *Avos* 1:16:

וְהִסְתַּלֵּק מִן הַסְּפֵיקוֹת — **Remove yourself from doubts,**[17] וְאַל תַּרְבֶּה לְעַשֵּׂר אוֹמָדוֹת — **and do not be in the habit of tithing by estimation.**[18]

---

can uproot it easily (*Meorei Ohr,* citing the commentaries).

14. [In *Avos,* "and purchase a friend for yourself" is not attributed to Rabban Gamliel in this Mishnah, but appears earlier (in Mishnah 6) as a teaching of Yehoshua ben Perachyah, who also said there "make a teacher for yourself."] I.e., acquire a friend even if you must spend money to "buy" his friendship (*Rav* to *Avos* 1:6). Often, friendship is "bought" not with money, but by forbearance, and a willingness to yield to the habits and preferences of one's friend (*R' Yonah* on the Mishnah there).

Although having a teacher is also very important, as stated first, it does not say to *purchase* a teacher. A teacher may not be "purchased," because one is forbidden to accept payment for teaching the Oral Torah [see *Nedarim* 37a; *Shulchan Aruch, Yoreh Deah* 246:5] (*Rav* ibid.). [Teachers may take money, however, as compensation for the business opportunities they forgo to devote their time to teaching (see *Nedarim* ibid. and *Shulchan Aruch* ibid.).]

15. Do not study by yourself, relying on your intellectual prowess to arrive at the correct understanding of the Torah; rather, learn the authentic tradition from a teacher (*Rashi* and *Magen Avos* to *Avos* 1:6).

16. See above, 8 §3.

17. By having a teacher and a friend with whom to study. For solitary study leads to multiple doubts (*Binyan Yehoshua*).

Alternatively, this is a self-contained teaching, and means that one must distance himself not just from definite sin but even from *possible* sin (*Machzor Vitri* to *Avos* 1:16, second explanation).

18. The Torah commands that certain portions be separated from produce grown in Eretz Yisrael. Some of these are *maaser* (a tithe) — one-tenth of the produce — such as *maaser rishon* (the first tithe, given to the Levi), and *maaser sheni* (the second tithe, brought to Jerusalem to be eaten there). Produce that has not been tithed is forbidden as *tevel.* Now, a "tithe" must be *exactly* one-tenth. Separate more than a tenth as *maaser,* and the excess remains *tevel* (since it has neither the status of *maaser,* nor the status of the produce for which the *maaser* was separated, since one did not intend his separation to exempt that excess). Separate less than a tenth, and there remains a portion of the crop for which *maaser* was not taken. In either case, *tevel* will be mixed in with his *maaser* or with his ordinary produce. Thus, Rabban Gamliel warns against tithing "by estimation" (see *Binyan Yehoshua*).

Meiri (on the Mishnah) finds this explanation difficult. The Mishnah states that one should not be *in the habit of* tithing by estimation, which implies that it is fine to do so *occasionally.* But separating *maaser* by estimation even one time might create the problematic situation described above! Because of this difficulty, *Meiri* suggests that "tithing" here refers to the farmer separating *terumah* for the Kohen, a portion that has

‏**ב.** שִׁמְעוֹן בְּנוֹ אוֹמֵר: כָּל יָמַי גָּדַלְתִּי בֵּין הַחֲכָמִים[19] וְלֹא מָצָאתִי לַגּוּף‏
‏טוֹב מִשְּׁתִיקָה[20]. אִם לַחֲכָמִים יָפָה שְׁתִיקָה קַל וָחוֹמֶר לַטִּיפְּשִׁים[21]:‏

‏**ג.** לֹא חָכְמָה מֵבִיא דְבָרִים וְלֹא דְבָרִים מֵבִיא חָכְמָה[22] אֶלָּא מַעֲשֶׂה[23].‏
‏כָּל הַמַּרְבֶּה דְבָרִים מֵבִיא חֵטְא, שֶׁנֶּאֱמַר (משלי י, יט) ״בְּרֹב דְּבָרִים לֹא‏
‏יֶחְדַּל פָּשַׁע״, וְאוֹמֵר (שם יז, כח) ״גַּם אֱוִיל מַחֲרִישׁ חָכָם יֵחָשֵׁב״:‏

---

§2 The Baraisa cites and elaborates *Avos* 1:17 (with some variations):
שִׁמְעוֹן בְּנוֹ אוֹמֵר — Shimon his son says: ‏כָּל יָמַי גָּדַלְתִּי בֵּין הַחֲכָמִים וְלֹא‏
‏מָצָאתִי לַגּוּף טוֹב מִשְּׁתִיקָה‏ — All my days I grew up among the sages,[19] and I
found nothing better for a person than silence.[20] ‏אִם לַחֲכָמִים יָפָה שְׁתִיקָה‏
‏קַל וָחוֹמֶר לַטִּיפְּשִׁים‏ — If silence is good for scholars, how much more so for
fools![21]

§3 ‏לֹא חָכְמָה מֵבִיא דְבָרִים וְלֹא דְבָרִים מֵבִיא חָכְמָה‏ — Wisdom does not bring
one to words — and words do not bring one to wisdom[22] — ‏אֶלָּא‏
‏מַעֲשֶׂה‏ — but to deeds.[23] ‏כָּל הַמַּרְבֶּה דְבָרִים מֵבִיא חֵטְא‏ — Whoever talks
excessively brings sin, ‏שֶׁנֶּאֱמַר ״בְּרֹב דְּבָרִים לֹא יֶחְדַּל פָּשַׁע״‏ — as it is stated,
In an abundance of words, offense will not be lacking (*Proverbs* 10:19),
‏וְאוֹמֵר ״גַּם אֱוִיל מַחֲרִישׁ חָכָם יֵחָשֵׁב״‏ — and it says, *Even a fool will be considered wise if he is silent* (ibid. 17:28).

---

no fixed Biblical limit. Alternatively, it refers
to tithing one's income; see Artscroll *Yad
Avraham, Avos* 1:16 at length.

This last maxim is seemingly out of place
in the Mishnah and Baraisa of *Avos,* which
are concerned with moral conduct, not legal
rulings. The commentators explain that the
Mishnah's injunction not to tithe by estimation follows from its previous maxim: that
one should remove himself from doubt. The
reason one should not tithe by estimation is
that, as explained above, the practice gives
rise to doubts concerning the permissibility of the remaining produce or the portion
designated as tithes (*Rambam* on *Avos* ad
loc.; see *Rashi* and *R' Yonah* there for other
explanations).

19. [As the son of the *Nasi,* Rabban Shimon
ben Gamliel grew up in a house in which Torah scholars were a constant presence.] By
observing their actions, he was able to learn
the proper, Torah-based mode of conduct
(see *Machzor Vitri*).

20. I.e., of all the character traits that a person can acquire, none is as beneficial as the
trait of silence (*R' Yonah, Meiri* to the Mishnah there).

21. Avoiding needless speech is good for
the wise, who are usually careful about what
they say; all the more so is it good for fools,
who are not careful about what they say (*Yefeh Mareh, Yerushalmi Pesachim* 9:9).

22. R' Shimon advocated silence both for the
wise and for fools. He now anticipates the
objection of both: The wise man will say that
his wisdom compels him to speak. The fool
will say that perhaps through speaking he will
attain wisdom. R' Shimon rejects both objections: To the wise he says, "Wisdom does not
bring words." And to the fool he says, "Words
do not bring wisdom" (*Magen Avos*).

23. This is the conclusion of the *first* statement, which thus reads: "Wisdom does not
bring [to] words, but [to] deeds." The words
‏וְלֹא דְבָרִים מֵבִיא חָכְמָה‏ were inserted parenthetically (see *Magen Avos*).

﴾ פֶּרֶק כג ﴿

א. בֶּן זוֹמָא אוֹמֵר: אֵיזֶהוּ חָכָם, הַלּוֹמֵד מִכָּל אָדָם, שֶׁנֶּאֱמַר (תהלים
קיט, צט) "מִכָּל מְלַמְּדַי הִשְׂכַּלְתִּי"[1], אֵיזוֹ עָלוּב שֶׁבָּעֲלוּבִים,
זֶה שֶׁהוּא עָלוּב כְּמשֶׁה רַבֵּינוּ, שֶׁנֶּאֱמַר (במדבר יב, ג) "וְהָאִישׁ
משֶׁה עָנָו מְאֹד"[3]. אֵיזוֹ עָשִׁיר שֶׁבָּעֲשִׁירִים, זֶה שֶׁשָּׂמֵחַ בְּחֶלְקוֹ[4],
שֶׁנֶּאֱמַר (תהלים קכח, ב) "יְגִיעַ כַּפֶּיךָ כִּי תֹאכֵל אַשְׁרֶיךָ וְטוֹב לָךְ".

﴾ CHAPTER 23 ﴿

§1 The Baraisa cites *Avos* 4:1 (with variations):
בֶּן זוֹמָא אוֹמֵר — Ben Zoma says: אֵיזֶהוּ חָכָם הַלּוֹמֵד מִכָּל אָדָם — Who is wise? He who learns from every person, שֶׁנֶּאֱמַר "מִכָּל מְלַמְּדַי הִשְׂכַּלְתִּי" — as it is stated, *From all my teachers I grew wise* (Psalms 119:99).[1] אֵיזוֹ עָלוּב זֶה שֶׁהוּא שֶׁבָּעֲלוּבִים — Who is the most unoffendable of the unoffendable?[2] עָלוּב כְּמשֶׁה רַבֵּינוּ — This is he who is as unoffendable as Moses our Teacher, שֶׁנֶּאֱמַר "וְהָאִישׁ משֶׁה עָנָו מְאֹד" — as it is stated: *Now, the man Moses was exceedingly humble, more than any person on the face of the earth!* (Numbers 12:3), so he did not take offense at what Miriam and Aaron had said about him.[3] אֵיזוֹ עָשִׁיר שֶׁבָּעֲשִׁירִים זֶה שֶׁשָּׂמֵחַ — Who is the richest of the rich? בְּחֶלְקוֹ — This is he who is happy with his lot,[4] שֶׁנֶּאֱמַר "יְגִיעַ כַּפֶּיךָ כִּי תֹאכֵל אַשְׁרֶיךָ וְטוֹב לָךְ" — as it is stated, *When you eat the labor of your hands, you are praiseworthy and all is well with you* (Psalms 128:2), which is

---

1. Learning from "every person" means even from those equal to him (*Rashi* to the Mishnah, cited in *Binyan Yehoshua*) and even from those lesser than he (*Kikar LaAden*) and even from someone who knows only one thing (see *R' Yonah* ibid.). *Rambam* writes: "Accept truth from whoever says it" (Preface to *Shemoneh Perakim*).

It can be said that for this reason a Torah scholar is referred to as a תַּלְמִיד חָכָם (which can be rendered: a student-sage), for if a person learns from every person, he becomes a sage (see *Hagahos Regel Yesharah* to *Avos DeRabbi Nassan*).

2. *Magen Avos,* second explanation.

3. One who is exceedingly humble is one who will not easily be offended (see *Rashi* on that verse). Possibly, the connection between Ben Zoma's previous teaching about learning from everyone and this one about

humility is that they are interrelated. It requires great humility for one to be willing to learn from every person (see *Tosefes Ohr,* based on *Meiri* and *Chida*).

4. *Magen Avos* [*Rashbatz*] (to the Mishnah there) explains: True wealth is not measured by the value of one's possessions, but rather by what one feels he is *lacking*: the less one lacks, the wealthier he is. Thus, one who feels he has everything he needs and lacks for nothing is truly wealthy. Conversely, one who is dissatisfied with his lot and constantly seeks to accumulate more riches is really a pauper, despite his vast fortune, since he cannot satisfy his desires. Someone who covets money can never have enough, so he can never be truly rich. As the Sages observed (see *Koheles Rabbah* 1 §13): "One who has 100 wants 200, and one who has 200 wants 400."

אֵיזֶו גִּבּוֹר שֶׁבַּגִּבּוֹרִים, זֶהוּ שֶׁכּוֹבֵשׁ אֶת יִצְרוֹ, שֶׁנֶּאֱמַר (משלי טז, לב) "טוֹב
אֶרֶךְ אַפַּיִם מִגִּבּוֹר וּמשֵׁל בְּרוּחוֹ מִלֹּכֵד עִיר". וְכָל הַכּוֹבֵשׁ אֶת יִצְרוֹ מַעֲלִין
עָלָיו כְּאִילוּ כָּבַשׁ עִיר מְלֵאָה גִּבּוֹרִים, שֶׁנֶּאֱמַר (שם כא, כב) "עִיר גִּבֹּרִים עָלָה
חָכָם"[6], וְאֵין גִּבֹּרִים אֶלָּא גִּבּוֹרֵי תוֹרָה[7], שֶׁנֶּאֱמַר (תהלים קג, כ) "גִּבֹּרֵי כֹחַ עֹשֵׂי

---

interpreted to mean: *You are praiseworthy — in this world; and all is well with you* — in the World to Come.[5] אֵיזֶו גִּבּוֹר שֶׁבַּגִּבּוֹרִים — **Who is the strongest of the strong?** זֶהוּ שֶׁכּוֹבֵשׁ אֶת יִצְרוֹ — **This is he who subdues his evil inclination,** שֶׁנֶּאֱמַר "טוֹב אֶרֶךְ אַפַּיִם מִגִּבּוֹר וּמשֵׁל בְּרוּחוֹ מִלֹּכֵד עִיר" — **as it is stated,** *He who is slow to anger is better than a strong man, and a master of his passions [is better] than a conqueror of a city* (Proverbs 16:32). וְכָל **הַכּוֹבֵשׁ אֶת יִצְרוֹ מַעֲלִין עָלָיו כְּאִילוּ כָּבַשׁ עִיר מְלֵאָה גִּבּוֹרִים — And anyone who subdues his personal inclination is considered** by Scripture **as if he conquered a city full of strong men,** שֶׁנֶּאֱמַר "עִיר גִּבֹּרִים עָלָה חָכָם" — **as it is stated,** *The wise one went up to the city of the strong* and brought down the strength in which it trusted (ibid. 21:22).[6] וְאֵין גִּבֹּרִים אֶלָּא גִּבּוֹרֵי תוֹרָה — **And "the strong" are none other than Torah warriors,**[7] שֶׁנֶּאֱמַר "גִּבֹּרֵי כֹחַ עֹשֵׂי

---

5. Since one who is satisfied with the share that God has granted him is self-reliant, he is spared the shame and embarrassment *in this world* that comes from having to rely on the goodwill of others. And since he does not crave excessive wealth, he is not tempted to gain money dishonestly, ensuring him a share in the World to Come (*Rashi* on the Mishnah there; *Machzor Vitri*; see *Rabbeinu Bachya* there).

6. [The "city of the strong" represents the fortress of the evil inclination; see *Malbim* ad loc.]

The evil inclination seems strong to those who regularly battle against it, but weak to those who yield to it. *Binyan Yehoshua* cites the Gemara's depiction of this phenomenon (*Succah* 52a): In the Future Era, when God will slaughter the evil inclination before the righteous and the wicked, to the righteous it will seem like a mountain; to the wicked like a strand of hair. Both will weep. The righteous will weep, wondering how they were able to overcome this high mountain. And the wicked will weep, wondering how they were unable to overcome this thin strand of hair. The commentators there explain: The righteous overcome their evil inclination

constantly and, as the Gemara there teaches later, the defeated evil inclination renews its attacks constantly with increased strength and vigor. Thus, their evil inclination develops into a formidable force that they nonetheless overcome. But the wicked succumb to the slightest temptation, and so their evil inclination never develops beyond being a slight urge, to which they yield nonetheless (*Rif* and *Geon Yaakov* to *Ein Yaakov*; *Chasam Sofer*, *Sfas Emes*).

7. This refers back to the original statement — "Who is the strongest of the strong?" "The strong" are the Torah scholars (as the Baraisa will demonstrate). The Baraisa now explains that when it speaks of someone "who subdues his inclination," it refers not to an unlearned person, but to a Torah scholar, for an unlearned person cannot be truly pious (see *Avos* 2:5). Subduing one's evil inclination requires both great strength of character *and* strength in Torah learning. Only one who is stronger than "the strong" — who is stronger than Torah scholars in that he brings strength of character to the fight as well, can subdue his evil inclination (see *Magen Avos* [though his reading here is: וְאֵין "גִּבֹּרֵי" גִּבּוֹרֵי אֶלָּא גִּבּוֹרֵי תוֹרָה]).

דְּבָרוֹ"[8]. וְיֵשׁ אוֹמְרִים: מַלְאֲכֵי הַשָּׁרֵת, שֶׁנֶּאֱמַר (שם) "בָּרְכוּ ה' מַלְאָכָיו
גִּבֹּרֵי כֹחַ וְגוֹ'[9]" וְיֵשׁ אוֹמְרִים: מִי שֶׁעוֹשֶׂה שׂוֹנֵא אוֹהֲבוֹ[10]:

ב. (רַבִּי נְהוֹרַאי אוֹמֵר: הֱוֵי גוֹלֶה לִמְקוֹם תּוֹרָה וְכוּ',) הוּא הָיָה
אוֹמֵר[12]: אַל תְּהִי בָז לְכָל אָדָם[13] (וְאַל תְּהִי מַפְלִיג לְכָל דָּבָר[14]),
שֶׁנֶּאֱמַר (משלי יג, יג) "בָּז לְדָבָר יֵחָבֶל לוֹ וִירֵא מִצְוָה הוּא יְשֻׁלָּם[15]",

"דְּבָרוֹ" — as it is stated, Bless HASHEM, O His angels; the strong warriors who do His bidding (Psalms 103:20).[8] וְיֵשׁ אוֹמְרִים מַלְאֲכֵי הַשָּׁרֵת — And some say that "the strong" who are meant are the ministering angels, שֶׁנֶּאֱמַר "בָּרְכוּ ה' — as it is stated in that very verse, Bless HASHEM, O "His angels," the strong warriors., etc.[9] וְיֵשׁ אוֹמְרִים מִי שֶׁעוֹשֶׂה שׂוֹנֵא אוֹהֲבוֹ — But some say that the reference is to the one who makes his enemy into his friend.[10]

§2 The Baraisa now turns to teachings of R' Nehorai:

רַבִּי נְהוֹרַאי אוֹמֵר — R' Nehorai says: הֱוֵי גוֹלֶה לִמְקוֹם תּוֹרָה וְכוּ' — Exile yourself to a place of Torah, etc., and do not assume it will come after you, [or] that your colleagues will cause it to remain with you; and do not rely on your own understanding (Proverbs 3:5).[11]

The Baraisa continues:

הוּא הָיָה אוֹמֵר — He used to say:[12] אַל תְּהִי בָז לְכָל אָדָם — Do not be disdainful of any person,[13] וְאַל תְּהִי מַפְלִיג לְכָל דָּבָר — and do not dismiss anything as unlikely,[14] שֶׁנֶּאֱמַר "בָּז לְדָבָר יֵחָבֶל לוֹ וִירֵא מִצְוָה הוּא יְשֻׁלָּם" — as

8. The Baraisa cites this verse to describe the one who has both strength of character and strength in Torah learning (see preceding note). The strong warriors are those who are strong in Torah learning; those who do His bidding are those who subdue their evil inclinations (Magen Avos).

9. That is, one who subdues his evil inclination is stronger even than the ministering angels (Magen Avos).

10. It takes great inner strength for a person to abandon his negative feelings toward his enemy and cultivate his friendship. People who do this are "the strong." But one who subdues his evil inclination is even stronger than they; he is "the strongest of the strong" (Magen Avos, first approach). Alternatively, "the one who makes his enemy into his friend" refers to one who transforms his evil inclination into his ally for good (see above, 16 §3 with note 36 there). And "the some say" of the Baraisa

here mean that the "strongest of the strong" is not the one who simply subdues his evil inclination, but rather the one who goes so far as to transform it into his friend (Magen Avos, second approach; Kikar LaAden).

11. [This appears in Avos 4:14.] The availability of Torah study and not physical comforts should determine where a person lives. If one cannot find a suitable Torah teacher in his hometown, he should uproot himself and move to where he can find one (Rav, Magen Avos [Rashbatz] ibid.).

12. [This teaching appears in Avos 4:3, where "he used to say" refers to Ben Azzai, mentioned in Mishnah 2 there. Ahavas Chesed here writes that our Baraisa means the same.]

13. Do not belittle anyone, even someone presently incapable of affecting you in any way. Rather, treat everyone with respect (Rav, Magen Avos [Rashbatz] to Avos there).

14. Do not disregard any legitimate warning

הוּא הָיָה אוֹמֵר: הַלּוֹמֵד תּוֹרָה בְּיַלְדוּתוֹ לָמָה הוּא דּוֹמֶה,לְעֶגְלָה
שֶׁבְּכָשׁוּהָ כְּשֶׁהִיא קְטַנָּה, שֶׁנֶּאֱמַר (הושע י, יא) "וְאֶפְרֵיִם עֶגְלָה מְלֻמָּדָה
אֹהַבְתִּי לָדוּשׁ". וְהַלּוֹמֵד תּוֹרָה בְּזִקְנוּתוֹ דּוֹמֶה לְפָרָה שֶׁלֹּא כְּבָשׁוּהָ אֶלָּא
בְּזִקְנוּתָהּ, שֶׁנֶּאֱמַר (שם ד, טז) "כִּי כְּפָרָה סֹרֵרָה סָרַר יִשְׂרָאֵל". הוּא הָיָה
אוֹמֵר: הַלּוֹמֵד תּוֹרָה בְּיַלְדוּתוֹ דּוֹמֶה לְאִשָּׁה שֶׁהִיא לָשָׁה בְּחַמִּין, וְהַלּוֹמֵד
תּוֹרָה בְּזִקְנוּתוֹ לָמָה הוּא דּוֹמֶה, לְאִשָּׁה שֶׁהִיא לָשָׁה בְּצוֹנֵן:

---

it is stated, *He who disdains something will be harmed [by it], but he who reveres a commandment will be rewarded* (ibid. 13:13).[15]

The Baraisa continues:

הוּא הָיָה אוֹמֵר — **He used to say:** הַלּוֹמֵד תּוֹרָה בְּיַלְדוּתוֹ לָמָה הוּא דּוֹמֶה — **One who studies Torah in his youth, to what is he compared?** לְעֶגְלָה שֶׁבְּכָשׁוּהָ — **To a calf that was tamed when it was small,** שֶׁנֶּאֱמַר "וְאֶפְרֵיִם כְּשֶׁהִיא קְטַנָּה — as it is stated, *Ephraim is a trained calf who loves to thresh* (Hosea 10:11).[16] וְהַלּוֹמֵד תּוֹרָה בְּזִקְנוּתוֹ דּוֹמֶה לְפָרָה שֶׁלֹּא — **But one who studies Torah in his old age is like a cow** בְּכָשׁוּהָ אֶלָּא בְּזִקְנוּתָהּ — **that was not tamed until its adulthood,** שֶׁנֶּאֱמַר "כִּי כְּפָרָה סֹרֵרָה סָרַר יִשְׂרָאֵל" — as it is stated, *For Israel has strayed like a wayward cow* (ibid. 4:16).[17]

The Baraisa adds several other comparisons on this point:

הוּא הָיָה אוֹמֵר — **He used to say:** הַלּוֹמֵד תּוֹרָה בְּיַלְדוּתוֹ דּוֹמֶה לְאִשָּׁה שֶׁהִיא לָשָׁה בְּחַמִּין — **One who studies Torah in his youth is like a woman who kneads** her dough with hot water. וְהַלּוֹמֵד תּוֹרָה בְּזִקְנוּתוֹ לָמָה הוּא דּוֹמֶה לְאִשָּׁה שֶׁהִיא לָשָׁה בְּצוֹנֵן — **But one who studies Torah in his old age is like a woman who kneads** her dough with cold water.[18]

---

of danger; rather, take appropriate precautions to protect yourself and those under your care (*Rav, Magen Avos* [*Rashbatz*] ibid.). The Mishnah there concludes: "For there is no person who does not have [his] hour, and no thing that does not have [its] place."

15. *Magen Avos* writes that this verse relates to R' Nehorai's opening statement as well: "Exile yourself to a place of Torah." If you disdain this possibility, going elsewhere to study, in the end you will be harmed by it, for in the end you will remain bereft of all that is good. But if you "revere the commandments" and make the pursuit of Torah study your primary consideration, lest you remain ignorant and violate the commandments, you will be amply rewarded.

16. When a cow is trained to bear a yoke when it is yet a young calf, it will get used to the yoke and eventually come to enjoy the threshing process. Similarly, a person who studied Torah when he was young will not diverge from it in his old age, for the habits of a lifetime become second nature (*Binyan Yehoshua*).

17. It rebels against the yoke (see *Binyan Yehoshua*).

Magen Avos connects this teaching to the preceding one: Do not say that you will — eventually — exile yourself to a place of Torah, but only when you are older, not when you are still young: For the yoke of Torah will be far more easily borne if you are trained in it from your youth.

18. Hot water helps the dough rise more quickly. A young person grasps new concepts more quickly; an old person requires

ג. רַבִּי אֱלִיעֶזֶר בֶּן יַעֲקֹב אוֹמֵר:[19] הַלּוֹמֵד תּוֹרָה בְּיַלְדוּתוֹ דּוֹמֶה לִכְתָב שֶׁנִּכְתַּב עַל נְיָיר חָדָשׁ[20], וְהַלּוֹמֵד תּוֹרָה בְּזִקְנוּתוֹ דּוֹמֶה לִכְתָב שֶׁנִּכְתַּב עַל נְיָיר יָשָׁן[21]:

ד. רַבָּן שִׁמְעוֹן בֶּן גַּמְלִיאֵל מוֹסִיף עַל דְּבָרָיו: הַלּוֹמֵד תּוֹרָה בְּיַלְדוּתוֹ דּוֹמֶה לְבָחוּר שֶׁנָּשָׂא בְתוּלָה, שֶׁהִיא הוֹגֶנֶת לוֹ וְהוּא הָגוּן לָהּ וְהִיא מִתְנַפֶּלֶת עָלָיו וְהוּא מִתְנַפֵּל עָלֶיהָ[22], הַלּוֹמֵד תּוֹרָה בְּזִקְנוּתוֹ לְמָה הוּא דּוֹמֶה, לְזָקֵן שֶׁנָּשָׂא בְתוּלָה, הִיא הוֹגֶנֶת לוֹ וְהוּא אֵינוֹ הָגוּן לָהּ[23]

---

§3 The Baraisa now cites the sayings of other Sages on this matter: הַלּוֹמֵד תּוֹרָה רַבִּי אֱלִיעֶזֶר בֶּן יַעֲקֹב אוֹמֵר — R' Eliezer ben Yaakov says:[19] בְּיַלְדוּתוֹ דּוֹמֶה לִכְתָב שֶׁנִּכְתַּב עַל נְיָיר חָדָשׁ — One who studies Torah in his youth is comparable to script written on new paper.[20] וְהַלּוֹמֵד תּוֹרָה בְּזִקְנוּתוֹ דּוֹמֶה לִכְתָב שֶׁנִּכְתַּב עַל נְיָיר יָשָׁן — And one who studies Torah in his old age is comparable to script written on old paper.[21]

§4 The Baraisa continues this theme: רַבָּן שִׁמְעוֹן בֶּן גַּמְלִיאֵל מוֹסִיף עַל דְּבָרָיו — Rabban Shimon ben Gamliel expands on his words: הַלּוֹמֵד תּוֹרָה בְּיַלְדוּתוֹ דּוֹמֶה לְבָחוּר שֶׁנָּשָׂא בְתוּלָה — One who studies Torah in his youth is like a young man who marries a young woman, שֶׁהִיא הוֹגֶנֶת לוֹ וְהוּא הָגוּן לָהּ — in which case she is suitable for him and he is suitable for her, וְהִיא מִתְנַפֶּלֶת עָלָיו וְהוּא מִתְנַפֵּל עָלֶיהָ — for she is desirous of him and he is desirous of her.[22] הַלּוֹמֵד תּוֹרָה בְּזִקְנוּתוֹ לְמָה הוּא דּוֹמֶה — But one who studies Torah in his old age, to what is he compared? לְזָקֵן שֶׁנָּשָׂא בְתוּלָה — To an old man who marries a young woman. הִיא הוֹגֶנֶת לוֹ וְהוּא אֵינוֹ הָגוּן לָהּ — She is suitable for him but he is not suitable

---

more time, like a dough kneaded in cold water (*Magen Avos*).

19. In *Avos* 4:20, a similar teaching is recorded in the name of Elisha ben Avuyah; see also below, 24 §4.

20. Ink written on fresh paper does not fade. So, too, material studied in one's youth will not be forgotten (*Rav*). Fresh paper has two advantages: It is bright, allowing even the finest line to show up clearly; and it is smooth, allowing the ink to bond securely. A young student possesses similar traits: He easily comprehends intricate subjects and he remembers his studies (*Tiferes Yisrael* §97).

21. *Avos* 4:20 has "erased" paper instead of "old" paper, but according to *Meiri*, the two terms refer to the same thing (cf. *Tiferes*

Yisrael §98 and *Lev Avos*, cited in *Midrash Shmuel*).

One who begins his studies when he is already advanced in years (*Rashi* and *Machzor Vitri* to *Avos* ad loc.) is prone to readily forget what he learns (*Rashi; Rambam Commentary; R' Yonah*). An elder's mind is cluttered with much worldly trivia that must be erased in order to make room for the new information. Since this process of erasing is imperfect, the new knowledge does not last (*Tos. Yom Tov* ad loc., citing *Midrash Shmuel*; this idea is developed further by *Magen Avos* [*Rashbatz*] ad loc.).

22. So too the youthful scholar is desirous of the Torah and the Torah is "desirous" of him, ensuring a strong, enduring bond.

הִיא מִתְנַפֶּלֶת עָלָיו וְהוּא מִתְרַחֵק מִמֶּנָּה[24], שֶׁנֶּאֱמַר (תהלים קכז, ד)
"כְּחִצִּים בְּיַד גִּבּוֹר כֵּן בְּנֵי הַנְּעוּרִים[25]", וּכְתִיב בַּתְרֵיהּ (שם פסוק ה)
"אַשְׁרֵי הַגֶּבֶר אֲשֶׁר מִלֵּא אֶת אַשְׁפָּתוֹ מֵהֶם[26]". שׁוֹנֶה וּמְשַׁכֵּחַ דּוֹמֶה
לְאִשָּׁה שֶׁיּוֹלֶדֶת בָּנִים וְקוֹבֶרֶת, שֶׁנֶּאֱמַר (הושע ט, יב) "כִּי אִם יְגַדְּלוּ אֶת
בְּנֵיהֶם וְשִׁכַּלְתִּים מֵאָדָם", אַל תִּקְרֵי "וְשִׁכַּלְתִּים" אֶלָּא "וְשִׁכַּחְתִּים",
(רַבִּי שִׁמְעוֹן בֶּן אֶלְעָזָר אוֹמֵר: הַלּוֹמֵד תּוֹרָה בְּיַלְדוּתוֹ דּוֹמֶה לְרוֹפֵא
שֶׁהֵבִיאוּ לְפָנָיו מַכָּה וְיֵשׁ לוֹ אִיזְמֵל לַחְתּוֹךְ וְסַמָּנֵי רְפוּאוֹת לְרַפְּאוֹת,

---

for her,[23]　הִיא מִתְנַפֶּלֶת עָלָיו וְהוּא מִתְרַחֵק מִמֶּנָּה — for she is desirous of
him, but he distances himself from her.[24]　שֶׁנֶּאֱמַר "כְּחִצִּים בְּיַד גִּבּוֹר כֵּן בְּנֵי
הַנְּעוּרִים" — It is as it is stated, *Like arrows in the hand of a warrior, so are
the children of youth* (Psalms 127:4).[25]　וּכְתִיב בַּתְרֵיהּ "אַשְׁרֵי הַגֶּבֶר אֲשֶׁר
מִלֵּא אֶת אַשְׁפָּתוֹ מֵהֶם" — And it is written directly afterward, *Praiseworthy is
the man who fills his quiver with them* (ibid. v. 5).[26]　שׁוֹנֶה וּמְשַׁכֵּחַ דּוֹמֶה
לְאִשָּׁה שֶׁיּוֹלֶדֶת בָּנִים וְקוֹבֶרֶת — And he who studies only when he is old studies and forgets and is like a woman who gives birth to children and buries
them,[27]　שֶׁנֶּאֱמַר "כִּי אִם יְגַדְּלוּ אֶת בְּנֵיהֶם וְשִׁכַּלְתִּים מֵאָדָם" — as it is stated,
For even if they rear their children I will bereave them ("v'shikaltim")
before manhood (Hosea 9:12).　אַל תִּקְרֵי "וְשִׁכַּלְתִּים" אֶלָּא "וְשִׁכַּחְתִּים" —
And we expound: **Do not read** this as *v'shikaltim* (I will bereave them);
rather, read it as though it were written: *v'shikachtim* (I will cause them
to forget).

The Baraisa continues this theme:

הַלּוֹמֵד תּוֹרָה　רַבִּי שִׁמְעוֹן בֶּן אֶלְעָזָר אוֹמֵר — R' Shimon ben Elazar says:
בְּיַלְדוּתוֹ דּוֹמֶה לְרוֹפֵא שֶׁהֵבִיאוּ לְפָנָיו מַכָּה — One who studies Torah in his youth
is like a doctor before whom a wound is brought,　וְיֵשׁ לוֹ אִיזְמֵל לַחְתּוֹךְ וְסַמָּנֵי
רְפוּאוֹת לְרַפְּאוֹת — and he has the scalpel with which to cut away the injured
tissue, as well as the medicinal herbs with which to heal the wound afterward.

---

23. She is capable of providing his needs,
but he cannot provide hers.

24. As he is too old to be desirous of such
matters. Similarly, one who "marries"
Torah study when he is old is likely to be
disinterested, even though the Torah always
remains available to and "desirous of" him
(*Magen Avos*).

25. A warrior's arrows are sharp and he is
able to shoot them with great force; this
combination causes them to penetrate deep
into their targets. So are "the children of
youth" — students who study Torah in their

youth — for their studies penetrate quickly
and deeply into the mind (see *Magen Avos*
and *Ben Avraham*).

26. Praiseworthy is the one who raises up
many young students of Torah (*Binyan
Yehoshua*).

27. Explanation follows *Ben Avraham*.
This is a continuation of Rabban Shimon
ben Gamliel's expansion on R' Eliezer ben
Yaakov (*Ben Avraham*; cf. *Magen Avos*, who
writes that these are the words of R' Eliezer
ben Yaakov himself).

הַלּוֹמֵד תּוֹרָה בְּזִקְנוּתוֹ דּוֹמֶה לְרוֹפֵא שֶׁהֵבִיאוּ לְפָנָיו מַכָּה וְיֵשׁ לוֹ אִיזְמֵל
לַחְתּוֹךְ וְאֵין לוֹ סַמָּנִין לְרַפְּאוֹת.28 אַף כָּךְ דִּבְרֵי תוֹרָה יִהְיוּ) מְצוּיָּינִין לְךָ
זֶה מִזֶּה29 וְיִהְיוּ מְצוּיָּינִין לְךָ זֶה בְּצַד זֶה,30 שֶׁנֶּאֱמַר (משלי ז, ג) ״קָשְׁרֵם עַל
אֶצְבְּעוֹתֶיךָ כָּתְבֵם עַל לוּחַ לִבֶּךָ״, וְאוֹמֵר (שם ו, כא) ״קָשְׁרֵם עַל לִבְּךָ תָמִיד
עָנְדֵם עַל גַּרְגְּרֹתֶךָ״:31

הַלּוֹמֵד תּוֹרָה בְּזִקְנוּתוֹ דּוֹמֶה לְרוֹפֵא שֶׁהֵבִיאוּ לְפָנָיו מַכָּה — One who studies Torah
in his old age is like a doctor before whom an injury is brought, וְיֵשׁ לוֹ
אִיזְמֵל לַחְתּוֹךְ וְאֵין לוֹ סַמָּנִין לְרַפְּאוֹת — and he has the scalpel with which to cut
away the injured tissue, but not the medicinal herbs with which to heal the
wound afterward.[28]

Having contrasted Torah that is studied and retained with that which is not,
the Baraisa concludes:

אַף כָּךְ דִּבְרֵי תוֹרָה יִהְיוּ מְצוּיָּינִין לְךָ זֶה מִזֶּה וְיִהְיוּ מְצוּיָּינִין לְךָ זֶה בְּצַד זֶה — So too,
you should have Torah concepts clearly marked, this teaching comes from
this sage;[29] and you should have them clearly marked, this teaching next to
this one.[30] שֶׁנֶּאֱמַר ״קָשְׁרֵם עַל אֶצְבְּעוֹתֶיךָ כָּתְבֵם עַל לוּחַ לִבֶּךָ״ — For it is stated
regarding the words of Torah, *Bind them on your fingers, inscribe them on*
the tablet of your heart (Proverbs 7:3). וְאוֹמֵר ״קָשְׁרֵם עַל לִבְּךָ תָמִיד עָנְדֵם עַל
גַּרְגְּרֹתֶךָ״ — and it states, *Tie them to your heart always; entwine them upon*
your neck (ibid. 6:21).[31]

---

28. The scalpel represents the faculty of
analysis. The medicinal herbs represent the
memory to make the analytical studies last.
The mature mind of an older person may
have the desire to learn and the analytical
skill of the younger mind, but he does not
have the "medicinal herbs" — the memory
— to make his learning permanent (*Magen
Avos*; see *Binyan Yehoshua*).

29. I.e., make a mnemonic for which sage
holds which opinion (*Mefaresh,* based on
Rashi to *Eruvin* 54b).

30. I.e., make a mnemonic for which case or
source, in a sequence of cases or sources,
follows the other (ibid.).

31. *Ben Avraham* writes that this last section
of the Baraisa is meant to encourage those
who have not studied until they are old and
forgetful: Do not despair that it is now difficult to remember what you study. Though

the greater effectiveness of youthful study is
an opportunity lost, with review and mne-
monics, you can still retain Torah knowledge, and whether one does much or a little,
God accepts it, provided that his intent is for
the sake of Heaven. The two verses cited last
by the Baraisa speak of placing the words
of Torah on your heart — the first one cited
does not mention "always," whereas the
second does. For the first one cited speaks
of one who has not studied until he is old,
whereas the second speaks of one who has
studied since his youth — always. And because this section of the Baraisa is intended
primarily as an encouragement to the older
student, the Baraisa cites the verse that refers to him first, even though it appears later
in the Book of *Proverbs* than the verse that
refers to the one who has studied always.
[For more on the importance of Torah study
in one's old age, see below, 24 §6.]

﴾ פֶּרֶק כד ﴿

א. אֱלִישָׁע¹ בֶּן אֲבוּיָה אוֹמֵר: אָדָם שֶׁיֵּשׁ בּוֹ מַעֲשִׂים טוֹבִים וְלָמַד תּוֹרָה הַרְבֵּה לְמָה הוּא דוֹמֶה, לְאָדָם שֶׁבּוֹנֶה אֲבָנִים מִלְּמַטָּה וְאַחַר כָּךְ לְבֵנִים³, אֲפִילוּ בָּאִים מַיִם הַרְבֵּה וְעוֹמְדִין בְּצִידָן אֵין מָחִין אוֹתָן מִמְּקוֹמָן:

﴾ CHAPTER 24 ﴿

§1 The Baraisa presents a series of teachings from Elisha ben Avuyah, most of them relating to Torah study and its preservation. The first four are analogies illustrating the proper relationship between Torah scholarship and mitzvah observance:[1]

אֱלִישָׁע בֶּן אֲבוּיָה אוֹמֵר — Elisha ben Avuyah says: אָדָם שֶׁיֵּשׁ בּוֹ מַעֲשִׂים טוֹבִים וְלָמַד תּוֹרָה הַרְבֵּה לְמָה הוּא דוֹמֶה — A person who has many[2] good deeds to his credit and has studied much Torah — to what is he comparable? לְאָדָם שֶׁבּוֹנֶה אֲבָנִים מִלְּמַטָּה וְאַחַר כָּךְ לְבֵנִים — To a person who, when erecting a structure, **builds in the stones** first at the base, **and afterward** adds the bricks on top.[3] אֲפִילוּ בָּאִים מַיִם הַרְבֵּה וְעוֹמְדִין בְּצִידָן — **Even if a great deal of water comes and stands next to [the stones]** at ground level, אֵין מָחִין אוֹתָן מִמְּקוֹמָן — **it will not dissolve them** and cause them to slide **from their place.**[4] Similarly, a person who builds for himself a strong foundation of good deeds[5] will not be overcome by the floodwaters of sinful ambitions and desires.[6]

---

1. Elisha ben Avuyah was one of four sages who entered the sublime "Orchard" [פַּרְדֵּס] (*Chagigah* 14b ff.); that is, he delved into spiritual mysteries that only the most saintly of Torah sages can contemplate. Unfortunately, this experience altered his mental state and caused him to stray from the path of Torah observance, and for this reason he is known throughout the Talmud as אַחֵר, *Acher* [lit., *Other*] (see ibid.). This Baraisa is one of the rare instances where he is called by his name.

Ben Avraham suggests that Elisha ben Avuyah presented these teachings after his defection, and after he had puzzled over the question of why his Torah scholarship had not protected him from spiritual ruin. These musings brought him to the ideas conveyed by the four upcoming analogies — ideas pointing to flaws in his spiritual makeup that made him unable to benefit from the Torah's protection. After reaching this conclusion,

he offered the fruits of his introspection to later generations (see below, note 14).

[The teachings in §5 below seem to be in this vein as well; see *Maharsha* to *Chagigah* 15a ד"ה שאל אחר.]

2. *Mefaresh.*

3. Stones are much stronger than bricks. According to *Hagahos Yaavetz*, the reference is to bricks that have not been kiln-fired, known as adobe bricks (cf. *Ahavas Chesed*).

4. Standing water permeates bricks and erodes them, but not stones (*Ahavas Chesed*). Thus, a structure with a stone base is an enduring one.

5. Including the development of fine character traits, such as humility, forbearance, and neighborly love (*Binyan Yehoshua*), as well as the active observance of such mitzvos as charity, kindness, Sabbath observance, reading the *Shema,* and prayer (*Kisei Rachamim*).

6. *Kisei Rachamim,* based on *Psalms* 124:5

ב. וְאָדָם שֶׁאֵין בּוֹ מַעֲשִׂים טוֹבִים וְלָמַד תּוֹרָה לְמָה הוּא דּוֹמֶה, לְאָדָם
שֶׁבּוֹנֶה לְבֵנִים תְּחִלָּה וְאַחַר כָּךְ אֲבָנִים, אֲפִילוּ בָּאִים מַיִם קִימְעָא
מִיָּד הוֹפְכִין אוֹתָן:

ג. הוּא הָיָה אוֹמֵר: אָדָם שֶׁיֵּשׁ בּוֹ מַעֲשִׂים טוֹבִים וְלָמַד תּוֹרָה הַרְבֵּה
לְמָה הוּא דּוֹמֶה, לְסִיד שָׁטוּחַ עַל גַּבֵּי לְבֵנִים, אֲפִילוּ יוֹרְדִין עָלָיו
גְּשָׁמִים אֵין מְזִיזִין אוֹתוֹ מִמְּקוֹמוֹ. אָדָם שֶׁאֵין בּוֹ מַעֲשִׂים טוֹבִים וְלָמַד
תּוֹרָה הַרְבֵּה דּוֹמֶה לְסִיד שֶׁנִּיטוֹחַ עַל גַּבֵּי לְבֵנִים, אֲפִילוּ יוֹרְדִין עָלָיו
מִיעוּט גְּשָׁמִים מִיָּד נִימוֹק וְנוֹפֵל:[8]

---

§2 The Baraisa presents the other side of this first analogy:
וְאָדָם שֶׁאֵין בּוֹ מַעֲשִׂים טוֹבִים וְלָמַד תּוֹרָה לְמָה הוּא דּוֹמֶה — **But a person who
does not have many**[7] **good deeds to his credit but has studied Torah — to
what is he comparable?**   **To a** — לְאָדָם שֶׁבּוֹנֶה לְבֵנִים תְּחִלָּה וְאַחַר כָּךְ אֲבָנִים **—
person who, when erecting a structure, lays the bricks first at the base, and
afterward** adds **the stones on top.**   אֲפִילוּ בָּאִים מַיִם קִימְעָא מִיָּד הוֹפְכִין אוֹתָן —
**Even if a small amount of water comes by and stands near the ground-level
bricks, it will immediately dissolve and overturn them.**

§3 The second analogy:
אָדָם שֶׁיֵּשׁ בּוֹ מַעֲשִׂים טוֹבִים וְלָמַד תּוֹרָה   **He used to say:** הוּא הָיָה אוֹמֵר —
הַרְבֵּה לְמָה הוּא דּוֹמֶה — **A person who has many good deeds to his credit and
has studied much Torah — to what is he comparable?** לְסִיד שָׁטוּחַ עַל גַּבֵּי
לְבֵנִים — **To lime plastered on bricks.**   אֲפִילוּ יוֹרְדִין עָלָיו גְּשָׁמִים אֵין מְזִיזִין אוֹתוֹ
מִמְּקוֹמוֹ — **Even if many rains descend upon it, they will not move it from its
place.** אָדָם שֶׁאֵין בּוֹ מַעֲשִׂים טוֹבִים וְלָמַד תּוֹרָה הַרְבֵּה — **By** contrast, **a person
who does not have many good deeds to his credit but has studied much
Torah** דּוֹמֶה לְסִיד שֶׁנִּיטוֹחַ עַל גַּבֵּי לְבֵנִים — **is comparable to lime that has
dripped onto bricks.** אֲפִילוּ יוֹרְדִין עָלָיו מִיעוּט גְּשָׁמִים מִיָּד נִימוֹק וְנוֹפֵל — **Even if
a little rain descends upon it, it will immediately dissolve and fall.**[8]

---

and *Sotah* 21a. According to *Binyan Yehoshua*, the intention is that a strong foundation of good deeds will preserve one's
Torah scholarship.

7. *Mefaresh.*

8. [The rain will wash away both the lime and
the bricks.] The first case speaks of lime that
is plastered properly [שָׁטוּחַ] onto the bricks.
This creates a proper and lasting seal. The
second case speaks of lime that has simply
dripped [שֶׁנִּיטוֹחַ] onto the bricks; the lime
will simply dissolve in the rain, leaving the

bricks exposed to damage (*Ahavas Chesed;
Ben Avraham*, first explanation). Alternatively, שֶׁנִּיטוֹחַ means that *it was peeled off
of* the bricks, leaving them exposed to the
rain (*Binyan Yehoshua*).

Magen Avos and *Gra*, however, emend the
text in the first case to read אֲבָנִים, *stones*,
rather than לְבֵנִים, *bricks*. [As the Baraisa
has just mentioned, stones are impervious
to water, whereas bricks are not.] This is
also the reading in *Avos DeRabbi Nassan,
Nusach* 2, Ch. 35.

ד . הוּא הָיָה אוֹמֵר: אָדָם שֶׁיֵּשׁ בּוֹ מַעֲשִׂים טוֹבִים וְלָמַד תּוֹרָה הַרְבֵּה דּוֹמֶה לְכוֹס שֶׁיֵּשׁ לוֹ פִּיסְפָּס[9], שֶׁכֵּיוָן שֶׁמַּנִּיחַ אוֹתוֹ מִיָּדוֹ אַף עַל פִּי שֶׁנֶּהֱפָךְ עַל צִידוֹ אֵין נִשְׁפָּךְ כָּל מַה שֶׁיֵּשׁ בּוֹ. וְאָדָם שֶׁאֵין בּוֹ מַעֲשִׂים טוֹבִים וְלָמַד תּוֹרָה הַרְבֵּה דּוֹמֶה לְכוֹס שֶׁאֵין לוֹ פִּיסְפָּס, שֶׁכֵּיוָן שֶׁהִנִּיחַ אוֹתוֹ מִיָּדוֹ מִיָּד נֶהֱפָךְ עַל צִידוֹ וְנִשְׁפָּךְ כָּל מַה שֶׁיֵּשׁ בּוֹ[11]. הוּא הָיָה אוֹמֵר: אָדָם שֶׁיֵּשׁ בּוֹ מַעֲשִׂים טוֹבִים וְלָמַד תּוֹרָה הַרְבֵּה דּוֹמֶה לְסוּס שֶׁיֵּשׁ לוֹ כֵּלִים נָאִים[12]. וְאָדָם שֶׁאֵין בּוֹ מַעֲשִׂים טוֹבִים וְלָמַד תּוֹרָה הַרְבֵּה דּוֹמֶה לְסוּס שֶׁאֵין לוֹ רֶסֶן לִבְלֹם, כֵּיוָן שֶׁאָדָם רוֹצֶה לִרוֹכְבוֹ זוֹרְקוֹ בְּבַת אַחַת[13,14].

§4 The third analogy:

הוּא הָיָה אוֹמֵר — He used to say: אָדָם שֶׁיֵּשׁ בּוֹ מַעֲשִׂים טוֹבִים וְלָמַד תּוֹרָה הַרְבֵּה — A person who has many good deeds to his credit and has studied much Torah דּוֹמֶה לְכוֹס שֶׁיֵּשׁ לוֹ פִּיסְפָּס — is like a goblet that has a wide and stable base.[9] שֶׁכֵּיוָן שֶׁמַּנִּיחַ אוֹתוֹ מִיָּדוֹ אַף עַל פִּי שֶׁנֶּהֱפָךְ עַל צִידוֹ אֵין נִשְׁפָּךְ כָּל מַה שֶׁיֵּשׁ בּוֹ — When one lets go of it, even if it tips to its side, it rights itself immediately and all its contents are not spilled out.[10] וְאָדָם שֶׁאֵין בּוֹ מַעֲשִׂים טוֹבִים וְלָמַד תּוֹרָה הַרְבֵּה — But a person who does not have many good deeds to his credit but has studied much Torah דּוֹמֶה לְכוֹס שֶׁאֵין לוֹ פִּיסְפָּס — is like a goblet that does not have a wide and stable base, שֶׁכֵּיוָן שֶׁהִנִּיחַ אוֹתוֹ מִיָּדוֹ מִיָּד נֶהֱפָךְ עַל צִידוֹ וְנִשְׁפָּךְ כָּל מַה שֶׁיֵּשׁ בּוֹ — so that once one lets go of it, it tips to its side and all its contents spill out.[11]

The fourth analogy:

הוּא הָיָה אוֹמֵר — He used to say: אָדָם שֶׁיֵּשׁ בּוֹ מַעֲשִׂים טוֹבִים וְלָמַד תּוֹרָה הַרְבֵּה — A person who has many good deeds to his credit and has studied much Torah דּוֹמֶה לְסוּס שֶׁיֵּשׁ לוֹ כֵּלִים נָאִים — is like a horse that has proper equipment.[12] וְאָדָם שֶׁאֵין בּוֹ מַעֲשִׂים טוֹבִים וְלָמַד תּוֹרָה הַרְבֵּה — But a person who does not have many good deeds to his credit but has studied much Torah דּוֹמֶה לְסוּס שֶׁאֵין לוֹ רֶסֶן לִבְלֹם — is like a horse without a bridle with which to restrain it. כֵּיוָן שֶׁאָדָם רוֹצֶה לִרוֹכְבוֹ זוֹרְקוֹ בְּבַת אַחַת — When a person tries to ride it, it throws him off at once.[13]

9. The term פִּיסְפָּס refers to cube-shaped stones (see 28 §9 below with *Ben Avraham*), which sit squarely on their flat bottoms and do not tip over.

10. [This would seem to be the meaning of this line. Other texts, however, have a different reading.]

11. Similarly, without good deeds as an anchor, a person is vulnerable to being swayed by evil influences, and that puts the "wine"

of his Torah in danger of being spilled from his heart (see *Binyan Yehoshua*).

12. Especially a bridle — the headgear (consisting of straps, a bit, and reins) used to control a horse (*Binyan Yehoshua*).

13. A horse is a strong animal and can act wildly. If it is controlled by means of a bridle, then it can be ridden safely and used to travel far and wide. Similarly, Torah scholarship has immense power, and if controlled

הוּא הָיָה אוֹמֵר: הַלּוֹמֵד תּוֹרָה בְּיַלְדוּתוֹ דִּבְרֵי תוֹרָה נִבְלָעִין בְּדָמָיו [15]
וְיוֹצְאִין מִפִּיו מְפוֹרָשִׁין [16]. וְהַלּוֹמֵד תּוֹרָה בְּזִקְנוּתוֹ אֵין דִּבְרֵי תוֹרָה נִבְלָעִין
בְּדָמָיו וְאֵין יוֹצְאִין מִפִּיו מְפוֹרָשִׁין וְכֵן מְתָלָא אוֹמֵר: אִם בִּנְעַרוּתֶיךָ לֹא
חֲפַצְתָּם אֵיךְ תַּשִּׂיגֵם בְּזִקְנוּתֶךָ [17]:

This concludes the four analogies.[14]

Elisha ben Avuyah identifies another factor in retaining one's achievements
in Torah study, aside from a strong foundation of good deeds:
הוּא הָיָה אוֹמֵר — He used to say: הַלּוֹמֵד תּוֹרָה בְּיַלְדוּתוֹ — Someone who
studies Torah in his youth has a great advantage. דִּבְרֵי תוֹרָה נִבְלָעִין בְּדָמָיו
וְיוֹצְאִין מִפִּיו מְפוֹרָשִׁין — The words of Torah seep into his blood[15] and emerge
from his mouth perfectly articulated.[16] וְהַלּוֹמֵד תּוֹרָה בְּזִקְנוּתוֹ — But someone who studies Torah only in his old age does not have this advantage. אֵין
דִּבְרֵי תוֹרָה נִבְלָעִין בְּדָמָיו וְאֵין יוֹצְאִין מִפִּיו מְפוֹרָשִׁין — The words of Torah do not
seep into his blood and do not emerge from his mouth perfectly articulated.
אִם בִּנְעַרוּתֶיךָ — And so the saying goes: וְכֵן מְתָלָא אוֹמֵר — אֵיךְ
לֹא חֲפַצְתָּם אֵיךְ — If in your youth you did not want them, how can you attain
them in your old age?[17]

---

by faithful mitzvah observance, it is safe
and can help a person make great strides,
in terms of spiritual and intellectual attainments. But if good deeds are lacking and
one's Torah is uncontrolled, the scholarship
itself can throw a person off in short order
(see *Magen Avos*).

14. In summary: If Elisha ben Avuyah is indeed sharing what he considers to be the lessons of his unfortunate life story (see above,
note 1), he is offering, through these four
analogies, an explanation for the collapse
of his own Torah stature, and a warning to
other Torah scholars wishing to avoid a similar fate. Elisha, it might therefore be said,
recognized in hindsight that he had failed
to lay a proper foundation for the edifice of
Torah knowledge that he worked so hard
to build. His character was not sufficiently
developed, and his commitment to turning all that he learned into a living reality (
"good deeds") was lacking. He now realized
that he had never insulated himself properly
from the spiritual challenges a sage of his
caliber would inevitably face, and that he
had always been at risk, like a goblet with an
unsteady base or a horseman with no reins

to hold. As a result, not only did his edifice of
Torah greatness come tumbling down, but
he fell along with it, for, as the Sages teach
(*Shabbos* 88b, *Yoma* 72b), Torah knowledge
has a two-sided nature: It is an elixir of life
for those who use it properly, and a potion of
death for those who do not.

15. Or, according to another text, into מֵעָיו,
his innards, an allusion to the verse, *it is
pleasant if you guard them in your innards*
(*Mefaresh,* quoting *Proverbs* 22:18).

16. This is a function of *girsa d'yankusa*, the
studies of one's youth (see *Shabbos* 21b).
A text that is reviewed constantly and committed to memory in one's youth becomes
lastingly ingrained in his mind, so much so
that years later, the precise wording rolls ef-
fortlessly off his tongue (*Binyan Yehoshua,*
from *Mefaresh*).

17. This statement is meant only as a general
rule. There can be, and have been, exceptions to the rule — perhaps most notably R'
Akiva, who was illiterate until he began learning at forty years old, and eventually rose to
become one of the greatest sages in history.
For him and others with an extraordinary

ה. הוּא הָיָה אוֹמֵר: קָשִׁין דִּבְרֵי תוֹרָה לִקְנוֹתָם כִּכְלֵי זְהָבִים. וְנוֹחִין לְאַבְּדָם כִּכְלֵי זְכוּכִית[18], שֶׁנֶּאֱמַר (איוב כח, יז) "לֹא יַעַרְכֶנָּה זָהָב וּזְכוּכִית", מַקִּישׁ זָהָב לִזְכוּכִית, מַה כְּלִי זָהָב לְאַחַר שֶׁנִּשְׁבַּר יֵשׁ לוֹ תַּקָּנָה, (וְכָל[19] כְּלִי זְכוּכִית אֵין לָהֶם תַּקָּנָה כְּשֶׁנִּשְׁבְּרוּ אֶלָּא אִם כֵּן חָזְרוּ לִבְרִיָּיתָן[20]. וּמָה אֲנִי מְקַיֵּים) (שם) "וּתְמוּרָתָה כְּלִי פָז"[21], לוֹמַר לְךָ כָּל הֶעָמֵל בָּהֶן וּמְקַיְּימָן פָּנָיו מַצְהִיבוֹת כְּפָז. וְכָל הֶעָמֵל בָּהֶם וְאֵין מְקַיְּימָן פָּנָיו מַשְׁחִירוֹת כִּזְכוּכִית:

---

§5 More on the theme of losing one's Torah knowledge.

הוּא הָיָה אוֹמֵר — **He used to say:** קָשִׁין דִּבְרֵי תוֹרָה לִקְנוֹתָם כִּכְלֵי זְהָבִים — **The words of Torah are as difficult to acquire as gold vessels, but as easy to lose** through forgetfulness **as glass vessels,**[18] שֶׁנֶּאֱמַר "לֹא יַעַרְכֶנָּה זָהָב וּזְכוּכִית" — **as it says,** *But as for wisdom ... mankind does not know its worth ... gold and glass cannot approximate it,* nor can its *exchange be [in] articles of fine gold* (Job 28:12,13,17). מַקִּישׁ זָהָב לִזְכוּכִית — But aside from teaching that Torah knowledge can be as fragile as glass, [Scripture] here also **compares gold to glass,** to teach that מַה כְּלִי זָהָב לְאַחַר שֶׁנִּשְׁבַּר יֵשׁ לוֹ תַּקָּנָה — **just as a gold vessel that has been broken can be repaired,** וְכָל כְּלִי זְכוּכִית אֵין לָהֶם תַּקָּנָה כְּשֶׁנִּשְׁבְּרוּ אֶלָּא אִם כֵּן חָזְרוּ לִבְרִיָּיתָן — **all**[19] **glass vessels that have been broken can be repaired, but only if they are remade from the beginning.**[20] וּמָה אֲנִי מְקַיֵּים "וּתְמוּרָתָה כְּלִי פָז" — **And how do I interpret** the end of the verse, *glass cannot approximate it, nor can its exchange be [in] articles of fine gold?*[21] לוֹמַר לְךָ כָּל הֶעָמֵל בָּהֶן וּמְקַיְּימָן פָּנָיו מַצְהִיבוֹת כְּפָז — **This** comparison to fine gold comes **to teach you** that **whoever toils in** the study of [Torah], and fulfills them in practice — his face **shines as** radiantly as fine gold; וְכָל הֶעָמֵל בָּהֶם וְאֵין מְקַיְּימָן פָּנָיו מַשְׁחִירוֹת כִּזְכוּכִית — **and** it tells you that **whoever toils in** studying [Torah], but does **not fulfill them** in practice, **his face becomes as black as** smoke-blackened **glass.**

---

measure of devotion to Torah study and drive to succeed, the teaching presented here does not apply (*Kisei Rachamim*).

For other teachings on the superiority of youthful learning, see previous chapter.

18. [If one is careless with a glass vessel, it will slip from one's hand and shatter. If one is careless with one's Torah knowledge, it will likewise slip away.] See Rabban Gamliel's parallel teaching below, 28 §5.

19. [In the margin of *Ahavas Chesed*, the word וְכָל, *all,* here is emended to כָּךְ, *so too.*]

20. The scholar who has forgotten his

learning through neglect can regain it, but the fix is not a simple one: He must "remake himself from the beginning," to concentrate and study anew with enthusiasm and exceptional desire, whereupon he can indeed regain his former learning (*Ahavas Chesed;* see also *Magen Avos;* see, however, *Nuschas HaGra,* who emends the text to make it conform with the parallel passage in *Chagigah* 15a).

21. The word "glass" appears between זָהָב and כְּלִי פָז and is compared, homiletically, to both the term before and the term after (*Binyan Yehoshua,* from *Mefaresh*).

ו. הוּא הָיָה אוֹמֵר: יָכוֹל אָדָם לִלְמוֹד תּוֹרָה בְּעֶשְׂרִים שָׁנָה וּלְשַׁכֵּחַ בִּשְׁתֵּי שָׁנִים. כֵּיצַד, יָשַׁב שִׁשָּׁה חֳדָשִׁים וְאֵין חוֹזֵר לְאַחֲרָיו [23] נִמְצָא אוֹמֵר עַל טָמֵא טָהוֹר וְעַל טָהוֹר טָמֵא. שְׁנֵים עָשָׂר חֳדָשִׁים וְלֹא חָזַר לְאַחֲרָיו נִמְצָא מַחֲלִיף חֲכָמִים זֶה בָּזֶה. שְׁמוֹנָה עָשָׂר חֳדָשִׁים וְלֹא חָזַר לְאַחֲרָיו נִמְצָא מְשַׁכֵּחַ רָאשֵׁי מַסֶּכְתּוֹתָיו. [24] עֶשְׂרִים וְאַרְבָּעָה חֳדָשִׁים וְאֵין חוֹזֵר לְאַחֲרָיו נִמְצָא מְשַׁכֵּחַ רָאשֵׁי פְּרָקִים, [25] וּמִתּוֹךְ שֶׁאָמַר עַל טָמֵא טָהוֹר וְעַל טָהוֹר טָמֵא וּמַחֲלִיף חָכָם בְּחָכָם וּמְשַׁכֵּחַ רָאשֵׁי מַסֶּכְתּוֹתָיו וְרָאשֵׁי פְּרָקָיו, סוֹף שֶׁיּוֹשֵׁב וְדוֹמֵם, וְעָלָיו אָמַר שְׁלֹמֹה (משלי כד, ל-לא) "עַל

---

§6 Having extolled the value and enduring nature of youthful study (above, §4), Elisha warns that even a scholar from youth can forfeit the benefits of his early study.[22]

יָכוֹל אָדָם לִלְמוֹד תּוֹרָה בְּעֶשְׂרִים שָׁנָה וּלְשַׁכֵּחַ הוּא הָיָה אוֹמֵר — **He used to say:** בִּשְׁתֵּי שָׁנִים — **What a person can learn in twenty years he can forget in two years.** כֵּיצַד — **How so?** יָשַׁב שִׁשָּׁה חֳדָשִׁים וְאֵין חוֹזֵר לְאַחֲרָיו — **If after** studying Torah for twenty years **a person sits** idly **for six months and does not go back to review** his learning,[23] נִמְצָא אוֹמֵר עַל טָמֵא טָהוֹר וְעַל טָהוֹר טָמֵא — he will, as a result, declare *tahor* (ritually pure) **that which is** *tamei* (impure) and *tamei* that which is *tahor*. שְׁנֵים עָשָׂר חֳדָשִׁים וְלֹא חָזַר לְאַחֲרָיו — **If he sits** idle **for twelve months and does not go back to review,** נִמְצָא מַחֲלִיף חֲכָמִים זֶה בָּזֶה — he will, as a result, **mix up the names of the Sages** with opposing views on a given matter, and invert who holds what. שְׁמוֹנָה עָשָׂר חֳדָשִׁים וְלֹא חָזַר לְאַחֲרָיו — **If he sits** idle **for eighteen months and does not go back to review,** נִמְצָא מְשַׁכֵּחַ רָאשֵׁי מַסֶּכְתּוֹתָיו — he will, as a result, **forget his tractate headings.**[24] עֶשְׂרִים וְאַרְבָּעָה חֳדָשִׁים וְאֵין חוֹזֵר לְאַחֲרָיו — **And if he sits idle for twenty-four months and does not go back to review,** נִמְצָא מְשַׁכֵּחַ רָאשֵׁי פְּרָקִים — he will, as a result, **forget even the chapter headings.**[25] וּמִתּוֹךְ שֶׁאָמַר עַל טָמֵא טָהוֹר וְעַל טָהוֹר טָמֵא וּמַחֲלִיף חָכָם בְּחָכָם וּמְשַׁכֵּחַ רָאשֵׁי מַסֶּכְתּוֹתָיו וְרָאשֵׁי פְּרָקָיו — **And once he declares** *tahor* **that which is** *tamei* **and** *tamei* **that which is** *tahor*, **and he mixes up the names of the Sages and forgets his tractate headings and his chapter headings,** סוֹף שֶׁיּוֹשֵׁב וְדוֹמֵם — he will, **in the end, sit and remain silent,** having nothing left to review or study. וְעָלָיו אָמַר שְׁלֹמֹה — **It is about [such a person] that King Solomon said:** "עַל

---

22. *Magen Avos*

23. By speaking of "going back" to review, the Baraisa hints that even if one does not leave his studies, but rather goes on to learn other Torah subjects, he can still suffer the miserable fate laid out here if he focuses

single-mindedly on his forward progress and does not continually "go back" to review his earlier studies (*Magen Avos*).

24. [I.e. the general outline of the tractate.]

25. [I.e., the general outline of each chapter.] Although it might seem that one would sooner

שְׂדֵה אִישׁ עָצֵל עָבַרְתִּי וְעַל כֶּרֶם אָדָם חֲסַר לֵב וְהִנֵּה עָלָה כֻלּוֹ קִמְּשֹׂנִים
כָּסּוּ פָנָיו חֲרֻלִּים וְגֶדֶר אֲבָנָיו נֶהֱרָסָה״.²⁶ וְכֵיוָן שֶׁנָּפַל כּוֹתְלוֹ שֶׁל כֶּרֶם מִיָּד
חָרֵב כָּל הַכֶּרֶם כּוּלּוֹ:

ז. הוּא הָיָה אוֹמֵר: כָּל הָעוֹשֶׂה מִצְוָה בַּחֲבֵירוֹ מַעֲלֶה עָלָיו הַכָּתוּב
כְּאִילּוּ לֹא עֲשָׂאוֹ אֶלָּא בְּגוּפוֹ²⁷. מָשָׁל לְמָה הַדָּבָר דּוֹמֶה, לְמֶלֶךְ

חֲסַר לֵב אָדָם כֶּרֶם וְעַל עָבַרְתִּי עָצֵל אִישׁ שְׂדֵה — *I passed by the field of a lazy
man, and by the vineyard of a man lacking [an understanding] heart,* וְהִנֵּה
״נֶהֱרָסָה אֲבָנָיו וְגֶדֶר חֲרֻלִּים פָנָיו כָּסּוּ קִמְּשֹׂנִים כֻלּוֹ עָלָה — *and, behold, it was all
overgrown with thorns; nettles had covered its surface; and its stone wall
was broken down* (*Proverbs* 24:30-31).[26] חָרֵב מִיָּד כֶּרֶם שֶׁל כּוֹתְלוֹ שֶׁנָּפַל וְכֵיוָן
כּוּלּוֹ הַכֶּרֶם כָּל — *Once the wall of a vineyard has fallen, the entire vineyard is
immediately* doomed to be **destroyed.**

§7 The Baraisa digresses to another teaching of Elisha ben Avuyah:
אוֹמֵר הָיָה הוּא — *He used to say:* בַּחֲבֵירוֹ מִצְוָה הָעוֹשֶׂה כָּל — *Whoever*
performs a mitzvah through his fellow, that is, he causes his fellow to perform
a mitzvah, בְּגוּפוֹ אֶלָּא עֲשָׂאוֹ לֹא כְּאִילּוּ הַכָּתוּב עָלָיו מַעֲלֶה — is regarded by
Scripture as if he had performed it with none other than **his own person.**[27]

The Baraisa returns to its previous discussion:[28]
דּוֹמֶה הַדָּבָר לְמָה מָשָׁל — *To illustrate* the importance of preserving one's Torah
knowledge, the Sages offered **an analogy: To what is the matter comparable?**

forget the chapter outlines than the tractate
outlines, since the former are more numerous
and specialized, the truth is that a scholar has
more use from the chapter outlines, which
point more closely to the subjects he needs
to investigate, and thus he is more likely to
remember them (*Magen Avos*). [Some texts,
however, have the negligent scholar forgetting the chapter headings before the tractate
headings, and this is the reading in *Tanna
DeVei Eliyahu Zuta* §16 as well.]

26. In the parallel passage in *Tanna DeVei
Eliyahu Zuta* §16, the text adds: *I passed by
the field of a lazy man* — he who sits idly and
does not review; *and by the vineyard of a
man lacking [an understanding] heart* — he
who becomes arrogant regarding his learning; *and, behold, it was all overgrown with
thorns* — ultimately, he seeks [to recall] a
detail from what he has learned, but cannot
summon it; *nettles had covered its face* —
ultimately, he feels humiliated; *and its stone*

wall was broken down — ultimately, he will
never see a favorable sign in his studies.

27. The Baraisa does not say where it finds
that Scripture regards him as if he performed
the mitzvah himself. But the Gemara in *Sanhedrin* cites a verse that describes Moses as
having struck the river in Egypt to bring on
the Plague of Blood (*Exodus* 17:5). Although
it was not Moses but Aaron who did the
actual striking, the verse attributes the act
to Moses because it was he who conveyed
the Divine command to Aaron, and thus
"caused" Aaron to perform the mitzvah. The
Midrash (*Shemos Rabbah* 35 §3) makes a
similar point regarding Moses, Bezalel, and
the construction of the Tabernacle.

28. *Ahavas Chesed*, who connects the following paragraph to the earlier discussion
about one who forgets his Torah studies.

[Forgetfulness in Torah is viewed with
such severity because it can cause a person

בָּשָׂר וָדָם שֶׁצָּד צִפּוֹר וּנְתָנוֹ לְאֶחָד מֵעֲבָדָיו, וְאוֹמֵר לוֹ: הֱוֵי זָהִיר בְּצִפּוֹר
זֶה, שֶׁאִם אַתָּה נִזְהָר בּוֹ, טוֹב, וְאִם לָאו אֲנִי נוֹטֵל נִשְׁמָתְךָ תַּחְתָּיו. כָּךְ
אָמַר הַקָּדוֹשׁ בָּרוּךְ הוּא לְיִשְׂרָאֵל: דִּבְרֵי תוֹרָה שֶׁנָּתַתִּי לָכֶם, אִם אַתֶּם
מְשַׁמְּרִים אוֹתָן, טוֹב, וְאִם לָאו אֲנִי נוֹטֵל נַפְשְׁכֶם תַּחְתֵּיהֶ,²⁹ שֶׁנֶּאֱמַר (דברים
ד, ט) ("רַק הִשָּׁמֶר לְךָ וּשְׁמֹר נַפְשְׁךָ מְאֹד פֶּן תִּשְׁכַּח אֶת הַדְּבָרִים אֲשֶׁר רָאוּ
עֵינֶיךָ"),³⁰ (שם לב, מז) "כִּי לֹא דָבָר רֵק הוּא מִכֶּם כִּי הוּא חַיֵּיכֶם"³¹:

לְמֶלֶךְ בָּשָׂר וָדָם שֶׁצָּד צִפּוֹר וּנְתָנוֹ לְאֶחָד מֵעֲבָדָיו — **To a flesh-and-blood king who captured a prized bird and gave it to one of his servants** for safekeeping, וְאוֹמֵר לוֹ: הֱוֵי זָהִיר בְּצִפּוֹר זֶה שֶׁאִם אַתָּה נִזְהָר בּוֹ טוֹב — **telling him, "Take good care of this bird, for if you are careful with it, all will be good;** וְאִם לָאו אֲנִי נוֹטֵל נִשְׁמָתְךָ תַּחְתָּיו — **but if not, I will take your life in its place."** כָּךְ אָמַר — **Similarly, the Holy One, Blessed is He, said to the Jewish people,** הַקָּדוֹשׁ בָּרוּךְ הוּא לְיִשְׂרָאֵל — דִּבְרֵי תוֹרָה שֶׁנָּתַתִּי לָכֶם, אִם אַתֶּם מְשַׁמְּרִים אוֹתָן טוֹב — **"The words of Torah that I have given you — if you preserve them, all will be good;** וְאִם לָאו אֲנִי נוֹטֵל נַפְשְׁכֶם תַּחְתֵּיהֶ — **but if not, I will take your life in its place,"[29]** שֶׁנֶּאֱמַר "רַק הִשָּׁמֶר לְךָ וּשְׁמֹר נַפְשְׁךָ מְאֹד פֶּן תִּשְׁכַּח אֶת הַדְּבָרִים אֲשֶׁר רָאוּ עֵינֶיךָ" — **as it says, Only beware for yourself, and greatly beware for your soul, lest you forget the things your eyes have seen [at Mount Sinai], and lest you remove them from your heart all the days of your life** (Deuteronomy 4:9).[30] "כִּי לֹא דָבָר רֵק הוּא מִכֶּם כִּי הוּא חַיֵּיכֶם" — **And it says, For it is not an empty thing for you, for it is your life** (ibid. 32:47).[31]

---

to reach the wrong conclusions on halachic questions and permit that which is forbidden. The error may have been inadvertent, but it is deemed intentional since it arose from inexcusable negligence, and he must therefore *bear guilt for his soul* (*Rav* to *Avos* 3:8 [first explanation], *R' Yonah*; see *Avos* 4:13, s.v. רַבִּי יְהוּדָה אוֹמֵר.).]

29. The king warns his servant that the bird is beyond price; if he fails to guard it, he will pay with his life. So too with Torah: Its value is such that its loss cannot be offset by money or any material thing. Therefore, one who fails to safeguard his Torah must pay with his life (see *Maharal, Chidushei Aggados* to *Menachos* 99b).

30. The "things your eyes have seen" are the Divine lessons of the Torah, which all Jews have "seen," whether they were alive and present at the Revelation, or live in later generations and perceived them with their

mind's eye through the study of Torah (*Tiferes Yisrael* §49 to *Avos* 3:8). The admonition *greatly beware for your soul* indicates that one's soul is designated as the collateral for this requirement to remember his Torah learning; if a Jew falls short in this regard, he forfeits his soul (*Machzor Vitri* ad loc.; see also *Rabbeinu Bachya* ad loc.).

Based on this verse, the Sages (*Menachos* 99b and *Avos* 3:8) teach that one who causes even one item of his Torah learning to be forgotten transgresses one or more Biblical prohibitions. The Gemara, however, excludes from the prohibition and its punishment those who forget their learning involuntarily; the verse speaks only of one who *removes [the teachings] from his heart.* See *Yoreh Deah* 246:3-4.

31. Since the Torah "is your life," it follows that without the Torah, you can have no life (*Binyan Yehoshua*, from *Mefaresh*).

﴾ פֶּרֶק כה ﴿

א. בֶּן עַזַּאי אוֹמֵר: כֹּל שֶׁדַּעְתּוֹ נוֹחָה מִפְּנֵי חָכְמָתוֹ סִימָן יָפֶה הוּא לוֹ. וְשֶׁאֵין דַּעְתּוֹ נוֹחָה מִפְּנֵי חָכְמָתוֹ סִימָן רַע הוּא לוֹ[1]. כֹּל שֶׁדַּעְתּוֹ נוֹחָה מִפְּנֵי יִצְרוֹ סִימָן יָפֶה לוֹ. וְשֶׁאֵין דַּעְתּוֹ נוֹחָה מִפְּנֵי יִצְרוֹ סִימָן רַע לוֹ[2]. כֹּל שֶׁרוּחַ חֲכָמִים נוֹחָה הֵימֶנּוּ (בִּשְׁעַת מִיתָה) סִימָן יָפֶה לוֹ. שֶׁאֵין רוּחַ חֲכָמִים נוֹחָה הֵימֶנּוּ סִימָן רַע לוֹ[4]. כֹּל שֶׁפָּנָיו זְקוּפוֹת לְמַעְלָה סִימָן יָפֶה לוֹ.

﴾ CHAPTER 25 ﴿

§1 The Baraisa presents a list of attributes that are seen as omens for those who have them.

בֶּן עַזַּאי אוֹמֵר — Ben Azzai says: כֹּל שֶׁדַּעְתּוֹ נוֹחָה מִפְּנֵי חָכְמָתוֹ — Anyone whose mind remains composed — humble and unassuming — in the face of his wisdom — סִימָן יָפֶה הוּא לוֹ — it is a good omen for him;   וְשֶׁאֵין דַּעְתּוֹ נוֹחָה מִפְּנֵי חָכְמָתוֹ — but anyone whose mind does not remain composed in the face of his wisdom — סִימָן רַע הוּא לוֹ — it is a bad omen for him.[1] כֹּל שֶׁדַּעְתּוֹ נוֹחָה מִפְּנֵי יִצְרוֹ סִימָן יָפֶה לוֹ — Anyone whose mind remains composed in the face of his evil inclination — it is a good omen for him;   וְשֶׁאֵין דַּעְתּוֹ נוֹחָה מִפְּנֵי יִצְרוֹ סִימָן רַע לוֹ — but anyone whose mind does not remain composed in the face of his evil inclination — it is a bad omen for him.[2]

Four more pairs of omens, arising from the circumstances surrounding one's death:[3]

כֹּל שֶׁרוּחַ חֲכָמִים נוֹחָה הֵימֶנּוּ בִּשְׁעַת מִיתָה סִימָן יָפֶה לוֹ — Anyone whom the Sages are pleased with at the time of his death — it is a good omen for him;   שֶׁאֵין רוּחַ חֲכָמִים נוֹחָה הֵימֶנּוּ סִימָן רַע לוֹ — anyone whom the Sages are not pleased with at the time of his death — it is a bad omen for him.[4] כֹּל שֶׁפָּנָיו זְקוּפוֹת לְמַעְלָה סִימָן יָפֶה לוֹ — Anyone whose face is directed upward when he dies —

---

1. If a person remains humble despite his superior wisdom, his humility is a sign that his wisdom will endure, and that he has found favor in the eyes of God and man (see *Bava Basra* 10b). Conversely, if a person takes undue pride in his wisdom, his arrogance is a sign that not only his wisdom but even his life will not endure, for "prominence tends to bury its masters" (*Magen Avos,* first explanation, echoed by *Kisei Rachamim*).

2. Although fighting the *yetzer hara* (evil inclination) is the central challenge of human life, one must wage the war in a restrained and prudent manner. Calm and indirect

maneuvers to outflank the *yetzer hara* are generally more successful than relentless frontal assaults that cause one's bodily nature to rise up in opposition. Therefore, the ability to remain "composed" while pursuing this epic struggle is a good sign of eventual success (*Magen Avos,* third approach; for further discussion of this idea, see *R' Yisrael Salanter, Igros U'Michtavim, Michtav 25,* and *R' Henach Leibowitz, Chidushei HaLev, Bamidbar* 5:18).

3. *Ben Avraham.*

4. A person is judged by the spiritual condition in which he ends his life. He may have

וְכֹל שֶׁפָּנָיו כְּבוּשׁוֹת לְמַטָּה סִימָן רַע לוֹ[5]. נָתַן עֵינָיו בִּבְנֵי אָדָם סִימָן
יָפֶה לוֹ. לֹא נָתַן עֵינָיו בִּבְנֵי אָדָם סִימָן רַע לוֹ[6]. כֹּל שֶׁפָּנָיו מַצְהִיבוֹת
סִימָן יָפֶה לוֹ. כֹּל שֶׁפָּנָיו מַשְׁחִירוֹת סִימָן רַע לוֹ[7]. בִּשְׁעַת פְּטִירָתוֹ שֶׁל
רַבָּן יוֹחָנָן בֶּן זַכַּאי[8] הָיָה מַגְבִּיהַּ קוֹלוֹ וּבוֹכֶה[9]. אָמְרוּ לוֹ תַּלְמִידָיו: רַבִּי,

it is a good omen for him; וְכֹל שֶׁפָּנָיו כְּבוּשׁוֹת לְמַטָּה סִימָן רַע לוֹ — and anyone whose face is directed downward when he dies — it is a bad omen for him.[5] נָתַן עֵינָיו בִּבְנֵי אָדָם סִימָן יָפֶה לוֹ — If [someone] looks at the people around him when he dies, it is a good omen for him; לֹא נָתַן עֵינָיו בִּבְנֵי אָדָם סִימָן רַע לוֹ — if he does not look at the people around him, it is a bad omen for him.[6] כֹּל שֶׁפָּנָיו מַצְהִיבוֹת סִימָן יָפֶה לוֹ — Anyone whose face is radiant when he dies — it is a good omen for him; כֹּל שֶׁפָּנָיו מַשְׁחִירוֹת סִימָן רַע לוֹ — anyone whose face darkens when he dies — it is a bad omen for him.[7]

An anecdote that centers on the concept that the dying are brought before the Divine Presence.

בִּשְׁעַת פְּטִירָתוֹ שֶׁל רַבָּן יוֹחָנָן בֶּן זַכַּאי הָיָה מַגְבִּיהַּ קוֹלוֹ וּבוֹכֶה — At the time of Rabban Yochanan ben Zakkai's passing,[8] he raised his voice and wept.[9] אָמְרוּ לוֹ תַּלְמִידָיו — Surprised, his students said to him, רַבִּי — "Teacher!

long been wicked, but if he repents later in life, his evil past is forgotten and his sins are forgiven (see Kiddushin 40b and Rambam, Hil. Teshuvah 2:1). Conversely, a person may have always been righteous, but if at the end he lapses into sin (like Yochanan the Kohen Gadol, who served faithfully in the Temple for eighty years but then defected to the Tzadokim), he is judged as a wicked person. Since the Sages' opinion of someone is a reliable indicator of his spiritual worth, that opinion at the end of one's life bodes well or ill for his eternal fate (Binyan Yehoshua).

5. The Midrash teaches that before a person dies, he is granted a vision of the Divine Presence. If he led a righteous life, he is told, "Come and meet the King Whom you served so faithfully and Who will be rewarding you!" If he led a wicked life, he is told, "Come and meet the King Whom you rebelled against and Who will be punishing you!" (Midrash Shocher Tov, end of §22, cited by Ben Avraham). Therefore, if a dying person is able to keep his gaze trained upward, toward the Divine Presence, and does not feel a need to turn away in fear or shame, he must have received an encouraging welcome. But if he

is facing downward, away from the Divine Presence, the indication is that his welcome was actually a ringing rebuke (Ben Avraham; see there further).

6. In light of the aforementioned pre-death vision (see previous note), it follows that if a dying person is looking at other people, he is obviously untroubled by what he has seen and by what lies in store for his soul after death. But if he is looking away, he may be discomfited by fear and embarrassment, thinking that those present can hear and see the same incriminating things that he can hear and see (Ben Avraham).

7. See note 5. The radiant face of a dying person reflects the brilliance of the Divine Presence, as well as his own joy in the warm greeting he is receiving from Heaven. A darkened visage, on the other hand, expresses a dread of the Divine Presence and dismay at where his future lies (Ben Avraham; see also Avos HaRosh).

8. On the day of his passing, but not immediately before his death (Ben Avraham); see below, note 29.

9. He "raised his voice" to ensure that his

עַמּוּד הַגָּבוֹהַ נֵר עוֹלָם פַּטִּישׁ הֶחָזָק‎10, מִפְּנֵי מָה אַתָּה בּוֹכֶה‎11. אָמַר
לָהֶם: וְכִי פְּנֵי מֶלֶךְ בָּשָׂר וָדָם אֲנִי הוֹלֵךְ לְהַקְבִּיל, שֶׁאִם יִכְעוֹס עָלַי אֵין
כַּעֲסוֹ אֶלָּא בָּעוֹלָם הַזֶּה, וְאִם אוֹסְרֵנִי אֵין °אֲסוּרִין‎13 אֶלָּא בָּעוֹלָם הַזֶּה
אִם מְמִיתֵנִי אֵין מִיתָתִי אֶלָּא בָּעוֹלָם הַזֶּה, וְעוֹד שֶׁאֲנִי יָכוֹל לְפַיְּיסוֹ
בִּדְבָרִים וּלְשַׁחֲדוֹ בְּמָמוֹן. הָא אֵינִי הוֹלֵךְ לְהַקְבִּיל אֶלָּא פְּנֵי מֶלֶךְ מַלְכֵי
הַמְּלָכִים הַקָּדוֹשׁ בָּרוּךְ הוּא, שֶׁאִם יִכְעוֹס עָלַי כַּעֲסוֹ בָּעוֹלָם הַזֶּה וְעוֹלָם
הַבָּא, וְעוֹד שֶׁאֵינִי יָכוֹל לְפַיְּיסוֹ בִּדְבָרִים וּלְשַׁחֲדוֹ בְּמָמוֹן‎14. וְעוֹד שֶׁיֵּשׁ

עַמּוּד הַגָּבוֹהַּ נֵר עוֹלָם פַּטִּישׁ הֶחָזָק — **Lofty Pillar, Lamp of the World, Mighty Hammer!**[10] מִפְּנֵי מָה אַתָּה בּוֹכֶה — **Why do you weep?"**[11] אָמַר לָהֶם — **He said to them,** וְכִי פְּנֵי מֶלֶךְ בָּשָׂר וָדָם אֲנִי הוֹלֵךְ לְהַקְבִּיל — **"Am I then going to meet a flesh-and-blood king?** שֶׁאִם יִכְעוֹס עָלַי אֵין כַּעֲסוֹ אֶלָּא בָּעוֹלָם הַזֶּה — **If I were, I would not weep**[12] at the thought of meeting a ruler who if he becomes angry at me, his anger is merely in this world; וְאִם אוֹסְרֵנִי אֵין אֲסוּרוֹ אֶלָּא בָּעוֹלָם הַזֶּה — **if he imprisons me, his imprisonment**[13] is merely in this world, אִם מְמִיתֵנִי אֵין מִיתָתִי אֶלָּא בָּעוֹלָם הַזֶּה — and if he puts me to death, my death is merely in this world. וְעוֹד שֶׁאֲנִי יָכוֹל לְפַיְּיסוֹ בִּדְבָרִים וּלְשַׁחֲדוֹ בְּמָמוֹן — **Fur**thermore, I can appease [a flesh-and-blood king] with words of conciliation and bribe him with money. הָא אֵינִי הוֹלֵךְ לְהַקְבִּיל אֶלָּא פְּנֵי מֶלֶךְ מַלְכֵי הַמְּלָכִים — **But** I am not going to meet a flesh-and-blood king. I am going to meet none other than the King Who reigns over kings, הַקָּדוֹשׁ בָּרוּךְ הוּא the Holy One, Blessed is He, שֶׁאִם יִכְעוֹס עָלַי כַּעֲסוֹ בָּעוֹלָם הַזֶּה וְעוֹלָם הַבָּא — **Who, if He be**comes angry at me, His anger is in this world and the World to Come. וְעוֹד שֶׁאֵינִי יָכוֹל לְפַיְּיסוֹ בִּדְבָרִים וּלְשַׁחֲדוֹ בְּמָמוֹן — **And what is more, I cannot appease Him with words or bribe him with money.**[14] That is why I weep! וְעוֹד שֶׁיֵּשׁ

students would hear him weeping and ask for an explanation, thus allowing him to teach them a final lesson in the fear of God (*Velo Od Ella, Ben Avraham*). Not only to them, in fact, but to Jews of all generations, as *Rosh* admonishes in his *Orchos Chaim* (§32): "Be mindful always of the day of death ... and let your thoughts alarm you when you recall the dread of Rabban Yochanan [ben Zakkai], of blessed memory."

10. "Lofty Pillar" of Jewish continuity, since he rescued many Torah sages during the Roman siege of Jerusalem (see Ch. 4 above); "Lamp of the World," due to his exemplary performance of the lamp-like mitzvos (based on *Proverbs* 6:23: *a mitzvah is a lamp*); and "Mighty Hammer," due to his

comprehensive knowledge of the hammer-like Torah (based on *Jeremiah* 23:2: *Are not My words ... like a hammer that shatters a rock*) (*Binyan Yehoshua*, from *Maharsha, Berachos* 28b).

11. Why would a person of such spiritual eminence have cause to weep in the face of death?

12. *Magen Avos*.

13. Emendation follows some manuscripts and *Nuschas HaGra*. Other texts have אֵין "יִסּוּרִין", *the "suffering" is merely ...*

14. During one's lifetime, it is possible to "bribe" God with words (of prayer and contrition, which can gain atonement for one's sins) and money (given as charity, which

לִי שְׁתֵּי דְרָכִים אַחַת לְגַן עֵדֶן וְאַחַת לְגֵיהִנָּם, וְאֵינִי יוֹדֵעַ אִם יַכְרִיעֵנִי
לְגֵיהִנָּם אוֹ אִם יַכְנִיסֵנִי לְגַן עֵדֶן¹⁵. וְעָלָיו הַכָּתוּב אוֹמֵר (תהלים כב, ל)
"לְפָנָיו יִכְרְעוּ כָּל יוֹרְדֵי עָפָר וְגוֹ'"¹⁶. (בְּמֹשֶׁה הוּא אוֹמֵר °וַיִּגְוַע וַיֵּמָת
(דברים לב, נ) "וַיֵּאָסֶף אֶל עַמָּיו"¹⁷,) וְאוֹמֵר (שמות לג, כג) "וַהֲסִרֹתִי אֶת כַּפִּי",
וְאוֹמֵר (יחזקאל ב, י) "וַיִּפְרֹשׂ אוֹתָהּ לְפָנַי °וְהִנֵּה כְתוּבָה פָּנִים וְאָחוֹר וְכוּ'"¹⁹,

אַחַת לְגַן עֵדֶן וְאַחַת — Moreover, I have two paths before me, לִי שְׁתֵּי דְרָכִים — one to Gan Eden and one to Gehinnom, וְאֵינִי יוֹדֵעַ אִם יַכְרִיעֵנִי לְגֵיהִנָּם — לְגֵיהִנָּם אוֹ אִם יַכְנִיסֵנִי לְגַן עֵדֶן — and I do not know whether He will decide my fate in favor of Gehinnom or whether He will bring me into Gan Eden."[15]

The Baraisa cites a number of related verses:

וְעָלָיו הַכָּתוּב אוֹמֵר "לְפָנָיו יִכְרְעוּ כָּל יוֹרְדֵי עָפָר וְגוֹ'" — Of [this final moment of one's life], it is stated, All who descend to the dust will kneel before Him, etc. (Psalms 22:30).[16] בְּמֹשֶׁה הוּא אוֹמֵר "וַיֵּאָסֶף אֶל עַמָּיו" — Similarly, regarding Moses it says, And he was gathered to his people (Deuteronomy 32:50).[17] וְאוֹמֵר "וַהֲסִרֹתִי אֶת כַּפִּי" — And it says further regarding Moses, Then I shall remove My hand and and you will see My back, but My face may not be seen (Exodus 33:23).[18] וְאוֹמֵר "וַיִּפְרֹשׂ אוֹתָהּ לְפָנַי וְהִיא כְתוּבָה פָּנִים — וְאָחוֹר וְכוּ'" — And it says, He spread [the scroll] before me; it was inscribed

can set aside a decree of death), but for a dying or dead person, these opportunities are no longer available (Binyan Yehoshua, from Maharsha).

15. That is, even if I am not at risk of losing my share in the World to Come, I am still vulnerable to a lesser judgment: the torment of a stay in Gehinnom (ibid.). Alternatively, Rabban Yochanan meant to say, "Not only do I fear the suffering to which God may subject me in retribution for my sins, but I also dread the anguish I will feel at squandering my eternal reward in Gan Eden — an anguish someone awaiting the judgment of a flesh-and-blood king, who punishes the disobedient but does not reward the obedient, need not be concerned about" (Kochvei Or §1).

[On why a saintly Torah sage like Rabban Yochanan ben Zakkai would entertain doubts about his eternal fate, see Kochvei Or ibid. and Sichos Mussar 5731:33.]

16. When anyone is in the process of descending to the dust (i.e., dying), but before he actually dies, he perceives the Divine Presence and "kneels" in submission to the

One Who will decide his fate (see Binyan Yehoshua [from Mefaresh] and Ahavas Chesed, both citing the Midrash [Bamidbar Rabbah 19 §22]).

17. This verse follows shortly after the command for Moses to ascend Mount Nebo, where he was to be shown, just before his death, the eternal blessings in store for the righteous (Binyan Yehoshua, based on Yalkut Shimoni, VeZos HaBerachah, end of §964). The fact that a dying tzaddik receives a glimpse of the Garden of Eden is taken as evidence that he meets with God, Who gives him this preview of his eternal reward (Ahavas Chesed).

18. "My face" refers to the first part of world history — this world, while "My back" refers to the latter part of history — the World to Come. [פָּנִים and אָחוֹר also mean "before" and "after."] Thus, God was telling Moses that he was not capable of perceiving Him during his lifetime, in this world, but he would be able to do so in the World to Come, and even just before his death (Midrash Lekach Tov, Devarim 34:10).

"פָּנִים" בָּעוֹלָם הַזֶּה "וְאָחוֹר" לָעוֹלָם הַבָּא.[20] דָּבָר אַחֵר, "פָּנִים" יִסּוּרִין
שֶׁל צַדִּיקִים בָּעוֹלָם הַזֶּה וְשַׁלְוָתָן שֶׁל רְשָׁעִים בָּעוֹלָם הַזֶּה. "וְאָחוֹר"
מַתַּן שְׂכָרָן שֶׁל צַדִּיקִים לֶעָתִיד לָבֹא וּפוּרְעֲנוּתָן שֶׁל רְשָׁעִים בְּגֵיהִנֹּם.[21]
(שם) [21]"וְכָתוּב אֵלֶיהָ קִנִים וָהֶגֶה וָהִי". "קִנִים" זוֹ פּוּרְעֲנוּתָן שֶׁל רְשָׁעִים
בָּעוֹלָם הַזֶּה, שֶׁנֶּאֱמַר (שם לב, טז) "קִינָה הִיא וְקוֹנְנוּהָ בְּנוֹת הַגּוֹיִם
תְּקוֹנֵנָּה אוֹתָה".[22] "וָהֶגֶה" זֶה מַתַּן שְׂכָרָן שֶׁל צַדִּיקִים לֶעָתִיד לָבֹא,

---

*on its **face** and on its **back**, etc.* (*Ezekiel* 2:10).[19] "פָּנִים" בָּעוֹלָם הַזֶּה "וְאָחוֹר"
לָעוֹלָם הַבָּא — *On its **face*** means that it was inscribed with an account of future
events **in this world**, and *on its **back*** means that it was inscribed with a description of **the World to Come**.[20]

The Baraisa delves further into the *Ezekiel* verse.

"פָּנִים" יִסּוּרִין שֶׁל צַדִּיקִים בָּעוֹלָם הַזֶּה — **Another interpretation:** דָּבָר אַחֵר
וְשַׁלְוָתָן שֶׁל רְשָׁעִים בָּעוֹלָם הַזֶּה — *"Face"* represents the **suffering of the righteous in this world and the tranquility of the wicked in this world;** "וְאָחוֹר"
מַתַּן שְׂכָרָן שֶׁל צַדִּיקִים לֶעָתִיד לָבֹא וּפוּרְעֲנוּתָן שֶׁל רְשָׁעִים בְּגֵיהִנֹּם — and *"back"*
represents the **reward of the righteous in the World to Come and the punish-
ment of the wicked in Gehinnom.**[21] "וְכָתוּב אֵלֶיהָ קִנִים וָהֶגֶה וָהִי" — The
verse continues, *and in [the scroll] was inscribed lamentations (kinnim),
rejoicing (hegeh), and woe (hi).* "קִנִים" זוֹ פּוּרְעֲנוּתָן שֶׁל רְשָׁעִים בָּעוֹלָם הַזֶּה
— *"Lamentations"* (*kinnim*) refers to the **punishments of the wicked in this
world,** שֶׁנֶּאֱמַר — as it is stated, *"קִינָה הִיא וְקוֹנְנוּהָ בְּנוֹת הַגּוֹיִם תְּקוֹנֵנָּה אוֹתָה"*
*It is a lamentation (kinah) and they shall lament it, the daughters of the
nations will lament it* (*Ezekiel* 32:16).[22] "וָהֶגֶה" זֶה מַתַּן שְׂכָרָן שֶׁל צַדִּיקִים
לֶעָתִיד לָבֹא — *"Rejoicing"* (*hegeh*) refers to the **reward of the righteous in**

Indeed, *Sifrei* (to *Numbers* 12:6) comments on another verse in the same passage, *for no human can see My face and live:*
"When [a human] is alive he cannot see, but
at the time of his death, he can see." *Sifrei*
then cites the aforementioned *Psalms* verse,
*All who descend to the dust will kneel before
Him.*

19. In a prophetic vision, Ezekiel saw a scroll
being spread out before him. According to
the plain meaning of the verse, he remarked
on the fact that the parchment was inscribed
on both sides. But since that detail does
not seem remarkable, the Sages perceived
a deeper meaning in the terms "face" and
"back."

20. The point of this quotation is to confirm

that the terms "face" and "back" can be
used to mean this world and the next, as
they do in the previous exposition (*Ahavas
Chesed*).

21. According to this approach, the scroll in
Ezekiel's vision answered the age-old question of why there are righteous people who
endure misfortune and wicked people who
enjoy good fortune (see *Magen Avos* and
Ben Avraham).

22. Ezekiel is told here of Egypt's eventual downfall at the hand of the Babylonians
shortly after the destruction of the First
Temple. From the verse's language it is
clear that the term *kinnim* connotes misfortune (see *Riaf* in *Ein Yaakov, Eruvin* 21a, for
a further nuance).

שֶׁנֶּאֱמַר (תהלים צב, ד) "עֲלֵי עָשׂוֹר וַעֲלֵי נָבֶל עֲלֵי הִגָּיוֹן בְּכִנּוֹר"[23]. "וָהִי" זֶה פּוּרְעָנוּתָן שֶׁל רְשָׁעִים לָעוֹלָם הַבָּא, שֶׁנֶּאֱמַר (יחזקאל ז, כו) "הֹוָה עַל הֹוָה תָּבוֹא וּשְׁמֻעָה °עַל שְׁמוּעָה תִּהְיֶה"[24]. הוּא הָיָה אוֹמֵר: פַּנּוּ הַבַּיִת מִפְּנֵי הַטֻּמְאָה[25] וְהָכִינוּ כִּסֵּא לְחִזְקִיָּה מֶלֶךְ יְהוּדָה[26]:

ב • הוּא הָיָה אוֹמֵר: מֵת מִתּוֹךְ הַיִּשּׁוּב סִימָן יָפֶה לוֹ. מִתּוֹךְ הַטֵּירוּף סִימָן

---

the World to Come,   שֶׁנֶּאֱמַר "עֲלֵי עָשׂוֹר וַעֲלֵי נָבֶל עֲלֵי הִגָּיוֹן בְּכִנּוֹר" — as it is stated, *Upon a ten-stringed instrument and upon a lyre, with singing (higayon) accompanied by a harp* (Psalms 92:4). [23]   "וָהִי" זֶה פּוּרְעָנוּתָן שֶׁל רְשָׁעִים לָעוֹלָם הַבָּא — "And woe" (*hi*) refers to the punishment of the wicked in the World to Come, שֶׁנֶּאֱמַר "הֹוָה עַל הֹוָה תָּבוֹא וּשְׁמֻעָה אֶל שְׁמוּעָה תִּהְיֶה" — as it is stated, *Disaster will come upon disaster, and report will be on report* (*Ezekiel* 7:26). [24]

The Baraisa concludes its account of Rabban Yochanan ben Zakkai's final words to his students:

הוּא הָיָה אוֹמֵר: פַּנּוּ הַבַּיִת מִפְּנֵי הַטֻּמְאָה — At the moment of his passing, **he was saying, "Clear the house** of utensils because of the *tumah*,[25]   וְהָכִינוּ כִּסֵּא לְחִזְקִיָּה מֶלֶךְ יְהוּדָה — **and prepare a seat for Hezekiah, King of Judah,** who has come to escort me."[26]

§2   The Baraisa cites further deathbed omens:

הוּא הָיָה אוֹמֵר — [Rabban Yochanan ben Zakkai][27] used to say: מֵת מִתּוֹךְ הַיִּשּׁוּב סִימָן יָפֶה לוֹ — **If one dies amid clarity of mind, it is a good omen for him;**   מִתּוֹךְ הַטֵּירוּף סִימָן רַע לוֹ — **amid confusion, it is a bad omen for**

---

23. The singing, or *higayon*, mentioned in this verse is occasioned by the recognition that *it is good to thank HASHEM and to sing praise to Your Name* — especially over *Your kindness in the dawn* (the World to Come) and *Your faith in the nights* (this world; see above, 1 §8, near the end). We thus learn that the term *hegeh,* based on the same root as *higayon,* is an expression of joy (see *Ahavas Chesed*).

24. Here Ezekiel is told of the ruinous events that would befall Jerusalem. The word הֹוָה, *happening* (in this context a disastrous happening), is similar to הִי. Thus, הִי connotes a disastrous happening of some kind.

25. A human corpse imparts *tumah* to everything under the same roof. Therefore, when Rabban Yochanan ben Zakkai sensed

that his soul was about to depart, he warned his students to remove all the utensils from the house so that they would not become defiled. [See Schottenstein ed. of *Kesubos,* 103b note 28, regarding the view (rejected by halachah) that corpses of the truly righteous do not generate *tumah*.]

26. Having dedicated his life to teaching Torah and promoting mitzvah observance among the Jewish people, Rabban Yochanan ben Zakkai was to be accompanied into the heavenly world by none other than King Hezekiah, who furthered God's cause in the same way, filling the Holy Land with Torah erudition "from Dan [in the north] to Beersheba [in the south]" (*Binyan Yehoshua,* from *HaKoseiv* to *Ein Yaakov, Berachos* 28b).

27. *Ben Avraham.*

רַע לוֹ. מִתּוֹךְ הַדִּבּוּר סִימָן יָפֶה לוֹ[28]. מִתּוֹךְ הַשְּׁתִיקָה סִימָן רַע לוֹ. מִתּוֹךְ
דִּבְרֵי תוֹרָה סִימָן יָפֶה לוֹ. מִתּוֹךְ דִּבְרֵי סְחוֹרָה סִימָן רַע לוֹ. מִתּוֹךְ דְּבַר
מִצְוָה סִימָן יָפֶה לוֹ. מִתּוֹךְ דְּבַר בַּטָּלָה סִימָן רַע לוֹ. מִתּוֹךְ שִׂמְחָה סִימָן יָפֶה
לוֹ. מִתּוֹךְ עַצְבוּת סִימָן רַע לוֹ. מִתּוֹךְ הַשְּׂחוֹק סִימָן יָפֶה לוֹ. מִתּוֹךְ בְּכִיָה
סִימָן רַע לוֹ[29]. מֵת בְּעֶרֶב שַׁבָּת סִימָן יָפֶה לוֹ. בְּמוֹצָאֵי שַׁבָּת סִימָן רַע לוֹ[30].

מִתּוֹךְ הַדִּבּוּר סִימָן יָפֶה לוֹ — amid speaking, it is a good omen for him; מִתּוֹךְ הַשְּׁתִיקָה סִימָן רַע לוֹ — amid silence, it is a bad omen for him;[28] מִתּוֹךְ דִּבְרֵי תוֹרָה סִימָן יָפֶה לוֹ — amid words of Torah, it is a good omen for him; מִתּוֹךְ דִּבְרֵי סְחוֹרָה סִימָן רַע לוֹ — amid discussion of business matters, it is a bad omen for him; מִתּוֹךְ דְּבַר מִצְוָה סִימָן יָפֶה לוֹ — amid discussion of a mitzvah matter, it is a good omen for him; מִתּוֹךְ דְּבַר בַּטָּלָה סִימָן רַע לוֹ — amid discussion of a trivial matter, it is a bad omen for him; מִתּוֹךְ שִׂמְחָה סִימָן יָפֶה לוֹ — amid joy, it is a good omen for him; מִתּוֹךְ עַצְבוּת סִימָן רַע לוֹ — amid sadness, it is a bad omen for him; מִתּוֹךְ הַשְּׂחוֹק סִימָן יָפֶה לוֹ — amid laughter, it is a good omen for him; מִתּוֹךְ בְּכִיָה סִימָן רַע לוֹ — amid weeping, it is a bad omen for him.[29] מֵת בְּעֶרֶב שַׁבָּת סִימָן יָפֶה לוֹ — If one dies on the eve of the Sabbath, it is a good omen for him; בְּמוֹצָאֵי שַׁבָּת סִימָן רַע לוֹ — on the night after the Sabbath, it is a bad omen for him.[30]

---

28. Sometimes, but not always (for some forms of speaking do not bode well for the departing soul, as the Baraisa goes on to say). But the point here is to draw a contrast with silence, which is *never* a good omen (*Ben Avraham*).

A person with clarity of mind and in command of his speech is able to make and disclose his final decisions regarding his property and legacy, recite a final *vidui* (confession) of his sins, and sanctify God's Name by leaving the world amid words of Torah and concern for the mitzvos. Dying in this way bodes well for a person (*Binyan Yehoshua*).

29. The Midrash, citing the verse וַתִּשְׂחַק לְיוֹם אַחֲרוֹן, *And she has joy at the last day* (*Proverbs* 31:25), teaches that God gives the righteous a preview of their Heavenly reward before they die, whereupon they die in a state of contentment (*Bereishis Rabbah* 62 §2). If someone is cheerful as he dies, he is likely rejoicing in the otherworldly bliss that he sees awaiting him in the Next World, with the opposite being true of someone who dies amid sadness and weeping (*Binyan Yehoshua*).

Although Rabban Yochanan ben Zakkai himself wept on his deathbed, as described above (§1), he did so hours before his actual death, when he still had time to impart a final lesson to his students. Indeed, by the time of his passing, he perceived that King Hezekiah had arrived to escort him to the Heavenly world, something that surely aroused in him a joyful confidence in the fate of his soul (*Ben Avraham*).

30. Sabbath eve is a time when even the souls of the wicked enter into a state of tranquility, since the torments of Gehinnom are suspended on the Sabbath. Thus, dying at this time is an omen that the departing soul will be led directly to its eternal rest, without a painful regimen of purification. Conversely, dying at the close of the Sabbath, when the souls of the wicked are returning to the fires of Gehinnom, is an omen that the departing soul is destined for the same fate (*Magen Avos*).

מֵת בְּעֶרֶב יוֹם הַכִּפּוּרִים סִימָן רַע לוֹ. בְּמוֹצָאֵי יוֹם הַכִּפּוּרִים סִימָן יָפֶה לוֹ:[31]

ג. כְּשֶׁחָלָה רַבִּי אֱלִיעֶזֶר, (אָמְרוּ) אוֹתוֹ הַיּוֹם עֶרֶב שַׁבָּת הָיָה. נִכְנַס רַבִּי עֲקִיבָא וַחֲבֵירָיו לְבַקְּרוֹ[33] וְהָיָה יָשֵׁן בְּתוֹךְ חַדְרוֹ וְהֵם יוֹשְׁבִין בַּטְּרַקְלִין שֶׁלּוֹ. נִכְנַס הוֹרְקָנוֹס בְּנוֹ לַחֲלוֹץ תְּפִילִין שֶׁלּוֹ[34] וְלֹא הִנִּיחוֹ וְהָיָה בּוֹכֶה[35], וְיָצָא הוֹרְקָנוֹס וְאָמַר לַחֲכָמִים: רַבּוֹתַי, דוֹמֶה לִי שֶׁנִּטְרְפָה דַּעְתּוֹ שֶׁל אַבָּא[36].

מֵת בְּעֶרֶב יוֹם הַכִּפּוּרִים סִימָן רַע לוֹ — If one dies on the eve of Yom Kippur, it is a bad omen for him;   בְּמוֹצָאֵי יוֹם הַכִּפּוּרִים סִימָן יָפֶה לוֹ — on the night after Yom Kippur, it is a good omen for him.[31]

§3 The Baraisa cites the example of an exceptional sage who died amid words of Torah:[32]

כְּשֶׁחָלָה רַבִּי אֱלִיעֶזֶר — When R' Eliezer fell deathly ill,   אוֹתוֹ הַיּוֹם עֶרֶב שַׁבָּת הָיָה — the day was the eve of the Sabbath,   נִכְנַס רַבִּי עֲקִיבָא וַחֲבֵירָיו לְבַקְּרוֹ — and R' Akiva and his colleagues[33] went in to visit him.   וְהָיָה יָשֵׁן בְּתוֹךְ חַדְרוֹ וְהֵם יוֹשְׁבִין בַּטְּרַקְלִין שֶׁלּוֹ — He was sleeping in his room, and they sat waiting in his parlor.   נִכְנַס הוֹרְקָנוֹס בְּנוֹ לַחֲלוֹץ תְּפִילִין שֶׁלּוֹ וְלֹא הִנִּיחוֹ וְהָיָה בּוֹכֶה — His son, Hyrkanos, went in to take off his [father's] tefillin before the Sabbath,[34] but he did not let him do so, and [Hyrkanos] was crying.[35]   וְיָצָא הוֹרְקָנוֹס וְאָמַר לַחֲכָמִים: רַבּוֹתַי, דוֹמֶה לִי שֶׁנִּטְרְפָה דַּעְתּוֹ שֶׁל אַבָּא — Hyrkanos came out and told the sages, "My teachers, it seems to me that my father's mind is muddled."[36]

---

31. If one dies just before experiencing the atonement of Yom Kippur, the timing is a sign that God wishes to maximize his punishment in the next world. Conversely, if one lives just long enough to receive that atonement, the timing indicates that God does not wish to punish him for his sins (*Magen Avos, Ben Avraham*).

32. *Magen Avos*. For another connection to the preceding segment, see note 35 below.

33. One of these colleagues was R' Elazar ben Azaryah (*Avos HaRosh*, citing *Seder HaDoros*), who is mentioned in connection with this incident above (19 §2) and later on in this account.

34. R' Eliezer held the opinion that the mitzvah to wear tefillin does not apply on the Sabbath (see *Menachos* 36b). [According to that view, the Sages forbade going from a private domain (רְשׁוּת הַיָּחִיד) to a public domain (רְשׁוּת הָרַבִּים) on the Sabbath while wearing tefillin, for in the absence of

a mitzvah to wear tefillin, wearing them is tantamount to carrying them.] Furthermore, the Sages forbade merely *wearing* tefillin on the Sabbath lest one inadvertently go outside while wearing them. Thus, as the Sabbath approached, Hyrkanos entered R' Eliezer's room to remove his tefillin (*Rashi, Tosafos* ibid. ד"ה לחלוץ).

35. R' Eliezer had rebuked him for trying to remove his tefillin, causing him to leave in shame (*Binyan Yehoshua*, from *Sanhedrin* 68a). Alternatively, Hyrkanos wept at the thought that his father had deteriorated to the point of senility (*Ben Avraham*; cf. *Magen Avos*), or because he thought that his father was dying מִתּוֹךְ הַטֵּרוּף, *amid confusion*, which is a bad omen, as taught in the previous segment (*Magen Avos*, who cites this connection to explain why the Baraisa retells this story here).

36. For if his mind were clear, he would have let me remove his tefillin (*Binyan Yehoshua*, from *Rashi* to *Sanhedrin* ibid.).

אָמַר לוֹ: בְּנִי, לֹא דַעְתִּי נִטְרְפָה[37] אֲבָל דַעְתָּךְ נִטְרְפָה שֶׁהַנַּחַת הַדְלָקַת
הַנֵּר שֶׁנִּתְחַיַּיבְתָּ עָלֶיהָ מִיתָה לַשָּׁמַיִם[38] וְהָיִיתָ מִתְעַסֵּק בִּתְפִלִּין
שֶׁאֵין אַתָּה מִתְחַיֵּיב עֲלֵיהֶן אֶלָּא מִשּׁוּם שְׁבוּת[39]. כֵּיוָן שֶׁרָאוּ חֲכָמִים
שֶׁדַּעְתּוֹ מְיוּשֶּׁבֶת עָלָיו (נִכְנְסוּ) יָשְׁבוּ לְפָנָיו בְּרָחוֹק אַרְבַּע אַמּוֹת[40].
אָמְרוּ לוֹ: רַבִּי, כֶּסֶת עֲגוּלָה וְהַכִּידוּר וְהָאֵימוּם וְהַקְּמֵיעַ וּתְפִלִּין

אָמַר לוֹ, בְּנִי, לֹא דַעְתִּי נִטְרְפָה אֲבָל — R' Eliezer overheard this and said to him,
דַעְתָּךְ נִטְרְפָה — "My son, it is not my mind that is muddled[37] but your mind
that is muddled, שֶׁהַנַּחַת הַדְלָקַת הַנֵּר שֶׁנִּתְחַיַּיבְתָּ עָלֶיהָ מִיתָה לַשָּׁמַיִם — for you
have neglected the lighting of the Sabbath candle, for which you will be liable
to death before the Heavenly Court if you do it too late,[38] וְהָיִיתָ מִתְעַסֵּק
בִּתְפִלִּין שֶׁאֵין אַתָּה מִתְחַיֵּיב עֲלֵיהֶן אֶלָּא מִשּׁוּם שְׁבוּת — and you occupied yourself
instead with removing my tefillin, for which you are liable only for violating
a Rabbinic prohibition at worst."[39] כֵּיוָן שֶׁרָאוּ חֲכָמִים שֶׁדַּעְתּוֹ מְיוּשֶּׁבֶת עָלָיו —
Once the sages realized that [R' Eliezer's] mind was composed, נִכְנְסוּ
יָשְׁבוּ לְפָנָיו בְּרָחוֹק אַרְבַּע אַמּוֹת — they entered his room and sat before him at
a distance of four amos, in accordance with the laws of excommunication.[40]

The visiting sages posed a series of questions concerning the laws of tumah
to R' Eliezer. The Baraisa recounts their discussion:
אָמְרוּ לוֹ — They said to him, רַבִּי, כֶּסֶת עֲגוּלָה וְהַכִּידוּר וְהָאֵימוּם וְהַקְּמֵיעַ וּתְפִלִּין

---

37. R' Eliezer was careful to point this out
because if his mind were muddled, it would
have been a bad omen for him, as mentioned in note 35 (Magen Avos).

38. When a Jew desecrates the Sabbath
with intent, but without a proper warning or
valid witnesses to testify against him in beis
din, he is liable to the Heaven-administered
penalty of kares (Kereisos 1:1). [According
to the version found in Yerushalmi Shabbos
2:7, R' Eliezer actually said that he would be
liable to kares.]

39. You have neglected to kindle the Sabbath lights, despite the fact that the Sabbath
is approaching and kindling them after the
holy day has begun is Biblically prohibited,
yet you are occupied with removing my
tefillin to ensure that I do not transgress a
Rabbinic prohibition. Wearing tefillin on the
Sabbath would not even lead to the transgression of a Biblical prohibition according
to R' Eliezer, for under Biblical law even if
one were to go out to a public domain on

the Sabbath while wearing tefillin, he would
not be deemed to be carrying the tefillin.
Since tefillin are worn during the week, they
are analogous to an article of clothing or
adornment that, when worn, is considered
an extension of the body (Binyan Yehoshua,
from Rashi to Sanhedrin ibid.).

Ordinarily, tefillin would be removed
before the Sabbath lights were kindled.
Hyrkanos thus acted in accordance with the
normal procedure. However, on that Friday,
the Sabbath preparations (including the
cooking — Rashi ibid.) had been delayed
due to R' Eliezer's illness. R' Eliezer therefore reproached him for attending to the
removal of his tefillin before other, more essential preparations (see Tosafos, Sanhedrin
ad loc. ד"ה היאך; Chidushei HaRan ad loc.).

40. The Gemara in Bava Metzia (59b) relates that R' Eliezer was excommunicated
by the other Sages because of his refusal to
accede to the opposing majority view in a
certain halachic matter (Binyan Yehoshua,
from Rashi ibid.).

שֶׁנִּקְרְעוּ מַהוּ (מְקַבְּלִין טוּמְאָה)‎42,41. אָמַר לָהֶם: מְקַבְּלִין טוּמְאָה וְהַטְבִּילוּ
אוֹתָן כְּמוֹ שֶׁהֵן וְהִזָּהֲרוּ בָּהֶן שֶׁהֵן הֲלָכוֹת גְּדוֹלוֹת שֶׁנֶּאֶמְרוּ לְמֹשֶׁה בְּסִינַי.

שֶׁנִּקְרְעוּ מַהוּ מְקַבְּלִין טוּמְאָה — "My teacher, what is the law concerning **a round pillow, a ball, a shoe-form, an amulet, and tefillin that became torn?**[41] Are they susceptible to *tumah*?[42] And in the event they tear open and contract *tumah,* can they be purified through immersion in a *mikveh* without being emptied of the matter inside them?"[43] אָמַר לָהֶם — [R' Eliezer] replied,

מְקַבְּלִין טוּמְאָה וְהַטְבִּילוּ אוֹתָן כְּמוֹ שֶׁהֵן — "They are all susceptible to *tumah* when whole, **and** if they contract *tumah,* **immerse them in a *mikveh* as they are,** i.e., without being emptied, even if they are torn.[44] וְהִזָּהֲרוּ בָּהֶן שֶׁהֵן — **And take care** to remember the things

41. In earlier times, all of these items consisted of a sealed leather casing with some inner component: (i) a "round pillow" containing unspecified stuffing, used by merchants and sewn together, leaving no opening (*Rambam, Commentary* to *Mikvaos* 10:2); (ii) a "ball" consisting of a leather skin stuffed with ram's wool, used for recreation (*Binyan Yehoshua,* from *Rashi*); (iii) an oblong leather skin shaped like a shoe, filled with hair and sewn shut ("shoe-form"), used by shoemakers as a template on which to craft new shoes (ibid.); (iv) a stuffed leather pendant ("amulet") worn as jewelry (ibid.); and (v) tefillin filled with sacred parchments.

The word שֶׁנִּקְרְעוּ, *that became torn,* refers to all five leather-covered items.

42. A leather article can contract *tumah* only if it has a hollow that can serve as a receptacle. This is derived from a Scriptural passage (*Leviticus* 11:32) dealing with *tumah,* in which leather articles are compared to a sack. Since a sack is a receptacle, we learn from the Scriptural comparison that an article of leather is susceptible to *tumah* only if it can serve as a receptacle (see *Keilim* 2:1 with *Rav*).

The Sages and R' Eliezer had debated whether the articles mentioned above are susceptible to *tumah.* The Sages had maintained that since the leather casing of these articles is sewn permanently shut after it is filled, it does not qualify as a receptacle. Accordingly, the articles are not susceptible to *tumah.* R' Eliezer had maintained that a

hollow that is permanently filled is a valid receptacle, and accordingly, these articles are susceptible to *tumah.*

The visiting sages now inquired of R' Eliezer, in the moments before his death, whether he still held his opinion (*Binyan Yehoshua,* from *Rashi*).

43. With this second question, R' Akiva and his colleagues referred to another point the Sages had debated with R' Eliezer. The Sages agreed that if any of the aforementioned leather articles tore open and its hollow became exposed, the article would be susceptible to *tumah.* There was a question, however, as to how such an article might be purified in a *mikveh.* The Sages maintained that the leather pouch would have to be emptied of all matter before it could be immersed. Otherwise, the matter would constitute a barrier [חֲצִיצָה] between the water of the *mikveh* and the leather receptacle. R' Eliezer maintained that it could be immersed while filled, because the pouch with its filling constituted one complete utensil that could be purified as a unit.

Here, too, the visiting sages wished to know whether R' Eliezer still held his opinion (ibid.).

[As noted, this elucidation follows *Rashi.* For a review of Rishonim who explain the dispute differently, see *Yad Avraham* edition of *Keilim* 23:1.]

44. Thus, R' Eliezer maintained his original opinion on both issues (ibid.). Regarding the significance of this fact, see above, 19 §4, note 20.

וְהָיוּ שׁוֹאֲלִים לוֹ בִּטְהָרוֹת בִּטְמָאוֹת בְּמִקְוָאוֹת. אָמְרוּ לוֹ: רַבִּי, מַה הוּא
זֶה. אָמַר לָהֶם: טָמֵא. מַה הוּא זֶה. אָמַר לָהֶם: טָהוֹר. וְהָיָה מֵשִׁיב עַל טָמֵא
טָמֵא וְעַל טָהוֹר טָהוֹר. אַחַר כָּךְ אָמַר רַבִּי אֱלִיעֶזֶר לַחֲכָמִים: תָּמֵהַּ אֲנִי
עַל תַּלְמִידֵי הַדּוֹר שֶׁמָּא יֵעָנְשׁוּ מִיתָה לַשָּׁמַיִם. אָמְרוּ לוֹ: רַבִּי, מִפְּנֵי מָה.
אָמַר לָהֶם: מִפְּנֵי שֶׁלֹּא בָאוּ וְשִׁמְּשׁוּ אוֹתִי[45]. וְאַחַר כָּךְ אָמַר לַעֲקִיבָא בֶּן
יוֹסֵף: עֲקִיבָא, מִפְּנֵי מָה לֹא בָּאתָ לְפָנַי וְשִׁמַּשְׁתָּ אוֹתִי. אָמַר לוֹ: רַבִּי, לֹא
נִפְנֵיתִי[46]. אָמַר לוֹ: תָּמֵהַּ אֲנִי עָלֶיךָ אִם תָּמוּת מִיתַת עַצְמְךָ[47]. וְיֵשׁ אוֹמְרִים:
לֹא אָמַר לוֹ כְּלוּם, אֶלָּא כֵּיוָן שֶׁאָמַר רַבִּי אֱלִיעֶזֶר לְתַלְמִידָיו כָּךְ, מִיַּד

I have told you, for they are important halachos that were transmitted to Moses at Sinai." וְהָיוּ שׁוֹאֲלִים לוֹ בִּטְהָרוֹת בִּטְמָאוֹת בְּמִקְוָאוֹת — After this opening exchange, they asked him more questions about *taharah, tumah,* and *mikveh* matters. אָמְרוּ לוֹ: רַבִּי, מַה הוּא זֶה. אָמַר לָהֶם: טָמֵא — They would say to him, "My teacher, what is the status of this object (or situation)?" and he would tell them, *"Tamei."* מַה הוּא זֶה. אָמַר לָהֶם: טָהוֹר — Then they would ask, "What is the status of that object?" and he would tell them, *"Tahor."* וְהָיָה מֵשִׁיב עַל טָמֵא טָמֵא וְעַל טָהוֹר טָהוֹר — He continued in this way, answering for a *tamei* object, *"Tamei,"* and for a *tahor* object, *"Tahor."*

R' Eliezer reflects on the fact that it had been many years since the sages have come to him for guidance:

אַחַר כָּךְ אָמַר רַבִּי אֱלִיעֶזֶר לַחֲכָמִים — Afterward, R' Eliezer said to the sages, תָּמֵהַּ אֲנִי עַל תַּלְמִידֵי הַדּוֹר שֶׁמָּא יֵעָנְשׁוּ מִיתָה לַשָּׁמַיִם — "I am surprised at the behavior of the students of the generation; I worry lest they be punished with death by Heaven." אָמְרוּ לוֹ: רַבִּי, מִפְּנֵי מָה — They said to him, "My teacher, why so?" אָמַר לָהֶם: מִפְּנֵי שֶׁלֹּא בָאוּ וְשִׁמְּשׁוּ אוֹתִי — He replied, "Because they did not come to study under me."[45] וְאַחַר כָּךְ אָמַר לַעֲקִיבָא בֶּן יוֹסֵף — Afterward, he said to Akiva ben Yosef, עֲקִיבָא, מִפְּנֵי מָה לֹא בָּאתָ לְפָנַי וְשִׁמַּשְׁתָּ אוֹתִי — "Akiva, why did *you* not come before me to study under me?" אָמַר לוֹ: רַבִּי, לֹא נִפְנֵיתִי — Said [R' Akiva] in reply, "My teacher, I did not have the opportunity."[46] אָמַר לוֹ: תָּמֵהַּ אֲנִי עָלֶיךָ אִם תָּמוּת מִיתַת עַצְמְךָ — [R' Eliezer] then said to him, "I would be surprised at you if you die a natural death."[47] וְיֵשׁ אוֹמְרִים: לֹא אָמַר לוֹ כְּלוּם — But some say that he said nothing to him. אֶלָּא כֵּיוָן שֶׁאָמַר רַבִּי אֱלִיעֶזֶר לְתַלְמִידָיו כָּךְ, מִיַּד

---

45. They have fallen short of their potential in Torah knowledge because they failed to study under me, and they are likely to suffer gravely for this (*Ben Yehoyada* to *Sanhedrin* 68a).

46. Rather than offend R' Eliezer by

mentioning the excommunication, his true reason for staying away, he gave this excuse (*Yad Ramah* ad loc.), which was not without merit, since R' Akiva was the teacher of 24,000 Torah scholars (*Magen Avos*).

47. See note 45.

נָמֵס דָּמוֹ בְּקִרְבּוֹ. אָמַר לוֹ רַבִּי עֲקִיבָא: רַבִּי, מִיתָתִי בַּמֶּה. אָמַר לוֹ: (רַבִּי)
עֲקִיבָא, שֶׁלְּךָ קָשָׁה מִכּוּלָּן[49]. נִכְנַס רַבִּי עֲקִיבָא וְיָשַׁב לְפָנָיו, וְאָמַר לוֹ: רַבִּי,
מֵעַתָּה שְׁנֵה לִי[50]. פָּתַח וְשָׁנָה לוֹ שְׁלֹשׁ מֵאוֹת הֲלָכוֹת בְּבַהֶרֶת[51]. בְּאוֹתָהּ
שָׁעָה הִגְבִּיהַּ רַבִּי אֱלִיעֶזֶר שְׁתֵּי זְרוֹעוֹתָיו וְהִנִּיחָן עַל חָזֵהוּ שֶׁלּוֹ[52], וְאָמַר:
אוֹי לִי עַל שְׁתֵּי זְרוֹעוֹתַי אֵלֶּה שְׁנֵי סִפְרֵי תוֹרוֹת שֶׁנִּפְטָרִין מִן הָעוֹלָם[53],
שֶׁאִם יִהְיוּ כָּל הַיַּמִּים דְּיוֹ וְכָל קָנִים קוֹלְמוֹסִים[54] וְכָל בְּנֵי אָדָם לַבְלָרִין

נָמֵס דָּמוֹ בְּקִרְבּוֹ — Rather, once R' Eliezer said what he said to his students, the blood drained[48] within [R' Akiva]. אָמַר לוֹ רַבִּי עֲקִיבָא: רַבִּי, מִיתָתִי בַּמֶּה — R' Akiva said to him, "My teacher, what will the circumstances of *my* death be?" אָמַר לוֹ: עֲקִיבָא, שֶׁלְּךָ קָשָׁה מִכּוּלָּן — He replied, "Akiva, yours will be worse than theirs."[49] נִכְנַס רַבִּי עֲקִיבָא וְיָשַׁב לְפָנָיו, וְאָמַר לוֹ — R' Akiva entered and sat before him and said, רַבִּי, מֵעַתָּה שְׁנֵה לִי — "My teacher, teach me from now on."[50] פָּתַח וְשָׁנָה לוֹ שְׁלֹשׁ מֵאוֹת הֲלָכוֹת בְּבַהֶרֶת — [R' Eliezer] began and taught him three hundred laws concerning a *baheres*.[51]

R' Eliezer despairs of transmitting all of his Torah knowledge and preserving it for posterity.

בְּאוֹתָהּ שָׁעָה הִגְבִּיהַּ רַבִּי אֱלִיעֶזֶר שְׁתֵּי זְרוֹעוֹתָיו וְהִנִּיחָן עַל חָזֵהוּ שֶׁלּוֹ — At that time, R' Eliezer took his two arms, placed them upon his chest[52] וְאָמַר: אוֹי לִי — and said, "Woe to me עַל שְׁתֵּי זְרוֹעוֹתַי אֵלֶּה שְׁנֵי סִפְרֵי תוֹרוֹת שֶׁנִּפְטָרִין מִן הָעוֹלָם — regarding these two arms of mine — two Torah scrolls that are departing from the world.[53] שֶׁאִם יִהְיוּ כָּל הַיַּמִּים דְּיוֹ וְכָל קָנִים קוֹלְמוֹסִים וְכָל בְּנֵי אָדָם — For if all the seas were black ink, and all the marshes were quills,[54] לַבְלָרִין — For if all the seas were black ink, and all the marshes were quills,[54]

---

48. Literally, *melted*.

49. For you have an especially broad mind, and if you had studied under me you could have grown immensely (*Binyan Yehoshua*, from *Rashi*). Indeed, R' Akiva was ultimately tortured to death by the Romans, who flayed his flesh with iron combs (see *Berachos* 61b).

50. [It seems that at this point, R' Akiva entered into R' Eliezer's four *amos*, demonstrating that the excommunication had ended. He was then at liberty to ask R' Eliezer to teach him Torah (see *Radal, Emek HaBerachah* [an introduction to *Pirkei De-Rabbi Eliezer*] §19).]

51. A *baheres* (a white skin-affliction) is a type of *tzaraas*. The three hundred laws defined which of the various shades of *baheres* are considered *tzaraas* (*Rashi, Sanhedrin* 68a).

52. A precedent for this is found in the Midrashic account of Moses' death: "God said to him, 'Place your hands upon your chest,' and he placed his hands upon his chest" (*Magen Avos*, citing *Devarim Rabbah* 11 §10). Indeed, the customary position for burial is with the hands folded over the chest (*Yerushalmi Nazir* 9:3, cited by *Radal* and *Eitz Yosef* to *Devarim Rabbah* ibid.).

53. Just as the words on a Torah Scroll are concealed when the scroll is rolled up, my wisdom will likewise be concealed when I die, for the scholars did not sufficiently partake of it (*Binyan Yehoshua*, from *Rashi*). R' Eliezer referred specifically to his arms because in Scriptural usage the term "arm" often alludes to strength and power. In R' Eliezer's case, his vast potential for teaching Torah had been left untapped (*Maharsha, Sanhedrin* ad loc.; cf. *Toras Chaim* ad loc.).

54. Reeds, which grow in marshes, are used for quills.

אֵינָן יְכוֹלִין לִכְתּוֹב כָּל מַה שֶּׁקָּרִיתִי וְשָׁנִיתִי וּמַה שֶּׁשִּׁמַּשְׁתִּי לַחֲכָמִים
בַּיְשִׁיבָה וְלֹא חָסַרְתִּי (מִכֹּל אֲשֶׁר שָׁאֲלוּ עֵינַי) אֶלָּא כְּאָדָם שֶׁטּוֹבֵל אֶצְבָּעוֹ
בַּיָּם[56] וְלֹא חָסַרְתִּי מִתַּלְמוּדִי אֶלָּא כְּדֵי שֶׁיִּכְחוֹל הַמִּכְחוֹל מִן הַשְּׁפוֹפֶרֶת[57],
וְעוֹד אֲנִי שׁוֹנֶה שָׁלֹשׁ מֵאוֹת הֲלָכוֹת (שמות כב, יז) בְּ״מְכַשֵּׁפָה לֹא תְחַיֶּה״, וְיֵשׁ
אוֹמְרִים: שְׁלֹשֶׁת אֲלָפִים (מֹשֶׁל) הֲלָכוֹת, וְלֹא שְׁאָלַנִי אָדָם בָּהֶם דָּבָר מֵעוֹלָם
חוּץ מֵעֲקִיבָא בֶן יוֹסֵף[58], שֶׁפַּעַם אַחַת אָמַר לִי: רַבִּי, לַמְּדֵנִי אֵיךְ נוֹטְעִים
קִישּׁוּאִין[60] (וְאֵיךְ עוֹקְרִין אוֹתָן). אָמַרְתִּי דָבָר אֶחָד נִתְמַלֵּא כָּל הַשָּׂדֶה

אֵינָן — and heaven and earth were scrolls,[55] and all the people were scribes, **יְכוֹלִין לִכְתּוֹב כָּל מַה שֶּׁקָּרִיתִי וְשָׁנִיתִי וּמַה שֶּׁשִּׁמַּשְׁתִּי לַחֲכָמִים בַּיְשִׁיבָה** — they would not suffice to record everything that I have studied in Scripture, in the Mishnah, and under the Sages in the academy. **וְלֹא חָסַרְתִּי אֶלָּא כְּאָדָם שֶׁטּוֹבֵל אֶצְבָּעוֹ בַּיָּם** — Yet I did not diminish my teachers' knowledge any more than a person who dips his finger in the sea diminishes the sea.[56] **וְלֹא חָסַרְתִּי מִתַּלְמוּדִי אֶלָּא כְּדֵי שֶׁיִּכְחוֹל הַמִּכְחוֹל מִן הַשְּׁפוֹפֶרֶת** — And, though I have taught much Torah, I have not diminished my learning any more than an applicator picks up from a tube of eye-powder."[57]

R' Eliezer continues:

וְעוֹד אֲנִי שׁוֹנֶה שָׁלֹשׁ מֵאוֹת הֲלָכוֹת בְּ״מְכַשֵּׁפָה לֹא תְחַיֶּה״ — "And furthermore, I have learned three hundred laws in regard to the verse, *You shall not permit a sorceress to live*" (*Exodus 22:17*).

The Baraisa interjects:

וְיֵשׁ אוֹמְרִים: שְׁלֹשֶׁת אֲלָפִים הֲלָכוֹת — And some say it was three thousand laws.

R' Eliezer continues:

וְלֹא שְׁאָלַנִי אָדָם בָּהֶם דָּבָר מֵעוֹלָם חוּץ מֵעֲקִיבָא בֶן יוֹסֵף — "And nobody ever questioned me about them at all,[58] except for Akiva ben Yosef, **שֶׁפַּעַם אַחַת אָמַר לִי: רַבִּי, לַמְּדֵנִי אֵיךְ נוֹטְעִים קִישּׁוּאִין** — for he said to me once as we were walking along a road,[59] 'My teacher, teach me how one plants cucumbers by means of sorcery.'[60] **אָמַרְתִּי דָבָר אֶחָד נִתְמַלֵּא כָּל הַשָּׂדֶה**

---

55. *Shir HaShirim Rabbah* 1 §20.

56. Despite all that I learned from my teachers, I did not narrow the gap between their knowledge and mine any more (proportionally) than someone reduces the sea-level when removing his finger from the water (see *Binyan Yehoshua,* from *Rashi*).

57. Despite all that I have taught my students, I did not narrow the gap between my knowledge and theirs any more than

someone reduces the amount of eye-powder in a tube with one dip of the applicator (ibid.).

58. Not only did the other sages not exhaust my knowledge, but they did not even think of asking me about certain areas of Torah law (*Yad Ramah, Sanhedrin* 68a).

59. *Binyan Yehoshua,* from *Sanhedrin* 68a.

60. This is among the sorcerous practices

קִישׁוּאִין[61]. אָמַר לִי: רַבִּי, לִמַּדְתַּנִי נְטִיעָתָן לַמְּדֵנִי עֲקִירָתָן. אָמַרְתִּי דָּבָר
אֶחָד נִתְכַּנְּסוּ כָּל הַקִּישׁוּאִין כּוּלָם לְמָקוֹם אֶחָד. אָמַר לוֹ רַבִּי אֶלְעָזָר
בֶּן עֲזַרְיָה: רַבִּי, מִנְעָל שֶׁעַל גַּבֵּי הָאִימוּם[62,63]. אָמַר לוֹ: טָהוֹר. וְהָיָה
מֵשִׁיב עַל טָמֵא טָמֵא וְעַל טָהוֹר טָהוֹר עַד שֶׁיָּצְתָה נִשְׁמָתוֹ בְּטָהֳרָה[64].
מִיָּד קָרַע רַבִּי אֶלְעָזָר בֶּן עֲזַרְיָה אֶת בְּגָדָיו וּבָכָה וְיָצָא וְאָמַר לַחֲכָמִים:
רַבּוֹתַי, בּוֹאוּ וּרְאוּ בְּרַבִּי אֱלִיעֶזֶר שֶׁטָּהוֹר הוּא לָעוֹלָם הַבָּא (לְפִי) שֶׁיָּצְתָה

קִישׁוּאִין — I said one word and the entire nearby field became filled with
cucumbers.[61]   אָמַר לִי: רַבִּי, לִמַּדְתַּנִי נְטִיעָתָן לַמְּדֵנִי עֲקִירָתָן — He said to me,
'My teacher, you have taught me how to plant them; now teach me how to
uproot them.'   אָמַרְתִּי דָּבָר אֶחָד נִתְכַּנְּסוּ כָּל הַקִּישׁוּאִין כּוּלָם לְמָקוֹם אֶחָד — I said
one word and they all were gathered to one place."

The sages departed. At the hour in which R' Eliezer died, R' Akiva was away
but R' Elazar ben Azaryah was present.

רַבִּי,   אָמַר לוֹ רַבִּי אֶלְעָזָר בֶּן עֲזַרְיָה — R' Elazar ben Azaryah asked him,
מִנְעָל שֶׁעַל גַּבֵּי הָאִימוּם — "My teacher, what is the law concerning a completed shoe that is still on the shoe-form?[62] Is it susceptible to tumah or
not?"[63]   אָמַר לוֹ: טָהוֹר — [R' Eliezer] replied, "It is tahor, i.e., it is not susceptible to tumah."   וְהָיָה מֵשִׁיב עַל טָמֵא טָמֵא וְעַל טָהוֹר טָהוֹר — More questions followed and [R' Eliezer] continued answering, "Tamei," for a tamei
object and "Tahor" for a tahor object,   עַד שֶׁיָּצְתָה נִשְׁמָתוֹ בְּטָהֳרָה — until
his soul departed in purity.[64]   מִיָּד קָרַע רַבִּי אֶלְעָזָר בֶּן עֲזַרְיָה אֶת בְּגָדָיו וּבָכָה
— Immediately, R' Elazar ben Azaryah tore his clothes and wept.   וְיָצָא
He — וְאָמַר לַחֲכָמִים: רַבּוֹתַי, בּוֹאוּ וּרְאוּ בְּרַבִּי אֱלִיעֶזֶר שֶׁטָּהוֹר הוּא לָעוֹלָם הַבָּא
went out and said to the sages, "My teachers! Come and see that R' Eliezer
is pure and ready to proceed directly to the World to Come,   שֶׁיָּצְתָה

---

for which a sorcerer can incur the death
penalty. Knowledge of these techniques
was transmitted by Moses at Sinai in order
for members of a sanhedrin to be able to
properly assess an act of supposed sorcery.
Such knowledge was also important for dis-
tinguishing between true prophets and sorcerers (Teshuvos HaGeonim, Mussafia §31).

61. The Gemara (Sanhedrin 68a) explains
how R' Eliezer was permitted to do this.

62. That is, a shoe that the shoemaker has
not yet removed from the shoe-form.

63. This was the subject of another debate
between the Sages and R' Eliezer (see
Keilim 26:4). The law is that an unfinished

utensil is not susceptible to tumah. R' Eliezer
maintained that a shoe is not considered
"finished" until it is removed from the shoe-
form. Thus, while on the shoe-form it is not
susceptible to tumah even if the rest of the
shoemaking process has been completed.
The Sages maintained that since removing
the shoe from the form does not require
skilled labor, a shoe that is otherwise complete is considered "finished," and is susceptible to tumah even while it is on the form.
In this case, too, R' Elazar ben Azaryah
inquired whether R' Eliezer still maintained
his original opinion (Binyan Yehoshua, from
Rashi).

64. He passed away with the word tahor

נִשְׁמָתוֹ בְּטָהֳרָה. לְאַחַר שַׁבָּת בָּא רַבִּי עֲקִיבָא וּמְצָאוֹ בָּאֲרִיסְרַטְיָא שֶׁבָּא
מְקַסְרִי לְלוֹד. מִיָּד קָרַע אֶת בְּגָדָיו וְתָלַשׁ בִּשְׂעָרוֹ וְהָיָה דָּמוֹ שׁוֹתֵת וְנוֹפֵל
לָאָרֶץ 65 וְהָיָה צוֹעֵק וּבוֹכֶה וְאוֹמֵר: אַלְלַי רַבִּי עָלֶיךָ, אַלְלַי רַבִּי עָלֶיךָ
מָרִי, שֶׁהִנַּחְתָּ כָּל הַדּוֹר יָתוֹם. פָּתַח עָלָיו בְּשׁוּרָה 66 וְאָמַר: אָבִי אָבִי רֶכֶב
יִשְׂרָאֵל וּפָרָשָׁיו 67, מָעוֹת יֵשׁ לִי עָלַי וְאֵין לִי שׁוּלְחָנִי לְרַצוֹתָן: 68

לְאַחַר שַׁבָּת בָּא רַבִּי — נִשְׁמָתוֹ בְּטָהֳרָה — for his soul departed amid purity." עֲקִיבָא וּמְצָאוֹ בָּאֲרִיסְרַטְיָא שֶׁבָּא מְקַסְרִי לְלוֹד — After the Sabbath, R' Akiva came and found the coffin of [R' Eliezer] on the public thoroughfare, as [his funeral procession] was going from Caesarea to Lod. מִיָּד קָרַע אֶת בְּגָדָיו — וְתָלַשׁ בִּשְׂעָרוֹ וְהָיָה דָּמוֹ שׁוֹתֵת וְנוֹפֵל לָאָרֶץ — Immediately, [R' Akiva] tore his clothes and pulled out some of his hair. His blood was dripping and falling to the ground,[65] וְהָיָה צוֹעֵק וּבוֹכֶה — and he was crying out and weeping, וְאוֹמֵר — say- ing, "Woe is to me regarding you, my teacher! Woe is to me regarding you, my teacher, my master! For you have left the entire generation orphaned!" פָּתַח עָלָיו בְּשׁוּרָה וְאָמַר — In the funeral line,[66] he opened his eulogy for [R' Eliezer] by saying, אָבִי אָבִי רֶכֶב יִשְׂרָאֵל וּפָרָשָׁיו — "My father, my fa- ther, chariot of Israel and its horsemen![67] מָעוֹת יֵשׁ לִי עָלַי וְאֵין לִי שׁוּלְחָנִי — I have money but I have no moneychanger to whom to proffer לְרַצוֹתָן — it!"[68]

("pure") on his lips, which indicated that his soul was pure (Yerushalmi Shabbos 2:7).

65. R' Akiva kept striking his flesh until his blood flowed to the ground (Binyan Yeho-shua, from Sanhedrin 68a). He did not thereby violate the Biblical prohibition against cutting one's flesh over the dead (Leviticus 19:28), because he was mourning the Torah knowledge that had been lost (as he would soon make clear), rather than the soul of R' Eliezer (Binyan Yehoshua, from Tosafos to Sanhedrin ibid. s.v. היה).

66. It was customary to form a line encir-cling the casket for the eulogy (ibid., from Rashi).

67. These words are borrowed from the cry uttered by the prophet Elisha (II Kings 2:12) when his mentor, Elijah the Prophet, ascended to Heaven. Bemoaning the loss of a great advocate for the Jewish people, Elisha meant to say, "My master, my master,

whose prayers accomplish more for Israel than chariots and horsemen!" (Binyan Ye-hoshau, from Targum ad loc.). When R' Akiva applied this lament to R' Eliezer, he was alluding to R' Eliezer's prowess (sym-bolized by that of chariots and horsemen) in debating matters of Torah law (ibid., from Maharsha).

68. [See Nuschas HaGra.] In other words, I have many questions in matters of Torah law but there is nobody left to present them to (Rashi, Sanhedrin 86a). In earlier times, people would bring coins to a moneychang-er to check their condition and assess their value. Thus, R' Akiva was comparing him-self to a layman who has many coins but does not know their value. He was saying, "I have much Torah knowledge, but I also have many questions and uncertainties about what I have learned, and now there is no expert who can resolve them for me" (Binyan Yehoshua, from Maharsha).

ד • בֶּן עַזַּאי אוֹמֵר: הֱוֵי רָץ לְמִצְוָה קַלָּה.[69] הוּא הָיָה אוֹמֵר: אִם עָשִׂיתָ
מִצְוָה אַחַת וְאֵין אַתָּה דּוֹאֵג מִמֶּנָּה מֵאוֹתָהּ מִצְוָה,[70] סוֹף שֶׁהִיא גּוֹרֶרֶת
מִצְוֹת הַרְבֵּה. הָעוֹבֵר עֲבֵירָה אַחַת וְאֵינוֹ דּוֹאֵג מֵאוֹתָהּ עֲבֵירָה, סוֹף שֶׁהִיא
גּוֹרֶרֶת עֲבֵירוֹת הַרְבֵּה. שֶׁמִּצְוָה גּוֹרֶרֶת מִצְוָה[71] וַעֲבֵירָה גּוֹרֶרֶת עֲבֵירָה.[72]

---

§4 The Baraisa returns to the teachings of Ben Azzai, echoing *Avos* 4:2:
בֶּן עַזַּאי אוֹמֵר — **Ben Azzai says:** הֱוֵי רָץ לְמִצְוָה קַלָּה — **Run to** perform
even a "minor" mitzvah.[69]

Ben Azzai continues:

הוּא הָיָה אוֹמֵר—**He used to say:** אִם עָשִׂיתָ מִצְוָה אַחַת וְאֵין אַתָּה דּוֹאֵג מִמֶּנָּה מֵאוֹתָהּ
מִצְוָה — **If you have performed** even **one mitzvah and you are not troubled,**
i.e., regretful, **about** performing **that mitzvah,**[70] סוֹף שֶׁהִיא גּוֹרֶרֶת מִצְוֹת הַרְבֵּה
— **in the end it will lead to many** other **mitzvos.** הָעוֹבֵר עֲבֵירָה אַחַת וְאֵינוֹ דּוֹאֵג
מֵאוֹתָהּ עֲבֵירָה—**Conversely, if someone commits one sin and he is not troubled**
about committing **that sin,** סוֹף שֶׁהִיא גּוֹרֶרֶת עֲבֵירוֹת הַרְבֵּה — **in the end it will**
lead to many other **sins,** שֶׁמִּצְוָה גּוֹרֶרֶת מִצְוָה וַעֲבֵירָה גּוֹרֶרֶת עֲבֵירָה — **because**
one mitzvah leads to another mitzvah[71] **and one sin leads to another sin;**[72]

---

69. That is, a mitzvah that appears minor to you (*Binyan Yehoshua*, from *Rashi* to *Avos* 4:2). Your assessment of a given mitzvah as "minor" may very well be wrong, since the Torah, which does not specify rewards for obeying its positive commands, gives us no yardstick with which to measure those commands. As another sage, Rebbi, taught in *Avos* (2:1), "Be as scrupulous with a 'minor' mitzvah as with a 'major' one, for you do not know the reward for the [respective] mitzvos" (*Ahavas Chesed*).

Moreover, the entire concept of favoring some mitzvos over others betrays a misguided emphasis on reward and self-interest. Proper mitzvah observance comes along with a desire to fulfill God's Will, and anyone filled with that desire will regard all mitzvos as equally binding revelations of God's Will (*Magen Avos*; see *Shaarei Teshuvah* 1 §38 regarding sins: "One should look not at the smallness of the transgression, but at the greatness of the One Who prohibited it").

70. Despite the expense or exertion it involved, or the ridicule it brought on you from those who scoff at acts of piety (*Binyan Yehoshua*).

71. Ben Azzai refers to a natural phenomenon: Performing one mitzvah, even a minor one, makes it easier to perform other mitzvos (*Rav, Avos* 4:2). Every act of mitzvah observance draws one closer to God and conditions him to His service. He will then be more inclined to fulfill the next mitzvah, even a more challenging one, and he will do so with greater spirit and devotion. Each succeeding mitzvah will build on this effect until serving God will become second nature to him (*R' Yonah ad loc.*; see also *R' Yitzchak of Toledo*).

Meiri adds that performing good deeds often leads to more opportunities to perform good deeds. [For example, an act of kindness may earn one a reputation for being a caring individual. People will then begin to turn to him in their time of need.]

72. This, too, is a natural phenomenon. When someone turns onto the path of sin [even if only for a "minor" transgression], it becomes hard to turn back (*Rav*). Every wrongful act distances the perpetrator from God and conditions him to follow his evil inclination. He will then be more inclined to commit the next sin, even if it is less

שֶׁשְּׂכַר מִצְוָה מִצְוָה וּשְׂכַר עֲבֵירָה עֲבֵירָה.[73] הוּא הָיָה אוֹמֵר: הַפְסֵק
מֵאֵלֶיךָ וִיהֵא שָׂכָר לְהֶפְסֵקֶךָ, וְאַל יַפְסִיקוּךָ אֲחֵרִים וִיהֵא שָׂכָר לְהֶפְסֵיקָם.

שֶׁשְּׂכַר מִצְוָה מִצְוָה וּשְׂכַר עֲבֵירָה עֲבֵירָה — and also because the reward for a mitzvah is another mitzvah and the punishment for a sin is another sin.[73]

The Baraisa presents another teaching of Ben Azzai:

הוּא הָיָה אוֹמֵר — He used to say: הַפְסֵק מֵאֵלֶיךָ וִיהֵא שָׂכָר לְהֶפְסֵקֶךָ — Pledge gifts of charity on your own so that there will be a reward for your pledge; וְאַל יַפְסִיקוּךָ אֲחֵרִים וִיהֵא שָׂכָר לְהֶפְסֵיקָם — and do not leave it to others to pledge on your behalf, for then there will be a reward for *their* pledge.[74]

tempting than the first one. In this way he will sink further and further into a sinful life until even the most abominable acts will become second nature to him (*R' Yonah*).

Furthermore, committing one sin, even a relatively minor one, will often leave the sinner with little choice but to commit other, more serious sins. For example, if a burglar is discovered breaking into a home, he will likely resort to violence and even murder to protect himself from the homeowner's wrath (*Meiri*).

73. [Elucidation follows *Rav*, first approach.] One who performs a mitzvah merits Divine assistance and will be afforded the opportunity to perform another mitzvah. God will then reward him [in the Afterlife] for *both* mitzvos (ibid.). This spiritual process is in addition to the natural one described above (*R' Yonah*).

In the Mishnah (4:2), the idea that one mitzvah leads to another is presented as a reason for Ben Azzai's *first* statement — that one should "run to perform a minor mitzvah." For even if the mitzvah itself is relatively minor, it is "major" in the sense that it brings another mitzvah in its wake. According to this approach, Ben Azzai's last statement can be understood differently: Another reason to "run to perform a minor mitzvah" is that performing a mitzvah with enthusiasm earns one a double reward, because "the reward for a mitzvah" — that is, the joy and pleasure derived from the mitzvah — is itself a mitzvah, since it is God's Will that we serve Him with joy. [Conversely, a sinner is punished not only for the sinful act, but also

for whatever pleasure and benefit ("reward") it brought him.] Thus every "minor" mitzvah is doubly significant, even for those concerned about reward (see *Binyan Yehoshua*, from *Rav*, second approach).

In a variation of this approach, some explain that earning a Heavenly reward for a good deed is itself a mitzvah, since God created the world to share His goodness and shower blessings on His creatures. Earning those blessings, by justifying the world's existence, fulfills God's Will and therefore is itself deserving of a reward (*Tiferes Yisrael* ad loc.; *Malbim* to *Deuteronomy* 6:18).

74. Elucidation follows *Binyan Yehoshua*, *Regel Yesharah*, *R' Yeshayah Berlin*, and *Ahavas Chesed*. The latter explains that for a premeditated good deed there are two rewards: one for the decision to do the mitzvah and one for the act of doing it. If a person motivates himself to give charity, for example, he is entitled to both rewards — for the "pledge" and for the actual gift. But if he remains idle until roused into action by others, he will forfeit the first reward to those who "pledge" on his behalf, though he will retain the second reward for himself.

Other commentators render הֶפְסֵק as "stop," yielding a different statement, but with the same underlying message: "**Stop your sinful ways on your own, so that there will be a reward for your stopping** yourself; **and do not leave it to others to stop you**, for then **there will be a reward for their stopping** you (*Magen Avos, Hagahos Yaavetz, Ben Avraham;* see *Chovos HaLevavos, Shaar HaTeshuvah*, Ch. 6).

הוּא הָיָה אוֹמֵר: רֵד מִמְּקוֹמְךָ שְׁתַּיִם וְשָׁלֹשׁ מַעֲלוֹת וְשֵׁב. טוֹב שֶׁיֹּאמְרוּ לְךָ
עֲלֵה מִשֶּׁיֹּאמְרוּ לְךָ רֵד[75], שֶׁנֶּאֱמַר (משלי כה, ז) "כִּי טוֹב אֲמָר לְךָ עֲלֵה הֵנָּה
מֵהַשְׁפִּילְךָ לִפְנֵי נָדִיב אֲשֶׁר רָאוּ עֵינֶיךָ":

ה. שְׁלֹשָׁה חַיֵּיהֶם אֵינָן חַיִּים[76]. אֵלּוּ הֵן: הַמְצַפֶּה לְשֻׁלְחַן חֲבֵירוֹ וְהַדָּר בַּעֲלִיָּיה[77]
וְכֹל שֶׁאִשְׁתּוֹ מוֹשֶׁלֶת עָלָיו. וְיֵשׁ אוֹמְרִים: שֶׁיִּסּוּרִין מוֹשְׁלִין בְּגוּפוֹ[78].

One more teaching of Ben Azzai: הוּא הָיָה אוֹמֵר — He used to say: רֵד מִמְּקוֹמְךָ שְׁתַּיִם וְשָׁלֹשׁ מַעֲלוֹת וְשֵׁב — Go down two or three levels from your rightful place and sit there. טוֹב שֶׁיֹּאמְרוּ לְךָ עֲלֵה מִשֶּׁיֹּאמְרוּ לְךָ רֵד — It is better that they should tell you, "Go up higher," than that they should tell you, "Go down lower,"[75] שֶׁנֶּאֱמַר "כִּי טוֹב אֲמָר לְךָ עֲלֵה הֵנָּה מֵהַשְׁפִּילְךָ לִפְנֵי נָדִיב אֲשֶׁר רָאוּ עֵינֶיךָ" — as it says, For it is better that it be said to you, "Come up here," than that you be demoted before the prince, as your eyes have seen [happen to others] (Proverbs 25:7).

§5 The Baraisa presents another teaching: שְׁלֹשָׁה חַיֵּיהֶם אֵינָן חַיִּים — There are three types of people whose lives are not lives.[76] אֵלּוּ הֵן: הַמְצַפֶּה לְשֻׁלְחַן חֲבֵירוֹ — They are: one who must look to another's table for sustenance; וְהַדָּר בַּעֲלִיָּיה — one who dwells on an upper floor;[77] וְכֹל שֶׁאִשְׁתּוֹ מוֹשֶׁלֶת עָלָיו — and one whose wife rules over him. וְיֵשׁ אוֹמְרִים: שֶׁיִּסּוּרִין מוֹשְׁלִין בְּגוּפוֹ — And some add: one whose body is racked with pain.[78]

---

75. In former times, Torah students would sit before their teacher in order of eminence (see, for example, Sanhedrin 37a, Bava Kamma 117a). Ben Azzai's advice for such students was to sit in a place lower than what they thought appropriate for their level of scholarship, until they are invited to sit in a higher one. Otherwise, they may take a more prestigious seat than they deserve and risk being told to move down lower (Matnos Kehunah, Eitz Yosef to Shemos Rabbah 45 §5). The Midrash (ibid.) quotes Hillel as saying in this context: הַשְׁפָּלָתִי זוֹ הַגְבָּהָתִי וְהַגְבָּהָתִי הִיא הַשְׁפָּלָתִי, "My self-abasement is my exaltation, while my self-exaltation is my abasement," for the one leads to the other. [Hillel spoke from personal experience on both counts; see Eitz Yosef ibid.]

76. That is, their lives are uncommonly miserable.

77. Living on an upper floor is one of the things that age a person before his time (Reishis Chochmah, Chupas Eliyahu Rabbah, Shaar 3; see also Eruvin 56a). The constant exertion of climbing the steps, the extra anxiety over being more exposed to the elements than a first-floor occupant, and the greater responsibility for keeping the building in good repair (full responsibility for the roof above him and shared responsibility for the floor-ceiling underneath him) combine to wear down an upper-floor occupant (Magen Avos).

78. See Eruvin 55b, Pesachim 113b, and Beitzah 32b for other examples of people whose lives are not lives.

Ben Avraham explains the connection between these last teachings: When it comes to a person's spirituality, he should be assertive, prompting himself to improve his behavior and not waiting for others to prompt him. However, when it comes to derech eretz, matters of social behavior, he should instead show a measure of humility, seating himself, for example, a couple of stations

הוּא הָיָה אוֹמֵר: נוֹחַ לִמְלוֹךְ עַל כָּל הָעוֹלָם כֻּלּוֹ מִלֵּישֵׁב (וְלִשְׁנוֹת) בִּפְנֵי בְּנֵי אָדָם הָעֲטוּפִים בְּסְדִינִין:[79]

A final teaching:

הוּא הָיָה אוֹמֵר — **He used to say:**   נוֹחַ לִמְלוֹךְ עַל כָּל הָעוֹלָם כֻּלּוֹ — **Better to rule over the entire world,** with all the difficulties and dangers that would involve,   מִלֵּישֵׁב וְלִשְׁנוֹת בִּפְנֵי בְּנֵי אָדָם הָעֲטוּפִים בְּסְדִינִין — **than to sit and teach Torah before** an audience of **people wrapped in linen cloaks,** pretending to be pious.[79]

---

beneath what he deserves. But not all interpersonal dealings are the same: One should strive for independence in regard to earning a living rather than be a perpetual guest at someone else's table. Also, one must be his own person within a marriage rather than allow his wife to control every aspect of his life. Someone who remains meek and unassertive even in these situations lives a life that is not a life.

79. For a teacher of such unworthy students, who may misunderstand and distort the Torah concepts he teaches them, can unwittingly create a spiritual menace to the Jewish people, as happened to Antigonus of Socho with his errant students (*Binyan*

Yehoshua, referring to the Baraisa above, 5 §2).

Some emend the text to read: נוֹחַ לַהֲלֹךְ עַל כָּל הָעוֹלָם כֻּלּוֹ — **Better to walk through the entire world** in search of a teacher of genuine character under whom to study, מִלֵּישֵׁב וְלִשְׁנוֹת בִּפְנֵי בְּנֵי אָדָם הָעֲטוּפִים בְּסְדִינִין — **than to sit and learn before people wrapped in linen cloaks,** pretending to be pious (*Mefaresh, Regel Yesharah,* and *R' Yeshayah Berlin*). Though it may be difficult for a person to travel, it is better for him to journey around the entire world to find a proper teacher than to study comfortably under men who are devout on the outside and something else on the inside (*Mefaresh*).

֎ פֶּרֶק כו ֎

א. רַבִּי[1] עֲקִיבָא אוֹמֵר: סְיָיג לַכָּבוֹד שְׂחוֹק[2]. סְיָיג לַחָכְמָה שְׁתִיקָה[3]. סְיָיג לַנְּדָרִים פְּרִישׁוּת[4]. סְיָיג לַטָּהֳרָה קְדוּשָׁה[5]. סְיָיג לָעֲנָוָה יִרְאַת חֵטְא[6]:

֎ CHAPTER 26 ֎

§1 The Baraisa cites a statement of R' Akiva that is similar in content to his teaching cited in *Avos* 3:13:[1]

רַבִּי עֲקִיבָא אוֹמֵר — R' Akiva says: סְיָיג לַכָּבוֹד שְׂחוֹק — A fence for one's honor is refraining from jest.[2] סְיָיג לַחָכְמָה שְׁתִיקָה — A fence for wisdom is silence.[3] סְיָיג לַנְּדָרִים פְּרִישׁוּת — A fence for vows is abstinence.[4] סְיָיג לַטָּהֳרָה קְדוּשָׁה — A fence for purity is holiness.[5] סְיָיג לָעֲנָוָה יִרְאַת חֵטְא — A fence for humility is fear of sin.[6]

---

1. We have followed the version that appears on the standard printed page of *Avos DeRabbi Nassan*, and which is followed by *Binyan Yehoshua*. Most of the commentators, however, prefer the alternative version cited by *Tummas Yesharim*, as it conforms with the Mishnah (see *Mefaresh*, *Ahavas Chesed*, *Nuschas HaGra*, and *Ben Avraham*). In the Vilna edition, this version can be found in *Hagahos HaGriv*.

The theme of this teaching is the סְיָיג, *fence*. Just as a person erects a fence in order to protect that which is within it, one should accustom himself to certain forms of behavior in order to protect his most essential qualities. [Compare 2:1 above, where the Baraisa discussed the necessity of erecting a protective fence for the Torah by enacting safeguards to ensure that one does not transgress it.]

2. In *Avos* 3:13, R' Akiva teaches: "Jest and levity accustom one to immorality." In the same vein, he teaches here that by avoiding such behavior, a person guards himself against immorality and thereby protects his honor (*Binyan Yehoshua*).

3. One should refrain from mundane conversation to the greatest extent possible, for he will thereby preserve whatever wisdom he has. This is as the verse states (*Proverbs* 17:28), *Even a fool will be considered wise if he is silent* (*Binyan Yehoshua*, citing *Rav* to *Avos* 3:13; see above, 22 §3).

4. This refers to a person who has undertaken certain stringencies in order to help him attain higher levels of piety. Such a person should accustom himself to abstaining from excessive social interaction, as it will be very difficult for him to maintain his standards in the company of other people. Thus, abstinence is the fence that will protect him from transgressing his vows (*Avos HaRosh*). [In the Mishnah, R' Akiva's words are inverted: "Vows are a fence for abstinence." See *Binyan Yehoshua*, who explains our Baraisa in this vein as well.]

5. One who sanctifies himself by abstaining even from permissible pleasures will be able to remain pure from sin (*Magen Avos*). Excessive involvement in the pleasures of this world, however, will invariably lead to sin (see *Mesillas Yesharim* Ch. 13). According to *Binyan Yehoshua*, however, the Baraisa means to say that purity *leads to* holiness. This conforms with the Baraisa of R' Pinchas ben Yair (cited in *Avodah Zarah* 20b and elsewhere), where purity is listed as one of the steps leading up to holiness. See *Mesillas Yesharim* Chs. 16 and 26, where Ramchal explains the essence of these two traits according to the approach of R' Pinchas ben Yair.

6. One who fears sin is aware of his own faults and of how short he has fallen in fulfilling his obligation toward God. This in turn

ב. הוּא הָיָה אוֹמֵר: אַל תָּבֹא לְבֵין הַלֵּצִים שֶׁמָּא תִּלְמַד מִמַּעֲשֵׂיהֶם.[8]
אַל תֹּאכַל לֶחֶם עִם כֹּהֵן עַם הָאָרֶץ שֶׁמָּא תִּמְעוֹל בַּקֳּדָשִׁים.[9] אַל
תִּפְרוֹץ בִּנְדָרִים שֶׁמָּא תִּמְעוֹל בִּשְׁבוּעוֹת.[10] אַל תַּרְגִּיל עַצְמְךָ לֶאֱכוֹל מִן
הַסְּעוּדָה שֶׁמָּא יְהֵא סוֹפְךָ לֶאֱכוֹל מִן הַקָּנִים.[11] וְאַל תָּבֹא לִידֵי סָפֵק שֶׁמָּא
תָּבֹא לִידֵי וַדַּאי.[12] וְאַל תֵּצֵא חוּצָה לָאָרֶץ שֶׁמָּא תַעֲבוֹד עֲבוֹדַת כּוֹכָבִים,

---

§2 R' Akiva continues with additional examples of protective fences:[7]
הוּא הָיָה אוֹמֵר — He used to say: אַל תָּבֹא לְבֵין הַלֵּצִים שֶׁמָּא תִּלְמַד
מִמַּעֲשֵׂיהֶם — Do not go among the scorners, lest you learn from their behavior.[8] אַל תֹּאכַל לֶחֶם עִם כֹּהֵן עַם הָאָרֶץ שֶׁמָּא תִּמְעוֹל בַּקֳּדָשִׁים — Do not eat
bread with an ignorant Kohen, lest you transgress the prohibition of eating
holy things, such as sacrificial portions and *terumah,* which are forbidden to
a non-Kohen.[9] אַל תִּפְרוֹץ בִּנְדָרִים שֶׁמָּא תִּמְעוֹל בִּשְׁבוּעוֹת — **Do not be free
with making vows, lest you transgress** the prohibition of oaths.[10] אַל תַּרְגִּיל
עַצְמְךָ לֶאֱכוֹל מִן הַסְּעוּדָה שֶׁמָּא יְהֵא סוֹפְךָ לֶאֱכוֹל מִן הַקָּנִים — **Do not accustom
yourself to partaking of a banquet, lest you ultimately be** reduced to eat-
ing reeds.[11] וְאַל תָּבֹא לִידֵי סָפֵק שֶׁמָּא תָּבֹא לִידֵי וַדַּאי — **And do not allow
yourself to transgress a doubtful [sin], lest you come to transgress a definite
sin.**[12] וְאַל תֵּצֵא חוּצָה לָאָרֶץ שֶׁמָּא תַעֲבוֹד עֲבוֹדַת כּוֹכָבִים — **And do not go**

---

brings him to humility (*Kisei Rachamim*).
According to *Binyan Yehoshua,* however, the
Baraisa is saying that humility *leads to* fear of
sin. [This too conforms with most versions of
the Baraisa of R' Pinchas ben Yair in *Avodah
Zarah* ibid.] A humble person realizes that
he is just a weak, lowly creature before the
ultimate exaltedness of the Almighty. He so
reveres God that he is eager to obey Him,
and cannot bring himself to wrong Him in
any way. This is the fear of sin that comes as
a result of humility — not fear that one will be
punished for sinning, but fear of the sin itself,
out of reverence for the One Who prohibited
it (see *Pnei Moshe* to *Yerushalmi Shabbos*
1:3; *Mesillas Yesharim* Ch. 24).

7. *Ben Avraham.*

8. As it states (*Psalms* 1:1), *Praiseworthy
is the man who ... sat not in the session of
scorners* (*Binyan Yehoshua*).

9. Ibid. Generally speaking, a Kohen is permitted to eat *terumah, terumas maaser,* and
the portions of offerings designated for the
Kohanim, but these are forbidden to non-
Kohanim. A Kohen who is an ignoramus

might be careless enough to serve his
non-Kohen guests *terumah* without their
knowledge.

10. That is, you might not only break your
vows, but even make oaths and violate
them. This is more severe than violating
vows, because the Torah states regarding
such a transgressor (*Exodus* 20:7), *Hashem
will not absolve [him]* (*Ran* and *Tosafos* to
Nedarim 20a, based on 18a there).

11. A person who feasts excessively at ban-
quets accustoms himself to an expensive
lifestyle and squanders his assets to support
his habit. Eventually he will become destitute, and will have to subsist on reeds and
other wild vegetation (*Magen Avos*).

12. If a person wishes to do something and
he is aware that it may not be permitted, he
might allow himself to be lenient since it is a
questionable matter. Our Baraisa warns him
not to do so, since this may ultimately lead
him to do something that is unquestionably
prohibited, based on the principle (*Avos*
4:2) that one sin leads to another (*Ben
Avraham*).

שֶׁכֵּן דָּוִד הוּא אוֹמֵר (שמואל א כו, יט) "כִּי גֵרְשׁוּנִי הַיּוֹם מֵהִסְתַּפֵּחַ בְּנַחֲלַת ה'
לֵאמֹר לֵךְ עֲבֹד אֱלֹהִים אֲחֵרִים". וְכִי תַעֲלֶה עַל דַּעְתְּךָ שֶׁדָּוִד הַמֶּלֶךְ עוֹבֵד
עֲבוֹדַת כּוֹכָבִים הָיָה. אֶלָּא כָּךְ אָמַר דָּוִד: כָּל הַמַּנִּיחַ אֶרֶץ יִשְׂרָאֵל וְיוֹצֵא חוּצָה
לָאָרֶץ מַעֲלֶה עָלָיו הַכָּתוּב כְּאִלּוּ עוֹבֵד עֲבוֹדַת כּוֹכָבִים¹³. הוּא הָיָה אוֹמֵר:
כָּל הַקָּבוּר בִּשְׁאָר אֲרָצוֹת כְּאִלּוּ קָבוּר בְּבָבֶל¹⁴. כָּל הַקָּבוּר בְּבָבֶל כְּאִלּוּ
קָבוּר בְּאֶרֶץ יִשְׂרָאֵל¹⁵. כָּל הַקָּבוּר בְּאֶרֶץ יִשְׂרָאֵל כְּאִלּוּ קָבוּר תַּחַת הַמִּזְבֵּחַ.

---

outside of the Land of Israel, lest you worship idols, כִּי — שֶׁכֵּן דָּוִד הוּא אוֹמֵר
גֵרְשׁוּנִי הַיּוֹם מֵהִסְתַּפֵּחַ בְּנַחֲלַת ה' לֵאמֹר לֵךְ עֲבֹד אֱלֹהִים אֲחֵרִים" — for thus did
David say regarding those who forced him to flee the Land of Israel, *"For they
have driven me away this day from attaching myself to the heritage of
HASHEM [as if] to say, 'Go worship the gods of others!' "* (I Samuel 26:19).
וְכִי תַעֲלֶה עַל דַּעְתְּךָ שֶׁדָּוִד הַמֶּלֶךְ עוֹבֵד עֲבוֹדַת כּוֹכָבִים הָיָה — Now, would it enter
your mind that King David would worship idols? Certainly not! אֶלָּא כָּךְ אָמַר
דָּוִד — What, then, did he mean by saying that they were inciting him to worship
idols? Rather, this is what David was saying: כָּל הַמַּנִּיחַ אֶרֶץ יִשְׂרָאֵל וְיוֹצֵא
חוּצָה לָאָרֶץ מַעֲלֶה עָלָיו הַכָּתוּב כְּאִלּוּ עוֹבֵד עֲבוֹדַת כּוֹכָבִים — Anyone who leaves
the Land of Israel and goes outside of the Land is considered by Scripture
as if he is worshiping idols.[13] Therefore, by driving him out of the Land (*the
heritage of HASHEM*), it is as if they were telling him to worship foreign gods.

R' Akiva shifts from living in the Land of Israel to being buried in the Land
of Israel:

כָּל הַקָּבוּר בִּשְׁאָר אֲרָצוֹת כְּאִלּוּ קָבוּר בְּבָבֶל — He used to say: הוּא הָיָה אוֹמֵר
— Whoever is buried in other lands is considered as if he were buried in
Babylonia.[14] כָּל הַקָּבוּר בְּבָבֶל כְּאִלּוּ קָבוּר בְּאֶרֶץ יִשְׂרָאֵל — Whoever is buried
in Babylonia is considered as if he were buried in the Land of Israel.[15] כָּל
הַקָּבוּר בְּאֶרֶץ יִשְׂרָאֵל כְּאִלּוּ קָבוּר תַּחַת הַמִּזְבֵּחַ — Whoever is buried in the Land
of Israel is considered as if he were buried under the Altar in the Temple,

---

13. This is because God exercises His direct
providence only in the Land of Israel, while
conducting the affairs of other lands through
the agency of angels (see *Ramban* to *Leviticus* 18:25 and *Deuteronomy* 31:16). One
who chooses to maintain his residence in
other lands has chosen angelic supervision
over God's, and therefore he is akin to one
who worships idols (*Maharsha* to *Kesubos*
110b, cited in part by *Binyan Yehoshua*).
Accordingly, when R' Akiva said not to leave
the Land of Israel "lest you worship idols," he
meant: lest it will be considered *as if* you had
worshiped idols (see *Kisei Rachamim*).

14. The Baraisa is referring to those who long
to be buried in the Land of Israel but are unable to have their wish fulfilled. God reckons
their good intentions as if they were actually
carried out, and it is considered as though
they were buried in Babylonia, which — as the
Baraisa goes on to say — is equivalent to being buried in the Land of Israel (*Avos HaRosh*).

15. In Talmudic times, Babylonia was considered equal in holiness to the Land of Israel
because it was home to great Torah institutions [see *Kesubos* 111a with *Rashi* ד"ה אלא
לעינן קבורה] (see *Ben Avraham* and *Avos
HaRosh*).

לְפִי שֶׁכָּל אֶרֶץ יִשְׂרָאֵל רְאוּיָה לְמִזְבֵּחַ.[16] וְכָל הַקָּבוּר תַּחַת הַמִּזְבֵּחַ[17] כְּאִלּוּ קָבוּר תַּחַת כִּסֵּא הַכָּבוֹד, שֶׁנֶּאֱמַר (ירמיה יז, יב) "כִּסֵּא כָבוֹד מָרוֹם מֵרִאשׁוֹן מְקוֹם מִקְדָּשֵׁנוּ"[18]:

ג. הוּא הָיָה אוֹמֵר:[19] אֵין עַם הָאָרֶץ חָסִיד[20] וְלֹא הַבַּיְישָׁן לָמֵד[21] וְלֹא הַקַּפְּדָן

לְפִי שֶׁכָּל אֶרֶץ יִשְׂרָאֵל רְאוּיָה לְמִזְבֵּחַ — for the entire Land of Israel is fit for building an Altar.[16]   וְכָל הַקָּבוּר תַּחַת הַמִּזְבֵּחַ כְּאִלּוּ קָבוּר תַּחַת כִּסֵּא הַכָּבוֹד — And whoever is buried under the Altar[17] is considered as if he were buried underneath the Throne of Glory, שֶׁנֶּאֱמַר "כִּסֵּא כָבוֹד מָרוֹם מֵרִאשׁוֹן מְקוֹם מִקְדָּשֵׁנוּ" — as it is stated, *Like the Throne of Glory, exalted of old, is the place of our Sanctuary* (*Jeremiah* 17:12).[18]

§3 The Baraisa cites Avos 2:5:

הוּא הָיָה אוֹמֵר — He used to say:[19]   אֵין עַם הָאָרֶץ חָסִיד — An unlearned person cannot be scrupulously pious;[20]   וְלֹא הַבַּיְישָׁן לָמֵד — a bashful person cannot learn;[21]   וְלֹא הַקַּפְּדָן מְלַמֵּד — and a short-tempered person cannot teach.[22]

16. During the periods when it was permitted to bring offerings on a private altar (see *Zevachim* 14:4-8), such altars could be erected anywhere in the Land of Israel (*Hagahos Yaavetz*).

Certainly, the Baraisa does not suggest that there would be a special merit in being buried under the Altar in a literal sense, as it is prohibited to bring a corpse into the Temple. Rather, *Maharsha* (to *Kesubos* ibid.) explains as follows: The earth that God used to create Adam, the first man, was taken from the future location of the Altar [in Jerusalem] (see *Rashi* to *Genesis* 2:7). Accordingly, the metaphor of being buried under the Altar means that the body returns to its original source on earth in a state of purity, just as the soul returns to its sublime source in a state of purity. One who is buried anywhere in the Land of Israel merits this distinction.

Indeed, we find great importance attached to burial in the Land of Israel since the earliest times: both Jacob and Joseph instructed that their bodies be taken to the Land of Israel and buried there (*Rambam, Hil. Melachim* 5:11).

17. I.e., he is buried in the Land of Israel, which is equivalent to being buried under the Altar (*Magen Avos*).

18. Thus, anyone who is (considered to be) buried underneath the Altar in the Sanctuary is considered as if he were buried beneath the Throne of Glory.

19. In *Avos*, this teaching is ascribed to Hillel. The Baraisa is saying that when R' Akiva would state his teaching about safeguards (cited in the first part of the previous section), he would also mention this teaching of Hillel, which similarly discusses the necessity of guarding oneself from those traits that prevent a person from achieving piety or scholarship, or impair his ability to teach students (*Ben Avraham*).

20. A scrupulously pious person is not satisfied doing the minimal requirement, but goes beyond the letter of the law. One who is ignorant in Torah might be able to fulfill the basic requirements if he is instructed by others, but lacks the refinement of character needed to attain piety, which can be achieved only through Torah study (*R' Yonah* on the Mishnah).

21. One who is ashamed to ask questions during his studies lest he be mocked by his fellow students will never be able to clarify his doubts, and will thus be unable to advance in his learning (*Rav* ad loc.).

22. A teacher who is impatient with his students and intolerant of their questions will never succeed at teaching. Rather, a teacher must exhibit a cheerful disposition

מְלַמֵּד[22]. הוּא הָיָה אוֹמֵר: מִפְּנֵי מָה תַּלְמִידֵי חֲכָמִים מֵתִים כְּשֶׁהֵן קְטַנִּים, לֹא מִפְּנֵי שֶׁהֵן מְנָאֲפִים וְלֹא מִפְּנֵי שֶׁהֵן גּוֹזְלִין אֶלָּא שֶׁפּוֹסְקִין מִדִּבְרֵי תוֹרָה וְעוֹסְקִים בְּדִבְרֵי שִׂיחָה[24]. וְעוֹד שֶׁאֵין מַתְחִילִין בַּמָּקוֹם שֶׁפּוֹסְקִים[25]:

ד. רַבִּי שִׁמְעוֹן בֶּן אֶלְעָזָר אוֹמֵר: יִשְׂרָאֵל שֶׁבְּחוּצָה לָאָרֶץ עוֹבְדִים עֲבוֹדַת כּוֹכָבִים בְּטָהֳרָה[26]. הָא כֵּיצַד, כּוּתִי שֶׁעָשָׂה מִשְׁתֶּה לִבְנוֹ שָׁלַח וְזִימֵּן כָּל הַיְּהוּדִים שֶׁבְּעִירוֹ אַף עַל פִּי שֶׁהֵן אוֹכְלִין וְשׁוֹתִין וְשַׁמָּשׁ שֶׁלָּהֶן עוֹמֵד וּמַשְׁקֶה עֲלֵיהֶן[27] מַעֲלֶה עֲלֵיהֶם כְּאִלּוּ אָכְלוּ מִזִּבְחֵי מֵתִים[28], שֶׁנֶּאֱמַר (שמות לד, טו)

Another teaching regarding Torah students:[23]

הוּא הָיָה אוֹמֵר — He used to say: מִפְּנֵי מָה תַּלְמִידֵי חֲכָמִים מֵתִים כְּשֶׁהֵן קְטַנִּים — Why do some Torah students die when they are young? לֹא מִפְּנֵי שֶׁהֵן מְנָאֲפִים וְלֹא מִפְּנֵי שֶׁהֵן גּוֹזְלִין — Not because they commit adultery or steal, for they are surely innocent of such misconduct. אֶלָּא שֶׁפּוֹסְקִין מִדִּבְרֵי תוֹרָה וְעוֹסְקִים בְּדִבְרֵי שִׂיחָה — Rather, it is because they interrupt their study of words of Torah and engage in idle chatter,[24] וְעוֹד שֶׁאֵין מַתְחִילִין בַּמָּקוֹם שֶׁפּוֹסְקִים — and moreover, when they resume their studies, they do not begin in the same place where they left off.[25]

§4 More on living outside the Land of Israel and idol worship:

רַבִּי שִׁמְעוֹן בֶּן אֶלְעָזָר אוֹמֵר — R' Shimon ben Elazar says: יִשְׂרָאֵל שֶׁבְּחוּצָה לָאָרֶץ עוֹבְדִים עֲבוֹדַת כּוֹכָבִים בְּטָהֳרָה — The Jews outside the Land of Israel serve idols with pure [intentions].[26] הָא כֵּיצַד — How so? כּוּתִי שֶׁעָשָׂה מִשְׁתֶּה לִבְנוֹ שָׁלַח וְזִימֵּן כָּל הַיְּהוּדִים שֶׁבְּעִירוֹ — An idolater makes a wedding feast for his son and extends an invitation to all the Jews in his town, and they participate. אַף עַל פִּי שֶׁהֵן אוֹכְלִין וְשׁוֹתִין — Even though they eat their own kosher food and drink their own kosher beverages, וְשַׁמָּשׁ שֶׁלָּהֶן עוֹמֵד וּמַשְׁקֶה עֲלֵיהֶן — and their own attendant waits upon them and serves them their food and drinks,[27] מַעֲלֶה עֲלֵיהֶם כְּאִלּוּ אָכְלוּ מִזִּבְחֵי מֵתִים — it is considered as if they ate from the "sacrifices of the dead," i.e., from idolatrous sacrifices,[28] שֶׁנֶּאֱמַר

---

toward his students, so that they will feel free to make any inquiries (Rav ad loc., cited by Binyan Yehoshua).

23. This teaching likewise concerns a safeguard that is critical for every Torah student (Ben Avraham).

24. See Avodah Zarah 3b (cited by Binyan Yehoshua) regarding the gravity of this behavior.

25. Since they interrupted their studies with chatter, they lose their place and skip over part of the text when they begin studying

again (Mefaresh).

26. That is, without meaning to do so. They fail to realize that seemingly innocent actions on their part cause them to transgress prohibitions relating to idolatry (Rashi to Avodah Zarah 8a).

27. [To make sure that their food and drink does not become mixed with nonkosher food and beverages from the other guests.]

28. Psalms 106:28 describes animals slaughtered in idolatrous rites as sacrifices of the dead.

"וְקָרָא לְךָ וְאָכַלְתָּ מִזִּבְחוֹ"[29]. [30]רַבִּי אֶלְעָזָר הַמּוֹדָעִי אוֹמֵר: הַמְחַלֵּל °שַׁבָּתוֹת[31]
וְהַמְבַזֶּה אֶת הַמּוֹעֲדוֹת[32] וְהַמֵּפֵר אֶת הַבְּרִית בַּבָּשָׂר[33] וְהַמְגַלֶּה פָּנִים בַּתּוֹרָה[34]
אַף עַל פִּי שֶׁיֵּשׁ בְּיָדוֹ תּוֹרָה וּמַעֲשִׂים טוֹבִים אֵין לוֹ חֵלֶק לָעוֹלָם הַבָּא[35].

"וְקָרָא לְךָ וְאָכַלְתָּ מִזִּבְחוֹ" — **as it is stated,** *And they will slaughter to their gods, and he will invite you and you will eat from his slaughter* (Exodus 34:15).[29]

The Baraisa cites *Avos* 3:11:[30]

הַמְחַלֵּל אֶת הַקֳּדָשִׁים — **R' Elazar the Modi'ite says:** רַבִּי אֶלְעָזָר הַמּוֹדָעִי אוֹמֵר — One who desecrates consecrated objects,[31] וְהַמְבַזֶּה אֶת הַמּוֹעֲדוֹת — one who disgraces the festivals,[32] וְהַמֵּפֵר אֶת הַבְּרִית בַּבָּשָׂר — one who nullifies the covenant of the flesh,[33] וְהַמְגַלֶּה פָּנִים בַּתּוֹרָה — and one who acts insolently with regard to the Torah[34] — אַף עַל פִּי שֶׁיֵּשׁ בְּיָדוֹ תּוֹרָה וּמַעֲשִׂים טוֹבִים אֵין לוֹ חֵלֶק לָעוֹלָם הַבָּא — **even though he may possess Torah and good deeds, has no share in the World to Come.**[35]

---

29. A previous verse (v. 12) prohibits the Jews from making a covenant with the Canaanite nations, lest they become a snare to them. Verse 15 goes on to warn that such association will lead the Jews to partake of the idolatrous sacrifices offered by the Canaanites. By saying the otherwise superfluous statement, *and he will invite you,* the Torah teaches that even just accepting an invitation to an idolater's banquet is prohibited, as it is regarded as eating from his idolatrous sacrifice (*Avodah Zarah* ibid.).

This prohibition applies specifically to a feast that is made in celebration of a wedding. Such festivities were generally accompanied by idolatrous sacrifices, and therefore eating at such a celebration is considered partaking of the sacrifice (see further, *Avodah Zarah* 8a-b with *Rashi* s.v. ובין; for further discussion, see *Shulchan Aruch,* Yoreh Deah 152:1 with commentators).

30. This teaching parallels the previous one, for it, too, lists grievous sins that people sometimes commit without realizing that these acts place them in the category of one who has *scorned the word of HASHEM* [as will be explained in note 35] (*Ben Avraham;* see note 26).

31. [Emendation follows *Binyan Yehoshua* and other commentators, and conforms with the Mishnah in *Avos.*] "One who desecrates consecrated objects" refers to someone who disregards the laws pertaining to sacrificial offerings, and thereby causes them to become unfit (*Binyan Yehoshua,* citing *Rashi* to the Mishnah).

32. This refers to one who either performs (unnecessary) work on Chol HaMoed (the intermediate days of the festivals of Pesach and Succos) or does not honor these days with the appropriate food and drink. Because the days of Chol HaMoed do not carry the same level of stringency as the Yom Tov itself, he disregards them (ibid.).

33. This refers to one who has (purposely) not undergone circumcision (ibid.), or who surgically undoes his circumcision so as to appear uncircumcised (*Binyan Yehoshua,* from *Rav* to the Mishnah).

34. This final category refers to a heretic who [deliberately] offers incorrect interpretations of the Torah or expounds on them in a ridiculing fashion, as well as somebody who unabashedly transgresses the commandments in public (ibid.).

35. The Gemara (*Sanhedrin* 99a) derives this from the verse (*Numbers* 15:31), *For*

וְרַבִּי[36] עֲקִיבָא אוֹמֵר: כָּל הַנּוֹשֵׂא אִשָּׁה שֶׁאֵינָהּ מְהוּגֶּנֶת לוֹ[37] עוֹבֵר מִשּׁוּם
חֲמִשָּׁה לָאוִין, מִשּׁוּם (ויקרא יט, יח) ”לֹא תִקֹּם״ וּמִשּׁוּם (שם) ”לֹא תִטֹּר״
וּמִשּׁוּם (שם שם יז) ”לֹא תִשְׂנָא אֶת אָחִיךָ בִּלְבָבֶךָ״ וּמִשּׁוּם (שם שם יח) ”וְאָהַבְתָּ
לְרֵעֲךָ כָּמוֹךָ״[38] וּמִשּׁוּם (שם כה, לו) ”וְחֵי אָחִיךָ עִמָּךְ״, מִתּוֹךְ שֶׁשּׂוֹנֵא אוֹתָהּ
רוֹצֶה הוּא שֶׁתָּמוּת[39], וְנִמְצָא מְבַטֵּל פְּרִיָּה וּרְבִיָּה מִן הָעוֹלָם[40]:

The Baraisa continues with another example of bad behavior with serious consequences:[36]

כָּל הַנּוֹשֵׂא אִשָּׁה שֶׁאֵינָהּ מְהוּגֶּנֶת לוֹ עוֹבֵר — וְרַבִּי עֲקִיבָא אוֹמֵר — R' Akiva says: מִשּׁוּם חֲמִשָּׁה לָאוִין — Anyone who marries a woman who is not appropriate for him[37] will ultimately commit five transgressions: מִשּׁוּם ”לֹא תִקֹּם״ — He will transgress the prohibitions: (1) *You shall not take revenge* (*Leviticus* 19:18), לֹא וּמִשּׁוּם ”לֹא תִטֹּר״ — (2) *you shall not bear a grudge* (ibid.), תִשְׂנָא אֶת אָחִיךָ בִּלְבָבֶךָ״ — and (3) *You shall not hate your brother in your heart* (ibid. v. 17); וּמִשּׁוּם ”וְאָהַבְתָּ לְרֵעֲךָ כָּמוֹךָ״ — and the positive commandments: (4) *You shall love your fellow as yourself* (ibid. v. 18),[38] וּמִשּׁוּם ”וְחֵי אָחִיךָ עִמָּךְ״ — and (5) *And let your brother live with you* (ibid. 25:36), מִתּוֹךְ שֶׁשּׂוֹנֵא אוֹתָהּ רוֹצֶה הוּא שֶׁתָּמוּת — for since he hates her, he wants her to die.[39] וְנִמְצָא מְבַטֵּל פְּרִיָּה וּרְבִיָּה מִן הָעוֹלָם — Moreover, it emerges that he negates a portion of procreation from the world.[40]

he scorned the word of HASHEM and nullified His commandment; that person will surely be cut off, his sin is upon him. One who *nullified His commandment* refers to a person who nullifies the covenant of circumcision (see *Genesis* 17:14), whereas the other three are included in *for he scorned the word of HASHEM*. Regarding all these sins, the verse states the double expression הִכָּרֵת תִּכָּרֵת (*he will surely be cut off*), to indicate that he will be cut off in this world (i.e., he will die prematurely) and in the World to Come (*Rashi* to the Mishnah). However, that is true only if he dies without repentance. If he repents, he does not forfeit his portion in the World to Come, for there is nothing that stands in the way of repentance (*Binyan Yehoshua*, citing *Rav* to the Mishnah).

36. Here too, *Ben Avraham* explains that people who are guilty of this conduct do not realize how many prohibitions they have violated.

37. I.e., he marries her for her money, even though she is not a suitable wife for him (see ibid.).

38. Because they are not a suitable match, the marriage deteriorates and he comes to hate her. All of these other interpersonal sins result: He does not treat her in a loving way, and he holds it against her and takes revenge if she ever wrongs him.

39. The verse, *And let your brother live with you*, contains a positive commandment to render financial assistance to one in need. If the Torah obligates a person to provide his fellow with a livelihood, then it is surely prohibited to seek his harm (*Magen Avos*).

40. Because he hates her, he refrains from procreating with her (see *Ben Avraham*). The Baraisa does not enumerate this as a sixth transgression, since it would not apply to a man who already has children or who is married to more than one wife (*Binyan Yehoshua*).

ה. הוּא הָיָה אוֹמֵר: הָאוֹכֵל אוֹכָלִין [שֶׁאֵינָם עוֹלִים עַל גּוּפוֹ] (שֶׁאֵינוּ
מְבָרֵךְ עֲלֵיהֶן) עוֹבֵר מִשּׁוּם שְׁלֹשָׁה לָאוִין[42], שֶׁבִּיזָּה אֶת עַצְמוֹ[43]
וּבִיזָּה אֶת הָאוֹכָלִין[44] וּמְבָרֵךְ בְּרָכָה שֶׁאֵינָהּ כְּתִיקוּנָהּ[45]:

ו. רַבִּי יְהוּדָה בֶּן אִילְעַאי אוֹמֵר: אָדָם שֶׁמֵּת וְהִנִּיחַ בֵּן וְלֹא לָמַד
תּוֹרָה מֵאָבִיו[46] וְהָלַךְ וְלָמַד תּוֹרָה מֵאֲחֵרִים הֲרֵי חֲנוּפָה מְבַקֵּשׁ[47].

---

§5 Another example of bad behavior that entails several transgressions:[41]

הוּא הָיָה אוֹמֵר — He used to say: הָאוֹכֵל אוֹכָלִין שֶׁאֵינָם עוֹלִים עַל גּוּפוֹ
עוֹבֵר מִשּׁוּם שְׁלֹשָׁה לָאוִין — One who eats foods that do not agree with his body
commits three transgressions:[42] שֶׁבִּיזָּה אֶת עַצְמוֹ — (1) He has demeaned
himself,[43] וּבִיזָּה אֶת הָאוֹכָלִין — (2) he has degraded the foods that he
ate,[44] וּמְבָרֵךְ בְּרָכָה שֶׁאֵינָהּ כְּתִיקוּנָהּ — and (3) he has recited a blessing
improperly.[45]

§6 A teaching concerning the conduct of a teacher toward his student:

רַבִּי יְהוּדָה בֶּן אִילְעַאי אוֹמֵר — R' Yehudah ben Il'ai says: אָדָם שֶׁמֵּת וְהִנִּיחַ
בֵּן וְלֹא לָמַד תּוֹרָה מֵאָבִיו — If a man died and left behind a son who never
learned Torah from his father,[46] וְהָלַךְ וְלָמַד תּוֹרָה מֵאֲחֵרִים — and [that son]
went and learned Torah from others, הֲרֵי חֲנוּפָה מְבַקֵּשׁ — it is because he is
seeking a compliment, i.e., he craves the warmth that he never received from
his father.[47]

---

41. And which people commonly commit due to a lack of awareness (*Ben Avraham*).

42. [Emendation follows *Nuschas HaGra*.] That is, he eats food that is repulsive to him (see the following note).

43. I.e., he has caused himself to become disgusted, and thereby transgressed the prohibition (*Leviticus* 11:43), *Do not make yourselves abominable* (*Binyan Yehoshua*, second explanation; see *Makkos* 16b and *Shulchan Aruch, Yoreh Deah* 116:6 with *Beur HaGra* §19).

44. And thereby violated the prohibition (*Deuteronomy* 20:19), *Do not destroy ...* (*Binyan Yehoshua*). This applies to any destructive or wasteful act (see *Shabbos* 129a, 140b, et al.). Since a different person who is not repulsed by the foods could have benefited from them, this person is considered to have wasted food.

45. One who eats food that is inedible to him does not recite a blessing (see *Shulchan*

Aruch, Orach Chaim 204:2; *Magen Avraham* ibid. §20). Therefore, if a person eats food that is repulsive to him and recites a blessing, he has transgressed the prohibition against reciting a blessing in vain [see *Berachos* 33a] (*Binyan Yehoshua*).

46. I.e., the father attempted to teach him during his lifetime but was unsuccessful.

47. Since the son learned from others successfully, he is clearly capable of studying Torah. Why then was he not successful in learning under his father? Because he needed his father to flatter and honor him in order to succeed, and frequently, a father does not do that for his son. When the son receives such warm encouragement from other teachers, he blossoms. Later on, when the son grows wiser, he will realize on his own that his motives should be pure. The lesson here is that one should flatter and honor such a student (*VeLo Od Ella*), and that a father should do the same for his son (*Rishon LeTzion*).

רַבִּי⁴⁸ אֶלְעָזָר הַקַּפָּר אוֹמֵר: אַל תְּהֵא כַּמַּשְׁקוֹף הָעֶלְיוֹן שֶׁאֵין יַד בְּנֵי אָדָם
יְכוֹלָה לִיגַּע בָּה⁴⁹. וְלֹא כָּאִסְקוּפָּה הָעֶלְיוֹנָה שֶׁמְּבַלַּעַת פַּרְצוּפוֹת⁵⁰. וְלֹא
כָּאִסְקוּפָּה הָאֶמְצָעִית שֶׁמְּנַגֶּפֶת הָרַגְלַיִם. אֶלָּא הֱוֵי כָּאִסְקוּפָּה תַּחְתּוֹנָה
שֶׁהַכֹּל דָּשִׁין בָּה, וְסוֹף כָּל הַבִּנְיָן נִסְתָּר וְהִיא בִּמְקוֹמָה עוֹמֶדֶת⁵¹:

A final teaching concerning the importance of humility:[48]

אַל תְּהֵא כַּמַּשְׁקוֹף הָעֶלְיוֹן רַבִּי אֶלְעָזָר הַקַּפָּר אוֹמֵר — R' Elazar HaKappar says: שֶׁאֵין יַד בְּנֵי אָדָם יְכוֹלָה לִיגַּע בָּה — Do not be like the lintel above the doorway that is inaccessible to people,[49] וְלֹא כָּאִסְקוּפָּה הָעֶלְיוֹנָה שֶׁמְּבַלַּעַת פַּרְצוּפוֹת — nor like the elevated stoop in front of the doorway that damages the faces of those who walk into it accidentally,[50] וְלֹא כָּאִסְקוּפָּה הָאֶמְצָעִית שֶׁמְּנַגֶּפֶת הָרַגְלַיִם — nor like the central (i.e., slightly elevated) stoop that stubs the feet and causes people to trip. אֶלָּא הֱוֵי כָּאִסְקוּפָּה תַּחְתּוֹנָה שֶׁהַכֹּל דָּשִׁין בָּה — Rather, be humble like the threshold at the bottom of the doorway that everyone steps on; וְסוֹף כָּל הַבִּנְיָן נִסְתָּר וְהִיא בִּמְקוֹמָה עוֹמֶדֶת — ultimately, the entire building is demolished, and it remains in its place.[51]

---

48. In *Avos* 4:21, R' Elazar HaKappar teaches that the pursuit of personal honor is one of three things that remove a man from the world. His statement here parallels that teaching (*Ahavas Chesed*).

49. Meaning, do not be arrogant and so disdainful of others that you wish to have

nothing to do with them (*Binyan Yehoshua*).

50. *Ahavas Chesed.* [Do not be so haughty that people will have a painful confrontation with you when they interact with you.]

51. Similarly, if you are humble you will endure, in contrast with the conceited person who is removed from this world (ibid.).

﴾ פֶּרֶק כז ﴿

א. רַבִּי יוֹסֵי אוֹמֵר: כָּל הַמְכַבֵּד אֶת הַתּוֹרָה גּוּפוֹ מְכוּבָּד עַל הַבְּרִיּוֹת,¹
שֶׁנֶּאֱמַר (שמואל א ב, ל) "כִּי מְכַבְּדַי אֲכַבֵּד וּבֹזַי יֵקָלּוּ".² ³"כִּי מְכַבְּדַי
אֲכַבֵּד" זֶה פַּרְעֹה מֶלֶךְ מִצְרַיִם שֶׁנּוֹהֵג כָּבוֹד לִפְנֵי מִי שֶׁאָמַר וְהָיָה
הָעוֹלָם, שֶׁיָּצָא בְּרֹאשׁ פָּמַלְיָא שֶׁלּוֹ.⁴ וְאָמְרוּ לוֹ עֲבָדָיו: מִנְהָג שֶׁבָּעוֹלָם
כָּל הַמְּלָכִים אֵינָם יוֹצְאִים אֶלָּא אַחַר פָּמַלְיָא שֶׁלָּהֶם, וְאַתָּה יוֹצֵא בְּרֹאשׁ
פָּמַלְיָא שֶׁלְּךָ. אָמַר לָהֶם: וְכִי פְּנֵי מֶלֶךְ בָּשָׂר וָדָם אֲנִי הוֹלֵךְ לְהַקְבִּיל,
אֵינִי הוֹלֵךְ לְהַקְבִּיל אֶלָּא פְּנֵי מֶלֶךְ מַלְכֵי הַמְּלָכִים הַקָּדוֹשׁ בָּרוּךְ הוּא.⁵

﴾ CHAPTER 27 ﴿

§1 The Baraisa quotes an expanded version of *Avos* 4:6:

רַבִּי יוֹסֵי אוֹמֵר — R' Yose says: כָּל הַמְכַבֵּד אֶת הַתּוֹרָה גּוּפוֹ מְכוּבָּד עַל
הַבְּרִיּוֹת — Whoever honors the Torah is himself honored by people; and whoever disgraces the Torah is himself disgraced by people,[1] שֶׁנֶּאֱמַר "כִּי מְכַבְּדַי
אֲכַבֵּד וּבֹזַי יֵקָלּוּ" — as it is stated, *For I honor those who honor Me, and those
that scorn Me will be disgraced* (*I Samuel* 2:30).[2]

The Baraisa cites another interpretation of this verse:[3]

"כִּי מְכַבְּדַי אֲכַבֵּד" — *For those who honor Me I will honor* — זֶה פַּרְעֹה מֶלֶךְ
מִצְרַיִם שֶׁנּוֹהֵג כָּבוֹד לִפְנֵי מִי שֶׁאָמַר וְהָיָה הָעוֹלָם — this is referring to Pharaoh,
king of Egypt, who acted with honor toward the One Who spoke and thereby
the world came into being, שֶׁיָּצָא בְּרֹאשׁ פָּמַלְיָא שֶׁלּוֹ — when he went forth
at the head of his retinue to pursue the Israelites.[4] וְאָמְרוּ לוֹ עֲבָדָיו — Upon
seeing this, his servants said to him, מִנְהָג שֶׁבָּעוֹלָם כָּל הַמְּלָכִים אֵינָם יוֹצְאִים
אֶלָּא אַחַר פָּמַלְיָא שֶׁלָּהֶם — "The way of the world is that all kings go out to battle
only *behind* their retinue; וְאַתָּה יוֹצֵא בְּרֹאשׁ פָּמַלְיָא שֶׁלְּךָ — and you are going
out to battle at the *head* of your retinue?!" אָמַר לָהֶם: וְכִי פְּנֵי מֶלֶךְ בָּשָׂר וָדָם
אֲנִי הוֹלֵךְ לְהַקְבִּיל — [Pharaoh] replied, "Am I going to confront a king of flesh
and blood? Certainly not! אֵינִי הוֹלֵךְ לְהַקְבִּיל אֶלָּא פְּנֵי מֶלֶךְ מַלְכֵי הַמְּלָכִים הַקָּדוֹשׁ
בָּרוּךְ הוּא — I am rather going to confront the King Who reigns over kings, the

---

1. One who treats a Torah Scroll with the
proper respect and accords respect to Torah
scholars honors the Torah, whereas one who
behaves in the opposite manner disgraces
the Torah (see *Binyan Yehoshua*).

2. The speaker in this verse is God Himself.
Because God is bound, so to speak, with the
Torah, one who honors the Torah is actu-
ally honoring God, and vice versa (see *Kisei*

Rachamim and *Ben Avraham*).

3. The forthcoming exposition of the first
half of the verse will continue into the next
section, followed by the exposition of the
second half.

4. Pharaoh brought himself close to the front
line of his army when he pursued the Jewish
people at the Sea of Reeds; see *Bamidbar
Rabbah* 8 §3.

לְפִיכָךְ נָהַג בּוֹ הַקָּדוֹשׁ בָּרוּךְ הוּא כָּבוֹד וְלֹא נִפְרַע מִמֶּנּוּ אֶלָּא הוּא בְּעַצְמוֹ[6], (שֶׁנֶּאֱמַר (שיר השירים א, ט) "לְסֻסָתִי בְּרִכְבֵי פַרְעה דִּמִּיתִיךְ רַעְיָתִי":

ב. רַבִּי פַּפְּיָיס אוֹמֵר: כְּנֶסֶת יִשְׂרָאֵל הָיְתָה מְשַׁבַּחַת עַל סוּס רֶכֶב פַּרְעה,) שֶׁנֶּאֱמַר (חבקוק ג, טו) "דָּרַכְתָּ בַיָּם סוּסֶיךָ". רַבִּי יְהוֹשֻׁעַ בֶּן קָרְחָה אוֹמֵר: כְּשֶׁבָּא פַרְעה לַיָּם בָּא עַל סוּס זָכָר, וְנִגְלָה עָלָיו הַקָּדוֹשׁ בָּרוּךְ הוּא בְּסוּסְיָא נְקֵיבָה, שֶׁנֶּאֱמַר (שיר השירים א, ט) "לְסֻסָתִי בְּרִכְבֵי

Holy One, Blessed is He!"[5] — לְפִיכָךְ נָהַג בּוֹ הַקָּדוֹשׁ בָּרוּךְ הוּא כָּבוֹד — Therefore, the Holy One, Blessed is He, accorded him honor, וְלֹא נִפְרַע מִמֶּנּוּ אֶלָּא הוּא בְּעַצְמוֹ — and exacted punishment from him only by Himself,[6] שֶׁנֶּאֱמַר — as it is stated, *To My steed against Pharaoh's chariot I have likened you, My beloved* (*Song of Songs* 1:9).[7]

§2 The Baraisa cites another teaching from which we see that God Himself exacted punishment from Pharaoh at the Sea of Reeds:[8]

רַבִּי פַּפְּיָיס אוֹמֵר — R' Papyas says: כְּנֶסֶת יִשְׂרָאֵל הָיְתָה מְשַׁבַּחַת עַל סוּס רֶכֶב פַּרְעה — The Congregation of Israel praised God for His miracles in battling the horses of Pharaoh's chariots, שֶׁנֶּאֱמַר "דָּרַכְתָּ בַיָּם סוּסֶיךָ" — as it is stated, *You have trodden the sea with Your steeds* (*Habakkuk* 3:15). The prophet is extolling God for arriving at the Sea of Reeds on a steed to defend the Jews against their Egyptian pursuers.

The Baraisa explains the role of God's "steed" in His battle against Egypt, based on the *Song of Songs* verse cited in the previous section. The opening word of the verse, לְסֻסָתִי (translated *to My steed*), is written in the feminine. The Baraisa therefore interprets it as *to My mare*:

רַבִּי יְהוֹשֻׁעַ בֶּן קָרְחָה אוֹמֵר — R' Yehoshua ben Korchah says: כְּשֶׁבָּא פַרְעה לַיָּם בָּא עַל סוּס זָכָר — When Pharaoh came to the Sea, he came on a stallion, וְנִגְלָה עָלָיו הַקָּדוֹשׁ בָּרוּךְ הוּא בְּסוּסְיָא נְקֵיבָה — and the Holy One, Blessed is He, was revealed to him as riding upon a mare, שֶׁנֶּאֱמַר "לְסֻסָתִי בְּרִכְבֵי

---

5. I.e., I am waging a battle against the Jewish people, and, by extension, God, and it is therefore only appropriate that I myself travel at the head of the camp.

[Although Pharaoh sinned by waging war against the Jewish people and against God, he was rewarded for this single act of honoring God.]

6. It is less humiliating to be shamed by a greater individual than it is to be shamed by a lesser individual. Thus, because of the honor he showed God, Pharaoh was accorded the "honor" of being punished by God

Himself instead of by one of His emissaries (*Rashi* to *Sanhedrin* 94a).

7. Translation follows the Baraisa's exposition. In this verse God likens His beloved (the Jewish people) to the steed that He mounted, as it were, in His battle against Pharaoh (see the following section for further discussion regarding God's "steed"). This proves that God Himself arrived at the Sea of Reeds to exact punishment from Pharaoh (see *Ben Avraham*).

8. See *Sanhedrin* 94b.

‫פַּרְעֹה". וַהֲלֹא לֹא רָכַב אֶלָּא עַל כְּרוּב, שֶׁנֶּאֱמַר (תהלים יח, יא) "וַיִּרְכַּב‬
‫עַל כְּרוּב וַיָּעֹף וַיֵּדֶא עַל כַּנְפֵי רוּחַ"⁹, אֶלָּא נִדְמָה הַכְּרוּב לְסוּסֵי פַרְעֹה‬
‫כִּנְקֵבָה וְנִכְנְסוּ כֻּלָּם לַיָּם¹⁰. (שמואל א ב, ל) "וּבֹזַי יֵקָלּוּ" זֶה סַנְחֵרִיב שֶׁנָּהַג‬
‫בִּזָּיוֹן לִפְנֵי מִי שֶׁאָמַר וְהָיָה הָעוֹלָם, (לְפִיכָךְ בִּיְזָהוּ הַקָּדוֹשׁ בָּרוּךְ הוּא,)‬
‫שֶׁנֶּאֱמַר (ישעיה לז, כד) "בְּיַד עֲבָדֶיךָ חֵרַפְתָּ (אֶת) אֲדֹנָי וַתֹּאמֶר בְּרֹב רִכְבִּי‬
‫אֲנִי עָלִיתִי מְרוֹם הָרִים יַרְכְּתֵי לְבָנוֹן וְאֶכְרֹת קוֹמַת אֲרָזָיו מִבְחַר בְּרֹשָׁיו‬
‫וְאָבוֹא מְלוֹן קִצֹּה יַעַר כַּרְמִלּוֹ", (וְאָמַר) (שם פסוק כה) "אֲנִי קַרְתִּי וְשָׁתִיתִי‬
‫מַיִם וְאַחְרִב בְּכַף פְּעָמַי כֹּל יְאֹרֵי מָצוֹר"¹¹. לְפִיכָךְ פָּרַע הַקָּדוֹשׁ בָּרוּךְ הוּא‬

‫וַהֲלֹא‬ **פַּרְעֹה"** — as it is stated, *To My mare against Pharaoh's chariot, etc.*
‫לֹא רָכַב אֶלָּא עַל כְּרוּב‬ — But why did Pharaoh perceive God as riding upon a mare? Why, we know that in reality, **[God] rode only upon a cherub,** ‫שֶׁנֶּאֱמַר‬
"וַיִּרְכַּב עַל כְּרוּב וַיָּעֹף וַיֵּדֶא עַל כַּנְפֵי רוּחַ" — as it is stated, *He mounted a cherub and flew; He swooped on the wings of the wind* (Psalms 18:11)![9] ‫אֶלָּא‬
‫נִדְמָה הַכְּרוּב לְסוּסֵי פַרְעֹה כִּנְקֵבָה‬ — Rather, the cherub appeared to Pharaoh's **stallions like a mare,** ‫וְנִכְנְסוּ כֻּלָּם לַיָּם‬ — and they all entered the sea in pursuit of it.[10]

The Baraisa proceeds to expound the second half of the *Samuel* verse cited in §1:

‫זֶה סַנְחֵרִיב שֶׁנָּהַג‬ **"וּבֹזַי יֵקָלּוּ"** — *And those that scorn Me will be disgraced* — ‫בִּזָּיוֹן לִפְנֵי מִי שֶׁאָמַר וְהָיָה הָעוֹלָם‬ — this is referring to **Sennacherib,** king of Assyria, **who treated the One Who spoke and** thereby **the world came into being with scorn** by sending a messenger to convey his blasphemous words to the Israelites. ‫לְפִיכָךְ בִּיְזָהוּ הַקָּדוֹשׁ בָּרוּךְ הוּא‬ — **Therefore, the Holy One, Blessed is He, disgraced him.** ‫שֶׁנֶּאֱמַר "בְּיַד עֲבָדֶיךָ חֵרַפְתָּ אֲדֹנָי וַתֹּאמֶר בְּרֹב רִכְבִּי אֲנִי‬
‫עָלִיתִי מְרוֹם הָרִים יַרְכְּתֵי לְבָנוֹן וְאֶכְרֹת קוֹמַת אֲרָזָיו מִבְחַר בְּרֹשָׁיו וְאָבוֹא מְלוֹן קִצֹּה יַעַר‬
כַּרְמִלּוֹ" — **We know that Sennacherib blasphemed through a messenger, as it is stated,** *By the hand of your servants you [Sennacherib] have insulted my Lord, and said, "With my multitude of chariots I climbed the highest mountains, [to] the ends of the Lebanon [forest]; I shall cut down its tallest cedars, its choicest cypresses, and I shall enter His ultimate height, the forest of His fruitful field"* (Isaiah 37:24). ‫וְאָמַר "אֲנִי קַרְתִּי וְשָׁתִיתִי מַיִם וְאַחְרִב‬
"בְּכַף פְּעָמַי כֹּל יְאֹרֵי מָצוֹר" — **And [Sennacherib] further said,** through the agency of his servants, *"I dug and drank waters, for the soles of my feet dried up all the rivers of the besieged area"* (ibid. v. 25).[11] ‫לְפִיכָךְ פָּרַע הַקָּדוֹשׁ בָּרוּךְ הוּא‬

---

9. The passage is referring to the Splitting of the Sea; see *Rashi* to v. 16 there.

10. God caused the cherub to appear as a mare so that Pharaoh's stallions would

follow it into the sea, dragging their riders to their deaths (*Magen Avos, Ben Avraham*).

11. In these verses, Sennacherib expresses his confidence in his ability to conquer

מִמֶּנּוּ עַל יְדֵי מַלְאָךְ[12], וְגִילַח רֹאשׁוֹ וּזְקָנוֹ וְחָזַר בְּבוֹשֶׁת פָּנִים אֶל
אַרְצוֹ[13]. (רַבִּי יִשְׁמָעֵאל בְּנוֹ שֶׁל רַבִּי יוֹחָנָן בֶּן בְּרוֹקָא אוֹמֵר: הַלּוֹמֵד
עַל מְנָת לְלַמֵּד וְכוּ'.) הוּא הָיָה אוֹמֵר[15]: לֹא כָל הַתּוֹרָה כּוּלָּה
אַתָּה מְקַבֵּל עָלֶיךָ לְגוֹמְרָהּ[16] וְאִי אַתָּה בֶּן חוֹרִין לִפְרוֹשׁ הֵימֶנָּה[17],

---

מִמֶּנּוּ עַל יְדֵי מַלְאָךְ — **Therefore, the Holy One, Blessed is He, exacted punishment from him through an angel.**[12] וְגִילַח רֹאשׁוֹ וּזְקָנוֹ וְחָזַר בְּבוֹשֶׁת פָּנִים אֶל אַרְצוֹ — **Moreover, the angel further demeaned Sennacherib when he shaved his head and beard, and he returned to his land in disgrace.**[13]

The Baraisa cites *Avos* 4:5:

רַבִּי יִשְׁמָעֵאל בְּנוֹ שֶׁל רַבִּי יוֹחָנָן בֶּן בְּרוֹקָא אוֹמֵר הַלּוֹמֵד עַל מְנָת לְלַמֵּד וְכוּ' — R' **Yishmael the son of R' Yochanan ben Beroka says: One who studies Torah in order to teach is given the means to study and to teach; but one who studies Torah in order to practice is given the means to study and to teach, to guard and to practice.**[14]

The Baraisa continues with a paraphrase of *Avos* 2:16:

הוּא הָיָה אוֹמֵר — **He used to say:**[15] לֹא כָל הַתּוֹרָה כּוּלָּה אַתָּה מְקַבֵּל עָלֶיךָ לְגוֹמְרָהּ — **You need not accept upon yourself to complete the entire Torah,**[16] וְאִי אַתָּה בֶּן חוֹרִין לִפְרוֹשׁ הֵימֶנָּה — **yet you are not free to withdraw from it.**[17]

Jerusalem and take the Temple, God's abode (see *Rashi* there). These blasphemous words were delivered to the Jewish people by his messenger Rabshakeh (see ibid. Ch. 36).

12. As it states (*II Kings* 19:35), *And it was that [very] night: An angel of HASHEM went out and struck down one hundred eighty-five thousand [people] of the Assyrian camp.* Since Sennacherib disgraced God through his messengers — which is even more insulting than if he had done so by himself — God also sent *His* messenger (an angel) to execute Sennacherib's punishment, instead of according Sennacherib the "honor" of being punished by God Himself (*Sanhedrin* 94b with *Rashi* ad loc.).

13. The Gemara (*Sanhedrin* 95b-96a) relates that after Sennacherib's defeat, God sent an angel to him in the guise of an elderly man. The old man asked Sennacherib how he intended to defend himself before the kings whose sons had served in his invading army and were stricken down by the angel. The "man" offered to help Sennacherib disguise himself by shaving his head. Since it was dark, he had Sennacherib bring a fire. The fire

caught hold of Sennacherib's beard, so that in the end, both his head and beard were shaven. [See *Maharal* and *Ben Yehoyada* ad loc. for the underlying themes of this narrative.]

14. The first case speaks of someone who wants to devote himself entirely to studying and teaching Torah. However, although he surely plans to fulfill all the precepts of the Torah, he does not intend to actively pursue acts of kindness and the like. The second case refers to a person who intends to devote himself to the study of Torah *and* to the performance of kind deeds. Each is given the means from Heaven to achieve his goal (see *Rav* to the Mishnah).

15. This teaching is cited there in the name of R' Tarfon.

16. God does not expect a person to master the entire Torah. Therefore, even if he is unable to complete his studies, his reward will not be diminished as a result (*Binyan Yehoshua*, citing *Rav* to the Mishnah).

17. Lest one think that he may be absolved from studying Torah if he is willing to forgo the reward, we are informed that one must

אֶלָּא כָּל הַמַּרְבֶּה וּמוֹסִיף מוֹסִיף שָׂכָר הַרְבֵּה[18]. רַבִּי אֶלְעָזָר בֶּן חִסְמָא
אוֹמֵר: קִינִּין[19] וּפִתְחֵי נִדָּה[20] הֵן הֵן גּוּפֵי הַהֲלָכוֹת[21]. רַבִּי יוֹחָנָן בֶּן נוּרִי
אוֹמֵר: הַהֲלָכוֹת[22] וְהַטָּהֲרוֹת[23] וְהַנִּדּוֹת וְהַקִּינִּין הֵן הֵן גּוּפֵי תוֹרָה[24].

אֶלָּא כָּל הַמַּרְבֶּה וּמוֹסִיף מוֹסִיף שָׂכָר הַרְבֵּה — **Rather, anyone who increases** his knowledge **greatly will increase** his **reward greatly.**[18]

The Baraisa cites *Avos* 3:18, as well as a similar teaching:

רַבִּי אֶלְעָזָר בֶּן חִסְמָא אוֹמֵר — **R' Elazar ben Chisma says:** קִינִּין וּפִתְחֵי נִדָּה הֵן הֵן גּוּפֵי הַהֲלָכוֹת — **The laws of bird offerings**[19] **and beginnings of menstrual cycles**[20] — **these are essential laws.**[21] רַבִּי יוֹחָנָן בֶּן נוּרִי אוֹמֵר — **R' Yochanan ben Nuri says:** הַהֲלָכוֹת וְהַטָּהֲרוֹת וְהַנִּדּוֹת וְהַקִּינִּין הֵן הֵן גּוּפֵי תוֹרָה — **The halachos**[22] **and the laws of purifications,**[23] **menstruants, and bird offerings are essentials of the Torah.**[24]

---

see himself as a servant, who is not free to do as he pleases, but must dedicate himself to his task (ibid.).

18. One might reason that since the reward for studying Torah is so great, he may study for only a brief time, as that will provide him with ample reward, and spend the rest of his time engaging in leisurely pursuits. The Baraisa therefore informs us that only one who studies as much as he can will be greatly rewarded. One who *chooses* to study for only a brief time, however, will be punished for the time he wasted from his studies (see *Tos. Yom Tov* ad loc.).

19. Certain laws concerning these offerings are very complex, such as what must be done when birds for an obligatory offering become intermingled with birds for a voluntary offering, or when birds set aside for an *olah* offering become intermingled with birds set aside for a *chatas* offering (*Binyan Yehoshua*, citing *Rav* to the Mishnah). There is a dedicated tractate, *Kinnim*, that details the formulas to be used in rectifying such situations.

20. A woman's halachic menstrual cycle consists of a seven-day *niddah* period and an eleven-day *zivah* period. By Biblical law, the two periods are treated differently with regard to how many days she needs to wait before immersing after she experiences bleeding, and whether those days must be clean (i.e., free of any blood flow). When a woman loses track of her calendar, the calculations needed

to determine the beginning of her next cycle can be very complex; see *Arachin* 8a-b.

21. Both sets of laws — bird offerings and menstrual cycles — are quintessential examples of Oral Torah, and the study of them will merit much reward (*Rav* to *Avos* 3:18). Since both appear to involve nothing more than trivial calculations, one might think that there is less reward for studying them than for studying other aspects of the Torah. R' Elazar therefore informs us that they are just as essential as any other part of the Oral Torah (*Binyan Yehoshua*).

22. These are laws taught orally to Moses at Sinai that have no Scriptural basis. Such laws have the force of Biblical law (*Ahavas Chesed*).

23. I.e., laws pertaining to ritual contamination and purification (ibid.).

24. These last two refer to the same items mentioned in the previous teaching. This teaching merely adds the first two: the halachos and the laws of purification (ibid.). R' Yochanan is telling us not to differentiate between the laws taught to Moses orally and those written in the Torah, as all of them were equally spoken by God. Likewise, one should not invest less effort into studying the laws of contamination and purification, which are not applicable in our times, than he does into the study of those laws that do apply nowadays, since all of them are fundamentals of the Torah (see *Ben Avraham*).

הוּא הָיָה אוֹמֵר: סִידּוּר שֶׁל שֻׁלְחָן [גָּדוֹל[25]] וַעֲשִׂיַּית בֵּית דִּין וְקִיּוּמֵיהֶן מְבִיאִין טוֹבָה לָעוֹלָם[27]:

ג. רַבִּי יוֹחָנָן בֶּן דַּהֲבַאי אוֹמֵר: הָאוֹמֵר אֵין הֲלָכָה זֹאת נִבְרֵאת אֵין לוֹ חֵלֶק לָעוֹלָם הַבָּא[28]. הוּא הָיָה אוֹמֵר: אַל תְּרַחֵק עַצְמְךָ מִמִּדָּה שֶׁאֵין לָהּ קִצְבָה וּמִמְּלָאכָה שֶׁאֵין לָהּ גְּמִירָא[30]. מָשָׁל לְמָה הַדָּבָר דּוֹמֶה, לְאֶחָד

The Baraisa continues:

הוּא הָיָה אוֹמֵר — He used to say: **סִידּוּר שֶׁל שֻׁלְחָן גָּדוֹל** — The setting of the great Table in the Temple with the new Show-bread every week,[25] **וַעֲשִׂיַּית בֵּית דִּין וְקִיּוּמֵיהֶן** — and the appointment of, and compliance with, a Rabbinic Court,[26] **מְבִיאִין טוֹבָה לָעוֹלָם** — bring good to the world.[27]

§3 The Baraisa makes a point regarding the disgrace of Torah:

רַבִּי יוֹחָנָן בֶּן דַּהֲבַאי אוֹמֵר — R' Yochanan ben Dahavai says: **הָאוֹמֵר אֵין הֲלָכָה זֹאת נִבְרֵאת אֵין לוֹ חֵלֶק לָעוֹלָם הַבָּא** — One who says regarding even one law of the Torah, "This law did not originate from God," has no portion in the World to Come.[28]

The Baraisa returns to the theme mentioned in the previous section — i.e., that one is not expected to complete the entire Torah, but the more one studies, the more reward he will receive:[29]

אַל תְּרַחֵק עַצְמְךָ מִמִּדָּה שֶׁאֵין לָהּ קִצְבָה Do — **הוּא הָיָה אוֹמֵר** — He used to say: not distance yourself from a measure that has no limit **וּמִמְּלָאכָה שֶׁאֵין לָהּ גְּמִירָא** — and from a task that has no end, i.e., the Torah and its study.[30] **מָשָׁל לְמָה הַדָּבָר דּוֹמֶה** — To what may this matter be compared? **לְאֶחָד**

---

25. *Binyan Yehoshua*. Every Sabbath, the twelve loaves of the Show-bread (*lechem hapanim*) would be removed from the Table in the Sanctuary and replaced with the new loaves that had been baked the day before (see *Leviticus* 24:5-9).

26. *Ben Avraham*.

27. The Table in the Temple, and the loaves of bread that lay upon it, served as the medium for the Divine blessings of satiety and wealth (*Binyan Yehoshua*; see *Bava Basra* 25b; *Zohar* Vol. I, 88b and Vol. II, 154b-155a; *Ramban* to *Exodus* 25:24). Regarding the establishment of a Rabbinic Court, the Baraisa in *Shabbos* 33a teaches that for the sin of failing to carry out justice properly, pestilence and famine come to the world. This implies that the world is preserved through properly administered justice (*Magen Avos*).

28. The Gemara (*Sanhedrin* 99a) teaches that one who claims that the Torah is not from Heaven, God forbid, is included in the verse (*Numbers* 15:31), *For he scorned the word of HASHEM and nullified His commandment; that person will surely be cut off, his sin is upon him.* This means that he will be eradicated from both this world and the World to Come (see above, 26 §4 note 35). The Gemara adds that this includes someone who says that the entire Torah is from Heaven except for one verse or even one halachic inference. Accordingly, our Baraisa states that one who claims that a certain law of the Torah did not originate from God has no share in the World to Come (*Binyan Yehoshua*).

29. Ibid.

30. Scripture describes the Torah by saying (*Job* 11:9), *Its measure is longer than the*

שֶׁהָיָה נוֹטֵל מֵי הַיָּם וּמֵטִיל לַיַּבָּשָׁה, יָם אֵינוֹ חָסֵר וְיַבָּשָׁה אֵינָהּ מִתְמַלְּאָה.
הָיָה מְקַצֵּר בְּדַעְתּוֹ. אָמַר לוֹ: רֵיקָה, מִפְּנֵי מָה אַתָּה מְקַצֵּר בְּדַעְתְּךָ,
בְּכָל יוֹם טוֹל שְׂכָרְךָ דִּינָר שֶׁל זָהָב:[31]

ד. רַבִּי אֶלְעָזָר בֶּן שַׁמּוּעַ אוֹמֵר: יְהִי כְּבוֹד תַּלְמִידְךָ חָבִיב עָלֶיךָ
כְּשֶׁלָּךְ, וּכְבוֹד חֲבֵירְךָ כְּמוֹרָא רַבָּךְ[32] וּמוֹרָא רַבָּךְ כְּמוֹרָא שָׁמַיִם.
°מְלַמֵּד שֶׁיְּהֵא כְּבוֹד תַּלְמִידוֹ חָבִיב עָלָיו °כִּכְבוֹד חֲבֵירוֹ[33], יִלְמְדוּ כָּל
אָדָם מִמֹּשֶׁה רַבֵּינוּ שֶׁאָמַר לִיהוֹשֻׁעַ (שמות יז, ט) "בְּחַר לָנוּ אֲנָשִׁים."

שֶׁהָיָה נוֹטֵל מֵי הַיָּם וּמֵטִיל לַיַּבָּשָׁה — To someone who was hired to take the water from the sea and pour it onto the dry land. יָם אֵינוֹ חָסֵר וְיַבָּשָׁה אֵינָהּ מִתְמַלְּאָה — He noticed that the sea never diminished and the dry land never filled. הָיָה מְקַצֵּר בְּדַעְתּוֹ — Seeing that he would never complete the task assigned to him, he became disheartened. אָמַר לוֹ — Thereupon [someone] said to him, רֵיקָה מִפְּנֵי מָה אַתָּה מְקַצֵּר בְּדַעְתְּךָ — "Empty one! Why are you becoming disheartened? בְּכָל יוֹם טֹל שְׂכָרְךָ דִּינָר שֶׁל זָהָב — For each day you work, you are being paid a gold *dinar!*"[31]

§4 The Baraisa cites *Avos* 4:12: רַבִּי אֶלְעָזָר בֶּן שַׁמּוּעַ אוֹמֵר — R' Elazar ben Shamua says: יְהִי כְּבוֹד תַּלְמִידְךָ חָבִיב עָלֶיךָ כְּשֶׁלָּךְ — Let the honor of your student be as dear to you as your own, וּכְבוֹד חֲבֵרְךָ כְּמוֹרָא רַבָּךְ — the honor of your colleague as the reverence for your teacher,[32] וּמוֹרָא רַבָּךְ כְּמוֹרָא שָׁמַיִם — and the reverence for your teacher as the reverence for Heaven.

The Baraisa explains the sources for these three teachings: מִנַּיִן שֶׁיְּהֵא כְּבוֹד תַּלְמִידוֹ חָבִיב עָלָיו כִּכְבוֹדוֹ — From where do we derive that the honor of one's student should be as dear to him as his own honor?[33] יִלְמְדוּ כָּל אָדָם מִמֹּשֶׁה רַבֵּינוּ שֶׁאָמַר לִיהוֹשֻׁעַ "בְּחַר לָנוּ אֲנָשִׁים" — Let every person learn it from Moses, our teacher, who said to his student Joshua, when instructing

---

earth and wider than the sea. Therefore, one might wonder: Why should I toil for nothing? Ultimately, I can never complete the Torah. R' Yochanan teaches us that this reasoning is wrong, as he will go on to explain (*Binyan Yehoshua*, citing *Mefaresh*).

31. Similarly, a person is rewarded for every moment that he spends studying Torah, despite the fact that it is virtually impossible to complete the entire task (ibid.).

32. This does not mean that one must actually honor his colleagues the same way he honors his teacher. Rather, it means that

one should *cherish* the honor due to his colleagues, i.e., he should desire to honor them — to the extent that they deserve — as much as he desires to show reverence to his teacher — to the extent that he deserves. The same applies to the previous statement and to the following one (*Binyan Yehoshua*, citing *Midrash Shmuel* to the Mishnah). Thus, the Mishnah is saying that one must be careful not to diminish the honor due to *anyone* — whether his student, colleague, or teacher (see *Rabbeinu Yonah* ad loc.).

33. Emendation follows *Nuschas HaGra*.

״בְּחַר לִי״ לֹא נֶאֱמַר אֶלָּא ״בְּחַר לָנוּ״, מְלַמֵּד שֶׁעֲשָׂאָהוּ כְּמוֹתוֹ אַף עַל
פִּי שֶׁהוּא רַבּוֹ וִיהוֹשֻׁעַ תַּלְמִידוֹ. וּמִנַּיִן שֶׁכְּבוֹד חֲבֵירוֹ יְהֵא חָבִיב עָלָיו
כְּרַבּוֹ, שֶׁנֶּאֱמַר (במדבר יב, יא) ״וַיֹּאמֶר אַהֲרֹן אֶל מֹשֶׁה בִּי אֲדֹנִי״. וַהֲלֹא
אָחִיו קָטָן מִמֶּנּוּ הָיָה אֶלָּא עֲשָׂאוֹ רַבּוֹ.[34] וּמִנַּיִן שֶׁכְּבוֹד רַבּוֹ [יְהֵא] חָבִיב
עָלָיו כִּכְבוֹד שָׁמַיִם, שֶׁנֶּאֱמַר (שם יא, כח) ״וַיַּעַן יְהוֹשֻׁעַ בִּן נוּן מְשָׁרֵת
מֹשֶׁה מִבְּחֻרָיו וַיֹּאמַר אֲדֹנִי מֹשֶׁה כְּלָאֵם״.[35] שְׁקָלוֹ כְּנֶגֶד שְׁכִינָה.

him to wage battle against Amalek, *Choose people for us* (Exodus 17:9).
״בְּחַר לִי״ לֹא נֶאֱמַר אֶלָּא ״בְּחַר לָנוּ״ — It is not stated that he said, "Choose
people for me," but, *Choose people for us.* מְלַמֵּד שֶׁעֲשָׂאָהוּ כְּמוֹתוֹ — This
teaches that [Moses] treated [Joshua] as himself, אַף עַל פִּי שֶׁהוּא רַבּוֹ וִיהוֹשֻׁעַ
תַּלְמִידוֹ — even though [Moses] was the teacher and Joshua was the student.
וּמִנַּיִן שֶׁכְּבוֹד חֲבֵירוֹ יְהֵא חָבִיב עָלָיו כְּרַבּוֹ — And from where do we derive that
the honor of one's colleague should be as dear to him as that of his teacher?
שֶׁנֶּאֱמַר ״וַיֹּאמֶר אַהֲרֹן אֶל מֹשֶׁה בִּי אֲדֹנִי״ — For it is stated, *Aaron said to Moses,
"I beg you, my lord, etc."* (Numbers 12:11). וַהֲלֹא אָחִיו קָטָן מִמֶּנּוּ הָיָה — But
was [Moses] not [Aaron's] younger brother? Indeed he was! Why then did
Aaron call him *my lord?* אֶלָּא עֲשָׂאוֹ רַבּוֹ — Rather, it is because he treated
him as his teacher, although in reality he was his colleague — and a younger
colleague at that.[34] וּמִנַּיִן שֶׁכְּבוֹד רַבּוֹ יְהֵא חָבִיב עָלָיו כִּכְבוֹד שָׁמַיִם — And from
where do we derive that the honor of one's teacher should be as dear to him
as the honor of Heaven? שֶׁנֶּאֱמַר ״וַיַּעַן יְהוֹשֻׁעַ בִּן נוּן מְשָׁרֵת מֹשֶׁה מִבְּחֻרָיו וַיֹּאמַר
אֲדֹנִי מֹשֶׁה כְּלָאֵם״ — For it is stated, *Joshua son of Nun, the servant of Moses
since his youth, spoke up and said, "My lord Moses, eliminate them!"* (ibid.
11:28).[35] שְׁקָלוֹ כְּנֶגֶד שְׁכִינָה — [Joshua] was thereby equating his teacher,
[Moses], with the Divine Presence, as if to say: Just as they would be liable to
death had they rebelled against God, so are they liable to death for rebelling
against you![36]

---

34. We know that Moses and Aaron were
equal, as the Sages derive from the fact
that when mentioning them both by name,
Scripture sometimes places Moses first and
at other times places Aaron first (*Mechilta*
to *Exodus* 12:1, cited by *Rashi* to ibid.
6:26). Since we see that Aaron referred to
his younger colleague as *my lord*, we may
derive that one should cherish the honor of
his colleague like that of his teacher, regardless of who is older (*Ben Avraham*).

35. [Translation follows *Rav* to *Avos* 4:12,
and is based on *Sifrei* to the verse, cited by

Rashi to *Exodus* 17:9.] The passage there
tells how God instructed Moses to gather
seventy elders and have them stand at the
Tent of Meeting. God would then speak with
Moses and impart some of Moses' spirit of
prophecy to the elders. Two of the chosen
men, Eldad and Medad, remained behind in
the camp, and the spirit of prophecy rested
upon them there. Joshua maintained that
they were deserving of death for having de-
fied Moses' instructions.

36. *Binyan Yehoshua.*

מִפְּנֵי שֶׁבָּרִאשׁוֹנָה הָיוּ אוֹמְרִין: דָּגָן בִּיהוּדָה וְתֶבֶן בַּגָּלִיל וּמוֹץ בְּעֵבֶר
הַיַּרְדֵּן[38]. חָזְרוּ לוֹמַר: אֵין דָּגָן בִּיהוּדָה וְאֵין תֶּבֶן בַּגָּלִיל אֶלָּא מוֹץ וּבְעֵבֶר
הַיַּרְדֵּן לֹא זֶה וְלֹא זֶה:[39]

The Baraisa concludes with a teaching concerning the deteriorating level of Torah scholarship in the various regions of the Land of Israel. The matter is illustrated using an analogy of the various components of grain:[37] דָּגָן בִּיהוּדָה וְתֶבֶן מִפְּנֵי שֶׁבָּרִאשׁוֹנָה הָיוּ אוֹמְרִין — Since [people] initially said: בַּגָּלִיל וּמוֹץ בְּעֵבֶר הַיַּרְדֵּן — Kernels of grain can be found in Judah, straw in the Galilee, and chaff in the Trans-Jordan,[38] חָזְרוּ לוֹמַר — they later retracted, saying: אֵין דָּגָן בִּיהוּדָה — There are no kernels of grain to be found in Judah, but only straw, וְאֵין תֶּבֶן בַּגָּלִיל אֶלָּא מוֹץ — and there is no straw to be found in the Galilee, but only chaff, וּבְעֵבֶר הַיַּרְדֵּן לֹא זֶה וְלֹא זֶה — and in the Trans-Jordan, none of these can be found.[39]

---

37. Our elucidation of this paragraph follows *Hagahos Yaavetz*; see also *Kisei Rachamim*. See the other commentators, however, who connect it to the previous teaching.

38. That is, Judah (the southern part of the Land) possessed a superior level of scholarship, represented by the wheat kernel, which is ultimately ground into flour and used as food. The level of scholarship in the Galilee (the northern part of the Land) was inferior to that of Judah (see *Eruvin* 53a-b), and it was therefore likened to the straw, which has many practical uses but is not fit for human

consumption. The lands on the east side of the Jordan, however, which were outside the Land of Israel proper, possessed the lowest degree of scholarship, like the chaff that is not used at all, but is thrown to the wind during winnowing.

39. The level of scholarship ultimately declined in all three regions. Thus, Judah deteriorated to the previous level of the Galilee, the Galilee deteriorated to the previous level of the Trans-Jordan, and the Trans-Jordan deteriorated even further.

෴ פֶּרֶק כח ෴

א. רַבִּי נָתָן אוֹמֵר אֵין לְךָ אַהֲבָה כְּאַהֲבָה שֶׁל תּוֹרָה¹. וְאֵין לְךָ חָכְמָה כְּחָכְמָה שֶׁל °דֶּרֶךְ אֶרֶץ² וְאֵין לְךָ יוֹפִי כְּיוֹפִי שֶׁל יְרוּשָׁלַיִם³. וְאֵין לְךָ עוֹשֶׁר כְּעוֹשֶׁר שֶׁל מָדַי⁴. וְאֵין לְךָ גְּבוּרָה כִּגְבוּרָה שֶׁל פָּרֵס. וְאֵין לְךָ זְנוּת כִּזְנוּת שֶׁל עַרְבִיִּים. וְאֵין לְךָ גַּסּוּת כְּגַסּוּת שֶׁל עֵילָם⁵. וְאֵין לְךָ חֲנוּפָּה כַּחֲנוּפָּה שֶׁל בָּבֶל שֶׁנֶּאֱמַר, (זכריה ה, יא) "וַיֹּאמֶר [אֵלַי] לִבְנוֹת לָהּ בַיִת בְּאֶרֶץ שִׁנְעָר"⁶.

෴ CHAPTER 28 ෴

§1 The Baraisa lists the exceptional nature of certain entities, nations, and lands:

רַבִּי נָתָן אוֹמֵר — **R' Nassan says:** אֵין לְךָ אַהֲבָה כְּאַהֲבָה שֶׁל תּוֹרָה — **There is no love like the love of Torah,**[1] וְאֵין לְךָ חָכְמָה כְּחָכְמָה שֶׁל אֶרֶץ יִשְׂרָאֵל — **and no wisdom like the wisdom of the Land of Israel,**[2] וְאֵין לְךָ יוֹפִי כְּיוֹפִי שֶׁל יְרוּשָׁלַיִם — **and no beauty like the beauty of Jerusalem,**[3] וְאֵין לְךָ עוֹשֶׁר כְּעוֹשֶׁר שֶׁל מָדַי — **and no wealth like the wealth of Media,**[4] וְאֵין לְךָ גְּבוּרָה כִּגְבוּרָה שֶׁל פָּרֵס — **and no might like the might of Persia,** וְאֵין לְךָ זְנוּת כִּזְנוּת שֶׁל עַרְבִיִּים — **and no immorality like the immorality of the Arabians,** וְאֵין לְךָ גַּסּוּת כְּגַסּוּת שֶׁל עֵילָם — **and no arrogance like the arrogance of Elam,**[5] חֲנוּפָּה כַּחֲנוּפָּה שֶׁל בָּבֶל — **and no false flattery like the false flattery of Babylonia,** שֶׁנֶּאֱמַר "וַיֹּאמֶר אֵלַי לִבְנוֹת לָהּ בַיִת בְּאֶרֶץ שִׁנְעָר" — **as it is stated,** *I said to the angel who was speaking to me, "Where are they taking the ephah?" He said to me, "To build her a house in the land of Shinar"* (Zechariah 5:10-11).[6]

---

1. Meaning, there is no love that can compare to the love that Torah scholars display toward the Torah (see *Ahavas Chesed*, citing *Eruvin* 54b).

2. [Emendation follows *Nuschas HaGra*.] Compare *Kiddushin* 49b, where the Gemara says: "Ten measures of wisdom descended to the world. The Land of Israel took nine of them, and all the rest of the world took one." As explained by *Rashi* there, "wisdom" refers to knowledge of Torah and the ways of the world (*Binyan Yehoshua*). The Gemara goes on to make similar statements regarding most of the nations and lands listed below and their respective character traits (in addition to many others not listed here).

3. Scripture (*Lamentations* 4:2) portrays the beauty of the residents of Jerusalem,

referring to them as *the precious children of Zion, who are comparable to fine gold* (*Binyan Yehoshua*, from *Mefaresh*).

4. In *Kiddushin*, however, the Gemara states that it was Rome that was blessed with outstanding wealth. [This was the original version in our Baraisa as well, and that is how it appeared in the first printing (Venice, 1546). In subsequent printings, however, it was changed to "Media."]

5. Elam was an ancient nation that dwelled in what is now the southwestern region of Iran.

6. In the previous verses, the prophet Zechariah relates how an angel showed him a vision in which two winged women lifted an *ephah* (a hollow utensil used for measuring) and carried it between heaven

וְאֵין לְךָ כְּשָׁפִים כִּכְשָׁפִים שֶׁל מִצְרָיִם:[7]

ב. רַבִּי שִׁמְעוֹן בֶּן אֶלְעָזָר אוֹמֵר: חָכָם הַדָּר בְּאֶרֶץ יִשְׂרָאֵל וְיוֹצֵא חוּצָה לָאָרֶץ פָּגַם[8]. (הַדָּר בָּהּ מְשׁוּבָּח הֵימֶנּוּ.) וְאַף עַל פִּי שֶׁפָּגַם מְשׁוּבָּח הוּא יוֹתֵר מִכָּל הַמְשׁוּבָּחִים שֶׁבַּמְּדִינוֹת. מָשְׁלוּ מָשָׁל לְמָה הַדָּבָר דּוֹמֶה, לְבַרְזֶל הַנְּדוּאִי שֶׁבָּא מִמְּדִינַת הַיָּם, שֶׁאַף עַל פִּי שֶׁנִּפְחַת מִמַּה שֶׁהָיָה הוּא מְשׁוּבָּח יוֹתֵר מִכָּל הַמְשׁוּבָּחִים שֶׁבַּמְּדִינוֹת:[10]

וְאֵין לְךָ כְּשָׁפִים כִּכְשָׁפִים שֶׁל מִצְרָיִם — And there is no witchcraft like the witchcraft of Egypt.[7]

§2 The Baraisa expands on the teaching above that "there is no wisdom like the wisdom of the Land of Israel":

רַבִּי שִׁמְעוֹן בֶּן אֶלְעָזָר אוֹמֵר — R' Shimon ben Elazar says: חָכָם הַדָּר בְּאֶרֶץ יִשְׂרָאֵל וְיוֹצֵא חוּצָה לָאָרֶץ פָּגַם — A scholar who lives in the Land of Israel and goes to live outside of the Land has thereby impaired his scholarship.[8] הַדָּר בָּהּ מְשׁוּבָּח הֵימֶנּוּ — And therefore one who dwells there and does not leave is superior to him. וְאַף עַל פִּי שֶׁפָּגַם מְשׁוּבָּח הוּא יוֹתֵר מִכָּל הַמְשׁוּבָּחִים שֶׁבַּמְּדִינוֹת — However, even though [the scholar] who left the Land of Israel has impaired his scholarship, he is still superior to all of the best [scholars] in other provinces, due to the wisdom that he gained before he left the Land. מָשְׁלוּ מָשָׁל לְמָה הַדָּבָר דּוֹמֶה — They illustrated this with a parable: To what can this matter be compared? לְבַרְזֶל הַנְּדוּאִי שֶׁבָּא מִמְּדִינַת הַיָּם — To Indian iron that arrives from overseas: שֶׁאַף עַל פִּי שֶׁנִּפְחַת מִמַּה שֶׁהָיָה הוּא מְשׁוּבָּח יוֹתֵר — Even though its quality has diminished as a result of being tossed about while in transit,[9] it is still superior to all the best iron מִכָּל הַמְשׁוּבָּחִים שֶׁבַּמְּדִינוֹת — found throughout the other provinces.[10]

§3 The Baraisa makes a point regarding the importance of harmony in the home:

and earth. The angel informed Zechariah that they were transporting it to the land of Shinar, a name for Babylonia. The Gemara (Kiddushin 49b) explains that the ephah symbolically contained the character traits of arrogance and false flattery (see Rashi ad loc.). The Gemara adds that while both of these traits descended to Babylonia, only false flattery remained there; arrogance made its way from there to Elam.

7. In ancient times, Egypt was reputed to be a land rife with sorcerers (see Rashi to Exodus 7:22).

8. Because he is no longer breathing in the wisdom-fostering air of the Land of Israel (Binyan Yehoshua; see Bava Basra 158b).

9. Shenei Eliyahu.

10. The comparison of a Torah scholar to iron is apt because the Gemara teaches: "Any Torah scholar who is not hard as iron is not a [true] Torah scholar" (Taanis 4a). "Hard as iron" means that he is wise and sharp, and cleaves through halachic doubts like an iron blade (Binyan Yehoshua).

ג. רַבָּן שִׁמְעוֹן בֶּן גַּמְלִיאֵל אוֹמֵר: כָּל הַמֵּשִׂים שָׁלוֹם בְּתוֹךְ בֵּיתוֹ מַעֲלֶה
עָלָיו הַכָּתוּב כְּאִילוּ מֵשִׂים שָׁלוֹם בְּיִשְׂרָאֵל עַל כָּל אֶחָד וְאֶחָד.[11] וְכָל
הַמֵּטִיל קִנְאָה וְתַחֲרוּת בְּתוֹךְ בֵּיתוֹ מַעֲלֶה עָלָיו הַכָּתוּב כְּאִילוּ מֵטִיל
קִנְאָה וְתַחֲרוּת בְּיִשְׂרָאֵל. לְפִי שֶׁכָּל אֶחָד וְאֶחָד מֶלֶךְ בְּתוֹךְ בֵּיתוֹ שֶׁנֶּאֱמַר
(אסתר א, כב) "לִהְיוֹת כָּל אִישׁ שֹׂרֵר בְּבֵיתוֹ":[12]

ד. רַבָּן גַּמְלִיאֵל אוֹמֵר: בְּאַרְבָּעָה דְּבָרִים מַלְכוּת כּוּתִים אוֹכֶלֶת,
בְּמִכְסָאוֹת בְּמֶרְחֲצָאוֹת וְתַרְטִיָאוֹת[13] וְאַרְנוֹנִיּוֹת שֶׁלָּהֶן:

ה. הוּא הָיָה אוֹמֵר: דִּבְרֵי תוֹרָה קָשִׁין לִקְנוֹתָן (כִּכְלֵי מִילָת[14]) וְנוֹחִין

כָּל הַמֵּשִׂים — **Rabban Shimon ben Gamliel says:** רַבָּן שִׁמְעוֹן בֶּן גַּמְלִיאֵל אוֹמֵר — **Anyone who establishes peace within his home** שָׁלוֹם בְּתוֹךְ בֵּיתוֹ מַעֲלֶה — **is considered by** עָלָיו הַכָּתוּב כְּאִילוּ מֵשִׂים שָׁלוֹם בְּיִשְׂרָאֵל עַל כָּל אֶחָד וְאֶחָד **Scripture as if he establishes peace for each and every Jewish person.**[11] וְכָל הַמֵּטִיל קִנְאָה וְתַחֲרוּת בְּתוֹךְ בֵּיתוֹ — **But anyone who provokes jealousy and rivalry within his home** מַעֲלֶה עָלָיו הַכָּתוּב כְּאִילוּ מֵטִיל קִנְאָה וְתַחֲרוּת בְּיִשְׂרָאֵל **is considered by Scripture as if he provokes jealousy and rivalry among the entire Jewish people.** לְפִי שֶׁכָּל אֶחָד וְאֶחָד מֶלֶךְ בְּתוֹךְ בֵּיתוֹ — **The responsibil**ity of ensuring peace in the home rests on the master of the house, **because each and every [man] is a king within his own home,** and his behavior will set the tone for his entire household, שֶׁנֶּאֱמַר "לִהְיוֹת כָּל אִישׁ שֹׂרֵר בְּבֵיתוֹ" — **as** it is stated, *That every man should rule in his own home* (*Esther 1:22*).[12]

§4 The Baraisa discusses the travails of the exorbitant taxes levied by the Romans:

בְּאַרְבָּעָה דְּבָרִים מַלְכוּת כּוּתִים **— Rabban Gamliel says:** רַבָּן גַּמְלִיאֵל אוֹמֵר
אוֹכֶלֶת — **The government of the Roman idolaters consumes** the people's money **through four things:** בְּמִכְסָאוֹת בְּמֶרְחֲצָאוֹת וְתַרְטִיָאוֹת וְאַרְנוֹנִיּוֹת שֶׁלָּהֶן — **through their income taxes,** their **bathhouse** fees, their **theater** assessments,[13] and their **taxes on livestock and produce.**

§5 Rabban Gamliel draws a contrast between words of Torah and words of foolishness:

דִּבְרֵי תוֹרָה קָשִׁין לִקְנוֹתָן כִּכְלֵי מִילָת וְנוֹחִין **— He used to say:** הוּא הָיָה אוֹמֵר

---

11. If one conducts his home with peace, his family members will follow his model in their respective homes, and his peaceful ways will extend to the entire Jewish people (*Binyan Yehoshua*, citing *Mefaresh*).

12. This was a decree of Ahasuerus, issued in the aftermath of Vashti's contemptuous refusal to obey the king's summons. The

Gemara in *Megillah* 12b states that this principle is obvious without a decree.

13. These public arenas served as venues for official meetings such as court proceedings and the like. The government would charge excessive taxes to fund the operation of these facilities (*Binyan Yehoshua*, based on *Rashi* to *Shabbos* 150a ד״ה טרטייאות).

לְאַבְּדָן בִּכְלֵי פִשְׁתָּן[15]. דִּבְרֵי שְׁטוּת וְדִבְרֵי תִּיפְלוּת נוֹחִין לִקְנוֹתָן וְקָשִׁין לְאַבְּדָם כְּשַׂק[16]. פְּעָמִים שֶׁאָדָם לוֹקֵחַ שַׂק מִן הַשּׁוּק בְּסֶלַע[17] וּמִשְׁתַּמֵשׁ בּוֹ וְהוֹלֵךְ אַרְבַּע אוֹ חָמֵשׁ שָׁנִים. רַבִּי יְהוּדָה הַנָּשִׂיא אוֹמֵר: כָּל הַמְקַבֵּל עָלָיו תַּעֲנוּגֵי הָעוֹלָם הַזֶּה מוֹנְעִין מִמֶּנּוּ תַּעֲנוּגֵי הָעוֹלָם הַבָּא[18]. וְכֹל שֶׁאֵינוֹ מְקַבֵּל תַּעֲנוּגֵי הָעוֹלָם הַזֶּה נוֹתְנִין לוֹ תַּעֲנוּגֵי הָעוֹלָם הַבָּא:

ו. הוּא הָיָה אוֹמֵר: צַדִּיקִים שֶׁרַע לָהֶם בָּעוֹלָם הַזֶּה לְמָה הוּא דוֹמֶה,

לְאַבְּדָן בִּכְלֵי פִשְׁתָּן — Torah concepts are as difficult to acquire as fine woolen garments,[14] but are as easy to lose through forgetfulness as linen garments;[15] דִּבְרֵי שְׁטוּת וְדִבְרֵי תִּיפְלוּת נוֹחִין לִקְנוֹתָן וְקָשִׁין לְאַבְּדָם כְּשַׂק — whereas matters of nonsense and folly are as easy to acquire and as difficult to lose as sackcloth,[16] which is extremely affordable and durable. פְּעָמִים שֶׁאָדָם לוֹקֵחַ שַׂק מִן הַשּׁוּק בְּסֶלַע — Indeed, a person will sometimes buy sackcloth from the market for a *sela*[17] וּמִשְׁתַּמֵשׁ בּוֹ וְהוֹלֵךְ אַרְבַּע אוֹ חָמֵשׁ שָׁנִים — and use it continuously for four or five years.

The Baraisa notes an inverse relationship between the delights of this world and the delights of the World to Come: רַבִּי יְהוּדָה הַנָּשִׂיא אוֹמֵר — R' Yehudah HaNasi says: כָּל הַמְקַבֵּל עָלָיו תַּעֲנוּגֵי הָעוֹלָם הַזֶּה — Anyone who receives the delights of this world unrestrainedly מוֹנְעִין מִמֶּנּוּ תַּעֲנוּגֵי הָעוֹלָם הַבָּא — will be deprived of the delights of the World to Come;[18] וְכֹל שֶׁאֵינוֹ מְקַבֵּל תַּעֲנוּגֵי הָעוֹלָם הַזֶּה — and anyone who does not receive the delights of this world with abandon נוֹתְנִין לוֹ תַּעֲנוּגֵי הָעוֹלָם הַבָּא — will be granted the delights of the World to Come.

§6 Another teaching of R' Yehudah HaNasi:

הוּא הָיָה אוֹמֵר — He used to say: צַדִּיקִים שֶׁרַע לָהֶם בָּעוֹלָם הַזֶּה לְמָה הוּא דוֹמֶה — To what may the righteous for whom it is bad in this world be

---

14. Which are very expensive (*Ben Avraham*).

15. Linen garments can come to ruin easily if one does not care for them properly. Similarly, words of Torah require vigilance to preserve them (*Magen Avos*). See the Baraisa's similar metaphor above, 24 §5.

16. The evil inclination makes them seem fascinating and fixes them in a person's mind (see *Binyan Yehoshua*).

17. A "*sela*" (plural "*sela'im*") was a silver coin used in the Land of Israel in ancient times.

18. If a person hurls himself into a life of materialism, it is inevitable that his indulgences

will draw him away from Torah study. Accordingly, he will be denied the pleasures of the Next World (*Ben Avraham*).

Furthermore, the blessings of this world are not for man to indulge in hedonistically; rather, they are tools for his service of God. They enable us to have the time and the peace of mind to live a life of Torah (see *Rambam, Hil. Teshuvah* 9:1). A person who abuses these pleasures by treating them as an end unto themselves is similar to one who misuses sacred property, since they are intended for a holy purpose (*Michtav MeiEliyahu* Vol. 1, pp. 5-6, cited by *Meorei Ohr, Miluim* §32).

לְטַבָּח שֶׁמְּתַקֵּן סְעוּדָה לְעַצְמוֹ, וְאַף שֶׁמִּצְטַעֵר בְּעַצְמוֹ אֵין מְתַקֵּן לַאֲחֵרִים
אֶלָּא לְעַצְמוֹ[19]. אֲבָל רְשָׁעִים שֶׁרַע לָהֶם בָּעוֹלָם הַזֶּה לְמָה הוּא דוֹמֶה,
לְטַבָּח שֶׁהִתְקִין סְעוּדָה לַאֲחֵרִים, וְאַף עַל פִּי שֶׁמִּצְטַעֵר בְּעַצְמוֹ אֵין מְתַקֵּן
לְעַצְמוֹ כְּלוּם אֶלָּא לַאֲחֵרִים[20]:

ז • הוּא הָיָה אוֹמֵר: יְהֶיֶה סִתְרְךָ עָלֶיךָ גָּלוּי[21]. וְדָבָר שֶׁאִי אֶפְשָׁר לִשְׁמוֹעַ
אַל תֹּאמַר לַחֲבֵירְךָ[22]:

ח • הִלֵּל אוֹמֵר: אַל תִּפְרוֹשׁ עַצְמְךָ מִן הַצִּבּוּר וְכוּ'[23]:

To a butcher who prepares a — לְטַבָּח שֶׁמְּתַקֵּן סְעוּדָה לְעַצְמוֹ **meal for himself;** — וְאַף שֶׁמִּצְטַעֵר בְּעַצְמוֹ אֵין מְתַקֵּן לַאֲחֵרִים אֶלָּא לְעַצְמוֹ **al- though he troubles himself** by doing so, he need not be distressed, for he is not preparing the meal for others, but for himself.[19] אֲבָל רְשָׁעִים שֶׁרַע לָהֶם **But to what may the wicked for whom it is bad in** — בָּעוֹלָם הַזֶּה לְמָה הוּא דוֹמֶה **this world be compared?** — לְטַבָּח שֶׁהִתְקִין סְעוּדָה לַאֲחֵרִים **To a butcher who prepared a meal for others;** — וְאַף עַל פִּי שֶׁמִּצְטַעֵר בְּעַצְמוֹ אֵין מְתַקֵּן לְעַצְמוֹ כְּלוּם **despite the fact that he troubles himself, he prepares nothing** — אֶלָּא לַאֲחֵרִים **for himself, but only for others.**[20]

§7 Another teaching of R' Yehudah HaNasi:

יְהֶיֶה סִתְרְךָ עָלֶיךָ גָּלוּי **Let your be-** — הוּא הָיָה אוֹמֵר **He used to say:** **havior in private be the same as your behavior in public;**[21] וְדָבָר שֶׁאִי אֶפְשָׁר **and do not tell even your trusted friend something** — לִשְׁמוֹעַ אַל תֹּאמַר לַחֲבֵירְךָ **that is not meant to be heard publicly.**[22]

§8 The Baraisa cites *Avos 2:4*:

Do not sepa- — אַל תִּפְרוֹשׁ עַצְמְךָ מִן הַצִּבּוּר וְכוּ' **Hillel says:** — הִלֵּל אוֹמֵר **rate yourself from the community, etc.**[23]

---

19. The butcher puts considerable effort into the meal's preparation, and he himself will enjoy the fruits of his labor. Similarly, when a person studies Torah and performs mitzvos amid suffering, the great reward that he thereby earns is his alone to enjoy in the World to Come (see *Binyan Yehoshua*).

20. His suffering would entitle the wicked person to a portion in the World to Come, but his wickedness precludes him from receiving it. Instead, a righteous person takes that portion in the Next World. This is in accordance with that which our Sages teach (*Chagigah* 15a), that a righteous person receives his portion and his [wicked] fellow's

portion in the Garden of Eden (*Binyan Yehoshua*).

21. One's fear of Heaven should, at the very least, equal his fear of people. Just as a person would be embarrassed to sin if he knew someone was watching him, he should be afraid to commit a sin in God's presence (*Binyan Yehoshua*, citing *Berachos* 28b).

22. See *Avos 2:4*. One should not make a statement if it is not intended to be heard by others, for the one to whom he said it is likely to repeat it, and eventually it will become public knowledge (*Binyan Yehoshua*, citing *Rav* ad loc.).

23. The full statement of the Mishnah reads:

ט. הוּא הָיָה אוֹמֵר: כָּל הַמַּרְבֶּה לֶאֱכוֹל מַרְבֶּה לְהוֹצִיא. וְכָל
הַמַּרְבֶּה בָּשָׂר מַרְבֶּה רִמָּה וְתוֹלֵעָה.²⁴ וְכָל הַמַּרְבֶּה מַעֲשִׂים טוֹבִים
מֵשִׂים שָׁלוֹם בְּגוּפוֹ.²⁵ רַבִּי אֶלְעָזָר בֶּן שַׁמּוּעַ אוֹמֵר: שָׁלשׁ מִדּוֹת
בְּתַלְמִידֵי חֲכָמִים, אֶבֶן גָּזִית אֶבֶן פִּנָּה אֶבֶן פִּסְפֵּס.²⁶ אֶבֶן גָּזִית
כֵּיצַד, זֶה תַּלְמִיד שֶׁשָּׁנָה מִדְרָשׁ, בִּזְמַן שֶׁתַּלְמִיד חָכָם נִכְנַס אֶצְלוֹ
שׁוֹאֲלוֹ בַּמִּדְרָשׁ אוֹמֵר לוֹ, זֶהוּ אֶבֶן גָּזִית שֶׁאֵין לָהּ אֶלָּא פֶּה אַחַת.

§9 The Baraisa cites a statement of Hillel that is similar in content to his teaching cited in *Avos* 2:7. Hillel contrasts the unfortunate results experienced by one who indulges in material pursuits with the beneficial results experienced by one engaged in spiritual pursuits:

כָּל הַמַּרְבֶּה לֶאֱכוֹל מַרְבֶּה לְהוֹצִיא — **He used to say:** הוּא הָיָה אוֹמֵר — Whoever **eats more, voids more;** וְכָל הַמַּרְבֶּה בָּשָׂר מַרְבֶּה רִמָּה וְתוֹלֵעָה — whoever **eats excessively so that he will have more flesh, will have more maggots and worms;**[24] וְכָל הַמַּרְבֶּה מַעֲשִׂים טוֹבִים מֵשִׂים שָׁלוֹם בְּגוּפוֹ — but whoever **increases good deeds establishes peace for his body.**[25]

The Baraisa cites a teaching concerning students who are in the process of becoming Torah scholars:

רַבִּי אֶלְעָזָר בֶּן שַׁמּוּעַ אוֹמֵר — **R' Elazar ben Shamua says:** שָׁלשׁ מִדּוֹת בְּתַלְמִידֵי חֲכָמִים — **There are three categories among Torah students:** אֶבֶן גָּזִית אֶבֶן פִּנָּה אֶבֶן פִּסְפֵּס — **a hewn stone, a cornerstone, and a cube-shaped stone.**[26] זֶה תַּלְמִיד — A Torah student is like **a hewn stone** — how so? אֶבֶן גָּזִית כֵּיצַד שֶׁשָּׁנָה מִדְרָשׁ — **This refers to a student who has studied Midrash,** i.e., the Sages' halachic expositions of Scripture. בִּזְמַן שֶׁתַּלְמִיד חָכָם נִכְנַס אֶצְלוֹ שׁוֹאֲלוֹ — When a Torah scholar visits him and asks him a question בַּמִּדְרָשׁ אוֹמֵר לוֹ — regarding Midrash, [the student] can answer him. זֶהוּ אֶבֶן גָּזִית שֶׁאֵין לָהּ אֶלָּא פֶּה אַחַת — This student **is** thus like **a hewn stone that has only one** smooth

Do not separate yourself from the community. Do not believe in yourself until the day you die. Do not judge your fellow until you have reached his place. Do not make a statement that is not meant to be heard, for it will be heard eventually. And do not say, "When I am free I will study," for perhaps you will not become free. See the commentators there.

24. I.e., there will be more flesh for the worms to consume when he goes to the grave. He will suffer greatly as a result, for the Talmud (*Berachos* 18b) teaches that maggots are as painful to the dead as sharp needles are to the living (*Rav* to *Avos* 2:7; see *Tos. Yom Tov* ad loc.).

25. There are 248 positive commandments corresponding to the 248 limbs of a person [enumerated in *Oholos* 1:8], and there are 365 negative commandments corresponding to a person's 365 nerves and sinews. When a person observes a mitzvah he gives life to the corresponding part of his body, and that limb will function properly in the World to Come (*Ben Avraham*, first explanation; see *Shaarei Kedushah* 1:1 and *Chafetz Chaim*, Introduction).

26. A hewn stone is a stone with one smooth surface, a cornerstone has two smooth surfaces, and a cube-shaped stone is smooth on all four sides (*Ben Avraham*; see below).

אֶבֶן פִּנָּה כֵּיצַד, זֶה תַּלְמִיד שֶׁשָּׁנָה מִדְרָשׁ וַהֲלָכוֹת, בִּזְמַן שֶׁתַּלְמִיד
חָכָם נִכְנָס אֶצְלוֹ שׁוֹאֲלוּ בַּמִּדְרָשׁ אוֹמֵר לוֹ בַּהֲלָכוֹת אוֹמֵר לוֹ, זֶהוּ אֶבֶן
פִּנָּה שֶׁיֵּשׁ לוֹ שְׁתֵּי פִיּוֹת בִּלְבַד. אֶבֶן פִּסְפֵּס כֵּיצַד, זֶה תַּלְמִיד שֶׁשָּׁנָה
מִדְרָשׁ וַהֲלָכוֹת וְאַגָּדוֹת וְתוֹסֶפְתּוֹת, כְּשֶׁתַּלְמִיד חָכָם נִכְנָס אֶצְלוֹ שׁוֹאֲלוּ
בַּמִּדְרָשׁ אוֹמֵר לוֹ בַּהֲלָכוֹת אוֹמֵר לוֹ בַּתּוֹסֶפְתּוֹת אוֹמֵר לוֹ בָּאַגָּדוֹת אוֹמֵר
לוֹ, וְזֶהוּ אֶבֶן פִּסְפֵּס שֶׁיֵּשׁ לָהּ אַרְבַּע פִּיּוֹת מֵאַרְבַּע רוּחוֹתֶיהָ:

י. רַבִּי יְהוּדָה בֶן אִילְעַי אוֹמֵר: כָּל הָעוֹשֶׂה דִּבְרֵי תוֹרָה עִיקָּר וְדֶרֶךְ אֶרֶץ
טָפֵל אוֹתוֹ עִיקָּר בָּעוֹלָם (הַזֶּה[27]). דֶּרֶךְ אֶרֶץ עִיקָּר וְדִבְרֵי תוֹרָה

אֶבֶן פִּנָּה כֵּיצַד — **surface,** for he has mastered only one area of the Torah.
זֶה תַּלְמִיד שֶׁשָּׁנָה מִדְרָשׁ A Torah student is like **a cornerstone — how so?**
וַהֲלָכוֹת — This refers to a student who has studied Midrash and Torah laws.
בִּזְמַן שֶׁתַּלְמִיד חָכָם נִכְנָס אֶצְלוֹ שׁוֹאֲלוּ בַּמִּדְרָשׁ אוֹמֵר לוֹ בַּהֲלָכוֹת אוֹמֵר לוֹ When —
a Torah scholar visits him and **asks him** a question **regarding Midrash, he**
can answer him; and when he asks him a question **regarding** Torah laws, he
can answer him as well. **זֶהוּ אֶבֶן פִּנָּה שֶׁיֵּשׁ לוֹ שְׁתֵּי פִיּוֹת בִּלְבַד** — This student
is thus like **a cornerstone, which has only two** smooth **surfaces,** for he has
mastered two areas of the Torah. **אֶבֶן פִּסְפֵּס כֵּיצַד** — A Torah student is
like **a cube-shaped stone— how so?** **זֶה תַּלְמִיד שֶׁשָּׁנָה מִדְרָשׁ וַהֲלָכוֹת וְאַגָּדוֹת**
וְתוֹסֶפְתּוֹת — This refers to a student who has studied Midrash, Torah laws,
Aggados (homiletical expositions), **and Toseftos** (Baraisos). **כְּשֶׁתַּלְמִיד חָכָם**
נִכְנָס אֶצְלוֹ שׁוֹאֲלוּ בַּמִּדְרָשׁ אוֹמֵר לוֹ בַּהֲלָכוֹת אוֹמֵר לוֹ בַּתּוֹסֶפְתּוֹת אוֹמֵר לוֹ בָּאַגָּדוֹת
אוֹמֵר לוֹ — When a Torah scholar visits him and asks him a question regard-
ing Midrash, he can answer him; regarding Torah laws, he can answer him;
regarding Toseftos, he can answer him; regarding Aggados, he can answer
him. **וְזֶהוּ אֶבֶן פִּסְפֵּס שֶׁיֵּשׁ לָהּ אַרְבַּע פִּיּוֹת מֵאַרְבַּע רוּחוֹתֶיהָ** — This student is
thus like **a cube-shaped stone, which has four** smooth **surfaces on its four**
sides, for he has mastered all four areas.

§10 The Baraisa presents a teaching related to *Avos* 1:15:
רַבִּי יְהוּדָה בֶן אִילְעַי אוֹמֵר — R' Yehudah ben Il'ai says: **כָּל הָעוֹשֶׂה דִּבְרֵי**
תוֹרָה עִיקָּר וְדֶרֶךְ אֶרֶץ טָפֵל — Whoever makes his study of **words of Torah** his
primary occupation **and** his pursuit of a **livelihood secondary** **אוֹתוֹ עוֹשִׂין**
עִיקָּר בָּעוֹלָם הַזֶּה — is treated as a **primary** person even **in this world.**[27] **דֶּרֶךְ**
אֶרֶץ עִיקָּר וְדִבְרֵי תוֹרָה טָפֵל — But whoever makes his **livelihood primary and** his

---

27. And certainly in the World to Come
(*Ben Avraham*). *R' Yonah* and *Rashbatz*
to *Avos* 1:15, however, quote our Baraisa
as saying that such a person is treated
as primary in the World to Come. This

conforms with the version in the Epstein
manuscript, which has בָּעוֹלָם הַבָּא, "in
the World to Come," here and below;
see also *Tummas Yesharim* and *Nuschas*
HaGra.

טָפֵל עוֹשִׂין אוֹתוֹ טָפֵל בָּעוֹלָם (הַזֶּה).[28] מָשְׁלוּ מָשָׁל לְמָה הַדָּבָר דּוֹמֶה, לְאִיסְטְרַטְיָא שֶׁהִיא עוֹבֶרֶת בֵּין שְׁנֵי דְרָכִים אַחַת שֶׁל אוּר וְאַחַת שֶׁל שֶׁלֶג. אִם מְהַלֵּךְ כְּנֶגֶד הָאוּר הֲרֵי נִכְוֶוה בָּאוּר וְאִם מְהַלֵּךְ נֶגֶד שֶׁלֶג הֲרֵי הוּא לוֹקֶה בַּצִּינָה. כֵּיצַד יַעֲשֶׂה, יֵלֵךְ בֵּינְתַּיִם וְיִזָּהֵר בְּעַצְמוֹ שֶׁלֹּא יִכָּוֶוה בָּאוּר וְשֶׁלֹּא יִלְקֶה בַּצִּינָה (רבי שמעון בן אלעזר אומר אל תרצה את חבירך וכו׳):

─────────

עוֹשִׂין אוֹתוֹ טָפֵל בָּעוֹלָם הַזֶּה study of **words of Torah secondary** — is treated as a **secondary** person even **in this world.**[28]

The Baraisa cites a parable to illustrate the importance of maintaining the correct balance between engaging in Torah and pursuing a livelihood:

מָשְׁלוּ מָשָׁל לְמָה הַדָּבָר דּוֹמֶה — [The Sages] illustrated this with a parable: To what may this matter be compared? לְאִיסְטְרַטְיָא שֶׁהִיא עוֹבֶרֶת בֵּין שְׁנֵי דְרָכִים — To a public road running between two paths, אַחַת שֶׁל אוּר וְאַחַת שֶׁל שֶׁלֶג — one of fire and the other of snow. אִם מְהַלֵּךְ כְּנֶגֶד הָאוּר הֲרֵי נִכְוֶוה בָּאוּר — Someone traveling on the road must remain constantly alert, for **if** he goes too close to the path of fire, he will be singed by the fire, וְאִם מְהַלֵּךְ נֶגֶד שֶׁלֶג הֲרֵי הוּא לוֹקֶה בַּצִּינָה — **and if** he goes too close to the path of snow, he will be frostbitten. כֵּיצַד יַעֲשֶׂה — How should he proceed? יֵלֵךְ בֵּינְתַּיִם — He should walk exactly in between them, וְיִזָּהֵר בְּעַצְמוֹ שֶׁלֹּא יִכָּוֶוה בָּאוּר וְשֶׁלֹּא יִלְקֶה בַּצִּינָה — taking care not to be singed by the fire nor stricken by the frost. Similarly, one must take heed not to become drawn after material pursuits to the point of abandoning the Torah, for that will cause him to be burned by the fire of Gehinnom; nor should he abandon his livelihood entirely, for that will cause him to be "frostbitten," i.e., it will bring him to the point of starvation. Rather, he should travel the middle road.[29]

─────────

28. [See the previous note.] This is as the Mishnah states (*Avos* 1:15): "Shammai says: Make your Torah fixed and your work incidental." See *R' Yonah* and other commentators there.

29. *Magen Avos.* This would seem to indicate that one should divide his time equally between the two. However, that would contradict the previous teaching, which indicates that one should make his Torah primary and his livelihood secondary. The *Mefaresh* explains that indeed, the Baraisa did not cite this analogy to convey that one should focus equally on Torah study and earning a livelihood, but only that he should not neglect his livelihood entirely. However, he must make his Torah study primary and his livelihood incidental, as explained above.

[We have removed the final line of the Baraisa — which appears again at the beginning of the following chapter — as per the emendation of *Gra*. It does not appear here in the manuscript versions, and seems to be the result of a printer's error.]

﴾ פֶּרֶק כט ﴿

א. רַבִּי שִׁמְעוֹן בֶּן אֶלְעָזָר אוֹמֵר מִשּׁוּם רַבִּי מֵאִיר: אַל תְּרַצֶּה אֶת חֲבֵירְךָ בְּשָׁעַת כַּעֲסוֹ. [וְאַל תְּנַחֲמֵהוּ בְּשָׁעַת אֶבְלוֹ.] וְאַל תִּשְׁאַל לוֹ בְּשָׁעַת נִדְרוֹ. וְאַל תָּבֹא לְבֵיתוֹ בְּיוֹם אֵידוֹ. וְאַל תִּשְׁתַּדֵּל לִרְאוֹתוֹ וְכוּ׳. °(יֵשׁ אוֹמְרִים) יֵשׁ לְךָ חֲבֵירִים מִקְצָתָן מוֹכִיחִין אוֹתְךָ וּמִקְצָתָן מְשַׁבְּחִין אוֹתָךְ, אֱהוֹב אֶת הַמּוֹכִיחֲךָ וּשְׂנָא אֶת הַמְשַׁבֵּחֲךָ, מִפְּנֵי

﴾ CHAPTER 29 ﴿

§1 The Baraisa cites a variation of *Avos* 4:18:

רַבִּי שִׁמְעוֹן בֶּן אֶלְעָזָר אוֹמֵר מִשּׁוּם רַבִּי מֵאִיר — R' Shimon ben Elazar says in the name of R' Meir: אַל תְּרַצֶּה אֶת חֲבֵירְךָ בְּשָׁעַת כַּעֲסוֹ — Do not appease your friend at the time of his anger,[1] וְאַל תְּנַחֲמֵהוּ בְּשָׁעַת אֶבְלוֹ — do not comfort him at the time of his sorrow,[2] וְאַל תִּשְׁאַל לוֹ בְּשָׁעַת נִדְרוֹ — do not question him at the time of his vow,[3] וְאַל תָּבֹא לְבֵיתוֹ בְּיוֹם אֵידוֹ — do not come to his house on the day of his calamity,[4] וְאַל תִּשְׁתַּדֵּל לִרְאוֹתוֹ וְכוּ׳ — and do not attempt to see him at the time of his degradation.[5]

The Baraisa discusses how a person should receive the opinions of others concerning him:

הוּא הָיָה אוֹמֵר — He used to say:[6] יֵשׁ לְךָ חֲבֵירִים מִקְצָתָן מוֹכִיחִין אוֹתְךָ וּמִקְצָתָן מְשַׁבְּחִין אוֹתָךְ — When you have friends, some of whom rebuke you for your behavior and some of whom praise you, אֱהוֹב אֶת הַמּוֹכִיחֲךָ וּשְׂנָא אֶת הַמְשַׁבֵּחֲךָ — love the one who rebukes you and dislike the one who praises you; מִפְּנֵי

1. Appeasing a person when he is enraged is an exercise in futility; he will remain impervious to conciliatory words until he calms down (*Rashi* to Mishnah). Indeed, one may provoke him into making discourteous statements, as he will become even angrier (*R' Yonah* ad loc.).

2. This means that one should not offer words of consolation to a mourner at a time when he is deeply immersed in his sorrow. As above, well-meant but ill-timed words of solace will be ineffective in bringing comfort to a mourner (*Mefaresh*; see *Rashbatz* to *Avos* ad loc.). [In *Avos*, the version is: "Do not comfort him at the time that his dead lies before him."]

3. It is often possible to annul a vow by determining that the original vow was contingent on certain conditions or circumstances that do not really apply to the vower's present situation. However, one should not immediately question the vower regarding the parameters of his declaration for, in the heat of the moment, he may take each suggested loophole and state that it was, in fact, incorporated into his original vow. Broadening the scope of the vow in this manner will make it almost impossible to annul it (*Binyan Yehoshua*, citing *Rav* ad loc.).

4. For he might think that you have come to rejoice in his misfortune (*Mefaresh*).

5. When someone has fallen spiritually and succumbed to sin, he is embarrassed to be seen by others. The Mishnah teaches that this desire for privacy should be respected (ibid.).

6. Emendation follows *Nuschas HaGra*.

שֶׁמּוֹכִיחֲךָ מְבִיאֲךָ לְחַיֵּי הָעוֹלָם הַבָּא[7] וְהַמְשַׁבֵּחֲךָ מוֹצִיאֲךָ מִן הָעוֹלָם.[8]
הוּא הָיָה אוֹמֵר: בְּכָל מָקוֹם שֶׁאָדָם הוֹלֵךְ, לִבּוֹ הוֹלֵךְ. עוֹמֵד, לִבּוֹ עוֹמֵד.
יוֹשֵׁב, דְּבָרִים מְיוּשָּׁבִים כְּנֶגְדּוֹ:[9]

ב. הוּא הָיָה אוֹמֵר: כָּל הַשּׁוֹקֵד עַצְמוֹ עַל דִּבְרֵי תוֹרָה מוֹסְרִין לוֹ

שֶׁמּוֹכִיחֲךָ מְבִיאֲךָ לְחַיֵּי הָעוֹלָם הַבָּא — for the one who rebukes you brings you to life in the World to Come,[7] וְהַמְשַׁבֵּחֲךָ מוֹצִיאֲךָ מִן הָעוֹלָם — while the one who praises you removes you from the world.[8]

Another teaching from the same sage:

הוּא הָיָה אוֹמֵר — He used to say: בְּכָל מָקוֹם שֶׁאָדָם הוֹלֵךְ לִבּוֹ הוֹלֵךְ — Wherever a person goes, his heart goes along with him; עוֹמֵד לִבּוֹ עוֹמֵד — when he stands, his heart stands; יוֹשֵׁב דְּבָרִים מְיוּשָּׁבִים כְּנֶגְדּוֹ — and when he sits, matters are settled before him in his heart.[9]

§2 The Mishnah in *Avos* 4:10 states: "If you are idle from Torah study, you will encounter many idle things." The Baraisa elaborates on this teaching:

כָּל הַשּׁוֹקֵד עַצְמוֹ עַל דִּבְרֵי תוֹרָה מוֹסְרִין לוֹ הוּא הָיָה אוֹמֵר — He used to say:

---

7. By pointing out your faults, he informs you of what needs rectification. This will motivate you to improve your ways and thereby earn a share in the World to Come (*Binyan Yehoshua*).

8. For he causes you to continue behaving as you did before, blissfully unaware of your wrongdoing (ibid.). Here the Baraisa does not specify that he removes you from "the World to Come," for in fact one who flatters a sinner and thereby reinforces his evil behavior causes him to be cut off from both this world *and* the World to Come (*Ben Avraham*).

9. The point of this teaching is that it is within a person's power to control his heart, rather than have his heart control him. This is the way of the righteous, as the Midrash teaches (*Bereishis Rabbah* 34 §10): "The wicked are controlled by their hearts, while the righteous are in control of their hearts." Thus, if one chooses to do what is right instead of allowing his decisions to be influenced by the desires of his heart, then on the contrary, his actions will influence his heart and it will desire to do the right thing.

To convey this idea, the Baraisa focuses on three phases of making and implementing a proper decision — initial intent, second thoughts, and deliberation — and demonstrates that on each of these levels, a person can see to it that his actions influence his desires rather than vice versa. Accordingly, this teaching should be understood as follows: "Wherever a person goes, his heart goes" — i.e., if a person intends ("goes") to embark on a virtuous endeavor, his heart will follow him and desire to perform that act. "When he stands, his heart stands" — i.e., if he subsequently reconsiders and concludes that this is not the right thing to do and refrains ("stands") from his intended course of action, his heart will likewise cease from its desire. "When he sits, matters are settled before him" — i.e., if he does things in a careful and deliberate manner, his heart will follow suit (*Binyan Yehoshua*, citing *Mefaresh*). [By contrast, if a wicked person considers taking an action and his base desires have no interest in it, he will not pursue that action; if he has started to do something and he begins to realize that it is not moral, his heart will carry him forward; and if he is engaged in a matter that requires deliberation, his heart will lead him to act impulsively.]

שֶׁקְּדָנִין כְּנֶגְדּוֹ[10]. וְכָל הַבּוֹטֵל מִדִּבְרֵי תוֹרָה מוֹסְרִין לוֹ בַּטְלָנִין כְּנֶגְדּוֹ, כְּגוֹן אֲרִי וּזְאֵב וְנָמֵר וּבַרְדְּלָס[11] וְנָחָשׁ, וְהַגַּיָּיסוֹת וְהַלִּיסְטִין בָּאִין וּמַקִּיפִין אוֹתוֹ וְנִפְרָעִין מִמֶּנוּ[12], שֶׁנֶּאֱמַר (תהלים נח, יב) "אַךְ יֵשׁ אֱלֹהִים שֹׁפְטִים בָּאָרֶץ"[13]:

ג. אַבָּא שָׁאוּל (בֶּן נַנָּס) אוֹמֵר: (יֵשׁ לְךָ) [אַרְבַּע מִדּוֹת בְּתַלְמִידֵי חֲכָמִים.]יֵשׁ (לְךָ)[14] אָדָם שֶׁלָּמֵד לְעַצְמוֹ וְאֵינוֹ מְלַמֵּד לַאֲחֵרִים. לַאֲחֵרִים וְאֵינוֹ מְלַמֵּד לְעַצְמוֹ. הַלָּמֵד לְעַצְמוֹ וְלַאֲחֵרִים. וְאֵינוֹ לָמֵד לֹא לְעַצְמוֹ וְלֹא לַאֲחֵרִים. הַלָּמֵד לְעַצְמוֹ וְאֵינוֹ לָמֵד לַאֲחֵרִים, כֵּיצַד, שָׁנָה

שֶׁקְּדָנִין כְּנֶגְדּוֹ — Whoever is diligent in studying words of Torah will be assigned diligent beings to stand before him.[10] וְכָל הַבּוֹטֵל מִדִּבְרֵי תוֹרָה מוֹסְרִין לוֹ בַּטְלָנִין כְּנֶגְדּוֹ — And whoever is idle from studying words of Torah will be assigned idle beings to stand before him, כְּגוֹן אֲרִי וּזְאֵב וְנָמֵר וּבַרְדְּלָס וְנָחָשׁ — such as a lion, a wolf, a leopard, a *bardelas*,[11] or a snake, וְהַגַּיָּיסוֹת וְהַלִּיסְטִין בָּאִין וּמַקִּיפִין אוֹתוֹ — or armies or highwaymen that will come and surround him, וְנִפְרָעִין מִמֶּנוּ שֶׁנֶּאֱמַר "אַךְ יֵשׁ אֱלֹהִים שֹׁפְטִים בָּאָרֶץ" — and these will exact punishment from him,[12] as it is stated, *Indeed, God has dispensers of justice in the land* (*Psalms* 58:12).[13]

§3 The Baraisa cites several statements regarding the study and teaching of Torah:

אַבָּא שָׁאוּל בֶּן נַנָּס אוֹמֵר — Abba Shaul ben Nannas says: אַרְבַּע מִדּוֹת בְּתַלְמִידֵי חֲכָמִים — There are four categories among Torah students:[14] אָדָם שֶׁלָּמֵד לְעַצְמוֹ וְאֵינוֹ מְלַמֵּד לַאֲחֵרִים — (1) a person who teaches himself but does not teach others; לַאֲחֵרִים וְאֵינוֹ מְלַמֵּד לְעַצְמוֹ — (2) one who teaches others but does not teach himself; הַלָּמֵד לְעַצְמוֹ וְלַאֲחֵרִים — (3) one who teaches both himself and others; וְאֵינוֹ לָמֵד לֹא לְעַצְמוֹ וְלֹא לַאֲחֵרִים — (4) and one who teaches neither himself nor others. הַלָּמֵד לְעַצְמוֹ וְאֵינוֹ לָמֵד לַאֲחֵרִים, כֵּיצַד — One who teaches himself but does not teach others — how so? שָׁנָה

---

10. I.e., he will be provided with angels that will be diligent in guarding him, just as he was diligent in studying Torah (*Kisei Rachamim*).

11. There is a wide-ranging dispute regarding the identity of the *bardelas*. Talmudic commentators have identified it as either a polecat, a viper, a hyena, or a cheetah. See the Schottenstein ed. of *Bava Kamma,* 16a note 33.

12. God will employ wild animals and/or wicked men, who are idle, meaning that they are not involved in any positive activity, to serve as agents to punish one who neglects Torah study (*Rav* to *Avos* 4:10).

Since he did not use his time productively, God unleashes these unproductive agents to mete out his punishment.

13. I.e., God has innumerable agents throughout the world with which to exact punishment, such as those mentioned above (*Binyan Yehoshua*).

The plain meaning of the verse is: *There is, indeed, a God Who judges in the land.* However, because it uses the term שֹׁפְטִים, in the plural, the Baraisa interprets it as referring to God's numerous *dispensers of justice* (see *Mefaresh*).

14. Emendation follows *Tummas Yesharim;*

אָדָם פֶּרֶק אֶחָד שְׁנַיִם וּשְׁלשָׁה וְלֹא הַשָּׁנָה אוֹתָם לְאַחֵר וְנִתְעַסֵּק בָּהֶן וְלֹא שְׁכָחָן, זֶה שֶׁלָּמֵד לְעַצְמוֹ וְאֵינוֹ לָמֵד לַאֲחֵרִים. לַאֲחֵרִים וְלֹא לָמֵד לְעַצְמוֹ, כֵּיצַד, שָׁנָה אָדָם סֵדֶר אֶחָד שְׁנַיִם וּשְׁלשָׁה פְּעָמִים¹⁵ ° וְשָׁנָה אוֹתָן לַאֲחֵרִים וְלֹא נִתְעַסֵּק בָּהֶם וּשְׁכָחָן¹⁶, זֶה שֶׁלָּמֵד לַאֲחֵרִים וְלֹא לָמֵד לְעַצְמוֹ. הַלָּמֵד לְעַצְמוֹ וְלַאֲחֵרִים, כֵּיצַד, שָׁנָה סֵדֶר אֶחָד שְׁנַיִם וּשְׁלשָׁה סְדָרִים וְהַשָּׁנָה אוֹתָן לַאֲחֵרִים וְנִתְעַסֵּק בָּהֶן וְלֹא שְׁכָחָן, נִתְפָּשָׁה וּתְפָשׂוּה, זֶהוּ שֶׁלָּמֵד לְעַצְמוֹ וְלַאֲחֵרִים. אֵינוֹ לָמֵד לֹא לְעַצְמוֹ וְלֹא לַאֲחֵרִים, כֵּיצַד, שָׁנָה אָדָם סֵדֶר אֶחָד שְׁנַיִם וּשְׁלשָׁה פְּעָמִים¹⁷ ° וְלֹא שְׁנָאָן לַאֲחֵרִים וְלֹא נִתְעַסֵּק בָּהֶן וּשְׁכָחָן, זֶהוּ שֶׁלֹּא לָמֵד לְעַצְמוֹ וְלֹא לַאֲחֵרִים. רַבִּי חֲנַנְיָא בֶּן יַעֲקֹב אוֹמֵר: הַנֵּעוֹר בַּלַּיְלָה

אָדָם פֶּרֶק אֶחָד שְׁנַיִם וּשְׁלשָׁה וְלֹא הַשָּׁנָה אוֹתָם לְאַחֵר וְנִתְעַסֵּק בָּהֶן וְלֹא שְׁכָחָן — If a person studied one, two, or three chapters, and did not teach them to anyone else, but he himself engaged in their [review] and therefore did not forget them, **זֶה שֶׁלָּמֵד לְעַצְמוֹ וְאֵינוֹ לָמֵד לַאֲחֵרִים** — that is the case of one who teaches himself but does not teach others. **לַאֲחֵרִים וְלֹא לָמֵד לְעַצְמוֹ, כֵּיצַד** — One who teaches others but does not teach himself — how so? **שָׁנָה אָדָם סֵדֶר אֶחָד שְׁנַיִם וּשְׁלשָׁה סְדָרִים וְשָׁנָה אוֹתָן לַאֲחֵרִים וְלֹא נִתְעַסֵּק בָּהֶם וּשְׁכָחָן** — If a person studied one, two, or three orders of the Mishnah[15] and taught them to others, but did not engage in their [review], so that he forgot them,[16] **זֶה שֶׁלָּמֵד לַאֲחֵרִים וְלֹא לָמֵד לְעַצְמוֹ** — that is the case of one who teaches others but does not teach himself. **הַלָּמֵד לְעַצְמוֹ וְלַאֲחֵרִים, כֵּיצַד** — One who teaches both himself and others — how so? **שָׁנָה סֵדֶר אֶחָד שְׁנַיִם וּשְׁלשָׁה סְדָרִים וְהַשָּׁנָה אוֹתָן לַאֲחֵרִים וְנִתְעַסֵּק בָּהֶן וְלֹא שְׁכָחָן** — If one studied one, two, or three orders of the Mishnah and taught them to others, and also engaged in their [review] so that he did not forget them, **נִתְפָּשָׁה וּתְפָשׂוּה** — and thus [the matter] was retained both by him and by [his pupils], **זֶהוּ שֶׁלָּמֵד לְעַצְמוֹ וְלַאֲחֵרִים** — that is the case of one who teaches both himself and others. **אֵינוֹ לָמֵד לֹא לְעַצְמוֹ וְלֹא לַאֲחֵרִים, כֵּיצַד** — One who teaches neither himself nor others — how so? **שָׁנָה אָדָם סֵדֶר אֶחָד שְׁנַיִם וּשְׁלשָׁה סְדָרִים וְלֹא שְׁנָאָן לַאֲחֵרִים וְלֹא נִתְעַסֵּק בָּהֶן וּשְׁכָחָן** — If one studied one, two, or three orders of the Mishnah[17] and he did not teach them to others, and he himself did not engage in their [review], so that he forgot them, **זֶהוּ שֶׁלֹּא לָמֵד לְעַצְמוֹ וְלֹא לַאֲחֵרִים** — that is the case of one who teaches neither himself nor others.

רַבִּי חֲנַנְיָא בֶּן יַעֲקֹב אוֹמֵר — R' Chananya ben Yaakov says: **הַנֵּעוֹר בַּלַּיְלָה**

---

see also *Nuschas HaGra.*

15. Emendation follows *Nuschas HaGra.*

16. Whereas his pupils did review their

studies and thus did not forget what they learned (*Binyan Yehoshua*).

17. Emendation follows *Nusachas HaGra.*

מִתּוֹךְ דִּבְרֵי תוֹרָה סִימָן יָפֶה לוֹ. מִתּוֹךְ דִּבְרֵי שִׂיחָה סִימָן רַע לוֹ[18]. רַבִּי
יַעֲקֹב בֶּן חֲנַנְיָה אוֹמֵר: הַנֵּעוֹר בַּלַּיְלָה וְאֵינוֹ פּוֹתֵחַ פִּיו בְּדִבְרֵי תוֹרָה,
רָאוּי לוֹ וּמוּטָב לוֹ שֶׁנֶּהְפְּכָה לוֹ שִׁלְיָתוֹ שֶׁל אִמּוֹ עַל פָּנָיו וְלֹא יָצָא לַאֲוִיר
הָעוֹלָם וְלֹא רָאָה אֶת הָעוֹלָם[19]:

ד. רַבִּי אֶלְעָזָר הַקַּפָּר אוֹמֵר: כָּל הַמְכַבֵּד חֲבֵירוֹ לְשׁוּם מָמוֹן סוֹף שֶׁנִּפְטָר
מִמֶּנּוּ בְּקָלוֹן. וְכָל הַבּוֹזֶה אֶת חֲבֵירוֹ לְשׁוּם מִצְוָה סוֹף שֶׁנִּפְטָר מִמֶּנּוּ
בְּכָבוֹד[20]. וּמִנַּיִן שֶׁכָּל הַמְכַבֵּד חֲבֵירוֹ לְשׁוּם מָמוֹן סוֹף שֶׁנִּפְטָר מִמֶּנּוּ בְּקָלוֹן,

---

מִתּוֹךְ דִּבְרֵי תוֹרָה סִימָן יָפֶה לוֹ — If a person awakens at night amid words of
Torah, it is an auspicious omen for him; מִתּוֹךְ דִּבְרֵי שִׂיחָה סִימָן רַע לוֹ — but
if he awakens amid words of idle conversation, it is an evil omen for him.[18]

The Baraisa cites a teaching that parallels *Avos* 3:4:

רַבִּי יַעֲקֹב בֶּן חֲנַנְיָה אוֹמֵר — R' Yaakov ben Chananyah says: הַנֵּעוֹר בַּלַּיְלָה
וְאֵינוֹ פּוֹתֵחַ פִּיו בְּדִבְרֵי תוֹרָה — If someone stays awake at night and does not
open his mouth to engage in words of Torah, רָאוּי לוֹ וּמוּטָב לוֹ שֶׁנֶּהְפְּכָה לוֹ
שִׁלְיָתוֹ שֶׁל אִמּוֹ עַל פָּנָיו וְלֹא יָצָא לַאֲוִיר הָעוֹלָם וְלֹא רָאָה אֶת הָעוֹלָם — it would
have been fitting and better for him if the amniotic sac of his mother had
overturned on his face and he had not emerged into the world as a viable
human being, and he had never seen the world.[19]

§4 The Baraisa returns to discussing interpersonal relations:
רַבִּי אֶלְעָזָר הַקַּפָּר אוֹמֵר — R' Elazar HaKappar says: כָּל הַמְכַבֵּד חֲבֵירוֹ
לְשׁוּם מָמוֹן סוֹף שֶׁנִּפְטָר מִמֶּנּוּ בְּקָלוֹן — Anyone who honors his fellow for the
sake of attaining money will ultimately depart from him in disgrace; וְכָל
הַבּוֹזֶה אֶת חֲבֵירוֹ לְשׁוּם מִצְוָה סוֹף שֶׁנִּפְטָר מִמֶּנּוּ בְּכָבוֹד — and anyone who slights
his fellow for the sake of performing a mitzvah, i.e., when it is a mitzvah to do
so,[20] will ultimately depart from him with honor.

The Baraisa cites Scriptural sources for both of these statements:
וּמִנַּיִן שֶׁכָּל הַמְכַבֵּד חֲבֵירוֹ לְשׁוּם מָמוֹן סוֹף שֶׁנִּפְטָר מִמֶּנּוּ בְּקָלוֹן — And from where
do we derive that whoever honors his fellow for the sake of attaining money

---

18. If he awakens thinking words of Torah, it
is an indication that while he was asleep, his
soul ascended to a place in Heaven where
they teach it Torah (see *Zohar Chadash*
28a); however, if he awakens thinking about
mundane matters, it is an indication that his
soul was not allowed to ascend to such a
place because it is not sufficiently pure (*Binyan Yehoshua*, citing *Mefaresh*).

19. Nighttime is particularly conducive to
lucid thought, as one is neither burdened

with his usual work nor distracted by other
people (*Binyan Yehoshua*, citing *Midrash
Shmuel* to *Avos* 3:4). If one refrains from
using this time for contemplation of Torah
matters, he would have been better off
had he never been born, for we are taught
(*Niddah* 30b) that during the period that
a fetus is in its mother's womb, its time is
spent studying Torah (*Binyan Yehoshua*,
citing *Mefaresh*).

20. For instance, he reproves his fellow for

שֶׁכֵּן מָצִינוּ בְּבִלְעָם הָרָשָׁע שֶׁכִּבֵּד בָּלָק לְשֵׁם מָמוֹן, שֶׁנֶּאֱמַר (במדבר כב,
יח) "וַיַּעַן בִּלְעָם וַיֹּאמֶר אֶל עַבְדֵי בָלָק אִם יִתֶּן לִי בָלָק מְלֹא בֵיתוֹ כֶּסֶף
וְזָהָב"²¹. וּמִנַּיִן שֶׁנִּפְטַר מִמֶּנּוּ בְּקָלוֹן, שֶׁנֶּאֱמַר (שם כד, יא) "וְעַתָּה בְּרַח לְךָ
אֶל מְקוֹמֶךָ וְגו' וְהִנֵּה מְנָעֲךָ ה' מִכָּבוֹד". וּמִנַּיִן שֶׁכָּל הַבּוֹזֶה אֶת חֲבֵירוֹ
לְשֵׁם מִצְוָה סוֹף שֶׁנִּפְטַר מִמֶּנּוּ בְּכָבוֹד, שֶׁכֵּן מָצִינוּ בְּמֹשֶׁה רַבֵּנוּ שֶׁבִּזָּה
פַּרְעֹה לְשׁוּם מִצְוָה, שֶׁנֶּאֱמַר (שמות יא, ח) "וְיָרְדוּ כָל עֲבָדֶיךָ אֵלֶּה אֵלַי
וְהִשְׁתַּחֲווּ לִי לֵאמֹר"²², וְכִי פַרְעֹה עוֹמֵד עַל הַגַּג וּמֹשֶׁה עוֹמֵד עַל הָאָרֶץ,

---

will ultimately depart from him in disgrace? שֶׁכֵּן מָצִינוּ בְּבִלְעָם הָרָשָׁע שֶׁכִּבֵּד
בָּלָק לְשֵׁם מָמוֹן — For we find that the wicked Balaam honored Balak for the
sake of the money that Balak might give him, שֶׁנֶּאֱמַר "וַיַּעַן בִּלְעָם וַיֹּאמֶר אֶל
עַבְדֵי בָלָק אִם יִתֶּן לִי בָלָק מְלֹא בֵיתוֹ כֶּסֶף וְזָהָב" — as it is stated, *Balaam an-*
swered and said to the servants of Balak, "If Balak will give me his house-
ful of silver and gold, I cannot transgress the word of HASHEM, etc." (*Numbers*
22:18).[21] וּמִנַּיִן שֶׁנִּפְטַר מִמֶּנּוּ בְּקָלוֹן — And from where do we know that
[Balaam] departed from [Balak] in disgrace? שֶׁנֶּאֱמַר "וְעַתָּה בְּרַח לְךָ אֶל
מְקוֹמֶךָ וְגו' וְהִנֵּה מְנָעֲךָ ה' מִכָּבוֹד" — For it is stated that after Balaam blessed the
Jewish people three times, Balak dismissed him with these words, *"Now, flee*
to your place. I said I would honor you, but — behold! HASHEM has withheld
you from honor" (ibid. 24:11).

וּמִנַּיִן שֶׁכָּל הַבּוֹזֶה אֶת חֲבֵירוֹ לְשֵׁם מִצְוָה סוֹף שֶׁנִּפְטַר מִמֶּנּוּ בְּכָבוֹד — And from where
do we derive that whoever slights his fellow for the sake of performing a
mitzvah will ultimately depart from him with honor? שֶׁכֵּן מָצִינוּ בְּמֹשֶׁה רַבֵּנוּ
שֶׁבִּזָּה פַּרְעֹה לְשׁוּם מִצְוָה — For we find that our teacher Moses slighted Pharaoh for the sake of a mitzvah, i.e., in order to deliver God's message to him,
שֶׁנֶּאֱמַר "וְיָרְדוּ כָל עֲבָדֶיךָ אֵלֶּה אֵלַי וְהִשְׁתַּחֲווּ לִי לֵאמֹר" — as it is stated that when
warning Pharaoh about the upcoming Plague of the Firstborn, Moses said:
"Then all these servants of yours will come down to me and bow to me,
saying, 'Leave — you and the entire people that follows you.' After that, I will
leave!" (*Exodus* 11:8). וְכִי פַרְעֹה עוֹמֵד עַל הַגַּג וּמֹשֶׁה עוֹמֵד עַל הָאָרֶץ — Now,
what did Moses mean when he said that the servants would *come down*? Was

---

his evil deeds. Although his fellow might
feel slighted by the words of reproof, they
will ultimately benefit him, as he will be
motivated to change his ways [provided that
the reproof is delivered in the proper way]
(*Binyan Yehoshua*).

21. Balaam said this to the second group of
messengers that Balak sent to implore him to
curse the Jewish people. With these words,

Balaam indicated that he truly desired to fulfill Balak's request, and that the only thing
stopping him was God's refusal to allow him
to go. With this, Balaam flattered and honored Balak. However, his true motive was
for the money that he hoped to receive from
Balak, as implied by his reference to a payment consisting of Balak's houseful of silver
and gold (*Mefaresh*; see *Binyan Yehoshua*).

אֶלָּא כָּךְ אָמַר מֹשֶׁה לְפַרְעֹה: אֲפִילוּ כָּל עֲבָדֶיךָ שֶׁעוֹמְדִין (ומשתחוים)
לְפָנֶיךָ עַל בָּמָה שֶׁלָךְ יַעַמְדוּ וִיבַקְשׁוּ מִמֶּנִּי אֵינִי שׁוֹמֵעַ לָהֶם[23]. וּמִנַּיִין שֶׁנִּפְטַר
מִמֶּנּוּ בְּכָבוֹד, שֶׁנֶּאֱמַר (שם יב, לא) "וַיִּקְרָא לְמֹשֶׁה וּלְאַהֲרֹן לַיְלָה"[24]. אָמְרוּ
לוֹ וְכִי גַּנָּבִים אָנוּ שֶׁנֵּצֵא בַּלַּיְלָה, אֶלָּא הַמְתֵּן לָנוּ עַד שֶׁיָּבִיא הַקָּדוֹשׁ בָּרוּךְ
הוּא לָנוּ שִׁבְעָה עַנְנֵי כָבוֹד[25] וְנֵצֵא בָּהֶם בְּשִׂמְחָה וּבְרֹאשׁ גָּלוּי[26], שֶׁנֶּאֱמַר
(במדבר לג, ג) "מִמָּחֳרַת הַפֶּסַח יָצְאוּ בְנֵי יִשְׂרָאֵל בְּיָד רָמָה":

Pharaoh standing on the roof and Moses standing on the ground, that Pharaoh and his servants would have to literally *come down* to speak to Moses?[22]
Surely not!   אֶלָּא כָּךְ אָמַר מֹשֶׁה לְפַרְעֹה — **Rather, this is what Moses said to
Pharaoh,**   אֲפִלּוּ כָּל עֲבָדֶיךָ שֶׁעוֹמְדִין לְפָנֶיךָ עַל בָּמָה שֶׁלָךְ יַעַמְדוּ וִיבַקְשׁוּ מִמֶּנִּי אֵינִי
שׁוֹמֵעַ לָהֶם — **"Even if all your servants who stand before you on your platform
will** descend from their grandeur, and **arise and prostrate themselves before
me and implore me** to leave, **I will not listen to them!"**[23]   וּמִנַּיִין שֶׁנִּפְטַר מִמֶּנּוּ
בְּכָבוֹד — **And from where** do we know that [Moses] **departed from him with
honor?**   שֶׁנֶּאֱמַר "וַיִּקְרָא לְמֹשֶׁה וּלְאַהֲרֹן לַיְלָה" — **For it is stated,** *He* [Pharaoh]
*called to Moses and Aaron at night and said, "Rise up, go out from among my
people, etc."* (ibid. 12:31).[24] However, as Moses had said, they did not leave
immediately.   אָמְרוּ לוֹ וְכִי גַּנָּבִים אָנוּ שֶׁנֵּצֵא בַּלַּיְלָה — **Thus, they replied, "But
are we thieves that we should go out at night?** Certainly not!   אֶלָּא הַמְתֵּן
לָנוּ עַד שֶׁיָּבִיא הַקָּדוֹשׁ בָּרוּךְ הוּא לָנוּ שִׁבְעָה עַנְנֵי כָבוֹד וְנֵצֵא בָּהֶם בְּשִׂמְחָה וּבְרֹאשׁ גָּלוּי
— **Rather, wait for us until the Holy One, Blessed is He, will bring the seven
Clouds of Glory,**[25] **whereupon we will leave** accompanied **by them, joyfully
and openly!"**[26]   שֶׁנֶּאֱמַר "מִמָּחֳרַת הַפֶּסַח יָצְאוּ בְנֵי יִשְׂרָאֵל בְּיָד רָמָה" — **And
indeed, they left only the next day, in full view of the Egyptians, as it is stated,**
*On the day after the pesach offering, the Children of Israel went forth with
an upraised hand, before the eyes of all Egypt* (Numbers 33:3).

---

22. Although Moses mentioned Pharaoh's
servants, the Baraisa mentions Pharaoh
himself because Moses was in fact referring
to him as well. However, out of respect for
the king, he specified only the servants (*Ben
Avraham*, citing *Yalkut Shimoni, Exodus*
§178; see also *Zevachim* 102a and *Rashi* to
the verse).

23. [Emendation follows *Nuschas HaGra*.]
Thus, when Moses said that Pharaoh's servants — and Pharaoh himself — would come
down to him, he did not mean it in the literal
sense, but meant that they would have to
lower themselves before him and beg him to

leave. And when he concluded, *"After that, I
will leave!,"* he meant that even then he would
not leave immediately, but only when he was
ready to go. This was of course a slight to
Pharaoh, delivered as part of the message
that God had instructed Moses to convey to
him (*Magen Avos*; see also *Mefaresh*).

24. Pharaoh accorded Moses great honor by
coming to him in person and imploring him
to leave (*Binyan Yehoshua*).

25. See *Rashi* to *Numbers* 10:34.

26. This is derived from the clause, *He
called to Moses and Aaron at night.* The term
at night is superfluous, as it already stated

ה. עַל אַרְבָּעָה חִלּוּקֵי כַפָּרָה[27] הָלַךְ רַבִּי מַתְיָא בֶּן חָרָשׁ אֵצֶל רַבִּי
יִשְׁמָעֵאל בֶּן אֶלְעָזָר הַקַּפָּר לְלוּדְקִיָּא לְבַקְּרוֹ, וְאָמַר לוֹ: שָׁמַעְתָּ בְּאַרְבַּע
חִלּוּקֵי כַפָּרָה שֶׁהָיָה רַבִּי יִשְׁמָעֵאל דּוֹרֵשׁ. אָמַר לוֹ: שָׁמַעְתִּי, וּשְׁלֹשָׁה הֵן
וּתְשׁוּבָה עַל כָּל אַחַת וְאַחַת.[28] כָּתוּב אֶחָד אוֹמֵר (ירמיה ג, יד) "שׁוּבוּ בָנִים
שׁוֹבָבִים נְאֻם ה' ", (שם פסוק כב) "אֶרְפָּא מְשׁוּבֹתֵיכֶם". וְכָתוּב אֶחָד אוֹמֵר
(ויקרא טז, ל) "כִּי בַיּוֹם הַזֶּה יְכַפֵּר עֲלֵיכֶם לְטַהֵר אֶתְכֶם". וְכָתוּב אֶחָד אוֹמֵר
(תהלים פט, לג) "וּפָקַדְתִּי בְשֵׁבֶט פִּשְׁעָם וּבִנְגָעִים עֲוֹנָם". וְכָתוּב אֶחָד אוֹמֵר

§5 The Baraisa turns to the subject of atonement:

עַל אַרְבָּעָה חִלּוּקֵי כַפָּרָה הָלַךְ רַבִּי מַתְיָא בֶּן חָרָשׁ אֵצֶל רַבִּי יִשְׁמָעֵאל בֶּן אֶלְעָזָר
הַקַּפָּר לְלוּדְקִיָּא לְבַקְּרוֹ — For the purpose of ascertaining the four divisions of
atonement,[27] R' Masya ben Charash went to R' Yishmael ben Elazar HaKappar in Ludkiya to visit him, וְאָמַר לוֹ — and said to him, שָׁמַעְתָּ בְּאַרְבַּע
חִלּוּקֵי כַפָּרָה שֶׁהָיָה רַבִּי יִשְׁמָעֵאל דּוֹרֵשׁ — "Have you heard of the four divisions of
atonement that R' Yishmael expounded?" אָמַר לוֹ שָׁמַעְתִּי — He replied to
him, "I have indeed **heard** of them. וּשְׁלֹשָׁה הֵן וּתְשׁוּבָה עַל כָּל אַחַת וְאַחַת — In
reality, **they are** only three, and repentance is required with each one."[28]

R' Yishmael ben Elazar proceeded to report R' Yishmael's teaching:

כָּתוּב אֶחָד אוֹמֵר "שׁוּבוּ בָנִים שׁוֹבָבִים נְאֻם ה' " " אֶרְפָּא מְשׁוּבֹתֵיכֶם" — One verse
states, *Repent, O wayward sons — the word of HASHEM* (*Jeremiah* 3:14);
Repent, O wayward sons, **and I will heal your waywardness** (ibid. v. 22),
indicating that "healing" (i.e., atonement) is achieved through repentance
alone. וְכָתוּב אֶחָד אוֹמֵר "כִּי בַיּוֹם הַזֶּה יְכַפֵּר עֲלֵיכֶם לְטַהֵר אֶתְכֶם" — And a
different verse states, *For on this day* [Yom Kippur] *He shall atone for you
to cleanse you* (*Leviticus* 16:30), indicating that atonement is not achieved
until Yom Kippur. וְכָתוּב אֶחָד אוֹמֵר "וּפָקַדְתִּי בְשֵׁבֶט פִּשְׁעָם וּבִנְגָעִים עֲוֹנָם"
— **Yet** [a third] verse states, *Then I will punish their transgression with
the rod, and their iniquity with plagues* (*Psalms* 89:33), indicating that afflictions are required in order to achieve atonement. וְכָתוּב אֶחָד אוֹמֵר

---

in the previous verse, *Pharaoh rose up at
night.* The Baraisa therefore understands
it as Moses' and Aaron's reply to Pharaoh,
saying, "Shall we leave *at night* like fleeing
thieves?!" (*Binyan Yehoshua*).

27. These are four processes that differ in
their capacity to provide atonement; each
process atones for a different type of sin.
[The forthcoming discussion appears, with
some variations, in *Bavli Yoma* 86a, and
Yerushalmi, Yoma 8:7 and *Shevuos* 1:6. See

Shaarei Teshuvah, Shaar 4, where this matter is discussed at length.]

28. Three of the four processes are required
only for certain categories of sin, as enumerated below. The exception is the first process (i.e., repentance), which is necessary
for the atonement of *every* sin. Hence, it is
not appropriate to call repentance a "division" of atonement, which implies a limited
application (*Binyan Yehoshua*, citing *Rashi*
to *Yoma* 86a).

(ישעיה כב, יד) "אִם יְכֻפַּר הֶעָוֹן הַזֶּה לָכֶם עַד תְּמֻתוּן". הָא כֵּיצַד, אִם
עָבַר אָדָם עַל מִצְוַת עֲשֵׂה וְעָשָׂה תְשׁוּבָה, אֵינוֹ זָז מִשָּׁם עַד שֶׁמּוֹחֲלִין
לוֹ מִיָּד.[29] עַל זֶה נֶאֱמַר "שׁוּבוּ בָּנִים שׁוֹבָבִים". עָבַר אָדָם עַל מִצְוַת לֹא
תַעֲשֶׂה וְעָשָׂה תְשׁוּבָה, הַתְּשׁוּבָה תּוֹלָה[30] וְיוֹם הַכִּפּוּרִים מְכַפֵּר. עַל זֶה
נֶאֱמַר "כִּי בַיּוֹם הַזֶּה יְכַפֵּר עֲלֵיכֶם". עָבַר אָדָם עַל כְּרֵיתוֹת וּמִיתוֹת
בֵּית דִּין וְעָשָׂה תְשׁוּבָה, תְּשׁוּבָה וְיוֹם הַכִּפּוּרִים תּוֹלִין[31] וְיִסּוּרִין מְמָרְקִין,
(וּבִשְׁאָר יְמוֹת הַשָּׁנָה מְכַפְּרִין.)[32] וְעַל זֶה נֶאֱמַר "וּפָקַדְתִּי בְשֵׁבֶט פִּשְׁעָם".

"אִם יְכֻפַּר הֶעָוֹן הַזֶּה לָכֶם עַד תְּמֻתוּן" — And another verse states, *This sin will not be atoned for you until you die* (Isaiah 22:14), indicating that a person is not forgiven for his sins until he dies. הָא כֵּיצַד — How are these seemingly contradictory verses to be reconciled? They are referring to different categories of sins, as follows: אִם עָבַר אָדָם עַל מִצְוַת עֲשֵׂה וְעָשָׂה תְשׁוּבָה — If a person transgressed a positive commandment and repented, אֵינוֹ זָז מִשָּׁם עַד שֶׁמּוֹחֲלִין לוֹ מִיָּד — he does not move from there until he is immediately forgiven.[29] עַל זֶה נֶאֱמַר "שׁוּבוּ בָּנִים שׁוֹבָבִים" — Regarding such a person it is stated, *Repent, O wayward sons, and I will heal your waywardness.* עָבַר אָדָם עַל מִצְוַת לֹא תַעֲשֶׂה וְעָשָׂה תְשׁוּבָה — If a person transgressed a negative commandment and repented, הַתְּשׁוּבָה תּוֹלָה וְיוֹם הַכִּפּוּרִים מְכַפֵּר — the repentance suspends punishment[30] and Yom Kippur atones for the sin. עַל זֶה נֶאֱמַר "כִּי בַיּוֹם הַזֶּה יְכַפֵּר עֲלֵיכֶם" — Regarding such a person it is stated, *For on this day He shall atone for you.* עָבַר אָדָם עַל כְּרֵיתוֹת וּמִיתוֹת בֵּית דִּין וְעָשָׂה תְשׁוּבָה — If a person committed sins that are punishable by excision or sins that are punishable by court-imposed death, and repented, תְּשׁוּבָה וְיוֹם הַכִּפּוּרִים תּוֹלִין וְיִסּוּרִין מְמָרְקִין — repentance and Yom Kippur suspend punishment[31] and suffering purges the sin; וּבִשְׁאָר יְמוֹת הַשָּׁנָה מְכַפְּרִין — and moreover, even during the rest of the year [suffering] atones for such sins.[32] וְעַל זֶה נֶאֱמַר "וּפָקַדְתִּי בְשֵׁבֶט פִּשְׁעָם" — Regarding such a person it is stated, *Then I will punish their transgression with the rod, and their iniquity with*

---

29. In other words, he is forgiven as soon as he repents; he does not even have time to move before forgiveness is granted.

30. I.e., it protects him from afflictions (*Magen Avos*; see *Rashi* to *Yoma* 85b, ד"ה אשם תלוי).

31. Here it cannot mean that they protect him from afflictions, for in this case he is afflicted. Rather, it means that they protect him from premature death (*Magen Avos*).

32. That is, when we said that repentance and Yom Kippur suspend punishment, that did not mean that Yom Kippur is required, but that *even* the combination of repentance and Yom Kippur does not achieve complete atonement. However, (repentance alone does suspend punishment, and) the combination of repentance and suffering achieves complete atonement, with or without Yom Kippur (*Magen Avos*; see *Minchas Chinuch* 364:22-23).

אֲבָל מִי שֶׁמְּחַלֵּל שֵׁם שָׁמַיִם[33] אֵין בּוֹ כֹּחַ לֹא לִתְשׁוּבָה לִתְלוֹת וְלֹא לְיִסּוּרִין לְמָרֵק וְלֹא לְיוֹם הַכִּפּוּרִים לְכַפֵּר, אֶלָּא תְּשׁוּבָה וְיִסּוּרִין תּוֹלִין[34] וּמִיתָה מְמָרֶקֶת עִמָּהֶן[35]. וְעַל זֶה נֶאֱמַר "אִם יְכֻפַּר הֶעָוֹן הַזֶּה לָכֶם עַד תְּמֻתוּן"[36]:

ו. אִיסִי בֶּן יְהוּדָה אוֹמֵר: מִפְּנֵי מָה תַּלְמִידֵי חֲכָמִים מֵתִים בְּלֹא זְמַנָּן, לֹא מִפְּנֵי שֶׁמְּנָאֲפִין וְלֹא מִפְּנֵי שֶׁגּוֹזְלִין[37] אֶלָּא מִפְּנֵי שֶׁהֵן בּוֹזִין בְּעַצְמָן[38]:

אֲבָל מִי שֶׁמְּחַלֵּל שֵׁם שָׁמַיִם אֵין בּוֹ כֹּחַ לֹא לִתְשׁוּבָה לִתְלוֹת וְלֹא לְיִסּוּרִין *plagues.* **לְמָרֵק וְלֹא לְיוֹם הַכִּפּוּרִים לְכַפֵּר** — But as for **one who desecrates the Name of Heaven,**[33] repentance does not have the capacity to suspend punishment, nor does **suffering** have the capacity **to purge** the sin, nor does **Yom Kippur** have the capacity **to atone;** **אֶלָּא תְּשׁוּבָה וְיִסּוּרִין תּוֹלִין וּמִיתָה מְמָרֶקֶת עִמָּהֶן** — rather, **repentance, Yom Kippur, and suffering** all **suspend** punishment,[34] and **death purges** the sin **together with them.**[35] **וְעַל זֶה נֶאֱמַר "אִם יְכֻפַּר הֶעָוֹן הַזֶּה לָכֶם עַד תְּמֻתוּן"** — Regarding such a person **it is stated,** *This sin will not be atoned for you until you die.*[36]

§6 Continuing its discussion from the previous section, the Baraisa cites a teaching concerning the severity of desecrating the Name of Heaven: **אִיסִי בֶּן יְהוּדָה אוֹמֵר** — **Issi ben Yehudah says:** **מִפְּנֵי מָה תַּלְמִידֵי חֲכָמִים מֵתִים בְּלֹא זְמַנָּן** — Why do some Torah students die before their time? **לֹא מִפְּנֵי שֶׁמְּנָאֲפִין וְלֹא מִפְּנֵי שֶׁגּוֹזְלִין** — **Not because they commit adultery or steal,** for they are surely innocent of such misconduct.[37] **אֶלָּא מִפְּנֵי שֶׁהֵן בּוֹזִין בְּעַצְמָן** — **Rather, it is because they disgrace themselves** with unbecoming behavior and thereby desecrate the Name of Heaven.[38]

---

33. He sins publicly, and thereby causes others to sin (*Rashi* to *Yoma* 86a; see also note 38 below).

34. I.e., they protect him from dying immediately (*Magen Avos*).

35. Here too, *Sheyarei Korban* (on *Yerushalmi Shevuos* 1:6) suggests that repentance and death alone are sufficient to atone for these sins, even without Yom Kippur or afflictions. R' Yishmael meant that *even* a combination of repentance, Yom Kippur, and suffering do not completely eradicate the sin until the sinner's death. [Likewise, when it says that repentance does not have the capacity to suspend punishment, it does not mean that repentance alone will not protect the person from immediate death, but that it does not have the power to suspend punishment *and* complete the atonement

together with Yom Kippur or afflictions. Rather, complete atonement is achieved only through death (see *Minchas Chinuch* 364:23).]

36. None of these verses specify the type of sin to which they refer. Logic dictates, however, that the more severe the transgression the more severe the process of atonement it requires (*Rashi* to *Yoma* 86a). [Some commentators, though, find allusions in the verses to the respective transgressions; see *Rif* on *Ein Yaakov*, *Maharsha*, *Tosefes Yom HaKippurim*, and *Menachem Meishiv Nefesh* ad loc.]

37. Compare 26 §3 above.

38. The Gemara (*Yoma* 86a) states that a Torah scholar who acts in a way that causes people to look down at those who study Torah is guilty of desecrating the Divine

ז. רַבִּי יִצְחָק בֶּן פִּנְחָס אוֹמֵר: כָּל מִי שֶׁיֵּשׁ בְּיָדוֹ מִדְרָשׁ וְאֵין בְּיָדוֹ הֲלָכוֹת
לֹא טָעַם טַעַם שֶׁל חָכְמָה40. כָּל מִי שֶׁיֵּשׁ בְּיָדוֹ הֲלָכוֹת וְאֵין בְּיָדוֹ
מִדְרָשׁ לֹא טָעַם טַעַם שֶׁל יִרְאַת חֵטְא41. הוּא הָיָה אוֹמֵר: כָּל שֶׁיֵּשׁ בְּיָדוֹ
מִדְרָשׁ וְאֵין בְּיָדוֹ הֲלָכוֹת זֶה גִבּוֹר וְאֵינוֹ מְזוּיָּין. כָּל שֶׁיֵּשׁ בְּיָדוֹ הֲלָכוֹת
וְאֵין בְּיָדוֹ מִדְרָשׁ חַלָּשׁ וְזַיִּין בְּיָדוֹ42. יֵשׁ בְּיָדוֹ זֶה וָזֶה גִבּוֹר וּמְזוּיָּין.
הוּא הָיָה אוֹמֵר: הֱוֵי זָהִיר בִּשְׁאִילַת שָׁלוֹם בֵּין אָדָם לַחֲבֵירוֹ43. וְאַל

---

§7 The Baraisa cites a teaching concerning the importance of studying the various branches of the Torah:

רַבִּי יִצְחָק בֶּן פִּנְחָס אוֹמֵר — R' Yitzchak ben Pinchas says: כָּל מִי שֶׁיֵּשׁ בְּיָדוֹ מִדְרָשׁ וְאֵין בְּיָדוֹ הֲלָכוֹת — Whoever has mastered **Midrash, i.e., Aggados** (homiletical expositions of Scripture)[39] **but has not** mastered **Torah laws** לֹא טָעַם טַעַם שֶׁל חָכְמָה — **has never savored the taste of wisdom.**[40] כָּל מִי שֶׁיֵּשׁ בְּיָדוֹ הֲלָכוֹת וְאֵין בְּיָדוֹ מִדְרָשׁ — Conversely, **whoever has** mastered Torah **laws but has not** mastered **Midrash** לֹא טָעַם טַעַם שֶׁל יִרְאַת חֵטְא — **has never savored the taste of fear of sin.**[41]

R' Yitzchak continues in the same vein:

הוּא הָיָה אוֹמֵר — He used to say: כָּל שֶׁיֵּשׁ בְּיָדוֹ מִדְרָשׁ וְאֵין בְּיָדוֹ הֲלָכוֹת זֶה גִבּוֹר וְאֵינוֹ מְזוּיָּין — **Whoever has** mastered **Midrash but has not** mastered Torah **laws is** likened to **a strong [warrior] who is unarmed.** כָּל שֶׁיֵּשׁ בְּיָדוֹ הֲלָכוֹת וְאֵין בְּיָדוֹ מִדְרָשׁ חַלָּשׁ וְזַיִּין בְּיָדוֹ — Conversely, **whoever has** mastered Torah **laws but has not** mastered **Midrash is** likened to **a weak [warrior] who is armed.**[42] יֵשׁ בְּיָדוֹ זֶה וָזֶה גִבּוֹר וּמְזוּיָּין — **If one has** mastered **both, he is** likened to **a strong [warrior] who is armed.**

Some final teachings, the first and last of which parallel *Avos* 4:15:

הוּא הָיָה אוֹמֵר — He used to say: הֱוֵי זָהִיר בִּשְׁאִילַת שָׁלוֹם בֵּין אָדָם לַחֲבֵירוֹ — **Be scrupulous with regard to the matter of greeting one's fellow.**[43] וְאַל

Name. Since this sin can be fully atoned only through death, students who are guilty of such behavior die before their time (*Mefaresh*; see *Binyan Yehoshua*, end of the previous section).

39. *Magen Avos*. [Usually, however, the term Midrash refers to halachic expositions (see e.g., above, 8 §1 and 28 §9).]

40. "Wisdom" refers to the in-depth analysis of Torah law, as in *Shabbos* 31a (*Binyan Yehoshua*, citing *Mefaresh*).

41. For the Aggados are replete with teachings whose purpose is to inspire character improvement and fear of God (ibid.).

42. The Torah laws are like weapons, for one who has mastered them is equipped to engage in the "combat" of halachic debate (*Magen Avos*). However, it is through the study of Aggados, which instills fear of Heaven, that one is defined as strong, as the Baraisa taught above (23 §1): "Who is the strongest of the strong? He who subdues his inclination" (*Binyan Yehoshua*).

43. That is, one should be the first one to greet his fellow when meeting him; and if someone else greets him first, he should make sure to return the greeting (*Binyan Yehoshua*, citing *Berachos* 6b). This is as

תָּבוֹא לְבֵין הַמַּחֲלוֹקֶת וְאַל תִּשְׁתַּדֵּל לִרְאוֹתוֹ.[44] שֵׁב בִּמְקוֹם חֲבֵרִים וֶהֱוֵי זָנָב לָאֲרָיוֹת וְאַל תְּהִי רֹאשׁ לַשּׁוּעָלִים:[45]

וְאַל תִּשְׁתַּדֵּל **Do not enter the scene of a quarrel,** — תָּבוֹא לְבֵין הַמַּחֲלוֹקֶת
לִרְאוֹתוֹ — **and do not attempt to see it.**[44]   שֵׁב בִּמְקוֹם חֲבֵרִים וֶהֱוֵי זָנָב לָאֲרָיוֹת
— Sit among your colleagues and be a tail to lions,   וְאַל תְּהִי רֹאשׁ לַשּׁוּעָלִים
— rather than a head to foxes.[45]

---

the Mishnah states (Avos 4:15): "Initiate a greeting to every person."

44. That is, do not be a spectator to a quarrel (Ahavas Chesed), unless your intent is to make peace between the two parties (Avos HaRosh, Vol. 2).

45. Do not leave the company of your colleagues in order to attain a higher position, for it is better to be subservient to the righteous than to be a leader over lowly people (Binyan Yehoshua, based on Rashi to Avos 4:15). One who follows the wise and righteous will become wise, for he will hear their words of wisdom and learn from their ways; whereas one who becomes a leader of the wicked will become evil like them (R' Yonah ad loc.; Peirush HaGra to Proverbs 13:20, in explanation of the verse there).

﴾ פֶּרֶק ל ﴿

א. רַבִּי נָתָן בֶּן יוֹסֵף אוֹמֵר: כָּל הַמְבַטֵּל דִּבְרֵי תוֹרָה מֵעוֹשֶׁר[1] סוֹפוֹ
לְבַטְּלָה מֵעוֹנִי[2], וְכָל הַמְקַיֵּים דִּבְרֵי תוֹרָה מֵעוֹנִי[3] סוֹפָה לְקַיְּימָה
מֵעוֹשֶׁר[4]. הוּא הָיָה אוֹמֵר: תַּנְחוּמֵי אֲבֵלִים וּבִקּוּר חוֹלִים וּגְמִילוּת חֲסָדִים[5]
מְבִיאִין טוֹבָה לָעוֹלָם[6]:

﴾ CHAPTER 30 ﴿

§1 The Baraisa cites a teaching from *Avos* 4:9:

רַבִּי נָתָן בֶּן יוֹסֵף אוֹמֵר — R' Nassan ben Yosef says: כָּל הַמְבַטֵּל דִּבְרֵי
תוֹרָה מֵעוֹשֶׁר סוֹפוֹ לְבַטְּלָה מֵעוֹנִי — Whoever neglects the words of the Torah in
wealth[1] will ultimately neglect it in poverty;[2] וְכָל הַמְקַיֵּים דִּבְרֵי תוֹרָה מֵעוֹנִי
סוֹפָה לְקַיְּימָה מֵעוֹשֶׁר — but whoever fulfills the words of the Torah in poverty[3]
will ultimately fulfill it in wealth.[4]

Another teaching from the same sage:

הוּא הָיָה אוֹמֵר — He used to say: תַּנְחוּמֵי אֲבֵלִים וּבִקּוּר חוֹלִים וּגְמִילוּת חֲסָדִים
— Comforting mourners, visiting the sick, and acts of
kindness[5] מְבִיאִין טוֹבָה לָעוֹלָם — all bring goodness to the world.[6]

---

1. That is, he becomes so involved in the management of his wealth that he finds no time for Torah study (*Binyan Yehoshua*, citing *Rav* to *Avos* ad loc.).

2. In the end he will become poor, and neglect Torah study for a different reason — because he will be preoccupied with his quest to acquire life's basic necessities (*Rambam*, commentary to *Avos* ad loc.).

3. That is, despite his poverty and need to labor for basic necessities, he steals time from his labors to study Torah (*Binyan Yehoshua*, citing *Rav* to *Avos* ad loc.).

4. He will be blessed with such wealth that he will no longer need to labor for his needs, giving him even more free time to study Torah (*R' Yonah* to *Avos* ad loc.).

The commentators ask that common experience, as well as incidents in the Gemara, show that this is not always true: Some people learn Torah in poverty their entire lives and never become wealthy. Conversely, some people neglect Torah in wealth throughout their lives, and are never reduced to poverty. *Binyan Yehoshua*

points to several commentators who present various answers. He also references *Alshich* (*Yarim Moshe* on *Avos* ad loc.), who offers a different understanding of this teaching, which eliminates the question: R' Nassan is not speaking about punishment or reward, but about a psychological reality that affects how a person should view various tests in life. Both wealth and poverty test a person's loyalty to God. R' Nassan is explaining why it is better to be tested with poverty than with wealth: One who neglects the Torah in wealth will do so even if the wealth is removed; the conceit one tends to develop when wealthy does not disappear with the wealth. The humility one can develop in poverty, however, will remain with him even in prosperity; if he has fulfilled the Torah in poverty, he will do so in wealth as well.

5. Comforting mourners and visiting the sick are forms of kindness that one performs with his body, whereas "acts of kindness" refers (in this context) to kindness performed with one's money (*Binyan Yehoshua*).

6. As elaborated above (4:5; see *Avos* 1:2), kindness is one of the pillars on which the

ב. רַבִּי מֵאִיר אוֹמֵר: כָּל הָעוֹבֵר עֲבֵירָה אַחַת בְּסָפֵק מַעֲלֶה עָלָיו
הַכָּתוּב כְּאִילוּ עֲשָׂאוֹ בְּוַדַּאי. כֵּיצַד, אָדָם חוֹטֵא וְנוֹדַע לוֹ חֶטְאוֹ
מֵבִיא חַטָּאת בְּסֶלַע[8] וַעֲשִׂירִית הָאֵיפָה בְּפוּנְדְּיוֹן[9]. סָפֵק חָטָא סָפֵק
לֹא חָטָא מֵבִיא (מְעִילָה וַחֲמִשָּׁה וּמֵבִיא) אָשָׁם בִּשְׁתֵּי סְלָעִים[10].

§2 The Baraisa cites a teaching that underscores the severity of sin:[7]

כָּל הָעוֹבֵר עֲבֵירָה אַחַת בְּסָפֵק מַעֲלֶה עָלָיו — R' Meir says: רַבִּי מֵאִיר אוֹמֵר
— Whoever has possibly transgressed a single sin הַכָּתוּב כְּאִילוּ עֲשָׂאוֹ בְּוַדַּאי
is considered by Scripture as if he definitely committed it, as will now be
demonstrated. — How so? כֵּיצַד, אָדָם חוֹטֵא וְנוֹדַע לוֹ חֶטְאוֹ מֵבִיא חַטָּאת בְּסֶלַע
If a person sins inadvertently and his sin became known to him, he brings in
some cases a chatas offering worth a sela,[8] וַעֲשִׂירִית הָאֵיפָה בְּפוּנְדְּיוֹן — and
in some cases as little as a tenth-ephah of flour worth a pundyon.[9] These are
the offerings that one brings if he knows he has committed the transgression.
סָפֵק חָטָא סָפֵק לֹא חָטָא מֵבִיא אָשָׁם בִּשְׁתֵּי סְלָעִים — But if in the case of a chatas-
bearing sin one is in doubt as to whether or not he has sinned, he must bring
an asham offering worth at least two selas.[10] Thus, we see that a person who

---

world stands. Thus, the various forms of
kindness listed here bring goodness to the
world, as it is they that enable it to stand
(Binyan Yehoshua). Moreover, when people
treat each other with kindness, God responds in kind and treats them with kindness rather than strictly, thus filling the world
with good (Mefaresh).

7. Magen Avos. [Presumably, this is cited
here in order to lead up to the later statement of R' Nassan ben Yosef (after note 14),
whose teachings were cited in the previous
section.]

8. This refers primarily to prohibitions that
carry the kares penalty if transgressed deliberately. If one transgresses one of them
inadvertently and then realizes what he
has done, he must bring a chatas offering
to atone. This offering is a female sheep or
goat in its first year (Leviticus Ch. 4), whose
value has no minimum, but must by Rabbinic law be worth at least a sela (Ahavas
Chesed, citing Tosafos to Menachos 107b).
[A sela is the Rabbinic term for the shekel
of the Torah.]

9. There are certain sins for which the Torah
prescribes a variable offering. This is a form
of chatas offering that varies according to

the sinner's financial situation. The smallest
offering that may be brought is a meal offering consisting of a tenth-ephah of fine flour
(Leviticus Ch. 5), whose value has no minimum, but must by Rabbinic law be worth at
least a pundyon, which is one forty-eighth
of a sela. See, however, Kereisos 10b, where
the Gemara states that it need cost only a
perutah [which is one-sixteenth of a pun-
dyon] (Binyan Yehoshua).

10. One who is unsure whether he committed a sin that would obligate him in a chatas
must bring an offering called an asham talui
(guilt offering of doubt), which must be a
ram worth at least two selas (Leviticus 5:17-
19). This offering achieves for him temporary atonement, effective as long as he does
not discover that he definitely committed the
sin. If he does discover that he is definitely
guilty, he must then bring a chatas offering, even though he has already brought an
asham offering.

We have followed the emendation of
Gra (see also Magen Avos), who removes
from the standard text the words מְעִילָה
וְחֻמְשָׁה, the misappropriated amount plus
its fifth. If these words are included, then the
Baraisa refers to the case of possible me'ilah

וְכִי אֵיזֶה מִדָּה מְרוּבָּה מִדָּה טוֹבָה אוֹ מִדַּת פּוּרְעָנוּת, הֱוֵי אוֹמֵר מִדָּה
טוֹבָה.[12] וַהֲרֵי דְּבָרִים קַל וָחֹמֶר, אִם מִדַּת פּוּרְעָנוּת מְעוּטָה הָעוֹבֵר
עֲבֵירָה בְּסָפֵק מַעֲלֶה עָלָיו הַכָּתוּב כְּאִילוּ עָשָׂה בְּוַדַּאי, קַל וָחֹמֶר

---

has possibly sinned must bring an atonement offering no less substantial than
the offering required for a *definite* sin.[11]

The Baraisa draws an inference from the above regarding the significance
of a mitzvah:

וְכִי אֵיזֶה מִדָּה מְרוּבָּה, מִדָּה טוֹבָה אוֹ מִדַּת פּוּרְעָנוּת — **Now, which measure is
greater, the measure of goodness or the measure of punishment?** הֱוֵי אוֹמֵר
מִדָּה טוֹבָה — **You must say that the measure of goodness is greater.**[12] וַהֲרֵי
דְּבָרִים קַל וָחֹמֶר — **The following matter, then, may be derived by means of a**
kal va'chomer: אִם מִדַּת פּוּרְעָנוּת מְעוּטָה הָעוֹבֵר עֲבֵירָה בְּסָפֵק מַעֲלֶה עָלָיו הַכָּתוּב
כְּאִילוּ עָשָׂה בְּוַדַּאי — **If regarding the measure of punishment, which is smaller, one who is in doubt as to whether he transgressed a sin is considered by
Scripture as if he definitely committed it** (as demonstrated above), קַל וָחֹמֶר

(misappropriation of sacred property). In
the case of definite *me'ilah*, the person must
bring an *asham me'ilos* in addition to paying
the misappropriated amount plus its fifth.
In the case of possible *me'ilah,* the person
would bring (according to some Tannaic
views — see *Kereisos* 5:2) an *asham talui*
in addition to paying the misappropriated
amount plus its fifth (should he wish for that
asham talui to count as his *asham me'ilos,*
in the event he realizes that he definitely
committed the *me'ilah*). This is the highest
amount that a person would bring for a possible transgression, a much higher amount
than the *chatas* brought for definitely having
committed an inadvertent sin of *kares* (see
Magen Avos and *Binyan Yehoshua*).

11. In fact, R' Meir has proven that the
atonement offering required for a possible
sin is *greater* than that required for a definite
sin. [A possible sin is in a sense worse in
that a person naturally feels less regret for a
doubtful sin. Therefore, he needs a greater
degree of repentance and atonement in order to achieve forgiveness (*Binyan Yehoshua,* from *Rama, Orach Chaim* 603:1).] The
reason R' Meir speaks only of the possible
sin being accounted "as if he committed the
definite sin" (and no more) is that he wishes

to extend this below to the analogous cases
of a possible and definite mitzvah, where it
is certain that the possible mitzvah cannot
be greater than the definite one (*Ahavas
Chesed*).

Actually, the language of the verse with
regard to *asham talui* indicates that the
possible sin is considered a sin, for the
verse there states, *but he did not know and
became guilty, he shall bear "his iniquity"*
(*Leviticus* 5:17). *Binyan Yehoshua* suggests
that this verse is indeed R' Meir's source
as well, and that his proof from the greater
value of the *asham talui* is meant to demonstrate the *additional* point that the possible
sin is in some ways *greater* than the definite
one. See also *Ben Avraham.*

12. This is based on the verse that states
among the Divine Attributes, *Preserver of
Kindness for thousands of generations ... recalling the iniquity of parents upon children
and grandchildren, to the third and fourth
generations* (*Exodus* 34:7). Thus we see that
whereas God recalls merit for thousands of
generations of one's descendants, He recalls
iniquity for only four generations; hence the
proof that the measure of goodness is greater than the measure of punishment (*Binyan
Yehoshua,* citing *Rashi* to *Makkos* 5b).

לְמִדַּת הַטוֹבָה מְרוּבָה. רַבִּי נָתָן בֶּן יוֹסֵף אוֹמֵר: כָּל הָעוֹבֵר עֲבֵירָה
בְּשׁוֹגֵג מַעֲלֶה עָלָיו הַכָּתוּב כְּאִילוּ עָשָׂה בְמֵזִיד[14]. כֵּיצַד, שׁוֹגֵג שֶׁהָרַג
אֶת הַנֶּפֶשׁ וְגוֹלֶה לָעִיר מִקְלָטוֹ[15] וּמְצָאוֹ גוֹאֵל הַדָּם[16] וַהֲרָגוֹ הֲרֵי זֶה
פָּטוּר[18]. הֲרָגוֹ בְּמֵזִיד וּמְצָאוֹ גוֹאֵל הַדָּם וַהֲרָגוֹ [הֲרֵי זֶה גוֹלֶה עַל יָדוֹ[19]].

לְמִדַּת הַטוֹבָה מְרוּבָה — **all the more so for the measure of goodness,** which is greater! Thus, we can infer that Scripture accounts even a possible mitzvah as if it were a definite one.[13]

The Baraisa cites another, similar teaching regarding the severity of sin and the significance of a mitzvah:

כָּל הָעוֹבֵר עֲבֵירָה בְּשׁוֹגֵג — רַבִּי נָתָן בֶּן יוֹסֵף אוֹמֵר — **R' Nassan ben Yosef says:** מַעֲלֶה עָלָיו הַכָּתוּב כְּאִילוּ עָשָׂה בְמֵזִיד — **Whoever transgresses a sin inadvertently is considered as if he committed it deliberately.**[14] כֵּיצַד, שׁוֹגֵג שֶׁהָרַג אֶת הַנֶּפֶשׁ וְגוֹלֶה לָעִיר מִקְלָטוֹ — **How so? One who kills a person inadvertently and is exiled to his city of refuge,**[15] וּמְצָאוֹ גוֹאֵל הַדָּם וַהֲרָגוֹ הֲרֵי זֶה פָּטוּר — **and** some time later he leaves the city and **the avenger of the blood**[16] **found him** outside the city of refuge[17] **and killed him, [the avenger] is exempt from** any punishment.[18] הֲרָגוֹ בְּמֵזִיד וּמְצָאוֹ גוֹאֵל הַדָּם וַהֲרָגוֹ הֲרֵי זֶה גוֹלֶה עַל יָדוֹ — **However, if he had killed [the person] deliberately and the avenger of the blood found him and killed him, [the avenger of the blood] would be exiled on his account.**[19] Thus, we see that sometimes the inadvertent murderer is treated

---

13. And this is so even if the mitzvah was not only uncertain but also inadvertent, as in the case of *asham talui* from which this is being proven (*Binyan Yehoshua, Avos HaRosh* [Vol. 2]). [In this vein, *Sifrei* (§283, on *Deuteronomy* 24:19, cited in *Rashi* there) teaches that one who loses a coin which is then found and used by a poor person to sustain himself is considered by Scripture as if he had intentionally given that benefit to the poor person.]

14. Before, the Baraisa discussed (with regard to inadvertent transgression) a *possible* sin versus a *definite* one. Now it discusses *inadvertent* versus *deliberate*.

15. As prescribed by the Torah in *Numbers* Ch. 35.

16. I.e., a close relative of the victim.

17. *Binyan Yehoshua*, citing *Makkos* 12a.

18. As it states, *But if the murderer will ever leave the border of the city of refuge to which*

he had fled, and the avenger of the blood shall find him outside of the border of his city of refuge, and the avenger of the blood will kill the murderer — he has no blood-guilt (*Numbers* 35:26-27).

19. If he killed the murderer unintentionally; if he killed the murderer deliberately, he would be liable to the death penalty (see *Binyan Yehoshua*). [*Gra* emends the text of the Baraisa to read, "he would be executed on his account."]

The Baraisa refers to where we do not have two witnesses testifying that the murderer committed the crime; rather, the murderer confessed to it or there is one witness who saw him do it. In this case, the murderer is exempt from any punishment, and if the avenger of the blood kills him, he is judged as if he has killed an innocent man (*Shenei Eliyahu*). This, then, is not exactly analogous to the first case, where there *were* two witnesses who saw the murderer kill unintentionally (which is why he had to be

וְכִי אֵיזוֹ מִדָּה מְרוּבָּה מִדַּת הַטוֹב אוֹ מִדַּת הַפּוּרְעָנוּת, הֱוֵי אוֹמֵר מִדַּת הַטוֹב. וְאִם מִדַּת פּוּרְעָנוּת מְעוּטָה הָעוֹבֵר עֲבֵירָה בְּשׁוֹגֵג מַעֲלִין עָלָיו כְּאִילוּ עָשָׂה עֲשָׂאָה בְּמֵזִיד, קַל וָחֹמֶר לְמִדַּת הַטּוֹב מְרוּבָּה:

ג. רַבִּי עֲקִיבָא אוֹמֵר: כָּל הַמִּדַּבֵּק בְּעוֹבְרֵי עֲבֵירָה אַף עַל פִּי שֶׁלֹּא עָשָׂה כְּמַעֲשֵׂיהֶם הֲרֵי זֶה מְקַבֵּל פּוּרְעָנוּת כַּיוֹצֵא בָּהֶן. וְכָל הַמִּדַּבֵּק בְּעוֹשֵׂי מִצְוָה אַף עַל פִּי שֶׁלֹּא עָשָׂה כְּמַעֲשֵׂיהֶם הֲרֵי זֶה מְקַבֵּל שָׂכָר כַּיוֹצֵא בָּהֶן. כֵּיצַד, שְׁנַיִם מְעִידִים בְּאֶחָד וְאוֹמְרִים: אָדָם זֶה הָרַג אֶת הַנֶּפֶשׁ. וְנִמְצְאוּ

---

no less stringently than the deliberate murderer.[20] וְכִי אֵיזוֹ מִדָּה מְרוּבָּה מִדַּת הַטוֹב אוֹ מִדַּת הַפּוּרְעָנוּת — Now, which measure is greater, the measure of goodness or the measure of punishment? הֱוֵי אוֹמֵר מִדַּת הַטוֹב — You must say that the measure of goodness is greater. וְאִם מִדַּת פּוּרְעָנוּת מְעוּטָה הָעוֹבֵר עֲבֵירָה בְּשׁוֹגֵג מַעֲלִין עָלָיו כְּאִילוּ עֲשָׂאָה בְּמֵזִיד — Now, if regarding the measure of punishment, which is smaller, one who transgresses a sin inadvertently is considered as if he committed it deliberately, קַל וָחֹמֶר לְמִדַּת הַטוֹב מְרוּבָּה — then all the more so for the measure of goodness, which is greater! Thus, we can infer that Scripture accounts even an inadvertent mitzvah as if it were a definite one.

§3 Continuing the theme of the previous section, the Baraisa cites a teaching regarding the severity of being an accomplice to transgressors, and the corresponding value of being an accomplice to the righteous: כָּל הַמִּדַּבֵּק בְּעוֹבְרֵי עֲבֵירָה אַף עַל פִּי שֶׁלֹּא — רַבִּי עֲקִיבָא אוֹמֵר R' Akiva says: עָשָׂה כְּמַעֲשֵׂיהֶם — Whoever attaches himself to transgressors, even if he did not do as they did, הֲרֵי זֶה מְקַבֵּל פּוּרְעָנוּת כַּיוֹצֵא בָּהֶן — receives punish- ment like they do. וְכָל הַמִּדַּבֵּק בְּעוֹשֵׂי מִצְוָה אַף עַל פִּי שֶׁלֹּא עָשָׂה כְּמַעֲשֵׂיהֶם — And similarly, whoever attaches himself to the performers of a mitzvah, even if he did not do as they did, הֲרֵי זֶה מְקַבֵּל שָׂכָר כַּיוֹצֵא בָּהֶן — receives reward like they do. כֵּיצַד, שְׁנַיִם מְעִידִים בְּאֶחָד וְאוֹמְרִים אָדָם זֶה הָרַג אֶת הַנֶּפֶשׁ — How so? We see it from the following cases: Two witnesses tes- tify against someone, saying, "This person committed murder," וְנִמְצְאוּ

---

exiled to the city of refuge). Nevertheless, we still see that certain instances of uninten- tional murder are treated more severely than certain instances of intentional murder; for in the first instance (the case of the uninten- tional murderer) the avenger of the blood is exempt from any punishment for killing him, whereas in the second instance (the case of the deliberate murderer) the avenger of

blood *is* liable (either to exile or to the death penalty).

[For further discussion of our Baraisa and its legal ramifications, see *Ben Avraham* here at length, and *Shiurei R' Shmuel* to *Makkos, Inyanim* §4.]

20. And even *more* stringently, as in the Baraisa's proof (*Binyan Yehoshua*; see above, note 11).

זוֹמְמִין[21] וְנִגְמַר דִּינָם לֵיהָרֵג. וּכְשֶׁהֵן מוֹצִיאִין אוֹתָן לְבֵית הַסְּקִילָה[22], אֶחָד
רָץ (וּבָא) אַחֲרֵיהֶם וְאוֹמֵר: יוֹדֵעַ אֲנִי בְּעֵדוּת זוֹ[23]. אוֹמְרִים לוֹ: בֹּא וְהָעֵד
עֵדוּתְךָ. אַף הוּא נִמְצָא זוֹמֵם וְנִגְמַר דִּינוֹ לֵיהָרֵג[24]. כְּשֶׁהֵן מוֹצִיאִין אוֹתוֹ לְבֵית
הַסְּקִילָה, אוֹמֵר: אוֹי לִי, שֶׁאִילּוּ לֹא בָאתִי אֲנִי כְּבָר לֹא נִגְמַר דִּינִי לֵיהָרֵג,

---

זוֹמְמִין וְנִגְמַר דִּינָם לֵיהָרֵג — **and they are found to be** *zomemin*,[21] **and they are sentenced to death** for conspiring to condemn an innocent man.   וּכְשֶׁהֵן מוֹצִיאִין אוֹתָן לְבֵית הַסְּקִילָה — **While [the agents of the court] are taking them out to the stoning place** to be killed,[22]   אֶחָד רָץ וּבָא אַחֲרֵיהֶם וְאוֹמֵר יוֹדֵעַ אֲנִי בְּעֵדוּת זוֹ — **someone comes running after them and says, "I know** something **regarding this testimony."**[23]   אוֹמְרִים לוֹ: בֹּא וְהָעֵד עֵדוּתְךָ — **So [the members of the court] tell him, "Come and state your testimony."**   אַף הוּא נִמְצָא זוֹמֵם וְנִגְמַר דִּינוֹ לֵיהָרֵג — **He then states his testimony, and he too is found to be a** *zomeim* **and is sentenced to death.**[24]   כְּשֶׁהֵן מוֹצִיאִין אוֹתוֹ לְבֵית הַסְּקִילָה, אוֹמֵר: אוֹי לִי — **As they take him out to the stoning place, he says, "Woe is me!** שֶׁאִילּוּ לֹא בָאתִי אֲנִי כְּבָר לֹא נִגְמַר דִּינִי לֵיהָרֵג — **For had I not come to join with the first two witnesses, I would not have been sentenced to death;**

---

21. Literally, *conspirers* (singular, *zomeim*). *Zomemin* are witnesses whose testimony has been discredited through the testimony of other witnesses who place them elsewhere at the time of the alleged incident, so that they could not possibly have witnessed it. The Torah rules, *You shall do to him* [the conspiring witnesses] *as he conspired to do to his fellow* (*Deuteronomy* 19:19). That is, whatever consequences the false witnesses conspired to inflict on their victim — execution, lashes, or monetary payment — is meted out to them instead. See *Makkos* Ch. 1.

22. The court had a designated place for stoning outside the city (*Sanhedrin* 42b). Now, the penalty for murder is not stoning, but beheading (ibid. 76b). Nevertheless, the Baraisa seems to assume that all forms of execution were carried out in the same location, since all must be done outside the city; see *Sifrei, Numbers* 15:36 and *Rambam, Hil. Sanhedrin* 12:3.

23. That is, I saw the same incident that the witnesses who are about to be executed claimed to have seen.

24. The commentators point out that our version of the Baraisa is problematic. For in the scenario just described the third witness would *not* be liable to execution, since even if his testimony had not been falsified, that testimony, which is the testimony of a single witness, could not have caused his victim to be executed! Accordingly, he could not be liable to the punishment of a *zomeim* (see *Shenei Eliyahu* and *Meorei Ohr*). *Gra* therefore emends the text so that the Baraisa refers to where the third witness came to testify before the verdict was pronounced against the original defendant, and before the other two witnesses were found to be *zomemin*. [In the Oxford Opp. 95 manuscript, the reading is: "שֶׁמּוֹצִיאִין אוֹתָן לְבֵית הַסְּקִילָה" rather than "וּכְשֶׁהֵן מוֹצִיאִין".] Thus, he joins an existing testimony of two witnesses and expands it to become a testimony of three. Then, all three witnesses were found to be *zomemin*. In this case, although the testimony of the third witness was not needed to convict the defendant, and thus accomplished nothing, he receives the same punishment as the other two (see *Makkos* 5b with *Rashi* ד"ה ר' עקיבא; see *Ben Avraham* for further discussion).

עַכְשָׁיו שֶׁבָּאתִי עִמָּהֶן נִגְמַר דִּינִי לֵיהָרֵג.[25] (אוֹמְרִים לוֹ: רֵיקָה, אֲפִילוּ מֵאָה בְּנֵי אָדָם בָּאִין אַחֲרֶיךָ וְנִמְצְאוּ זוֹמְמִין כּוּלָן נֶהֱרָגִין[26]). וְכִי אֵיזֶהוּ מִדָּה מְרוּבָּה מִדַּת הַטּוֹב אוֹ מִדַּת פּוּרְעָנוּת, הֱוֵי אוֹמֵר מִדַּת הַטּוֹב. אִם פּוּרְעָנוּת מְעוּטָה הַמִּדַּבֵּק בְּעוֹבְרֵי עֲבֵירָה אַף עַל פִּי שֶׁלֹּא עָשָׂה כְּמַעֲשֵׂיהֶם הֲרֵי זֶה מְקַבֵּל פּוּרְעָנוּת, קַל וָחֹמֶר לְמִדַּת הַטּוֹב מְרוּבָּה:

עַכְשָׁיו שֶׁבָּאתִי עִמָּהֶן נִגְמַר דִּינִי לֵיהָרֵג — now that I have come to join with them, I have been sentenced to death!"[25] אוֹמְרִים לוֹ: רֵיקָה, אֲפִילוּ מֵאָה בְּנֵי אָדָם בָּאִין — But they answer him, "Empty one! Even if one hundred people had come after you and testified, and they would have been found to be zomemin, they would have all been killed!"[26]

The Baraisa draws an inference from the above regarding one who collaborates with others in performing a mitzvah: וְכִי — Now, אֵיזֶהוּ מִדָּה מְרוּבָּה מִדַּת הַטּוֹב אוֹ מִדַּת פּוּרְעָנוּת, הֱוֵי אוֹמֵר מִדַּת הַטּוֹב — which measure is greater, the measure of goodness or the measure of punishment? You must say that the measure of goodness is greater. אִם פּוּרְעָנוּת מְעוּטָה הַמִּדַּבֵּק בְּעוֹבְרֵי עֲבֵירָה אַף עַל פִּי שֶׁלֹּא עָשָׂה כְּמַעֲשֵׂיהֶם הֲרֵי זֶה מְקַבֵּל פּוּרְעָנוּת — Now, if regarding the measure of punishment, which is smaller, one who attaches himself to transgressors, even though he did not do as they did, receives punishment just like they do, קַל וָחֹמֶר לְמִדַּת הַטּוֹב מְרוּבָּה — then all the more so is this true regarding the measure of good, which is greater, that one who adheres to those who perform a mitzvah, even if he does not do as they did,[27] is rewarded just like they are!

---

25. From the court's response to this (see Baraisa further), it is evident that this is not merely the third witness's cry of despair, but rather an argument as to why he should not be executed. The essence of his argument is that he does not deserve to be killed because his testimony did not play any role in the victim's conviction (Ben Avraham). Thus, he argues (as per the words of the Baraisa): Had I not come and testified, I would certainly not have been killed; thus, even now that I did testify, it should be as though I never came, since my testimony did not contribute to the original conviction! [Perhaps the Baraisa text might be emended to read: שֶׁאִלּוּ לֹא בָּאתִי אֲנִי כְּבָר לֹא נִגְמַר "דִּינוֹ" לֵיהָרֵג, For had I not come, would "he" not have been sentenced to death (anyway)?]

26. For they would all be considered part of the same original "group" of witnesses. See Makkos ibid., where R' Akiva derives this from a verse.

In this illustration of the Baraisa, the third witness actually did exactly what the original transgressors did. Nevertheless, R' Akiva refers to the third witness as one who attaches himself to transgressors "even though he does not do as they did," because although he did testify falsely, his testimony, unlike theirs, had no practical effect on the victim. And still, this third witness receives punishment just like they do (see Ben Avraham at the beginning of this section).

27. [I.e., he collaborates with them in a mitzvah endeavor, even if his role is not as active as theirs.]

ד. רַבִּי שִׁמְעוֹן אוֹמֵר: כָּךְ עוֹנֶשׁ שֶׁל בַּדַּאי שֶׁאֲפִילוּ דוֹבֵר אֱמֶת אֵין שׁוֹמְעִין לוֹ. שֶׁכֵּן מָצִינוּ בְּבָנָיו שֶׁל יַעֲקֹב שֶׁכִּזְּבוּ לַאֲבִיהֶן, בַּתְּחִלָּה הֶאֱמִין לָהֶם, שֶׁנֶּאֱמַר (בראשית לז, לא) "וַיִּקְחוּ אֶת כְּתֹנֶת יוֹסֵף וַיִּשְׁחֲטוּ שְׂעִיר עִזִּים", וּכְתִיב (שם שם לג) "וַיַּכִּירָהּ וַיֹּאמֶר כְּתֹנֶת בְּנִי".[29] אֲבָל בָּאַחֲרוֹנָה אַף עַל פִּי שֶׁדִּבְּרוּ אֱמֶת לְפָנָיו לֹא הֶאֱמִין לָהֶם, שֶׁנֶּאֱמַר (שם מה, כו) [וַיָּפָג לִבּוֹ כִּי לֹא הֶאֱמִין לָהֶם] "וַיַּגִּדוּ לוֹ לֵאמֹר עוֹד יוֹסֵף חַי", וְלֹא הֶאֱמִין לָהֶם.[30]

---

§4 Apropos of its discussion regarding false witnesses, the Baraisa informs us of a particular consequence of lying:[28]

כָּךְ עוֹנֶשׁ שֶׁל בַּדַּאי שֶׁאֲפִילוּ דוֹבֵר אֱמֶת אֵין — R' Shimon says: — רַבִּי שִׁמְעוֹן אוֹמֵר שׁוֹמְעִין לוֹ — Such is the punishment of a liar, that even when he speaks the truth, he is not believed. שֶׁכֵּן מָצִינוּ בְּבָנָיו שֶׁל יַעֲקֹב — For thus do we find regarding the sons of the Patriarch Jacob, שֶׁכִּזְּבוּ לַאֲבִיהֶן, בַּתְּחִלָּה הֶאֱמִין לָהֶם — who lied to their father; originally, he believed them, שֶׁנֶּאֱמַר "וַיִּקְחוּ אֶת כְּתֹנֶת יוֹסֵף וַיִּשְׁחֲטוּ שְׂעִיר עִזִּים" — as it says, *They took Joseph's tunic, slaughtered a young goat, and dipped the tunic in the blood. They dispatched the fine woolen tunic and they brought it to their father, and said, "We found this; identify, if you please: Is it your son's tunic or not?"* וּכְתִיב "וַיַּכִּירָהּ וַיֹּאמֶר כְּתֹנֶת בְּנִי" — And it is written there further, *He recognized it and he said, "My son's tunic! A savage beast devoured him! Joseph has surely been torn to bits!"* (*Genesis* 37:31-33).[29] אֲבָל בָּאַחֲרוֹנָה אַף עַל פִּי שֶׁדִּבְּרוּ אֱמֶת לְפָנָיו לֹא הֶאֱמִין לָהֶם — But later, even though they spoke the truth before him, he did not believe them, שֶׁנֶּאֱמַר "וַיַּגִּדוּ לוֹ לֵאמֹר עוֹד יוֹסֵף חַי" — as it says, *And they told him, saying, "Joseph is still alive,"* and that he is ruler over all the land of Egypt, וְלֹא הֶאֱמִין לָהֶם — and he did not believe them, as it says further in that verse, *but his heart rejected it, for he did not believe them* (ibid. 45:26).[30]

---

28. *Binyan Yehoshua.*

29. Jacob's sons lied to him by saying that they had found Joseph's tunic covered in blood, when in truth they had sold him and dipped his tunic in blood. Jacob believed what they said, and therefore assumed that Joseph had been killed by a wild beast.

30. [The Vilna edition (which follows the Frankfort edition of 1720) has these words of the verse (וַיָּפָג לִבּוֹ כִּי לֹא הֶאֱמִין לָהֶם) inserted into the text in brackets, but in the wrong place; *Binyan Yehoshua* and *Gra* move them to the end of the sentence, where they belong, and we have added them in the English translation.]

Many commentators assume that the

"liar's punishment" meant by the Baraisa is a *natural* consequence: Once a person has shown himself to be liar, nothing he says will be trusted (see *Magen Avos, Ahavas Chesed, Ben Avraham,* et al.). Accordingly, the Baraisa's proof seems difficult on the surface, as we do not see that Jacob had *realized* that they lied the first time. The answer may be that while Jacob might not have known for sure that his sons had lied to him the first time, he had long suspected that they were the ones who had caused Joseph's disappearance; see *Bereishis Rabbah* 91 §9. Therefore, when they told him that Joseph was still alive and ruling in the land of Egypt, he did not believe them (*Ahavas Chesed* and

וְיֵשׁ אוֹמְרִים: רוּחַ הַקּוֹדֶשׁ שֶׁנִּסְתַּלְּקָה מִיַּעֲקֹב אָבִינוּ שָׁרְתָה עָלָיו בְּאוֹתָהּ
שָׁעָה, שֶׁנֶּאֱמַר (שם פסוק כז) "וַתְּחִי רוּחַ יַעֲקֹב אֲבִיהֶם"[31]:

The Baraisa concludes:

וְיֵשׁ אוֹמְרִים: רוּחַ הַקּוֹדֶשׁ שֶׁנִּסְתַּלְּקָה מִיַּעֲקֹב אָבִינוּ שָׁרְתָה עָלָיו בְּאוֹתָהּ שָׁעָה — **And some say** that **the Holy Spirit that had departed from Jacob, our forefather, rested on him** once more **at that time** that his sons informed him that Joseph was alive, שֶׁנֶּאֱמַר "וַתְּחִי רוּחַ יַעֲקֹב אֲבִיהֶם" — **as it says** in the very next verse, *However, when they related to him all the words that Joseph had spoken to them, and he saw the wagons that Joseph had sent to transport him, **the spirit of their father Jacob was revived*** (ibid. v. 27).[31]

Avos HaRosh [Vol. 2], citing *Yefeh To'ar* to *Bereishis Rabbah* 94 §3).

31. I.e., the Divine Spirit of prophecy returned to him. Some explain that the Baraisa now comes to answer an unspoken question: If Jacob suspected his sons of lying when they said that Joseph was still alive, why did he then (in the verse now cited) believe that Joseph *was* alive? The Baraisa answers that it was the Divine Spirit that rested upon him and revealed the truth to him (*Mefaresh, Binyan Yehoshua*).

﴾ פֶּרֶק לא ﴿

א. רַבִּי¹ אֲחַאי בֶּן יֹאשִׁיָּה אוֹמֵר: הַלּוֹקֵחַ תְּבוּאָה מִן הַשּׁוּק² לְמָה הוּא
דּוֹמֶה, לְתִינוֹק שֶׁמֵּתָה אִמּוֹ וּמַחֲזִירִין אוֹתוֹ עַל פִּתְחֵי מֵינִיקוֹת
אֲחֵרוֹת וְאֵינוֹ שָׂבֵעַ³. הַלּוֹקֵחַ פַּת מִן הַשּׁוּק⁴ לְמָה הוּא דוֹמֶה, כְּאִילּוּ
חָפוּר וְקָבוּר⁵. הָאוֹכֵל מִשֶּׁלּוֹ דּוֹמֶה לְתִינוֹק הַמִּתְגַּדֵּל עַל שְׁדֵי אִמּוֹ⁶.

﴾ CHAPTER 31 ﴿

§1 The Baraisa cites a teaching regarding various degrees of poverty and the
advantages of self-sufficiency:[1]

הַלּוֹקֵחַ תְּבוּאָה מִן — **R' Achai ben Yoshiyah says:** רַבִּי אֲחַאי בֶּן יֹאשִׁיָּה אוֹמֵר
הַשּׁוּק לְמָה הוּא דוֹמֶה — **One who buys produce from the marketplace,**[2] **to what
is he comparable?** לְתִינוֹק שֶׁמֵּתָה אִמּוֹ וּמַחֲזִירִין אוֹתוֹ עַל פִּתְחֵי מֵינִיקוֹת אֲחֵרוֹת
וְאֵינוֹ שָׂבֵעַ — **To an infant whose mother died, and he is passed around the
entrances** to the houses of other nursing mothers, **but he is not satiated.**[3]
הַלּוֹקֵחַ פַּת מִן הַשּׁוּק לְמָה הוּא דוֹמֶה — **One who buys bread from the marketplace,**[4] **to what is he comparable?** כְּאִילּוּ חָפוּר וְקָבוּר — **He is considered
as if [his grave] has been dug and he is buried** inside of it.[5] הָאוֹכֵל מִשֶּׁלּוֹ
דּוֹמֶה לְתִינוֹק הַמִּתְגַּדֵּל עַל שְׁדֵי אִמּוֹ — **One who eats** the produce **of his own field,**
however, **is comparable to an infant who is nurtured at his mother's breasts.**[6]

---

1. According to *Binyan Yehoshua*, this teaching is connected to that of R' Nassan ben Yosef
cited at the beginning of the previous chapter,
where it states that one who fulfills the Torah
in poverty will merit to fulfill it in wealth. In
the forthcoming teaching, the Baraisa defines
what constitutes "poverty" in this regard.

2. I.e., he does not own land on which to
grow his own produce, so he is forced to buy
his food from the marketplace (as per *Rashi*
to *Menachos* 103b).

3. An infant who nurses from someone other
than his mother is never satiated. Similarly,
someone who must buy his food from the
marketplace is never satiated. The Gemara
(*Menachos* 103b with *Rashi*), in explanation
of *Deuteronomy* 28:66, states that one who
buys grain from year to year is constantly
worrying that he may not have enough
money to make his purchase next year,
and one who has only enough money to
purchase grain for a week at a time is even
more worried, for he may not have enough

money for the next week. Our Baraisa
teaches that these people are not satiated
no matter how much they eat, based on
the principle that "one who has bread in his
basket is not comparable to one who does
not have bread in his basket" (*Yoma* 18b).
His constant fear of starvation prevents him
from being satiated (see *Magen Avos*).

4. He does not even have enough to purchase a few days' supply of grain, but
instead lives a hand-to-mouth existence,
earning money each day and using it to buy
bread from the baker the next morning.

5. With no stockpile of grain whatsoever, his
situation is the bleakest of all, for starvation
stares him in the face.

6. A child that nurses from its mother is satiated with a small amount of milk. Similarly,
one who eats the produce grown on his own
land is satiated with whatever amount his
field produces [for he is free of worry, as he
knows that his field will be there for him year
after year] (*Magen Avos*).

הוּא הָיָה אוֹמֵר: בִּזְמַן שֶׁאָדָם אוֹכֵל מִשֶּׁלּוֹ דַּעְתּוֹ מְיוּשֶׁבֶת עָלָיו, וַאֲפִילוּ
אוֹכֵל אָדָם מִשֶּׁל אָבִיו וּמִשֶּׁל אִמּוֹ וּמִשֶּׁל בָּנָיו אֵין דַּעְתּוֹ מְיוּשֶׁבֶת עָלָיו,
וְאֵין צָרִיךְ לוֹמַר מִשֶּׁל אֲחֵרִים:[7]

ב. בַּעֲשָׂרָה מַאֲמָרוֹת נִבְרָא הָעוֹלָם.[8] וְכִי מַה צוֹרֶךְ לְבָאֵי עוֹלָם בְּכָךְ,[9]
אֶלָּא לְלַמֶּדְךָ שֶׁכָּל הָעוֹשֶׂה מִצְוָה אַחַת וְכָל הַמְשַׁמֵּר שַׁבָּת אֶחָד וְכָל
הַמְקַיֵּים נֶפֶשׁ אַחַת [מַעֲלֶה עָלָיו הַכָּתוּב] כְּאִילוּ קִיֵּים עוֹלָם מָלֵא שֶׁנִּבְרָא
בַּעֲשָׂרָה מַאֲמָרוֹת. וְכָל הָעוֹבֵר עֲבֵירָה אַחַת וְכָל הַמְחַלֵּל שַׁבָּת אֶחָד וְכָל
הַמְאַבֵּד נֶפֶשׁ אַחַת מַעֲלִין עָלָיו כְּאִילוּ אִיבֵּד עוֹלָם מָלֵא שֶׁנִּבְרָא בַּעֲשָׂרָה

A related teaching:

הוּא הָיָה אוֹמֵר — He used to say: בִּזְמַן שֶׁאָדָם אוֹכֵל מִשֶּׁלּוֹ דַּעְתּוֹ מְיוּשֶׁבֶת עָלָיו
— When a person eats the produce of his own field, his mind is at ease.
וַאֲפִילוּ אוֹכֵל אָדָם מִשֶּׁל אָבִיו וּמִשֶּׁל אִמּוֹ וּמִשֶּׁל בָּנָיו — But if a person must resort to
others, even if he eats the food of his father, of his mother, or of his children,
אֵין דַּעְתּוֹ מְיוּשֶׁבֶת עָלָיו — his mind is not at ease. וְאֵין צָרִיךְ לוֹמַר מִשֶּׁל אֲחֵרִים
— And it goes without saying that his mind is not at ease if he must eat the
food of others who are not related to him.[7]

§2 The Baraisa cites *Avos* 5:1 (with variations) and elaborates upon it:
בַּעֲשָׂרָה מַאֲמָרוֹת נִבְרָא הָעוֹלָם — The world was created through ten Divine utterances.[8] וְכִי מַה צוֹרֶךְ לְבָאֵי עוֹלָם בְּכָךְ — Now, what purpose does
this serve for mankind to know this?[9] אֶלָּא לְלַמֶּדְךָ שֶׁכָּל הָעוֹשֶׂה מִצְוָה אַחַת
— Rather, it is to teach you that וְכָל הַמְשַׁמֵּר שַׁבָּת אֶחָד וְכָל הַמְקַיֵּים נֶפֶשׁ אַחַת
anyone who performs one mitzvah, anyone who observes one Sabbath, or
anyone who preserves one human life, מַעֲלֶה עָלָיו הַכָּתוּב כְּאִילוּ קִיֵּים עוֹלָם
מָלֵא שֶׁנִּבְרָא בַּעֲשָׂרָה מַאֲמָרוֹת — is considered by Scripture as though he upheld the entire world that was created through ten utterances; וְכָל הָעוֹבֵר
עֲבֵירָה אַחַת וְכָל הַמְחַלֵּל שַׁבָּת אֶחָד וְכָל הַמְאַבֵּד נֶפֶשׁ אַחַת — and anyone who
transgresses one sin, anyone who desecrates one Sabbath, or anyone who
destroys one human life, מַעֲלִין עָלָיו כְּאִילוּ אִיבֵּד עוֹלָם מָלֵא שֶׁנִּבְרָא בַּעֲשָׂרָה

---

7. For he is ashamed to receive handouts
from them (*Binyan Yehoshua*).

8. Everything in the world was created by
an "utterance" of God, Who decreed that it
should come into existence. God employed
ten such utterances in the course of the
six days of Creation, as evident from the
verses at the beginning of *Genesis*, which
state "God said." [Actually, the expression,
God said, appears only nine times in the
Scriptural account of Creation in *Genesis*

Ch. 1. The Gemara (*Megillah* 21b) explains
that the very first verse of the Torah, *In the
beginning God created the heavens and the
earth*, represents a Divine utterance. For the
heavens and the earth were also created
through the word of God, as it states (*Psalms*
33:6), *By the word of HASHEM the heavens
were made* (*Binyan Yehoshua*, citing *Rashi*
to *Avos* 5:1).]

9. That is, what lesson does God teach His
creatures by creating the world with ten

מַאֲמָרוֹת[10] שֶׁכֵּן[11] מָצִינוּ בְּקַיִן שֶׁהָרַג אֶת הֶבֶל[12] אָחִיו, שֶׁנֶּאֱמַר (בראשית ד,
י) "קוֹל דְּמֵי אָחִיךָ". דָּם אֶחָד שָׁפַךְ, דָּמִים רַבִּים נֶאֱמַר. אֶלָּא מְלַמֵּד שֶׁדַּם
בָּנָיו וּבְנֵי בָנָיו וְכָל תּוֹלְדוֹתָיו עַד סוֹף כָּל הַדּוֹרוֹת שֶׁעֲתִידִין לָצֵאת מִמֶּנּוּ
כֻּלָּם הָיוּ עוֹמְדִין וְצוֹעֲקִין לִפְנֵי הַקָּדוֹשׁ בָּרוּךְ הוּא. (הָא לָמַדְתָּ שֶׁאָדָם
אֶחָד שָׁקוּל כְּנֶגֶד מַעֲשֵׂה בְרֵאשִׁית כֻּלּוֹ[13].):

מַאֲמָרוֹת — is considered as though he destroyed the entire world that was created through ten utterances.[10]

The Baraisa cites a proof from Scripture for its assertion that the destruction of one human life is equal to that of the entire world, and vice versa:[11] שֶׁכֵּן מָצִינוּ בְּקַיִן שֶׁהָרַג אֶת הֶבֶל אָחִיו — We know this to be so, for thus do we find regarding Cain who killed his brother Abel,[12] that he was considered to have destroyed an entire world, שֶׁנֶּאֱמַר "קוֹל דְּמֵי אָחִיךָ" — as it says that God said to Cain, *"What have you done? The voice of your brother's 'bloods' cry out to Me from the ground!"* (Genesis 4:10). דָּם אֶחָד שָׁפַךְ, דָּמִים רַבִּים נֶאֱמַר — Now, [Cain] had spilled only one person's blood; yet it is stated, your brother's *"bloods,"* in the plural. Why the plural? אֶלָּא מְלַמֵּד שֶׁדַּם בָּנָיו וּבְנֵי — Rather, this teaches בָּנָיו וְכָל תּוֹלְדוֹתָיו שֶׁעֲתִידִין לָצֵאת מִמֶּנּוּ — that the blood of [Abel's] unborn children, grandchildren, and all his offspring until the end of all generations, which were destined to issue forth from him were it not for his murder, כֻּלָּם הָיוּ עוֹמְדִין וְצוֹעֲקִין לִפְנֵי הַקָּדוֹשׁ בָּרוּךְ הוּא — were all standing and crying out before the Holy One, Blessed is He. הָא לָמַדְתָּ שֶׁאָדָם אֶחָד שָׁקוּל כְּנֶגֶד מַעֲשֵׂה בְרֵאשִׁית כֻּלּוֹ — Thus you may learn that one person is equal to the entirety of creation.[13]

---

utterances instead of one? (*Binyan Yehoshua,* based on *Avos* ibid. with *Rashi*).

10. God's purpose in creating the world with ten utterances was to underscore its importance, and thus the significance of even one human deed or misdeed, which can be the cause of preserving or destroying the entire world (see the next note), as well as the significance of a human life, whose value is equivalent to that of the entire world, as the Baraisa will proceed to demonstrate.

11. *Magen Avos, Ben Avraham.* The Baraisa does not, however, support its assertion that the world can be upheld or destroyed through the observance or transgression of a single Sabbath or mitzvah. That assertion, though, is based on the Gemara (*Kiddushin* 40b), which teaches that the world is judged

according to the deeds of its inhabitants; if mankind's deeds are mostly worthy, the world is sustained. If mostly wicked, the world is condemned. When the world's sins or merits are equal, a person's single good deed has the power to tip the scales favorably for the entire world; his single sin can tip the balance unfavorably (*Binyan Yehoshua,* first explanation, from *Rav* to *Avos* ibid.).

12. See *Genesis* 4:8.

13. Had Abel lived, an entire world would have emerged from him, just as it eventually did from his brothers Cain and Seth. Since we see that Cain was held accountable not only for the one person that he murdered but for all the generations that Abel would have produced, we may learn that anyone who destroys a human life will be held

ג. רַבִּי נְחֶמְיָה אוֹמֵר: מִנַּיִן שֶׁאָדָם אֶחָד שָׁקוּל כְּנֶגֶד כָּל מַעֲשֵׂה בְרֵאשִׁית,
שֶׁנֶּאֱמַר (שם ה, א) "זֶה סֵפֶר תּוֹלְדֹת אָדָם", וּלְהַלָּן הוּא אוֹמֵר (שם ב,
ד) "אֵלֶּה תוֹלְדוֹת הַשָּׁמַיִם וְהָאָרֶץ בְּהִבָּרְאָם". מַה לְהַלָּן בְּרִיאָה וַעֲשִׂיָּה
אַף כָּאן בְּרִיאָה וַעֲשִׂיָּה. מְלַמֵּד שֶׁהֶרְאָהוּ הַקָּדוֹשׁ בָּרוּךְ הוּא כָּל הַדּוֹרוֹת
שֶׁעֲתִידִין לָצֵאת מִמֶּנּוּ[17] כְּאִלּוּ הֵם עוֹמְדִין (וּמְשַׂחֲקִין) לְפָנָיו[18]. וְיֵשׁ אוֹמְרִים:
לֹא הֶרְאָהוּ אֶלָּא צַדִּיקִים בִּלְבַד, שֶׁנֶּאֱמַר (ישעיה ד, ג) "כָּל הַכָּתוּב לַחַיִּים

---

§3 Another proof that one human life is equal to the entire world:

רַבִּי נְחֶמְיָה אוֹמֵר: מִנַּיִן שֶׁאָדָם אֶחָד שָׁקוּל כְּנֶגֶד כָּל מַעֲשֵׂה בְרֵאשִׁית — **R'**
Nechemyah says: From where do we know **that one person is equal to**
the entirety of creation? שֶׁנֶּאֱמַר "זֶה סֵפֶר תּוֹלְדֹת אָדָם" וּלְהַלָּן הוּא אוֹמֵר
"אֵלֶּה תוֹלְדוֹת הַשָּׁמַיִם וְהָאָרֶץ בְּהִבָּרְאָם" — **For it says,** *This is the book of the*
"toldos" [descendants] *of Adam* — on the day that God "created" Man, He
"made" him in the likeness of God (ibid. 5:1); **and elsewhere it states,** *These*
are the "toldos" [products] *of the heaven and the earth when they were*
"created" on the day that HASHEM *God "made" earth and heaven* (ibid. 2:4).
מַה לְהַלָּן בְּרִיאָה וַעֲשִׂיָּה אַף כָּאן בְּרִיאָה וַעֲשִׂיָּה — **Just as there,** with regard to
the "toldos" of heaven and earth, Scripture uses the terms **"creation" and**
"making," so too here, with regard to *the "toldos" of Adam,* it uses the terms
"creation" and "making."[14] The similar wording teaches us that each of *the*
descendants of Adam is equal in value to all of the products of heaven and
earth.[15]

Tangentially, the Baraisa expounds the clause, *This is the book of the descen-*
dants of Adam, in *Genesis 5:1:*[16]

מְלַמֵּד שֶׁהֶרְאָהוּ הַקָּדוֹשׁ בָּרוּךְ הוּא כָּל הַדּוֹרוֹת שֶׁעֲתִידִין לָצֵאת מִמֶּנּוּ — **This**
teaches that the Holy One, Blessed is He, showed [Adam] all the gen-
erations that were destined to issue forth from him,[17] כְּאִלּוּ הֵם
עוֹמְדִין וּמְשַׂחֲקִין לְפָנָיו — **as though they were standing and reveling be-**
fore him.[18] וְיֵשׁ אוֹמְרִים: לֹא הֶרְאָהוּ אֶלָּא צַדִּיקִים בִּלְבַד — **And some say**
that [God] showed [Adam] only the righteous, שֶׁנֶּאֱמַר "כָּל הַכָּתוּב לַחַיִּים

---

accountable for all the generations that he
prevented his victim from producing (see
Magen Avos).

14. Elucidation follows *Mefaresh*.

15. *Ben Avraham.*

16. *Ahavas Chesed.*

17. I.e., when the verse states, *This is the*
book of the descendants of Adam, it is referring to a book that God showed to Adam,
in which were written the names of all of

Adam's descendants until the end of time
(see *Bereishis Rabbah* 24 §2).

18. That is, He showed Adam both the righteous, who "stand" in awe and fear before
God, and the wicked, who are constantly
"reveling" (*Ben Avraham*; see also *Magen*
Avos).

[Other commentators find difficulty explaining the word וּמְשַׂחֲקִין, *and reveling*; and
indeed *Gra* deletes it from the text.]

בִּירוּשָׁלָיִם"[19]. רַבִּי יְהוֹשֻׁעַ בֶּן קָרְחָה אוֹמֵר: הֲרֵי הוּא אוֹמֵר (תהלים
קלט, טז) "גָּלְמִי רָאוּ עֵינֶיךָ וְעַל סִפְרְךָ וְגוֹ' ". מְלַמֵּד שֶׁהֶרְאָהוּ הַקָּדוֹשׁ
בָּרוּךְ הוּא לְאָדָם הָרִאשׁוֹן דּוֹר דּוֹר וְדוֹרְשָׁיו דּוֹר דּוֹר וּפַרְנָסָיו דּוֹר דּוֹר
וּמַנְהִיגָיו דּוֹר דּוֹר וּנְבִיאָיו דּוֹר דּוֹר וְגִבּוֹרָיו דּוֹר דּוֹר וּפוֹשְׁעָיו דּוֹר דּוֹר
וַחֲסִידָיו[21]. בְּדוֹר פְּלוֹנִי עָתִיד לִהְיוֹת מֶלֶךְ פְּלוֹנִי בְּדוֹר פְּלוֹנִי עָתִיד לִהְיוֹת
חָכָם פְּלוֹנִי[22]. רַבִּי אֱלִיעֶזֶר בְּנוֹ שֶׁל רַבִּי יוֹסֵי הַגְּלִילִי אוֹמֵר: תְּשַׁע מֵאוֹת
וְשִׁבְעִים וְאַרְבָּעָה דוֹרוֹת קוֹדֶם שֶׁנִּבְרָא הָעוֹלָם הָיְתָה תּוֹרָה כְּתוּבָה

בִּירוּשָׁלָיִם" — as it is stated, *Of every remnant that will be in Zion and every remaining one in Jerusalem, "Holy" will be said of him, everyone who is
inscribed for life in Jerusalem* (Isaiah 4:3).[19]　　רַבִּי יְהוֹשֻׁעַ בֶּן קָרְחָה אוֹמֵר:
הֲרֵי הוּא אוֹמֵר "גָּלְמִי רָאוּ עֵינֶיךָ וְעַל סִפְרְךָ וְגוֹ' " — R' Yehoshua ben Korchah
says: Behold it states, *Your eyes saw my unfinished form, and in Your book
all were recorded* (Psalms 139:16).　　מְלַמֵּד שֶׁהֶרְאָהוּ הַקָּדוֹשׁ בָּרוּךְ הוּא לְאָדָם
הָרִאשׁוֹן — **This teaches that the Holy One, Blessed is He, showed Adam, the
first man,** while he was still lying **as an unfinished form before Him,**[20]　דּוֹר
דּוֹר וּפַרְנָסָיו דּוֹר דּוֹר — each generation with its expounders,　דּוֹר וְדוֹרְשָׁיו
וּמַנְהִיגָיו — **each generation with its patrons, each generation with its leaders,**　דּוֹר דּוֹר וּנְבִיאָיו דּוֹר דּוֹר וְגִבּוֹרָיו — **each generation with its prophets,
each generation with its mighty ones,**　דּוֹר דּוֹר וּפוֹשְׁעָיו דּוֹר דּוֹר וַחֲסִידָיו —
each generation with its sinners, and each generation with its pious ones.[21]
בְּדוֹר פְּלוֹנִי עָתִיד לִהְיוֹת מֶלֶךְ פְּלוֹנִי בְּדוֹר פְּלוֹנִי עָתִיד לִהְיוֹת חָכָם פְּלוֹנִי — And He
informed him: **In such and such a generation, So-and-so will be king; in such
and such a generation, So-and-so will be a sage.**[22]

The Baraisa discusses another "book" that was in existence prior to the
creation of Adam:

רַבִּי אֱלִיעֶזֶר בְּנוֹ שֶׁל רַבִּי יוֹסֵי הַגְּלִילִי אוֹמֵר — R' Eliezer the son of R' Yose HaGlili
says:　תְּשַׁע מֵאוֹת וְשִׁבְעִים וְאַרְבָּעָה דוֹרוֹת קֹדֶם שֶׁנִּבְרָא הָעוֹלָם — **Nine hundred
seventy-four generations before the world was created,**　הָיְתָה תּוֹרָה כְּתוּבָה

---

19. This verse speaks of those "inscribed
for life," but *where* are they inscribed? Our
Baraisa understands that it is in the book
that was shown to Adam. And the verse
says, *"Holy" will be said of him,* which indicates that only the "holy" — the righteous
descendants of Adam — were written in the
book shown to Adam (*Magen Avos, Ahavas Chesed*). Alternatively, the indication is
from the expression לַחַיִּים, *for life,* itself, for
true "life" exists only with reference to the
righteous (*Ahavas Chesed,* from *Bereishis*

Rabbah 24 §3; *Binyan Yehoshua*).

20. *Bereishis Rabbah* 24 §2.

21. R' Yehoshua ben Korchah follows the first
opinion above, which maintains that God
showed Adam the righteous *and* the wicked
that would arise from him (*Ben Avraham*).

22. The Baraisa is interpreting the *Psalms*
verse as follows: At the time that *Your eyes
saw my* (i.e., Adam's) *unfinished form, all
[future generations]* were recorded *in Your
book* that You showed me. The term *all*

וּמוּנַּחַת בְּחֵיקוֹ שֶׁל הַקָּדוֹשׁ בָּרוּךְ הוּא[23] וְאוֹמֶרֶת שִׁירָה עִם מַלְאֲכֵי הַשָּׁרֵת,[24] שֶׁנֶּאֱמַר (משלי ח, ל-לא) "וָאֶהְיֶה אֶצְלוֹ אָמוֹן וָאֶהְיֶה שַׁעֲשׁוּעִים יוֹם יוֹם ... מְשַׂחֶקֶת בְּתֵבֵל אַרְצוֹ"[26]. מָשְׁלוּ מָשָׁל[28] לְמָה הַדָּבָר דּוֹמֶה,

וּמוּנַּחַת בְּחֵיקוֹ שֶׁל הַקָּדוֹשׁ בָּרוּךְ הוּא — the Torah was already written and lay in the bosom of the Holy One, Blessed is He,[23]   וְאוֹמֶרֶת שִׁירָה עִם מַלְאֲכֵי הַשָּׁרֵת — and it was uttering songs of praise before God together with the ministering angels,[24]   שֶׁנֶּאֱמַר "וָאֶהְיֶה אֶצְלוֹ אָמוֹן וָאֶהְיֶה שַׁעֲשׁוּעִים יוֹם יוֹם ... מְשַׂחֶקֶת בְּתֵבֵל אַרְצוֹ" — as it says in the Torah's description of its relation to God before the creation of the world,[25] *I was then His nursling, I was then His delight day after day, playing before Him at all times, playing in the inhabited areas of His earth, my delights are with the sons of man* (Proverbs 8:30-31).[26]

Earlier, the Baraisa asserted that one person is equal to the entire world. It will now elaborate further on this idea by demonstrating that Man is a microcosm of the universe:[27]

מָשְׁלוּ מָשָׁל לְמָה הַדָּבָר דּוֹמֶה — An analogy was made:[28] To what is the matter

---

indicates both the righteous *and* the wicked (*Ben Avraham*).

23. The Sages teach that the Torah [which preceded the world; see below, note 26] was destined to be given at the end of 1,000 generations, as it states, *the word He commanded for the thousandth generation* (Psalms 105:8). However, we find only 26 generations from Adam until Moses. There must have been, then, 974 generations [1000-26=974] before Adam that were never created. This was because God saw that the world could not endure for 1,000 generations without receiving the Torah. Therefore, He did not create the first 974 generations and began the actual creation with Adam, so that no more than 26 generations would elapse before the Torah was given. Those generations that never came into being were destined to be created during the period by which the Torah preceded the world (*Binyan Yehoshua*, from *Rashi* to *Shabbos* 88b; see note 26). That period is therefore referred to as "974 generations."

24. *Ahavas Chesed* notes that this Baraisa seems to presume that the angels were created long before the world itself. Elsewhere, however (*Bereishis Rabbah* 1 §3 et al.), the Sages posit that the angels were created on the second day of Creation at the earliest.

25. See the verses in *Proverbs* (8:22ff) leading

up to the verses now cited by the Baraisa.

26. As expounded elsewhere, the expression *day after day* indicates two days, and the day of the Holy One, Blessed is He, is 1,000 years (see *Psalms* 90:4). This refers to the 2,000 years that the Torah preceded the creation of the world (*Bereishis Rabbah* 8 §2). The aforementioned 974 generations were to have been created during those 2,000 years (*Rashi* to *Shabbos* 88b, cited by *Binyan Yehoshua*). *Ahavas Chesed* refers us to *Yefeh To'ar's* commentary on *Bereishis Rabbah* [see there on 8 §2] for a discussion of how 974 generations can be compressed into 2,000 years. [However, verse 31, the first part of which — *playing in the inhabited areas of His earth* — is also cited by the Baraisa, must apparently refer to what the Torah did *after* the creation of man. Alternatively, it refers to the Torah's *waiting* during those times until it would be able to become the delight of man with the Giving of the Torah; see *Binyan Yehoshua*.]

The Baraisa quotes the *Proverbs* verse only to prove that the Torah preceded the world's creation by 2,000 years, and not to support any other of the Baraisa's assertions here (*Ben Avraham*).

27. *Ahavas Chesed, Ben Avraham*. See further, note 57.

28. In one manuscript (Oxford Opp. 95),

לְאֶחָד שֶׁנָּטַל אֶת הָעֵץ וּמְבַקֵּשׁ לָצוּר צוּרוֹת הַרְבֵּה וְאֵין לוֹ מָקוֹם לָצוּר
וְיֵשׁ לוֹ צַעַר, אֲבָל מְצַיֵּיר בָּאָרֶץ וְהוֹלֵךְ וּמַבְדִּיל הַרְבֵּה הַרְבֵּה. אַף כָּךְ
הַקָּדוֹשׁ בָּרוּךְ הוּא יְהֵא שְׁמוֹ הַגָּדוֹל מְבוֹרָךְ לְעוֹלָם וּלְעוֹלְמֵי עוֹלָמִים,
בְּחָכְמָתוֹ וּבִתְבוּנָתוֹ בָּרָא אֶת כָּל הָעוֹלָם כּוּלוֹ וּבָרָא אֶת הַשָּׁמַיִם וְאֶת
הָאָרֶץ עֶלְיוֹנִים וְתַחְתּוֹנִים. וְיָצַר בָּאָדָם כָּל מַה שֶׁבָּרָא בְּעוֹלָמוֹ.[30] בָּרָא
חוֹרְשִׁים בָּעוֹלָם וּבָרָא חוֹרְשִׁים בָּאָדָם, זֶה שְׂעָרוֹת שֶׁל אָדָם. בָּרָא חַיָּה
רָעָה בָּעוֹלָם בָּרָא חַיָּה רָעָה בָּאָדָם, זֶה (בְּנֵי מֵעָיו) שֶׁל אָדָם.[31] (בָּרָא

of God's creation of Man comparable? לְאֶחָד שֶׁנָּטַל אֶת הָעֵץ וּמְבַקֵּשׁ לָצוּר
צוּרוֹת הַרְבֵּה — To someone who takes a block of wood and wishes to sculpt
many images on it, וְאֵין לוֹ מָקוֹם לָצוּר וְיֵשׁ לוֹ צַעַר — but he does not have
much room on the block to sculpt all of those images, so he must take great
pains to miniaturize all those images, and as a result they are not as clear and
distinct as he would like them to be.[29] אֲבָל מְצַיֵּיר בָּאָרֶץ וְהוֹלֵךְ וּמַבְדִּיל הַרְבֵּה הַרְבֵּה
— But when he sculpts in the earth, he can keep on sculpting and
widely separate the images from one another, so each is clear and distinct.
אַף כָּךְ הַקָּדוֹשׁ בָּרוּךְ הוּא יְהֵא שְׁמוֹ הַגָּדוֹל מְבוֹרָךְ לְעוֹלָם וּלְעוֹלְמֵי עוֹלָמִים — So too,
the Holy One, Blessed is He, may His great Name be blessed forever and for
all eternity, בְּחָכְמָתוֹ וּבִתְבוּנָתוֹ בָּרָא אֶת כָּל הָעוֹלָם כּוּלוֹ — with His wisdom
and understanding He created the entire world, וּבָרָא אֶת הַשָּׁמַיִם וְאֶת הָאָרֶץ
— and He created the heavens and the earth, the upper עֶלְיוֹנִים וְתַחְתּוֹנִים
and lower spheres, without any limitations; וְיָצַר בָּאָדָם כָּל מַה שֶׁבָּרָא בְּעוֹלָמוֹ
— yet He formed in Man a clear representation of all that He created in His
world.[30]

The Baraisa supports its assertion by enumerating various parts of the
human body and their corresponding components of the world:
בָּרָא חוֹרְשִׁים בָּעוֹלָם וּבָרָא חוֹרְשִׁים בָּאָדָם, זֶה שְׂעָרוֹת שֶׁל אָדָם — [God] created forests in the world, and correspondingly, He created "forests" in Man, namely,
a person's hair, which are like the trees of a forest. בָּרָא חַיָּה רָעָה בָּעוֹלָם בָּרָא
חַיָּה רָעָה בָּאָדָם, זֶה בְּנֵי מֵעָיו שֶׁל אָדָם — He created wild beasts in the world,
and He created "wild beasts" in Man, namely, a person's innards.[31] בָּרָא

---

this analogy is prefaced with the line: "R'
Yose HaGlili says: Whatever the Holy One,
Blessed is He, created on earth, He created
in Man."

29. *Ben Avraham.*

30. Although Man is small in size, like a
wooden block, the Holy One, Blessed is He,
with His infinite wisdom and unlimited capa-
bility, is able to form in him the vastness of the

images He formed in the entirety of the world,
with each one clear and distinct — just as a
human artist would be able to do if he were
sculpting in the earth (*Ben Avraham*). [In the
Oxford Opp. 95 manuscript, the reading is
אֲבָל, *However*, in place of אַף, *So, too*, which
makes the intent of the Baraisa even clearer.]

31. A person's innards resemble wild beasts
in that they devour and consume anything

קוּרְצִין בָּעוֹלָם וּבָרָא קוּרְצִין בָּאָדָם, זֶה אָזְנָיו שֶׁל אָדָם). בָּרָא רֵיחַ בָּעוֹלָם בָּרָא רֵיחַ בָּאָדָם, זֶה חוֹטְמוֹ שֶׁל אָדָם.[33] חַמָּה בָּעוֹלָם חַמָּה בָּאָדָם, זֶה אוֹרוֹ שֶׁל אָדָם. מַיִם סְרוּחִים בָּעוֹלָם מַיִם סְרוּחִים בָּאָדָם, זֶהוּ מֵימֵי חוֹטְמוֹ שֶׁל אָדָם. מַיִם מְלוּחִים בָּעוֹלָם מַיִם מְלוּחִים בָּאָדָם, זֶהוּ דִּמְעוֹת שֶׁל עֵינָיו. נְחָלִים בָּעוֹלָם נְחָלִים בָּאָדָם, אֵלּוּ דִּמְעוֹת.[34] חוֹמוֹת בָּעוֹלָם חוֹמוֹת בָּאָדָם, אֵלּוּ שִׂפְתוֹתָיו שֶׁל אָדָם. דְּלָתוֹת בָּעוֹלָם דְּלָתוֹת בָּאָדָם, זֶה שִׁנָּיו שֶׁל אָדָם.[35] (רְקִיעִים בָּעוֹלָם רְקִיעִים בָּאָדָם, זֶה לְשׁוֹנוֹ שֶׁל אָדָם[36]).

בָּרָא רֵיחַ **קוּרְצִין בָּעוֹלָם וּבָרָא קוּרְצִין בָּאָדָם, זֶה אָזְנָיו שֶׁל אָדָם** — He created caves in the world,[32] and He created caves in Man, namely, a person's ears. חַמָּה **בָּעוֹלָם בָּרָא רֵיחַ בָּאָדָם, זֶה חוֹטְמוֹ שֶׁל אָדָם** — He created odors in the world, and He created an organ of smell in Man, namely, a person's nose.[33] מַיִם סְרוּחִים בָּעוֹלָם **בָּעוֹלָם חַמָּה בָּאָדָם, זֶה אוֹרוֹ שֶׁל אָדָם** — He created a sun in the world, and He created a "sun" in Man, namely, a person's sight. **סְרוּחִים בָּאָדָם, זֶהוּ מֵימֵי חוֹטְמוֹ שֶׁל אָדָם** — He created putrid fluids in the world, and He created putrid fluids in Man, namely, the fluid excreted by a person's nose. **מַיִם מְלוּחִים בָּעוֹלָם מַיִם מְלוּחִים בָּאָדָם, זֶהוּ דִּמְעוֹת שֶׁל עֵינָיִם** — He created salty waters in the world, and He created salty waters in Man, namely, the tears of the eyes. **נְחָלִים בָּעוֹלָם נְחָלִים בָּאָדָם, אֵלּוּ דִּמְעוֹת** — He created streams in the world, and He created streams in Man, namely, the tears.[34] דְּלָתוֹת בָּעוֹלָם **חוֹמוֹת בָּעוֹלָם חוֹמוֹת בָּאָדָם, אֵלּוּ שִׂפְתוֹתָיו שֶׁל אָדָם** — He created walls in the world, and He created walls in Man, namely, a person's lips. **דְּלָתוֹת בָּאָדָם, זֶה שִׁנָּיו שֶׁל אָדָם** — He created doors in the world, and He created doors in Man, namely, a person's teeth.[35] רְקִיעִים בָּעוֹלָם רְקִיעִים בָּאָדָם, **זֶה לְשׁוֹנוֹ שֶׁל אָדָם** — He created what stretches out in the world (the skies), and He created what stretches out in Man, namely, a person's tongue.[36]

---

that comes into contact with them (see Yaavetz).

[The commentators suggest various explanations of this analogy. Note, however, that *Tummas Yesharim* cites an alternative version that reads: זֶה הַכִּנִּים שֶׁבּוֹ, *namely, the lice in his [hair].* This version is followed by *Gra* as well; see *Ben Avraham.*]

32. Translation follows *Shevet Mussar,* cited in *Binyan Yehoshua.*

33. [The correspondence here is not precise. *Ben Avraham* suggests emending the text to רוּחַ, *wind,* and this is indeed the reading in the Oxford Opp. 95 ms. Accordingly, the correspondence is that a person's nose,

through breathing, also produces a wind.]

34. [The composition of the salty tears resembles seawater, while their flow resembles a stream.]

35. The lips and the teeth act as walls and doors for the mouth, as they guard the tongue from uttering evil speech (*Arachin* 15b, cited by *Binyan Yehoshua*).

36. The word רָקִיעַ is a form of the verb root רקע, which means *stretch out.* The firmament is thus called רָקִיעַ because it is stretched out above the earth. Therefore, the tongue, which can be stretched out and extended from the mouth, corresponds to the firmaments (*Binyan Yehoshua*).

מַיִם מְתוּקִים בָּעוֹלָם וּמַיִם מְתוּקִים בָּאָדָם, זֶהוּ רוּקוֹ שֶׁל אָדָם. לְסָתוֹת
בָּעוֹלָם לְסָתוֹת בָּאָדָם, זֶה לְחָיָיו שֶׁל אָדָם.[37] מִגְדָּלִים מִגְדָּלִים בָּעוֹלָם
בָּאָדָם, זֶה צַוָּארוֹ שֶׁל אָדָם.[39] סְתִידְרָאוֹת בָּעוֹלָם סְתִידְרָאוֹת בָּאָדָם, זֶה
זְרוֹעוֹתָיו שֶׁל אָדָם.[41] יְתֵידוֹת בָּעוֹלָם יְתֵידוֹת בָּאָדָם, זֶה אֶצְבְּעוֹתָיו שֶׁל
אָדָם.[42] מֶלֶךְ בָּעוֹלָם מֶלֶךְ בָּאָדָם, רֹאשׁוֹ.[43] (אַשְׁכּוֹלוֹת בָּעוֹלָם אַשְׁכּוֹלוֹת
בָּאָדָם, דָּמוֹ.[44]) יוֹעֲצִים בָּעוֹלָם יוֹעֲצִים בָּאָדָם, כְּלָיוֹתָיו.[45] רֵיחַיִם בָּעוֹלָם

מַיִם מְתוּקִים בָּעוֹלָם וּמַיִם מְתוּקִים בָּאָדָם, זֶהוּ רוּקוֹ שֶׁל אָדָם — He created sweet waters in the world, and He created sweet waters in Man, namely, a person's saliva. לְסָתוֹת בָּעוֹלָם לְסָתוֹת בָּאָדָם, זֶה לְחָיָיו שֶׁל אָדָם — He created "cheeks" in the world, and He created cheeks in Man, namely, a person's cheekbones.[37] מִגְדָּלִים בָּעוֹלָם מִגְדָּלִים בָּאָדָם, זֶה צַוָּארוֹ שֶׁל אָדָם — He created towers in the world, i.e., mountains,[38] and He created towers in Man, namely, a person's neck.[39] סְתִידְרָאוֹת בָּעוֹלָם סְתִידְרָאוֹת בָּאָדָם, זֶה זְרוֹעוֹתָיו שֶׁל אָדָם — He created powerful officers[40] in the world, and He created powerful "officers" in Man, namely, a person's arms.[41] יְתֵידוֹת בָּעוֹלָם יְתֵידוֹת בָּאָדָם, זֶה אֶצְבְּעוֹתָיו שֶׁל אָדָם — He created spikes in the world, and He created spikes in Man, namely, a person's fingers.[42] מֶלֶךְ בָּעוֹלָם מֶלֶךְ בָּאָדָם, רֹאשׁוֹ — He created a king in the world, and He created a king in Man, namely, his head.[43] אַשְׁכּוֹלוֹת בָּעוֹלָם אַשְׁכּוֹלוֹת בָּאָדָם, דָּמוֹ — He created clusters of fruits in the world, and He created "clusters" (אֶשְׁכֹּלוֹת) in Man, namely, his blood.[44] יוֹעֲצִים בָּעוֹלָם יוֹעֲצִים בָּאָדָם, כְּלָיוֹתָיו — He created advisers in the world, and He created advisers in Man, namely, his kidneys.[45] רֵיחַיִם בָּעוֹלָם

---

37. The reference is to the stars, which stand out as points of light against the night sky. So, too, a man's hairless cheekbones stand out shining as spots against the darker beard that frames them (see *Binyan Yehoshua*, second explanation, citing *Shabbos* 151b, and *Rashi* to Ecclesiastes 12:2).

38. *Binyan Yehoshua* ד"ה לסתות בעולם.

39. Which stands straight and tall like a tower (see *Song of Songs* 7:5, cited by *Ben Avraham*).

40. Translation follows *Ahavas Chesed*, cited by *Ben Avraham*.

41. For they perform acts that require strength (*Ben Avraham*).

42. Which are tapered like spikes; see *Kesubos* 5b.

43. Which is the "king" of the body by virtue of its location and its function (see *Kisei Rachamim*).

44. The word אֶשְׁכֹּל is an acronym for שֶׁהַכֹּל בּוֹ, *it contains all* (see *Temurah* 16b). This is a fitting description of blood, which contains all the essential elements of life (*Ahavas Chesed, Binyan Yehoshua*).

["Blood" is mentioned below in another analogy. *Gra* deletes the present analogy entirely, and it is indeed absent from most other texts. The Oxford Opp. 95 ms. here דַּדָּיו שֶׁל אָדָם", *a person's "breasts."* See also *Ben Avraham*, who makes a similar emendation.]

45. The kidneys act as a source of guidance and instruction, as stated in *Berachos* 61a; see also below, 33 §1, referenced by *Binyan Yehoshua*.

רֵיחַיִם בָּאָדָם, זֶה קֻרְקְבָנוֹ שֶׁל אָדָם[46]. נִימְסִים בָּעוֹלָם נִימְסִים בָּאָדָם, זֶה טְחוֹלוֹ שֶׁל אָדָם[47]. אַשְׁפַּתּוֹת בָּעוֹלָם אַשְׁפַּתּוֹת בָּאָדָם, זֶה כְּרֵיסוֹ שֶׁל אָדָם[48]. בּוֹרוֹת בָּעוֹלָם בּוֹרוֹת בָּאָדָם, זֶה טִיבּוּרוֹ שֶׁל אָדָם[49]. מַיִם חַיִּים בָּעוֹלָם מַיִם חַיִּים בָּאָדָם, זֶה (מֵי רַגְלָיו שֶׁל אָדָם[50]. חַיִּים בָּעוֹלָם חַיִּים בָּאָדָם, זֶה) דָּמוֹ שֶׁל אָדָם[51]. עֵצִים בָּעוֹלָם עֵצִים בָּאָדָם, זֶה עַצְמוֹתָיו שֶׁל אָדָם[52]. גְּבָעוֹת בָּעוֹלָם גְּבָעוֹת בָּאָדָם, זֶה עַגְבוֹתָיו שֶׁל אָדָם[53]. עֱלִי וּמַכְתֶּשֶׁת בָּעוֹלָם עֱלִי וּמַכְתֶּשֶׁת בָּאָדָם, זֶה אַרְכֻּבּוֹתָיו שֶׁל אָדָם[54]. סוּסִים בָּעוֹלָם סוּסִים בָּאָדָם, זֶה שׁוֹקָיו שֶׁל אָדָם[55]. (מַלְאַךְ הַמָּוֶת בָּעוֹלָם מַלְאַךְ הַמָּוֶת

רֵיחַיִם בָּאָדָם, זֶה קֻרְקְבָנוֹ שֶׁל אָדָם — He created a mill in the world, and He created a "mill" in Man, namely, a person's stomach.[46] **נִימְסִים בָּעוֹלָם נִימְסִים בָּאָדָם, זֶה טְחוֹלוֹ שֶׁל אָדָם** — He created dissolvable matter in the world, and He created dissolvable matter in Man, namely, a person's spleen.[47] **אַשְׁפַּתּוֹת בָּעוֹלָם אַשְׁפַּתּוֹת בָּאָדָם, זֶה כְּרֵיסוֹ שֶׁל אָדָם** — He created refuse heaps in the world, and He created refuse heaps in Man, namely, a person's abdomen.[48] **בּוֹרוֹת בָּעוֹלָם בּוֹרוֹת בָּאָדָם, זֶה טִיבּוּרוֹ שֶׁל אָדָם** — He created cisterns in the world, and He created cisterns in Man, namely, a person's navel.[49] **מַיִם חַיִּים בָּעוֹלָם חַיִּים בָּאָדָם, זֶה מֵי רַגְלָיו שֶׁל אָדָם** — He created spring water in the world, and He created "spring water" in Man, namely, a person's urine.[50] **חַיִּים בָּעוֹלָם בָּאָדָם, זֶה דָּמוֹ שֶׁל אָדָם** — He created sources of life in the world, and He created a source of life in Man, namely, a person's blood.[51] **עֵצִים בָּעוֹלָם עֵצִים בָּאָדָם, זֶה עַצְמוֹתָיו שֶׁל אָדָם** — He created wood in the world, and He created "wood" in Man, namely, a person's bones.[52] **גְּבָעוֹת בָּעוֹלָם גְּבָעוֹת בָּאָדָם, זֶה עַגְבוֹתָיו שֶׁל אָדָם** — He created hills in the world, and He created "hills" in Man, namely, a person's buttocks.[53] **עֱלִי וּמַכְתֶּשֶׁת בָּעוֹלָם עֱלִי וּמַכְתֶּשֶׁת בָּאָדָם, זֶה אַרְכֻּבּוֹתָיו שֶׁל אָדָם** — He created a pestle and mortar in the world, and He created a pestle and mortar in Man, namely, a person's knees.[54] **סוּסִים בָּעוֹלָם סוּסִים בָּאָדָם, זֶה שׁוֹקָיו שֶׁל אָדָם** — He created horses in the world, and He created "horses" in Man, namely, a person's legs.[55] **מַלְאַךְ הַמָּוֶת בָּעוֹלָם מַלְאַךְ הַמָּוֶת**

---

46. Which grinds the food just like millstones grind grain (*Binyan Yehoshua*, citing *Berachos* 61b).

47. The spleen is capable of disintegrating; see *Rama, Yoreh Deah* 43:2 (*Ben Avraham*).

48. Which holds the waste matter until it is excreted from the body (*Magen Avos*).

49. Which, in a fetus, is open like a cistern to receive nourishment from his mother through the umbilical cord, as stated in *Niddah* 30b (*Binyan Yehoshua*, second explanation).

50. Which flows regularly like spring water (*Ben Avraham*, first explanation).

51. See above, note 44.

52. Which have a consistency similar to wood.

53. Which are shaped like hills.

54. Where the thighbone and the shin connect, just as a pestle fits into a mortar (see *Magen Avos* and *Chullin* 52a).

55. With which one runs like a horse, as it states (*Psalms* 147:10), *Not in the strength of*

בָּאָדָם, זֶה עֲקֵיבָיו שֶׁל אָדָם[56]). הָרִים וּבְקָעוֹת בָּעוֹלָם הָרִים וּבְקָעוֹת
בָּאָדָם, עוֹמֵד דּוֹמֶה לְהַר, נוֹפֵל דּוֹמֶה לִבְקָעָה. הָא לָמַדְתָּ שֶׁכָּל מַה
שֶׁבָּרָא הַקָּדוֹשׁ בָּרוּךְ הוּא בְּעוֹלָמוֹ בָּרָא בָּאָדָם[57]:

בָּאָדָם, זֶה עֲקֵיבָיו שֶׁל אָדָם — He created **the Angel of Death in the world,** and
He created **an angel of death in Man, namely, the soles of a person's feet.**[56]

He — הָרִים וּבְקָעוֹת בָּעוֹלָם הָרִים וּבְקָעוֹת בָּאָדָם, עוֹמֵד דּוֹמֶה לְהַר, נוֹפֵל דּוֹמֶה לִבְקָעָה
created **mountains and valleys in the world,** and He created **mountains and
valleys in Man;** for when **one stands, he resembles a** high **mountain,** and when
he falls he resembles a low valley.

The Baraisa concludes:

הָא לָמַדְתָּ שֶׁכָּל מַה שֶׁבָּרָא הַקָּדוֹשׁ בָּרוּךְ הוּא בְּעוֹלָמוֹ בָּרָא בָּאָדָם — **Thus you learn
that whatever the Holy One, Blessed is He, created in His world, He created
in Man.**[57]

---

*the horse does He desire, and not in the legs
of man does He favor (Ben Avraham).*

56. As stated in the Gemara (*Succah* 53a
with *Rashi*): A person's feet are his guaran-
tors; to the place where he is summoned to
die, they lead him. Thus, his feet play a role
in bringing about his death (*Ben Avraham,
Binyan Yehoshua*).

57. *Binyan Yehoshua* cites *Shevet Mussar*
(Ch. 1), who explains that the purpose of
this teaching is to make known to us that
the universe and all that it contains were
created for the sake of Man. Moreover, the
way a person acts with part of his body has

an impact on the corresponding component
of the universe. If he sins with a particular
part of his body, thereby impairing it spiritually, he damages its counterpart in the larger
world. And if he transgresses all the mitzvos
of the Torah, Heaven forbid, he damages his
entire body, and thereby brings destruction
upon the whole world. Conversely, when a
person improves one part of his body spiritually by using it to fulfill the Will of God, he
brings improvement to its counterpart in
the larger world, and when he improves his
entire body by observing all the mitzvos, he
improves and maintains the entire world.

﴾ פֶּרֶק לב ﴿

א. עֲשָׂרָה דוֹרוֹת מֵאָדָם וְעַד נֹחַ¹. וְכִי מָה הוּצְרַךְ לְבָאֵי עוֹלָם לְכָךְ,
אֶלָּא לְלַמֶּדְךָ שֶׁכָּל הַדּוֹרוֹת הָיוּ מַכְעִיסִין וּבָאִין³ וְלֹא הֵבִיא הַקָּדוֹשׁ
בָּרוּךְ הוּא עֲלֵיהֶם אֶת מֵי הַמַּבּוּל בִּשְׁבִיל צַדִּיקִים וַחֲסִידִים שֶׁהָיוּ בָּהֶם⁴.
וְיֵשׁ אוֹמְרִים: כָּל זְמַן שֶׁהָיָה מְתוּשֶׁלַח חַי לֹא יָרַד מַבּוּל לָעוֹלָם⁵, וּכְשֶׁמֵּת
מְתוּשֶׁלַח עוֹד נִתְלָה לָהֶם שִׁבְעַת יָמִים לְאַחַר מִיתָתוֹ, שֶׁנֶּאֱמַר (בראשית ז, י)

﴾ CHAPTER 32 ﴿

§1 The Baraisa paraphrases *Avos* 5:2 and elaborates on it:

עֲשָׂרָה דוֹרוֹת מֵאָדָם וְעַד נֹחַ — The Torah records that there were **ten generations from Adam until Noah.**[1] וְכִי מָה הוּצְרַךְ לְבָאֵי עוֹלָם לְכָךְ — **Now,
what purpose does it serve for those who have come to the world** to know
that there were ten generations from the creation of man until Noah? Why
did the Torah record this?[2] אֶלָּא לְלַמֶּדְךָ שֶׁכָּל הַדּוֹרוֹת הָיוּ מַכְעִיסִין וּבָאִין — It
is **only to teach you that all the generations** of that time **were continuously
provoking** God,[3] וְלֹא הֵבִיא הַקָּדוֹשׁ בָּרוּךְ הוּא עֲלֵיהֶם אֶת מֵי הַמַּבּוּל בִּשְׁבִיל
צַדִּיקִים וַחֲסִידִים שֶׁהָיוּ בָּהֶם — **but the Holy One, Blessed is He, did not** yet
**bring the Flood-waters upon them because of the merit of the righteous and
pious ones that were among them.**[4] וְיֵשׁ אוֹמְרִים: כָּל זְמַן שֶׁהָיָה מְתוּשֶׁלַח
חַי לֹא יָרַד מַבּוּל לָעוֹלָם — **And some say** that **as long as Methuselah was
alive, the Flood did not descend onto the world.**[5] וּכְשֶׁמֵּת מְתוּשֶׁלַח עוֹד נִתְלָה
לָהֶם שִׁבְעַת יָמִים לְאַחַר מִיתָתוֹ — **And** furthermore, **when Methuselah died, their
punishment was delayed for another seven days after his death,** שֶׁנֶּאֱמַר

---

1. These ten generations, from Adam until
and including Noah, are listed in *Genesis*
Ch. 5. They are: Adam, Seth, Enosh, Ke-
nan, Mahalalel, Jared, Enoch, Methuselah,
Lamech, and Noah.

2. *Mefaresh.*

3. From the earliest time, human beings
angered God, beginning with Cain, who
murdered his brother Abel (*Genesis* 4:8),
and continuing into the generation of Enosh,
which initiated idolatry (ibid. v. 26), and concluding with the generations just before the
Flood, which degenerated into immorality
(*Rashbatz* in *Magen Avos* on *Avos* ad loc.).

4. It is important for us to know how long
it took until God finally punished mankind,
so that we should appreciate how forbearing

He is in the merit of even a minority of
righteous individuals, such as Seth, Enoch,
and Methuselah, who lived in those first ten
generations (*Ahavas Chesed* and *Binyan Yehoshua*). When He did ultimately bring the
Flood, it was because there were no longer
any righteous people left, other than Noah
and his family (*Mefaresh*; see the next note).

5. From a calculation of the years of Methuselah, Lamech, and Noah given in *Genesis*
Ch. 5, it emerges that Methuselah died when
Noah was 600 years old, in the same year
as the Flood (*Rashi* to *Genesis* 7:4; see v.
6 ad loc.). This opinion maintains that Methuselah was the only one whose merit was
powerful enough to stop the Flood. According to both opinions, Noah's merit was not
as great, for he was able to save only himself

"וַיְהִי לְשִׁבְעַת הַיָּמִים". מַה טִיבָן שֶׁל שִׁבְעַת הַיָּמִים הַלָּלוּ[6] אֵלּוּ יְמֵי
אֶבְלוֹ שֶׁל צַדִּיק שֶׁעִיכֵּב אֶת הַפּוּרְעָנוּת[7]. לְפִיכָךְ נֶאֱמַר "וַיְהִי לְשִׁבְעַת
הַיָּמִים". דָּבָר אַחֵר, "וַיְהִי לְשִׁבְעַת הַיָּמִים", מְלַמֵּד שֶׁקָּבַע הַקָּדוֹשׁ
בָּרוּךְ הוּא לָהֶם זְמַן לְאַחַר מֵאָה וְעֶשְׂרִים שָׁנָה שֶׁמָּא יַעֲשׂוּ תְּשׁוּבָה וְלֹא
עָשׂוּ[8]. וּלְכָךְ נֶאֱמַר "וַיְהִי לְשִׁבְעַת הַיָּמִים". דָּבָר אַחֵר, מְלַמֵּד שֶׁשִּׁינָה
עֲלֵיהֶם הַקָּדוֹשׁ בָּרוּךְ הוּא סִידּוּרוֹ שֶׁל עוֹלָם וְהָיְתָה חַמָּה יוֹצֵאת מִמַּעֲרָב

"וַיְהִי לְשִׁבְעַת הַיָּמִים" — as it is stated, *And it came to pass after the seven-day period that the waters of the Flood were upon the earth* (Genesis 7:10). מַה טִיבָן שֶׁל שִׁבְעַת הַיָּמִים הַלָּלוּ — What was the special nature of this seven-day period?[6] אֵלּוּ יְמֵי אֶבְלוֹ שֶׁל צַדִּיק שֶׁעִיכֵּב אֶת הַפּוּרְעָנוּת — These were the seven days of mourning for the righteous Methuselah, which held back the punishment from coming.[7] לְפִיכָךְ נֶאֱמַר "וַיְהִי לְשִׁבְעַת הַיָּמִים" — Therefore it says, *And it came to pass after the seven-day period.*

Other opinions regarding the nature of these seven days:

דָּבָר אַחֵר, "וַיְהִי לְשִׁבְעַת הַיָּמִים" — Another explanation: *And it came to pass after the seven-day period.* What was the significance of these seven days? מְלַמֵּד שֶׁקָּבַע הַקָּדוֹשׁ בָּרוּךְ הוּא לָהֶם זְמַן לְאַחַר מֵאָה וְעֶשְׂרִים שָׁנָה — This teaches that the Holy One, Blessed is He, allotted them another period after the period of one hundred twenty years allotted previously, שֶׁמָּא יַעֲשׂוּ תְּשׁוּבָה וְלֹא עָשׂוּ — in the hope that perhaps they would repent; but they did not do so.[8] וּלְכָךְ נֶאֱמַר "וַיְהִי לְשִׁבְעַת הַיָּמִים" — And that is why it says, *And it came to pass after the seven-day period.*

Yet another explanation of these words:

דָּבָר אַחֵר — Another explanation: מְלַמֵּד שֶׁשִּׁינָה עֲלֵיהֶם הַקָּדוֹשׁ בָּרוּךְ הוּא סִידּוּרוֹ שֶׁל עוֹלָם — This teaches that during those seven days, the Holy One, Blessed is He, altered for them the natural order of the world, וְהָיְתָה חַמָּה יוֹצֵאת מִמַּעֲרָב

---

and his family, but not the rest of the world (see *Magen Avos* here and at the end of this section; see also *Sanhedrin* 108a; but see *Ramban* to Genesis 6:9).

6. Since the verse refers to these seven days as *"the"* seven-day period, with the definite article, the indication is that these were unique days. The Baraisa therefore asks what was special about them (see *Ahavas Chesed*; *Binyan Yehoshua*, citing *Maharsha* to *Sanhedrin* 108b).

7. God held back the Flood for these seven days in the hope that the people would realize that Methuselah's merit no longer

protected them and they would be moved to repent. When the period of mourning concluded and they had not been moved, all hope of repentance was extinguished (*Maharsha* ibid.).

8. Earlier, when God observed the corruption of the world, He said of mankind, *his days shall be a hundred and twenty years* (Genesis 6:3), meaning that He would give that generation 120 years in which to repent. When that period passed without repentance, God allotted to them a final seven-day period in which to repent. The purpose of these additional seven days was

וְשׁוֹקַעַת בְּמִזְרָח, שֶׁמָּא יָבִינוּ וְיִתְיָירְאוּ וְיַעֲשׂוּ תְשׁוּבָה, וְלֹא עָשׂוּ[9]. לְכָךְ נֶאֱמַר ״וַיְהִי לְשִׁבְעַת הַיָּמִים״. דָּבָר אַחֵר, מְלַמֵּד שֶׁהֶאֱרִיךְ לָהֶם הַקָּדוֹשׁ בָּרוּךְ הוּא אֶת שׁוּלְחָנוּ וְהֶרְאָה לָהֶם טוּבוֹ מֵעֵין הָעוֹלָם הַבָּא[10], כְּדֵי שֶׁיְדַקְדְּקוּ הֵן בְּעַצְמָן וְיֹאמְרוּ: אוֹי לָנוּ, טוֹבָה זוּ שֶׁאָבַדְנוּ[11] וְשֶׁשִּׁיחַתְנוּ זַרְעֵנוּ (מִן הָאָרֶץ[12]), שֶׁנֶּאֱמַר (שם ו, יב) ״וַיַּרְא אֱלֹהִים אֶת הָאָרֶץ וְהִנֵּה נִשְׁחָתָה וְגוֹ׳ ״[13]:

וְשׁוֹקַעַת בְּמִזְרָח — and the sun would rise in the west and set in the east. שֶׁמָּא יָבִינוּ וְיִתְיָירְאוּ וְיַעֲשׂוּ תְשׁוּבָה, וְלֹא עָשׂוּ — Perhaps in this way they would contemplate this sudden reversal of nature, and become afraid of what it might portend and repent; but they did not do so.[9] לְכָךְ נֶאֱמַר ״וַיְהִי לְשִׁבְעַת הַיָּמִים״ — Therefore it is stated, *And it came to pass after the seven-day period.*

One final explanation:

דָּבָר אַחֵר, מְלַמֵּד שֶׁהֶאֱרִיךְ לָהֶם הַקָּדוֹשׁ בָּרוּךְ הוּא אֶת שׁוּלְחָנוּ — Another explanation: This teaches that during those seven days, the Holy One, Blessed is He, "set His table" for them וְהֶרְאָה לָהֶם טוּבוֹ מֵעֵין הָעוֹלָם הַבָּא — and showed them His goodness, allowing them to experience a semblance of the World to Come,[10] כְּדֵי שֶׁיְדַקְדְּקוּ הֵן בְּעַצְמָן וְיֹאמְרוּ — in order that they should ponder this sublime goodness and say, אוֹי לָנוּ, טוֹבָה זוּ שֶׁאָבַדְנוּ וְשֶׁשִּׁיחַתְנוּ זַרְעֵנוּ מִן הָאָרֶץ — "Woe to us that we have forfeited this goodness,[11] and that we have destroyed our seed from the earth!"[12] שֶׁנֶּאֱמַר ״וַיַּרְא אֱלֹהִים אֶת הָאָרֶץ וְהִנֵּה נִשְׁחָתָה וְגוֹ׳ ״ — As it says, *And God saw the earth and behold it was corrupted, etc.,* for all flesh had corrupted its way upon the earth (ibid. 6:12).[13]

---

to warn those who had been born during the previous 120 years [and thus had not heard the first warning] (*Binyan Yehoshua*, citing *Rashi* and *Maharsha* to *Sanhedrin* ibid.).

9. By altering the natural order of creation, God conveyed His intention to destroy the world and all that was in it. Had the people taken this message to heart, they would have realized that their doom was imminent, and repented (*Magen Avos*).

10. I.e., He showered them with extraordinary goodness, and granted them pleasure resembling that of the World to Come.

11. By allowing them to experience a semblance of the World to Come, God was hinting to them that they stood to forfeit all that goodness, and that if they did not repent now it would be too late (*Ben Avraham*).

Indeed, the generation of the Flood forfeited their share in the World to Come, as stated in the Mishnah, *Sanhedrin* 10:3.

12. One of the sins that brought on the Flood was that of wasting seed (see *Rashi* to *Niddah* 13a, *Pirkei DeRabbi Eliezer* Ch. 22, and *Bereishis Rabbah* 26 §4). They committed this sin in order to prevent themselves from having children. Now they would bemoan that they had deprived not only themselves of the goodness of the World to Come, but also the children they had refrained from having (*Magen Avos*).

13. The Baraisa cites this verse to prove that the generation of the Flood was guilty of the sin of wasting seed (*Magen Avos*). The phrase הִשְׁחִית ... אֶת דַּרְכּוֹ עַל הָאָרֶץ, *corrupted* (lit., *destroyed*) *its way on the earth*, is understood to mean that they destroyed their

ב. רַבִּי אֶלְעָזָר בֶּן פַּרְטָא אוֹמֵר: הֲרֵי הוּא אוֹמֵר (שם פסוק ג) "לֹא יָדוֹן
רוּחִי בָאָדָם לְעֹלָם"[14]. אָמַר הַקָּדוֹשׁ בָּרוּךְ הוּא: אֵינִי דָן אוֹתָם עַד
שֶׁאֶכְפּוֹל לָהֶם שְׂכָרָן[15], שֶׁנֶּאֱמַר (איוב כא, יג) "יְבַלּוּ בַטּוֹב יְמֵיהֶם (ושנותיהם
בנעימים) וּבְרֶגַע שְׁאוֹל יֵחָתוּ"[16]. **רַבִּי יוֹסֵי הַגְּלִילִי אוֹמֵר:** הֲרֵי הוּא אוֹמֵר
"לֹא יָדוֹן". אָמַר הַקָּדוֹשׁ בָּרוּךְ הוּא: אֵינִי מַשְׁוֶה יֵצֶר הָרַע עַל יֵצֶר הַטּוֹב[17].

---

§2 The Baraisa continues discussing God's conduct toward mankind in the days leading up to the Flood:

רַבִּי אֶלְעָזָר בֶּן פַּרְטָא אוֹמֵר: הֲרֵי הוּא אוֹמֵר "לֹא יָדוֹן רוּחִי בָאָדָם לְעֹלָם" — R' Elazar ben Parta says: [The Torah] says, *And HASHEM said, "My spirit shall not contend evermore concerning Man since he is but flesh; his days shall be a hundred and twenty years"* (ibid. v. 3).[14] **אָמַר הַקָּדוֹשׁ בָּרוּךְ הוּא: אֵינִי דָן אוֹתָם עַד שֶׁאֶכְפּוֹל לָהֶם שְׂכָרָן — The Holy One, Blessed is He, said, "I shall not punish them until I double their reward for them."**[15] **שֶׁנֶּאֱמַר "יְבַלּוּ בַטּוֹב יְמֵיהֶם וּבְרֶגַע שְׁאוֹל יֵחָתוּ" — And this is as it says,** *They spend their days with good fortune, and they descend to the grave in a moment* (Job 21:13).[16]

Another approach to *Genesis 6:3*:

רַבִּי יוֹסֵי הַגְּלִילִי אוֹמֵר: הֲרֵי הוּא אוֹמֵר "לֹא יָדוֹן" — R' Yose HaGlili says: It states, *And HASHEM said, "My spirit shall not contend evermore concerning Man."* **אָמַר הַקָּדוֹשׁ בָּרוּךְ הוּא: אֵינִי מַשְׁוֶה יֵצֶר הָרַע עַל יֵצֶר הַטּוֹב — The Holy One, Blessed is He, said, "I do not equate the evil inclination with the good**

---

seed by emitting it in vain onto the ground (see *Rashi* and *Pirkei DeRabbi Eliezer* ibid., and *Kli Yakar* to the verse).

14. The verse in full reads: וַיֹּאמֶר ה' לֹא יָדוֹן רוּחִי בָאָדָם לְעֹלָם בְּשַׁגַּם הוּא בָשָׂר וְהָיוּ יָמָיו מֵאָה וְעֶשְׂרִים שָׁנָה. This was stated in the period preceding the Flood. According to the plain meaning of the verse, God was saying that He would not deliberate indefinitely whether or not to punish Man, since he refuses to be humbled before God despite his being nothing but flesh; rather, he would be given no longer than 120 years to repent (*Rashi* ad loc.). R' Elazar ben Parta will expound the beginning of the verse differently.

15. This was in order to reward them in this world for any good deeds they had done, so that nothing would be left for them in the World to Come (see *Mefaresh*, who references *Deuteronomy* 7:10, where this concept is indicated). R' Elazar ben Parta thus expounds the *Genesis* verse as follows:

My spirit shall not punish [יָדוֹן] *Man until [I have paid him his share in] eternity* [לְעֹלָם] by doubling his reward in this world (see *Ben Avraham*).

[*Magen Avos*, however, explains that the purpose of the double reward was to induce them to repent. And R' Elazar ben Parta expounds the verse to mean: *My spirit shall not punish Man in all worlds* (i.e., this world and the next) at this time. Rather, I will give them now the reward that should be due them in the World to Come.]

16. [The first word of this verse is written יְבַלּוּ, but is read יְכַלּוּ. Also, many texts have the words וּשְׁנוֹתֵיהֶם בַּנְּעִימִים added to the citation, but those words are erroneously included based on a different but similar verse in *Job* 36:11.]

This passage, in which Job describes the tranquility enjoyed by "the wicked," is taken as a specific reference to the Generation of the Flood; see *Sanhedrin* 108a,

אֵימָתַי, עַד שֶׁלֹּא נֶחְתַּם גְּזַר דִּינָם. אֲבָל נֶחְתַּם גְּזַר דִּינָם שְׁנֵיהֶם שָׁוִין
(בַּעֲבֵירָה)‏:[18]

ג. הוּא הָיָה אוֹמֵר: צַדִּיקִים נוֹטֵל מֵהֶם יֵצֶר הָרַע וְנוֹתֵן לָהֶם יֵצֶר טוֹב,
שֶׁנֶּאֱמַר (תהלים קט, כב) ‏"‏לִבִּי חָלַל בְּקִרְבִּי‏"‏.[19] רְשָׁעִים נוֹטֵל מֵהֶם
יֵצֶר טוֹב וְנוֹתֵן לָהֶם יֵצֶר הָרַע, שֶׁנֶּאֱמַר (שם לו, ב) ‏"‏נְאָם פֶּשַׁע לָרָשָׁע
בְּקֶרֶב לִבִּי אֵין פַּחַד אֱלֹהִים לְנֶגֶד עֵינָיו‏"‏.[20] בֵּינוֹנִים נוֹתְנִין לָהֶם זֶה וָזֶה,

---

inclination.[17] אֵימָתַי, עַד שֶׁלֹּא נֶחְתַּם גְּזַר דִּינָם — However, when is that? As long as [the sinners'] verdict has not yet been sealed. אֲבָל נֶחְתַּם גְּזַר דִּינָם — But once their verdict of guilt has been sealed, both שְׁנֵיהֶם שָׁוִין בַּעֲבֵירָה — inclinations are equal in condemning the sinners for their transgression."[18]

§3 The Baraisa cites another, related, teaching from R' Yose HaGlili:
הוּא הָיָה אוֹמֵר — He used to say: צַדִּיקִים נוֹטֵל מֵהֶם יֵצֶר הָרַע וְנוֹתֵן לָהֶם יֵצֶר טוֹב — With regard to the completely righteous, [God] removes the evil inclination from them and gives them only the good inclination, שֶׁנֶּאֱמַר ‏"‏לִבִּי חָלַל בְּקִרְבִּי‏"‏ — as it says that King David declared, *My heart has died within me* (*Psalms* 109:22).[19] רְשָׁעִים נוֹטֵל מֵהֶם יֵצֶר טוֹב וְנוֹתֵן לָהֶם יֵצֶר הָרַע — With regard to the completely wicked, [God] removes from them the good inclination and gives them only the evil inclination, שֶׁנֶּאֱמַר ‏"‏נְאָם פֶּשַׁע לָרָשָׁע בְּקֶרֶב לִבִּי אֵין פַּחַד אֱלֹהִים לְנֶגֶד עֵינָיו‏"‏ — as it says, *Transgression's word to the wicked is in my heart, that there should be no dread of God before his eyes* (ibid. 36:2).[20] בֵּינוֹנִים נוֹתְנִין לָהֶם זֶה וָזֶה — With regard to average people,

---

Bereishis Rabbah 36 §1, and *Vayikra Rabbah* 5 §1. The passage portrays the bounty and peacefulness that they experienced, which led them to rebel against God. The cited verse tells us that they enjoyed a life replete with good fortune, and when the time for their death arrived, they did not endure prolonged suffering, but died quickly (*Rashi* on the verse). The Baraisa cites this verse to show that God doubled their reward in this world.

17. When God judges a person for his deeds, the evil inclination prosecutes the defendant, and the good inclination argues in his defense. The good inclination is never equated with the evil inclination; that is, he never joins him in accusing the defendant (*Ben Avraham*).

18. Once a guilty verdict has been handed down, the good inclination no longer shows

the sinner any favor, but joins the evil inclination in pronouncing him deserving of punishment. According to R' Yose HaGlili, God was saying: *My spirit shall nevermore judge,* i.e., vanquish, the Attribute of Justice (represented by the evil inclination) before the Attribute of Mercy (represented by the good inclination) *with regard to Man;* for now that the verdict to bring a Flood has been sealed, the Attribute of Mercy shall concur with the Attribute of Justice in condemning Man (ibid., citing R' Yose HaGlili's similar exposition of the verse in *Bereishis Rabbah* 26 §6 and *Matnos Kehunah* ad loc.).

19. *My heart* refers to his evil inclination. Because King David was completely righteous, God neutralized the power of his evil inclination (*Magen Avos*).

20. In this verse King David says: I think *in my heart*: The evil inclination (*transgression*)

אֶת שֶׁבָּא לַיֵּצֶר הָרָע יֵצֶר הָרָע שׁוֹפְטוֹ אֶת שֶׁבָּא לַיֵּצֶר טוֹב יֵצֶר טוֹב
שׁוֹפְטוֹ, שֶׁנֶּאֱמַר (שם קט, לא) "כִּי יַעֲמֹד לִימִין אֶבְיוֹן לְהוֹשִׁיעַ מִשֹּׁפְטֵי
נַפְשׁוֹ"22. רַבִּי שִׁמְעוֹן בֶּן אֶלְעָזָר אוֹמֵר: הֲרֵי הוּא אוֹמֵר "לֹא יָדוֹן". אָמַר
הַקָּדוֹשׁ בָּרוּךְ הוּא: (אֵינִי דָן אוֹתָם עַד שֶׁאֲשַׁלֵּם שָׂכָר לַצַּדִּיקִים. אֵימָתַי,
בָּעוֹלָם הַזֶּה24. אֲבָל בָּעוֹלָם הַבָּא אָמַר הַכָּתוּב (שם קמו, ד) "תֵּצֵא רוּחוֹ יָשֻׁב
לְאַדְמָתוֹ"25. רַבִּי עֲקִיבָא אוֹמֵר: הֲרֵי הוּא אוֹמֵר "לֹא יָדוֹן רוּחִי בָאָדָם
לְעֹלָם". אָמַר הַקָּדוֹשׁ בָּרוּךְ הוּא:) הֵם לֹא דָנוּ בְּעַצְמָן שֶׁהֵן בָּשָׂר וָדָם

אֶת — one — אֶת שֶׁבָּא לַיֵּצֶר הָרָע יֵצֶר הָרָע שׁוֹפְטוֹ [God] gives them both inclinations; one who is drawn toward the evil inclination is ruled by the evil inclination, שֶׁבָּא לַיֵּצֶר טוֹב יֵצֶר טוֹב שׁוֹפְטוֹ — and one who is drawn toward the good inclination is ruled by the good inclination,[21] שֶׁנֶּאֱמַר "כִּי יַעֲמֹד לִימִין אֶבְיוֹן לְהוֹשִׁיעַ מִשֹּׁפְטֵי נַפְשׁוֹ" — as it says, *For [God] stands at the right of the destitute, to save [him] from the rulers of his soul* (ibid. 109:31).[22]

The *Baraisa* resumes citing other expositions of *Genesis* 6:3:

רַבִּי שִׁמְעוֹן בֶּן אֶלְעָזָר אוֹמֵר: הֲרֵי הוּא אוֹמֵר "לֹא יָדוֹן" — R' Shimon ben Elazar says: It states, *And* HASHEM *said, "My spirit* **shall not contend** *evermore concerning Man."* אָמַר הַקָּדוֹשׁ בָּרוּךְ הוּא: אֵינִי דָן אוֹתָם עַד שֶׁאֲשַׁלֵּם שָׂכָר לַצַּדִּיקִים — The Holy One, Blessed is He, said, "I shall not punish them as long as I am still paying reward to the righteous.[23] אֵימָתַי, בָּעוֹלָם הַזֶּה — When will this be? As long as I am rewarding them in this world."[24] אֲבָל בָּעוֹלָם הַבָּא אָמַר הַכָּתוּב "תֵּצֵא רוּחוֹ יָשֻׁב לְאַדְמָתוֹ" — But once the righteous die and are being rewarded in the World to Come, Scripture states concerning them, *When his spirit departs he returns to his earth* (ibid. 146:4).[25]

Another exposition of the verse:

רַבִּי עֲקִיבָא אוֹמֵר: הֲרֵי הוּא אוֹמֵר "לֹא יָדוֹן רוּחִי בָאָדָם לְעֹלָם" — R' Akiva says: It states, *And* HASHEM *said, "My spirit shall not contend evermore concerning Man since he is but flesh."* אָמַר הַקָּדוֹשׁ בָּרוּךְ הוּא: הֵם לֹא דָנוּ בְּעַצְמָן שֶׁהֵן בָּשָׂר וָדָם — The Holy One, blessed is He, said, "[The people] did not contemplate

---

causes the wicked to lose sight of the fear of Heaven completely [for the good inclination no longer has any influence on them] (*Rashi* to *Berachos* 61b, cited by *Binyan Yehoshua*).

21. Elucidation follows *Magen Avos*.

22. The verse speaks of an average person, who is torn between the two rulers of his soul — the good and evil inclinations — and who therefore needs God's support in order for his good inclination to emerge victorious.

23. Elucidation follows *Ben Avraham*.

24. I.e., as long as the righteous of the generation (such as Methuselah) are alive, and I am still rewarding them in this world, I will not punish the rest of mankind, for the merit of the righteous will protect them [as was expounded at the beginning of §1] (*Ben Avraham*).

25. And his merit no longer protects his generation (*Ben Avraham*). Accordingly, the *Genesis* verse means: *My spirit will not*

אֶלָּא הֵגִיסוּ אֶת רוּחָן כְּלַפֵּי מַעְלָה, (איוב כא, יד) "וַיֹּאמְרוּ לָאֵל סוּר
מִמֶּנּוּ".²⁶ רַבִּי מֵאִיר אוֹמֵר: הֲרֵי הוּא אוֹמֵר "לֹא יָדוֹן". אָמַר הַקָּדוֹשׁ בָּרוּךְ
הוּא: אָמְרוּ הַדּוֹר הַהוּא: לֹא יָדוֹן ה', אֵין דַּיָּין בָּעוֹלָם, נָטַשׁ הַמָּקוֹם אֶת
הָעוֹלָם.²⁷ רַבִּי אוֹמֵר: הֲרֵי הוּא אוֹמֵר "לֹא יָדוֹן". אָמַר הַקָּדוֹשׁ בָּרוּךְ הוּא:
הֵם לֹא הוֹשִׁיבוּ סַנְהֶדְרִין בָּאָרֶץ,²⁸ אֲנִי מוֹשִׁיב לָהֶם סַנְהֶדְרִין בַּמָּרוֹם:²⁹

---

that they are mere **flesh and blood**, which would have led them to humble themselves before Me"; אֶלָּא הֵגִיסוּ אֶת רוּחָן כְּלַפֵּי מַעְלָה, "וַיֹּאמְרוּ לָאֵל סוּר מִמֶּנּוּ" — rather, they were haughty toward God on High, as it says, *And they said to God, "Go away from us! We have no desire to know Your ways!"* (*Job* 21:14).[26]

Another exposition of the verse:

רַבִּי מֵאִיר אוֹמֵר: הֲרֵי הוּא אוֹמֵר "לֹא יָדוֹן" — R' Meir says: It states, *And HASHEM said, "My spirit* **shall not contend** *evermore concerning Man."* אָמַר הַקָּדוֹשׁ בָּרוּךְ הוּא אָמְרוּ הַדּוֹר הַהוּא לֹא יָדוֹן ה' — The Holy One, Blessed is He, said, "That generation has said, 'God will not judge us. אֵין דַּיָּין בָּעוֹלָם, נָטַשׁ הַמָּקוֹם אֶת הָעוֹלָם — There is no Judge in the world; the Omnipresent has abandoned the world!' "[27]

A final exposition of the verse:

רַבִּי אוֹמֵר: הֲרֵי הוּא אוֹמֵר "לֹא יָדוֹן" — Rebbi says: It states, *And HASHEM said, "My spirit* **shall not contend** *evermore concerning Man since he is but flesh."* אָמַר הַקָּדוֹשׁ בָּרוּךְ הוּא: הֵם לֹא הוֹשִׁיבוּ סַנְהֶדְרִין בָּאָרֶץ — The Holy One, Blessed is He, said: "They did not convene a court on earth;[28] אֲנִי מוֹשִׁיב לָהֶם סַנְהֶדְרִין בַּמָּרוֹם — therefore, I shall convene a court to judge them on High."[29]

---

punish Man [as long as the righteous are] in the world [לְעֹלָם].

26. This passage refers to the generation of the Flood; see §1 above with note 16. According to this approach, the *Genesis* verse is read as follows: *My spirit that is within Man* [רוּחִי בָאָדָם] *never contemplates* [... לֹא יָדוֹן לְעֹלָם] *that he is but flesh* (see *Magen Avos*).

27. R' Meir reads the verse as follows: *HASHEM said, "[They think that] My spirit will never judge Man"* (*Magen Avos*).

28. I.e., they did not practice justice.

29. The *Genesis* verse is being expounded as though the words יָדוֹן רוּחִי בָאָדָם were repeated, and thus interpreted as follows: *My spirit [that is placed] in Man* (i.e., his soul) *never judges* (i.e., he never carries out justice); *[therefore,] My spirit* (i.e., God's decree) *shall judge Man* (*Yefeh To'ar* and *Eitz Yosef* to *Bereishis Rabbah* 26 §6). This is based on the principle that wherever there is no judgment below, there is judgment above. In other words, if mankind does not perform justice on earth, this incites Heavenly prosecution (Midrash ibid. with *Eitz Yosef*).

❊ פֶּרֶק לג ❊

א. עֲשָׂרָה דוֹרוֹת מִנֹּחַ וְעַד אַבְרָהָם.¹ וְכִי מַה צּוֹרֶךְ לְבָאֵי עוֹלָם בְּכָךְ,²
אֶלָּא לְלַמֵּד שֶׁכָּל אוֹתָן הַדּוֹרוֹת הָיוּ מַכְעִיסִין לְפָנָיו,³ וְלֹא הָיָה אֶחָד
מֵהֶם שֶׁיְהַלֵּךְ בְּדַרְכֵי הַקָּדוֹשׁ בָּרוּךְ הוּא עַד שֶׁבָּא אַבְרָהָם אָבִינוּ וְהָלַךְ
בְּדַרְכֵי הַקָּדוֹשׁ בָּרוּךְ הוּא,⁴ שֶׁנֶּאֱמַר (בראשית כו, ה) "עֵקֶב אֲשֶׁר שָׁמַע

❊ CHAPTER 33 ❊

§1 The Baraisa paraphrases and elaborates the next part of Avos 5:2:

עֲשָׂרָה דוֹרוֹת מִנֹּחַ וְעַד אַבְרָהָם — **The Torah records that there were ten generations from Noah until Abraham.**[1] וְכִי מַה צּוֹרֶךְ לְבָאֵי עוֹלָם בְּכָךְ — **Now,
what purpose does it serve for mankind** to know that there were ten generations from Noah until Abraham? Why did the Torah record this?[2] אֶלָּא לְלַמֵּד
שֶׁכָּל אוֹתָן הַדּוֹרוֹת הָיוּ מַכְעִיסִין לְפָנָיו — It is **only to teach that all those generations were** continuously **provoking [God],**[3] וְלֹא הָיָה אֶחָד מֵהֶם שֶׁיְהַלֵּךְ בְּדַרְכֵי
הַקָּדוֹשׁ בָּרוּךְ הוּא — **and there was not one** person **from among them who would
walk in the ways of the Holy One, Blessed is He,** עַד שֶׁבָּא אַבְרָהָם אָבִינוּ
וְהָלַךְ בְּדַרְכֵי הַקָּדוֹשׁ בָּרוּךְ הוּא — **until our forefather Abraham came** along and
walked in the ways of the Holy One, Blessed is He,[4] שֶׁנֶּאֱמַר "עֵקֶב אֲשֶׁר שָׁמַע

---

1. These ten generations are enumerated in *Genesis* Ch. 11. They are: Shem, Arpach-shad, Shelah, Eber, Peleg, Reu, Serug, Nahor, Terah, Abraham. [The Baraisa (and Mishnah) above (32 §1) listed the first ten generations of mankind as spanning from "the first generation (Adam) to the tenth (Noah)." One would have expected our Baraisa (and Mishnah) to follow the same pattern and list the next ten generations as spanning from "the eleventh generation (Shem) to the twentieth (Abraham)." Nevertheless, it describes this second group of ten generations as spanning from "Noah" until Abraham in order to connect the two lists by starting this one with the last person of the previous one (*Binyan Yehoshua*, from *Tos. Yom Tov* to *Avos* ad loc.; for further discussion, see *Avos HaRosh* [Vol. 2]).]

2. *Mefaresh*.

3. Throughout those ten generations, idolatry was rampant. In addition, among those generations was the Generation of the Dispersion (דּוֹר הַפַּלָגָה) [when virtually the entire

generation united to battle God] (*Rashbatz* in *Magen Avos* to *Avos* ad loc.).

4. There were certainly a number of righteous individuals in the generations between Noah and Abraham, such as Shem and Eber, who were faithful to God and observed the part of the Torah that was given to them, i.e., the Seven Noahide Laws. However, none of them "walked in the ways of the Holy One, Blessed is He" like Abraham, who observed *all* of God's Torah, i.e., the entire Torah that would be given on Mount Sinai, both the Written Torah and the Oral Torah, as the Baraisa teaches next (*Binyan Yehoshua; Avos HaRosh* [Vol. 2]).

Kisei Rachamim, however, explains the Baraisa to mean that there was none who walked in the ways of God *on his own* except for Abraham. Shem and Eber and others, however, received the traditions of God's service from Noah, who in turn received them from Methusaleh. *Ben Avraham* explains the Baraisa to mean that there was none other than Abraham who succeeded in

אַבְרָהָם בְּקֹלִי וְגוֹ' ". (וְכִי תּוֹרָה אַחַת שָׁמַר וַהֲלֹא תּוֹרוֹת הַרְבֵּה שָׁמַר,)
אֶלָּא מְלַמֵּד שֶׁזִּימֵּן הַקָּדוֹשׁ בָּרוּךְ הוּא לְאַבְרָהָם אָבִינוּ שְׁתֵּי כְלָיוֹתָיו
כִּשְׁנֵי חֲכָמִים וְהָיוּ מְבִינוֹת אוֹתוֹ וְיוֹעֲצוֹת אוֹתוֹ וּמְלַמְּדוֹת אוֹתוֹ חָכְמָה
כָּל הַלַּיְלָה, שֶׁנֶּאֱמַר (תהלים טז, ז) "אֲבָרֵךְ אֶת ה' אֲשֶׁר יְעָצָנִי אַף לֵילוֹת
יִסְּרוּנִי כִלְיוֹתָי".6 וְלֹא עוֹד אֶלָּא שֶׁהָיָה אַבְרָהָם אָבִינוּ עוֹשֶׂה צְדָקָה
תְּחִלָּה וְאַחַר כָּךְ מִשְׁפָּט, שֶׁנֶּאֱמַר (בראשית יח, יט) "כִּי יְדַעְתִּיו לְמַעַן אֲשֶׁר
יְצַוֶּה וְגוֹ' ". בִּזְמַן שֶׁשְּׁנֵי בַּעֲלֵי דִינִין בָּאִין לִפְנֵי אַבְרָהָם אָבִינוּ בַּדִּין

אַבְרָהָם בְּקֹלִי וְגוֹ' " — as it is stated, *Because Abraham obeyed My voice, and observed My safeguards, My commandments, My decrees, and My Torahs* (*Genesis* 26:5). וְכִי תּוֹרָה אַחַת שָׁמַר — Now, does this verse say that **he guarded** only *one* **Torah?** וַהֲלֹא תּוֹרוֹת הַרְבֵּה שָׁמַר — No, it says that **he guarded** *multiple* **Torahs** ("*and my Torahs*").[5] This teaches us that Abraham observed everything God commanded, in both the Written Torah and the Oral Torah. But how did Abraham know the Written and Oral Torahs if the Torah had not been given yet? אֶלָּא מְלַמֵּד שֶׁזִּימֵּן הַקָּדוֹשׁ בָּרוּךְ הוּא לְאַבְרָהָם אָבִינוּ שְׁתֵּי כְלָיוֹתָיו כִּשְׁנֵי חֲכָמִים — Rather, [this verse] **teaches** us that the Holy One, Blessed is He, arranged for our forefather Abraham that **his two kidneys** should be like two sages, וְהָיוּ מְבִינוֹת אוֹתוֹ וְיוֹעֲצוֹת אוֹתוֹ וּמְלַמְּדוֹת אוֹתוֹ חָכְמָה כָּל הַלַּיְלָה — and **they gave him** the ability **to understand; they advised him, and they taught him wisdom throughout the night,** שֶׁנֶּאֱמַר "אֲבָרֵךְ אֶת ה' אֲשֶׁר יְעָצָנִי אַף לֵילוֹת יִסְּרוּנִי כִלְיוֹתָי" — as it is stated, *I will bless Hashem Who has advised me, also in the nights my kidneys instruct me* (*Psalms* 16:7).[6]

An additional way in which Abraham proved to be more worthy than others: וְלֹא עוֹד אֶלָּא שֶׁהָיָה אַבְרָהָם אָבִינוּ עוֹשֶׂה צְדָקָה תְּחִלָּה וְאַחַר כָּךְ מִשְׁפָּט — What is more, **our forefather Abraham would perform charity first, and only afterward administer justice,** שֶׁנֶּאֱמַר "כִּי יְדַעְתִּיו לְמַעַן אֲשֶׁר יְצַוֶּה וְגוֹ' " — as it is stated, *For I have loved him, because he commands his children and his household after him that they keep the way of Hashem, doing charity and justice* (*Genesis* 18:19). The Baraisa illustrates Abraham's practice: בִּזְמַן שֶׁשְּׁנֵי בַּעֲלֵי דִינִין בָּאִין לִפְנֵי אַבְרָהָם אָבִינוּ בַּדִּין — **When two litigants would come**

---

causing others to walk in the ways of God.

5. Several commentaries emend this line to read: תּוֹרָה אַחַת אֵין כְּתִיב כָּאן אֶלָּא תּוֹרוֹת הַרְבֵּה, מִנַּיִן לוֹ, "Torah," implying one, is not written here, but rather "Torahs," implying multiple. How did he know [all these Torahs]? (*Tummas Yesharim, Kisei Rachamim, Mesores Ha-Shas*, citing other texts and *Nuschas HaGra*).

6. We can now understand the answer to

the Baraisa's original question: For what purpose did the Torah record the ten generations from Noah until Abraham? It is to allow us to understand why Abraham, more than all the righteous people before him, merited to have so many miracles performed for him by God and merited to become a great nation. It is because even while the generations before him engaged in idolatry

וְאָמַר אֶחָד עַל חֲבֵירוֹ: זֶה חַיָּיב לִי מָנֶה, הָיָה אַבְרָהָם אָבִינוּ מוֹצִיא מָנֶה מִשֶׁלּוֹ וְנוֹתֵן לוֹ, וְאָמַר לָהֶם: סַדְּרוּ דִינְכֶם לְפָנַי, וְסִדְּרוּ דִינָן. כֵּיוָן שֶׁאֶחָד מִתְחַיֵּיב לַחֲבֵירוֹ, אָמַר לְזֶה שֶׁבְּיָדוֹ הַמָּנֶה: תֵּן הַמָּנֶה לַחֲבֵירְךָ. וְאִם לָאו, אָמַר לָהֶם: חִילְקוּ (מַה שֶׁעֲלֵיכֶם) וְהִפָּטְרוּ לְשָׁלוֹם.⁹ אֲבָל דָּוִד הַמֶּלֶךְ לֹא עָשָׂה כֵן, אֶלָּא עוֹשֶׂה מִשְׁפָּט תְּחִלָּה וְאַחַר כָּךְ עוֹשֶׂה צְדָקָה, שֶׁנֶּאֱמַר (שמואל ב ח, טו) "וַיְהִי דָוִד עֹשֶׂה מִשְׁפָּט וּצְדָקָה לְכָל עַמּוֹ". בִּזְמַן שֶׁבַּעֲלֵי דִינִין בָּאִין לְדִין לִפְנֵי דָוִד הַמֶּלֶךְ, אוֹמֵר הָאֶחָד: זֶה נִתְחַיֵּיב לִי מָנֶה,

---

before our forefather Abraham for judgment, וְאָמַר אֶחָד עַל חֲבֵירוֹ: זֶה חַיָּיב — and one of them would say about his fellow, "This man owes me a *maneh*," and the borrower happened to be poor,[7] לִי מָנֶה הָיָה אַבְרָהָם אָבִינוּ מוֹצִיא — our forefather Abraham would take out a *maneh* of his מָנֶה מִשֶׁלּוֹ וְנוֹתֵן לוֹ own and give it to [the defendant], so that even if he would lose the case, he would have the funds to pay. Abraham thus performed charity before justice. **He would then say to them, "Present your case** וְאָמַר לָהֶם: סַדְּרוּ דִינְכֶם לְפָנַי **before me,"** וְסִדְּרוּ דִינָן — and they would present their case. כֵּיוָן שֶׁאֶחָד מִתְחַיֵּיב לַחֲבֵירוֹ — Then, if one of them (i.e., the defendant) was declared liable to pay the money to his fellow, אָמַר לְזֶה שֶׁבְּיָדוֹ הַמָּנֶה: תֵּן הַמָּנֶה לַחֲבֵירְךָ — [Abraham] would say to the defendant, who was holding the *maneh* that he had given him, **"Give the *maneh* you are holding to your fellow."** וְאִם לָאו — If, however, it could not be determined that the defendant was liable, for he had some counterclaim against the plaintiff,[8] אָמַר לָהֶם: חִילְקוּ מַה שֶׁעֲלֵיכֶם וְהִפָּטְרוּ לְשָׁלוֹם — then [Abraham] would say to them, **"Split the claims that are upon you, and part in peace."**[9]

The Baraisa contrasts Abraham's practice with a practice of another great man:

אֲבָל דָּוִד הַמֶּלֶךְ לֹא עָשָׂה כֵן — **King David,** however, **did not conduct himself in this way.** אֶלָּא עוֹשֶׂה מִשְׁפָּט תְּחִלָּה וְאַחַר כָּךְ עוֹשֶׂה צְדָקָה — **Rather, he would administer justice first, and** only **afterward** perform charity, שֶׁנֶּאֱמַר "וַיְהִי — **as it is stated,** *David administered justice* דָוִד עֹשֶׂה מִשְׁפָּט וּצְדָקָה לְכָל עַמּוֹ" *and charity to his entire people* (*II Samuel* 8:15). בִּזְמַן שֶׁבַּעֲלֵי דִינִין בָּאִין לְדִין לִפְנֵי דָוִד הַמֶּלֶךְ — **When two litigants would come before King David for judgment,** אוֹמֵר הָאֶחָד: זֶה נִתְחַיֵּיב לִי מָנֶה — **and one** of them **would say, "This**

---

and rebelliousness against God, he achieved the greatest level of commitment to Hashem and His Torah (see *Mefaresh*).

7. *Ben Avraham.* [A *maneh* is 100 *dinars*, which is a significant amount of money.]

8. *Ben Avraham.*

9. That is, Abraham would advise them to arrive at some compromise and use the funds from the *maneh* he had given to pay the settlement. In that way, the case would be settled without resentment and they would part in peace (see *Ben Avraham*). [See

אָמַר לָהֶם: סַדְּרוּנוּ דִינְכֶם, וְסִדְּרוּ דִינָם. כֵּיוָן שֶׁנִּתְחַיֵּיב אֶחָד מֵהֶם לַחֲבֵירוֹ
מָנֶה, הָיָה מוֹצִיא מָנֶה מִשֶּׁלּוֹ וְנוֹתֵן לוֹ. וְאִם לָאו, אָמַר לָהֶם: (חִלְקוּ מַה
שֶּׁעֲלֵיכֶם וְ)תִּפָּטְרוּ בְּשָׁלוֹם:[10]

ב. עֶשֶׂר נִסְיוֹנוֹת נִתְנַסָּה אַבְרָהָם אָבִינוּ לִפְנֵי הַקָּדוֹשׁ בָּרוּךְ הוּא וּבְכוּלָּן
נִמְצָא שָׁלֵם.[11] וְאֵלּוּ הֵן: שְׁנַיִם (בראשית יב, א) בְּ״לֶךְ לְךָ״.[12] שְׁנַיִם בִּשְׁתֵּי

---

man owes me a *maneh*,"   אָמַר לָהֶם: סַדְּרוּנוּ דִינְכֶם — [King David] would say to them, "Present your case before us,"   וְסִדְּרוּ דִינָם — and they would present their case.   כֵּיוָן שֶׁנִּתְחַיֵּיב אֶחָד מֵהֶם לַחֲבֵירוֹ מָנֶה — Then, if one of them (i.e., the defendant) was declared liable to pay the money to his fellow, הָיָה מוֹצִיא מָנֶה מִשֶּׁלּוֹ וְנוֹתֵן לוֹ — [King David] would take out a *maneh* of his own and give it to him. King David thus performed charity after administering justice.   וְאִם לָאו — And if it could not be determined that the defendant was liable, for he had some counterclaim against the plaintiff, אָמַר לָהֶם: — חִלְקוּ מַה שֶּׁעֲלֵיכֶם וְתִּפָּטְרוּ בְּשָׁלוֹם — then [King David] would say to them, "Use my money, if you need it, to split the claims that are upon you, and part in peace."[10]

§2 This Baraisa paraphrases and elaborates on *Avos* 5:3: עֶשֶׂר נִסְיוֹנוֹת נִתְנַסָּה אַבְרָהָם אָבִינוּ לִפְנֵי הַקָּדוֹשׁ בָּרוּךְ הוּא — Our forefather Abraham was tested with ten trials before the Holy One, Blessed is He, וְאֵלּוּ — וּבְכוּלָּן נִמְצָא שָׁלֵם — and in all of them he was found to be whole.[11] הֵן — These are the ten trials: שְׁנַיִם בְּ״לֶךְ לְךָ״ — (i-ii) Two that are associated with God's instruction to him, "*Go for yourself* from your land ... to the land that I will show you" (*Genesis* 12:1);[12] שְׁנַיִם בִּשְׁתֵּי בָנָיו — (iii-iv) two

---

Binyan Yehoshua, Magen Avos, and *Kisei Rachamim* for alternative explanations.]

10. See *Ben Avraham* and previous note.

According to the *Mefaresh,* the Baraisa is not suggesting that David's approach was inferior to Abraham's; it is merely contrasting the difference of their respective approaches. Abraham's primary attribute was kindness and charity (see *Micah* 7:20), and so he gave precedence to charity. David, on the other hand, was bidden by God to judge the Jewish people (see *Jeremiah* 21:12), and so he placed judgment before charity (*Mefaresh*).

11. Not only did Abraham withstand all the tests God placed before him, he also never asked why he was being subjected to these

difficulties, demonstrating that his love toward God was wholehearted (*Binyan Yehoshua,* from *Rashi* to the Mishnah).

12. The first one was when God said these words to Abraham, commanding him to leave his family and his homeland and go to an unknown land. The second one was when shortly after arriving at the destination that God showed him, he had to pick up once again and move from his new home in Canaan because of a famine that had stricken that area (*Genesis* 12:10). [This test was additionally trying because the famine struck no other land, and it was a challenge for Abraham not to wonder why God had done this to him (*Binyan Yehoshua,* based on *Pirkei DeRabbi Eliezer* Ch. 26).]

בָּנָיו¹³. שְׁנַיִם בִּשְׁתֵּי נָשָׁיו¹⁴. אֶחָד עִם הַמְּלָכִים¹⁵. וְאֶחָד בֵּין הַבְּתָרִים¹⁶. אֶחָד בְּאוּר כַּשְׂדִּים¹⁷. וְאֶחָד בִּבְרִית מִילָה¹⁸ (בֵּין הבתרים). וְכָל כָּךְ לָמָה¹⁹, כְּדֵי שֶׁכְּשֶׁיָּבֹא אַבְרָהָם אָבִינוּ לִיטוֹל שְׂכָרוֹ, שֶׁיִּהְיוּ הַמַּלְאָכִים אוֹמְרִים: יוֹתֵר מִכּוּלָּנוּ יוֹתֵר מִכֹּל שָׁוֶה אַבְרָהָם אָבִינוּ לִיטוֹל שְׂכָרוֹ²⁰, שֶׁנֶּאֱמַר (קהלת ט, ז) "לֵךְ אֱכֹל בְּשִׂמְחָה לַחְמֶךָ וּשְׁתֵה בְּלֶב טוֹב יֵינֶךָ"²¹.

---

with his two sons;[13] שְׁנַיִם בִּשְׁתֵּי נָשָׁיו — (v-vi) **two with his two wives;**[14] וְאֶחָד בֵּין — (vii) **one with the war against the four kings;**[15] הַבְּתָרִים — (viii) **one with the Covenant Between the Parts;**[16] אֶחָד בְּאוּר — (ix) **one in Ur Kasdim,**[17] וְאֶחָד בִּבְרִית מִילָה — (x) **and one with the covenant of circumcision.**[18] וְכָל כָּךְ לָמָה — **And why did God test Abraham so much?**[19] כְּדֵי שֶׁכְּשֶׁיָּבֹא אַבְרָהָם אָבִינוּ לִיטוֹל שְׂכָרוֹ — **So that when our forefather Abraham would come to take his reward** for all his loyalty to God, שֶׁיִּהְיוּ הַמַּלְאָכִים אוֹמְרִים — **the angels would say,** יוֹתֵר מִכּוּלָּנוּ יוֹתֵר מִכֹּל שָׁוֶה אַבְרָהָם אָבִינוּ לִיטוֹל שְׂכָרוֹ — **"Indeed, more than any of us or anyone else, Abraham, our forefather, is worthy of accepting his reward."**[20] שֶׁנֶּאֱמַר "לֵךְ אֱכֹל בְּשִׂמְחָה לַחְמֶךָ וּשְׁתֵה בְּלֶב טוֹב יֵינֶךָ" — **Abraham** would then be able to enjoy his reward without any objections, **as it is stated, Go, eat your bread with joy**

---

13. One when God had him send away his son Yishmael [*Genesis* 21:10-11], and one when God instructed him to sacrifice his son Isaac [ibid. 22:2] (*Binyan Yehoshua*).

14. One when his wife Sarah was kidnaped by Pharaoh [*Genesis* 12:14-15] and subsequently by Abimelech [ibid. 20:2]; and one when God instructed him to send away his wife Hagar [ibid. 21:10-12] (*Binyan Yehoshua; Magen Avos*).

15. The kings captured Abraham's nephew Lot, and Abraham was forced to go to war to rescue him [*Genesis* Ch. 14] (*Magen Avos*).

16. God informed him at this time that his children would be in exile for many years and oppressed by other nations [*Genesis* 15:13] (*Magen Avos, Mefaresh*).

17. This refers to where Nimrod threw the young Abraham into a fiery furnace (from which he was miraculously saved) for believing in God rather than in Nimrod's idols. It is alluded to in the words, אוּר כַּשְׂדִּים, since אוּר means *fire,* and כַּשְׂדִּים refers to the [land of the] Chaldeans, where this incident took

place; see *Genesis* 11:28 with *Rashi* and *Ramban.*

18. This was a test for Abraham, since he was already a man of advanced age — 99 years old — when God commanded him to circumcise himself. (see *Binyan Yehoshua*).

Note that aside from the Baraisa's list here, there are several other opinions as to exactly which experiences in Abraham's life are counted in the ten trials. See commentaries to the Mishnah; see also *Meorei Ohr, Miluim* §36 for a summary of the different opinions.

19. Since, after all, God knew from the outset that Abraham would pass all of the tests (*Kisei Rachamim*).

20. [Obviously, the angels do not call him "Abraham, our forefather." It is the Baraisa that is citing what is said about Abraham, *our* forefather.] God would perform many miracles for Abraham through angels. Had the tests not demonstrated how truly worthy Abraham was, the angels might have objected that it was not fitting for them to serve a mere mortal. Now, however, they understood how he was more exalted

כְּנֶגֶד עֶשֶׂר נִסְיוֹנוֹת שֶׁנִּתְנַסָּה אַבְרָהָם אָבִינוּ וּבְכוּלָן נִמְצָא שָׁלֵם, וּכְנֶגְדָן
עָשָׂה הַקָּדוֹשׁ בָּרוּךְ הוּא עֲשָׂרָה נִסִּים לְבָנָיו בְּמִצְרַיִם‎22‎, כְּנֶגְדָן הֵבִיא עֶשֶׂר
מַכּוֹת‎23‎, כְּנֶגְדָן נַעֲשׂוּ לְיִשְׂרָאֵל עֲשָׂרָה נִסִּים עַל הַיָּם‎24‎, כְּנֶגְדָן הֵבִיא עֶשֶׂר
מַכּוֹת עַל הַמִּצְרִיִּים בַּיָּם. ‎25‎מִצְרִיִּים הִרְעִימוּ עֲלֵיהֶם בְּקוֹלָם, אַף הַקָּדוֹשׁ

---

and drink your wine with a glad heart, for God has already approved your deeds (*Ecclesiastes* 9:7).[21]

The Baraisa (see also *Avos* 5:4) now draws a connection between Abraham's successful ten trials and other sets of tens — miracles that occurred at the time of the Exodus:

כְּנֶגֶד עֶשֶׂר נִסְיוֹנוֹת שֶׁנִּתְנַסָּה אַבְרָהָם אָבִינוּ וּבְכוּלָן נִמְצָא שָׁלֵם — Corresponding to the ten trials with which our forefather Abraham was tested and in all of which he was found to be whole, וּכְנֶגְדָן עָשָׂה הַקָּדוֹשׁ בָּרוּךְ הוּא עֲשָׂרָה — corresponding to them the Holy One, Blessed is He, נִסִּים לְבָנָיו בְּמִצְרַיִם — performed ten miracles for his descendants in Egypt,[22] כְּנֶגְדָן הֵבִיא עֶשֶׂר מַכּוֹת — corresponding to them He brought Ten Plagues upon the Egyptians in Egypt.[23] כְּנֶגְדָן נַעֲשׂוּ לְיִשְׂרָאֵל עֲשָׂרָה נִסִּים עַל הַיָּם — And also corresponding to [those ten trials], ten miracles were performed for the people of Israel at the Sea,[24] כְּנֶגְדָן הֵבִיא עֶשֶׂר מַכּוֹת עַל הַמִּצְרִיִּים בַּיָּם — corresponding to them He brought ten blows upon the Egyptians at the Sea, blows that the Baraisa will now enumerate.

The Baraisa enumerates these blows and how each was retribution, measure for measure, for something the Egyptians did to the Israelites they were attacking at the Sea:[25]

מִצְרִיִּים הִרְעִימוּ עֲלֵיהֶם בְּקוֹלָם — The Egyptians thundered with their voices against [the Israelites] as they bore down on them at the Sea, אַף הַקָּדוֹשׁ

---

than they (see *Binyan Yehoshua*, citing *Mefaresh*).

21. This verse is expounded elsewhere as God's words to Abraham following the *Akeidah*, assuring him that his actions were deemed worthy in God's eyes [*Bamidbar Rabbah* 17 §2, and *Koheles Rabbah* 9 §2b] (*Ahavas Chesed*; see also *Magen Avos* and *Ben Avraham*). He would now be able to receive his reward — "eat his bread and drink his wine" — with joy and a glad heart.

22. By saving them from any of the negative effects of the Ten Plagues that He brought upon the Egyptians who lived in close proximity to them, which the Baraisa mentions

next (*Binyan Yehoshua*, citing *Rav* to the Mishnah).

23. These are the famous "Ten Plagues" that He brought upon the Egyptians in Egypt to repay them for the suffering that they inflicted on Abraham's descendants.

24. Enumerated below in the Baraisa (at note 36 ff.).

25. The specifics of what the Egyptians did to the Israelites at the Sea are not explicit in the verse; the Baraisa infers them from the retribution meted out to the Egyptians, which must have been "measure for measure" for some particular thing they did to the Israelites (*Binyan Yehoshua*).

בָּרוּךְ הוּא הָרְעִים עֲלֵיהֶם בְּקוֹל עַל הַיָּם, שֶׁנֶּאֱמַר (איוב לז, ה) "יַרְעֵם אֵל
בְּקוֹלוֹ נִפְלָאוֹת". מִצְרִיִּים בָּאוּ עַל הַיָּם בְּקֶשֶׁת וּבַחִצִּים, וְהַקָּדוֹשׁ בָּרוּךְ הוּא
נִגְלָה עֲלֵיהֶם בְּקֶשֶׁת וּבַחִצִּים, שֶׁנֶּאֱמַר (חבקוק ג, ט) "עֶרְיָה תֵעוֹר קַשְׁתֶּךָ"²⁷,
וְאוֹמֵר (תהלים יח, טו) "וַיִּשְׁלַח °חִצָּיו וַיְפִיצֵם"²⁸. מִצְרִיִּים בָּאוּ עַל הַיָּם
בַּחֲרָבוֹת, אַף הַקָּדוֹשׁ בָּרוּךְ הוּא בָּא עֲלֵיהֶם בַּחֲרָבוֹת (וּרְמָחִים), שֶׁנֶּאֱמַר
(שם) "וַיִּשְׁלַח °חִצָּיו וַיְפִיצֵם", (שמואל ב כב, טו) "בָּרָק וַיָּהֹם"³⁰. וְאֵין בָּרָק

בָּרוּךְ הוּא הָרְעִים עֲלֵיהֶם בְּקוֹל עַל הַיָּם — so the Holy One, Blessed is He, also thundered with His voice upon the Egyptians at the Sea, יַרְעֵם" שֶׁנֶּאֱמַר אֵל בְּקוֹלוֹ נִפְלָאוֹת" — as it is stated, *God thunders marvelously with His voice* (Job 37:5), referring to the Splitting of the Sea.[26] מִצְרִיִּים בָּאוּ עַל הַיָּם בְּקֶשֶׁת וּבַחִצִּים — The Egyptians came upon the people of Israel at the Sea with bows and arrows, וְהַקָּדוֹשׁ בָּרוּךְ הוּא נִגְלָה עֲלֵיהֶם בְּקֶשֶׁת וּבַחִצִּים — so the Holy One, Blessed is He, also revealed Himself upon [the Egyptians] at the Sea with a bow and arrows, שֶׁנֶּאֱמַר "עֶרְיָה תֵעוֹר קַשְׁתֶּךָ" — as it is stated, *Your bow bared itself* (Habakkuk 3:9),[27] וְאוֹמֵר "וַיִּשְׁלַח חִצִּים וַיְפִיצֵם" — and it also says, *He sent forth arrows and scattered them* (II Samuel 22:15).[28] מִצְרִיִּים בָּאוּ עַל הַיָּם בַּחֲרָבוֹת — The Egyptians came upon the people of Israel at the Sea with swords and lances,[29] אַף הַקָּדוֹשׁ בָּרוּךְ הוּא בָּא עֲלֵיהֶם בַּחֲרָבוֹת וּרְמָחִים — so the Holy One, Blessed is He, also revealed Himself upon [the Egyptians] at the Sea with swords and lances, שֶׁנֶּאֱמַר "וַיִּשְׁלַח חִצִּים וַיְפִיצֵם בָּרָק וַיָּהֹם" — as it is stated, *He sent forth arrows and scattered them; a "barak," and He terrified them* (ibid.).[30] וְאֵין בָּרָק אֶלָּא חֶרֶב — The word *barak* [בָּרָק] in this verse means nothing

---

26. *Ahavas Chesed.*

27. The preceding *Habakkuk* verse (v. 8) states, *Was HASHEM angry with the rivers; was Your wrath with the rivers, or your fury against the Sea? Rather, You rode upon your horses, Your chariots were [our] salvation* — which the Baraisa understands as a clear reference to the occasion of the Splitting of the Sea (God split the waters as if He were a savior riding to save Israel). Thus, the Baraisa expounds other verses in that passage as referring to the same event (*Ahavas Chesed, Ben Avraham*; see also *Targum* and *Radak* there, v. 8 ff.).

28. [Emendation follows *Tummas Yesharim.*] This section of the chapter is speaking about the Splitting of the Sea (see *Rashi* ad loc.,

vv. 10-16; see also *Ahavas Chesed*). "Bow" and "arrows" are counted as two retributions, since a bow may at times be used as a weapon by itself. This is indicated in the two verses that the Baraisa cites, one speaking of a bow and the other speaking of arrows (*Magen Avos* ד"ה ועתה הרי לך י' ניסים).

29. [We have added the words "and lances" in accordance with *Ben Avraham*, who adds the word וּרְמָחִים to the Hebrew text. This parallels the corresponding retribution "swords and lances" stated next in the Baraisa, both of which are counted separately in the ten blows that were brought upon the Egyptians at the Sea (see below, note 35).]

30. [Emendation follows *Tummas Yesharim.*]

אֶלָּא חֶרֶב[31], שֶׁנֶּאֱמַר (יחזקאל כא, יד-טו) "חֶרֶב חֶרֶב הוּחַדָּה וְגַם מְרוּטָה
לְמַעַן טְבֹחַ טֶבַח הוּחַדָּה לְמַעַן הֱיֵה לָהּ בָּרָק מֹרָטָה". מִצְרִיִּים נִתְגָּאוּ
בְּמָגֵן וְצִנָּה, וְהַקָּדוֹשׁ בָּרוּךְ הוּא עָשָׂה כְּמוֹ כֵן, שֶׁנֶּאֱמַר (תהלים לה, ב)
"הַחֲזֵק מָגֵן וְצִנָּה וְקוּמָה בְּעֶזְרָתִי"[32]. מִצְרִיִּים בָּאוּ בַּחֲנִית, וְכָךְ הַקָּדוֹשׁ
בָּרוּךְ הוּא, שֶׁנֶּאֱמַר (חבקוק ג, יא) "לְנֹגַהּ בְּרַק חֲנִיתֶךָ"[33]. מִצְרִיִּים בָּאוּ
בַּאֲבָנִים בִּקְלָעִים, וְהַקָּדוֹשׁ בָּרוּךְ הוּא נִתְגָּאָה עֲלֵיהֶם בְּאַבְנֵי אֶלְגָּבִישׁ[34],
שֶׁנֶּאֱמַר (תהלים יח, יג) "(מִנֹּגַהּ נֶגְדּוֹ) עָבָיו עָבְרוּ בָּרָד וְגַחֲלֵי אֵשׁ"[35].

שֶׁנֶּאֱמַר "חֶרֶב חֶרֶב הוּחַדָּה וְגַם מְרוּטָה לְמַעַן טְבֹחַ טֶבַח הוּחַדָּה — but the sword,[31] as it is stated, *A sword, a sword has been sharp-ened and even polished. That it may make a slaughter has it been polished, and that it may have a flash* [בָּרָק] *has it been polished* (Ezekiel 21:14-15). מִצְרִיִּים נִתְגָּאוּ בְּמָגֵן וְצִנָּה — The Egyptians exalted themselves over the Isra-elites with the **shields and bucklers** that they held while coming to attack, וְהַקָּדוֹשׁ בָּרוּךְ הוּא עָשָׂה כְּמוֹ כֵן — so the Holy One, Blessed is He, did the same against the Egyptians, שֶׁנֶּאֱמַר "הַחֲזֵק מָגֵן וְצִנָּה וְקוּמָה בְּעֶזְרָתִי" — as it is stated, *Take hold of shield and buckler, and rise up in my defense* (Psalms 35:2).[32] מִצְרִיִּים בָּאוּ בַּחֲנִית — The Egyptians came against the people of Israel **with spears,** וְכָךְ הַקָּדוֹשׁ בָּרוּךְ הוּא — and so did the Holy One, Blessed is He, against the Egyptians, שֶׁנֶּאֱמַר "לְנֹגַהּ בְּרַק חֲנִיתֶךָ" — as it is stated, *[Israel] would travel ... by the lightning flash of Your spear* (Habak-kuk 3:11).[33] מִצְרִיִּים בָּאוּ בַּאֲבָנִים בִּקְלָעִים — The Egyptians came against the people of Israel **with stones and slingshots,** וְהַקָּדוֹשׁ בָּרוּךְ הוּא נִתְגָּאָה עֲלֵיהֶם בְּאַבְנֵי אֶלְגָּבִישׁ — and so the Holy One, Blessed is He, exalted Himself over them with large, glistening and fiery hailstones,[34] שֶׁנֶּאֱמַר "מִנֹּגַהּ נֶגְדּוֹ עָבָיו עָבְרוּ בָּרָד וְגַחֲלֵי אֵשׁ" — as it is stated, *From out of the brilliance that is before Him, His clouds passed over, with hail and fiery coals* (Psalms 18:13).[35]

---

31. The word בָּרָק literally refers to a flash of lightning. The Baraisa, however, is expound-ing it as referring to (the flash of) a sword.

[For possible explanation as to how the Baraisa derived that God struck the Egyp-tians with lances, see *Avos HaRosh* (Vol. 2).]

32. The Egyptians came to attack the Isra-elites while relying on their shields to protect them. God showed them that the Israelites, too, had the same form of protection from Above (*Magen Avos*, third approach).

33. See note 27 above.

34. See *Rashi* on *Ezekiel* 13:11. The Gemara

in *Berachos* (54b) explains that this refers to the type of hailstones that rained down on Egypt during the Plague of Hail — flaming hailstones (see *Exodus* 9:24 with *Rashi*).

35. [This chapter of *Psalms* parallels *II Samu-el* Ch. 22. This part of the chapter speaks of the Splitting of the Sea.] Thus, the ten retri-butions with which God punished the Egyp-tians at the Sea were the "weapons" that He used against them, namely: (i) a thundering voice, (ii) a bow, (iii) arrows, (iv) swords, (v) lances, (vi) shields, (vii) bucklers, (viii) spears, (ix) hailstones, and (x) fiery coals

בְּשָׁעָה שֶׁעָמְדוּ אֲבוֹתֵינוּ עַל הַיָּם, אָמַר לָהֶם מֹשֶׁה: קוּמוּ עִבְרוּ. אָמְרוּ לוֹ: לֹא נַעֲבֹר עַד שֶׁנִּרְאֶה הַיָּם נְקָבִים נְקָבִים.[37] נָטַל מֹשֶׁה מַטֵּהוּ וְהִכָּה עַל הַיָּם וְנַעֲשָׂה הַיָּם נְקָבִים נְקָבִים, שֶׁנֶּאֱמַר (חבקוק ג, יד) "נָקַבְתָּ בְמַטָּיו רֹאשׁ פְּרָזָיו".[38] אָמַר לָהֶם מֹשֶׁה: קוּמוּ עִבְרוּ. אָמְרוּ לוֹ: לֹא נַעֲבֹר עַד שֶׁנַּעֲשָׂה הַיָּם בִּקְעָה לְפָנֵינוּ.[39] הִכָּה מֹשֶׁה עַל הַיָּם וְנַעֲשָׂה בִּקְעָה לִפְנֵיהֶם, שֶׁנֶּאֱמַר (תהלים עח, יג) "בָּקַע יָם וַיַּעֲבִירֵם",[40] וְנֶאֱמַר (ישעיה סג, יד) "כַּבְּהֵמָה בַּבִּקְעָה

The Baraisa mentioned above that God performed ten miracles for the people of Israel at the Sea. The Baraisa now identifies these miracles, and shows how each was performed in response to a request made by the people:[36] בְּשָׁעָה שֶׁעָמְדוּ אֲבוֹתֵינוּ עַל הַיָּם — At the time that our forefathers stood at the shore of the Sea, אָמַר לָהֶם מֹשֶׁה: קוּמוּ עִבְרוּ — Moses said to them, "Arise and cross the Sea!" אָמְרוּ לוֹ: לֹא נַעֲבֹר עַד שֶׁנִּרְאֶה הַיָּם נְקָבִים נְקָבִים — They replied, "We shall not cross until the Sea is seen to be full of holes!"[37] נָטַל מֹשֶׁה מַטֵּהוּ וְהִכָּה עַל הַיָּם וְנַעֲשָׂה הַיָּם נְקָבִים נְקָבִים — So Moses took his staff and hit the Sea, and the Sea indeed became full of holes, שֶׁנֶּאֱמַר "נָקַבְתָּ בְמַטָּיו רֹאשׁ פְּרָזָיו" — as it is stated, With his own staffs You pierced the head of his outspread troops (Habakkuk 3:14).[38] אָמַר לָהֶם מֹשֶׁה: קוּמוּ עִבְרוּ — Once again Moses said to them, "Arise and cross the Sea!" אָמְרוּ לוֹ: לֹא נַעֲבֹר — They replied, "We shall not cross until עַד שֶׁנַּעֲשָׂה הַיָּם בִּקְעָה לְפָנֵינוּ — the bed of the Sea becomes a plain [בִּקְעָה] before us!"[39] הִכָּה מֹשֶׁה עַל הַיָּם וְנַעֲשָׂה בִּקְעָה לִפְנֵיהֶם — So Moses hit the bed of the Sea once more and it became a plain before them, שֶׁנֶּאֱמַר "בָּקַע יָם וַיַּעֲבִירֵם" — as it is stated, He split [בָּקַע] the sea and brought them across (Psalms 78:13),[40] וְנֶאֱמַר "כַּבְּהֵמָה בַּבִּקְעָה

(Magen Avos, Ahavas Chesed, Avos HaRosh [Vol. 2]).

36. The Children of Israel had a tradition that the miracle of the Splitting of the Sea would take place in the merit of Abraham (see Mechilta to Exodus 14:15). For this reason, they realized on their own that there would be ten miracles performed at the time of the Splitting of the Sea, corresponding to the ten trials that Abraham passed. This is why they unabashedly requested these miracles, as the Baraisa goes on to describe (Binyan Yehoshua, citing Mefaresh).

37. That is, tunnels that stretch across the seabed, with walls of water on the side and a dome of water on top (Binyan Yehoshua, based on Rambam to the Mishnah here; see also Midrash Tanchuma, Beshalach §10).

Walking through this crystalline edifice of water, designed specially for the Jews' passage, would be a source of glory for the Children of Israel (see Tos. Yom Tov to the Mishnah here).

38. [See note 27.] The Baraisa interprets the verse as saying that God used Moses' staff to make holes ("pierce") in the ["troops" of] water (see Magen Avos; see also Targum to the verse).

39. That is, the ground that we are to walk on through the Sea should be like a smooth plain (Binyan Yehoshua), and full of grass and plants that both the people and the animals can eat (see Avos DeRabbi Nassan, Nusach 2, Ch. 38; Avos HaRosh [Vol. 2], citing Shocher Tov 114 [§7]; see also Magen Avos).

40. Interpreting the words בָּקַע יָם as "He

תֵּרֵד"⁴¹. אָמַר לָהֶם מֹשֶׁה: קוּמוּ עִבְרוּ. אָמְרוּ: לֹא נַעֲבוֹר עַד שֶׁנַּעֲשֶׂה
לְפָנֵינוּ גְזָרִים גְזָרִים⁴², שֶׁנֶּאֱמַר (תהלים קלו, יג) "לְגֹזֵר יַם סוּף לִגְזָרִים". אָמַר
לָהֶם מֹשֶׁה: קוּמוּ עִבְרוּ. אָמְרוּ: לֹא נַעֲבוֹר עַד שֶׁנַּעֲשֶׂה לְפָנֵינוּ חוֹמֶר⁴³. נָטַל
מֹשֶׁה הַמַּטֶּה וְהִכָּה הַיָּם וְנַעֲשָׂה לִפְנֵיהֶם טִיט, שֶׁנֶּאֱמַר (חבקוק ג, טו) "דָּרַכְתָּ
בַיָּם סוּסֶיךָ חֹמֶר מַיִם רַבִּים"⁴⁴. אָמַר לָהֶם מֹשֶׁה: קוּמוּ עִבְרוּ. אָמְרוּ: לֹא
נַעֲבוֹר עַד שֶׁיֵּעָשֶׂה לְפָנֵינוּ מִדְבָּר⁴⁵. נָטַל מֹשֶׁה אֶת הַמַּטֶּה וְהִכָּה עַל הַיָּם,

---

תֵּרֵד" — and it is further stated, *As an animal descends into a plain* [בְּקְעָה],
so the spirit of HASHEM led them (Isaiah 63:14).[41] אָמַר לָהֶם מֹשֶׁה: קוּמוּ עִבְרוּ
— Once again Moses said to them, "Arise and cross the Sea!" אָמְרוּ: לֹא
נַעֲבוֹר עַד שֶׁנַּעֲשֶׂה לְפָנֵינוּ גְזָרִים גְזָרִים — They replied, "We shall not cross until
[the Sea] turns into many divided parts before us!"[42] And so it was, שֶׁנֶּאֱמַר
"לְגֹזֵר יַם סוּף לִגְזָרִים" — as it is stated, *To Him Who divided the Sea of Reeds
into parts* (Psalms 136:13). אָמַר לָהֶם מֹשֶׁה: קוּמוּ עִבְרוּ — Once again Moses
said to them, "Arise and cross the Sea!" אָמְרוּ: לֹא נַעֲבוֹר עַד שֶׁנַּעֲשֶׂה לְפָנֵינוּ
חוֹמֶר — They replied, "We shall not cross until [the Sea] becomes like a wet
mortar before us!"[43] נָטַל מֹשֶׁה הַמַּטֶּה וְהִכָּה הַיָּם וְנַעֲשָׂה לִפְנֵיהֶם טִיט — So
Moses took the staff and hit the bed of the Sea, and it became wet clay
before them, שֶׁנֶּאֱמַר "דָּרַכְתָּ בַיָּם סוּסֶיךָ חֹמֶר מַיִם רַבִּים" — as it is stated,
You made Your horses tread in the sea, [in] the mortar of abundant water
(Habakkuk 3:15).[44] אָמַר לָהֶם מֹשֶׁה: קוּמוּ עִבְרוּ — Once again Moses said to
them, "Arise and cross the Sea!" אָמְרוּ: לֹא נַעֲבוֹר עַד שֶׁיֵּעָשֶׂה לְפָנֵינוּ מִדְבָּר —
They replied, "We shall not cross until it becomes like a desert before us!"[45]
נָטַל מֹשֶׁה אֶת הַמַּטֶּה וְהִכָּה עַל הַיָּם — So Moses took the staff and hit the bed of

---

made the sea into a plain" [בְּקְעָה] (*Avos Ha-Rosh* [Vol. 2]).

41. This is a reference to God leading the Israelites through the Sea, as indicated in the preceding verses (vv. 12-13), *Who split the Sea before them to make Himself eternal renown? Who led them through the depths as a horse in the desert*, etc. (*Ben Avraham*; see also *Binyan Yehoshua*).

42. Meaning, a separate path for each one of the Tribes of Israel to pass though (*Binyan Yehoshua*).

43. They wanted the seabed behind them to be muddy so that the Egyptians would get stuck in it while chasing them (see *Rashbatz* in *Magen Avos* to *Avos* 5:4; see also *Magen Avos* here). For themselves, however, they

later requested that it be dry (see below). Accordingly, when they said "before *us*," they meant before our eyes, not in the path in front of us. (For an alternative explanation, see *Ahavas Chesed*; *Avos HaRosh* [Vol. 2].)

44. [See note 27.] Accordingly, the term "Your horses" means the Egyptians' horses over which God wielded full control (*Rashbatz* in *Magen Avos* ibid.; see also *R' Yonah* to that Mishnah).

45. Presumably, this means that the seabed should be dry like a desert and easy to walk on. However, it is unclear how this is different from their subsequent request that the seabed should become "dry land" [יַבָּשָׁה] (see *Avos HaRosh* [Vol. 2]). See further, note 56 below.

שֶׁנֶּאֱמַר (תהלים קו, ט) "וַיּוֹלִיכֵם בַּתְּהֹמוֹת כַּמִּדְבָּר". אָמַר לָהֶם מֹשֶׁה: קוּמוּ עִבְרוּ. אָמְרוּ: לֹא נַעֲבוֹר עַד שֶׁיֵּעָשֶׂה לְפָנֵינוּ פֵּירוּרִים פֵּירוּרִים.[46] נָטַל מֹשֶׁה אֶת הַמַּטֶּה וְהִכָּה עַל הַיָּם, שֶׁנֶּאֱמַר (שם עד, יג) "אַתָּה פוֹרַרְתָּ בְעָזְּךָ יָם". אָמַר לָהֶם מֹשֶׁה: קוּמוּ עִבְרוּ. אָמְרוּ: לֹא נַעֲבוֹר עַד שֶׁיֵּעָשֶׂה לְפָנֵינוּ סְלָעִים סְלָעִים.[47] נָטַל הַמַּטֶּה וְהִכָּה עַל הַיָּם, שֶׁנֶּאֱמַר (שם) "שִׁבַּרְתָּ רָאשֵׁי תַנִּינִים עַל הַמָּיִם".[48] הֱוֵי אוֹמֵר רָאשֵׁי תַנִּינִים אֵין מִשְׁתַּבְּרִין אֶלָּא עַל הַסְּלָעִים. אָמַר לָהֶם מֹשֶׁה: קוּמוּ עִבְרוּ. אָמְרוּ: לֹא נַעֲבוֹר עַד שֶׁיֵּעָשֶׂה לָנוּ יַבָּשָׁה.[49]

---

as — שֶׁנֶּאֱמַר "וַיּוֹלִיכֵם בַּתְּהֹמוֹת כַּמִּדְבָּר" the Sea, and it became like a desert, it is stated, *And He led them through the depths as through a desert* (Psalms 106:9). אָמַר לָהֶם מֹשֶׁה: קוּמוּ עִבְרוּ — Once again Moses said to them, "Arise and cross the Sea!" אָמְרוּ: לֹא נַעֲבוֹר עַד שֶׁיֵּעָשֶׂה לְפָנֵינוּ פֵּירוּרִים פֵּירוּרִים — They replied, "We shall not cross until [the Sea] becomes separated into fragments before us."[46] נָטַל מֹשֶׁה אֶת הַמַּטֶּה וְהִכָּה עַל הַיָּם — So Moses took the staff and hit the Sea, and it became separated into fragments, שֶׁנֶּאֱמַר "אַתָּה פוֹרַרְתָּ בְעָזְּךָ יָם" — as it is stated, *You fragmented the sea with Your might* (ibid. 74:13). אָמַר לָהֶם מֹשֶׁה: קוּמוּ עִבְרוּ — Once again Moses said to them, "Arise and cross the Sea!" אָמְרוּ: לֹא נַעֲבוֹר עַד שֶׁיֵּעָשֶׂה לְפָנֵינוּ סְלָעִים סְלָעִים — They replied, "We shall not cross until [the Sea] becomes like rocks!"[47] נָטַל הַמַּטֶּה וְהִכָּה עַל הַיָּם — So Moses took the staff and hit the Sea, and it became like rocks, שֶׁנֶּאֱמַר "שִׁבַּרְתָּ רָאשֵׁי תַנִּינִים עַל הַמָּיִם" — as it is stated, *You smashed the heads of sea serpents* [the Egyptians] *upon the water* (ibid.).[48] הֱוֵי אוֹמֵר רָאשֵׁי תַנִּינִים אֵין מִשְׁתַּבְּרִין אֶלָּא עַל הַסְּלָעִים — Say that this is indeed a proof, for the heads of sea serpents do not get "smashed" unless they are thrown against rocks. אָמַר לָהֶם מֹשֶׁה: קוּמוּ עִבְרוּ — Once again Moses said to them, "Arise and cross the Sea!" אָמְרוּ: לֹא נַעֲבוֹר עַד שֶׁיֵּעָשֶׂה לָנוּ יַבָּשָׁה — They replied, "We shall not cross until it becomes dry land for us!"[49]

---

46. They requested that the water — which had formed into walls between the paths, and domes over their heads (see above) — take the form of separated bricks stacked on top of one another rather than one large block (*Binyan Yehoshua*, from *Rambam* to the Mishnah here). This would make the Sea more aesthetically pleasing for them as they passed through it, and would be a source of glory for the Children of Israel (*Tos. Yom Tov* to the Mishnah here [cited also in note 37, above, in regard to the dome shape]; for an alternative explanation, see *Meiri* to the Mishnah).

47. Meaning, until the waters of the Sea become hard like rocks, so that when the water comes down on the Egyptians it will smash their heads (*Binyan Yehoshua*, citing *Rambam* to the Mishnah here).

48. The term תַּנִּינִים, *sea serpents*, is an allusion to the Egyptians, as they were the nation of Pharaoh, who is called by the prophet, הַתַּנִּים הַגָּדוֹל, *the great sea-serpent* [Ezekiel 29:3] (*Binyan Yehoshua*, from *Rashi* to the verse).

49. *Ahavas Chesed*. Although they wanted the land *behind* them to become muddy for the Egyptians, they wanted the land *in front of*

נָטַל מֹשֶׁה אֶת הַמַּטֶּה וְהִכָּה עַל הַיָּם, שֶׁנֶּאֱמַר (שם סו, ו) "הָפַךְ יָם לְיַבָּשָׁה", וְאוֹמֵר (שמות יד, כט) "וּבְנֵי יִשְׂרָאֵל הָלְכוּ בַיַּבָּשָׁה בְּתוֹךְ הַיָּם". אָמַר לָהֶם מֹשֶׁה: קוּמוּ עִבְרוּ. אָמְרוּ: לֹא נַעֲבוֹר עַד שֶׁיֵּעָשֶׂה לְפָנֵינוּ חוֹמוֹת[50] נָטַל מֹשֶׁה אֶת הַמַּטֶּה וְהִכָּה עַל הַיָּם, שֶׁנֶּאֱמַר (שם) "וְהַמַּיִם לָהֶם חֹמָה מִימִינָם וּמִשְּׂמֹאלָם". אָמַר לָהֶם מֹשֶׁה: קוּמוּ עִבְרוּ. אָמְרוּ: לֹא נַעֲבוֹר עַד שֶׁיֵּעָשׂוּ לְפָנֵינוּ נֹאדוֹת.[51] נָטַל מֹשֶׁה אֶת הַמַּטֶּה וְהִכָּה עַל הַיָּם, שֶׁנֶּאֱמַר (שם טו, ח) "נִצְּבוּ כְמוֹ נֵד נֹזְלִים". (וּמִנַּיִן שֶׁבֵּין הַגְּזָרִים יָרְדָה אֵשׁ וְלִיחֲכָתָן[52], שֶׁנֶּאֱמַר (ישעיה סד, א) "כִּקְדֹחַ אֵשׁ הֲמָסִים מַיִם תִּבְעֶה אֵשׁ לְהוֹדִיעַ שִׁמְךָ לְצָרֶיךָ".[53])

נָטַל מֹשֶׁה אֶת הַמַּטֶּה וְהִכָּה עַל הַיָּם — So Moses took the staff and hit the Sea, and it indeed became dry land, שֶׁנֶּאֱמַר "הָפַךְ יָם לְיַבָּשָׁה" — as it is stated, *He changed the sea into dry land* (ibid. 66:6), וְאוֹמֵר "וּבְנֵי יִשְׂרָאֵל הָלְכוּ בַיַּבָּשָׁה בְּתוֹךְ הַיָּם" — and it says further, *The Children of Israel went on dry land in the midst of the sea* (*Exodus* 14:29). אָמַר לָהֶם מֹשֶׁה: קוּמוּ עִבְרוּ — Once again Moses said to them, "Arise and cross the Sea!" אָמְרוּ: לֹא נַעֲבוֹר עַד שֶׁיֵּעָשֶׂה לְפָנֵינוּ חוֹמוֹת — They replied, "We shall not cross until [the Sea] becomes walls before us!"[50] נָטַל מֹשֶׁה אֶת הַמַּטֶּה וְהִכָּה עַל הַיָּם — So Moses took the staff and hit the Sea, and it became walls, שֶׁנֶּאֱמַר "וְהַמַּיִם לָהֶם חֹמָה — took the staff and hit the Sea, and it became walls, מִימִינָם וּמִשְּׂמֹאלָם" — as it is stated, *The water was a wall for them, on their right and on their left* (*Exodus* ibid.). אָמַר לָהֶם מֹשֶׁה: קוּמוּ עִבְרוּ — Once again Moses said to them, "Arise and cross the Sea!" אָמְרוּ: לֹא נַעֲבוֹר עַד שֶׁיֵּעָשׂוּ לְפָנֵינוּ נֹאדוֹת — They replied, "We shall not cross until flasks form before us!"[51] נָטַל מֹשֶׁה אֶת הַמַּטֶּה וְהִכָּה עַל הַיָּם — So Moses took the staff and hit the Sea, and flasks were formed, שֶׁנֶּאֱמַר "נִצְּבוּ כְמוֹ נֵד נֹזְלִים" — as it is stated, *As a flask stood the running waters* (ibid. 15:8). וּמִנַּיִן שֶׁבֵּין הַגְּזָרִים יָרְדָה אֵשׁ וְלִיחֲכָתָן — From where do we know that a fire descended between the passageways and licked [the waters], thereby forming the flasks?[52] שֶׁנֶּאֱמַר "כִּקְדֹחַ אֵשׁ הֲמָסִים מַיִם תִּבְעֶה אֵשׁ לְהוֹדִיעַ שִׁמְךָ לְצָרֶיךָ" — For it is stated,

---

them to be dry so that they themselves could walk on it easily (see notes 43 and 45 above).

50. That is, walls on either side of us. The people of Israel wanted there to be a semblance of solid walls [between them and the huge mounds of water on either side of them] to "block" the water from crashing down on them as they would walk through (see *Ahavas Chesed*; for an alternative explanation, see *Binyan Yehoshua*).

51. From which we will be able to drink [as the Baraisa describes below] (*Ahavas*

Chesed; Ben Avraham).

52. See *Magen Avos* ד"ה וי"א היה יוצא.

Some replace the word וּמִנַּיִן, *and from where*, with the word וּמַיִם, *and the waters* (*Ahavas Chesed, Ben Avraham*; see also editorial note added into the commentary of *Rashi* to *Avos* here, and *Machzor Vitri* ad loc.). Accordingly, the phrase is read as a statement rather than as a question: *A fire descended and licked the waters in the passageways* [thereby forming the flasks], as it is stated, etc.

וְהָיוּ הַנּוֹדוֹת מוֹשְׁכִין שֶׁמֶן וּדְבַשׁ לְתוֹךְ פִּיהֶן שֶׁל תִּינוֹקוֹת[54] וְהֵן יוֹנְקִין
מֵהֶם, שֶׁנֶּאֱמַר (דברים לב, יג) "וַיֵּנִקֵהוּ דְבַשׁ מִסֶּלַע". וְיֵשׁ אוֹמְרִים: הָיָה יוֹצֵא
לָהֶם מַיִם חַיִּים מִן הַיָּם וְשׁוֹתִין בְּתוֹךְ הַגְּזָרִים[55] לְפִי שֶׁמֵּימֵי הַיָּם מְלוּחִים
הֵם, שֶׁנֶּאֱמַר (שמות טו, ח) "נֹזְלִים", וְאֵין "נֹזְלִים" אֶלָּא מְתוּקִים, שֶׁנֶּאֱמַר
(שיר השירים ד, טו) "בְּאֵר מַיִם חַיִּים וְנֹזְלִים מִן לְבָנוֹן"[56]. וְעַנְנֵי כָבוֹד לְמַעְלָה
מֵהֶם שֶׁלֹּא יִשְׁלוֹט בָּהֶם הַשֶּׁמֶשׁ, וְעָבְרוּ יִשְׂרָאֵל כֵּן כְּדֵי שֶׁלֹּא יִצְטַעֲרוּ.

---

*As a melting fire burned — a fire that caused water to bubble — to make
Your Name known to Your enemies (Isaiah 64:1).*[53] וְהָיוּ הַנּוֹדוֹת מוֹשְׁכִין שֶׁמֶן
וּדְבַשׁ לְתוֹךְ פִּיהֶן שֶׁל תִּינוֹקוֹת — And those "flasks" would stream oil and honey
into the mouths of the Israelite children,[54] וְהֵן יוֹנְקִין מֵהֶם — and they would
suckle from them, שֶׁנֶּאֱמַר "וַיֵּנִקֵהוּ דְבַשׁ מִסֶּלַע" — as it is stated, *He* [God]
would suckle him [the nation of Israel] *with honey from a stone, and oil
from a flinty rock (Deuteronomy 32:13).* וְיֵשׁ אוֹמְרִים: הָיָה יוֹצֵא לָהֶם מַיִם חַיִּים
מִן הַיָּם וְשׁוֹתִין בְּתוֹךְ הַגְּזָרִים — And some say: Fresh water would issue from
the Sea for them, and they would drink in the passageways,[55] לְפִי שֶׁמֵּימֵי
הַיָּם מְלוּחִים הֵם — which is a great miracle, since sea water is salty. שֶׁנֶּאֱמַר
"נֹזְלִים" — The proof that fresh water issued from the walls of the Sea is as it is
stated, *running water (Exodus 15:8),* וְאֵין "נֹזְלִים" אֶלָּא מְתוּקִים — and the
term "running water" [נֹזְלִים] in this verse means nothing other than sweet
water, שֶׁנֶּאֱמַר "בְּאֵר מַיִם חַיִּים וְנֹזְלִים מִן לְבָנוֹן" — as it is stated, *a well of
fresh waters streams* [נֹזְלִים] *from Lebanon (Song of Songs 4:15).*[56]

The Baraisa adds:

וְעַנְנֵי כָבוֹד לְמַעְלָה מֵהֶם — The Clouds of Glory were above [the Israelites]
שֶׁלֹּא יִשְׁלוֹט בָּהֶם הַשֶּׁמֶשׁ — so that the hot sun should not affect them. וְעָבְרוּ
יִשְׂרָאֵל כֵּן כְּדֵי שֶׁלֹּא יִצְטַעֲרוּ — And this is how the people of Israel crossed

---

53. The verse would thus means that the effect of the fire causing the water to "bubble"
— and thereby creating the miraculous
flasks — was to make God's Name and
power known to his enemies, the Egyptians.

54. And certainly water and milk [as in the
verse cited next by the Baraisa], which are
their basic needs (see *Magen Avos*).

55. This opinion maintains that rather than
providing flasks which gave forth drinks,
God made it possible for the Israelites to
drink fresh water directly from the walls of
seawater that separated between the divisions of the Sea (ibid., ד"ה וי"א היה יוצא).

56. Thus, the ten miracles God performed

for the people of Israel at the Sea of Reeds
were that He made it into: (i) tunnels,
(ii) a plain, (iii) divided parts, (iv) mortar,
(v) a desert, (vi) fragments, (vii) rocks,
(viii) dry land, (ix) walls, and (x) flasks (or,
fresh water).

[*Avos HaRosh* (Vol. 2) does not count
"dry land" as a separate miracle (see note
45 above), but rather counts the Clouds of
Glory (see immediately below) in its place.
Ben Avraham, however, argues that the
Clouds of Glory are not counted in this list of
ten, since they accompanied the Children of
Israel throughout their sojourn in the Wilderness, and were not specific to the Splitting
of the Sea.]

רַבִּי אֱלִיעֶזֶר אוֹמֵר: תְּהוֹם כָּפָה עֲלֵיהֶם מִלְמַעְלָה וְעָבְרוּ בּוֹ יִשְׂרָאֵל
כְּדֵי שֶׁלֹּא יִצְטַעֲרוּ⁵⁷. רַבִּי אֶלְעָזָר וְרַבִּי שִׁמְעוֹן אוֹמְרִים: מַיִם הָעֶלְיוֹנִים
וְהַתַּחְתּוֹנִים הָיוּ מְנַעֲרִין אֶת הַמִּצְרִיִּים, שֶׁנֶּאֱמַר (שמות יד, כז) "וַיְנַעֵר ה'
אֶת מִצְרַיִם בְּתוֹךְ הַיָּם"⁵⁸:

---

the Sea, **because** God wanted that **they should not suffer** discomfort.   **רַבִּי**
אֱלִיעֶזֶר אוֹמֵר — R' Eliezer says: **תְּהוֹם כָּפָה עֲלֵיהֶם מִלְמַעְלָה וְעָבְרוּ בּוֹ יִשְׂרָאֵל**
— [God] bent the waters over them from above, and the people of **Israel**
crossed under it,   **כְּדֵי שֶׁלֹּא יִצְטַעֲרוּ** — so that they should not have to suffer
discomfort.[57]

The Baraisa concludes with a detail about the punishment of the Egyptians
in the Sea:

מַיִם הָעֶלְיוֹנִים   **רַבִּי אֶלְעָזָר וְרַבִּי שִׁמְעוֹן אוֹמְרִים** — R' Elazar and R' Shimon say:
וְהַתַּחְתּוֹנִים הָיוּ מְנַעֲרִין אֶת הַמִּצְרִיִּים — The upper and lower waters churned
the Egyptians between them,   **שֶׁנֶּאֱמַר "וַיְנַעֵר ה' אֶת מִצְרַיִם בְּתוֹךְ הַיָּם"** — as
it is stated, And HASHEM churned Egypt in the midst of the sea (Exodus
14:27).[58]

---

57. This Tanna is of the opinion that while
they passed through the Sea, there was
no need for the Cloud of Glory above their
heads, for the water itself served as the
protection against the sun (Magen Avos;
see also Ahavas Chesed and Avos HaRosh
[Vol. 2]). [R' Eliezer seems to be referring
to the domelike shape of the water mentioned above as one of the ten miracles (at
note 37).]

58. The word בְּתוֹךְ, in the midst, implies that
the Egyptians were in between two bodies of
water that came together, namely, the upper and lower waters [of the sea] (Ahavas
Chesed).

Ben Avraham connects this piece with

R' Eliezer's statement above, which mentioned the idea that there was water above
the heads of the Israelites as they were passing through. That, too, is perhaps alluded to
in the verse, The Children of Israel went on
dry land "in the midst" of the sea (Exodus
14:29), implying that there was water above
them as well on their sides. In that vein, the
Baraisa concludes with the statement of R'
Elazar and R' Shimon, that when the Egyptians then came into the Sea in pursuit of the
Israelites, the waters on the side came crashing down and the Egyptians were thrashed
around between the "upper waters" (which
originally served as a cover over the heads
of the Israelites) and the now "lower waters."

﴾ פֶּרֶק לד ﴿

א. עֲשָׂרָה נִסְיוֹנוֹת נִסָּה הַקָּדוֹשׁ בָּרוּךְ הוּא אֶת אֲבוֹתֵינוּ וּבְכוּלָן לֹא נִמְצְאוּ שְׁלֵמִים¹. וְאֵלּוּ הֵן: (דברים א, א) "בַּמִּדְבָּר בָּעֲרָבָה מוֹל סוּף [בֵּין פָּארָן וּבֵין תֹּפֶל וְלָבָן וַחֲצֵרוֹת וְדִי זָהָב]²". "בַּמִּדְבָּר" שֶׁעָשׂוּ אֶת הָעֵגֶל, שֶׁנֶּאֱמַר (שמות לב, ח) "עָשׂוּ לָהֶם עֵגֶל מַסֵּכָה"³. "בָּעֲרָבָה" עַל הַמַּיִם, שֶׁנֶּאֱמַר (שם יז, ג) "וַיִּצְמָא שָׁם הָעָם לַמַּיִם"⁴. "מוֹל סוּף" עַל שֶׁהִמְרוּ

﴾ CHAPTER 34 ﴿

§1 The Baraisa paraphrases the second half of *Avos* 5:4 and elaborates on it:

עֲשָׂרָה נִסְיוֹנוֹת נִסָּה הַקָּדוֹשׁ בָּרוּךְ הוּא אֶת אֲבוֹתֵינוּ וּבְכוּלָן לֹא נִמְצְאוּ שְׁלֵמִים — The Holy One, Blessed is He, tested our forefathers with ten tests, and they were not found to be complete in any of them.[1] וְאֵלּוּ הֵן — And they are as follows: "בַּמִּדְבָּר בָּעֲרָבָה מוֹל סוּף בֵּין פָּארָן וּבֵין תֹּפֶל וְלָבָן וַחֲצֵרוֹת וְדִי זָהָב" — Seven are listed in the verse: *Concerning the Wilderness, concerning the Arabah, opposite the Sea of Reeds, between Paran and Tophel, and Laban, and Hazeroth, and Di-zahab* (*Deuteronomy* 1:1).[2] "בַּמִּדְבָּר" שֶׁעָשׂוּ אֶת הָעֵגֶל שֶׁנֶּאֱמַר "עָשׂוּ לָהֶם עֵגֶל מַסֵּכָה" — (i) *Concerning the Wilderness* — this refers to that which they made the Golden Calf, as it is stated, *They made themselves a molten calf* (*Exodus* 32:8).[3] "בָּעֲרָבָה" עַל הַמַּיִם שֶׁנֶּאֱמַר "וַיִּצְמָא שָׁם הָעָם לַמַּיִם" — (ii) *Concerning the Arabah* — this refers to their complaints regarding the lack of water, as it is stated, *The people thirsted there for water, and the people complained against Moses, etc.* (ibid. 17:3).[4] "מוֹל סוּף" עַל שֶׁהִמְרוּ

---

1. That is, they did not pass the tests. The reference here is to the generation of the Wilderness.

In *Avos*, and in 9 §2 above, the order of this teaching is reversed, as it says there, "With ten tests *our forefathers* tested *the Holy One*, Blessed is He, in the Wilderness, as it states (*Numbers* 14:22), *They have tested Me these ten times and have not heeded My voice.*" *Magen Avos* explains that in fact both are true: Our forefathers tested God ten times, and God tested their faith ten times. See further there, where he explains that this accounts for the discrepancies between the list given below and the one given in 9 §2, as there are some incidents that would fall under one category but not the other.

2. This verse introduces Moses' admonition of the Jewish people shortly before

his death, in which he rebukes them for their behavior during the forty years in the Wilderness. As the Baraisa will go on to explain, these enigmatic phrases are veiled references to seven of the sins that the Jews committed throughout that period.

3. Although all ten tests took place in *the Wilderness*, this term is interpreted as an allusion to the Golden Calf in particular, based on the verse (*Numbers* 24:1), *He set his face toward the Wilderness*, which Onkelos interprets to mean that Balaam turned his face [i.e., his attention] toward the [sin of the] Golden Calf that the Israelites had committed in the Wilderness (*Binyan Yehoshua*).

4. The term *Arabah* denotes a land of desolation without water — see *Jeremiah* 2:6 and elsewhere (see *Mefaresh*).

The verse cited here is from the Torah's

עַל יַם סוּף[5]. (וְיֵשׁ אוֹמְרִים: זֶה פִּסְלוֹ שֶׁל מִיכָה[6]). רַבִּי יְהוּדָה אוֹמֵר: הִמְרוּ
עַל הַיָּם הִמְרוּ בְּתוֹךְ הַיָּם[7], שֶׁנֶּאֱמַר (תהלים קו, ז) "וַיַּמְרוּ עַל יָם בְּיַם סוּף"[8].
"בֵּין פָּארָן" בַּמְרַגְּלִים, (במדבר יג, ג) "וַיִּשְׁלַח אֹתָם מֹשֶׁה מִמִּדְבַּר פָּארָן".

עַל יַם סוּף — (iii) *Opposite the Sea of Reeds* — this refers to their rebellious behavior at the Sea of Reeds.[5] וְיֵשׁ אוֹמְרִים: זֶה פִּסְלוֹ שֶׁל מִיכָה — And some say that this is referring to Micah's carved image, which the Jews carried with them as they crossed the Sea of Reeds.[6] רַבִּי יְהוּדָה אוֹמֵר: הִמְרוּ עַל הַיָּם הִמְרוּ בְּתוֹךְ הַיָּם — R' Yehudah says: They rebelled at the Sea and they rebelled while they were in the midst of the Sea,[7] שֶׁנֶּאֱמַר "וַיַּמְרוּ עַל יָם בְּיַם סוּף" — as it is stated, *And they rebelled by the sea, at the Sea of Reeds* (Psalms 106:7).[8] "בֵּין פָּארָן" בַּמְרַגְּלִים "וַיִּשְׁלַח אֹתָם מֹשֶׁה מִמִּדְבַּר פָּארָן" — (iv) *Between Paran*

---

account of the complaint that took place at Rephidim regarding the lack of water there. However, the Baraisa cannot be referring to this incident, as that is the sin at *Massah* mentioned below (*Shenei Eliyahu*; but see *Binyan Yehoshua*). *Magen Avos* explains that although the Baraisa cites the verse from the Rephidim passage, it is in fact referring to the earlier episode at Marah, where they complained regarding the bitterness of the waters; see further there (see *Nuschas HaGra*, who emends the text of the Baraisa accordingly).

5. This occurred when they saw the Egyptians chasing after them, as it states (*Exodus* 14:11), *They said to Moses, "Were there no graves in Egypt that you took us to die in the Wilderness? etc."* (*Binyan Yehoshua*).

6. As it states (*Zechariah* 10:11), *The rival* [צָרָה] *passed through the sea* (*Sanhedrin* 103b, cited by *Binyan Yehoshua*). This term is normally used to refer to a co-wife; in our context it refers to the idol that was worshiped as a rival to God, so to speak (*Mefaresh*).

Judges Ch. 17 relates that a man named Micah fashioned an idol and set it up in his home, where people would come to worship it. Although the incident there took place several generations later, the Gemara (see *Sanhedrin* 101b) maintains that Micah himself was born during the slavery in Egypt. Evidently, the details of the fashioning of the idol described there in *Judges* actually happened while the Jews were still in Egypt,

after which Micah secretly carried it along with him when the Jews passed through the Sea. However, it was not until much later, in the days when "there was no king in Israel, [and] a man would do whatever seemed proper in his eyes" (see ibid. v. 6), that Micah was brazen enough to actually set it up for public worship (*Yefeh To'ar* to *Shemos Rabbah* 41 §1; for further discussion, see *Rashi* to *Sanhedrin* 103b, ד"ה זה). [According to *Gra* (*Aderes Eliyahu* to *Deuteronomy* 29:17), it was not Micah's actual idol that crossed the Sea, but the *roots* of this sin in the hearts of certain individuals. In due course, these produced their evil fruit.]

7. I.e., before they emerged from the Sea, after crossing it on dry land. The rebellion "at the Sea" refers to their complaints against Moses when they saw the Egyptians chasing after them (see note 5), and the rebellion "in the midst of the Sea" refers to that which we are taught in the Gemara (*Arachin* 15a), that after they crossed the Sea, the Israelites exhibited a lack of faith and said, "Just as we are ascending from this side of the Sea, so are the Egyptians ascending safely from the other side." They did not believe that God had destroyed the Egyptians until He ordered the Sea to spit their bodies out onto the dry land (*Magen Avos*).

8. The repetitive language of the verse indicates two incidents of rebellion at the Sea of Reeds (see *Mefaresh* and *Binyan Yehoshua*).

"בֵּין תֹּפֶל" אֵלּוּ דִּבְרֵי תִיפְלוֹת שֶׁתִּפְּלוּ עַל הַמָּן9. "וְלָבָן" זֶה מַחֲלוּקְתּוֹ שֶׁל
קֹרַח10. "וַחֲצֵרוֹת" עַל הַשְּׂלָיו11, הֲרֵי שִׁבְעָה. וּבְמָקוֹם אַחֵר הוּא אוֹמֵר (דברים
ט, כב) "וּבְתַבְעֵרָה12 וּבְמַסָּה13 וּבְקִבְרֹת הַתַּאֲוָה"14. "וְדִי זָהָב", אָמַר לָהֶם

— this refers to the incident **with the Spies,** of whom it states, *Moses sent them forth from the Wilderness of Paran* (Numbers 13:3). **"בֵּין תֹּפֶל" אֵלּוּ** — (v) *And Tophel* [תֹּפֶל] — this refers to **the words of folly** [תִּפְלוֹת] **that they uttered regarding the manna.**[9] **"וְלָבָן" זֶה מַחֲלוּקְתּוֹ** **שֶׁל קֹרַח** — (vi) *And Laban* — **this is a reference to the dispute** instigated **by Korah.**[10] **"וַחֲצֵרוֹת" עַל הַשְּׂלָיו, הֲרֵי שִׁבְעָה** — (vii) *And Hazeroth* — this refers to the incident **involving the quail.**[11] Thus we have **seven.** **וּבְמָקוֹם** **אַחֵר הוּא אוֹמֵר "וּבְתַבְעֵרָה וּבְמַסָּה וּבְקִבְרֹת הַתַּאֲוָה"** — And **the other three are enumerated elsewhere, as it states** that Moses told the Israelites, *And* **(viii)** *in Taberah,*[12] **(ix)** *in Massah,*[13] and **(x)** *in Kibroth-hataavah*[14] *you* *were provoking HASHEM* (Deuteronomy 9:22). Hence we have a total of ten.

The Baraisa expounds the final phrase in *Deuteronomy 1:1:* **אָמַר לָהֶם אַהֲרֹן:** [וְדִי זָהָב]. *And Di-zahab* [וְדִי זָהָב] — The verse concludes, — **"וְדִי זָהָב"**

---

9. When they said (*Numbers* 21:5), *"Our soul is disgusted with the insubstantial food!"* (*Binyan Yehoshua*). The Baraisa is connecting תֹּפֶל with the similar word תִּפְלוֹת, *folly.*

10. The word לָבָן means *white*. As taught by the Sages (*Sanhedrin* 110a and elsewhere), one of the mitzvos that Korah disputed was that of affixing *techeiles* (blue-dyed) threads together with the *white* (i.e., undyed) tzitzis threads on a four-cornered garment. Therefore, the word *white* alludes to Korah's dispute (*Tummas Yesharim, Binyan Yehoshua*).

11. This conforms with Onkelos, who translates this phrase as: "In Hazeroth where they angered [God] with regard to meat" (see *Avos HaRosh*). Presumably, this refers to the incident recorded in *Numbers* 11:4 ff., in which the Jews complained regarding their lack of meat, to which God responded by providing them with quail. This occurred in the vicinity of Hazeroth (see ibid. v. 35; *Chizkuni* and *Gur Aryeh* to the *Deuteronomy* verse). However, the Baraisa below mentions this incident separately, as the test of Kibroth-hataavah. *Magen Avos* therefore explains that here it is referring to an earlier complaint regarding a lack of meat that took place in the Wilderness of Sin — recorded

in *Exodus* 16:3 — to which God likewise responded by providing quail (ibid. vv. 12-13). He points out, however, that there is no apparent explanation as to why the verse refers to the Wilderness of Sin as Hazeroth. See *Mefaresh* for a different version of the text.

12. Referring to that which it states (*Numbers* 11:1-3), *The people took to seeking complaints; it was evil in the ears of HASHEM, and HASHEM heard and His wrath flared, and a fire of HASHEM burned against them, and it consumed at the edge of the camp ... He named that place Taberah [Conflagration], for the fire of HASHEM had burned against them.*

13. Referring to the incident at Rephidim, where the people complained regarding their lack of water. The verse states regarding that incident (*Exodus* 17:7), *He called the place Massah U'Meribah [Test and Contention], because of the contention of the Children of Israel and because of their test of HASHEM, saying, "Is HASHEM among us or not?"*

14. Referring to the second incident of complaint regarding meat (see note 11 above), recounted in *Numbers* Ch. 11. God provided quail in response to this complaint, but also struck the complainers down with a plague. The verse states later (ibid. v. 34), *He named*

(אַהֲרֹן): דַּיֵּיכֶם חֵטְא זָהָב שֶׁהֲבֵאתֶם לָעֵגֶל¹⁵. וְרַבִּי אֱלִיעֶזֶר בֶּן יַעֲקֹב אוֹמֵר: דַּי הוּא עָוֹן זֶה שֶׁלָּקוּ יִשְׂרָאֵל בּוֹ מִכָּאן וְעַד שֶׁיִּחְיוּ הַמֵּתִים¹⁶:

ב. עֲשָׂרָה שֵׁמוֹת שֶׁל שֶׁבַח נִקְרָא הַקָּדוֹשׁ בָּרוּךְ הוּא. אֵלּוּ הֵן: שֵׁם אָלֶ"ף דָּלֶ"ת, וְיוֹ"ד הֵ"א, יָ"הּ, אֱלֹהִי"ם, אֱלוֹ"הַּ, אֱלֹהֶי"ךָ, אֱלֹהֵיכֶם¹⁸, אֵל, אֶהְיֶ"ה אֲשֶׁ"ר אֶהְיֶ"ה¹⁹, שַׁדַּ"י²⁰, צְבָאוֹת²¹. אָמַר רַבִּי יוֹסֵי: חָלְקֵנוּ

דַּיֵּיכֶם חֵטְא זָהָב שֶׁהֲבֵאתֶם לָעֵגֶל — This refers to the sin of the Golden Calf mentioned earlier, and means that after this incident **Aaron said to [the Israelites],** "**It is enough [דַּי]** of a sin for you that **you brought gold [זָהָב]** for the making of the calf."[15] **וְרַבִּי אֱלִיעֶזֶר בֶּן יַעֲקֹב אוֹמֵר: דַּי הוּא עָוֹן זֶה שֶׁלָּקוּ יִשְׂרָאֵל בּוֹ מִכָּאן וְעַד שֶׁיִּחְיוּ הַמֵּתִים** — R' Eliezer ben Yaakov says: It means that **this sin** of the Golden Calf **is** severe **enough for** the people of **Israel to be punished for it from now until the Revivification of the Dead.**[16]

§2 The Baraisa cites additional teachings involving the number ten:[17]

עֲשָׂרָה שֵׁמוֹת שֶׁל שֶׁבַח נִקְרָא הַקָּדוֹשׁ בָּרוּךְ הוּא — **The Holy One, Blessed is He, is called** by ten Names of praise. **אֵלּוּ הֵן** — **They are as follows:** **שֵׁם אָלֶ"ף דָּלֶ"ת, וְיוֹ"ד הֵ"א, יָ"הּ, אֱלֹהִי"ם, אֱלוֹ"הַּ, אֱלֹהֶי"ךָ, אֱלֹהֵיכֶם, אֵל, אֶהְיֶ"ה אֲשֶׁ"ר אֶהְיֶ"ה, שַׁדַּ"י, צְבָאוֹת** — (i) **The Name** that begins with the letters *aleph dalet* [אֲדֹנָי]; (ii) the Name that begins with the letters *yud hei* [יְ־הֹ־וֹ־ה]; (iii) *Yah* [יָהּ]; (iv) *Elohim* [אֱלֹהִים]; (v) *Eloah* [אֱלוֹהַּ]; (vi) *Elohecha* [אֱלֹהֶיךָ]; (vii) *Eloheichem* [אֱלֹהֵיכֶם];[18] (viii) *El* [אֵל]; (ix) *Ehyeh Asher Ehyeh* [אֶהְיֶה אֲשֶׁר אֶהְיֶה];[19] (x) *Shaddai* [שַׁדַּי];[20] and (xi) *Tzevaos* [צְבָאוֹת].[21] **אָמַר רַבִּי יוֹסֵי: חָלְקֵנוּ**

that place Kibroth-Hataavah [Graves of the Craving], because there they buried the people who had been craving.

15. See *Exodus* 32:1-4. The Baraisa is interpreting וְדִי זָהָב as though it were vowelized וְדַי זָהָב, *the gold is enough*. Aaron rebuked the people for compelling him to fashion an image, and told them that even the mere act of donating their gold for this purpose was enough to be regarded as a great sin on their part (see *Binyan Yeshoshua* and *Avos HaRosh*).

16. For the Gemara (*Sanhedrin* 102a) states that there is no punishment that comes upon the Jews that does not include a small measure of retribution for the sin of the Golden Calf (*Binyan Yehoshua*). [R' Eliezer ben Yaakov also interprets the phrase וְדִי זָהָב as, "the gold is enough," but explains the intent of this statement differently.]

17. *Binyan Yehoshua.*

18. The four Names just listed are different forms of the same Name: אֱלוֹהַּ is in the singular, אֱלֹהִים is in the plural (following the rule that terms connoting mastery or divinity are often written in the plural), אֱלֹהֶיךָ means *your* (singular) God, and אֱלֹהֵיכֶם means *your* (plural) God. The Baraisa enumerates only these forms of the Name (and not others such as אֱלֹהֵינוּ, *our God*) because they are all found in verses that extol God's praises; e.g., *Deuteronomy* 10:14,17 (*Ben Avraham*).

19. This Name is found in *Exodus* 3:14. Its meaning is *I Shall Be As I Shall Be.* See the commentators there.

20. *The Almighty.*

21. *The [Lord of] Hosts.*

Several of the commentators point out that although the Baraisa begins by stating that there are ten Divine Names, it actually

עַל צְבָאוֹת, שֶׁנֶּאֱמַר (דברים כ, ט) "וּפָקְדוּ שָׂרֵי צְבָאוֹ'ת בְּרֹאשׁ הָעָם"²²:

ג. עֲשָׂרָה שֵׁמוֹת נִקְרְאוּ לְעַבוּ"ם שֵׁם גְּנַאי²³. אֵלּוּ הֵן: שִׁקּוּצִים, גִּלּוּלִים, מַסֵּכוֹת, פְּסִילִים, אֱלִילִים, אֲשֵׁירִים, חַמָּנִים, עֲצַבִּים, אָוֶן, וּתְרָפִים:

ד. שְׁנֵי²⁴ סְמָנִיּוֹת אֲמוּרוֹת בַּתּוֹרָה בְּפָרָשָׁה קְטַנָּה²⁵. וְאֵיזוֹ פָרָשָׁה קְטַנָּה, (במדבר י, לה) "וַיְהִי בִּנְסֹעַ הָאָרֹן וְכוּ'"²⁶. רַבָּן שִׁמְעוֹן בֶּן גַּמְלִיאֵל אוֹמֵר:

עַל צְבָאוֹת — R' Yose said: I disagree regarding *Tzevaos*, for I maintain that it is not a Divine Name, שֶׁנֶּאֱמַר "וּפָקְדוּ שָׂרֵי צְבָאוֹ'ת בְּרֹאשׁ הָעָם" — but should be understood in the same manner as that which is stated, *The leaders of the legions* [צְבָאוֹת] *should take command at the head of the people* (*Deuteronomy* 20:9).[22]

§3 עֲשָׂרָה שֵׁמוֹת נִקְרְאוּ לְעַבוּ"ם שֵׁם גְּנַאי — There are ten terms of disgrace by which idols are called.[23] אֵלּוּ הֵן — They are as follows: שִׁקּוּצִים, גִּלּוּלִים, מַסֵּכוֹת, פְּסִילִים, אֱלִילִים, אֲשֵׁירִים, חַמָּנִים, עֲצַבִּים, אָוֶן, וּתְרָפִים — (i) *Abominations*, (ii) *detestable [idols]*, (iii) *molten images*, (iv) *carved images*, (v) *nothings*, (vi) *idolatrous trees*, (vii) *sun-idols*, (viii) *designed [idols]*, (ix) *iniquity*, and (x) *icons*.

§4(a) The Baraisa discusses a Scriptural passage that has markings inserted on either side:[24]

שְׁנֵי סְמָנִיּוֹת אֲמוּרוֹת בַּתּוֹרָה בְּפָרָשָׁה קְטַנָּה — In the Torah Scroll, there are two markings in a certain small section, one marking before the section and one after it. These signs take the form of inverted *nuns*.[25] וְאֵיזוֹ פָרָשָׁה קְטַנָּה, "וַיְהִי בִּנְסֹעַ הָאָרֹן וְכוּ'" — And which small section is this? The one that begins, *When the Ark would journey, etc.* (*Numbers* 10:35).[26] רַבָּן שִׁמְעוֹן בֶּן גַּמְלִיאֵל אוֹמֵר:

---

lists eleven; see *Ahavas Chesed* and *Ben Avraham* for discussion. In fact, however, the Name יָה does not appear in earlier prints of *Avos DeRabbi Nassan*; it was inserted in later prints based on the emendation of *Tummas Yesharim* (see *Avos HaRosh*; and see *Beur HaGra, Yoreh Deah* 276:19).

22. In this verse, the word צְבָאוֹת certainly does not refer to God, but to the legions of the Israelite army. In the same manner, R' Yose maintains, since צְבָאוֹת is never used in Scripture as a Name on its own, but is always preceded by an actual Name of God (e.g., אֱלֹהֵי צְבָאוֹת, *God of Hosts*), it does not refer to God but to the *legions* or *hosts* under His dominion (see *Toras Chaim* to *Shevuos* 35b).

23. [Some are general descriptions of idol-

atry, whereas others refer to specific idols.]

24. [The Vilna ed. numbers both this section and the next as "4".] This teaching does not seem to have any relevance here. According to *Magen Avos*, it belongs in the following section, after the Baraisa concludes its discussion of the ten dots found in the Torah. At that point, it is relevant to cite a similar discussion regarding the markings found in the Torah.

25. Although the Baraisa itself does not describe the shape of the signs, making them as inverted *nuns* has been the custom for many centuries. For further discussion, see the Schottenstein ed. of *Shabbos*, 115b note 22.

26. This section consists of two verses that describe what Moses said each time the Ark would travel when the camp was about

רְאוּיָה הָיְתָה פָּרָשָׁה זוֹ שֶׁתֵּעָקֵר מִמְּקוֹמָהּ וְתִכָּתֵב בְּמָקוֹם אַחֵר.²⁷ כַּיּוֹצֵא בּוֹ,
(שופטים יח, ל) ״וִיהוֹנָתָן בֶּן גֵּרְשֹׁם בֶּן מְנַשֶּׁה״.²⁹ וְכִי בֶן מְנַשֶּׁה הָיָה, וַהֲלֹא בֶן
מֹשֶׁה הָיָה.³⁰ אֶלָּא לְפִי שֶׁלֹּא נִדְמוּ מַעֲשָׂיו לְמֹשֶׁה אָבִיו לְפִיכָךְ תּוֹלִין בִּמְנַשֶּׁה.

רְאוּיָה הָיְתָה פָּרָשָׁה זוֹ שֶׁתֵּעָקֵר מִמְּקוֹמָהּ וְתִכָּתֵב בְּמָקוֹם אַחֵר — **Rabban Shimon ben Gamliel says:** The purpose of the inverted *nuns* is to inform us that in principle, **this section should have been uprooted from its** current **place and written in a different place.**[27]

Having discussed an instance of inverted *nuns*, the Baraisa discusses an instance of a hanging *nun*:[28]

כַּיּוֹצֵא בּוֹ, ״וִיהוֹנָתָן בֶּן גֵּרְשֹׁם בֶּן מְנַשֶּׁה״ — **Similarly,** it is written, *The children of Dan set up for themselves the carved image,* **and Jonathan son of Gershom son of Manasseh** — *he and his children* — *were priests for the tribe of the Danite, up until the day the land was exiled (Judges 18:30).*[29] וְכִי בֶן מְנַשֶּׁה הָיָה, וַהֲלֹא בֶן מֹשֶׁה הָיָה — **Now, was he** (Gershom, the father of Jonathan), really **the son of Manasseh? Why, he was the son of Moses!**[30] אֶלָּא לְפִי שֶׁלֹּא נִדְמוּ מַעֲשָׂיו לְמֹשֶׁה אָבִיו לְפִיכָךְ תּוֹלִין בִּמְנַשֶּׁה — It must be that the verse does not mean that he was actually a son of Manasseh; **but because his deeds did not resemble those of his ancestor Moses,** but were similar to those of the idolatrous king Manasseh,[31] **therefore he is connected with Manasseh.** This follows the rule that Scripture connects evil with evil people.[32]

---

to journey and when it was ready to camp.

27. That is, the purpose of these signs is to indicate that this was not really the appropriate place for the Torah to include this section. These verses more appropriately belong in *Numbers* Ch. 2, where the Torah describes how each tribe camped under its banner (*Binyan Yehoshua*, citing *Shabbos* 115b-116a with *Rashi* ad loc.). The reason it was placed further on is in order to separate between the narrative of one punishment and the narrative of another punishment. See further in the Gemara there (with *Rashi* s.v. מאחרי ה' and *Tosafos* s.v. פורענות) regarding which two narratives of punishment the Torah is coming to separate.

28. *Mefaresh.*

29. *Judges* Ch. 17-18 relates that Micah fashioned a carved image that was then stolen from him by the children of Dan, who proceeded to set up a house of idol worship for the image and elected a man named Jonathan as its priest. The *nun* in the word

מְנַשֶּׁה (Manasseh) is left hanging, i.e., it is slightly above the other letters. The Baraisa will explain the reason for this.

30. As stated (*I Chronicles* 23:15), *The sons of Moses: Gershom and Eliezer* (*Bava Basra* 109b; see *Maharsha* there, cited by *Binyan Yehoshua*, regarding why the Gemara cites this verse). Although there certainly could have been a Jonathan who was the son of another Gershom, the fact that the name מְנַשֶּׁה was written with a hanging *nun* — allowing us to read it *without* the *nun*, rendering it מֹשֶׁה (Moses) — combined with Scripture's identification of this Jonathan as a Levite (*Judges* 17:7), indicates that he was indeed the grandson of Moses, who was a Levite (*Rashbam* to *Bava Basra* ibid.).

31. Gemara ibid., cited by *Binyan Yehoshua*.

32. Gemara ibid. In other words, a verse will sometimes attribute ancestry of an evil person to those who are not his blood relatives, but who are "related" to him in terms of their deeds.

כַּיּוֹצֵא בוֹ (זכריה ד, יד) "אֵלֶּה שְׁנֵי בְנֵי הַיִּצְהָר הָעֹמְדִים עַל אֲדוֹן כָּל הָאָרֶץ"[34], זֶה אַהֲרֹן וּמָשִׁיחַ[35]. וְאֵינִי יוֹדֵעַ אֵיזֶה מֵהֶן חָבִיב, כְּשֶׁהוּא אוֹמֵר (תהלים קי, ד) "נִשְׁבַּע ה' וְלֹא יִנָּחֵם אַתָּה כֹהֵן לְעוֹלָם"[36], הֱוֵי יוֹדֵעַ שֶׁמֶּלֶךְ הַמָּשִׁיחַ חָבִיב יוֹתֵר מִכֹּהֵן צֶדֶק. הֲרֵי הוּא אוֹמֵר (תהלים פ, יד) "יְכַרְסְמֶנָּה חֲזִיר מִיָּעַר"[37], וְ"יְכַרְסְמֶנָּה חֲזִיר מִיאוֹר" (כְּתִיב)[38]. "יְכַרְסְמֶנָּה חֲזִיר מִיָּעַר", שֶׁבִּזְמַן שֶׁאֵין יִשְׂרָאֵל עוֹשִׂין רְצוֹנוֹ שֶׁל מָקוֹם, כּוֹתִים דוֹמוֹת עֲלֵיהֶם כַּחֲזִיר מִיָּעַר.

Tangentially, the Baraisa cites an exposition from which we may derive that Scripture also connects greatness with great people:[33]

כַּיּוֹצֵא בוֹ, "אֵלֶּה שְׁנֵי בְנֵי הַיִּצְהָר הָעֹמְדִים עַל אֲדוֹן כָּל הָאָרֶץ" — In a similar manner, it is written, *These are the two anointed men who are standing by the Lord of all the land* (Zechariah 4:14).[34] זֶה אַהֲרֹן וּמָשִׁיחַ — This is a reference to **Aaron and the Messiah.**[35] וְאֵינִי יוֹדֵעַ אֵיזֶה מֵהֶן חָבִיב — Now, from this verse, which places the two together, I would not know which of them is more beloved before God. כְּשֶׁהוּא אוֹמֵר "נִשְׁבַּע ה' וְלֹא יִנָּחֵם אַתָּה כֹהֵן לְעוֹלָם" — When it states elsewhere, *HASHEM has sworn and will not relent, "You shall hold authority forever, beyond that of Malchizedek"* (Psalms 110:4),[36] הֱוֵי יוֹדֵעַ שֶׁמֶּלֶךְ הַמָּשִׁיחַ חָבִיב יוֹתֵר מִכֹּהֵן צֶדֶק — you know that the King Messiah is more beloved than a righteous priest such as Aaron.

Apropos of its earlier discussion of the hanging *nun*, the Baraisa discusses an instance of another hanging letter: הֲרֵי הוּא אוֹמֵר "יְכַרְסְמֶנָּה חֲזִיר מִיָּעַר" — It states, *The boar of the forest* [מִיָּעַר] *ravages it* (ibid. 80:14),[37] וְ"יְכַרְסְמֶנָּה חֲזִיר מִיאוֹר" כְּתִיב — but it is written so that it may be read as, *The boar of the river* [מִיאוֹר] *ravages it.*[38] "יְכַרְסְמֶנָּה חֲזִיר מִיָּעַר" שֶׁבִּזְמַן שֶׁאֵין יִשְׂרָאֵל עוֹשִׂין רְצוֹנוֹ שֶׁל מָקוֹם, כּוֹתִים דוֹמוֹת עֲלֵיהֶם כַּחֲזִיר מִיָּעַר — The plain meaning of the verse, *The boar of the forest ravages it,*

33. *Binyan Yehoshua*, citing *Mefaresh*.

34. In this verse, an angel is telling Zechariah the significance of the images that he was shown in a prophetic vision.

35. Aaron was anointed by Moses, and the Messiah will be the anointed king from the House of David, as indicated by his very name, מָשִׁיחַ, which means *anointed one*.

The vision of Zechariah did not actually concern Aaron the Kohen and the King Messiah, but pertained to Joshua and Zerubbabel, the Kohen Gadol and governor of Judah (respectively) at the beginning of the Second Temple era. [See earlier in the passage there.] In Zechariah's prophetic vision, these leaders were depicted as *two anointed*

men, corresponding to Aaron and the Messiah. Thus, we see that Scripture connects greatness — the positions of Joshua and Zerubbabel — with great people — Aaron and the Messiah (ibid.).

36. This psalm is speaking with regard to the Messiah. In the cited verse, God swears that the Messiah will have greater authority than Malchizedek, who was a priest of God, as stated in *Genesis* 14:18 (*Ben Avraham*, based on *Rashi* to the *Psalms* verse in his second approach).

37. The verse portrays Israel's plight under foreign dominion as that of a vineyard that is abandoned to the ravages of the wild beasts.

38. The *ayin* of מִיָּעַר is hanging, to indicate

מָה חֲזִיר מִיַּעַר הוֹרֵג נְפָשׁוֹת וּמַזִּיק אֶת הַבְּהֵמוֹת וּמַלְקֶה בְּנֵי אָדָם, כָּךְ כָּל
זְמַן שֶׁאֵין יִשְׂרָאֵל עוֹשִׂים רְצוֹנוֹ שֶׁל מָקוֹם, כּוּתִים הוֹרְגִין וּמַלְקִין וּמַזִּיקִין
אוֹתָם. וְכָל זְמַן שֶׁיִּשְׂרָאֵל עוֹשִׂים רְצוֹנוֹ שֶׁל מָקוֹם, אֵין כּוּתִים מוֹשְׁלִין
בָּהֶם כַּחֲזִיר שֶׁל יְאוֹר.[39] מָה חֲזִיר שֶׁל יְאוֹר אֵינוּ הוֹרֵג נְפָשׁוֹת וְאֵינוּ מַזִּיק
לַבְּרִיּוֹת, כָּךְ כָּל זְמַן שֶׁיִּשְׂרָאֵל עוֹשִׂין רְצוֹנוֹ, אֵין אוּמָּה וְלָשׁוֹן הוֹרְגִין בָּהֶן
וּמַזִּיקִין בָּהֶן וְלֹא מַלְקִין אוֹתָן. לְכָךְ נִכְתַּב "חֲזִיר מִיאוֹר":

[בוֹילְנא הַצִּיּוּן לבריתא ד נכפל]

ד • עֶשֶׂר נְקוּדוֹת בַּתּוֹרָה.[40] אֵלּוּ הֵן: (בראשית טז, ה) "יִשְׁפֹּט ה' בֵּינִי וּבֵינֶיךָ",[41]
עַל י' שֶׁ"בֵּינֶיךָ" נָקוּד, מְלַמֵּד שֶׁלֹא אָמְרָה לוֹ אֶלָּא עַל הָגָר.[42]

---

is teaching us that **when the people of Israel do not perform the Will of the Omnipresent, the idolaters are to them like a boar of the forest:** מָה חֲזִיר מִיַּעַר הוֹרֵג נְפָשׁוֹת וּמַזִּיק אֶת הַבְּהֵמוֹת וּמַלְקֶה בְּנֵי אָדָם — **Just as a boar of the forest kills people, harms other animals, and hurts human beings,** כָּךְ כָּל זְמַן שֶׁאֵין יִשְׂרָאֵל עוֹשִׂים רְצוֹנוֹ שֶׁל מָקוֹם, כּוּתִים הוֹרְגִין וּמַלְקִין וּמַזִּיקִין אוֹתָם — **so too whenever the people of Israel do not perform the Will of the Omnipresent, the idolaters kill, hurt, and harm them.** וְכָל זְמַן שֶׁיִּשְׂרָאֵל עוֹשִׂים רְצוֹנוֹ שֶׁל מָקוֹם, אֵין כּוּתִים מוֹשְׁלִין בָּהֶם — **But whenever the people of Israel perform the Will of the Omnipresent, the idolaters do not have dominion over them,** כַּחֲזִיר שֶׁל יְאוֹר — **but are rendered as a boar of the river:**[39] מָה חֲזִיר שֶׁל יְאוֹר אֵינוּ הוֹרֵג נְפָשׁוֹת וְאֵינוּ מַזִּיק לַבְּרִיּוֹת — **Just as a boar of the river does not kill people and does not harm creatures,** כָּךְ כָּל זְמַן שֶׁיִּשְׂרָאֵל עוֹשִׂין רְצוֹנוֹ, אֵין אוּמָּה וְלָשׁוֹן הוֹרְגִין בָּהֶן וּמַזִּיקִין בָּהֶן וְלֹא מַלְקִין אוֹתָן — **so too whenever the people of Israel perform [God's] Will, no nation or tongue can kill, harm, or hurt them.** לְכָךְ נִכְתַּב "חֲזִיר מִיאוֹר" — **Therefore it is written so that it can be read,** *The boar of the river.*

§4(b) The Baraisa continues citing teachings involving the number ten: עֶשֶׂר נְקוּדוֹת בַּתּוֹרָה — **There are ten places where there are dots on top of letters in the Torah.**[40] אֵלּוּ הֵן — **They are as follows:** "יִשְׁפֹּט ה' בֵּינִי וּבֵינֶיךָ" — (i) In the verse, *Sarai said to Abram ... "Let HASHEM judge between me and you!"* (Genesis 16:5),[41] עַל י' שֶׁ"בֵּינֶיךָ" נָקוּד — **there is a dot on the second yud of the word "u'veinecha"** [וּבֵינֶיךָ], *and [between] you.* מְלַמֵּד שֶׁלֹא אָמְרָה לוֹ אֶלָּא עַל הָגָר — **It is teaching us that [Sarah] was saying this to [Abraham]**

---

that it may be read as an *aleph* (*Binyan Yehoshua,* citing *Rashi* ad loc.).

39. I.e., they are like a sea-creature that has emerged onto the dry land, which is rendered harmless and submissive (see *Vayikra Rabbah* 13 §5).

40. The dot or dots above a word in Scripture

indicate that the word is not to be understood in its full sense; either the dotted letters, or part of the implication of the word, should be viewed as "omitted" (see *Binyan Yehoshua*).

41. When Sarah, who had never conceived, gave her maidservant Hagar to her husband Abraham in marriage, Hagar conceived

וְיֵשׁ אוֹמְרִים: עַל הַמְטִילִין מְרִיבָה בֵּינִי וּבֵינֶיךָ"[43]. (שם יח, ט) "וַיֹּאמְרוּ
אֵלָיו אַיֵּה שָׂרָה"[44], נָקוֹד עַל אי"ו, שֶׁיּוֹדְעִין בָּהּ וּמְבַקְּרִין אַחֲרֶיהָ[45].
(נָקוֹד עַל) (שם יט, לג) "בְּשִׁכְבָהּ וּבְקוּמָהּ"[46], נָקוֹד עַל וָי"ו שֶׁ"בְּקוּמָהּ"
הָרִאשׁוֹן[47], מְלַמֵּד שֶׁלֹּא הִרְגִּישׁ אֶלָּא בַּעֲמִידָתָהּ (שֶׁל צְעִירָה)[48].

---

only in reference to Hagar, not in reference to him.[42]   וְיֵשׁ אוֹמְרִים: עַל הַמְטִילִין
מְרִיבָה בֵּינִי וּבֵינֶיךָ — **And others say** that Sarah's intent was, "Let Hashem pass
judgment **upon those who are causing argument between me and you!**"[43]
"וַיֹּאמְרוּ אֵלָיו אַיֵּה שָׂרָה" — (ii) Similarly, in the verse, *They said to him, "Where
is Sarah your wife?"* (ibid. 18:9),[44]   נָקוֹד עַל אי"ו — **there are dots above**
the letters *aleph, yud,* and *vav* of the word "*eilav*" [אֵלָיו], *to him.*   שֶׁיּוֹדְעִין בָּהּ
וּמְבַקְּרִין אַחֲרֶיהָ — **It is teaching us that [the angels] knew of her whereabouts,**
and were merely checking after her.[45]
נָקוֹד עַל "בְּשִׁכְבָהּ וּבְקוּמָהּ" נָקוֹד עַל וָי"ו שֶׁ"בְּקוּמָהּ" הָרִאשׁוֹן — (iii) Similarly, **there**
is a dot in (lit., *above*) the verse, *And he was not aware of her lying down*
and of her rising (ibid. 19:33),[46] i.e., **there is a dot above the** letter *vav* in
the middle of the word "*uv'kumah*" [וּבְקוּמָהּ], *and of her rising,* **the first** time
it is written.[47]   מְלַמֵּד שֶׁלֹּא הִרְגִּישׁ אֶלָּא בַּעֲמִידָתָהּ שֶׁל צְעִירָה — **It is teaching**
us that [Lot] realized what had happened **only when the younger one rose.**[48]

---

immediately, whereupon Sarah's esteem
became lowered in Hagar's eyes. Sarah
complained to Abraham for not taking up
her cause (*Genesis* 16:2-5).

42. The dot on the *yud* teaches us that
Sarah's concluding statement, *"Let HASHEM*
judge between me and you," was not directed at Abraham, as were her preceding
words, but at Hagar (*Ben Avraham*).

43. This opinion maintains that Sarah's concluding statement *was* addressed to Abraham. However, the dot on the *yud* tells us
not to understand the verse according to its
plain meaning, but that Sarah was saying,
"Let HASHEM judge [those who are causing
argument] between me and you!," referring
to Hagar (ibid.). Thus, both opinions agree
that despite her indignation, Sarah did not
wish evil upon her husband.

44. In this verse, the angels whom Abraham hosted were asking him as to Sarah's
whereabouts.

45. The dots above the letters of the word
teach us that the angels did not need to ask

their question, as they knew the answer already (*Eshed HaNechalim* to *Bamidbar Rab-*
bah 3 §13). However, they asked Abraham
about Sarah's whereabouts for the purpose
of endearing her to him by drawing his attention to her modesty, or in order to send
her the cup of wine over which Grace After
Meals was recited (*Binyan Yehoshua*, citing
Bava Metzia 87a with *Rashi*).

46. After their homeland of Sodom was
completely destroyed, and only they and
their father were spared, Lot's two daughters
intoxicated their father and lay with him so
that they could bear children. The first night
his older daughter did so, and the second
night the younger one (*Genesis* 19:30-36).

47. With regard to the younger daughter,
this phrase is also written in v. 35. The dot
is on the *vav* in the first occurrence of this
phrase, written with regard to the older one
(*Binyan Yehoshua*).

48. In all other sources of this teaching
(e.g., *Nazir* 23a, *Bereishis Rabbah* 51 §8),
it states, "he was unaware of her lying
down, but was aware of her rising." Many

כַּיּוֹצֵא בוֹ, (שם לג, ד) "וַיָּרָץ עֵשָׂו לִקְרָאתוֹ וַיְחַבְּקֵהוּ וַיִּפֹּל עַל צַוָּארוֹ
וַיִּשָּׁקֵהוּ", כּוּלוֹ נָקוּד, מְלַמֵּד שֶׁלֹּא נְשָׁקוֹ בֶּאֱמֶת.[49] רַבִּי שִׁמְעוֹן בֶּן
אֶלְעָזָר אוֹמֵר: נְשִׁיקָה זוֹ שֶׁל אֱמֶת וְכוּלָן אֵינָן שֶׁל אֱמֶת.[50] כַּיּוֹצֵא בוֹ,
(שם לז, יב) "וַיֵּלְכוּ אֶחָיו לִרְעוֹת אֶת צֹאן אֲבִיהֶם בִּשְׁכֶם", נָקוּד עַל
"אֶת", מְלַמֵּד שֶׁלֹּא לִרְעוֹת הַצֹּאן הָלְכוּ אֶלָּא לֶאֱכוֹל וְלִשְׁתּוֹת[51]

(iv) Similarly, — כַּיּוֹצֵא בוֹ, "וַיָּרָץ עֵשָׂו לִקְרָאתוֹ וַיְחַבְּקֵהוּ וַיִּפֹּל עַל צַוָּארוֹ וַיִּשָּׁקֵהוּ"
in the verse, *Esau ran toward [Jacob], embraced him, fell upon his neck,
and kissed him* (ibid. 33:4),   כּוּלוֹ נָקוּד — the entire [word] *"vayishakeihu"*
[וַיִּשָּׁקֵהוּ], *and he kissed him*, is dotted,   מְלַמֵּד — teaching
us that he did not kiss him sincerely.[49]   רַבִּי שִׁמְעוֹן בֶּן אֶלְעָזָר אוֹמֵר: נְשִׁיקָה זוֹ
שֶׁל אֱמֶת וְכוּלָן אֵינָן שֶׁל אֱמֶת — R' Shimon ben Elazar, however, **says:** On the
contrary, it is coming to teach us that *only* this kiss was sincere, but all other
ones were not sincere.[50]

(v) Similarly, in — כַּיּוֹצֵא בוֹ, "וַיֵּלְכוּ אֶחָיו לִרְעוֹת אֶת צֹאן אֲבִיהֶם בִּשְׁכֶם"
the verse, *Now, [Joseph's] brothers went to pasture their father's flock*
[אֶת צֹאן אֲבִיהֶם] *in Shechem* (ibid. 37:12),   נָקוּד עַל "אֶת" — there are dots
above the word *"es"* [אֶת].   מְלַמֵּד שֶׁלֹּא לִרְעוֹת הַצֹּאן הָלְכוּ אֶלָּא לֶאֱכוֹל וְלִשְׁתּוֹת

---

of the commentators emend the text of
our Baraisa accordingly. That is, since the
dot on the word minimizes the implication of the verse, it is teaching us that in
reality, after the older one rose Lot *was*
aware of what had transpired. Despite this
awareness, he did not resist his daughters' attempts to intoxicate him again the
following night, although he realized the
potential results (*Binyan Yehoshua*, citing
Nazir ibid. with *Tosafos* ד"ה למה). When it
states, *And he was not aware of her lying
down and of her rising*, it means that he
did not have a complete awareness of what
happened; but he did have a sense that
something suspicious had transpired (*Yefeh
To'ar* to *Bereishis Rabbah* ibid., cited by
Mefaresh).

Velo Od Ella reconciles our version of the
text by explaining that when it states, "he
realized only when the younger one rose," it
is not referring to when she rose from lying
with him. Rather, it means that when she
arose on the second night to ply him with
wine, he was able to discern her intent. That
is, our Baraisa agrees with the Gemara and

Bereishis Rabbah, which explain the dot
on the *vau* of וּבְקוּמָהּ as coming to teach us
that when the *older* one rose from lying with
Lot, he had a partial awareness of what had
happened. However, the Baraisa is coming
to tell us the Torah's purpose in stating this
information. Therefore, it adds that since
Lot knew that something had happened, he
surely should have understood why
the younger one was plying him with wine
on the second night. Nonetheless, he allowed himself to become intoxicated once
again.

49. The dots above the word serve to minimize the implication of Esau's gesture. Thus,
we may infer that he did not kiss Jacob with
a full heart (*Binyan Yehoshua*).

50. R' Shimon maintains that when the
Torah wishes to minimize the implication
of the word, only part of the word is dotted.
Since here the entire word is dotted, it must
be that on the contrary, it is coming to *reinforce* the word, and to teach us that Esau
kissed Jacob wholeheartedly. And since we
see that it was necessary for the Torah to inform us of this, we may derive that any other

(וּלְהִתְפַּתּוֹת[52]). כַּיּוֹצֵא בוֹ, (במדבר ג, לט) "כָּל פְּקוּדֵי הַלְוִיִּם אֲשֶׁר פָּקַד מֹשֶׁה וְאַהֲרֹן", נָקוּד עַל אַהֲרֹן. לָמָּה, מְלַמֵּד שֶׁלֹּא הָיָה אַהֲרֹן מִן הַמִּנְיָן[53]. כַּיּוֹצֵא בוֹ, (שם ט, י) "אוֹ בְדֶרֶךְ רְחֹקָה"[54], נָקוּד עַל ה' שֶׁבִּ"רְחֹקָה". מְלַמֵּד שֶׁלֹּא הָיְתָה דֶרֶךְ רְחוֹקָה אֶלָּא מִן אִסְקוּפַּת עֲזָרָה וְלַחוּץ[55]. כַּיּוֹצֵא בוֹ, (שם כא, ל) "וַנָּשִׁים עַד נָפַח אֲשֶׁר עַד מֵידְבָא"[56],

וּלְהִתְפַּתּוֹת — It is teaching us that they did not truly go with intention to pasture the flock, but to eat and to drink[51] and to be persuaded.[52]

כַּיּוֹצֵא בוֹ, "כָּל פְּקוּדֵי הַלְוִיִּם אֲשֶׁר פָּקַד מֹשֶׁה וְאַהֲרֹן" — (vi) Similarly, in the verse, *All the countings of the Levites, which Moses and Aaron counted, etc.* (Numbers 3:39), נָקוּד עַל "אַהֲרֹן" — there is a dot above the word *"ve'Aharon"* [וְאַהֲרֹן], *and Aaron.* לָמָּה, מְלַמֵּד שֶׁלֹּא הָיָה אַהֲרֹן מִן הַמִּנְיָן — Why is this? It teaches us that Aaron was not part of the counting.[53]

כַּיּוֹצֵא בוֹ, "אוֹ בְדֶרֶךְ רְחֹקָה" — (vii) Similarly, in the verse, *If any man will become contaminated through a human corpse or [will be] on a distant road, whether you or your generations, etc.* (ibid. 9:10),[54] נָקוּד עַל ה' שֶׁבִּ"רְחֹקָה" — there is a dot above the letter *hei* of the word *"rechokah"* [רְחֹקָה], *distant.* מְלַמֵּד שֶׁלֹּא הָיְתָה דֶרֶךְ רְחוֹקָה אֶלָּא מִן אִסְקוּפַּת עֲזָרָה וְלַחוּץ — It is teaching us that it is not necessary to actually be on a distant road; rather, it is sufficient if one was merely located somewhere from the threshold of the Temple Courtyard and outward.[55]

כַּיּוֹצֵא בוֹ, "וַנָּשִׁים עַד נָפַח אֲשֶׁר עַד מֵידְבָא" — (viii) Similarly, in the verse, *And*

---

kisses from Esau to Jacob were not sincere (*Magen Avos*, first explanation, based on *Bereishis Rabbah* 78 §9).

51. The Hebrew word אֶת usually functions as a preface to a direct object. Here, as in the previous cases, the dots serve to "remove" the אֶת from the verse; the result of this is that *their father's flock* cannot be considered the direct object of the verb *pasture*. Accordingly, we interpret the verse as two separate clauses: *His brothers went to pasture; their father's flock [was] in Shechem.* Accordingly, the verse is saying that they went to pasture (i.e., indulge) *themselves* (*Yefeh To'ar* to *Bereishis Rabbah* 84 §13, cited in part by *Binyan Yehoshua*).

52. I.e., under the influence of food and drink, they would persuade one another to do something about Joseph (*Ben Avraham*).

53. The commentators (on *Rashi* ad loc.) disagree as to whether this means that

Aaron, who was a Levite, was nonetheless omitted from the Levite count, or that he did not participate with Moses in counting the Levites. *Ahavas Chesed* maintains that both are true; see further there, and see *Avos HaRosh*.

54. The verse states that one who was contaminated by coming in contact with a human corpse or one who was distant from the Temple, and could thus not make the *pesach* offering in its proper time, on the 14th day of Nissan, can make it instead on the 14th day of Iyar. The qualification of the term "distant" is the topic of discussion.

55. The dot over the *hei* serves to minimize the distance, telling us that one does not have to actually be on a distant road in order to be exempt from bringing the *pesach* offering in its time; it suffices that he is outside the Temple Courtyard (*Binyan Yehoshua*, citing *Peachim* 93b with *Rashi*).

נָקוּד עַל רֵי"שׁ שֶׁבַּ"אֲשֶׁ"ר". לָמָּה, מְלַמֵּד שֶׁהֶחֱרִיבוּ °הָעוֹבְדֵי כּוֹכָבִים
וְלֹא הֶחֱרִיבוּ הַמְּדִינוֹת, שֶׁלֹּא הֶחֱרִיבוּ °עוֹבְדֵי כּוֹכָבִים אֶלָּא הַמְּדִינוֹת.[58]
(שם כט, טו) "וְעִשָּׂרוֹן עִשָּׂרוֹן" שֶׁל יוֹם טוֹב הָרִאשׁוֹן שֶׁל חַג הַסֻּכּוֹת,[59] נָקוּד
עַל "עִשָּׂרוֹן" בַּוָּי"ו. לָמָּה, מְלַמֵּד שֶׁלֹּא יְהֵא שָׁם אֶלָּא עִשָּׂרוֹן אֶחָד.[60]
כַּיּוֹצֵא בוֹ, (דברים כט, כח) "הַנִּסְתָּרֹת לַה' אֱלֹהֵינוּ וְהַנִּגְלֹת לָנוּ וּלְבָנֵינוּ",[61]

---

we laid waste to Nophah, which reaches up to Medeba (ibid. 21:30),[56]
"אֲשֶׁ"ר" שֶׁבַּ"רֵי"שׁ עַל נָקוּד — there is a dot above the letter *reish* that is in
the word "*asher*" [אֲשֶׁר], *which.* הֶחֱרִיבוּ וְלֹא הָאֻמּוֹת שֶׁהֶחֱרִיבוּ מְלַמֵּד, לָמָּה,
us teaching is It — Why is this? הַמְּדִינוֹת, אֻמּוֹת אֶלָּא הַמְּדִינוֹת שֶׁלֹּא הֶחֱרִיבוּ
that they destroyed the nations but they did not destroy the provinces,
or vice versa,[57] that they did not destroy the nations, but only the provinces.[58]

הַסֻּכּוֹת חַג שֶׁל הָרִאשׁוֹן טוֹב יוֹם שֶׁל עִשָּׂרוֹן" "וְעִשָּׂרוֹן — (ix) Similarly, in the verse,
And one tenth-ephah, one tenth-ephah, for each lamb of the fourteen lambs
(ibid. 29:15), written in the description of the offerings brought on **the first day
of the Festival of Succos,**[59] בַּוָּי"ו "עִשָּׂרוֹן" עַל נָקוּד — there is a dot above
the *vav* in the first of the two occurrences of the word "*issaron*" [עִשָּׂרוֹן], *one
tenth-ephah.* אֶחָד עִשָּׂרוֹן אֶלָּא שָׁם יְהֵא שֶׁלֹּא מְלַמֵּד לָמָּה, — Why? It is teaching us that there was to be only one measuring utensil in the size of a single
tenth-*ephah* there.[60]

וּלְבָנֵינוּ" לָנוּ וְהַנִּגְלֹת אֱלֹהֵינוּ לַה' "הַנִּסְתָּרֹת בוֹ, כַּיּוֹצֵא — (x) Similarly, in the verse,
*The hidden ones are for HASHEM, our God, but the revealed ones are for
us and our children forever* [עַד עוֹלָם] (*Deuteronomy* 29:28),[61] עַל נָקוּד

---

56. In this verse, the poets describe Sihon's
victory over Moab.

57. *Magen Avos.*

58. The dot on the *reish* of the word אֲשֶׁר
serves to minimize the implication of the
verse, which states that Sihon's army lay
waste to the land of Moab until Nophah and
Medeba. This may be teaching us either that
they destroyed only the lands but not the nations that dwelled upon them, or vice versa
(see ibid., first approach).

59. The cited verse is discussing the meal offering that accompanied the lambs brought
as part of the *mussaf* offering on the first day
of Succos. Each lamb was accompanied by
a meal offering consisting of a tenth-*ephah*
of flour.

60. The dot serves to minimize the number
of measuring utensils used in the Temple,
informing us that there should be no three-
tenth-*ephah* or two-tenth-*ephah* measuring
cups for the meal offerings that accompanied the offerings of bulls and rams respectively. Rather, all measurements were to be
done by using the one-tenth-*ephah* utensil
as many times as needed (*Binyan Yehoshua*, citing *Menachos* 87b).

61. According to the plain meaning of the
verse, the Jewish people are told that the
community bears responsibility for the
sins of the individual, provided that his sins
were revealed. However, they do not bear
responsibility for the hidden sins of individuals; those are God's domain (*Rashi* ad
loc.).

נָקוּד עַל ״לָנוּ וּלְבָנֵינוּ״ וְעַל ע׳ שֶׁבְּ״עַד״.‏62 לָמָּה, אֶלָּא כָּךְ אָמַר עֶזְרָא:‏ אִם יָבֹא אֵלִיָּהוּ וְיֹאמַר לִי מִפְּנֵי מָה כָּתַבְתָּ כָּךְ,‏64 אוֹמֵר אֲנִי לוֹ: כְּבָר נָקַדְתִּי עֲלֵיהֶן.‏65 וְאִם אוֹמֵר לִי: יָפֶה כָּתַבְתָּ,‏66 אַעֲבִיר נְקוּדָה מֵעֲלֵיהֶן.‏67

"לָנוּ וּלְבָנֵינוּ״ וְעַל ע׳ שֶׁבְּ״עַד״ — there are dots above all the letters of the words "lanu ul'vaneinu" [לָנוּ וּלְבָנֵינוּ], for us and our children, and above the letter ayin of the word "ad" [עַד], lit., until. This too is coming to minimize the connotation of the verse.[62]

An alternative explanation for the dotting in the cited verses:[63]

לָמָּה, אֶלָּא כָּךְ אָמַר עֶזְרָא: אִם יָבֹא אֵלִיָּהוּ וְיֹאמַר לִי מִפְּנֵי מָה כָּתַבְתָּ כָּךְ — Why are these verses dotted? Rather, Ezra the Scribe reasoned the following:[64] If Elijah the Prophet will come to me in the Future and say, "Why did you write [these words] in the Torah?," אוֹמֵר אֲנִי לוֹ: כְּבָר נָקַדְתִּי עֲלֵיהֶן — then I will reply to him, "I have already preempted this question when I made dots above [these letters]."[65] וְאִם אוֹמֵר לִי: יָפֶה כָּתַבְתָּ — And if he will say to me, "It was good that you wrote those letters,"[66] אַעֲבִיר נְקוּדָה מֵעֲלֵיהֶן — then I will remove the dots from above them.[67]

---

62. According to our version of the Baraisa, the explanation for the dots in this verse is omitted. However, in *Sanhedrin* 43b, the Gemara cites R' Nechemyah, who says that the dots serve to minimize the time in which the community would be liable for the revealed sins of the individual. R' Nechemyah explains this to mean that the rule of collective responsibility did not go into effect until they crossed the Jordan into the Land of Israel. *Nuschas HaGra* (as emended by *Shenei Eliyahu*) inserts this explanation into our Baraisa as well. For the dissenting opinion of R' Yehudah, see *Sanhedrin* ibid., and see *Bamidbar Rabbah* 3 §13 with the commentators there.

63. *Ahavas Chesed*.

We are following the majority of the commentators, who explain that the forthcoming discussion pertains to all ten places where words or letters are dotted. However, *Binyan Yehoshua* understands it to be referring only to the *Deuteronomy* verse just cited. See *Kisei Rachamim*.

64. Ezra was the spiritual leader of the Jewish nation at the beginning of the Second Temple era. A Torah Scroll written by him and preserved for many generations is mentioned by the Sages in several places (see

e.g., *Moed Katan* 18b, end, two versions cited by *Rashi*). Our Baraisa presumes that Ezra originated the aforementioned dots, apparently because he was unsure whether those letters actually belonged in the Torah; see, however, note 67 below.

65. That is, I intentionally placed the dots above these words to indicate that they may not belong in the text (*Binyan Yehoshua*).

66. And therefore you should not have dotted them (*Ben Avraham*).

67. And they will appear no different from any other word in Scripture.

Magen Avos wonders how Ezra could have doubted whether or not to include these words which are found in our received Torah. Moreover, deleting these words in the *Deuteronomy* verse (as well as most of the other verses) would make the verse unintelligible (*Mas'as HaMelech*, *Ohel Yehoshua* to *Deuteronomy* ad loc.). Indeed, R' Moshe Feinstein (*Igros Moshe, Yoreh Deah*, Vol. 3 §114) emphatically rejects the notion that Ezra was uncertain whether to include these words. Accordingly, he maintains that the version of this statement as it appears here is erroneous, and the correct version is the one cited in *Piskei Tosafos* (*Menachos* §231,

אַחַת עֶשְׂרֵה "הִיא" ["וְהִיא,"] כְּתִיב בְּיוּ"ד בַּתּוֹרָה.[68] הָרִאשׁוֹן הוּא (בראשית יד, ב) "מֶלֶךְ בֶּלַע הִיא צֹעַר". (שם כ, ה) "הֲלֹא הוּא אָמַר לִי אֲחֹתִי הִוא וְהִיא גַם הוּא אָמְרָה אָחִי הוּא". (שם לח, כה) "הִוא מוּצֵאת וְהִיא שָׁלְחָה אֶל חָמִיהָ לֵאמֹר". (ויקרא יא, לט) "וְכִי יָמוּת מִן הַבְּהֵמָה אֲשֶׁר הִיא לָכֶם לְאָכְלָה". (שם יג, י) "וְהִיא הָפְכָה שֵׂעָר לָבָן". (שם פסוק כא) "וְאִם יִרְאֶנָּה הַכֹּהֵן [וְגוֹ'] וְהִיא כֵהָה". (שם כ, יז) "וְהִיא תִרְאֶה אֶת עֶרְוָתוֹ". (שם כא, ט) "אֶת אָבִיהָ הִיא מְחַלֶּלֶת". (בְּקְנָאֹת,) (במדבר ה, יג-יד) "וְנִסְתְּרָה וְהִיא נִטְמָאָה ... (וְהִיא לֹא נִתְפָּשָׂה) ... אוֹ עָבַר עָלָיו רוּחַ קִנְאָה וְקִנֵּא אֶת אִשְׁתּוֹ וְהִיא לֹא נִטְמָאָה":[69,70]

Having discussed the ten places in the Torah where letters are dotted, the Baraisa discusses another anomaly that appears in eleven places in the Torah: אַחַת עֶשְׂרֵה "הִיא" "וְהִיא" כְּתִיב בְּיוּ"ד בַּתּוֹרָה — **There are eleven** places in the Torah where the word *"hi"* [הִיא] or *"vehi"* [וְהִיא] is written with a *yud* as opposed to a *vav*.[68] They are as follows: הָרִאשׁוֹן הוּא "מֶלֶךְ בֶּלַע הִיא צֹעַר" — **(i) The first is:** *And the king of Bela, which is* [הִיא] *Zoar* (*Genesis* 14:2). "הֲלֹא הוּא אָמַר לִי אֲחֹתִי הִוא וְהִיא גַם הוּא אָמְרָה אָחִי הוּא" — **(ii)** *"Did not he himself tell me, 'She is my sister'? And she* [וְהִיא]*, too, herself said, 'He is my brother!'"* (ibid. 20:5). "הִוא מוּצֵאת וְהִיא שָׁלְחָה אֶל חָמִיהָ לֵאמֹר" — **(iii)** *As she was taken out, she* [וְהִיא] *sent word to her father-in-law, saying* (ibid. 38:25). "וְכִי יָמוּת מִן הַבְּהֵמָה אֲשֶׁר הִיא לָכֶם לְאָכְלָה" — **(iv)** *If an animal that* [הִיא] *you may eat has died* (*Leviticus* 11:39). "וְהִיא הָפְכָה שֵׂעָר לָבָן" — **(v)** *And it* [וְהִיא] *has changed hair to white* (ibid. 13:10). "וְאִם יִרְאֶנָּה הַכֹּהֵן — **(vi)** *But if the Kohen looks as it, etc., and it* [וְהִיא] *is dim* וְגוֹ' וְהִיא כֵהָה" (ibid. v. 21). "וְהִיא תִרְאֶה אֶת עֶרְוָתוֹ" — **(vii)** *And she* [וְהִיא] *shall see his nakedness* (ibid. 20:17). "אֶת אָבִיהָ הִיא מְחַלֶּלֶת" — **(viii)** *She* [הִיא] *desecrates her father* (ibid. 21:9). בְּקְנָאֹת, "וְנִסְתְּרָה וְהִיא נִטְמָאָה ... וְהִיא לֹא נִתְפָּשָׂה ... אוֹ עָבַר עָלָיו רוּחַ קִנְאָה וְקִנֵּא אֶת אִשְׁתּוֹ וְהִיא לֹא נִטְמָאָה" — And **there are three in the passage of the jealousies:**[69] **(ix-xi)** *And she became*

---

quoted by *Taz, Yoreh Deah* 274:7), which states merely that Ezra reasoned that if he will be asked why he dotted these letters, he will reply that he did not delete them. (That is, he will reply that he did not dot them because he was in doubt about including them [but only to indicate that they should be expounded as minimizing the implication of the word].) Thus, Ezra was not concerned that he might be asked why he wrote the words altogether, but only that he might be asked why he dotted them. [According to this version, the only difference between

the present opinion and the preceding one is that the preceding one maintains that the Torah Scrolls always contained these dots to indicate the expositions, whereas this opinion holds that the dots indicating the expositions were added by Ezra.]

68. הִיא is the Hebrew pronoun for "she." In most places where this word or its conjunctive form appears in the Torah, it is spelled הוּא, with a *vav* instead of a *yud*. In eleven places, however, it is spelled as it is pronounced (*Binyan Yehoshua*).

69. I.e., the passage dealing with the *sotah*,

ה. עֶשֶׂר יְרִידוֹת יָרְדָה שְׁכִינָה עַל הָעוֹלָם.[71] אַחַת בְּגַן עֵדֶן, שֶׁנֶּאֱמַר
(בראשית ג, ח) "וַיִּשְׁמְעוּ אֶת קוֹל ה' אֱלֹהִים מִתְהַלֵּךְ בַּגָּן".[72] וְאַחַת בְּדוֹר
הַמִּגְדָּל, שֶׁנֶּאֱמַר (שם יא, ה) "וַיֵּרֶד ה' לִרְאֹת אֶת הָעִיר וְאֶת הַמִּגְדָּל".[73]
וְאַחַת בִּסְדוֹם, שֶׁנֶּאֱמַר (שם יח, כא) "אֵרְדָה נָּא וְאֶרְאֶה הַכְּצַעֲקָתָהּ הַבָּאָה
אֵלַי".[74] וְאַחַת בְּמִצְרַיִם,[75] שֶׁנֶּאֱמַר (שמות ג, ח) "וָאֵרֵד לְהַצִּילוֹ מִיַּד מִצְרַיִם".

---

secluded and she [וְהִיא] could have been defiled ... and she [וְהִיא] had not
been forced ... or a spirit of jealousy had passed over him and he had warned
his wife and she [וְהִיא] had not become defiled (Numbers 5:13-14).[70]

§5 The Baraisa resumes citing teachings involving the number ten:

עֶשֶׂר יְרִידוֹת יָרְדָה שְׁכִינָה עַל הָעוֹלָם — On ten occasions, the Divine Presence descended onto the world below:[71] אַחַת בְּגַן עֵדֶן, שֶׁנֶּאֱמַר "וַיִּשְׁמְעוּ אֶת
קוֹל ה' אֱלֹהִים מִתְהַלֵּךְ בַּגָּן" — (i) One was in the Garden of Eden, as it is stated,
[Adam and his wife] heard the sound of HASHEM God moving in the garden
(Genesis 3:8).[72] וְאַחַת בְּדוֹר הַמִּגְדָּל, שֶׁנֶּאֱמַר "וַיֵּרֶד ה' לִרְאֹת אֶת הָעִיר וְאֶת
הַמִּגְדָּל" — (ii) One was in the generation that built the Tower of Babel, as it is
stated, HASHEM descended to look at the city and the tower (ibid. 11:5).[73]
וְאַחַת בִּסְדוֹם, שֶׁנֶּאֱמַר "אֵרְדָה נָּא וְאֶרְאֶה הַכְּצַעֲקָתָהּ הַבָּאָה אֵלַי" — (iii) One was in
Sodom, as it is stated that God said, "I will descend and see: If they act in
accordance with its outcry which has come to Me — then destruction!" (ibid.
18:21).[74] וְאַחַת בְּמִצְרַיִם, שֶׁנֶּאֱמַר "וָאֵרֵד לְהַצִּילוֹ מִיַּד מִצְרַיִם" — (iv) One was
in Egypt,[75] as it is stated that God said to Moses at the Burning Bush, "I have
descended to rescue [My people] from the hand of Egypt" (Exodus 3:8).

---

a woman whose husband suspects her of
adultery and warns her not to seclude herself with a certain man.

70. Binyan Yehoshua points out that in the
Masoretic text, the second occurrence of וְהִיא
(in the phrase, and she had not been forced)
is spelled with a vav, not a yud. Instead, the
word היא in the verse (Leviticus 16:31), It
[הִיא] is a Sabbath of complete rest for you, is
written with a yud. See Nuschas HaGra, who
emends the text of our Baraisa accordingly.

71. The commentators note that although
the Baraisa states "ten" occasions, it then
enumerates only nine. They therefore suggest various ways of emending the text. We
will cite one of these emendations in note 75.

72. God descended to the Garden of Eden in
order to pass judgment on Adam, Eve, and the
serpent for disobeying His injunction against

eating the fruit of the Tree of Knowledge.

73. The builders of the Tower did so with the
intention of rebelling against God (see Rashi
to v. 1 there, and see Bereishis Rabbah 38
§6). God descended in order to punish them
(see Targum Onkelos to the cited verse).

74. God descended to judge the residents of
Sodom and Gomorrah for their terrible deeds,
and to destroy them if they were found guilty.

75. Avos HaRosh (see also Binyan Yehoshua) inserts the following lines into the text
at this point, based on Pirkei DeRabbi Eliezer
Chs. 39-40: שֶׁנֶּאֱמַר "אָנֹכִי אֵרֵד עִמְּךָ מִצְרַיְמָה" —
as it is stated that God said to Jacob, "I
shall descend with you to Egypt" (Genesis
46:4). ... וְאַחַת בַּסְּנֶה — And one was in the
Burning Bush, as it is stated, etc. This accounts for the missing tenth descent in our
Baraisa; see note 71.

וְאַחַת עַל הַיָּם, שֶׁנֶּאֱמַר (תהלים יח, י) "וַיֵּט שָׁמַיִם וַיֵּרַד"‎[76]. וְאַחַת בְּסִינַי, שֶׁנֶּאֱמַר (שמות יט, כ) "וַיֵּרֶד ה' עַל הַר סִינַי, (שם פסוק יא) "לְעֵינֵי כָל הָעָם"‎[77]. וְאַחַת בַּמִּקְדָּשׁ, שֶׁנֶּאֱמַר‎[78] (יחזקאל מד, ב) "וַיֹּאמֶר אֵלַי ה' הַשַּׁעַר הַזֶּה סָגוּר יִהְיֶה לֹא יִפָּתֵחַ וְגוֹ' כִּי ה' אֱלֹהֵי יִשְׂרָאֵל בָּא בוֹ". וְאַחַת בְּעַמּוּד הֶעָנָן‎[79], שֶׁנֶּאֱמַר (במדבר יא, כה) "וַיֵּרֶד ה' בֶּעָנָן"‎[78]. וְאַחַת שֶׁעֲתִידָה לִהְיוֹת בִּימֵי גּוֹג וּמָגוֹג, שֶׁנֶּאֱמַר (זכריה יד, ד) "וְעָמְדוּ רַגְלָיו בַּיּוֹם הַהוּא עַל הַר הַזֵּיתִים"‎[80]:

ו. עֲשָׂרָה מַעֲלוֹת נִסְתַּלְּקָה שְׁכִינָה מִמָּקוֹם לְמָקוֹם‎[81]. מִכַּפֹּרֶת לִכְרוּב‎[82],

וְאַחַת עַל הַיָּם, שֶׁנֶּאֱמַר "וַיֵּט שָׁמַיִם וַיֵּרַד"‎ — (v) One was at the Sea of Reeds, as it is stated, *He bent down the heavens and descended* (Psalms 18:10).[76] וְאַחַת בְּסִינַי, שֶׁנֶּאֱמַר "וַיֵּרֶד ה' עַל הַר סִינַי", "... לְעֵינֵי כָל הָעָם"‎ — (vi) One was at Mount Sinai, as it is stated, *HASHEM descended upon Mount Sinai* (Exodus 19:20), and earlier, "*For on the third day HASHEM shall descend in the sight of the entire people on Mount Sinai*" (ibid. v. 11).[77] וְאַחַת בַּמִּקְדָּשׁ, שֶׁנֶּאֱמַר "וַיֹּאמֶר אֵלַי ה' הַשַּׁעַר הַזֶּה סָגוּר יִהְיֶה לֹא יִפָּתֵחַ וְגוֹ' כִּי ה' אֱלֹהֵי יִשְׂרָאֵל בָּא בוֹ"‎ — (vii) One will be in the Third Temple, as it is stated,[78] *HASHEM said to me, "This gate shall be closed; it shall not be opened; no man may come through it, because HASHEM, the God of Israel, has come through it"* (Ezekiel 44:2). וְאַחַת בְּעַמּוּד הֶעָנָן, שֶׁנֶּאֱמַר "וַיֵּרֶד ה' בֶּעָנָן"‎ — (viii) One was in the pillar of cloud in the Tabernacle, as it is stated, *HASHEM descended in a cloud* and spoke to *[Moses], etc.* (Numbers 11:25).[79] וְאַחַת שֶׁעֲתִידָה לִהְיוֹת בִּימֵי גּוֹג וּמָגוֹג, שֶׁנֶּאֱמַר "וְעָמְדוּ רַגְלָיו בַּיּוֹם הַהוּא עַל הַר הַזֵּיתִים"‎ — (ix) And one is destined to be in the days of Gog and Magog, as it is stated, *His feet will stand on that day on the Mount of Olives, etc.* (Zechariah 14:4).[80]

§6 עֲשָׂרָה מַעֲלוֹת נִסְתַּלְּקָה שְׁכִינָה מִמָּקוֹם לְמָקוֹם‎ — The Divine Presence departed from the Temple during the period of the destruction of the First Temple in ten stages, journeying from place to place until it returned to Heaven:[81] מִכַּפֹּרֶת לִכְרוּב‎ — (i) It first went from its established station on the

---

76. See Ch. 33 above, where the Baraisa expounds this passage in connection with the Splitting of the Sea of Reeds (*Ben Avraham*).

77. [Actually, the words לְעֵינֵי כָל הָעָם, *in the sight of the entire people,* do not appear in the early texts of *Avos DeRabbi Nassan,* but were added based on an emendation that appears in *Tummas Yesharim*.]

78. This verse is from the prophet Ezekiel's vision of the future Third Temple. See *Avos HaRosh*.

79. God descended into the Tent of Meeting

in order to impart some of the spirit of prophecy that was on Moses to the seventy elders.

80. The passage there foretells a climactic battle that will take place in Jerusalem in the era of the Future Redemption. God Himself will descend, so to speak, onto the Mount of Olives and battle Israel's enemies. Elsewhere (*Ezekiel* Chs. 38-39), it states that Israel's enemies will be led at that time by Gog, king of Magog.

81. [See *Rosh Hashanah* 31a and *Eichah Rabbah, Pesichta* §25, for alternative

וּמִכְּרוּב לְמִפְתַּן הַבַּיִת83, וּמִמִּפְתַּן הַבַּיִת לִשְׁנֵי כְּרוּבִים84, וּמִשְׁנֵי כְּרוּבִים
לְגַג הַהֵיכָל, וּמִגַּג הַהֵיכָל לְחוֹמַת עֲזָרָה, וּמֵחוֹמַת עֲזָרָה לְמִזְבֵּחַ,
וּמִמִּזְבֵּחַ לָעִיר, וּמֵעִיר לְהַר (הַבַּיִת86), וּמֵהַר (הַבַּיִת) לַמִּדְבָּר. מִכַּפּוֹרֶת
לִכְרוּב, דִּכְתִיב (שמואל ב כב, יא) "וַיִּרְכַּב עַל כְּרוּב וַיָּעֹף"88. מִכְּרוּב לְמִפְתָּן,

---

Ark-cover to a Cherub,[82] וּמִכְּרוּב לְמִפְתַּן הַבַּיִת — (ii) then from the Cherub
to the threshold of the Temple.[83] וּמִמִּפְתַּן הַבַּיִת לִשְׁנֵי כְּרוּבִים — (iii) It then
returned from the threshold of the Temple to the two Cherubim,[84] וּמִשְׁנֵי
כְּרוּבִים לְגַג הַהֵיכָל — (iv) and then traveled from the two Cherubim to the roof
of the Sanctuary, וּמִגַּג הַהֵיכָל לְחוֹמַת עֲזָרָה — (v) then from the roof of the
Sanctuary to the wall of the Courtyard, וּמֵחוֹמַת עֲזָרָה לְמִזְבֵּחַ — (vi) then
from the wall of the Courtyard to the Outer Altar,[85] וּמִמִּזְבֵּחַ לָעִיר — (vii)
then from the Outer Altar to the city of Jerusalem, וּמֵעִיר לְהַר הַבַּיִת — (viii)
then from the city to the Temple Mount,[86] וּמֵהַר הַבַּיִת לַמִּדְבָּר — (ix) then
from the Temple Mount to the wilderness, (x) and from the wilderness, It
ascended to its place in Heaven.[87]

The Baraisa cites the Scriptural source for each of these journeys:
מִכַּפּוֹרֶת לִכְרוּב, דִּכְתִיב "וַיִּרְכַּב עַל כְּרוּב וַיָּעֹף" — We know that the Divine Presence journeyed from the Ark-cover to a Cherub, for it is written with regard
to God, *He mounted a cherub and flew* (II Samuel 22:11).[88] מִכְּרוּב לְמִפְתָּן,

---

versions of this teaching.]

During the latter years of the First Temple
era, as the Jews sank ever deeper into sin,
the Divine Presence gradually departed the
Temple. It did so agonizingly and incremen-
tally, in the hope that the Jews would repent
(*Rashi to Rosh Hashanah* ibid., cited in part
by *Binyan Yehoshua*).

82. There were two sets of Cherubim in the
First Temple — one set was hammered from
the top of the Ark-cover in Moses' times,
and another set, crafted by order of King
Solomon, stood on the Temple floor on either side of the Ark (see *I Kings* 6:23). Originally, the Divine Presence resided on top of
the Ark-cover, between the two Cherubim.
In its first "journey," the Divine Presence left
the Ark-cover and alighted on one of the
Cherubim that had been crafted by Solomon
(*Rashi* loc. cit.).

83. I.e., the threshold of the Holy of Holies
(*Rashi to Ezekiel* 9:3).

84. Although the Divine Presence was in the
process of *departing* from the Sanctuary,

it returned to the Cherubim one more time
as a way of bidding farewell to the Temple,
so to speak. See *Eichah Rabbah* ibid. for a
poignant description of this episode.

85. *Rashi to Rosh Hashanah* ibid.

86. In *Rosh Hashanah* ibid., the Gemara
does not specify to which mountain the Divine Presence traveled. *Rashi* says that it is
referring to the Mount of Olives, and *Eichah
Rabbah* ibid. states this explicitly. See *Nuschas HaGra*, who emends the Baraisa here
to conform with the Gemara. [According to
our version of the Baraisa, we would have
to explain that the Divine Presence returned
from the city to the Temple Mount to bid
farewell, just as when it returned from the
threshold of the Holy of Holies to the Cherubim, as explained in note 84.]

87. See below; see *Mefaresh* and *Nuschas
HaGra*, who insert this into the text of the
Baraisa itself.

88. That the Divine Presence initially dwelled
on the Ark-cover is derived from *Exodus*

דְּכְתִיב (יחזקאל ט, ג) ‏"(וַיַּעַל כְּבוֹד ה') ° מֵעַל הַכְּרוּב אֲשֶׁר °יִהְיֶה עָלָיו אֶל מִפְתַּן הַבָּיִת‏"‏[89]. וּמִמִּפְתַּן הַבַּיִת לִשְׁנֵי כְּרוּבִים, דְּכְתִיב (שם י, יח) ‏"וַיֵּצֵא כְּבוֹד ה' מֵעַל מִפְתַּן הַבַּיִת וַיַּעֲמֹד עַל הַכְּרוּבִים‏"‏[90]. מִכְּרוּב לְגַג הַהֵיכָל, דְּכְתִיב (משלי כא, ט) ‏"טוֹב לָשֶׁבֶת עַל פִּנַּת גָּג‏"‏[91]. מִגַּג לְחוֹמַת הָעֲזָרָה, דְּכְתִיב (עמוס ז, ז) ‏"וְהִנֵּה ה' נִצָּב עַל חוֹמַת אֲנָךְ‏"‏[92]. וּמֵחוֹמַת הָעֲזָרָה לַמִּזְבֵּחַ,

---

It — דְּכְתִיב ‏"וּכְבוֹד אֱלֹהֵי יִשְׂרָאֵל נַעֲלָה מֵעַל הַכְּרוּב אֲשֶׁר הָיָה עָלָיו אֶל מִפְתַּן הַבָּיִת‏" journeyed from the Cherub to the threshold of the Temple, as it is written, *Then the glory of the God of Israel ascended from atop the Cherub on which it had been, going to the threshold of the Temple* (Ezekiel 9:3).[89] וּמִמִּפְתַּן

It — הַבַּיִת לִשְׁנֵי כְּרוּבִים, דְּכְתִיב ‏"וַיֵּצֵא כְּבוֹד ה' מֵעַל מִפְתַּן הַבַּיִת וַיַּעֲמֹד עַל הַכְּרוּבִים‏" journeyed from the threshold of the Temple to the two Cherubim, as it is written, *The glory of HASHEM then went forth from upon the threshold of the Temple and stood upon the Cherubim* (ibid. 10:18).[90] מִכְּרוּב לְגַג הַהֵיכָל,

דְּכְתִיב ‏"טוֹב לָשֶׁבֶת עַל פִּנַּת גָּג‏" — It journeyed from the Cherub(im) to the roof of the Sanctuary, as it is written, *Better is dwelling on a corner of a roof* than [dwelling with] a contentious wife in a house of associates (Proverbs 21:9).[91]

מִגַּג לְחוֹמַת הָעֲזָרָה, דְּכְתִיב ‏"וְהִנֵּה ה' נִצָּב עַל חוֹמַת אֲנָךְ‏" — It journeyed from the roof of the Sanctuary to the wall of the Courtyard, as it is written, *Behold, the Lord standing on a plumbed wall* (Amos 7:7).[92] וּמֵחוֹמַת הָעֲזָרָה לַמִּזְבֵּחַ,

---

25:22, where God tells Moses, *It is there that I will set My meetings with you, and I shall speak with you from atop the Cover* (*Rosh Hashanah* ibid.). The verse from *II Samuel* is understood as alluding to the period before the destruction of the Temple, and saying that the Divine Presence would depart from its place on the Ark-cover and alight on one of Solomon's Cherubim before ultimately ascending back to Heaven. [Cf. *Rashi* to *Rosh Hashanah* ibid.]

89. [Emendation follows *Nuschas HaGra*.] Ezekiel prophesied in the period of the destruction of the First Temple. In this vision, which he was shown some time before the destruction, he saw the Divine Presence travel from the Cherub to the threshold of the Holy of Holies.

90. Although in this journey the Divine Presence actually *returned* to the Holy of Holies, the verse uses the term *went forth* since its reentry was for the purpose of taking leave (*Eichah Rabbah, Pesichta* §25 with *Eitz Yosef*).

91. This verse foretells God's eventual departure from the Temple in the wake of Israel's sins. The "contentious wife" is the congregation of Israel, who abandoned God by placing an idol in the Sanctuary (see *Sanhedrin* 103b). The "house of associates" describes the Temple after Israel introduced the idol into it in an attempt to associate the idol with God. King Solomon, who authored the Book of *Proverbs*, predicted that the Divine Presence would at some point dwell on the roof rather than tolerate this association (*Rashi* to *Rosh Hashanah* ibid.).

92. The word אֲנָךְ, *plumbed*, has a numerical value of 71 [א=1, נ=50, ך=20]. This alludes to the Great Sanhedrin of seventy-one judges that convened in the Chamber of Hewn Stone, which bordered on the wall of the Courtyard. Hence, when the verse states that God stood on the "אֲנָךְ wall," it alludes to the wall of the Temple Courtyard (*Ahavas Chesed*, citing *Eichah Rabbah* ibid. with *Yefeh Anaf* ad loc.).

Amos prophesied during the reign of Uzziah, king of Judah, many generations before

שֶׁנֶּאֱמַר (שם ט, א) "רָאִיתִי אֶת ה' נִצָּב עַל הַמִּזְבֵּחַ". וּמִמִּזְבֵּחַ לָעִיר,
שֶׁנֶּאֱמַר (מיכה ו, ט) "קוֹל ה' לָעִיר יִקְרָא"[93]. וּמֵעִיר לָהַר, דִּכְתִיב (יחזקאל יא,
כג) "וַיַּעַל כְּבוֹד ה' מֵעַל תּוֹךְ הָעִיר וַיַּעֲמֹד עַל הָהָר וְגו' ". מֵהַר לַמִּדְבָּר,
דִּכְתִיב (משלי כא, יט) "טוֹב שֶׁבֶת בְּאֶרֶץ מִדְבָּר". וְאַחַת שֶׁנִּסְתַּלְּקָה כְּלַפֵּי
מַעְלָה, שֶׁנֶּאֱמַר (הושע ה, טו) "אֵלֵךְ אָשׁוּבָה אֶל מְקוֹמִי":

ז. עֲשָׂרָה שֵׁמוֹת נִקְרָא נָבִיא. אֵלּוּ הֵן: צִיר. נֶאֱמָן. עֶבֶד. שָׁלִיחַ[94]. חוֹזֶה.
צוֹפֶה[95]. רוֹאֶה. חוֹלֵם[96]. נָבִיא. אִישׁ הָאֱלֹהִים:

"רָאִיתִי אֶת ה' נִצָּב עַל הַמִּזְבֵּחַ" שֶׁנֶּאֱמַר — It journeyed from the wall of the Court-yard to the Outer Altar, as it is stated, *I saw the Lord standing upon the Altar* (ibid. 9:1).   "קוֹל ה' לָעִיר יִקְרָא" שֶׁנֶּאֱמַר ,לָעִיר וּמִמִּזְבֵּחַ — It journeyed from the Outer **Altar** to the city of Jerusalem, as it is stated, *The voice of HASHEM calls out to the [people of the] city* (*Micah* 6:9).[93]   ה' כְּבוֹד "וַיַּעַל דִּכְתִיב ,לָהַר וּמֵעִיר " וְגו' הָהָר עַל וַיַּעֲמֹד הָעִיר תּוֹךְ מֵעַל — It journeyed from the city of Jerusalem to the Temple **Mount,** as it is written, *And the glory of HASHEM ascended from over the midst of the city and stood upon the mountain* that is east of the city (*Ezekiel* 11:23).   "מִדְבָּר בְּאֶרֶץ שֶׁבֶת "טוֹב דִּכְתִיב ,לַמִּדְבָּר מֵהַר — It journeyed from the Temple **Mount** to the wilderness, as it is written, *Better to dwell in a desert land* than [with] *a woman of contention and anger* (*Proverbs* 21:19).   מַעְלָה כְּלַפֵּי שֶׁנִּסְתַּלְּקָה וְאַחַת — And one last journey was when it departed from this world entirely and returned to its place **on High,**   אָשׁוּבָה "אֵלֵךְ שֶׁנֶּאֱמַר "מְקוֹמִי אֶל — as it is stated, *I will go, I will return to My place* (*Hosea* 5:15).

נָבִיא נִקְרָא שֵׁמוֹת עֲשָׂרָה — **§7** There are ten terms used to describe a prophet.   הֵן אֵלּוּ — **They are as follows:**   רוֹאֶה. צוֹפֶה. חוֹזֶה. שָׁלִיחַ. עֶבֶד. נֶאֱמָן. צִיר. — (i) *Messenger,* (ii) *trusted one,* (iii) *servant,* (iv) *agent,*[94] (v) *viewer,* (vi) *lookout,*[95] (vii) *seer,* (viii) *one who dreams,*[96] (ix) *prophet,* and (x) *man of God.*   הָאֱלֹהִים אִישׁ נָבִיא. חוֹלֵם. —

Ezekiel (see *Amos* 1:1). However, Amos stated this verse as a prophecy of future events. The Baraisa assumes that it represents the fifth journey, since logic dictates that the Divine Presence gradually made its way out of the Temple area (see *Rashi* to *Rosh Hashanah* ibid., and see *Ben Avraham*).

93. *"The"* city is a reference to Jerusalem (*Metzudas David* ad loc.).

94. The first four terms describe the prophet's relationship with God. A prophet is a servant of God, whom He trusts to act as His emissary and convey His message to its

intended recipient.

95. In *Ezekiel* Ch. 33, God compares the task of a prophet to that of a sentinel who is responsible to warn the residents of a city in the event that an enemy approaches. In the same manner, it is the responsibility of a prophet to convey the word of God to the people, and to warn them if He has foretold evil about them, so that they may save themselves by repenting.

96. The terms *viewer, seer,* and *one who dreams* describe the prophet's perception of the Divine vision that he is shown.

ח. עֲשָׂרָה שֵׁמוֹת נִקְרָא רוּחַ הַקֹּדֶשׁ[97]. אֵלּוּ הֵן: מָשָׁל. מְלִיצָה. חִידָה[98].
דִּיבּוּר. אֲמִירָה. תִּפְאֶרֶת[99]. צִיווּי[100]. מַשָּׂא[101]. נְבוּאָה. חִזָּיוֹן:

ט. עֲשָׂרָה שֵׁמוֹת נִקְרָא שִׂמְחָה. אֵלּוּ הֵן: שָׂשׂוֹן. שִׂמְחָה. גִּילָה. רִינָה.
דִּיצָה. צָהֳלָה. עֲלִיזָה. חֶדְוָה. תִּפְאֶרֶת[102]. עֲלִיצָה:

י. עֲשָׂרָה נִקְרְאוּ חַיִּים. הַקָּדוֹשׁ בָּרוּךְ הוּא, (ירמיה י, י) "וַה' אֱלֹהִים אֱמֶת
הוּא אֱלֹהִים חַיִּים". תּוֹרָה נִקְרֵאת חַיִּים, שֶׁנֶּאֱמַר (משלי ג, יח) "עֵץ חַיִּים
הִיא לַמַּחֲזִיקִים בָּהּ וְתוֹמְכֶיהָ מְאֻשָּׁר". יִשְׂרָאֵל נִקְרְאוּ חַיִּים, שֶׁנֶּאֱמַר (דברים

§8 עֲשָׂרָה שֵׁמוֹת נִקְרָא רוּחַ הַקֹּדֶשׁ — *The Holy Spirit* of prophecy is called by ten
descriptions:[97]   אֵלּוּ הֵן — They are as follows: מָשָׁל. מְלִיצָה. חִידָה.
חִזָּיוֹן נְבוּאָה. מַשָּׂא. צִיווּי. תִּפְאֶרֶת. אֲמִירָה. דִּיבּוּר — (i) *Parable*, (ii) *metaphor*,
(iii) *riddle*,[98] (iv) *speech*, (v) *saying*, (vi) *splendor*,[99] (vii) *command*,[100]
(viii) *burden*,[101] (ix) *prophecy*, and (x) *vision*.

§9 עֲשָׂרָה שֵׁמוֹת נִקְרָא שִׂמְחָה — There are ten terms used to describe joy.
אֵלּוּ הֵן — They are as follows: שָׂשׂוֹן. שִׂמְחָה. גִּילָה. רִינָה. דִּיצָה. צָהֳלָה.
עֲלִיצָה. תִּפְאֶרֶת. חֶדְוָה. עֲלִיזָה — (i) *Joy*, (ii) *gladness*, (iii) *mirth*, (iv) *glad
song*, (v) *pleasure*, (vi) *jubilation*, (vii) *exultation*, (viii) *delight*, (ix) *splendor*,[102] and (x) *elation*.

§10 עֲשָׂרָה נִקְרְאוּ חַיִּים — There are ten beings that are called "living" or
"life":   הַקָּדוֹשׁ בָּרוּךְ הוּא, "וַה' אֱלֹהִים אֱמֶת הוּא אֱלֹהִים חַיִּים" — (i) The
Holy One, Blessed is He, is referred to as living, as it states, *But HASHEM,
God, is True; He is the living God* (*Jeremiah* 10:10).   תּוֹרָה נִקְרֵאת
חַיִּים, שֶׁנֶּאֱמַר "עֵץ חַיִּים הִיא לַמַּחֲזִיקִים בָּהּ וְתוֹמְכֶיהָ מְאֻשָּׁר" — (ii) The Torah is
called life, as it is stated, *It is a tree of life to those who grasp it, and its
supporters are praiseworthy* (*Proverbs* 3:18).   יִשְׂרָאֵל נִקְרְאוּ חַיִּים, שֶׁנֶּאֱמַר

---

97. *Bereishis Rabbah* 44 §6 indicates that
these terms refer to various types of prophetic visions.

98. The prophets (with the exception of
Moses) did not perceive their prophecy with
absolute clarity; often it would be conveyed
to them in the form of a parable or a riddle,
which they would then have to interpret
in order to discern God's message (see
Numbers 12:6-8).

99. The commentators point out that we do
not find this term used anywhere in reference to prophecy. Most of them prefer the
alternative version of סוֹכָה, *gazing*, cited by
Tummas Yesharim, who explains that this is

based on the verse (*Genesis* 11:29) where
Sarah is called by the name יִסְכָּה, alluding to
her ability to *gaze* through the Divine Spirit
of prophecy (*Rashi* ad loc., from *Megillah*
14a).

100. The terms *speak*, *say*, and *command*
are used countless times in Scripture in
reference to God's communication with the
prophets.

101. This term for prophecy appears frequently in the Books of the Prophets; see
e.g., *II Kings* 9:25.

102. The joy that a person feels in his
heart is reflected in the splendor of his face
(*Magen Avos*).

ד, ד) ״וְאַתֶּם הַדְּבֵקִים בַּה׳ אֱלֹהֵיכֶם חַיִּים כֻּלְּכֶם הַיּוֹם״. צַדִּיק נִקְרָא חַיִּים,
שֶׁנֶּאֱמַר (משלי יא, ל) ״פְּרִי צַדִּיק עֵץ חַיִּים״[103]. גַּן עֵדֶן נִקְרָא חַיִּים, ([שנאמר
(תהלים קטז) אֶתְהַלֵּךְ לִפְנֵי ה׳ בְּאַרְצוֹת הַחַיִּים. עֵץ נִקְרָא חַיִּים]) שֶׁנֶּאֱמַר
(בראשית ב, ט) ״וְעֵץ הַחַיִּים בְּתוֹךְ הַגָּן״[104]. אֶרֶץ יִשְׂרָאֵל נִקְרֵאת חַיִּים,
שֶׁנֶּאֱמַר (יחזקאל כו, כ) ״וְנָתַתִּי צְבִי בְּאֶרֶץ חַיִּים״. (יְרוּשָׁלַיִם נִקְרֵאת חַיִּים,
שֶׁנֶּאֱמַר (תהלים קטז, ט) ״אֶתְהַלֵּךְ לִפְנֵי ה׳ בְּאַרְצוֹת הַחַיִּים״[105]). גְּמִילוּת
חֲסָדִים נִקְרָא חַיִּים, שֶׁנֶּאֱמַר (תהלים סג, ד) ״כִּי טוֹב חַסְדְּךָ מֵחַיִּים שְׂפָתַי
יְשַׁבְּחוּנְךָ״. חָכָם נִקְרָא חַיִּים, שֶׁנֶּאֱמַר (משלי יג, יד) ״תּוֹרַת חָכָם מְקוֹר
חַיִּים״. מַיִם נִקְרָא חַיִּים, שֶׁנֶּאֱמַר (זכריה יד, ח) ״בַּיּוֹם הַהוּא יֵצְאוּ מַיִם חַיִּים
מִירוּשָׁלַיִם״:

״וְאַתֶּם הַדְּבֵקִים בַּה׳ אֱלֹהֵיכֶם חַיִּים כֻּלְּכֶם הַיּוֹם״ — (iii) The people of Israel are called living, as it is stated, *But you who cling to HASHEM, your God — you are all alive today* (Deuteronomy 4:4). צַדִּיק נִקְרָא חַיִּים, שֶׁנֶּאֱמַר ״פְּרִי צַדִּיק עֵץ חַיִּים״ — (iv) A righteous person is called life, as it is stated, *The fruit of a righteous one is a tree of life* (Proverbs 11:30).[103] גַּן עֵדֶן נִקְרָא חַיִּים, שֶׁנֶּאֱמַר ״וְעֵץ הַחַיִּים בְּתוֹךְ הַגָּן״ — (v) The Garden of Eden is called life, as it is stated, *And the Tree of life in the midst of the garden* (Genesis 2:9).[104] אֶרֶץ יִשְׂרָאֵל נִקְרֵאת חַיִּים, שֶׁנֶּאֱמַר ״וְנָתַתִּי צְבִי בְּאֶרֶץ חַיִּים״ — (vi) The Land of Israel is called life, as it is stated, *But I will bestow splendor upon the Land of Life* (Ezekiel 26:20). יְרוּשָׁלַיִם נִקְרֵאת חַיִּים, שֶׁנֶּאֱמַר ״אֶתְהַלֵּךְ לִפְנֵי ה׳ בְּאַרְצוֹת הַחַיִּים״ — (vii) Jerusalem is called life, as it is stated, *I shall walk before HASHEM in the lands of life* (Psalms 116:9).[105] גְּמִילוּת חֲסָדִים נִקְרָא חַיִּים, שֶׁנֶּאֱמַר ״כִּי טוֹב חַסְדְּךָ מֵחַיִּים שְׂפָתַי יְשַׁבְּחוּנְךָ״ — (viii) Acts of kindness are called life, as it is stated, *For Your kindness is better than life, my lips shall praise You* (ibid. 63:4). חָכָם נִקְרָא חַיִּים, שֶׁנֶּאֱמַר ״תּוֹרַת חָכָם מְקוֹר חַיִּים״ — (ix) A wise person is called life, as it is stated, *The teaching of the wise man is a source of life* (Proverbs 13:14). מַיִם נִקְרָא חַיִּים, שֶׁנֶּאֱמַר ״בַּיּוֹם הַהוּא יֵצְאוּ מַיִם חַיִּים מִירוּשָׁלַיִם״ — Water is called living, as it is stated, *On that day living water will flow out of Jerusalem* (Zechariah 14:8).

---

103. Through his virtuous deeds, the righteous individual brings life to the entire world (*Rashi* ad loc.).

104. [Emendation of the text follows *Binyan Yehoshua* and most other commentators, and conforms with earlier prints.] Since the Garden of Eden contains the Tree of Life, it itself is called "life" (*Binyan Yehoshua*, from

Zayis Raanan to *Yalkut Shimoni, Tehillim* §874).

105. Jerusalem is referred to as *the lands of life*, in the plural, in accordance with the teaching of the Sages (*Taanis* 5a) that there is a celestial city of Jerusalem corresponding to the earthly city. The plural *lands* refers to both of these cities (*Magen Avos*).

﴾ פֶּרֶק לה ﴿

א. עֲשָׂרָה[1] נִסִּים נַעֲשׂוּ לַאֲבוֹתֵינוּ בְּבֵית הַמִּקְדָּשׁ. [°מֵעוֹלָם לֹא הִסְרִיחַ בְּשַׂר הַקֹּדֶשׁ[.5] °וְלֹא הִפִּילָה אִשָּׁה מֵרֵיחַ בְּשַׂר הַקּוֹדֶשׁ[6]. °(עֲשָׂרָה נִסִּים נַעֲשׂוּ לַאֲבוֹתֵינוּ בִּירוּשָׁלַיִם.) לֹא נִזּוֹק אָדָם בִּירוּשָׁלַיִם מֵעוֹלָם.[7]

﴾ CHAPTER 35 ﴿

§1 Continuing to discuss sets of ten,[1] the Baraisa cites and elaborates *Avos* 5:5:

עֲשָׂרָה נִסִּים נַעֲשׂוּ לַאֲבוֹתֵינוּ בְּבֵית הַמִּקְדָּשׁ — **Ten miracles were performed** regularly **for our ancestors in the Holy Temple.** עֲשָׂרָה נִסִּים נַעֲשׂוּ לַאֲבוֹתֵינוּ בִּירוּשָׁלַיִם — And **ten miracles were performed** regularly **for our ancestors in Jerusalem:**[2]

The Baraisa starts by enumerating the ten miracles in Jerusalem.[3] Later, it will return to discuss those of the Temple:[4]

מֵעוֹלָם לֹא הִסְרִיחַ בְּשַׂר הַקֹּדֶשׁ — (i) **Never did the sacrificial meat become putrid;**[5] וְלֹא הִפִּילָה אִשָּׁה מֵרֵיחַ בְּשַׂר הַקּוֹדֶשׁ — (ii) **no woman** in Jerusalem ever **miscarried because of the aroma of the sacrificial meat;**[6] לֹא נִזּוֹק אָדָם בִּירוּשָׁלַיִם מֵעוֹלָם — (iii) **no person ever got injured** by a snake or

---

1. *Magen Avos.*

2. In many texts, this sentence appears below, after the first two examples. It has been moved here based on *Binyan Yehoshua, Ahavas Chesed,* and *Avos HaRosh* [Vol. 2]; see also *Kisei Rachamim.* For a slightly different emendation, see *Magen Avos* and *Hagahos HaGra.*

3. [For a discussion of whether these ten miracles occurred only during the time of the Temple or even after it was destroyed, see *Avos HaRosh* [Vol. 2, ד״ה לא ניזוק]. And for a discussion of whether these miracles were contingent upon the behavior of the Jewish people, see *Ahavas Chesed* in marginal note.]

4. See *Binyan Yehoshua.*

5. This was true even of *kodashim kalim,* whose meat may (in some cases) be eaten until sundown the day after slaughter (*R' Yonah* to *Avos* here; see note 37). The meat never spoiled during the interim, even on hot summer days.

Since the meat of *kodashim kalim* may be eaten anywhere in Jerusalem, the Baraisa associates this miracle with the Holy City, unlike the parallel Mishnah in *Avos,* which

associates it with the Temple (*Mefaresh, Binyan Yehoshua;* see also *Ahavas Chesed*).

6. The portions of *kodshei kodashim,* most-holy offerings, given to the Kohanim were eaten in the Temple Courtyard, where they were commonly roasted. Furthermore, the sacrificial parts of all animal offerings were burned on the open flames of the Altar there. Thus, the Temple area was constantly permeated with the pungent aroma of roasting meat — meat that was forbidden to be eaten by non-Kohanim. This tantalizing aroma could arouse in a pregnant woman such a compelling desire to taste some of the meat that she could miscarry, and be in mortal danger herself, when prevented from sampling it at all. Miraculously, though, this never occurred (*Rashi* and *R' Yonah* to *Avos* here), even though the aroma could be smelled throughout the city and beyond (*Machzor Vitri* ad loc.).

[In truth, a woman in such circumstances would be permitted to eat from the sacrificial meat to save herself from danger (just as she would be allowed to eat from any forbidden food for the same reason). Practically speaking, though, many God-fearing women

וְלֹא נִפְגַּע אָדָם בִּירוּשָׁלַיִם[8]. וְלֹא נִכְשַׁל אָדָם בִּירוּשָׁלַיִם מֵעוֹלָם[9]. וְלֹא נָפְלָה דְלֵיקָה בִּירוּשָׁלַיִם מֵעוֹלָם[10]. לֹא הָיְתָה מַפּוֹלֶת בִּירוּשָׁלַיִם מֵעוֹלָם[11]. לֹא אָמַר אָדָם לַחֲבֵירוֹ: לֹא מָצָאתִי תַנּוּר לִצְלוֹת פְּסָחִים בִּירוּשָׁלַיִם[12]. מֵעוֹלָם לֹא אָמַר אָדָם לַחֲבֵירוֹ: לֹא מָצָאתִי מִטָּה שֶׁאִישַׁן עָלֶיהָ בִּירוּשָׁלַיִם[13]. מֵעוֹלָם לֹא אָמַר אָדָם לַחֲבֵירוֹ: צַר לִי הַמָּקוֹם שֶׁאָלִין בִּירוּשָׁלַיִם[14]:

---

scorpion[7] in Jerusalem; וְלֹא נִפְגַּע אָדָם בִּירוּשָׁלַיִם — (iv) no person ever became insane in Jerusalem;[8] וְלֹא נִכְשַׁל אָדָם בִּירוּשָׁלַיִם מֵעוֹלָם — (v) no person ever stumbled in Jerusalem;[9] וְלֹא נָפְלָה דְלֵיקָה בִּירוּשָׁלַיִם מֵעוֹלָם — (vi) no fire ever spread in Jerusalem;[10] לֹא הָיְתָה מַפּוֹלֶת בִּירוּשָׁלַיִם מֵעוֹלָם — (vii) no building ever collapsed in Jerusalem;[11] לֹא אָמַר אָדָם לַחֲבֵירוֹ: לֹא מָצָאתִי תַנּוּר — לִצְלוֹת פְּסָחִים בִּירוּשָׁלַיִם — (viii) no person ever said to his fellow, "I did not find an oven in Jerusalem in which to roast the *pesach* offerings";[12] מֵעוֹלָם לֹא אָמַר אָדָם לַחֲבֵירוֹ: לֹא מָצָאתִי מִטָּה שֶׁאִישַׁן עָלֶיהָ בִּירוּשָׁלַיִם — (ix) never did a person say to his fellow, "I did not find a bed in Jerusalem to sleep on";[13] מֵעוֹלָם לֹא אָמַר אָדָם לַחֲבֵירוֹ: צַר לִי הַמָּקוֹם שֶׁאָלִין בִּירוּשָׁלַיִם — (x) and never did a person say to his fellow, "The space is too restrictive for me to stay in Jerusalem."[14]

---

would not want to express their desire to eat the meat for fear of having to eat something that is usually strictly prohibited (see *Yoma* 82b-83a). The Baraisa teaches that the aroma of the sacrificial meat never caused this type of situation to arise (*Mefaresh*).]

7. *Binyan Yehoshua* (see *Avos* here). No one was harmed by a snake or scorpion in Jerusalem, even if they were occasionally bitten (ibid., citing *Tos. Yom Tov*).

Even though Jerusalem naturally abounded with such poisonous creatures (*Avos HaRosh* [Vol. 2], citing *Meiri*), the sanctity of the city protected its inhabitants from harm (*Machzor Vitri* to *Avos* here).

8. That is, no one was ever driven mad by evil spirits, because the forces of impurity harnessed by such spirits hold no sway in the Holy City (*Magen Avos*).

9. No one ever stumbled into sinning unintentionally (*Binyan Yehoshua*, as explained by *Kisei Rachamim*). Alternatively, no one ever tripped over physical obstacles, like stones or branches (*Kisei Rachamim, Ben Avraham*), or over any of the countless visitors who thronged the city during the three Pilgrimage Festivals (*Mefaresh*).

10. This was in the merit of the fire that burned constantly on the Outer Altar in the Temple Courtyard [see *Leviticus* 6:6] (*Binyan Yehoshua*, from *Mefaresh*).

11. The reference is to sturdy buildings, which sometimes collapse in other places. It was the merit of the *Shesiyah* Stone, which underlay the Temple (see *Yoma* 53b, 54b), that served to protect the [predominantly stone] structures of the city (*Binyan Yehoshua*, from *Mefaresh*). Alternatively, no buildings in Jerusalem were ever felled by an earthquake (*Kisei Rachamim*, citing *Maharitatz*).

12. Even though large furnaces were banned in Jerusalem (see *Bava Kamma* 82b), the smaller ovens miraculously sufficed (*Binyan Yehoshua*, from *Mefaresh*) for the myriads of *pesach* offerings that had to be roasted, all in one afternoon, on the 14th of Nissan (*Magen Avos*).

13. God arranged for everyone to find suitable accommodations in Jerusalem (ibid.).

14. None of Jerusalem's inhabitants ever had to move elsewhere to seek a livelihood, for God made special provisions for the city's inhabitants (*Rashi* and *Rav* to *Avos* here; *Magen Avos*).

ב.

אֵין¹⁵ יְרוּשָׁלַיִם מְטַמְּאָה בִּנְגָעִים¹⁶. וְאֵין נִדּוֹנִית בְּעִיר הַנִּדַּחַת¹⁷. וְאֵין מוֹצִיאִין בָּהּ זִיזִין וּגְזֻוְזְטְרָאוֹת וְצִינּוֹרוֹת לִרְשׁוּת הָרַבִּים מִפְּנֵי אֹהֶל הַמֵּת¹⁸ (וְ)הַטּוּמְאָה¹⁹. וְאֵין מְלִינִין בָּהּ אֶת הַמֵּת²⁰. וְאֵין מַעֲבִירִין

§2 Having described the special qualities of Jerusalem, the Baraisa now presents a list of special laws that apply exclusively to Jerusalem.[15]

אֵין יְרוּשָׁלַיִם מְטַמְּאָה בִּנְגָעִים — The houses in **Jerusalem are not** susceptible to becoming **contaminated through** *tzaraas* afflictions.[16] וְאֵין נִדּוֹנִית בְּעִיר הַנִּדַּחַת — [Jerusalem] **cannot be judged as a "subverted city."**[17] וְאֵין מוֹצִיאִין בָּהּ זִיזִין וּגְזֻוְזְטְרָאוֹת וְצִינּוֹרוֹת לִרְשׁוּת הָרַבִּים — **We may not extend beams, balconies, or gutters into a public domain in [Jerusalem],** מִפְּנֵי אֹהֶל הַמֵּת וְהַטּוּמְאָה — **because of** the possibility that they will form **a tent over a corpse**[18] or over some other kind of *tumah*.[19] וְאֵין מְלִינִין בָּהּ אֶת הַמֵּת — **We may not keep**

---

15. The Gemara (*Bava Kamma* 82b) records a variation of the coming list and introduces it as a set of ten. See *Avos HaRosh* [Vol. 2, beginning of the chapter], who explains how our Baraisa's list can also be considered a set of ten; but cf. *Magen Avos*.

16. Even if one of these afflictions (described in *Leviticus* 14:34-53) appears on a house in Jerusalem, the house will not be deemed *tamei* and will not be treated in the way afflicted houses usually are.

This is because the rules of *tzaraas* apply only to houses "in the land of your possession" (*Leviticus* 14:34). Since Jerusalem was not apportioned to any tribe (according to the opinion followed here; see *Yoma* 12a and below, note 36), but rather remained public property to some extent, it does not qualify as a "land of your possession," and therefore is not subject to the laws of *tzaraas* (*Binyan Yehoshua*, from *Bava Kamma* 82b).

[The Tannaic opinion that there is no truly private land ownership in Jerusalem figures prominently in this chapter. *Chazon Ish* (*Orach Chaim* 126:8) clarifies the meaning of this concept. He explains that initially, when the Land of Israel was divided into tribal provinces, Jerusalem *was* apportioned to the tribes that received the adjacent areas (Judah and Benjamin), since at that time the eventual site of the Temple was unknown. Later, when Jerusalem was designated as the Temple city, equal access was granted

to all the tribes. It is only in this narrow sense that Jerusalem was not apportioned among the tribes. Thus, the original property owners retained their ownership even after the Temple was built. The rest of Israel merely received the right to use these properties when visiting the city.]

17. If more than half of a city's inhabitants are enticed to worship idols, the entire city is declared a "subverted city"; the guilty parties are executed, and the property of all the inhabitants is destroyed. The city itself must also be razed and left as a desolate heap, never to be rebuilt (see *Deuteronomy* 13:13-19). Since the Torah specifies "your cities" (ibid. v. 13) as the ones subject to this law, it implicitly excludes Jerusalem, which (as explained in the previous note) is not anyone's city (*Binyan Yehoshua*, from *Bava Kamma* 82b).

18. One way to contract *tumah* from a corpse is by being together with it under the same roof ("tent"). Thus, if a small, unnoticed portion of a corpse were to lie under one of these protruding structures, many people could pass by and become *tamei* without realizing it (*Binyan Yehoshua*, from *Rashi* ad loc.). Since Jerusalem abounds with consecrated items and people eating consecrated food, all of which must be kept clear of *tumah*, the Sages took extra precautions to limit the spread of *tumah* there.

19. Another kind of *tumah* that can be transmitted to someone under the same roof is

בְּתוֹכָהּ עַצְמוֹת אָדָם.[21] וְאֵין עוֹשִׂין בָּהּ מָקוֹם לְגֵר °וְתוֹשָׁב.[22] וְאֵין
מְקַיְּימִין בָּהּ קְבָרוֹת,[23] חוּץ מִקִּבְרֵי בֵּית דָּוִד וְחוּלְדָּה הַנְּבִיאָה שֶׁהָיוּ שָׁם
מִימוֹת נְבִיאִים הָרִאשׁוֹנִים (וּכְשֶׁפִּינּוּ אֶת הַקְּבָרוֹת מִפְּנֵי מָה לֹא פִּינּוּם,)
אָמְרוּ: מְחִילָה הָיְתָה שָׁם שֶׁהָיְתָה מוֹצִיאָה הַטּוּמְאָה לְנַחַל קִדְרוֹן.[24]

We — וְאֵין מַעֲבִירִין בְּתוֹכָהּ עַצְמוֹת אָדָם a corpse overnight in [Jerusalem].[20]
may not transport human bones through [Jerusalem].[21] וְאֵין עוֹשִׂין בָּהּ מָקוֹם
We may not make a place in [Jerusalem] for a "resident alien."[22] — לְגֵר תּוֹשָׁב
חוּץ **We do not maintain graves in [Jerusalem],**[23] — וְאֵין מְקַיְּימִין בָּהּ קְבָרוֹת
except for the graves belonging to the House — מִקִּבְרֵי בֵּית דָּוִד וְחוּלְדָּה הַנְּבִיאָה
of David and the grave of Huldah the Prophetess, שֶׁהָיוּ שָׁם מִימוֹת נְבִיאִים
הָרִאשׁוֹנִים **— which were there since the days of the early prophets.**

A parenthetical comment about those graves:
וּכְשֶׁפִּינּוּ אֶת הַקְּבָרוֹת מִפְּנֵי מָה לֹא פִּינּוּם **— And when they removed all the other**
graves from Jerusalem, why did they not remove these? אָמְרוּ: מְחִילָה
הָיְתָה שָׁם שֶׁהָיְתָה מוֹצִיאָה הַטּוּמְאָה לְנַחַל קִדְרוֹן **— [The Sages] said: It is because**
there was a tunnel there, which would lead the *tumah* out toward the Kidron
Valley.[24]

---

a person or object afflicted with *tzaraas*
(*Keilim* 1:4). [See alternative explanation in
Magen Avos.]

20. Rather, we either bury it on the day of
death (ibid.) or remove the corpse to a holding place outside the city (*Meiri, Bava Kamma*
82b). The Gemara ascribes this law to an oral
tradition passed down from earlier generations (*Bava Kamma* ibid.). Although delaying
a burial unnecessarily is always forbidden,
it is normally permitted when doing so will
bring more honor to the deceased (such as
by allowing for more people to attend the
funeral). In Jerusalem, however, keeping a
corpse overnight is forbidden even for such a
worthy purpose (*Shitah Mekubetzes* ad loc.).

This law, too, was intended to limit the
spread of *tumah* in Jerusalem, since the
longer a corpse remains unburied, the more
likely it is that people will contract *tumah*
from it (*Mefaresh*).

21. Bones from a human corpse can transmit *tumah* to a person who touches or carries even one bone as small as a barleycorn
(*Oholos* 2:3). If the bones constitute the
greater part of a human skeleton, either in

number of bones or in total volume, they
can transmit *tumah* to a person under the
same roof as them (ibid. 2:1). Therefore, the
Sages forbade transporting bones through
Jerusalem, so as not to spread *tumah* there
(*Ahavas Chesed, Ben Avraham*).

22. Emendation based on *Mefaresh* and
Nuschas HaGra; see also *Magen Avos* and
Avos HaRosh [Vol. 2, beginning of chapter].

A "resident alien" is a non-Jew who has
undertaken to observe the seven Noahide
commandments, but continues to eat the
meat of *neveilos,* animals that were not
properly slaughtered. Since he eats *neveilah*
meat, and such meat, being *tamei,* is capable of transmitting *tumah,* the Sages feared
that if he were allowed to take up residence
in Jerusalem, his constant presence would
lead to the spread of *tumah* there (*Mefaresh*).

23. Because they can spread *tumah* when
people walk over them and become *tamei*
(*Magen Avraham* to *Tosefta, Bava Basra* 2:7).

24. Standard graves, which are buried in the
ground with no openings, project their *tumah*
straight upward and contaminate anyone
or anything passing directly over them (see

וְאֵין נוֹטְעִים בָּהּ נְטִיעוֹת[25]. וְאֵין עוֹשִׂין בָּהּ גַּנּוֹת וּפַרְדְּסִין[26], חוּץ מִגַּנּוֹת
וְוֶרְדִים שֶׁהָיוּ שָׁם מִימוֹת נְבִיאִים רִאשׁוֹנִים[27]. וְאֵין מְגַדְּלִין בָּהּ (אֲוָוזִין
וְ)תַרְנְגוֹלִין[28], וְאֵין צָרִיךְ לוֹמַר חֲזִירִים[29]. אֵין מְקַיְּמִין בָּהּ אַשְׁפַּתּוֹת
מִפְּנֵי הַטּוּמְאָה[30]. וְאֵין מְקַיְּמִין בָּהּ סוֹרֵר וּמוֹרֶה, דִּבְרֵי רַבִּי נָתָן[31],

---

The Baraisa resumes the list:

וְאֵין נוֹטְעִים בָּהּ נְטִיעוֹת — We do not plant trees in [Jerusalem].[25] וְאֵין עוֹשִׂין בָּהּ גַּנּוֹת וּפַרְדְּסִין — We may not create or maintain gardens and orchards in [Jerusalem],[26] חוּץ מִגַּנּוֹת וְוֶרְדִים שֶׁהָיוּ שָׁם מִימוֹת נְבִיאִים רִאשׁוֹנִים — except for the "Rose Gardens," which were there since the days of the early prophets.[27] וְאֵין מְגַדְּלִין בָּהּ אֲוָוזִין וְתַרְנְגוֹלִין — We may not raise geese or chickens in [Jerusalem],[28] וְאֵין צָרִיךְ לוֹמַר חֲזִירִים — and it goes without saying that we may not raise swine there.[29] אֵין מְקַיְּמִין בָּהּ אַשְׁפַּתּוֹת מִפְּנֵי הַטּוּמְאָה — We may not let garbage dumps remain in [Jerusalem] because of the tumah they might spread.[30] וְאֵין מְקַיְּמִין בָּהּ סוֹרֵר וּמוֹרֶה, דִּבְרֵי רַבִּי נָתָן — We do not fulfill the law of a wayward and rebellious son in [Jerusalem][31]

Oholos 7:1). These graves were different; each one had an opening on one side that led to the Kidron Valley, and that channeled its tumah in that direction (where people were not commonly found), instead of upward. Hence, there was no concern that these graves would contaminate anyone (ibid.).

25. For the beauty of the city is enhanced by open expanses that have no trees obstructing the view (Mefaresh; cf. Bava Basra 24b and Rashi, Numbers 35:2). Alternatively, trees were unwanted because the overhanging branches could serve as a "tent" capable of spreading tumah [see note 18] (Binyan Yehoshua).

26. Maintaining a garden involves uprooting and discarding the dead plants and weeds. Piles of such decayed matter around Jerusalem would mar the beauty of the city. In addition, cultivating garden plants requires fertilizer, which would spread its foul smell throughout the city (Binyan Yehoshua, citing Bava Kamma 82b with Rashi).

27. These gardens were spared because they provided "Jordan amber," a rose extract that was needed for the incense used in the Temple service [see Kereisos 6a] (Binyan Yehoshua, from Rashi to Bava Kamma 82b).

28. Since these birds habitually pick at dung

heaps, the Sages were concerned that they would emerge from those heaps carrying a (lentil-sized) piece of a dead sheretz (any of eight crawling creatures enumerated in Leviticus 11:29-30), which is a source of tumah and could defile any of the numerous consecrated items that were prevalent in Jerusalem (ibid.)

[This decree forbids raising chickens (or geese) only when they are allowed to roam free. It does not apply to raising the birds when they are confined in coops (Binyan Yehoshua, citing Responsa Menachem Azaryah §85).]

29. Just as we may not raise swine anywhere, due to a Rabbinic decree [see Bava Kamma 82b] (Mefaresh, Binyan Yehoshua).

30. Creeping creatures [some of which can contaminate people and utensils by contact (see Leviticus ibid. vv. 31-32)] naturally thrive in garbage dumps, and the Sages were concerned that when these creatures would die, their remains would become a source of defilement for the sacred offerings brought to Jerusalem. For this reason, they banned garbage dumps in the city (Binyan Yehoshua, from Rashi to Bava Kamma 82b).

31. [A "wayward and rebellious son" (ben sorer u'moreh) is a boy who commits certain

שֶׁנֶּאֱמַר (דברים כא, יט) "וְתָפְשׂוּ בוֹ אָבִיו וְאִמּוֹ וְהוֹצִיאוּ אֹתוֹ אֶל זִקְנֵי עִירוֹ
וְאֶל שַׁעַר מְקֹמוֹ", וְאֵין זֶה עִירוֹ וְאֵין זֶה מְקוֹמוֹ[32]. אֵין מוֹכְרִין בָּהּ בָּתִּים
[אֶלָּא] מִן הַקַּרְקָעוֹת וּלְמַעְלָה[33]. וְאֵין [מוֹכְרִין הַבַּיִת לַצְמִיתוּת] בְּתוֹכָהּ
לְאַחַר שְׁנֵים עָשָׂר חֹדֶשׁ[34]. וְאֵין לוֹקְחִין בָּהּ שְׂכַר מִטּוֹת וּמַצָּעוֹת[35].
רַבִּי יְהוּדָה אוֹמֵר: אַף שְׂכַר הַמִּטּוֹת וְהַמַּצָּעוֹת [°לֹא הָיוּ לוֹקְחִין בָּהּ[36].]

שֶׁנֶּאֱמַר "וְתָפְשׂוּ בוֹ אָבִיו וְאִמּוֹ וְהוֹצִיאוּ — these are **the words of R' Nassan.**
אֹתוֹ אֶל זִקְנֵי עִירוֹ וְאֶל שַׁעַר מְקֹמוֹ"— For it is stated regarding such a son, *Then
his father and mother shall grasp him and take him out to the elders of his
city and the gate of his place (Deuteronomy 21:19),* וְאֵין זֶה עִירוֹ וְאֵין זֶה
מְקוֹמוֹ — and this is neither *his* city nor *his* place.[32] אֵין מוֹכְרִין בָּהּ בָּתִּים
— except אֶלָּא מִן הַקַּרְקָעוֹת וּלְמַעְלָה — We may not sell houses in [Jerusalem],
from the ground up.[33] וְאֵין מוֹכְרִין הַבַּיִת לַצְמִיתוּת בְּתוֹכָהּ לְאַחַר שְׁנֵים עָשָׂר
חֹדֶשׁ — We may not sell houses in [Jerusalem] permanently, that is, with the
understanding that the sale will become irreversible after twelve months.[34]
וְאֵין לוֹקְחִין בָּהּ שְׂכַר מִטּוֹת וּמַצָּעוֹת — We may not take rental fees in [Jerusa-
lem] for beds and bedding.[35] רַבִּי יְהוּדָה אוֹמֵר: אַף שְׂכַר הַמִּטּוֹת וְהַמַּצָּעוֹת הָיוּ
לוֹקְחִין בָּהּ — R' Yehudah disagrees and says: They would even take rental

---

sins associated with theft and gluttony. As a
general rule, if such a boy is admonished by
his parents and he ignores their warnings,
he is flogged in court. If he nevertheless
persists in his behavior, he is put to death
through stoning (*Deuteronomy* 21:18-21).]
In Jerusalem, these rules do not apply. Even
if a boy in Jerusalem fulfills all the criteria
of a *ben sorer u'moreh,* he is not judged and
treated as such (*Binyan Yehoshua*).

32. For Jerusalem is considered (to some
extent) public property and cannot be called
"his" [see note 16] (*Magen Avos, Ben Avraham, Avos HaRosh* [Vol. 2]).

33. When one sells a house in Jerusalem,
he may sell what is "above ground" [i.e., not
part of the ground, such as the house itself],
but he cannot sell the land under and around
the house, for the land in Jerusalem never
belongs exclusively to any one person [see
note 16] (*Ahavas Chesed, Kisei Rachamim*).

34. The general rule for walled cities in Eretz
Yisrael is that someone who sells a house
has twelve months to buy the house back.
After that time, the sale is irreversible; the
house becomes the buyer's for eternity and

it does not return to the seller in the Jubilee
(*Yovel*) Year (as do houses in unwalled cities). This rule does not apply to Jerusalem,
even though it is a walled city. Thus, someone who sells a house in Jerusalem may
buy it back at any time, during or after the
first twelve months, and if he does not buy it
back, it returns to him automatically in the
Jubilee Year [see *Leviticus* 25:29-31].

The reason Jerusalem is excluded from
the law for walled cities is that the verse
dealing with that law speaks of a house
being "purchased" (ibid. v. 30). Due to the
limited rights of ownership in Jerusalem, a
conventional purchase can never take place
there [see note 16] (*Binyan Yehoshua,* from
Bava Kamma 82b with *Rashi*).

35. Homeowners in Jerusalem may not rent
out these items to people who visit the city
during the festivals, because the ground on
which the beds stand belongs not only to the
homeowner but also to the public (*Magen
Avos,* citing *Tosafos, Megillah* 26a; see note
16). The homeowners must therefore provide these amenities to their festival guests
without charge (but see below, note 37).

עוֹרוֹת קָדָשִׁים מֶה הָיוּ עוֹשִׂין בָּהֶן, נוֹתְנִין אוֹתָן לְבַעֲלֵי אוּשְׁפִּיזִין[37]. רַבָּן שִׁמְעוֹן בֶּן גַּמְלִיאֵל אוֹמֵר: אַכְסְנָיִים הָיוּ שְׁרוּיִים מִבִּפְנִים וּבַעֲלֵי אוּשְׁפִּיזִין מִבַּחוּץ. אַכְסְנָיִים הָיוּ מַעֲרִימִין וְנוֹטְלִין כְּבָשִׂים הַמְצוּיָירִין[39] שֶׁעוֹרוֹתֵיהֶן יָפֶה בְּאַרְבָּעָה וַחֲמִשָּׁה סְלָעִים וְנוֹתְנִין לְבַעֲלֵי אַנְשֵׁי יְרוּשָׁלַיִם, וּבָהּ [בַּעֲלֵי בָתִּים] הָיוּ מִשְׂתַּכְּרִין:

---

fees in [Jerusalem] for beds and bedding.[36]   עוֹרוֹת קָדָשִׁים מֶה הָיוּ עוֹשִׂין

בָּהֶן — Yet even according to the first opinion, those who provided lodging to the people coming to Jerusalem received some compensation: The hides of the sacrificial offerings — what would [the people] do with them? נוֹתְנִין

אוֹתָן לְבַעֲלֵי אוּשְׁפִּיזִין — They would give them to the innkeepers who host-ed them.[37]   רַבָּן שִׁמְעוֹן בֶּן גַּמְלִיאֵל אוֹמֵר: אַכְסְנָיִים הָיוּ שְׁרוּיִים מִבִּפְנִים וּבַעֲלֵי

אוּשְׁפִּיזִין מִבַּחוּץ — Rabban Shimon ben Gamliel says: In addition to not pay-ing rent for their lodgings, the guests in Jerusalem during the festivals would reside inside the houses while the hosts would remain outside![38]   אַכְסְנָיִים

הָיוּ מַעֲרִימִין וְנוֹטְלִין כְּבָשִׂים הַמְצוּיָירִין — And to repay their hosts for this extraor-dinary gesture, the guests would craftily take beautiful sheep[39] שֶׁעוֹרוֹתֵיהֶן

יָפֶה בְּאַרְבָּעָה וַחֲמִשָּׁה סְלָעִים — whose hides were each worth as much as four or five sela'im,   וְנוֹתְנִין לְבַעֲלֵי אַנְשֵׁי יְרוּשָׁלַיִם — and give them to the people who owned homes in Jerusalem.   וּבָהּ בַּעֲלֵי בָתִּים הָיוּ מִשְׂתַּכְּרִין — And it was through this that the homeowners in Jerusalem would profit.

---

36. Emendation based on *Ahavas Chesed*, *Avos HaRosh* [Vol. 2], and alternative ver-sion cited by *R' Yeshayah Berlin*; cf. *Nuschas HaGra*.

  R' Yehudah disagrees with the author of the earlier part of the Baraisa; he maintains that Jerusalem *was* apportioned to specific tribes [namely, to Judah and Benjamin; see note 16] (*Ahavas Chesed*, *Avos HaRosh* [Vol. 2]). Thus, R' Yehudah is saying that not only does he reject the previous law, which prohibits selling a house for eternity, but he also rejects this prohibition against taking rental fees for beds and beddings from people coming to the Temple (*Avos HaRosh* [Vol. 2]).

  [It follows that R' Yehudah also disagrees with the other laws explained above as based on the same reasoning. In his opinion, then, Jerusalem is susceptible to the laws of *tzara-as*; it can be judged as a "subverted city"; its boys can be punished as "wayward and re-bellious sons"; and its residents can sell plots of land together with the houses on them.]

37. As mentioned, the homeowners were not entitled to charge a conventional fee for use of their beds, since the ground supporting the beds was not really theirs (according to the first opinion in the preceding dispute; see note 35). Nevertheless, because the beds and bedding did belong to them and were being used for free, the accepted practice was for the visitors to give the hides of their sacrificial animals to the homeowners as a quasi-payment. Indeed, the Gemara (ibid.) says that the homeowners were even al-lowed to take the hides by force (see *Binyan Yehoshua*, from *Megillah* 26a with *Tosafos*).

  [The hides of *kodashim kalim* (offerings of "lesser" sanctity) were not considered to be part of the offering. After being flayed, they were returned to the owners and could be put to mundane uses (*Zevachim* 103a).]

38. *Mefaresh*.

39. Literally, *artistically formed sheep*. Some emend the text to read כְּבְשֵׂי מִצְרַיִם, *Egyptian*

ג. כָּתוּב אֶחָד אוֹמֵר (דברים יב, יד) "בְּאַחַד שְׁבָטֶיךָ", וְכָתוּב אֶחָד
אוֹמֵר (שם פסוק ה) "מִכָּל שִׁבְטֵיכֶם". "בְּאַחַד שְׁבָטֶיךָ" זוֹ שֵׁבֶט
יְהוּדָה וּבִנְיָמִין.[40] "מִכָּל שִׁבְטֵיכֶם" (זוֹ יְרוּשָׁלַיִם) שֶׁכָּל יִשְׂרָאֵל שׁוּתָּפִין
בָּהּ.[41] מֶה הָיָה בְּחֶלְקוֹ שֶׁל יְהוּדָה, הַר הַבַּיִת[42] וְהַלְּשָׁכוֹת[43] וְהָעֲזָרוֹת.[44]

---

§3 Having mentioned several laws that hinge on the question of who owns Jerusalem, the Baraisa now examines this issue directly:

כָּתוּב אֶחָד אוֹמֵר "בְּאַחַד שְׁבָטֶיךָ" — One verse says in its description of the Temple, *the place that HASHEM will choose among "one" of your tribes* (Deuteronomy 12:14); וְכָתוּב אֶחָד אוֹמֵר "מִכָּל שִׁבְטֵיכֶם" — but another verse says, *from among "all" your tribes* (ibid. v. 5). בְּאַחַד שְׁבָטֶיךָ זוֹ שֵׁבֶט יְהוּדָה וּבִנְיָמִין — These two descriptions of Jerusalem seem to contradict each other, but they can be reconciled as follows: When the verse speaks of Jerusalem as being *among "one" of your tribes,* it is referring to the tribes of Judah and Benjamin;[40] מִכָּל שִׁבְטֵיכֶם זוֹ יְרוּשָׁלַיִם שֶׁכָּל יִשְׂרָאֵל שׁוּתָּפִין בָּהּ — and when the verse speaks of the city being *from among "all" your tribes,* it is referring to the part of **Jerusalem** in which all the tribes of **Israel are partners** — namely, the Temple.[41]

We have seen that the Temple, like the rest of Jerusalem, was in the territories of Judah and Benjamin. This implies that each of them had a distinct portion in it. The Baraisa elaborates:

מֶה הָיָה בְּחֶלְקוֹ שֶׁל יְהוּדָה — Which parts of the Temple complex were in Judah's territory? הַר הַבַּיִת וְהַלְּשָׁכוֹת וְהָעֲזָרוֹת — The Temple Mount,[42] the

---

sheep (*Tummas Yesharim*, R' Yeshayah Berlin), which were presumably known for their superior quality.

40. The Baraisa is now following the opinion that Jerusalem was apportioned to specific tribes, and is *not* the property of all the Jewish people (see note 36). Thus, the place that God chose for His Temple was in the city that was apportioned to the tribes of Judah and Benjamin (see *Rashi* to *Deuteronomy* 12:14, cited by *Binyan Yehoshua*; see also *Ahavas Chesed* and *Nuschas HaGra*).

Although the Baraisa says that Jerusalem belonged to *two* tribes, the verse says, "*one*" of your tribes, because the city was predominantly in Benjamin's portion, with only a small section (underlying part of the Temple; see below) located in Judah's portion (*Avos HaRosh* [Vol 2]).

41. Although the Temple site, like the rest

of Jerusalem, was located in the portions of Judah and Benjamin, it belonged in a sense to all of the tribes. For when King David identified this plot of land as the proper site for the Temple, he collected money from all the tribes in order to buy the land from its non-Jewish occupant. In this sense, the Temple was situated *among "all" your tribes* (*Binyan Yehoshua*, from *Rashi* to *Deuteronomy* 12:14).

42. [The Baraisa lists the different parts of the Temple complex in the basic order that one encounters them upon entering the eastern gate of the Temple Mount. For a clearer picture of the Temple complex and its numerous subdivisions, as discussed below, see Introduction to the Schottenstein ed. of *Middos* with diagrams there.]

The "Temple Mount" in this context refers not to the entire Temple complex, but only

וּמֶה הָיָה בְחֶלְקוֹ שֶׁל בִּנְיָמִין, הַהֵיכָל וְהָאוּלָם וּבֵית קָדְשֵׁי הַקֳּדָשִׁים.[45]
וּכְרֹאשׁ תּוֹר הָיָה יוֹצֵא וְנִכְנָס[46] וְהָיָה חוֹזֵר לַאֲחוֹרָיו, [וְעָלָיו מִזְבֵּחַ בָּנוּי[47]].

Chambers[43] and the Courtyards.[44]   וּמֶה הָיָה בְחֶלְקוֹ שֶׁל בִּנְיָמִין — And which
parts were in Benjamin's portion?   הַהֵיכָל וְהָאוּלָם וּבֵית קָדְשֵׁי הַקֳּדָשִׁים — The
Sanctuary, the Antechamber, and the chamber of the Holy of Holies.[45]
וּכְרֹאשׁ תּוֹר הָיָה יוֹצֵא וְנִכְנָס וְהָיָה חוֹזֵר לַאֲחוֹרָיו — There was a piece of land
like the tip of a triangle that projected outward from Benjamin's portion and
reached into Judah's portion,[46] and went back again toward Benjamin's
portion,   וְעָלָיו מִזְבֵּחַ בָּנוּי — and on that spot the Outer Altar was built.[47]

---

to the open area inside the eastern gate of
the Temple complex, stretching westward
until the eastern wall of the Temple Courtyard (Binyan Yehoshua, from Rashi to Megillah 26a).

43. These chambers were located outside
the Temple Courtyards, between its eastern
wall (which was, to be more precise, the
eastern wall of the Women's Courtyard) and
the low wooden wall known as the soreg.
This latter wall encompassed the Temple
Courtyards at a distance of ten amos from
the Courtyard walls. The ten-amah space
it fenced in was known as the חֵיל, cheil
(see Middos 2:3), and it was in this space,
to the east of the Temple Courtyards,
that the Chambers mentioned here were
located (Binyan Yehoshua, from Rashi
ibid.).

44. Three Courtyards were situated on the
east side of the Temple building, arranged
one behind the other from east to west. The
Womens' Courtyard, the largest of the three,
measured 135x135 amos and extended all
the way to the east wall of the main courtyard area. The Israelites' Courtyard, on the
other side of the wall just mentioned, measured 11 amos from east to west and 135
amos from north to south, its length extending along the entire width of the courtyard
area. Finally, the Kohanim's Courtyard was
sandwiched between the Israelites' Courtyard and the Outer Altar, and measured 11
amos from east to west by 135 amos from
north to south [see Middos 2:5-6] (Binyan
Yehoshua).

45. These were the three sections of the

Temple building. The Antechamber was
actually first in the sense that it was closest to the entrance; for this reason, some
emend the text so that it lists the Antechamber before the Sanctuary, as do the
parallel Baraisa texts in Megillah 26a and
Yoma 12a (Binyan Yehoshua, Avos HaRosh
[Vol. 2]).]

Thus far, the Baraisa has essentially said
that Judah's territory held the eastern part
of the Temple complex, extending to the
east wall of the Altar, while Benjamin's territory held the western part of the Temple
complex, starting from the opening of
the Antechamber. The Baraisa will now
discuss the area in between. This area
was 54 amos wide; the eastern 32 amos
contained the Altar, and the western 22
amos was an open area separating the Altar
from the Antechamber [see Middos 3:1,6]
(Binyan Yehoshua, from Rashi to Megillah
26a).

46. A תּוֹר was a triangularly shaped piece
of women's jewelry worn in Talmudic times.
When a corner of something [whether of a
triangle, square, or any other angled object]
jutted out toward something else, it was
called a רֹאשׁ תּוֹר, because it was reminiscent
of the tip of this piece of jewelry [see, for
example, Kilayim 2:7] (Mefaresh, Binyan
Yehoshua).

47. The line dividing the territories of Judah and Benjamin ran through the Temple
Courtyard, from north to south, corresponding to the eastern edge of the Altar. This
line, however, did not cut straight across
the entire Courtyard, for once it extended

זָכָה בִּנְיָמִין[48] וְנַעֲשָׂה אוּשְׁפִּיזִכְנָא לַגְּבוּרָה[49], שֶׁנֶּאֱמַר (שם לג, יב) "וּבֵין כְּתֵפָיו שָׁכֵן":

ד. אָמַר °רַבִּי יְהוֹשֻׁעַ[50] °בֶּן לֵוִי בְּאוֹתָהּ שָׁעָה: °שֶׁיּוֹדֵעַ[52] אֲנִי שֶׁבֵּית הַבְּחִירָה עֲתִידָה לִיקָבַע בֵּין תְּחוּמוֹ שֶׁל יְהוּדָה לְבִנְיָמִין. אֵלֵךְ וַאֲתַקֵּן

זָכָה בִּנְיָמִין וְנַעֲשָׂה אוּשְׁפִּיזִכְנָא לַגְּבוּרָה — **Benjamin was found deserving,**[48] and therefore **became host to the mighty Presence** of God,[49] שֶׁנֶּאֱמַר "וּבֵין כְּתֵפָיו שָׁכֵן" — **as it is stated,** *and between his* (Benjamin's) *shoulders does He rest* (*Deuteronomy* 33:12).

§4 We have seen that Judah and Benjamin provided the land on which the Temple was built. The Baraisa discusses how this "loss" of territory was made up to them. אָמַר יְהוֹשֻׁעַ בְּאוֹתָהּ שָׁעָה — **At the time** that **Joshua**[50] was dividing up the Land of Israel among the tribes,[51] he **said,** יוֹדֵעַ אֲנִי שֶׁבֵּית הַבְּחִירָה עֲתִידָה לִיקָבַע בֵּין תְּחוּמוֹ שֶׁל יְהוּדָה לְבִנְיָמִין — **"I know**[52] that the House of God's Choice (i.e., the Temple) **is destined to be established between the boundaries of** the tribes of **Judah and Benjamin,** thus diminishing their portions. אֵלֵךְ וַאֲתַקֵּן

---

one *amah* south of the Altar's northeastern corner, it turned west for one *amah* and then proceeded south again. In addition, when the line reached the southeastern corner of the Altar, it turned again to the west, creating a strip of Judaean territory running along the south edge of the Altar, ending one *amah* short of the southwest corner. Thus, the land adjacent to both the eastern and southern walls of the Altar (except for one *amah* of each) belonged to Judah.

It emerges, then, that while the entire square area covered by the Altar (roughly measuring 32x32 *amos*) was in Benjamin's portion, it was flanked by Judah's portion on two sides (east and south). This part of Judah's territory formed a right angle wrapping around the southeastern corner of the Altar. Into the inside corner of that right angle, the square-shaped part of Benjamin's territory that underlay the Altar projected its southeastern corner "like the tip of a triangle." Beyond that projection to the south, Benjamin's territory retreated westward (in our Baraisa's language, it "went back toward Benjamin's portion") to accommodate the strip of Judaean territory that

extended westward along the southern wall of the Altar (see *Binyan Yehoshua,* citing *Mefaresh*).

48. Benjamin deserved the privilege of hosting the most sacred parts of the Temple in his territory. Among his merits was that he was the only one of the tribes born in Eretz Yisrael, and the only one not involved in selling his brother Joseph (*Binyan Yehoshua,* from *Yalkut Shimoni* to *Deuteronomy* 33:12). Benjamin was also one of only four people who never sinned, and who died only because of the curse pronounced on Adam and Eve and their descendants (*Avos HaRosh* [Vol. 2]; see there for many other reasons).

49. The Holy Ark [upon which the Divine Presence rested] was located in Benjamin's portion (*Binyan Yehoshua,* from *Rashi* to *Megillah* 26a).

50. Emendation based on many commentaries.

51. *Mefaresh.*

52. Emendation based on many commentaries.

דוֹשְׁנָה שֶׁל יְרִיחוֹ[53]. וּמִי אָכַל כָּל אוֹתָן הַשָּׁנִים[54], בְּנֵי קֵינִי חוֹתֵן
מֹשֶׁה[55]. שֶׁנֶּאֱמַר (שופטים א, טז) "וּבְנֵי קֵינִי חֹתֵן מֹשֶׁה עָלוּ מֵעִיר הַתְּמָרִים
וְגוֹ' "[56]. °אָמַר: כְּשֶׁיִּגָּלֶה הַקָּדוֹשׁ בָּרוּךְ הוּא אֶת שְׁכִינָתוֹ, עָתִיד לְשַׁלֵּם
שָׂכָר טוֹב לְיִתְרוֹ וּלְבָנָיו[58]. [וּמִנַּיִן] הֵם מִתְפַּרְנְסִין בָּנָיו שֶׁל יִתְרוֹ, מִן
הַצְּדָקָה, שֶׁנֶּאֱמַר (דברי הימים א ב, נה) "וּמִשְׁפְּחוֹת סוֹפְרִים יֹשְׁבֵי יַעְבֵּץ"[60].

דוֹשְׁנָה שֶׁל יְרִיחוֹ — To compensate them, I shall go and prepare an area of
equal size to the Temple Mount in the most fertile land of Jericho."[53] וּמִי
אָכַל כָּל אוֹתָן הַשָּׁנִים — And who consumed the produce of that area in Jericho all those years?[54] בְּנֵי קֵינִי חֹתֵן מֹשֶׁה — The children of the Kenite,[55]
father-in-law of Moses, שֶׁנֶּאֱמַר "וּבְנֵי קֵינִי חֹתֵן מֹשֶׁה עָלוּ מֵעִיר הַתְּמָרִים וְגוֹ' "
— as it is stated, The children of the Kenite, Moses' father-in-law, ascended
from [Jericho,] the City of Date Palms, etc. (Judges 1:16).[56]

    Having mentioned that Jethro's descendants left Jericho, the Baraisa dis-
cusses why they left and what became of them:
אָמְרוּ — [The Sages][57] said: When the
Holy One, Blessed is He, will reveal His Divine Presence in the Future, עָתִיד
לְשַׁלֵּם שָׂכָר טוֹב לְיִתְרוֹ וּלְבָנָיו — He will pay a goodly reward to Jethro and his
descendants for their noble deeds.[58] For these descendants did something
extraordinary: They abandoned their comfortable life in the "most fertile land
of Jericho" and moved to a place where they could study Torah. וּמִנַּיִן הֵם
מִתְפַּרְנְסִין בָּנָיו שֶׁל יִתְרוֹ — And where did the descendants of Jethro receive
their sustenance after they left Jericho and took on their new occupation?[59]
שֶׁנֶּאֱמַר "וּמִשְׁפְּחוֹת סוֹפְרִים יֹשְׁבֵי יַעְבֵּץ" This — מִן הַצְּדָקָה — From charity.
historical episode is alluded to in Scripture, for it is stated, And the families
of scholars who dwelt at Jabez ... these were the Kenites (I Chronicles 2:55).[60]

---

53. Since the Temple Mount would take away
an area measuring 500 amos by 500 amos
from the territories of Judah and Benjamin (as
the Temple was to belong to all the tribes; see
note 41), Joshua designated an equal-sized
portion to be given to them when the Temple
would be built (Binyan Yehoshua, based on
Yalkut Shimoni, Vezos HaBerachah §957).

54. I.e., the 440 years that passed from
Israel's entry into the Holy Land until the
Temple was built (Magen Avos).

55. "Kenite" is another name for Jethro
(Mechilta to Exodus 18:1).

56. This verse describes how some of Jethro's descendants left the city of Jericho,
where they were living. Appearing in a

passage describing the conquest of Israel, the
verse shows that Jethro's family was living
in Jericho long before the Temple was built.

57. Binyan Yehoshua. [The version in standard editions of the Baraisa, which reads
אָמַר, seems to be a relatively recent printer's
error, as all of the commentators have the
word אָמְרוּ in its place.]

58. [When God will reveal His Presence,
He will repay all those who clung faithfully
to His ways even when His Presence was
concealed.]

59. Avos HaRosh [Vol. 2]; see also the second explanation of Radak to Judges 1:16,
in the name of Sifrei to Deuteronomy 33:12.

60. By describing the Kenites as dwelling

וְאוֹמֵר (שם ד, כג) "הֵמָּה הַיּוֹצְרִים וְיֹשְׁבֵי נְטָעִים וְגוֹ' ". (בְּנֵי אָדָם גְּדוֹלִים הָיוּ וּבַעֲלֵי בָתִּים וּבַעֲלֵי שָׂדוֹת וּכְרָמִים הָיוּ⁶². וּבִשְׁבִיל מְלַאכְתּוֹ שֶׁל מֶלֶךְ מַלְכֵי הַמְּלָכִים הַקָּדוֹשׁ בָּרוּךְ הוּא יָשְׁבוּ שָׁם,) (שם) "עִם הַמֶּלֶךְ °בִּמְלַאכְתּוֹ יָשְׁבוּ שָׁם"⁶³. לְהֵיכָן הָלְכוּ, אֵצֶל יַעְבֵּץ לִלְמוֹד תּוֹרָה⁶⁴, וְנַעֲשׂוּ עַם לַמָּקוֹם⁶⁵

" וְגוֹ' נְטָעִים וְיֹשְׁבֵי הַיּוֹצְרִים "הֵמָּה וְאוֹמֵר — And it further states, *They were the potters, who dwelt as planters and fence-makers, etc.* (ibid. 4:23).[61] הָיוּ וּכְרָמִים שָׂדוֹת וּבַעֲלֵי בָתִּים וּבַעֲלֵי הָיוּ גְּדוֹלִים אָדָם בְּנֵי — These verses teach us that [the descendants of Jethro] were important people, and while living in Jericho, they were the owners of houses, and the owners of fields and vineyards,[62] יָשְׁבוּ הוּא בָּרוּךְ הַקָּדוֹשׁ הַמְּלָכִים מַלְכֵי מֶלֶךְ שֶׁל מְלַאכְתּוֹ וּבִשְׁבִיל שָׁם — yet for the sake of engaging in the service of the King Who reigns over kings, the Holy One, Blessed is He, they left all their wealth behind and went to reside "there" — in the place referred to later in the same verse: "עִם שָׁם יָשְׁבוּ בִּמְלַאכְתּוֹ הַמֶּלֶךְ — *They resided "there" in the service of the King* (ibid.).[63] הָלְכוּ לְהֵיכָן — What does "there" refer to? **Where did they go?** תּוֹרָה לִלְמוֹד יַעְבֵּץ אֵצֶל — To the vicinity of Jabez to study Torah from him,[64] שָׁעָה בְּאוֹתָהּ לַמָּקוֹם עַם וְנַעֲשׂוּ — and by so doing, **they became a nation for God**[65]

"at Jabez," this verse indicates that Jethro's descendants went to study Torah under Jabez (as the Baraisa will soon say). Having no source of income, they relied on the support of others. Thus, we see that they were so driven to study God's Torah that in order to do so, they were ready to give up their wealth and subsist on whatever would come to hand. This presumably meant that they subsisted on charity, since they had no other source of income (see *Ben Avraham;* cf. *Magen Avos*).

An alternative version of the Baraisa replaces the above phrase הַצְּדָקָה מִן, *from charity*, with the words הַיְצִירָה מִן, *from the [profession of] pottery.* In other words, for the sake of studying Torah, they were ready to give up their prestige as wealthy landowners and accept the working-class status of "potters," as they are called in the next-quoted verse (*Kisei Rachamim, Ben Avraham, Avos HaRosh* [Vol. 2]).

[See further in *Avos HaRosh,* who suggests that these two versions are divided on the question of whether a Torah scholar is permitted to rely on others for his financial support.]

61. Translation based on *Rashi* and *Radak* ad loc.

[It is not clear why the Baraisa assumes that this verse relates to the Kenites. It is also not clear how the Baraisa explains the verse's reference to "potters" according to the version that they subsisted on charity. Possibly it is referring to another of the Kenites' original occupations when they were independently wealthy: They were master craftsmen who made ceramic utensils of the highest quality; see *Rashi's* commentary to the verse.]

62. As is evident from the fact that the verse calls them *planters and fence-makers* (see *Ben Avraham*).

63. Emendation follows *Nuschas HaGra.*

64. [See note 60.] "Jabez" is another name for the famous Judge of Israel, Osniel son of Kenaz [see *Judges 3:9*] (*Binyan Yehoshua,* from *Rashi* to *Judges* 1:16; *Sifrei* to *Deuteronomy* 33:12), who was a great Torah scholar (see *Temurah* 16a).

65. Here the Baraisa is interpreting the last clause of the *Judges* verse, which began, *The children of the Kenite ... ascended from*

(בְּאוֹתָהּ שָׁעָה) הָיָה. יַעְבֵּץ אִישׁ טוֹב וְכָשֵׁר וְאִישׁ אֱמֶת וְחָסִיד וְיוֹשֵׁב
וְדוֹרֵשׁ בַּתּוֹרָה, שֶׁנֶּאֱמַר (שם פסוק י) "וַיִּקְרָא יַעְבֵּץ לֵאלֹהֵי יִשְׂרָאֵל לֵאמֹר
[אִם בָּרֵךְ תְּבָרְכֵנִי וְגוֹ' וַיָּבֵא אֱלֹהִים אֵת אֲשֶׁר שָׁאַל"[67]]:

ה. עֲשָׂרָה נִסִּים נַעֲשׂוּ לַאֲבוֹתֵינוּ בְּבֵית הַמִּקְדָּשׁ. מֵעוֹלָם לֹא נִרְאָה זְבוּב
בְּבֵית הַמִּטְבָּחַיִם.[68] וְלֹא אֵרַע קֶרִי לְכֹהֵן גָּדוֹל בְּיוֹם הַכִּפּוּרִים,[70] חוּץ

הָיָה יַעְבֵּץ אִישׁ טוֹב וְכָשֵׁר וְאִישׁ אֱמֶת וְחָסִיד — This Jabez was a good and proper man, a truthful and pious man, at that time.[66] **וְיוֹשֵׁב וְדוֹרֵשׁ בַּתּוֹרָה** — and he would constantly sit and expound the Torah, **שֶׁנֶּאֱמַר "וַיִּקְרָא יַעְבֵּץ לֵאלֹהֵי יִשְׂרָאֵל לֵאמֹר אִם בָּרֵךְ תְּבָרְכֵנִי וְגוֹ' וַיָּבֵא אֱלֹהִים אֵת אֲשֶׁר שָׁאַל"** — as it is stated, *Jabez called out to the God of Israel, saying, "If You bless me and expand my borders, and Your hand is with me, and You keep me from harm, that I not be saddened ...." And God granted him that which he requested* (ibid. v. 10).[67]

§5 The Baraisa returns to elaborate the opening statement of this chapter: **עֲשָׂרָה נִסִּים נַעֲשׂוּ לַאֲבוֹתֵינוּ בְּבֵית הַמִּקְדָּשׁ** — Ten miracles were performed regularly for our ancestors in the Holy Temple: **מֵעוֹלָם לֹא נִרְאָה זְבוּב בְּבֵית הַמִּטְבָּחַיִם** — (i) Never was a fly seen in the Temple butchering-area.[68] **וְלֹא אֵרַע קֶרִי לְכֹהֵן גָּדוֹל בְּיוֹם הַכִּפּוּרִים** — (ii) No seminal emission, nor any other contamination,[69] ever occurred to a High Priest on Yom Kippur,[70] **חוּץ**

---

the City of Date Palms. The verse concludes, וַיֵּלֶךְ וַיֵּשֶׁב אֶת הָעָם, *they went and settled with the "nation"* (Magen Avos). According to the Baraisa, this clause is saying that by leaving their beautiful and prosperous land to go study Torah, they became genuine Torah scholars, joining the ranks of those who are referred to as God's nation (Avos HaRosh [Vol. 2], referencing Bava Metzia 33b with Rashi ד"ה לעמי).

66. Our understanding of the phrase בְּאוֹתָהּ שָׁעָה as the conclusion of this sentence is based on the Baraisa text followed by, and printed with, the Magen Avos commentary. Some commentators delete the phrase entirely; see Ben Avraham and Avos HaRosh [Vol. 2].

67. The Gemara (Temurah 16a) interprets this verse as alluding to Jabez's various prayers for success in studying and teaching Torah: With the words *and expand my borders*, Jabez was asking to be blessed with many disciples. As a result of this appeal, HASHEM granted him that which

he had requested, sending him, the pious teacher, a new group of students, the pious descendants of Jethro (Magen Avos, citing Mechilta; Avos HaRosh [Vol. 2], citing Sifrei to Numbers 10:29; see also Nuschas HaGra). Accordingly, this verse demonstrates that Jabez "would sit and expound the Torah," and that the descendants of Jethro were among his disciples.

68. I.e. in the Courtyard section north of the Altar, where the offerings were butchered on marble tables [see Middos 3:8]. The fact that no fly was ever attracted to the blood, intestines, or meat was a clear indication of the Divine Presence that resided in the Temple (see Binyan Yehoshua, from Rashi to Avos here).

69. See Avos HaRosh [Vol. 2].

70. Such a contamination would temporarily disqualify the High Priest and force him to pass on the honor of performing the Yom Kippur service to a replacement (see Rashbatz to Avos 5:5).

Although many precautions were taken to

מֵרַבִּי יִשְׁמָעֵאל בֶּן קִמְחִית שֶׁיָּצָא[71] לְהָסִיחַ עִם שַׂר אֶחָד[72] וְנִתְזָה צִינוֹרָא
מִפִּיו וְנָפַל עַל בְּגָדָיו[73] וְנִכְנַס אָחִיו וְשִׁמֵּשׁ בִּכְהוּנָה גְּדוֹלָה תַּחְתָּיו, וְרָאֲתָה
אוֹתָן אִמָּן בּוֹ בַּיּוֹם שְׁנֵי כֹּהֲנִים גְּדוֹלִים[74]. רָאוּהָ חֲכָמִים וְאָמְרוּ: מַה זְּכוּת
הָיָה בְּיָדֵךְ. וְאָמְרָה: מֵעוֹלָם לֹא רָאוּ קוֹרוֹת בֵּיתִי שַׂעֲרוֹת רֹאשִׁי[75].

מֵרַבִּי יִשְׁמָעֵאל בֶּן קִמְחִית — **except for R' Yishmael ben Kimchis.**

The Baraisa interrupts the list of miracles to retell the story involving R' Yishmael ben Kimchis:[71]

שֶׁיָּצָא לְהָסִיחַ עִם שַׂר אֶחָד — **It once happened that he left** the Temple on Yom Kippur **to speak with a certain** non-Jewish **officer,**[72] וְנִתְזָה צִינוֹרָא מִפִּיו וְנָפַל עַל בְּגָדָיו — **and some spittle flew from [the officer's] mouth onto [R' Yishmael's] garments,** thereby rendering him *tamei*.[73] וְנִכְנַס אָחִיו וְשִׁמֵּשׁ בִּכְהוּנָה גְּדוֹלָה תַּחְתָּיו — **And so, his brother entered and served in the** position of **High Priest in his stead.** וְרָאֲתָה אוֹתָן אִמָּן בּוֹ בַּיּוֹם שְׁנֵי כֹּהֲנִים גְּדוֹלִים — **As a result of** this incident, **their mother saw them** serving **on that day as two High Priests** — a very rare privilege.[74] רָאוּהָ חֲכָמִים וְאָמְרוּ: מַה זְּכוּת הָיָה בְּיָדֵךְ — **Later, the Sages saw her and asked her, "What merit did you have** to make you worthy of this great honor?" וְאָמְרָה: מֵעוֹלָם לֹא רָאוּ קוֹרוֹת בֵּיתִי שַׂעֲרוֹת רֹאשִׁי — **And** she replied, "**Never did the beams of my house see the hairs of my head!"**[75]

---

prevent the High Priest from being in a contaminated state on Yom Kippur (see *Yoma* 6a-b and 18a-19b), it was still considered a miracle that it did not occur. This is because the evil inclination is like a warrior who, on the verge of being vanquished, summons all of his energy reserves to overcome his enemy. In the same way, the evil inclination, when seeing all the precautions being taken, surely rose to the challenge and endeavored mightily to confound the Yom Kippur service by causing the High Priest to become contaminated (*Midrash Shmuel* to *Avos* here).

[Conversely, the precautions were taken even after the miracle became evident, because it is not proper to rely on miracles (*Maharsha* to *Yoma* 18a, first answer).]

71. The story will implicitly explain why the miracle did not protect R' Yishmael from being contaminated; see below, end of note 75.

72. He left the Temple during a pause between two parts of the service to discuss an important matter with the officer (*Meiri* to *Yoma* 47a). According to some versions of this incident (see *Tosefta, Yoma* 3:15, et

al.), he walked out to speak with an Arab king whom he felt obliged to honor. Other sources imply that this incident occurred not on Yom Kippur *day*, but on the previous evening (when there was no service to be performed). See *Avos HaRosh* [Vol. 2] for a lengthy discussion of the matter.

73. The officer was an idolater, whose saliva is considered by Rabbinic law to be like that of a *zav*, which ritually contaminates anyone who touches or carries it (see *Niddah* 34a).

74. Only great and scholarly men were worthy of serving as High Priest. The fact that two of her sons were qualified for this position was indeed a rare honor for her. [In fact, *Yerushalmi* (*Yoma* 1:1) tells us that she merited to see all *seven* of her sons serving in this position (without any of them having to die to enable this; *Tos. Yeshanim* to *Yoma* 47a).]

75. When it was possible for me to keep them covered (*Tos. Yeshanim* ibid.).

Although a married woman is not required, under the letter of the law, to keep her hair covered inside her home (see *Even HaEzer* 21:2 and 115:4; see also *Orach*

(מֵעוֹלָם לֹא נִפְגַּע אָדָם בִּירוּשָׁלַיִם וְלֹא נִיזּוֹק אָדָם‎ ‏76 וְלֹא נִכְשַׁל
בַּמִּקְדָּשׁ מֵעוֹלָם.) לֹא הִפִּילָה אִשָּׁה מֵרֵיחַ בְּשַׂר הַקֹּדֶשׁ מֵעוֹלָם‎‏78.
וְלֹא פִּיגְּלוּ הַכֹּהֲנִים בַּקֳּדָשִׁים מֵעוֹלָם. וּכְשֶׁהָיוּ מַרְבִּים לֶאֱכוֹל בְּשַׂר

The Baraisa returns to its list of miracles that occurred in the Temple:
לֹא נִיזּוֹק אָדָם וְלֹא נִכְשַׁל בַּמִּקְדָּשׁ מֵעוֹלָם — (iii) **Never did any person**[76] **get
injured** by a snake or scorpion **or stumble in the Temple.**[77] לֹא הִפִּילָה
אִשָּׁה מֵרֵיחַ בְּשַׂר הַקֹּדֶשׁ מֵעוֹלָם — (iv) **No woman ever miscarried because of
the aroma of the sacrificial meat.**[78] וְלֹא פִּיגְּלוּ הַכֹּהֲנִים בַּקֳּדָשִׁים מֵעוֹלָם —
(v) **The Kohanim never disqualified the sacrificial offerings** by having improper thoughts[79] during the sacrificial process. וּכְשֶׁהָיוּ מַרְבִּים לֶאֱכוֹל בְּשַׂר

Chaim 75:2 with *Mishnah Berurah*), it is a time-honored custom for women to keep their hair covered at all times even in their own homes (see *Beur Halachah* ad loc. s.v. מחוץ לצמתן). Kimchis attributed her good fortune in having such illustrious sons to her meticulous observance of this custom.

Yerushalmi (*Yoma* 1:1) explains the connection between Kimchis's practice and her reward. It is based on a verse in *Psalms* (45:14): *All her glory — the daughter of a king — is inside, her raiment is of golden settings.* This verse can be expounded to mean that a Jewish woman (a "daughter of the King") who modestly conceals herself ("all her glory is inside") is worthy of a son who wears the vestments of the Kohen Gadol, which contain golden settings [on the Breastplate and *Ephod*] (*Binyan Yehoshua,* from *Rashi* to *Yoma* 47a).

Having described the righteousness of Kimchis, the Baraisa hints at the reason why God suspended the miracle in this case and allowed R' Yishmael to become contaminated on Yom Kippur: His intention was to reward Kimchis with the rare honor of having two sons serve as the Kohen Gadol on the same day (*Magen Avos*).

76. Emendation follows *Nuschas HaGra* and *Binyan Yehoshua.*

77. [In counting this miracle among those based in the Temple, we have followed the opinion of *Magen Avos,* ד״ה עשרה נסים, and *Ben Avraham,* end of the chapter; see also *Mefaresh* and *Binyan Yehoshua.*]

As mentioned earlier (note 9), the term "stumble" can mean stumble into sin or trip over an obstacle. Either way, this miracle is distinct from the similar one associated there with the entire city of Jerusalem. The miracle in Jerusalem (according to the first interpretation) was that no one ever stumbled accidentally into transgressing a mitzvah that applied there (or anywhere), whereas the additional miracle counted here was that no one transgressed a Temple-specific prohibition (*Binyan Yehoshua*).

Alternatively, the miracle in both places was that no one tripped over anything or anyone. In the Temple, however, this miracle was especially noteworthy given the large festival crowds that squeezed into the relatively small space of the Temple complex (*Ben Avraham,* end of chapter).

78. See note 6. [In counting this as one of the ten miracles that occurred in the Temple, we have followed the opinion of *Ben Avraham* at the end of the chapter.]

Although this miracle was already counted (above, §1) among those that occurred in Jerusalem, the miracle primarily occurred in the Temple, where the meat sat on the fire and produced the aroma. Nevertheless, the Baraisa earlier associates the miracle with the city at large because the miracle's beneficial effect was felt there as well (*Ben Avraham*).

79. Specifically, thoughts of eating the meat of the offering past the allotted time (ibid.).

הַקֳּדָשִׁים[80] הָיוּ שׁוֹתִים אֶת מֵי הַשִּׁילוֹחַ, וּמִתְעַכֵּל בְּמֵעֵיהֶן כְּדֶרֶךְ שֶׁהַמָּזוֹן מִתְעַכֵּל:[81]

ו. מֵעוֹלָם לֹא נִמְצָא פְּסוּל[82] בָּעוֹמֶר[83] וּבִשְׁתֵּי הַלֶּחֶם[84] וְלֶחֶם הַפָּנִים:[85]

הַקֳּדָשִׁים — (vi) When [the Kohanim] would eat a lot of sacrificial meat,[80] הָיוּ שׁוֹתִים אֶת מֵי הַשִּׁילוֹחַ — they would drink from the waters of the Shiloah River, וּמִתְעַכֵּל בְּמֵעֵיהֶן כְּדֶרֶךְ שֶׁהַמָּזוֹן מִתְעַכֵּל — and [the large amounts of meat] would be digested in their innards with miraculous ease, just as regular food is digested with ease.[81]

§6 The next of the ten miracles that occurred regularly in the Temple: מֵעוֹלָם לֹא נִמְצָא פְּסוּל בָּעוֹמֶר וּבִשְׁתֵּי הַלֶּחֶם וְלֶחֶם הַפָּנִים — (vii) Never was any disqualification[82] found in the *Omer* offering,[83] the *Two Loaves*,[84] or the *Show-bread*.[85]

---

80. As they would often do, since their consumption of certain meat portions was necessary for the offering's owner to gain full atonement [*Yevamos* 90a] (*Ahavas Chesed*). Moreover, it is forbidden to leave over any sacrificial meat past the time allowed for its consumption (see *Nuschas HaGra*).

81. Whatever amount of sacrificial meat the Kohanim had eaten would become digested with miraculous ease because of the Shiloah waters they drank afterward (*Ahavas Chesed*). Alternatively, it was the Shiloah waters themselves that were digested with miraculous ease, sparing the Kohanim any of the physical discomfort that digestive aids often bring (*Kisei Rachamim*).

[Our inclusion of this miracle in the count of ten follows the opinion of *Ahavas Chesed* at the end of the chapter; see also *Magen Avos* ד"ה עשרה נסים.]

82. Among the possible disqualifications were contact with a dead *sheretz* (one of eight creeping creatures whose corpses are a source of *tumah*), being removed from the Temple Courtyard (*Binyan Yehoshua*, from *Rashi* to *Avos* here), or being neglected overnight (*R' Yonah* ad loc.).

83. The *Omer* was the communal meal offering brought on the second day of Pesach. It was brought from the very first grain harvested from the new crop, and it served to permit consumption of the new crop (see

Leviticus 23:9-14). If the prepared *Omer* offering had been disqualified one year, it would have been impossible to bring another in its place, because the grain for the *Omer* offering had to be harvested the night before it was to be offered, and no extra grain was harvested at that time (*Binyan Yehoshua*, from *Rashi* to *Avos* here).

84. The *Two Loaves* (*Shtei HaLechem*) was a communal offering brought on Shavuos. It served to permit use of the new crops for private offerings (*Leviticus* 23:15-18). The loaves had to be baked before Yom Tov because the baking of these sacrificial loaves did not override the Yom Tov prohibition against labor, and thus, if they had ever been disqualified there would have been no *Two Loaves* offering that year (ibid.).

85. The *Show-bread* was arranged on the *Shulchan* (Table) in the Temple each Sabbath and removed the following Sabbath (ibid. 24:5-9). Since it had to be baked before the Sabbath (see *Menachos* 95b), if it had been disqualified, the *Shulchan* would have stood empty of Show-bread until the following Sabbath, which was the next suitable day for arranging it (ibid.).

[In combining all three of these miracles (i.e., no disqualification for the *Omer* offering, for the *Two Loaves*, or for the Show-bread) into one entry in the Baraisa's list of ten miracles, we have followed *Ahavas*

ז . כְּלִי חֶרֶס שֶׁנִּשְׁבַּר בִּמְקוֹמוֹ נִבְלָעִין שְׁבָרָיו.[86] לֹא נִצְחָה הָרוּחַ בְּעַמּוּד עָשָׁן (הַקְּטוֹרֶת).[87] וּבִזְמַן שֶׁיָּצָא [עַמּוּד עָשָׁן] מִן הַמִּזְבֵּחַ [הָעוֹלָה הָיָה] מִתַּמֵּר וְעוֹלֶה כְּמַקֵּל עַד שֶׁמַּגִּיעַ לָרָקִיעַ.[88] [וּבִזְמַן שֶׁעַמּוּד הַקְּטוֹרֶת יוֹצֵא מִמִּזְבֵּחַ הַזָּהָב הָיָה נִכְנָס כְּדַרְכּוֹ לְבֵית קָדְשֵׁי הַקֳּדָשִׁים:[89]

---

§7 The eighth and ninth miracles that occurred regularly in the Temple: כְּלִי חֶרֶס שֶׁנִּשְׁבַּר — (viii) **Any earthenware utensil that was broken** in the Temple — בִּמְקוֹמוֹ נִבְלָעִין שְׁבָרָיו — **its shards would be swallowed in its place.**[86] לֹא נִצְחָה הָרוּחַ בְּעַמּוּד עָשָׁן —(ix) **The wind did not disperse the vertical column of smoke**[87] **rising from the Outer Altar,** וּבִזְמַן שֶׁיָּצָא עַמּוּד עָשָׁן מִן הַמִּזְבֵּחַ — **and thus, when the column of smoke would rise from the Outer Altar,** also known as the *Olah* Altar, הָיָה מִתַּמֵּר וְעוֹלֶה כְּמַקֵּל עַד שֶׁמַּגִּיעַ לָרָקִיעַ — **it would rise straight up like a staff until it reached the sky.**[88] וּבִזְמַן שֶׁעַמּוּד הַקְּטוֹרֶת יוֹצֵא מִמִּזְבֵּחַ הַזָּהָב — Similarly, **when the column of incense** smoke **would leave** the area above **the Golden** (Inner) **Altar,** הָיָה נִכְנָס כְּדַרְכּוֹ לְבֵית קָדְשֵׁי הַקֳּדָשִׁים — **it would enter directly into the chamber of the Holy of Holies.**[89]

Chesed here and *Ben Avraham* at the end of the chapter; see also *Magen Avos* to §5 ד"ה עשרה נסים.]

86. [Sacrificial meat that is left over past the time it was to be eaten becomes *nossar* ("leftover") and is henceforth forbidden for consumption.] When sacrificial meat was cooked in an earthenware vessel, the juices that were absorbed in the walls of the vessel eventually became *nossar*. Since it is impossible to purge an earthenware vessel of the flavors absorbed in it (see below, 41 §6), the Torah requires that such vessels be broken — inside the Courtyard (see *Zevachim* 93b, 94b). This requirement could have resulted in the Courtyard becoming filled with heaps of shards [since even the shards could not be removed (*Ritva* to *Yoma* 21a)]. Miraculously, however, the shards sank into the ground and disappeared (*Binyan Yehoshua*, from *Rashi* to *Yoma* ibid.).

87. Emendation follows *Tummas Yesharim*, *Nuschas HaGra*, and *Binyan Yehoshua*. [The omitted word, הַקְּטוֹרֶת, is problematic because the *ketores*, or incense, was burned inside the Sanctuary, on the Inner Altar, where there was no wind; see *Binyan Yehoshua*.]

88. No matter how strong the wind was, it could not disperse the column of smoke rising from the pyre, despite the fact that the Outer Altar stood in the unroofed Courtyard and was exposed to the elements. As a result, the air in the Courtyard remained clear, even though smoke always rose from the Altar (*Rambam* to *Avos* here).

Midrash Shmuel (ad loc., cited by *Binyan Yehoshua*) notes a profound lesson that can be drawn from this particular miracle. Wind is among the strongest natural forces, while a pillar of smoke is among the weakest. Nevertheless, the holiness of the Altar's smoke prevented it from being overpowered by the mighty wind. In the same vein, if a person — no matter how physically feeble he may be — sanctifies himself with Torah study and mitzvah observance, he will be able to withstand the mightiest of forces and no one will be able to triumph over him.

89. When the incense was placed on top of the coals on the Inner Altar, the smoke would rise straight up like a staff (see *Yoma* 38a). Our Baraisa is telling us that at some point afterward this pillar of smoke would miraculously change course

ח. (עוֹמְדִין צְפוּפִין וּמִשְׁתַּחֲוִין רְוָחִים.[90] בִּזְמַן שֶׁיִּשְׂרָאֵל עוֹלִין לְהִשְׁתַּחֲוֹות לַאֲבִיהֶן שֶׁבַּשָּׁמַיִם, כְּשֶׁהֵן יוֹשְׁבִין יוֹשְׁבִין דְּחוּקִים, אֵין כָּל בְּרִיָּה יְכוֹלָה לְהוֹשִׁיט אֶצְבָּעוֹ בֵּינֵיהֶם. [וּכְשֶׁהֵם מִשְׁתַּחֲוִים מִשְׁתַּחֲוִים רְוָחִים.]) נֵס גָּדוֹל מִכּוּלָם, אֲפִילוּ מֵאָה בְּנֵי אָדָם נִכְפָּפִים בְּבַת אַחַת אֵין חַזַּן הַכְּנֶסֶת מַכְרִיז וְאוֹמֵר: פַּנּוּ מָקוֹם לַאֲחֵיכֶם. (נִסִּים נַעֲשׂוּ בָעֲזָרָה שֶׁאֲפִילוּ כָּל יִשְׂרָאֵל נִכְנָסִין בָּעֲזָרָה[91] עֲזָרָה מַחֲזִקְתָּן.) נֵס גָּדוֹל מִכּוּלָן

---

§8 The Baraisa counts the tenth of the Temple-based miracles:

עוֹמְדִין צְפוּפִין וּמִשְׁתַּחֲוִין רְוָחִים — (x) In the Temple Courtyard, [the people] would stand **crowded together**, and yet they would **prostrate themselves** all **spread out.**[90]

The Baraisa elaborates on this miracle:

בִּזְמַן שֶׁיִּשְׂרָאֵל עוֹלִין לְהִשְׁתַּחֲוֹות לַאֲבִיהֶן שֶׁבַּשָּׁמַיִם — When the people of Israel would **ascend** to the Temple **to prostrate themselves before their Father in heaven** — כְּשֶׁהֵן יוֹשְׁבִין יוֹשְׁבִין דְּחוּקִים — **when they** would **sit, they would sit crammed together,** אֵין כָּל בְּרִיָּה יְכוֹלָה לְהוֹשִׁיט אֶצְבָּעוֹ בֵּינֵיהֶם — so much so that **no person would be able to extend his finger between** any two **of them** because of the lack of space. וּכְשֶׁהֵם מִשְׁתַּחֲוִים מִשְׁתַּחֲוִים רְוָחִים — **And** yet **when they** would **prostrate themselves, they** would be **able to prostrate themselves all spread out.** נֵס גָּדוֹל מִכּוּלָם — **An even bigger miracle than all of that** אֲפִילוּ מֵאָה בְּנֵי אָדָם נִכְפָּפִים בְּבַת אַחַת — was that **even if one hundred people were bending over at the same time,** אֵין חַזַּן הַכְּנֶסֶת מַכְרִיז וְאוֹמֵר: פַּנּוּ מָקוֹם לַאֲחֵיכֶם — **the synagogue attendant** of the Temple **would never have to call out** instructions **and say, "Everyone, make room from your brethren!"** נִסִּים נַעֲשׂוּ בָעֲזָרָה — **Similarly, miracles occurred** regularly **in the Temple Courtyard;** שֶׁאֲפִילוּ כָּל יִשְׂרָאֵל נִכְנָסִין בָּעֲזָרָה עֲזָרָה מַחֲזִקְתָּן — **one of which was that even if all the people of Israel would enter the Courtyard** simultaneously,[91] **the Courtyard would hold them all.** נֵס גָּדוֹל מִכּוּלָן — **An even greater miracle than all of that**

---

and head for the Holy of Holies (*Binyan Yehoshua*).

90. This would occur on the three Pilgrimage Festivals, when all Jewish males would make their obligatory appearance in the Temple (see *Magen Avos,* citing *Yoma* 21a).

The word צְפוּפִין literally means "floating," indicating that the people in the Temple were sometimes pressed together so tightly that their feet were lifted off the ground.

Nevertheless, when they bowed, the space opened up for them, creating room for four *amos* between each person, and ensuring that no one would hear the private confessions of his neighbor (ibid., from *Rashi* to *Yoma* 21a).

[Our inclusion of this miracle in the count of ten follows *Magen Avos* to §5, ד"ה עשרה נסים, and *Ben Avraham,* end of the chapter.]

91. On the afternoon of Erev Pesach, when

כְּשֶׁיִּשְׂרָאֵל עוֹמְדִים בַּתְּפִלָּה דְּחוּקִים, וְאֵין כָּל בְּרִיָּה יָכוֹל לְהוֹשִׁיט אֶצְבְּעוֹ
בֵּינֵיהֶם (כִּמְלֹא קוֹמָתוֹ)· וּכְשֶׁהֵן מִשְׁתַּחֲוִין נַעֲשֶׂה רֶיַח בֵּינֵיהֶם כִּמְלֹא
קוֹמַת אָדָם:[92]

ט· רַבָּן שִׁמְעוֹן בֶּן גַּמְלִיאֵל אוֹמֵר: עֲתִידָה יְרוּשָׁלַיִם שֶׁיִּתְקַבְּצוּ בְּתוֹכָהּ
כָּל הָאוּמּוֹת וְכָל הַמַּמְלָכוֹת[94], שֶׁנֶּאֱמַר (ירמיה ג, יז) "וְנִקְווּ אֵלֶיהָ כָל
הַגּוֹיִם לְשֵׁם ה' ", וּלְהַלָּן הוּא אוֹמֵר (בראשית א, ט) "יִקָּווּ הַמַּיִם". מַה [קִוּוּי
הָאָמוּר לְהַלָּן לִיכָּנֵס] כָּל מֵימֵי בְרֵאשִׁית לְמָקוֹם אֶחָד[95], אַף קִוּוּי הָאָמוּר

כְּשֶׁיִּשְׂרָאֵל עוֹמְדִים בַּתְּפִלָּה דְּחוּקִים — was that when the people of Israel would stand to pray the *Shemoneh Esrei*, they would be crammed together, וְאֵין — כָּל בְּרִיָּה יָכוֹל לְהוֹשִׁיט אֶצְבְּעוֹ בֵּינֵיהֶם — so that no person would be able to extend his finger between any two of them. וּכְשֶׁהֵן מִשְׁתַּחֲוִין נַעֲשֶׂה רֶיַח בֵּינֵיהֶם כִּמְלֹא קוֹמַת אָדָם — And yet when they would prostrate themselves, a space would be created between them equal to the full height of a person![92]

§9 Having discussed the Temple's miraculous capacity to hold its Jewish visitors, the Baraisa mentions a similar miracle:[93]

עֲתִידָה — רַבָּן שִׁמְעוֹן בֶּן גַּמְלִיאֵל אוֹמֵר — Rabban Shimon ben Gamliel says: יְרוּשָׁלַיִם שֶׁיִּתְקַבְּצוּ בְּתוֹכָהּ כָּל הָאוּמּוֹת וְכָל הַמַּמְלָכוֹת — Jerusalem is destined to have all the nations and all the kingdoms gathered into it in the Future Era,[94] שֶׁנֶּאֱמַר "וְנִקְווּ אֵלֶיהָ כָל הַגּוֹיִם לְשֵׁם ה' " — as it is stated, *And all the nations will be gathered to her* (Jerusalem) *in the Name of HASHEM* (Jeremiah 3:17). וּלְהַלָּן הוּא אוֹמֵר "יִקָּווּ הַמַּיִם" — And elsewhere, a similar term is used when it says, *Let the waters beneath the heaven be gathered into one area* (Genesis 1:9). מַה קִוּוּי הָאָמוּר לְהַלָּן לִיכָּנֵס כָּל מֵימֵי בְרֵאשִׁית לְמָקוֹם אֶחָד — Just as the term "gathering" that is said over there (in the *Genesis* verse) refers to having all the waters of Creation gathered into one place,[95] אַף קִוּוּי הָאָמוּר

the Courtyard would fill with Jews bringing their *pesach* offerings (*Magen Avos*).

92. Since the Baraisa has said this already, it possibly is now saying that the same miracle would occur in ordinary synagogues (*Magen Avos*).

93. *Magen Avos, Ben Avraham*.

94. For in this era, the city of Jerusalem will expand immeasurably (*Binyan Yehoshua*; see *Bava Basra* 75b). It will then be able to receive all the world's nations, who will

come to witness the glory of Israel (*Velo Od Ella*).

95. This "gathering" was itself miraculous, because the waters originally covered the entire surface of the earth. In the natural order of things, it is not possible to empty a full vessel into another full vessel (as the Midrash [*Vayikra Rabbah* 10 §9] puts it). Thus, the same kind of miracle that enabled the waters of Creation to gather in one place will also enable the world's nations and kingdoms to come together in Jerusalem (*Velo Od Ella*).

כָּאן לְקַבֵּץ כָּל הָאומות וְהַמַּמְלָכות לְתוכָהּ, שֶׁנֶּאֱמַר ״וְנִקְוּוּ אֵלֶיהָ כָּל הַגּויִם״:[96]

כָּאן לְקַבֵּץ כָּל הָאומות וְהַמַּמְלָכות לְתוכָהּ — so does the "gathering" that is said over here (in the *Jeremiah* verse) refer to having all the nations and the royal houses of the world **gathered into** one place, namely, [the city of Jerusalem], שֶׁנֶּאֱמַר ״וְנִקְוּוּ אֵלֶיהָ כָּל הַגּויִם״ — as it is stated, *And all the nations will be gathered to her in the Name of HASHEM.*[96]

---

96. Even if the verse had simply stated "And the nations will be gathered to her," without the word "all," we would have known that it means *all* the nations, based on the similar word used in the *Genesis* verse. The word "all," then, is added to teach that not only all the nations, but all the royal houses, too, will be gathered there. This is why the Baraisa cites this verse a second time: to stress the word כָּל, *all* (*Ben Avraham*).

﷽ פֶּרֶק לו ﷽

א. אַנְשֵׁי[1] סְדוֹם לֹא חַיִּין וְלֹא נִדּוֹנִין[2], שֶׁנֶּאֱמַר (בראשית יג, יג) "וְאַנְשֵׁי סְדֹם רָעִים וְחַטָּאִים וְגוֹ' "[3]. "רָעִים" זֶה עִם זֶה[4]. "וְחַטָּאִים" בְּגִלּוּי עֲרָיוֹת[5].

﷽ CHAPTER 36 ﷽

§1 The Baraisa presents a series of teachings about several groups of wicked people who have no portion in the World to Come, beginning with the people of Sodom:[1]

אַנְשֵׁי סְדוֹם לֹא חַיִּין וְלֹא נִדּוֹנִין — **The people of Sodom will not live in the World to Come, nor will they be judged,**[2] שֶׁנֶּאֱמַר "וְאַנְשֵׁי סְדֹם רָעִים וְחַטָּאִים וְגוֹ' " — **for it is stated,** *Now the people of Sodom were wicked and sinful toward Hashem, exceedingly* (Genesis 13:13).[3] "רָעִים" זֶה עִם זֶה — Each term used here teaches us a different aspect of their wickedness. They were *wicked* in their behavior **toward one another;**[4] "וְחַטָּאִים" בְּגִלּוּי עֲרָיוֹת — *and sinful* in that they were guilty of **immorality;**[5] "לה' "

---

1. Much of this chapter parallels parts of the eleventh and last chapter of *Sanhedrin* (according to the order of *Bavli*; according to the order followed in Mishnayos and *Yerushalmi*, it is the tenth chapter). The Mishnah that parallels the present teaching (107b-108a) begins its list of those who have no portion in the World to Come with the generation of the Flood and the generation of the Dispersion. Our Baraisa, however, omits the first two and begins with the people of Sodom. See *Binyan Yehoshua* for discussion.

There is a dispute among the Rishonim as to whether the term "World to Come" refers to the world of resurrected life after the Revivification of the Dead or to the Afterlife (see *Ramban, Shaar HaGemul*, end). For the purpose of our elucidation, we will follow the view that it refers — at least here — to the period after the Revivification. For further discussion, see Appendix to the Schottenstein ed. of *Talmud Bavli, Sanhedrin* Vol. III, and Introduction to Chapter 11 there.

2. They have no share in the World to Come, but on the other hand, they will not be resurrected to receive a punishment for their sins on the Final Day of Judgment that precedes the World to Come, because they already received their punishment when

God destroyed them [as recorded in *Genesis* Ch. 19] (see *Yad Ramah* to *Sanhedrin* 107b).

3. I.e., they are banned from the World to Come *because* they were wicked and sinful, as stated in the *Genesis* verse. The *source* of R' Eliezer's opinion, however, is the very verse cited by R' Yehoushua just below (Psalms 1:5): *Therefore the wicked shall not stand up in judgment, nor the sinful in the assembly of the righteous* (*Mefaresh*, based on the Mishnah, *Sanhedrin* 107b-108a). The first half of the verse is understood as referring to the generation of the Flood (who are called *wicked* in *Genesis* 6:5 — *Rashi* to *Sanhedrin* 108a), whereas the second half of the verse refers to the people of Sodom (who are called *sinful* in *Genesis* 13:13 — *Rashi* ibid.). The *Psalms* verse states that neither of these groups will rise (*stand up*) at the time of the Revivification, even for judgment. See *Nuschas HaGra*, who inserts this proof into the actual text of the Baraisa.

4. I.e., they were evil with regard to money matters (Baraisa cited in *Sanhedrin* 109a).

5. See *Sanhedrin* ibid. for the Scriptural sources linking the term *evil* to monetary sins and the term *sinful* to immoral behavior.

"לַהּ" זֶה חִלּוּל הַשֵּׁם.6 "מְאֹד" שֶׁהָיוּ מִתְכַּוְּונִין לַעֲבֵירוֹת, דִּבְרֵי רַבִּי
אֱלִיעֶזֶר. רַבִּי יְהוֹשֻׁעַ אוֹמֵר: בָּאִין הֵן לַדִּין, שֶׁנֶּאֱמַר (תהלים א, ה) "עַל כֵּן
לֹא יָקֻמוּ רְשָׁעִים בַּמִּשְׁפָּט וְחַטָּאִים) בַּעֲדַת צַדִּיקִים". בַּעֲדַת צַדִּיקִים אֵינָן
עוֹמְדִין אֲבָל עוֹמְדִין הֵן בַּעֲדַת רְשָׁעִים.8 רַבִּי נְחֶמְיָה אוֹמֵר: אֲפִילוּ בַּעֲדַת
רְשָׁעִים אֵינָן בָּאִים, שֶׁנֶּאֱמַר (שם קד, לה) "יִתַּמּוּ חַטָּאִים מִן הָאָרֶץ וּרְשָׁעִים
עוֹד אֵינָם".9 קְטַנִּים בְּנֵי רְשָׁעִים10 לֹא חַיִּין וְלֹא נִידוֹנִים, שֶׁנֶּאֱמַר (מלאכי ג, יט)
"כִּי הִנֵּה הַיּוֹם בָּא בֹּעֵר כַּתַּנּוּר [וְגו'] [אֲשֶׁר לֹא יַעֲזֹב לָהֶם שֹׁרֶשׁ וְעָנָף11]",

זֶה חִלּוּל הַשֵּׁם — *toward Hashem* — this is referring to desecration of the Name of God;[6] "מְאֹד" שֶׁהָיוּ מִתְכַּוְּונִין לַעֲבֵירוֹת — *exceedingly* — this means that they deliberately [committed] sins. דִּבְרֵי רַבִּי אֱלִיעֶזֶר — These are the words of R' Eliezer. רַבִּי יְהוֹשֻׁעַ אוֹמֵר — R' Yehoshua says: בָּאִין הֵן לַדִּין — They will come to judgment, שֶׁנֶּאֱמַר "עַל כֵּן לֹא יָקֻמוּ רְשָׁעִים בַּמִּשְׁפָּט וְחַטָּאִים בַּעֲדַת צַדִּיקִים" — as it is stated, *Therefore the wicked shall not stand up in judgment, nor the sinful in the assembly of the righteous* (Psalms 1:5). The second half of the verse refers to the people of Sodom,[7] and implies merely that בַּעֲדַת צַדִּיקִים אֵינָן עוֹמְדִין — they shall not stand in the assembly of the righteous, אֲבָל עוֹמְדִין הֵן בַּעֲדַת רְשָׁעִים — but they shall stand for judgment in the assembly of the wicked.[8] רַבִּי נְחֶמְיָה אוֹמֵר — R' Nechemyah says in support of R' Eliezer's view: אֲפִילוּ בַּעֲדַת רְשָׁעִים אֵינָן בָּאִים — They will not come even in the assembly of the wicked, שֶׁנֶּאֱמַר "יִתַּמּוּ חַטָּאִים מִן הָאָרֶץ וּרְשָׁעִים עוֹד אֵינָם" — as it is stated, *The sinful shall cease from the earth, and the wicked shall be no more* (ibid. 104:35).[9]

The Baraisa turns to another group of people whose fate in the future is the subject of a dispute between R' Eliezer and R' Yehoshua: קְטַנִּים בְּנֵי רְשָׁעִים לֹא חַיִּין וְלֹא נִידוֹנִים — The minor children of the wicked[10] will not live in the World to Come, nor will they be judged, שֶׁנֶּאֱמַר "כִּי הִנֵּה הַיּוֹם בָּא בֹּעֵר כַּתַּנּוּר וְגו' אֲשֶׁר לֹא יַעֲזֹב לָהֶם שֹׁרֶשׁ וְעָנָף" — as it is stated, *For behold, the day is coming, burning like an oven,* when all the wicked people and all the evildoers will be like straw; and that coming day will burn them

---

6. I.e., they blasphemed the Divine Name (see *Sanhedrin* ibid., and see *Nuschas HaGra*).

7. As explained in note 3.

8. I.e., they will be resurrected and brought to judgment [among all the other sinners] (*Rashi* to *Sanhedrin* 108a). According to R' Yehoshua, it is only *the wicked* (the generation of the Flood) that *shall not stand up in judgment.* However, *the sinful* (the people of Sodom) are not excluded from standing

in judgment, but only from standing *in the assembly of the righteous.*

9. As in the verse cited previously, *the sinful* refers to the people of Sodom whereas *the wicked* refers to the generation of the Flood (see *Shenei Eliyahu*). This verse tells us that both groups will have ceased from the earth, never to return.

10. I.e., the children of the wicked who died before reaching maturity.

דִּבְרֵי רַבִּי אֱלִיעֶזֶר. רַבִּי יְהוֹשֻׁעַ אוֹמֵר: (אינם) בָּאִים.[12] וַעֲלֵיהֶם הוּא אוֹמֵר
(דניאל ד, יא) "קָרֵא בְחַיִל וְכֵן אָמַר גֹּדּוּ אִילָנָא וְקַצִּצוּ עַנְפֽוֹהִי אַתַּרוּ עָפְיֵהּ
וּבַדַּרוּ אִנְבֵּהּ". וְאוֹמֵר (שם פסוק יב) "בְּרַם עִקַּר שָׁרְשֽׁוֹהִי בְּאַרְעָא שְׁבֻקוּ
וּבֶאֱסוּר דִּי פַרְזֶל וּנְחָשׁ".[13] נֶאֱמַר כָּאן שָׁרָשָׁיו וְנֶאֱמַר לְהַלָּן שָׁרָשָׁיו. מַה
שָׁרָשָׁיו הָאָמוּר לְהַלָּן בְּגוּפוֹ שֶׁל אִילָן אַף שֹׁרֶשׁ הָאָמוּר כָּאן בְּגוּפוֹ שֶׁל
אָדָם הַכָּתוּב מְדַבֵּר.[14] אִם כֵּן מַה אֲנִי מְקַיֵּים "אֲשֶׁר לֹא יַעֲזֹב לָהֶם שֹׁרֶשׁ

---

up, says HASHEM, Master of Legions, **so that it will not leave them a root or
branch** (Malachi 3:19). The wicked will not be left with a root — in this world,
or branch — in the World to Come.[11]   דִּבְרֵי רַבִּי אֱלִיעֶזֶר — These are the
words of R' Eliezer.   רַבִּי יְהוֹשֻׁעַ אוֹמֵר: בָּאִים — R' Yehoshua says: **They will
enter the World to Come.**[12]   וַעֲלֵיהֶם הוּא אוֹמֵר "קָרֵא בְחַיִל וְכֵן אָמַר גֹּדּוּ אִילָנָא
"וְקַצִּצוּ עַנְפֽוֹהִי אַתַּרוּ עָפְיֵהּ וּבַדַּרוּ אִנְבֵּהּ — Regarding them it states, **He cried
out loudly, and said thus, "Chop down the tree and cut off its branches;
cast down its foliage and scatter its fruit"** (Daniel 4:11);   וְאוֹמֵר "בְּרַם עִקַּר
"שָׁרְשֽׁוֹהִי בְּאַרְעָא שְׁבֻקוּ וּבֶאֱסוּר דִּי פַרְזֶל וּנְחָשׁ — and it states further, **"However,
leave its major roots in the ground, [secured] with a band of iron and cop-
per"** (ibid. v. 12).[13]   נֶאֱמַר כָּאן שָׁרָשָׁיו וְנֶאֱמַר לְהַלָּן שָׁרָשָׁיו — Now, [a wicked
person's] roots are spoken of here in the Malachi verse, and [a tree's] roots
are spoken of there in the Daniel verse.   מַה שָׁרָשָׁיו הָאָמוּר לְהַלָּן בְּגוּפוֹ שֶׁל
אִילָן אַף שֹׁרֶשׁ הָאָמוּר כָּאן בְּגוּפוֹ שֶׁל אָדָם הַכָּתוּב מְדַבֵּר — The similar wording
in the two verses teaches us that **just as [the tree's roots] spoken of there
are referring to a part of the tree itself, so too in regard to the root spoken
of here** in Malachi, **the verse is referring to the wicked man himself.** That is,
the evildoers themselves will be completely destroyed in the World to Come,
but their children will live.[14]   אִם כֵּן מַה אֲנִי מְקַיֵּים "אֲשֶׁר לֹא יַעֲזֹב לָהֶם שֹׁרֶשׁ

---

11. *Sanhedrin* 110b. That the wicked themselves have no share in the World to Come
is undisputed, and is derived from a different
verse (see *Kesubos* 111b). However, this view
maintains that even their small children, who
are too young to have sinned themselves, will
die young (see *Sifrei* to *Deuteronomy* 24:16,
which states that small children sometimes
die for their fathers' sins) and will be excluded
from the World to Come. This is indicated by
the verse's reference to "roots" and "branches," which are metaphors for children (*Rashi*
to *Sanhedrin* ibid.). However, since they
themselves did not sin, R' Eliezer posits that
they will not be judged either (*Ben Avraham*).

12. [Emendation follows virtually all of the
commentators.] Although we do find that

minor children die for their parents' sins (see
the previous note), that is only in this world;
but they will merit the World to Come.

13. The passage there tells how King Nebuchadnezzar of Babylon dreamed that an
angel descended from Heaven and ordered
that a great tree — which symbolized Nebuchadnezzar — be chopped down, but
that care be taken not to uproot it. On the
contrary, the roots were to be protected by
a covering of iron and copper. The meaning of this dream was that Nebuchadnezzar
himself was to be removed temporarily from
his throne ("chopped down"), but his "roots"
were to be protected; that is, the throne
would revert to him.

14. In the Gemara (*Sanhedrin* 110b),

וְעָנָף״, שֶׁלֹּא תִמָּצֵא לָהֶם זְכוּת שֶׁיִּסְמְכוּ עָלֶיהָ15. וַאֲחֵרִים אוֹמְרִים: בָּאִים הֵם. וַעֲלֵיהֶם הַכָּתוּב הוּא אוֹמֵר (ישעיה מד, ה) ״זֶה יֹאמַר לַה׳ אֲנִי וְזֶה יִקְרָא בְשֵׁם יַעֲקֹב וְזֶה יִכְתֹּב יָדוֹ לַה׳ וּבְשֵׁם יִשְׂרָאֵל יְכַנֶּה״. ״זֶה יֹאמַר לַה׳ אֲנִי״, אֵלּוּ צַדִּיקִים גְּמוּרִים. ״וְזֶה יִקְרָא בְשֵׁם יַעֲקֹב״, אֵלּוּ קְטַנִּים בְּנֵי רָשָׁע17. ״וְזֶה יִכְתֹּב יָדוֹ לַה׳ ״, אֵלּוּ רְשָׁעִים שֶׁפֵּירְשׁוּ מִדַּרְכֵיהֶם וְחָזְרוּ בָהֶם וְעָשׂוּ תְשׁוּבָה18. ״וּבְשֵׁם יִשְׂרָאֵל יְכַנֶּה״, אֵלּוּ גֵּרֵי אוּמּוֹת הָעוֹלָם:

_____

״וְעָנָף״ — **How, then, do we account for** the words, _so that it will not leave them a root or branch_? **What parts of the wicked themselves is the verse** calling a _root_ and a _branch_? שֶׁלֹּא תִמָּצֵא לָהֶם זְכוּת שֶׁיִּסְמְכוּ עָלֶיהָ — **It means that no merit will be found for them upon which to rely.**[15]

Another Tanna supports R' Yehoshua's opinion, based on a different verse:
וַאֲחֵרִים אוֹמְרִים: בָּאִים הֵם — **And others say** in support of this view: [The minor children of the wicked] **will enter the World to Come.** וַעֲלֵיהֶם הַכָּתוּב הוּא אוֹמֵר ״זֶה יֹאמַר לַה׳ אֲנִי וְזֶה יִקְרָא בְשֵׁם יַעֲקֹב וְזֶה יִכְתֹּב יָדוֹ לַה׳ וּבְשֵׁם יִשְׂרָאֵל יְכַנֶּה״ — **Regard**ing them Scripture states, _This one will say: "I am Hashem's," and the other one will call [himself] by the name of Jacob; this one will sign his allegiance to HASHEM, and adopt the name of Israel_ (Isaiah 44:5). **The verse mentions four distinct groups that will be present in the World to Come:** ״זֶה יֹאמַר לַה׳ אֲנִי״, אֵלּוּ צַדִּיקִים גְּמוּרִים — (i) _This one will say: "I am Hashem's"_ — these **are** referring to **the perfectly righteous, who were always dedicated to God;**[16] ״וְזֶה יִקְרָא בְשֵׁם יַעֲקֹב״, אֵלּוּ קְטַנִּים בְּנֵי רָשָׁע — (ii) _and the other one will call [himself] by the name of Jacob_ — these **are** referring to **the minor children of a wicked person;**[17] ״וְזֶה יִכְתֹּב יָדוֹ לַה׳ ״, אֵלּוּ רְשָׁעִים שֶׁפֵּירְשׁוּ מִדַּרְכֵיהֶם וְחָזְרוּ בָהֶם וְעָשׂוּ תְשׁוּבָה — _this one will sign his allegiance to HASHEM_ — these **are** refer**ring to the wicked who abandoned and turned back from their evil ways and repented;**[18] ״וּבְשֵׁם יִשְׂרָאֵל יְכַנֶּה״, אֵלּוּ גֵּרֵי אוּמּוֹת הָעוֹלָם — _and adopt the name of Israel_ — these **are** referring to **the proselytes of the nations of the world.**

_____

however, the inference that the children of the wicked have a share in the World to Come is drawn directly from the _Daniel_ verse; see there with _Rashi_. See _Magen Avos,_ who reconciles our Baraisa with the Gemara.

15. I.e., they will have the reward of neither a major mitzvah (_root_) nor a minor mitzvah (_branch_). God will reward the wicked while they are still alive for any good deed that they may have performed — whether major or minor — to ensure that they lose the World to Come. Since they have already received full reward for whatever good they

accomplished during their lifetimes, they cannot claim any reward after death. Only punishment remains (_Sanhedrin_ 110b with _Rashi_ there, cited by _Binyan Yehoshua_).

16. _Magen Avos._

17. Jacob experienced the travails of raising children more than any of the other Patriarchs (see _Shabbos_ 89b). Therefore, he will protect the minor children of the wicked (whose fathers will not be present with them) in the World to Come (_Magen Avos_).

18. These people will sign their allegiance to God by dedicating themselves entirely to

ב. קֹרַח וַעֲדָתוֹ לֹא חַיִּין וְלֹא נִדּוֹנִין, שֶׁנֶּאֱמַר (במדבר טז, לג) "וַתְּכַס עֲלֵיהֶם הָאָרֶץ וַיֹּאבְדוּ מִתּוֹךְ הַקָּהָל"[19], דִּבְרֵי רַבִּי אֱלִיעֶזֶר. רַבִּי יְהוֹשֻׁעַ אוֹמֵר: בָּאִין הֵן. וַעֲלֵיהֶם הוּא אוֹמֵר (שמואל א ב, ו) "ה׳ מֵמִית וּמְחַיֶּה מוֹרִיד שְׁאוֹל וַיָּעַל". נֶאֱמַר כָּאן שְׁאוֹל, (במדבר טז, לג) "וַיֵּרְדוּ הֵם וְכָל אֲשֶׁר לָהֶם חַיִּים שְׁאֹלָה", וְנֶאֱמַר לְהַלָּן שְׁאוֹל. מַה שְׁאוֹל שֶׁנֶּאֱמַר לְהַלָּן מוֹרִיד וּמַעֲלֶה, אַף שְׁאוֹל הָאָמוּר כָּאן יָרְדוּ וַעֲתִידִין לַעֲלוֹת. אָמַר לוֹ רַבִּי אֱלִיעֶזֶר: מָה אֲנִי מְקַיֵּם "וַתְּכַס עֲלֵיהֶם הָאָרֶץ וַיֹּאבְדוּ מִתּוֹךְ הַקָּהָל". אָמַר לוֹ: מִתּוֹךְ הַקָּהָל אָבְדוּ, מִן הָעוֹלָם הַבָּא לֹא אָבְדוּ[20]:

§2 The Baraisa turns to another group of sinners:

קֹרַח וַעֲדָתוֹ לֹא חַיִּין וְלֹא נִדּוֹנִין — **Korah and his congregation will not live in the World to Come, nor will they be judged,** שֶׁנֶּאֱמַר "וַתְּכַס עֲלֵיהֶם הָאָרֶץ וַיֹּאבְדוּ מִתּוֹךְ הַקָּהָל" — **as it is stated,** *The earth covered them over and they were lost from among the congregation* (Numbers 16:33).[19] דִּבְרֵי רַבִּי אֱלִיעֶזֶר — **These are the words of R' Eliezer.** רַבִּי יְהוֹשֻׁעַ אוֹמֵר: בָּאִין הֵן — **R' Yehoshua says: They will enter the World to Come.** וַעֲלֵיהֶם הוּא אוֹמֵר "ה׳ מֵמִית וּמְחַיֶּה מוֹרִיד שְׁאוֹל וַיָּעַל" — **Regarding them it states,** *Hashem brings death and gives life, He lowers to the pit and raises up* (I Samuel 2:6). נֶאֱמַר כָּאן שְׁאוֹל, "וַיֵּרְדוּ הֵם וְכָל אֲשֶׁר לָהֶם חַיִּים שְׁאֹלָה" — **Now, the term** *pit* **is stated here** regarding the congregation of Korah, *They and all that was theirs descended alive to the pit* (Numbers ibid.); וְנֶאֱמַר לְהַלָּן שְׁאוֹל — **and** **the term** *pit* **is stated there** in the *I Samuel* verse. מַה שְׁאוֹל שֶׁנֶּאֱמַר לְהַלָּן מוֹרִיד וּמַעֲלֶה — **Just as in the case of the** *pit* **mentioned there,** the verse states clearly that [God] lowers to it **and raises up** from it, אַף שְׁאוֹל הָאָמוּר כָּאן יָרְדוּ וַעֲתִידִין לַעֲלוֹת — **so too in the case of the** *pit* **stated here** regarding the congregation of Korah, **they descended to it and they are destined to arise** from it. אָמַר לוֹ רַבִּי אֱלִיעֶזֶר — **R' Eliezer said to him:** מָה אֲנִי מְקַיֵּם "וַתְּכַס עֲלֵיהֶם הָאָרֶץ וַיֹּאבְדוּ מִתּוֹךְ הַקָּהָל" — **But according to your opinion, how do we account for** the words, *The earth covered them over and they were lost from among the congregation?* אָמַר לוֹ: מִתּוֹךְ הַקָּהָל אָבְדוּ — **[R' Yehoshua] replied to him: They were** indeed **lost from among the congregation** in this world, מִן הָעוֹלָם הַבָּא לֹא אָבְדוּ — **but they were not lost from the World to Come.**[20]

---

the pursuit of good deeds (see *Magen Avos*).

19. The Mishnah in *Sanhedrin* (108a) expounds the verse as follows: *The earth covered them over* — in this world; *and they were lost from among the congregation* — for the World to Come.

20. According to R' Eliezer, the term *from*

among the congregation indicates that they were permanently excluded from the congregation of Israel. R' Yehoshua, however, maintains that on the contrary, it implies that they were excluded only from that particular congregation, but not from the Jewish nation as a whole (see *Magen Avos*).

‫ג. דּוֹר הַמִּדְבָּר לֹא חַיִּין וְלֹא נִדּוֹנִין‬²¹, שֶׁנֶּאֱמַר ‫)שם יד, לה(‬ "בַּמִּדְבָּר הַזֶּה
‫יִתַּמּוּ וְשָׁם יָמֻתוּ‬"²². וְאוֹמֵר ‫)תהלים צה, יא(‬ "אֲשֶׁר נִשְׁבַּעְתִּי בְאַפִּי אִם
‫יְבֹאוּן אֶל מְנוּחָתִי‬"²³, דִּבְרֵי רַבִּי אֱלִיעֶזֶר. רַבִּי יְהוֹשֻׁעַ אוֹמֵר: בָּאִין הֵן
‫וַעֲלֵיהֶן הוּא אוֹמֵר ‫)שם נ, ה(‬ "אִסְפוּ לִי חֲסִידָי כֹּרְתֵי בְרִיתִי עֲלֵי זָבַח‬"²⁴.
‫אָמַר לוֹ: קַבֵּל דְּבָרַי. מָה אַתָּה מְקַיֵּים "אֲשֶׁר נִשְׁבַּעְתִּי בְאַפִּי‬"²⁵. אָמַר
‫לוֹ: אֵלוּ מְרַגְּלִים כָּל רִשְׁעֵי הַדּוֹר)כוּלָן(. אָמַר לוֹ רַבִּי יְהוֹשֻׁעַ: וּמָה אַתָּה‬

---

§3 The Baraisa turns to another group:

‫דּוֹר הַמִּדְבָּר לֹא חַיִּין וְלֹא נִדּוֹנִין‬ — **The generation of the Wilderness will not live** in the World to Come, **nor will they be judged,**[21] ‫שֶׁנֶּאֱמַר "בַּמִּדְבָּר הַזֶּה יִתַּמּוּ‬ ‫וְשָׁם יָמֻתוּ‬" — **as it is stated** that God said of them, *"In this Wilderness shall they cease, and there they shall die!"* (Numbers 14:35).[22] ‫וְאוֹמֵר "אֲשֶׁר נִשְׁבַּעְתִּי‬ ‫בְאַפִּי אִם יְבֹאוּן אֶל מְנוּחָתִי‬" — **And it states,** *Therefore, I have sworn in My anger that they shall not enter My place of contentment* (Psalms 95:11).[23] ‫דִּבְרֵי רַבִּי אֱלִיעֶזֶר‬ — These are **the words of R' Eliezer.** ‫רַבִּי יְהוֹשֻׁעַ אוֹמֵר: בָּאִין‬ ‫הֵן‬ — **R' Yehoshua says: They will enter** the World to Come. ‫וַעֲלֵיהֶן הוּא‬ ‫אוֹמֵר "אִסְפוּ לִי חֲסִידָי כֹּרְתֵי בְרִיתִי עֲלֵי זָבַח‬" — **Regarding them it states,** *Gather My devout ones unto Me, sealers of My covenant through sacrifice* (ibid. 50:5).[24] ‫אָמַר לוֹ קַבֵּל דְּבָרַי‬ — **[R' Eliezer] said to him: Accept my opinion;** ‫מָה אַתָּה מְקַיֵּים "אֲשֶׁר נִשְׁבַּעְתִּי בְאַפִּי‬" — **for according to your opinion, how will you account for** the verse, *Therefore, I have sworn in My anger that they shall not enter My place of contentment?*[25] ‫אָמַר לוֹ‬ — **[R' Yehoshua] replied to him:** ‫אֵלוּ מְרַגְּלִים כָּל רִשְׁעֵי הַדּוֹר כוּלָן‬ — **Those** people that God swore to exclude **were the Spies** themselves, **and all the wicked people of that generation.** ‫אָמַר לוֹ רַבִּי יְהוֹשֻׁעַ‬ — **R' Yehoshua** then asked [R' Eliezer]: ‫וּמָה אַתָּה‬

---

21. The reference is to the generation that left Egypt, whose male members died in the Wilderness as punishment for following the evil counsel of the Spies.

22. The Baraisa in *Sanhedrin* 110b expounds the verse as follows: *In this Wilderness shall they shall cease* — in this World; *and there they shall die* — for the World to Come.

23. Earlier verses in this psalm indicate that it is speaking of the generation of the Wilderness (*Binyan Yehoshua*). The term *My place of contentment* refers to the World to Come (*Tosafos* to *Chagigah* 10a, ‫ד"ה באפי‬).

24. This refers to the generation of the Wilderness, which entered the covenant with

God at Sinai by bringing offerings and sprinkling the blood, as stated in *Exodus* 24:5-8 (*Rashi* to *Sanhedrin* 110b). God's statement that they are to be gathered unto Him implies that they will be with Him in the World to Come.

25. R' Eliezer did not ask R' Yehoshua how he would deal with his proof from the *Numbers* verse, as that can be explained away easily by saying that both expressions (*In this Wilderness they shall cease, and there they shall die*) are referring to their physical demise in the Wilderness, and that the purpose of the double expression was to convey an oath [see *Shevuos* 36a] (*Avos HaRosh*, based on *Rif* in *Ein Yaakov* to *Sanhedrin* 110b).

מְקַיֵּים ״אִסְפוּ לִי חֲסִידָי״. אָמַר לוֹ: זֶה מֹשֶׁה וְאַהֲרֹן וְכָל חֲסִידֵי הַדּוֹר
מִשֵּׁבֶט לֵוִי[26]. ° מְשִׁיבִין עַל דְּבָרָיו: רְשָׁעִים נֶאֱמַר בָּהֶם ״שָׁם״ וְצַדִּיקִים לֹא
נֶאֱמַר בָּהֶם ״שָׁם״, וַהֲלֹא כְּבָר[28] ° (בראשית מט, לא) ״שָׁמָּה קָבְרוּ אֶת אַבְרָהָם
וְאֵת שָׂרָה אִשְׁתּוֹ״, וְאוֹמֵר °נֶאֱמַר (שם נ, ה) ״בְּקִבְרִי אֲשֶׁר כָּרִיתִי לִי בְּאֶרֶץ
כְּנַעַן שָׁמָּה תִּקְבְּרֵנִי״, וְאוֹמֵר (במדבר כ, א) ״וַתָּמָת שָׁם מִרְיָם וַתִּקָּבֵר שָׁם״,

---

מְקַיֵּים ״אִסְפוּ לִי חֲסִידָי״ — **And how do you account for** the verse, *Gather My*
devout ones unto Me, etc.? — אָמַר לוֹ — [R' Eliezer] **replied to him:** זֶה מֹשֶׁה
וְאַהֲרֹן וְכָל חֲסִידֵי הַדּוֹר מִשֵּׁבֶט לֵוִי — **This is** referring to **Moses, Aaron, and all**
the devout ones of the generation from the tribe of Levi.[26]

Another Tanna supports R' Eliezer's opinion, based on a different proof from
the *Numbers* verse cited by R' Eliezer:[27]

רַבִּי יוֹסֵי הַגְּלִילִי אוֹמֵר: אֵינָן בָּאִין — R' Yose HaGlili **says: They will not enter**
the World to Come, שֶׁנֶּאֱמַר ״בַּמִּדְבָּר הַזֶּה יִתַּמּוּ וְשָׁם יָמֻתוּ״ — **as it is stated,**
"In this Wilderness shall they cease, and there they shall die!" (*Numbers*
14:35), וְאוֹמֵר ״וְעָרְפוּ שָׁם אֶת הָעֶגְלָה בַּנָּחַל״ — **and it states** elsewhere, *And*
they shall axe the back of the calf's neck there in the valley (*Deuteronomy*
21:4). מַה ״שָׁם״ הָאָמוּר לְהַלָּן בְּעֶגְלָה עֲרוּפָה שֶׁתָּמוּת וְלֹא תְזוּז מִמְּקוֹמָהּ — **Just**
as the word *there* **stated there in the passage of the Axed Heifer** (*eglah aru-*
fah) **means that [the calf] will die** there, **never to** come back to life and **move**
from its place, אַף ״שָׁם״ הָאָמוּר כָּאן יָמוּתוּ וְלֹא יָזוּזוּ מִמְּקוֹמָן — **so too** the word
there **stated here** with regard to the generation of the Wilderness means that
they would die there, **never to** come back to life and **move from their place.**

This inference is challenged:

מְשִׁיבִין עַל דְּבָרָיו — However, **an objection was raised to [R' Yose HaGlili's]**
argument: רְשָׁעִים נֶאֱמַר בָּהֶם ״שָׁם״ וְצַדִּיקִים לֹא נֶאֱמַר בָּהֶם ״שָׁם״ — **Is the**
word *there* used only in reference to the death of **the wicked,** who will never
be revivified, **and never in** reference to the death of **the righteous?** וַהֲלֹא
שָׁמָּה קָבְרוּ אֶת אַבְרָהָם כְּבָר נֶאֱמַר — Why, **it has already been stated,**[28]
וְאֵת שָׂרָה אִשְׁתּוֹ — *There they buried Abraham and Sarah his wife* (*Genesis*
49:31); וְאוֹמֵר ״בְּקִבְרִי אֲשֶׁר כָּרִיתִי לִי בְּאֶרֶץ כְּנַעַן שָׁמָּה תִּקְבְּרֵנִי״ — **and it states**
that Jacob said, *"In my grave, which I have hewn for myself in the land of*
Canaan — there you are to bury me" (ibid. 50:5); וְאוֹמֵר ״וַתָּמָת שָׁם מִרְיָם
וַתִּקָּבֵר שָׁם״ — **and it states,** *Miriam died there and she was buried there*

---

26. The righteous tribe of Levi was excluded
from the decree that God issued against
the generation of the Wilderness (*Ahavas*
Chesed, citing *Bava Basra* 121b).

27. In the standard Hebrew text, the next two
paragraphs are inverted. Our emendation

follows *Nuschas HaGra.*

28. We have moved the word נֶאֱמַר that appears below in Vilna edition (between וְאוֹמֵר
and בְּקִבְרִי) back to this line. This is how it
appears in most editions; the Vilna edition, from which our Hebrew text is taken,

[וַהֲלֹא כְּבָר נֶאֱמַר (שם לג, לח) "וַיַּעַל אַהֲרֹן הַכֹּהֵן וְגוֹ' וַיָּמָת שָׁם",] וְאוֹמֵר (דברים לד, ה) "וַיָּמָת שָׁם מֹשֶׁה עֶבֶד ה' בְּאֶרֶץ מוֹאָב עַל פִּי ה' ". רַבִּי יוֹסֵי הַגְּלִילִי אוֹמֵר: אֵינָן בָּאִין, שֶׁנֶּאֱמַר (במדבר יד, לה) "בַּמִּדְבָּר הַזֶּה יִתַּמּוּ וְשָׁם יָמֻתוּ". וְאוֹמֵר (דברים כא, ד) "וְעָרְפוּ שָׁם אֶת הָעֶגְלָה בַּנָּחַל". מַה "שָׁם" הָאָמוּר לְהַלָּן בָּעֶגְלָה עֲרוּפָה שֶׁתָּמוּת וְלֹא תָזוּז מִמְּקוֹמָהּ, אַף "שָׁם" הָאָמוּר כָּאן יָמוּתוּ וְלֹא יָזוּזוּ מִמְּקוֹמָן. (וַאֲחֵרִים אוֹמְרִין: בָּאִים הֵן וַעֲלֵיהֶן הוּא אוֹמֵר (ירמיה ב, ב) "הָלֹךְ וְקָרָאתָ בְאָזְנֵי יְרוּשָׁלַיִם לֵאמֹר [וְגוֹ' זָכַרְתִּי לָךְ חֶסֶד נְעוּרַיִךְ] וְגוֹ' "):[29]

ד. עֲשֶׂרֶת הַשְּׁבָטִים לֹא חַיִּין וְלֹא נִדּוֹנִין, שֶׁנֶּאֱמַר (דברים כט, כז) "וַיִּתְּשֵׁם ה' מֵעַל אַדְמָתָם ... [וַיַּשְׁלִכֵם אֶל אֶרֶץ אַחֶרֶת כַּיּוֹם הַזֶּה]".[30]

וַהֲלֹא כְּבָר נֶאֱמַר "וַיַּעַל אַהֲרֹן הַכֹּהֵן וְגוֹ' וַיָּמָת שָׁם" — and it it is already stated, *Then Aaron the Kohen went up, etc., and died there* (Numbers 20:1); וְאוֹמֵר "וַיָּמָת שָׁם מֹשֶׁה עֶבֶד ה' בְּאֶרֶץ מוֹאָב עַל פִּי ה' " — and it states, *So Moses, servant of HASHEM, died there, in the Land of Moab, by the mouth of HASHEM* (Deuteronomy 34:5). In all these cases, the word *there* is used, but it certainly cannot mean that these righteous persons will remain there and not come back to life! Accordingly, the use of the word *there* with regard to the generation of the Wilderness is no proof either.

Another Tanna supports R' Yehoshua's view, based on a different verse: וַאֲחֵרִים אוֹמְרִין: בָּאִים הֵן — And others say: [The generation of the Wilderness] will enter the World to Come. וַעֲלֵיהֶן הוּא אוֹמֵר "הָלֹךְ וְקָרָאתָ בְאָזְנֵי יְרוּשָׁלַיִם לֵאמֹר וְגוֹ' זָכַרְתִּי לָךְ חֶסֶד נְעוּרַיִךְ וְגוֹ' " — Regarding them it states, *"Go and call out in the ears of Jerusalem, saying: Thus said HASHEM: I recall for you the kindness of your youth,* the love of your nuptials, your following Me into the Wilderness, into an unsown land" (Jeremiah 2:2).[29]

§4 The Baraisa discusses the fate of the Ten Tribes of Israel, who were carried off to exile by the king of Assyria (II Kings 17:6): עֲשֶׂרֶת הַשְּׁבָטִים לֹא חַיִּין וְלֹא נִדּוֹנִין — The Ten Tribes will not live in the World to Come, nor will they be judged, שֶׁנֶּאֱמַר "וַיִּתְּשֵׁם ה' מֵעַל אַדְמָתָם ... וַיַּשְׁלִכֵם אֶל אֶרֶץ אַחֶרֶת כַּיּוֹם הַזֶּה" — as it is stated, *And HASHEM uprooted them from upon their soil,* with anger, with wrath, and with great fury, and He cast them to

---

contains a printing error.

29. [God declares that the people of Jerusalem would have a share in the World to Come — not in their own merit, but in the merit of the generation of the Wilderness, who in the "love of their bridal days" were willing to

follow God out into the desert wastelands.] Now, if others will enter the World to Come through the merit of the generation of the Wilderness, then certainly they themselves will enter the World to Come! (Sanhedrin 110b).

רַבִּי שִׁמְעוֹן בֶּן יְהוּדָה אוֹמֵר: מָה הַיּוֹם ([הַזֶּה אֲשֶׁר מָרְדוּ בוֹ][31]) הוֹלֵךְ וְאֵינוֹ
חוֹזֵר אַף הֵם אֵינָם חוֹזְרִין[31]. רַבִּי עֲקִיבָא אוֹמֵר: מָה הַיּוֹם מַאֲפִיל וּמֵאִיר
אַף אֲפֵילָה שֶׁלָּהֶן עֲתִידָה לְהָאִיר. (רַבָּן גַּמְלִיאֵל אוֹמֵר: הֲרֵי הוּא אוֹמֵר
(דברים יא, כא) "לְמַעַן יִרְבּוּ יְמֵיכֶם וִימֵי בְנֵיכֶם"[32], וְאוֹמֵר (שם כד, טז) "לֹא
יוּמְתוּ אָבוֹת עַל בָּנִים"[33]. כָּל זְמַן שֶׁהָאָב מַאֲרִיךְ יָמִים הַבֵּן מַאֲרִיךְ יָמִים.

רַבִּי שִׁמְעוֹן בֶּן יְהוּדָה[30] *another land, as this very day* (Deuteronomy 29:27). —
אוֹמֵר — R' Shimon ben Yehudah says: It is derived from the concluding words
of the verse, *as this very day:* מָה הַיּוֹם הוֹלֵךְ וְאֵינוֹ חוֹזֵר אַף הֵם אֵינָם חוֹזְרִין —
Just as the day goes, never to return,[31] **so will [the Ten Tribes] never return.**
רַבִּי עֲקִיבָא אוֹמֵר — R' Akiva says: מָה הַיּוֹם מַאֲפִיל וּמֵאִיר אַף אֲפֵילָה שֶׁלָּהֶן
עֲתִידָה לְהָאִיר — **On the contrary, they will enter the World to Come; for the**
phrase *as this very day* implies that **just as the day darkens and** then **becomes**
light again, so will the darkness of [the Ten Tribes] give way to light.

The Baraisa returns to its discussion in the previous section regarding
the generation of the Wilderness, citing another Tanna who agrees with
R' Yehoshua and maintains that they will enter the World to Come:
הֲרֵי הוּא אוֹמֵר "לְמַעַן יִרְבּוּ יְמֵיכֶם — רַבָּן גַּמְלִיאֵל אוֹמֵר — **Rabban Gamliel says:**
"וִימֵי בְנֵיכֶם — **It states** that God said to the generation of the Wilderness, *In*
order to prolong your days and the days of your children (ibid. 11:21),
indicating that the fathers, like their children, will merit the World to Come.[32]
כָּל זְמַן שֶׁהָאָב מַאֲרִיךְ יָמִים הַבֵּן מַאֲרִיךְ — **Moreover, it states,** *Fathers shall not be put*
to death because of sons (ibid. 24:16). וְאוֹמֵר "לֹא יוּמְתוּ אָבוֹת עַל בָּנִים"
יָמִים — **This may be understood to mean that in the World to Come, fathers**
will be saved from death in the merit of their righteous sons.[33] Thus, **as long**

---

30. In this passage, Moses warns the Jews
that if they stray into idolatry, the Land will
be laid waste; and when outsiders inquire as
to the reason for the desolation, they will be
told that God had punished the Jews for their
idolatry, driving them from their homeland
into exile, where they remain to this day. A
Baraisa (*Sanhedrin* 110b, cited by *Binyan*
Yehoshua) expounds this verse as follows:
And HASHEM uprooted them from upon their
soil — in this world; *and He cast them to an-*
other land — in the World to Come.

The phrase *to another land* (in its simple
meaning) indicates that all the exiles were
sent to a single land. This can only refer to the Ten Tribes, who were exiled to
Assyria, because the two tribes of Judah
and Benjamin, who were exiled later, were

(ultimately) dispersed across many lands
(*Rashi* to *Sanhedrin* ibid.).

31. Emendation follows *Nuschas HaGra*.

32. Although the Book of *Deuteronomy* was
addressed to the *children* of the generation
that died in the Wilderness, the entire Torah
— including this statement — was given to
the generation of the Wilderness as well.
This verse compares the men of that generation to their children, indicating that just
as the children's days would be prolonged in
the World to Come (see *Kiddushin* 39b), for
they did not sin, so would the fathers' days
be prolonged in the World to Come (*Binyan*
Yehoshua).

33. The plain meaning of the verse is that
fathers may not be put to death for the *sins*

[אֵין הָאָב מַאֲרִיךְ יָמִים אֵין הַבֵּן מַאֲרִיךְ יָמִים[34]] רַבִּי יוֹסֵי הַגְּלִילִי מְסַיֵּיעַ
לְרַבִּי אֱלִיעֶזֶר וְרַבָּן גַּמְלִיאֵל מְסַיֵּיעַ לְרַבִּי יְהוֹשֻׁעַ:

ה. שִׁבְעָה אֵין לָהֶם חֵלֶק לָעוֹלָם הַבָּא. וְאֵלוּ הֵן[35]: לַבְלָר[36]. וְסוֹפֵר[37]. וְטוֹב

אֵין הָאָב — as the father's days are prolonged, the son's days are prolonged; מַאֲרִיךְ יָמִים אֵין הַבֵּן מַאֲרִיךְ יָמִים — and if the father's days are not prolonged, the son's days are not prolonged.[34]

The Baraisa concludes:

רַבִּי יוֹסֵי הַגְּלִילִי מְסַיֵּיעַ לְרַבִּי אֱלִיעֶזֶר — R' Yose HaGlili (cited in the previous section) **supports R' Eliezer,** who maintains that the generation of the Wilderness has no portion in the World to Come; וְרַבָּן גַּמְלִיאֵל מְסַיֵּיעַ לְרַבִּי יְהוֹשֻׁעַ — and **Rabban Gamliel supports R' Yehoshua,** who maintains that they do have a portion in the World to Come.

§5 The Baraisa lists certain professions whose members are at risk of losing their share in the World to Come:

שִׁבְעָה אֵין לָהֶם חֵלֶק לָעוֹלָם הַבָּא וְאֵלוּ הֵן — There are **seven** professionals who are liable to **have no share in the World to Come,** as these occupations contain potential spiritual pitfalls:[35] וְסוֹפֵר — לַבְלָר — a **scribe** of Torah Scrolls;[36] a **writer of documents;**[37] וְטוֹב שֶׁבְּרוֹפְאִין — even **the best of physicians;**[38]

---

of their sons. However, Rabban Gamliel interprets it to mean that fathers will not be put to death (in the World to Come) in the *merit* of their sons. This is in accordance with the principle (*Sanhedrin* 104a) that a son can earn merit for his father (*Binyan Yehoshua*).

34. In other words, it is inconceivable that the son's days should be prolonged in the World to Come and the father should forfeit his portion. The only way it is possible for the father's days not to be prolonged is if the son's days are not prolonged — i.e., if the son was wicked. However, if the son was righteous, his merit will ensure his father a share in the World to Come. Thus, the generation of the Wilderness will surely enter the World to Come in the merit of their righteous children (*Ben Avraham*, second explanation).

35. These professions all share one quality: Those who are engaged in them are often faced with a powerful temptation to mislead people, as it is unlikely that their deception will ever be discovered (see *Binyan Yehoshua*).

36. At times, if a scribe adds or deletes a letter, he may lead people into heresy. For example, if when writing the verse (*Jeremiah* 10:10), וַה׳ אֱלֹהִים אֱמֶת, *And Hashem God is true,* he were to omit the א of אֱמֶת, the result would be the word מֵת, *dead,* instead of *true,* which is blasphemous. Similarly, if a scribe were to add a final ו to the word בָּרָא in the verse (*Genesis* 1:1), בְּרֵאשִׁית בָּרָא אֱלֹהִים, *In the beginning God created,* the resulting word בָּרְאוּ, *they created,* would convey a polytheistic impression (*Binyan Yehoshua,* citing *Sotah* 20a with *Rashi* ad loc.).

37. I.e., if he forges documents (*Mefaresh,* cited by *Binyan Yehoshua*), or if he is a court scribe and he is careless in the way he records the claims of the litigants, resulting in an incorrect ruling (*Ben Avraham*).

38. They might be inclined to make critical decisions affecting the very life of a patient without seeking a second opinion, sometimes with tragic results (*Binyan Yehoshua*). See further, *Rashi* to *Kiddushin* 82a.

שֶׁבְּרוֹפְאִין[38]. וְדַיָּין לְעִירוֹ[39]. וְקוֹסֵם[40]. חַזָּן[41]. וְטַבָּח[42]:

ו. שְׁלֹשָׁה[43] מְלָכִים וְאַרְבָּעָה הֶדְיוֹטוֹת אֵין לָהֶם חֵלֶק לָעוֹלָם הַבָּא[44]. שְׁלֹשָׁה מְלָכִים, יָרָבְעָם[45] אַחְאָב[46] מְנַשֶּׁה[47]. אַרְבָּעָה הֶדְיוֹטוֹת,

---

חַזָּן — וְדַיָּין לְעִירוֹ — a judge for his city;[39] וְקוֹסֵם — a user of divinations;[40] — an agent of the court;[41] וְטַבָּח — and an animal slaughterer.[42]

§6 The Baraisa resumes listing specific individuals in history who forfeited their share in the World to Come:[43]

שְׁלֹשָׁה מְלָכִים וְאַרְבָּעָה הֶדְיוֹטוֹת אֵין לָהֶם חֵלֶק לָעוֹלָם הַבָּא — Three kings and four commoners have no share in the World to Come.[44] שְׁלֹשָׁה מְלָכִים, יָרָבְעָם — אַחְאָב מְנַשֶּׁה — The three kings are: Jeroboam,[45] Ahab,[46] and Manasseh.[47]

---

39. Judges who do not fulfill their role with integrity bring Divine retribution upon their community (see *Shabbos* 139a). Additionally, the singular "judge" indicates one who judges alone. Such a person is particularly liable to err and issue unlawful rulings, as we are taught in *Avos* (4:8): "Do not judge alone, for none judges alone except One" (*Binyan Yehoshua*).

40. He utilizes the power of divination to mislead people into thinking that he is a prophet (ibid.).

41. The agent of the court projects and enforces the court's authority (e.g., by delivering summons or seizing property). However, he can misuse his authority. The Gemara (*Shabbos* 139a, as explained by *Rashi* there) refers to an unfortunate situation in which the agent threatens the abandonment of his duties, crippling the court's effectiveness, if certain demands, such as a raise in his salary, are not met (*Binyan Yehoshua*).

42. One who slaughters animals is constantly faced with questions of *kashrus*, and he can often make wrong decisions to prevent himself from suffering a financial loss, resulting in Jews eating nonkosher meat (*Rashi* to *Kiddushin* 82a, cited by *Binyan Yehoshua*).

43. The first part of this section (until רַבִּי מֵאִיר אוֹמֵר) is an almost exact quote of the Mishnah in *Sanhedrin* 90a. [Vilna numbers this section "5" in error.]

44. Many other wicked people have forfeited

their share in the World to Come. The Mishnah singles out these individuals, however, for one might have thought that they *do* have a share in the merit of their broad and profound Torah knowledge. Therefore, the Mishnah teaches us that they nonetheless forfeited their share in the World to Come (*Rambam, Commentary to the Mishnah, Sanhedrin* 10:2). [Regarding Balaam, see note 48.]

45. Jeroboam revolted against the sovereignty of Rehoboam, the son of King Solomon, and led the Ten Tribes in a break from the kingdom of the House of David. He then became their king, in compliance with the prophetic instruction he had received from Ahijah the Shilonite. Fearing that if his subjects would go to the Temple in Jerusalem to bring offerings to God on the three festivals they would gradually resume their loyalty to the House of David, he established two golden calves within his kingdom for his people to serve, and thus led them to idolatry (see *I Kings* 11:29-39 and 12:25-33). For this, he lost his share in the World to Come (see *Sanhedrin* 101b).

46. Ahab was king of the Ten Tribes who, together with his wicked wife Jezebel, introduced Baal worship to Israel (see *Radak* to *I Kings* 21:25; *Sanhedrin* 102b).

47. Manasseh, the son of the righteous King Hezekiah, was an idolatrous king of Judah who is compared by Scripture to Ahab (see *II Kings* 21:2-3; *Sanhedrin* 102b).

בִּלְעָם[48] דּוֹאֵג[49] וַאֲחִיתוֹפֶל[50] וְגֵיחֲזִי[51]. רַבִּי יְהוּדָה אוֹמֵר: מְנַשֶּׁה כְּבָר שָׁב
שֶׁנֶּאֱמַר (דברי הימים ב לג, יג) "וַיִּתְפַּלֵּל אֵלָיו וַיֵּעָתֶר לוֹ"[52]. אָמַר לוֹ: אִילּוּ
כְּתִיב "וַיְשִׁיבֵהוּ לִירוּשָׁלַיִם" וְשָׁתַק, הָיִינוּ [אוֹמְרִים] כִּדְבָרֶיךָ. כְּשֶׁהוּא
אוֹמֵר "לְמַלְכוּתוֹ", לְמַלְכוּתוֹ הֱשִׁיבוֹ וְלֹא הֱשִׁיבוֹ לְחַיֵּי הָעוֹלָם הַבָּא. רַבִּי
מֵאִיר אוֹמֵר: אַבְשָׁלוֹם אֵין לוֹ חֵלֶק לָעוֹלָם הַבָּא[53]. רַבִּי שִׁמְעוֹן בֶּן אֶלְעָזָר

אַרְבָּעָה הֶדְיוֹטוֹת, בִּלְעָם דּוֹאֵג וַאֲחִיתוֹפֶל וְגֵיחֲזִי — The four commoners are: Balaam,[48] Doeg,[49] Ahithophel,[50] and Gehazi.[51] רַבִּי יְהוּדָה אוֹמֵר — R' Yehudah says: מְנַשֶּׁה כְּבָר שָׁב, שֶׁנֶּאֱמַר "וַיִּתְפַּלֵּל אֵלָיו וַיֵּעָתֶר לוֹ" — Manasseh had already repented long before he died and therefore has a portion in the World to Come, as it is stated, *[Manasseh] prayed to [God], and He was entreated by him* and heard his supplication, and He returned him to Jerusalem, to his kingship (II Chronicles 33:13).[52] אָמַר לוֹ — [Another sage] replied to him: אִילּוּ כְּתִיב "וַיְשִׁיבֵהוּ לִירוּשָׁלַיִם", וְשָׁתַק, הָיִינוּ אוֹמְרִים כִּדְבָרֶיךָ — Were it to be written, *and He returned him to Jerusalem*, and remained silent, without adding anything further, we would agree with your view. כְּשֶׁהוּא אוֹמֵר "לְמַלְכוּתוֹ", לְמַלְכוּתוֹ הֱשִׁיבוֹ וְלֹא הֱשִׁיבוֹ לְחַיֵּי הָעוֹלָם הַבָּא — However, when it says further *to his kingship*, this teaches us that only to his *kingship* [God] returned him, but He did not return him to the life of the World to Come. רַבִּי מֵאִיר אוֹמֵר — R' Meir says: אַבְשָׁלוֹם אֵין לוֹ חֵלֶק לָעוֹלָם הַבָּא — Absalom has no portion in the World to Come.[53] רַבִּי שִׁמְעוֹן בֶּן אֶלְעָזָר אוֹמֵר — R' Shimon ben Elazar

---

48. As expounded in *Sanhedrin* 105a, the righteous among the nations of the world have a share in the World to Come. Lest one think that Balaam was among them (as we see that he had the power to foretell the future — *Meiri, Sanhedrin* 90a), the Mishnah informs us that to the contrary, he was among the wicked men of the nations (*Rambam, Commentary to the Mishnah, Sanhedrin* 10:2; *Binyan Yehoshua*, citing *Rav* ad loc.).

49. Doeg the Edomite was the adviser of King Saul who slandered David to him and thereby brought about the destruction of Nob, the city of Kohanim (see *I Samuel* 22:9-22; *Sanhedrin* 106b).

50. Ahithophel was the highly regarded sage and adviser to King David who deserted the king in favor of his renegade son, Absalom (see *II Samuel*, Ch. 17; *Sanhedrin* 106b).

51. Gehazi was the attendant of the prophet Elisha, but he sinned and led others to sin (see *Sanhedrin* 107b).

52. Scripture states there that God punished Manasseh and delivered him into the hands of the Assyrians, who brought him in chains to Babylon. There, in his pain, he called out to God *and he humbled himself greatly before the God of his fathers* (v. 12 ad loc.). God accepted his prayer and returned him to his throne in Jerusalem. R' Yehudah infers from God's acceptance of his prayer that his penitence was accepted and he regained his share in the World to Come.

53. David's son Absalom rebelled against him, ultimately leading to Absalom's death at the hands of David's general Joab, as recorded in *II Samuel* Chs. 15-19. Absalom also had relations with his father's concubines (ibid. 16:22). [See *Tosafos* to *Yoma* 66b, ד״ה פלוני and *Tosafos* to *Sotah* 10b, ד״ה דקרב for further discussion of Absalom's sin and his punishment.]

אוֹמֵר: יָרָבְעָם אַחְאָב מְנַשֶּׁה בַּעְשָׁא[54] וַאֲחַזְיָה[55] וְכָל מַלְכֵי יִשְׂרָאֵל
שֶׁהִרְשִׁיעוּ אֵין לָהֶן חֵלֶק לָעוֹלָם הַבָּא[56]. רַבִּי יוֹחָנָן בֶּן נוּרִי אוֹמֵר: אַף
הַהוֹגֶה אֶת הַשֵּׁם בְּאוֹתִיּוֹתָיו אֵין לוֹ חֵלֶק לָעוֹלָם הַבָּא[57]. הוּא הָיָה אוֹמֵר:
הַמְנַעְנֵעַ קוֹלוֹ בְּשִׁיר הַשִּׁירִים[58] (וְהַלּוֹחֵשׁ עַל הַמַּכָּה) וְהָרוֹקֵק עַל הַמַּכָּה

יָרָבְעָם אַחְאָב מְנַשֶּׁה בַּעְשָׁא וַאֲחַזְיָה וְכָל מַלְכֵי יִשְׂרָאֵל שֶׁהִרְשִׁיעוּ אֵין לָהֶן חֵלֶק says:
לָעוֹלָם הַבָּא — Jeroboam, Ahab, Manasseh, Baasa,[54] Ahaziah,[55] and all the
kings of Israel (i.e., the Ten Tribes) who acted wickedly have no portion in the
World to Come.[56]

The Baraisa continues with certain behaviors that cause one to forfeit his
share in the World to Come:

אַף הַהוֹגֶה אֶת הַשֵּׁם — רַבִּי יוֹחָנָן בֶּן נוּרִי אוֹמֵר — R' Yochanan ben Nuri says:
בְּאוֹתִיּוֹתָיו אֵין לוֹ חֵלֶק לָעוֹלָם הַבָּא — Also one who pronounces the Name of
God according to its letters does not have a share in the World to Come.[57]
הוּא הָיָה אוֹמֵר — He used to say: הַמְנַעְנֵעַ קוֹלוֹ בְּשִׁיר הַשִּׁירִים — One who
modulates his voice in reading Song of Songs by singing it with a common
melody,[58]   וְהַלּוֹחֵשׁ עַל הַמַּכָּה וְהָרוֹקֵק עַל הַמַּכָּה — and one who utters an

---

54. A king of the Ten Tribes who assassinated the previous king, Nadab the son of Jeroboam. He then took over the throne and exterminated all of Jeroboam's descendants. Nevertheless, he followed Jeroboam's idolatrous ways. See I Kings 15:16-16:7.

55. There were two idolatrous kings named Ahaziah: one of the Ten Tribes (see I Kings 22:52-II Kings 1:17) and one of Judah (see II Kings 8:25-9:29). It is not clear which of the two our Baraisa is referring to (see Magen Avos and Ben Avraham, and see the next note).

56. This includes every king of the Ten Tribes aside from Jehu (Yad Ramah to Sanhedrin 103b).

R' Shimon's mention by name of some of the Israelite kings seems redundant, since he ultimately includes them all. Indeed, the commentators note that a parallel teaching cited in Bavli Sanhedrin 103b names only Ahaz (an idolatrous king of Judah; see II Kings 16:1-20) and Ahaziah (king of Judah — Rashi ad loc.); and Yerushalmi Sanhedrin 10:1 names Ahaz alone. See Gra and Avos HaRosh (Vol. 2),

who suggest various ways of emending our Baraisa; see also Magen Avos, who seems to have had a different version of the text.

57. According to Rashi (Sanhedrin 101b), this refers to one who utters the forty-two-letter Name of God that was used only in the Temple. According to Rav (Sanhedrin 10:1; see also Yerushalmi ad loc.), it refers to one who utters the Tetragrammaton [יהו-ה] according to the way it is written — as opposed to the way we commonly pronounce it [אדנ-י] (Binyan Yehoshua). See Sanhedrin 101b and Tosafos to Avodah Zarah 18a, ד"ה הוגה for further discussion.

58. I.e., any melody other than that indicated by the traditional notes of cantillation. Although the essence of this Book is song, one may not sing it as an ordinary song; rather, it is part of Scripture and must be recited with the same reverence and attention to tradition with which one recites any other part of the Torah (Binyan Yehoshua, citing Rashi to Sanhedrin 101a). For further discussion, see Yad Ramah and Yad David ad loc., and Sdei Chemed (Asifas Dinim, Zayin §12).

וְאוֹמֵר (שמות טו, כו) "כָּל הַמַּחֲלָה וְגוֹ'"⁵⁹, "אֵין לוֹ חֵלֶק לָעוֹלָם הַבָּא. וַחֲכָמִים
אוֹמְרִים: כָּל תַּלְמִיד חָכָם שֶׁשָּׁנָה וּפֵירַשׁ אֵין לוֹ חֵלֶק לָעוֹלָם הַבָּא, שֶׁנֶּאֱמַר
(במדבר טו, לא) "כִּי דְבַר ה' בָּזָה"⁶⁰. וְאוֹמֵר (ירמיה ב, ה) "מַה מָּצְאוּ אֲבוֹתֵיכֶם
בִּי עָוֶל כִּי רָחֲקוּ מֵעָלָי"⁶¹. רַבִּי מֵאִיר אוֹמֵר: כֹּל שֶׁיֵּשׁ לוֹ בֵית הַמִּדְרָשׁ
בְּעִירוֹ וְאֵינוּ הוֹלֵךְ לְשָׁם אֵין לוֹ חֵלֶק לָעוֹלָם הַבָּא⁶². וְרַבִּי עֲקִיבָא אוֹמֵר:
אַף מִי שֶׁאֵינוּ מְשַׁמֵּשׁ לְתַלְמִידֵי חֲכָמִים אֵין לוֹ חֵלֶק לָעוֹלָם הַבָּא⁶³:

incantation and spits on a wound, "כָּל הַמַּחֲלָה וְגוֹ'" — saying the
verse, *Any of the diseases* that I placed in Egypt, I will not bring upon you, for
I am HASHEM, your Healer (Exodus 15:26),[59] אֵין לוֹ חֵלֶק לָעוֹלָם הַבָּא — has
no share in the World to Come. וַחֲכָמִים אוֹמְרִים — And the Sages say:
כָּל תַּלְמִיד חָכָם שֶׁשָּׁנָה וּפֵירַשׁ אֵין לוֹ חֵלֶק לָעוֹלָם הַבָּא — Any Torah scholar who
studies and then departs from those studies has no share in the World to
Come, שֶׁנֶּאֱמַר "כִּי דְבַר ה' בָּזָה" — as it is stated, *For he scorned the word
of HASHEM and nullified His commandment; that person will surely be cut off,
his sin is upon him* (Numbers 15:31).[60] וְאוֹמֵר "מַה מָּצְאוּ אֲבוֹתֵיכֶם בִּי עָוֶל כִּי
רָחֲקוּ מֵעָלָי" — And regarding such an individual it states, *What wrong did
your forefathers find in Me, that they distanced themselves from Me, and
pursued futility, and became futile?* (Jeremiah 2:5).[61] רַבִּי מֵאִיר אוֹמֵר — R'
Meir says: כֹּל שֶׁיֵּשׁ לוֹ בֵית הַמִּדְרָשׁ בְּעִירוֹ וְאֵינוּ הוֹלֵךְ לְשָׁם אֵין לוֹ חֵלֶק לָעוֹלָם
הַבָּא — Anyone who has a study hall in his city but does not go there has no
portion in the World to Come.[62] וְרַבִּי עֲקִיבָא אוֹמֵר — R' Akiva says: אַף
מִי שֶׁאֵינוּ מְשַׁמֵּשׁ לְתַלְמִידֵי חֲכָמִים אֵין לוֹ חֵלֶק לָעוֹלָם הַבָּא — Also one who does
not serve Torah scholars has no portion in the World to Come.[63]

---

59. It was the custom of incantation healers to spit on the wound before uttering their incantations. If one recites a verse containing the Name of God (such as the verse cited), he may not spit before doing so [for such an act is extremely disrespectful] (*Binyan Yehoshua*, citing *Sanhedrin 101a*).

60. One who abandons the study of Torah has scorned the word of God (see *Sanhedrin 99a*). The phrase, *that person will surely be cut off*, means that he will be destroyed in both worlds; see above, 26 §4 note 35.

61. Only one who was previously close to God can be said to subsequently distance himself. The verse refers specifically to a former Torah scholar, as borne out by another verse in that passage (v. 8): *those who had grasped the Torah did not know Me* (*Maharsha* to *Chagigah 9b*).

62. Such a person is also included in the verse, *For he has scorned the word of HASHEM* (*Mefaresh*).

63. Even if one has studied Scripture and Mishnah, he needs to serve Torah scholars in order to understand the Talmudic analyses of the Mishnah's reasoning. [This discipline is known as "Talmud" (see *Rashi* to *Sotah 20*, ד"ה והדר), and is acquired by attending Torah scholars.] Understanding the reasoning behind the Mishnah's rulings is essential for proper application of those rulings. The Gemara (*Sotah 22a*) refers to those who issue halachic rulings based on their knowledge of the Mishnah without the benefit of Talumdic analysis as "ruiners of the world" (*Mefaresh*). Thus, one who does not engage in the study of Talmud also scorns the word of God.

﴾ פֶּרֶק לז ﴿

א. שִׁבְעָה בְּרִיּוֹת זוֹ לְמַעְלָה מִזּוֹ וְזוֹ לְמַעְלָה מִזּוֹ². לְמַעְלָה מִכּוּלָם בָּרָא רָקִיעַ³. לְמַעְלָה מִן הָרָקִיעַ בָּרָא כּוֹכָבִים שֶׁמְּאִירִין לָעוֹלָם⁴. לְמַעְלָה מִכּוֹכָבִים בָּרָא אִילָנוֹת שֶׁאִילָנוֹת עוֹשִׂין פֵּירוֹת וְכוֹכָבִים אֵינָם עוֹשִׂין פֵּירוֹת. וּלְמַעְלָה מִן הָאִילָנוֹת בָּרָא רוּחוֹת רָעוֹת⁵ שְׁרוּחוֹת רָעוֹת הוֹלְכוֹת לְכָאן וּלְכָאן וְאִילָנוֹת אֵינָם זָזִים מִמְּקוֹמָן⁶. לְמַעְלָה מֵרוּחוֹת רָעוֹת בָּרָא בְּהֵמָה

✺﴾ CHAPTER 37 ﴿✺

§1 The Baraisa presents a series of teachings organized around groups of seven:[1]

שִׁבְעָה בְּרִיּוֹת זוֹ לְמַעְלָה מִזּוֹ וְזוֹ לְמַעְלָה מִזּוֹ — **There are seven creations** that God created to be **one higher than the other.**[2] לְמַעְלָה מִכּוּלָם בָּרָא רָקִיעַ — **(i) Above all of them, [God] created the heaven.**[3] לְמַעְלָה מִן הָרָקִיעַ בָּרָא כּוֹכָבִים שֶׁמְּאִירִין לָעוֹלָם — **(ii) Higher than the heaven He created stars, which give light to the world.**[4] לְמַעְלָה מִכּוֹכָבִים בָּרָא אִילָנוֹת — **(iii) Higher than stars He created trees,** which are superior to stars, שֶׁאִילָנוֹת עוֹשִׂין פֵּירוֹת — **in that trees produce fruit,** whereas stars do not וְכוֹכָבִים אֵינָם עוֹשִׂין פֵּירוֹת — produce fruit. וּלְמַעְלָה מִן הָאִילָנוֹת בָּרָא רוּחוֹת רָעוֹת — **(iv) Higher than the trees He created bad winds,**[5] which are superior to trees, שְׁרוּחוֹת רָעוֹת הוֹלְכוֹת לְכָאן וּלְכָאן וְאִילָנוֹת אֵינָם זָזִים מִמְּקוֹמָן — **in that bad winds can go here and there while trees cannot move from their place.**[6] לְמַעְלָה מֵרוּחוֹת רָעוֹת בָּרָא בְּהֵמָה — **(v) Higher than bad winds He created** domestic **animals,** which

---

1. Our Baraisa continues the theme of *Avos* 5:7: *Seven things [are found] in a crude person ...* (which our Baraisa includes, in an expanded form, below §11-12) by presenting other lists of "seven" (*Binyan Yehoshua*).

2. That is, each successive creation was made with a superior quality that the one preceding it does not have (*Binyan Yehoshua*).

3. This line is problematic: If the Baraisa is listing the seven things in *ascending* order (as it states next: *Above the heaven He created ...*), then how does it say here that the heaven is *higher* than all of them? Some suggest that this "higher" (in contrast to the other ones) means *physically* higher (*Tosefes Ohr*). *Magen Avos* (based on the reading found in *Avos DeRabbi Nassan, Nusach 2*, Ch. 43) emends the text to read לְמַעְלָה "מִן הָאָרֶץ" בָּרָא רָקִיע, *Higher than "the earth" He*

created the heaven. Accordingly, the Baraisa is listing, in ascending order, seven creations that are higher than the earth.

4. Thus, their advantage over the heaven itself is that they give light to the world. [The sun and the moon are included in "stars."]

5. *Hagahos Yaavetz* suggests that this should be רוּחוֹת סְעָרוֹת, *stormy winds* [see *Ezekiel* 13:11,13].

6. Mobility is an advantage over being fixed in one place.

According to *Ben Avraham,* our Baraisa refers to winds that are "bad" in the sense that they blow from all directions, so that one cannot shield himself from them. *Magen Avos* removes the word רָעוֹת, *bad,* altogether, based on the reading in *Avos DeRabbi Nassan, Nusach 2*, Ch. 43.

שֶׁבְּהֵמָה עוֹשָׂה וְאוֹכֶלֶת וְרוּחוֹת רָעוֹת לֹא עוֹשׂוֹת וְלֹא אוֹכְלוֹת. וּלְמַעְלָה
מִן הַבְּהֵמָה בָּרָא אָדָם שֶׁבָּאָדָם יֵשׁ בּוֹ דֵּעָה וּבַבְּהֵמָה אֵין בָּהּ דֵּעָה. לְמַעְלָה
מִן הָאָדָם בָּרָא מַלְאֲכֵי הַשָּׁרֵת שֶׁמַּלְאֲכֵי הַשָּׁרֵת הוֹלְכִין מִסּוֹף הָעוֹלָם וְעַד
סוֹפוֹ[7] וּבְנֵי אָדָם אֵינָן כֵּן[8]:

ב. שִׁשָּׁה דְּבָרִים נֶאֶמְרוּ בִּבְנֵי אָדָם, שְׁלֹשָׁה כַּבְּהֵמָה וּשְׁלֹשָׁה כְּמַלְאֲכֵי
הַשָּׁרֵת. שְׁלֹשָׁה כַּבְּהֵמָה: אוֹכְלִין וְשׁוֹתִין כַּבְּהֵמָה פָּרִין וְרָבִין
כַּבְּהֵמָה וּמוֹצִיאַין רְעִי רֵיעִי כַּבְּהֵמָה[10]. שְׁלֹשָׁה כְּמַלְאֲכֵי הַשָּׁרֵת: יֵשׁ בָּהֶן בִּינָה

שֶׁבְּהֵמָה עוֹשָׂה וְאוֹכֶלֶת וְרוּחוֹת רָעוֹת לֹא עוֹשׂוֹת וְלֹא — are superior to bad winds, אוֹכְלוֹת — in that an animal works and eats, whereas bad winds neither work nor eat. וּלְמַעְלָה מִן הַבְּהֵמָה בָּרָא אָדָם — (vi) Higher than animals He created man, who is superior to the animal, שֶׁבָּאָדָם יֵשׁ בּוֹ דֵּעָה וּבַבְּהֵמָה — in that man has intellect, whereas an animal does not have intellect. אֵין בָּהּ דֵּעָה — (vii) Higher than man He לְמַעְלָה מִן הָאָדָם בָּרָא מַלְאֲכֵי הַשָּׁרֵת created the ministering angels, which are superior to man, שֶׁמַּלְאֲכֵי הַשָּׁרֵת הוֹלְכִין מִסּוֹף הָעוֹלָם וְעַד סוֹפוֹ וּבְנֵי אָדָם אֵינָן כֵּן — in that the ministering angels can go from one end of the world to the other,[7] whereas people cannot do so.[8]

§2 Having placed man as higher than the animal and lower than the angel, the Baraisa now lists the characteristics man shares with each:[9]

שִׁשָּׁה דְּבָרִים נֶאֶמְרוּ בִּבְנֵי אָדָם — Six characteristics were said regarding human beings; שְׁלֹשָׁה כַּבְּהֵמָה וּשְׁלֹשָׁה כְּמַלְאֲכֵי הַשָּׁרֵת — in three they are like an animal and in three they are like the ministering angels. שְׁלֹשָׁה כַּבְּהֵמָה — These are the three in which human beings are like an animal: אוֹכְלִין וְשׁוֹתִין כַּבְּהֵמָה פָּרִין וְרָבִין כַּבְּהֵמָה וּמוֹצִיאַין רְעִי כַּבְּהֵמָה — (i) They eat and drink like an animal; (ii) they reproduce like an animal; (iii) and they eliminate bodily waste like an animal.[10] שְׁלֹשָׁה כְּמַלְאֲכֵי הַשָּׁרֵת — And these are the three characteristics in which human beings are like ministering angels: יֵשׁ בָּהֶן בִּינָה

---

7. See below, note 14.

8. It is in this respect that the ministering angels are superior to man. But in terms of importance, righteous people are greater than the angels, as taught in the Gemara [*Sanhedrin* 93a and *Chullin* 91b, based on Scripture] (*Binyan Yehoshua*).

[*Ben Avraham* interprets this cryptic Baraisa as a collection of seven metaphors for man, each highlighting a specific positive quality that a God-fearing person should seek to attain. See there at length.]

9. Even though they are six and not seven (*Ben Avraham*).

[This Baraisa and the one that follows are cited by the Gemara in *Chagigah* 16a, and the commentators there elaborate on them.]

10. The Baraisa does *not* list the fact that people also *die* like animals. For it is indeed not so: The spirit of a man ascends above whereas the spirit of an animal descends below (*Binyan Yehoshua*, citing *Rosh*; cf. *HaRif* in *Ein Yaakov* cited there).

כְּמַלְאֲכֵי הַשָּׁרֵת וּמְהַלְּכִין בְּקוֹמָה זְקוּפָה כְּמַלְאֲכֵי הַשָּׁרֵת וּמְסַפְּרִין בִּלְשׁוֹן
הַקּוֹדֶשׁ כְּמַלְאֲכֵי הַשָּׁרֵת:[11]

ג. שִׁשָּׁה דְבָרִים נֶאֶמְרוּ בַּשֵּׁדִים[12], שְׁלֹשָׁה כִּבְנֵי אָדָם וּשְׁלֹשָׁה כְּמַלְאֲכֵי
הַשָּׁרֵת. שְׁלֹשָׁה כִּבְנֵי אָדָם: אוֹכְלִין וְשׁוֹתִין כִּבְנֵי אָדָם פָּרִין וְרָבִין
כִּבְנֵי אָדָם וּמֵתִים כִּבְנֵי אָדָם. שְׁלֹשָׁה כְּמַלְאֲכֵי הַשָּׁרֵת: יֵשׁ לָהֶם
כְּנָפַיִם כְּמַלְאֲכֵי הַשָּׁרֵת וְיוֹדְעִים מַה עָתִיד לִהְיוֹת כְּמַלְאֲכֵי הַשָּׁרֵת[13]

כְּמַלְאֲכֵי הַשָּׁרֵת — (i) They have understanding like ministering angels;
וּמְהַלְּכִין בְּקוֹמָה זְקוּפָה כְּמַלְאֲכֵי הַשָּׁרֵת — (ii) and they walk erect like the ministering angels; וּמְסַפְּרִין בִּלְשׁוֹן הַקּוֹדֶשׁ כְּמַלְאֲכֵי הַשָּׁרֵת — (iii) and they speak in
the Holy Tongue like ministering angels.[11]

§3 Having listed the ways in which human beings combine aspects of both
animals and angels, the Baraisa continues with the ways in which demons
combine aspects of both human beings and angels:
שִׁשָּׁה דְבָרִים נֶאֶמְרוּ בַּשֵּׁדִים — Six characteristics were said regarding demons;[12]
שְׁלֹשָׁה כִּבְנֵי אָדָם וּשְׁלֹשָׁה כְּמַלְאֲכֵי הַשָּׁרֵת — in three they are like human beings
and in three they are like the ministering angels. שְׁלֹשָׁה כִּבְנֵי אָדָם — These
are the three in which demons are like human beings: אוֹכְלִין וְשׁוֹתִין כִּבְנֵי
אָדָם פָּרִין וְרָבִין כִּבְנֵי אָדָם וּמֵתִים כִּבְנֵי אָדָם — (i) They eat and drink like human
beings; (ii) they reproduce like human beings; (iii) and they die like human
beings. שְׁלֹשָׁה כְּמַלְאֲכֵי הַשָּׁרֵת — And these are the three characteristics
in which demons are like the ministering angels: יֵשׁ לָהֶם כְּנָפַיִם כְּמַלְאֲכֵי
הַשָּׁרֵת — (i) They have wings like the ministering angels; וְיוֹדְעִים מַה עָתִיד
לִהְיוֹת כְּמַלְאֲכֵי הַשָּׁרֵת — (ii) they know the future like the ministering angels;[13]

---

11. Of course they speak other languages as
well. The Baraisa's point is that both humans
and angels have the gift of speech, and their
common language is Hebrew, as angels do
not speak Aramaic [which was the other
main language spoken by Jews in Mishnaic
times] (*Maharsha* to *Chagigah* 16a, cited
here by *Ben Avraham*). Alternatively, our
Baraisa is speaking about characteristics
with which these creatures *were created*.
Hebrew is the natural language of man and
of the angels (see *Binyan Yehoshua*).

Magen Avos sees an important lesson for
us in this Baraisa: We were created to share
characteristics with the animals and the angels. It is up to us to decide whether we will
be like one or like the other.

12. *Rambam* contends that demons are not
actual phenomena, but the great majority of
Rishonim and Acharonim maintain that they
are (see discussion in *Nishmas Chaim* 3:12
by *R' Menashe ben Yisrael*). [For insights
into how *Rambam* would understand the
many passages in the Talmudic literature
that discuss demons, see *Michtav MeEli-
yahu* V, p. 346; see also *Teshuvos Chasam
Sofer, Yoreh Deah* §7; see also *Chidushei Ha-
Meiri* to *Pesachim* 109b-114a, published by
R' Moshe Blau at the end of *Sefer HaBattim*.]

13. The Gemara (*Chagigah* loc. cit.) explains that they do not know the future on
their own. [Even ministering angels do
not know the future on their own.] Rather,
the Baraisa means that they hear what is

וּמְהַלְּכִין מִסּוֹף הָעוֹלָם וְעַד סוֹפוֹ כְּמַלְאֲכֵי הַשָּׁרֵת.[14] וְיֵשׁ אוֹמְרִים: אַף
הוֹפְכִין פְּנֵיהֶן לְכָל דְּמוּת שֶׁיִּרְצוּ וְרוֹאִין וְאֵינָם נִרְאִין:[15]

ד. °שְׁמוֹנָה פְרוּשִׁין הֵם:[16] פָּרוּשׁ שִׁכְמִי.[17] פָּרוּשׁ °נִכְפַּאי.[18] פָּרוּשׁ

כְּמַלְאֲכֵי הַשָּׁרֵת וְעַד סוֹפוֹ הָעוֹלָם מִסּוֹף וּמְהַלְּכִין — (iii) **and they can go from one
end of the world to the other like the ministering angels.**[14] וְיֵשׁ אוֹמְרִים —
And some say: אַף הוֹפְכִין פְּנֵיהֶן לְכָל דְּמוּת שֶׁיִּרְצוּ — **In addition, they can
transform their faces to any look they wish,** וְרוֹאִין וְאֵינָם נִרְאִין — **and they
can see without being seen.**[15]

§4 The Baraisa presents another list of seven:

שִׁבְעָה פְרוּשִׁין הֵם — **There are seven** types of *Perushim:*[16] פָּרוּשׁ שִׁכְמִי —
(i) **a Shechemite** *Parush;*[17] פָּרוּשׁ — (ii) **a knocking** *Parush;*[18]

---

announced from behind the Partition [which
shields the Divine Presence (*Rashi* to *Berachos* 18b)] like ministering angels. That is,
they hear announcements regarding the
immediate future, but they are ignorant of
what will happen beyond that (*Ramban* to
Leviticus 17:7).

14. This means that they are capable of
living anywhere on earth, even in places
whose harsh environments do not permit
human habitation (*Maharsha* to *Chagigah*
loc. cit.).

15. *Ben Avraham* takes this to be a continuation of the preceding: Because demons can
assume any guise they wish, they can see
people without the people realizing that they
are being observed by demons.

16. [The standard editions of *Avos De-
Rabbi Nassan* have here "שְׁמוֹנָה פְרוּשִׁין הֵם",
There are "eight" Perushim. See end of this
note.]

[*Perushim* (literally, *removed*), or Pharisees, were pious, God-fearing Jews of the
Second Temple era who supported the Rabbis and opposed the heretical Sadducean
sect (Tzadokim).] The true *Perushim* were
so called because they distanced themselves
from the unrefined character and immoderate material pursuits of the common people,
and set their sights on elevated matters and
on that which leads to the life of the World
to Come (*Rambam, Mishnah Commentary,
Sotah* 3:3, cited here in *Binyan Yehoshua*).

Our Baraisa enumerates various types of
insincere *Perushim,* who adopt exaggerated
externalities of the true *Perushim* in order
to feign piety so as to attain some type of
worldly benefit (*Rambam* ibid.).

[Other versions of this Baraisa, with some
significant differences, appear in *Avos De-
Rabbi Nassan, Nusach* 2, Ch. 45; in *Bavli Sotah* 22b and *Yerushalmi Berachos* 9:5. The
commentators here emend the language
of our Baraisa in some places to conform
with one of the other versions. Our elucidation will follow that of the Gemara in *Sotah.
Yerushalmi's* reading and understanding
(which is very close to that of *Avos DeRabbi
Nassan, Nusach* 2) will be presented at the
end of note 23 below.]

17. He acts in the manner of Shechem
(*Sotah* loc. cit.), who circumcised himself
for ulterior motives (see *Bereishis* Ch. 34).
So too, the "Shechemite *Parush*" adopts pious practices for selfish reasons — so that
people will accord him honor — rather than
for the sake of Heaven (*Rashi* ad loc.).

18. He knocks his feet (*Sotah* loc. cit.). That
is, he displays false humility by shuffling
along humbly. Because he never lifts his
feet from the ground, he knocks his toes
against the stones strewn along the path
(*Rashi* ad loc.). [The standard reading נִכְפַּאי
can also mean the same, as the letters כ and
ק are sometimes interchangeable (*Binyan
Yehoshua*).]

°מַקְצוֹאִי¹⁹. פָּרוּשׁ °מְכוֹבַאִי²⁰. פָּרוּשׁ מְלָאכָה הָיְתָה לוֹ²¹. פָּרוּשׁ °מֶחוּפָּתוֹ
עֲשָׂאֲנִי²². וּפָרוּשׁ מִן °הָיִצְרָא. וּפָרוּשׁ מִן הַיִּרְאָה²³:

קִיזָאִי — (iii) a bloodletting *Parush*;[19]   פָּרוּשׁ מְדוֹכְיָא — (iv) a pestle *Pa-rush*;[20]   פָּרוּשׁ מְלָאכָה הָיְתָה לוֹ (21) — a *Parush* who had work;)[21]   פָּרוּשׁ מַה חוֹבָתִי וְאֶעֱשֶׂנָה — (v) a "What is my obligation and I will do it" *Parush*;[22]   וּפָרוּשׁ מִן הָאַהֲבָה וּפָרוּשׁ מִן הַיִּרְאָה — (vi) a *Parush* out of love; (vii) and a *Parush* out of fear.[23]

19. He lets blood against the walls (*Sotah* loc. cit.). That is, he pretends to close his eyes as he walks, so as to appear to be someone who avoids looking at women. As part of his pretense, he bangs into walls, causing his head to bleed (*Rashi* ad loc.) and the blood to spatter onto the walls (*Meiri* ad loc.). [The standard reading מַקְצוֹאִי can also mean the same, as the letters צ and ז are sometimes interchangeable (*Binyan Yehoshua*).]

20. He is bent like a pestle (*Sotah* loc. cit.). That is, he feigns modesty by walking bent over like a pestle, which has a bent head (*Rashi* ad loc.). [Perhaps the standard reading מְכוֹבַאִי can also be rendered in this way: "hammerlike."]

Actually, a person is *supposed* to walk with his head bent and not arrogantly with his head held high. Perhaps, then, the reference here is to one who walks with his head bent excessively (*Maharsha* ad loc.). [*Maharsha* there also suggests that the references in this Baraisa are to those who *adopt* these behaviors insincerely. But those who behave in these manners out of true piety are indeed praiseworthy. However, *Chida* (*Kisei Rachamim* here) argues at length that a truly pious person is obligated to hide his pious deeds.]

21. He quits his job, claiming that he wishes to focus instead on mitzvos (*Ahavas Chesed*) or that he cannot tolerate the crookedness of the business world (*Avos HaRosh*).

[This kind of *Parush* does not appear in the parallel Baraisa texts (and we have placed it in parentheses and have not numbered it in the text). Consistent with its inclusion of this kind of *Parush* here, the Vilna version

of *Avos DeRabbi Nassan* states above that there are *eight* types of *Perushim*.]

22. This is the reading in *Sotah* loc. cit. He says, "What *further* obligation is there that I have not done and I will do it?" implying that he is perfect in his observance (Gemara there with *Rashi*). [The standard reading מֶחוּפָּתוֹ can also mean something similar, as the letters פ and ב are sometimes interchangeable (*Binyan Yehoshua*).]

23. The Gemara (*Sotah* ibid.) indicates that these refer to one who perfroms mitzvos out of "love for the Divine reward" or who refrains from sin for "fear of Divine punishment." Even these are deemed to be impure motivations for serving God. [Regarding the standard reading מִן הַיִּצְרָא, see end of this note.]

The Gemara there, however, relates further that Abaye and Rava said to the teacher of Baraisos to remove "the *Parush* out of love and ... fear" from the Baraisa, since such behavior is *not* to be criticized. For Rav taught that a person should serve God even out of ulterior motives, so that he will eventually come to serve Him out of pure motives. See note 11 in the Schottenstein ed. there at length.

As related in *Sotah* (loc. cit.), even the wicked King Yannai, who had murdered so many of the Sages, recognized the difference between the true *Parush* and his insincere imitator. On his deathbed, he reassured his wife that she had no reason to fear retaliation from the true *Perushim*. She would have to be wary only of the pretenders, "who do the [wicked] deeds of Zimri, but seek the reward of Phinehas."

We have explained this Baraisa according

ה. °שְׁמוֹנָה[25] דְּבָרִים רוּבָּן קָשֶׁה וּמִיעוּטָן יָפֶה[26]. יַיִן מְלָאכָה שֵׁינָה[27] וְעוֹשֶׁר[28] וְדֶרֶךְ אֶרֶץ[29] וּמַיִם חַמִּין[30] (וְתַשְׁמִישׁ[31]) וְהַקָּזַת דָּם[32]:

§5 Another list of seven:[24]

שִׁבְעָה דְּבָרִים רוּבָּן קָשֶׁה וּמִיעוּטָן יָפֶה — Seven[25] things are harmful in abundance but beneficial in moderation:[26] יַיִן מְלָאכָה שֵׁינָה — (i) wine, (ii) labor, (iii) sleep,[27] וְעוֹשֶׁר וְדֶרֶךְ אֶרֶץ — (iv) wealth,[28] (v) "the way of the world,"[29] וּמַיִם חַמִּין (וְתַשְׁמִישׁ) וְהַקָּזַת דָּם — (vi) hot water,[30] (conjugal relations),[31] (vii) and bloodletting.[32]

to the Gemara in *Sotah* as explained by *Rashi*. *Yerushalmi's* reading and understanding (see above, note 15) as explained (except as otherwise noted) by *Chareidim* (ad loc.) is: There are seven *Perushim*: פְּרוּשׁ שִׁכְמִי, a *Parush* of "shoulders" [who will expend labor, but not money, for mitzvos]; וּפְרוּשׁ נִקְפִּי, a *Parush* of "credit" [who borrows money to perform mitzvos, but does not repay it in a timely way]; וּפְרוּשׁ קִיזַאי, a *Parush* of "balancing" [who commits a sin and then a mitzvah to balance it out (*Pnei Moshe* there)]; פְּרוּשׁ מָה הַנְּכַיֶּיה, a *Parush* of "what benefit?" [who performs mitzvos only for benefit]; פְּרוּשׁ אֲדַע חוֹבָתִי וְאֶעֱשֶׂנָה, a *Parush* of "shall I know my sin and do [a mitzvah to offset] it?" [who says: What sin have I done that I should have to do a mitzvah to offset it? (see *Pnei Moshe*)]; פְּרוּשׁ יִרְאָה, a *Parush* out of fear [like Job]; פְּרוּשׁ אַהֲבָה, a *Parush* out of love [for God] (like Abraham). *Yerushalmi* there concludes: *Of all these, there is none dearer [to God] than a Parush out of love like Abraham.* [*Ahavas Chesed* explains that the standard reading מִן הַיְצָרָא is the same as *Yerushalmi's* understanding of "*Parush* out of love like Avraham," for the *Yerushalmi* there relates that Avraham made a covenant with his יֵצֶר, *inclination,* that it would not cause him to sin.]

24. [See, however, *Magen Avos* cited in note 31 below.] A parallel passage appears in *Gittin* 70a.

25. Emendation follows *Tummas Yesharim* (see below, note 31).

26. A moderate amount of each of them is better for one's health than none at all, but too much is harmful (*Rashi* to *Gittin* 70a).

27. Through sleeping a bit, a person regains his strength, and subsequently he can arise and toil in Torah study (*Bereishis Rabbah* 9 §6, cited in *Binyan Yehoshua*).

28. A moderate degree of wealth is beneficial. Vast wealth, however, tends to distract a person from Torah study and make him haughty (*Rashi* ibid.). Moreover, it robs one's peace of mind (as the Mishnah [*Avos* 2:7] states: מַרְבֶּה נְכָסִים מַרְבֶּה דְאָגָה, *Increasing possessions, increasing anxiety*), and it invites envy (*Ben Yehoyada* to *Gittin* 70a).

29. I.e., conjugal relations (see note 31). [See *Rambam, Hil. Deios* 4:19; and *Orach Chaim* 240:1,14.]

30. I.e., drinking hot water and bathing in it (*Rashi* ibid.).

31. Emendation follows *Tummas Yesharim*. [The standard reading (which we have enclosed in parentheses without numbering) has here תַּשְׁמִישׁ (which is the common term for conjugal relations) listed distinctly from the earlier mention of דֶרֶךְ אֶרֶץ [see note 29] (and thus lists "eight" things here rather than "seven"). According to that reading, דֶרֶךְ אֶרֶץ would mean "commerce" (*Magen Avos*; cf. *Binyan Yehoshua*). The reason this list of "eight" would be included here is that it follows from the preceding Baraisa, which spoke about *Perushim* (who are removed from immoderate physical pursuits — see above, note 15). Accordingly, the Baraisa lists things that are good in moderation and should not be entirely neglected by *Perushim* (*Magen Avos*).]

32. See *Shabbos* 129b; see also *Rambam* ibid. §18.

ו. בְּשִׁבְעָה דְבָרִים בָּרָא הַקָּדוֹשׁ בָּרוּךְ הוּא אֶת עוֹלָמוֹ, אֵלּוּ הֵן: בְּדֵיעָה בְּבִינָה וּבִגְבוּרָה (בִּגְעָרָה בְּדִין) בְּחֶסֶד וּבְרַחֲמִים:[33]

ז. וּכְעִנְיָן שִׁבְעָה דְבָרִים שֶׁבָּרָא אֶת עוֹלָמוֹ כָּךְ בָּרָא שִׁבְעָה. אָבוֹת שְׁלֹשָׁה וְאִמָּהוֹת אַרְבַּע:[34]

ח. שֶׁבַע מִדּוֹת שֶׁמְשַׁמְּשׁוֹת לִפְנֵי כִּסֵּא הַכָּבוֹד[35], אֵלּוּ הֵן: חָכְמָה צֶדֶק וּמִשְׁפָּט חֶסֶד וְרַחֲמִים אֱמֶת וְשָׁלוֹם, שֶׁנֶּאֱמַר (הושע ב, כא־כב) "וְאֵרַשְׂתִּיךְ לִי לְעוֹלָם וְאֵרַשְׂתִּיךְ לִי בְּצֶדֶק וּבְמִשְׁפָּט וּבְחֶסֶד וּבְרַחֲמִים וְאֵרַשְׂתִּיךְ לִי בֶּאֱמוּנָה וְיָדַעַתְּ אֶת ה' ".[36]

---

§6 Another list of seven:
בְּשִׁבְעָה דְבָרִים בָּרָא הַקָּדוֹשׁ בָּרוּךְ הוּא אֶת עוֹלָמוֹ — The Holy One, Blessed is He, created His world with seven things. אֵלּוּ הֵן — They are: בְּדֵיעָה בְּבִינָה וּבִגְבוּרָה — (i) with understanding, (ii) with insight, (iii) and with might; בִּגְעָרָה בְּדִין — (iv) with rebuke, (v) with justice; בְּחֶסֶד וּבְרַחֲמִים — (vi) with kindness, (vii) and with mercy.[33]

§7 A related list of seven:
וּכְעִנְיָן שִׁבְעָה דְבָרִים שֶׁבָּרָא אֶת עוֹלָמוֹ — And similar to the seven things with which He created His world, כָּךְ בָּרָא שִׁבְעָה — He likewise created seven foundational persons: אָבוֹת שְׁלֹשָׁה וְאִמָּהוֹת אַרְבַּע — the three Patriarchs and the four Matriarchs.[34]

§8 Another list of seven:
שֶׁבַע מִדּוֹת שֶׁמְשַׁמְּשׁוֹת לִפְנֵי כִּסֵּא הַכָּבוֹד, אֵלּוּ הֵן — There are seven attributes that serve before the Throne of Glory,[35] and they are: חָכְמָה — (i) wisdom, צֶדֶק — (ii) righteousness, וּמִשְׁפָּט — (iii) justice, חֶסֶד — (iv) kindness, וְרַחֲמִים — (v) mercy, אֱמֶת — (vi) truth, וְשָׁלוֹם — (vii) and harmony; שֶׁנֶּאֱמַר "וְאֵרַשְׂתִּיךְ לִי לְעוֹלָם וְאֵרַשְׂתִּיךְ לִי בְּצֶדֶק וּבְמִשְׁפָּט וּבְחֶסֶד וּבְרַחֲמִים — as it is stated, *I will betroth you to Me* וְאֵרַשְׂתִּיךְ לִי בֶּאֱמוּנָה וְיָדַעַתְּ אֶת ה' "

---

33. The Gemara in *Chagigah* 12a mentions *ten* things — the seven mentioned here in the Baraisa (some worded differently) and three more. [The Gemara there cites verses that mention all ten things in reference to the creation of the world.] The three that our Baraisa omits are: חָכְמָה, כֹּחַ, צֶדֶק, *Wisdom, strength, righteousness*. *Ahavas Chesed* suggests that the Baraisa considers each one of those three to be included in one of the other seven — "wisdom" in "understanding," "strength" in "might," and "righteousness" in "mercy."

[*Ben Avraham* suggests a different reason for why our Baraisa omits these three.]

34. The three Patriarchs are Abraham, Isaac, and Jacob; the four Matriarchs are Sarah, Rebecca, Rachel, and Leah (see *Berachos* 16b with *Rashi*). These seven correspond to the seven with which God created the world, indicating that it is they who sustained the world by keeping the ways of God (*Magen Avos*).

35. That is, they argue in defense of man [despite his shortcomings] before the Throne of Glory (*Binyan Yehoshua*).

[רַבִּי מֵאִיר אוֹמֵר: מַה תַּלְמוּד לוֹמַר "וְיָדַעַתְּ אֶת ה' " אֶלָּא] מְלַמֵּד שֶׁכָּל
אָדָם שֶׁיֵּשׁ בּוֹ כָּל מִדּוֹת הַלָּלוּ יוֹדֵעַ דַּעְתּוֹ שֶׁל מָקוֹם:[37]

ט. שִׁבְעָה מְדוֹרוֹת הֵן, אֵלּוּ הֵן: מָדוֹר עֶלְיוֹן וּמָדוֹר תַּחְתּוֹן[38] וַאֲוִיר
הָעוֹלָם וְאַרְבָּעָה עֶלְיוֹנִים.[40] רַבִּי מֵאִיר אוֹמֵר:[41] שֶׁבַע רְקִיעִין הֵן,

---

forever; and I will betroth you to Me with righteousness, with justice, with kindness, and with mercy; and I will betroth you to Me with fidelity, and you will know HASHEM (Hosea 2:21-22).[36] רַבִּי מֵאִיר אוֹמֵר — R' Meir says: מַה תַּלְמוּד לוֹמַר "וְיָדַעַתְּ אֶת ה' " — What does Scripture mean by saying at the end, *and you will know HASHEM?* אֶלָּא מְלַמֵּד שֶׁכָּל אָדָם שֶׁיֵּשׁ בּוֹ כָּל מִדּוֹת הַלָּלוּ יוֹדֵעַ דַּעְתּוֹ שֶׁל מָקוֹם — Rather, this teaches us that whoever possesses all these attributes knows the mind of the Omnipresent.[37]

§9 The Baraisa presents three related teachings about groups of seven: שִׁבְעָה מְדוֹרוֹת הֵן, אֵלּוּ הֵן — There are seven realms, and they are: מָדוֹר עֶלְיוֹן — (i) the upper realm, וּמָדוֹר תַּחְתּוֹן — (ii) the lower realm,[38] וַאֲוִיר הָעוֹלָם — (iii) the open space of the world,[39] וְאַרְבָּעָה עֶלְיוֹנִים — (iv-vii) and the four upper regions.[40] רַבִּי מֵאִיר אוֹמֵר — R' Meir says:[41] שֶׁבַע רְקִיעִין הֵן,

---

36. [Since these attributes, which argue in defense of man (see preceding note), are what enable us to live before God, He has, in effect, "betrothed us" to Him through them.]

Numbers 2,3,4, and 5 are mentioned explicitly in the words, *and I will betroth you to Me with* **righteousness,** *with* **justice,** *with* **kindness,** *and with* **mercy.** The next words, *and I will betroth you to Me with* **fidelity** [אֱמוּנָה], indicate number 6: אֱמֶת, *truth.* The next words, *and you will* **know** *HASHEM,* indicate number 1, "wisdom." Number 7 ("harmony") is indicated by the beginning of the verse, *I will betroth you to Me forever,* which continues from the end of the previous verse, *I will banish bow and sword and warfare from the land; and I will lay them down in safety* (Magen Avos).

37. That is, whoever employs these attributes in his interaction with people knows the Will of the Omnipresent, Who also deals with His creatures in this manner (Magen Avos). Alternatively, it means that he merits Divine Inspiration (Mefaresh).

38. This Tanna follows the view (see Chagigah 12b) that there are two heavens, as

it says (Deuteronomy 10:14), *Behold! To Hashem, your God, are the heavens and the heavens of the heavens.* When this verse mentions *"the heavens,"* that is one, and *"the heavens of the heavens"* is two (see Ahavas Chesed). The upper heavens contain the Seraphim and Ophanim, while the lower heavens contain the sun, the moon, the planets and the constellations (see Tosafos, Avodah Zarah 43b, ד"ה לא, cited in Mefaresh; cf. Ahavas Chesed, Ben Avraham). See note 42 below.

39. Alternatively, the [higher part of the] atmosphere (see Pesikta Zutresa to Exodus 2:8; Pisron Torah, Vayelech, p. 297), or the vacuum of space (see Sifrei, Pinchas §134).

40. Magen Avos suggests that these "four upper regions" are references to areas of the World to Come, but he does not know what they are. See a different suggestion in Ben Avraham. Gra emends the Baraisa here to read: וְאַרְבַּע "רוּחוֹת", *and the four "directions"* — north, south, east, and west. This would refer to the habitable regions of the four directions (see Shenei Eliyahu).

41. The following appears in Chagigah 12b as well.

אֵלוּ הֵן: וִילוֹן רָקִיעַ שְׁחָקִים זְבוּל מָעוֹן מָכוֹן עֲרָבוֹת.⁴². כְּנֶגְדָּן קָרָא לָאָרֶץ
שִׁבְעָה שֵׁמוֹת,⁴³ אֵלוּ הֵן: אֶרֶץ⁴⁴ אֲדָמָה⁴⁵ אַרְקָא⁴⁶ חָרָבָה⁴⁷ יַבָּשָׁה⁴⁸ תֵּבֵל⁴⁹
חֶלֶד.⁵⁰ לָמָּה נִקְרָא שְׁמָהּ תֵּבֵל, עַל שֵׁם שֶׁהִיא מְתוּבֶּלֶת בַּכֹּל.⁵¹ דָּבָר אַחֵר:

אֵלוּ הֵן — There are seven heavens, and they are: רָקִיעַ — (i) Curtain, וִילוֹן — (i) Curtain,
— (ii) Sky,   שְׁחָקִים — (iii) Mills,   זְבוּל — (iv) Residence,   מָעוֹן — (v)
Abode,   מָכוֹן — (vi) Arsenal,   עֲרָבוֹת — (vii) and Plains.[42]   כְּנֶגְדָּן קָרָא
לָאָרֶץ שִׁבְעָה שֵׁמוֹת, אֵלוּ הֵן — Corresponding to these seven heavens, He called
the earth by seven names,[43] and they are: אֶרֶץ אֲדָמָה אַרְקָא — (i) Eretz,[44]
(ii) Adamah,[45] (iii) Arka,[46]   חָרָבָה יַבָּשָׁה תֵּבֵל — (iv) Charavah,[47] (v) Yabashah,[48] (vi) Teiveil,[49]   חֶלֶד — (vii) and Cheled.[50]   לָמָּה נִקְרָא שְׁמָהּ
תֵּבֵל — And why is it called Teiveil?   עַל שֵׁם שֶׁהִיא מְתוּבֶּלֶת בַּכֹּל — Because
it is spiced [מְתוּבֶּלֶת] with all manner of good.[51]   דָּבָר אַחֵר — An alternative

42. The Gemara in Chagigah describes each of these seven heavens. The following excerpt from the Gemara omits the supporting verses cited there and follows Rashi (and other commentators) ad loc.: [The first heaven,] Curtain, serves no purpose except that it enters [its enclosure] in the morning and emerges [to cover the sky] in the evening and [thus] renews the work of Creation every day. Sky [is the second heaven], in which the sun, moon, stars, and constellations are fixed. Mills [is the third heaven], in which millstones stand and grind manna for the righteous. Residence [is the fourth heaven], in which are [the Heavenly] Jerusalem, the [Heavenly] Holy Temple and [its] built Altar, and Michael the great prince stands and offers an offering upon it. Abode [is the fifth heaven], in which are bands of ministering angels who utter song at night, but keep silent during the day out of respect for the Jewish people. [The sixth heaven is] Arsenal, in which [are prepared various forms of tribulation:] storehouses of snow, storehouses of hail, an attic full of destructive dews, and an attic full of beads [of water], a chamber of whirlwind and storm, and a cave of vapor. And the doors of [all these rooms] are fire. Plains [is the seventh heaven], in which are righteousness, justice, and charity; treasuries of life, treasuries of peace, and treasuries of blessing; the souls of the righteous; the spirits and souls that are destined to be created; and the dew that the Holy One, Blessed is He, is destined

to use to resurrect the dead. There [also] are Ophanim, Seraphim, Holy Chayos, and ministering angels, and the Throne of Glory. The King, the living God — exalted and uplifted — rests [His Presence] upon them, שֶׁנֶּאֱמַר „סֹלּוּ — as it says, Extol He לָרֹכֵב בָּעֲרָבוֹת בְּיָהּ שְׁמוֹ" Who rides upon Plains, with His Name Yah.

For further discussion of this topic, see sources cited in the Schottenstein ed. of Chagigah 12b.

43. Whereas there are seven distinct heavens, there is only one earth, but that earth has seven names (Avos HaRosh, first explanation). Alternatively, they refer to distinct regions of the earth (ibid. from the Zohar and other sources; see also Ben Avraham here).

44. Numerous verses refer to it by this name, including the first verse: בְּרֵאשִׁית בָּרָא אֱלֹהִים אֵת הַשָּׁמַיִם וְאֵת הָאָרֶץ, In the beginning of God's creating the heavens and the earth (Binyan Yehoshua).

45. See, e.g., Genesis 1:25 and 2:5.

46. See Jeremiah 10:11.

47. See Genesis 7:22.

48. See ibid. 1:9.

49. See, e.g., I Samuel 2:8.

50. See Psalms 49:2.

51. [According to Ben Avraham (who explains that each of the seven names refers to a different region — see above, note 43), Teiveil refers to Eretz Yisrael, which contains every manner of bounty and lacks nothing (see Deuteronomy 8:9).]

שֶׁדַּרְכָּהּ לְהַכְנִיס וְאֵינָהּ דַּרְכָּהּ לְהוֹצִיא52. (שֶׁבַע מַעֲלוֹת בֵּין צַדִּיק לְצַדִּיק:
אִשְׁתּוֹ נָאָה מִשֶּׁל חֲבֵירוֹ בָּנָיו נָאִים מִשֶּׁל חֲבֵירוֹ שְׁנַיִם אוֹכְלִין בִּקְעָרָה
אַחַת זֶה טוֹעֵם לְפִי מַעֲשָׂיו וְזֶה טוֹעֵם לְפִי מַעֲשָׂיו שְׁנַיִם צוֹבְעִים בְּיוֹרָה
אַחַת לָזֶה עוֹלָה נָאָה וְלָזֶה עוֹלָה כִּיעוּר. בְּחָכְמָתוֹ וּבִתְבוּנָתוֹ וּבְדַעְתּוֹ53

---

explanation: שֶׁדַּרְכָּהּ לְהַכְנִיס וְאֵינָהּ דַּרְכָּהּ לְהוֹצִיא — Because its way is to take in and not to send out.[52]

Another set of seven:

שֶׁבַע מַעֲלוֹת בֵּין צַדִּיק לְצַדִּיק — There are seven advantages enjoyed by one righteous man over the other: אִשְׁתּוֹ נָאָה מִשֶּׁל חֲבֵירוֹ — (i) One's wife is nicer than the other's; בָּנָיו נָאִים מִשֶּׁל חֲבֵירוֹ — (ii) one's children are nicer than the other's; שְׁנַיִם אוֹכְלִין בִּקְעָרָה אַחַת — (iii) both righteous men may eat out of the same bowl, זֶה טוֹעֵם לְפִי מַעֲשָׂיו וְזֶה טוֹעֵם לְפִי מַעֲשָׂיו — but this one tastes the food according to his deeds and the other one tastes it according to his deeds; שְׁנַיִם צוֹבְעִים בְּיוֹרָה אַחַת — (iv) both of them may dye wool in the same pot, לָזֶה עוֹלָה נָאָה וְלָזֶה עוֹלָה כִּיעוּר — but for this one, [the wool] comes out beautiful and for this one it comes out ugly; בְּחָכְמָתוֹ וּבִתְבוּנָתוֹ וּבְדַעְתּוֹ — (v) one righteous man can also differ from another in his wisdom, (vi) in his understanding (vii) and in his intellect;[53]

---

52. According to this interpretation, the word תֵּבֵל is from the root יבל, meaning "to bring" (Ben Avraham).

[According to the explanation that these names refer to the earth as a whole (see above, note 43),] the meaning is that the earth receives the bodies that are buried in it; it does not (without the miracle of revivification of the dead) send them out [see Job 21:32] (Magen Avos). In keeping with his explanation that Teiveil refers specifically to Eretz Yisrael, Ben Avraham explains this line in accordance with the Mishnah in Kesubos (110b) that teaches: One can force all [members of his household] to move to Eretz Yisrael, but he can force none of them to leave.]

Gra emends the text, removing the words שֶׁדַּרְכָּהּ לְהַכְנִיס וְאֵין דַּרְכָּהּ לְהוֹצִיא and replacing them with שֶׁמְּבַלָּה אֶת הַכֹּל, because it withers [i.e., outlasts] everything.

While our Baraisa explains only one of earth's seven names, the Midrash (Midrash Mishlei §8) offers explanations for all of them:

□ אֶרֶץ, Eretz, because people "run" (רצין) within it;

□ אֲדָמָה, Adamah, because Adam (אדם) the first man was created from it;

□ אַרְקָא, Arka, because the earth "fled" (ערק) from before the Holy One, Blessed is He, when He came to give the Torah on Mt. Sinai;

□ חָרָבָה, Charavah, because the water "lays waste" (חרב) to it;

□ יַבָּשָׁה, Yabashah, because the earth "swallowed up" (יבש, dried) Abel's blood after Cain murdered him (see Genesis 4:1-11 with Rashi);

□ תֵּבֵל, Teiveil, because it is "spiced" (מתובלת) with its fruits;

□ חֶלֶד, Cheled, because people "decay" (חלד, rust) in it [i.e., after burial (Mahari Kohen ad loc.)].

[Some different explanations for these names are offered in Avos DeRabbi Nassan, Nusach 2, Ch. 43.]

53. According to Binyan Yehoshua, בְּדַעְתּוֹ here refers to Divine Inspiration.

Some texts have here as well: וּבְקוֹמָתוֹ, and

‏(ובקומתו) שֶׁנֶּאֱמַר (משלי יב, כו) "יָתֵר מֵרֵעֵהוּ צַדִּיק וְגוֹ' "‎54:

‏י. שֶׁבַע מִדּוֹת דָּרַשׁ הִלֵּל הַזָּקֵן לִפְנֵי בְּנֵי בְּתֵירָה, אֵלּוּ הֵן56: קַל וָחֹמֶר, וּגְזֵרָה שָׁוָה57, בִּנְיַן אָב (מִכָּתוּב אֶחָד וּבִנְיַן אָב מִשְּׁנֵי כְּתוּבִים58),

‏שֶׁנֶּאֱמַר "יָתֵר מֵרֵעֵהוּ צַדִּיק וְגוֹ' " — as it is stated, *A righteous one has an advantage over his fellow, etc.* (*Proverbs* 12:26).[54]

§10 Another set of seven:

‏שֶׁבַע מִדּוֹת דָּרַשׁ הִלֵּל הַזָּקֵן לִפְנֵי בְּנֵי בְּתֵירָה, אֵלּוּ הֵן — Hillel the Elder expounded seven rules of hermeneutic interpretation of Scripture in the presence of the sons of Beseirah,[55] and they are: ‏קַל וָחֹמֶר — (i) *kal va'chomer*;[56] ‏וּגְזֵרָה שָׁוָה — (ii) *gezeirah shavah*;[57] ‏בִּנְיַן אָב מִכָּתוּב אֶחָד וּבִנְיַן אָב מִשְּׁנֵי כְּתוּבִים — (iii) *binyan av* from one verse, and *binyan av* from two verses;[58]

in his [physical] stature, but then there would be *eight* advantages enumerated rather than seven. Possibly, however, "both eat out of the same bowl" and "both dye in the same pot" are to be counted as one, so that "in his stature" would be the seventh advantage (*Ben Avraham*).

54. The simple meaning of this Baraisa is that some *tzaddikim* are granted more comfortable lives than others. Thus has God decreed their lots in life. The tribulations of the one and the triumphs of the other are not indications of who is the more righteous man (*Velo Od Ella*).

Avos HaRosh (based on *Menachos* 29b), however, explains the Baraisa to mean that these differences between *tzaddikim* stem from the differences between their deeds. [This approach would seem to be supported by the words "this one tastes according to his deeds and the other one tastes according to his deeds."]

55. [This Baraisa also appears in *Tosefta, Sanhedrin*, end of Ch. 7, and in *Sifra, Baraisa of R' Yishmael* §7. The commentary below will draw on some of the commentators to *Sifra* there.]

The sons of Beseirah were the heads of the Sanhedrin. One year, they encountered a dilemma. Erev Pesach, the day on which the *pesach* offering is to be slaughtered, fell on the Sabbath, and they were unable to decide whether the requirement to slaughter the *pesach* offering supersedes the laws of

the Sabbath. Hillel the Elder (founder of the School of Hillel) had recently arrived from Babylonia and he proceeded to demonstrate to them at length that the *pesach* offering is indeed to be slaughtered even on the Sabbath. Recognizing the superior scholarship of Hillel, the sons of Beseirah immediately resigned their positions and appointed Hillel to be the head of the Sanhedrin in their stead (*Pesachim* 66a). Our Baraisa lists the seven rules of interpretation that Hillel expounded before the sons of Beseirah on that occasion.

Actually, there are *thirteen* rules of Scriptural interpretation, as detailed in the famous Baraisa of R' Yishmael, found at the beginning of *Sifra*, and recited daily by many at the beginning of the morning prayers. It might be that our Baraisa is listing only those seven rules *employed by Hillel to support his ruling* in his arguments before the sons of Beseirah. Alternatively, Hillel's seven encapsulates all thirteen of R' Yishmael (*Middos Aharon* [at beginning of *Korban Aharon*] on *Sifra* loc. cit.; see also *Raavad* ad loc.; see also *Collected Writings of R' Samson Raphael Hirsch*, Vol. 5, Ch. 4).

56. Literally, *lenient and strict.* This is the logical argument that if a lenient case has a stringency, the same stringency must also apply to a stricter case.

57. Literally, *a common expression.* The Torah often uses the same expression in two different contexts to indicate that laws regarding them are to be derived from one another.

58. *Binyan Av* — literally, *building on a*

מִכְּלָל וּפְרָט‎⁵⁹, וּמִפְּרָט וּכְלָל‎⁶⁰, כַּיּוֹצֵא בּוֹ בְּמָקוֹם אַחֵר‎⁶¹, דָּבָר הַלָּמֵד מֵעִנְיָנוֹ‎⁶², אֵלּוּ שֶׁבַע מִדּוֹת שֶׁדָּרַשׁ הִלֵּל הַזָּקֵן לִפְנֵי בְּנֵי בְּתֵירָה‎⁶³:

יא. שִׁבְעָה דְבָרִים בַּגּוֹלֶם וְשִׁבְעָה בֶחָכָם וְכוּ'‎⁶⁴ עַל מַה שֶׁלֹּא שָׁמַע

מִכְּלָל וּפְרָט — (iv) **through a general statement followed by a specification;**[59] וּמִפְּרָט וּכְלָל — (v) **through a specification followed by a general statement;**[60] כַּיּוֹצֵא בּוֹ בְּמָקוֹם אַחֵר — (vi) **something similar in another place;**[61] דָּבָר הַלָּמֵד מֵעִנְיָנוֹ — (vii) **a matter elucidated from its context.**[62] אֵלּוּ שֶׁבַע מִדּוֹת שֶׁדָּרַשׁ הִלֵּל הַזָּקֵן לִפְנֵי בְּנֵי בְּתֵירָה — **These are the seven rules that Hillel the Elder expounded in the presence of the sons of Beseirah.**[63]

§11 The Baraisa cites *Avos 5:7*, which contains another set of seven: שִׁבְעָה דְבָרִים בַּגּוֹלֶם וְשִׁבְעָה בֶחָכָם וְכוּ' — **Seven things are found in a crude person and seven in a wise person, etc.**[64] [חָכָם אֵינוֹ מְדַבֵּר בִּפְנֵי מִי שֶׁהוּא

---

model. According to this rule, a general principle derived from one context ("one verse") is applied to similar contexts. Sometimes, however, the principles must be drawn from *two* contexts ("two verses"). [The specifics of these two rules and whether or not they are identical to the rule known as מַה מָּצִינוּ, *what do we find,* are discussed by the commentators to the *Baraisa of R' Yishmael* §5-6; see *Raavad, Sefer HaKerisus* and *Middos Aharon* there.]

The reading here of the *Baraisa of R' Yishmael* §7, as found in the commentaries of *Raavad* and *Rabbeinu Hillel* there, is: בְּנְיַן אָב וּשְׁנֵי כְתוּבִים, *binyan av and two verses,* which they explain to be two distinct rules — a *binyan av* [whether from one verse or from two], and the rule that *two verses* that are in apparent conflict can be resolved by a third verse (which is the same as the thirteenth rule of R' Yishmael). [That does not add to the "seven" rules of this Baraisa, since in that reading what appears here as rule 5 (מִפְּרָט וּכְלָל) is omitted.]

59. When a general statement in the verse is followed by a specification, the law applies only to the specific case of the specification.

60. This is the reverse of the above case: where a specification is *followed* by the general statement. The concluding general statement expands the application of the law to *all* cases, not just to the specification.

61. That is, an additional verse cited in support. This is not actually a "rule of interpretation" but was a proof adduced by Hillel in his arguments before the sons of Beseirah. The Baraisa nevertheless includes it under the heading of "seven rules" since the other six are indeed rules of interpretation (*Raavad* loc. cit.). Alternatively, "something similar in another place" refers to all the various *other* forms of "general and specific" [כְּלָל וּפְרָט] enumerated in R' Yishmael's thirteen rules (*Rabbeinu Hillel* loc. cit.).

62. That is, a verse whose intent is clarified by what is stated in a nearby verse.

63. A Baraisa in *Pesachim* 66a recounts some of the arguments offered by Hillel in support of his ruling.

64. [Our versions of *Avos DeRabbi Nassan* have an abbreviated quote from the Mishnah here. We have expanded that (in brackets) to include the full quote of the Mishnah. This expansion is also added by *Gra.*]

The term גּוֹלֶם, *golem,* is a Hebrew word for a crude or unfinished product (as in *Psalms* 139:16; *Keilim* 12:6). In contrast to a בּוּר, *boor* (see *Avos* 2:5), who lacks both wisdom and manners, and an עַם הָאָרֶץ, *am haaretz* (ibid.), who is ignorant of Torah, but well-mannered enough to contribute to society, the *golem* is somewhat learned and semi-developed in character. He is, however, not *fully* developed in either area, leaving him

אוֹמֵר לֹא שָׁמַעְתִּי[66] וְאֵינוֹ מִתְבַּיֵּישׁ[67] וּמוֹדֶה עַל הָאֱמֶת וּכְנֶגְדּוֹ נֶאֶמְרוּ בְּגוֹלֶם (בְּחִילוּפִין):[68]

יב. חָכָם אֵינוֹ מְדַבֵּר לִפְנֵי מִי שֶׁגָּדוֹל מִמֶּנּוּ בְּחָכְמָה וּבְמִנְיָן, זֶה מֹשֶׁה, שֶׁנֶּאֶמַר (שמות ד, ל) "וַיְדַבֵּר אַהֲרֹן אֶת כָּל הַדְּבָרִים אֲשֶׁר דִּבֶּר ה' אֶל מֹשֶׁה וַיַּעַשׂ הָאֹתֹת לְעֵינֵי הָעָם" וְכִי מִי רָאוּי לְדַבֵּר מֹשֶׁה אוֹ אַהֲרֹן,

---

גָּדוֹל מִמֶּנּוּ בְּחָכְמָה וּבְמִנְיָן — (i) A wise person does not speak in the presence of someone greater than he in wisdom or in number;[65] וְאֵינוֹ נִכְנָס לְתוֹךְ דִּבְרֵי חֲבֵרוֹ — (ii) he does not interrupt the words of his friend; וְאֵינוֹ נִבְהָל לְהָשִׁיב — (iii) he does not hasten to answer; שׁוֹאֵל כָּעִנְיָן וּמֵשִׁיב כַּהֲלָכָה — (iv) he asks what is relevant and answers appropriately; וְאוֹמֵר עַל רִאשׁוֹן רִאשׁוֹן עַל מַה וְעַל אַחֲרוֹן אַחֲרוֹן — (v) he says first things first and last things last; שֶׁלֹּא שָׁמַע אוֹמֵר לֹא שָׁמַעְתִּי וְאֵינוֹ מִתְבַּיֵּישׁ — (vi) about that which he has not heard he says, "I have not heard"[66] and he is not embarrassed;[67] וּמוֹדֶה עַל הָאֱמֶת — (vii) and he concedes the truth. וּכְנֶגְדּוֹ נֶאֶמְרוּ בְּגוֹלֶם בְּחִילוּפִין — And the corresponding things are said in reverse about a crude person.[68]

§12 The Baraisa elaborates on this last list of seven attributes. The first attribute:

חָכָם אֵינוֹ מְדַבֵּר לִפְנֵי מִי שֶׁגָּדוֹל מִמֶּנּוּ בְּחָכְמָה וּבְמִנְיָן — A wise person does not speak in the presence of someone greater than he in wisdom or in number: זֶה מֹשֶׁה, שֶׁנֶּאֶמַר "וַיְדַבֵּר אַהֲרֹן אֶת כָּל הַדְּבָרִים אֲשֶׁר דִּבֶּר ה' אֶל מֹשֶׁה וַיַּעַשׂ הָאֹתֹת לְעֵינֵי הָעָם" — This is exemplified by Moses, as it is stated, *Aaron spoke all the words that HASHEM had spoken to Moses; and he performed the signs in the sight of the people* (Exodus 4:30). וְכִי מִי רָאוּי לְדַבֵּר מֹשֶׁה אוֹ אַהֲרֹן — Now, let us examine this: Who would have been more fit to speak those words

---

noticeably lacking in wisdom and proper etiquette (*Rambam Commentary* and *R' Yonah* to the Mishnah).

65. "Greater in number" can mean that he is older [number of years] or that he has a greater number of disciples (*Rashi* on the Mishnah). [Our Baraisa takes it in the sense of "years," as seen below.]

One should remain silent in the presence of those greater than he only when it comes to offering an answer or taking some initiative. But when it comes to asking questions, on the contrary, we say, "The shy one does not learn" (*Binyan Yehoshua* on §12, from *Tos. Yom Tov*).

66. He does not say what he has not heard

from his teachers in a way that would suggest that he says it on their authority (*R' Yonah; Meiri; Rav*). Alternatively, he does not pretend to be knowledgeable about matters that he does not know (*Rambam* to the Mishnah; *Ahavas Chesed* here). See note 97 below.

67. He is not embarrassed to admit his lack of learning (*Ahavas Chesed,* and *Avos Ha-Rosh,* who demonstrates that these words are part of the preceding attribute and not the beginning of the one that follows; see, however, *Magen Avos*).

68. He blurts out his opinion in the presence of greater people, he interrupts when other people are speaking, he hastens to reply without careful consideration, he asks

הֱוֵי אוֹמֵר מֹשֶׁה, שֶׁמֹּשֶׁה שָׁמַע מִפִּי הַגְּבוּרָה וְאַהֲרֹן שָׁמַע מִפִּי מֹשֶׁה,
אֶלָּא כָּךְ אָמַר מֹשֶׁה: אֶפְשָׁר שֶׁאֲדַבֵּר בְּמָקוֹם שֶׁאָחִי גָדוֹל מִמֶּנִּי עוֹמֵד
שָׁם[69], לְפִיכָךְ אָמַר לוֹ לְאַהֲרֹן: דַּבֵּר, שֶׁנֶּאֱמַר (שם) "וַיְדַבֵּר אַהֲרֹן אֶת
כָּל הַדְּבָרִים אֲשֶׁר דִּבֶּר ה' אֶל מֹשֶׁה"[70]. וְאֵינוּ נִכְנָס לְתוֹךְ דִּבְרֵי חֲבֵירוֹ,
זֶה אַהֲרֹן, [שֶׁנֶּאֱמַר (ויקרא י, יט) "וַיְדַבֵּר אַהֲרֹן וְגוֹ' הֵן הַיּוֹם הִקְרִיבוּ
אֶת חַטָּאתָם וְאֶת עֹלָתָם וְגוֹ' " אֶלָּא] שֶׁשָּׁתַק עַד שֶׁסִּיֵּם מֹשֶׁה אֶת

---

to the people at that time, **Moses or Aaron?** הֱוֵי אוֹמֵר מֹשֶׁה, שֶׁמֹּשֶׁה שָׁמַע מִפִּי
הַגְּבוּרָה וְאַהֲרֹן שָׁמַע מִפִּי מֹשֶׁה — One must say it would have been Moses, for
Moses heard that message directly from the mouth of the Almighty, whereas
Aaron heard it from the mouth of Moses. אֶלָּא כָּךְ אָמַר מֹשֶׁה — **But this
is what Moses,** who was a wise man, **said** to himself: אֶפְשָׁר שֶׁאֲדַבֵּר בְּמָקוֹם
שֶׁאָחִי גָדוֹל מִמֶּנִּי עוֹמֵד שָׁם — "**Is it possible that I should speak where my older
brother is standing?!"**[69] לְפִיכָךְ אָמַר לוֹ לְאַהֲרֹן: דַּבֵּר — **Therefore, he said to
Aaron, "You speak** to the people," שֶׁנֶּאֱמַר "וַיְדַבֵּר אַהֲרֹן אֶת כָּל הַדְּבָרִים אֲשֶׁר
דִּבֶּר ה' אֶל מֹשֶׁה" — **as it is stated,** *Aaron spoke all the words that* HASHEM
had spoken to Moses (ibid.).[70]

The second attribute of a wise person :

וְאֵינוּ נִכְנָס לְתוֹךְ דִּבְרֵי חֲבֵירוֹ — **He does not interrupt the words of his friend:**
זֶה אַהֲרֹן, שֶׁנֶּאֱמַר "וַיְדַבֵּר אַהֲרֹן וְגוֹ' הֵן הַיּוֹם הִקְרִיבוּ אֶת חַטָּאתָם וְאֶת עֹלָתָם וְגוֹ' " —
This is exemplified by **Aaron, as it is stated,** *Aaron spoke* to Moses: *"Was it
they who this day offered their sin offering and their burnt offering* before
HASHEM? (Leviticus 10:19). Aaron said this in response to Moses, who had accused Aaron's sons at some length of violating the sacrificial procedures. Now,
Aaron knew all along that Moses was mistaken, אֶלָּא שֶׁשָּׁתַק עַד שֶׁסִּיֵּם מֹשֶׁה אֶת

---

irrelevant questions and gives answers that
are inappropriate and out of sequence, he
says what he has not heard as if he has, and
does not admit when he is wrong.

69. Though Moses was greater than Aaron in
wisdom, as evidenced by the fact that God
had spoken to him and not to Aaron, Moses
did not think it appropriate to speak in his
older brother's presence (*Ahavas Chesed*).
Certainly, then, we can learn from this that
it is inappropriate to speak in the presence
of one who is greater both in wisdom *and*
in age, even if we say that Moses deferred
to Aaron's age because of Moses' exceeding
humility (*Kisei Rachamim*). Others explain
that the Baraisa means that it is inappropriate to speak in the presence of someone

who is greater in wisdom *or in years* (*Midrash Shmuel* on the Mishnah, cited by *Tos.
Yom Tov* there), and where there is a conflict
between the two (as in the case of Moses
and Aaron) age takes precedence over wisdom (see *Tosefes Ohr*).

70. *Magen Avos* raises an obvious question: How can the Baraisa prove that Moses
deferred to Aaron's age from the fact that
Aaron spoke to the people? Why, God had
explicitly *commanded* (in v. 16 there) that
Aaron should be the one to speak to the
people! *Magen Avos* (in one answer) suggests that Moses could have construed that
command as a censure for his unwillingness to accept the mission, but that God
really wanted *him* to speak to Pharaoh.

דְּבָרוֹ וְלֹא אָמַר לוֹ: קַצֵּר דְּבָרֶיךָ, וְאַחַר כָּךְ אָמַר אֶל מֹשֶׁה: "הֵן הַיּוֹם
הִקְרִיבוּ [וְגוֹ']"‎[71] וְאוֹנְנִים אֲנַחְנוּ‎, וְיֵשׁ אוֹמְרִים: מְשָׁכוֹ אַהֲרֹן מִתּוֹךְ הַצִּבּוּר
לַחוּץ וְאָמַר לוֹ‎[72]: מֹשֶׁה אָחִי, וּמָה מַעֲשֵׂר הַקַּל אָסוּר לְאוֹנֵן לֶאֱכוֹל מִמֶּנּוּ,

קַצֵּר דְּבָרֶיךָ דְּבָרוֹ וְלֹא אָמַר לוֹ: — but, nevertheless, [Aaron] remained silent
until Moses finished speaking and did not say to him right away, "Cut short
your words." ‏וְאַחַר כָּךְ אָמַר אֶל מֹשֶׁה: "הֵן הַיּוֹם הִקְרִיבוּ וְגוֹ'" וְאוֹנְנִים אֲנַחְנוּ
— Only afterward did he say to Moses, "Was it they who this day offered,
etc., and we are thus onenim and therefore forbidden to have done what you
are suggesting."[71]   ‏וְיֵשׁ אוֹמְרִים — And some say: Not only did Aaron wait
until Moses finished speaking, but to avoid embarrassing him,   ‏מְשָׁכוֹ אַהֲרֹן
he also drew him away from the public to the   ‏מִתּוֹךְ הַצִּבּוּר לַחוּץ וְאָמַר לוֹ
outside and said to him,[72]   ‏מֹשֶׁה אָחִי, וּמָה מַעֲשֵׂר הַקַּל אָסוּר לְאוֹנֵן לֶאֱכוֹל מִמֶּנּוּ.

That Moses allowed Aaron to speak instead
was because he did not wish to speak in
the presence of his older brother. *Magen
Avos* also notes that *Avos DeRabbi Nassan,
Nusach* 2, Ch. 40, presents Moses' reasoning ("Is it possible that I should speak where
my older brother is standing?!") as being
said to God immediately when He initially
told him (*Exodus* 3:10) to go to Pharaoh and
demand that the Children of Israel be sent
out of Egypt. Accordingly, God's command
that Aaron should speak instead was a *result*
of Moses' unwillingness to speak in the presence of his older brother, and the question
raised above is avoided entirely. (See also
Ben Avraham, who offers a different resolution of this difficulty.)

71. On the eighth day of the Inauguration of
the Tabernacle in the Wilderness, Aaron's two
sons, Nadab and Abihu, died, placing Aaron
and his remaining sons into a state of *aninus*
(the state of mourning that begins immediately upon the death of one's seven closest
relatives). Normally, an *onein* is prohibited
to partake of sacrificial foods. However, on
that day there were exceptions. The verses in
Leviticus 10:12-18 speak of three offerings:
a *minchah*, a *shelamim*, and a *chatas*. The
minchah and the *shelamim* were one-time
offerings brought specifically for the Inauguration service (as commanded, ibid. 9:4).
The *chatas* was the regular *chatas* of Rosh
Chodesh, which was brought because that

day was Rosh Chodesh Nissan. The Torah
relates that Moses commanded Aaron and
his sons to eat the *minchah* (although they
were in a state of *aninus*). Subsequently,
Moses discovered that the *chatas* had been
burned, and he became angry at his brother
and nephews, but directed his rebuke to his
nephews alone. He asked them, *"Why did
you not eat the chatas?"* He reprimanded
them: You should have assumed that the
same instruction I gave you for the *minchah*
applied to the *chatas* as well.

In fact, Moses was mistaken in his analogy. While God had instructed that the *aninus*
prohibition be overridden for the sake of the
Inauguration *minchah*, that was an offering
unique to one occasion [‏קָדְשֵׁי שָׁעָה]. It could
not be assumed that the same law held true
for the regular Rosh Chodesh *chatas*, which
was an offering common to all generations
[‏קָדְשֵׁי דּוֹרוֹת]. This was Aaron's response to
Moses cited in our Baraisa, and Moses (in
v. 20) conceded his error (see *Yoma* 5b with
Rashi).

72. Perhaps this is indicated by the verse,
which begins: *Aaron spoke "to Moses"* (instead of simply "Aaron spoke"), implying
that what he said was heard *only* by Moses.
Moreover, this may be indicated by the
next verse, which says, *Moses "heard" and
he approved* (instead of simply "Moses approved"), implying that *only* Moses heard
(*Ben Avraham*).

חַטָּאת חָמוּר לֹא כָּל שֶׁכֵּן שֶׁתְּהֵא אֲסוּרָה לְאוֹנֵן[73]. מִיָּד הוֹדָה לוֹ,
שֶׁנֶּאֱמַר (שם פסוק כ) ״וַיִּשְׁמַע מֹשֶׁה וַיִּיטַב בְּעֵינָיו״[74] (וּבְעֵינֵי הַגְּבוּרָה)[75].
כַּיּוֹצֵא בּוֹ (שם פסוק טז) ״וַיִּקְצֹף עַל אֶלְעָזָר וְעַל אִיתָמָר בְּנֵי אַהֲרֹן״.
מִכַּאן אָמְרוּ: כְּשֶׁאָדָם [עוֹשֶׂה מִשְׁתֶּה] לְתַלְמִידָיו אֵינוֹ נוֹתֵן פָּנָיו אֶלָּא
בַּגָּדוֹל. וּכְשֶׁהוּא קוֹצֵף אֵינוֹ קוֹצֵף אֶלָּא עַל הַקָּטָן, שֶׁנֶּאֱמַר ״וַיִּקְצֹף
עַל אֶלְעָזָר וְעַל אִיתָמָר״ מְלַמֵּד שֶׁאַף אַהֲרֹן הָיָה בַּקְּצָפוֹן[78]. אַהֲרֹן

חַטָּאת חָמוּר לֹא כָּל שֶׁכֵּן שֶׁתְּהֵא אֲסוּרָה לְאוֹנֵן — "Moses, my brother: If *maaser sheni*, which is a more lenient matter than *chatas*, is forbidden for an *onein* to eat, then is it not surely so that a *chatas*, which is a more stringent matter, is forbidden for an *onein* to eat?"[73] מִיָּד הוֹדָה לוֹ, שֶׁנֶּאֱמַר ״וַיִּשְׁמַע מֹשֶׁה וַיִּיטַב בְּעֵינָיו״ — Immediately, [Moses] conceded the point to him, as it is stated, *Moses heard and he approved* (ibid. v. 20).[74] This can also be read: *and He approved,* meaning that וּבְעֵינֵי הַגְּבוּרָה — indeed, the Almighty approved.[75]

The Baraisa notes parenthetically:

כַּיּוֹצֵא בּוֹ — Similarly, we may glean another lesson in proper etiquette from this same episode.[76] ״וַיִּקְצֹף עַל אֶלְעָזָר וְעַל אִיתָמָר בְּנֵי אַהֲרֹן״ — It says, *And [Moses] was wrathful with Elazar and Ithamar, the sons of Aaron* (ibid. v. 16). Wasn't Aaron equally to blame? מִכַּאן אָמְרוּ: כְּשֶׁאָדָם עוֹשֶׂה מִשְׁתֶּה לְתַלְמִידָיו אֵינוֹ נוֹתֵן פָּנָיו אֶלָּא בַּגָּדוֹל — Based on this they said: When a person makes a banquet for his students, he directs his attention primarily to the greatest of the students; וּכְשֶׁהוּא קוֹצֵף אֵינוֹ קוֹצֵף אֶלָּא עַל הַקָּטָן — but when he is angry with them, he directs his anger primarily to the least of his students, שֶׁנֶּאֱמַר ״וַיִּקְצֹף עַל אֶלְעָזָר וְעַל אִיתָמָר״ — as it is stated, *and he was wrathful with Elazar and Ithamar, the sons of Aaron.* What does the Torah teach by adding: *the sons of Aaron*?[77] Do we not already know that they were the sons of Aaron? מְלַמֵּד שֶׁאַף אַהֲרֹן הָיָה בַּקְּצָפוֹן — This teaches that Aaron too was included in the wrath of Moses. And still, Moses directed his anger primarily to the lesser ones — Elazar and Ithamar — rather than to Aaron.[78] אַהֲרֹן

---

73. See *Zevachim* 101a.

74. Which demonstrates the seventh attribute of a wise man — that he admits his mistakes; see Baraisa at the end of this chapter (and note 95 there).

75. In the the previous verse, Aaron had said to Moses, *Were I to eat a sin offering this day, would Hashem approve?* implying that Hashem approved (Aaron maintained) of his *not* eating the *chatas.* The next verse thus concludes that Hashem had indeed approved (see *Ahavas Chesed*).

76. *Binyan Yehoshua.* See below, note 78.

77. *Korban Aharon* on *Sifra* there. [*Gra* and *Avos HaRosh* emend the text of our Baraisa to contain these words.]

78. *Magen Avos* adds that the Baraisa *had* to include this additional teaching to anticipate an objection to its earlier teaching: How can the Baraisa prove from that which Aaron did not interrupt Moses that "a wise man does not interrupt the words of his friend"? Perhaps the reason Aaron did not interrupt is that Moses was not addressing him but

הָיָה גָדוֹל מִמֹּשֶׁה, וְגָדוֹל מֵאַהֲרֹן הַקָּדוֹשׁ בָּרוּךְ הוּא[79], וְלָמָּה לֹא דִבֵּר עִם אַהֲרֹן[80], עַל שֶׁלֹּא הָיוּ לוֹ בָנִים עוֹמְדִים בַּפֶּרֶץ, שֶׁאִילוּ הָיָה לוֹ בָּנִים עוֹמְדִים בַּפֶּרֶץ אֶלְעָזָר וְאִיתָמָר לֹא גָרַם חֵטְא לְנָדָב וַאֲבִיהוּא[81]).

הָיָה גָדוֹל מִמֹּשֶׁה וְגָדוֹל מֵאַהֲרֹן הַקָּדוֹשׁ בָּרוּךְ הוּא — Aaron was greater (i.e., older) than Moses, but the Holy One, Blessed is He, is greater than Aaron.[79]

The Baraisa asks:

וְלָמָּה לֹא דִבֵּר עִם אַהֲרֹן — And why did he not simply speak to Aaron?[80] עַל שֶׁלֹּא הָיוּ לוֹ בָנִים עוֹמְדִים בַּפֶּרֶץ — Because [Aaron] did not have sons who would stand in the breach. שֶׁאִילוּ הָיָה לוֹ בָּנִים עוֹמְדִים בַּפֶּרֶץ אֶלְעָזָר וְאִיתָמָר לֹא גָרַם — For if he did have sons who would stand in the breach חֵטְא לְנָדָב וַאֲבִיהוּא — namely, Elazar and Ithamar — the sin would not have caused Nadab and Abihu to die.[81]

only his sons! The Baraisa therefore cites a teaching from which it emerges that Moses was indeed speaking to Aaron as well, albeit indirectly.

79. The Baraisa is explaining how Moses could have been angry [albeit indirectly] with his older brother. It explains that although Aaron was greater (i.e., older) than he, God is even greater, and Moses was standing up for the honor of God, Who (in Moses' opinion) had commanded that the *chatas* should be eaten (*Magen Avos*, second explanation).

Other commentators explain this line as belonging to the next part of the Baraisa; see below, end of note 81.

80. Why did Moses speak angrily to Elazar and Ithamar? Why did he not simply speak *without* anger directly to Aaron to ask him why the *chatas* was not eaten? (*Magen Avos*, second explanation). [Others explain this line altogether differently; see below, end of note 81.]

81. [In the aftermath of the sin of the Golden Calf, when God wished to wipe out the Jewish people, Moses "stood in the breach" to forestall that calamity through his earnest prayers on their behalf, as it says (*Psalms* 106:23), *He said He would destroy them — had not Moses, His chosen one, stood in the breach before Him to turn away His wrath from destroying* (see *Ben Avraham*).] Had Elazar and Ithamar similarly "stood in the breach" to protest against Nadab and Abihu when they were about to

sin, they might have saved their two brothers from dying. Therefore, Moses reacted angrily to them, rather than speaking to Aaron, their father (*Magen Avos*).

Other commentators, however, [remove the words וְגָדוֹל מֵאַהֲרֹן הַקָּדוֹשׁ בָּרוּךְ הוּא, *but the Holy One, Blessed is He, is greater than Aaron,* and] read the Baraisa as follows: *If Aaron was greater than Moses, then why did [God] not speak to Aaron?* That is, since the Baraisa has just taught that *When a person makes a banquet for his students, he directs his attention to the greatest [of them],* then why didn't God, too, give the Torah through Aaron instead of through Moses? On this the Baraisa answers that Aaron did not have sons who would stand in the breach, etc. (*Avos HaRosh*). According to the emendation of *Gra,* the Baraisa answers that *Aaron did not stand in the breach* [as did Moses] to pray on behalf of Israel (see *Ben Avraham* in explanation of that reading).

[It should be noted that in a parallel passage in *Derech Eretz Zuta, Perek HaShalom* (as found in the Epstein ms., cited in the notes to *Avos DeRabbi Nassan Bishtei Nuschaos, Nusach* 2, Ch. 40), the words גָדוֹל מֵאַהֲרֹן הקב"ה, *Greater than Aaron is the Holy One, Blessed is He,* appear at a different point. The passage first mentions the example of Aaron, who did not interrupt Moses, and then continues that God is greater than Aaron, and He did not interrupt Abraham (as detailed in our Baraisa below).]

כַּיּוֹצֵא בוֹ בְּאַבְרָהָם אָבִינוּ כְּשֶׁהָיָה מִתְפַּלֵּל עַל אַנְשֵׁי סְדוֹם, אָמַר לוֹ
הַקָּדוֹשׁ בָּרוּךְ הוּא: (בראשית יח, כו) "אִם אֶמְצָא בִסְדֹם חֲמִשִּׁים צַדִּיקִם
וְנָשָׂאתִי לְכָל הַמָּקוֹם בַּעֲבוּרָם" גָּלוּי וְיָדוּעַ לִפְנֵי מִי שֶׁאָמַר וְהָיָה הָעוֹלָם
שֶׁאִילוּ הָיוּ מְצוּיִין בִּסְדוֹם שְׁלֹשָׁה אוֹ חֲמִשָּׁה צַדִּיקִים לֹא גָּרַם בָּהּ עָוֹן[82],
אֶלָּא הִמְתִּין הַקָּדוֹשׁ בָּרוּךְ הוּא אֶת אַבְרָהָם עַד שֶׁסִּיֵּם דְּבָרָיו וְאַחַר כָּךְ
הֱשִׁיבוֹ[83], שֶׁנֶּאֱמַר (שם פסוק לג) "וַיֵּלֶךְ ה' כַּאֲשֶׁר כִּלָּה לְדַבֵּר אֶל אַבְרָהָם"
(כִּבְיָכוֹל אָמַר לוֹ: הֲרֵי אֲנִי נִפְטָר, שֶׁנֶּאֱמַר) (שם) "וְאַבְרָהָם שָׁב לִמְקֹמוֹ"[84]:

The Baraisa returns to the second attribute of a wise person, not to interrupt someone who is speaking:

כַּיּוֹצֵא בוֹ בְּאַבְרָהָם אָבִינוּ — We find a similar thing with regard to our forefather Abraham: כְּשֶׁהָיָה מִתְפַּלֵּל עַל אַנְשֵׁי סְדוֹם אָמַר לוֹ הַקָּדוֹשׁ בָּרוּךְ הוּא — When he prayed on behalf of the people of Sodom, the Holy One, Blessed is He, said to him, "אִם אֶמְצָא בִסְדֹם חֲמִשִּׁים צַדִּיקִם וְנָשָׂאתִי לְכָל הַמָּקוֹם בַּעֲבוּרָם" — "If I find in Sodom fifty righteous people in the midst of the city, then I would spare the entire place on their account" (Genesis 18:26). גָּלוּי וְיָדוּעַ לִפְנֵי מִי שֶׁאָמַר וְהָיָה הָעוֹלָם שֶׁאִילוּ הָיוּ מְצוּיִין בִּסְדוֹם שְׁלֹשָׁה אוֹ חֲמִשָּׁה צַדִּיקִים לֹא גָּרַם בָּהּ עָוֹן — Now, it was known and revealed before He Who spoke and the world came into being that if there were even three or five righteous people found in Sodom, sin would not have caused [the city] to be destroyed.[82] So God could have cut Abraham short and informed him right away that there were simply not enough righteous people in Sodom to save it. אֶלָּא הִמְתִּין הַקָּדוֹשׁ בָּרוּךְ הוּא אֶת אַבְרָהָם עַד שֶׁסִּיֵּם דְּבָרָיו וְאַחַר כָּךְ הֱשִׁיבוֹ — However, the Holy One, Blessed is He, waited for Abraham to finish his statements, and only afterward did He respond to him,[83] שֶׁנֶּאֱמַר "וַיֵּלֶךְ ה' כַּאֲשֶׁר כִּלָּה לְדַבֵּר אֶל אַבְרָהָם" — as it is stated, HASHEM departed when He had finished speaking to Abraham (ibid. v. 33). כִּבְיָכוֹל אָמַר לוֹ: הֲרֵי אֲנִי נִפְטָר — He told him, as it were, "I am taking leave of you," שֶׁנֶּאֱמַר "וְאַבְרָהָם שָׁב לִמְקֹמוֹ" — as it is stated in the next words of the verse, And Abraham returned to his place.[84]

---

82. I.e., because they would have influenced the rest of the populace to be better people (Mefaresh).

83. Actually, God responded to Abraham several times in the course of the conversation — saying, each time Abraham lowered the number of righteous people that might be found in Sodom, that He would not destroy the city if that number were to be found. So God could have told Abraham during His first response that righteous people were not to be found, and that would not have

entailed interrupting Abraham's comments! Nevertheless, since God knew that Abraham had in mind to continue speaking after each response, cutting the conversation short prematurely would have been tantamount to "interrupting his words." Therefore, God waited until Abraham had finished speaking completely (Magen Avos).

84. Since with regard to God it says that He "went," whereas with regard to Abraham it says that he "returned to his place" (i.e., he resumed what he was doing), the implication

יג. וְאֵינוּ נִבְהָל לְהָשִׁיב זֶה אֱלִיהוּ בֶּן בַּרַכְאֵל הַבּוּזִי שֶׁנֶּאֱמַר (איוב לב, ז)

"אָמַרְתִּי יָמִים יְדַבֵּרוּ"[86] מְלַמֵּד[87] שֶׁהָיוּ יוֹשְׁבִין וְשׁוֹתְקִין לִפְנֵי אִיוֹב

עָמַד הָיוּ עוֹמְדִין יָשַׁב הָיוּ יוֹשְׁבִין אָבַל הָיוּ אוֹכְלִין שָׁתָה הָיוּ שׁוֹתִין[88]

---

§13 The third attribute of a wise person: זֶה אֱלִיהוּ בֶּן — וְאֵינוּ נִבְהָל לְהָשִׁיב — **He does not hasten to answer:** בַּרַכְאֵל הַבּוּזִי — This is exemplified by **Elihu ben Barachel the Buzite,** who remained silent as Job and his three friends discussed Job's suffering at great length,[85] שֶׁנֶּאֱמַר "אָמַרְתִּי יָמִים יְדַבֵּרוּ" — **as it is stated,** *Elihu the son of Bara-chel the Buzite then spoke up and said: I am young in years and you are elderly; therefore, I trembled and feared to express my opinion to you.* **I had thought, "Let days speak out;** *let abundant years teach wisdom"* (*Job 32:6-7*).[86]

The Baraisa continues:

מְלַמֵּד שֶׁהָיוּ יוֹשְׁבִין וְשׁוֹתְקִין לִפְנֵי אִיוֹב — **This teaches**[87] that the three friends of Job exhibited the first three attributes of a wise person: When they came to visit the suffering Job, **they** initially **sat and were silent before Job;** עָמַד הָיוּ עוֹמְדִין, יָשַׁב הָיוּ יוֹשְׁבִין — **if [Job] stood, they would stand;** אָבַל הָיוּ אוֹכְלִין, שָׁתָה הָיוּ שׁוֹתִין — **if he ate, they would eat; if he drank, they would drink.**[88] This continued for seven days,

---

is that it was God Who, as it were, took leave of Abraham (*Magen Avos*). [From *Tanchuma* (*Vayeira* §8), it would seem that the proof is simply from the fact that God's leaving is mentioned first, implying that it was He Who took leave.] God's "taking leave" of Abraham only when the latter finished speaking indicates that He did not interrupt the conversation and end it prematurely, which proves that a person should not interrupt one who is talking (see *Magen Avos*).

85. These discussions between Job and his three friends — Eliphaz the Temanite, Bildad the Shuhite, and Zophar the Naamathite (*Job 2:11*) — are recounted in detail in the earlier chapters of *Job*.

86. This verse shows that Elihu exhibited the wise attribute of not hastening to answer, as well as the first two attributes of the wise mentioned above — not speaking in the presence of those greater than he [unless compelled to do so] and not interrupting the words of his friend (*Magen Avos*). However, as Elihu saw that they did not answer properly, he now spoke up and voiced his opinion, as related in the verses that follow.

87. It is not clear what "this" refers to, and some suggest that there is something missing in the text (see *Meorei Ohr*). *Ahavas Chesed* explains that the reference is to the first part of the verse cited next — *[They sat with him on the ground ...] After that, Job opened his mouth ...* [Alternatively, the Baraisa might mean as follows: The Baraisa has just cited that Elihu said to the three older friends that he had remained silent until now because he thought: *let abundant years teach wisdom,* i.e., he had thought that the three older friends (who possessed "abundant years") would eventually teach the truth, as they had been speaking in the manner of wisdom; that is, they had exhibited the first three attributes of the wise, as the Baraisa proceeds to detail. Thus, the Baraisa means that Elihu's statement *let abundant words teach wisdom* teaches that they had been speaking in the manner of the wise.]

88. The Baraisa infers this from the wording of the verse: *they sat "with him" on the ground for seven days and seven nights; none of them spoke a word ...* (*Job 2:13*); "with him" implies that they did exactly

עַד שֶׁנָּטַל מֵהֶם רְשׁוּת שֶׁנֶּאֱמַר (שם ב, יד) "אַחֲרֵי כֵן פָּתַח אִיּוֹב אֶת פִּיהוּ
וַיְקַלֵּל אֶת יוֹמוֹ"[89] וְאָמַר: (שם ג, ב) "יֹאבַד יוֹם אִוָּלֶד בּוֹ וְהַלַּיְלָה אָמַר הֹרָה
גָבֶר". יֹאבַד יוֹם שֶׁבָּא אָבִי אֵצֶל אִמִּי וְאָמְרָה לוֹ: אֲנִי הָרָה[90]. וּמִנַּיִן שֶׁלֹּא
עָנוּ בְּעִרְבּוּבְיָא שֶׁנֶּאֱמַר (שם ג, א; ו, א; ט, א; יב, א; טז, א; יט, א; כא, א; כג, א; כו, א) "וַיַּעַן
אִיּוֹב וַיֹּאמַר". (שם ד, א; טו, א; כב, א) "וַיַּעַן אֱלִיפַז הַתֵּימָנִי וַיֹּאמַר". (שם ח, א;
יח, א; כה, א) "וַיַּעַן בִּלְדַּד הַשּׁוּחִי וַיֹּאמַר". (שם יא, א; כ, א) "וַיַּעַן צֹפַר הַנַּעֲמָתִי
וַיֹּאמַר". (שם לב, ו) "וַיַּעַן אֱלִיהוּא בֶן בַּרַכְאֵל הַבּוּזִי וַיֹּאמַר". סִדְרָן הַכָּתוּב
אֶחָד אֶחָד (אֶלָּא) לְהוֹדִיעַ לְכָל בָּאֵי עוֹלָם שֶׁאֵין חָכָם מְדַבֵּר לִפְנֵי מִי

שֶׁנֶּאֱמַר — עַד שֶׁנָּטַל מֵהֶם רְשׁוּת — until [Job] asked their permission to speak,
"אַחֲרֵי כֵן פָּתַח אִיּוֹב אֶת פִּיהוּ וַיְקַלֵּל אֶת יוֹמוֹ" — as it is stated, *They sat with him
on the ground for a period of seven days and seven nights ... After that, Job
opened his mouth and cursed his day* (ibid. 2:13-14).[89] וְאָמַר: "יֹאבַד יוֹם
אִוָּלֶד בּוֹ וְהַלַּיְלָה אָמַר הֹרָה גָבֶר" — In this vein [Job] said, *Lost be the day when I
was born, and the night when it was announced: A man has been conceived*
(ibid. 3:2). יֹאבַד יוֹם שֶׁבָּא אָבִי אֵצֶל אִמִּי וְאָמְרָה לוֹ: אֲנִי הָרָה — What is meant
by *Lost be the day when I was born?* Lost be the day that my father came to
my mother and she told him, "I am pregnant."[90] וּמִנַּיִן שֶׁלֹּא עָנוּ בְּעִרְבּוּבְיָא
— And from where do we see that they did not answer him in a disorderly
fashion? שֶׁנֶּאֱמַר "וַיַּעַן אִיּוֹב וַיֹּאמַר" ... "וַיַּעַן אֱלִיפַז הַתֵּימָנִי וַיֹּאמַר" ... "וַיַּעַן בִּלְדַּד
הַשּׁוּחִי וַיֹּאמַר" ... "וַיַּעַן צֹפַר הַנַּעֲמָתִי וַיֹּאמַר" ... "וַיַּעַן אֱלִיהוּא בֶן בַּרַכְאֵל הַבּוּזִי וַיֹּאמַר"
— For it is stated: *Job then spoke up and said ...* (ibid. 3:1; 6:1; 9:1; 12:1;
16:1; 19:1; 21:1; 23:1; 26:1); *Eliphaz the Temanite then spoke up and said
...* (ibid. 4:1; 15:1; 22:1); *Bildad the Shuhite then spoke up and said ...* (ibid.
8:1; 18:1; 25:1); *Zophar the Naamathite then spoke up and said ...* (ibid. 11:1;
20:1); *Elihu the son of Barachel the Buzite then spoke up and said ...* (ibid.
32:6). סִדְרָן הַכָּתוּב אֶחָד אֶחָד לְהוֹדִיעַ לְכָל בָּאֵי עוֹלָם שֶׁאֵין חָכָם מְדַבֵּר לִפְנֵי מִי

---

what he did (*Ben Avraham*; see also *Magen
Avos*). Their silence exhibited the attribute
of not hastening to answer.

89. [In some Bible editions, *Job* 2:14 is
numbered as 3:1, and there is a one-verse
discrepancy in the numbering of the balance of Ch. 3.] The Baraisa expounds the
seemingly unnecessary expression *after that*
to mean "after he had received permission
to speak" (*Magen Avos*). Alternatively, it
is expounding the seemingly unnecessary
expression *[he] opened his mouth* to mean
that he did so in order to ask their permission to speak (*Ben Avraham*).

The wise man makes himself small and
his fellow great. Thus, by asking their permission to speak, Job exhibited the attribute
of not speaking [without permission] in the
presence of those greater than he (*Ben
Avraham*).

90. The Baraisa is explaining the verse's
use of the future tense אִוָּלֶד בּוֹ, which means
literally "when I *would be* born." He was
cursing not only the day of his birth but the
day on which it was first said that he *would
be born* — the day on which his mother told
his father that she had conceived (*Magen
Avos, Ben Avraham*).

שֶׁגָּדוֹל הֵימֶנּוּ בְּחָכְמָה. וְאֵינוֹ נִכְנָס לְתוֹךְ דִּבְרֵי חֲבֵירוֹ[91]. וְאֵינוֹ נִבְהָל לְהָשִׁיב.
שׁוֹאֵל כָּעִנְיָן זֶה יְהוּדָה שֶׁנֶּאֱמַר (בראשית מג, ט) "אָנֹכִי אֶעֶרְבֶנּוּ"[92]. שׁוֹאֵל
שֶׁלֹּא כָּעִנְיָן זֶה רְאוּבֵן שֶׁנֶּאֱמַר (שם מב, לז) "וַיֹּאמֶר רְאוּבֵן אֶל אָבִיו אֶל שְׁנֵי
בָנַי תָּמִית"[93]. וְאוֹמֵר עַל רִאשׁוֹן רִאשׁוֹן זֶה יַעֲקֹב[94], וְיֵשׁ אוֹמְרִים: זוֹ שָׂרָה[95]

שֶׁגָּדוֹל הֵימֶנּוּ בְּחָכְמָה — Scripture ordered each person's lengthy discourse by itself to teach all who come into the world that a wise person does not speak before someone who is greater than he in wisdom or in number; וְאֵינוֹ נִכְנָס לְתוֹךְ דִּבְרֵי חֲבֵירוֹ — and he does not interrupt the words of his friend, as evidenced by all of Job's friends;[91] וְאֵינוֹ נִבְהָל לְהָשִׁיב — and he does not hasten to answer, as evidenced most strikingly by Elihu.

The fourth attribute of a wise person: זֶה יְהוּדָה שׁוֹאֵל כָּעִנְיָן — He asks what is relevant and answers appropriately: שֶׁנֶּאֱמַר "אָנֹכִי אֶעֶרְבֶנּוּ" — This is exemplified by Judah, as it is stated that he said to his father Jacob: *"I will personally guarantee him; of my own hand you can demand him. If I do not bring him back to you and stand him before you, then I will have sinned to you for all time"* (Genesis 43:9).[92] On the other hand, the opposite trait, שׁוֹאֵל שֶׁלֹּא כָּעִנְיָן, זֶה רְאוּבֵן — he asks what is irrelevant and answers inappropriately, is exemplified by Reuben, שֶׁנֶּאֱמַר "וַיֹּאמֶר רְאוּבֵן אֶל אָבִיו אֶת שְׁנֵי בָנַי תָּמִית" — as it is stated that Reuben proposed to Jacob, *"You may slay my two sons if I fail to bring him back to you"* (ibid. 42:37).[93]

The fifth attribute: וְאוֹמֵר עַל רִאשׁוֹן רִאשׁוֹן, זֶה יַעֲקֹב — He discusses first things first and last things last: This is exemplified by Jacob,[94] וְיֵשׁ אוֹמְרִים: זוֹ שָׂרָה — and some say:

---

91. That each one waited until the one before him had finished is evident from a simple reading of the narrative. That each waited for the one greater than he to speak can be seen from the fact that each friend spoke several times, always in the same order — Eliphaz, Bildad, and Zophar; evidently this was the descending order of their greatness (see *Ben Avraham*).

92. As narrated in that chapter, Jacob needed his sons to go to Egypt to buy food, but refused to send Benjamin with them, as demanded by the Master of Egypt (Joseph). To break the impasse, Judah proposed this guarantee, which Jacob accepted. [This is called "asking" what is relevant because it was a *proposal* to Jacob; Jacob's response was the "answer." Alternatively, it might be that the Baraisa means to bring an example

of the *second* aspect of this attribute: he asks what is relevant *and answers appropriately*.]

93. This was an inappropriate proposal, because Jacob obviously would not kill Reuben's two sons should Benjamin fail to return (see *Bereishis Rabbah* 91:9, cited in *Rashi* to the verse).

94. When Jacob sent a tribute to his brother, Esau (see *Genesis* 32:4-22), he instructed the servants bringing it, *"When my brother Esau meets you and asks you, saying, 'Whose are you, where are you going, and whose are these that are before you?' — You shall say, 'Your servant, Jacob's. It is a tribute sent to my lord, to Esau, and behold he himself is behind us.'"* (vv. 18-19). Thus, Jacob arranged for the servants to answer Esau's first question first, and the last questions last (*Binyan Yehoshua*, first explanation, citing *Rashi* ad

וְעַל אַחֲרוֹן אַחֲרוֹן[96], אֵלּוּ אַנְשֵׁי חָרָן[97]. וּמוֹדֶה[98] עַל הָאֱמֶת, זֶה מֹשֶׁה,

וְעַל אַחֲרוֹן אַחֲרוֹן, אֵלּוּ אַנְשֵׁי חָרָן — **And last things last:[96]** This is exemplified by **the men of Haran** in the answers they gave to Jacob's questions, when he first came to Haran and met them at the well.[97]

This is exemplified by **Sarah.**[95]

---

loc.). Alternatively, the reference is to when Laban overtook the fleeing Jacob and said, *"What have you done that you have deceived me and led my daughters away like captives of the sword? Why have you fled so stealthily ... why did you steal my gods?"* (Genesis 31:26-30). Jacob responded: *"Because I was afraid, for I thought, perhaps you might steal your daughters from me. With whomever you find your gods, he shall not live ..."* (ibid. 31-32), answering first things first, as noted by *Rashi* there (*Ben Avraham*).

95. It is not clear where this attribute is exemplified by Sarah. *Ahavas Chesed* suggests that it is in the following. Scripture tells us that when one of the three men who came to visit Abraham said to him in earshot of Sarah that she would bear a son within the year, *Sarah laughed inside, saying, "After I have withered shall I again have delicate skin? And my husband is old!."* Then Hashem said to Abraham, *"Why is it that Sarah laughed, saying: 'Shall I in truth bear a child, though I have aged?' Is anything beyond Hashem?! At the appointed time I will return to you at this time next year, and Sarah will have a son."* Sarah denied it, saying, *"I did not laugh,"* for she was frightened. But he said, *"No, you laughed indeed"* (Genesis 18:12-15). As *Ramban* explains there, Sarah laughed initially because she did not realize that the "man" who said that she would bear a son was in fact an angel. But when Abraham made it clear to her that he was aware that she "had laughed inside," she realized that all this had been a prophecy to Abraham — a prophecy that she would finally bear a son! — and still she did nothing more than respond exactly to what she had been asked: "Why did you laugh?" This exemplifies the attribute of answering "first things first" — i.e., tailoring the response to what has been asked. *Binyan Yehoshua* attempts a different explanation (see also a third explanation proposed by *Ben Avraham*), but concludes

that it is likely that the text here should be emended to read "Rebecca" rather than "Sarah." (This emendation is made by *Gra* and *Magen Avos* as well, and is the reading found in *Avos DeRabbi Nassan, Nusach 2,* Ch. 40.) Scripture tells us that Abraham's servant asked Rebecca, *"Whose daughter are you? Pray tell me. Is there room in your father's house for us to spend the night?"* Whereupon Rebecca answered, in order of the questions, *"I am the daughter of Bethuel the son of Milcah whom she bore to Nahor... Even straw and feed is plentiful with us, as well as place to lodge"* (Genesis 24:23-25). This exemplifies answering first things first, as noted by *Rashi* there on v. 24.

96. According to our reading (which presents a separate example for "last things last"), it would seem that "first things first" and "last things last" are distinct attributes, and not simply different sides of the same coin (*Ben Avraham*). See next note.

97. *Ahavas Chesed* suggests that the Baraisa means the following. Scripture states there, *Jacob said to them, "My brothers, where are you from?" And they said, "We are from Haran."* He said to them, *"Do you know Laban the son of Nahor?" And they said, "We know."* Then he said to them, *"Is it well with him?" They answered, "It is well; and see — his daughter Rachel is coming with the flock!"* (Genesis 29:4-6). The Midrash tells us that they mentioned that Rachel was coming to say that she is more talkative than we, and you can find out many more details from her (*Bereishis Rabbah* 70 §11). The question, then, is why did they not say this to Jacob immediately after his first question? The answer is that there is a virtue in the attribute of "last things last" — that is, one should not answer the first thing in a way that closes the door to further questions, but in a way that allows the questioner to probe further and receive answers on "last things last." (See

שֶׁנֶּאֱמַר (דברים ה, כה) "וַיֹּאמֶר ה' אֵלַי [וְגוֹ'] הֵיטִיבוּ (אֶת) [כָּל] אֲשֶׁר
דִּבֵּרוּ"[99]. וְכֵן הַקָּדוֹשׁ בָּרוּךְ הוּא הוֹדָה עַל הָאֱמֶת, שֶׁנֶּאֱמַר (במדבר כז, ז)
"כֵּן בְּנוֹת צְלָפְחָד דֹּבְרֹת"[100]:

The seventh attribute:[98]

וּמוֹדֶה עַל הָאֱמֶת — And he concedes the truth: זֶה מֹשֶׁה, שֶׁנֶּאֱמַר "וַיֹּאמֶר ה'
אֵלַי וְגוֹ' הֵיטִיבוּ כָּל אֲשֶׁר דִּבֵּרוּ" — This is exemplified by Moses, as it is stated,
HASHEM said to me ... they have done well in all that they spoke (Deuter-
onomy 5:25).[99]   וְכֵן הַקָּדוֹשׁ בָּרוּךְ הוּא הוֹדָה עַל הָאֱמֶת, שֶׁנֶּאֱמַר "כֵּן בְּנוֹת צְלָפְחָד
דֹּבְרֹת" — And the Holy One, Blessed is He, conceded the truth as well, as it
is stated, *The daughters of Zelophehad speak properly* (Numbers 27:7).[100]

---

another explanation in *Ben Avraham*.)

Ahavas Chesed points out, however, that
from *Rav's* commentary on the Mishnah, it
appears that he followed a reading according
to which the men of Haran exemplify the *sixth*
attribute of the wise — "about that which he
has not heard he says, 'I have not heard.' "
That is, they could tell Jacob no more about
Laban, and referred Jacob instead to Laban's
daughter Rachel. [This is indeed the reading
of our Baraisa quoted in *Machzor Vitri* to the
Mishnah, and is also found in *Avos DeRabbi
Nassan, Nusach 2, Ch. 40*. See a different
emendation in *Nuschas HaGra*.]

98. [Our version of the Baraisa skips the illustration of the sixth attribute. According to
the alternative reading mentioned at the end
of the preceding note, however, the Baraisa
illustrates the sixth attribute as well. (See
also *Nuschas HaGra* for a different emendation.) See, however, the last comments of
Ben Avraham on this chapter.]

99. This was said in response to the people,
who were afraid to hear the overwhelming
voice of God directly and asked that God
should speak only to Moses, and he would
relay the words of God to them.

[Although the Baraisa above (at note 75)
already cited a *different* verse that demonstrates that Moses conceded the truth, it
could be that the earlier verse was a conces-
sion of truth that Moses had made in private
(as indeed suggested by one opinion in the
Baraisa there). The present verse, however, was spoken by Moses before the entire
people (*Binyan Yehoshua*, first explanation).

Alternatively, the verse cited above might
mean that Moses conceded the truth mental-
ly, not verbally (ibid., second explanation).]

The commentators ask, however, that
these were the words of *God*, not of Moses.
How, then, can the Baraisa use this to say
that the attribute of "conceding the truth" is
exemplified by *Moses*? (*Magen Avos; Avos
HaRosh*). [Perhaps it is for this reason that
the Baraisa cites the *second* occurrence of
this statement (*Deuteronomy 18:17*), where
Moses is relating what he already said [in
verse 5:25] (with a very slight change in
wording). The reason Moses reiterated this
statement of God was his desire to "concede
the truth," that the people had indeed been
correct in their complaint to him.]

Some commentators, therefore, emend the
text of the Baraisa so that the verse cited is
indeed the same verse that the Baraisa cited
above in this regard, namely: וַיִּשְׁמַע מֹשֶׁה וַיִּיטַב
בְּעֵינָיו, *Moses heard and he approved* (Leviticus 10:20). [This is indeed the reading cited
in *Machzor Vitri* to the Mishnah.] Other commentators retain the verse cited in our Baraisa, but place it after the words below, *And the
Holy One, Blessed is He, conceded the truth as
well,* so that the Baraisa there cites *two* proofs
to that assertion, and no proof to the assertion
regarding Moses, since it has already stated
that above (*Ahavas Chesed; Avos HaRosh;
Ben Avraham*; see also *Nuschas HaGra*).

100. God conceded that the daughters of
Zelophehad were correct in their claim that
they should inherit their father's share in the
Land, since he had left no sons.

⁂ פֶּרֶק לח ⁂

א. שִׁבְעָה מִינֵי פּוּרְעָנִיּוֹת בָּאוֹת לָעוֹלָם וְכוּ׳.[1] מִקְצָתָן מְעַשְּׂרִין
וּמִקְצָתָן אֵינָן מְעַשְּׂרִין רָעָב שֶׁל בַּצּוֹרֶת בָּאָה.[2] מִקְצָתָן תּוֹרְמִים
וּמִקְצָתָן אֵינָן תּוֹרְמִים רָעָב שֶׁל מְהוּמָה בָּאָה.[3] מִקְצָתָן מַפְרִישִׁין חַלָּה
וּמִקְצָתָן אֵינָן מַפְרִישִׁין חַלָּה רָעָב שֶׁל כְּלָיָה בָּא.[4] גָּמְרוּ שֶׁלֹּא לְעַשֵּׂר[5]

⁂ CHAPTER 38 ⁂

§1 This chapter, which continues the previous chapter's theme of sevens, is a variation of *Avos* 5:8-9, with some elaboration:

שִׁבְעָה מִינֵי פּוּרְעָנִיּוֹת בָּאוֹת לָעוֹלָם וְכוּ׳ — **Seven types of calamities come to the world, etc.** [on account of seven kinds of transgressions].[1] The Baraisa enumerates the seven transgressions and their corresponding calamities: מִקְצָתָן מְעַשְּׂרִין וּמִקְצָתָן אֵינָן מְעַשְּׂרִין — **(i) When** only **some** of the **people separate** *maaser* **from their produce to give to the Levite, but others do not,** רָעָב שֶׁל בַּצּוֹרֶת בָּאָה — then **a famine caused by lack of rain comes** to the world.[2] מִקְצָתָן תּוֹרְמִים וּמִקְצָתָן אֵינָן תּוֹרְמִים — **(ii) When** only **some** of the **people separate** *terumah* **from their produce to give to the Kohen, but others do not,** רָעָב שֶׁל מְהוּמָה בָּאָה — then **a famine caused by unrest comes** to the world.[3] מִקְצָתָן מַפְרִישִׁין חַלָּה וּמִקְצָתָן אֵינָן מַפְרִישִׁין חַלָּה — **(iii) When** only **some** of the **people separate** *challah* **from their dough to give to the Kohen, but others do not,** רָעָב שֶׁל כְּלָיָה בָּא — then **a famine of depletion comes** to the world.[4] גָּמְרוּ שֶׁלֹּא לְעַשֵּׂר — **(iv) When they cease to tithe entirely** (i.e.,

---

1. The premise of the following chapter is that nothing happens by chance. Even world events that may seem "natural," such as drought, are in reality punishments sent by God to arouse people to repent. Since punishment is meted out מִדָּה כְּנֶגֶד מִדָּה, *measure for measure*, the nature of the punishment is instructive in helping man determine where he has erred, thus allowing him to correct his ways. Indeed, the seven calamities enumerated below are "measure for measure" for the transgressions associated with them [as will be briefly indicated in the notes] (see *Meiri* to the Mishnah).

2. The lack of adequate rain means the fields yield less crops, and with food in short supply, the prices go up and many cannot afford to buy.

This is "measure for measure": people did not give their tithes to sustain the Levites,

so God withholds rain, and by extension, people's sustenance.

3. "Unrest" refers to the disruptive presence of foreign armies, which prevents people from planting and harvesting (*Mefaresh*; see *Binyan Yehoshua* for an additional explanation). It is a more severe famine than a famine of drought, where food is available, though in short supply.

Why does withholding *terumah* from the Kohen result in a more severe famine than that caused by withholding *maaser*? Whereas *maaser* involves separating a significant amount of the produce (one tenth), the obligation of *terumah* can technically be fulfilled with a portion of negligible size. It thus requires a greater degree of stinginess to withhold it, and so, the punishment it carries is more severe (*Mefaresh*).

4. That is, even the grain that people might

עָצְרוּ הַשָּׁמַיִם לְהוֹרִיד טַל וּמָטָר[6] וּבְנֵי אָדָם יְגֵעִים וְאֵין מִסְתַּפְּקִין[7]. רַבִּי
יֹאשִׁיָה אָמַר: בַּעֲוֹן חַלָּה אֵין הַבְּרָכָה נִכְנָס בַּפֵּירוֹת וּבְנֵי אָדָם יְגֵעִים
וְאֵינָן מִסְתַּפְּקִין[9]. (בַּעֲוֹן תְּרוּמוֹת וּמַעַשְׂרוֹת נֶעֶצְרוּ הַשָּׁמַיִם לְהוֹרִיד טַל
וּמָטָר וְהָעָם נִמְסָרוֹת לְאוֹיְבֵיהֶם[10]):

עָצְרוּ הַשָּׁמַיִם לְהוֹרִיד טַל — no one separates *maaser*, *terumah*, or *challah*),[5] וּבְנֵי אָדָם וּמָטָר — the heavens completely **stop letting down rain and dew,**[6] יְגֵעִים וְאֵין מִסְתַּפְּקִין — **and people toil** to earn a living **but cannot provide** food **for themselves.**[7]

The Baraisa interrupts the set of seven to cite a dissenting opinion as to the misfortunes that occur on account of the sins just mentioned:[8] רַבִּי יֹאשִׁיָה אָמַר — R' Yoshiyah said: בַּעֲוֹן חַלָּה — **Due to the sin of not separating** *challah* **the produce,** אֵין הַבְּרָכָה נִכְנָס בַּפֵּירוֹת — **God's blessing is not imparted to** וּבְנֵי אָדָם יְגֵעִים וְאֵינָן מִסְתַּפְּקִין — **and people toil but do not have enough.**[9] בַּעֲוֹן תְּרוּמוֹת וּמַעַשְׂרוֹת — **And due to the sin of not separating** *terumah* **and tithes,** נֶעֶצְרוּ הַשָּׁמַיִם לְהוֹרִיד טַל וּמָטָר — **the heavens hold back rain and dew,** וְהָעָם נִמְסָרוֹת לְאוֹיְבֵיהֶם — **and the Jewish nation is delivered into the hands of its enemies.**[10]

---

have in their storehouses from the *previous* crop will be confiscated by the enemy, and certainly the food they have in their homes, leaving the people with nothing to eat (*Ben Avraham*).

Withholding *challah* carries a more severe consequence than withholding *terumah* or *maaser* because, whereas *terumah* and *maaser* are separated when the grain is yet unprocessed, *challah* is separated at the kneading of the dough, just before it is baked into edible bread. Since the benefit from the grain is more tangible at this point, there is a greater expectation that one should feel a sense of gratitude to Hashem for His blessing, and express this gratitude by sharing the blessing with others (*Magen Avos*; for another explanation, see *Ben Avraham*).

5. [Some render גָּמְרוּ שֶׁלֹא לְעַשֵׂר as: when *"they decide" not to tithe* (*Magen Avos*; *Ben Avraham*.] The word לְעַשֵׂר here is a generic term referring to the three types of separations mentioned earlier (*Binyan Yehoshua*, from *Tos. Yom Tov*).

6. As long as only some of the populace neglected the separation of tithes, the famines described above affected only some parts of the land. However, if withholding tithes has become a widespread practice, the entire land suffers the consequences (*Ben Avraham*).

7. Even if they can earn money, they cannot use it to buy food, as there is no food available to buy (ibid.)

8. *Ahavas Chesed* and *Ben Avraham*.

9. The separation of *challah* has the power to evoke Hashem's blessings, as it is stated: *And you shall give the first portion of your dough to the Kohen, to bring a blessing to rest upon your home* (Ezekiel 44:30). Withholding it, therefore, causes those blessings — whether in produce or in livelihood — to be withheld from Above (see *Shabbos* 32b).

10. The people did not wish to give a portion of their possessions to those in need, so God delivers them into the hands of their enemies, who rob them of all their possessions (*Magen Avos*).

R' Yoshiyah's main point of contention with the first Tanna (Tanna Kamma) is that according to R' Yoshiyah, even if only some

ב. דֶּבֶר בָּא לָעוֹלָם בַּעֲוֹן לֶקֶט שִׁכְחָה וּפֵאָה[11] וּמַעְשַׂר עָנִי[12]. מַעֲשֶׂה בְּאִשָּׁה אַחַת שֶׁהָיְתָה יוֹשֶׁבֶת בִּשְׁכוּנָה שֶׁל בַּעַל הַשָּׂדֶה וְיָצְאוּ שְׁנֵי בָנֶיהָ לְלַקֵּט וְלֹא הִנִּיחָן בַּעַל הַשָּׂדֶה. אִמָּן הָיְתָה אוֹמֶרֶת: מָתַי יָבוֹאוּ בָנַי מִן הַשָּׂדֶה, שֶׁמָּא אִמְצָא אֶמְצָא בְּיָדָם כְּלוּם לֶאֱכוֹל. וְהֵם הָיוּ אוֹמְרִים: מָתַי נֵלֵךְ אֶל אִמֵּנוּ שֶׁמָּא נִמְצָא בְּיָדָהּ כְּלוּם לֶאֱכוֹל הִיא לֹא מָצְאָה בְיָדָם כְּלוּם וְהֵם לֹא מָצְאוּ בְיָדָהּ כְּלוּם לֶאֱכוֹל. וְהִנִּיחוּ רָאשֵׁיהֶם בֵּין בִּרְכֵּי אִמָּם

§2 The fifth type of calamity that comes to the world on account of a specific sin: בַּעֲוֹן לֶקֶט שִׁכְחָה דֶּבֶר בָּא לָעוֹלָם — (v) **Pestilence comes to the world** וּפֵאָה וּמַעְשַׂר עָנִי — **for the sins of** not leaving *leket, shich'chah,* and *peah,*[11] **and** for not giving **the tithe of the poor** (*maasar ani*).[12]

One might argue that pestilence, which involves the sudden death of many people, is too harsh a consequence of withholding gifts from the poor. In truth, however, the poor rely on these gifts for their very sustenance, and withholding the gifts from them may be akin to taking their lives, as the following incident shows: מַעֲשֶׂה בְּאִשָּׁה אַחַת שֶׁהָיְתָה יוֹשֶׁבֶת בִּשְׁכוּנָה שֶׁל בַּעַל הַשָּׂדֶה — There was an incident with a certain woman who lived in the neighborhood of a wealthy landowner. וְיָצְאוּ שְׁנֵי בָנֶיהָ לְלַקֵּט — Her two young sons went out to collect *leket, shich'chah,* and *peah* in the landowner's field, וְלֹא הִנִּיחָן בַּעַל הַשָּׂדֶה — but the landowner did not allow them to collect. אִמָּן הָיְתָה אוֹמֶרֶת: מָתַי יָבוֹאוּ בָנַי מִן הַשָּׂדֶה — During this time, their starving mother was saying, "When will my sons return from the field? שֶׁמָּא אֶמְצָא בְּיָדָם כְּלוּם לֶאֱכוֹל — Perhaps I will find that they have something for me to eat." וְהֵם הָיוּ אוֹמְרִים: מָתַי נֵלֵךְ אֶל אִמֵּנוּ — They, too, having been rejected by the landowner, were saying to themselves, "When will we return to our mother? שֶׁמָּא נִמְצָא בְּיָדָהּ כְּלוּם לֶאֱכוֹל — Perhaps we will find that she has something for us to eat from the tithe of the poor she may have collected from the landowner's home."[13] הִיא לֹא מָצְאָה בְיָדָם כְּלוּם וְהֵם לֹא מָצְאוּ בְיָדָהּ כְּלוּם לֶאֱכוֹל — When they returned home, however, she did not find that they had anything for them to eat, and they did not find that she had anything for them to eat. וְהִנִּיחוּ רָאשֵׁיהֶם בֵּין בִּרְכֵּי אִמָּם — In despair, [the two sons] placed their heads between their mother's knees,

---

of the people neglect the various tithes, this can result in "the heavens holding back rain and dew" or in "the people toiling but not being able to provide for themselves," whereas according to the Tanna Kamma, these occur only if everybody stops tithing (*Ben Avraham*; see *Ahavas Chesed* for an alternative explanation).

11. I.e., fallen stalks, forgotten sheaves, and a corner of the field that is being harvested (respectively), all of which are to be left for the poor to collect.

12. I.e., a tenth of the produce that is to be given to the poor on the third and sixth year of the *Shemittah* cycle.

13. *Ben Avraham.*

וּמֵתוּ שְׁלָשְׁתָּן בְּיוֹם אֶחָד. אָמַר (לָהֶן) הַקָּדוֹשׁ בָּרוּךְ הוּא: (אֵין) אַתֶּם
גּוֹבִין מֵהֶן אֶלָּא נְפָשׁוֹת. חַיֵּיכֶם אַף אֲנִי אֶגְבֶּה מִכֶּם נַפְשׁוֹתֵיכֶם. וְכֵן הוּא
אוֹמֵר (משלי כב, כב-כג) "אַל תִּגְזָל דָּל כִּי דַל הוּא וְאַל תְּדַכֵּא עָנִי בַשָּׁעַר כִּי
ה' יָרִיב רִיבָם וְקָבַע אֶת קֹבְעֵיהֶם נָפֶשׁ":

ג. חֶרֶב בָּא לָעוֹלָם עַל עִנּוּיֵי הַדִּין[14] וְעַל עִיווּת הַדִּין וּמִפְּנֵי הַמּוֹרִין
בַּתּוֹרָה שֶׁלֹּא כַּהֲלָכָה.[15] וּכְשֶׁתָּפְשׂוּ אֶת רַבָּן שִׁמְעוֹן בֶּן גַּמְלִיאֵל וְאֶת
רַבִּי יִשְׁמָעֵאל לְיהָרֵג,[16] הָיָה רַבָּן שִׁמְעוֹן בֶּן גַּמְלִיאֵל יוֹשֵׁב וְתוֹהֶה בְּדַעְתּוֹ

וּמֵתוּ שְׁלָשְׁתָּן בְּיוֹם אֶחָד — and all three of them died of starvation in one day.
אָמַר הַקָּדוֹשׁ בָּרוּךְ הוּא — The Holy One, Blessed is He, therefore says to those
who withhold from the poor the gifts mandated by the Torah, אֵין אַתֶּם גּוֹבִין
מֵהֶן אֶלָּא נְפָשׁוֹת — "When you withhold the gifts from the poor, you are taking
from them nothing less than their souls! חַיֵּיכֶם אַף אֲנִי אֶגְבֶּה מִכֶּם נַפְשׁוֹתֵיכֶם
— By your lives! I swear that I, too, will take from you your souls!" וְכֵן
הוּא אוֹמֵר — Thus it states, "אַל תִּגְזָל דָּל כִּי דַל הוּא וְאַל תְּדַכֵּא עָנִי בַשָּׁעַר כִּי
ה' יָרִיב רִיבָם וְקָבַע אֶת קֹבְעֵיהֶם נָפֶשׁ" — Do not rob the destitute because he is
destitute, and do not oppress the poor man in the gate [of judgment]. For
HASHEM will take up their grievance; He will rob the soul of those who
would rob from them (Proverbs 22:22-23).

§3 The sixth type of misfortune that comes to the world on account of a
specific sin:

חֶרֶב בָּא לָעוֹלָם — (vi) The sword comes to the world on account of the following
sins: עַל עִנּוּיֵי הַדִּין — for the delay of justice;[14] וְעַל עִיווּת הַדִּין — for the perversion of justice, i.e., when judges purposely absolve the guilty and condemn
the innocent; וּמִפְּנֵי הַמּוֹרִין בַּתּוֹרָה שֶׁלֹּא כַּהֲלָכָה — and for those who render
decisions in Torah matters that are not in accordance with the halachah.[15]
The Baraisa records an incident illustrating the calamity of the sword:
וּכְשֶׁתָּפְשׂוּ אֶת רַבָּן שִׁמְעוֹן בֶּן גַּמְלִיאֵל וְאֶת רַבִּי יִשְׁמָעֵאל לְיהָרֵג — When [the Ro-
mans] seized Rabban Shimon ben Gamliel and R' Yishmael ben Elisha for
the purpose of killing them,[16] הָיָה רַבָּן שִׁמְעוֹן בֶּן גַּמְלִיאֵל יוֹשֵׁב וְתוֹהֶה בְּדַעְתּוֹ

---

14. When the judges know what the verdict
will be, yet refrain from taking any legal action,
and instead delay the case (Rav to Avos 5:8).
The sin is termed עִנּוּי הַדִּין, literally, affliction of
justice, since the litigant suffers the anxiety of
being kept in suspense until the judges render
a decision (Machzor Vitri ad loc.).

15. In the case of all these sins, there exists a
real concern that the victim who was judged
unfairly or unlawfully may want to avenge

the wrong by killing his disputant. These sins
unleash one man's "sword" against his fellow, and so they are the cause for tragedies
brought on by the sword (Meiri to Avos 5:8).

16. Rabban Shimon ben Gamliel and R'
Yishmael ben Elisha were among the ten
Sages (known as the עֲשָׂרָה הֲרוּגֵי מַלְכוּת, the
Ten Martyrs) who were brutally put to death
by a Roman ruler. [For lengthy treatment of
the historical context of this incident, see

וְאוֹמֵר: אוֹי לָנוּ שֶׁאָנוּ נֶהֱרָגִין כִּמְחַלְּלֵי שַׁבָּתוֹת וּכְעוֹבְדֵי כּוֹכָבִים וְכִמְגַלֵּי
עֲרָיוֹת וּכְשׁוֹפְכֵי דָמִים‏17. אָמַר לוֹ רַבִּי יִשְׁמָעֵאל בֶּן אֱלִישָׁע: רְצוֹנְךָ שֶׁאוֹמַר
לְפָנֶיךָ דָּבָר אֶחָד. אָמַר לוֹ: אֱמוֹר. אָמַר לוֹ: שֶׁמָּא כְּשֶׁהָיִיתָ מֵיסֵב בִּסְעוּדָה
בָּאוּ עֲנִיִּים וְעָמְדוּ עַל פִּתְחֲךָ וְלֹא הִנַּחְתָּם שֶׁיִּכָּנְסוּ וְיֹאכֵלוּ. אָמַר לוֹ:
הַשָּׁמַיִם אִם עָשִׂיתִי כֵּן, אֶלָּא שׁוֹמְרִים הָיוּ לִי יוֹשְׁבִין עַל הַפֶּתַח, כְּשֶׁהָיוּ
עֲנִיִּים בָּאִים הָיוּ מַכְנִיסִין אוֹתָן אֶצְלִי וְאוֹכְלִין וְשׁוֹתִין אֶצְלִי וּמְבָרְכִין
לְשֵׁם שָׁמַיִם. אָמַר לוֹ: שֶׁמָּא כְּשֶׁהָיִיתָ יוֹשֵׁב וְדוֹרֵשׁ בְּהַר הַבַּיִת וְהָיוּ כָּל
אוּכְלוּסֵי יִשְׂרָאֵל יוֹשְׁבִין לְפָנֶיךָ זָחָה דַעְתְּךָ עָלֶיךָ‏18. אָמַר לוֹ: יִשְׁמָעֵאל אָחִי,

---

וְאוֹמֵר — Rabban Shimon ben Gamliel sat, his mind wondering about his impending fate, and he exclaimed, אוֹי לָנוּ שֶׁאָנוּ נֶהֱרָגִין כִּמְחַלְּלֵי שַׁבָּתוֹת וּכְעוֹבְדֵי כּוֹכָבִים וְכִמְגַלֵּי עֲרָיוֹת וּכְשׁוֹפְכֵי דָמִים — "Woe to us that we are being put to death like those who desecrate the Sabbath, like idolaters, like adulterers, and like murderers!"[17] אָמַר לוֹ רַבִּי יִשְׁמָעֵאל בֶּן אֱלִישָׁע — R' Yishmael ben Elisha said to him, רְצוֹנְךָ שֶׁאוֹמַר לְפָנֶיךָ דָּבָר אֶחָד — "May I say something to you?" אָמַר לוֹ: אֱמוֹר — [Rabban Shimon] replied to him, "You may speak." שֶׁמָּא כְּשֶׁהָיִיתָ מֵיסֵב בִּסְעוּדָה בָּאוּ עֲנִיִּים וְעָמְדוּ עַל פִּתְחֲךָ — So [R' Yishmael] said to him, "Perhaps when you were once reclining during your meal, poor people came and stood at your door, וְלֹא הִנַּחְתָּם שֶׁיִּכָּנְסוּ וְיֹאכֵלוּ — and you did not allow them to enter and eat with you." אָמַר לוֹ: הַשָּׁמַיִם אִם עָשִׂיתִי כֵּן — [Rabban Shimon] replied to him, "By Heaven! I swear that I never did that! אֶלָּא שׁוֹמְרִים הָיוּ לִי יוֹשְׁבִין עַל הַפֶּתַח — On the contrary, I had watchmen constantly sitting at my door, כְּשֶׁהָיוּ עֲנִיִּים בָּאִים הָיוּ מַכְנִיסִין אוֹתָן אֶצְלִי — and when poor people would come to the door, [the watchmen] would immediately bring them in to me, וְאוֹכְלִין וְשׁוֹתִין אֶצְלִי וּמְבָרְכִין לְשֵׁם שָׁמַיִם — and [those poor people] would eat and drink with me and bless the Name of God in Heaven!" אָמַר לוֹ: שֶׁמָּא כְּשֶׁהָיִיתָ יוֹשֵׁב וְדוֹרֵשׁ בְּהַר הַבַּיִת — [R' Yishmael] said to him further, "Then perhaps when you were sitting and expounding Torah thoughts on the Temple Mount, וְהָיוּ כָּל אוּכְלוּסֵי יִשְׂרָאֵל יוֹשְׁבִין לְפָנֶיךָ — with the entire Jewish population sitting before you, זָחָה דַעְתְּךָ עָלֶיךָ — you became high-spirited because of your honored position."[18] אָמַר לוֹ: יִשְׁמָעֵאל אָחִי,

---

Avos HaRosh (Vol. 2).] Rabban Shimon ben Gamliel was the *Nasi* (Prince) — the head of the Sanhedrin and leader of the people. R' Yishmael ben Elisha was the Kohen Gadol.

17. Rabban Shimon ben Gamliel examined his deeds to see if he could find a sin that would warrant the punishment he was about to receive, but could not find any (*Magen Avos*). He was especially distressed by the

fact that this punishment of death by execution is generally reserved for the worst sinners (*Machzor Vitri* to the Mishnah; see also *Maseches Semachos* Ch. 8 §9).

18. This would be a form of "exploiting the crown of Torah," and it states in *Avos* 1:13 and above, 12 §1, *he who exploits the crown [of Torah] shall fade away* (*Avos HaRosh* [Vol. 2]).

מוּכָן אָדָם שֶׁיְּקַבֵּל אֶת פְּגָעוֹ.[19] וְהָיוּ מִתְחַנְּנִין לָאִסְפַּקְלָטוֹר, זֶה אָמַר: אֲנִי כֹהֵן בֶּן כֹּהֵן גָּדוֹל, הָרְגֵנִי תְּחִלָּה וְאַל אֶרְאֶה בְּמִיתַת חֲבֵירִי. [וְזֶה אָמַר לוֹ: אֲנִי נָשִׂיא בֶּן נָשִׂיא, הָרְגֵנִי תְּחִלָּה וְאַל אֶרְאֶה בְּמִיתַת חֲבֵירִי.] אָמַר לָהֶם: הַפִּילוּ גוֹרָלוֹת. וְהִפִּילוּ וְנָפַל הַפּוּר עַל רַבָּן שִׁמְעוֹן בֶּן גַּמְלִיאֵל.

מוּכָן אָדָם שֶׁיְּקַבֵּל אֶת פְּגָעוֹ — [Rabban Shimon] replied, "Yishmael, my brother. A person is always **ready to receive his affliction** from God."[19]

The Baraisa continues to recount the incident:

וְהָיוּ מִתְחַנְּנִין לָאִסְפַּקְלָטוֹר — When the time of their execution arrived, **each of them pleaded with the executioner.** זֶה אָמַר: אֲנִי כֹהֵן בֶּן כֹּהֵן גָּדוֹל — **This** one (R' Yishmael) said, "I am a Kohen Gadol only because I am **the son of a Kohen Gadol,** but Rabban Shimon is greater than I.[20] הָרְגֵנִי תְּחִלָּה וְאַל אֶרְאֶה בְּמִיתַת חֲבֵירִי — **Kill me first,** so that I will not have to **witness my great colleague's death."** וְזֶה אָמַר לוֹ: אֲנִי נָשִׂיא בֶּן נָשִׂיא — **And this one** (Rabban Shimon ben Gamliel) similarly **said to [the executioner], "I am a prince** only because I am the son of a prince, but R' Yishmael is greater than I. הָרְגֵנִי תְּחִלָּה וְאַל אֶרְאֶה בְּמִיתַת חֲבֵירִי — **Kill** me **first** so that I will not have to **witness my great colleague's death."** אָמַר לָהֶם: הַפִּילוּ גוֹרָלוֹת — **[The executioner] said to them, "Cast lots** to see who will be killed first." וְהִפִּילוּ וְנָפַל הַפּוּר עַל רַבָּן שִׁמְעוֹן בֶּן גַּמְלִיאֵל — **They cast** lots, **and the lottery fell out on Rabban**

---

19. Some explain Rabban Shimon ben Gamliel's response to mean that he humbly accepted the truth of R' Yishmael's keen insight, and remarked that a person is constantly at the mercy of God, Who may decide at any given moment to give him the punishment he deserves for his sin (*Magen Avos*). Others, however, explain that Rabban Shimon ben Gamliel meant to deny this explanation as well, as he was not guilty of that charge either. Rather, he declared, we do not have an explanation of why we are suffering. Even if we cannot think of what we have done wrong, God's ways are just and it is we who have sinned (see *Binyan Yehoshua*).

According to a different version of our Baraisa, Rabban Shimon ben Gamliel explicitly denied the second charge as well. Whereupon R' Yishmael pressed further and asked, "Have you ever forced someone who came to you for judgment to wait while you finished your drink or donned your *tallis* (in preparation for judgment)? The Torah

states, *If you [dare to] cause him pain... My wrath shall blaze and I shall kill you by the sword* (Exodus 22:22-23), which implies that *any* pain that one causes a widow or orphan [and, by extension, any person in distress], whether it be major or minor [such as delaying his judgment], is punished severely." Hearing this, Rabban Shimon ben Gamliel realized that R' Yishmael's conjecture was correct, and that he was indeed deserving of this punishment. He said to R' Yishmael, "You have comforted me!" (see *Ahavas Chesed* and *Ben Avraham;* see also *Machzor Vitri* to *Avos* 5:8) According to this version, the Baraisa cites this incident to illustrate that the sword comes to the world for the sin of delaying justice [and certainly for the sins of perverting justice and of rendering incorrect Torah rulings, which are more severe (*Machzor Vitri* ibid.)] (*Ahavas Chesed*). See further, note 23 below.

20. *Ben Avraham,* based on the version of this incident cited in *Tanna DeVei Eliyahu (Rabbah)* §30.

מִיָּד נָטַל הַחֶרֶב וְחָתַךְ אֶת רֹאשׁוֹ. נְטָלוֹ רַבִּי יִשְׁמָעֵאל בֶּן אֱלִישָׁע וְהִנִּיחוֹ בְּחֵיקוֹ
וְהָיָה בּוֹכֶה וְצוֹעֵק: פֶּה קָדוֹשׁ פֶּה נֶאֱמָן פֶּה קָדוֹשׁ פֶּה נֶאֱמָן²¹, פֶּה שֶׁמּוֹצִיא
סַנְדַּלְפוֹנִין טוֹבוֹת וַאֲבָנִים טוֹבוֹת וּמַרְגָּלִיּוֹת, מִי הִטְמִינְךָ בֶּעָפָר וּמִי מִילֵּא
לְשׁוֹנְךָ עָפָר וָאֵפֶר. עָלֶיךָ הַכָּתוּב אוֹמֵר (זכריה יג, ז) "חֶרֶב עוּרִי עַל רֹעִי וְעַל
גֶּבֶר עֲמִיתִי"²². לֹא הִסְפִּיק לִגְמוֹר הַדָּבָר עַד שֶׁנָּטְלוּ הַחֶרֶב וְחָתְכוּ אֶת רֹאשׁוֹ.
(וַעֲלֵיהֶם אָמַר הַכָּתוּב (שמות כב, כג) "וְחָרָה אַפִּי וְהָרַגְתִּי אֶתְכֶם בֶּחָרֶב"²³,

---

Shimon ben Gamliel. מִיָּד נָטַל הַחֶרֶב וְחָתַךְ אֶת רֹאשׁוֹ — Immediately, [the executioner] took the sword and beheaded [Rabban Shimon ben Gamliel], whose head rolled off into the dirt. נְטָלוֹ רַבִּי יִשְׁמָעֵאל בֶּן אֱלִישָׁע וְהִנִּיחוֹ בְּחֵיקוֹ — R' Yishmael ben Elisha took [the severed head] and held it to his chest, וְהָיָה בּוֹכֶה וְצוֹעֵק: פֶּה קָדוֹשׁ פֶּה נֶאֱמָן פֶּה קָדוֹשׁ פֶּה נֶאֱמָן — and began weeping and crying out, "Holy mouth, faithful mouth! Holy mouth, faithful mouth![21] פֶּה שֶׁמּוֹצִיא סַנְדַּלְפוֹנִין טוֹבוֹת וַאֲבָנִים טוֹבוֹת וּמַרְגָּלִיּוֹת — O mouth that would express precious gems, precious stones, and pearls of Torah wisdom! מִי הִטְמִינְךָ בֶּעָפָר וּמִי מִילֵּא לְשׁוֹנְךָ עָפָר וָאֵפֶר — Who has pressed you ino the dirt?! Who has filled your tongue with dirt and ashes?! עָלֶיךָ הַכָּתוּב אוֹמֵר "חֶרֶב עוּרִי עַל רֹעִי וְעַל גֶּבֶר עֲמִיתִי" — Regarding you Scripture states, *O sword, arouse yourself against My shepherd, the man who is My colleague! — says Hashem, Master of Legions*" (*Zechariah* 13:7).[22] לֹא הִסְפִּיק לִגְמוֹר הַדָּבָר עַד שֶׁנָּטְלוּ הַחֶרֶב וְחָתְכוּ אֶת רֹאשׁוֹ — [R' Yishmael] had not finished the matter of this eulogy, before they took the sword and beheaded him as well. וַעֲלֵיהֶם אָמַר הַכָּתוּב "וְחָרָה אַפִּי וְהָרַגְתִּי אֶתְכֶם בֶּחָרֶב" — Regarding the tragic deaths of [these two Sages] Scripture states, *My wrath shall blaze and I shall kill you by the sword* (*Exodus* 22:23).[23]

---

21. Rabban Shimon ben Gamliel's mouth spoke only holy words of Torah, and it was faithful to each one of those words that it uttered, fulfilling every last one completely (*Velo Od Ella* [§37], second approach).

22. This verse is understood here as an allusion to Rabban Shimon ben Gamliel's death by the sword, for as *Nasi* of the Jewish people, he could fittingly be titled the "shepherd" of God's children (*Ahavas Chesed; Ben Avraham*; see also *Avos DeRabbi Nassan, Nusach 2, Ch. 41; cf. Binyan Yehoshua*).

23. It is unclear why the Baraisa associates the death of Rabban Shimon ben Gamliel and R' Yishmael ben Elisha with this verse. *Ben Avraham* suggests that the verse is

expounded to read, *My wrath shall blaze* against the Jewish people *and I shall kill you by the sword.* In other words, the Baraisa is saying that these great men were killed to atone for the sins of the nation. [This may be related to the verse that R' Yishmael associated with the death of Rabban Shimon, *O sword, arouse yourself against My shepherd,* i.e., the one in charge of my flock (see previous note). There, too, the idea may be that Rabban Shimon was held accountable for the sins of his people.]

However, according to the emended version of this Baraisa cited above in note 19, the verse, *My wrath shall blaze, etc.,* is the same verse that R' Yishmael cited to show that delaying justice results in the retribution

[מִמַּשְׁמַע שֶׁנֶּאֱמַר "וְהָרַגְתִּי אֶתְכֶם בֶּחָרֶב"] אֵינִי יוֹדֵעַ שֶׁהַנָּשִׁים נַעֲשׂוּ
אַלְמָנוֹת וּבָנִים יְתוֹמִים. אֶלָּא אַלְמָנוֹת וְלֹא אַלְמָנוֹת כְּגוֹן שֶׁלֹּא יִמָּצְאוּ
לָהֶן עֵדִים לְהַתִּירָם לְהִנָּשֵׂא²⁵ כְּגוֹן בֵּיתָר שֶׁלֹּא נִמְלַט מִמֶּנָּה נְשָׁמָה²⁶
לְהַתִּיר אֵשֶׁת אִישׁ. וּמִמַּשְׁמַע שֶׁנֶּאֱמַר (שם) "וְהָיוּ נְשֵׁיכֶם אַלְמָנוֹת" אֲנִי
יוֹדֵעַ שֶׁהַבָּנִים יְתוֹמִים²⁷, אֶלָּא יְתוֹמִים וְשֶׁאֵינָן יְתוֹמִים, שֶׁהָיוּ נִכְסֵיהֶם

Having cited this verse in the context of the above incident, the Baraisa now proceeds to expound it further.[24] The verse, which states the consequence for causing anguish to widows and orphans, reads in its entirety: *My wrath shall blaze and I shall kill you by the sword, and your wives will be widows and your children orphans.* The Baraisa expounds: מִמַּשְׁמַע שֶׁנֶּאֱמַר "וְהָרַגְתִּי אֶתְכֶם בֶּחָרֶב" — **From the plain meaning of what is stated** in the verse, *and I shall kill you by the sword,* אֵינִי יוֹדֵעַ שֶׁהַנָּשִׁים נַעֲשׂוּ אַלְמָנוֹת וּבָנִים יְתוֹמִים — **do I not** already **know that the wives** of the people killed **will be widows and the children orphans?!** Why, then, does Scripture have to state it explicitly? אֶלָּא אַלְמָנוֹת וְלֹא אַלְמָנוֹת — **Rather,** it is saying that their wives will be "**widows**" in that they have no husband, **yet "not widows,"** in that they cannot remarry; כְּגוֹן שֶׁלֹּא יִמָּצְאוּ לָהֶן עֵדִים — **such as where they will not find witnesses** to their husbands' deaths לְהַתִּירָם לְהִנָּשֵׂא — **to permit them to remarry,**[25] כְּגוֹן בֵּיתָר שֶׁלֹּא נִמְלַט מִמֶּנָּה — **as in the case of** the city of **Beitar, from which not** נְשָׁמָה לְהַתִּיר אֵשֶׁת אִישׁ — **one** Jewish **soul was spared,**[26] so that there were no survivors **to** testify that they had seen the corpses and thereby **permit** the massacred **men's wives to remarry.** וּמִמַּשְׁמַע שֶׁנֶּאֱמַר "וְהָיוּ נְשֵׁיכֶם אַלְמָנוֹת" אֲנִי יוֹדֵעַ שֶׁהַבָּנִים יְתוֹמִים — **Likewise, from the plain meaning of what is stated,** *and your wives will be widows,* indeed I already **know that the children will be orphans.**[27] Why then is it stated explicitly? אֶלָּא יְתוֹמִים וְשֶׁאֵינָן יְתוֹמִים — **Rather,** it is saying that the children will be "**orphans**" in that they will have no father, **yet "not orphans,"** שֶׁהָיוּ נִכְסֵיהֶם

---

of the sword, and Rabban Shimon conceded that this is why he was punished. Concluding the incident with this verse is thus appropriate (*Ahavas Chesed*).

24. *Binyan Yehoshua.*

25. Even if a man disappears and is presumed dead, his wife cannot remarry without the testimony of someone who has actually seen that he is dead.

[By repeating that the wives will be widows, the verse indicates that they will be a different kind of widow — one that has no husband,

but who nevertheless cannot remarry.]

26. Beitar was a large city in Eretz Yisrael whose entire population was massacred by the Romans following the destruction of the Second Temple (see *Gittin* 57a-58).

27. [Actually, this is already known from the earlier part of the verse — *and I shall kill you by the sword* — as the Baraisa stated earlier with regard to knowing that the wives will be widows, and is indeed the reading in *Bava Metzia* 38b and in *Mechilta* to the verse (see *Ahavas Chesed*).]

עוֹמְדִים בְּחֶזְקַת אֲבוֹתָם וְלֹא הָיוּ מַנִּיחִין אוֹתָן לִירַשׁ וְלִישָׂא וְלִיתֵּן בָּהֶן[28]:

ד. גָּלוּת בָּא לָעוֹלָם עַל עֲבוֹדַת כּוֹכָבִים וְעַל גִּלּוּי עֲרָיוֹת וְעַל שְׁפִיכוּת דָּמִים וְעַל שְׁמִיטַת הָאָרֶץ. עַל עֲבוֹדַת כּוֹכָבִים שֶׁנֶּאֱמַר (ויקרא כו, ל) "וְהִשְׁמַדְתִּי אֶת בָּמֹתֵיכֶם". אָמַר הַקָּדוֹשׁ בָּרוּךְ הוּא: הוֹאִיל וְאַתֶּם רוֹצִין בַּעֲבוֹדַת כּוֹכָבִים אַף אֲנִי מַגְלֶה אֶתְכֶם לְמָקוֹם שֶׁיֵּשׁ שָׁם עֲבוֹדַת כּוֹכָבִים, לְכָךְ נֶאֱמַר "וְהִשְׁמַדְתִּי אֶת בָּמֹתֵיכֶם". עַל שְׁמִיטַת הָאָרֶץ מִנַּיִן, שֶׁנֶּאֱמַר (שם פסוק לד) "אָז תִּרְצֶה הָאָרֶץ אֶת שַׁבְּתֹתֶיהָ", אָמַר לָהֶן הַקָּדוֹשׁ

עוֹמְדִים בְּחֶזְקַת אֲבוֹתָם — for, in the absence of witnesses to their fathers' deaths, **the properties** that they should rightfully inherit **will remain under the titles of their fathers,** וְלֹא הָיוּ מַנִּיחִין אוֹתָן לִירַשׁ וְלִישָׂא וְלִיתֵּן בָּהֶן — and [the court] will not allow them to inherit those properties and do business with them.[28]

§4 The seventh and final type of calamity that comes to the world on account of a specific sin:

גָּלוּת בָּא לָעוֹלָם — (vii) **Exile comes to the world** on account of the following sins: עַל עֲבוֹדַת כּוֹכָבִים וְעַל גִּלּוּי עֲרָיוֹת וְעַל שְׁפִיכוּת דָּמִים וְעַל שְׁמִיטַת הָאָרֶץ — **for** the sin of **idolatry, for** the sin of **immorality, for** the sin of **murder, and for** not allowing **the land to rest** during the Sabbatical (*Shemittah*) year. The relationship between these sins and the consequence of exile is expressed in the following verses:

שֶׁנֶּאֱמַר "וְהִשְׁמַדְתִּי אֶת בָּמֹתֵיכֶם" עַל עֲבוֹדַת כּוֹכָבִים — **"Because of idolatry,"** — as it is stated, *I will destroy your lofty buildings and decimate your sun-idols, I will cast your carcasses upon the carcasses of your idols ... And you, I will scatter among the nations* (*Leviticus* 26:30-33). אָמַר הַקָּדוֹשׁ בָּרוּךְ הוּא — **The Holy One, Blessed is He, said** to the Jewish people, הוֹאִיל וְאַתֶּם **"Since you have chosen idolatry,** רוֹצִין בַּעֲבוֹדַת כּוֹכָבִים אַף אֲנִי מַגְלֶה אֶתְכֶם לְמָקוֹם שֶׁיֵּשׁ שָׁם עֲבוֹדַת כּוֹכָבִים — **I too shall exile you to a place where there is idolatry** (i.e., foreign lands)." לְכָךְ נֶאֱמַר "וְהִשְׁמַדְתִּי אֶת בָּמֹתֵיכֶם" — Thus it is stated, *I will destroy your lofty buildings and decimate your sun-idols ... And you, I will scatter among the nations.*

עַל שְׁמִיטַת הָאָרֶץ מִנַּיִן — **"For not allowing the land to rest** during the Sabbatical year" — how do we know this? שֶׁנֶּאֱמַר "אָז תִּרְצֶה הָאָרֶץ אֶת שַׁבְּתֹתֶיהָ" — For it is stated, *Then the land will be appeased for its sabbaticals ... while you are in the land of your foes* (ibid. v. 34). אָמַר לָהֶן הַקָּדוֹשׁ בָּרוּךְ

---

28. [Here too, the verse's additional statement that the children of these men will be orphans indicates that they will be a different kind of orphan — one that undergoes the suffering of orphanhood but who nevertheless is not given the rights to his father's property.]

בָּרוּךְ הוּא: הוֹאִיל וְאֵין אַתֶּם מַשְׁמִיטִין אוֹתָהּ הִיא תַּשְׁמֵט אֶתְכֶם, וּמִסְפַּר
יְרָחִים שֶׁאֵי אַתֶּם מַשְׁמִיטִין אוֹתָהּ הִיא תִּשָּׁמֵט מֵאֵלֶיהָ, לְכָךְ נֶאֱמַר (שם
פסוקים לד-לה) "אָז תִּרְצֶה הָאָרֶץ ... כָּל יְמֵי הָשַׁמָּה".²⁹ (עַל גִּלּוּי עֲרָיוֹת,
כֵּיצַד, אָמַר רַבִּי יִשְׁמָעֵאל בְּרַבִּי יוֹסֵי: כָּל זְמַן שֶׁיִּשְׂרָאֵל פְּרוּצִים בָּעֲרָיוֹת
שְׁכִינָה מִסְתַּלֶּקֶת מִבֵּינֵיהֶם, שֶׁנֶּאֱמַר (דברים כג, טו) "וְלֹא יִרְאֶה בְךָ עֶרְוַת
דָּבָר וְשָׁב מֵאַחֲרֶיךָ"³⁰):

הוֹאִיל — הוֹאִיל — The Holy One, Blessed is He, said to [the Jewish people], הוּא
וְאֵין אַתֶּם מַשְׁמִיטִין אוֹתָהּ — "Since you do not allow [the land] to rest during
the Sabbatical year, הִיא תַּשְׁמֵט אֶתְכֶם — it will cause you to take a rest
from living on it, i.e., it will expel you. וּמִסְפַּר יְרָחִים שֶׁאֵי אַתֶּם מַשְׁמִיטִין אוֹתָהּ
— And then, for the same number of months that you did not allow the land
to rest during the Sabbatical years, הִיא תִּשָּׁמֵט מֵאֵלֶיהָ — it will rest on its
own while you are banished from it." לְכָךְ נֶאֱמַר "אָז תִּרְצֶה הָאָרֶץ ... כָּל יְמֵי
הָשַׁמָּה" — Thus it is stated, *Then the land will be appeased for its sabbaticals*
during all the years of its desolation, while you are in the land of your foes; then
the land will rest and it will appease for its sabbaticals. **All the years of its**
desolation *it will rest, whatever it did not rest during your sabbaticals when*
you dwelled upon it (ibid. verses 34-35).[29]
אָמַר רַבִּי — "Because of immorality" — how so? עַל גִּלּוּי עֲרָיוֹת, כֵּיצַד
יִשְׁמָעֵאל בְּרַבִּי יוֹסֵי — R' Yishmael the son of R' Yose said: כָּל זְמַן שֶׁיִּשְׂרָאֵל
פְּרוּצִים בָּעֲרָיוֹת — Any time that the Jewish people are unrestrained in the
area of immorality, שְׁכִינָה מִסְתַּלֶּקֶת מִבֵּינֵיהֶם — the Divine Presence removes
itself from their midst, שֶׁנֶּאֱמַר "וְלֹא יִרְאֶה בְךָ עֶרְוַת דָּבָר וְשָׁב מֵאַחֲרֶיךָ" — as
it is stated, *So that He will not see an immoral matter among you and turn*
away from behind you (Deuteronomy 23:15). And when the Divine Presence
is removed from the Jewish people, the result is exile.[30]

---

29. See *Rashi* on v. 35 there, who shows
how the length of the exile corresponded exactly to the time that they had not observed
the *Shemittah*.

30. *Binyan Yehoshua*.
   Our Baraisa does not give a source for the
fourth sin that brings exile, namely, murder.
The Gemara (*Shabbos* 33a), however, provides the source from that which is stated
with reference to murder, *You shall not bring*

guilt upon the land in which you are, for the
blood will bring guilt upon the Land, and
in the very next verse it says, *You shall not*
contaminate the Land in which you dwell,
in whose midst I rest (*Numbers* 35:33-34).
The implication is that if the Jewish people
do contaminate the Land through murder,
they will cease to dwell in it, and the Divine
Presence will cease to rest in their midst, i.e.,
they will be exiled to a foreign land.

﴾ פֶּרֶק לט ﴿

א. חֲמִשָּׁה אֵין לָהֶם סְלִיחָה[1]: הַמַּרְבֶּה (לָשׁוּב[2] וּמַרְבֶּה) לַחֲטוֹא[3].
וְהַחוֹטֵא (בְּדוֹר זַכַּאי[4]. וְחוֹטֵא) עַל מְנָת לָשׁוּב[5]. וְכָל שֶׁיֵּשׁ
בְּיָדוֹ חִלּוּל הַשֵּׁם (בַּעֲוֹנוֹ[6]. אֵין סִפֵּק לָאָדָם לֵידַע מַה דְּמוּת לְמַעְלָה[7])

﴾ CHAPTER 39 ﴿

§1 In the preceding chapters, the Baraisa presented sets of ten and seven. In this chapter it presents sets of five and six. First, a set of five: חֲמִשָּׁה אֵין לָהֶם סְלִיחָה — There are **five** types of people who **do not earn Divine forgiveness** easily:[1] הַמַּרְבֶּה לָשׁוּב — (i) **One who repents repeatedly;**[2] וּמַרְבֶּה לַחֲטוֹא — (ii) and one who **sins repeatedly;**[3] וְהַחוֹטֵא בְּדוֹר זַכַּאי — (iii) **one who sins** despite living **in a righteous generation;**[4] וְחוֹטֵא עַל מְנָת — (iv) **one who sins intending to repent;**[5] לָשׁוּב וְכָל שֶׁיֵּשׁ בְּיָדוֹ חִלּוּל הַשֵּׁם — (v) **and anyone who has a desecration of God's Name** in his sin.[6] בַּעֲוֹנוֹ
The Barasia continues: אֵין סִפֵּק לָאָדָם לֵידַע מַה דְּמוּת לְמַעְלָה — It **is not within man's capacity to know**

---

1. They require an extraordinary degree of repentance to obtain forgiveness (*Binyan Yehoshua*). It does not mean, however, that they can never be forgiven, for there is nothing that stands in the way of sincere repentance (*Kisei Rachamim*).

2. He commits and repents the same sin repeatedly. This indicates that his repentance each time was incomplete, as he never abandoned the sin (*Kisei Rachamim*; see also *Binyan Yehoshua*).

3. Doing the same sin repeatedly makes the sin seem acceptable in the person's eyes, which makes it so much more difficult for him to repent for it (see *Binyan Yehoshua*).

4. Such a sinner is faulted not only for his sin, but for his failure to learn righteous conduct from those around him. Moreover, in a righteous generation his sin stands out for its brazenness (*Velo Od Ella*; see also *Binyan Yehoshua*, first approach).

5. He sins only because he knows that repentance atones. The possibility of atonement, then, is the *cause* of his sin, so God does not help him repent; see below, 40 §4 note 13.

6. That is, even if his sin in and of itself is not so severe, if it brings about a desecration of God's Name, the *chillul Hashem* aspect of his sin does not allow for full forgiveness. Rather, as stated above (29 §5), even repentance, suffering and Yom Kippur do not fully atone for his sin; only death does (see *Magen Avos*; see also *Ahavas Chesed* and *Kisei Rachamim*).

Why does the Baraisa state that he has "a desecration of God's Name *in his sin*"? Why does it not state simply that he has caused a desecration of God's Name? *Binyan Yehoshua* (first approach) answers that the Baraisa wishes to emphasize that the *chillul Hashem* must have come about as a result of the person's *sin*. This excludes a case in which people misrepresented what he did, while in truth he did nothing wrong. In a similar vein, *Ben Avraham* explains that the Baraisa wishes to limit the incompleteness of forgiveness to where a *chillul Hashem* was caused through the commission of an *actual* sin. But a *chillul Hashem* that does not involve an actual sin, such as where an exceptionally righteous man buys on credit (see *Yoma* 86a) *does* allow for full

וְאִלְמָלֵא כֵּן הָיוּ מוֹסְרִין לוֹ מַפְתְּחוֹת וְיוֹדֵעַ בַּמֶּה נִבְרְאוּ שָׁמַיִם וָאָרֶץ.[8] (הוּא הָיָה אוֹמֵר:[9] הַכֹּל צָפוּי וְהַכֹּל גָּלוּי וְהַכֹּל לְפִי דַעְתּוֹ שֶׁל אָדָם).[10]

וְאִלְמָלֵא כֵּן הָיוּ מוֹסְרִין לוֹ מַפְתְּחוֹת — And were it not so (i.e., if he *did* have this capacity), he would be handed "keys" **וְיוֹדֵעַ** what "likeness" is above.[7] **בַּמֶּה נִבְרְאוּ שָׁמַיִם וָאָרֶץ** — through which he would be able to know how the heaven and earth were created.[8]

The Baraisa cites some teachings of R' Akiva: **הַכֹּל צָפוּי וְהַכֹּל גָּלוּי** — Everything is seen by God and everything is revealed before Him, **וְהַכֹּל לְפִי דַעְתּוֹ שֶׁל אָדָם** — and everything follows the will of the person.[10] **הוּא הָיָה אוֹמֵר** — He used to say:[9]

---

forgiveness (see, however, *Binyan Yehoshua*, first approach, according to which this *is* the case of the Baraisa). [*Nuschas HaGra*, however, omits the word בַּעֲוֹנוֹ, *in his sin*, entirely.]

7. It is not clear what the Baraisa means here [or the connection it has to what preceded it] (*Velo Od Ella*). [דְּמוּת, *likeness*, cannot mean "image" when used in reference to God, as He has no form or image whatsoever, perceivable to man or otherwise. *Rambam* devotes the first chapter of *Moreh Nevuchim* to explaining the term דְּמוּת.]

Some suggest it means that man is incapable of understanding the *nature* of God (see *Binyan Yehoshua* and *Magen Avos*, first approach), with "likeness" being used in the sense of "clear idea" (see *Ahavas Chesed*). Because man does not have this capacity, he is forbidden to contemplate "what is above," for he will inevitably be led to erroneous and even heretical ideas (see *Chagigah* 11b). Such forbidden contemplation is akin to the sins for which one does not easily receive forgiveness (mentioned previously), which is why the Baraisa places this teaching here (*Magen Avos*, first approach). [See next note for other explanations.]

8. A true understanding of God would endow a person with such powerful intelligence that with it he would be able to perceive even the greatest mysteries of Creation (*Binyan Yehoshua*).

Others explain "what likeness is above" as

referring to the secrets of *Maaseh Merkavah*, a clear understanding of the concepts alluded to by the visions of the Divine Chariot shown to the prophet Ezekiel [see *Chagigah* loc. cit.] (*Magen Avos*, second approach; see also *Ahavas Chesed*).

Ben Avraham suggests a different meaning, according to which the Baraisa is explaining *why* a person falls prey to the sins enumerated above. "What likeness is above" is a reference to the Mishnah in *Avos* (2:1) that teaches: *Consider three things and you will not come into the grip of sin: Know what is above you: a watchful Eye, an attentive Ear, and all your deeds are recorded in a book.* The "likeness above" is the reality of an All-seeing and All-knowing God. Our Baraisa means that a person *considers himself* unable to fully appreciate that reality, and so he does not internalize those truths. For if he did allow himself to grasp that reality, he would not fall prey to sin; morever, he would be handed the keys — the wisdom, understanding, and knowledge — with which to comprehend the creation of heaven and earth.

9. The reference is to R' Akiva, mentioned in *Avos* 3:13; the first teaching cited here is a variation of Mishnah 15 there.

10. The all-knowing God sees all, including the future and what a person will choose. Still, "everything follows the will of the person"; a person has free will to do good or evil (*Binyan Yehoshua, Mefaresh, Ahavas Chesed, Velo Od Ella* [first approach], *Avos HaRosh*, from *Rambam* to *Avos* ad

הוּא הָיָה אוֹמֵר[11]: הַכֹּל נָתוּן בְּעֵרָבוֹן וּמְצוּדָה פְּרוּסָה עַל כָּל הַחַיִּים וְכוּ'[13].

The Baraisa continues its citation of R' Akiva's teachings:

הוּא הָיָה אוֹמֵר — He also used to say:[11]   הַכֹּל נָתוּן בְּעֵרָבוֹן — Everything is given on collateral,[12]   וּמְצוּדָה פְּרוּסָה עַל כָּל הַחַיִּים וְכוּ' — and a net is spread over all the living, etc.[13]

The chapter began by teaching that there are five who do not earn forgiveness easily. The Baraisa now presents a series of teachings to emphasize that

loc.). [The idea that God's foreknowledge does not preclude free will is difficult to grasp. The key to understanding it is the recognition that God's knowledge and way of knowing things differ fundamentally from ours. For further exploration of this profound topic, see *Tos. Yom Tov, Magen Avos,* and *Tiferes Yisrael* to *Avos* ad loc.; *Rambam, Introduction to Avos,* Ch. 8, *Hil. Teshuvah* 5:5, and *Moreh Nevuchim* 3:20.]

[Perhaps this teaching is cited here to emphasize that it is in a person's power to resist "the sins that are not easily forgiven" mentioned earlier in the Baraisa.]

Other commentators, though, explain this teaching as referring to something other than the coexistence of foreknowledge and free will; see *Magen Avos, Velo Od Ella* (second approach), and *Ben Avraham.*

11. This citation is from *Avos* 3:16.

12. This continues the theme of the previous citation, and anticipates the following question: If God sees all, then why are sinners not punished immediately for their misdeeds? The answer is that all is as if given on collateral. True, God may not punish immediately [giving sinners the opportunity to repent], but it is as if He has collateral in His hand for everything, and is sure to collect His "debt" at the time of His choosing (*Binyan Yehoshua,* from *Tos. Yom Tov,* citing earlier commentators). [For different explanations of this teaching, see commetaries on *Avos* ad loc.]

13. The net is death and the Day of Judgment, which no man can escape (*Binyan Yehoshua*).

The Vilna and other printed editions, as well as virtually all the available

manuscripts, abbreviate the citation here with וכו', etc. The balance of the Mishnah there reads: הַחֲנוּת פְּתוּחָה וְהַחֶנְוָנִי מַקִּיף, וְהַפִּנְקָס פָּתוּחַ וְהַיָּד כּוֹתֶבֶת, וְכָל הָרוֹצֶה לִלְווֹת יָבוֹא וְיִלְוֶה, וְהַגַּבָּאִים מַחֲזִירִים תָּדִיר בְּכָל יוֹם, וְנִפְרָעִין מִן הָאָדָם מִדַּעְתּוֹ וְשֶׁלֹּא מִדַּעְתּוֹ, וְיֵשׁ לָהֶם עַל מַה שֶׁיִּסְמוֹכוּ, וְהַדִּין דִּין אֱמֶת, וְהַכֹּל מְתֻקָּן לַסְּעוּדָה, *The store is open and the storekeeper gives credit, and the account book is open and the [storekeeper's] hand writes [what is owed]; and anyone who wants to borrow can come and borrow; and the collectors make their rounds frequently each day, and collect from a person, whether he realizes it or not, but they have something to rely on, and the judgment is a true judgment and everything is prepared for the banquet.* In This World, man is offered the opportunity to find all types of pursuits ("the store is open"), pure and impure alike, and even if he chooses a path of evil for himself, God still does not exact immediate retribution ("the storekeeper gives credit") [see below, note 24]. A person, though, should not mistakenly think that God is not watching his every action, for He *is* recording everything, and He has many messengers through which He can mete out the punishment He deems worthy ("and the collectors make their rounds ..."). And although a person does not always remember the infraction for which he is being punished ("whether he realizes it or not"), which might cause him to question the fairness of God's ways, nevertheless, God is always righteous in His judgment, and He punishes sin in this world to prepare the sinner for the banquet in the World to Come (see *Rav* to *Avos* ad loc.).

תְּשׁוּבַת רְשָׁעִים מְעַכֶּבֶת וּגְזַר דִּינָם מְחוּתָם[15]. וְשַׁלְוַת רְשָׁעִים סוֹפָהּ רָעָה[16].
וְהָרְשׁוּת קוֹבֶרֶת אֶת בְּעָלֶיהָ[17]. תְּשׁוּבָה תּוֹלָה וְיוֹם הַכִּפּוּרִים מְכַפֵּר[18].
תְּשׁוּבָה מְכַפֶּרֶת עַד יוֹם הַמִּיתָה. וְיוֹם הַמִּיתָה (בִּתְשׁוּבָה) [מְמָרֵק].

---

one should nevertheless never despair of repenting, for it is effective in many respects:[14] תְּשׁוּבַת רְשָׁעִים מְעַכֶּבֶת — **The repentance of the wicked forestalls** their punishment, וּגְזַר דִּינָם מְחוּתָם — **even though their decree is** already **sealed.**[15] וְשַׁלְוַת רְשָׁעִים סוֹפָהּ רָעָה — **The tranquility of the wicked is ultimately bad for them,**[16] וְהָרְשׁוּת קוֹבֶרֶת אֶת בְּעָלֶיהָ — **and a position of authority buries the one who holds it.**[17] תְּשׁוּבָה תּוֹלָה וְיוֹם הַכִּפּוּרִים מְכַפֵּר — **For some sins, repentance suspends** punishment **and Yom Kippur atones.**[18] תְּשׁוּבָה מְכַפֶּרֶת עַד יוֹם הַמִּיתָה — **For other sins, repentance atones** temporarily **until the day of the** person's **death,** וְיוֹם הַמִּיתָה בִּתְשׁוּבָה — **and then the day of death** together with the previous **repentance** erases the sin completely.[19]

---

14. *Magen Avos; Ben Avraham.*

15. [This teaching of the Baraisa, together with the two that follow, are cited (with slightly different wording) in *Yoma* 86b.] Even if Heaven has judged a person wicked and sealed his decree of punishment, that decree can be forestalled by his repentance. Some say an individual's repentance will actually *nullify* the decree against him, whereas others say it will only *delay* its implementation (*Tos. HaRosh* to *Yoma* 86b, from *Rosh Hashanah* 18b; *Ahavas Chesed*; see, however, *Magen Avos*).

16. Their tranquility and leisure lead them to indulge in sinful pursuits (*Binyan Yehoshua*, from *Rashi* to *Yoma* ad loc.), which is ultimately to their detriment. [The converse, then, is that challenge and difficulty can ultimately be for a person's benefit.]

17. That is, it causes him to die prematurely. This is learned from Joseph, ruler of Egypt, who died before his brothers, though he was the second youngest (*Binyan Yehoshua*, from *Rashi* ad loc.), because "he conducted himself with authority" (*Berachos* 55b; *Sotah* 13b). [The converse, then, is that remaining in a subordinate position results in a longer life.]

18. [We have rendered this in accordance with *Magen Avos* and *Ben Avraham*.] For some sins, repentance alone will not actually wipe away the sin, but merely suspend punishment until Yom Kippur arrives and atones, thus wiping away the sin. (See above, 29 §5, for elaboration.)

19. *Ben Avraham,* second explanation. According to this explanation, the expression "repentance atones" does not mean actual atonement, but only that it "suspends" punishment (ibid.). [We have followed the reading found in the manuscripts and early prints of *Avos DeRabbi Nassan*: וְיוֹם הַמִּיתָה בִּתְשׁוּבָה. In the Vilna edition, the word בִּתְשׁוּבָה, *with repentance,* here is placed in parentheses, to be replaced with the bracketed word מְמָרֵק, *erases.*]

The Baraisa thus lists here some of the various combinations of repentance, Yom Kippur, and death that it discussed in greater detail above in 29 §5 (*Ben Avraham*).

Others explain the last two clauses of the Baraisa as independent (albeit related) statements, teaching that one must never consider it too late to repent. The first clause teaches that "repentance atones until the day of death" — even if one has lived nearly his entire life in sin, repentance will atone. And the second clause teaches "and even the day of death with repentance" — even if the [start of the] day of death arrived *before* his repentance. That is, even if one did not repent until the final day of his life, his repentance is accepted (*Magen Avos*).

מְשַׁלְּמִין לָרְשָׁעִים וּמַקִּיפִין לַצַּדִּיקִים‎[21]. מְשַׁלְּמִין לָרְשָׁעִים [בָּעוֹלָם הַזֶּה]
בִּבְנֵי אָדָם שֶׁעָשׂוּ אֶת הַתּוֹרָה בְּעַיִן רָעָה וְלֹא נִמְצָא בָהֶם דָּבָר טוֹב מֵעוֹלָם‎[22].
וּמַקִּיפִין לַצַּדִּיקִים בִּבְנֵי אָדָם שֶׁעָשׂוּ אֶת הַתּוֹרָה בְּעַיִן יָפָה וְלֹא נִמְצָא
בָהֶם דָּבָר רָע‎[23], נוֹתְנִין לְאֵלּוּ וָאֵלּוּ קִמְעָה וְהַשְּׁאָר מוֹנֶה לָהֶם (מְרוּבֶּה‎[24].

The Baraisa elaborates on the teaching, "the shop is open and the shop-keeper gives credit," mentioned above:[20] מְשַׁלְּמִין לָרְשָׁעִים וּמַקִּיפִין לַצַּדִּיקִים — The wicked are paid, but the righteous are given credits.[21] The Baraisa elaborates: מְשַׁלְּמִין לָרְשָׁעִים בָּעוֹלָם הַזֶּה — When we say "the wicked are paid in this world," בִּבְנֵי אָדָם שֶׁעָשׂוּ אֶת הַתּוֹרָה בְּעַיִן רָעָה — it refers to people who did the mitzvos of the Torah stingily and there was no good thing to be found in them ever.[22] וּמַקִּיפִין לַצַּדִּיקִים — And when we say "but the righteous are given credits," בִּבְנֵי אָדָם — it refers to people who did the mitzvos of the Torah generously and there was no bad thing to be found in them.[23] נוֹתְנִין לְאֵלּוּ וָאֵלּוּ קִמְעָה — Both these and those (the wicked and the righteous) are given a little good in this world, וְהַשְּׁאָר מוֹנֶה לָהֶם מְרוּבֶּה — while the remainder of their due is counted out to them in great measure in the World to Come.[24]

---

20. *Magen Avos.* [This teaching appears in that part of the Mishnah whose citation was abridged above — see note 13.]

21. The "open shop" refers to the bounty and blessings of this world (*Magen Avos*). These are "paid" to the wicked, in that they receive in this world the full measure of whatever good they have done; no reward is left for them to receive in the World to Come. [See *Kisei Rachamim* here, who cites several reasons why the wicked are rewarded only in this world.] The righteous, too, receive some of the bounty and blessings of this world, but for them it is not "payment." It is but a small measure of what they deserve. The vastness of their reward is given to them as credits, which they will redeem in the World to Come (*Mefaresh; Ben Avraham*). Thus, they eat the "fruits" of their righteousness in this world, but the "principal" is reserved for them in the World to Come (*Mefaresh* below).

22. Whatever mitzvos they did do were done "stingily" — always tainted with ulterior motives, never for the sake of Heaven ("no good thing to be found in them ever") (*Mefaresh*). Alternatively, these are two distinct things:

They did few mitzvos ("stingily"), and even the few they did do were done for ulterior motives (*Ben Avraham*). Such people do not deserve to bask in the glory of the World to Come even for the limited mitzvos they have performed. Therefore, God repays them for their few good deeds while they are still alive (see further, *Kisei Rachamim*). These wicked people are paid fully in this world.

23. Their mitzvos were done "generously" — for the sake of Heaven, with no ulterior motives ("no bad thing to be found in them") (*Mefaresh*). Alternatively, these are two distinct things: They did numerous mitzvos ("generously") and they were done purely for the sake of Heaven (*Ben Avraham*). These people deserve to have their main reward reserved for the World to Come, a moment of whose happiness is superior to all the life of this world (see *Binyan Yehoshua* below).

24. The rewards of the righteous and the punishments of the wicked meted out to them in the World to Come completely dwarf the relatively negligible good they enjoy in this world. Whatever good they enjoy in this world, then, is only "a little" in the ultimate

הוּא הָיָה אוֹמֵר: הַכֹּל יוֹצֵא וְהוֹלֵךְ עָרוֹם וְהַלְוַאי שֶׁתְּהֵא יְצִיאָה
כְּבִיאָה.[25] רַבִּי מֵאִיר אוֹמֵר: חָבִיב אָדָם שֶׁנִּבְרָא בְּצֶלֶם אֱלֹהִים, שֶׁנֶּאֱמַר
(בראשית ט, ו) "כִּי בְּצֶלֶם אֱלֹהִים עָשָׂה אֶת הָאָדָם".[26] חֲבִיבִין יִשְׂרָאֵל
שֶׁנִּקְרְאוּ בָנִים לַמָּקוֹם, שֶׁנֶּאֱמַר (דברים יד, א) "בָּנִים אַתֶּם לַיָי אֱלֹהֵיכֶם".[27]

Additional teachings of R' Akiva on this theme:
הוּא הָיָה אוֹמֵר — He also used to say: הַכֹּל יוֹצֵא וְהוֹלֵךְ עָרוֹם — Everyone
emerges and comes into this world unclothed; וְהַלְוַאי שֶׁתְּהֵא יְצִיאָה כְּבִיאָה
— if only one's leaving this world would be like his entering it![25]

The Baraisa continues, with a variation of Avos 3:14:
רַבִּי מֵאִיר אוֹמֵר — R' Meir says: Beloved is
man, for he was created in the image of God, שֶׁנֶּאֱמַר "כִּי בְּצֶלֶם אֱלֹהִים
עָשָׂה אֶת הָאָדָם" — as it is stated, For in the image of God He made man
(Genesis 9:6).[26] חֲבִיבִין יִשְׂרָאֵל שֶׁנִּקְרְאוּ בָנִים לַמָּקוֹם — Beloved are the people
of Israel, for they are described as children of the Omnipresent, שֶׁנֶּאֱמַר
"בָּנִים אַתֶּם לַיָי אֱלֹהֵיכֶם" — as it is stated, You are children of HASHEM, your

---

scheme of things (see Binyan Yehoshua and
Ahavas Chesed).

The Baraisa uses the expression "counted
out to them" to indicate that everything is
meted out precisely, according to a person's
deeds (Ben Avraham). [The text printed in
Kisei Rachamim, though, has the reading:
וְהַשְׁאָר "מוּנָח" לָהֶם מְרוּבֶּה, while the remainder
"is reserved" for them in great measure.]

Magen Avos cites approvingly the significantly different reading of Avos DeRabbi
Nassan, Nusach 2, Ch. 44, according to
which the "credit" refers to credit extended,
i.e., the customer is allowed to take goods
from the shop without the apparent means
to pay for them. The reading is as follows:
מַקִּיפִין לָרְשָׁעִים וְאֵין מַקִּיפִין לַצַּדִּיקִים — Credit is extended to the wicked but credit is not extended
to the righteous. מַקִּיפִין לָרְשָׁעִים בָּעוֹלָם הַזֶּה
כְּבְנֵי אָדָם שֶׁעָשׂוּ אֶת הַתּוֹרָה — Credit is extended
to the wicked in this world, as [if they were]
people who fulfilled the Torah כְּדֵי שֶׁיִּפָּרַע
מֵהֶם לֶעָתִיד לָבֹא וְאֵין זוֹכֵר לָהֶם כָּל מַעֲשֵׂיהֶם — (in
order to exact retribution from them in the Fu-
ture) without [apparent] remembrance of their
[evil] deeds. כָּל כַּךְ לָמָה, בִּשְׁבִיל לִיתֵּן לָהֶן שָׂכָר
מִצְוָה קַלָּה שֶׁעָשׂוּ בָּעוֹלָם הַזֶּה כְּדֵי שֶׁיִּפָּרַע מֵהֶם לֶעָתִיד
לָבֹא — Why all this? In order to give them in
this world the reward for the few mitzvos they

did, so that they will be punished [fully] in
the Future. וּמְיַסְּרִין לַצַּדִּיקִים בָּעוֹלָם הַזֶּה כִּבְנֵי
אָדָם שֶׁשָּׂרְפוּ אֶת הַתּוֹרָה — And the righteous
are given suffering in this world, as if [they
were] people who burned the Torah, וְאֵין
זוֹכֵר לָהֶם כָּל מַעֲשִׂים טוֹבִים — without [apparent]
remembrance of all their good deeds. כָּל כַּךְ
לָמָה, בִּשְׁבִיל לְהִפָּרַע מֵהֶם הֶפְסֵד עֲבֵירָה שֶׁעָשׂוּ בָּעוֹלָם
הַזֶּה — Why all this? In order to punish them
in this world for the few sins they did, כְּדֵי
שֶׁיִּתֵּן לָהֶם שָׂכָר טוֹב מֻשְׁלָם לֶעָתִיד לָבֹא — so that
they will be given the good reward in full in
the Future. אֵלּוּ וָאֵלּוּ נוֹטְלִין שְׂכָרָן וְהַקֶּרֶן קַיֶּימֶת לוֹ
לָעוֹלָם הַבָּא — These and those take reward [in
this world] while the principal [recompense] is
reserved for him in the World to Come.

25. The pristine state of the newborn's unclothed body represents his pure, unblem-
ished state. Oh, that one would leave the
world as free of sin as he entered it! (Magen
Avos, Binyan Yehoshua; see Bava Metzia
107a [end]).

26. God has no physical form or image.
When the verse says that man is made in the
"image" of God, it means that he is endowed
with some Godly quality that sets him apart
from all other creatures, such as intellectual
perception (Rambam, Moreh Nevuchim 1:1;
Magen Avos to Avos there; see above, note

חֲבִיבִין יִשְׂרָאֵל שֶׁנִּיתַּן לָהֶם כְּלִי חֶמְדָּה שֶׁבּוֹ נִבְרָא הָעוֹלָם[28], שֶׁנֶּאֱמַר (משלי ד, ב) ״כִּי לֶקַח טוֹב נָתַתִּי לָכֶם תּוֹרָתִי אַל תַּעֲזֹבוּ״[29]). רַבִּי אֶלְעָזָר בַּר צָדוֹק אוֹמֵר: לְמָה הַצַּדִּיקִים דּוֹמִים בָּעוֹלָם הַזֶּה, לְאִילָן שֶׁעוֹמֵד בִּמְקוֹם טָהֳרָה וְסוֹכָה יוֹצֵא מִמֶּנּוּ לִמְקוֹם טָמֵא, מַה הֵם אוֹמְרִים: קִצּוּ סוֹכָה זוֹ מִן הָאִילָן וְיִהְיֶה כֻּלּוֹ טָהוֹר כְּדַרְכּוֹ[30]. לְמָה רְשָׁעִים דּוֹמִים בָּעוֹלָם הַזֶּה, לְאִילָן שֶׁעוֹמֵד בִּמְקוֹם טָמֵא וְסוֹכָה יוֹצֵא מִמֶּנּוּ לִמְקוֹם טָהוֹר, מַה הֵן אוֹמְרִים: קִצּוּ סוֹכָה זוֹ מִן הָאִילָן וִיהֵא הָאִילָן כֻּלּוֹ כְּדַרְכּוֹ טָמֵא[31]:

God (Deuteronomy 14:1).[27]   חֲבִיבִין יִשְׂרָאֵל שֶׁנִּיתַּן לָהֶם כְּלִי חֶמְדָּה שֶׁבּוֹ נִבְרָא הָעוֹלָם — Beloved are the people of Israel, for they were given the cherished utensil with which the world was created,[28]   שֶׁנֶּאֱמַר ״כִּי לֶקַח טוֹב נָתַתִּי לָכֶם תּוֹרָתִי אַל תַּעֲזֹבוּ״ — as it is stated, *For I have given you a good teaching, do not forsake My Torah* (Proverbs 4:2).[29]

The Baraisa cites a parable related to the earlier discussion of some of the righteous ones suffering in this world while some of the evil ones flourish:

רַבִּי אֶלְעָזָר בַּר צָדוֹק אוֹמֵר: לְמָה הַצַּדִּיקִים דּוֹמִים בָּעוֹלָם הַזֶּה — R' Elazar bar Tzadok says: To what can the righteous people who suffer in this world be compared?   לְאִילָן שֶׁעוֹמֵד בִּמְקוֹם טָהֳרָה — To a tree that stands rooted in a pure place,   וְסוֹכָה יוֹצֵא מִמֶּנּוּ לִמְקוֹם טָמֵא — with a single branch extending from it into an impure place.   מַה הֵם אוֹמְרִים — What do people say about such a tree?   קוֹצוּ סוֹכָה זוֹ מִן הָאִילָן — "Cut this abnormal branch off the tree,   וְיִהְיֶה כֻּלּוֹ טָהוֹר כְּדַרְכּוֹ — and then the entire [tree] will be in a pure place, as is normal for it."[30]   לְמָה רְשָׁעִים דּוֹמִים בָּעוֹלָם הַזֶּה — And to what can the wicked people who prosper in this world be compared?   לְאִילָן שֶׁעוֹמֵד בִּמְקוֹם טָמֵא — To a tree that stands rooted in an impure place,   וְסוֹכָה יוֹצֵא מִמֶּנּוּ — with a single branch extending from it into a pure place.   לִמְקוֹם טָהוֹר — What do people say about such a tree?   מַה הֵן אוֹמְרִים — What do people say about such a tree?   קִצּוּ סוֹכָה זוֹ מִן הָאִילָן — "Cut this abnormal branch off the tree   וִיהֵא הָאִילָן כֻּלּוֹ כְּדַרְכּוֹ טָמֵא — and then the entire tree will be standing in an impure place, as is normal for it."[31]

---

7) or free will (*Tiferes Yisrael* to *Avos* ad loc. §89; *Nefesh HaChaim* 1:1-3).

27. Although all people are created in the image of God, the Chosen People have the special status of being deemed God's children.

28. Meaning, the most precious gift of all, the Torah, which God used as His blueprint when creating the world (*Rashi* to *Avos* ad loc.; see *Bereishis Rabbah* 1 §1).

29. The Torah is called a *"good"* teaching, alluding to the "good" world that was created based on it, as stated many times in

the passages of Creation, that God saw what He had made and it was "good" (*Rav* and *Magen Avos* to *Avos* loc. cit.).

30. A righteous person, who is almost entirely pure, stands rooted in the World to Come. His few sins are the anomaly. Therefore, it is only fitting that those "irregular branches" of impurity be removed in this world through suffering, so that he will remain entirely pure in the World to Come (*Binyan Yehoshua*, from *Kiddushin* 40b).

31. A wicked person, who is almost entirely

ב. שִׁשָּׁה שֵׁמוֹת נִקְרָא הָאַרְיֵה. אַרְיֵה[32] כְּפִיר[33] לָבִיא[34] לַיִשׁ[35] שַׁחַל[36] שַׁחַץ[37]:

ג. שִׁשָּׁה שֵׁמוֹת נִקְרָא נָחָשׁ. [נָחָשׁ[38]] שָׂרָף.[39] תַּנִּין.[40] צִפְעוֹנִי.[41] אֶפְעֶה.[42] עַכְשׁוּב[43]:

ד. שִׁשָּׁה שֵׁמוֹת נִקְרָא שְׁלֹמֹה.[44] יְדִידְיָה.[45] קֹהֶלֶת.[46] בֶּן יָקֶה.[47] אָגוּר.[48] לְמוּאֵל[49]:

---

§2 The Baraisa resumes its presentation of groups of six:

שִׁשָּׁה שֵׁמוֹת נִקְרָא הָאַרְיֵה — By **six names** is a **lion** referred to in Scripture: אַרְיֵה כְּפִיר לָבִיא לַיִשׁ שַׁחַל שַׁחַץ — (i) *Aryeh*,[32] (ii) *Kefir*,[33] (iii) *Lavi*,[34] (iv) *Layish*,[35] (v) *Shachal*,[36] (vi) and *Shachatz*.[37]

§3 שִׁשָּׁה שֵׁמוֹת נִקְרָא נָחָשׁ — By **six names** is a **snake** referred to in Scripture: נָחָשׁ שָׂרָף. תַּנִּין. צִפְעוֹנִי. אֶפְעֶה. עַכְשׁוּב — (i) *Nachash*,[38] (ii) *Saraf*,[39] (iii) *Tanin*,[40] (iv) *Tzif'oni*,[41] (v) *Ef'eh*,[42] (vi) and *Achshuv*.[43]

§4 שִׁשָּׁה שֵׁמוֹת נִקְרָא שְׁלֹמֹה — By **six names** is King **Solomon** referred to in Scripture: In addition to (i) Shlomo,[44] we find: יְדִידְיָה. קֹהֶלֶת. בֶּן יָקֶה. אָגוּר. לְמוּאֵל — (ii) *Yedidiah*,[45] (iii) *Koheles*,[46] (iv) *Bin Yakeh*,[47] (v) *Agur*,[48] (vi) and *Lemuel*.[49]

---

impure, stands rooted in this world of impurity. His few good deeds are the anomaly. Therefore, it is only fitting that those "irregular branches" of purity be removed in this world through prosperity, so that nothing of him shall stand in the World to Come (ibid.).

32. *Genesis* 49:9, et al. [Most texts have here אֲרִי, *Ari*, which also appears many times in Scripture; see *Proverbs* 22:13, et al.]

33. *Isaiah* 31:4, et al.

34. *Genesis* 49:9, et al.

35. *Proverbs* 30:30; *Job* 4:11.

36. *Hosea* 13:7, et al.

37. *Job* 28:8 and 41:25.

See *Avos DeRabbi Nassan, Nusach 2*, Ch. 43 (cited also by *Magen Avos* here) regarding the distinct connotation of each name. See also *Avos HaRosh*.

38. *Genesis* 3:1, et. al.

39. *Deuteronomy* 8:15, et al.

40. *Isaiah* 51:9.

41. Ibid. 11:8 and 59:5.

42. Ibid. 30:6 and 59:5; *Job* 20:16.

43. *Psalms* 140:4.

See *Avos DeRabbi Nassan, Nusach 2*, Ch. 43 (cited also by *Magen Avos*) regarding the distinct connotation of each name.

44. *II Samuel* 12:24, et al.

45. Ibid. v. 25.

46. *Ecclesiastes* 1:1, et al.

47. *Proverbs* 30:1.

48. Ibid.

49. Ibid. 31:1.

See *Targum Sheni* to *Esther* 1:2, where reasons are given for Solomon's various names.

﴾ פֶּרֶק מ ﴿

א. אַרְבָּעָה דְבָרִים אָדָם הָעוֹשֶׂה אוֹתָן אוֹכֵל פֵּירוֹתֵיהֶן בָּעוֹלָם הַזֶּה וְהַקֶּרֶן קַיֶּמֶת לָעוֹלָם הַבָּא.¹ אֵלּוּ הֵן: כִּבּוּד אָב וָאֵם וּגְמִילוּת חֲסָדִים וַהֲבָאַת שָׁלוֹם בֵּין אָדָם לַחֲבֵירוֹ וְתַלְמוּד תּוֹרָה כְּנֶגֶד כֻּלָּם.² אַרְבָּעָה דְבָרִים אָדָם הָעוֹשֶׂה אוֹתָן נִפְרָעִין מִמֶּנּוּ בָּעוֹלָם הַזֶּה וְלָעוֹלָם הַבָּא.³ עֲבוֹדַת כּוֹכָבִים וְגִילּוּי עֲרָיוֹת וּשְׁפִיכוּת דָּמִים⁴

﴾ CHAPTER 40 ﴿

§1 The Baraisa continues presenting numerical sets, beginning with a set of four that is taken from the first Mishnah in *Peah*:

אַרְבָּעָה דְבָרִים — There are **four things** (i.e., mitzvos) אָדָם הָעוֹשֶׂה אוֹכֵל פֵּירוֹתֵיהֶן בָּעוֹלָם הַזֶּה — **for which a person who fulfills them eats their fruits in this world,** וְהַקֶּרֶן קַיֶּמֶת לָעוֹלָם הַבָּא — but **the principal** reward **remains intact** for him to enjoy in **the World to Come.**[1] אֵלּוּ הֵן — **They are:** כִּבּוּד אָב וָאֵם — (i) **honoring one's father and mother;** וּגְמִילוּת חֲסָדִים — (ii) **performing** acts of **kindness;** וַהֲבָאַת שָׁלוֹם בֵּין אָדָם לַחֲבֵירוֹ — (iii) **bringing about peace between one person and his fellow;** וְתַלְמוּד תּוֹרָה כְּנֶגֶד כֻּלָּם — (iv) and **Torah study is equal to them all.**[2]

Another set of four that parallels the preceding one:

אַרְבָּעָה דְבָרִים — There are **four** sinful **things** אָדָם הָעוֹשֶׂה אוֹתָן נִפְרָעִין מִמֶּנּוּ בָּעוֹלָם הַזֶּה וְלָעוֹלָם הַבָּא — **for which a person who does them is punished in** both **this world and the World to Come.**[3] They are: עֲבוֹדַת כּוֹכָבִים — (i) **idolatry;** וְגִילּוּי עֲרָיוֹת — (ii) **immorality;** וּשְׁפִיכוּת דָּמִים — (iii) **bloodshed;**[4]

---

1. Generally speaking, God does not grant reward in this world for performing the mitzvos, but reserves it for the World to Come. However, the four mitzvos listed here are unique in that they have two aspects to them: one who performs them fulfills God's Will, and he also benefits others. [Studying Torah is counted among these, since it leads to the fulfillment of all the commandments, including those that cause one to benefit others (see the following note).] Therefore, aside from the reward that he will receive for having fulfilled God's Will, which is reserved entirely for the World to Come, it is only right that he be rewarded in this world for having brought benefit to the other inhabitants of the world. It is this additional reward that the Mishnah refers to as "fruits," whereas the

reward for the actual mitzvah is called "principal" (*Rambam, Mishnah Commentary* to *Peah* 1:1, cited by *Binyan Yehoshua*).

2. Through studying Torah, a person knows how to properly perform all the other mitzvos (ibid.). In addition, Torah study is an antidote to the evil inclination (*Kiddushin* 30b), allowing the person to follow his innate desire to fulfill God's will (*Kisei Rachamim*).

3. That is, even the wicked, who enjoy relative serenity in this world so as to receive their due punishment in the next world (see above, 39 §1), are punished for these sins in this world as well (*Binyan Yehoshua*).

4. These are the three cardinal sins for which one must give his life rather than transgress (*Sanhedrin* 74a).

וְלָשׁוֹן הָרַע יוֹתֵר מִכּוּלָם:[5]

ב. זְכוּת יֵשׁ לָהּ קֶרֶן וְיֵשׁ לָהּ פֵּירוֹת[6], שֶׁנֶּאֱמַר (ישעיה ג, י) "אִמְרוּ צַדִּיק כִּי טוֹב כִּי פְרִי מַעַלְלֵיהֶם יֹאכֵלוּ". עֲבֵירָה יֵשׁ לָהּ קֶרֶן וְאֵין לָהּ פֵּירוֹת[7], שֶׁנֶּאֱמַר (שם פסוק יא) "אוֹי לְרָשָׁע רָע וְגוֹ' ". וְיֵשׁ אוֹמְרִים: יֵשׁ לָהֶם לַעֲבֵירוֹת פֵּירוֹת, שֶׁנֶּאֱמַר (משלי א, לא) "וְיֹאכְלוּ מִפְּרִי דַרְכָּם וּמִמֹּעֲצֹתֵיהֶם יִשְׂבָּעוּ"[9]:

וְלָשׁוֹן הָרַע יוֹתֵר מִכּוּלָם — (iv) and *lashon hara* is more severe than all of them.[5]

§2 The Baraisa discusses further the topic of principal and fruits of one's actions:

זְכוּת יֵשׁ לָהּ קֶרֶן וְיֵשׁ לָהּ פֵּירוֹת — A meritorious act has both principal reward and fruits,[6] שֶׁנֶּאֱמַר "אִמְרוּ צַדִּיק כִּי טוֹב כִּי פְרִי מַעַלְלֵיהֶם יֹאכֵלוּ" — as it is stated, *Tell [each] righteous man that it is good; for they shall eat the fruit of their deeds* (Isaiah 3:10). עֲבֵירָה יֵשׁ לָהּ קֶרֶן וְאֵין לָהּ פֵּירוֹת — A sin, however, has principal punishment but no fruit,[7] שֶׁנֶּאֱמַר "אוֹי לְרָשָׁע רָע וְגוֹ' " — as it says, *But woe to the wicked person who does evil,* for the recompense of his hands will be dealt to him (ibid. v. 11).[8] וְיֵשׁ אוֹמְרִים: יֵשׁ לָהֶם לַעֲבֵירוֹת פֵּירוֹת — However, some say that sins *do* have fruits, שֶׁנֶּאֱמַר "וְיֹאכְלוּ מִפְּרִי דַרְכָּם וּמִמֹּעֲצֹתֵיהֶם יִשְׂבָּעוּ" — as it says regarding sinners, *They will eat of the fruit of their way and will be sated with their own schemes* (Proverbs 1:31).[9]

5. See, similarly, *Arachin* 15b. Although one is not obligated to give his life in the case of *lashon hara* (evil speech), it is more serious than the other three in certain respects: For example, *lashon hara* is more likely to become a habit and to be spoken often and without restraint, leading to multiple transgressions every day. It also more difficult to repent for *lashon hara*, since people often do not realize the gravity of the sin, and also, because it is often impossible to ask forgiveness from all the people one spoke about (see further, *Shaarei Teshuvah* 3:202-207, pp. 546-556 in the Jaffa ed.; see also Introduction to *Chafetz Chaim*).

6. In this context, "fruits" does not refer to reward in this world, which is granted only for the four mitzvos listed in the previous section. Rather, it refers to additional reward (in the World to Come) beyond what a person deserves for performing the mitzvah. Every meritorious act has such "fruits" (*Anaf Yosef* to *Kiddushin* 40a, from *Shevus*

Yaakov there, based on *Rashi* [cited in the following note]).

7. That is, one is not punished over and above what he deserves for the wickedness of his act (*Rashi* to *Kiddushin* 40a, ד"ה אין לו פירות).

8. The verse implies that he will be repaid *only* for the acts of his hands ("principal") but not more than that.

9. This does not mean that a sinner will receive a greater punishment than he deserves. Rather, it is as the Gemara (*Kiddushin* 40a) explains, that when one's sins do not "bear fruit" [i.e., they do not cause others to follow his ways and further desecrate God's Name (*Rashi* ad loc.)], then the punishment also has no "fruit," meaning, it is no greater than what is appropriate for the sin itself. If, however, the sin *does* bear fruits, then the punishment, too, has "fruits," in that it is greater than what is deserved for the sin alone, as the perpetrator bears responsibility

ג. כָּל הַמְזַכֶּה אֶת הָרַבִּים אֵין מְגַלְגְּלִין עֲבֵירָה עַל יָדוֹ שֶׁלֹּא יְהֵא
תַּלְמִידָיו נוֹחֲלִין הָעוֹלָם הַבָּא וְהוּא יוֹרֵד לִשְׁאוֹל, שֶׁנֶּאֱמַר (תהלים טז,
י) "כִּי לֹא תַעֲזֹב נַפְשִׁי לִשְׁאוֹל"[10]. וְכָל הַמַּחֲטִיא אֶת הָרַבִּים אֵין מַסְפִּיקִין
בְּיָדוֹ לַעֲשׂוֹת תְּשׁוּבָה[11] כְּדֵי שֶׁלֹּא יִהְיוּ תַלְמִידָיו יוֹרְדִים לִשְׁאוֹל וְהוּא
נוֹחֵל הָעוֹלָם הַבָּא, שֶׁנֶּאֱמַר (משלי כח, יז) "אָדָם עָשֻׁק בְּדַם נָפֶשׁ עַד בּוֹר
יָנוּס"[12]:

ד. הָאוֹמֵר: אֶחֱטָא וְאָשׁוּב, אֵין מַסְפִּיקִין בְּיָדוֹ לַעֲשׂוֹת תְּשׁוּבָה.[13]

---

§3 The Baraisa elaborates upon *Avos* 5:18:

אֵין — כָּל הַמְזַכֶּה אֶת הָרַבִּים — Whoever causes the public to do good,
מְגַלְגְּלִין עֲבֵירָה עַל יָדוֹ — will not have the opportunity to sin come his way,
שֶׁלֹּא יְהֵא תַלְמִידָיו נוֹחֲלִין הָעוֹלָם הַבָּא וְהוּא יוֹרֵד לִשְׁאוֹל — so that there should
not be a situation where his disciples inherit a share in the World to Come
while he, who elevated them, descends to Gehinnom. He is therefore given
Divine protection from sin, שֶׁנֶּאֱמַר "כִּי לֹא תַעֲזֹב נַפְשִׁי לִשְׁאוֹל" — as it says,
*Because You will not abandon my soul to the netherworld, You will not al-
low Your devout one to witness destruction* (Psalms 16:10).[10] וְכָל הַמַּחֲטִיא
אֶת הָרַבִּים — But whoever causes the public to sin אֵין מַסְפִּיקִין בְּיָדוֹ לַעֲשׂוֹת
תְּשׁוּבָה — will not be given the opportunity to repent for his sins,[11] כְּדֵי שֶׁלֹּא
יִהְיוּ תַלְמִידָיו יוֹרְדִים לִשְׁאוֹל וְהוּא נוֹחֵל הָעוֹלָם הַבָּא — so that his disciples do not
descend to Gehinnom while he, who caused them to sin, inherits a share in
the World to Come, שֶׁנֶּאֱמַר "אָדָם עָשֻׁק בְּדַם נָפֶשׁ עַד בּוֹר יָנוּס" — as it says,
A man guilty of bloodshed will flee until the grave; no one will support him
(Proverbs 28:17).[12]

§4 The Baraisa mentions other cases in which one forfeits the privilege to
earn forgiveness for his sins (paraphrasing the Mishnah, *Yoma* 85b):
הָאוֹמֵר: אֶחֱטָא וְאָשׁוּב — If one says, "I will sin and then I will repent," and he
proceeds to sin, אֵין מַסְפִּיקִין בְּיָדוֹ לַעֲשׂוֹת תְּשׁוּבָה — he will not be given the

---

for the effects of his behavior (see *Binyan Yehoshua, Ben Avraham*).

10. The verse teaches that God prevents the righteous from falling into Gehinnom. [Since God does not generally interfere with a person's free will, it must be that] this goal is achieved by ensuring that the opportunity to sin does not come their way (*Rashi* to *Yoma* 87a, cited by *Binyan Yehoshua*).

11. I.e., God will not help such a person repent. If, however, he *does* repent despite the lack of Divine aid, his repentance will

be accepted and he will be given a share in the World to Come (*Rambam, Hil. Teshuvah* 4:1,6).

12. The verse is understood as saying that one who is guilty of spiritually "murdering" his friend by causing him to sin may try to repent and thereby achieve atonement for his sin ["*will flee*"] his entire life ["*until the grave*"], but the Heavenly Court will not afford him this opportunity ["*no one will support him*"] (*Binyan Yehoshua*, citing *Rashi* to the verse; see also *Rashi* to *Yoma* 87a).

אֶחֱטָא וְיוֹם הַכִּפּוּרִים מְכַפֵּר, אֵין יוֹם הַכִּפּוּרִים מְכַפֵּר.[14] אֶחֱטָא וְיוֹם
הַמִּיתָה מְמָרֵק, אֵין יוֹם הַמִּיתָה מְמָרֵק:[15]

ה. רַבִּי אֶלְעָזָר בְּרַבִּי יוֹסֵי אוֹמֵר: הַחוֹטֵא וְשָׁב וְהוֹלֵךְ לְתוּמּוֹ[16], אֵינוּ זָז
מִמְּקוֹמוֹ עַד שֶׁמּוֹחֲלִין לוֹ[17]. וְהָאוֹמֵר: אֶחֱטָא וְאָשׁוּב, מוֹחֲלִין לוֹ עַד
שְׁלֹשָׁה פְעָמִים וְלֹא יוֹתֵר:[18]

---

opportunity to repent.[13]   אֶחֱטָא וְיוֹם הַכִּפּוּרִים מְכַפֵּר — Similarly, if one says,
"I will sin and Yom Kippur will atone for my sin,"   אֵין יוֹם הַכִּפּוּרִים מְכַפֵּר —
Yom Kippur will not atone for his sin.[14]   אֶחֱטָא וְיוֹם הַמִּיתָה מְמָרֵק — And
similarly, if one says, "I will sin and the day of my death will purge the sin,"
אֵין יוֹם הַמִּיתָה מְמָרֵק — the day of his death will not purge his sin.[15]

§5 The Baraisa cites another teaching concerning repentance:
הַחוֹטֵא   רַבִּי אֶלְעָזָר בְּרַבִּי יוֹסֵי אוֹמֵר — R' Elazar the son of R' Yose says:
וְשָׁב וְהוֹלֵךְ לְתוּמּוֹ — If one sins and then repents and proceeds to act with integrity,[16]   אֵינוּ זָז מִמְּקוֹמוֹ עַד שֶׁמּוֹחֲלִין לוֹ — he does not move from his place
until he is forgiven.[17]   וְהָאוֹמֵר: אֶחֱטָא וְאָשׁוּב — But if one says, "I will sin
and then I will repent," and proceeds to sin,   מוֹחֲלִין לוֹ עַד שְׁלֹשָׁה פְעָמִים וְלֹא
יוֹתֵר — he is forgiven up to three times, but not more.[18]

---

13. This too means that God will not help him
repent; but if he does repent, his repentance
is accepted (*Rambam,* cited in note 11).

14. There are numerous levels of sin: the
least severe sins require only repentance to
be erased; the more severe ones require Yom
Kippur as well; those that are even more severe require afflictions; and there are some
that are so severe that they are not completely purged until the sinner's death. However,
neither Yom Kippur, afflictions, nor death can
achieve atonement for any sin unless the sinner has repented. See above, 29 §5.

When it says that Yom Kippur will
atone, it carries the same connotation as
the previous phrase, "he will not be given
the opportunity to repent"; that is, God will
not help him accomplish that which must be
done on Yom Kippur for his sin to be atoned
(*Rambam, Mishnah Commentary, Yoma*
8:9, cited by *Binyan Yehoshua*).

15. [I.e., he will not be given the opportunity
to repent before he dies, and therefore his
death will not atone for his sin; see the previous note.] In whatever form it is attained,

atonement is a gift from God. Accordingly,
when one sins and relies on the fact that his
sin will be forgiven, he is using the gift of
atonement to *increase* his sin, for had it not
been for the concept of atonement, he would
have been afraid to sin. Such a person does
not deserve to benefit from this kindness
(see *Meiri, Chibbur HaTeshuvah, Maamar* 1,
Ch. 3).

16. That is, he accepts upon himself to avoid
repeating the transgression (*Ben Avraham*).

17. This refers to the sins for which repentance alone is sufficient (ibid.; see similar
usage of this phrase above, 29 §5).

18. I.e., he is forgiven the first two times that
he does this, but not the third time (*Ahavas
Chesed, Ben Avraham*). R' Elazar seems to
disagree with the opinion cited in the previous section, which maintains that such a
person is not given the opportunity to repent
even after one repeat transgression. In R'
Elazar's view, however, this does not apply until three times (see *Mefaresh* and *Ben
Avraham;* but see *Magen Avos* and *Ahavas
Chesed,* who reconcile the two teachings).

ו. אַרְבַּע מִדּוֹת בָּאָדָם. הָאוֹמֵר: שֶׁלִּי שֶׁלְּךָ וְשֶׁלְּךָ שֶׁלִּי וְכוּ'.[19] אַרְבַּע מִדּוֹת בַּתַּלְמִידִים.[20] הָרוֹצֶה °שֶׁיִּלְמוֹד °וְיִלְמְדוּ אֲחֵרִים עַיִן טוֹבָה.[21] °יִלְמוֹד וְלֹא °יִלְמְדוּ אֲחֵרִים עַיִן רָעָה.[22] °יִלְמְדוּ אֲחֵרִים וְהוּא לֹא °יִלְמוֹד זוֹ מִדָּה בֵּינוֹנִית[23] וְיֵשׁ אוֹמְרִים: זוֹ מִדַּת סְדוֹם.[24] לֹא °יִלְמוֹד וְלֹא °יִלְמְדוּ אֲחֵרִים הֲרֵי זֶה רָשָׁע גָּמוּר.[25] אַרְבַּע[26] מִדּוֹת בַּהוֹלְכֵי לְבֵית הַמִּדְרָשׁ.

---

§6 The Baraisa resumes presenting sets of four. The following set is from *Avos* 5:10:

אַרְבַּע מִדּוֹת בָּאָדָם — **There are four types of people:** הָאוֹמֵר: שֶׁלִּי שֶׁלְּךָ וְשֶׁלְּךָ שֶׁלִּי וְכוּ' — **One who says, "What is mine is yours and** what is **yours is mine,"** is an ignoramus, etc.[19]

Another set of four:

אַרְבַּע מִדּוֹת בַּתַּלְמִידִים — **There are four types of students:**[20] הָרוֹצֶה שֶׁיִּלְמַד וְיִלְמְדוּ אֲחֵרִים — **(i) One who desires that he** himself **should teach** Torah and **that others should** also **teach** Torah עַיִן טוֹבָה — **has a good eye.**[21] יִלְמַד וְלֹא יִלְמְדוּ אֲחֵרִים — **(ii) One who desires that he** himself **should teach** Torah **but that others should not** עַיִן רָעָה — **has an evil eye.**[22] יִלְמְדוּ אֲחֵרִים וְהוּא לֹא יִלְמַד — **(iii) One who desires that others should teach** Torah **but that he** himself **should not —** זוֹ מִדָּה בֵּינוֹנִית — **this is average behavior.**[23] וְיֵשׁ אוֹמְרִים: זוֹ מִדַּת סְדוֹם — **But some say, this is the behavior of Sodom.**[24] לֹא יִלְמַד וְלֹא יִלְמְדוּ אֲחֵרִים — **(iv) One who desires that neither he nor others should teach** Torah הֲרֵי זֶה רָשָׁע גָּמוּר — **is completely wicked.**[25]

The Baraisa now presents another set of four, also dealing with the topic of Torah study. The discussion continues into the following section:[26] אַרְבַּע מִדּוֹת בַּהוֹלְכֵי לְבֵית הַמִּדְרָשׁ — **There are four types among those who go**

---

19. The full statement of the Mishnah reads: (i) One who says, "What is mine is mine and what is yours is yours," this is average behavior; but some say, this is the behavior of Sodom. (ii) "What is mine is yours and what is yours is mine" is an ignoramus. (iii) "What is mine is yours and what is yours is yours" is a pious person. (iv) "What is mine is mine and what is yours is mine" is a wicked person. See the commentators there.

20. Our version of this teaching follows *Nuschas HaGra*.

21. I.e., a positive, generous attitude. This type of student generously shares his Torah knowledge with others, and is not jealous of others who do the same.

22. I.e., a negative and grudging attitude. Although he imparts of his knowledge to others, he does not want anyone else to have this merit.

23. He himself studies Torah and wants others to teach, but he is not willing to take the trouble to teach others.

24. The people of Sodom were not willing to benefit others even when doing so involved no loss to themselves (see *Avos* 5:10, cited in note 19; *Eruvin* 49a with *Rashi* ד"ה מדת סדום). This person is likewise not willing to teach others, even at no loss to himself (*Ahavas Chesed*).

25. He begrudges other people to such an extent that he does not want *anyone* — himself or his fellow students — to teach Torah to others.

26. Our version of this teaching follows *Nuschas HaGra*; see also *Ahavas Chesed*.

מִתְקָרֵב וְיוֹשֵׁב יֵשׁ לוֹ חֵלֶק°[27]. מִתְקָרֵב °וְאֵינוּ יוֹשֵׁב אֵין לוֹ חֵלֶק. מִתְרַחֵק
וְיוֹשֵׁב יֵשׁ לוֹ חֵלֶק מִתְרַחֵק °וְאֵינוּ יוֹשֵׁב אֵין לוֹ חֵלֶק:

ז. °שׁוֹאֵל וּמֵשִׁיב יֵשׁ לוֹ חֵלֶק. ° יוֹשֵׁב וְשׁוֹתֵק אֵין לוֹ חֵלֶק. מִתְקָרֵב
וְיוֹשֵׁב בִּשְׁבִיל שֶׁיִּשְׁמַע וְיִלְמוֹד יֵשׁ לוֹ חֵלֶק. מִתְקָרֵב וְיוֹשֵׁב
מִפְּנֵי שֶׁיֹּאמְרוּ: אִישׁ פְּלוֹנִי מִתְקָרֵב וְיוֹשֵׁב לִפְנֵי חָכָם, אֵין לוֹ חֵלֶק.
מִתְרַחֵק וְיוֹשֵׁב בִּשְׁבִיל שֶׁיִּנְהוֹג כָּבוֹד בְּמִי שֶׁהוּא גָּדוֹל יֵשׁ לוֹ חֵלֶק.

---

to the study hall, each of which has two subdivisions: מִתְקָרֵב וְיוֹשֵׁב יֵשׁ לוֹ
חֵלֶק — (i) There is **one who seats himself close** to the scholars in the study
hall and thereby **has a portion** among them,[27] מִתְקָרֵב וְיוֹשֵׁב אֵין לוֹ חֵלֶק
— and there is **one who seats himself close** to the scholars in the study hall
but **has no portion** among them. מִתְרַחֵק וְיוֹשֵׁב יֵשׁ לוֹ חֵלֶק — (ii) There is
one who seats himself far away from the scholars in the study hall, **who has
a portion** among them, מִתְרַחֵק וְיוֹשֵׁב אֵין לוֹ חֵלֶק — and there is **one who
seats himself far away** from the scholars in the study hall, **who has no portion**
among them.

§7 The latter two pairs of this set of four groups:
יוֹשֵׁב וְשׁוֹאֵל יֵשׁ לוֹ חֵלֶק — (iii) There is **one who sits** with the scholars in the
study hall **and asks** questions, **who has a portion** among them, יוֹשֵׁב וְשׁוֹאֵל
אֵין לוֹ חֵלֶק — and there is **one who sits** with the scholars **and asks** questions,
who has no portion among them. יוֹשֵׁב וְשׁוֹתֵק יֵשׁ לוֹ חֵלֶק — (iv) There is
one who sits with the scholars **and remains silent, who has a portion** among
them, יוֹשֵׁב וְשׁוֹתֵק אֵין לוֹ חֵלֶק — and there is **one who sits** with the scholars
and remains silent, who has no portion among them.

The Baraisa explains each of the four pairs just presented. The first pair:
מִתְקָרֵב וְיוֹשֵׁב בִּשְׁבִיל שֶׁיִּשְׁמַע וְיִלְמוֹד — If **one seats himself close** to the scholars
in the study hall **so that he should hear** their words of Torah **and learn** from
them, יֵשׁ לוֹ חֵלֶק — **he has a portion** among them. מִתְקָרֵב וְיוֹשֵׁב מִפְּנֵי
שֶׁיֹּאמְרוּ: אִישׁ פְּלוֹנִי מִתְקָרֵב וְיוֹשֵׁב לִפְנֵי חָכָם — However, if **one seats himself
close** to the scholars just **so that [people] should say** about him, **"So-and-so
seats himself close to** that **scholar** because he wants to learn Torah from
him," but he does not genuinely desire to do so, אֵין לוֹ חֵלֶק — **he has no
portion** among them.

The second pair:
מִתְרַחֵק וְיוֹשֵׁב בִּשְׁבִיל שֶׁיִּנְהוֹג כָּבוֹד בְּמִי שֶׁהוּא גָּדוֹל — If **one seats himself far
away** from the scholars in the study hall **because he wishes to show respect
for those greater** than him by seating himself below them, יֵשׁ לוֹ חֵלֶק — **he**

---

27. I.e., he is considered one of them (see *Binyan Yehoshua*).

מִתְרַחֵק וְיוֹשֵׁב בִּשְׁבִיל שֶׁיֹּאמְרוּ: אִישׁ פְּלוֹנִי אֵין צָרִיךְ לְחָכָם, זֶה אֵין לוֹ
חֵלֶק. יוֹשֵׁב וְשׁוֹאֵל בִּשְׁבִיל שֶׁיֹּאמְרוּ: אִישׁ פְּלוֹנִי יוֹשֵׁב וְשׁוֹאֵל וּמְשַׁמֵּשׁ
לִפְנֵי חֲכָמִים, (זֶה) אֵין לוֹ חֵלֶק יוֹשֵׁב וְשׁוֹאֵל בִּשְׁבִיל שֶׁיִּשְׁמַע וְיִלְמוֹד יֵשׁ
לוֹ חֵלֶק.[28] יוֹשֵׁב וְשׁוֹתֵק בִּשְׁבִיל שֶׁיִּשְׁמַע וְיִלְמוֹד יֵשׁ לוֹ חֵלֶק. יוֹשֵׁב וְשׁוֹתֵק
בִּשְׁבִיל שֶׁיֹּאמְרוּ: אִישׁ פְּלוֹנִי יוֹשֵׁב וְשׁוֹתֵק לִפְנֵי חֲכָמִים, (זֶה) אֵין לוֹ חֵלֶק:[29]

ח ▪ אַרְבַּע מִדּוֹת בַּיּוֹשְׁבִים לִפְנֵי חֲכָמִים. יֵשׁ דּוֹמֶה לִסְפוֹג יֵשׁ דּוֹמֶה לְנָפָה

---

has a portion among the scholars. מִתְרַחֵק וְיוֹשֵׁב בִּשְׁבִיל שֶׁיֹּאמְרוּ: אִישׁ פְּלוֹנִי
אֵין צָרִיךְ לְחָכָם — However, if **one seats himself far away** from the scholars
in the study hall **so that [people] should say** about him, "So-and-so is so
knowledgeable that he **does not need** to learn Torah from a **scholar**," זֶה אֵין
לוֹ חֵלֶק — **he has no portion** among them.

The third pair:

יוֹשֵׁב וְשׁוֹאֵל בִּשְׁבִיל שֶׁיֹּאמְרוּ: אִישׁ פְּלוֹנִי יוֹשֵׁב וְשׁוֹאֵל וּמְשַׁמֵּשׁ לִפְנֵי חֲכָמִים — If one
sits in the study hall **and asks** questions just **so that [people] should say** about
him, "So-and-so sits before the scholars, asks them questions, **and serves**
them," זֶה אֵין לוֹ חֵלֶק — **he has no portion** among them. יוֹשֵׁב וְשׁוֹאֵל
בִּשְׁבִיל שֶׁיִּשְׁמַע וְיִלְמוֹד — However, if **one sits** in the study hall **and asks** questions so that he should hear words of Torah **and learn** from the scholars, יֵשׁ
לוֹ חֵלֶק — **he has a portion** among them.

The fourth pair:

יוֹשֵׁב וְשׁוֹתֵק בִּשְׁבִיל שֶׁיִּשְׁמַע וְיִלְמוֹד — If one sits in the study hall **and remains**
silent so that he should hear and learn from the Torah scholars, יֵשׁ לוֹ חֵלֶק
— **he has a portion** among them.[28] יוֹשֵׁב וְשׁוֹתֵק בִּשְׁבִיל שֶׁיֹּאמְרוּ: אִישׁ פְּלוֹנִי
יוֹשֵׁב וְשׁוֹתֵק לִפְנֵי חֲכָמִים — However, if **one sits** in the study hall **and remains**
silent just **so that [people] should say** about him, "So-and-so sits silently
before the scholars in order to learn from them," זֶה אֵין לוֹ חֵלֶק — **he has no
portion** among them.[29]

§8 The next set of four is cited from *Avos* 5:15:

אַרְבַּע מִדּוֹת בַּיּוֹשְׁבִים לִפְנֵי חֲכָמִים — **There are four types** among [the stu-
dents] **who sit before** Torah **scholars:** יֵשׁ דּוֹמֶה לִסְפוֹג — **(i) There is one
who is like a sponge;** יֵשׁ דּוֹמֶה לְנָפָה — **(ii) there is one who is like a sieve;**

---

28. At times, one can gain more knowledge
by asking questions of the teacher, while at
other times he will gain more by listening
silently. The previous statement refers to the
former instance, while this statement refers
to the latter (see *Ben Avraham*).

29. The point of this teaching is that a

person's intentions determine how his actions are viewed. Two people can perform
identical acts, but because of the drastically
different purposes that they have in mind,
one of them has a portion among the great
scholars, whereas the other has no portion
among them at all (see *Binyan Yehoshua*).

יֵשׁ דּוֹמֶה לְמַשְׁפֵּךְ יֵשׁ דּוֹמֶה לִמְשַׁמֶּרֶת. דּוֹמֶה לִסְפוֹג, כֵּיצַד, זֶה תַּלְמִיד
חָכָם שֶׁיּוֹשֵׁב לִפְנֵי חֲכָמִים וְלָמֵד מִקְרָא וּמִשְׁנָה וּמִדְרָשׁ הֲלָכוֹת וְאַגָּדוֹת.[30]
כְּשֵׁם שֶׁסְּפוֹג סוֹפֵג אֶת הַכֹּל כָּךְ הוּא סוֹפֵג אֶת הַכֹּל.[31] לְנָפָה, כֵּיצַד,
תַּלְמִיד חָכָם פִּקֵּחַ שֶׁיּוֹשֵׁב לִפְנֵי (תַּלְמִידֵי) חֲכָמִים וְשָׁמַע מִקְרָא וּמִשְׁנָה
מִדְרָשׁ הֲלָכוֹת וְאַגָּדוֹת, כְּשֵׁם שֶׁנָּפָה מוֹצִיאָה אֶת הַקֶּמַח וְקוֹלֶטֶת
אֶת הַסֹּלֶת כָּךְ הוּא מוֹצִיא אֶת הָרַע וְקוֹלֵט אֶת הַיָּפֶה.[32] לְמַשְׁפֵּךְ,
כֵּיצַד, זֶה תַּלְמִיד טִפֵּשׁ שֶׁיּוֹשֵׁב לִפְנֵי תַּלְמִידֵי חֲכָמִים שָׁמַע מִקְרָא
וּמִשְׁנָה הֲלָכוֹת וְאַגָּדוֹת, כְּשֵׁם שֶׁהַמַּשְׁפֵּךְ מֵטִיל מִכָּאן וְיוֹצֵא מִכָּאן

יֵשׁ דּוֹמֶה לְמַשְׁפֵּךְ — (iii) there is one who is like a funnel; יֵשׁ דּוֹמֶה לִמְשַׁמֶּרֶת
— (iv) and there is one who is like a strainer.

The Baraisa explains each type:

זֶה תַּלְמִיד חָכָם שֶׁיּוֹשֵׁב לִפְנֵי — How is one like a sponge? דּוֹמֶה לִסְפוֹג, כֵּיצַד — This refers to a Torah student who sits before scholars וְלָמֵד חֲכָמִים — and learns from them Scripture, Mish- מִקְרָא וּמִשְׁנָה וּמִדְרָשׁ הֲלָכוֹת וְאַגָּדוֹת nah, Midrash, Halachos, and Aggados.[30] כְּשֵׁם שֶׁסְּפוֹג סוֹפֵג אֶת הַכֹּל — Just as a sponge absorbs all liquid with which it comes into contact, whether it is clean or murky, כָּךְ הוּא סוֹפֵג אֶת הַכֹּל — so does [this student] absorb everything that he learns, whether it is worthy of being remembered or not.[31] תַּלְמִיד חָכָם פִּקֵּחַ שֶׁיּוֹשֵׁב לִפְנֵי תַּלְמִידֵי — How is one like a sieve? לְנָפָה, כֵּיצַד — This refers to a wise Torah student who sits before scholars וְשָׁמַע חֲכָמִים — and hears from them Scripture, Mishnah, מִקְרָא וּמִשְׁנָה מִדְרָשׁ הֲלָכוֹת וְאַגָּדוֹת Midrash, Halachos, and Aggados. כְּשֵׁם שֶׁנָּפָה מוֹצִיאָה אֶת הַקֶּמַח וְקוֹלֶטֶת אֶת — Just as a sieve allows the flour dust to pass through and retains הַסֹּלֶת only the valuable, fine flour, כָּךְ הוּא מוֹצִיא אֶת הָרַע וְקוֹלֵט אֶת הַיָּפֶה — so does [this student] allow the undesirable material to pass through and retains only the desirable material.[32] זֶה תַּלְמִיד טִפֵּשׁ שֶׁיּוֹשֵׁב לִפְנֵי תַּלְמִידֵי — How is one like a funnel? לְמַשְׁפֵּךְ, כֵּיצַד — This refers to a dull student who sits before scholars שָׁמַע מִקְרָא חֲכָמִים — and hears from them Scripture, Mishnah, Midrash, וּמִשְׁנָה הֲלָכוֹת וְאַגָּדוֹת Halachos, and Aggados. כְּשֵׁם שֶׁהַמַּשְׁפֵּךְ מֵטִיל מִכָּאן וְיוֹצֵא מִכָּאן — Just as

---

30. "Scripture" is the entire Bible. "Mish-nah" is a general term for the Oral Tradition explaining the laws of the Torah; "Midrash" refers to the [Halachic] expositions of Scrip-ture; "Halachos" are the various rulings and halachic discussions; and "Aggados" are the ethical and homiletic teachings.

31. Even when studying Torah, some false explanations may occasionally come up during the discussion, and such things would be better forgotten. This student is fortunate enough to have a good memory, but lacks the ability to differentiate between truth and error (Binyan Yehoshua, citing Rav to Avos ibid.).

32. The best of all the types, such a student possesses the skill to select only the truth before committing it to memory (ibid.).

כָּךְ הוּא כָּל דָּבָר וְדָבָר שֶׁמְּטִילִין בְּאָזְנָיו נִכְנָסִים מִכָּאן וְיוֹצְאִין מִכָּאן,
רִאשׁוֹן רִאשׁוֹן נִשְׁמָט וְהוֹלֵךְ לוֹ. לְמִשְׁמֶרֶת, כֵּיצַד, זֶה תַּלְמִיד רָשָׁע
שֶׁיּוֹשֵׁב לִפְנֵי חָכָם וְשָׁמַע מִקְרָא וּמִשְׁנָה מִדְרָשׁ הֲלָכוֹת וְאַגָּדוֹת, כְּשֵׁם
שֶׁהַמְּשַׁמֶּרֶת מוֹצִיאָה הַיַּיִן וְקוֹלֶטֶת הַשְּׁמָרִים כָּךְ הוּא מוֹצִיא אֶת הַיָּפֶה
וְקוֹלֵט אֶת הָרַע[33]. רַבִּי אֱלִיעֶזֶר בֶּן יַעֲקֹב קוֹרֵא אוֹתוֹ קֶרֶן נָקוּב[34] קִיטוֹעָה[35].
קִיטוֹעָה, כֵּיצַד, זֶה תִּינוֹק שֶׁנּוֹתְנִין לוֹ מַרְגָּלִית וְחוֹזְרִין וְנוֹתְנִין לוֹ פַּת, זוֹרֵק
אֶת הַמַּרְגָּלִית וְנוֹטֵל אֶת הַפַּת. חוֹזְרִין וְנוֹתְנִין לוֹ כְּלִי חֶרֶס, זוֹרֵק אֶת
הַפַּת וְנוֹטֵל אֶת הַחֶרֶס, לֹא נִמְצָא בְּיָדוֹ כִּי אִם כְּלִי חֶרֶס בִּלְבַד[36]:

with a funnel, one pours in liquid on one side and it all comes out from the other side, כָּךְ הוּא — so it is with this student: כָּל דָּבָר וְדָבָר שֶׁמְּטִילִין — all the Torah matters that [the scholars] place in his ears בְּאָזְנָיו נִכְנָסִים מִכָּאן וְיוֹצְאִין מִכָּאן go in on this side and come out from the other side, רִאשׁוֹן רִאשׁוֹן נִשְׁמָט וְהוֹלֵךְ לוֹ — slipping away from him one by one.

לְמִשְׁמֶרֶת, כֵּיצַד — How is one like a strainer? זֶה תַּלְמִיד רָשָׁע שֶׁיּוֹשֵׁב לִפְנֵי חָכָם — This refers to a wicked student who sits before a scholar וְשָׁמַע מִקְרָא וּמִשְׁנָה מִדְרָשׁ הֲלָכוֹת וְאַגָּדוֹת and hears from him Scripture, Mishnah, Midrash, Halachos, and Aggados. כְּשֵׁם שֶׁהַמְּשַׁמֶּרֶת מוֹצִיאָה הַיַּיִן וְקוֹלֶטֶת הַשְּׁמָרִים — Just as a strainer allows the wine to pass through and retains only the dregs, כָּךְ הוּא מוֹצִיא אֶת הַיָּפֶה וְקוֹלֵט אֶת הָרַע — so does he allow the desirable material to pass through and retains only the undesirable material.[33]

Another sage's comments on some of the types of students just discussed: רַבִּי אֱלִיעֶזֶר בֶּן יַעֲקֹב קוֹרֵא אוֹתוֹ קֶרֶן נָקוּב קִיטוֹעָה — R' Eliezer ben Yaakov would call the dull student a "perforated horn,"[34] and the wicked student a "severed one."[35] זֶה קִיטוֹעָה, כֵּיצַד — How can the "severed one" be described? תִּינוֹק שֶׁנּוֹתְנִין לוֹ מַרְגָּלִית וְחוֹזְרִין וְנוֹתְנִין לוֹ פַּת — He is like a child that was given a precious stone and then bread, זוֹרֵק אֶת הַמַּרְגָּלִית וְנוֹטֵל אֶת הַפַּת — and he throws away the precious stone and keeps the bread. חוֹזְרִין וְנוֹתְנִין לוֹ כְּלִי — They then give him an earthenware utensil, חֶרֶס, זוֹרֵק אֶת הַפַּת וְנוֹטֵל אֶת — and he throws away the bread and keeps the earthenware utensil. הַחֶרֶס לֹא נִמְצָא בְּיָדוֹ כִּי אִם כְּלִי חֶרֶס בִּלְבַד — In the end, he is left with nothing but the earthenware utensil, which has the least value of all the items that he received.[36]

---

33. Such a student forgets everything he learns in the study hall, but exhibits good retention skills when it comes to idle matters (ibid.).

34. Blowing into a horn [used to create musical sounds] that is perforated is a futile endeavor, as no sound will come out of it.

Similarly, teaching a student who forgets all that he is taught is of no purpose (*Binyan Yehoshua*).

35. I.e., one who is severed from everything good (see *Ahavas Chesed*).

36. R' Eliezer ben Yaakov prefers this description over the earlier metaphor of a

ט. לְעִנְיַן תַּלְמִידִים דָּרַשׁ רַבָּן גַּמְלִיאֵל הַזָּקֵן אַרְבָּעָה דְבָרִים, דָּג טָמֵא דָּג טָהוֹר דָּג מִן הַיַּרְדֵּן דָּג מִן הַיָּם הַגָּדוֹל. דָּג טָמֵא, כֵּיצַד, בֶּן עֲנִיִּים שֶׁלָּמֵד מִקְרָא וּמִשְׁנָה הֲלָכוֹת וְאַגָּדוֹת וְאֵין בּוֹ דֵעָה[38]. דָּג טָהוֹר, כֵּיצַד, זֶה בֶּן עֲשִׁירִים שֶׁלָּמֵד מִקְרָא וּמִשְׁנָה הֲלָכוֹת וְאַגָּדוֹת וְיֵשׁ בּוֹ דֵעָה[40]. דָּג מִן הַיַּרְדֵּן, כֵּיצַד, זֶה תַּלְמִיד חָכָם שֶׁלָּמֵד מִקְרָא וּמִשְׁנָה מִדְרָשׁ הֲלָכוֹת וְאַגָּדוֹת וְאֵין בּוֹ דַעַת לְהָשִׁיב[41]. דָּג מִן הַיָּם הַגָּדוֹל, כֵּיצַד,

§9 Another set of four, also relating to types of students: לְעִנְיַן תַּלְמִידִים דָּרַשׁ רַבָּן גַּמְלִיאֵל הַזָּקֵן אַרְבָּעָה דְבָרִים — Regarding students, Rabban Gamliel the Elder expounded four [analogies]: דָּג טָמֵא — (i) There is a type of student who is like **a nonkosher fish;** דָּג טָהוֹר — (ii) one that is like **a kosher fish;** דָּג מִן הַיַּרְדֵּן — (iii) one that is like **a fish from the Jordan River;** דָּג מִן הַיָּם הַגָּדוֹל — (iv) and one that is like **a fish from the Great Sea.**

The Baraisa explains what each type symbolizes: דָּג טָמֵא, כֵּיצַד — **How** is one like **a nonkosher fish?** בֶּן עֲנִיִּים — This refers to **a student who is poor** in intelligence,[37] שֶׁלָּמֵד מִקְרָא וּמִשְׁנָה הֲלָכוֹת וְאַגָּדוֹת — who learns **Scripture, Mishnah, Halachos, and Aggados,** וְאֵין בּוֹ דֵעָה — but **lacks the intelligence** to understand what he has been taught.[38] דָּג טָהוֹר, כֵּיצַד — **How** is one like **a kosher fish?** זֶה בֶּן עֲשִׁירִים — This refers to **a student who is rich** in intelligence,[39] שֶׁלָּמֵד מִקְרָא וּמִשְׁנָה הֲלָכוֹת וְאַגָּדוֹת — who learns **Scripture, Mishnah, Halachos, and Aggados,** וְיֵשׁ בּוֹ דֵעָה — and **has the intelligence** to understand what he has been taught.[40] כֵּיצַד — **How** is one like **a fish from the Jordan River?** זֶה תַּלְמִיד חָכָם שֶׁלָּמֵד — This refers to **a Torah student who learns** מִקְרָא וּמִשְׁנָה מִדְרָשׁ הֲלָכוֹת וְאַגָּדוֹת — **Scripture, Mishnah, Midrash, Halachos, and Aggados,** וְאֵין בּוֹ דַעַת לְהָשִׁיב — **and** though he may have the intelligence to understand what he has been taught, he **does not have** enough **intelligence to respond** to all queries that are posed to him.[41] דָּג מִן הַיָּם הַגָּדוֹל, כֵּיצַד — **How** is one like **a fish from the**

---

strainer, for the sediments retained by a strainer absorb a bit of the wine, whereas this student is left *completely* without Torah knowledge, like the child who is left with nothing other than the item with the least value (*Binyan Yehoshua*).

37. *Binyan Yehoshua*, citing *Mefaresh*.

38. Such a student is likened to a nonkosher fish because he does not possess the "fins" [one of the signs of a kosher fish (see *Leviticus* 11:9-12)] necessary to navigate the sea of Torah successfully (*Magen Avos*, second approach).

[The vastness of the sea is a Scriptural metaphor used to give us an inkling of the Torah's tremendous breadth and scope (see below), as the verse says in describing the Torah (*Job* 11:9), *Its measure is longer than the earth and wider than the sea* (*Binyan Yehoshua*, citing *Mefaresh*).]

39. *Binyan Yehoshua*.

40. Thus possessing the "fins" to navigate smoothly through the sea of Torah, making him rightfully comparable to a kosher fish (*Magen Avos*, second approach).

41. This type of scholar is not capable of

זֶה תַּלְמִיד חָכָם שֶׁלָּמֵד מִקְרָא וּמִשְׁנָה מִדְרָשׁ הֲלָכוֹת וְאַגָּדוֹת וְיֵשׁ בּוֹ
דַעַת לְהָשִׁיב:[42]

י. אַרְבַּע מִדּוֹת הֵם. יֵשׁ רוֹאֶה וְנִרְאֶה רוֹאֶה וְאֵינוֹ רוֹאֶה רוֹאֶה וְאֵינוֹ
נִרְאֶה אֵינוֹ רוֹאֶה וְאֵינוֹ נִרְאֶה. רוֹאֶה וְנִרְאֶה כְּגוֹן הַזְּאֵב וְהָאֲרִי
וְהַנָּמֵר וְהַדּוֹב הַבַּרְדְּלָס[43] וְהַנָּחָשׁ וְהַלִּיסְטִין וְהַגְּיָיסוֹת, אֵלּוּ רוֹאִין וְנִרְאִין.
נִרְאֶה וְאֵינוֹ רוֹאֶה כְּגוֹן הַסַּיִּיף וְהַקֶּשֶׁת וְהָרוֹמַח וְהַסַּכִּין וּמַקֵּל וְקִינוּקְנוֹת,
נִרְאִין וְאֵינָן רוֹאִין. רוֹאֶה וְאֵינוֹ נִרְאֶה זוֹ מַכַּת רוּחַ רַע.[44] אֵינוֹ נִרְאֶה וְלֹא

Great Sea? זֶה תַּלְמִיד חָכָם שֶׁלָּמֵד מִקְרָא וּמִשְׁנָה מִדְרָשׁ הֲלָכוֹת וְאַגָּדוֹת — **This** refers to a Torah student who learns Scripture, Mishnah, Midrash, Halachos, and Aggados, וְיֵשׁ בּוֹ דַעַת לְהָשִׁיב — **and** not only has the intelligence to understand what he has been taught, but also **has** enough **intelligence to respond** to all queries that are posed to him.[42]

§10 Another set of four:

אַרְבַּע מִדּוֹת הֵם — **There are four types** of harmful entities: יֵשׁ רוֹאֶה וְנִרְאֶה — (i) **There is** one type **that can see and can be seen,** רוֹאֶה וְאֵינוֹ נִרְאֶה — (ii) one **that can be seen but cannot see,** רוֹאֶה וְאֵינוֹ נִרְאֶה — (iii) one **that can see but cannot be seen,** אֵינוֹ רוֹאֶה וְאֵינוֹ נִרְאֶה — (iv) and one **that can neither see nor be seen.**

The Baraisa explains each type:

רוֹאֶה וְנִרְאֶה — "**One that can see and can be seen**" refers to creatures כְּגוֹן הַזְּאֵב וְהָאֲרִי וְהַנָּמֵר וְהַדּוֹב הַבַּרְדְּלָס וְהַנָּחָשׁ וְהַלִּיסְטִין וְהַגְּיָיסוֹת — such as the wolf, lion, leopard, bear, *bardelas*,[43] snake, highwaymen, and armies; אֵלּוּ רוֹאִין וְנִרְאִין — these can see and can be seen. נִרְאֶה וְאֵינוֹ רוֹאֶה — "**One that can be seen but cannot see**" refers to weapons כְּגוֹן הַסַּיִּיף וְהַקֶּשֶׁת וְהָרוֹמַח וְהַסַּכִּין וּמַקֵּל וְקִינוּקְנוֹת — such as the sword, bow, spear, knife, club, and cane; נִרְאִין וְאֵינָן רוֹאִין — these can be seen but cannot see. רוֹאֶה וְאֵינוֹ נִרְאֶה — "**One that can see but cannot be seen**" — זוֹ מַכַּת רוּחַ רַע — this refers to the afflictions brought on by an **evil spirit.**[44] אֵינוֹ נִרְאֶה וְלֹא

---

swimming through the endless expanse of the enormous sea of Torah [as is the scholar described next], and is therefore symbolized by a fish who can live only in the relatively small Jordan River (*Binyan Yehoshua*, citing *Mefaresh*).

[This scholar and the one described next are not distinct types from the two students described above. Rather, these two scholars are two possible outcomes of the second type of student, who possesses the

intelligence to understand what he has been taught (see *Magen Avos*).]

42. Such a scholar is marked by his distinguished level of knowledge in all areas of Torah, and is thus aptly represented by a fish who can nimbly maneuver through the entirety of the Great Sea (*Binyan Yehoshua*, citing *Mefaresh*).

43. See above, 29 §2 note 11.

44. The evil spirits are celestial agents of

רוֹאֶה זֶה מַכַּת חוֹלִי מֵעַיִים:⁴⁵

יא. אַרְבָּעָה⁴⁶ חֲכָמִים הֵם. הָרוֹאֶה רַבִּי יוֹחָנָן בֶּן נוּרִי בַּחֲלוֹם יְצַפֶּה לְיִרְאַת חֵטְא⁴⁷. רַבִּי אֶלְעָזָר בֶּן עֲזַרְיָה יְצַפֶּה לִגְדוּלָה וְלַעֲשִׁירוּת.⁴⁸ רַבִּי יִשְׁמָעֵאל יְצַפֶּה לַחָכְמָה.⁴⁹ רַבִּי עֲקִיבָא יִדְאַג מִן הַפּוּרְעָנוּת:⁵⁰

יב. שְׁלֹשָׁה תַּלְמִידֵי חֲכָמִים הֵם.⁵¹ הָרוֹאֶה בֶּן עַזַּאי בַּחֲלוֹם יְצַפֶּה לַחֲסִידוּת.⁵²

זֶה מַכַּת חוֹלִי מֵעַיִים — this רוֹאֶה — "One that can neither see nor be seen" — refers to ailments such as stomach illness.[45]

§11 The final set of four presented by the Baraisa:[46] אַרְבָּעָה חֲכָמִים הֵם — There are four Sages whose appearance in a dream has special meaning: הָרוֹאֶה רַבִּי יוֹחָנָן בֶּן נוּרִי בַּחֲלוֹם — (i) One who sees R' Yochanan ben Nuri in a dream יְצַפֶּה לְיִרְאַת חֵטְא — may anticipate acquiring the trait of fearing sin;[47] רַבִּי אֶלְעָזָר בֶּן עֲזַרְיָה יְצַפֶּה לִגְדוּלָה וְלַעֲשִׁירוּת — (ii) if he sees R' Elazar ben Azaryah, he may anticipate attaining prominence and wealth;[48] רַבִּי יִשְׁמָעֵאל יְצַפֶּה לַחָכְמָה — (iii) if he sees R' Yishmael, he may anticipate acquiring wisdom;[49] רַבִּי עֲקִיבָא יִדְאַג מִן הַפּוּרְעָנוּת — (iv) and if he sees R' Akiva, he should fear Heavenly retribution.[50]

§12 Having discussed a set of four that relates to dreams, the Baraisa discusses some sets of three that relate to the same topic. The first set: שְׁלֹשָׁה תַּלְמִידֵי חֲכָמִים הֵם — There are three students of the Sages[51] whose appearance in a dream has special meaning: הָרוֹאֶה בֶּן עַזַּאי בַּחֲלוֹם יְצַפֶּה לַחֲסִידוּת — (i) One who sees Ben Azzai in a dream may anticipate attaining piety;[52]

---

retribution such as demons and the like, which can see but cannot be seen. See above, 36 §3 note 15.

45. The significance of this information is that if one has a dream in which he is told that he will be harmed by something that "can see and be seen," he should know that he must pray to be spared from the lion, the wolf, or their like, and so on (*Binyan Yehoshua*, citing *Mefaresh*).

46. The teachings cited in the following four sections appear in *Berachos 57b*, with several variations.

47. R' Yochanan ben Nuri was a scrupulously pious person (*Magen Avos*).

48. R' Elazar ben Azaryah was raised to the prominent position of *Nasi* of the Jewish people at a young age, and was also very

wealthy [see *Berachos 28a* and *Shabbos 54b*] (*Binyan Yehoshua*).

49. R' Yishmael was a leading sage (*Magen Avos*).

50. R' Akiva was martyred [by the Romans] in a particularly barbaric way, as described in *Berachos 61b* (*Binyan Yehoshua*).

51. The scholars listed in this group are termed "*students* of the Sages" [as opposed to being called "Sages," like those in the previous group] because they never officially received Rabbinic ordination [סְמִיכָה], and were therefore never given the title רַבִּי, *Rabbi* (*Rashi* to *Berachos 57b*; *Ben Avraham*).

52. Ben Azzai maintained the highest level of sanctity despite the fact that he was unmarried (see *Yevamos 63b*). This is the epitome of piety (*Binyan Yehoshua*, citing *Mefaresh*).

בֶּן זוֹמָא יְצַפֶּה לַחָכְמָה.[53] אֱלִישָׁע בֶּן אֲבוּיָה יִדְאַג מִן הַפּוּרְעָנוּת:[54]

יג. שְׁלֹשָׁה נְבִיאִים הֵם. הָרוֹאֶה סֵפֶר מְלָכִים בַּחֲלוֹם יְצַפֶּה לִגְדוּלָה
וְלַעֲשִׁירוּת.[55] יְשַׁעְיָה יְצַפֶּה לְנֶחָמָה.[56] יִרְמְיָה יִדְאַג מִן הַפּוּרְעָנוּת:[57]

יד. שָׁלֹשׁ כְּתוּבִים הֵם. הָרוֹאֶה סֵפֶר תְּהִלִּים בַּחֲלוֹם יְצַפֶּה לַעֲנָוָה.[58]
מִשְׁלֵי יְצַפֶּה לַחָכְמָה.[59] אִיּוֹב יִדְאַג מִן הַפּוּרְעָנוּת:[60]

בֶּן זוֹמָא יְצַפֶּה לַחָכְמָה — (ii) if he sees **Ben Zoma**, he may anticipate acquiring wisdom;[53] אֱלִישָׁע בֶּן אֲבוּיָה יִדְאַג מִן הַפּוּרְעָנוּת — (iii) and if he sees **Elisha ben Avuyah**, he should fear Heavenly retribution.[54]

§13 Another set of three pertaining to dreams:

שְׁלֹשָׁה נְבִיאִים הֵם — There are three Books of **Prophets** whose appearance in a dream has special meaning: הָרוֹאֶה סֵפֶר מְלָכִים בַּחֲלוֹם יְצַפֶּה לִגְדוּלָה וְלַעֲשִׁירוּת — (i) **One who sees the Book of *Kings*** in a dream may anticipate rising to **prominence and wealth**;[55] יְשַׁעְיָה יְצַפֶּה לְנֶחָמָה — (ii) if he sees the Book of *Isaiah*, he may anticipate **consolation**;[56] יִרְמְיָה יִדְאַג מִן הַפּוּרְעָנוּת — (iii) and if he sees the Book of *Jeremiah*, **he should fear** Heavenly retribution.[57]

§14 Yet another set of three pertaining to dreams:

שָׁלֹשׁ כְּתוּבִים הֵם — There are three Books of **Writings** whose appearance in a dream has special meaning: הָרוֹאֶה סֵפֶר תְּהִלִּים בַּחֲלוֹם יְצַפֶּה לַעֲנָוָה — (i) **One who sees the Book of *Psalms*** in a dream may anticipate acquiring the trait of **humility**;[58] מִשְׁלֵי יְצַפֶּה לַחָכְמָה — (ii) if he sees the Book of *Proverbs*, **he may anticipate** acquiring **wisdom**;[59] אִיּוֹב יִדְאַג מִן הַפּוּרְעָנוּת — (iii) and if he sees the Book of *Job*, **he should fear** Heavenly retribution.[60]

---

53. Ben Zoma was one of the two most outstanding scholars of his generation (see *Kiddushin* 49b with *Rashi* ד״ה בן עזאי ובן זומא). He had expert knowledge of the underlying meanings of Scriptural verses, as indicated in *Berachos* 12b (*Magen Avos*; see also *Sotah* 49a with *Rashi* ד״ה הדרשנים).

54. Elisha ben Avuyah, the mentor of R' Meir, became a heretic later in his life. From that time onward, he was known simply as *Acher*, the "other" (see *Chagigah* 15a-b and above, Ch. 24). Since he broke away from the path of Torah, it is deemed a bad omen should one perceive him in a dream.

55. The Book of *Kings* mentions David, Solomon, and other prominent and wealthy kings of Israel (*Binyan Yehoshua*).

56. The dominant theme of Isaiah's prophecy is consolation to the Jewish people. The prophet assures them that God's wrath

is not permanent; rather, He will eventually redeem them (see *Bava Basra* 14b).

57. Jeremiah lived just before and during Nebuchadnezzar's conquest of Jerusalem. The dominant theme of his prophecy was that the Kingdom of Judah would be defeated if its people do not return to God (see *Bava Basra* 14b).

58. *Psalms* was authored by King David, who was an extremely humble person, as evident from the way he speaks about himself (*Psalms* 22:7), *But I am a worm and not a man* (*Binyan Yehoshua*).

59. *Proverbs* was written by King Solomon, whom Scripture describes as the wisest of all men (*II Kings* 5:10). The book offers Solomon's counsel on various spiritual and practical matters (see *Rashi* to *Bava Basra* 14b, ד״ה משלי קהלת).

60. The Book of *Job* chronicles the

‏**טו.** מִיתָה לָרְשָׁעִים נָאֶה לָהֶם וְנָאֶה לָעוֹלָם.[62] לַצַּדִּיקִים רַע לָהֶם וְרַע‏
‏לָעוֹלָם.[63] שֶׁקֶט לָרְשָׁעִים רַע לָהֶם וְרַע לָעוֹלָם לַצַּדִּיקִים טוֹב לָהֶם‏
‏וְטוֹב לָעוֹלָם.[64] אַל[65] יַעֲמוֹד אָדָם עָרוֹם כְּנֶגֶד בֵּית קָדְשֵׁי הַקֳּדָשִׁים:[66]‏

‏**טז.** הַנִּכְנָס לְבֵית הַכִּסֵּא לֹא יַחֲזִיר פָּנָיו לֹא לַמִּזְרָח וְלֹא לַמַּעֲרָב‏

---

§15 The Baraisa enumerates two things that have opposite effects on the righteous and the wicked:[61]

‏מִיתָה לָרְשָׁעִים נָאֶה לָהֶם וְנָאֶה לָעוֹלָם‏ — Death for the wicked is beneficial to them and beneficial to the world,[62] ‏לַצַּדִּיקִים רַע לָהֶם וְרַע לָעוֹלָם‏ — but death for the righteous is detrimental to them and detrimental to the world.[63] ‏שֶׁקֶט‏ ‏לָרְשָׁעִים רַע לָהֶם וְרַע לָעוֹלָם‏ — Tranquility for the wicked is detrimental to them and detrimental to the world, ‏לַצַּדִּיקִים טוֹב לָהֶם וְטוֹב לָעוֹלָם‏ — but tranquility for the righteous is beneficial to them and beneficial to the world.[64]

The Baraisa records a seemingly unrelated law by way of introduction to the set of three presented afterward:[65]

‏אַל יַעֲמוֹד אָדָם עָרוֹם כְּנֶגֶד בֵּית קָדְשֵׁי הַקֳּדָשִׁים‏ — A person should not stand unclothed opposite the gateway to the Holy of Holies.[66]

§16 The Baraisa presents another set of three, pertaining to proper conduct when attending to one's bodily needs:[67]

‏הַנִּכְנָס לְבֵית הַכִּסֵּא לֹא יַחֲזִיר פָּנָיו לֹא לַמִּזְרָח וְלֹא לַמַּעֲרָב‏ — (i) One who enters a latrine in an area that is to the east or west of the Temple should not face toward the east nor toward the west while relieving himself, for then he would

---

extraordinary suffering endured by Job, and recounts debates between Job and his colleagues as to the meaning of these afflictions.

61. [Vilna has these next two sections numbered erroneously.] These are part of a larger list that appears in the Mishnah, *Sanhedrin* 71b. [In the Vilna edition, the final three sections are misnumbered as ‏'ח‏ through ‏'י‏.]

62. Death benefits the wicked because it prevents them from further sinning (thus sparing them from even greater punishment in the World to Come — see *Yevamos* 63b). Their death also benefits society by sparing it from any more of their destructive actions (*Binyan Yehoshua*, citing *Rashi* to *Sanhedrin* 71b).

63. When the righteous die, they lose the opportunity to acquire for themselves even greater merit and reward (through their Torah study and mitzvah performance). In addition, they are no longer available to protect the world with their merit or to teach

people to act correctly (ibid.).

64. Tranquility allows a person time and peace of mind to pursue the endeavors he considers worthy. Therefore, it is detrimental when granted to the wicked, who use their time for evil purposes, but beneficial when enjoyed by the righteous, who study Torah and perform mitzvos (*Binyan Yehoshua*, citing *Rashi* to *Sanhedrin* 72a).

65. *Magen Avos.* This law is related to the first of the three laws cited in the following section.

66. This is based on the ruling of the Mishnah (*Berachos* 54a) that one should not act in a lightheaded manner opposite the Eastern Gate of the Temple Mount, since that gate is directly opposite the gateway to the Holy of Holies. Standing unclothed when facing this sacred location is certainly a gross form of lightheaded behavior, and therefore a prime example of this prohibition (*Ben Avraham*).

67. *Magen Avos.*

אֶלָּא לַצְּדָדִין.[68] לֹא יִפְרַע עַצְמוֹ מְעוֹמָד אֶלָּא מְיוּשָּׁב.[69] וְלֹא יְקַנֵּחַ אָדָם עַצְמוֹ בְּיָמִין אֶלָּא בִּשְׂמֹאל. וּמִפְּנֵי מָה אָמְרוּ לֹא יְקַנֵּחַ אָדָם עַצְמוֹ בְּיָמִין אֶלָּא בִּשְׂמֹאל, רַבִּי אֱלִיעֶזֶר אוֹמֵר: מִפְּנֵי שֶׁמַּרְאִין בָּהּ דִּבְרֵי תוֹרָה.[70] רַבִּי יְהוֹשֻׁעַ אוֹמֵר: מִפְּנֵי שֶׁאוֹכֵל וְשׁוֹתֶה בָּהּ:

יז. כָּל[71] אַהֲבָה שֶׁהִיא תְלוּיָה בְדָבָר וְכוּ׳. אֵיזוֹ הִיא אַהֲבָה שֶׁהִיא תְלוּיָה

---

be presenting the exposed part of his body to the Temple.   אֶלָּא לַצְּדָדִין — Rather, he should face **toward** one of the other **sides,** i.e., north or south, so as to present only the side of his body to the Temple.[68]   לֹא יִפְרַע עַצְמוֹ מְעוֹמָד אֶלָּא מְיוּשָּׁב — (ii) He should not uncover himself while standing, but only once seated.[69]   וְלֹא יְקַנֵּחַ אָדָם עַצְמוֹ בְּיָמִין אֶלָּא בִּשְׂמֹאל — (iii) And a person should not wipe himself with his right hand, but only with his left hand.

The Baraisa elaborates on the third law:

וּמִפְּנֵי מָה אָמְרוּ לֹא יְקַנֵּחַ אָדָם עַצְמוֹ בְּיָמִין אֶלָּא בִּשְׂמֹאל — Why did [the Sages] say that **a person should not wipe himself with his right hand, but only with his left hand?**   רַבִּי אֱלִיעֶזֶר אוֹמֵר: מִפְּנֵי שֶׁמַּרְאִין בָּהּ דִּבְרֵי תוֹרָה — R' Eliezer says: **Because one shows Torah words with [his right hand].**[70] The hand used for a holy purpose should not be used for this base purpose.   רַבִּי יְהוֹשֻׁעַ אוֹמֵר: מִפְּנֵי שֶׁאוֹכֵל וְשׁוֹתֶה בָּהּ — R' Yehoshua says: **Because one** generally **eats and drinks with [the right hand],** and it would be inappropriate to use that same hand for this purpose.

§17 The Baraisa presents a set of three things that can endure only if they are done for the right purpose:[71]

כָּל אַהֲבָה שֶׁהִיא תְלוּיָה בְדָבָר וְכוּ׳ — (i) **Any love that depends on a** particular **thing,** when that thing ceases, the love ceases;[72] but a love that does not depend on any particular thing will never cease.   אֵיזוֹ הִיא אַהֲבָה שֶׁהִיא תְלוּיָה בְדָבָר וְכוּ׳ — What is an example of **love that depends on a** particular **thing?** The love of Amnon and Tamar.[73] And what is an example of love that does not depend

---

68. For discussion of this law, see *Berachos* 61b-62a; *Tur* and *Shulchan Aruch, Orach Chaim* 3:5 with commentators.

69. For reasons of modesty (see *Shulchan Aruch, Orach Chaim* 3:2). Likewise, one should not first rise and then cover himself, but first cover himself and then rise (*Mishnah Berurah* ad loc. §2; see *Tamid* 27b).

70. The Gemara in *Berachos* 62a says that one shows the *cantillation notes* of the Torah with it. That is, those who followed the custom to indicate the shape and/or pitch of the cantillation notes with their hands as

they read the Torah would use their right hand to do so (see *Rashi* to *Berachos* 62a).

71. *Magen Avos.* They are collected from various Mishnayos in *Avos.*

72. If one's love for another is based on anything besides the sincere desire for closeness and true friendship, the love will not endure. When the factor upon which one's love depends ceases to exist, the relationship will also cease (*Rashi* and *Meiri* to *Avos* 5:16).

73. Amnon loved his sister Tamar and ultimately violated her; afterward, his love turned to a hate that was far more intense

בְּדָבָר כו'. כָּל מַחֲלוֹקֶת שֶׁהִיא לְשֵׁם שָׁמַיִם כו'. אֵיזוֹ הִיא מַחֲלוֹקֶת שֶׁהִיא לְשֵׁם שָׁמַיִם כו'. כָּל כְּנֵסִיָּה שֶׁהִיא לְשֵׁם מִצְוָה כו'. כָּל כְּנֵסִיָּה שֶׁהָיְתָה לְשֵׁם מִצְוָה זוֹ כְּנֶסֶת אַנְשֵׁי ° הַגְּדוֹלָה[77]. וְשֶׁלֹּא לְשֵׁם מִצְוָה זוֹ כְּנֶסֶת אַנְשֵׁי דוֹר הַפַּלָּגָה[78]:

---

on any particular thing? The love between David and Jonathan (*Avos* 5:16).[74] כָּל מַחֲלוֹקֶת שֶׁהִיא לְשֵׁם שָׁמַיִם כו' — (ii) **Any dispute that is for the sake of Heaven** will endure; but one that is not for the sake of Heaven will not endure. אֵיזוֹ הִיא מַחֲלוֹקֶת שֶׁהִיא לְשֵׁם שָׁמַיִם כו' — **What is an example of a dispute that is for the sake of Heaven?** The dispute between Hillel and Shammai.[75] And what is an example of a dispute that is not for the sake of Heaven? The dispute of Korah and his entire company (*Avos* 5:17).[76]

כָּל כְּנֵסִיָּה שֶׁהִיא לְשֵׁם מִצְוָה כו' — (iii) **Any gathering that is** convened **for the sake of a mitzvah** will endure; but one that is not for the sake of a mitzvah will not endure (see *Avos* 4:11). כָּל כְּנֵסִיָּה שֶׁהָיְתָה לְשֵׁם מִצְוָה — "**Any gathering that is** convened **for the sake of a mitzvah**" — זוֹ כְּנֶסֶת אַנְשֵׁי כְּנֶסֶת הַגְּדוֹלָה — this is the gathering of the Men of the Great Assembly.[77] וְשֶׁלֹּא לְשֵׁם מִצְוָה — And a gathering that was not for the sake of a mitzvah — זוֹ כְּנֶסֶת אַנְשֵׁי דוֹר הַפַּלָּגָה — — this is the gathering of the men of the generation of the Dispersion.[78]

---

than the original love (see *II Samuel* Ch. 13). His love did not endure because it was motivated only by physical desire. Once he satisfied his desire, his love for her dissipated (*Rashi* and *Rashbatz* to *Avos* 5:16).

74. Scripture describes the bond between David and Jonathan, the son of King Saul (*I Samuel* 18:1): *Jonathan's soul became attached to David's soul and Jonathan loved him as himself.* This relationship was not based on personal interests or ulterior motives, but on their shared desire to fulfill God's Will that David succeed Saul as king of Israel; see ibid. 23:17 (*Rav* to *Avos* 5:16). Therefore, their love never ceased, even when Jonathan incurred Saul's wrath and endangered his life as a result this friendship (see ibid. Ch. 20); and it endured until Jonathan was killed in battle (see *II Samuel* Ch. 1).

75. Hillel and Shammai are the prototypes of disputants engaged in debate for the sake of Heaven. In their halachic disputes, they were concerned only with arriving at a true understanding of the Torah; and they succeeded in their quest for the truth. Therefore, the Mishnah says that their dispute — i.e.,

the objective of their dispute — endured (*Rav* to *Avos* 5:17, second interpretation).

76. Korah, together with Dathan, Abiram, and a group of 250 men, incited the Jewish people to rebel openly against Moses and Aaron (see *Numbers* Chs. 16-17). They were not motivated by the pursuit of truth, but by a desire for power and a lust for victory. Therefore, they did not accomplish their goal, but instead died an ignominious death (*Rav* ibid.).

77. [Emendation follows *Nuschas HaGra*.] The Men of the Great Assembly were the leaders of the Jewish nation at the beginning of the Second Temple era. They convened to help guide the people on the proper path, by formulating the wording for all their prayers and by instituting many enactments to ensure compliance with the Torah (*Magen Avos*). Their enactments endure forever, as they are used and practiced to this very day (*Ben Avraham*).

78. These men united for a wicked purpose, building the Tower of Babel in order to wage "war" against God (see *Sanhedrin* 109a). Their unity did not last, as they were dispersed among the nations (*Ben Avraham*).

﴾ פֶּרֶק מא ﴿

א. רַבִּי שִׁמְעוֹן אוֹמֵר: שְׁלֹשָׁה כְּתָרִים הֵם[1], אֵלּוּ הֵן: כֶּתֶר תּוֹרָה[2] וְכֶתֶר כְּהוּנָה[3] וְכֶתֶר מַלְכוּת[4] וְכֶתֶר שֵׁם טוֹב עוֹלֶה עַל גַּבֵּיהֶן[5]. כֶּתֶר כְּהוּנָה, כֵּיצַד, אֲפִילּוּ נוֹתֵן (לוֹ) כָּל כֶּסֶף וְזָהָב שֶׁבָּעוֹלָם אֵין נוֹתְנִין לוֹ כֶּתֶר כְּהוּנָה, שֶׁנֶּאֱמַר (במדבר כה, יג) "וְהָיְתָה לּוֹ וּלְזַרְעוֹ אַחֲרָיו בְּרִית כְּהֻנַּת עוֹלָם". כֶּתֶר מַלְכוּת אֲפִילּוּ נוֹתֵן כָּל כֶּסֶף וְזָהָב שֶׁבָּעוֹלָם[6] אֵין נוֹתְנִין לוֹ כֶּתֶר מַלְכוּת,

﴾ CHAPTER 41 ﴿

§1 This chapter continues presenting sets of three and four, beginning with the set of three mentioned in *Avos* 4:13:

רַבִּי שִׁמְעוֹן אוֹמֵר: שְׁלֹשָׁה כְּתָרִים הֵם — R' Shimon says: There are three crowns of honor alluded to in the Torah.[1] אֵלּוּ הֵן — They are: כֶּתֶר תּוֹרָה וְכֶתֶר כְּהוּנָה וְכֶתֶר מַלְכוּת — the crown of Torah,[2] the crown of priesthood[3] and the crown of kingship.[4] וְכֶתֶר שֵׁם טוֹב עוֹלֶה עַל גַּבֵּיהֶן — And there is another crown, **the crown of a good name**, which surpasses them all.[5]

The Baraisa discusses who is qualified to receive each of these three crowns: כֶּתֶר כְּהוּנָה, כֵּיצַד — How does one acquire **the crown of priesthood?** אֲפִילּוּ נוֹתֵן לוֹ כָּל כֶּסֶף וְזָהָב שֶׁבָּעוֹלָם — Even if someone would offer to give [a Kohen][6] all the silver and gold in the world in exchange for his priestly status, אֵין נוֹתְנִין לוֹ כֶּתֶר כְּהוּנָה — he is not given the crown of priesthood, שֶׁנֶּאֱמַר "וְהָיְתָה לּוֹ וּלְזַרְעוֹ אַחֲרָיו בְּרִית כְּהֻנַּת עוֹלָם" — as it is stated, *And it shall be for [Phinehas] and his offspring after him a covenant of eternal priesthood* (*Numbers* 25:13), indicating that this honor is to remain forever reserved for those born into the family of Kohanim. כֶּתֶר מַלְכוּת — Regarding **the crown of kingship** as well, אֲפִילּוּ נוֹתֵן כָּל כֶּסֶף וְזָהָב שֶׁבָּעוֹלָם — even if someone would offer to **give all the silver and gold in the world** in exchange for it, אֵין נוֹתְנִין לוֹ כֶּתֶר מַלְכוּת — he is not given **the crown of kingship,**

---

1. That is, three distinctions that confer noble status on their bearers, and that demand respect from other Jews (*Binyan Yehoshua*).

2. As it is written, *And you shall honor the presence of a sage* (ibid., citing *Leviticus* 19:32).

3. *You shall sanctify [the Kohen] ... he shall remain holy to you* (*Rav* to *Avos* 4:13, citing *Leviticus* 21:8).

4. *You shall surely set over yourself a king* — meaning that the awe of the king shall be upon you (*Rav* ibid., citing Mishnah, *Sanhedrin* 2:8).

5. The crown of a good name adorns someone whose sterling character and good deeds earn him the respect and affection of his fellows. This crown is not in the same category as the others, since the Torah does not require us to show honor to all Jews with a "good name" (hence, there are "three crowns" and not four). On the other hand, it surpasses the other crowns, because even Torah scholars, priests, and kings are undeserving of honor when their deeds do not earn them this additional crown (*Rav* ibid.).

6. *Magen Avos*.

שֶׁנֶּאֱמַר (יחזקאל לז, כה) "וְדָוִד עַבְדִּי נָשִׂיא לָהֶם לְעוֹלָם", אֲבָל כֶּתֶר תּוֹרָה אֵינוֹ כֵן, עֲמָלָה שֶׁל תּוֹרָה כָּל הָרוֹצֶה לִיטוֹל יָבוֹא וְיִטוֹל, שֶׁנֶּאֱמַר (ישעיה נה, א) "הוֹי כָּל צָמֵא לְכוּ לַמַּיִם"[9] הֱוֵי[10] עָמֵל בְּדִבְרֵי תוֹרָה וְאַל תִּתְעַסֵּק בִּדְבָרִים בְּטֵילָה. מַעֲשֶׂה בְּרַבִּי שִׁמְעוֹן בֶּן יוֹחַאי שֶׁהָיָה מְבַקֵּר אֶת הַחוֹלִים וּמָצָא אָדָם אֶחָד שֶׁתָּפוּחַ וּמוּטָל בְּחוֹלִי מֵעַיִם וְאוֹמֵר גִּידוּפִין לִפְנֵי הַקָּדוֹשׁ בָּרוּךְ הוּא, אָמַר לוֹ: רֵיקָה, הָיָה לְךָ שֶׁתְּבַקֵּשׁ רַחֲמִים עַל עַצְמְךָ[11] וְאַתָּה אוֹמֵר גִּידוּפִין. אָמַר לוֹ: הַקָּדוֹשׁ בָּרוּךְ הוּא

שֶׁנֶּאֱמַר "וְדָוִד עַבְדִּי נָשִׂיא לָהֶם לְעוֹלָם" — as it is stated, *And My servant David will be a leader for them forever* (Ezekiel 37:25), implying that kings would always be of Davidic descent.[7]   אֲבָל כֶּתֶר תּוֹרָה אֵינוֹ כֵן — However, the crown of Torah is not that way.   עֲמָלָה שֶׁל תּוֹרָה כָּל הָרוֹצֶה לִיטוֹל יָבוֹא וְיִטוֹל — Rather, anyone who wishes to take the crown obtained through the toil of Torah study may come and take it,[8]   שֶׁנֶּאֱמַר "הוֹי כָּל צָמֵא לְכוּ לַמַּיִם" — as it is stated, *Ho, everyone who is thirsty, go to the water* (Isaiah 55:1).[9]

Having discussed the idea of toiling in the study of Torah, the Baraisa records a related teaching and anecdote:[10]

הֱוֵי עָמֵל בְּדִבְרֵי תוֹרָה — Toil in studying the words of Torah,   בִּדְבָרִים בְּטֵילָה — and do not occupy yourself with idle matters.   מַעֲשֶׂה בְּרַבִּי שִׁמְעוֹן בֶּן יוֹחַאי — An incident once happened with R' Shimon ben Yochai,   שֶׁהָיָה מְבַקֵּר אֶת הַחוֹלִים — in which he was visiting the sick.   וּמָצָא אָדָם אֶחָד שֶׁתָּפוּחַ וּמוּטָל בְּחוֹלִי מֵעַיִם — He encountered one sick person who was bloated and bedridden with a stomach illness,   וְאוֹמֵר גִּידוּפִין לִפְנֵי הַקָּדוֹשׁ בָּרוּךְ הוּא — and, being embittered by his plight, was uttering blasphemies toward the Holy One, Blessed is He.   אָמַר לוֹ: רֵיקָה, הָיָה לְךָ שֶׁתְּבַקֵּשׁ רַחֲמִים — [R' Shimon ben Yochai] said to him, "Empty one! You should be pleading for Heavenly mercy on your own behalf,[11]   עַל עַצְמְךָ — וְאַתָּה אוֹמֵר גִּידוּפִין — and instead you are uttering blasphemies?!"   אָמַר לוֹ: הַקָּדוֹשׁ בָּרוּךְ הוּא

---

7. See *Binyan Yehoshua*.

8. Thus, the crown of Torah is different in two ways: It can be acquired only through great effort, unlike the other two crowns, which are inherited automatically at birth; and it can be acquired by any Jew prepared to toil for it, regardless of his ancestry or station in life (*Ben Avraham*). [Moreover, no payment is needed to acquire this crown, as the *Isaiah* verse concludes, *Go and buy without money and without price, etc.*]

9. Using water as a metaphor for Torah, the verse proclaims that everyone who has

a thirst for Torah is urged to go study it. Clearly, the crown of Torah is not reserved for any exclusive group.

Indeed, this is one reason why water is a fitting symbol for Torah: Both are essential to life, and are readily and cheaply available to anyone who desires them (*Kisei Rachamim*). [For many other interpretations of this metaphor, see *Yalkut Shimoni, Yeshayah* §479).]

10. See *Magen Avos*.

11. The prayer of a sick person for himself is more effective than the prayer of others

יְסַלְּקֵנוּ מִמֶּנִּי וְיַנִּיחֵנוּ עָלֶיךָ. אָמַר: יָפֶה עָשָׂה לִי הַקָּדוֹשׁ בָּרוּךְ הוּא
שֶׁהִנַּחְתִּי דִּבְרֵי תוֹרָה וְהָיִיתִי מִתְעַסֵּק בִּדְבָרִים בְּטֵלִים.[12] מַעֲשֶׂה בְּרַבִּי
שִׁמְעוֹן בֶּן אֶלְעָזָר שֶׁבָּא מִמִּגְדַּל עֵדֶר מִבֵּית רַבּוֹ וְהָיָה רוֹכֵב עַל הַחֲמוֹר
וּמְטַיֵּיל עַל שְׂפַת הַיָּם, רָאָה אָדָם אֶחָד שֶׁהָיָה מְכוֹעָר בְּיוֹתֵר,[15] אָמַר
לוֹ: רֵיקָה, כַּמָּה מְכוֹעָר אַתָּה, שֶׁמָּא כָּל בְּנֵי עִירְךָ מְכוֹעָרִים כְּמוֹתְךָ.[16]

יְסַלְּקֵנוּ מִמֶּנִּי וְיַנִּיחֵנוּ עָלֶיךָ — Angered by R' Shimon ben Yochai's sharp rebuke, [the sick person] replied, "May the Holy One, Blessed is He, remove [this illness] from me and place it upon you!" אָמַר: יָפֶה עָשָׂה לִי הַקָּדוֹשׁ בָּרוּךְ הוּא — [R' Shimon ben Yochai] then said, "It is fitting what the Holy One, Blessed is He, has done to me in causing me to be cursed, שֶׁהִנַּחְתִּי דִּבְרֵי תוֹרָה וְהָיִיתִי מִתְעַסֵּק בִּדְבָרִים בְּטֵלִים — for I have set aside the words of Torah and occupied myself with idle matters."[12]

The Baraisa tangentially relates another story about a sage who referred to someone as an "empty one."[13]

מַעֲשֶׂה בְּרַבִּי שִׁמְעוֹן בֶּן אֶלְעָזָר — An incident happened with R' Shimon ben Elazar, שֶׁבָּא מִמִּגְדַּל עֵדֶר מִבֵּית רַבּוֹ — in which he was coming home from Migdal Eder, from studying Torah in the house of his teacher, and feeling overly proud of all that he had learned there.[14] וְהָיָה רוֹכֵב עַל הַחֲמוֹר וּמְטַיֵּיל עַל שְׂפַת הַיָּם — He was riding on his donkey and traveling along the sea-shore רָאָה אָדָם אֶחָד שֶׁהָיָה מְכוֹעָר בְּיוֹתֵר — when he saw a person who was exceedingly ugly.[15] אָמַר לוֹ: רֵיקָה, כַּמָּה מְכוֹעָר אַתָּה — [R' Shimon ben Elazar] said to him, "Empty one! How ugly you are! שֶׁמָּא כָּל בְּנֵי עִירְךָ מְכוֹעָרִים כְּמוֹתְךָ — Are all the people of your city perhaps as ugly as you?"[16]

(Avos HaRosh, based on Rashi, Bereishis 21:17).

12. After being cursed by the sick man, R' Shimon ben Yochai took himself to task for speaking harshly to someone in such a miserable state, and for expecting a pointed rebuke to be effective in these circumstances (see Avos 4:18). By admonishing the sick person to no avail, he had wasted precious time that he could have spent learning Torah (Yaavetz). Alternatively, R' Shimon was regretting his act of visiting the sick. Since he and his colleagues were so preoccupied with Torah study that they were exempt from interrupting even for prayer (Shabbos 11a), he concluded that someone of his caliber should not have taken time away from his study to visit the sick (Binyan Yehoshua).

In a completely different approach, some

explain that it was not R' Shimon ben Yochai but the sick person who said these words after calming down and giving the matter some thought. In his contrition, he acknowledged exposing himself to suffering by neglecting his spiritual mission and pursuing instead the idle distractions of this world (Magen Avos; Ben Avraham, second explanation).

13. Ahavas Chesed.

14. From Taanis 20a.

15. Some sources state that this man was actually Elijah the Prophet, who was sent to teach R' Shimon ben Elazar a lesson in humility (Binyan Yehoshua, citing Rashi and Tosafos to Taanis ibid.).

16. It is inconceivable that R' Shimon's sharp words were occasioned solely by the man's appearance. Rather, because the man was

אָמַר לוֹ: מָה אֶעֱשֶׂה, לֵךְ לָאוֹמָן שֶׁעֲשָׂאַנִי וֶאֱמוֹר לוֹ: כַּמָּה מְכוֹעָר כְּלִי זֶה שֶׁעָשִׂיתָ[17]. כֵּיוָן שֶׁיָּדַע רַבִּי שִׁמְעוֹן שֶׁחָטָא יָרַד מִן הַחֲמוֹר וְהָיָה מִשְׁתַּטֵּחַ לְפָנָיו, אָמַר לוֹ: נַעֲנֵיתִי לָךְ, מְחוֹל לִי[19]. אָמַר לוֹ: אֵינִי מוֹחֵל לָךְ עַד שֶׁתֹּאמַר לָאוֹמָן שֶׁעֲשָׂאַנִי: כַּמָּה מְכוֹעָר כְּלִי זֶה שֶׁעָשִׂיתָ[20], רָץ אַחֲרָיו שְׁלֹשָׁה מִילִין. יָצְאוּ אַנְשֵׁי הָעִיר לִקְרָאתוֹ, אָמְרוּ לוֹ: שָׁלוֹם עָלֶיךָ רַבִּי, אָמַר לָהֶם: לְמִי אַתֶּם קוֹרְאִים רַבִּי, אָמְרוּ: לְמִי שֶׁמְטַיֵּיל אַחֲרֶיךָ, אָמַר לָהֶם: אִם רַבִּי זֶה אַל יִרְבּוּ כְּמוֹתוֹ בְּיִשְׂרָאֵל. אָמְרוּ לוֹ: חָס וְשָׁלוֹם, מֶה עָשָׂה לְךָ,

---

אָמַר לוֹ: מָה אֶעֱשֶׂה — Slighted by these words, [the man] replied, "What shall I do? לֵךְ לָאוֹמָן שֶׁעֲשָׂאַנִי וֶאֱמוֹר לוֹ: כַּמָּה מְכוֹעָר כְּלִי זֶה שֶׁעָשִׂיתָ — Go to the Craftsman Who made me, and say to Him, 'How ugly is this vessel that You made!' "[17] כֵּיוָן שֶׁיָּדַע רַבִּי שִׁמְעוֹן שֶׁחָטָא — When [R' Shimon ben Elazar] realized that he had sinned by insulting the man, יָרַד מִן הַחֲמוֹר וְהָיָה מִשְׁתַּטֵּחַ לְפָנָיו — he got down from the donkey, prostrated himself before him, אָמַר לוֹ: נַעֲנֵיתִי לָךְ, מְחוֹל לִי — and said to him, "I have spoken out of turn to you,[18] and I regret what I said. Please forgive me!"[19] אָמַר לוֹ: אֵינִי מוֹחֵל לָךְ עַד שֶׁתֹּאמַר לָאוֹמָן שֶׁעֲשָׂאַנִי: כַּמָּה מְכוֹעָר כְּלִי זֶה שֶׁעָשִׂיתָ — [The man] answered him, "I will not forgive you until you say to the Craftsman Who made me, 'How ugly is this vessel that You made!' "[20] רָץ אַחֲרָיו שְׁלֹשָׁה מִילִין — [R' Shimon ben Elazar] ran after him while seeking his forgiveness for a distance of three mil, until they reached R' Shimon ben Elazar's city. יָצְאוּ אַנְשֵׁי הָעִיר לִקְרָאתוֹ — Upon their arrival, all the people of the city came out to greet [R' Shimon ben Elazar], אָמְרוּ לוֹ: שָׁלוֹם עָלֶיךָ רַבִּי — saying to him, "Peace be upon you, Teacher!" אָמַר לָהֶם: לְמִי אַתֶּם קוֹרְאִים רַבִּי — [The man] asked them, "Whom are you calling, 'Teacher'?" אָמְרוּ: לְמִי שֶׁמְטַיֵּיל אַחֲרֶיךָ — They answered him, "We are speaking to the one traveling behind you." אָמַר לָהֶם: אִם רַבִּי זֶה אַל יִרְבּוּ כְּמוֹתוֹ בְּיִשְׂרָאֵל — He said to them, "If this person is a teacher, may there not be many like him in Israel!" אָמְרוּ לוֹ: חָס וְשָׁלוֹם מֶה עָשָׂה לְךָ — They

---

unusually ugly, R' Shimon concluded that his unsightly appearance was not a natural phenomenon, but an external manifestation of a severe spiritual malady. When R' Shimon said, "Are all the people of your city perhaps as ugly as you?" he meant that while a person's appearance often reflects his place of origin, it is unlikely that such a degree of ugliness is characteristic of everyone in your region. It must therefore be a reflection of your evil character (Ben Avraham).

17. In other words, my ugliness is not a sign of my spiritual level, but rather an inborn

physical trait. Therefore, your complaints are directed at God, not at me (ibid.).

18. See Rashi to Kesubos 67b, s.v. נענתי.

19. [R' Shimon ben Elazar realized that he had been too quick to make assumptions about the man and his character (see note 16), and that his overly prideful feelings (after having learned so much Torah) had caused him to place undue confidence in his own judgment.]

20. If you say these words before God and He forgives you for criticizing His handiwork, then I too will forgive you (Ben Avraham).

אָמַר לָהֶם: כָּךְ וְכָךְ עָשָׂה לִי, אָמְרוּ לוֹ: אַף עַל פִּי כֵן מָחוּל לוֹ. אָמַר
לָהֶם: הֲרֵינִי מוֹחֵל [לוֹ] וּבִלְבַד שֶׁלֹּא יְהֵא רָגִיל לַעֲשׂוֹת כֵּן.²¹ אוֹתוֹ הַיּוֹם
נִכְנַס רַבִּי שִׁמְעוֹן לְבֵית הַמִּדְרָשׁ גָּדוֹל שֶׁלּוֹ וְדָרַשׁ: לְעוֹלָם יְהֵא אָדָם רַךְ
בְּקָנֶה וְלֹא יְהֵא קָשֶׁה כְּאֶרֶז, מַה קָּנֶה זֶה כָּל הָרוּחוֹת בָּאוֹת וְנוֹשְׁבוֹת בּוֹ
הוֹלֵךְ וּבָא עִמָּהֶם, דָּמְמוּ הָרוּחוֹת חוֹזֵר הַקָּנֶה עוֹמֵד בִּמְקוֹמוֹ, לְפִיכָךְ זָכָה
קָנֶה לִיטּוֹל הֵימֶנּוּ קוּלְמוֹס לִכְתּוֹב סֵפֶר תּוֹרָה.²³ אֲבָל אֶרֶז אֵינוֹ עוֹמֵד
בִּמְקוֹמוֹ אֶלָּא כֵּיוָן שֶׁנָּשְׁבָה רוּחַ דְּרוֹמִית עוֹקַרְתּוֹ וְהוֹפַכְתּוֹ עַל פָּנָיו.

replied, "Heaven forbid! Why do you say this? **What did he do to you** that led **you to say such a thing?"** אָמַר לָהֶם: כָּךְ וְכָךְ עָשָׂה לִי — **He answered them,** **"He did such and such to me,"** i.e., he related the entire incident to them. אָמְרוּ לוֹ: אַף עַל פִּי כֵן מָחוּל לוֹ — **They said to him, "Forgive him nevertheless,** for he is a great sage." אָמַר לָהֶם: הֲרֵינִי מוֹחֵל לוֹ — **He replied,** **"For your sake,** **I shall forgive him,** וּבִלְבַד שֶׁלֹּא יְהֵא רָגִיל לַעֲשׂוֹת כֵּן — **provided that he does** **not make a habit of doing this."**[21]

R' Shimon derives a lesson from this incident: אוֹתוֹ הַיּוֹם נִכְנַס רַבִּי שִׁמְעוֹן לְבֵית הַמִּדְרָשׁ גָּדוֹל שֶׁלּוֹ וְדָרַשׁ: — **That very day, R' Shimon ben Elazar entered his large study hall and expounded:** לְעוֹלָם יְהֵא אָדָם רַךְ בְּקָנֶה וְלֹא יְהֵא קָשֶׁה כְּאֶרֶז — **A person should always be soft like a reed** in his approach toward others, **and not hard like a cedar** (as he had been to the ugly man).

Reeds are better than cedars as models of human behavior in another way:[22] מַה קָּנֶה זֶה כָּל הָרוּחוֹת בָּאוֹת וְנוֹשְׁבוֹת בּוֹ הוֹלֵךְ וּבָא עִמָּהֶם — **Just as a reed,** which, even when **all the winds in the world** are **blowing on it, sways back and forth** **with them,** דָּמְמוּ הָרוּחוֹת חוֹזֵר הַקָּנֶה עוֹמֵד בִּמְקוֹמוֹ — but as soon as the **winds subside, it returns to its** upright **position** — so too a person who is flexible and compromising will ultimately emerge victorious. לְפִיכָךְ זָכָה קָנֶה לִיטּוֹל הֵימֶנּוּ קוּלְמוֹס לִכְתּוֹב סֵפֶר תּוֹרָה — **Indeed, because it represents this ad-** mirable trait, **the reed therefore merited to have pens drawn from its** ranks to be used **to write Torah Scrolls.**[23] אֲבָל אֶרֶז אֵינוֹ עוֹמֵד בִּמְקוֹמוֹ — **The** **cedar, on the other hand, does not** always **remain in its place** for very long; אֶלָּא כֵּיוָן שֶׁנָּשְׁבָה רוּחַ דְּרוֹמִית — **rather, as soon as the** powerful **south wind blows,** עוֹקַרְתּוֹ וְהוֹפַכְתּוֹ עַל פָּנָיו — **it uproots [the** rigid **cedar] and overturns it.**

---

21. One might have expected the man to say, "provided that he does not do it again," for even one more insult of this kind would be too many. Rather, the man was saying that R' Shimon ben Elazar should not make a habit of behaving in ways that can breed haughtiness and lead a person to act disdainfully toward others (*Binyan Yehoshua* [to *Derech Eretz Rabbah* 4:1], from *Maharsha*).

22. See *Taanis* 20a; see also *Magen Avos*.

23. The stems of certain varieties of reeds were fashioned into quill-like pens and used in writing scrolls of Scripture.

וּמַה סּוֹפוֹ שֶׁל אֶרֶז [בָּאִים עָלָיו סַתָּתִין וּמְסַתְּתִין אוֹתוֹ °[24] וּמְסַבְּבִין מִמֶּנּוּ
בָּתִּים [25] וְהַשְׁאָר] מַשְׁלִיכִין אוֹתוֹ לָאוּר. מִכָּאן אָמְרוּ יְהֵא אָדָם רַךְ כְּקָנֶה
וְאַל יְהֵא קָשֶׁה כְּאֶרֶז:[26]

ב. וּשְׁלֹשָׁה דְבָרִים נֶאֶמְרוּ בִּבְנֵי אָדָם: הַנּוֹתֵן צְדָקָה תָּבֹא עָלָיו בְּרָכָה.[27]
וְהַמַּלְוֶה טוֹב מִמֶּנּוּ. הַנּוֹתֵן מֶחֱצָה מְמוּתָר זֶהוּ לְמַעֲלָה מִכּוּלָן:[29]

ג. שָׁלֹשׁ מִדּוֹת בְּתַלְמִיד חָכָם. שׁוֹאֵל וּמֵשִׁיב חָכָם. שׁוֹאֵל וְאֵינוֹ מֵשִׁיב

בָּאִים עָלָיו וּמַה סּוֹפוֹ שֶׁל אֶרֶז — Moreover, what is the fate of the cedar?
סַתָּתִין וּמְסַתְּתִין אוֹתוֹ — Ultimately, lumbermen set upon it and chop it down;[24]
וּמְסַבְּבִין מִמֶּנּוּ בָּתִּים — then people use part of it to cover their houses,[25]
וְהַשְׁאָר מַשְׁלִיכִין אוֹתוֹ לָאוּר — and using the rest as firewood, they throw it into
the fire. Similarly, those who are harsh and unyielding will ultimately be defeated and broken.   מִכָּאן אָמְרוּ: יְהֵא אָדָם רַךְ כְּקָנֶה וְאַל יְהֵא קָשֶׁה כְּאֶרֶז — From
here [the Sages] concluded that a person should be soft like a reed and not
hard like a cedar.[26]

§2 The Baraisa turns back to listing various sets of three:
וּשְׁלֹשָׁה דְבָרִים נֶאֶמְרוּ בִּבְנֵי אָדָם — Three things are said about people who
help the poor: הַנּוֹתֵן צְדָקָה תָּבֹא עָלָיו בְּרָכָה — (i) One who gives charity to
a poor person — blessing shall come upon him.[27]   וְהַמַּלְוֶה טוֹב מִמֶּנּוּ —
(ii) One who lends money to a poor person is even better than that, since
he causes less embarrassment to the recipient.[28]   הַנּוֹתֵן מֶחֱצָה מְמוּתָר זֶהוּ
לְמַעֲלָה מִכּוּלָן — (iii) And one who gives a poor person capital to invest and
receive half of the profits — this one is superior to them all.[29]

§3 שָׁלֹשׁ מִדּוֹת בְּתַלְמִיד חָכָם — There are three types among the Torah scholars in training: שׁוֹאֵל וּמֵשִׁיב חָכָם — (i) One who can ask questions of
his own and can also answer the questions of others is a scholar.   שׁוֹאֵל וְאֵינוֹ

---

24. The root סתת actually refers to stone-
cutting (as in 6 §2 above), but the Baraisa
applies it to cutting the cedar to emphasize
the "stonelike" hardness of cedarwood (Ben
Avraham).

25. Emendation follows R' Yeshayah Berlin
and several earlier editions. Due to the superior strength of cedarwood, people fashion
it into beams and lay them across the top
of their houses and buildings, because such
beams can reliably bear the weight of a roof
(ibid.).

26. The reed's flexibility allows it to withstand even the mightiest winds, for it simply

gives way until the gale spends itself. By
contrast, the cedar's rigidity makes it vulnerable to breakage, for by standing up to
every opposing force, it is liable to crack
when overpowered (see ibid.).

27. As it is written, You shall surely give him
... for in return for this matter HASHEM, your
God, will bless you in all your deeds and in
your every undertaking (Binyan Yehoshua,
citing Deuteronomy 15:10).

28. Ibid., from Rashi to Shabbos 63a.

29. For he causes the recipient no shame
at all. On the contrary, he infuses him with

לְמַטָּה הֵימֶנּוּ. אֵינוֹ שׁוֹאֵל וְאֵינוֹ מֵשִׁיב זֶהוּ לְמַטָּה מִכּוּלָם:

ד. שָׁלֹשׁ זֵיעוֹת הֵן יָפוֹת לַגּוּף: זֵיעַת חוֹלִי זֵיעַת מֶרְחָץ זֵיעַת מְלָאכָה. זֵיעַת חוֹלִי מַרְפֵּא. זֵיעַת מֶרְחָץ אֵין לְךָ כַּיּוֹצֵא בּוֹ:

ה. שֵׁשׁ דְּמָעוֹת הֵן, שָׁלֹשׁ יָפוֹת וְשָׁלֹשׁ רָעוֹת. שֶׁל בֶּכִי וְשֶׁל עָשָׁן וְשֶׁל בֵּית הַכִּסֵּא רָעוֹת, שֶׁל סַם וְשֶׁל שְׂחוֹק וְשֶׁל פֵּירוֹת[34] יָפוֹת:

ו. שְׁלֹשָׁה דְבָרִים בִּכְלִי חֶרֶס: בּוֹלֵעַ וְאֵינוֹ פוֹלֵט[35] וְאֵינוֹ מַבְאִישׁ כָּל מַה

הֵימֶנּוּ לְמַטָּה מֵשִׁיב — (ii) **One who can ask** questions of his own, **but cannot answer** the questions of others **is one level below him.** מֵשִׁיב וְאֵינוֹ שׁוֹאֵל אֵינוֹ מִכּוּלָם לְמַטָּה זֶהוּ — (iii) **And one who can neither ask** questions of his own nor **answer** the questions of others **is the lowest of them all.**

§4 לַגּוּף יָפוֹת הֵן זֵיעוֹת שָׁלֹשׁ — **There are three** kinds of **sweat that are good for the body:** חוֹלִי זֵיעַת — (i) **the sweat** induced **by illness;** זֵיעַת מֶרְחָץ — (ii) **the sweat** induced **by a bathhouse;** מְלָאכָה זֵיעַת — (iii) **and the sweat** induced **by labor.** מַרְפֵּא חוֹלִי זֵיעַת — **The sweat** induced **by illness is therapeutic,** בּוֹ כַּיּוֹצֵא לְךָ אֵין מֶרְחָץ זֵיעַת — **and the sweat** induced **by a bathhouse has no parallel** with respect to its healthful benefit.

§5 The Baraisa now presents a double set of three.
הֵן דְּמָעוֹת שֵׁשׁ — **There are six** kinds of **tears.** רָעוֹת וְשָׁלֹשׁ יָפוֹת שָׁלֹשׁ — **Three are good** for the eyes **and three are bad** for the eyes:[30] בֶּכִי שֶׁל — **Three are good** for the eyes **and three are bad** for the eyes:[30] רָעוֹת הַכִּסֵּא בֵּית וְשֶׁל עָשָׁן וְשֶׁל — **Tears** induced **by crying** over one's sorrow or misfortune,[31] **by smoke,** or **by** stomach pains in **the lavatory**[32] **are bad for the eyes.** יָפוֹת פֵּירוֹת וְשֶׁל שְׂחוֹק וְשֶׁל סַם שֶׁל — **But tears** caused **by a strong eye medicine,**[33] **by laughter,** or **by** smelling pungent **produce**[34] **are good for the eyes.**

§6 Two contrasting sets of three:
חֶרֶס בִּכְלִי דְבָרִים שְׁלֹשָׁה — **Three things** are said **about** the nature of an **earthenware vessel:** בּוֹלֵעַ — (i) **It absorbs,** פוֹלֵט וְאֵינוֹ — (ii) **it does not emit,**[35] שֶׁבְּתוֹכוֹ מַה כָּל מַבְאִישׁ וְאֵינוֹ — **and** (iii) **it does not allow any of its**

---

pride in his ability to earn his own income (ibid., from *Mefaresh*).

30. *Avos DeRabbi Nassan, Nusach 2,* Ch. 48.

31. *Ben Avraham,* from *Rashi, Shabbos* 151b.

32. *Binyan Yehoshua,* from *Rashi* ibid.

33. *Ben Avraham.*

34. Such as onions (see *Avos DeRabbi Nassan, Nusach 2,* Ch. 48) or mustard (*Binyan Yehoshua;* see also *R' Yeshayah Berlin*).

35. Earthenware is distinct from other materials in that it absorbs the flavor of a food cooked in it but can never fully eject that flavor. [As a result, if an earthenware vessel was used to cook nonkosher food, it cannot be purged and rendered kosher (as other vessels can) by boiling water in it (*hagalah*).] It does, however, emit the absorbed flavor little by little, and it can therefore no longer be used for cooking kosher food (*Binyan Yehoshua*).

שֶׁבְּתוֹכוֹ[36]. שְׁלֹשָׁה דְבָרִים בִּכְלִי זְכוּכִית: אֵינוֹ בּוֹלֵעַ (וְאֵינוֹ פוֹלֵט[37]) וּמַרְאֶה כָּל מַה שֶּׁבְּתוֹכוֹ, בִּמְקוֹם חַם חַם בִּמְקוֹם צוֹנֵן צוֹנֵן[38]:

ז. אַרְבָּעָה דְבָרִים קָשִׁין לְתַשְׁמִישׁ הַמִּטָּה. הַבָּא מִן הַדֶּרֶךְ וְהָעוֹמֵד מִלִּפְנֵי הַסַּפָּר (וְהָעוֹמֵד מִלִּפְנֵי הַחוֹלִי) וְהַיּוֹצֵא מִבֵּית הָאֲסוּרִין[41]:

ח. כָּל הַמְקַבֵּל עָלָיו אַרְבָּעָה דְבָרִים [מְקַבְּלִין אוֹתוֹ] לִהְיוֹת חָבֵר[42]:

---

contents to spoil.[36] שְׁלֹשָׁה דְבָרִים בִּכְלִי זְכוּכִית — Three things are said about the nature of a glass vessel: אֵינוֹ בּוֹלֵעַ — (i) It does not absorb, וְאֵינוֹ פוֹלֵט — (ii) it does not emit,[37] וּמַרְאֶה כָּל מַה שֶּׁבְּתוֹכוֹ — and (iii) it allows all of its contents to be seen, בִּמְקוֹם חַם חַם בִּמְקוֹם צוֹנֵן צוֹנֵן — so that when it is in a hot place, they get hot, and when it is in a cold place, they get cold.[38]

§7 The Baraisa briefly returns to the theme of the previous chapter, which listed various sets of four.[39]

אַרְבָּעָה דְבָרִים קָשִׁין לְתַשְׁמִישׁ הַמִּטָּה — Four things cause difficulty for marital relations performed immediately afterward: הַבָּא מִן הַדֶּרֶךְ — (i) returning from a journey; וְהָעוֹמֵד מִלִּפְנֵי הַסַּפָּר — (ii) arising from before a bloodletter;[40] וְהָעוֹמֵד מִלִּפְנֵי הַחוֹלִי — (iii) arising from an illness; וְהַיּוֹצֵא מִבֵּית הָאֲסוּרִין — and (iv) coming out of prison.[41]

§8 Another set of four:

כָּל הַמְקַבֵּל עָלָיו אַרְבָּעָה דְבָרִים מְקַבְּלִין אוֹתוֹ לִהְיוֹת חָבֵר — Anyone who

---

36. The thick and opaque walls of the earthenware vessel serve to insulate its contents to some degree, thereby protecting them from spoilage (*Ben Avraham*).

37. That is, although glass does absorb a trace amount of flavor, it does not emit any of it during subsequent uses. Accordingly, if a glass vessel was used to cook nonkosher food, it may still be used for kosher foods as long as it is rinsed out (*Ben Avraham*, citing *Ran* to *Pesachim* folio 9a; *Beis Yosef* and *Shulchan Aruch, Orach Chaim* 451:26; but see dissenting opinion of *Rama* there with *Beur HaGra*).

38. Because of its thin and transparent walls, the contents of a glass vessel quickly take on the temperature of the surrounding area (*Ben Avraham*; see also *Magen Avos*).

[Our enumeration of the three qualities of glass follows the approach of *Ben Avraham*. For a different way of counting them, see *Magen Avos*.]

39. It is not clear why these sets of four are placed here rather than in the previous chapter. Apparently for this reason, *Gra* emends the text in this and the next paragraph so that they present sets of three, not four. *Ben Avraham* (to Ch. 40) adopts a different solution: He moves these paragraphs to the previous chapter.

40. See *Magen Avos* (comparing *Gittin* 70a); see also *Nuschas HaGra*.

Alternatively, הַסַּפָּר means "the barber" (*Yaavetz*). A third approach is that the word should be vowelized הַסֵּפֶר, "the [holy] book," so that the phrase וְהָעוֹמֵד מִלִּפְנֵי הַסֵּפֶר refers to the act of rising from a session of Torah study, which tends to sap a person of his strength (see *Ben Avraham* to Ch. 40; see also *Binyan Yehoshua* and *Avos HaRosh* [Vol. 2]).

41. In each of these cases, the person is worn and weak in one way or another (see *Ben Avraham* ibid.).

(אֵינוֹ הוֹלֵךְ לְבֵית הַקְּבָרוֹת,[43] וְאֵינוֹ מְגַדֵּל בְּהֵמָה דַקָּה,[44]) [אֵינוֹ נוֹתֵן תְּרוּמָה לְכֹהֵן עַם הָאָרֶץ,[45] אֵינוֹ עוֹשֶׂה טָהֳרוֹת אֵצֶל עַם הָאָרֶץ[46] אוֹכֵל חֻלִּין בְּטָהֳרָה]:

ט. °כֶּסֶף מִצְרַיִם חָזַר לִמְקוֹמָהּ, שֶׁנֶּאֱמַר (שמות יב, לו) "וַיְנַצְּלוּ אֶת מִצְרָיִם"

---

undertakes to be meticulous about **four matters is accepted as a** *chaver*.[42] וְאֵינוֹ מְגַדֵּל — (i) **He may not go to the cemetery,**[43] אֵינוֹ הוֹלֵךְ לְבֵית הַקְּבָרוֹת בְּהֵמָה דַקָּה — (ii) **nor raise small livestock,**[44] אֵינוֹ נוֹתֵן תְּרוּמָה לְכֹהֵן עַם הָאָרֶץ — (iii) **nor give** *terumah* **to an ignorant Kohen,**[45] אֵינוֹ עוֹשֶׂה טָהֳרוֹת אֵצֶל עַם הָאָרֶץ — (iv) **nor work with ritually pure items near an ignorant person,**[46] אוֹכֵל חֻלִּין בְּטָהֳרָה — **even one who** attempts to **eat his own** *chullin* (nonsacred foods) **in a state of ritual purity.**[47]

§9 The Baraisa now lists another set of three:

יִשְׂרָאֵל חָזְרוּ לִמְקוֹמָן — (i) **The Jewish people** eventually **returned to their place** of origin,[48] שֶׁנֶּאֱמַר "בָּבֶלָה יוּבָאוּ וְגוֹ' " — as it is stated, *They will be brought to Babylonia, etc. (Jeremiah 27:22).*[49] כֶּסֶף מִצְרַיִם חָזַר לִמְקוֹמָה — (ii) **The money** that the Jewish people took with them out **of Egypt** (at the time of the Exodus) eventually **returned to its place** of origin, שֶׁנֶּאֱמַר "וַיְנַצְּלוּ אֶת מִצְרָיִם" — for when the Jews went free, they took all of Egypt's riches, **as it is stated,** *[The Children of Israel] emptied Egypt (Exodus 12:36).*

---

42. Someone given the title of *chaver* was certified as trustworthy in matters of *tumah* and *taharah* (ritual purity and impurity). [In general usage, the title of *chaver* (literally, *friend*) was used to designate Torah scholars. Here the term has a more specific meaning (*Binyan Yehoshua;* see *Bechoros* 30a-b).]

43. Because doing so would render him *tamei*, ritually impure. A *chaver* must not become *tamei* unnecessarily because of the risk of contaminating other people and things.

44. In keeping with the Rabbinic prohibition against raising such animals, which are notoriously liable to graze in other people's fields (*Binyan Yehoshua,* from *Rav* to *Demai* 2:3; see *Bava Kamma* 79b). Although this matter has no connection to *tumah* and *taharah,* the Sages reasoned that if a person is lax regarding this Rabbinic enactment, he is likely to have a similar attitude toward the numerous Rabbinic laws that regulate *tumah* and *taharah* (see *Demai* 2:3).

45. The term "ignorant" in this context refers

to anyone who has not been accepted as a *chaver* (*Tiferes Yisrael* to *Demai* 2:3). Since he cannot be trusted with regard to the purity of food items, there is a concern that he might contaminate the *terumah*.

46. Since doing so is prone to lead to the contamination of the *chaver's* food or utensils (*Binyan Yehoshua*).

47. *Binyan Yehoshua,* second approach; *Ben Avraham.* Even if the ignorant neighbor has accepted upon himself the pious custom of eating his everyday food in a state of purity, there is no guarantee that he is actually successful in maintaining such a state, since he may not be versed in the relevant laws (ibid.).

48. The first entry in this list, which appears in the Talmudic version of this teaching in *Pesachim* 87b, has been added here based on *Magen Avos, Binyan Yehoshua,* and many others.

49. When the Jews went to exile in Babylonia, they were actually returning to their ancestral home, as their forefather Abraham was born in that region [see *Joshua* 24:2-3]

וְאוֹמֵר (בראשית מז, יד) "וַיְלַקֵּט יוֹסֵף אֶת כָּל הַכֶּסֶף" [וְאוֹמֵר (מלכים-א יד,
כה-כו) "וַיְהִי בַּשָּׁנָה הַחֲמִישִׁית לַמֶּלֶךְ רְחַבְעָם עָלָה שִׁישַׁק מֶלֶךְ מִצְרַיִם
וְגוֹ' וַיִּקַּח אֶת אֹצְרוֹת בֵּית ה' וְגוֹ' "].[51] כְּתָב שָׁמַיִם חָזְרָה לִמְקוֹמָהּ,[52]
שֶׁנֶּאֱמַר (משלי כג, ה) "הֲתָעִיף עֵינֶיךָ בּוֹ וְאֵינֶנּוּ [כִּי עָשֹׂה יַעֲשֶׂה לּוֹ כְנָפַיִם
כְּנֶשֶׁר יָעוּף °בַּשָּׁמָיִם]":

י. רַבִּי יְהוּדָה בֶּן תֵּימָא אוֹמֵר: הֱוֵי עַז כַּנָּמֵר[54] וְקַל כַּנֶּשֶׁר[55] וְרָץ כַּצְּבִי[56]

וְאוֹמֵר "וַיְלַקֵּט יוֹסֵף אֶת כָּל הַכֶּסֶף" — **And** among these riches was a vast store of
money, as [Scripture] states, *Joseph gathered all the money that was to be
found in the land of Egypt and in the land of Canaan ... and Joseph brought the
money into Pharaoh's palace* (Genesis 47:14). וְאוֹמֵר "וַיְהִי בַּשָּׁנָה הַחֲמִישִׁית
לַמֶּלֶךְ רְחַבְעָם עָלָה שִׁישַׁק מֶלֶךְ מִצְרַיִם וְגוֹ' וַיִּקַּח אֶת אֹצְרוֹת בֵּית ה' וְגוֹ' " — The Jews
took this money out of Egypt with them,[50] but centuries later, it all came back
to Egypt, as it states, *It was in King Rehoboam's fifth year that Shishak
king of Egypt* ascended against Jerusalem. *He took away the treasures of the
Temple of HASHEM and the treasures of the king's palace* (I Kings 14:25-26).[51]
כְּתָב שָׁמַיִם חָזְרָה לִמְקוֹמָהּ — (iii) And **the Heavenly inscription** that was carved
into the First Tablets **returned to its place** of origin,[52] שֶׁנֶּאֱמַר "הֲתָעִיף עֵינֶיךָ בּוֹ
וְאֵינֶנּוּ כִּי עָשֹׂה יַעֲשֶׂה לּוֹ כְנָפַיִם כְּנֶשֶׁר יָעוּף הַשָּׁמָיִם" — as it is stated, *You blinked
your eyes at [the writing on the Tablets] and it is gone, for it makes wings
for itself [and], like an eagle, it soars to the Heavens* (Proverbs 23:5).[53]

§10 The Baraisa cites *Avos* 5:20:

רַבִּי יְהוּדָה בֶּן תֵּימָא אוֹמֵר — R' Yehudah ben Teima says: הֱוֵי עַז כַּנָּמֵר
— **Be bold as a leopard,**[54] וְקַל כַּנֶּשֶׁר — **swift as an eagle,**[55] וְרָץ כַּצְּבִי

(*Magen Avos* and *Tumas Yesharim*, from
Pesachim 87b; see also *Avos DeRabbi Nassan*, Nusach 2, Ch. 37).

50. *Binyan Yehoshua*.

51. Included in this loot was the money
originally gathered by Joseph on Pharaoh's
behalf. That money was now brought back
to Egypt (see *Ben Avraham*).

52. The Talmud states that when Moses set
eyes on the Golden Calf and shattered the
Tablets at the foot of Mount Sinai, the letters
did not cease to exist. Rather, they floated
off the broken stones and rose Heavenward
(*Pesachim* 87b).

53. Translation based on *Binyan Yehoshua*;
see also *Ben Avraham*.

54. Employ the brazenness of a leopard

and shamelessly ask your teacher to clarify
anything you do not understand, since we
are taught (*Avos* 2:5 and above, 26 §3) that
"a bashful person cannot learn" (*Binyan
Yehoshua*, citing *Rav* to *Avos* 5:20). You
should likewise have the courage to perform
the mitzvos when necessary in the face of
scoffers who will deride you for your religious devotion (*Magen Avos*).

55. Approach your study and review of Torah with the untiring diligence characteristic
of eagles, as it is written (*Isaiah* 40:31),
*Those whose hope is in HASHEM will have
renewed strength; they will grow wings like
eagles; they will run and not grow tired, they
will walk and not grow weary* (*Binyan Ye-
hoshau*, citing *Rav* to *Avos* 5:20).

וְגִבּוֹר כָּאֲרִי[57] לַעֲשׂוֹת רְצוֹן אָבִיךְ שֶׁבַּשָּׁמָיִם:

יא. הוּא הָיָה אוֹמֵר: אָהוּב (מִן) הַשָּׁמַיִם הַדְּרוּשׁ שֶׁל כָּל הַמִּצְוֹת[58].
וְאִם עָשִׂיתָ לַחֲבֵרְךָ רַע קִימְעָא יְהֵא בְּעֵינֶיךָ הַרְבֵּה[59]. וְאִם עָשִׂיתָ
לַחֲבֵרְךָ טוֹבָה הַרְבֵּה יְהֵא בְּעֵינֶיךָ מְעַט[60]. וְאִם עָשָׂה לְךָ חֲבֵרְךָ טוֹבָה
קִימְעָא יְהֵא בְּעֵינֶיךָ הַרְבֵּה [אִם עָשָׂה לְךָ רָעָה רַבָּה יְהֵא בְּעֵינֶיךָ קִימְעָא][61].

לַעֲשׂוֹת רְצוֹן — fast as a deer,[56] וְגִבּוֹר כָּאֲרִי — and strong as a lion,[57]
אָבִיךְ שֶׁבַּשָּׁמַיִם — to do the will of your Father in Heaven.

§11 Additional teachings from R' Yehudah ben Teima:
הוּא הָיָה אוֹמֵר: אָהוּב מִן הַשָּׁמַיִם הַדְּרוּשׁ שֶׁל כָּל הַמִּצְוֹת — He used to say:
Beloved to Heaven is the expounding of all the commandments.[58] וְאִם
יְהֵא — עָשִׂיתָ לַחֲבֵרְךָ רַע קִימְעָא — If you did a little evil against your fellow,
בְּעֵינֶיךָ הַרְבֵּה — it should be considered in your eyes as a lot;[59] וְאִם עָשִׂיתָ
יְהֵא בְּעֵינֶיךָ — לַחֲבֵרְךָ טוֹבָה הַרְבֵּה — and if you did a lot of good for your fellow,
מְעַט — it should be considered in your eyes as only a little.[60] וְאִם עָשָׂה לְךָ
חֲבֵרְךָ טוֹבָה קִימְעָא — On the other hand, if your fellow did a little good for you,
יְהֵא בְּעֵינֶיךָ הַרְבֵּה — it should be considered in your eyes as a lot; אִם עָשָׂה לְךָ
יְהֵא בְּעֵינֶיךָ — רָעָה רַבָּה — and if your fellow committed much evil against you,
קִימְעָא — it should be considered in your eyes as only a little.[61]

---

56. Run like a deer to seek out and perform the commandments (ibid.).

57. Build up your spiritual fortitude for the purpose of overcoming your evil inclination (ibid.; see above, 23 §1).

58. Many of the Torah's mitzvos apply only in the Temple, or only in the Land of Israel, or only at certain times, to certain people, or in certain circumstances. Thus, for anyone who cannot observe these mitzvos, the only way to connect to them is by expounding their halachic details and moral lessons — with the hope of one day being able to put this knowledge into practice. This kind of study is beloved to God, and is considered tantamount to actual observance of the mitzvos being studied (Ahavas Chesed, first approach; Ben Avraham to Ch. 40; see also Magen Avos).

Alternatively, the Baraisa refers to the study of the reasons, benefits, and thought system associated with each mitzvah. God takes special pleasure when His children expound the deeper meanings of His

commandments (Ahavas Chesed, second approach; see also Kisei Rachamim).

59. Just as you cannot fathom the reward of even a "small" mitzvah (see Avos 2:1), you also cannot fathom the punishment incurred by a "small" sin. Therefore, always view your interpersonal offenses as much graver than they may seem (Binyan Yehoshua).

60. There is no limit to your obligation to help out other people (Peah 1:1). In this light, even a great act of kindness pales in significance (ibid.).

61. If you humbly consider yourself as deficient and unworthy, you will view any favor done for you as an extraordinary kindness, and any offense committed against you as less than you deserved (see Binyan Yehoshua to Derech Eretz Zuta, end of Ch. 2).

When a person internalizes this attitude in his interpersonal relationships — he is demanding of himself but forbearing and appreciative toward others — he will be able to develop the same attitude in his relationship with God (Magen Avos).

סְפוֹג וְקַנְקַנָּה זְפוּתָה, אֵלּוּ תַּלְמִידֵי חֲכָמִים.[62] מַשְׁפֵּךְ וְשִׁפּוֹפֶרֶת, אֵלּוּ
הָרְשָׁעִים.[63] הֱוֵי כְּנוֹד שֶׁאֵין בּוֹ פֶּתַח לְהַכְנִיס אֶת הָרוּחַ.[65] הֱוֵי לָמוּד לְקַבֵּל
אֶת הַצַּעַר,[66] וֶהֱוֵי מוֹחֵל עַל עֶלְבּוֹנְךָ:[67]

יב. דְּבָרִים הָעֲשׂוּיִין וּגְנוּזִין אֵלּוּ הֵן: אֹהֶל מוֹעֵד וְכֵלִים שֶׁבּוֹ[69] וְאָרוֹן

The Baraisa presents two sets of metaphors, representing two types of people.

סְפוֹג וְקַנְקַנָּה זְפוּתָה, אֵלּוּ תַּלְמִידֵי חֲכָמִים — (i) The "sponge" and (ii) the "tarred barrel" — these are the scholars.[62]   מַשְׁפֵּךְ וְשִׁפּוֹפֶרֶת, אֵלּוּ הָרְשָׁעִים — (iii) The "funnel" and (iv) the "tube" — these are the wicked.[63]

A set of three teachings on accepting insults with forbearance.[64]

הֱוֵי כְּנוֹד שֶׁאֵין בּוֹ פֶּתַח לְהַכְנִיס אֶת הָרוּחַ — (i) Be like a leather flask that has no opening to let in air.[65]   הֱוֵי לָמוּד לְקַבֵּל אֶת הַצַּעַר — (ii) Become used to accepting pain.[66]   וֶהֱוֵי מוֹחֵל עַל עֶלְבּוֹנְךָ — And (iii) forgive the offender for your shame.[67]

§12 The Baraisa presents two lists of holy objects, divided by where they have been stored during the exile.

דְּבָרִים הָעֲשׂוּיִין וּגְנוּזִין אֵלּוּ הֵן — The things that were made for sacred use and eventually hidden away due to their great sanctity[68] are the following: אֹהֶל מוֹעֵד וְכֵלִים שֶׁבּוֹ — The Tent of Meeting and the vessels in it;[69] וְאָרוֹן

---

62. Sponges soak up any liquids they encounter, whereas tarred barrels resist seepage and spoilage. Torah scholars combine the traits of both: They absorb Torah wisdom from any available source (for "Who is a wise man? He who learns from every person" — *Avos* 4:1; above, 23 §1), and then review it constantly so that nothing gets lost or distorted over time (*Magen Avos, Mefaresh*).

63. Funnels hold nothing back; they allow everything to pass through indiscriminately (see above, 40 § 8). Tubes allow the good wine to pass through while retaining some of the sediment that adheres to its walls. A wicked person is like a funnel with respect to Torah learning, allowing all of what he hears to be forgotten, but is like a tube when it comes to letting worthless ideas and information linger in his mind (*Mefaresh*; see also *Velo Od Ella*).

64. See *Velo Od Ella*.

65. Skins used as containers are limp and flat when empty, and do not even appear to be anything useful. Only when inflated do they stand tall and present themselves as strong and valuable utensils. When a person is censured or insulted, he should accept the criticism meekly, as if he were a deflated flask with no opening to take in air, rise to its true form, and display its full worth (*Mefaresh, VeLo Od Ella*).

66. Instead of attempting to vindicate yourself, accept the verbal abuse with equanimity (ibid.).

67. Rather than nursing a grudge and seeking revenge, forgive the speaker for his offense and erase the incident from your heart (ibid.).

68. See *Ben Avraham* to Ch. 40.

69. When the Temple was established as the national Sanctuary, it rendered the Tent of Meeting obsolete. The Tent's structural

וְשִׁבְרֵי לוּחוֹת [70] וְצִנְצֶנֶת הַמָּן [71] וְהַמַּטֶּה [72] [צְלוֹחִית שֶׁל שֶׁמֶן הַמִּשְׁחָה [73]]
וּמַקְלוֹ שֶׁל אַהֲרֹן שְׁקֵדֶיהָ וּפְרָחֶיהָ [74] וּבִגְדֵי כְהוּנָה וּבִגְדֵי כֹהֵן מָשִׁיחַ [75],
אֲבָל מַכְתֶּשֶׁת שֶׁל בֵּית אַבְטִינַס [76] שֻׁלְחָן וּמְנוֹרָה וּפָרוֹכֶת וְצִיץ עֲדַיִין
מוּנָּחִין בְּרוֹמִי:

וְשִׁבְרֵי לוּחוֹת — the Holy Ark and the fragments of the First Tablets that were placed inside it;[70]   וְצִנְצֶנֶת הַמָּן — the jar of manna;[71]   וְהַמַּטֶּה — the staff of Moses;[72]   צְלוֹחִית שֶׁל שֶׁמֶן הַמִּשְׁחָה — the jug of Anointing Oil;[73]   וּמַקְלוֹ שֶׁל אַהֲרֹן שְׁקֵדֶיהָ וּפְרָחֶיהָ — the staff of Aaron, with its almonds and blossoms;[74]   וּבִגְדֵי כְהוּנָה — the priestly vestments;   וּבִגְדֵי כֹהֵן — and the vestments of the Anointed Kohen.[75]   אֲבָל מַכְתֶּשֶׁת שֶׁל מָשִׁיחַ — However, the spice-mill of the House of Avtinas,[76]   בֵּית אַבְטִינַס   שֻׁלְחָן — the Table, the Menorah, the Partition, and the Head- וּמְנוֹרָה וּפָרוֹכֶת וְצִיץ plate   עֲדַיִין מוּנָּחִין בְּרוֹמִי — are still lying in Rome, where the conquerors

---

components were then stored away in a special chamber under the Temple (Magen Avos, from Sotah 9a).

70. The Gemara records that when King Josiah realized that the collapse of Jewish independence was not long in coming, he hid the Ark along with the jar of manna, the jug of Anointing Oil, and the stick of Aaron with its almonds and blossoms (Yoma 52b, Horayos 12a), all of which had previously resided near the Ark in the Holy of Holies (Tosefta, Sotah 13:2). He took this step to protect the Ark from being exiled along with the Jewish people, because he understood, based on Scriptural allusions, that if the Ark would be exiled, it would never return (see Yerushalmi Shekalim 6:1).

71. See previous note. God had told Moses to save this jar as a memorial, to remind future generations of how He sustained the Jews in the barren Wilderness for forty years; see Exodus 16:33-34.

72. Which was used to bring about the Ten Plagues in Egypt and to split the Sea of Reeds.

After passing down through the generations, this staff was used by King David and his royal descendants. It was hidden away before the First Temple was destroyed, but it will be used again by the Messiah when

he redeems the Jewish people and presides over them as king (Avos HaRosh [Vol. 2], citing Yalkut Shimoni to Psalms 119:2).

73. This oil, mixed with a special blend of spices, was used to anoint, and thereby inaugurate, the Tabernacle with its vessels, and then to anoint high priests and kings until it was hidden away alongside the Holy Ark (see note 70). It too will be recovered for further use in the Messianic era (Horayos 11a).

74. See note 70. The almonds and blossoms on this staff sprouted miraculously in the aftermath of Korah's rebellion against Moses and campaign to win the High Priesthood for himself. The blossoming staff demonstrated that it was God Who had chosen Aaron to be the Kohen Gadol and the tribe of Levi in general for a special role in serving Him; see Numbers 17:21-26.

75. I.e., the Kohen Gadol, who is elevated to his office through anointment (Binyan Yehoshua; see Leviticus 4:3).

Unlike the other items on this list, the Kohanic vestments were placed into hiding only at the end of the Second Temple era, to protect them from falling into enemy hands (Magen Avos).

76. The family of Avtinas possessed a guarded tradition concerning how to prepare

יג. (מַעֲשֶׂה בְּרַבִּי טַרְפוֹן שֶׁיָּשַׁב וְשָׁנָה לַתַּלְמִידִים וְעָבְרָה כַּלָּה לְפָנָיו,
צִוָּה עָלֶיהָ וְהִכְנִיסָהּ בְּתוֹךְ בֵּיתוֹ וְאָמַר לְאִמּוֹ וּלְאִשְׁתּוֹ: רַחֲצוּהָ
וְסוּכוּהָ וְקַשְּׁטוּהָ וְרִקְדוּ לְפָנֶיהָ עַד שֶׁתֵּלֵךְ לְבֵית בַּעְלָהּ)[78]:

יד. אֵלּוּ (שֶׁתִּקְּנוּ חֲכָמִים) שֶׁאֵין לָהֶם חֵלֶק לָעוֹלָם הַבָּא: חֲמִשָּׁה
מְלָכִים[79] וְשִׁשָּׁה (מְבַקְשֵׁי גְדוֹלָה) הֶדְיוֹטוֹת[80] קַיִן וְקֹרַח[81] וּבִלְעָם[82]

---

of Jerusalem brought them after destroying the Second Temple.

§13 A story that involves a set of four:[77]
מַעֲשֶׂה בְּרַבִּי טַרְפוֹן שֶׁיָּשַׁב וְשָׁנָה לַתַּלְמִידִים — There was an incident with R'
Tarfon in which he was sitting and teaching Torah to his students, וְעָבְרָה
כַּלָּה לְפָנָיו — when a bride passed before him. צִוָּה עָלֶיהָ וְהִכְנִיסָהּ בְּתוֹךְ בֵּיתוֹ
— Immediately, he interrupted his lecture and ordered that she be brought
into his house. וְאָמַר לְאִמּוֹ וּלְאִשְׁתּוֹ — Then he said to his mother and his
wife, רַחֲצוּהָ וְסוּכוּהָ וְקַשְּׁטוּהָ וְרִקְדוּ לְפָנֶיהָ — "Bathe her, anoint her, adorn her,
and dance before her עַד שֶׁתֵּלֵךְ לְבֵית בַּעְלָה — until she is ready to go to the
house of her new husband."[78]

§14 Another set:
אֵלּוּ שֶׁאֵין לָהֶם חֵלֶק לָעוֹלָם הַבָּא — These are the people who have
no portion in the World to Come: חֲמִשָּׁה מְלָכִים וְשִׁשָּׁה הֶדְיוֹטוֹת — The
five kings discussed elsewhere,[79] and six commoners; קַיִן וְקֹרַח וּבִלְעָם

---

the spice mixture used as incense in the
Temple (see *Yoma* 38a). The instrument
they used for grinding the herbs was considered a sacred vessel.

77. Namely, the four things R' Tarfon told
his mother and sister to do for the bride,
as mentioned below (*Ben Avraham* to
Ch. 40).

[Note that according to *Nuschas HaGra*,
this anecdote belongs in chapter 4 (§2), together with two other anecdotes of a similar
nature.]

78. When R' Tarfon noticed a bride who
was not properly beautified for her wedding, he understood that her family did
not have the means to provide for her. He
therefore spent his own funds and called
on his own family to prepare her for the occasion — not only to supply the resources
she lacked, but also to raise her image in
her groom's eyes by associating his famous

and respected name with her (*Velo Od Ella*).

79. It is not clear who these five kings are.
Three of them were named earlier in Ch.
36 (§6, and in Mishnah, *Sanhedrin* 10:1):
Jeroboam son of Nebat, Ahab son of Omri,
and Manasseh son of Hezekiah (*Mefaresh*).
The other two may be Ahaz son of Jotham
and Amon son of Manasseh, since the
Gemara (*Sanhedrin* 104a) indicates (according to one opinion) that they should
have been included in the Mishnah's list,
and were omitted only to protect the honor
of their righteous sons — Hezekiah and Josiah, respectively (cf. *Hagahos Yaavetz* and
Ahavas Chesed).

Alternatively, some emend the text to
read שְׁלֹשָׁה, *three*, instead of חֲמִשָּׁה, *five*
(*Nuschas HaGra*). According to this reading,
it is understandable why the Baraisa does
not name the kings, since it already named
them in Ch. 36 (*Ben Avraham*).

וַאֲחִיתוֹפֶל[83] וְדוֹאֵג[84] וְגֵיחֲזִי[85]׃

טו. רַבִּי יוֹסֵי אוֹמֵר: צַדִּיקִים גְּמוּרִים אֵין °מִצְטָרְפִין אוֹתָם[89] רְשָׁעִים גְּמוּרִים אֵין °מִצְטָרְפִין אוֹתָם אֶת מִי הֵן °מִצְטָרְפִין, בֵּינוֹנִים[90]׃

וַאֲחִיתוֹפֶל וְדוֹאֵג וְגֵיחֲזִי — namely, **Cain,**[80] **Korah,**[81] **Balaam,**[82] **Ahitophel,**[83] **Doeg**[84] and **Gehazi.**[85]

§15 The Baraisa presents a final set of three.[86]

רַבִּי יוֹסֵי אוֹמֵר צַדִּיקִים גְּמוּרִים אֵין מְצָרְפִין אוֹתָם — **R' Yose says:** In the Future Era,[87] **the completely righteous** (i.e., those with more mitzvos than sins[88]) **will not be purified** in fire,[89] since they are worthy of entering the World to Come as they are. רְשָׁעִים גְּמוּרִים אֵין מְצָרְפִין אוֹתָם — **The completely wicked** (those with more sins than mitzvos) **will not be purified** in fire, since they cannot be helped. אֶת מִי הֵן מְצָרְפִין — Who then will [the Heavenly Court] **purify** in fire? בֵּינוֹנִים — **The intermediate** people (those whose mitzvos and sins

---

80. In his anger over God's rejection of his offering, Cain committed history's first act of murder and became a heretic as well (see *Genesis* Ch. 4 with *Targum Yonason* to v. 8).

81. Korah led a rebellion against Moses in the Wilderness. By accusing Moses of speaking and acting without Divine sanction, he effectively cast doubt on the Torah's divinity. See *Numbers* Ch. 17 with *Malbim* to v. 28).

82. Balaam was the non-Jewish prophet who sought Israel's downfall, first by attempting to curse them and then by drawing them into sin. See ibid., Chs. 22-23.

83. Ahitophel was the highly regarded sage and adviser to King David who deserted the king in favor of David's renegade son, Absalom. See *II Samuel* Ch. 16 and *Sanhedrin* 106b.

84. Doeg was the adviser of King Saul who slandered David and brought about the destruction of Nob, the city of Kohanim. See *Sanhedrin* ibid.

[*Tummas Yesharim* places Doeg's name before Ahitophel's, presumably in keeping with the chronological order.]

85. Gehazi was the attendant of the prophet Elisha. He blocked Torah scholars from gaining access to the prophet and promoted the worship of Jeroboam's golden calves. See *II Kings* Ch. 5 and *Sanhedrin* 107a.

86. *Ben Avraham.*

87. When it is time, that is, for the Great Judgment at the end of days, when all men are judged to determine whether they are worthy of revivification and entry into the World to Come (*Magen Avos*, citing *Rashi* to *Rosh Hashanah* 16b).

88. *Ben Avraham*

This determination of whether one's merits or sins are in the majority does not depend on sheer numbers. One merit can outweigh many sins and one sin can outweigh many merits. Only God Himself, Who knows man's every thought, can make this determination (*Rambam, Hil. Teshuvah* 3:2).

89. Emendation follows *Tummas Yesharim, Yaavetz, Nuschas HaGra,* and *Regel Yesharah.*

The prophet Zechariah discusses (in the verse cited below) the concept that at the end of days, God will purify "one-third" of the Jewish people by means of fire (i.e., the torments of Gehinnom, as the Baraisa will soon make clear). R' Yose comes to identify which third of the nation this will be.

(תהלים קטז, ד) "אָנָּה ה' מַלְּטָה נַפְשִׁי" מְדִינָה שֶׁל גֵּיהִנֹּם[91]. שֶׁמָּא °אִם יוֹרְדִין לְתוֹכָה °וּמִסְתַּפְּסְכִין[92] וְעוֹלִין מִמֶּנּוּ °וּמִסְתַּפְּסְכִין, שֶׁנֶּאֱמַר (זכריה יג, ט) "וְהֵבֵאתִי אֶת הַשְּׁלִשִׁית[93] בָּאֵשׁ וּצְרַפְתִּים כִּצְרֹף אֶת הַכֶּסֶף וּבְחַנְתִּים כִּבְחֹן אֶת הַזָּהָב". בֵּית הִלֵּל אוֹמְרִים: אֵין רוֹאִין אוֹתָה כָּל עִיקָּר[94], שֶׁנֶּאֱמַר (תהלים סג, ד) "כִּי טוֹב חַסְדְּךָ מֵחַיִּים שְׂפָתַי יְשַׁבְּחוּנְךָ"[95] וְאוֹמֵר (נחמיה יג, כב) "וְחוּסָה

are equally balanced).[90]   "אָנָּה ה' מַלְּטָה נַפְשִׁי" — And it is with this group in mind that King David prayed, *"Please, HASHEM, save my soul"* (Psalms 116:4),   מְדִינָה שֶׁל גֵּיהִנֹּם — meaning, from the punishment of Gehinnom.[91]

This subject was actually debated by the Sages of an earlier generation: בֵּית שַׁמַּאי אוֹמְרִים — Beis Shammai say in agreement with R' Yose's view:[92] [The intermediate people] will descend into [Gehinnom], become purified in it, and immediately emerge and rise out of it,   שֶׁנֶּאֱמַר "וְהֵבֵאתִי אֶת הַשְּׁלִשִׁית בָּאֵשׁ וּצְרַפְתִּים כִּצְרֹף אֶת הַכֶּסֶף וּבְחַנְתִּים כִּבְחֹן אֶת הַזָּהָב" — as it is stated, *I will bring that third[93] into fire and purify it as one purifies silver, and I will refine it as one refines gold* (Zechariah 13:9).   בֵּית הִלֵּל אוֹמְרִים: אֵין רוֹאִין אוֹתָה כָּל עִיקָּר — Beis Hillel say: They will not have to witness [Gehinnom] at all,[94] שֶׁנֶּאֱמַר — as it is stated, *For Your kindness is better than life, my lips shall praise You* (Psalms 63:4).[95]   וְאוֹמֵר "וְחוּסָה

---

90. The group of people destined to be purified in fire before entering the World to Come are neither the righteous nor the wicked, but rather the intermediate group, who are not so virtuous as to not need purification, yet not so unworthy as to be excluded unconditionally from the life of eternity (*Magen Avos*).

91. King David was pleading with God that he should not be made to suffer in Gehinnom like the intermediate-level Jews; or he was praying on behalf of those very Jews, asking that they not be left to suffer in Gehinnom indefinitely. Either way, R' Yose derives from this verse that intermediate-level Jews must descend to Gehinnom for purification (ibid.)

92. Emendations follow *Tummas Yesharim*; see also *R' Yeshayah Berlin, Binyan Yeho-shua,* and *Nuschas HaGra.*

93. I.e., the intermediate third of the nation, as explained above by R' Yose.

94. In Beis Hillel's view, God "tips the scales" of the intermediate group toward leniency, so that they do not have to descend into

Gehinnom at all (*Binyan Yehoshua*, citing *Rosh Hashanah* 17a). Who, then, belongs to the "third" that God will purify in the fire of Gehinnom, as foreseen by Zechariah? The Gemara (*Rosh Hashanah* ibid.) answers that this cleansing process is reserved for people whose sins not only equal their merits but also include at least one sin that places them in the category of "transgressors of Israel who sin through their bodies" (פּוֹשְׁעֵי יִשְׂרָאֵל בְּגוּפָן), such as if they never put on tefillin [out of disdain for the mitzvah — *Tosafos* ad loc.] (*Ben Avraham*).

95. The future kindness that God will perform for those intermediate-level Jews — sparing them from Gehinnom and granting them immediate life in the World to Come — will be even greater than the kindness that He performs by granting life to the creatures of this world — for "one hour of spiritual bliss in the World to Come is better than the entire life of this world" [*Avos* 4:17] (*Binyan Yehoshua*). That this verse is referring to the subject at hand is evident from the previous

עָלַי(הם) כְּרֹב חַסְדֶּךָ" (כְּדֵי שֶׁיִּנָּצְלוּ מִדִּינָה שֶׁל גֵּיהִנֹּם):

טז. כָּל מַה שֶׁבָּרָא הַקָּדוֹשׁ בָּרוּךְ הוּא בְּעוֹלָמוֹ לֹא בָּרָא אֶלָּא לִכְבוֹדוֹ, שֶׁנֶּאֱמַר (ישעיה מג, ז) "כֹּל הַנִּקְרָא בִשְׁמִי וְלִכְבוֹדִי בְּרָאתִיו יְצַרְתִּיו אַף עֲשִׂיתִיו"[97] וְאוֹמֵר (שמות טו, יח) "ה' יִמְלֹךְ לְעוֹלָם וָעֶד"[98]:

יז. אָמַר רַבִּי חֲנַנְיָא בֶּן עֲקַשְׁיָא רָצָה הַקָּדוֹשׁ בָּרוּךְ הוּא לְזַכּוֹת אֶת יִשְׂרָאֵל לְפִיכָךְ הִרְבָּה לָהֶם תּוֹרָה וּמִצְוֹת[100] שֶׁנֶּאֱמַר (ישעיה מב, כא)

"עָלַי כְּרֹב חַסְדֶּךָ — And [Scripture] states further, *And be compassionate toward me according to Your abundant kindness* (Nehemiah 13:22). כְּדֵי שֶׁיִּנָּצְלוּ מִדִּינָה שֶׁל גֵּיהִנֹּם — This verse expresses the plea that every intermediate Jew will put forward in the future[96] so that they may be spared from the punishment of Gehinnom.

§16 Nearing the end of the book, the Baraisa presents (as *Pirkei Avos* does) the underlying theme of its many teachings on Torah ethics. כָּל מַה שֶׁבָּרָא הַקָּדוֹשׁ בָּרוּךְ הוּא בְּעוֹלָמוֹ — All that the Holy One, Blessed is He, created in His world, לֹא בָּרָא אֶלָּא לִכְבוֹדוֹ — He created solely for His glory, שֶׁנֶּאֱמַר "כֹּל הַנִּקְרָא בִשְׁמִי וְלִכְבוֹדִי בְּרָאתִיו יְצַרְתִּיו אַף עֲשִׂיתִיו" — as it is stated, *All that is called by My Name, indeed, it is for My glory that I have created it, formed it, and made it* (Isaiah 43:7).[97] וְאוֹמֵר "ה' יִמְלֹךְ לְעוֹלָם וָעֶד" — And it further **states,** *God shall reign for all eternity* (Exodus 15:18).[98]

§17 Although God created all of us to honor Him, the true beneficiary of our Divine service is not Him but us.[99] אָמַר רַבִּי חֲנַנְיָא בֶּן עֲקַשְׁיָא — R' Chananya ben Akashya said: רָצָה הַקָּדוֹשׁ בָּרוּךְ הוּא לְזַכּוֹת אֶת יִשְׂרָאֵל — The Holy One, Blessed is He, wished to bestow merit upon the people of Israel; לְפִיכָךְ הִרְבָּה לָהֶם תּוֹרָה וּמִצְוֹת — therefore, He gave them Torah and mitzvos in abundance,[100] שֶׁנֶּאֱמַר

---

verses: *My soul thirsts for You, my flesh longs for You, in a parched and thirsty land with no water.* "As I stand at the brink of Gehinnom, that parched and thirsty land," says the Psalmist, "I yearn to be spared from punishment there and instead to be found worthy of approaching You in the World to Come ... *to have beheld You in the Sanctuary, to see Your might and glory* (ibid.).

96. Ibid.

97. With this teaching, the Baraisa conveys a powerful message: If a person exists solely for the purpose of according honor to God, then every moment he is not somehow

engaged in this mission, there is no justification for his existence (*Magen Avos*).

98. There will come a time when mankind will recognize God, once and for all, as King of the universe. With their eyes open as never before, they will see how even those phenomena that had always seemed to contradict this teaching were actually serving, in some hidden way, to ultimately establish God's sovereignty and enhance His glory (*Tiferes Yisrael* to *Avos* 6:11).

99. *Magen Avos.*

100. The Torah forbids many things that people would have avoided anyway (like

"ה׳ חָפֵץ לְמַעַן צִדְקוֹ יַגְדִיל תּוֹרָה וְיַאְדִיר":

"ה׳ חָפֵץ לְמַעַן צִדְקוֹ יַגְדִיל תּוֹרָה וְיַאְדִיר" — as it is stated, *HASHEM desired, for the sake of [Israel's] righteousness, that the Torah be made great and glorious* (Isaiah 42:21).

---

eating vermin, carrion, etc.), or that they would have surely outlawed as a society (like theft and murder). In His kindness, God incorporated these laws into the Torah in order to reward us when we observe them (*Binyan Yehoshua*, citing *Rav*, end of *Makkos*; see *Tiferes Yisrael* there).

Alternatively, there is a Torah principle that if a person fulfills even one mitzvah properly, with perfect adherence to the mitzvah's specifications and with complete devotion to God, he will earn the merit, through that mitzvah act alone, for a blissful life in the World to Come. In His desire to help us make this ideal a reality, God gave us a great variety of mitzvos, so that every Jew can find at least one area of Torah, at least one mitzvah, that he can fulfill in this pure and complete fashion, and thereby earn his eternal reward (*Rambam ad loc.*).